HANDBOOK OF POSITIVE PSYCHOLOGY

HANDBOOK OF
POSITIVE PSYCHOLOGY

Edited by

C. R. Snyder

Shane J. Lopez

OXFORD
UNIVERSITY PRESS
2002

OXFORD
UNIVERSITY PRESS

Oxford   New York

Athens   Auckland   Bangkok   Bogotá   Buenos Aires   Cape Town
Chennai   Dar es Salaam   Delhi   Florence   Hong Kong   Istanbul   Karachi
Kolkata   Kuala Lumpur   Madrid   Melbourne   Mexico City   Mumbai   Nairobi
Paris   São Paulo   Shanghai   Singapore   Taipei   Tokyo   Toronto   Warsaw

and associated companies in
Berlin   Ibadan

Library of Congress Cataloging-in-Publication Data
Handbook of positive psychology / edited by C. R. Snyder and Shane J. Lopez.
p.   cm.
Includes bibliographical references and indexes.
ISBN 0–19–513533–4
1. Psychology.   2. Health.   3. Happiness.   4. Optimism.
I. Snyder, C. R.   II. Lopez, Shane J.
BF121 6.H212 2002
150.19'8—dc21   2001021584

1 3 5 7 9 8 6 4 2

Printed in the United States of America
on acid-free paper

To the positive in all of us . . .

Foreword

It gives me great joy to know that so many scientists—many of whom have contributed to this landmark volume—are striving to inspire people to develop a more wholesome focus on the *positive* aspects of life. I am convinced that one day these scientists will be recognized as visionary leaders, whose research helped to identify, elevate, and celebrate the creative potential of the human spirit.

Until recently, I had rarely heard about scientific research that examined the life-enhancing power of "spiritual principles"—positive character traits and virtues such as love, hope, gratitude, forgiveness, joy, future-mindedness, humility, courage, and noble purpose. Perhaps my long-standing interest in these spiritual principles and character traits is best understood by sharing with you the following perspective. My grandfather was a physician during the Civil War, and several of my own children are physicians today. I think we would all agree that my children, because of the enormous number of dollars earmarked for medical research during this past century, know a hundred times—perhaps a thousand times—more about the human body than my grandfather ever did. But I have always wondered: *Why is it that we know so little about the human spirit?*

The research highlighted in this volume provides overwhelming evidence that many talented scholars and award-winning researchers are reclaiming what was once at the core of their discipline: the psyche, the study and understanding of the power of the human spirit to benefit from life's challenges. The men and women who have written chapters for this handbook, as well as countless more inspired by their research, are courageously gathering data and testing hypotheses to help us learn more about an essential question that perhaps serves as the North Star for a positive psychology: What enables us to override our biological inclinations to be selfish and instead find meaning, purpose, and value in nurturing and upholding the positive qualities of our human nature?

In fact, I am more optimistic than ever that one day soon a group of scientists will publish findings that will advance humankind's understanding of a spiritual principle that has been at the core of my own life's purpose: *agape love.* One of my favorite sayings is, "Love hoarded dwindles, but love given grows." Love is more powerful than money; unlike money, the more love we give away, the more we have left. Perhaps, dear reader, you will be the researcher who studies a spiritual principle such as agape love scientifically or empirically. Wouldn't all of humankind benefit from knowing more about this fundamental "law of life," and many others?

Finally, I am hopeful that as current and future researchers catch the vision of a positive psychology, and as foundations and governments initiate programs to support this groundbreaking and beneficial work, we will all forge ahead in a spirit of humility. We know so little, my friends, about the many gifts that God has given to each and every human being. As the truly wise tell us, "How little we know, how eager to learn."

Radnor, Pennsylvania   Sir John Templeton

Preface

How often does one have the opportunity to edit the first handbook for a new approach to psychology? We had a "once-in-a-lifetime" scholarly adventure in preparing this *Handbook of Positive Psychology*. There was never a question in our minds about editing this volume. We were at the right place at the right time, and the book simply had to happen.

Fortunately, our superb editors at Oxford University Press, Joan Bossert and Catharine Carlin, shared our enthusiasm about the necessity of this volume, and they made this huge editorial undertaking seamless in its unfolding. The authors we invited to write chapters readily agreed. Much to our delight, this handbook almost took on a life of its own. We attribute this to the vitality of the authors, along with the power of their positive psychology ideas and science.

We complemented each other as an editorial team. Snyder was a stickler for detail and yet sought ingenuity in thought and expression. Lopez saw linkages in ideas, would call upon the related literatures, and brought unbridled enthusiasm to the editorial process. What this combination produced was a line-by-line analysis and feedback in every chapter. In short, we were "hands-on" editors. Given the stature of the contributing scholars, with numerous awards, distinguished professorships, and honorary degrees, they certainly could have balked at such editorial scrutiny. But they did not. Instead, they used our feedback and revised their already superb first drafts into stellar subsequent chapters. We are indebted to this

remarkable group of authors for their patience in this process. Their dedication to excellence can be seen in the chapters of this handbook.

In order to help readers in gaining a sense of the topics contained in each chapter, we have asked our expert authors to identify sources that provide excellent overviews of their areas. Therefore, in the reference section of each chapter, the authors have placed an asterisk in front of such key readings. We encourage our readers to use these background sources when more detailed descriptions of a topic are desired.

Now, before you peruse the contributions of the outstanding scholars, consider the following . . . Imagine a planet where the inhabitants are self-absorbed, hopeless, and filled with psychological problems and weaknesses. Confusion, anxiety, fear, and hostility race through their minds. These creatures "communicate" with each other by lying, faking, torturing, fighting, and killing. They hurt each other, and they hurt themselves. Of course, this imaginary planet is not far away—we call it Earth. Although these problems do exist, they are made to loom even larger because of the propensities of psychology and its sister disciplines to focus on the weaknesses in humankind. Now let us imagine another planet where the inhabitants are caring, hopeful, and boundless in their psychological strengths. Their thoughts and feelings are clear, focused, and tranquil. These creatures communicate by spending time talking and listening to each other. They are kind to each other and to themselves. Again, this imaginary, not-so-far-away planet is Earth. These positive descriptions aptly fit many of the people on Earth. In this regard, hardly anyone (including some cynics) quibbles with this latter conclusion. *But no science, including psychology, looks seriously at this positive side of people.* It is this latter troubling void that positive psychology addresses. As such, this handbook provides an initial scientific overview of the positive in humankind. As with any new and promising paradigm, the reactions of people such as you will determine the fate of positive psychology. Although science certainly advances on the merits of particular ideas and facts, it also is true that the success of a new theory rests, in part, upon its ability to gather supporters. On this point, this handbook may enable you to cast a more informed vote as to the enduring viability of positive psychology.

Lawrence, Kansas   C. R. Snyder
                                      Shane J. Lopez

Contents

Contributors

GLENN AFFLECK, Professor, Department of Psychiatry, University of Connecticut Health Center

NADIA AHMAD, Doctoral Student, Social Psychology Program, Department of Psychology, University of Kansas

LISA ASPINWALL, Associate Professor, Department of Psychology, University of Utah

JENNIFER L. AUSTENFELD, Doctoral Student, Clinical Psychology Program, Department of Psychology, University of Kansas

JAMES R. AVERILL, Professor, Department of Psychology, University of Massachusetts, Amherst

PAUL B. BALTES, Director, Center for Lifespan Psychology, Max Planck Institute for Human Development, Berlin, Germany

JULIAN BARLING, Associate Dean, Research and Graduate Programs, School of Business, Queen's University, Kingston, Ontario, Canada

C. DANIEL BATSON, Professor, Social Psychology Program, Department of Psychology, University of Kansas

ROY F. BAUMEISTER, Elsie B. Smith Chair in Liberal Arts, and Professor, Department of Psychology, Case Western Reserve University

KERI G. BROWN, Doctoral Student, Clinical Child Psychology, Departments of Psychol-

ogy and Human Development and Family Life, University of Kansas

DAVID CARUSO, President, Work-Life Strategies, New Canaan, Connecticut

CHARLES S. CARVER, Professor, Department of Psychology, University of Miami

ERIC J. CASSELL, Clinical Professor of Public Health, Weill Medical College of Cornell University

MIHALY CSIKSZENTMIHALYI, C. S. and C. J. Davidson Professor of Psychology, Peter Drucker School of Management, Claremont Graduate University

CHRISTOPHER G. DAVIS, Associate Professor, Department of Psychology, St. Francis Xavier University

SALLY S. DICKERSON, Master's Student, Department of Psychology, University of California, Los Angeles

ED DIENER, Distinguished Professor, Department of Psychology, University of Illinois at Champaign-Urbana

RICHARD A. DIENSTBIER, Professor, Department of Psychology, University of Nebraska, Lincoln

LISA M. EDWARDS, Doctoral Student, Counseling Psychology Program, Department of Psychology and Research in Education, University of Kansas

TIMOTHY R. ELLIOTT, Associate Professor and Psychologist, Department of Physical Medicine and Rehabilitation, University of Alabama–Birmingham Medical School

ROBERT A. EMMONS, Professor, Department of Psychology, University of California, Davis

BARBARA L. FREDRICKSON, Associate Professor, Department of Psychology, University of Michigan

JUDITH GLECK, Max Planck Institute for Human Development, Berlin, Germany

MICHAEL C. GOTTLIEB, Private Practice, Dallas, Texas

JON HAIDT, Assistant Professor, Department of Psychology, University of Virginia, Charlottesville

MITCHELL M. HANDELSMAN, Professor of Psychology and Colorado University President's Teaching Scholar, Department of Psychology, University of Colorado

SUSAN HARTER, Professor, Department of Psychology, University of Denver

JOHN H. HARVEY, Professor, Department of Psychology, University of Iowa

CLYDE HENDRICK, Paul Whitfield Horn Professor of Psychology, Department of Psychology, Texas Tech University

SUSAN HENDRICK, Associate Dean, College of Arts and Sciences, and Professor, Department of Psychology, Texas Tech University

P. PAUL HEPPNER, Professor, Department of Educational and Counseling Psychology, University of Missouri–Columbia

JOHN P. HEWITT, Professor, Department of Sociology, University of Massachusetts, Amherst

RAYMOND L. HIGGINS, Professor, Clinical Psychology Program, Department of Psychology, University of Kansas

ALICE M. ISEN, Samuel Curtis Johnson Professor of Marketing and Professor of Behavioral Science, Johnson Graduate School of Management and Department of Psychology, Cornell University

REBECCA J. JOHNSON, Doctoral Student, Clinical Child Psychology, Departments of Psychology and Human Development and Family Life, University of Kansas

DACHER KELTNER, Associate Professor, Department of Psychology, University of California, Berkeley

COREY L. M. KEYES, Assistant Professor, Department of Sociology and the Rollins School of Public Health, Emory University

LAURA COUSINO KLEIN, Department of Biobehavioral Health, Pennsylvania State University

SAMUEL KNAPP, Director of Professional Affairs, Pennsylvania Psychological Association

UTE KUNZMANN, Max Planck Institute for Human Development, Berlin, Germany

MONICA KURYLO, Rehabilitation Psychologist, Department of Physical Medicine and Rehabilitation, University of Alabama–Birmingham Medical School

ELLEN LANGER, Professor, Department of Psychology, Harvard University

DOUG-GWI LEE, Doctoral Student, Counseling Psychology Program, Department of Educational and Counseling Psychology, University of Missouri–Columbia

HERBERT M. LEFCOURT, Distinguished Professor Emeritus, Department of Psychology, University of Waterloo

DAVID A. LISHNER, Doctoral Student, Social Psychology Program, Department of Psychology, University of Kansas

EDWIN A. LOCKE, Dean's Professor Emeritus of Leadership and Motivation, R. H. Smith School of Business, University of Maryland, College Park

SHANE J. LOPEZ, Assistant Professor, Counseling Psychology Program, Department of Psychology and Research in Education, University of Kansas

RICHARD E. LUCAS, Assistant Professor, Department of Psychology, Michigan State University

MICHAEL LYNN, Professor, School of Hotel Administration, Cornell University

JAMES E. MADDUX, Professor and Associate Chair for Graduate Studies, Department of Psychology, George Mason University

JEANA L. MAGYAR-MOE, Doctoral Student, Counseling Psychology Program, Department of Psychology and Research in Education, University of Kansas

ANNETTE MAHONEY, Associate Professor, Department of Psychology, Bowling Green State University

MICHAEL J. MAHONEY, Professor, Clinical Psychology Program, Department of Psychology, University of North Texas

ANN S. MASTEN, Director, Institute of Child Development, and Emma M. Birkmaier Professor in Educational Leadership, University of Minnesota

JOHN D. MAYER, Professor of Psychology, Department of Psychology, University of New Hampshire

MICHAEL E. MCCULLOUGH, Associate Professor, Department of Psychology, Southern Methodist University

JEANNE NAKAMURA, Research Director, Quality of Life Research Center, Claremont Graduate University

JASON E. NEUFELD, Doctoral Student, Counseling Psychology Program, Department of Psychology and Research in Education, University of Kansas

KATE G. NIEDERHOFFER, Doctoral Student, Social Psychology Program, Department of Psychology, University of Texas

SUSAN NOLEN-HOEKSEMA, Professor, Department of Psychology, University of Michigan

SHIGEHIRO OISHI, Assistant Professor, Department of Psychology, University of Minnesota

KENNETH I. PARGAMENT, Professor, Department of Psychology, Bowling Green State University

ANITA PARSA, Doctoral Student, Clinical Psychology Program, Department of Psychology, University of Kansas

BRIAN G. PAUWELS, Doctoral Student, Personality and Social Psychology, Department of Psychology, University of Iowa

BRETT W. PELHAM, Associate Professor, Department of Psychology, State University of New York at Buffalo

JAMES W. PENNEBAKER, Professor, Department of Psychology, University of Texas

CHRISTOPHER PETERSON, Professor of Psychology and Arthur F. Thurnau Professor, Clinical Psychology Program, University of Michigan

ELLIE C. PROSSER, Doctoral Student, Counseling Psychology Program, Department of Psychology and Research in Education, University of Kansas

KEVIN L. RAND, Doctoral Student, Clinical Psychology Program, Department of Psychology, University of Kansas

HEATHER N. RASMUSSEN, Doctoral Student, Counseling Psychology Program, Department of Psychology and Research in Education, University of Kansas

MARIE-GABRIELLE J. REED, Research Assistant, Institute of Child Development, University of Minnesota

JANNETTE REINKE, Doctoral Student, Clinical Child Psychology, Departments of Psychology and Human Development and Family Life, University of Kansas

PATRICIA RIVERA, Postdoctoral Fellow, Department of Physical Medicine and Rehabilitation, University of Alabama–Birmingham Medical School

MICHAEL C. ROBERTS, Professor and Director, Clinical Child Psychology Program, University of Kansas

CHRISTINE ROBITSCHEK, Associate Professor, Counseling Psychology Program, Department of Psychology, Texas Tech University

CAROL D. RYFF, Director, Institute on Aging and Professor of Psychology, Department of Psychology, University of Wisconsin, Madison

PETER SALOVEY, Professor of Psychology and of Epidemiology and Public Health, Department of Psychology, Yale University

CRAIG SANTERRE, Doctoral Student, Clinical Psychology Program, Department of Psychology, University of Arizona

MICHAEL F. SCHEIER, Professor, Department of Psychology, Carnegie-Mellon University

MICHAEL SCHULMAN, Clinical Department, Leake and Watts Services, Bronx, New York

GARY E. R. SCHWARTZ, Professor of Psychology, Neurology, Psychiatry, and Medicine, Director, Human Energy Systems Lab, Department of Psychology, University of Arizona

MARTIN E. P. SELIGMAN, Fox Leadership Professor of Psychology, Department of Psychology, University of Pennsylvania

SHAUNA L. SHAPIRO, Doctoral Student, Clinical Psychology Program, Department of Psychology, University of Arizona

CHARLES M. SHELTON, Professor of Psychology, Department of Psychology, Regis University

DAVID R. SIGMON, Doctoral Student, Clinical Psychology Program, Department of Psychology, University of Kansas

DEAN KEITH SIMONTON, Professor, Department of Psychology, University of California, Davis

BURTON SINGER, Professor of Demography and Public Affairs and the Charles and Marie Robertson Professor of Public and International Affairs, Office of Population Research, Princeton University

C. R. SNYDER, M. Erik Wright Distinguished Professor of Clinical Psychology, Department of Psychology, University of Kansas

ANNETTE L. STANTON, Professor, Clinical Psychology Program, Department of Psychology, University of Kansas

TRACY A. STEEN, Doctoral Student, Clinical Psychology Program, Department of Psychology, University of Michigan

WILLIAM B. SWANN, William Howard Beasley Professor, Department of Psychology, University of Texas

JUNE PRICE TANGNEY, Professor, Department of Psychology, James Madison University

SHELLEY E. TAYLOR, Professor, Department of Psychology, University of California, Los Angeles

SIR JOHN TEMPLETON, Founder of Templeton Foundation, Radnor Pennsylvania

HOWARD TENNEN, Professor, Department of Psychiatry, University of Connecticut Health Center

SUZANNE C. THOMPSON, Professor, Department of Psychology, Pomona College

JO-ANN TSANG, Postdoctoral Fellow, Department of Psychology, Southern Methodist University

NICK TURNER, Doctoral Student, Institute of Work Psychology, The University of Sheffield

KATHLEEN D. VOHS, Postdoctoral Fellow, Department of Psychology, Case Western Reserve University

DAVID WATSON, Professor, Department of Psychology, University of Iowa

MICHAEL WEHMEYER, Courtesy Associate Professor, Special Education Department, University of Kansas

GAIL M. WILLIAMSON, Professor and Chair, Life-Span Developmental Psychology, Department of Psychology, University of Georgia

CHARLOTTE VANOYEN WITVLIET, Associate Professor, Department of Psychology, Hope College

BEATRICE A. WRIGHT, Professor Emerita, University of Kansas

AMY WRZESNIEWSKI, Assistant Professor, Department of Management and Organizational Behavior, New York University

ANTHEA ZACHARATOS, Doctoral Student, School of Business, Queen's University, Kingston, Ontario, Canada

SUSAN ZICKMUND, Assistant Professor, Department of Internal Medicine, University of Iowa College of Medicine

LISA M. PYTLIK ZILLIG, Doctoral Student, Clinical Psychology Program, Department of Psychology, University of Nebraska

I

Introductory and Historical Overview

1

Positive Psychology, Positive Prevention, and Positive Therapy

Martin E. P. Seligman

Positive Psychology

Psychology after World War II became a science largely devoted to healing. It concentrated on repairing damage using a disease model of human functioning. This almost exclusive attention to pathology neglected the idea of a fulfilled individual and a thriving community, and it neglected the possibility that building strength is the most potent weapon in the arsenal of therapy. The aim of positive psychology is to catalyze a change in psychology from a preoccupation only with repairing the worst things in life to also building the best qualities in life. To redress the previous imbalance, we must bring the building of strength to the forefront in the treatment and prevention of mental illness.

The field of positive psychology at the subjective level is about positive subjective experience: well-being and satisfaction (past); flow, joy, the sensual pleasures, and happiness (present); and constructive cognitions about the future—optimism, hope, and faith. At the individual level it is about positive personal traits—the capacity for love and vocation, courage, interpersonal skill, aesthetic sensibility, perseverance, forgiveness, originality, future-mindedness, high talent, and wisdom. At the group level it is about the civic virtues and the institutions that move individuals toward better citizenship: responsibility, nurturance, altruism, civility, moderation, tolerance, and work ethic (Gillham & Seligman, 1999; Seligman & Csikszentmihalyi, 2000).

The notion of a positive psychology movement began at a moment in time a few months after I had been elected president of the American Psychological Association. It took place in my garden while I was weeding with my 5-year-old daughter, Nikki. I have to confess that even though I write books about children, I'm really not all that good with them. I am goal-oriented and time-urgent, and when I am weeding in the garden, I am actually trying to get the weeding done. Nikki, however, was throwing weeds into the air and dancing around. I yelled at her. She walked away, came back, and said, "Daddy, I want to talk to you."

"Yes, Nikki?"

"Daddy, do you remember before my fifth birthday? From the time I was three to the time I was five, I was a whiner. I whined every day. When I turned five, I decided not to whine anymore. That was the hardest thing I've ever done. And if I can stop whining, you can stop being such a grouch."

This was for me an epiphany, nothing less. I learned something about Nikki, something about raising kids, something about myself, and a great deal about my profession. First, I realized that raising Nikki was not about correcting whining. Nikki did that herself. Rather, I realized that raising Nikki was about taking this marvelous skill—I call it "seeing into the soul"—and amplifying it, nurturing it, helping her to lead her life around it to buffer against her weaknesses and the storms of life. Raising children, I realized, is more than fixing what is wrong with them. It is about identifying and nurturing their strongest qualities, what they own and are best at, and helping them find niches in which they can best live out these positive qualities.

As for my own life, Nikki hit the nail right on the head. I was a grouch. I had spent 50 years mostly enduring wet weather in my soul, and the last 10 years being a nimbus cloud in a household of sunshine. Any good fortune I had was probably not due to my grouchiness but in spite of it. In that moment, I resolved to change.

But the broadest implication of Nikki's lesson was about the science and practice of psychology. Before World War II, psychology had three distinct missions: curing mental illness, making the lives of all people more productive and fulfilling, and identifying and nurturing high talent. Right after the war, two events—both economic—changed the face of psychology. In 1946, the Veterans Administration was founded, and thousands of psychologists found out that they could make a living treating mental illness. At that time the profession of clinical psychologist came into its own. In 1947, the National Institute of Mental Health (which was based on the American Psychiatric Association's disease model and is better described as the National Institute of Mental Illness) was founded, and academics found out that they could get grants if their research was described as being about pathology.

This arrangement brought many substantial benefits. There have been huge strides in the understanding of and therapy for mental illness: At least 14 disorders, previously intractable, have yielded their secrets to science and can now be either cured or considerably relieved (Seligman, 1994). But the downside was that the other two fundamental missions of psychology—

making the lives of all people better and nurturing genius—were all but forgotten. It was not only the subject matter that altered with funding but also the currency of the theories underpinning how we viewed ourselves. Psychology came to see itself as a mere subfield of the health professions, and it became a victimology. We saw human beings as passive foci: stimuli came on and elicited responses (what an extraordinarily passive word). External reinforcements weakened or strengthened responses, or drives, tissue needs, or instincts. Conflicts from childhood pushed each of us around.

Psychology's empirical focus then shifted to assessing and curing individual suffering. There has been an explosion in research on psychological disorders and the negative effects of environmental stressors such as parental divorce, death, and physical and sexual abuse. Practitioners went about treating mental illness within the disease-patient framework of repairing damage: damaged habits, damaged drives, damaged childhood, and damaged brains.

The message of the positive psychology movement is to remind our field that it has been deformed. Psychology is not just the study of disease, weakness, and damage; it also is the study of strength and virtue. Treatment is not just fixing what is wrong; it also is building what is right. Psychology is not just about illness or health; it also is about work, education, insight, love, growth, and play. And in this quest for what is best, positive psychology does not rely on wishful thinking, self-deception, or hand waving; instead, it tries to adapt what is best in the scientific method to the unique problems that human behavior presents in all its complexity.

Positive Prevention

What foregrounds this approach is the issue of prevention. In the last decade psychologists have become concerned with prevention, and this was the theme of the 1998 American Psychological Association meeting in San Francisco. How can we prevent problems like depression or substance abuse or schizophrenia in young people who are genetically vulnerable or who live in worlds that nurture these problems? How can we prevent murderous schoolyard violence in children who have poor parental supervision, a mean streak, and access to weapons? What we have learned over 50 years is that the disease model does not move us closer to the prevention of these serious problems. Indeed, the major strides in prevention have largely come from a perspective focused on systematically building competency, not correcting weakness.

We have discovered that there are human strengths that act as buffers against mental illness: courage, future-mindedness, optimism, interpersonal skill, faith, work ethic, hope, honesty, perseverance, the capacity for flow and insight, to name several. Much of the task of prevention in this new century will be to create a science of human strength whose mission will be to understand and learn how to foster these virtues in young people.

My own work in prevention takes this approach and amplifies a skill that all individuals possess but usually deploy in the wrong place. The skill is called disputing (Beck, Rush, Shaw, & Emery, 1979), and its use is at the heart of "learned optimism." If an external person, who is a rival for your job, accuses you falsely of failing at your job and not deserving your position, you will dispute him. You will marshal all the evidence that you do your job very well. You will grind the accusations into dust. But if you accuse yourself falsely of not deserving your job, which is just the content of the automatic thoughts of pessimists, you will not dispute it. If it issues from inside, we tend to believe it. So in "learned optimism" training programs, we teach both children and adults to recognize their own catastrophic thinking and to become skilled disputers (Peterson, 2000; Seligman, Reivich, Jaycox, & Gillham, 1995; Seligman, Schulman, DeRubeis, & Hollon, 1999).

This training works, and once you learn it, it is a skill that is self-reinforcing. We have shown that learning optimism prevents depression and anxiety in children and adults, roughly halving their incidence over the next 2 years. I mention this work only in passing, however. It is intended to illustrate the Nikki principle: that building a strength, in this case, optimism, and teaching people when to use it, rather than repairing damage, effectively prevents depression and anxiety. Similarly, I believe that if we wish to prevent drug abuse in teenagers who grow up in a neighborhood that puts them at risk, the effective prevention is not remedial. Rather, it consists of identifying and amplifying the strengths that these teens already have. A teenager who is future-minded, who is interpersonally skilled, who derives flow from sports, is not at risk for substance abuse. If we wish to prevent schizophrenia in a young person at genetic risk, I would propose that the repairing of damage is not going to work. Rather, I suggest that a young person who learns effective interpersonal skills, who has a strong work ethic, and who has learned persistence under adversity is at lessened risk for schizophrenia.

This, then, is the general stance of positive psychology toward prevention. It claims that there is a set of buffers against psychopathology: the positive human traits. The Nikki principle holds that by identifying, amplifying, and concentrating on these strengths in people at risk, we will do effective prevention. Working exclusively on personal weakness and on damaged brains, and deifying the Diagnostic and Statistical Manual (DSM), in contrast, has rendered science poorly equipped to do effective prevention. We now need to call for massive research on human strength and virtue. We need to develop a nosology of human strength— the "UNDSM-I", the opposite of *DSM-IV*. We need to measure reliably and validly these strengths. We need to do the appropriate longitudinal studies and experiments to understand how these strengths grow (or are stunted; Vaillant, 2000). We need to develop and test interventions to build these strengths.

We need to ask practitioners to recognize that much of the best work they already do in the consulting room is to amplify their clients' strengths rather than repair their weaknesses. We need to emphasize that psychologists working with families, schools, religious communities, and corporations develop climates that foster these strengths. The major psychological theories now undergird a new science of strength and resilience. No longer do the dominant theories view the individual as a passive vessel "responding" to "stimuli"; rather, individuals now are seen as decision makers, with choices, preferences, and the possibility of becoming masterful, efficacious, or, in malignant circumstances, helpless and hopeless. Science and practice that relies on the positive psychology worldview may have the direct effect of preventing many of the major emotional disorders. It also may have two side effects: making the lives of our clients physically healthier, given all we are learning about the effects of mental well-being on the body; and reorienting psychology to its two neglected missions, making normal people stronger and more productive, as well as making high human potential actual.

Positive Therapy

I am going to venture a radical proposition about why psychotherapy works as well as it does. I am going to suggest that positive psychology, albeit intuitive and inchoate, is a major effective ingredient in therapy as it is now done; if it is recognized and honed, it will become an even more effective approach to psychotherapy. But before doing so, it is necessary to say what I believe about "specific" ingredients in therapy. I believe there are some clear specifics in psychotherapy. Among them are

- Applied tension for blood and injury phobia
- Penile squeeze for premature ejaculation
- Cognitive therapy for panic
- Relaxation for phobia
- Exposure for obsessive-compulsive disorder
- Behavior therapy for enuresis

(My book *What You Can Change and What You Can't* [1994] documents the specifics and reviews the relevant literature.) But specificity of technique to disorder is far from the whole story.

There are three serious anomalies on which present specificity theories of the effectiveness of psychotherapy stub their toes. First, effectiveness studies (field studies of real-world delivery), as opposed to laboratory efficacy studies of psychotherapy, show a substantially larger benefit of psychotherapy. In the *Consumer Reports* study, for example, over 90% of respondents reported substantial benefits, as opposed to about 65% in efficacy studies of specific psychotherapies (Seligman, 1995, 1996). Second, when one active treatment is compared with another active treatment, specificity tends to disappear or becomes quite a small effect. Lester Luborsky's corpus and the National Collaborative Study of Depression are examples. The lack of robust specificity also is apparent in much of the drug literature. Methodologists argue endlessly over flaws in such outcome studies, but they cannot hatchet away the general lack of specificity. The fact is that almost no psychotherapy technique that I can think of (with the

exceptions mentioned previously) shows big, specific effects when it is compared with another form of psychotherapy or drug, adequately administered. Finally, add the seriously large "placebo" effect found in almost all studies of psychotherapy and of drugs. In the depression literature, a typical example, around 50% of patients will respond well to placebo drugs or therapies. Effective specific drugs or therapies usually add another 15% to this, and 75% of the effects of antidepressant drugs can be accounted for by their placebo nature (Kirsch & Sapirstein, 1998).

So why is psychotherapy so robustly effective? Why is there so little specificity of psychotherapy techniques or specific drugs? Why is there such a huge placebo effect?

Let me speculate on this pattern of questions. Many of the relevant ideas have been put forward under the derogatory misnomer *nonspecifics*. I am going to rename two classes of nonspecifics as *tactics* and *deep strategies*. Among the *tactics* of good therapy are

- Attention
- Authority figure
- Rapport
- Paying for services
- Trust
- Opening up
- Naming the problem
- Tricks of the trade (e.g., "Let's pause here," rather than "Let's stop here")

The *deep strategies* are not mysteries. Good therapists almost always use them, but they do not have names, they are not studied, and, locked into the disease model, we do not train our students to use them to better advantage. I believe that the deep strategies are all techniques of positive psychology and that they can be the subject of large-scale science and of the invention of new techniques that maximize them. One major strategy is instilling hope (Snyder, Ilardi, Michael, & Cheavens, 2000). But I am not going to discuss this one now, as it is often discussed elsewhere in the literature on placebo, on explanatory style and hopelessness, and on demoralization (Seligman, 1994).

Another is the "building of buffering strengths," or the Nikki principle. I believe that it is a common strategy among almost all competent psychotherapists to first identify and then help their patients build a large variety of strengths, rather than just to deliver specific damage-healing techniques. Among the strengths built in psychotherapy are

- Courage
- Interpersonal skill
- Rationality
- Insight
- Optimism
- Honesty
- Perseverance
- Realism
- Capacity for pleasure
- Putting troubles into perspective
- Future-mindedness
- Finding purpose

Assume for a moment that the buffering effects of strength-building strategies have a larger effect than the specific "healing" ingredients that have been discovered. If this is true, the relatively small specificity found when different active therapies and different drugs are compared and the massive placebo effects both follow.

One illustrative deep strategy is "narration." I believe that telling the stories of our lives, making sense of what otherwise seems chaotic, distilling and discovering a trajectory in our lives, and viewing our lives with a sense of agency rather than victimhood are all powerfully positive (Csikszentmihalyi, 1993). I believe that all competent psychotherapy forces such narration, and this buffers against mental disorder in just the same way hope does. Notice, however, that narration is not a primary subject of research on therapy process, that we do not have categories of narration, that we do not train our students to better facilitate narration, that we do not reimburse practitioners for it.

The use of positive psychology in psychotherapy exposes a fundamental blind spot in outcome research: The search for empirically validated therapies (EVTs) has in its present form handcuffed us by focusing only on validating the specific techniques that repair damage and that map uniquely into *DSM-IV* categories. The parallel emphasis in managed care organizations on delivering only brief treatments directed solely at healing damage may rob patients of the very best weapons in the arsenal of therapy—making our patients stronger human beings. That by working in the medical model and looking solely for the salves to heal the wounds, we have misplaced much of our science and much of our training. That by embracing the disease model of psychotherapy,

we have lost our birthright as psychologists, a birthright that embraces both healing what is weak and nurturing what is strong.

Conclusions

Let me end this introduction to the *Handbook of Positive Psychology* with a prediction about the science and practice of psychology in the 21st century. I believe that a psychology of positive human functioning will arise that achieves a scientific understanding and effective interventions to build thriving individuals, families, and communities.

You may think that it is pure fantasy, that psychology will never look beyond the victim, the underdog, and the remedial. But I want to suggest that the time is finally right. I well recognize that positive psychology is not a new idea. It has many distinguished ancestors (e.g., Allport, 1961; Maslow, 1971). But they somehow failed to attract a cumulative and empirical body of research to ground their ideas.

Why did they not? And why has psychology been so focused on the negative? Why has it adopted the premise—without a shred of evidence—that negative motivations are authentic and positive emotions are derivative? There are several possible explanations. Negative emotions and experiences may be more urgent and therefore override positive ones. This would make evolutionary sense. Because negative emotions often reflect immediate problems or objective dangers, they should be powerful enough to force us to stop, increase vigilance, reflect on our behavior, and change our actions if necessary. (Of course, in some dangerous situations, it will be most adaptive to respond without taking a great deal of time to reflect.) In contrast, when we are adapting well to the world, no such alarm is needed. Experiences that promote happiness often seem to pass effortlessly. So, on one level, psychology's focus on the negative may reflect differences in the survival value of negative versus positive emotions.

But perhaps we are oblivious to the survival value of positive emotions precisely because they are so important. Like the fish that is unaware of the water in which it swims, we take for granted a certain amount of hope, love, enjoyment, and trust because these are the very conditions that allow us to go on living (Myers, 2000). They are the fundamental conditions of existence, and if they are present, any amount of objective obstacles can be faced with equanimity, and even joy. Camus wrote that the foremost question of philosophy is why one should not commit suicide. One cannot answer that question just by curing depression; there must be positive reasons for living as well.

There also are historical reasons for psychology's negative focus. When cultures face military threat, shortages of goods, poverty, or instability, they may most naturally be concerned with defense and damage control. Cultures may turn their attention to creativity, virtue, and the highest qualities in life only when they are stable, prosperous, and at peace. Athens during the 5th century B.C., Florence of the 15th century, and England in the Victorian era are examples of cultures that focused on positive qualities. Athenian philosophy focused on the human virtues: What is good action and good character? What makes life most worthwhile? Democracy was born during this era. Florence chose not to become the most important military power in Europe but to invest its surplus in beauty. Victorian England affirmed honor, discipline, and duty as important human virtues.

I am not suggesting that our culture should now erect an aesthetic monument. Rather, I believe that our nation—wealthy, at peace, and stable—provides a similar world historical opportunity. We can choose to create a scientific monument—a science that takes as its primary task the understanding of what makes life worth living. Such an endeavor will move the whole of social science away from its negative bias. The prevailing social sciences tend to view the authentic forces governing human behavior as self-interest, aggressiveness, territoriality, class conflict, and the like. Such a science, even at its best, is by necessity incomplete. Even if utopianly successful, it would then have to proceed to ask how humanity can achieve what is best in life.

I predict that in this new century positive psychology will come to understand and build those factors that allow individuals, communities, and societies to flourish. Such a science will not need to start afresh. It requires for the most part just a refocusing of scientific energy. In the 50 years since psychology and psychiatry became healing disciplines, they have developed a highly useful and transferable science of mental illness. They have developed a taxonomy, as well as reliable and valid ways of measuring such fuzzy concepts as schizophrenia, anger, and depression. They have developed sophisticated methods—both experimental and longitudinal—for understanding the causal pathways that lead to such undesirable outcomes. Most important, they have developed pharmacological and psychological interventions that have moved many of the mental disorders from "untreatable" to "highly treatable" and, in a couple of cases, "curable." These same methods, and in many cases the same laboratories and the next two generations of scientists, with a slight shift of emphasis and funding, will be used to measure, understand, and build those characteristics that make life most worth living. As a side effect of studying positive human traits, science will learn how to better treat and prevent mental, as well as some physical, illnesses. As a main effect, we will learn how to build the qualities that help individuals and communities not just endure and survive but also flourish.

Acknowledgment This research was supported by grants MH19604 and MH52270 from the National Institute of Mental Health. Please send reprint requests to Dr. M. E. P Seligman, Department of Psychology, University of Pennsylvania, 3815 Walnut Street, Philadelphia, PA 19104, or e-mail (seligman@psych.upenn.edu). This chapter draws heavily on Seligman and Csikszentmihalyi (2000).

References

Allport, G. W. (1961). *Pattern and growth in personality*. New York: Holt, Rinehart, & Winston.
Beck, A., Rush, J., Shaw, B., & Emery, G. (1979). *Cognitive therapy*. New York: Guilford.
Csikszentmihalyi, M. (1993). *The evolving self*. New York: HarperCollins.
Gillham, J. E., & Seligman, M. E. P. (1999). Footsteps on the road to positive psychology. *Behaviour Research and Therapy, 37*, S163–S173.
Kirsch, I., & Sapirstein, G. (1998). Listening to Prozac but hearing placebo: A meta-analysis of antidepressant medication. *Prevention & Treatment, 1*, Article 0002a, posted June 26, 1998. http://journals.apa.org/prevention/volume1.
Maslow, A. (1971). *The farthest reaches of human nature*. New York: Viking.
Myers, D. G. (2000). The funds, friends, and faith of happy people. *American Psychologist, 55*, 56–67.

Peterson, C. (2000). The future of optimism. *American Psychologist, 55,* 44–55.

Schwartz, B. (2000). Self-determination: The tyranny of freedom. *American Psychologist, 55,* 79–88.

Seligman, M. (1991). *Learned optimism.* NY: Knopf.

Seligman, M. (1994). *What you can change and what you can't.* New York: Knopf.

Seligman, M. E. P. (1995). The effectiveness of psychotherapy: The Consumer Reports study. *American Psychologist, 50,* 965–974.

Seligman, M. E. P. (1996). Science as an ally of practice. *American Psychologist, 51,* 1072–1079.

Seligman, M., & Csikszentmihalyi, M. (2000). Positive psychology: An introduction. *American Psychologist, 55,* 5–14.

Seligman, M. E. P., Reivich, K., Jaycox, L., & Gillham, J. (1995). *The optimistic child.* New York: Houghton Mifflin.

Seligman, M. E. P., Schulman, P., DeRubeis, R. J., & Hollon, S. D. (1999). The prevention of depression and anxiety. *Prevention and Treatment, 2.* http://journals.apa.org/prevention/

Snyder, C., Ilardi, S., Michael, S., & Cheavens, J. (2000). Hope theory: Updating a common process for psychological change. In C. R. Snyder & R. E. Ingram (Eds.), *Handbook of psychological change: Psychotherapy processes and practices for the 21st century* (pp. 128–153). New York: Wiley.

Vaillant, G. (2000). The mature defenses: Antecedents of joy. *American Psychologist, 55,* 89–98.

II

Identifying Strengths

2

Stopping the "Madness"

Positive Psychology and the Deconstruction of the Illness Ideology and the *DSM*

James E. Maddux

The ancient roots of the term *clinical psychology* continue to influence our thinking about the discipline long after these roots have been forgotten. *Clinic* derives from the Greek *klinike*, or "medical practice at the sickbed," and *psychology* derives from the Greek *psyche*, meaning "soul" or "mind" (*Webster's Seventh New Collegiate Dictionary*, 1976). How little things have changed since the time of Hippocrates. Although few clinical psychologists today literally practice at the bedsides of their patients, too many of its practitioners ("clinicians") and most of the public still view clinical psychology as a kind of "medical practice" for people with "sick souls" or "sick minds." It is time to change clinical psychology's view of itself and the way it is viewed by the public. Positive psychology, as represented in this handbook, provides a long-overdue opportunity for making this change.

How Clinical Psychology Became "Pathological"

The short history of clinical psychology suggests, however, that any such change will not

come easily. The field began with the founding of the first "psychological clinic" in 1896 at the University of Pennsylvania by Lightner Witmer (Reisman, 1991). Witmer and the other early clinical psychologists worked primarily with children who had learning or school problems—not with "patients" with "mental disorders" (Reisman, 1991; Routh, 2000). Thus, they were influenced more by psychometric theory and its attendant emphasis on careful measurement than by psychoanalytic theory and its emphasis on psychopathology. Following Freud's visit to Clark University in 1909, however, psychoanalysis and its derivatives soon came to dominate not only psychiatry but also clinical psychology (Barone, Maddux, & Snyder, 1997; Korchin, 1976).

Several other factors encouraged clinical psychologists to devote their attention to psychopathology and to view people through the lens of the disease model. First, although clinical psychologists' academic training took place in universities, their practitioner training occurred primarily in psychiatric hospitals and clinics (Morrow, 1946, cited in Routh, 2000). In these settings, clinical psychologists worked primarily as psychodiagnosticians under the direction of psychiatrists trained in medicine and psycho-analysis. Second, after World War II (1946), the Veterans Administration (VA) was founded and soon joined the American Psychological Association in developing training centers and standards for clinical psychologists. Because these early centers were located in VA hospitals, the training of clinical psychologists continued to occur primarily in psychiatric settings. Third, the National Institute of Mental Health was founded in 1947, and "thousands of psychologists found out that they could make a living treating mental illness" (Seligman & Csikszentmihalyi, 2000, p. 6).

By the 1950s, therefore, clinical psychologists had come "to see themselves as part of a mere subfield of the health professions" (Seligman & Csikszentmihalyi, 2000, p. 6). By this time, the practice of clinical psychology was characterized by four basic assumptions about its scope and about the nature of psychological adjustment and maladjustment (Barone, Maddux, & Snyder, 1997). First, clinical psychology is concerned with psychopathology—deviant, abnormal, and maladaptive behavioral and emotional conditions. Second, psychopathology, clinical problems, and clinical populations differ in kind, not just in degree, from normal problems in living, nonclinical problems and nonclinical populations. Third, psychological disorders are analogous to biological or medical diseases and reside somewhere *inside* the individual. Fourth, the clinician's task is to identify (diagnose) the disorder (disease) inside the person (patient) and to prescribe an intervention (treatment) that will eliminate (cure) the internal disorder (disease).

Clinical Psychology Today: The Illness Ideology and the *DSM*

Once clinical psychology became "pathologized," there was no turning back. Albee (2000) suggests that "the uncritical acceptance of the medical model, the organic explanation of mental disorders, with psychiatric hegemony, medical concepts, and language" (p. 247), was the "fatal flaw" of the standards for clinical psychology training that were established at the 1950 Boulder Conference. He argues that this fatal flaw "has distorted and damaged the development of clinical psychology ever since" (p. 247). Indeed, things have changed little since 1950. These basic assumptions about clinical

psychology and psychological health described previously continue to serve as implicit guides to clinical psychologists' activities. In addition, the language of clinical psychology remains the language of medicine and pathology—what may be called the language of the *illness ideology*. Terms such as *symptom, disorder, pathology, illness, diagnosis, treatment, doctor, patient, clinic, clinical,* and *clinician* are all consistent with the four assumptions noted previously. These terms emphasize abnormality over normality, maladjustment over adjustment, and sickness over health. They promote the dichotomy between normal and abnormal behaviors, clinical and nonclinical problems, and clinical and nonclinical populations. They situate the locus of human adjustment and maladjustment inside the person rather than in the person's interactions with the environment or in sociocultural values and sociocultural forces such as prejudice and oppression. Finally, these terms portray the people who are seeking help as passive victims of intrapsychic and biological forces beyond their direct control who therefore should be the passive recipients of an expert's "care and cure." This illness ideology and its medicalizing and pathologizing language are inconsistent with positive psychology's view that "psychology is not just a branch of medicine concerned with illness or health; it is much larger. It is about work, education, insight, love, growth, and play" (Seligman & Csikszentmihalyi, 2000, p. 7).

This pathology-oriented and medically oriented clinical psychology has outlived its usefulness. Decades ago the field of medicine began to shift its emphasis from the treatment of illness to the prevention of illness and later from the prevention of illness to the enhancement of health (Snyder, Feldman, Taylor, Schroeder, & Adams, 2000). Health psychologists acknowledged this shift over two decades ago (e.g., Stone, Cohen, & Adler, 1979) and have been influential ever since in facilitating it. Clinical psychology needs to make a similar shift, or it will soon find itself struggling for identity and purpose, much as psychiatry has for the last two or three decades (Wilson, 1993). The way to modernize is not to move even closer to pathology-focused psychiatry but to move closer to mainstream psychology, with its focus on understanding human behavior in the broader sense, and to join the positive psychology movement to build a more positive clinical psychology. Clinical psychologists always have been "more heavily invested in intricate theories of failure than in theories of success" (Bandura, 1998, p. 3). They need to acknowledge that "much of the best work that they already do in the counseling room is to amplify strengths rather than repair the weaknesses of their clients" (Seligman & Csikszentmihalyi, 2000).

Building a more positive clinical psychology will be impossible without abandoning the language of the illness ideology and adopting a language from positive psychology that offers a new way of thinking about human behavior. In this new language, ineffective patterns of behaviors, cognitions, and emotions are problems in living, not disorders or diseases. These problems in living are located not inside individuals but in the interactions between the individual and other people, including the culture at large. People seeking assistance in enhancing the quality of their lives are clients or students, not patients. Professionals who specialize in facilitating psychological health are teachers, counselors, consultants, coaches, or even social activists, not clinicians or doctors. Strategies and techniques for enhancing the quality of lives are educational, relational, social, and political interventions, not medical treatments. Finally, the facilities to which people will go for assistance with problems in living are centers, schools, or resorts, not clinics or hospitals. Such assistance might even take place in community centers, public and private schools, churches, and people's homes rather than in specialized facilities.

Efforts to change our language and our ideology will meet with resistance. Perhaps the primary barrier to abandoning the language of the illness ideology and adopting the language of positive psychology is that the illness ideology is enshrined in the most powerful book in psychiatry and clinical psychology—the *Diagnostic and Statistical Manual of Mental Disorders*, or, more simply, the *DSM*. First published in the early 1950s (American Psychiatric Association [APA], 1952) and now in either its fourth or sixth edition (APA, 2000) (depending on whether or not one counts the revisions of the third and fourth editions as "editions"), the *DSM* provides the organizational structure for virtually every textbook and course on abnormal psychology and psychopathology for undergraduate and graduate students, as well as almost every professional book on the assessment and treatment of psychological problems. So revered is the *DSM* that in many clinical programs (including mine), students are required to memorize parts of it line by line, as if it were a book of mathematical formulae or a sacred text.

The *DSM*'s categorizing and pathologizing of human experience is the antithesis of positive psychology. Although most of the previously noted assumptions of the illness ideology are explicitly disavowed in the *DSM-IV*'s introduction (APA, 1994), practically every word thereafter is *in*consistent with this disavowal. For example, in the *DSM-IV* (APA, 1994), "mental disorder" is defined as "a clinically significant behavioral or psychological syndrome or pattern that occurs *in* an individual" (p. xxi, emphasis added), and numerous common problems in living are viewed as "mental disorders." So steeped in the illness ideology is the *DSM-IV* that affiliation, anticipation, altruism, and humor are described as "defense mechanisms" (p. 752).

As long as clinical psychology worships at this icon of the illness ideology, change toward an ideology emphasizing human strengths will be impossible. What is needed, therefore, is a kind of iconoclasm, and the icon in need of shattering is the *DSM*. This iconoclasm would be figurative, not literal. Its goal is not *DSM*'s destruction but its *deconstruction*—an examination of the social forces that serve as its power base and of the implicit intellectual assumptions that provide it with a pseudoscientific legitimacy. This deconstruction will be the first stage of a reconstruction of our view of human behavior and problems in living.

The Social Deconstruction of the *DSM*

As with all icons, powerful sociocultural, political, professional, and economic forces built the illness ideology and the *DSM* and continue to sustain them. Thus, to begin this iconoclasm, we must realize that our conceptions of psychological normality and abnormality, along with our specific diagnostic labels and categories, are not facts about people but *social constructions*—abstract concepts that were developed collaboratively by the members of society (individuals and institutions) over time and that represent a shared view of the world. As Widiger and Trull (1991) have said, the *DSM* "is not a scientific document. . . . It is a *social* document" (p. 111, emphasis added). The illness ideology and the conception of mental disorder that have guided the evolution of the *DSM* were constructed through the implicit and explicit collaborations of theorists, researchers, professionals, their clients, and the culture in which all are embedded. For this reason, "mental disorder" and the numerous diagnostic categories of the *DSM* were not "discovered" in the same manner that an archaeologist discovers a buried artifact or a medical researcher discovers a virus. Instead, they were invented. By describing mental disorders as inventions, however, I do not mean that they are "myths" (Szasz, 1974) or that the distress of people who are labeled as mentally disordered is not real. Instead, I mean that these disorders do not "exist" and "have properties" in the same manner that artifacts and viruses do. For these reasons, a taxonomy of mental disorders such as the *DSM* "does not simply describe and classify characteristics of groups of individuals, but . . . actively *constructs* a version of both normal and abnormal . . . which is then applied to individuals who end up being classified as normal or abnormal" (Parker, Georgaca, Harper, McLaughlin, & Stowell-Smith, 1995, p. 93).

The illness ideology's conception of "mental disorder" and the various specific *DSM* categories of mental disorders *are not reflections and mappings of psychological facts about people.* Instead, they are social artifacts that serve the same sociocultural goals as our constructions of race, gender, social class, and sexual orientation—that of maintaining and expanding the power of certain individuals and institutions and maintaining social order, as defined by those in power (Beall, 1993; Parker et al., 1995; Rosenblum & Travis, 1996). Like these other social constructions, our concepts of psychological normality and abnormality are tied ultimately to social values—in particular, the values of society's most powerful individuals, groups, and institutions—and the contextual rules for behavior derived from these values (Becker, 1963; Parker et al., 1995; Rosenblum & Travis, 1996). As McNamee and Gergen (1992) state: "The mental health profession is not politically, morally, or valuationally neutral. Their practices typically operate to sustain certain values, political arrangements, and hierarchies or privilege" (p. 2). Thus, the debate over the definition of "mental disorder," the struggle over who gets to define it, and the continual revisions of the *DSM* are not searches for truth. Rather, they are debates over the definition of a set of abstractions and struggles for the personal, political, and economic power that derives from the authority to define these abstractions and thus to determine what and whom society views as normal and abnormal.

Medical philosopher Lawrie Resnek (1987) has demonstrated that even our definition of physical disease "is a normative or evaluative concept" (p. 211) because to call a condition a disease "is to judge that the person with that condition is less able to lead a good or worthwhile life" (p. 211). If this is true of physical disease, it is certainly also true of psychological "disease." Because they are social constructions that serve sociocultural goals and values, our notions of psychological normality-abnormality and health-illness are linked to our assumptions about how people should live their lives and about what makes life worth living. This truth is illustrated clearly in the American Psychiatric Association's 1952 decision to include homosexuality in the first edition of the *DSM* and its 1973 decision to revoke homosexuality's disease status (Kutchins & Kirk, 1997; Shorter, 1997). As stated by psychiatrist Mitchell Wilson (1993), "The homosexuality controversy seemed to show that psychiatric diagnoses were clearly wrapped up in social constructions of deviance" (p. 404). This issue also was in the forefront of the controversies over post-traumatic stress disorder, paraphilic rapism, and masochistic personality disorder (Kutchins & Kirk, 1997), as well as caffeine dependence, sexual compulsivity, low-intensity orgasm, sibling rivalry, self-defeating personality, jet lag, pathological spending, and impaired sleep-related painful erections, all of which were proposed for inclusion in *DSM-IV* (Widiger & Trull, 1991). Others have argued convincingly that "schizophrenia" (Gilman, 1988), "addiction" (Peele, 1995), and "personality disorder" (Alarcon, Foulks, & Vakkur, 1998) also are socially constructed categories rather than disease entities.

Therefore, Widiger and Sankis (2000) missed the mark when they stated that "social and political concerns might be hindering a recognition of a more realistic and accurate estimate of the *true rate* of psychopathology" (p. 379, emphasis added). A "true rate" of psychopathology does not exist apart from the social and political concerns involved in the construction of the definition of psychopathology in general and specific psychopathologies in particular. Lopez and Guarnaccia (2000) got closer to the truth by stating that "psychopathology is as much pathology of the social world as pathology of the mind or body" (p. 578).

With each revision, the *DSM* has had more to say about how people should live their lives and about what makes life worth living. The number of pages has increased from 86 in 1952 to almost 900 in 1994, and the number of mental disorders has increased from 106 to 297. As the boundaries of "mental disorder" have expanded with each *DSM* revision, life has become increasingly pathologized, and the sheer numbers of people with diagnosable mental disorders has continued to grow. Moreover, we mental health professionals have not been content to label only obviously and blatantly dysfunctional patterns of behaving, thinking, and feeling as "mental disorders." Instead, we gradually have been pathologizing almost every conceivable human problem in living.

Consider some of the "mental disorders" found in the *DSM-IV*. Premenstrual emotional change is now premenstrual dysphoric disorder. Cigarette smokers have nicotine dependence. If you drink large quantities of coffee, you may develop caffeine intoxication or caffeine-induced sleep disorder. Being drunk is alcohol intoxication. If you have "a preoccupation with a defect in appearance" that causes "significant distress or impairment in . . . functioning" (p. 466), you have a body dysmorphic disorder. A child whose academic achievement is "substantially below that expected for age, schooling, and level of intelligence" (p. 46) has a learning disorder. Toddlers who throw tantrums have oppositional defiant disorder. Even sibling relational problems, the bane of parents everywhere, have found a place in *DSM-IV*, although not yet as an official mental disorder.

Human sexual behavior comes in such variety that determining what is "normal" and "adaptive" is a daunting task. Nonetheless, sexual behavior has been ripe for pathologization in the *DSM-IV*. Not wanting sex often enough is hypoactive sexual desire disorder. Not wanting sex at all is sexual aversion disorder. Having sex but not having orgasms or having them too late or too soon is considered an orgasmic disorder. Failure (for men) to maintain "an adequate erection . . . that causes marked distress or interpersonal difficulty" (p. 504) is a male erectile disorder. Failure (for women) to attain or maintain "an adequate lubrication or swelling response of sexual excitement" (p. 502) accom-

panied by distress is female sexual arousal disorder. Excessive masturbation used to be considered a sign of a mental disorder (Gilman, 1988). Perhaps in *DSM-V* not masturbating at all, if accompanied by "marked distress or interpersonal difficulty," will become a mental disorder ("autoerotic aversion disorder").

Most recently we have been inundated with media reports of epidemics of Internet addiction, road rage, and pathological stockmarket day trading. Discussions of these new disorders have turned up at scientific meetings and are likely to find a home in the *DSM-V* if the media and mental health professions continue to collaborate in their construction, and if treating them and writing books about them becomes lucrative.

The trend is clear. First we see a pattern of behaving, thinking, feeling, or desiring that deviates from some fictional social norm or ideal; or we identify a common complaint that, as expected, is displayed with greater frequency or severity by some people than others; or we decide that a certain behavior is undesirable, inconvenient, or disruptive. We then give the pattern a medical-sounding name, preferably of Greek or Latin origin. Eventually, the new term may be reduced to an acronym, such as OCD (obsessive-compulsive disorder), ADHD (attention-deficit/hyperactive disorder), and BDD (body dysmorphic disorder). The new disorder then takes on a life of its own and becomes a diseaselike entity. As news about "it" spreads, people begin thinking they have "it"; medical and mental health professionals begin diagnosing and treating "it"; and clinicians and clients begin demanding that health insurance policies cover the "treatment" of "it."

Over the years, my university has constructed something called a "foreign-language learning disability." Our training clinic gets five or six requests each year for evaluations of this "disorder," usually from seniors seeking an exemption from the university's foreign-language requirement. These referrals are usually prompted by a well-meaning foreign-language instructor and our center for student disability services. Of course, our psychology program has assisted in the construction of this "disorder" by the mere act of accepting these referrals and, on occasion, finding "evidence" for this so-called disorder. Alan Ross (1980) referred to this process as the *reification* of the disorder. In light of the awe with which mental health professionals view their diagnostic terms and the power that such terms exert over both professional and client, a better term for this process may be the *deification* of the disorder.

We are fast approaching the point at which everything that human beings think, feel, do, and desire that is not perfectly logical, adaptive, or efficient will be labeled a mental disorder. Not only does each new category of mental disorder trivialize the suffering of people with severe psychological difficulties, but each new category also becomes an opportunity for individuals to evade moral and legal responsibility for their behavior (Resnek, 1997). *It is time to stop the "madness."*

The Intellectual Deconstruction of the *DSM:* An Examination of Faulty Assumptions

The *DSM* and the illness ideology it represents remain powerful because they serve certain social, political, and professional interests. Yet the *DSM* also has an intellectual foundation, albeit an erroneous one, that warrants our examination. The developers of the *DSM* have made a number of assumptions about human behavior and how to understand it that do not hold up very well to logical scrutiny.

Faulty Assumption I: Categories Are Facts About the World

The basic assumption of the *DSM* is that a system of socially constructed categories is a set of facts about the world. At issue here is not the reliability of classifications in general or of the *DSM* in particular—that is, the degree to which we can define categories in a way that leads to consensus in the assignment of things to categories. Instead, the issue is the validity of such categories. As noted previously, the validity of a classification system refers not to the extent to which it provides an accurate "map" of reality but, instead, to the extent to which it serves the goals of those who developed it. For this reason, all systems of classification are arbitrary. This is not to say that all classifications are capricious or thoughtless but that, as noted earlier, *they are constructed to serve the goals of those who develop them.* Alan Watts (1951) once asked whether it is better to classify rabbits according to the characteristics of their fur or according to the characteristics of their meat. He

answered by saying that it depends on whether you are a furrier or a butcher. How you choose to classify rabbits depends on what you want to *do* with them. Neither classification system is more valid or "true" than the other. We can say the same of all classification systems. They are not "valid" (true) or "invalid" (false). Instead, they are social constructions that are only more or less useful. Thus, we can evaluate the "validity" of a system of representing reality only by evaluating its utility, and its utility can be evaluated only in reference to a set of chosen goals, which in turn are based on values. Therefore, instead of asking, "How true is this system of classification?" we have to ask, "What do we value? What goals do we want to accomplish? How well does this system help us accomplish them?" Thus, we cannot talk about "diagnostic validity *and* utility" (Nathan & Langenbucher, 1999, p. 88, emphasis added) as if they are different constructs. They are one and the same.

Most proponents of traditional classification of psychological disorders justify their efforts with the assumption that "classification is the heart of any science" (Barlow, 1991, p. 243). Categorical thinking is not the only means, however, for making sense of the world, although it is a characteristically Western means for doing so. Western thinkers always have expended considerable energy and ingenuity dividing the world into sets of separate "things," dissecting reality into discrete categories and constructing either-or and black-or-white dichotomies. Westerners seem to believe that the world is held together by the categories of human thought (Watts, 1951) and that "making sense out of life is impossible unless the flow of events can somehow be fitted into a framework of rigid forms" (Watts, 1951, pp. 43–44). Unfortunately, once we construct our categories, we see them as representing "things," and we confuse them with the real world. We come to believe that, as Gregory Kimble (1995) said, "If there is a word for it, there must be a corresponding item of reality. If there are two words, there must be two realities and they must be different" (p. 70). What we fail to realize is that, as the philosopher Alan Watts (1966) said, "However much we divide, count, sort, or classify [the world] into particular things and events, this is no more than a way of thinking about the world. It is never *actually* divided" (p. 54). Also, as a result of confusing our categories with the real world, we too often *confuse classifying with understanding, and labeling with explaining* (Ross, 1980; Watts, 1951). We forget that agreeing on the names of things does *not* mean that we understand and can explain the things named.

Faulty Assumption II: We Can Distinguish Between Normal and Abnormal

The second faulty assumption made by the developers of the *DSM* is that we can establish clear criteria for distinguishing between normal and abnormal thinking, feeling, and behaving and between healthy and unhealthy psychological functioning. Although the *DSM-IV*'s developers claim that "there is no assumption that each category of mental disorder is a completely discrete entity with absolute boundaries dividing it from other mental disorders or from no mental disorder" (APA, 1994, p. xxii), the subsequent 800 pages that are devoted to descriptions of categories undermine the credibility of this claim. This discontinuity assumption is mistaken for at least three reasons. First, it ignores the legions of essentially healthy people who seek professional help before their problems get out of hand (and who have good health insurance coverage), as well as the vast numbers of people who experience problems that are similar or identical to those experienced by those relatively few people who appear in places called clinics, yet who never seek professional help (Wills & DePaulo, 1991). As Bandura (1978) stated, "No one has ever undertaken the challenging task of studying how the tiny sample of clinic patrons differs from the huge population of troubled nonpatrons" (p. 94).

The normal-abnormal and clinical-nonclinical dichotomies are encouraged by our service delivery system. Having places called "clinics" encourages us to divide the world into clinical and nonclinical settings, to differentiate psychological problems into clinical (abnormal) problems and nonclinical (normal) problems, and to categorize people into clinical (abnormal) and nonclinical (normal) populations. Yet, just as the existence of organized religions and their churches cannot be taken as proof of the existence of God, the existence of the mental health professions and their clinics is not proof of the existence of clinical disorders and clinical populations. The presence of a person in a facility called a "clinic" is not sufficient reason for assuming that residing within that person is a psychological pathology that differs in either kind or degree from the problems experienced by most people in the courses of their lives.

Second, this discontinuity assumption runs counter to an assumption made by virtually every major personality theorist—*that adaptive and maladaptive psychological phenomena differ not in kind but in degree and that continuity exists between normal and abnormal and between adaptive and maladaptive functioning*. A fundamental assumption made in behavioral and social cognitive approaches to personality and psychopathology is that the adaptiveness or maladaptiveness of a behavior rests not in the nature of the behavior itself but in the effectiveness of that behavior in the context of the person's goals and situational norms, expectations, and demands (Barone et al., 1997). Existential theorists reject the dichotomy between mental health and mental illness, as do most of the theoreticians in the emerging constructivist psychotherapy movement (e.g., Neimeyer & Mahoney, 1994; Neimeyer & Raskin, 1999). Even the psychoanalytic approaches, the most pathologizing of all theories, assume that psychopathology is characterized not by the presence of underlying unconscious conflicts and defense mechanisms but by the degree to which such conflicts and defenses interfere with functioning in everyday life (Brenner, 1973).

Third, the normal-abnormal dichotomy runs counter to yet another basic assumption made by most contemporary theorists and researchers in personality, social, and clinical psychology—*that the processes by which maladaptive behavior is acquired and maintained are the same as those that explain the acquisition and maintenance of adaptive behavior*. No one has yet demonstrated that the psychological processes that explain the problems of people who present themselves to mental health professionals ("clinical populations") and those who do not ("nonclinical populations") differ from each other. That is to say, there are no reasons to assume that behaviors judged to be "normal" and behaviors that violate social norms and are judged to be "pathological" are governed by different processes (Leary & Maddux, 1987).

Fourth, the assumption runs counter to the growing body of empirical evidence that normality and abnormality, as well as effective and ineffective psychological functioning, lie along a continuum, and that so-called psychological disorders are simply extreme variants of normal psychological phenomena and ordinary problems in living (Keyes & Lopez, this volume).

This *dimensional approach* is concerned not with classifying people or disorders but with identifying and measuring individual differences in psychological phenomena such as emotion, mood, intelligence, and personality styles (e.g., Lubinski, 2000). Great differences among individuals on the dimensions of interest are expected, such as the differences we find on formal tests of intelligence. As with intelligence, any divisions made between normality and abnormality are socially constructed for convenience or efficiency but are not to be viewed as indicative of true discontinuity among "types" of phenomena or "types" of people. Also, statistical deviation is not viewed as necessarily pathological, although extreme variants on either end of a dimension (e.g., introversion-extraversion, neuroticism, intelligence) may be maladaptive if they signify inflexibility in functioning.

Empirical evidence for the validity of a dimensional approach to psychological adjustment is strongest in the area of personality and personality disorders. Factor analytic studies of personality problems among the general population and a population with "personality disorders" demonstrate striking similarity between the two groups. In addition, these factor structures are not consistent with the *DSM*'s system of classifying disorders of personality into categories (Maddux & Mundell, 1999). The dimensional view of personality disorders also is supported by cross-cultural research (Alarcon et al., 1998).

Research on other problems supports the dimensional view. Studies of the varieties of normal emotional experiences (e.g., Oatley & Jenkins, 1992) indicate that "clinical" emotional disorders are not discrete classes of emotional experience that are discontinuous from everyday emotional upsets and problems. Research on adult attachment patterns in relationships strongly suggests that dimensions are more useful descriptions of such patterns than are categories (Fraley & Waller, 1998). Research on self-defeating behaviors has shown that they are extremely common and are not by themselves signs of abnormality or symptoms of "disorders" (Baumeister & Scher, 1988). Research on children's reading problems indicates that "dyslexia" is not an all-or-none condition that children either have or do not have but occurs in degrees without a natural break between "dyslexic" and "nondyslexic" children (Shawitz, Escobar, Shaywitz, Fletcher, & Makuch,

1992). Research on attention deficit/hyperactivity disorder (Barkley, 1997) and post-traumatic stress disorder (Anthony, Lonigan, & Hecht, 1999) demonstrates this same dimensionality. Research on depression and schizophrenia indicates that these "disorders" are best viewed as loosely related clusters of dimensions of individual differences, not as diseaselike syndromes (Claridge, 1995; Costello, 1993a, 1993b; Persons, 1986). Finally, biological researchers continue to discover continuities between socalled normal and abnormal (or pathological) psychological conditions (Claridge, 1995; Livesley, Jang, & Vernon, 1998).

Faulty Assumption III: Categories Facilitate Clinical Judgment

To be most useful, diagnostic categories should facilitate sound clinical judgment and decision making. In many ways, however, diagnostic categories can cloud professional judgments by helping set into motion a vicious circle in which error and bias are encouraged and maintained despite the professional's good intentions.

This vicious circle begins with four beliefs that the professional brings to the initial encounter with a client: first, that there is a dichotomy between normal and abnormal psychological functioning; second, that distinct syndromes called mental disorders actually exist and have real properties; third, that the people who come to "clinics" must have a "clinical problem" and that problem must fit one of these syndromes; and fourth, that he or she is an accurate perceiver of others, an unbiased and objective gatherer and processor of information about others, and an objective decision maker.

These beliefs lead to a biased and error-prone style of interacting with, thinking about, and gathering information about the client. One of the biggest myths about clinical psychology training is that professionals with graduate educations are more accurate, less error-prone, and less biased in gathering information about and forming impressions of other people than are persons without such training. Research suggests otherwise (Garb, 1998). Especially pernicious is a bias toward confirmatory hypothesis testing in which the professional seeks information supportive of the assumption that the client has a clinically significant dysfunction or mental disorder. The use of this strategy increases the probability of error and bias in perception and judgment. Furthermore, the criteria for normality and abnormality (or health and pathology) and for specific mental disorders are so vague that they almost guarantee the commission of the errors and biases in perception and judgment that have been demonstrated by research on decision making under uncertainty (Dawes, 1998). Finally, because the *DSM* describes only categories of disordered or unhealthy functioning, it offers little encouragement to search for evidence of healthy functioning. Thus, a fundamental negative bias is likely to develop in which the professional pays close attention to evidence of pathology and ignores evidence of health (Wright & Lopez, this volume). From the standpoint of positive psychology, this is one of the greatest flaws of the *DSM* and the illness ideology for which it stands.

Next, these errors and biases lead the professional to gather information about and form impressions of the client that, although not highly accurate, are consistent with the professional's hypotheses. Accordingly, the professional gains a false sense of confidence in her social perception and judgment abilities. In turn, she comes to believe that she *knows* pathology when she sees it and that people indeed do fit the categories described by the *DSM*. Because clients readily agree with the professional's assessments and pronouncements (Snyder, Shenkel, & Lowery, 1977), the professional's confidence is bolstered by this "evidence" that she is correct. Thus, together they construct a "collaborative illusion."

Finally, because of this false feedback and subsequent false sense of accuracy and confidence, over time the professional becomes increasingly confident and yet increasingly error-prone, as suggested by research showing a positive correlation between professional experience and error and bias in perceiving and thinking about clients (e.g., Garb, 1998). Thus, the professional plunges confidently into the next clinical encounter even more likely to repeat the error-prone process.

Faulty Assumption IV: Categories Facilitate Treatment

As noted previously, the validity of classification schemes is best evaluated by considering their utility or "how successful they are at achieving their specified goals" (Follete & Houts, 1996, p. 1120). The ultimate goal of a system for organizing and understanding human behavior and its "disorders" is the development of methods for relieving suffering and, in the spirit of positive psychology, enhancing well-being. Therefore, to determine the validity of a system for classifying "mental disorders," we need to ask not "How true is it?" but "How well does it facilitate the design of effective ways to help people live more satisfying lives?" As Gergen and McNamee (2000) have stated, "The discourse of 'disease' and 'cure' is itself optional. . . . If the goal of the profession is to aid the client . . . then the door is open to the more pragmatic questions. In what senses is the client assisted and injured by the demand for classification?" (pp. 336–337). As Raskin and Lewandowski (2000) state, "If people cannot reach the objective truth about what disorder really is, then viable constructions of disorder must compete with one another on the basis of their use and meaningfulness in particular clinical situations" (p. 26).

Because effective interventions must be guided by theories and concepts, designing effective interventions requires a conceptualization of human functioning that is firmly grounded in a theory of how patterns of behavior, thought, and emotion develop and how they are maintained despite their maladaptiveness. By design, the *DSM* is purely descriptive and atheoretical. Because it is atheoretical, it does not deal with the etiology of the disorders it describes. Thus, it cannot provide theory-based conceptualizations of the development and maintenance of adjustment problems that might lead to intervention strategies. Because a system of descriptive categories includes only lists of generic problematic behaviors ("symptoms"), it may suggest somewhat vaguely *what* needs to be changed, but it cannot provide guidelines for *how* to facilitate change.

Beyond the Illness Ideology and the *DSM*

The deconstruction of the illness ideology and the *DSM* leaves us with the question, But what will replace them? The positive psychology described in the rest of this handbook offers a replacement for the illness ideology. Positive psychology emphasizes well-being, satisfaction, happiness, interpersonal skills, perseverance, talent, wisdom, and personal responsibility. It is concerned with understanding what makes life worth living, with helping people become more self-organizing and self-directed, and with recognizing that "people and experiences are embedded in a social context" (Seligman & Csikszentmihalyi, 2000, p. 8). Unlike the illness ideology, which is grounded in certain social values that implicitly and explicitly tell people how to live their lives, positive psychology "would inform individuals' choices along the course of their lives, but would take no stand on the desirability of life courses" (Seligman & Csikszentmihalyi, 2000, p. 12).

What will replace the *DSM* is more difficult to predict, although three contenders have been on the scene for some time. The *dimensional approach* noted previously is concerned with describing and measuring continua of individual differences rather than constructing categories. It assumes that people will display considerable statistical deviation in behavioral, cognitive, and emotional phenomena and does not assume that such deviation is, per se, maladaptive or pathological.

Interpersonal approaches begin with the assumption that "maladjusted behavior resides in a person's recurrent transactions with others . . . [and] results from . . . an individual's failure to attend to and correct the self-defeating, interpersonally unsuccessful aspects of his or her interpersonal acts" (Kiesler, 1991, pp. 443–444). These approaches focus not on the behavior of individuals but on the behavior of individuals interacting in a system with others (Benjamin, 1996; Kiesler, 1991). For example, *relational diagnosis* is concerned with "understanding the structure function and interactional patterns of couples and families" (Kaslow, 1996, p. v). Despite its sometimes excessive concern for developing typologies of relationship patterns, its assumption that "theoretical formulations and clinical interventions must be informed by an understanding of ethnicity, culture, religion, gender, [and] sexual preference" (Kaslow, 1996, p. v) is nonetheless a stark contrast to the *DSM*'s assumption that mental disorders exist inside the individual.

The *case formulation approach* posits that the most useful way to understand psychological and behavioral problems is not to assign people and their problems to categories but to formulate hypotheses "about the causes, precipitants, and maintaining influences of a person's psychological, interpersonal, and behavioral problems" (Eells, 1997, p. 1). Because case formulations are guided by theory, they are the antithesis of the *DSM*'s atheoretical, descriptive approach. Case formulation has been given the

most attention by behavioral and cognitive theorists, but it also has advocates from psychoanalytic, time-limited psychodynamic, interpersonal, and experiential perspectives (Eells, 1997). Despite their diversity, case formulation approaches share an avoidance of diagnostic categories and labels; a concern with understanding not what the person *is* or what the person *has* but with what the person does, thinks, and feels; and an emphasis on developing theory-guided interventions tailored to the individual's specific needs and goals.

Despite their differences, these three approaches share a rejection of the illness ideology's emphasis on pathology, its assumption that pathology resides inside of people, and its rigid system of categorization and classification. Also, because they set the stage for an examination of both adaptive and maladaptive functioning, they share a basic compatibility with the principles and goals of positive psychology.

Conclusions

The illness ideology has outlived its usefulness. It is time for a change in the way that clinical psychologists view their discipline and in the way the discipline and its subject matter are viewed by the public. The positive psychology movement offers a rare opportunity for a reorientation and reconstruction of our views of clinical psychology through a reconstruction of our views of psychological health and human adaptation and adjustment. We need a clinical psychology that is grounded not in the illness ideology but in a positive psychology ideology that rejects: (a) the categorization and pathologization of humans and human experience; (b) the assumption that so-called mental disorders exist in individuals rather than in the relationships between the individual and other individuals and the culture at large; and (c) the notion that understanding what is worst and weakest about us is more important than understanding what is best and bravest.

This change in ideology must begin with a change in the language we use to talk about human behavior and the problems that human beings experience in navigating the courses of their lives—a change from the language of the illness ideology to the language of positive psychology. Because the language of the illness ideology is enshrined in the *DSM*, this reconstruction must begin with a deconstruction of this icon of the illness ideology. As long as we revere the *DSM*, a change in the way we talk about people and problems in living will come slowly, if at all.

The illness ideology and the *DSM* were constructed to serve and continue to serve the social, political, and economic goals of those of us who shared in their construction. They are sustained not only by the individuals and institutions whose goals they serve but also by an implicit set of logically flawed and empirically unsupported assumptions about how best to understand human behavior—both the adaptive and the maladaptive. Psychologists need to become aware of both the socially constructed nature of the assumptions about psychological disorders that guide their professional activities and the logical and empirical weaknesses of these assumptions. We need to continue to question the often unquestioned sociocultural forces and philosophical assumptions that provide the foundation for the illness ideology, the *DSM*, and our "distorted and damaged" clinical psychology. Finally, we need to encourage our students, the public, and our policy makers to do the same.

References

Alarcon, R. D., Foulks, E. F., & Vakkur, M. (1998). *Personality disorders and culture: Clinical and conceptual interactions.* New York: Wiley.

Albee, G. W. (2000). The Boulder model's fatal flaw. *American Psychologist, 55,* 247–248.

American Psychiatric Association. (1952). *Diagnostic and statistical manual of mental disorders.* Washington, DC: Author.

American Psychiatric Association. (1994). *Diagnostic and statistical manual of mental disorders* (4th ed.). Washington, DC: Author.

American Psychiatric Association. (2000). *Diagnostic and statistical manual of mental disorders* (4th ed., text revision). Washington, DC: Author.

Anthony, J. L., Lonigan, C. J., & Hecht, S. A. (1999). Dimensionality of post-traumatic stress disorder symptoms in children exposed to disaster: Results from a confirmatory factor analysis. *Journal of Abnormal Psychology, 108,* 315–325.

Bandura, A. (1978). On paradigms and recycled ideologies. *Cognitive Therapy and Research, 2,* 79–103.

Bandura, A. (1998, August). *Swimming against the mainstream: Accenting the positive aspects of humanity.* Invited address presented at the annual meeting of the American Psychological Association, San Francisco, CA.

Barkley, R. A. (1997). *ADHD and the nature of self-control.* New York: Guilford.

Barlow, D. H. (1991). Introduction to the special issue on diagnosis, dimensions, and *DSM-IV:* The science of classification. *Journal of Abnormal Psychology, 100,* 243–244.

Barone, D. F., Maddux, J. E., & Snyder, C. R. (1997). *Social cognitive psychology: History and current domains.* New York: Plenum.

Baumeister, R. F., & Scher, S. J. (1988). Self-defeating behavior patterns among normal individuals: Review and analysis of common self-destructive tendencies. *Psychological Bulletin, 104,* 3–22.

Beall, A. E. (1993). A social constructionist view of gender. In A. E. Beall & R. J. Sternberg (Eds.), *The psychology of gender* (pp. 127–147). New York: Guilford.

Becker, H. S. (1963). *Outsiders.* New York: Free Press.

Benjamin, L. S. (1996). *Interpersonal diagnosis and treatment of personality disorders* (2nd ed.). New York: Guilford.

Brenner, C. (1973). *An elementary textbook of psychoanalysis.* New York: Anchor Books.

*Claridge, G. (1995). *The origins of mental illness.* Cambridge, MA: Malor Books.

Costello, C. G. (1993a). *Symptoms of depression.* New York: Wiley.

Costello, C. G. (1993b). *Symptoms of schizophrenia.* New York: Wiley.

Costello, C. G. (1996). *Personality characteristics of the personality disordered.* New York: Wiley.

Dawes, R. M. (1998). Behavioral decision making and judgment. In D. T. Gilbert, S. T. Fiske, & G. Lindzey (Eds.), *Handbook of social psychology* (Vol. 1, pp. 497–548). New York: McGraw-Hill.

*Eells, T. D. (1997). Psychotherapy case formulation: History and current status. In T. D. Eells (Ed.), *Handbook of psychotherapy case formulation* (pp. 1–25). New York: Guilford.

Follete, W. C., & Houts, A. C. (1996). Models of scientific progress and the role of theory in taxonomy development: A case study of the *DSM. Journal of Consulting and Clinical Psychology, 64,* 1120–1132.

Fraley, R. C., & Waller, N. G. (1998). Adult attachment patterns: A test of the typological model. In J. A. Simpson & W. S. Rholes (Eds.), *Attachment theory and close relationships* (pp. 77–114). New York: Guilford.

*Garb, H. N. (1998). *Studying the clinician: Judgment research and psychological assessment.*

Washington, DC: American Psychological Association.

Gergen, K. J., & McNamee, S. (2000). From disordering discourse to transformative dialogue. In R. A. Neimeyer & J. D. Raskin (Eds.), *Constructions of disorder* (pp. 333–350). Washington, DC: American Psychological Association.

Gilman, S. L. (1988). *Disease and representation.* Ithaca, NY: Cornell University Press.

Kaslow, F. W. (Ed.). (1996). *Handbook of relational diagnosis and dysfunctional family patterns.* New York: Wiley.

Kiesler, D. J. (1991). Interpersonal methods of assessment and diagnosis. In C. R. Snyder & D. R. Forsyth (Eds.), *Handbook of social and clinical psychology* (pp. 438–468). New York: Pergamon.

Kimble, G. (1995). Psychology stumbling down the road to hell. *The General Psychologist, 31,* 66–71.

Korchin, S. J. (1976). *Modern clinical psychology.* New York: Basic Books.

*Kutchins, H., & Kirk, S. A. (1997). *Making us crazy: DSM: The psychiatric bible and the creation of mental disorders.* New York: Free Press.

Leary, M. R., & Maddux, J. E. (1987). Toward a viable interface between social and clinical/counseling psychology. *American Psychologist, 42,* 904–911.

Livesley, W. J., Jang, K. L., & Vernon, P. A. (1998). Phenotypic and genotypic structure of traits delineating personality disorder. *Archives of General Psychiatry, 55,* 941–948.

Lopez, S. R., & Guarnaccia, P. J. J. (2000). Cultural psychopathology: Uncovering the social world of mental illness. *Annual Review of Psychology, 51,* 571–598.

Lubinski, D. (2000). Scientific and social significance of assessing individual differences: "Sinking shafts at a few critical points." *Annual Review of Psychology, 51,* 405–444.

*Maddux, J. E., & Mundell, C. E. (1999). Disorders of personality: Diseases or individual differences? In V. J. Derlega, B. A. Winstead, & W. H. Jones (Eds.), *Personality: Contemporary theory and research* (pp. 541–571). Chicago: Nelson-Hall.

McNamee, S., & Gergen, K. J. (1992). *Therapy as social construction.* Thousand Oaks, CA: Sage.

Morrow, W. R. (1946). The development of psychological internship training. *Journal of Consulting Psychology, 10,* 165–183.

Nathan, P. E., & Langenbucher, J. W. (1999). Psychopathology: Description and classification. *Annual Review of Psychology, 50,* 79–107.

Neimeyer, R. A., & Mahoney, M. J. (Eds.). (1994).

Constructivism in psychotherapy. Washington, DC: American Psychological Association.

Neimeyer, R. A., & Raskin, J. D. (1999). *Constructions of disorder: Meaning-making frameworks for psychotherapy.* Washington, DC: American Psychological Association.

Oatley, K., & Jenkins, J. M. (1992). Human emotion: Function and dysfunction. *Annual Review of Psychology, 43,* 55–86.

*Parker, I., Georgaca, E., Harper, D., McLaughlin, T., & Stowell-Smith, M. (1995). *Deconstructing psychopathology.* London: Sage.

Peele, S. (1995). *Diseasing of America.* San Francisco: Lexington Books.

Persons, J. (1986). The advantages of studying psychological phenomena rather than psychiatric diagnosis. *American Psychologist, 41,* 1252–1260.

Raskin, J. D., & Lewandowski, A. M. (2000). The construction of disorder as human enterprise. In R. A. Neimeyer & J. D. Raskin (Eds.), *Constructions of disorder: Meaning making frameworks for psychotherapy* (pp. 15–40). Washington, DC: American Psychological Association.

Reisman, J. M. (1991). *A history of clinical psychology.* New York: Hemisphere.

Resnek, L. (1987). *The nature of disease.* New York: Routledge and Kegan Paul.

Resnek, L. (1997). *Evil or ill? Justifying the insanity defense.* London: Routledge.

*Rosenblum, K. E., & Travis, T. C. (Eds.). (1996). *The meaning of difference: American constructions of race, sex and gender, social class, and sexual orientation.* New York: McGraw-Hill.

Ross, A. O. (1980). *Psychological disorders of children: A behavioral approach to theory, research, and therapy* (2nd ed.). New York: McGraw-Hill.

Routh, D. K. (2000): Clinical psychology training: A history of ideas and practices prior to 1946. *American Psychologist, 55,* 236–240.

Seligman, M. E. P., & Csikszentmihalyi, M. (2000). Positive psychology: An introduction. *American Psychologist, 55,* 5–14.

Shaywitz, S. E., Escobar, M. D., Shaywitz, B. A., Fletcher, J. M., & Makuch, R. (1992). Evidence that dyslexia may represent the lower tail of normal distribution of reading ability. *New England Journal of Medicine, 326,* 145–150.

Shorter, E. (1997). *A history of psychiatry.* New York: Wiley.

Snyder, C. R., Feldman, D. B., Taylor, J. D., Schroeder, L. L., & Adams, V. (2000). The roles of hopeful thinking in preventing problems and enhancing strengths. *Applied & Preventive Psychology: Current Scientific Perspectives, 15,* 262–295.

Snyder, C. R., Shenkel, R. J., & Lowery, C. (1977). Acceptance of personality interpretations: The "Barnum effect" and beyond. *Journal of Consulting and Clinical Psychology, 45,* 104–114.

Stone, G. C., Cohen, F., & Adler, N. E. (Eds.). (1979). *Health psychology: A handbook.* San Francisco: Jossey-Bass.

Szasz, T. J. (1974). *The myth of mental illness.* New York: Harper and Row.

Watts, A. (1951). *The wisdom of insecurity.* New York: Vintage.

Watts, A. (1966). *The book: On the taboo against knowing who you are.* New York: Vintage.

Widiger, T. A., & Sankis, L. M. (2000). Adult psychopathology: Issues and controversies. *Annual Review of Psychology, 51,* 377–404.

Widiger, T. A., & Trull, T. J. (1991). Diagnosis and clinical assessment. *Annual Review of Psychology, 42,* 109–134.

Wills, T. A., & DePaulo, B. M. (1991). Interpersonal analysis of the help-seeking process. In C. R. Snyder & D. R. Forsyth (Eds.), *Handbook of social and clinical psychology* (pp. 350–375). New York: Pergamon.

*Wilson, M. (1993). *DSM-III* and the transformation of American psychiatry: A history. *American Journal of Psychiatry, 150,* 399–410.

3

Widening the Diagnostic Focus

A Case for Including Human Strengths and Environmental Resources

Beatrice A. Wright & Shane J. Lopez

In positive psychology we must challenge a common error of professional psychology today: making diagnostic, treatment, and policy decisions primarily on deficiencies of the person instead of giving serious consideration to *deficits* and *strengths* of both person and environment. This mission may seem disheartening in that it requires greater rather than less cognitive complexity. Yet this multifaceted focus is crucial if two system concepts—whole person and behavior as a function of person in interaction with environment—are to be taken seriously (Lewin, 1935). Practice and research that falls short of attending to this person-environment interaction does a disservice to remedial possibilities and personal integrity. We have divided this chapter into two parts. In the first part, we present enlightening concepts together with supporting research. In the second part, we apply the insights gained to professional practice and research and make specific recommendations regarding each of the issues raised.

Enlightening Concepts

Labeling, Distinctiveness, and Deindividuation

The problem of labeling always will be a problem. This assertion embraces two quite different meanings of the word *problem*. In the first instance, the problem refers to perplexing questions proposed for investigation and academic discussion. In the second instance, the reference is to problems that add to disadvantagement caused by negative labeling.

Labeling literature and the body of related research are vast. They range over work on impression formation (interpersonal perception), prejudice (attitudes), discrimination (behavior), deviancy (social edicts), ethnocentrism (in-group vs. out-group), semantics and semiotics (meaning of speech and symbols), labels (identity, diagnosis), and stereotypes (beliefs). Even research on categorizing objects (object perception) is relevant.

To label is to give a name to things grouped together according to a shared characteristic(s). Because labels stand for something, they are abstractions. They organize and simplify the world and seemingly make it more understandable. For labeling purposes, differences among members of the labeled group are secondary, if not unimportant, so long as they do not violate the rules of inclusion. Thus, the label "American" or the label "fruit" encompasses an enormous diversity within each of these categories.

Grouping and labeling also require differentiating an out-group. "American" and "fruit" are communicable labels because there are other people and edibles that are excluded from these classifications. It can be expected, therefore, that labeling groups leads to a muting of perceived within-group differences and a highlighting of perceived between-group differences. Such muting and highlighting of differences have received considerable support in a variety of laboratory studies. Two experiments are described here; one involves objects and the other, people. They were selected to underscore the fact that the process of grouping (labeling, categorizing) involves basic dynamic properties regardless of whether the grouping is of people or objects.

In the first experiment by Tajfel and Wilkes (1963), research participants were shown a series of eight lines whose lengths differed from each other by a constant ratio. In one condition, the letter A appeared above each of the four shorter lines, and the letter B appeared above each of the four longer lines. In other conditions, the four As and the four Bs either were attached to the lines indiscriminately or did not appear. The participants estimated the length of the lines in random order, and they reported that lines belonging to the two systematically labeled classes A and B were farther apart in length than in the unclassified or haphazardly classified conditions. Moreover, with the repeated experience of estimating the lines in successive trials, participants increased the judged similarity of stimuli belonging to the same systematically labeled class, as compared with the other two conditions. In short, the participants overestimated differences in adjacent lines across categories A and B and underestimated differences in length within the categories.

The second experiment by Doise, Deschamps, and Meyer (1978) concerns social perception. The research participants were asked to describe photographs of children using a list of trait adjectives. There were two conditions. In one condition, the participants were presented with six photographs at one time, grouped according to sex (three boys, three girls), and described each photograph. In the second condition, the research participants were initially presented with only three same-sex photographs (boys or girls) to describe. Following that, they were shown the three photographs of the other sex to describe. Thus, these participants did not know in advance that they would rate photographs of both sexes, whereas the participants in the first condition realized this from the beginning. The researchers reported that those participants who had the two sexes in mind at the outset tended to perceive smaller intrasex differences and larger intersex differences than those participants who did not anticipate rating the photographs of the other sex.

Based on these two experiments, we can conclude that the perception of within-group differences was diminished, whereas between-group differences were exaggerated. Another way to put this is that group members are perceived as more similar to each other and more dissimilar to out-group members than when they remain as unclassified objects or individuals.

A different type of evidence for within-group deindividuation (attenuation of differences) emerges when "the stream of behavior" of group members is divided into meaningful units. Wilder (1984) took advantage of the idea that behavior, rather than being perceived as a continuous stream, is "chunked" in order to impart meaning (Barker, 1963; Barker & Wright, 1955). He reasoned that behavior would be divided into larger chunks when the person is viewed as a member of a group rather than as an individual. In the experiment, research participants were asked to divide the videotaped behaviors of one of four people into meaningful action units. In the group condition, the four people were identified as a group, whereas in the nongroup condition they were described as having come together by chance. The results showed that research participants chunked the behavior of group members into fewer meaningful units than when the people were seen as aggregates of individuals. Our inference is that the behavior of an individual who is perceived as a member of a group is less informative.

Deindividuation has yet other consequences. Experimenters have shown that the beliefs as well as the behavior of people perceived as members of a group tend to be seen as more similar than in the case of people viewed as individuals (Wilder, 1978). Also, more information that is consistent than inconsistent with the group label will tend to be remembered. In one study, for example, more "librarian-like" behavior was recalled about the person when she was presented as a librarian instead of a waitress (Cohen, 1981). For further research on the implications of the categorization process, the reviews by Tajfel (1978) and by Wilder (1986) are recommended.

What needs to be emphasized is that human perception is coerced by the mere act of grouping things together. Within-group attenuation and between-group accentuation of differences are a product of categorization and may well be a general law that operates in the case of classification of both objects and people. Moreover, inasmuch as labeling identifies group membership, the mere act of labeling leads to both deindividuation of group members and accentuation of differences with outgroups. Such influence poses an enormous challenge to psychology, whether with respect to clinical practice or research. Fundamental questions surface: Does deindividuation have negative consequences? When, what are they, and for whom? What are the costs of emphasizing distinctiveness between groups? If differences are accentuated, what happens to the similarities between groups? And where is the environment in all this? The challenge to psychology will be explored further and partial solutions formulated in the second part of this chapter.

Labeling and the Fundamental Negative Bias

The discussion thus far has dealt with the effects of perceiving something as a member of a group (category, class of things) regardless of whether the affixed label is neutral or evokes a value-laden train of thought. But labels that identify group memberships of people (or of objects, for that matter) are usually not neutral but instead signal positive or negative evaluations. These value differentials, as compared with "neutral" categories, have been shown to enhance still further the perceived similarities within categories and the perceived differences between categories (Tajfel, 1978, p. 62). Accordingly, the problem of within-group deindividuation is compounded.

Basic Proposition

The fundamental negative bias involves basic propositions regarding the concepts of saliency, value, and context (Wright, 1988): If something stands out sufficiently (saliency); and if, for whatever reason, it is regarded as negative (value); and if its context is vague or sparse (context), then the negative value of the object of observation will be a major factor in guiding perception, thinking, and feeling to fit its negative character. This proposition has a parallel in the positive side of bias; namely, where something is perceived as salient, positive, and in a sparse context, then positivity will be a major factor in guiding subsequent cognitive-affective events. Because the fundamental negative bias contributes so insidiously to prejudice and disadvantagement, the focus is on this bias in the following discussion.

That the affective value of something, in the absence of counteracting contextual factors, can become a potent force in influencing what a person thinks and feels about it can be understood in terms of the concept of similarity as a unit-forming factor (Heider, 1958; Wertheimer, 1923). Similarity between entities, be they external objects or intrapsychic events, is a powerful factor in perceiving them as a unit, that is, as belonging together. An especially salient type of similarity among entities is their affective quality. Things that are positive are alike in engendering a force toward them; negative things, a force away from them. Combining positive and negative qualities subjects the person to forces in opposing directions.

Experiments on Context

External Context Context refers to the set of conditions within which something is perceived and that influences that thing's meaning. The context can refer to conditions external to the perceiver or to intrapsychic predispositions of various sorts. A few experiments bearing on the significance of external context with regard to the fundamental negative bias are presented in the following.

In an important yet simple experiment, reactions to the label "blindness" as compared with "blind people," and "physical handicap" as compared with "physically handicapped people" were examined (Whiteman & Lukoff, 1965). That the condition itself was evaluated far more negatively than were people with the condition is not surprising. Still, the question remains as to how to account for the difference. The explanation can be found in the fundamental negative bias. Blindness, the salient condition, generally is valued negatively. When no context existed to alter its meaning, its negativity guided the reaction accordingly. When, however, the positive concept "person" was added, a context was provided that moderated the dominant position of the negative condition. It was the context that in effect changed the concept to be rated. And that is just the point. Contexts bring about diverse structures of meaning. Also noteworthy here is the classic work of Asch (1952), where he clearly demonstrated the importance of context in perception of people.

The context can be positive or negative. In the previous example, the concept of "person" provided a positive context and therefore constrained the negative spread. Researchers also have shown that, as the positive character of the context becomes even more salient, attitudes become more favorable. This was demonstrated, for example, in an experiment in which attitudes toward a person who was labeled with a particular problem (e.g., former mental patient, amputee) became more positive when that person was described as functioning adequately than when the negatively labeled person stood alone (Jaffe, 1966).

If a positive context can constrain negative evaluation, we might surmise that a negative context could increase the negativity of the object of observation, augmenting the fundamental negative bias in controlling attitudes. Thus, in one experiment, attitudes toward a person described as physically disabled and as having undesirable personality traits tended to be more negative than those toward a comparably described, able-bodied person (Leek, 1966). Such intensified reactions also have been demonstrated with respect to race (Dienstbier, 1970) and people with mental disorders (Gergen & Jones, 1963).

Besides affecting the *processing* of information presented about a person, the fundamental negative bias also influences information *sought* about a person. This was demonstrated in a study specifically designed to explore implications of the fundamental negative bias (Pierce, 1987). The research participants, simulating the role of a counselor, were asked what they would like to know about a client. The client, Joan, was identified either as just having been released from a psychiatric ward (salient negative) or as just having graduated from college (salient positive). In both cases, she was described further as seeking help because she was "feeling somewhat anxious and uncertain about her future, including her job and other issues in her life." The research participants selected 24 items of information they would like to know about Joan the client, from a list of 68 items, half of which referred to something positive (e.g., "Is Joan intelligent?") and half to something negative (e.g., "Is Joan cruel?"). Significantly more negative items were selected in the case of the former psychiatric patient than the college graduate, apparently reflecting the belief that the negative information would be more relevant. Although there may be some basis in fact for this belief, the differential preference for negatives in the two cases poses a particular challenge for those who believe in the importance of calling special attention to positive personal traits. Bear in mind that the only revealed difference between the clients was identification as former psychiatric patient versus college graduate. Parenthetically, the subjects also rated Joan, as they believed the helping agency would, less positively in the former case.

The meaning of *external context* should be clarified. External context is not limited to a network of externally presented personal attributes but includes the external situation as well. The fact that the meaning of observations can be altered by the situation in which person perception takes place is well known. In the previous study (Pierce, 1987), two simulated situations were compared. One was that of a counseling center that "seeks out the strengths and assets of people"; the other was a psychological clinic that "deals with the emotional and behavioral problems of people." When the client was identified as attending a psychological clinic, whether as a former mental patient or as a college student, the research participants checked significantly more negative-information items that would be sought by the agency, and the client was evaluated less positively than when she was identified as attending a counseling center. In this experiment, the orienting function of the helping agency (the external situational context) played an important role in determining the affective course that cognition would take.

Intrapsychic Context   In addition to conditions externally imposed, factors internal to the person also can provide the main context for influencing perception. A variety of personal dispositions, such as personality traits and values, are potentially important in this regard. With respect to the fundamental negative bias, it is known that people who are more ethnocentric are more likely to view minority group members negatively than people who are less ethnocentric (English, 1971a, 1971b). This personality trait could provide the kind of internal context that maximizes the saliency of any negative attribute presented by the external stimulus conditions of an out-group; it could even have the power to lead the perceiver to ignore positive attributes. The same line of reasoning holds for values. It seems plausible that a strong value placed on human dignity, for example, would have the potential to exert a significant influence in organizing perception in a way that forestalls the fundamental negative bias.

Motivation should be mentioned as still another potentially important internal factor that can affect the potency of the fundamental negative bias. For example, the evaluator might benefit in some way by devaluating another, as when there is a need to feel superior. Such a motive could easily reinforce the fundamental negative bias, even to the extent of discrediting what would ordinarily be regarded as positive aspects of the other person. The converse also is true. Thus, humanistic and religious concerns could be a motivating force that creates a positive context of beliefs and principles in which to view people. These are a few examples of personal dispositions that conceivably support or compete with the power of the fundamental negative bias.

Insider Versus Outsider Perspectives

The contrasting viewpoints of the *insider* and *outsider* corral a different set of context conditions in terms of which judgments are made (Dembo, 1964, 1970). The insider (also referred to as the "actor") is the person experiencing his or her own behavior, feelings, or problems. The outsider is the person observing or evaluating someone else. Both clinicians and researchers are outsiders with respect to the views and feelings of the clients and participants they are studying. Several types of investigations involving insider-outsider perspectives are described subsequently.

Research on the *mine-thine problem* is especially revealing because the research participant is placed in the position of both insider and outside observer as he or she engages the assigned task (Wright, 1983). A simple way to conduct the experiment is to ask participants to list the initials of five people they know well in one column and beside each initial to indicate that person's worst handicap (limitation, shortcoming, disability, or problem). Then, next to each of the five handicaps they are asked to write what they regard as their own worst handicap. They are then asked to circle the one from each pair they would choose for themselves if they had a choice. Next, they are asked to write two numbers on a slip of paper to indicate the number of times their own and the others' worst handicaps were chosen, the sum of the two normally being five. These slips are then collected so that the number frequencies can be displayed and discussed.

The results are dramatic and consistent. The number of times one's own handicap or problem is reclaimed clearly exceeds the frequency of choosing the others'. Among the five choices, it is common for subjects to select their own handicap five, four, or three times—rarely less frequently.

The difference between what is taken into account by the insider and outsider becomes appreciated in a personally direct way in the group's attempt to explain the results. Explanations include the following: They are used to their own handicap (familiarity); they have learned how to deal with it (coping); it is a part of the self and one's history (self-identity). Keep in mind that the subject is an insider when considering his or her own handicap and an outsider when regarding the other person's. Consequently, the other person's handicap more or less stands alone as a labeled negative condition and is therefore perceptually more insulated from context factors that could check the spread of its negative affect.

Other investigators have shown that patients (the insiders) tend to have a more positive outlook than do others viewing their situation (Hamera & Shontz, 1978; Mason & Muhlenkamp, 1976). Still other researchers have shown that mental hospital patients, mothers on welfare, and clients at a rehabilitation center (i.e., the insiders) tend to rate themselves as above average in how fortunate they are, whereas people viewing their situation from the outside judge them to be below average (Wright & Howe, 1969). This phenomenon, known as the "fortune phenomenon," was first noted by Dembo, Leviton, and Wright (1956/1975).

Based on our knowledge of research bearing on the perspectives of insiders and outsiders, not only does the meaning of the experience or label appear to differ, but so, too, are insiders generally more inclined than outsiders to take into account positives in their troubling situations. It seems clear that the context in which the judgments are made differs greatly in the two cases. Insiders place the significance of the problem in a life context so that the span of realities connected with it is wide. Only some aspects are negative; others are clearly positive (e.g., coping, identity), and it is this broad context that restrains the spread of negative effects. On the other hand, to outsiders the other person's problem more or less tends to stand alone, especially when it is represented by a label. In this case, the context is sparse or simplified, and the negativity of the problem dominates the train of thought.

Relative Potency of Positives Versus Negatives

The problem of context raises the question of the relative potency of positive and negative attributes. There is strong and accumulating evidence that under many conditions people tend to weigh negative aspects more heavily than positive aspects (Kanouse & Hanson, 1971). The following experiment is illustrative (Feldman, 1966). Research participants rated each of 25 statements containing a different adjective to describe the person, given the context "He is a (e.g., wise) man." A 9-point rating scale was used, ranging from good to bad. The participants also rated the statement when it included both a positive and a negative adjective (e.g., wise and corrupt). The potency of each adjective was determined by comparing the ratings of the statement when the adjective was used alone and when it appeared as a pair. The results were clear. The most powerful trait adjectives were negative. That is, overall ratings of people described by both a positive and a negative label were more negative than would be predicted by simply averaging the scale values assigned to each used singly.

From the study previously described on the fundamental negative bias (Pierce, 1987), we also can glean evidence concerning the potency value of negatives. Recall that in that study, subjects sought information about a client from the perspective of a counseling center that focused on strengths and assets, or a psychological clinic that focused on emotional and behavior problems. At the end of the experiment, the subjects were asked to write an essay expressing their views as to whether the kind of information sought about the client would have been different had the client gone to the alternate agency for help (the psychological clinic in the case of the client at the counseling center, and vice versa). Whereas none of the subjects spontaneously indicated that the problem-oriented psychological clinic would have been less adequate than the counseling center to meet the client's needs, some subjects questioned whether a strength-focused agency could help the client resolve her problems even though she might feel better about herself for a short while.

Several explanations of the greater potency (weight) given to negatives than positives have been proposed. First, negative information may become more salient because it arouses vigilance. Also, negative experiences do not "let go" of the person; the person ruminates about them, thereby increasing their presence and potency. Moreover, the norms of society are positive. Any negative deviation stands out and is given added weight because of its normative violation. Another explanation for the disproportionate weight given to negative attributes is that they are more likely to reduce or cancel the value of positive attributes than vice versa. Finally, Kogan and Wallach (1967) have suggested that the special saliency of negatives may have a physiological basis insofar as evidence exists for the relative independence of reward and punishment systems in the brain. These separate systems may have evolved in the Darwinian sense, producing approach and avoidance tendencies of unequal strength.

The greater potency of negatives, however, should not be taken to mean that negatives facilitate a broader, more flexible, or more integrated organization of cognitive material. On the contrary, it appears that positive affect is superior in this regard. For example, in a variety of studies it has been shown that both positive affect and positive material cue a wider range of associations than negative material (Isen, 1987). This point is especially relevant when considering action to change matters for the better, as in the case of treatment settings. A further point needs to be emphasized, namely, that the added potency of negatives places a heavy demand on context factors in holding the fundamental negative bias in check.

Labeling and Neglect of Environmental Considerations

Thus far, we have dealt with the general effects of grouping people and objects by some labeling device and the effects when the label connotes something negative. As we have seen, within-group deindividuation and between-group accentuation of differences tend to occur. Additionally, when a label is both negative and salient within a sparse context, it tends to invite more negative associations than when the context is expanded to include positive aspects. The insider versus outsider perspective is important in this regard. Furthermore, the negative preoccupation is exacerbated by the added weight ordinarily given to negatives. The point was stressed that the negative preoccupation can be checked by embedding the label in a cognitive-affective context (external/intrapsychic) that alters the significance of the label. We now turn our attention to the obscurity of the environment in the labeling process.

Person and Environment as Figure and Ground

We begin by noting that people frequently are labeled (grouped) solely by personal attributes: race, gender, age, intellectual level, physical condition, emotional status, and so forth. These attributes describe the person, not the environment. Even in cases where the label alludes to a particular environment, the label is generally interpreted as providing information about the person. Thus, such labels as mental hospital patients, rehabilitation clients, librarians, prisoners, and third graders essentially define the kind of person one is referring to, not the kind of environment. The label directs attention to patients, not hospitals; prisoners, not prisons; librarians, not libraries. At best, the environment remains as a vague background against which the person is featured.

The prominence of the person as figure and the vagueness of the environment are further supported by the nature of environments and people. People are active, moving in space, commanding attention by their behavior. Environments are less visible when perceiving persons and therefore less apprehendable. The environment provides the medium that allows the person to act, just as sound waves are the medium that allows the person to hear (Heider, 1926). In both cases, the sound heard and the person behaving are more easily apprehended than the mediating conditions. Unless the environment stands out because it is the object of study (in ecology, for example), or because of some commanding event, as when an earthquake strikes (physical environment) or a child is sexually abused (social environment), the environment overwhelmingly remains hidden in our thinking about and evaluating a person.

An additional factor contributing to the saliency of the person and the eclipse of the environment is that the person and his or her behavior are tied together by proximity; that is, the person is present whenever the behavior occurs. Proximity, like similarity, has long been recognized as a unit-forming factor. Thus, closeness in time and space between person and behavior creates a strong force toward accounting for the person's behavior in terms of properties of the person to the neglect of the environment. Even the expression "the person's behavior" uses the possessive case to tie the behavior to the person and not to the environment. Moreover, as the person moves from place to place, the constancy is the person, not the environment.

Causal Attribution

Major consequences for seeking and understanding the causes of behavior follow from the figure-ground relationship between person and environment. Despite the fact that most people would agree that both physical and social environments affect behavior, the role of the environment is easily neglected because of its obscurity. The aforementioned study of information sought about a client bears on this point (Pierce, 1987). When the research participants were asked to indicate which of the initial pool of about 100 information items were irrelevant to the problems presented, a much larger percentage of environmental than person-attribute items were so judged (77% vs. 17%), with this occurring in spite of the fact that the contents of these items were not trivial. They touched on crime, pollution, standard of living, and education—environmental areas that clearly could be considered significant.

Additional factors affecting the relative saliency of person and environment in causal attribution are discussed subsequently. In order, they are insider versus outsider perspectives, covariation, just world phenomenon, focal task, and values and motivation.

Insider Versus Outsider Perspectives The difference in the two perspectives was introduced in connection with the fundamental negative bias, where it was shown that the insider is relatively more inclined than the outsider to take positives in a troubling situation into account. Now let us examine how the two perspectives influence the saliency of person versus environment and therefore causal attribution.

The overall conclusion, based on several lines of investigation, is that the insider is more apt than the outsider to attribute his or her own behavior to properties of the environment, whereas the outside observer more frequently sees the other person's traits as the source of the behavior (Goldberg, 1978). This general result is nicely shown in an experiment in which the research participants were asked to describe five people, including themselves, by selecting from each of 20 pairs of trait opposites (e.g., energetic vs. relaxed) the trait that most nearly applied to the person, or by checking the alternative option, "depends on the situation" (Nisbett, Caputo, Legant, & Maracek, 1973). The participants more frequently checked "depends on the situation" when describing themselves (the insider) than when they were in the position of observers describing someone else (e.g., best friend, peer acquaintance).

In a second study, it was demonstrated that the weight given to person and environment depends on the focus of attention of the insider and outsider (Storms, 1973). In this experiment, the focus of the insider's attention was shifted to approximate the visual focus of an observer. There were two parts to this experiment. The first part was a live situation in which two participants conversed with each other. This session was videotaped, with separate cameras focused on each of the conversants. In the second part, each member of the dyad watched the videotape that had been focused on himself or herself, thereby assuming the visual vantage point of an outsider observer.

In both the live and video situations, the participants indicated the degree to which they felt their own behavior (how friendly, talkative, nervous, and domineering they were) was affected (a) by their own personality and (b) by the nature of the situation (e.g., other person's behavior). In the live situation, the subjects as insiders attributed their behavior significantly more frequently to the environment than in the videotape situation, where their visual attention approximated that of an observer. It also should be pointed out that in this experiment, as well as the preceding one in which five persons were rated, the research participants attributed their own behavior to personal traits more frequently than to the situation whether they were in the position of insiders or outside observers. This is because behavior still remains "attached to the person" even when the person is the insider, although in this position the person is more sensitive to the environment than when in the position of an outsider.

In a third study, the insider and outsider roles were simulated (Snyder, Shenkel, & Schmidt, 1976). Research participants assumed the role of counselor (outsider) or client (insider) as they listened to a taped therapy interview ostensibly of a client who either was seen for the first time or was chronic (in counseling five different times). In the interview, the client asserted that her situation caused her problems. Once again, the problems of the client were seen as significantly more personality based when the ratings were made from the point of view of the counselor than of the client, a difference that held in the case of both the first-time and the chronic client.

Covariation The perception of "what varies with what" is a powerful factor in the determination of causes (Kelley, 1973). That is, where behavior is seen to vary with the person, explanation is sought in terms of personal attributes. Where behavior is seen to vary with the situation, characteristics of the situation are held accountable. It is now proposed that because of the saliency of the person in understanding a person's behavior, the attributes of the person initially become the arena for the explanatory search (Wright, 1983). Only when this probe proves unrewarding is the search expanded to include the environment.

As an illustration, consider the difference in attribution outcome when the behavior under scrutiny is atypical or typical. In his classic work, Heider (1958) pointed out, "If we know that only one person succeeded or only one person failed out of a large number in a certain endeavor, then we shall ascribe success or failure to this person—to his great ability or to his lack of ability. On the other hand, if we know that practically everyone who tries, succeeds, we shall attribute the success to the task" (p. 89). We then say that the task was easy or, in the case of general failure, that the task was hard.

The inferential process in the two cases can be described as follows. The judgment that a particular behavior is typical or deviant requires comparing the behavior of people at the start, simply because behavior is "tied to" people. At this stage, the environment does not enter. If an adequate explanation of the behavior can be found in person characteristics, person attribution takes place. In the interest of parsimony, the explanatory process then stops because there is no felt need to seek further explanation by examining the environment. It is only when cogent personal characteristics do not readily surface that the need to explain shifts attention to the environment, thus ushering in an additional stage in the inferential process.

It is further proposed that in the case of *atypical behavior*, personal characteristics more readily emerge than in the case of *typical behavior*. It is relatively easy to account for a child's inattentiveness, for example, in terms of presumed hyperactivity, mental retardation, or some other characteristic of the child when most children are able to attend to the task. With such closure in the attribution search, there is no need to pursue the matter further by inquiring about possible contributing situational factors, such as class size or home difficulties. There is even no felt need to ask whether the child is inattentive in other situations, such as on the playground. In short, the atypical behavior is seen to covary with the person, not with the situation. Snyder (1977) has shown that a person-based attribution of behavior correlates significantly and positively with the perceived degree of the person's maladjustment.

In the case of typical behavior, however, the course of events often takes a different turn. Consider the case where almost all members of a classroom are inattentive. It is not ordinarily concluded that the class is hyperactive or mentally retarded or delinquent. An observer would tend to reserve such judgment for special classes of labeled children. Instead, the teacher's skill in keeping order might be questioned or the overcrowded classroom noted. These probes enlarge the causal network to include the situation. Thus, when the search for personal traits is not

adequate to the task of accounting for common behavior, the perceiver moves to the next possible explanatory source—namely, the situation.

Apparently, once attention is directed to the situation, other situations are drawn into the comparative process. If an observer holds overcrowding accountable for the inattentiveness, it is because the inattentiveness is felt to contrast with behavior in less crowded classes. Similarly, behavior typical at a tennis match is ascribed to the nature of the situation, only because the behavior is understood to change with the situation. The side-to-side head turning occurs when the ball is volleyed from court to court, not during interludes; or it occurs at tennis matches, not at concerts. However, if a few individuals were observed to be engaged in "nontennis"-oriented activity, the behavior would likely be attributed to boredom or some other personal attribute.

The covariation process described previously is particularly threatening to atypical groups, however they are labeled (e.g., mentally ill, disabled). This is because once they and their behavior are identified as atypical—nonnormative, deviant—the covariation process captures many seemingly plausible personal traits in its causal net, thereby aborting the causal search. The result is that environmental considerations are effectively screened out.

The Just World Phenomenon   A third factor in causal attribution involves consideration of both reality and what ought to be. Theory and research support the idea that human beings are inclined to feel that suffering and punishment, like joys and rewards, should be deserved (Asch, 1952; Heider, 1958). This sentiment is aptly referred to as the "just world phenomenon" (Lerner, 1970). Belief in a just world can be maintained by *blaming the victim*. This has been shown in a series of laboratory experiments summarized by Lerner (1970). Blaming is manifested when the suffering is viewed as a consequence or punishment of some form of sin, wrongdoing, or irresponsibility. Because of the need to bring "ought" and "reality" into balance, the poor tend to be blamed for their poverty, and the person who is raped is blamed for the rape.

A scale has been developed to measure individual differences concerning belief in a just world (Rubin & Peplau, 1975). Results indicate that believers are more likely than nonbelievers to admire fortunate people and derogate victims, thus maintaining the notion that people in fact get what they deserve.

To be sure, "ought and reality" can be aligned by altering reality to fit what ought to be. Such is the goal of reformers and activists whose efforts are directed at environmental change (e.g., legal, political, social, economic). Yet, as we have seen, because it is the suffering of a person (or people) that is being explained, the focus quite naturally becomes the person, not the environment. It takes a broader view to be able to scan other situations and to recognize the possible covariation between suffering and situations.

Although the just world phenomenon applies equally to advantaged and disadvantaged groups, it adds to the problems of those who are already burdened. Whenever the suffering is justified by perceiving the person as its main cause, possible environmental circumstances are overlooked.

Task Focus   The explanatory search in understanding behavior also is guided by the task undertaken by the investigator. Where the task is to form an impression of the person, to understand the person's behavior, to characterize the person in terms of descriptions, labels, or diagnoses, the task itself directs the perceiver's attention to the person. Where the task is to describe the environment in which people function, however, the focus of attention shifts to families, homes and schools, neighborhoods and parks, places of work and worship, and so forth. A vocabulary then emerges to describe and label the characteristics of situations that influence behavior (Stokols & Altman, 1987). Ecological psychology is one representative of this focus (Barker, 1963; Schoggen, 1989). Its vocabulary includes such phrases as *behavior settings* and *penetration* which refers to the power of different functional positions in the setting. Another representative of systematic environmental attention is behavior modification approaches that focus on the connection between environmental contingencies and the reinforcement and extinction of behavior. Terms used are *schedules of reinforcement, chaining,* and *conditioned reinforcers.* There also are studies in which the focus is upon socioeconomic-behavioral correlates of broad environmental categories such as urban and rural.

The focus of helping agencies varies. Some concentrate on changing the person's situation, as is the case of social service and employment agencies. Others focus on changing the person:

Schools and treatment centers are examples. People are referred to one or another agency according to whether the problem is seen to be intrinsic to the person or to the environment.

Thus, the perceived source of difficulties critically affects referral decisions. This was clearly shown in an experiment in which participants, serving as counselors in a simulated referral agency, assigned clients to one or another agency after learning of the problem (Batson, 1975). When the client's situation was held primarily accountable for the problem, referrals were more likely to be directed to social service agencies than to institutions oriented toward changing the person, whereas the reverse was true when the problem was judged to reside in the client.

Where the primary mission of a treatment center is to change the person, assessment procedures will be directed toward describing and labeling person attributes. The danger is that the environment scarcely enters the equation in understanding behavior.

Other Factors in Neglect of Environmental Considerations   Just as intrapsychic factors were mentioned as supporting or diminishing the power of the fundamental negative bias, so do these factors need to be recognized in the mix of factors that influence the figure-ground relationship between person and environment. The ideology of rugged individualism, for example, focuses on the person as the responsible agent. On the other hand, values and ideology can direct attention to the environment, as in the case of reformers and activists who argue for integration or segregation. Also, ego-defensive forces may create a need to blame the person or the environment. By blaming the poor, for example, one may feel personally competent or unobliged to contribute to remediation. By blaming the environment, one may see a way to assuage personal guilt by shifting responsibility from the self to others. Snyder (1990) has drawn attention to the need to preserve a sense of control, this being a principal motivation on the part of both society and the individual in holding people responsible for their actions.

Additionally, the environment may be perceived as fixed, as too difficult to change. Effort may therefore be expended on changing the person. A case in point is the misperception that job tasks and the work environment are immutable. Instead of trying to modify them, the potential worker may be denied employment, directed elsewhere, or trained for a different oc-cupation. The net effect is that the person, not the environment, needs to change. The concept of "reasonable accommodations," however, shifts the focus to the environment. Increas-ingly, modifying the work environment, phys-ically or through rule change, is becoming evi-dent.

Further clarification of basic conceptual and methodological issues is sorely needed to re-solve the problem of environmental neglect. Without that, corrective measures will remain limited, a basic reason being that the forces to-ward perceiving people and their attributes are overpowering. Conyne and Clack (1981), who referred to the environment as an "untapped force for change," constructed an environmental classification matrix that offers diverse concep-tualizations of environmental factors. In a text that resulted from a 1989 national conference that focused on organism-environment inter-action, Wachs and Plomin (1991) clear the path to a better understanding of the environment by addressing conceptual and methodological roadblocks frequently encountered in behavioral research. Fortunately, the volume edited by Friedman and Wachs (1999) presents a compre-hensive review of insights and proposals con-cerned with conceptualizing and measuring organism-environment integration that should help stimulate ways of overcoming environ-mental neglect. Bear in mind that the forces to-ward perceiving people and not environments in causal attribution are so strong that it will take a counteracting commitment to overcome them.

Implications for Professional Practice and Research

The wide array of factors discussed thus far alert us to psychological decoys that easily lead the professional astray in practice and research. Recommendations based on this understanding are offered as safeguards in each case.

Clinical Settings

Clinical settings are established to help solve problems—physical, mental, or emotional. And that is part of the problem. Being problem ori-ented, the clinician easily concentrates on pa-thology, dysfunction, and troubles, to the ne-glect of discovering those important assets in the person and resources in the environment

that must be drawn upon in the best problem-solving efforts (Wright & Fletcher, 1982).

Consider the following example. A counselor, seeking consultation concerning the rehabilita-tion of a delinquent youth, presented the case of 14-year-old John to the first author of this chapter. The following 10 symptoms were listed: assault, temper tantrums, stealing (car theft), fire setting, self-destructive behavior (jumped out of a moving car), threats of harm to others, insatiable demand for attention, van-dalism, wide mood swings, and underachieve-ment in school. On the basis of these symp-toms, the diagnosis on Axis I of the *Diagnostic and Statistical Manual of Mental Disorders* (*DSM-III-R*; American Psychiatric Association, 1987) was conduct disorder, undersocialized, ag-gressive, and with the possibility of a dysthymic disorder; on Axis II, passive aggressive person-ality. No physical disorders were listed on Axis III. The psychosocial stressors, rated as extreme on Axis IV, noted the death of his mother when John was a baby and successive placement with various relatives and homes. On Axis V, John's highest level of adaptive functioning was rated as poor.

Following perusal of this dismal picture, Wright asked the counselor whether John had anything going for him. The counselor then mentioned that John kept his own room in or-der, took care of his personal hygiene, liked to do things for others (although on his own terms), liked school, and had an IQ of 140. No-tice how quickly the impression of John changes once positives in the situation are brought out to share the stage with the problems. Before that, the fundamental negative bias reigned su-preme. Whereas the fact of John's delinquency had led to the detection of all sorts of negatives about his conduct and situation, the positives remained unconsidered. Is this case atypical? Only in its extreme neglect of strengths, we venture to say. Even a casual review of psycho-logical reports of cases at mental health facili-ties will reveal how common it is for trouble-some aspects to overshadow those that hold promise.

Notice also that the positives in John's case had been neglected with respect to both personal characteristics and significant environments. Environmental stresses are briefly noted on Axis IV, the axis that requires such specifica-tion. But the counselor did not indicate any en-vironmental supports that could be provided by John's relatives, school, or community. Were such environmental resources nonexistent, or did they remain hidden and unexplored?

There are at least two reasons that contribute to the elusiveness of environmental resources in the assessment procedures of person-centered treatment settings. Because it is the person who is to be treated, attention is focused on the person. The consequence is that assessment procedures are inclined toward the person, not the environment. Adequate attention to resources in the environment also is made more difficult by the fundamental negative bias. Just as the negative train of thought gives short shrift to assets of the person, so it also does to resources in the environment. The affective shift required makes it more "natural" to disregard positives in the environment when trying to understand problems.

Hardly anyone would argue that the environment should be ignored, and yet we know how easily the environment fades into oblivion. Some may take the position that no one profession can do the entire job of assessment, pointing out that it is the psychologist's responsibility to examine people, whereas social workers are specifically trained to examine circumstances in the home, school, and other community settings. However, the conclusion that psychologists are therefore absolved from seriously considering environmental factors is not warranted.

The covariation principle discussed earlier provides a readily available self-monitoring check to assist in bringing environmental issues to the foreground. The general question, "Does this behavior or problem occur in all situations?" forces one to review the many types of situations in the person's life.

The Four-Front Approach to Assessment

Once the power of the fundamental negative bias and the forces that keep the environment at bay are recognized, it becomes clear that the assessment and diagnostic processes need to be engaged on four fronts. Professionals must give serious attention to: (a) deficiencies and undermining characteristics of the person; (b) strengths and assets of the person; (c) lacks and destructive factors in the environment; and (d) resources and opportunities in the environment.

Highlighting positives as well as negatives in both the person and the environment serves vital purposes. It provides a framework to counteract deindividuation. It affects the significance of the negatives and enlarges remediation possibilities. It also encourages the *discovery* of assets and resources that can be developed in serving human potential.

A brief example of the efficacy of using assets to remediate deficits involves the case of a middle-aged man whose visual-spatial skills were impaired by a stroke (Chelune, 1983). The neuropsychologist was able to demonstrate the potential utility of using the client's intact verbal skills as a means of compensating for his considerable difficulty with copying a cross. When the man was instructed to "talk himself through" such tasks, he was able to do them without difficulty. If only the impaired side of his functioning had been attended to, remediation possibilities would have been limited.

In accord with the approach on four fronts, an attempt was made to correct common oversights that appeared in the behavior checklists on children's intake forms at mental health centers (Fletcher, 1979). These checklists essentially pointed out child problems but rarely, if at all, included items pertaining to child assets or the environment. A checklist was therefore constructed consisting of four separate parts: (a) Child Problems (39 items; e.g., temper outbursts, mean to others); (b) Child Assets (39 items; e.g., affectionate, finishes tasks); (c) Environmental Problems (21 items; e.g., family fights, lack of recreational opportunities); and (d) Environmental Resources (21 items; e.g., grandparent(s), school). Notice that the problems and assets on the child side were made equal in number, as were the problems and resources on the environmental side, but that the child items far exceeded the environmental items. This disparity, which occurred in spite of a serious attempt to correct it, reflects the greater availability of person categories in our lexicon than environmental categories.

Information bearing on the four fronts can be obtained through the many types of assessment procedures available. It is essential that psychological tests are selected that are designed to uncover personal strengths and assets just as tests are selected that are sensitive to deficits and pathology. Systematic identification of environmental restraints and resources can be achieved via questionnaires, observation, and collateral sources of information. Recent advancements in the development of environment models and assessment tools (see Friedman & Wachs, 1999) make measurement of the objective, subjective, and temporal components of the environment possible.

The task of integrating data from four fronts is a challenging one. It is challenging because the four domains represent a dynamic whole in which the client's functioning needs to be grasped. Not only do the strengths and limitations of the client influence each other, but also the client's behavior and environment are mutually interdependent. Assessment is a cyclical process of building tentative understanding of issues involving the client within this complex network of factors.

Throughout the assessment process, the psychologist is urged to remain on guard lest positives in the person and situation remain overlooked because of the intrusion of the fundamental negative bias and environmental neglect. In this regard, recommendations have been made on how to interview for client strengths and minimize bias in clinical work (Spengler, Strohmer, Dixon, & Shivey, 1995).

To ensure that positives are not submerged by negatives, it was proposed (Wright, 1991) that assets and deficits approximate an equal amount of space in psychological reports and equal time at case conferences. This "equal space and time" guideline serves as a concrete reminder of the importance of seriously attending to both aspects. Observing this rule of equity is quite challenging. Adding a strengths section to a verbal or written report may be the first step toward being able to interweave information about pathology and strengths in psychological assessment.

Finally, it is imperative when presenting psychological data that the clinician demonstrate respect for the client's struggle with problems in daily living or more severe dysfunction. Focusing on how the repertoire of client strengths and environmental resources can enable the client in that struggle is the best way to ensure fundamental support and regard for the client.

The Diagnostic and Statistical Manual of Mental Disorders

The *Diagnostic and Statistical Manual of Mental Disorders* has been widely accepted in the United States as the diagnostic tool of mental health clinicians and researchers. The last revision, *DSM-IV* (American Psychiatric Association, 1994), describes over 400 categories of mental disorder grouped according to 16 major classes. The disorders are typically described in terms of diagnostic features, prevalence, course, cultural considerations, and so forth. Five axes are provided for recording information to help the clinician plan treatment and predict outcome (Axis I, Clinical Disorders and Other Conditions That May Be a Focus of Attention; Axis II, Personality Disorders and Mental Retardation; Axis III, General Medical Conditions; Axis IV, Psychosocial and Environmental Problems; and Axis V, Global Assessment of Functioning).

An enormous amount of research and care have gone into the *DSM*s. Because *DSM* is such an important document, it is fitting that we examine some of the ideas that have determined its nature. The recommendations offered center around the problems of deindividuation, the fundamental negative bias, and environmental neglect.

Deindividuation   The evidence is clear. Affixing a label (diagnosis in the present instance) leads to a muting of differences within the labeled group. *DSM-IV* developers remind the clinician that "individuals sharing a diagnosis are likely to be heterogeneous even in regard to the defining features of the diagnosis." They emphasize the need to "capture additional information that goes far beyond diagnosis" in order to accent the unique characteristics of individuals that may influence how they manage their lives (American Psychiatric Association, 1994, p. xxii).

But within-group deindividuation is so insidious that all too readily it reaches the ultimate point of dehumanization in which the person is then made equivalent to the disorder. The devaluative implication of such terminological equivalence was first recognized by Wright (1960). The *DSM* developers also caution, "A common misconception is that a classification of mental disorders classifies people, when actually what are being classified are disorders that people have" (American Psychiatric Association, 1994, p. xxii), and clinicians should avoid labeling people as schizophrenics or alcoholics and instead should use the more accurate but admittedly more cumbersome "an individual with Schizophrenia" or "an individual with Alcohol Dependence" (American Psychiatric Association, 1994, xxii). It is our belief, however, that the two caveats concerning homogenization of individuality and dehumanization, wise as they are, cannot stem the tide of deindividuation so long as a few diagnostic labels dominate perception. What is needed is greater individuation in terms of the four-front approach.

The Fundamental Negative Bias   So long as the main diagnostic categories are disorders, relatively little effort will be expended on personal assets and environmental resources. The *DSM* working group made an attempt to offset this danger by including the Global Assessment of Functioning Scale (Axis V). It is provided to assist this assessment, yet it actually serves as a global assessment of dysfunction, namely, the extent to which individuals are languishing or suffering. That is, only a small range of scores on the 100-point scale (approximately 75–100) describes functioning that is adequate, good, or superior. The remainder of the scale is coordinated to functioning, ranging from slightly impaired to harming self or others. Lopez, Prosser, LaRue, Ulven, and Vehige (2000) proposed that the Global Assessment Scale be restructured by having anchors of 1, 50, and 100 reflective of severely impaired functioning, good health, and thriving, respectively. It also should be noted that a *scant few pages* are devoted to Axis V, in contrast to the *hundreds of pages* devoted to diagnosing mental disorders. Small wonder that the aforementioned report of the delinquent youth was so negatively one-sided, and small wonder that attention to deficits and pathology so commonly overwhelms the reporting of strengths and assets in mental health agencies.

The rejoinder may be that it is the job of mental health agencies to diagnose and deal with problems, and that problems refer to dysfunction, not to well-functioning areas. But the rejoinder to this point of view is that inasmuch as the person functions as a whole system in which healthy and dysfunctional characteristics affect each other, both aspects must be given serious attention in diagnosis and treatment plans. Surely it makes a difference to both diagnosis and treatment if a client is aware of his or her difficulties, is willing to accept help, is responsible, is kind, and gets along with others. Systematic research can help to clarify which personal assets need to be singled out, how they cluster, and how to present them: on profiles, checklists, rating scales, for example.

Neglect of Environmental Considerations   Axis IV, *DSM-IV*, bears the title "Psychosocial and Environmental Problems." It was devised in recognition of the fact that the environment is not inconsequential in understanding and diagnosing mental disorder. Still, Axis IV must be considered barely a first step in meeting the challenge of addressing environmental influences on human behavior. First to be observed is that this axis refers to psychosocial and environmental *problems, not resources.* The neglect of the positive is so profound that *DSM-IV* developers caution users against listing "so-called positive stressors, such as a job promotion" on this axis unless they "constitute or lead to a problem" (American Psychiatric Association, 1994, p. 29). Again, positive attributes or characteristics of the person or situation are relegated to the background. Axis IV is helpful insofar as its guidelines draw attention to the environment—problems regarding family, occupation, living circumstances, and so forth. Even so, very little space and attention are devoted to this axis, and no axis directs attention to environmental supports.

Recommendations for the DSM and Its Alternatives   The themes of this chapter, with its focus on the problems of deindividuation, the fundamental negative bias, and environmental neglect, strongly suggest that the four-front approach become the model for future *DSM* revisions. How else can positives as well as negatives in both the person and the environment be made sufficiently salient to allow an integrated assessment of the whole person-in-environment? Is it too impractical to envision a diagnostic manual consisting of four volumes, one addressing each front? Can anything short of that do justice to the goal of optimizing diagnostic and remediation efforts on behalf of the client? An added benefit would be the likely impetus given to conceptually clarifying significant aspects of the person-in-environment.

There are other recommendations regarding the current diagnostic system. We already have argued for the inclusion of environmental resources on Axis IV and for modifications to Axis V of the current five-axis system. Also, Lopez et al. (2000) present the outline for what could constitute an Axis VI designed to guide the clinician in identifying client strengths, resources, and virtues.

Finally, the Developmental Diagnostic Classification System (Ivey & Ivey, 1998) constitutes a reengineering of the diagnostic classification framework that is grounded in a developmental focus and the assumption that all behavior is adaptive. This new system focus emphasizes detection of what is working in the client's life and capitalizes on human strengths.

Revisions of the *DSM* have been based on research garnered from extensive reviews of the literature and on consultation with experts from different disciplines. The developers state, "More than any other nomenclature of mental disorders, *DSM-IV* is grounded in empirical evidence" (American Psychiatric Association, 1994, xvi). They also point out that "to formulate an adequate treatment plan, the clinician will invariably require considerable information about the person being evaluated beyond that required to make a *DSM-IV* diagnosis" (American Psychiatric Association, 1994, xxv). What is not recognized is that the additional information required also must be buttressed by research that details personal strengths as well as difficulties. These are the domains of the fourfront approach. Greater conceptual clarification of the nature of this interdependent network requires continuing investigation.

Whether or not the *DSM* is used, the recommendations proposed here can be applied in clinical practice. These recommendations refer to the four-front approach, approximating equal time and space to assets as to deficits in psychological reports and at case conferences, and to uncovering the environment by covarying problematic behavior with situations in the person's life.

The main themes argued in the present chapter also raise issues bearing on the conduct and interpretation of research. A few examples are discussed in the following.

Research Practices

Comparing Conditions and Groups in Research

The difference in perspectives of the outsider and insider, as well as the power of the fundamental negative bias alert us to certain pitfalls that need to be avoided in interpreting research. Consider an experiment that compared reactions of able-bodied persons to confederate interviewers with and without a simulated disability. (Because there is no need to indict a particular researcher, this study is not identified here.) All things were kept equal in the two conditions except for the independent variable. Although the main finding was that the interviewer with the disability was consistently rated more favorably on a variety of personality characteristics (e.g., more likable, better attitude), the results were interpreted as supporting research indicating the operation of a sympathy effect to avoid the appearance of rejection or prejudice.

A number of points need to be emphasized. First, the investigator was seduced into attending to the disability variable as the salient factor in the experiment because "all other things were kept equal." Second, these controls kept the investigator, as observer, from attending to the context of the interview as *experienced by the research participants*. Instead, the negative value attributed to the disability stood alone in determining the negative flow of thoughts and feelings, leaving the investigator to become trapped by the fundamental negative bias, even to the extent of treating findings favoring the interviewer with the disability as if they were negative.

For the research participants, however, the situation appeared very different. They knew nothing about the behavior of the interviewer being held constant in two experimental conditions in which only the interviewer's physical appearance varied. All they were aware of was an interviewer whose status and behavior were positive. Thus, instead of the context being obliterated, the context was decidedly positive. Under these circumstances, response intensification occurred, a finding that fits with other research. The research participants may have appreciated the interviewer's apparent success in meeting the challenges of his or her disability and therefore perceived the interviewer as having special qualities as a cause or consequence of such success. The conclusion is compelling that two vastly different situations were evaluated, one as perceived by the research participants and a very different one by the experimenter.

Researchers must become sensitized to possible differences in perspective between themselves and subjects, especially in terms of the saliency and context of variables under study. They also must become aware of the power of the fundamental negative bias to influence their own thinking when the independent variable carries a negative connotation or label (disability in this experiment).

The preceding discussion relates to research in which participants are assigned to different conditions, not to research in which the behavior of distinct groups of people is compared. In the latter case, special precautions need to be taken lest the label identifying the groups controls the investigator's thinking. In countless studies, there are comparisons of males and females, blacks and whites, people with and without disabilities, heterosexuals and homosexuals, and so forth. All too often, between-group differences are attributed solely to the group characteristic made visible by the label (e.g., gender, race). Other factors such as the generally large overlap in behavior between groups, within-group differences, and differences in the groups' life circumstances are frequently ignored or discounted. The consequent between-group distinctiveness, within-group deindividuation, and environmental neglect have serious societal implications that need to be thought through by researchers. At the very least, the "something else perhaps" notion, proposed by the philosopher Herbert Feigl (1953), bears reemphasizing to avoid "nothing but" interpretations based on a salient, labeled variable. Feigl also reminded us that the investigator must be pressed to discover "what's what" by systematic research.

The Problem of Statistical Significance

The fact that the null hypothesis cannot be proven statistically (Fisher, 1955) adds to the complexity of the issues raised here. Similarities between groups, typically regarded as null findings, are therefore discounted. The consequence for understanding different groups is serious, and in the case of groups that are already disadvantaged, ignoring similarities adds to the disadvantagedness.

A variety of statistical procedures to help eliminate the bias against accepting the null hypothesis (i.e., similarities between groups) have been proposed. Traditionally, researchers use the .01 or .05 alpha level of significance to refer to the small probability that the obtained difference between groups could be due to chance. One proposal is that the high end of the probability range could be used to suggest the likelihood of similarity (rather than exact equivalence) between groups (Wright, 1988, p. 16). While it is true that the null hypothesis cannot logically be proven and can "at most be confirmed or strengthened" (Fisher, 1955), it should be noted that large p values do in fact "confirm or strengthen" the hypothesis that group differences are small or nonexistent. In that case, one could conclude that the obtained difference is unreliable as a difference but reliable as a similarity. The similarity, then, would have to be judged to determine whether it is of psychological importance, just as a statistically

significant difference has to be so judged. Of course, relevant research criteria, such as reliability and validity of measures used, would have to be evaluated.

The point is that investigators, by giving weight to similarities as well as to differences between groups, achieve better understanding of the data and help to stem the automatic slide toward between-group accentuation of differences. A further fact that should not be overlooked is that perceived similarities promote positive intergroup relations. Additional arguments, evidence, and procedures to counteract prejudice against accepting the null hypothesis can be found in Greenwald (1975).

The Problem of Attitude Tests of Stereotypes

When measuring attitudes toward a particular group, the intent is to get at stereotypes, attitudes that are tied to the label designating the group. If the label connotes something negative to the respondent, as is often the case, for example, with regard to mental disorder, disability, poverty, and homosexuality, then the label is likely to give rise to a negative mind-set in answering the items, especially because the label, as an abstraction, is separated from particular people and circumstances.

Contributing to this mind-set is a preponderance of negatively focused items that frequently, although not always, characterize attitude tests about groups stigmatized in some way. This negative loading may be a manifestation of the fundamental negative bias inasmuch as the test constructor may be led by the group's stigmatized status to formulate items that imply devaluation. It also may be considered a way to minimize the influence of "social desirability," that is, a subject's inclination to respond favorably to items expressing what is proper.

In any case, the negative loading can have several unacceptable consequences. First, we should be concerned lest a preponderance of negatively worded items orients thinking toward the negative side of possibilities, thereby strengthening a negative-response bias. Also, rejecting a negative statement is not the same, affectively and cognitively, as affirming a positive statement. Rejecting the idea, for example, that a particular group is often conniving or lazy does not imply the opposite belief, that the group is often honest or eager to work. Both types of statements are needed to guard against a negative bias and to offer respondents the opportunity to express attitudes that reflect genuinely positive, as well as negative, feelings and beliefs.

In addition, an overload of negatively worded items could provide a misleading educational experience, leading the respondent to begin to believe disparaging statements that had not been entertained before. The possibility of this happening is increased by evidence showing that people tend to give more weight to negative aspects of something than to positive aspects. To counteract the excessive weight that might be given to negative items, the most obvious suggestion is to include at least the same number, and preferably a greater number, of positively worded items.

Another concern relates to the nature of stereotyping itself. Although it is understandable that attitude tests avoid differentiations among group members captured by the label, the possible deleterious effects of an ostensible scientific instrument that homogenizes people in this way are of concern. Deindividuation flies in the face of decades of research showing that a label or diagnosis tells us very little about what a person is like inasmuch as individuals are unique in their combination of interests, values, abilities, circumstances, and so forth. Because of the nature of stereotypes, however, the tests themselves have to ignore this uniqueness. To minimize stereotyping effects of such tests, it is recommended that research participants be cautioned against this possibility during debriefing.

Another urgently needed recommendation is that researchers spend at least as much effort searching for and uncovering positive attitudes as they do negative ones. To agree with this recommendation depends on believing that positive attitudes toward disadvantaged groups not only exist but also are as important as negative attitudes, for two reasons. First, attitudes are typically ambivalent, and when evaluated within this more complex matrix, the perception of the group is likely to change. A telling example discussed earlier is the attitude change that took place toward the delinquent youth as soon as positive traits were brought to the fore. Second, positive attitudes are also important because it is these attitudes that have to be drawn on, built upon, and spread in the effort to overcome disparaging beliefs and feelings of one group toward another.

Positive Psychology: Just Another Label?

The label of *positive psychology* represents those efforts of professionals to help people optimize human functioning by acknowledging strengths as well as deficiencies, and environmental *resources* in addition to stressors. Label us hopeful optimists (please) because we believe that this enlarged focus is essential in clarifying what works in people's lives. Many issues were raised in this chapter. We hope that readers will be encouraged to consider the conceptual reasoning, evidence, and recommendations in both their ongoing scholarly work and their clinical practice.

Note

This chapter updates Wright, B. A. (1991). Labeling: The need for greater person-environment individuation. In C. R. Snyder & D. R. Forsyth (Ed.), *The handbook of social and clinical psychology: A health perspective.* New York: Pergamon.

References

American Psychiatric Association. (1987). *Diagnostic and statistical manual of mental disorders* (3rd ed., rev.). Washington, DC: Author.

American Psychiatric Association. (1994). *Diagnostic and statistical manual of mental disorders* (4th ed.). Washington, DC: Author.

Asch, S. E. (1952). Forming impressions of personality. *Journal of Abnormal and Social Psychology, 41,* 258–290.

Barker, R. G. (Ed.). (1963). *The stream of behavior.* New York: Appleton-Century-Crofts.

Barker, R. G., & Wright, H. F. (1955). *Midwest and its children.* New York: Harper and Row.

Batson, C. D. (1975). Attribution as a mediator of bias in helping. *Journal of Personality and Social Psychology, 32,* 455–466.

Chelune, G. J. (1983, August). *Neuropsychological assessment: Beyond deficit testing.* Paper presented at the 91st annual convention of the American Psychological Association, Anaheim, CA.

Cohen, C. E. (1981). Person categories and social perception: Testing some boundaries of the processing effects of prior knowledge. *Journal of Personality and Social Psychology, 40,* 441–452.

Conyne, R. K., & Clack, R. J. (1981). *Environmental assessment and design: A new tool for the applied behavioral scientist*. New York: Praeger.

Dembo, T. (1964). Sensitivity of one person to another. *Rehabilitation Literature, 25*, 231–235.

Dembo, T. (1970). The utilization of psychological knowledge in rehabilitation. *Welfare Review, 8*, 1–7.

Dembo, T., Leviton, G. L., & Wright, B. A. (1956/1975). Adjustment to misfortune: A problem of social-psychological rehabilitation. *Artificial Limbs, 3* (2), 4–62. (Reprinted in *Rehabilitation Psychology, 2* (1975), 1–100.)

Dienstbier, R. A. (1970). Positive and negative prejudice with race and social desirability. *Journal of Personality, 38*, 198–215.

Doise, W., Deschamps, J. C., & Meyer, G. (1978). The accentuation of intracategory similarities. In H. Tajfel (Ed.), *Differentiation between social groups: Studies in the social psychology of intergroup relations* (pp. 159–168). (European Monographs in Social Psychology 14.) London: Academic Press.

English, R. W. (1971a). Assessment, modification and stability of attitudes toward blindness. *Psychological Aspects of Disability, 18* (2) 79–85.

English, R. W. (1971b). Correlates of stigma toward physically disabled persons. *Rehabilitation Research and Practice Review, 2*, 1–17.

Feigl, H. (1953). The scientific outlook: Naturalism and humanism. In H. Feigl & M. Brodbeck (Eds.), *Readings in the philosophy of science* (pp. 8–18). New York: Appleton-Century-Crofts.

Feldman, S. (1966). Motivational aspects of attitudinal elements and their place in cognitive interaction. In S. Feldman (Ed.), *Cognitive consistency: Motivational antecedents and behavioral consequences* (pp. 75–108). New York: Academic Press.

Fisher, R. (1955). Statistical method and scientific induction. *Journal of the Royal Statistical Society, 17*, 69–78.

Fletcher, B. L. (1979). *Creating a child intake form for use in a mental health center*. Unpublished manuscript, University of Kansas, Lawrence.

*Friedman, S. L., & Wachs, T. D. (Eds.). (1999). *Measuring environment across the lifespan*. Washington, DC: American Psychological Association.

Gergen, K. L., & Jones, E. E. (1963). Mental illness, predictability and affective consequences as stimulus factors in person perception. *Journal of Abnormal and Social Psychology, 67*, 95–104.

Goldberg, L. R. (1978). Differential attribution to trait-descriptive terms to oneself as compared to well-liked, neutral, and disliked others: A psychometric analysis. *Journal of Personality and Social Psychology, 36*, 1012–1028.

Greenwald, A. G. (1975). Consequences of prejudice against the null hypothesis. *Psychological Bulletin, 82*, 1–20.

Hamera, E. K., & Shontz, F. C. (1978). Perceived positive and negative effects of life-threatening illness. *Journal of Psychosomatic Research, 22*, 419–424.

Heider, F. (1926). Ding und medium. *Symposion, 1*, 109–157.

Heider, F. (1958). *The psychology of interpersonal relations*. New York: Wiley.

Isen, A. M. (1987). Positive affect, cognitive processes, and social behavior. In L. Berkowitz (Ed.), *Advances in experimental social psychology* (Vol. 20, pp. 203–254). Orlando, FL: Academic Press.

*Ivey, A. E., & Ivey, M. B. (1998). Reframing DSM-IV: Positive strategies from developmental counseling and therapy. *Journal of Counseling and Development, 76*, 334–350.

Jaffe, J. (1966). Attitudes of adolescents toward the mentally retarded. *American Journal of Mental Deficiency, 70*, 907–912.

Kanouse, D. E., & Hanson, L. R., Jr. (1971). Negativity in evaluations. In E. E. Jones et al. (Eds.), *Attribution: Perceiving the causes of behavior* (pp. 47–62). Morristown, NJ: General Learning Press.

Kelley, H. H. (1973). Process of causal attribution. *American Psychologist, 28*, 107–128.

Kogan, N., & Wallach, M. A. (1967). Risk taking as a function of the situation, the person, and the group. In G. Mandler, P. N. Kogan, & M. A. Wallach (Eds.), *New directions in psychology III* (pp. 111–278). New York: Holt, Rinehart, and Winston.

Leek, D. F. (1966). *Formation of impressions of persons with a disability*. Unpublished master's thesis, University of Kansas, Lawrence.

Lerner, M. J. (1970). The desire of justice and reactions to victims. In J. Macaulay & L. Berkowitz (Eds.), *Altruism and helping behavior* (pp. 205–229). New York: Academic Press.

Lewin, K. (1935). *A dynamic theory of personality*. New York: McGraw-Hill.

Lopez, S. J., Prosser, E. C., LaRue, S., Ulven, J. C., & Vehige, S. (2000). *Practicing positive psychology*. Unpublished manuscript.

Mason, L., & Muhlenkamp, A. (1976). Patients' self-reported affective states following loss and caregivers' expectations of patients' affective states. *Rehabilitation Psychology, 23*, 72–76.

Nisbett, R. E., Caputo, C., Legant, P., & Maracek, J. (1973). Behavior as seen by the actor and as seen by the observer. *Journal of Personality and Social Psychology, 27,* 154–164.

Pierce, D. L. (1987). *Negative bias and situation: Perception of helping agency on information seeking and evaluation of clients.* Unpublished master's thesis, University of Kansas, Lawrence.

Rubin, Z., & Peplau, L. A. (1975). Who believes in a just world? *Journal of Social Issues, 31,* 65–89.

Schoggen, P. (1989). *Behavior settings: A revision of Barker's ecological psychology.* Stanford, CA: Stanford University Press.

Snyder, C. R. (1977). "A patient by any other name" revisited: Maladjustment or attributional locus of problem? *Journal of Consulting and Clinical Psychology, 45,* 101–103.

Snyder, C. R. (1990). Self-handicapping processes and sequelae: On the taking of a psychological dive. In R. L. Higgins, C. R. Snyder, & S. Berglas, *Self-handicapping: The paradox that isn't* (pp. 107–150). New York: Plenum.

Snyder, C. R., Shenkel, R. J., & Schmidt, A. (1976). Effects of role perspective and client psychiatric history on locus of problem. *Journal of Consulting and Clinical Psychology, 44,* 467–472.

Spengler, P. M., Strohmer, D. C., Dixon, D. N., & Shivy, V. A. (1995). A scientist-practitioner model of psychological assessment: Implications for training, practice and research. *The Counseling Psychologist, 23,* 506–534.

Stokols, D., & Altman, I. (Eds.). (1987). *Handbook of environmental psychology* (Vols. 1–2). New York: Wiley.

Storms, M. D. (1973). Videotape and the attribution process: Reversing actors' and observers' points of view. *Journal of Personality and Social Psychology, 27,* 165–175.

Tajfel, H. (Ed.). (1978). *Differentiation between social groups: Studies in the social psychology of intergroup relations.* (European Monographs in Social Psychology 14.) London: Academic Press.

Tajfel, H., & Wilkes, A. (1963). Classification and quantitative judgment. *British Journal of Psychology, 54,* 101–114.

Wachs, T. D., & Plomin, R. (1991). *Conceptualization and measurement of organism-environment interaction.* Washington, DC: American Psychological Association.

Wertheimer, M. (1923). Untersuehungen zur Lehre von der gestalt [Examination of the lessons of gestalt]. II. *Psychologishe Forschung, 4,* 301–350.

Whiteman, M., & Lukoff, I. F. (1965). Attitudes toward blindness and other physical handicaps. *Journal of Social Psychology, 65,* 135–145.

Wilder, D. A. (1978). Perceiving persons as a group: Effects on attributions of causality and beliefs. *Social Psychology, 1,* 13–23.

Wilder, D. A. (1984). *Effects of perceiving persons as a group on the information conveyed by their behavior.* Unpublished manuscript, Rutgers University, New Brunswick, NJ.

Wilder, D. A. (1986). Social categorization: Implications for creation and reduction of intergroup bias. In L. Berkowitz (Ed.), *Advances in experimental social psychology* (Vol. 19, pp. 291–355). Orlando, FL: Academic Press.

Wright, B. A. (1960). *Physical disability: A psychological approach.* New York: Harper and Row.

*Wright, B. A. (1983). *Physical disability: A psychosocial approach* (2nd ed.). New York: Harper and Row.

Wright, B. A. (1988). Attitudes and the fundamental negative bias. In H. E. Yuker (Ed.), *Attitudes toward persons with disabilities* (pp. 3–21). New York: Springer.

Wright, B. A. (1991). Labeling: The need for greater person-environment individuation. In C. R. Snyder & D. R. Forsyth (Ed.), *The handbook of social and clinical psychology* (pp. 469–487). New York: Pergamon.

Wright, B. A., & Fletcher, B. L. (1982). Uncovering hidden resources: A challenge in assessment. *Professional Psychology, 13,* 229–235.

Wright, B. A., & Howe, M. (1969). *The fortune phenomenon as manifested in stigmatized and non-stigmatized groups.* Unpublished manuscript, University of Kansas, Lawrence.

4

Toward a Science of Mental Health

Positive Directions in Diagnosis and Interventions

Corey L. M. Keyes & Shane J. Lopez

The science of mental illness diagnosis and its treatment has taken shape over the last half of the 20th century (see U.S. Department of Health and Human Services, 1995). Sophisticated talk and drug therapies are now available to treat many mental illnesses. Most of these treatments remain ephemeral and only partially effective, however, and mental illness continues to disable individuals, families, and communities. The investment of capital into the study of the etiology and treatment of mental disorders has not reduced the inflow of patients and has not led to the alleviation of widespread suffering. Clearly, this nation must find ways to prevent the early onset of mental disorders and to suggest new techniques for prolonging remission and preventing disorder.

For these reasons, we argue in this chapter that the utility of a positive approach to the diagnosis and treatment of mental health remains an unrealized tool. Toward that end, we will summarize the literature on the conception and measurement of subjective well-being. Although this review is not exhaustive (see Diener, Suh, Lucas, & Smith, 1999; Keyes, 1998; Keyes & Ryff, 1999; Ryff, 1989b; Ryff &

Keyes, 1995), our purpose is to describe the symptoms of well-being so that we can make informed suggestions about how social scientists may begin to diagnose and study mental health.

Additionally, we argue that the study of mental health is distinct from and complementary to the long-standing interest in mental illness, its prevalence, and its remedies. In the second part of this chapter, we link the diagnosis of mental health to the budding science of positive therapies and treatments. After reviewing these treatments, we marshal evidence to argue that some positive therapies can promote well-being that acts as a buffer against subsequent adversity, and yet other therapies may be used to prevent depression relapse.

Mental Illness: The Current State of Treatment and Prevalence

We believe that it is the best and the worst of times for the science of mental illness. Scientific advances have led to etiological discoveries, diagnostic tools that contribute to greater specificity in diagnosis, and a variety of effective talk therapies for reducing the severity and number of patient symptoms (Seligman, 1995). Additionally, the advent of selective serotonin reuptake inhibitors (SSRIs) has reduced the number and severity of symptoms, as well as side effects, in relation to the previous class of psychopharmaceuticals (U.S. Department of Health and Human Services, 1999).

Despite these accomplishments, the burden of mental disorders appears to be becoming more prevalent (Klerman & Weissman, 1989). Mental health practitioners struggle with scientific and practical limitations, and mental illness continues to cast a daunting shadow on the well-being of people. In our opinion, the science of mental illness has produced effective treatments for more "broken-down" people; it remains ineffective for preventing more people from "breaking down."

For example, the remission of depressive symptoms among many patients taking an SSRI is partial or short-lived, and nearly a third of patients do not respond to drug treatments (see, e.g., O'Reardon, Brunswick, & Amsterdam, 2000). Moreover, the period of remission from most therapies is brief. As many as 60% to 70% of patients with unipolar major depression relapse within six months of symptom remission (Keller, Shapiro, Lavori, & Wolfe, 1982; Ramana et al., 1995). Continuation and maintenance phase therapies, which involve providing treatment for a period of time following initial symptom remission, have helped to reduce depression relapse (see U.S. Department of Health and Human Services, 1999, p. 261).

Based on epidemiological studies conducted in the 1990s, there appears to be an astonishing amount of mental illness in the U.S. population. The estimates are that between one quarter and one third of adults will experience a serious mental disorder in their lifetimes. As much as one-quarter of individuals aged eighteen years old or older will experience a mental disorder annually; moreover, many of these persons will have comorbid disorders (e.g., addictive disorders) that complicate treatment and compound suffering (Kessler et al., 1994; Robins & Regier, 1991; U.S. Department of Health and Human Services, 1999).

Studies also reveal that the age of first onset of unipolar depression has decreased during the last century (Burke, Burke, Rae, & Regier, 1991; Cross-National Collaborative Group, 1992; Lewinsohn, Rohde, Seeley, & Fischer, 1993;

Wittchen, Knauper, & Kessler, 1994). Whereas depression used to first strike adults during midlife, it has become the "common cold" of young adulthood. Likewise, a prior episode of depression has been shown to be a risk factor for the recurrence of depression (Gonzales, Lewinsohn, & Clarke, 1985; Lewinsohn, Hoberman, & Rosenbaum, 1988). In short, more individuals at earlier ages are experiencing a mental disorder that is likely to lead to other comorbid illnesses (i.e., physical and mental) and increases the odds of a lifetime of recurrent mental illness.

Mental illness is a yoke to the quality and productivity of families, communities, and the workplace. The Global Burden of Disease study and report (Murray & Lopez, 1996) opened the eyes of policy makers to the disabling nature of mental illness. This study palpably expressed the burden to society of "diseases" in terms of the reduction of healthy life years through premature death and reduced productivity. Unipolar depression ranked second only to ischemic heart disease as the most potent cause of reduced healthy years of life for adults of all ages; unipolar depression was the leading cause of disability life years among adults under the ages of 44 in developed and developing countries.

Mental illness reduces productivity and costs billions of dollars each year due to lost wages, medical costs, and disability claims (Mrazek & Haggerty, 1994). During fiscal year 1999, the National Institutes of Health estimated that mental disorders amounted to approximately $160 billion in direct and indirect costs to society (U.S. Department of Health and Human Services, 1999). As shown in Figure 4.1, the burden of mental disorder is not far behind that of heart disease, the leading burden to society, amounting to about $180 billion annually.

Mental illness abbreviates lives. Major depression has been linked to increased risk for developing chronic physical diseases such as coronary heart disease (Musselman, Evans, & Nemeroff, 1998) and addictive disorders (Kessler, et al., 1996) that are implicated in premature mortality. Mood disorders such as unipolar and bipolar depression are a leading cause of suicide, contributing to nearly one third of all suicides. The rate of "successful" suicides is about 12 per 100,000, and it has remained stable over the past 40 years. During that same period, the suicide rate within some age-groups changed in concert with the decreased age of first onset of depression. That is, whereas the suicide rate has decreased among the elderly (viz., white elderly

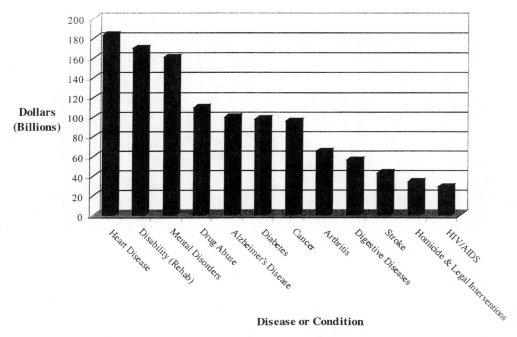

Disease or Condition

Figure 4.1 National Institutes of Health estimates of the combined direct and indirect costs of diseases and conditions in fiscal year 1999.

men), the suicide rate among adolescents and young adults nearly tripled between 1952 and 1996 (Koening & Blazer, 1992; Rebellon, Brown, & Keyes, in press; U.S. Department of Health and Human Services, 1998).

In sum—the good news—the national investment in the science of mental illness has created effective talk and drug therapies. These treatments are highly effective for ameliorating proximal causes of mental illness that reside in brain chemistry or mental function, yet remission is brief. There is a growing and effective branch of prevention science that aims to ameliorate distal causes (e.g., poverty) of mental illness. However, most prevention efforts usually are directed toward "at-risk" populations (e.g., youth living in poverty), and they seek to identify the factors that protect such individuals— those risks that usually result in physical disease or mental disorder.

To date, very little scholarly attention or federal research money has been directed toward mental health promotion as an end in itself, or as another avenue for preventing physical disease and mental disorder. The challenges that lie ahead are to (a) reduce the prevalence of mental illness, (b) prevent its early onset in young adults' lives, (c) prolong remission fol-

lowing therapies, and (d) reduce the recurrence of mental illness throughout the life course. Toward that end, we envision a science in the 21st century of mental health promotion and treatment that will complement the reigning science of mental illness prevention and treatment. To foster more mental health in adults, social scientists must articulate the diagnosis and interventions that directly aim to promote mental *health*.

Mental Health: Positive Diagnosis

Symptoms of Mental Health

Mental health, similar to its counterpart mental illness, is an emergent condition based on the notion of a syndrome. That is, health, like illness, is indicated when a set of symptoms at a specific level are present for a specified duration, and this health coincides with distinctive brain and social functioning (American Psychiatric Association [APA], 1980; Keyes, in press; Mechanic, 1999). To study mental health, researchers must move toward the operationalization of mental health as a syndrome of symptoms of well-being.

Subjective well-being reflects individuals' perceptions and evaluations of their own lives in terms of their affective states, psychological functioning, and social functioning. Well-being researchers often use positive mental health synonymously with subjective well-being (see Diener, Lucas, & Oishi, this volume). However, we argue that no one has studied an aggregated notion of mental health, *because scholars investigate variation in the quantity of specific facets of well-being that are symptoms of mental health.* That is, scholars investigate the predictors of dimensions of emotional well-being (e.g., happiness or satisfaction), of psychological well-being (e.g., personal growth), or of social well-being (e.g., social integration).

In this regard, the elements of subjective well-being appear to fall into two clusters of symptoms that parallel the symptom clusters for major depression. The first cluster reflects measures of emotional vitality, while the second consists of measures of positive functioning. In the same way that depression consists of depressed mood (or anhedonia) and malfunctioning (e.g., over- or undereating), subjective well-being has been operationalized in terms of emotional well-being and positive functioning.

As operationalized in the MacArthur Foundation's Successful Midlife in the U.S. (MIDUS) study conducted in 1995, symptoms of emotional well-being include scales of positive affect, negative affect, and satisfaction with life overall. Studies reveal that measures of the avowal of emotional well-being in terms of satisfaction and happiness are related but distinct dimensions (e.g., Andrews & Withey, 1976). Measures of the expression of emotional well-being in terms of positive and negative affect are related but distinct dimensions (e.g., Bradburn, 1969; Watson & Tellegen, 1985). Last, measures of avowed and expressed emotional well-being are related but distinct dimensions (Bryant & Veroff, 1982; Diener, 1984; Diener, Sandvik, & Pavot, 1991; Diener et al., 1999).

Beginning with Ryff's (1985, 1989b) operationalization of syntheses of clinical and personality theorists' conceptions of positive functioning (Jahoda, 1958; Ryff, 1989a), the study of subjective well-being has moved toward a broader set of measures of positive functioning. Positive functioning consists of six dimensions of psychological well-being: self-acceptance, positive relations with others, personal growth, purpose in life, environmental mastery, and autonomy (see Table 4.1 for a definition and ex-

emplary item of each dimension). The psychological well-being scales are well validated and reliable (Ryff, 1989b), and the six-factor structure has been confirmed in the MIDUS study (Ryff & Keyes, 1995).

Keyes (1998) reasoned that well-being as a form of positive functioning also is social and proposed five dimensions of social well-being. Whereas psychological well-being represents more private and personal criteria for evaluation of one's functioning, social well-being epitomizes many of the more public and social criteria whereby people evaluate their life functioning. These social dimensions, again validated and reliable, were tested in the MacArthur MIDUS national study as well as a representative sample of adults in Dane County, Wisconsin. Both studies validated the proposed five-factor theory of social well-being, which consists of the dimensions of social coherence, social actualization, social integration, social acceptance, and social contribution (see Table 4.1 for a definition and exemplary item of each dimension).

Mental Illness and Mental Health: Toward Rapprochement

Measures of mental illness symptoms correlate modestly and negatively with measures of subjective well-being (i.e., symptoms of mental health). Thus, as stated in *Mental Health: A Report of the Surgeon General* (U.S. Department of Health and Human Services, 1999), mental health and mental illness are not at opposite ends of a single health continuum. Specifically, measures of psychological well-being (in two separate studies reviewed in Ryff & Keyes, 1995) correlate on average $-.51$ with the Zung depression inventory and $-.55$ with the Center for Epidemiological Studies depression scale. Indicators and scales of life satisfaction and happiness (i.e., emotional well-being) also tend to correlate around $-.40$ to $-.50$ with scales of depression (see, e.g., Frisch, Cornell, Villanueva, & Retzlaff, 1992).

Based on these findings, we can discern support for the enduring proposal that health is a complete state (World Health Organization, 1948). Mental health is not merely the absence of mental illness, nor is it merely the presence of high well-being. Rather, we defined mental health as a complete state consisting of (a) the absence of mental illness and (b) the presence of high-level well-being. The model of complete

Table 4.1 Conceptions and Operationalizations of Dimensions of Psychological and Social Well-Being

Psychological Well-Being	Social Well-Being
Self-Acceptance: possess positive attitude toward the self; acknowledge and accept multiple aspects of self; feel positive about past life. *When I look at the story of my life, I am pleased with how things have turned out so far.*	*Social Acceptance*: have positive attitudes toward people; acknowledge others and generally accept people, despite others' sometimes complex and perplexing behavior. *I believe people are kind.*
Personal Growth: have feeling of continued development and potential and are open to new experience; feel increasingly knowledgeable and effective. *For me, life has been a continuous process of learning, changing, and growth.*	*Social Actualization*: care about and believe society is positive; think society has potential to grow positively; think self-society is realizing potential. *The world is becoming a better place for everyone.*
Purpose in Life: have goals and a sense of direction in life; present and past life are meaningful; hold beliefs that give purpose to life. *Some people wander aimlessly through life, but I am not one of them.*	*Social Contribution*: feel they have something valuable to give to society; think their daily activities are valued by their community. *I have something valuable to give to the world.*
Environmental Mastery: feel competent and able to manage a complex environment; choose or create personally suitable contexts. *I am good at managing the responsibilities of daily life.*	*Social Coherence*: see a social world that is intelligible, logical, and predictable; care about and are interested in society and community. *I find it easy to predict what will happen next in society.*
Autonomy: self-determining, independent, and regulate behavior internally; resist social pressures to think and act in certain ways; evaluate self by personal standards. *I have confidence in my own opinions, even if they are different from the way most other people think.*	*Social Integration*: feel part of community; think they belong, feel supported, and share commonalities with community. *My community is a source of comfort.*
Positive Relations With Others: have warm, satisfying, trusting relationships; are concerned about others' welfare; capable of strong empathy, affection, and intimacy; understand give-and-take of human relationships. *People would describe me as a giving person, willing to share my time with others.*	

Note: Exemplary items are italicized.

mental health (depicted in Figure 4.2) combines the mental illness and mental health dimensions, thereby yielding two states of mental illness and two states of mental health. In this model, mental health consists of a complete and an incomplete state; mental illness also consists of an incomplete and a complete state.

Complete mental health is the syndrome that combines high levels of symptoms of emotional well-being, psychological well-being, and social well-being, as well as the absence of recent mental illness. Thus, mentally healthy adults will exhibit emotional vitality (e.g., high happiness and satisfaction), will be functioning well psychologically and socially, and will be free of recent (i.e., 12-month) mental illness. Incomplete mental health, on the other hand, is a condition in which individuals may be free of recent mental illness, but they also have low levels of emotional, psychological, and social well-being (Keyes, in preparation).

Complete mental illness is the syndrome that combines low levels of symptoms of emotional well-being, psychological well-being, and social well-being and includes the diagnosis of a recent mental illness such as depression. Thus, mentally unhealthy adults not only will exhibit the classic signs of depression, but also will not feel good about their lives and will not be functioning well psychologically or socially. In contrast, adults with incomplete mental illness may be depressed, but they also will show signs of moderate or high levels of psychological and social functioning and will feel relatively satisfied and

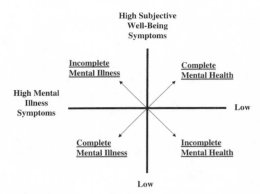

Figure 4.2 Mental health and mental illness: The complete state model.

happy with their lives. Conceptually, adults with incomplete mental health are similar to high-functioning individuals who have a serious alcohol problem but can successfully hold onto their jobs.

Put differently, mentally healthy adults are free of "pathologies." However, some adults without mental illness also will have low levels of well-being, which is a condition described as *languishing* by Keyes (in preparation). In contrast, adults who are free of mental illness but who have high levels of emotional well-being and high levels of psychological and social well-being, are *flourishing* (Keyes, in preparation). Mentally unhealthy adults will possess a recent mental illness. Some of these adults are described as *floundering* in life because they not only have a mental illness but also have very low levels of emotional, psychological, and social well-being. However, many adults who have a mental illness also may be filled with moderate or high levels of emotional, psychological, and social well-being, which may be described as a state of *struggling* with life (Keyes and Haidt, in preparation).

Penninx et al. (1998) were among the first to use a diagnostic approach that approximates the operationalization of mental health as a complete state. These researchers investigated the prevalence and predictors of emotional vitality of older women (65 and older) with physical disabilities. Emotional vitality was operationalized as high levels of perceived mastery and avowed happiness, and few symptoms of depression and anxiety. Penninx et al. found that 35% of these older women with physical disabilities met the criteria of emotional vitality. One third of these older women fit the criteria of incomplete mental health—that is, they were

free of depression but also were low in emotional vitality. In turn, 32% of the older women exhibited a version of complete mental illness, reporting low emotional vitality and a high number of symptoms of depression.

In sum, mental health is a syndrome of symptoms. These symptoms include emotional well-being, which reflects individuals' evaluations of their happiness and satisfaction with life, and the balance of their positive to negative affect. Symptoms of mental health also indicate levels of positive functioning as exhibited by the various dimensions of psychological well-being and social well-being. Mental health and illness are complete states that are best diagnosed as the absence and the presence of symptoms of mental disorders and subjective well-being.

The ability to diagnose complete and incomplete states of mental illness and mental health may lead to more effective prevention and treatment programs. For instance, incomplete mental health (e.g., languishing in life) may be a "way station" at which individuals reside prior to the onset of depression, or a place where many people reside following traditional psychotherapeutic treatments. Preventively, the diagnosis of languishing among youth may be used to identify individuals who require treatments and therapies to elevate well-being and prevent slippage into mental illness. For interventions, the diagnosis of mental health may be used to complete traditional regimens for reduction of depressive symptoms. If relapse is likely to occur within months of remission from treatments, mental health diagnosis may identify individuals who are languishing and require additional treatments to launch them into the realm of mental health. We would hypothesize that interventions and treatments that launch people toward the state of flourishing, as opposed to leaving them at the condition of languishing, should decrease the rate and amount of relapse.

Mental Health: Positive Treatments and Interventions

Positive treatments are those where the objective is to promote levels of well-being or build upon or draw out a person's existing strengths. Because most current treatments target the presence and absence of mental illness, the objective of symptom reduction has been their primary goal. The ephemeral nature of remission among depression patients (Ramana et al., 1995), however, strongly suggests that symptom reduction may be only a first step in treatment. The ability to measure patient well-being and to diagnose states and conditions of mental health suggests that treatment may fruitfully pursue loftier goals of promotion of quality of life and, possibly, flourishing in life (see e.g., Frisch et al., 1992; Gladis, Gosch, Dishuk, & Crits-Christoph, 1999). In this section, we lay the groundwork for the reconceptualization of clients, treatment, and outcome; moreover, we review the small but growing literature on the nature and utility of interventions that are believed to be "positive" and "additive" in nature.

Connecting Diagnosis and Treatment

Members of many factions of professional psychology (e.g., constructivist psychotherapists, counseling psychologists, clinical health psychologists) have attempted to shield their clients and research participants from the stigmatization associated with being identified as "a client with a disorder." Movement away from the overreliance on the *DSM-IV* as a comprehensive conceptual framework leaves postmodern psychologists asking, "How can we conceptualize this client's struggles in a way that is therapeutically useful and still communicate intelligibly with colleagues and case managers?" (Neimeyer & Raskin, 2000, p. 4). This gap between intention and practicality, however, remains unresolved. The heightened sensitivity to clients' human experiences and the acknowledgment of the expanse between best practice and usual practice signify movement in a desirable direction. Nevertheless, in most diagnostic approaches (most definitely the *DSM* system, but others as well), there is a failure to facilitate the conceptualization of struggles as well as strengths (see Wright & Lopez, this volume). Moreover, it is assumed that individuals do not seek psychological support unless they are struggling and lack other appropriate resources. The Keyes classification system of complete mental health provides a framework for conceptualizing clients' cognitive, behavioral, and emotional repertoire in a dynamic fashion, and it reflects a move to connect diagnosis and treatment.

Shifts in the diagnostic systems, or the mere introduction of alternatives, potentially will be accompanied by reconceptualizations of (a) who are candidates for psychotherapeutic interventions; (b) what stimulates change, growth, and well-being; and (c) what are considered as successful treatment outcomes. Psychological prevention, intervention, and health promotion could become woven into the fabrics of families and schools. Mindfulness of the positive effects of small gestures of kindness (Isen, 1987), awe-inspiring stories (Haidt, 2000), and other everyday occurrences could become a focus of psychological change approaches. Thus, we would create an additive change process rather than an enterprise focused on problem management and symptom relief. Attempts at therapeutic change therefore could target optimal human functioning and mental health.

Reconceptualizing Clients, Therapy, and Outcome

Clients as Active Seekers of Health

Much has been written about the role of the client in the diagnostic and change processes (see Petry, Tennen, and Affleck, 2000, for a review of "the elusive client variable in psychotherapy research"), and it seems that practice and science slowly have formed the views of clients as being their personal change agents. Views of clients as "passive receptacles" and therapists as purveyors of magical change techniques have become antiquated. Strupp (1980) asserted that psychotherapy can be beneficial to an individual "provided the patient is willing and able to avail himself of the essential ingredients" (p. 602). Bohart and Tallman (1999) contend that clients go beyond "availing" and are self-healers capable of realizing their optimal health status. Robitschek (1998), building on Ryff and Keyes's (1995) well-being dimension of positive growth, suggests that people possess a "personal growth initiative" that facilitates their abilities to be "fully aware of and intentionally engaged in the process of growth" (p. 183).

Meta-analytic outcome research suggests that "client factors" may contribute to change. Lambert (1992) demonstrated that the array of client variables associated with extratherapeutic change is the fodder that fuels the change process. More specifically, therapeutic techniques, expectancy and placebo effects, therapeutic relationship, and extratherapeutic change factors account for 15%, 15%, 30%, and 40%, respectively, of the improvement in client lives. Clearly, clinical interventions provide only one portion of the fuel for change.

The bulk of the "change responsibility" falls on active self-healers, and change is realized through developing a working alliance with a socially sanctioned healer, hoping and expecting change (see Snyder, Rand, & Sigmon, this volume), and availing oneself of the "extratherapeutic" strengths and strategies for living. Attributing such a large percentage of change responsibility to the client reinforces Bohart and Tallman's (1999) notion of "client as self-healer" and reaffirms the often-cited words of Hoyt (1994) regarding a "new direction" in the psychotherapy movement that allows people to "create their own realities": "This new direction focuses more on the strengths and resources that patients/clients bring to the enterprise than on their weaknesses and limitations. Similarly, more emphasis is put on where people want to go than on where they have been" (p. 8).

Therapy: Prevention, Intervention, and Health Promotion

Psychotherapy, the linguistic equivalent of "mental treatment," has taken on generally negative connotations in everyday parlance. Most certainly the word implies that the client is a passive recipient of "change magic." Reconceptualizing what mental health professionals do *to collaborate with clients* is needed. Our view is grounded in the belief that people are self-healers (Bohart & Tallman, 1999) who may have multiple and sometimes conflicting standards for evaluating the implications of self-change (Keyes & Ryff, 2000). Predicating a view of therapy on the Keyes classification model fosters the idea that therapy should help people move through stages of "being" (i.e., complete or incomplete mental illness and mental health).

Psychological treatment traditionally has been thought of as the practice of remediating illness. Although the fields of disease prevention and psychotherapy share some common principles (e.g., the promotion of competencies as protective factors), fundamental differences are more apparent. Clinicians remain focused on individual cases and try to invoke personal change in the client. In contrast, prevention is an attempt to reduce the number of cases (i.e., prevalence) and the number of new cases (i.e., incidence) of a disorder in a population by invoking changes in the environment as well as in the individuals (see Heller, Wyman, & Allen, 2000). To lay claim to one of the "birthrights" of psychology, that is, the nurturing of health and genius (Seligman, 1998), psychology must develop treatments that reduce the incidence of mental disorders and embrace environmental

change as well as individual change. Practitioners, as well as process and outcome researchers, should begin to conceptualize psychological treatment as being three-pronged, based on the acronym PIP: prevention, intervention, and promotion.

Outcome: Going Beyond the Baseline

Much of the research on effectiveness and efficacy, including the Consumer Reports Survey, has focused on the extent to which clients realize therapeutic goals of symptom relief and improved functioning in life domains (Seligman, 1995). Changes in symptomatology and vitality are the ingredients of therapeutic movement; premorbid baseline functioning, however, seldom is considered. (See Ingram, Hayes, and Scott, 2000, for a more detailed discussion of dimensions of outcome assessment.)

Outcome measures of convenience often are used by practitioners and researchers; one of these, the Global Assessment of Functioning (GAF) Scales (*DSM-IV*; APA, 1994), serves as an example of how symptoms and vigor are included in a conceptualization of improvement in psychological functioning, but in a manner that is quite limited. The GAF as currently constructed provides a user-friendly means of determining the extent to which symptoms of disorder are affecting the lives of people. Theoretically, if an assessment of an individual's behavior yields little evidence of symptomatology and associated effects on functioning, a high GAF score is given. In essence, the individual has moved toward what may be identified as a baseline state of "freedom from disorder and poor functioning." This, however, provides only some of the information clinicians should want to know about how well an individual is functioning. Furthermore, baseline functioning is not identified, and the "default" end goal of therapeutic movement, within a conceptual system with a GAF of 100 being optimal health, is at best at the baseline—with the person being asymptomatic for a mental illness.

Although there are more sophisticated outcome measures than the GAF, assessment of the effectiveness of positive treatments may be limited because of the focus on the alleviation of symptoms in our current system for measuring outcomes. Therefore, adoption of new diagnostic and treatment paradigms will influence approaches to outcome research. The view of the client as poised for movement into another health stage or quadrant suggests how prevention could ward off health declines, how intervention could eliminate barriers to growth and well-being, and how health promotion could help people go beyond their baseline functioning (i.e., prior to psychological struggles that precipitated treatment).

To extend this "beyond the baseline" view of therapeutic movement and outcome to the Keyes classification system, the two axes of the diagnostic framework need to be thought of as baselines for mental illness symptomatology and aspects of subjective well-being (the x- and y-axis, respectively). The classification criteria provide "built-in" outcome criteria because movement beyond the baseline involves movement from one diagnostic category to another as symptomatology decreases and/or vitality increases. Figure 4.3 depicts this positive change starting in each of the quadrants.

Positive Therapeutic Systems

In a body of emerging research, investigators are suggesting that the sole attention to the reduction of negative thinking and associated symptomatology does not necessarily lead to optimal functioning (e.g., Riskind, Sarampote, & Mercier, 1996; Snyder & McCollough, 2000). As Lopez, Prosser, LaRue, Ulven, & Vehige (2000) point out, "something else" appears to be essential to effective psychological functioning. What type of therapeutic interventions could increase the presence of functioning associated with mental health?

Positive therapeutic systems can promote well-being that may act as a buffer against subsequent stress, and other therapies may be used to prevent risk factors associated with illness (Kaplan, 2000), or posttreatment relapses, or to promote general health and well-being. In these systems, it is assumed that clients have a psychological focus rather than a problem. Subsequently, we describe exemplars of positive therapies with prevention, intervention, and promotion foci (see Snyder, Feldman, Taylor, Schroeder, & Adams, 2000, for a discussion of integrating hope training into prevention, intervention, and promotion).

Prevention

Attributional training for optimism inoculates children against depression. Learned optimism training (Seligman, Reivich, Jaycox, & Gillham,

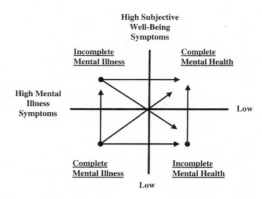

Figure 4.3 Making changes beyond baselines.

1995) is designed to transform negative thinking into positive cognitive processes that promote flexible thought and resiliency. In learned optimism interventions, the three components of explanatory style (i.e., permanence, pervasiveness, and personalization) are modified with cognitive techniques so that people are able to respond in a more healthy manner to both positive and negative outcomes of daily events.

Evidence supporting the prevention benefits of learned optimism training comes from Seligman et al. (1995). In a study of 70 fifth- and sixth-grade students who were at risk for depression, the children were taught techniques for changing their style of explaining situations. In comparison with children in a control group, the children who completed the learned optimism intervention experienced a significant decrease in depressive symptoms immediately following the study. Furthermore, in 6-month follow-ups for 2 years subsequent to the training, children were half as likely to develop depression.

Intervention

Snyder (1994, 2000) and his colleagues are studying various approaches for using the hope components (see Snyder, Rand, & Sigmon, this volume for a detailed discussion of the hope theory and model) to improve psychological and perhaps even physical health. Two groups of clinical researchers (Irving et al., 1997; Klausner, Snyder, & Cheavens, 2000) have conducted intervention studies that examined the effects of hope training on presenting symptomatology. Klausner et al. demonstrated that depressed older adults benefited from group therapy that focused on goal setting and increasing the production of pathways and agency thoughts through actual work on reasonable goals, discussion of the process, and weekly homework assignments. Participants' reports of hopelessness and anxiety lessened significantly, whereas the state of hope increased. Moreover, in comparison with members of a reminiscence therapy group, members of the hope-focused group substantially decreased their depressive symptomatology.

In another hope application study, Irving et al. demonstrated that a 5-week pretreatment hope-focused orientation group had benefits for incoming clients to a community mental health center. Furthermore, these researchers found that those clients who were lower in hope reported the greater responsiveness to the hope orientation on measures of well-being, level of functioning, coping, and symptomatology. A third intervention, scheduled for completion in 2001 (Cheavens et al. at the University of Kansas), examines the effectiveness of a 5-week hope intervention group designed to decrease anxiety and improve overall functioning in individuals who present to a psychological clinic with stress-related problems. Initial analyses suggest that this intervention is effective.

A hope therapy system has been developed, but to date its effectiveness has not been examined (see Lopez, Floyd, Ulven, & Snyder, 2000, for a detailed description of the systems underlying assumptions and associated clinical techniques). Hope therapy is based on the prerequisite skills necessary to produce well-conceptualized goal thoughts, along with the requisite associated pathway and agency thoughts. Accordingly, it helps clients in conceptualizing clearer goals, producing numerous pathways to attainment, summoning the mental energy to maintain pursuit, and reframing insurmountable obstacles as challenges to be overcome. The system may be most effective as an intervention for mild depression, anxiety, and adjustment problems (see Worthington et al., 1997; Worthington, 1999, for a discussion of hope intervention for couples).

Promoting Health

The dimensions of psychological well-being (Ryff, 1989b; Ryff & Keyes, 1995) serve as the foundation for the development of a psychotherapeutic treatment designed by Fava (1999). Well-being therapy is an 8-session treatment that utilizes a structured, problem-oriented approach, with emphasis on self-observation and the therapeutic relationship. The therapist's primary health-promoting responsibility is to help the client cognitively restructure his or her views on concepts pivotal to well-being (i.e., environmental mastery, personal growth, purpose in life, autonomy, self-acceptance, and positive relations with others). Consciousness of health is raised, and episodes of well-being are identified and highlighted. Once the client learns to hone in on mastery, growth, and positive relationships, intermediate sessions focus on the identification of processes that disrupt well-being, and later sessions promote progression beyond the baseline and induce greater psychological well-being.

Based on preliminary validation studies, this approach to therapy is equally or more effective than other techniques in reducing residual symptoms in people recovering from affective disorders (Rafanelli et al., 1998)—taking people beyond the baseline of previous functioning. Fava (1999) focuses on the value of the well-being intervention, but he has not addressed the health promotion benefits of his techniques. Future application and examination of well-being therapy should highlight the other dimensions of well-being (e.g., social well-being and emotional well-being) and investigate the health benefits (relapse prevention, coping resources, etc.) of this work.

This is not an exhaustive list of therapeutic systems and interventions designed to help clients achieve functioning beyond their idiographic baseline. Increasing "developmental assets" (Benson, Leffert, Scales, & Blyth, 1998; Scales, Benson, Leffert, & Blyth, 2000) appears to make children less vulnerable to dysfunction. Hope treatments provide preventative assistance as well as intervention (Lopez et al. at the University of Kansas, in progress). Outcome research focusing on positive psychotherapy, a system developed by Pesechkian (Pesechkian, 1997; Pesechkian & Tritt, 1998), has provided support for its effectiveness. Health promotion treatments that seem to be effective include those focusing on forgiveness (see McCullough and Witvliet, this volume) and emotional intelligence training (see Salovey, Mayer, and Caruso, this volume).

The Heart and Soul of Change

Psychological change processes often mystify even the most experienced researchers and clinicians, but the scientific spotlight has begun to illuminate the active ingredients of human potentialities. Hubble, Duncan, and Miller made strides in demystifying the psychological change process in their 1999 volume, *The Heart and Soul of Change*. Bergin and Garfield (1994) stated, "As therapists have depended more upon the client's resources, more change seems to occur" (p. 826). Helping clients marshal their strengths and resources in the change process begins with the mental health professionals' attitude about the client's role in the change process, and with the sharing of strategies that help get people where they want to go. On this note, we suggest that the heart and soul of change lies in the heart and soul of active self-healers and in prevention, intervention, and promotion strategies. That is to say we must capitalize on the resources of the people with whom we work. Likewise, researchers must avail themselves of the techniques and measures that reveal positive change.

Conclusions

These are indeed the best and the worst of times for the study and treatment of mental illness. If we continue to focus on the proximal causes and patient inflow, we will have more talk and drug therapies that provide statistically significant but short-lived remission from the symptoms of mental illness. Given the burden of mental illness to society, family, and the individual, it behooves us to continue to invest in the study of the etiology and treatment of mental illness.

We would strongly argue, however, that this country requires a more comprehensive approach to the etiology and treatment of mental illness. This new approach would recognize that health is not merely the absence of illness symptoms but also the presence of symptoms of well-being. To achieve the goal of genuine or complete mental health, we must begin to diagnose and study the etiology and treatments associated with mental health, and we must develop a science of mental health. The data clearly show that mental illness and mental health are correlated but distinct dimensions. Consequently, to achieve its goal of "improving this nation's health," the National Institute of Mental Health must marshal the political support and economic infrastructure to build a science of mental health in the same way it built the science of mental illness over the past 45

years (U.S. Department of Health and Human Services, 1995).

As the surgeon general (U.S. Department of Health and Human Services, 1999) states, "Mental health is a state of successful performance of mental function, resulting in productive activities, fulfilling relationships with people, and the ability to adapt to change and to cope with adversity" (p. 4). This state of mental function includes the presence and absence of symptoms of emotional, psychological, and social well-being, as well as the presence and absence of symptoms of mental illness.

Acknowledgment The first author acknowledges the support of the John D. and Catherine T. MacArthur Foundation, through membership in the Successful Midlife Research Network (directed by Dr. Orville Gilbert Brim, Jr.), as well as the financial and intellectual support of the Center for Child Well-Being, funded by the Robert Wood Johnson Foundation through the Taskforce for Child Survival and Development, an affiliated institute of the Rollins School of Public Health of Emory University.

Notes

1. Mental disorder is a persistent deviation from normal functioning that is sufficient to cause emotional suffering and to impair individuals' ability to execute their role responsibilities (e.g., as a parent, a spouse, or an employee; Spitzer & Wilson, 1976).
2. The High Scope/Perry Preschool Project (Schweinhart & Weikart, 1989; Wortman, 1995) is an excellent example of the cost-effectiveness of early interventions aimed at prevention through risk reduction.
3. Average correlations are based on the average of z-transformed Pearson correlations that are converted back into estimates of the Pearson correlation.

References

American Psychiatric Association. (1980). *Diagnostic and statistical manual of mental disorders* (3rd ed.). Washington, DC: Author.
American Psychiatric Association (1994). *Diagnostic and statistical manual of mental disorders* (4th ed.). Washington, DC: Author.

Andrews, F. M., & Withey, S. B. (1976). *Social indicators of well-being: Americans' perceptions of life quality.* New York: Plenum.

Benson, P. L., Leffert, N., Scales, P. C., & Blyth, D. A. (1998). Beyond the village rhetoric: Creating healthy communities for children and adolescents. *Applied Developmental Science, 2,* 138–159.

Bergin, A. E., & Garfield, S. L. (1994). Overview, trends, and future issues. In A. E. Bergin & S. L. Garfield (Eds.), *Handbook of psychotherapy and behavior change* (4th ed., pp. 821–830). New York: Wiley.

Bohart, A., & Tallman, K. (1999). *How clients make therapy work: The process of active self-healing.* Washington, DC: American Psychological Association.

Bradburn, N. M. (1969). *The structure of psychological well-being.* Chicago: Aldine.

Bryant, F. B., & Veroff, J. (1982). The structure of psychological well-being: A sociohistorical analysis. *Journal of Personality and Social Psychology, 43,* 653–673.

Burke, K. C., Burke, J. D., Rae, D. S., & Regier, D. A. (1991). Comparing age at onset of major depression and other psychiatric disorders by birth cohorts in five U.S. community populations. *Archives of General Psychiatry, 48,* 789–795.

Cross-National Collaborative Group. (1992). The changing rate of major depression: Cross-national comparisons. *Journal of the American Medical Association, 268,* 3098–3105.

Diener, E. (1984). Subjective well-being. *Psychological Bulletin, 95,* 542–575.

Diener, E., Sandvik, E., & Pavot, W. (1991). Happiness is the frequency, not the intensity, of positive versus negative affect. In F. Strack, M. Argyle, & N. Schwarz (Eds.), *Subjective well-being: An interdisciplinary perspective* (pp. 119–139). Oxford: Pergamon.

Diener, E., Suh, E. M., Lucas, R. E., & Smith, H. L. (1999). Subjective well-being: Three decades of progress. *Psychological Bulletin, 125,* 276–302.

Fava, G. A. (1999). Well-being therapy: Conceptual and technical issues. *Psychotherapy and Psychosomatics, 68,* 171–179.

Frisch, M. B., Cornell, J., Villanueva, M., & Retzlaff, P. J. (1992). Clinical validation of the Quality of Life Inventory: A measure of life satisfaction for use in treatment planning and outcome assessment. *Psychological Assessment, 4,* 92–101.

Gladis, M. M., Gosch, E. A., Dishuk, N. M., & Crits-Christoph, P. (1999). Quality of life: Expanding the scope of clinical significance. *Journal of Consulting and Clinical Psychology, 67,* 320–331.

Gonzales, L., Lewinsohn, P. M., & Clarke, G. (1985). Longitudinal follow-up of unipolar depressives: An investigation of predictors of relapse. *Journal of Consulting and Clinical Psychology, 53,* 461–469.

Haidt, J. (2000, January). *Awe and elevation.* Paper presented at the Akumal II: A Positive Psychology Summit, Akumal, Mexico.

Heller, K., Wyman, M. F., & Allen, S. M. (2000). Future directions for prevention science: From research to adoption. In C. R. Snyder & R. E. Ingram (Eds.), *Handbook of psychological change* (pp. 660–680). New York: Wiley.

Hoyt, M. F. (1994). Introduction: Competency-based future-oriented therapy. In M. F. Hoyt (Ed.), *Constructive therapies* (pp. 1–10). New York: Guilford.

Hubble, M. A., Duncan, B. L., & Miller, S. D. (Eds.). (1999). *The heart and soul of change: What works in therapy.* Washington, DC: American Psychological Association.

Ingram, R. E., Hayes, A., & Scott, W. (2000). Empirically supported treatments: A critical analysis. In C. R. Snyder & R. E. Ingram (Eds.), *Handbook of psychological change* (pp. 40–60). New York: Wiley.

Irving, L., Snyder, C. R., Gravel, L., Hanke, J., Hilberg, P., & Nelson, N. (1997). *Hope and effectiveness of a pre-therapy orientation group for community mental health center clients.* Paper presented at the Western Psychological Association Convention, Seattle, WA.

Isen, A. M. (1987). Positive affect, cognitive processes, and social behavior. In L. Berkowitz (Ed.)., *Advancements in social psychology* (Vol. 20, pp. 203–254). Orlando, FL: Academic Press.

Jahoda, M. (1958). *Current concepts of positive mental health.* New York: Basic Books.

Kaplan, R. M. (2000). Two pathways to prevention. *American Psychologist, 55,* 382–396.

Keller, M. B., Shapiro, R. W., Lavori, P. W., & Wolfe, N. (1982). Relapse in major depressive disorder: Analysis with the life event table. *Archives of General Psychiatry, 39,* 911–915.

Kessler, R. C., McGonagle, K. A., Zhao, S., Nelson, C. B., Hughes, M., Eshleman, S., Wittchen, H. U., & Kendler, K. S. (1994). Lifetime and 12 month prevalence of *DSM-III-R* psychiatric disorders in the United States: Results from the National Comorbidity Survey. *Archives of General Psychiatry, 51,* 8–19.

Kessler, R. C., Nelson, C. B., McGonagle, K. A., Edlund, M. J., Frank, R. G., & Leaf, P. J. (1996). The epidemiology of co-occurring addictive and mental disorders: Implications for prevention and service utilization. *American Journal of Orthopsychiatry, 66*(1), 17–31.

Keyes, C. L. M. (1998). Social well-being. *Social Psychology Quarterly, 61*, 121–140.

Keyes, C. L. M. (in press). Definition of mental disorders. In C. E. Faupel & P. M. Roman (Eds.), *The encyclopedia of criminology and deviant behavior* (Vol. 4). London: Taylor and Francis.

Keyes, C. L. M. (in preparation). *Mental health: The diagnosis and epidemiology of flourishing and languishing in the U.S.* Manuscript submitted for publication.

Keyes, C. L. M., & Haidt, J. (Ed.). (in preparation). *Flourishing: The positive person and the good life.* Washington, DC: American Psychological Association.

Keyes, C. L. M., & Ryff, C. D. (1998). Generativity in adult lives: Social structural contours and quality of life consequences. In D. McAdams & E. de St. Aubin (Eds.), *Generativity and adult development: Perspectives on caring for and contributing to the next generation* (pp. 227–263). Washington, DC: American Psychological Association.

Keyes, C. L. M., & Ryff, C. D. (1999). Psychological well-being in midlife. In S. L. Willis & J. D. Reid (Eds.), *Middle aging: Development in the third quarter of life* (pp. 161–180). Orlando, FL: Academic Press.

Keyes, C. L. M., & Ryff, C. D. (2000). Subjective change and mental health: A self-concept theory. *Social Psychology Quarterly, 63*, 264–279.

Klausner, E., Snyder, C. R., & Cheavens, J. (2000). A hope-based group treatment for depressed older outpatients. In G. M. Williamson, P. A. Parmalee, & D. R. Shaffer (Eds.), *Physical illness and depression in older adults: A handbook of theory, research, and practice* (pp. 295–310). New York: Plenum.

Klerman, G. L., & Weissman, M. M. (1989). Increasing rates of depression. *Journal of the American Medical Association, 261*, 2229–2235.

Koening, H. G., & Blazer, D. G. (1992). Mood disorders and suicide. In J. E. Birren & R. B. Sloane (Eds.), *Handbook of mental health and aging* (2nd ed., pp. 379–407). San Diego, CA: Academic Press.

Lambert, M. J. (1992). Psychotherapy outcome research. In J. C. Norcross & M. R. Goldfried (Eds.), *Handbook of psychotherapy integration* (pp. 94–129). New York: Basic Books.

Lewinsohn, P. M., Hoberman, H. M., & Rosenbaum, M. (1988). A prospective study of risk factors for unipolar depression. *Journal of Abnormal Psychology, 97*, 251–264.

Lewinsohn, P. M., Rohde, P., Seeley, J. R., & Fischer, S. A. (1993). Age-cohort changes in the lifetime occurrence of depression and other mental disorders. *Journal of Abnormal Psychology, 102*, 110–120.

Lopez, S. J., Floyd, R. K., Ulven, J. C., & Snyder, C. R. (2000). Hope therapy: Building a house of hope. In C. R. Snyder (Ed.), *The handbook of hope: Theory, measures, and applications* (pp. 123–148). New York: Academic Press.

Lopez, S. J., Prosser, E. C., LaRue, S., Ulven, J. C., & Vehige, S. (2000). *Practicing positive psychology.* Unpublished manuscript, University of Kansas, Lawrence.

Mechanic, D. (1999). Mental health and mental illness: Definitions and perspectives. In A. V. Horwitz & T. L. Scheid (Eds.), *A handbook for the study of mental health: Social contexts, theories, and systems* (pp. 12–28). New York: Cambridge University Press.

Mrazek, P. J., & Haggerty, R. J. (Eds.). (1994). *Reducing risks for mental disorders.* Washington, DC: National Academy Press.

Murray, C. J. L., & Lopez, A. D. (Eds.). (1996). *The global burden of disease: A comprehensive assessment of mortality and disability from diseases, injuries, and risk factors in 1990 and projected to 2020.* Cambridge, MA: Harvard School of Public Health.

Musselman, D. L., Evans, D. L., & Nemeroff, C. B. (1998). The relationship of depression to cardiovascular disease: Epidemiology, biology, and treatment. *Archives of General Psychiatry, 55*, 580–592.

Neimeyer, R. A., & Raskin, J. A. (Eds.). (2000). *Construction of disorder: Meaning-making frameworks for psychotherapy.* Washington, DC: American Psychological Association.

O'Reardon, J. P., Brunswick, D. J., & Amsterdam, J. D. (2000). Treatment-resistant depression in the age of serotonin: Evolving strategies. *Current Opinion in Psychiatry, 13*, 93–98.

Penninx, B. W. J. H, Guralnik, J. M., Simonsick, E. M., Kasper, J. D., Ferrucci, L., & Fried, L. P. (1998). Emotional vitality among disabled older women: The Women's Health and Aging Study. *Journal of the American Geriatrics Society, 46*, 807–815.

Pesechkian, N. (1977). *Positive psychotherapy: Theory and practice of a new method.* Berlin: Springer-Verlag.

Pesechkian, N., & Tritt, K. (1998). Positive psychotherapy: Effectiveness study and quality assurance. *European Journal of Psychotherapy, Counseling, and Health, 1*, 93–104.

Petry, N. M., Tennen, H., & Affleck, G. (2000). Stalking the elusive client variable in psychotherapy research. In C. R. Snyder & R. E. Ingram (Eds.), *Handbook of psychological change* (pp. 89–108). New York: Wiley.

Rafanelli, C., Conti, S., Ruini, C., Ottolini, F., Grandi, S., & Fava, G. A. (1998). A new psychotherapeutic strategy: Well-being therapy. In E. Sanavio (Ed.), *Behavior and cognitive therapy today: Essays in honor of Hans J. Eysenck* (pp. 223–228). Oxford: Elsevier Science.

Ramana, R., Paykel, E. S., Cooper, Z., Hayhurst, H., Saxty, M., & Surtees, P. G. (1995). Remission and relapse in major depression: A two-year prospective follow-up study. *Psychological Medicine, 25,* 1161–1170.

Rebellon, C., Brown, J., & Keyes, C. L. M. (in press). Suicide and mental illness. In C. E. Faupel & P. M. Roman (Eds.), *The encyclopedia of criminology and deviant behavior: (Vol. 4). Self-destructive behavior and disvalued identity.* London: Taylor and Francis.

Riskind, J. D., Sarampote, C., & Mercier, M. (1996). For every malady a sovereign cure: Optimism training. *Journal of Cognitive Psychotherapy: An International Quarterly, 10,* 105–117.

Robins, L. N., & Regier, D. A. (Eds.) (1991). *Psychiatric disorders in America: The Epidemiological Catchment Area study.* New York: Free Press.

Robitschek, C. (1998). Personal growth initiative: The construct and its measure. *Measurement and Evaluation in Counseling and Development, 30,* 183–198.

Ryff, C. D. (1985). Adult personality development and the motivation for personal growth. In D. Kleiber & M. Maher (Eds.), *Advances in motivation and achievement: Motivation and adulthood* (Vol. 4, pp. 55–92). Greenwich, CT: JAI Press.

Ryff, C. D. (1989a). Beyond Ponce de Leon and life satisfaction: New directions in quest of successful ageing. *International Journal of Behavioral Development, 12,* 35–55.

Ryff, C. D. (1989b). Happiness is everything, or is it? Explorations on the meaning of psychological well-being. *Journal of Personality and Social Psychology, 57,* 1069–1081.

Ryff, C. D., & Keyes, C. L. M. (1995). The structure of psychological well-being revisited. *Journal of Personality and Social Psychology, 69,* 719–727.

Scales, P. C., Benson, P. L., Leffert, N., & Blyth, D. A. (2000). Contribution of developmental assets to the prediction of thriving among adolescents. *Applied Developmental Science, 4,* 27–46.

Schweinhart, L. J., & Weikart, D. P. (1989). The High/Scope Perry Preschool study: Implications for early childhood care and education. *Prevention in Human Services, 7,* 109–132.

Seligman, M. E. P. (1995). The effectiveness of psychotherapy: The Consumer Reports study. *American Psychologist, 50,* 965–974.

Seligman, M. E. P. (1998). *Learned optimism: How to change your mind and your life.* New York: Pocket Books.

Seligman, M. E. P., Reivich, K., Jaycox, L., & Gillham, J. (1995). *The optimistic child.* New York: Houghton Mifflin.

Snyder, C. R. (1994). *The psychology of hope: You can get there from here.* New York: Free Press.

Snyder, C. R. (Ed.). (2000). *The handbook of hope: Theory, measures, and applications.* New York: Academic Press.

Snyder, C. R., Feldman, D. B., Taylor, J. D., Schroeder, L. L., & Adams, V., III. (2000). The roles of hopeful thinking in preventing problems and promoting strengths. *Applied & Preventive Psychology: Current Scientific Perspectives, 15,* 262–295.

Snyder, C. R., & McCullough, M. E. (2000). A positive psychology field of dreams: "If you build it, they will come . . ." *Journal of Social and Clinical Psychology, 19,* 151–160.

Spitzer, R. L., & Wilson, P. T. (1975). Nosology and the official psychiatric nomenclature. In A. Freedman, H. Kaplan, & B. Sadock (Eds.), *Comprehensive textbook of psychiatry* (pp. 826–845). Baltimore: Williams and Wilkins.

Strupp, H. H. (1980). Success and failure in time-limited psychotherapy. *Archives of General Psychiatry, 37,* 595–603.

U.S. Department of Health and Human Services. (1995). *Basic behavioral science research for mental health: A report of the national advisory mental health council.* Rockville, MD: Author.

U.S. Department of Health and Human Services. (1998). *Suicide: A report of the Surgeon General.* Rockville, MD: Author.

U.S. Department of Health and Human Services. (1999). *Mental health: A report of the Surgeon General.* Rockville, MD: Author.

U.S. Department of Health and Human Services. (2000). *Disease-specific estimates of direct and indirect costs of illness and NIH support.* Rockville, MD: Author.

Watson, D., & Tellegen, A. (1985). Toward a consensual structure of mood. *Psychological Bulletin, 98,* 219–235.

Wittchen, H. U., Knauper, B., & Kessler, R. C. (1994). Lifetime risk of depression. *British Journal of Psychiatry, 165* (Suppl.), 16–22.

World Health Organization. (1948). World Health Organization constitution. In *Basic Documents.* Geneva: Author.

Worthington, E. L., Jr. (1999). *Hope-focused marriage counseling.* Downers Grove, IL: Intervarsity Press.

Worthington, E. L., Jr., Hight, T. L., Ripley, J. S., Perrone, K. M., Kurusu, T. A., & Jones, D. R. (1997). Strategic hope-focused relationship-enrichment counseling with individual couples. *Journal of Counseling Psychology, 44,* 381–389.

Wortman, P. M. (1995). An exemplary evaluation of a program that worked: The High/Scope Perry Preschool Project. *Evaluation Practice, 16,* 257–265.

III

Emotion-Focused Approaches

5

Subjective Well-Being

The Science of Happiness and Life Satisfaction

Ed Diener, Richard E. Lucas, & Shigehiro Oishi

Definition of Subjective Well-Being

Since ancient times humans have wondered about what makes a good life. Scientists who study subjective well-being assume that an essential ingredient of the good life is that the person herself likes her life. Subjective well-being is defined as a person's cognitive and affective evaluations of his or her life. These evaluations include emotional reactions to events as well as cognitive judgments of satisfaction and fulfillment. Thus, subjective well-being is a broad concept that includes experiencing pleasant emotions, low levels of negative moods, and high life satisfaction. The positive experiences embodied in high subjective well-being are a core concept of positive psychology because they make life rewarding.

History

Throughout history, philosophers and religious leaders have suggested that diverse characteristics, such as love, wisdom, and nonattachment, are the cardinal elements of a fulfilled existence.

Utilitarians such as Jeremy Bentham, however, argued that the presence of pleasure and the absence of pain are the defining characteristics of a good life (1789/1948). Thus, the Utilitarians were the intellectual forerunners of subjective well-being researchers, focusing on the emotional, mental, and physical pleasures and pains that individuals experience. Although there are other desirable personal characteristics beyond whether a person is happy, the individual with abundant joy has one key ingredient of a good life.

Early in the 20th century, empirical studies of subjective well-being began to take shape. As early as 1925, Flugel studied moods by having people record their emotional events and then summing emotional reactions across moments. Flugel's work was the forerunner of modern experience sampling approaches to measuring subjective well-being on-line as people go about their everyday lives. After World War II, survey researchers began polling people about their happiness and life satisfaction using simple global survey questionnaires. The pollsters studied large numbers of people who were often selected to produce representative samples of nations. George Gallup, Gerald Gurin and his colleagues, and Hadley Cantril pioneered the use of large-scale surveys as an assessment technique. They asked people questions such as "How happy are you?" with simple response options varying from "very happy" to "not very happy." Recently, Diener (2000a) proposed that a national index be created in which subjective well-being would be tracked over time.

Although early subjective well-being studies were characterized by very short scales, many important discoveries were made. In 1969, for example, Norman Bradburn showed that pleasant and unpleasant affect are somewhat independent and have different correlates—they are not simply opposites of one another. Thus, the two affects must be studied separately to gain a complete picture of individuals' well-being. This finding had important implications for the field of subjective well-being: It showed that clinical psychology's attempts to eliminate negative states would not necessarily foster positive states. The elimination of pain may not result in a corresponding increase in pleasure; ridding the world of sadness and anxiety will not necessarily make it a happy place.

Wilson reviewed the meager amount of research on "avowed happiness" in 1967, and Diener (1984) provided a review of the much larger database on subjective well-being that had accumulated by the mid-1980s. By that time, the field was becoming a science. Since Diener's review was published, a number of books have appeared on the topic of subjective well-being (e.g., Argyle, 1987; Myers, 1982; Strack, Argyle, & Schwarz, 1991), and in 1999, Diener, Suh, Lucas, and Smith authored a new review of the literature in *Psychological Bulletin*. A handbook volume of chapters related to hedonic psychology (Kahneman, Diener, & Schwarz, 1999) and a book dedicated to cross-cultural differences in subjective well-being (Diener & Suh, 2000) also provide more thorough reviews of this area.

The scientific discipline of subjective well-being grew rapidly. One reason for this is that people in the Western nations have achieved a level of material abundance and health that allows them to go beyond mere survival in seeking the good life. People around the globe are entering a "postmaterialistic" world, in which they are concerned with issues of quality of life beyond economic prosperity. Subjective well-being also is popular because it is particularly democratic—it grants respect to what people think and feel about their lives. People are not content to have experts evaluate their lives; they believe that their opinions matter. In addition, the study of subjective well-being flourished because of the growing trend toward individualism around the globe. Individualists are concerned with their own feelings and beliefs, and thus the study of subjective well-being corresponds well with the Western zeitgeist. Finally, the field increased in popularity because researchers succeeded in developing scientific methods for studying subjective well-being. For these reasons the scientific study of subjective well-being is now poised to grow into a major scholarly and applied discipline.

Measurement

Early survey instruments usually posed a single question about people's happiness or life satisfaction. Psychometric evaluations of these simple scales showed that they possess a degree of validity. For example, Andrews and Withey (1976) found that global questions about people's overall evaluation of their lives yielded scores that converged well with one another. As the field matured, more multi-item scales appeared, with greater reliability and validity than the single-item instruments. Lucas, Diener, and Suh (1996) demonstrated that multi-item life satisfaction, pleasant affect, and unpleasant affect scales formed factors that were separable from each other, as well as from other constructs such as self-esteem. A number of happiness, affect, and life satisfaction measures are now available (see Andrews & Robinson, 1992, for a review), and we present the five-item Satisfaction With Life Scale (Diener, Emmons, Larsen, & Griffin, 1985; Pavot & Diener, 1993) in the appendix.

A major concern of researchers in the field is whether self-report instruments are valid. After all, people might report that they are happy yet not truly experience high subjective well-being. Sandvik, Diener, and Seidlitz (1993) found that the self-report measures converge with other types of assessment, including expert ratings based on interviews with respondents, experience sampling measures in which feelings are reported at random moments in everyday life, participants' memory for positive versus negative events in their lives, the reports of family and friends, and smiling. Despite the positive psychometric qualities of global subjective well-being measures, however, we recommend a multimethod battery to assess subjective well-being when this is possible. Additional assessment devices based on memory, informant reports, and experience sampling are likely to supplement the information obtained from global measures and guard against response artifacts, and in some cases the alternative measures may yield different answers about who is happiest (e.g., Oishi, 2000).

The use of multiple methods also allows researchers to understand how people construct subjective well-being judgments. Schwarz, Strack, and their colleagues, for example, showed that situational variables can exert a substantial impact on life satisfaction and mood reports (Schwarz & Strack, 1999). Schwarz and Strack's findings illustrate that life satisfaction judgments are not immutable, stored values that are reported when requested. Instead, respondents seem to use currently salient information to construct life satisfaction judgments. Building on this finding, Diener and his colleagues (e.g., Diener & Diener, 1995; Suh, Diener, Oishi, & Triandis, 1998) showed that certain information is chronically salient to some individuals but not to others (Suh & Diener, 1999). Thus, any single piece of information may or may not be used by an individual to construct her or his life satisfaction judgments. For instance, people in individualistic nations may base their life satisfaction judgments on the extent to which they feel high self-esteem, whereas people in collectivistic cultures may base their judgments on the opinions of other people (Diener & Diener, 1995). Thus, a person may use both situationally induced and chronically salient information to construct life satisfaction judgments.

People also may use different metastrategies in seeking the information upon which to base their life satisfaction judgments. For example, some people may search for information about the positive aspects of their lives, whereas others might seek information about problematic areas (Diener et al., in press). Likewise, people differ in the degree to which they weigh their moods and emotions when calculating life satisfaction judgments (Suh & Diener, 1999). Thus, life satisfaction reflects different information for different people and can change depending on what is salient at the moment.

When participants report on any aspect of global subjective well-being, they must construct a judgment about their well-being. This constructed judgment may not faithfully correspond to the average mood or level of satisfaction experienced across many different moments. Thomas and Diener (1990) found only a modest match between people's reports of momentary moods and their recall of those moods. Thus, estimates of happiness and reports of affect over time are likely to be influenced by a person's current mood, his or her beliefs about happiness, and the ease of retrieving positive and negative information.

A fascinating picture of subjective well-being is emerging in which we can differentiate between a person's momentary feelings and thoughts about well-being, and larger, more global constructions. At the momentary level, we can examine people's reports of moods, pleasures, pains, and satisfactions recorded on-line through the experience sampling method. For example, in our laboratory we use palm-sized computers to signal people randomly. When signaled, respondents complete a survey of their feelings at that moment. Kahneman (1999) suggested that these types of data offer the most accurate estimate of subjective well-being because they are less distorted by artifacts and biases.

Global reports of subjective well-being also are valuable, however, because they offer an insight into the fascinating psychological processes by which people construct global judgments about their lives. In global reports of subjective well-being, we discover how a person summarizes her or his life as a whole, and this synopsis may only be moderately correlated with on-line reports. For example, we find that people in cultures where subjective well-being is valued are more likely to weight their most positive domains in calculating a global life satisfaction judgment; people in cultures in which happiness is not an important value are more likely to weight their most negative domains in calculating a life satisfaction judgment (Diener, 2000b). If people believe that life satisfaction is desirable, they may be more likely to search for positive information when reporting global life satisfaction judgments. Thus, the relation between satisfaction with specific domains such as work and satisfaction with life as a whole is likely to be dependent on people's beliefs about what types of information should be considered when judging life in its entirety. In a sense, then, these are two varieties of happiness and satisfaction—evaluations of specific aspects of life and on-line at-the-moment feelings of well-being versus larger, global judgments about one's happiness and satisfaction.

Theoretical Approach

Many theories of happiness have been proposed since Aristotle's brilliant insights. These theories can be categorized into three groups: (1) need and goal satisfaction theories, (2) process or activity theories, and (3) genetic and personality predisposition theories. The first constellation of theories centers around the idea that the reduction of tensions (e.g., the elimination of pain and the satisfaction of biological and psychological needs) leads to happiness. Freud's (1933/1976) pleasure principle and Maslow's (1970) hierarchical needs model represent this approach. In support of this view, Omodei and Wearing (1990) found that the degree to which individuals' needs were met was positively associated with the degree of their life satisfaction.

Goal theorists argue that individuals attain subjective well-being when they move toward an ideal state or accomplish a valued aim (the standard). Other researchers have extended this idea to incorporate the degree of discrepancy from other potential comparison standards. For example, Michalos (1985) postulated that happiness is inversely related to the degree of discrepancy from multiple standards, including what one wants, what one has had in the past, and what relevant others have. Likewise, Higgins (1987) posited that discrepancies from one's "ideal self" and one's "ought self" lead to the experiences of negative emotions. Need and goal satisfaction theorists argue that the reduction of tension and satisfaction of biological and psychological needs and goals will cause happiness.

One implication of tension-reduction theories is that happiness occurs after needs are met and goals are fulfilled. In other words, happiness is a desired end state toward which all activity is directed. These theories can be compared with models of happiness in which engagement in an activity itself provides happiness. Most notably, Csikszentmihalyi (1975) suggested that people are happiest when they are engaged in interesting activities that match their level of skill. He called the state of mind that results from this matching of challenges and skill "flow," and argued that people who often experience flow tend to be very happy. Similarly, Cantor and her colleagues (Cantor & Blanton, 1996; Harlow &

Cantor, 1996) emphasized the importance of active participation in life tasks. For instance, Harlow and Cantor (1996) found that social participation was a strong predictor of life satisfaction for retired elders. Sheldon, Ryan, and Reis (1996) found that people were happiest on days when they engaged in activities for intrinsic reasons (because of the fun and enjoyment). Goal researchers (e.g., Emmons, 1986; Little, 1989) agree that having important goals and pursuing them are reliable indicators of well-being, and therefore goal theories can combine the elements of tension reduction and pleasurable activity in explaining subjective well-being. People who have important goals tend to be more energetic, experience more positive emotions, and feel that life is meaningful (e.g., McGregor & Little, 1998).

Both needs theorists and activity theorists argue that subjective well-being will change with the conditions in people's lives. When individuals are approaching their goals or are engaged in interesting activities, they should experience positive well-being. However, other theorists argue that there is an element of stability in people's levels of well-being that cannot be explained by the stability in the conditions of people's lives. These theorists argue that subjective well-being is strongly influenced by stable personality dispositions.

Subjective well-being judgments reflect cognitive and emotional reactions to life circumstances. Because circumstances can be short-lived and changeable or relatively stable, researchers study both momentary and long-term subjective well-being. Not surprisingly, momentary levels of affect fluctuate quite a bit. For example, Diener and Larsen (1984) found that when people's emotions were sampled at random times throughout the day, a single report of momentary pleasant affect on average correlated only about .10 with pleasant affect in other random moments. People react to changing circumstances, and these reactions are reflected in momentary reports of subjective well-being.

Although it is difficult to predict how happy an individual will be at any given moment, when affect is averaged across many occasions, stable patterns of individual differences emerge. For example, Diener and Larsen (1984) reported that mean levels of pleasant affect experienced in work situations correlated .74 with average levels of pleasant affect experienced in recreation situations. Similarly, average life satisfaction in social situations correlated .92 with average life satisfaction when alone. Based on these results, it appears that although emotions fluctuate, individuals do have characteristic emotional responses to a variety of situations and life circumstances. These characteristic emotional responses are also moderately to strongly stable across long periods of time. Magnus and Diener (1991) found a correlation of .58 between life satisfaction measures assessed over a 4-year interval. Costa and McCrae (1988) reported substantial stability coefficients for affective components of subjective well-being over a period of 6 years.

These results have led some theorists to suggest that although life events can influence subjective well-being, people eventually adapt to these changes and return to biologically determined "set points" or "adaptation levels" (e.g., Headey & Wearing, 1992). For instance, Diener, Sandvik, Seidlitz, and Diener (1993) found that stability in subjective well-being was comparable among people whose income went up, down, or stayed the same over 10 years. Similarly, Costa, McCrae, and Zonderman (1987) reported that people who lived in stable circumstances were no more stable than people who experienced major life changes (e.g., divorce, widowhood, or job loss).

One reason for the stability and consistency of subjective well-being is that there is a substantial genetic component to it; to some degree people are born prone to be happy or unhappy. Tellegen et al. (1988), for example, examined monozygotic twins who were reared apart and compared them with dizygotic twins who were reared apart, as well as with monozygotic and dizygotic twins who were raised together. After comparing the similarities of the various types of twins, Tellegen et al. estimated that 40% of the variability in positive emotionality and 55% of the variability in negative emotionality could be predicted by genetic variation. These estimates allow for environmental influences, but genes do appear to influence characteristic emotional responses to life circumstances.

When one examines personality influences in more detail, the traits that are most consistently linked to subjective well-being are extraversion and neuroticism (Diener & Lucas, 1999). Lucas and Fujita (2000) used meta-analytic and confirmatory factor analytic techniques to show that extraversion is consistently correlated moderately to strongly with pleasant affect; and Fujita (1991) found that neuroticism and nega-

tive affect are indistinguishable after controlling for measurement error. While other personality traits from the Five Factor Model (e.g., agreeableness, conscientiousness, and openness to experience) do correlate with subjective well-being, these relations are smaller and less consistent (see, e.g., Watson & Clark, 1992). Thus, it can be said that an extraverted non-neurotic has a head start in achieving happiness, but that other traits, as well as life circumstances, matter as well.

Differences in subjective well-being also result from stable individual differences in how people think about the world. Differences in the accessibility of pleasant versus unpleasant information, as well as the accuracy and efficiency with which people process pleasant versus unpleasant information influence subjective well-being. Certain people attend to and recall the pleasant aspects of life more than others. Similarly, certain cognitive dispositions such as hope (Snyder et al., 1991), dispositional optimism (e.g., Scheier & Carver, 1993), and expectancy for control (Grob, Stetsenko, Sabatier, Botcheva, & Macek, 1999) appear to influence subjective well-being. It is not just who we are that matters to happiness, but how we think about our lives.

Current Findings

Demographic Correlates of Subjective Well-Being

The strong association between temperament and subjective well-being does not mean that events and circumstances are irrelevant to people's subjective well-being. In the first major review of happiness, Wilson (1967) showed that both personality and demographic factors correlate with subjective well-being. He stated that the happy person is a "young, healthy, well-educated, well-paid, extroverted, optimistic, worry-free, religious, married person with high self-esteem, job morale, modest aspirations, of either sex and of a wide range of intelligence" (p. 294). However. Campbell, Converse, and Rodgers (1976) studied the well-being of Americans and found that demographic variables such as age, income, and education did not account for much variance in reports of well-being, echoing earlier findings by Bradburn (1969) and others. In the past 30 years, researchers systematically cataloged the various demographic correlates of subjective well-being (Diener et al., 1999), with a number of replicable findings emerging: (a) demographic factors such as age, sex, and income are related to subjective well-being; (b) these effects are usually small; and (c) most people are moderately happy, and thus, demographic factors tend to distinguish between people who are moderately happy and those who are very happy (Diener & Diener, 1996).

Income, for example, is consistently related to subjective well-being in both within-nation (e.g., Diener et al., 1993; Haring, Stock, & Okun, 1984) and between-nation analyses (e.g., Diener et al., 1993); but at both the individual and the national level, income change over time has little net effect on subjective well-being (Diener et al., 1993; Diener & Suh, 1998). Goals and expectations must be taken into account to understand the relation between income and subjective well-being; the benefits of a rising income are offset if one's material desires increase even faster than wealth.

Age and sex are related to subjective well-being, but these effects are small, too, and depend on the component of subjective well-being being measured. For example, in an international sample of 40 nations, Diener and Suh (1998) found that although pleasant affect declined across age cohorts, life satisfaction and unpleasant affect showed little change. In two separate international samples consisting of approximately 40 nations each, Lucas and Gohm (2000) found that sex differences in subjective well-being were small (only about one fifth of a standard deviation difference), with women reporting greater unpleasant *and* pleasant affect (though only significant differences in unpleasant affect were replicated across both international samples). Based on these results, one could not simply say that men are happier than women or that the young are happier than the old. The conclusion depends on the component of subjective well-being that is measured. Diener et al. (1999) argued that if theory in this area is to progress, researchers must study the separable components of subjective well-being— "happiness" is not a single thing.

Similarly, researchers must be careful about the conceptualization and measurement of independent variables. For example, Wilson (1967) concluded that physical health is correlated with subjective well-being. However, recent findings qualify this conclusion: The relation depends on whether self-report or objective ratings of health are assessed. Although self-reported health correlates positively with subjective well-being (e.g., Okun, Stock, & Haring, 1984), the correlation is weak when objective health ratings are examined (Watten, Vassend, Myhrer, & Syversen, 1997). Subjective well-being influences the subjective perception of health, and this inflates the correlation between subjective well-being and subjective health. *It appears that the way people perceive the world is much more important to happiness than objective circumstances.*

Other demographic characteristics such as marital status and religious activity are also positively correlated with subjective well-being; but the effects of marriage can differ for men and women, and the effects of religious activity may depend on the specific type of religiosity being assessed. Thus, the answer to whether particular demographic factors increase subjective well-being is likely dependent on people's values and goals, personality, and culture.

Culture and Subjective Well-Being

In recent years, cultural differences in subjective well-being (see Diener & Suh, 2000) have been explored, with a realization that there are profound differences in what makes people happy. Self-esteem, for example, is less strongly associated with life satisfaction (Diener & Diener, 1995), and extraversion is less strongly associated with pleasant affect (Lucas, Diener, Grob, Suh, & Shao, 2000) in collectivist cultures than in individualist cultures. Similarly, Suh (1999) found that there are cultural differences in the importance of personality congruence. Personality congruence reflects the extent to which a person's behaviors are consistent across situations and with the person's inner feelings. Although the importance of personality congruence is often emphasized in Western psychology, it is not universally important. Suh found that collectivists are less congruent than individualists, and that congruence is less strongly related to subjective well-being among collectivists. Suh et al. (1998) also found that among collectivists, the extent to which one's life accords with the wishes of significant others is more important than the emotions that the person feels in predicting his or her life satisfaction.

By examining between-nation differences in wealth and subjective well-being, researchers have arrived at a more complete understanding of the relation between income and happiness.

Some argue that wealth leads to higher subjective well-being only within the poorest nations. According to this idea, wealth influences subjective well-being when basic needs are in danger of not being met. However, Diener, Diener, and Diener (1995) found that even when levels of basic needs were controlled, income had a significant and moderate effect on national subjective well-being. Thus, people in the wealthiest nations tend to be the happiest. This might be because they possess more material goods, but it also could be because the wealthiest nations experience higher levels of human rights, greater longevity, and more equality.

Because demographic variables have different consequences in different cultures, these correlates can vary in importance. For example, marriage is an important demographic correlate of subjective well-being (Diener, Gohm, Suh, & Oishi, 2000). However, it is unclear whether the benefits of marriage result from the love and companionship that accompany long-term relationships or from the social approval that married couples receive. Diener, Gohm, Suh, and Oishi (2000) found that unmarried individuals who lived together were happier than married or single individuals in individualist cultures (suggesting that in these cultures companionship is more important than social approval), but unmarried partners who lived together were less happy than married or single individuals in collectivist cultures (suggesting that in these cultures social approval is an important benefit of marriage). Thus, cultural norms can change the correlates of subjective well-being.

Interventions

Interventions to increase subjective well-being are important not only because it feels good to be happy but also because happy people tend to volunteer more, have more positive work behavior, and exhibit other desirable characteristics. Because of the roots of the field of subjective well-being in survey research, few direct intervention efforts have been implemented. However, Fordyce (1977, 1983) published several studies in which he evaluated a program designed to boost people's happiness. The program is based on the idea that people's subjective well-being can be increased if they learn to imitate the traits of happy people, characteristics such as being organized, keeping busy, spending more time socializing, developing a positive

outlook, and working on a healthy personality. Fordyce found that the program produced increases in happiness compared with a placebo control, as well as compared with participants in conditions receiving only partial information. In a follow-up 9 to 28 months after the study, Fordyce found that there were lasting effects of his intervention.

Seligman, Reivich, Jaycox, and Gillham (1995) performed an experimental study with children in which the treatment groups were exposed to optimism training. Through cognitive training and social-problem solving, elementary school children who were at risk for depression were taught to see the bright side of events. After the intervention, the treatment groups were significantly less depressed than the control group, and this effect grew over the period of the study's 2-year follow-up.

Clearly, more efforts to enhance subjective well-being are needed, along with rigorous methods to evaluate these interventions. For example, more diverse dependent variables and measuring instruments would be salutary, as well as explorations of which interventions are most beneficial, and why. The positive benefits of the few existing experiments, however, suggest that programs designed to enhance subjective well-being can be quite effective.

Future Research

In terms of measurement and research methods, many researchers have relied solely on global retrospective self-reports. A series of construct validation studies by Diener and colleagues (e.g., Lucas et al., 1996; Sandvik et al., 1993) illustrated that global self-reports have a degree of validity. However, it is still unclear to what extent individual and cultural differences found in global reports are accurate reflections of differences in on-line experiences or are manifestations of processes related to global ways people see themselves. What is needed is a battery of subjective well-being measures based on on-line experiences, informant reports, biological measures, and cognitive measures that assess the accessibility of positive events in memory. In addition to better measures, we need many more longitudinal studies in order to assess variables in a temporal order.

In terms of substantive areas, more attention should be paid to developmental processes involving subjective well-being. In particular, given recent advances in infant/child temperament research (e.g., Goldsmith, 1996; Rothbart & Ahadi, 1995), the link between positive affectivity in infancy and childhood and subjective well-being in adulthood should be explored, not only in terms of stability but also with respect to the mechanisms that operate in maintaining or changing one's susceptibility to positive stimuli throughout life. Similarly, a longitudinal approach should be taken in an investigation of society and culture. Specifically, the way in which changes in macro systems (e.g., political, economic, and cultural) have an impact on people's well-being should be examined more carefully to create the happy societies Bentham and others envisioned.

In 1949, Henry Murray and Clyde Kluckhohn claimed that "Aristotle's assertion that the only rational goal of goals is happiness has never been successfully refuted as far as we know, but, as yet no scientist has ventured to break ground for a psychology of happiness" (p. 13). As demonstrated in this chapter, scientists have now begun the scientific study of happiness. Although the happy person is more likely to be from a wealthy nation and have enough resources to pursue his or her particular goals, characteristics such as a positive outlook, meaningful goals, close social relationships, and a temperament characterized by low worry are very important to high subjective well-being. We look to the day when effective interventions based on scientific findings will provide a readily available way to increase happiness.

APPENDIX

Satisfaction with Life Scale

Below are five statements that you may agree or disagree with. Using the 1–7 scale below indicate your agreement with each item by placing the appropriate number on the line preceding that item. Please be open and honest in your responding.

7 Strongly agree
6 Agree
5 Slightly agree
4 Neither agree nor disagree
3 Slightly disagree
2 Disagree
1 Strongly disagree

____ In most ways my life is close to my ideal
____ The conditions of my life are excellent
____ I am satisfied with my life
____ So far I have gotten the important things I want in life
____ If I could live my life over, I would change almost nothing

Scoring and Interpretation of the Scale

Add up your answers to the five items and use the following normative information to help in "interpretation:"

5–9   Extremely dissatisfied with your life
10–14 Very dissatisfied with your life
15–19 Slightly dissatisfied with your life
20   About neutral
21–25 Somewhat satisfied with your life
26–30 Very satisfied with your life
31–35 Extremely satisfied with your life

Most Americans score in the 21–25 range. A score above 25 indicates that you are more satisfied than most people. *The Satisfaction with Life Scale* (Diener, Emmons, Larsen, & Griffin, 1985).

References

Andrews, F. M., & Robinson, J. P. (1992). Measures of subjective well-being. In J. P. Robinson, P. R. Shaver, & L. S. Wrightsman (Eds.), *Measures of personality and social psychological attitudes* (pp. 61–114). San Diego, CA: Academic Press.
Andrews, F. M., & Withey, S. B. (1976). *Social indicators of well-being.* New York: Plenum.
*Argyle, M. (1987). *The psychology of happiness.* London: Methuen.
Bentham, J. (1789/1948). *Introduction to the principles and morals of legislation.* London: University of London Athlone Press.
Bradburn, N. M. (1969). *The structure of psychological well-being.* Chicago: Aldine.
Campbell, A., Converse, P. E., & Rodgers, W. L. (1976). *The quality of American life.* New York: Russell Sage Foundation.
Cantor, N., & Blanton, H. (1996). Effortful pursuit of personal goals in daily life. In J. A. Bargh & P. M. Gollwitzer (Eds.), *The psychology of ac-*

tion: *Linking cognition and motivation to behavior* (pp. 338–359). New York: Guilford.

Costa, P. T., & McCrae, R. R. (1988). Personality in adulthood: A six-year longitudinal study of self-reports and spouse ratings on the NEO Personality Inventory. *Journal of Personality and Social Psychology, 54,* 853–863.

Costa, P. T., Jr., McCrae, R. R., & Zonderman, A. (1987). Environmental and dispositional influences on well-being: Longitudinal follow-up of an American national sample. *British Journal of Psychology, 78,* 299–306.

Csikszentmihalyi, M. (1975). *Beyond boredom and anxiety.* San Francisco: Jossey-Bass.

*Diener, E. (1984). Subjective well-being. *Psychological Bulletin, 93,* 542–575.

Diener, E. (2000a). Subjective well-being: The science of happiness and a proposal for a national index. *American Psychologist, 55,* 34–43.

Diener, E. (2000b, April). Subjective well-being across cultures. Paper presented at the annual meeting of Social and Personality Psychologists Around the Midwest.

Diener, E., & Diener, C. (1996). Most people are happy. *Psychological Science, 7,* 181–185.

Diener, E., & Diener, M. (1995). Cross-cultural correlates of life satisfaction and self-esteem. *Journal of Personality and Social Psychology, 68,* 653–663.

Diener, E., Diener, M., & Diener, C. (1995). Factors predicting the subjective well-being of nations. *Journal of Personality and Social Psychology, 69,* 851–864.

Diener, E., Emmons, R. A., Larsen, R. J., & Griffen, S. (1985). The Satisfaction With Life Scale. *Journal of Personality Assessment, 49,* 71–75.

Diener, E., Gohm, C. L., Suh, E., & Oishi, S. (2000). Similarity of the relations between marital status and subjective well-being across cultures. *Journal of Cross-Cultural Psychology, 31,* 419–436.

Diener, E., & Larsen, R. J. (1984). Temporal stability and cross-situational consistency of affective, behavioral, and cognitive responses. *Journal of Personality and Social Psychology, 47,* 580–592.

Diener, E., & Lucas, R. E. (1999). Personality and subjective well-being. In D. Kahneman, E. Diener, & N. Schwarz (Eds.), *Well-being: The foundations of hedonic psychology* (pp. 213–229). New York: Russell Sage Foundation.

Diener, E., Lucas, R. E., Oishi, S., & Suh, E. M. (in press). Looking up and looking down: Weighting good and bad information in life satisfaction judgments. *Personality and Social Psychology Bulletin.*

Diener, E., Sandvik, E., Seidlitz, L., & Diener, M. (1993). *The relationship between income and subjective well-being: Relative or absolute? Social Indicators Research, 28,* 195–223.

Diener, E., & Suh, E. M. (1998). Subjective well-being and age: An international analysis. In K. W. Schaie & M. P. Lawton (Eds.), *Annual review of gerontology and geriatrics* (Vol. 17, pp. 304–324). New York: Springer.

*Diener, E., & Suh, E. M. (Eds.). (2000). *Subjective well-being across cultures.* Cambridge, MA: MIT Press.

*Diener, E., Suh, E., Lucas, R., & Smith, H. (1999). Subjective well-being: Three decades of progress. *Psychological Bulletin, 125,* 276–302.

Emmons, R. A. (1986). Personal strivings: An approach to personality and subjective well-being. *Journal of Personality and Social Psychology, 51,* 1058–1068.

Flugel, J. C. (1925). A quantitative study of feeling and emotion in everyday life. *British Journal of Psychology, 9,* 318–355.

Fordyce, M. W. (1977). Development of a program to increase personal happiness. *Journal of Counseling Psychology, 24,* 511–520.

Fordyce, M. W. (1983). A program to increase happiness: Further studies. *Journal of Counseling Psychology, 30,* 483–498.

Freud, S. (1976). New introductory lectures on psychoanalysis. In J. Strachey (Ed. & Trans.), *The complete psychological works* (Vol. 16). New York: Norton. (Original work published 1933).

Fujita, F. (1991). *An investigation of the relation between extraversion, neuroticism, positive affect, and negative affect.* Unpublished master's thesis, University of Illinois, Urbana-Champaign.

Goldsmith, H. H. (1996). Studying temperament via construction of the toddler behavior assessment questionnaire. *Child Development, 67,* 218–235.

Grob, A., Stetsenko, A., Sabatier, C., Botcheva, L., & Macek, P. (1999). A cross-national model of subjective well-being in adolescence. In F. D. Alsaker & A. Flammer (Eds.). (1999). *The adolescent experience: European and American adolescents in the 1990s. Research monographs in adolescence* (pp. 115–130). Mahwah, NJ: Erlbaum.

Haring, M. J., Stock, W. A., & Okun, M. A. (1984). A research synthesis of gender and social class as correlates of subjective well-being. *Human Relations, 37,* 645–657.

Harlow, R. E., & Cantor, N. (1996). Still participating after all these years: A study of life task participation in later life. *Journal of Personality and Social Psychology, 71,* 1235–1249.

Headey, B., & Wearing. A. (1992). *Understanding happiness: A theory of subjective well-being.* Melbourne: Longman Cheshire.

Higgins, E. T. (1987). Self-discrepancy: A theory relation self and affect. *Psychological Review, 94,* 319–340.

Kahneman, D. (1999). Objective happiness. In D. Kahneman, E. Diener, & N. Schwarz (Eds.), *Well-being: The foundations of hedonic psychology* (pp. 3–25). New York: Russell Sage Foundation.

*Kahneman, D., Diener, E., & Schwarz, N. (Eds.). (1999). *Well-being: The foundations of hedonic psychology.* New York: Russell Sage Foundation.

Little, B. R. (1989). Personal projects analysis: Trivial pursuits, magnificent obsessions, and the search for coherence. In D. Buss & N. Cantor (Eds.), *Personality psychology: Recent trends and emerging directions* (pp. 15–31). New York: Springer-Verlag.

Lucas, R. E., Diener, E., Grob, A., Suh, E. M., & Shao, L. (2000). Cross-cultural evidence for the fundamental features of extraversion. *Journal of Personality and Social Psychology, 79,* 452–468.

Lucas, R. E., Diener, E., & Suh, E. (1996). Discriminant validity of well-being measures. *Journal of Personality and Social Psychology, 71,* 616–628.

Lucas, R. E., & Fujita, F. (2000). Factors influencing the relation between extraversion and pleasant affect. *Journal of Personality and Social Psychology, 79,* 1039–1056.

Lucas, R. E., & Gohm, C. (2000). Age and sex differences in subjective well-being across cultures. In E. Diener & E. M. Suh (Eds.), *Subjective well-being across cultures.* Cambridge, MA: MIT Press.

Magnus, K., & Diener, E. (1991, April). *A longitudinal analysis of personality, life events, and subjective well-being.* Paper presented at the 63rd Annual Meeting of the Midwestern Psychological Association, Chicago.

Maslow, A. H. (1970). *Motivation and personality.* New York: Harper and Row.

McGregor, I., & Little, B. R. (1998). Personal projects, happiness, and meaning: On doing well and being yourself. *Journal of Personality and Social Psychology, 74,* 494–512.

Michalos, A. C. (1985). Multiple discrepancies theory (MDT). *Social Indicators Research, 16,* 347–413.

Murray, H. A., & Kluckhohn, C. (1949). Outline of a conception of personality. In H. A. Murray & C. Kluckhohn (Eds.), *Personality in nature, society, and culture* (pp. 3–32). New York: Knopf.

*Myers, D. G. (1992). *The pursuit of happiness: Who is happy and why.* New York: William Morrow.

Oishi, S. (2000). *Culture and memory for emotional experiences: On-line vs. retrospective judgments of subjective well-being.* Unpublished doctoral dissertation, University of Illinois, Urbana-Champaign.

Okun, M. A., Stock, W. A., & Haring, M. J. (1984). Health and subjective well-being: A meta-analysis. *International Journal of Aging and Human Development, 19,* 111–132.

Omodei, M. M., & Wearing, A. J. (1990). Need satisfaction and involvement in personal projects: Toward an integrative model of subjective well-being. *Journal of Personality and Social Psychology, 59,* 762–769.

Pavot, W., & Diener, E. (1993). Review of the satisfaction with life scale. *Psychological Assessment, 5,* 164–172.

Rothbart, M. K., & Ahadi, S. A. (1995). Temperament and the development of personality. *Journal of Abnormal Psychology, 103,* 55–66.

Sandvik, E., Diener, E., & Seidlitz, L. (1993). Subjective well-being: The convergence and stability of self-report and non-self-report measures. *Journal of Personality, 61,* 317–342.

Scheier, M. F., & Carver, C. S. (1993). On the power of positive thinking: The benefits of being optimistic. *Current Directions in Psychological Science, 2,* 26–30.

Schwarz, N., & Strack, F. (1999). Reports of subjective well-being: Judgmental processes and their methodological implications. In D. Kahneman, E. Diener, & N. Schwarz (Eds.), *Well-being: The foundations of hedonic psychology* (pp. 61–84). New York: Russell Sage Foundation.

Seligman, M. E. P., Reivich, K., Jaycox, L., & Gillham, J. (1995). *The optimistic child.* New York: Harper Perennial.

Sheldon, K. M., Ryan, R., & Reis, H. T. (1996). What makes for a good day? Competence and autonomy in the day and in the person. *Personality and Social Psychology Bulletin, 22,* 1270–1279.

Snyder, C. R., Harris, C., Anderson, J. R., Holleran, S. A., Irving, L. M., Sigmon, S. T., Yoshinobu, L., Gibb, J., Langelle, C., & Harney, P. (1991). The will and the ways: Development and validation of an individual differences measure of hope. *Journal of Personality and Social Psychology, 60,* 570–585.

*Strack, F., Argyle, M., & Schwarz, N. (Eds.). (1991). *Subjective well-being: An interdisciplinary perspective*. Oxford: Pergamon.

Suh, E. M. (1999). *Culture, identity, consistency, and subjective well-being*. Unpublished doctoral dissertation, University of Illinois, Urbana–Champaign.

Suh, E. M., & Diener, E. (1999). *The use of emotion information across cultures, individuals and persons: The case of life satisfaction*. Manuscript submitted for publication, University of Illinois, Urbana–Champaign.

Suh, E. M., Diener, E., Oishi, S., & Triandis, H. (1998). The shifting basis of life satisfaction judgments across cultures: Emotions versus norms. *Journal of Personality and Social Psychology, 74*, 482–493.

Tellegen, A., Lykken, D. T., Bouchard. T. J., Wilcox, K. J., Segal, N. L., and Rich, S. (1988). Personality similarity in twins reared apart and together. *Journal of Personality and Social Psychology, 54*, 1031–1039.

Thomas, D., & Diener, E. (1990). Memory accuracy in the recall of emotion. *Journal of Personality and Social Psychology, 59*, 291–297.

*Veenhoven, R. (1993). *Bibliography of happiness: 2472 contemporary studies on subjective appreciation of life*. Rotterdam, Netherlands: RISBO.

*Veenhoven, R. World Database of Happiness Web site, Erasmus University, Rotterdam, Netherlands: *http://www.eur.nl/fsw/research/happiness*.

Watten, R. G., Vassend, D., Myhrer, T., & Syversen, J. L. (1997). Personality factors and somatic symptoms. *European Journal of Personality, 11*, 57–68.

Watson, D., & Clark, L. A. (1992). On traits and temperament: General and specific factors of emotional experience and their relation to the five-factor model. *Journal of Personality, 60*, 441–476.

Wilson, W. (1967). Correlates of avowed happiness. *Psychological Bulletin, 67*, 294–306.

6

Resilience in Development

Ann S. Masten & Marie-Gabrielle J. Reed

Around 1970, a pioneering group of developmental scientists turned their attention to the observable phenomenon of children at risk for problems and psychopathology who nonetheless succeed in life (Masten, 1999). These investigators argued that understanding such phenomena, the study of "resilience," held the potential to inform programs, policies, and interventions directed at promoting competence and preventing or ameliorating problems in the lives of children. These pioneers inspired three decades of research on resilience in development that has provided models, methods, and data with implications for theory, research, and intervention.

The goal of this chapter is to highlight the results of this first generation of work and its implications and to consider where it is leading researchers, practitioners, and policy makers. We begin with a brief history of resilience research in psychology. In the next section, we describe the conceptual models and corresponding methods that have characterized the research on resilience to date. Results of this research then are summarized in terms of the protective factors and processes suggested by diverse studies of resilience, which bear a striking resemblance to many of the chapter titles of this volume. We conclude that resilience arises from human adaptational systems and discuss implications of these findings for theory, interventions, policy, and future research.

History of the Study of Resilience in Psychology

The idea of individual resilience in the face of adversity has been around for a very long time, as evident in myths, fairy tales, art, and literature over the centuries that portray heroes and heroines (Campbell, 1970). When psychology began to develop as a systematic science in the 19th and early 20th centuries, there clearly was an interest in individual adaptation to the environment, which can be seen in theories ranging from natural selection to psychoanalytic ego psychology (Masten & Coatsworth, 1995). Freud (1928), for example, noted the remarkable human capacity to triumph over adversity even on the way to execution, describing gallows humor as "the ego's victorious assertion of its own invulnerability." In addition to the ego, early concepts of mastery motivation, competence, and self-efficacy in 20th-century psychology focused on positive aspects of adaptation in development (Masten & Coatsworth, 1995). In contrast, the study of children and adolescents with problems or hazardous environments during much of the 20th century was dominated by research on risk and the treatment of symptoms. In 1962, Lois Murphy decried the negative focus of research on individual differences in children: "It is something of a paradox that a nation which has exulted in its rapid expansion and its scientific-technological achievements should have developed in its studies of childhood so vast a 'problem' literature" (p. 2).

Murphy's words were a harbinger of change. A decade later, the systematic study of resilience in psychology emerged from the study of children at risk for problems and psychopathology (Masten, 1999; Masten & Garmezy, 1985). By the 1960s, psychologists and psychiatrists interested in the etiology of psychopathology had begun to study children over time who were believed to be at risk for serious problems because of their biological heritage (e.g., a parent with schizophrenia), perinatal hazards (e.g, premature birth), or their environments (e.g., poverty). Some of these investigators were struck by the observation that there were children purportedly at high risk for problems who were developing quite well. Subsequently, these psychiatrists and psychologists began to write and speak about the significance of these children (Anthony, 1974; Garmezy, 1971, 1974; Murphy, 1974; Murphy & Moriarty, 1976; Rutter, 1979; Werner & Smith, 1982). Their observations were a call to action for research on the phenomenon of doing well in the context of risk.

In the early publications on resilience and in the press about such phenomena, successful high-risk children were referred to variously as "invulnerable," "stress-resistant," or "resilient." Eventually, *resilient* became the most prominent term for describing such individuals.

Conceptual Models of Resilience

Defining Resilience

In research on children over the past three decades, resilience generally refers to *a class of phenomena characterized by patterns of positive adaptation in the context of significant adversity or risk.* Resilience must be inferred because two major judgments are required to identify individuals as belonging in this class of phenomena. First, there is a judgment that individuals are "doing OK" or better than OK with respect to a set of expectations for behavior. Second, there is a judgment that there have been extenuating circumstances that posed a threat to good outcomes. Therefore, the study of this class of phenomena requires defining the criteria or method for ascertaining good adaptation and the past or current presence of conditions that pose a threat to good adaptation.

The meaning of resilience and its operational definition have been the subject of considerable debate and controversy over the years (Luthar, Cicchetti, & Becker, 2000; Masten, 1999; Wang & Gordon, 1994). Nonetheless, there is little dispute that there are individuals whom most people would consider "resilient" by almost any definition. Moreover, despite considerable variation in operational definitions of resilience, findings from a diverse literature point to the same conclusions with compelling consistency. Given the considerable degree of debate and confusion about defining resilience and related concepts, a glossary of how these terms are used in this chapter is provided in Table 6.1.

Defining and Assessing Good Developmental Outcomes

Diverse criteria have been used for judging good adaptation in studies of resilience. These include positive behavior such as the presence of social and academic achievements, the presence of other behaviors desired by society for people of this age, happiness or life satisfaction, or the absence of undesirable behavior, including mental illness, emotional distress, criminal behavior, or risk-taking behaviors. In the developmental literature, many investigators define good outcomes on the basis of a track record of success meeting age-related standards of behavior widely known as *developmental tasks*.

Developmental tasks refer to expectations of a given society or culture in historical context for the behavior of children in different age periods and situations (Elder, 1998; Masten & Coatsworth, 1995, 1998). These are the social milestones for development, presumed to guide socialization practices. They may vary from one culture to another to some degree, but these broad tasks presumably depend on human capabilities and societal goals that will be widely shared across cultures. For example, toddlers are expected to learn to walk and talk and to obey simple instructions of parents. In most societies older children are expected to learn at school, to get along with other children, and to follow the

Table 6.1 Glossary of Key Terms

Resilience. Good adaptation under extenuating circumstances. From a developmental perspective, meeting age-salient developmental tasks in spite of serious threats to development.

Developmental tasks. Expectations of a given society or culture in historical context for the behavior of children in different age periods and situations, the criteria by which progress in individual development is judged.

Risk. An elevated probability of an undesirable outcome.

Risk factor. A measurable characteristic in a group of individuals or their situation that predicts negative outcome in the future on a specific outcome criterion. Stressful life events (stressors) are one type of risk factor.

Cumulative risk. The total effect of multiple risk factors combined or the piling up in time of multiple risk factors.

Risk gradient. A visual depiction of risk or cumulative risk showing how a negative criterion of outcome rises as a function of rising risk level.

Asset. A measurable characteristic in a group of individuals or their situation that predicts positive outcome in the future on a specific outcome criterion. *Resource* is often used as a synonym for asset, referring to the human, social, or material capital utilized in adaptive processes.

Protective factor. A measurable characteristic in a group of individuals or their situation that predicts positive outcome in the context of risk or adversity. Purists reserve this term for predictors that work *only* under adversity (like an air bag in an automobile) or that have a larger positive effect on outcome when risk is high compared with when risk is low (to distinguish a protective factor from an asset that works the same way at all levels of risk).

Cumulative protection. The presence of multiple protective factors in an individual's life, either within or across time. A common goal of comprehensive prevention programs.

---

rules of classroom, home, and community. In the United States and many other economically developed countries, successful youth are expected to graduate from high school and gain the education and occupational skills needed for economic independence, to abide by the law, to have close friends and romantic relationships, and to begin to contribute to society. Resilient children and youth manage to meet developmental task expectations even though they have faced significant obstacles to success in life.

One of the ongoing debates in the resilience literature has focused on whether the criteria should include good *internal* adaptation (positive psychological well-being versus emotional distress and problems) as well as good *external* adaptation. Both camps agree that external adaptation standards define resilience. Some investigators, however, include indicators of emotional health and well-being as additional defining criteria, whereas others study the internal dimensions of behavior as concomitants or predictors of resilience. This debate reflects the dual nature of living systems (Masten & Coatsworth, 1995, 1998). Human individuals are living organisms that must maintain coherence and organization as a unit and also function as part of larger systems, such as families and communities. Almost a century ago, Freud described the role of the ego in dualistic terms, with the goal of maintaining internal well-being (self-

preservation) while also tending to the expectations of life in society (Freud, 1923/1960).

A second issue is whether to expect resilient children to function in the normative range (OK or better) or to excel. Stories of heroic survival or media accounts of resilient people tend to highlight outstanding achievements in the face of adversity. However, most investigators have set the bar at the level of the normal range, no doubt because their goal is to understand how individuals maintain or regain normative levels of functioning and avoid significant problems in spite of adversity—a goal shared by many parents and societies.

In studies of resilient children and youth, typical measures of good outcome assess the following: academic achievement (e.g., grades and test scores, staying in school, graduating from high school); conduct (rule-abiding behavior vs. antisocial behavior); peer acceptance and friendship; normative mental health (few symptoms of internalizing or externalizing behavior problems); and involvement in age-appropriate activities (extracurricular activities, sports, community service). Most studies also include multiple indicators of good functioning or outcome, rather than a single domain of functioning.

Until recently, there has been little empirical attention given to the criteria by which parents, teachers, researchers, and societies decide if a child is "doing OK," even though these criteria are likely to have a critical role in socialization practices and policies or interventions designed to promote good development (Durbrow, Pena, Masten, Sesma, & Williams, in press). It is possible to study the implicit criteria by which people assess the progress of children and compare those criteria to the standards used by investigators, and more work is needed in this area. Nonetheless, there is considerable agreement about what should be assessed in studies of resilience, and these tend to include the domains widely viewed as developmental tasks in the developmental literature.

Good outcomes are not enough to define resilience, however. Such children could be called competent, well-adjusted, or simply "normal." Resilient children must have overcome some kind of threat to good adaptation, which requires a second kind of criterion.

Defining and Assessing Threats to Good Adaptation or Development

Many different kinds of threats and hazards to individual functioning and development have been the target of investigation in studies of resilience (Masten, Best, & Garmezy, 1990; Glantz & Johnson, 1999). These include premature birth, divorce, maltreatment, motherhood in unwed teenagers, parental illness or psychopathology, poverty, homelessness, and the massive (community-level) trauma of war and natural disasters. Such threats are well-established *risk factors* for development; there is good evidence that such experiences or conditions elevate the probability of one or more problems in the development of children.

Initially, in the study of resilience, many investigators focused on a single indicator to define risk. It was quickly apparent, however, that risk factors often co-occur and pile up over time, and that different risk factors often predict similar problems, partly because they tend to co-occur over time (Masten & Wright, 1998). As a result, there was a shift to studying *cumulative risk*.

Cumulative risk assessment has taken two major forms: risk indices and stressful life experience scores. Cumulative risk scores often sum the number of risk factors present in a child's life, whereas life stress scores typically add up the number of negative life events or experiences encountered during a period of time. On the adversity side of the resilience equation, resilient children often are defined by high levels of cumulative risk in their distant or recent histories.

Issues abound in the assessment of adversity and risk, and most are beyond the scope of this chapter. Examples of controversies include whether to count stressful experiences that depend on the behavior of the individual, whether to assign severity weights to events or simply add them up, whether to consider subjective perceptions or objective judgments about the stressfulness of experiences, and whether life-event reports are reliable (Dohrenwend, 1998; Zimmerman, 1983).

Assessing Assets, Resources, and Protective Factors

The study of resilience also must address the question of what makes a difference. To do so requires examination of the qualities of individuals and their environments that might explain why some people fare better than others in the context of adversity. The concepts of assets, resources, protective factors, and related processes have been operationalized and studied in efforts to explain resilience (see glossary of terms in Table 6.1). *Assets* are the opposite of risk factors, in that there is evidence that their presence predicts better outcomes for one or more domains of good adaptation, regardless of level of risk. *Resource* is a generic term for the human, social, and material capital utilized in adaptive processes. *Protective factors* are the qualities of persons or contexts that predict better outcomes under high-risk conditions; in effect, they are assets that matter when risk or adversity is high. *Protective processes* refer to how protective factors work; theoretically, these are the processes by which good outcomes happen when development is threatened.

Models of Resilience

Two major approaches have characterized the research on resilience in development. *Variable-focused* approaches examine the linkages among characteristics of individuals, environments, and experiences to try to ascertain what accounts for good outcomes on indicators of adaptation when risk or adversity is high. This method effectively draws on the power of the whole sample or the entire risk group, as well as the strengths of multivariate statistics. It is well suited to searching for specific protective factors for particular aspects of adaptation. *Person-focused* approaches identify resilient people and try to understand how they differ from others who are not faring well in the face of adversity or who have not been challenged by threats to development. This approach reflects the perspective that resilience is configural, in that individuals are viewed as resilient because they are doing well in multiple ways, rather than just one. This approach is well suited to studying diverse lives through time.

Variable-Focused Models of Resilience

Illustrated in Figure 6.1 are several variable-focused models of resilience that have been tested in the empirical literature: additive models, interactive models, and indirect models. In the simplest model, the additive effects of risk factors, asset/resource factors, and bipolar asset/risk variables are examined in relation to a positive outcome. This kind of model is illustrated in the upper right quadrant of Figure 6.1. In this model, the assets and risks contribute independently to how well a child is doing in life on the outcome variable or criterion of interest. Pure risk factors have a negative effect on the outcome of interest when they occur but no effect if they are absent (like the loss of a parent). Pure assets have positive influences if they are present, but do not have negative effects if they are absent (like a fairy godmother or a musical talent). Many attributes operate along a continuum of risk-asset where more is good and less is bad for the outcome of interest (such as the ways intellectual skills and the quality of parenting may work for academic achievement). Assets can theoretically counterbalance high levels of risk in such models, hence the idea of "compensatory effects" (Garmezy, Masten, & Tellegen, 1984). Interventions that attempt to boost the presence of assets or reduce the number of risk factors are based on these additive models.

Risk/asset gradients also reflect additive models of this kind. A typical cumulative risk gradient is shown on the left side of Figure 6.2, where the level of a negative outcome is plotted as a function of the number of risk factors. Risk factors in such models often include well-established risks, such as a single-parent household, a mother who did not finish high school, a large family size, or income below the poverty level. Other gradients are formed by various

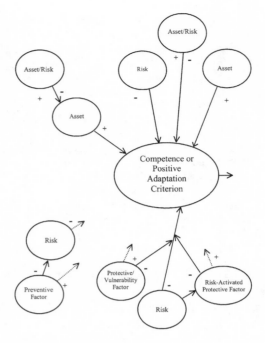

Figure 6.1 Models of resilience illustrating additive, interactive, and indirect models of how risks, assets, and protective factors could influence a desired outcome of interest.

levels on a single major indicator of disadvantage, such as socioeconomic status. Such risk indices predict a wide range of public health outcomes, including mortality rates, academic attainment, and physical and mental health, across many societies (Keating & Hertzman, 1999).

Risk gradients can be inverted to produce asset gradients, as illustrated on the right in Figure 6.2. This is because most of the risk indicators are actually risk/asset predictors that have high and low ends and are arbitrarily labeled by the negative end of a continuum. A positive psychology perspective would emphasize that the children low on such risk gradients typically are those with more assets and advantages, with two better educated parents, good income, the benefits that go along with higher socioeconomic status, and so forth. Even in studies that measure pure risk factors (negative life events, for example), the low-risk children are likely to have unmeasured assets because negative events are less likely to occur in advantaged families with effective parenting, more education, safer neighborhoods, good medical care, and so on.

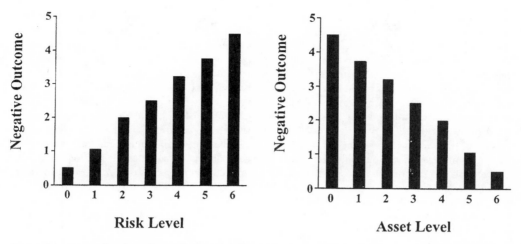

Figure 6.2 A typical risk gradient showing negative outcome as a function of risk level (on the left) and its inverse, plotting negative outcome as a function of assets (on the right), a hypothetical "asset gradient."

Interactive models can be seen in the bottom right quadrant of Figure 6.1. In these cases, there are moderating effects in which one variable alters the impact of the risk/adversity variable. Such moderators have been called "vulnerability" and "protective" factors. Two kinds of interaction effects are illustrated. One stems from the idea of an enduring quality of the individual or environment that increases or decreases the susceptibility of the individual to the threatening situation, the simple moderator. One of the most investigated moderator effects in the literature is the possibility that temperament or personality predisposes individuals to react with more or less distress or negative emotion to a given threat. Another kind of moderator portrayed in Figure 6.1 is the threat-activated protective system, akin to air bags in automobiles or emergency social services, that are triggered by the occurrence of threatening experiences. Effective parents who appear to buffer their children from the full impact of adversity as it occurs can be viewed as risk-activated in this way. A child's own coping efforts could operate this way as well, in that special attempts are made to reduce the impact of a particular threat to one's self. Interventions that attempt to improve how systems respond to threat in order to ameliorate the impact of hazards on the lives of individuals are based on this kind of model.

Indirect models of resilience are illustrated on the left side of figure 6.1. Not all possibilities are included. The upper left quadrant illustrates the phenomenon of mediated effects, where a powerful influence on outcome is itself affected by risks and resources. A good example of this effect involves studies where the determinants of parenting are examined, as are the outcomes of parenting. Interventions in which there is an attempt to improve the quality of key predictors of child outcome, such as parental effectiveness, often are based on such mediator models. In a sense, these models include all of the direct effect models moved out a step from the target individual. The assumption here is that protection provided by the mediator can be changed in ways that will have consequences for the child's life.

One other indirect model, illustrated in the lower left quadrant of Figure 6.1, is the invisible effect of total prevention, when a powerful protective factor prevents the risk/threatening condition from occurring at all. For example, if premature birth were prevented by excellent prenatal care, then the risks associated with premature birth would be totally alleviated. Similarly, an alert parent may intervene to head off a negative event prior to its occurrence.

Figure 6.1 is a convenient way to illustrate various models of resilience, but it is a vastly oversimplified depiction of how resilience unfolds in lives through time. First, it is static. In life, the systems represented by the variable labels of risks and assets are continually interacting and often influencing each other. Thus, a child's behavior influences the quality of parenting she receives and the behavior of her teachers; subsequently, the behavior of parents or teachers toward the child influences the child's behavior, and so on. In reality, there are few "one-way arrows" in life. Transactional models that capture the mutual influences over time resulting from the continual interaction of living systems, their environments, and their experiences are difficult to depict in static two-dimensional pictures.

Second, the variable-focused models that focus on a single aspect of "outcome" or one dimension of the criterion for good adaptation, will not capture the overall pattern of resilience in a person's life, which is multidimensional and configural. Person-focused models attempt to get a handle on the holistic patterns.

Person-Focused Models of Resilience

Three types of person-focused models have played a key role in resilience research. One model derives from the single case study of individuals who have inspired larger scale investigations and illustrate findings from larger studies in which they are embedded. Case studies are not true conceptual models of resilience, but they do serve as models in the sense of demonstrating natural phenomena that serve a heuristic purpose. Case reports can be found throughout the resilience literature.

A second person-focused model of resilience is based on identifying very high-risk individuals who do well, a resilient subgroup. This is a classic approach in the resilience field, exemplified by the most important longitudinal study of resilience to date, the Kauai longitudinal study by Werner and Smith (1982, 1992). In this study of a large birth cohort that began in 1955, a high-risk group of children was identified according to multiple risk indicators that were present before the age of 2. Then the outcomes of these children, how well they were doing on multiple developmental and mental health markers at around 10 and 18, were examined to identify a subgroup of resilient children. Resilient children could then be compared with their peers in the high-risk group who did not fare well. Results indicated many differences beginning at an early age that favored the resilient group, including better quality of care in infancy, higher self-worth and intellectual functioning in childhood, and more support from "kith and kin."

This approach often results in evidence of striking differences in the assets, human and so-

cial capital, characterizing the lives of resilient versus maladaptive children from risky backgrounds; however, two key issues limit the contributions of such studies. First, the results often suggest that the resilient subgroup actually has been exposed to lower levels of risk or adversity; in effect, they come from a lower-risk level of a risk gradient. Second, even when risk levels are comparable, it is not clear whether the correlates of resilience are general predictors of good outcome, regardless of risk, or specifically protective moderators of risk, because the low-risk groups are missing from the analyses. This led to a third approach, which includes children from a general population, with the goal of comparing the resilient to lower risk peers as well as high-risk, maladaptive peers.

Full diagnostic models of resilience classify children on the two major aspects of individual lives: good outcomes and adversity/risk. Figure 6.3 illustrates this model. In the Project Competence study of resilience (Masten et al., 1999), this strategy was used to complement the variable-focused analyses. Youth from a normative urban sample were classified as high, middle, or low on competence based on the pat-

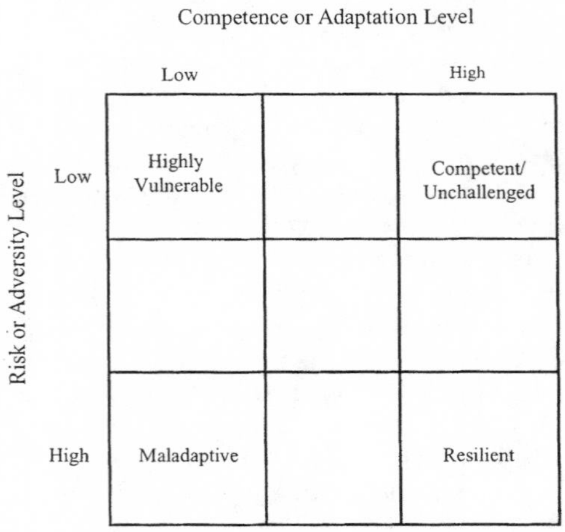

Competence or Adaptation Level

Figure 6.3 A full diagnostic model of resilience that identifies groups by two sets of criteria for (a) adversity level and (b) good outcome or competence on one or more criteria. Of greatest interest are comparisons of the "corner" groups: the resilient, who are high on both adversity and good outcomes; the maladaptive, who are high on adversity but have negative outcomes; the competent-unchallenged, who are low on adversity with good outcomes; and the vulnerable, who do not do well even though adversity is low.

tern of success for three main developmental tasks for their age-group, including academic achievement, rule-abiding conduct versus anti-social behavior, and social competence with peers. Youth classified as high in competence had achieved at least average success on all three developmental tasks. They also were classified on the basis of lifetime adversity exposure, based on life histories of negative experiences out of their control (such as death of a parent or close friend, marital conflict, violence of an alcoholic parent, accidents or health crises of family members). Lifetime adversity was rated as high (severe to catastrophic exposure), average, or low (below-average levels of exposure for the cohort). The goal was to compare the four corner groups (see Figure 6.3). As found in other studies, however, there was nearly an "empty cell" for low adversity exposure and low competence. Thus, resilient youth were compared with two other groups, their mal-adaptive peers who shared a history of severe-to catastrophic-level adversity but differed markedly in outcome, and their competent peers who were like them in achievements but dif-fered markedly in having low adversity back-grounds. Results indicated that resilient youth have much in common with competent youth who have not faced adversity, in that they share many of the same assets, both personal ones like good intellectual skills and family ones like ef-fective parenting. Both groups differed dramat-ically in resources from their maladaptive peers, who faced great adversity with much less hu-man and social capital. Results of this study suggest that there are fundamental processes that not only lead to normative competence but also protect development in the context of ad-versity.

Pathway Models

Both the classic and the full diagnostic models of resilience implicitly span considerable amounts of time because the risks and achieve-ments by which resilience is judged are not mo-mentary phenomena but rather characterize ex-periences and functioning that unfold over time. Currently, there is growing interest in more systematic pathway models of resilience that address patterns of behavior over time in more explicit ways. This interest reflects a general trend in developmental theory toward more complex, dynamic system models that account for major patterns in the life course. This trend

can be seen in studies of antisocial behavior (Loeber & Stouthamer-Loeber, 1998), as well as in normative life-span theory and research (Giele & Elder, 1998) and family systems the-ory and research (Burr & Klein, 1994).

Figure 6.4 illustrates three resilient pathways that could result from a host of cumulative in-fluences. Life course is plotted over time with respect to how an individual is doing on a sim-ple or complex index of good versus maladap-tive development. Path A reflects a child grow-ing up in a high-risk environment who nonetheless steadily functions well in life. Path B reflects a child who is doing well, is diverted by a major blow (perhaps a traumatic experi-ence), and recovers. Path C reflects a late-bloomer pattern, in which a high-risk child who is not doing well is provided with life-altering chances or opportunities. Many Romanian chil-dren adopted into other countries from pro-found privation to normative or enriched rear-ing environments follow path C. Rutter and colleagues (1998) have described the consequent changes in their functioning as "spectacular." There are also reports of maladaptive high-risk youth who seek or respond to "second-chance opportunities," such as military service, positive romantic relationships, or religious conversions, and turn their lives in new directions (Rutter, 1990; Werner & Smith, 1992).

Developmental pathways are difficult to study, as lives unfold from myriad transactions among systems and in idiosyncratic ways. How-ever, investigators are attempting to character-

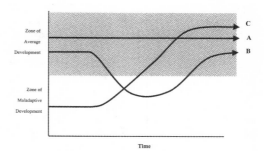

Figure 6.4 Resilient pathways over the life course. Path A illustrates the developmental course of a high-risk child who consistently does well in life. Path B shows the course of a child who initially does well and then is diverted by a major blow and later recovers to good functioning. Path C illus-trates the late-bloomer pattern where a child bur-dened by disadvantage begins to do well after ma-jor improvements in rearing conditions.

ize major patterns through time by "longitudinal classification diagnosis" (Bergman & Magnusson, 1997) and utilization of new statistical methods, such as growth curve modeling.

Summary of Findings on Resilience in Development

Findings from a wide-ranging and diverse literature on resilience in children and youth converge with striking regularity on a set of individual and environmental attributes associated with good adjustment and development under a variety of life-course-threatening conditions across cultural contexts. This "short list" of candidates for salient protective factors in development was evident in earlier reviews and discussions of this class of phenomena in the 1970s and 1980s (Anthony, 1974; Garmezy, 1971, 1974, 1985; Masten, 1989; Masten & Garmezy, 1985; Murphy, 1974; Murphy & Moriarty, 1976; Rutter, 1979, 1985; Sameroff & Chandler, 1975; Werner & Smith, 1982) and has held up remarkably well since that time (Cicchetti & Garmezy, 1993; Egeland, Carlson, & Sroufe, 1993; Luthar & Zigler, 1991; Luthar et al., 2000; Masten, 1994, 1999; Masten, Best, & Garmezy, 1990; Masten & Coatsworth, 1995, 1998; Rutter, 1990; Werner & Smith, 1992; Wyman, Sandler, Wolchik, & Nelson, 2000).

A list of the most commonly reported potential protective factors against developmental hazards found in studies of psychosocial resilience is presented in Table 6.2. These protective factors measure differential attributes of the child, the family, other relationships, and the major contexts in which children and youth develop, such as school and neighborhood. The most salient individual characteristics index cognitive capabilities of the child and personality traits that suggest effective problem solving and adaptability to stress (e.g., IQ scores, attentional skills, a not-readily upset or "easy" temperament). It is worth noting that many of these characteristics that have been found to predict good adaptation in the context of risk are addressed by chapters in this volume, including, for example, self-efficacy, self-worth, problem solving, positive relationships, faith or spirituality, and humor.

The most widely reported family attributes are related to the quality of parenting available to the child and the socioeconomic status (SES) of the family and all the advantages conveyed by high SES. Parenting adults who provide love and support, as well as structure and high expectations, appear to protect child development across a wide variety of situations and cultures. Relationship bonds to other competent and involved adults and also to prosocial peers are widely reported correlates and predictors of resilience. And, in the larger arenas in which children grow up, there are protective factors representing multiple contexts providing structure, safety, opportunities to learn and to develop talent, adult role models, support for cultural and religious traditions, and many other social capital resources. "Collective efficacy" refers to neighborhoods that combine social cohesion with informal social control (Sampson, Raudenbush, & Earls, 1997).

The attributes on this list, many of which have been implicated as predictors of good development in low-risk children as well, strongly suggest that there are fundamental human adaptational systems that serve to keep behavioral development on course and facilitate recovery from adversity when more normative conditions are restored (Masten & Coatsworth, 1998). Some of these systems have been the subject of extensive theoretical and empirical study in psychology, whereas others have been left to other disciplines or neglected. Systems that have received some attention in psychology would include the following: *attachment relationships and parenting; pleasure-in-mastery motivational systems; self-regulatory systems for regulating emotion, arousal, and behavior; families; and formal education systems, cultural belief systems, and religious organizations.* In the case of some systems, such as cultural beliefs and organizations, other disciplines may have contributed more than psychology to date, including anthropology and sociology.

Within the resilience field of study, the processes underlying specific protective factors identified in resilience research have not been the subject of much systematic study to date, though there have been numerous calls for such research (Luthar et al., 2000; Masten et al., 1990; Rutter, 1990). The most powerful tests of the processes implicated by the list will be found in efforts to change the course of development by influencing hypothesized processes, in well-designed prevention and intervention trials. Pioneering examples are provided in the next section. However, as the present volume attests, there is an extensive foundation of work on some of the processes that may be behind the

Table 6.2 Protective Factors for Psychosocial Resilience in
Children and Youth

Within the Child

Good cognitive abilities, including problem-solving and attentional skills
Easy temperament in infancy; adaptable personality later in development
Positive self-perceptions; self-efficacy
Faith and a sense of meaning in life
A positive outlook on life
Good self-regulation of emotional arousal and impulses
Talents valued by self and society
Good sense of humor
General appeal or attractiveness to others

Within the Family

Close relationships with caregiving adults
Authoritative parenting (high on warmth, structure/monitoring, and expectations)
Positive family climate with low discord between parents
Organized home environment
Postsecondary education of parents
Parents with qualities listed as protective factors with the child (above)
Parents involved in child's education
Socioeconomic advantages

Within Family or Other Relationships

Close relationships to competent, prosocial, and supportive adults
Connections to prosocial and rule-abiding peers

Within the Community

Effective schools
Ties to prosocial organizations, including schools, clubs, scouting, etc.
Neighborhoods with high "collective efficacy"
High levels of public safety
Good emergency social services (e.g., 911 or crisis nursery services)
Good public health and health care availability

list. Resilience appears to arise from the operation of many of the same systems that foster normative development and that have been studied under rubrics other than "resilience."

Fostering Resilience: Implications for Policy and Practice

The findings on resilience suggest that the greatest threats to children are those adversities that undermine the basic human protective systems for development. It follows that efforts to promote competence and resilience in children at risk should focus on strategies that prevent damage to, restore, or compensate for threats to these basic systems. For example, prenatal care, nutritional programs, early childhood education, adequate medical care, and good schools all

promote the protection of brain development, attention, thinking, and learning that appear to play a powerful role in the lives of children who successfully negotiate challenges to development.

Programs and policies that support effective parenting and the availability of competent adults in the lives of children also are crucial. The best-documented asset of resilient children is a strong bond to a competent and caring adult, who need not be a parent. For children who do not have such an adult involved in their lives, this is the first order of business.

Resilience models and findings suggest that programs will be most effective when they tap into powerful adaptational systems. One example is provided by the mastery motivational system. When development is proceeding normally, humans are motivated to learn about the environment and derive pleasure from mastering new skills. This is why infants delight in flinging food off the high chair and glow with pride when they toddle across the room for the first time. Children need opportunities to experience success at all ages. This means that families, schools, and communities have a responsibility to provide such opportunities and to ensure that the talents of an individual child are developed. One of the great differences in the lives of children growing up in the middle class versus poverty is in the richness of opportunities for achievement that feed the mastery motivation system. Feelings of self-confidence and self-efficacy grow from mastery experiences. Children who feel effective persist in the face of failure and achieve greater success because of their efforts (Bandura, 1997).

Much has been written about programs that work for children at risk, such as Lisbeth Shorr's 1988 book, *Within Our Reach: Breaking the Cycle of Disadvantage*. Based on the resilience literature, we would hypothesize that a careful look at programs that work for children at risk would reveal that they tap into basic but powerful protective systems for human development. Recent prevention efforts to promote "wellness" in children and youth reflect this belief as well (Cicchetti, Rappaport, Sandler, & Weissberg, in press; Cowen, in press).

Strategies for Fostering Resilience

The models and lessons arising from research on resilience suggest a new framework for planning prevention and intervention programs, as well as three major kinds of change strategies. Conceptually, the work on resilience suggests that we need to move positive goals front and center. *Promoting healthy development and competence is at least as important as preventing problems and will serve the same end.* As a society, we will do well to nurture human capital, to invest in the competence of our children. This means understanding how the capacity for academic achievement, rule-abiding behavior, or good citizenship develops. It is important to identify risks and prevent them whenever possible, but it is also important to identify assets and protective systems and to support these to the best of our knowledge. Three basic strategies for intervention are suggested by resilience research, as illustrated in Table 6.3.

Table 6.3 Strategies for Promoting Resilience in Children and Youth

Risk-Focused Strategies: Preventing/Reducing Risk and Stressors

Prevent or reduce the likelihood of low birth weight or prematurity through prenatal care
Prevent child abuse or neglect through parent education
Reduce teenage drinking, smoking, or drug use through community programs
Prevent homelessness through housing policy or emergency assistance
Reduce neighborhood crime or violence through community policing

Asset-Focused Strategies: Improving Number or Quality of Resources or Social Capital

Provide a tutor
Organize a Girls or Boys Club
Offer parent education classes
Build a recreation center

Process-Focused Strategies: Mobilizing the Power of Human Adaptational Systems

Build self-efficacy through graduated success model of teaching
Teach effective coping strategies for specific threatening situations, such as programs to prepare children for surgery
Foster secure attachment relationships between infants and parents through parental-sensitivity training or home visit program for new parents and their infants
Nurture mentoring relationships for children through a program to match children with potential mentors, such as Big Brothers/Big Sisters of America
Encourage friendships of children with prosocial peers in healthy activities, such as extracurricular activities
Support cultural traditions that provide children with adaptive rituals and opportunities for bonds with prosocial adults, such as religious education or classes for children where elders teach ethnic traditions of dance, meditation, etc.

Risk-Focused Strategies

These strategies aim to reduce the exposure of children to hazardous experiences. Examples of risk-focused strategies include prenatal care to prevent premature births, as well as school reforms to reduce the stressfulness of school transitions for young adolescents or community efforts to prevent homelessness through housing policies. Here the intent is to remove or reduce threat exposure.

Asset-Focused Strategies

These approaches aim to increase the amount of, access to, or quality of resources children need for the development of competence. Examples of resources that are assumed to have direct effects on children are providing a tutor or building a recreation center with programs for children. Other assets are assumed to operate indirectly on children, through strengthening the social or financial capital in a child's life. Examples include the establishment of literacy or job programs for parents, programs to foster parenting skills, and programs to provide teachers with more training or resources so they can be more effective in the classroom. The Search Institute has done extensive research and program development directed at this *asset-building* strategy (Benson, Galbraith, & Espeland, 1995).

Process-Focused Strategies

These strategies aim to mobilize the fundamental protective systems for development. In this case, efforts go beyond simply removing risk or adding assets but instead attempt to influence *processes* that will change a child's life. Examples include programs designed to improve the quality of attachment relationships and efforts to activate the mastery motivation system through a sequence of graduated mastery experiences that enable a child to experience success and build self-efficacy and motivation to succeed in life.

Comprehensive intervention efforts to change the life chances of children at risk include all three of these strategies. Examples include Head Start (Zigler, Taussig, & Black, 1992), the Abecedarian Project (Ramey & Ramey, 1998), the large-scale Fast Track prevention trial for conduct problems (Conduct Problems Prevention Research Group, 1999), and

the Seattle Social Development Project (Hawkins, Catalano, Kosterman, Abbott, & Hill, 1999). In effect, these programs aim to prevent or reduce problems in development by promoting good adaptation. Each has a different model and emphasis, yet they all utilize multiple strategies to reduce risk and increase protection in children's lives. Findings from successful interventions, such as these, corroborate the findings from the resilience literature, implicating highly similar protections and processes.

Conclusions and Future Directions for Resilience Research

The most striking conclusion arising from all the research on resilience in development is that the extraordinary resilience and recovery power of children arises from *ordinary processes*. The evidence indicates that the children who "make it" have basic human protective systems operating in their favor. Resilience does not come from rare and special qualities but from the operations of ordinary human systems, arising from brains, minds, and bodies of children, from their relationships in the family and community, and from schools, religions, and other cultural traditions.

Positive psychology, the focus of this handbook, represents a return to the study of how these systems and their interactions give rise to good adaptation and development, as well as resilience. The interest in positive adaptation evident in the early history of psychology is enjoying a renaissance that was rekindled in part by the study of resilient children in the 1970s and 1980s; now positive psychology is likely to inform theories and applications about resilience to the benefit of society.

The study of resilience in development has produced a "sea change" in the frameworks for understanding and helping children at risk or already in trouble. This shift is evident in changing conceptualization of the goals of prevention and intervention that now address competence as well as problems. It is also apparent in assessments that include strengths in addition to risks and problems. Theories about the etiology of behavior problems and mental illness must now account for why some people who share the risks and hazards believed to cause psychopathology nevertheless develop into competent and healthy individuals. Policy makers concerned about the large numbers of children at risk for problems, now ask, What works? to prevent such problems and to promote favorable youth development; they also ask how this knowledge can be effectively harnessed to enhance the human capital of society.

Fortified by the groundwork of a first generation of work, investigators of resilience now must address some tough questions about how naturally occurring resilience works and whether these processes can be initiated or facilitated by design in policies or practice (Masten, 1999). The biological underpinnings of resilience, in brain development and functions, for example, are just beginning to be considered (Luthar et al., 2000; Maier & Watkins, 1998; Nelson, 1999). The study of healthy physical development must be integrated with the study of healthy psychological development, for children growing up under favorable and unfavorable conditions. There is little information linking psychological and physical resilience, though studies at the biopsychosocial interface suggest important connections (Maier & Watkins, 1998). It also has become evident that the classification systems for psychopathology need an overhaul to address the role of positive adaptation more effectively in defining, assessing, and treating disorder (see Masten & Curtis, 2000).

It is not possible to prevent all of the hazards that jeopardize the lives and well-being of children and youth. Therefore, we must learn how to preserve, protect, and recover good adaptation and development that has been or will be threatened by adversity and risk exposure. That is the ongoing goal of resilience studies in psychology.

Acknowledgments   The authors are deeply grateful to Norman Garmezy, Auke Tellegen, and many members of the Project Competence research team over the years, who influenced their thinking about resilience. Preparation of this chapter was facilitated by grants to the first author from the National Science Foundation (NSF/SBR-9729111) and the William T. Grant Foundation (97-1845-97), and by her participation in the John D. and Catherine T. MacArthur Foundation Research Network on Psychopathology and Development.

References

Anthony, E. J. (1974). The syndrome of the psychologically invulnerable child. In E. J. Anthony & C. Koupernik (Eds.), *The child in his family: Children at psychiatric risk* (pp. 529–545). New York: Wiley.

Bandura, A. (1997). *Self-efficacy: The exercise of control.* New York: Freeman.

*Benson, P. L., Galbraith, J., & Espeland, P. (1995). *What kids need to succeed.* Minneapolis, MN: Free Spirit.

Bergman, L. A., & Magnusson, D. (1997). A person-oriented approach in research on developmental psychopathology. *Development and Psychopathology, 9,* 291–319.

Burr, W. R., & Klein, S. R. (Eds.). (1994). *Reexamining family stress: New theory and research.* Thousand Oaks, CA: Sage.

Campbell, J. (1970). *The hero with a thousand faces.* New York: World.

*Cicchetti, D., & Garmezy, N. (Eds.). (1993). Milestones in the development of resilience [Special issue]. *Development and Psychopathology, 5,* 497–774.

*Cicchetti, D., Rappaport, J., Sandler, I., & Weissberg, R. P. (Eds). (in press). *The promotion of wellness in children and adolescents.* Thousand Oaks, CA: Sage.

Conduct Problems Prevention Research Group. (1999). Initial impact of the Fast Track prevention trial for conduct problems: I. The high-risk sample. *Journal of Consulting and Clinical Psychology, 5,* 631–647.

Cowen, E. L. (in press). Psychological wellness: Some hopes for the future. In D. Cicchetti, J. Rappaport, I. Sandler, & R. P. Weissberg (Eds.), *The promotion of wellness in children and adolescents.* Thousand Oaks, CA: Sage.

Dohrenwend, B. P. (Ed.). (1998). *Adversity, stress, and psychopathology.* New York: Oxford University Press.

Durbrow, E. H., Pena, L. F., Masten, A. S., Sesma, A., & Williams, I. (in press). Mothers' perceptions of child competence in context of poverty: The Philippines, St. Vincent, and the United States. *International Journal of Behavioral Development.*

*Egeland, B., Carlson, E., & Sroufe, L. A. (1993). Resilience as process. *Development and Psychopathology, 5,* 517–528.

Elder, G. H. (1998). The life course as developmental theory. *Child Development, 69,* 1–12.

Freud, S. (1923/1960). *The ego and the id.* New York: Norton.

Freud, S. (1928). Humour. *The International Journal of Psycho-analysis, 9* (1), 1–6.

Garmezy, N. (1971). Vulnerability research and the issue of primary prevention. *American Journal of Orthopsychiatry, 41,* 101–116.

Garmezy, N. (1974). The study of competence in children at risk for severe psychopathology. In E. J. Anthony & C. Koupernik (Eds.), *The child in his family: Vol. 3. Children at psychiatric risk* (pp. 77–97). New York: Wiley.

*Garmezy, N. (1985). Stress-resistant children: The search for protective factors. In J. E. Stevenson (Ed.), *Recent research in developmental pathopathology: Journal of Child Psychology and Psychiatry Book Supplement No. 4* (pp. 213–233). Oxford: Pergamon.

Garmezy, N., Masten, A. S., & Tellegen, A. (1984). The study of stress and competence in children: A building block for developmental psychopathology. *Child Development, 55,* 97–111.

Giele, A. Z., & Elder, G. H., Jr. (Eds.). (1998). *Methods of life course research: Qualitative and quantitative approaches.* Thousand Oaks, CA: Sage.

*Glantz, M. D., & Johnson, J. L. (Eds.). (1999). *Resilience and development: Positive life adaptations.* New York: Plenum.

*Hawkins, J. D., Catalano, R. F., Kosterman, R., Abbott, R., & Hill, K. G. (1999). Preventing adolescent health-risk behavior by strengthening protection during childhood. *Archives of Pediatrics and Adolescent Medicine, 153,* 226–234.

Keating, D., & Hertzman, C. (Eds.). (1999). *Developmental health and the wealth of nations: Social, biological and educational dynamics.* New York: Guilford.

Loeber, R., & Stouthamer-Loeber, M. (1998). Development of juvenile aggression and violence: Some common misconceptions and controversies. *American Psychologist, 53,* 242–259.

*Luthar, S. S., Cicchetti, D., & Becker, B. (2000). The construct of resilience: A critical evaluation and guidelines for future work. *Child Development, 71,* 543–562.

Luthar, S. S., & Zigler, E. (1991). Vulnerability and competence: A review of research on resilience in childhood. *Journal of American Orthopsychiatry, 61,* 6–22.

Maier, S. F., & Watkins, L. R. (1998). Cytokines for psychologists: Implications of bidirectional immune-to-brain communication for understanding behavior, mood, and cognition. *Psychological Review, 105,* 83–107.

Masten, A. S. (1989). Resilience in development: Implications of the study of successful adaptation for developmental psychopathology. In D. Cicchetti (Ed.), *The emergence of a discipline: Rochester Symposium on Developmental Psychopathology* (Vol. 1, pp. 261–294). Hillsdale, NJ: Erlbaum.

Masten, A. S. (1994). Resilience in individual development: Successful adaptation despite risk and adversity. In M. Wang & E. Gordon (Eds.), *Risk and resilience in inner-city America: Challenges and prospects* (pp. 3–25). Hillsdale, NJ: Erlbaum.

Masten, A. S. (1999). Resilience comes of age: Reflections on the past and outlook for the next generation of research. In M. D. Glantz, J. Johnson, & L. Huffman (Eds.), *Resilience and development: Positive life adaptations* (pp. 282–296). New York: Plenum.

*Masten, A. S., Best, K. M., & Garmezy, N. (1990). Resilience and development: Contributions from the study of children who overcome adversity. *Development and Psychopathology, 2,* 425–444.

Masten, A. S., & Coatsworth, J. D. (1995). Competence, resilience, and psychopathology. In D. Cicchetti & D. Cohen (Eds.), *Developmental psychopathology: Vol 2. Risk, disorder, and adaptation* (pp. 715–752). New York: Wiley.

Masten, A. S., & Coatsworth, J. D. (1998). The development of competence in favorable and unfavorable environments: Lessons from successful children. *American Psychologist, 53,* 205–220.

Masten, A. S., & Curtis, W. J. (2000). Integrating competence and psychopathology: Pathways toward a comprehensive science of adaptation in development. *Development and Psychopathology, 12,* 529–550.

Masten, A. S., & Garmezy, N. (1985). Risk, vulnerability, and protective factors in developmental psychopathology. In B. B. Lahey & A. E. Kazdin (Eds.), *Advances in clinical child psychology* (Vol. 8, pp. 1–51). New York: Plenum.

*Masten, A. S., Hubbard, J. J., Gest, S. D., Tellegen, A., Garmezy, N., & Ramirez, M. (1999). Competence in the context of adversity: Pathways to resilience and maladaptation from childhood to late adolescence. *Development and Psychopathology, 11,* 143–169.

Masten, A. S., & Wright, M. O. D. (1998). Cumulative risk and protection models of child maltreatment. In B. B. R. Rossman & M. S. Rosenberg (Eds.), *Multiple victimization of children: Conceptual, developmental, research and treatment issues* (pp. 7–30). Binghamton, NY: Haworth.

Murphy, L. B. (1962). *The widening world of childhood: Paths toward mastery.* New York: Basic Books.

Murphy, L. B. (1974). Coping, vulnerability, and resilience in childhood. In G. V. Coelho, D. A. Hamburg, & J. E. Adams (Eds.), *Coping and adaptation* (pp. 69–100). New York: Basic Books.

Murphy, L. B., & Moriarty, A. E. (1976). *Vulnerability, coping, and growth: From infancy to ad-*

olescence. New Haven, CT: Yale University Press.

Nelson, C. A. (1999). Neural plasticity and human development. *Current Directions in Psychological Science, 8,* 42–45.

Ramey, C. T., & Ramey, S. L. (1998). Early intervention and early experience. *American Psychologist, 53,* 109–120.

Rutter, M. (1979). Protective factors in children's responses to stress and disadvantage. In M. W. Kent & J. E. Rolf (Eds.), *Primary prevention of psychopathology: Vol. 3. Social competence in children* (pp. 49–74). Hanover, NH: University Press of New England.

Rutter, M. (1985). Resilience in the face of adversity: Protective factors and resistance to psychiatric disorder. *British Journal of Psychiatry, 147,* 598–611.

*Rutter, M. (1990). Psychosocial resilience and protective mechanisms. In J. Rolf, A. S. Masten, D. Cicchetti, K. H. Nuechterlein, & S. Weintraub (Eds.), *Risk and protective factors in the development of psychopathology* (pp. 181–214). New York: Cambridge University Press.

Rutter, M., & the English and Romanian Adoptees (ERA) Study Team. (1998). Developmental catch-up and deficit, following adoption after severe global early privation. *Journal of Child Psychology and Psychiatry, 39,* 465–476.

Sameroff, A. J., & Chandler, M. J. (1975). Reproductive risk and the continuum of caretaking casualty. *Review of Child Development Research, 4,* 187–244.

Sampson, R., Raudenbush, S., & Earls, F. (1997). Neighborhoods and violent crime: A multilevel study of collective efficacy. *Science, 277,* 918–924.

Schorr, L. (1988). *Within our reach: Breaking the cycle of disadvantage.* New York: Doubleday.

*Wang, M., & Gordon, E. (Eds.). (1994). *Risk and resilience in inner-city America: Challenges and prospects.* Hillsdale, NJ: Erlbaum.

Werner, E. E., & Smith, R. S. (1982). *Vulnerable but invincible: A study of resilient children.* New York: McGraw-Hill.

*Werner, E. E., & Smith, R. S. (1992). *Overcoming the odds: High risk children from birth to adulthood.* Ithaca, NY: Cornell University Press.

Wyman, P. A., Sandler, I., Wolchik, S., & Nelson, K. (2000). Resilience as cumulative competence promotion and stress protection: Theory and intervention. In D. Cicchetti, J. Rappaport, I. Sandler, & R. P. Weissberg (Eds.), *The promotion of wellness in children and adolescents.* Thousand Oaks, CA: Sage.

Zigler, E., Taussig, C., & Black, K. (1992). A promising preventative for juvenile delinquency. *American Psychologist, 47,* 997–1006.

Zimmerman, M. (1983). Methodological issues in the assessment of life events: A review of issues and research. *Clinical Psychology Review, 3,* 339–370.

7

The Concept of Flow

Jeanne Nakamura & Mihaly Csikszentmihalyi

What constitutes a good life? Few questions are of more fundamental importance to a positive psychology. Flow research has yielded one answer, providing an understanding of experiences during which individuals are fully involved in the present moment. Viewed through the experiential lens of flow, *a good life is one that is characterized by complete absorption in what one does.* In this chapter, we describe the flow model of optimal experience and optimal development, explain how flow and related constructs have been measured, discuss recent work in this area, and identify some promising directions for future research.

Optimal Experience and Its Role in Development

The Flow Concept

Studying the creative process in the 1960s (Getzels & Csikszentmihalyi, 1976), Csikszentmihalyi was struck by the fact that when work on a painting was going well, the artist persisted single-mindedly, disregarding hunger, fatigue, and discomfort—yet rapidly lost interest in the artistic creation once it had been completed.

Flow research and theory had their origin in a desire to understand this phenomenon of intrinsically motivated, or *autotelic*, activity: activity rewarding in and of itself (*auto* = self, *telos* = goal), quite apart from its end product or any extrinsic good that might result from the activity.

Significant research had been conducted on the intrinsic motivation concept by this period (summarized in Deci & Ryan, 1985). Nevertheless, no systematic empirical research had been undertaken to clarify the *subjective phenomenology* of intrinsically motivated activity. Csikszentmihalyi (1975/2000) investigated the nature and conditions of enjoyment by interviewing chess players, rock climbers, dancers, and others who emphasized enjoyment as the main reason for pursuing an activity. The researchers focused on play and games, where intrinsic rewards are salient. Additionally, they studied work—specifically, surgery—where the extrinsic rewards of money and prestige could by themselves justify participation. They formed a picture of the general characteristics of optimal experience and its proximal conditions, finding that the reported phenomenology was remarkably similar across play and work settings. The conditions of flow include:

- Perceived challenges, or opportunities for action, that stretch (neither overmatching nor underutilizing) existing skills; a sense that one is engaging challenges at a level appropriate to one's capacities
- Clear proximal goals and immediate feedback about the progress that is being made.

Being "in flow" is the way that some interviewees described the subjective experience of engaging just-manageable challenges by tackling a series of goals, continuously processing feedback about progress, and adjusting action based on this feedback. Under these conditions, experience seamlessly unfolds from moment to moment, and one enters a subjective state with the following characteristics:

- Intense and focused concentration on what one is doing in the present moment
- Merging of action and awareness
- Loss of reflective self-consciousness (i.e., loss of awareness of oneself as a social actor)
- A sense that one can control one's actions; that is, a sense that one can in principle deal with the situation because one knows how to respond to whatever happens next
- Distortion of temporal experience (typically, a sense that time has passed faster than normal)
- Experience of the activity as intrinsically rewarding, such that often the end goal is just an excuse for the process.

When in flow, the individual operates at full capacity (cf. de Charms, 1968; Deci, 1975; White, 1959). The state is one of dynamic equilibrium. Entering flow depends on establishing a balance between perceived action capacities and perceived action opportunities (cf. optimal arousal, Berlyne, 1960; Hunt, 1965). The balance is intrinsically fragile. If challenges begin to exceed skills, one first becomes vigilant and then anxious; if skills begin to exceed challenges, one first relaxes and then becomes bored. Shifts in subjective state provide feedback about the changing relationship to the environment. Experiencing anxiety or boredom presses a person to adjust his or her level of skill and/or challenge in order to escape the aversive state and reenter flow.

The original account of the flow state has proven remarkably robust, confirmed through studies of art and science (Csikszentmihalyi, 1996), aesthetic experience (Csikszentmihalyi & Robinson, 1990), sport (Jackson, 1995, 1996),

literary writing (Perry, 1999), and other activities. The experience is the same across lines of culture, class, gender, and age, as well as across kinds of activity.

Flow research was pursued throughout the 1980s and 1990s in the laboratories of Csikszentmihalyi and colleagues in Italy (e.g., Csikszentmihalyi & Csikszentmihalyi, 1988; Inghilleri, 1999; Massimini & Carli, 1988; Massimini & Delle Fave, 2000). The research in Italy employed the Experience Sampling Method (ESM), using pagers to randomly sample everyday experience. It yielded several refinements of the model of experiential states and dynamics in which the flow concept is embedded. The ESM and the theoretical advances that it made possible are discussed in the section on measuring flow.

During the 1980s and 1990s, the flow concept also was embraced by researchers studying optimal experience (e.g., leisure, play, sports, art, intrinsic motivation) and by researchers and practitioners working in contexts where fostering positive experience is especially important (in particular, formal schooling at all levels). In addition, the concept of flow had growing impact outside academia, in the spheres of popular culture, professional sport, business, and politics.

In the 1980s, work on flow was assimilated by psychology primarily within the humanistic tradition of Maslow and Rogers (McAdams, 1990) or as part of the empirical literature on intrinsic motivation and interest (e.g., Deci & Ryan, 1985; Renninger, Hidi, & Krapp, 1992). In recent years, a model of the individual as a proactive, self-regulating organism interacting with the environment has become increasingly central in psychology (for reviews, see Brandstädter, 1998; Magnusson & Stattin, 1998). This is highly compatible with the model of psychological functioning and development formed in concert with the flow concept (Csikszentmihalyi & Rathunde, 1998; Inghilleri, 1999).

A key characteristic that the flow model shares with these other contemporary theories is *interactionism* (Magnusson & Stattin, 1998). Rather than focusing on the person, abstracted from context (i.e., traits, personality types, stable dispositions), flow research has emphasized the dynamic system composed of person and environment, as well as the phenomenology of person-environment interactions. Rock climbers, surgeons, and others who routinely find deep enjoyment in an activity illustrate how an organized set of challenges and a corresponding set of skills result in optimal experience. The activities afford rich opportunities for action. Complementarily, effectively engaging these challenges depends on the possession of relevant capacities for action. The effortless absorption experienced by the practiced artist at work on a difficult project always is premised upon earlier mastery of a complex body of skills.

Because the direction of the unfolding flow experience is shaped by both person and environment, we speak of *emergent motivation* in an open system (Csikszentmihalyi, 1985): what happens at any moment is responsive to what happened immediately before within the interaction, rather than being dictated by a preexisting intentional structure located within either the person (e.g., a drive) or the environment (e.g., a tradition or script). Here, motivation is emergent in the sense that *proximal goals* arise out of the interaction; later we will consider the companion notion of emergent long-term goals, such as new interests.

In one sense, an asymmetry characterizes the person-environment equation. It is the *subjectively perceived* opportunities and capacities for action that determine experience. That is, there is no objectively defined body of information and set of challenges within the stream of the person's experience, but rather the information that is selectively attended to and the opportunities for action that are perceived. Likewise, it is not meaningful to speak about a person's skills and attentional capacities in objective terms; what enters into lived experience are those capacities for action and those attentional resources and biases (e.g., trait interest) that are engaged by this presently encountered environment.

Sports, games, and other *flow activities* provide goal and feedback structures that make flow more likely. A given individual can find flow in almost any activity, however—working a cash register, ironing clothes, driving a car. Similarly, under certain conditions and depending on an individual's history with the activity, almost any pursuit—a museum visit, a round of golf, a game of chess—can bore or create anxiety. *It is the subjective challenges and subjective skills, not objective ones, that influence the quality of a person's experience.*

Flow, Attention, and the Self

To understand what happens in flow experiences, we need to invoke the more general model of experience, consciousness, and the self that was developed in conjunction with the flow concept (Csikszentmihalyi & Csikszentmihalyi, 1988). According to this model, people are confronted with an overwhelming amount of information. *Consciousness* is the complex system that has evolved in humans for selecting information from this profusion, processing it, and storing it. Information appears in consciousness through the selective investment of *attention*. Once attended to, information enters *awareness*, the system encompassing all of the processes that take place in consciousness, such as thinking, willing, and feeling about this information (i.e., cognition, motivation, and emotion). The *memory* system then stores and retrieves the information. We can think of *subjective experience* as the content of consciousness.

The *self* emerges when consciousness comes into existence and becomes aware of itself as information about the body, subjective states, past memories, and the personal future. Mead (1934; cf. James, 1890/1981) distinguished between two aspects of the self, the knower (the "I") and the known (the "me"). In our terms, these two aspects of the self reflect (a) the sum of one's conscious processes and (b) the information about oneself that enters awareness when one becomes the object of one's own attention. The self becomes organized around goals (see Locke, this volume; Snyder, Rand, & Sigmon, this volume).

Consciousness gives us a measure of control, freeing us from complete subservience to the dictates of genes and culture by representing them in awareness, thereby introducing the alternative of rejecting rather than enacting them. Consciousness thus serves as "a clutch between programmed instructions and adaptive behaviors" (Csikszentmihalyi & Csikszentmihalyi, 1988, p. 21). Alongside the genetic and cultural guides to action, it establishes a *teleonomy of the self*, a set of goals that have been freely chosen by the individual (cf. Brandstädter, 1998; Deci & Ryan, 1985). It might, of course, prove dangerous to disengage our behavior from direct control by the genetic and cultural instructions that have evolved over millennia of adapting to the environment. On the other hand, doing so may increase the chances for adaptive fit with the present environment, particularly under conditions of radical or rapid change.

Attentional processes shape a person's experience. The ability to regulate one's attention is underappreciated. As we have noted elsewhere, "What to pay attention to, how intensely and for how long, are choices that will determine the content of consciousness, and therefore the experiential information available to the organism. Thus, William James was right in claiming, *'My experience is what I agree to attend to. Only those items which I notice shape my mind'* " (Csikszentmihalyi, 1978, p. 339). The choices made are critical because attention is finite, limiting the amount of information that can be processed in consciousness (Csikszentmihalyi & Csikszentmihalyi, 1988). This information is the medium of exchange between person and environment, as well as the material out of which the self is formed.

Attention thus plays a key role in entering and staying in flow. *Entering flow* is largely a function of how attention has been focused in the past and how it is focused in the present by the activity's structural conditions. Interests developed in the past will direct attention to specific challenges. Clear proximal goals, immediate feedback, and just-manageable levels of challenge orient the organism, in a unified and coordinated way, so that attention becomes completely absorbed into the stimulus field defined by the activity.

The phenomenology of flow reflects attentional processes. Intense concentration, perhaps the defining quality of flow, is just another way of saying that attention is wholly invested in the present exchange. Action and awareness merge in the absence of spare attention that might allow objects beyond the immediate interaction to enter awareness. One such object is the self; the loss of self-consciousness in flow marks the fading of Mead's "me" from awareness, as attention is taken up entirely by the challenges being engaged. The passage of time, a basic parameter of experience, becomes distorted because attention is so fully focused elsewhere.

Staying in flow requires that attention be held by this limited stimulus field. Apathy, boredom, and anxiety, like flow, are largely functions of how attention is being structured at a given time. In boredom, and even more so in apathy, the low level of challenge relative to skills allows attention to drift. In anxiety, perceived challenges exceed capacities. Particularly in contexts of extrinsic motivation, attention shifts to the self and its shortcomings, creating a self-consciousness that impedes engagement of the challenges.

Flow, Complexity, and Development

When attention is completely absorbed in the challenges at hand, the individual achieves an ordered state of consciousness. Thoughts, feelings, wishes, and action are in concert. Subjective experience is both differentiated and integrated, the defining qualities of a complex phenomenon.

The notion of complexity applies in a second sense, as well. The flow state is intrinsically rewarding and leads the individual to seek to replicate flow experiences; this introduces a selective mechanism into psychological functioning that fosters growth. As people master challenges in an activity, they develop greater levels of skill, and the activity ceases to be as involving as before. In order to continue experiencing flow, they must identify and engage progressively more complex challenges. The teleonomy of the self is thus a growth principle; the optimal level of challenge stretches existing skills (cf. Vygotsky, 1978), resulting in a more complex set of capacities for action. This factor distinguishes the flow model from theories that define optimal challenge in terms of either a homeostatic equilibrium point to be returned to or a maximum level of challenge to be reached (Moneta & Csikszentmihalyi, 1996). A flow activity not only provides a set of challenges or opportunities for action but it typically also provides a system of graded challenges, able to accommodate a person's continued and deepening enjoyment as skills grow.

The teleonomy of the self is a source of new goals and interests, as well as new capacities for action in relation to existing interests (Csikszentmihalyi & Nakamura, 1999). That is, previously we observed that possessing skills and interest in an activity is one precondition for finding flow in it. Descending a staircase is an almost unnoticed means to an end for the person on foot, but it might be a beckoning opportunity for flow to the person on a skateboard. The phenomenon of emergent motivation means we can come to experience a new or previously unengaging activity as intrinsically motivating if we once find flow in it. The motivation to persist in or return to the activity arises out of the experience itself. The flow experience is thus a force for expansion in relation to the individual's goal and interest structure, as well as for growth of skills in relation to an existing interest.

The Autotelic Personality

As noted previously, flow theory and research have focused on phenomenology rather than personality. The goal has been to understand the dynamics of momentary experience and the conditions under which it is optimal. The capacity to experience flow appears to be nearly universal. Nevertheless, people vary widely in the frequency of reported flow. People also differ in the quality of their experience, and in their desire to be doing what they are doing, when their capacities and their opportunities for action are simultaneously high. This suggests that the latter balance represents an important but not a sufficient condition for flow.

From the beginning, Csikszentmihalyi (1975/2000) recognized the possibility of an *autotelic personality*, a person who tends to enjoy life or "generally does things for their own sake, rather than in order to achieve some later external goal" (Csikszentmihalyi, 1997, p. 117). This kind of personality is distinguished by several *metaskills* or competencies that enable the individual to enter flow and stay in it. These metaskills include a general curiosity and interest in life, persistence, and low self-centeredness, which result in the ability to be motivated by intrinsic rewards. Despite the importance of the topic, little theory or research was devoted to autotelic personality prior to 1990. Later in this chapter, we will discuss research in this area conducted during the past decade.

Measuring Flow and Autotelic Personality

Researchers have developed means of measuring intraindividual (e.g., cross-context) and interindividual differences in the frequency of flow. More recently, increased attention has been paid to measuring individual differences in autotelic personality, the disposition to experience flow. Next, we briefly summarize the measures used in flow research.

Measuring Flow

Psychology has devoted limited attention to developing methods for the systematic investigation of subjective experience. The phenomenon has been viewed as falling outside the sphere of scientific inquiry throughout many of the years since the decline of introspectionist psychology. Attention to subjective experience has grown recently (Richardson, 1999), however, increasing interest in the methods used in flow research. Several self-report tools have been fashioned in order to study this inherently unstable, un-self-conscious, subjective phenomenon, including interviews, paper-and-pencil measures, and the Experience Sampling Method.

Interview

As described, the flow concept emerged out of qualitative interviews about the nature of the experience when a particular activity is going well (Csikszentmihalyi, 1975/2000). The semistructured interview provides a holistic, emic account of the flow experience in real-life context. It was a critical tool in initially identifying and delineating dimensions and dynamics of the flow experience. It continues to be the approach of choice in studies directed toward rich, integrated description. For example, Jackson (1995) has asked elite athletes to describe a flow experience, distinguishing the characteristics of the state, factors that help and hinder entry into the state, factors that disrupt it, and degree of control over it. Perry (1999) has focused writers on the most recent occasion when they lost track of time while writing, asking them to describe what led up to the experience and how they deal with blocks that keep them out of flow.

Questionnaire

One-time paper-and-pencil measures have been used when the goal is not to identify but instead to measure dimensions of the flow experience and/or differences in its occurrence across contexts or individuals. The Flow Questionnaire presents respondents with several passages describing the flow state and asks (a) whether they have had the experience, (b) how often, and (c) in what activity contexts (Csikszentmihalyi & Csikszentmihalyi, 1988). The quotations used were drawn from the original interviews about flow activities (Csikszentmihalyi, 1975/2000), one each from a dancer, a rock climber, and a composer. Allison and Duncan (1988) presented a sample of working women with an additional composite description of "anti-flow" experience encompassing the aversive states of anxiety, boredom, and apathy.

The Flow Scale (Mayers, 1978) elicits an estimate of the frequency with which a person experiences each of ten dimensions of the flow experience (e.g., "I get involved," "I get direct clues as to how well I am doing"). The instrument has been used as a repeated measure to assess differences across activity contexts in the extent to which the flow dimensions are experienced. Delle Fave and Massimini (1988) utilized the Flow Questionnaire and Flow Scale in tandem to identify a person's flow activities and then compare the person's rating of the flow dimensions for primary flow activities with those for a standardized set of everyday activities (e.g., work, TV viewing). More recently, paper-and-pencil scales have been developed to measure the flow state in specific contexts, including sport (Jackson & Marsh, 1996) and psychotherapeutic practice (Parks, 1996).

The Experience Sampling Method

Interview and questionnaire approaches are limited by (a) their reliance on retrospective reconstruction of past experience and (b) the requirement that respondents first average across many discrete experiences to compose a picture of the typical subjective experience when things are going well, and then estimate the frequency and/or intensity of this experience. The study of flow has progressed in large part because researchers in the late 1970s developed a tool uniquely suited to the study of situated experience, including optimal experience. Full descriptions of the Experience Sampling Method (ESM) can be found elsewhere (e.g., Csikszentmihalyi & Larson, 1987). Subjects are equipped with paging devices (pagers, programmable watches, or handheld computers); these signal them, at preprogrammed times, to complete a questionnaire describing the moment at which they were paged. The method takes samples from the stream of actual everyday experience. Unlike diaries and time budgets, use of the ESM from the beginning focused on sampling not only activities but also cognitive, emotional, and motivational states, providing a tool for building a systematic phenomenology. Contents of the questionnaire vary depending on the research goals, as do paging schedules and study duration. A quasi-random schedule with data collected for one week has been widely used to provide a representative picture of daily life. ESM studies of flow have focused on the sampled moments when (a) the *conditions for flow*

exist, based on the balance of challenges (or opportunities for action) and skills (abilities to deal with the situation) and/or (b) the *flow state* is reported. The latter usually is measured by summing the self-reported levels of concentration, involvement, and enjoyment, which are typically measured on 10-point scales. These three dimensions provide a good proxy for what is in reality a much more complex state of consciousness.

The first mapping of the phenomenological landscape in terms of perceived challenges and skills identified three regions of experience (Csikszentmihalyi, 1975/2000): a *flow* channel along which challenges and skills matched; a region of *boredom*, as opportunities for action relative to skills dropped off; and a region of *anxiety*, as challenges increasingly exceeded capacities for action. This mapping was based on the original accounts of deep flow (see Figure 7.1a).

Initial analyses of ESM data were not consistent with this mapping, however. Simply balancing challenges and skills did not optimize the quality of experience. As Massimini and his colleagues clarified, inherent in the flow concept is the notion of skill stretching. Activities providing minimal opportunities for action do not lead to flow, regardless of whether the actor experiences a balance between perceived challenge and skill. Much of TV viewing exemplifies the less than optimal experience when low skills match low challenges (Kubey & Csikszentmihalyi, 1990). Operationally, the Milan group re-

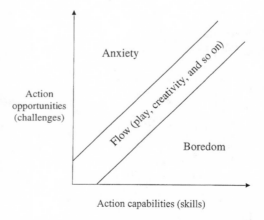

Figure 7.1a The original model of the flow state. Flow is experienced when perceived opportunities for action are in balance with the actor's perceived skills. Adapted from Csikszentmihalyi (1975/2000).

defined flow as the balance of challenges and skills *when both are above average levels for the individual*. That is, flow is expected to occur when individuals perceive greater opportunities for action than they encounter on average in their daily lives, and have skills adequate to engage them. This shift led to an important re-mapping of the phenomenological terrain, revealing a fourth state, apathy, associated with low challenges and correspondingly low skills. Experientially, it is a sphere of stagnation and attentional diffusion, the inverse of the flow state.

The Milan group subsequently showed that the resolution of this phenomenological map can be made finer by differentiating the challenge/skill terrain into eight experiential channels rather than four quadrants (see Figure 7.1b). The quality of experience intensifies within a channel or quadrant as challenges and skills move away from a person's average levels. Operationally, they divided the challenge/skill space into a series of concentric rings, associated with increasing intensity of experience. A researcher might decide to focus only on the outer rings of the flow channel, theoretically the region of the deep flow experiences described in the early interviews. Subsequent researchers have experimented with different challenge/skill formulas (e.g., Hektner & Csikszentmi-

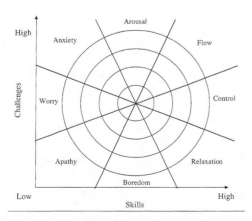

Figure 7.1b The current model of the flow state. Flow is experienced when perceived challenges and skills are above the actor's average levels; when they are below, apathy is experienced. Intensity of experience increases with distance from the actor's average levels of challenge and skill, as shown by the concentric rings. Adapted from Csikszentmihalyi (1997).

halyi, 1996; Moneta & Csikszentmihalyi, 1996), retaining the essential insight that perceived challenges and skills must be relative to a person's own average levels.

Measuring the Autotelic Personality

As interest in the autotelic personality has grown, researchers have sought a way to measure it with the naturalistic data provided by the ESM. *Time spent in flow* has been the most widely used measure of the general propensity toward flow (Adlai-Gail, 1994; Hektner, 1996). However, time in flow also reflects the range of action opportunities that happen to be available in the individual's environment during the sampling period. Other researchers therefore have operationalized the disposition as *intrinsic motivation in high-challenge, high-skill situations*, reflected in low mean scores on the item "I wish to be doing something else" when subjective challenges and skills are both above average (Abuhamdeh, 2000; Csikszentmihalyi & Le-Fevre, 1989).

A more traditional paper-and-pencil measure was utilized by Csikszentmihalyi, Rathunde, and Whalen (1993). They defined autotelic personality as the conjunction of receptive and active qualities, one measured by the Jackson PRF factors of Sentience and Understanding and the other by Achievement and Endurance (Jackson, 1984). They theorized that jointly these qualities would account for autotelic individuals' openness to new challenges and readiness to engage and persist in high-challenge activities, key aspects of the metaskills that contribute to getting into flow and staying there (Csikszentmihalyi & Nakamura, 1989; Csikszentmihalyi et al., 1993; Inghilleri, 1999).

Recent Directions in Flow Research

The past decade has seen developments on several fronts in the understanding of flow. In large part this has been due to longitudinal ESM studies of adolescent and adult samples being conducted at the University of Chicago.

Consequences of Flow

According to the flow model, experiencing flow encourages a person to persist at and return to an activity because of the experiential rewards it promises, and thereby fosters the growth of skills over time. In several studies, flow was associated with commitment and achievement during the high school years (Carli, Delle Fave, & Massimini, 1988; Mayers, 1978; Nakamura, 1988). More recently, a longitudinal ESM study of talented high school students provided evidence of a relationship between quality of experience and persistence in an activity. Students still committed to their talent area at age 17 were compared with peers who already had disengaged. Four years earlier, those currently still committed had experienced more flow and less anxiety than their peers when engaged in school-related activities; they also were more likely to have identified their talent area as a source of flow (Csikszentmihalyi et al., 1993). In a longitudinal study of students talented in mathematics (Heine, 1996), those who experienced flow in the first part of a course performed better in the second half, controlling for their initial abilities and grade point average. Because the self grows through flow experiences, we also might expect time spent in flow to predict self-esteem. Correlational studies with ESM data support this expectation (Adlai-Gail, 1994; Wells, 1988).

In addition to enhancing positive outcomes, longitudinal research suggests that mastering challenges in daily life may protect against negative outcomes (Schmidt, 2000). For American adolescents who had experienced high adversity at home and/or at school, the availability of challenging activities, involvement in these activities, and sense of success when engaged in them were all associated with diminished delinquency two years later.

Teenagers' quality of experience in everyday life, understood in terms of the subjective challenge/skill landscape, also may have consequences for physical health (Patton, 1999). In the same representative national sample of adolescents, time spent in relaxation (low-challenge, high-skill) situations was associated with greater freedom from physical pain 2 and 4 years later as well as concurrently. Apparent risk factors with respect to quality of experience differed by gender. The amount of physical pain reported 2 and 5 years later (and concurrently) was correlated with time spent in anxiety (high-challenge, low-skill) situations for girls, but with time spent in apathy (low-challenge, low-skill) situations for boys.

The Nature and Dynamics of Flow

The accumulating evidence for positive correlates and outcomes of the flow experience un-doubtedly accounts for a portion of the interest paid to flow in recent years. However, this interest, in a sense, misses the point. From the perspective of the individual, the flow state is a self-justifying experience; it is, by definition, an end in itself. We continue to be reminded of this by studies of flow in particular activity contexts.

That is, a distinct strand of flow research can be traced forward through the 1980s and 1990s from the original study of flow activities. In this line of research, qualitative interviews have yielded domain-specific descriptions of deep flow in diverse activities: elite and nonelite sport (Jackson & Csikszentmihalyi, 1999; Kimiecik & Harris, 1996); literary writing (Perry, 1999) and artistic and scientific creativity more generally (Csikszentmihalyi, 1996); social activism (Colby & Damon, 1992); and aesthetic experience (Csikszentmihalyi & Robinson, 1990). As noted earlier, these studies confirm the basic contours of the flow state, demonstrating how universal they are across activity contexts. Research also is yielding a differentiated picture of the sources of flow within particular contexts. For example, Trevino and Trevino (1992), Webster and Martocchio (1993), and others have explored how flow can be facilitated in software design and computer-mediated communication. Shernoff, Knauth, and Makris (2000) examined levels of flow across academic and nonacademic classes and across different types of classroom activity, in an ESM study of adolescents using a national sample. Paralleling well-documented differences in quality of experience between active and passive leisure pursuits (e.g., sports vs. TV viewing), levels of flow were higher in "active" classwork (taking tests, participating in groups, working individually) than in "passive" classwork (listening to lectures, watching videos or television).

As new ESM studies are conducted, we continue to clarify the general features of the experiential landscape defined by the interaction of challenges and skills. Selected data from a recent large-scale ESM study of adolescents illustrate the current picture (see Figure 7.2). For each challenge/skill combination, Figure 7.2 shows the mean ratings for several key experiential variables: concentration, enjoyment, wish to be doing the activity, self-esteem, and perceived importance to the future. Schoolwork is prevalent in the high-challenge, low-skill (anxiety) quadrant; structured leisure, schoolwork, and work in the high-challenge, high-skill (flow) quadrant; socializing and eating in the low-challenge, high-skill (relaxation) quadrant;

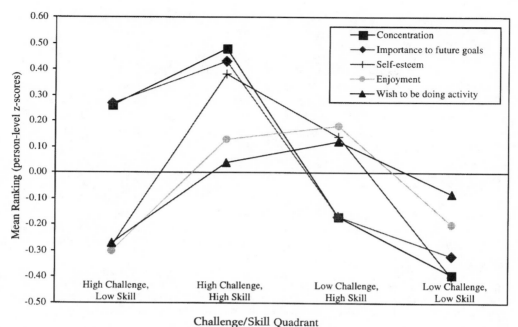

Figure 7.2 Quality of experience in each flow quadrant for a national sample of American adolescents (*n* = 824). Adapted from Hektner and Asakawa (2000).

and passive leisure and chores in the low-challenge, low-skill (apathy/boredom) quadrant.

The anxiety quadrant is characterized, as expected, by high stakes but low enjoyment and low motivation. Only in the flow quadrant are all of the selected variables simultaneously above the personal mean. In contrast, all are below average in the apathy/boredom quadrant. Concentration, self-esteem, and importance to future goals peak in the flow quadrant, whereas enjoyment and wish to be doing the activity are actually somewhat higher in the relaxation quadrant. The quality of experience in the relaxation quadrant is thus partially positive even though the stakes are not high and attention is unfocused. Marking a shift in the model, the current mapping of the experiential landscape labels the low-challenge, high-skill quadrant as *relaxation* to capture the mixed nature of the subjective state, which is less aversive than originally thought.

We speculate that two kinds of experiences might be intrinsically rewarding: one involving conservation of energy (relaxation), the other involving the use of skills to seize ever-greater opportunities (flow). It is consistent with current understandings of evolution to suppose that both of these strategies for coping with the environment, one conservative and the other

expansive, were selected over time as important components of the human behavioral repertoire, even though they motivate different—in some sense, opposite—behaviors. The two distinctly aversive situations, which organisms are presumably programmed to avoid, are those in which one feels overwhelmed by environmental demands (anxiety) or left with nothing to do (apathy).

Obstacles and Facilitators to Flow

Studies conducted in the late 1980s and 1990s, including longitudinal ESM studies, have enabled advances in knowledge about the conditions of flow. We look first at obstacles to optimal experience; we then turn to research on facilitators and causes of flow. We focus on two impediments to flow that concern the subjective construction of experience.

Preference for Relaxation Versus Flow

As noted previously, the quality of experience appears to be more positive than originally expected in the low-challenge, high-skill space adjacent to the flow channel or quadrant. One possible cause is that, at least for American adolescents, it is not uncommon in the context of schoolwork to feel overchallenged when stakes are high. The situation induces self-consciousness (cf. ego orientation), challenge becomes a stress rather than an opportunity for action, and reducing the level of challenge becomes an attractive option. This interpretation appeared to be borne out in comparisons of normal American adolescents, Italian adolescents at an elite school, and talented high school students in the United States. For the sample of normal American adolescents, motivation (Csikszentmihalyi & Nakamura, 1989) and happiness (Csikszentmihalyi & Rathunde, 1993) were greater in low-challenge, high-skill situations than when challenges and skills were simultaneously high.

Attitudes Toward Work and Play

The work-play distinction as it relates to subjective experience has been an important thread running through flow research. The original flow study showed that work, as well as play, can occasion deep flow (Csikszentmihalyi, 1975/ 2000; see also Delle Fave & Massimini, 1988). Haworth's (1997) ESM research on unemployed youth in the United Kingdom underlined this similarity between work and play. Whereas unemployment provides few opportunities for flow because the perceived challenges are low in everyday life, both work and play can provide a structured source of challenges in one's life.

Beginning with LeFevre (1988), however, research revealed a paradox about work that perhaps could be detected only with ESM data. In a heterogeneous sample of adult workers, multiple dimensions of subjective experience (e.g., concentrating, feeling happy, strong, creative, and satisfied) were significantly more positive in high-challenge, high-skill situations than elsewhere, and this was true both at work and at leisure. Furthermore, significantly more time was spent in high-challenge, high-skill situations at work than at leisure, whereas the opposite was true of time spent in low-challenge, low-skill situations. Work life was dominated by efficacy experiences and leisure time by moments of apathy. *Despite this experiential pattern*, workers wished to be doing something else when they were working and wished to be doing just what they were doing when at leisure (LeFevre, 1988). Motivation seemed insensitive to the actual data of the workers' own experience, being driven instead by their cultural prejudices about work (viewed as what one has to do) versus leisure (viewed as what one freely chooses).

An ESM study of students in grades 6 through 12 revealed that these attitudes toward work and play are already in place by sixth grade and intensify across the adolescent years (Csikszentmihalyi, 1997). Motivation in experiences characterized as "work" (academic classes and, later, paid jobs) was lower than in experiences characterized as "play" (e.g., passive activities like TV viewing), even though the worklike experiences were associated with higher concentration, importance to the future, and self-esteem. On a positive note, 10% of the time sampled, students reported engaging in extracurricular activities and pursuing art, games, and hobbies outside of formal settings. They labeled these activities as simultaneously worklike and playlike and experienced them as both important and enjoyable. In addition, both "play" and "work" were more positive than experiences that were labeled neither worklike nor playlike (e.g., maintenance activities like chores).

We turn next to facilitators of flow. Our interest here is in extrasituational factors; we focus on autotelic personality and autotelic families.

Autotelic Personality

Individuals vary in the time spent in flow. Over one third of those surveyed in U.S. and German polls (responding to slightly different questions) estimated that they rarely or never experienced involvement so intense that they lose track of time (42% of Americans, 35% of Germans), whereas about one fifth (16% of Americans, 23% of Germans) reported having such experiences daily (Gallup Poll, 1998; Noelle-Neumann, 1995). Adopting a different metric, LeFevre (1988) found that a sample of adult workers included about 40% who were most motivated in high-challenge, high-skill situations and about 40% who were most motivated in low-challenge, low-skill situations; the former might be called *autotelic individuals*. Measuring autotelic personality similarly with young adults, Hektner (1996) confirmed that autotelics were least happy and motivated in apathy (low-challenge, low-skill) situations, whereas nonautotelics (those least motivated in high-challenge, high-skill situations) did not find the apathy condition aversive. Individual differences thus clearly exist. What correlates and consequences do they have?

Studying a national sample of American teenagers, Adlai-Gail (1994) showed that autotelic personality, measured by time in flow, has positive correlates. Autotelic students had more well-defined future goals and reported more positive cognitive and affective states. For a sample of American adults, Abuhamdeh (2000) compared autotelics and nonautotelics, defined by preference for high-action-opportunity, high-skill situations. His research begins to suggest how high-action-opportunity, high-skill situations are distinctively experienced by autotelics, showing that autotelics experience less stress and strain in the flow quadrant than outside of it, whereas the reverse is true for nonautotelics.

Autotelic Families

The question thus becomes how autotelic personality is shaped. Rathunde (1988, 1996) demonstrated with data from an ESM study of talented adolescents that autotelic personality is fostered in what he has called a "complex" family environment, one that simultaneously provides support and challenge. Students from complex families spent significantly more time in high-challenge, high-skill situations and less time in low-challenge, low-skill situations than did the students from other types of families (e.g., ones that provided support or challenge alone). They also felt more in control of their actions and better about themselves generally, and they reported more positive experience in productive activities (e.g., studying).

We might speculate that early schooling experiences are another critical contributor to the development of autotelic personality. The Key School described in the next section represents one educational program deliberately designed to foster skills and propensity for flow, as well as identification of interests.

Interventions and Programs to Foster Flow

Flow researchers have discussed how their findings might be applied by practitioners and people in general (e.g., Csikszentmihalyi, 1990, 1996; Csikszentmihalyi & Robinson, 1990; Jackson & Csikszentmihalyi, 1999; Perry, 1999). The relevance of the flow concept is increasingly noted in applied settings, such as the Montessori schools (Kahn, 2000) and the field of oc-

cupational therapy (Emerson, 1998; Rebeiro & Polgar, 1998).

Flow principles have been translated into practice in a variety of contexts. Two types of intervention can be distinguished: (a) those seeking to shape activity structures and environments so that they foster flow or obstruct it less and (b) those attempting to assist individuals in finding flow. The former include interventions to make work a greater source of flow, such as efforts by the Swedish police to identify obstacles to flow in the organization of police work and then to restructure it along lines more conducive to flow on the beat. Likewise, factory work has been evaluated and reorganized to enhance flow at a Volvo automotive plant. Several art museums, including the Getty Museum in Los Angeles, have incorporated flow principles during their design of exhibits and buildings. Flow principles have informed product design at Nissan USA, with the goal of making the use of the product more enjoyable.

Educational settings present an opportunity to apply the results of flow research most directly. One experiment deserving mention is the 13-year-old Key School in Indianapolis, where the goal is to foster flow by influencing both environment and individual (Whalen, 1999). This public elementary and middle school seeks to (a) create a learning environment that fosters flow experiences and (b) help students form interests and develop the capacity and propensity to experience flow. In the Flow Activities Center, students have regular opportunities to actively choose and engage in activities related to their own interests and then pursue these activities without imposed demands or pacing. The teacher supports children's selection and enjoyment of activities that challenge and stretch them and helps the students to identify new challenges as their capacities grow. Based on observations of the Flow Activities Center and conversations with teachers, Whalen concluded that the center is effectively fostering "serious play" (Csikszentmihalyi et al., 1993) and that it has introduced values of flow and intrinsic motivation into the life of the school more generally.

The most direct efforts to assist individuals in finding flow lie in the sphere of psychotherapy. The Milan group built on its extensive program of basic research to develop therapeutic interventions aimed at transforming the structure of daily life toward more positive experience. Psychiatric interventions informed by flow theory have been successful in diverse cultural settings, including Nicaragua and northern Somalia (Inghilleri, 1999). In Italy, the ESM, guided by flow theory, has provided a tool for identifying patterns in everyday experience and ways in which these might be transformed (Inghilleri, 1999; Massimini, Csikszentmihalyi, & Carli, 1987). Additionally, it provides a means for monitoring one's success in transforming these patterns—a form of feedback about the extent of change. ESM data reveal to patient and therapist the disjunctions between attitudes and actual experience (as in the paradox of work described earlier, wherein work is disliked despite being absorbing), and between professed and enacted preferences (i.e., strength of professed commitment vs. actual time allocation). Likewise, by identifying activities that are intrinsically motivating, it pinpoints areas where optimal experience can be increased.

Delle Fave and Massimini (1992) reported a case study involving the 1-year psychotherapy of a young woman struggling with agoraphobia. She feared being alone in public and experienced anxiety symptoms in crowds. Despite drug therapy, the woman's life structure had become narrowly circumscribed around work, accompanied travel, and home, containing her agoraphobia but at the expense of enjoyment and growth. At the outset, the Flow Questionnaire was administered in order to identify activities that had ever been sources of flow in the woman's daily life. Therapy focused on supporting redirection of her time and attention into these activities. During the year, nine weeklong ESM samples were collected. The ESM data constituted an integral part of treatment: Experiential patterns (time use and associated quality of experience) were discussed with the client, along with strategies for transforming her life structure. The young woman's symptoms disappeared over the course of treatment, as registered in the reallocation of time away from TV viewing (i.e., homebound passive leisure) and toward activities in public places (e.g., volunteer work and socializing). Time spent alone also increased because of reduced need for accompanied travel. Improvement in quality of experience was marked, with decreased time in the low-challenge, low-skill conditions conducive to apathy and increased time in the high-challenge, high-skill conditions conducive to flow. Drug treatment was discontinued after 10 months.

Many therapies focus on conflict, under the assumption that once this is worked through, happiness will take care of itself. The therapeutic approach described here reverses figure and ground. Use of flow principles allows therapy to be reoriented toward building on interests and strengths, taking advantage of the growth of skill and confidence (cf. Wells, 1988) that attends flow experience, and enabling the individual to reduce dysphoric experience as a by-product of this growth.

The ESM also may provide the nonclinical population with a tool for personalized intervention directed toward prevention by optimizing (vs. rehabilitating) patterns of everyday experience (cf. Snyder, Feldman, Taylor, Schroeder, & Adams, 2000). The case example just described raises the possibility of structuring the evaluation and transformation of one's daily life more like a flow activity, making the change process itself more enjoyable by endowing it with clear goals, clear and rapid feedback, and manageable challenges. As a tool for insight, there should be many important applications of individual ESM use informed by flow principles.

A common theme of the educational and the therapeutic application of flow principles bears underlining. Their goal is not to foster the state of flow directly but rather to help individuals identify activities that they enjoy and learn how to invest their attention in these activities.

Directions for Future Research

The interventions just described represent promising directions for future applied efforts. In this section, we touch upon directions for future research.

Autotelic Personality: Attentional Processes and Meaningful Goals

Much remains to be learned about the nature of the autotelic personality and what qualities, metaskills, and dispositions characterize individuals inclined and able to find flow in daily life. Beyond Rathunde's (1988) work on the family environment, research is needed on the critical contributors and obstacles to the development of autotelic personality.

For both basic knowledge and intervention, fundamental and urgent questions concern the nature of the attentional processes that foster flow and the way in which optimal attentional practices are formed (Hamilton, 1983). Being able to control one's attention is what makes unified action and experience possible. The capacity to direct and regulate one's own attention is always critical; whatever occupies attention shapes experience and, through it, consciousness, the self, and the culture. Under contemporary social conditions, the importance of the self-regulation of attention is amplified. Individuals encounter exponentially growing amounts of information from an ever-rising number of sources, and they must decide how to invest their attention among these many possible claimants. Because attention is recognized as a precious commodity, others compete aggressively to attract, control, and direct it.

Elsewhere, we have reflected on the amorality of flow, acknowledging that it is possible for people to seek flow in activities that are neutral or destructive to the self and/or the culture (e.g., Csikszentmihalyi & Larson, 1978; Csikszentmihalyi & Rathunde, 1993). As the flow concept is taken up in applied settings, it becomes increasingly clear that flow experiences also can be used to beguile others' attention. Creating settings and objects that foster flow becomes a means of controlling scarce attentional resources. For each individual, the best defense against the manipulation of one's limited attention by others is to determine for oneself how one wants to invest it and then attempt to do so efficiently and wisely.

A related issue is the question of how children and adolescents learn what goals deserve attention. Individual differences in preference for flow, as well as ruptures within the unity of absorption and motivation (the "paradox of work"), emerge by early adolescence. We need to extend flow research downward into childhood in order to identify the endowments and experiences that differentiate those who reach adolescence with a propensity for flow from peers who prefer states of control, relaxation, and even apathy to the risk and rigors of challenging activities. Autotelic persons are attracted to goals that require effort to achieve; those who prefer relaxation are not. How does such a difference become habitual? The data suggest that the two strategies may be equally positive in the short term but that children who learn to enjoy investing effort in meaningful goals can count on more positive outcomes in the long run, compared with children who learn to enjoy less demanding goals. Longitudinal research would be especially helpful here, as would observational studies in flow-promoting early settings.

Measurement of Flow

ESM researchers have developed multiple ways of operationalizing the flow experience or defining when an individual is "in flow." As described, these include various state measures (usually composite variables, including cognitive, affective, and motivational components) and situational measures (indices of relative challenge and skill). We may be nearing the point when it will be advantageous to assess the pros and cons of different operationalizations and move toward a consensual ESM measure to facilitate the accumulation of knowledge.

A larger issue is the division of labor that has grown up within flow research between (a) ESM studies of daily experience, in which deep flow is represented only occasionally, and (b) interview studies of deep flow, in which the dynamics of experience are accessible only through retrospection. The reasons for the division of labor are clear—interrupting deep flow, as the ESM would do, destroys the phenomenon—but we should recognize the attendant limitations on what we can learn and generalize from ESM data. We may want to explore existing and conceivable alternatives. Some ESM research in fact has been undertaken with strategically selected samples engaged in flow activities, such as in the mountaineers studied by Delle Fave (personal communication, 2000) and colleagues during a Himalayan expedition. A hands-free version of the ESM might be helpful. Secondary analysis of existing ESM data sets, isolating all instances of opportunistically sampled deep flow, is also possible. Beyond this, alternative methods merit consideration, such as analysis of videotaped sequences of individuals in flow. This might encompass tracking a set of observable markers of flow, collecting self-reports about the associated course of subjective experience, and/or combining the two data sources. For example, working within the flow paradigm, Rathunde (1997) asked families to comment on audio playbacks of conversations immediately after they ended.

Forms of Flow

Research has focused most intensively on the individual's experience of flow in sports, games, and other kinds of structured leisure; in educational pursuits; and in artistic and other types of work. Other important areas remain relatively unexplored, and their investigation might contribute to further development of the flow model. For example, no research has addressed the category of *microflow activities* (Csikszentmihalyi, 1975/2000): activities like doodling that are short in duration, interstitial and subordinated within the stream of action, and often so routinized as to occur almost outside awareness. The early flow research suggested that they might play an important role in optimizing attentional regulation, and we suspect that further research into their dynamics and function would prove fruitful.

Relatively little research has addressed the experience of flow when attention is trained on internal sources of information (e.g., in psychotherapy, life-planning, life-review, and other forms of existential reflection; fantasy; spiritual experience). For many people, the inner life is vulnerable to chaos. ESM research shows that solitude is strenuous; the train of thought breaks down or becomes ruminative. Intrapsychic activities may foster development of a capacity for attentional self-regulation, however; research in this area is therefore important. These activities span a continuum from culturally defined domains (e.g., prayer), which may be understandable in terms of existing flow theory, to spheres that are largely unstructured by culturally provided rules and tools (e.g., life review), where research might extend the bounds of existing theory.

At the other end of the spectrum, flow has been studied in some group activities (e.g., team sports and classroom learning), but typically treating the individual as the focus of analysis. Other participants are conceptualized as sources of challenge (e.g., competitors) or of feedback about performance. Fewer studies have identified forms of what might be called *shared flow* (e.g., Csikszentmihalyi & Csikszentmihalyi, 1988; Csikszentmihalyi & Larson, 1984). This latter notion characterizes the inspired jam session (Csikszentmihalyi & Rich, 1998) or animated conversation; the *communitas* (Turner, 1974) experienced in expressive ritual; and the intense excitement of "hot groups" (Lipman-Blumen, 1999). Shared flow appears to be distinguishable from optimal individual experience in group settings where one's coparticipants may or may not be in flow. We lack an analysis of the phenomenon that addresses the possibility of emergent qualities, whether with respect to dimensions, dynamics, conditions, or functions and effects.

Conclusions

Research on flow contributes knowledge to several topics that are of central importance to positive psychology. In the first place, it illuminates the phenomenology of optimal experience, answering the question, What is it like to live fully, to be completely involved in the moment? Second, this perspective leads to questions about the long-term consequences of optimal experience: Does the sum of flow over time add up to a good and happy life? Or only under certain conditions, that is, if the person develops an autotelic personality and learns to enjoy high challenges? Furthermore, this line of research tries to unravel the conditions that act as obstacles or facilitators to optimal experience, focusing especially on the most prominent institutions such as the family, schools, and the workplace. Although it seems clear that flow serves as a buffer against adversity and prevents pathology, its major contribution to the quality of life consists in endowing momentary experience with value.

References

Abuhamdeh, S. (2000). *The autotelic personality: An exploratory investigation.* Unpublished manuscript, University of Chicago.

Adlai-Gail, W. (1994). *Exploring the autotelic personality.* Unpublished doctoral dissertation, University of Chicago.

Allison, M., & Duncan, M. (1988). Women, work, and flow. In M. Csikszentmihalyi & I. Csikszentmihalyi (Eds.), *Optimal experience* (pp. 118–137). Cambridge, England: Cambridge University Press.

Berlyne, D. E. (1960). *Conflict, arousal, and curiosity.* New York: McGraw-Hill.

Brandstadter, J. (1998). Action perspectives in human development. In R. M. Lerner (Ed.), *Handbook of child psychology* (Vol. 1, pp. 807–863). New York: Wiley.

*Carli, M., Delle Fave, A., & Massimini, F. (1988). The quality of experience in the flow channels: Comparison of Italian and U.S. students. In M. Csikszentmihalyi & I. Csikszentmihalyi (Eds.), *Optimal experience* (pp. 288–306). Cambridge, England: Cambridge University Press.

Colby, A., & Damon, W. (1992). *Some do care.* New York: Free Press.

Csikszentmihalyi, M. (1978). Attention and the holistic approach to behavior. In K. S. Pope & J. L. Singer (Eds.), *The stream of consciousness* (pp. 335–358). New York: Plenum.

Csikszentmihalyi, M. (1985). Emergent motivation and the evolution of the self. *Advances in Motivation and Achievement, 4*, 93–119.

Csikszentmihalyi, M. (1990). *Flow.* New York: Harper and Row.

Csikszentmihalyi, M. (1996). *Creativity.* New York: HarperCollins.

Csikszentmihalyi, M. (1997). *Finding flow.* New York: Basic.

*Csikszentmihalyi, M. (2000). *Beyond boredom and anxiety.* San Francisco: Jossey-Bass. (Original work published 1975)

*Csikszentmihalyi, M., & Csikszentmihalyi, I. (Eds.). (1988). *Optimal experience.* Cambridge, England: Cambridge University Press.

Csikszentmihalyi, M., & Larson, R. (1978). Intrinsic rewards in school crime. *Crime and Delinquency, 24*, 322–335.

Csikszentmihalyi, M., & Larson, R. (1984). *Being adolescent.* New York: Basic Books.

Csikszentmihalyi, M., & Larson, R. (1987). Validity and reliability of the experience sampling method. *Journal of Nervous and Mental Disease, 175*, 526–536.

*Csikszentmihalyi, M., & LeFevre, J. (1989). Optimal experience in work and leisure. *Journal of Personality and Social Psychology, 56*, 815–822.

Csikszentmihalyi, M., & Nakamura, J. (1989). The dynamics of intrinsic motivation: A study of adolescents. In R. Ames & C. Ames (Eds.), *Research on motivation in education: Goals and cognitions* (pp. 45–71). New York: Academic Press.

Csikszentmihalyi, M., & Nakamura, J. (1999). Emerging goals and the self-regulation of behavior. In R. S. Wyer (Ed.), *Advances in social cognition: Vol. 12. Perspectives on behavioral self-regulation* (pp. 107–118). Mahwah, NJ: Erlbaum.

Csikszentmihalyi, M., & Rathunde, K. (1993). The measurement of flow in everyday life. *Nebraska Symposium on Motivation, 40*, 57–97.

*Csikszentmihalyi, M., & Rathunde, K. (1998). The development of the person: An experiential perspective on the ontogenesis of psychological complexity. In R. M. Lerner (Ed.), *Handbook of child psychology* (pp. 635–685). New York: Wiley.

*Csikszentmihalyi, M., Rathunde, K., & Whalen, S. (1993). *Talented teenagers.* Cambridge, England: Cambridge University Press.

Csikszentmihalyi, M., & Rich, G. (1998). Musical improvisation: A systems approach. In K. Sawyer (Ed.), *Creativity in performance* (pp. 43–66). Greenwich, CT: Ablex.

Csikszentmihalyi, M., & Robinson, R. (1990). *The art of seeing.* Malibu, CA: J. Paul Getty Museum and the Getty Center for Education in the Arts.

de Charms, R. (1968). *Personal causation.* New York: Academic Press.

Deci, E. (1975). *Intrinsic motivation.* New York: Plenum.

Deci, E., & Ryan, R. (1985). *Intrinsic motivation and self-determination in human behavior.* New York: Plenum.

Delle Fave, A., & Massimini, F. (1988). Modernization and the changing contexts of flow in work and leisure. In M. Csikszentmihalyi & I. Csikszentmihalyi (Eds.), *Optimal experience* (pp. 193–213). Cambridge, England: Cambridge University Press.

*Delle Fave, A., & Massimini, F. (1992). The ESM and the measurement of clinical change: A case of anxiety disorder. In M. deVries (Ed.), *The experience of psychopathology* (pp. 280–289). Cambridge, England: Cambridge University Press.

Emerson, H. (1998). Flow and occupation: A review of the literature. *Canadian Journal of Occupational Therapy, 65*, 37–43.

Gallup Poll. (1998, November). Omnibus, III.

Getzels, J. W., & Csikszentmihalyi, M. (1976). *The creative vision.* New York: Wiley.

Hamilton, J. A. (1983). Development of interest and enjoyment in adolescence. *Journal of Youth and Adolescence, 12*, 355–372.

Haworth, J. T. (1997). *Work, leisure and well-being.* London: Routledge.

Heine, C. (1996). *Flow and achievement in mathematics.* Unpublished doctoral dissertation, University of Chicago.

Hektner, J. (1996). *Exploring optimal personality development: A longitudinal study of adolescents.* Unpublished doctoral dissertation, University of Chicago.

Hektner, J., & Asakawa, K. (2000). Learning to like challenges. In M. Csikszentmihalyi & B. Schneider, *Becoming adult* (pp. 95–112). New York: Basic Books.

Hektner, J., & Csikszentmihalyi, M. (1996, April). *A longitudinal exploration of flow and intrinsic motivation in adolescents.* Paper presented at the annual meeting of the American Educational Research Association, New York City.

Hunt, J. (1965). Intrinsic motivation and its role in development. *Nebraska Symposium on Motivation, 12*, 189–282.

*Inghilleri, P. (1999). *From subjective experience to cultural change*. Cambridge, England: Cambridge University Press.

Jackson, D. (1984). *Personality Research Form manual*. Goshen, NY: Research Psychologists Press.

Jackson, S. (1995). Factors influencing the occurrence of flow state in elite athletes. *Journal of Applied Sport Psychology, 7*, 138–166.

Jackson, S. (1996). Toward a conceptual understanding of the flow experience in elite athletes. *Research Quarterly for Exercise and Sport, 67*, 76–90.

Jackson, S., & Csikszentmihalyi, M. (1999). *Flow in sports*. Champaign, IL: Human Kinetics.

Jackson, S., & Marsh, H. W. (1996). Development and validation of a scale to measure optimal experience: The flow state scale. *Journal of Sport and Exercise Psychology, 18*, 17–35.

James, W. (1981). *The principles of psychology*. Cambridge, MA: Harvard University Press. (Original work published 1890)

Kahn, D. (2000). Montessori's positive psychology: A lasting imprint. *NAMTA Journal, 25* (2), 1–5.

Kimiecik, J. C., & Harris, A. T. (1996). What is enjoyment? A conceptual/definitional analysis with implications for sport and exercise psychology. *Journal of Sport and Exercise Psychology, 18*, 247–263.

Kubey, R., & Csikszentmihalyi, M. (1990). *Television and the quality of life*. Hillsdale, NJ: Erlbaum.

LeFevre, J. (1988). Flow and the quality of experience during work and leisure. In M. Csikszentmihalyi & I. Csikszentmihalyi (Eds.), *Optimal experience* (pp. 307–318). Cambridge, England: Cambridge University Press.

Lipman-Blumen, J. (1999). *Hot groups*. New York: Oxford University Press.

Magnusson, D., & Stattin, H. (1998). Person-context interaction theories. In R. M. Lerner (Ed.), *Handbook of child psychology* (Vol. 1, pp. 685–759). New York: Wiley.

*Massimini, F., & Carli, M. (1988). The systematic assessment of flow in daily experience. In M. Csikszentmihalyi & I. Csikszentmihalyi (Eds.), *Optimal experience* (pp. 266–287). Cambridge, England: Cambridge University Press.

Massimini, F., Csikszentmihalyi, M., & Carli, M. (1987). The monitoring of optimal experience: A tool for psychiatric rehabilitation. *Journal of Nervous and Mental Disease, 175* (9), 545–549.

Massimini, F., & Delle Fave, A. (2000). Individual development in a bio-cultural perspective. *American Psychologist, 55*, 24–33.

Mayers, P. (1978). *Flow in adolescence and its relation to school experience*. Unpublished doctoral dissertation, University of Chicago.

McAdams, D. P. (1990). *The person*. San Diego, CA: Harcourt Brace Jovanovich.

Mead, G. H. (1934). *Mind, self and society*. Chicago: University of Chicago Press.

*Moneta, G., & Csikszentmihalyi, M. (1996). The effect of perceived challenges and skills on the quality of subjective experience. *Journal of Personality, 64*, 275–310.

Nakamura, J. (1988). Optimal experience and the uses of talent. In M. Csikszentmihalyi & I. Csikszentmihalyi (Eds.), *Optimal experience* (pp. 319–326). Cambridge, England: Cambridge University Press.

Noelle-Neumann, E. (1995, Spring). Allensbach Archives, AWA.

Parks, B. (1996). *"Flow," boredom, and anxiety in therapeutic work*. Unpublished doctoral dissertation, University of Chicago.

Patton, J. (1999). *Exploring the relative outcomes of interpersonal and intrapersonal factors of order and entropy in adolescence: A longitudinal study*. Unpublished doctoral dissertation, University of Chicago.

Perry, S. K. (1999). *Writing in flow*. Cincinnati, OH: Writer's Digest Books.

Rathunde, K. (1988). Optimal experience and the family context. In M. Csikszentmihalyi & I. Csikszentmihalyi (Eds.), *Optimal experience* (pp. 342–363). Cambridge, England: Cambridge University Press.

Rathunde, K. (1996). Family context and talented adolescents' optimal experience in school-related activities. *Journal of Research on Adolescence, 6*, 605–628.

Rathunde, K. (1997). Parent-adolescent interaction and optimal experience. *Journal of Youth and Adolescence, 26*, 669–689.

Rebeiro, K. L., & Polgar, J. M. (1998). Enabling occupational performance: Optimal experiences in therapy. *Canadian Journal of Occupational Therapy, 66*, 14–22.

Renninger, K. A., Hidi, S., & Krapp, A. (1992). *The role of interest in learning and development*. Hillsdale, NJ: Erlbaum.

Richardson, A. (1999). Subjective experience: Its conceptual status, method of investigation, and psychological significance. *Journal of Personality, 133*, 469–485.

Schmidt, J. (2000). *Overcoming challenges: The role of opportunity, action, and experience in fostering resilience among adolescents*. Manuscript submitted for publication.

Shernoff, D., Knauth, S., & Makris, E. (2000). The quality of classroom experiences. In M. Csikszentmihalyi & B. Schneider (Eds.), *Becoming adult* (pp. 141–164). New York: Basic Books.

Snyder, C. R., Feldman, D. B., Taylor, J. D., Schroeder, L. L., & Adams, V. A. (2000). The roles of hopeful thinking in preventing problems and promoting strengths. *Applied and Preventive Psychology: Current Scientific Perspectives, 15,* 262–295.

Trevino, L., & Trevino, J. (1992). Flow in computer-mediated communication. *Communication Research, 19,* 539–573.

Turner, V. (1974). Liminal to liminoid in play, flow, and ritual: An essay in comparative symbology. *Rice University Studies, 60*(3), 53–92.

Vygotsky, L. (1978). *Mind in society.* Cambridge, MA: Harvard University Press.

Webster, J., & Martocchio, J. (1993). Turning work into play: Implications for microcomputer software training. *Journal of Management, 19,* 127–146.

Wells, A. (1988). Self-esteem and optimal experience. In M. Csikszentmihalyi & I. Csikszentmihalyi (Eds.), *Optimal experience* (pp. 327–341). Cambridge, England: Cambridge University Press.

Whalen, S. (1999). Challenging play and the cultivation of talent: Lessons from the Key School's flow activities room. In N. Colangelo & S. Assouline (Eds.), *Talent development III* (pp. 409–411). Scottsdale, AZ: Gifted Psychology Press.

White, R. (1959). Motivation reconsidered: The concept of competence. *Psychological Review, 66,* 297–333.

8

Positive Affectivity

The Disposition to Experience Pleasurable Emotional States

David Watson

In this chapter, I examine the broad disposition of positive affectivity, a trait that reflects stable individual differences in positive emotional experience. Individuals high on this dimension experience frequent and intense episodes of pleasant, pleasurable mood; generally speaking, they are cheerful, enthusiastic, energetic, confident, and alert. In contrast, those persons who are low in positive affectivity report substantially reduced levels of happiness, excitement, vigor, and confidence. Reflecting the general neglect of the larger field of positive psychology, positive affectivity was overlooked until the 1980s. Based on the past two decades of accrued research, however, a clear scholarly overview of the positive affectivity construct can be given.

Emergence of the Concept of Positive Affectivity

Throughout most of the 20th century, affect researchers typically studied basic negative emotions such as fear/anxiety, sadness/depression,

and anger/hostility; positive emotional states such as joy and excitement were largely ignored. The dominant role of the negative emotions reflected, in part, the seminal influence of Freud, who made the concept of anxiety a cornerstone of psychoanalytic thought (e.g., Freud, 1936). This focus on negative emotionality also was reinforced by Cannon (1929) and Selye (1936), who established the adverse health consequences of prolonged fear and anger. Finally, this preoccupation with the negative emotions can be attributed to their obvious survival value (e.g., Nesse, 1991): For instance, fear motivates organisms to escape from situations of potential threat or danger, whereas disgust helps to keep them away from noxious and toxic substances. The evolutionary functions of the positive emotions are less obvious, however, and took much longer to establish.

Gradually, however, interest in positive emotionality emerged during the latter half of the century. The first major theoretical breakthrough occurred in 1975, with the publication of Paul Meehl's landmark examination of "hedonic capacity." Meehl argued forcefully that "clinicians and theoreticians ought to consider seriously the possibility that not only are some persons born with more cerebral 'joy-juice' than others but also that this variable is fraught with clinical consequences" (p. 299). As this statement suggests, Meehl proposed that individual differences in hedonic capacity were present at birth and partly heritable. Furthermore, he posited that these innate, genotypic differences were associated with substantial phenotypic variations in positive emotionality and the related trait of surgency (now typically called "extraversion"). Of additional importance, Meehl assumed that individual differences in hedonic capacity/positive emotionality were largely distinct and separable from individual differences in negative emotions such as anxiety and anger.

In support of Meehl's argument, subsequent researchers have established that two largely independent factors—negative affect and positive affect—constitute the basic dimensions of emotional experience. These two broad dimensions have been identified in both intra- and interindividual analyses, and they emerge consistently across diverse descriptor sets, time frames, response formats, languages, and cultures (Mayer & Gaschke, 1988; Watson, 1988; Watson & Clark, 1997b). In brief, the Negative Affect dimension represents the extent to which an individual experiences negative emotional states such as fear, anger, sadness, guilt, contempt, and disgust; conversely, positive affect reflects the extent to which one experiences positive states such as joy, interest, confidence, and alertness. Both of these dimensions can be assessed either as a short-term state or as a long-term trait (in which case they typically are referred to as "negative affectivity" and "positive affectivity," respectively).

These two affect dimensions represent the subjective components of more general biobehavioral systems that have evolved to address very different evolutionary tasks (Tomarken & Keener, 1998; Watson, Wiese, Vaidya, & Tellegen, 1999). Specifically, negative affect is a component of the withdrawal-oriented behavioral inhibition system. The essential purpose of this system is to keep the organism out of trouble by inhibiting behavior that might lead to pain, punishment, or some other undesirable consequence. In sharp contrast, positive affect is a component of the approach-oriented behavioral facilitation system, which directs organisms toward situations and experiences that po-

tentially may yield pleasure and reward. This system is adaptive in that it ensures the procuring of resources (e.g., food and water, warmth and shelter, the cooperation of others, sexual partners) that are essential to the survival of both the individual and the species.

Given that they reflect very different evolutionary pressures, it is not surprising that negative and positive affect naturally are highly distinctive dimensions that are associated with fundamentally different classes of variables. For instance, as I will detail subsequently, they correlate quite differently with general traits of personality. In light of these differential correlates, it is essential that these dimensions be assessed and analyzed separately.

The Hierarchical Structure of Positive Affectivity

Self-rated affect is hierarchically structured and must be viewed at two fundamentally different levels: a higher order level that consists of the general Negative and Positive Affect dimensions and a lower order level that represents specific types of affect (Watson & Clark, 1992a, 1992b, 1997b). In other words, each of these broad dimensions can be decomposed into several correlated yet ultimately distinct affective states, much like general intelligence can be subdivided into specific abilities. In this hierarchical model, the upper level reflects the overall *valence* of the affects (i.e., whether they represent pleasant or unpleasant mood states), whereas the lower level reflects the specific *content* of mood descriptors (i.e., the distinctive qualities of each specific type of affect).

Researchers have had little trouble identifying specific types of negative emotionality. Most theories of emotion recognize several different negative affects, and virtually every model includes at least three basic negative mood states: fear/anxiety, sadness/depression, and anger/hostility (Watson & Clark, 1992a, 1997b). In contrast, little agreement exists regarding the specific positive affects. The Differential Emotions Scale (DES; Izard, Libero, Putnam, & Haynes, 1993), for instance, contains scales assessing Interest (i.e., feeling excited, interested, alert, and curious) and Enjoyment (i.e., feeling happy and joyful). The Multiple Affect Adjective Checklist-Revised (MAACL-R; Zuckerman & Lubin, 1985) also has two lower order positive mood scales but subdivides the domain rather differently; specifically, it includes a relatively broad measure of positive affect containing descriptors relevant to both DES scales (e.g., *happy, glad, interested*), as well as a measure of sensation seeking that assesses feelings of energy, adventurousness, and daring that are not systematically measured in the DES. Finally, the Profile of Mood States (POMS; McNair, Lorr, & Droppleman, 1971) simply includes a single broad measure of vigor (i.e., feeling cheerful, lively, alert, and energetic) and does not subdivide the domain at all.

I will emphasize a structural model that is based on extensive factor analyses that I have conducted in collaboration with Lee Anna Clark. We consistently have found three subcomponents of positive affect that are moderately to strongly intercorrelated. We therefore included scales assessing each of these facets in our own instrument, the Expanded Form of the Positive and Negative Affect Schedule: (PANAS-X; Watson & Clark, 1994): Joviality (8 items; e.g., *cheerful, happy, lively, enthusiastic*), Self-Assurance (6 items; e.g., *confident, strong, daring*), and Attentiveness (4 items; e.g., *alert, concentrating, determined*).

Table 8.1 reports correlations among these specific positive affects—along with the general Negative Affect scale of the PANAS-X—in a combined sample of more than 3,000 undergraduates (1,375 from Southern Methodist University, 1,761 from the University of Iowa). All of the respondents rated the extent to which they generally experienced each affect descriptor. Two aspects of these data are noteworthy. First, the Joviality, Self-Assurance, and Attentiveness scales are strongly interrelated, with correlations ranging from .48 to .57; from this, we can infer that these scales all reflect a common higher order factor. Second, the positive mood scales all are weakly related to general Negative Affect, with correlations ranging from only −.14 (Self-Assurance) to −.21 (Joviality).

Based on these data, we again can observe (a) the distinctiveness of positive and negative emotional experience and (b) the importance of assessing them separately.

Measures of Positive Affectivity

Positive Affectivity Scales

The assessment literature in this area is difficult to summarize briefly. This literature has never been subjected to a thorough review, and convergent and discriminant validity data are lacking for many measures. Consequently, the conclusions drawn from these data must be tentative.

For the sake of convenience, measures of positive affectivity can be divided into two basic types. First, many widely used affect inventories have a "general" form (in which respondents rate their typical, average feelings) that can be used to measure this trait. For instance, the DES, the MAACL-R, and the PANAS-X all have trait versions that allow one to assess various aspects of the dimension. Unfortunately, researchers have failed to examine the convergence among these different trait instruments.

Second, many multitrait personality inventories contain scales relevant to the construct; examples include the Activity and Positive Emotions facet scales of the Revised NEO Personality Inventory (NEO-PI-R; Costa & McCrae, 1992a), the Well-Being scale of the Multidimensional Personality Questionnaire (MPQ; Tellegen, in press), and the Positive Temperament scale of the General Temperament Survey (GTS; Clark & Watson, 1990). My colleagues and I have collected data establishing moderate to strong links among several of these measures. For instance, in a sample of 328 college students, we found that the GTS Positive Temperament scale correlated .62 and .48 with the

Table 8.1 Correlations among General Negative Affectivity and Specific Types of Positive Affectivity

Scale	Joviality	Self-Assurance	Attentiveness
Joviality	—		
Self-Assurance	.57	—	
Attentiveness	.53	.48	—
General negative affect	−.21	−.14	−.17

Note: N = 3,136. All correlations are significant at *p* < .01, two-tailed.

NEO-PI-R Activity and Positive Emotions scales, respectively. Relatedly, Clark (1993) reported a correlation of .73 between the GTS Positive Temperament and MPQ Well-Being scales in a sample of 251 college students. Based on these data, one can conclude that these scales reflect the same basic domain of personality; however, these correlations are not high enough to suggest that these measures are completely interchangeable.

My colleagues and I also have collected data demonstrating that these personality measures converge moderately to strongly with trait versions of the PANAS-X scales. For example, in a sample of 985 undergraduates, Watson and Clark (1993) reported that the GTS Positive Temperament scale correlated .55 with general Positive Affect, .57 with Joviality, .43 with Self-Assurance, and .36 with Attentiveness. Similarly, in an unpublished study of 898 college students, I found that the NEO-PI-R Activity facet scale correlated .46 with general Positive Affect and .40 with Joviality; parallel correlations for the NEO-PI-R Positive Emotions facet were .44 and .60, respectively. Again, from these data, I conclude that although the two types of measures are systematically interrelated, they are not so highly correlated as to be completely interchangeable.

Thus, several existing measures assess the general trait of positive affectivity and its various subcomponents. As we have seen, however, although the convergence among these measures is reasonably good (with correlations generally falling in the .40 to .65 range), it is not extraordinarily high. Because of this, it is somewhat hazardous to collapse results obtained using different instruments. At this stage of the literature, unfortunately, it is necessary to do so.

Measures of Related Constructs

Wherever possible, I will rely on data from pure, established measures of positive affectivity in the following sections. Because of gaps in the existing literature, however, it also will be necessary to draw on evidence based on closely related constructs. For instance, measures of happiness and subjective well-being tend to be strongly correlated with positive affectivity scales. However, they also have a secondary component of low negative affectivity (in other words, happy people tend to report both high positive affectivity and low negative affectivity),

so these indices do not represent pure measures of positive affectivity (Myers & Diener, 1995; Watson & Clark, 1997b). Similarly, global self-esteem scales tend to be complex mixtures of high positive affectivity and low negative affectivity (Joiner, 1996; Lucas, Diener, & Suh, 1996).

Positive affectivity scales also are strongly and systematically related to general traits of personality, particularly extraversion (Watson & Clark, 1992b, 1997a; Watson et al., 1999). It will be helpful, in this regard, to examine positive affectivity in relation to the complete five-factor (or "Big Five") model of personality. Researchers developed this model in studies in which they were attempting to understand the natural language of trait descriptors (Goldberg, 1993; John & Srivastava, 1999). Extensive structural analyses of these descriptors consistently revealed five broad factors: Extraversion, Agreeableness, Conscientiousness, Neuroticism, and Openness to Experience. This structure is remarkably robust, with the same five factors emerging in both self-ratings and peer ratings (McCrae & Costa, 1987), in analyses of both children and adults (Digman, 1997), and across a wide variety of languages and cultures (Jang, McCrae, Angleitner, Riemann, & Livesley, 1998; McCrae & Costa, 1997).

I computed correlations between trait affectivity and the Big Five in the combined undergraduate sample that was described earlier in connection with Table 8.1. All respondents completed trait forms of the general Negative Affect scale and the various positive affectivity scales of the PANAS-X. In addition, they were administered one of several different Big Five instruments, including the NEO-PI-R (Costa & McCrae, 1992a), the NEO Five-Factor Inventory (Costa & McCrae, 1992a), and the Big Five Inventory (John, Donahue, & Kentle, 1991).

I present the resulting correlations in Table 8.2. Replicating previous findings in this area (Watson & Clark, 1992b), negative affectivity is very strongly related to Neuroticism (overall $r = .58$) and more modestly correlated with the other traits. In contrast, the general Positive Affect scale is most strongly linked ($r = .49$) with Extraversion. Consistent with earlier research (Watson & Clark, 1992b), however, we also observe considerable specificity at the lower order level. That is, Extraversion is strongly correlated with Joviality ($r = .60$), moderately correlated with Self-Assurance ($r = .47$), and only modestly related to Attentiveness ($r = .28$). In-

Table 8.2 Correlations between Positive and Negative Affectivity and Measures of the Big Five Personality Traits

Affect Scale	Extroversion	Agreeableness	Conscientiousness	Neuroticism	Openness
Negative affectivity					
General negative affect	−.26	−.33	−.23	**.58**	−.14
Positive affectivity					
General positive affect	**.49**	.22	.39	−.35	.23
Joviality	**.60**	.31	.22	−.36	.15
Self-assurance	**.47**	−.05	.16	**−.41**	.21
Attentiveness	.28	.23	**.53**	−.26	.19

Note: N = 3,136. All correlations are significant at $p < .01$, two-tailed. Correlations of .40 and greater are shown in boldface.

deed, Attentiveness scores are much more highly related to Conscientiousness ($r = .53$) than to Extraversion.

Extraversion obviously is highly relevant to any discussion of positive affectivity; accordingly, I will make use of Extraversion-based results in subsequent sections. Extraverts report substantially greater cheerfulness, enthusiasm, and energy (Joviality) than do introverts, as well as elevated levels of boldness and confidence (Self-Assurance). I subsequently will show how these data are consistent with a broad array of evidence linking positive affectivity to individual differences in social and interpersonal activity.

Summary of Research Findings

Temporal Stability and Cross-Situational Consistency

Temporal Stability

Does positive affectivity represent a meaningful dimension of individual differences? Two characteristics are crucial in establishing the existence of a trait. First, an individual's standing on the trait should be relatively stable over time, such that people maintain a relatively consistent rank order across assessments. Second, scores on the trait should manifest some consistency or generality across different situations and contexts.

First I will consider the issue of temporal stability. Considerable evidence suggests that personality continues to develop and evolve throughout the 20s; accordingly, stability estimates are significantly lower prior to age 30

(Costa & McCrae, 1994). Consequently, one must distinguish between data collected on young adults (e.g., college students) versus older adults in analyzing the stability of traits.

Data from young adult samples establish that positive affectivity scores are strongly stable across short-term time spans of a few weeks to a few months, with retest correlations typically falling in the .50 to .70 range (for reviews, see Watson, 2000; Watson & Walker, 1996). For instance, in a sample of 399 undergraduates, Watson and Clark (1994) reported stability correlations of .64 (general Positive Affect), .64 (Joviality), .68 (Self-Assurance), and .55 (Attentiveness). However, studies using much longer retest intervals have reported more moderate stabilities, with correlations typically falling in the .30 to .60 range. For example, Watson and Walker obtained 6- to 7-year retests of .42 and .36 in two young adult samples assessed between the ages of 18 and 25.

Consistent with the broader personality literature, studies of older adults have yielded impressive levels of stability (i.e., correlations in the .60 to .80 range), even across extremely long time spans. For example, Costa and McCrae (1992b) obtained a 24-year stability coefficient of .64 on the General Activity scale of the Guilford-Zimmerman Temperament Survey (Guilford & Zimmerman, 1949). Similarly, Helson and Klohnen (1998) reported a 25-year stability coefficient of .62 on a Positive Emotionality scale derived from the Adjective Check List (Gough & Heilbrun, 1983). On the basis of these data, one can conclude that positive affectivity scores become strongly stable after the age of 30.

It also is worth noting that positive affectivity scores show no systematic variation with age.

For instance, mean levels of positive affectivity did not change significantly between the ages of 18 and 25 (Watson & Walker, 1996) or between the ages of 20 and 30 (McGue, Bacon, & Lykken (1993). Helson and Klohnen (1998) reported that positive affectivity scores increased significantly between the ages of 27 and 43 but showed no further change between 43 and 52. In contrast, Costa and McCrae (1992b) found that the NEO-PI-R Positive Emotions facet scale showed no consistent age-related effects, whereas scores on the NEO-PI-R Activity scale declined significantly over time. These inconsistent results contrast sharply with the evidence for negative affectivity, which peaks in late adolescence and then shows a significant age-related decline that continues at least into middle adulthood (see Clark & Watson, 1999).

Cross-Situational Consistency

There are only sparse data regarding cross-situational consistency; nevertheless, based on the available evidence, it appears that positive affectivity is quite consistent across various situations and contexts. In the earliest investigation of this issue, Diener and Larsen (1984) had 42 participants rate their current, momentary mood twice per day over a period of 6 weeks. At each assessment, the participants reported the current situation or activity in which they were engaged (e.g., working vs. recreating; socially engaged vs. alone). Diener and Larsen then computed mean positive affect scores for each student in each type of situation. Correlational analyses indicated that the students were highly consistent across dissimilar situations. For instance, mean positive affect levels while socializing correlated .58 with the corresponding values obtained when the students were alone; similarly, mean positive affect scores while working correlated .70 with the average scores while recreating.

I have replicated these results in a much larger college student sample ($N = 339$; Watson, 2000). The participants in this sample rated their current mood over 40 to 50 different occasions and also indicated whether or not they had interacted socially during the previous hour. I computed separate mean positive affect scores for each student across those occasions in which they reported socializing versus those in which they reported no recent social activity. These two sets of scores correlated .75 with one another. Thus, the individuals who tended to be

more cheerful and enthusiastic while they were socializing also tended to be more cheerful and enthusiastic when they were alone.

Characteristic Variability

Thus far, I have focused solely on individual differences in the overall *mean level* of positive emotionality. There is a second dispositional parameter, however, that is related to the operation of the behavioral facilitation system; this concerns individual differences in positive mood *variability*. It is well established that some individuals are consistently more labile than others (Larsen, 1987; Penner, Shiffman, Paty, & Fritzsche, 1994). For example, Watson (2000) reports corroborative data from 379 college students who completed 42 daily mood ratings; the data for each student were split into a first half (weeks 1 through 3) and a second half (weeks 4 through 6). A mean score and a standard deviation were computed for each student on the general Positive Affect scale of the PANAS-X across each 3-week period. Correlational analyses of these scores yielded two important findings. First, variability across the first half of the study was strongly correlated ($r = .68$) with variability during the second half, demonstrating once again that some people consistently show greater positive mood variability than others. Second, this variability was entirely unrelated to mean levels of positive mood (rs ranged from only $-.05$ to $.08$).

What could cause these stable individual differences in the variability of positive affect? As I discussed earlier, this mood dimension is a component of the approach-oriented behavioral facilitation system, which evolved to ensure that organisms obtain necessary resources (e.g., food, water, shelter). From an evolutionary perspective, these approach behaviors are most adaptive if they are performed when the potential for reward is relatively high (e.g., when food is plentiful) and the risk of danger is low (e.g., when predators are absent); at other times, it is preferable for organisms to conserve their precious store of energy. This evolutionary pressure encouraged the development of endogenous cycles that regulate the system's level of activation and promote the efficient expenditure of energy (Watson, 2000; Watson et al., 1999). For example, positive mood—but not negative mood—shows a well-defined, endogenous circadian cycle over the course of the day.

Consequently, variability is an innate, pre-designed feature of the system. This, in turn, suggests that over the course of evolution, control mechanisms developed to regulate this variability and to ensure that it remains within reasonable bounds. If so, then the stable individual differences we observe in positive mood variability may reflect variations in the quality and functioning of these control mechanisms (Depue, Krauss, & Spoont, 1987; Watson, 2000).

Causes and Correlates of Positive Affectivity

Genetic Evidence

What causes mean-level differences in positive affectivity? First, this trait clearly is strongly heritable. Most of the available data are based on measures of Extraversion. Heritability estimates for Extraversion derived from twin studies generally fall in the .40 to .60 range, with a median value of approximately .50 (Clark & Watson, 1999). Adoption studies yield somewhat lower heritability estimates, but this largely may be due to their failure to assess nonadditive genetic variance (i.e., the combined, interactive effects of multiple genes; Plomin, Corley, Caspi, Fulker, & DeFries, 1998). Finally, based on results from both twin and adoption studies, it appears that the common rearing environment (i.e., the effects of living together in the same household) exerts little influence on this trait (Clark & Watson, 1999).

Although the literature involving pure measures of positive affectivity is much smaller, it has yielded very similar results. Researchers using the MPQ Well-Being scale have reported heritability estimates in the .40 to .50 range (Finkel & McGue, 1997; Tellegen et al., 1988). Similarly, Jang et al. (1998) obtained heritabilities of .38 and .38, respectively, for the NEO-PI-R Activity and Positive Emotions scales. Moreover, consistent with the data for Extraversion, these studies indicate that the common rearing environment essentially has no effect on the development of positive affectivity.

Neurobiological Basis of Positive Affectivity

How do these innate genotypic differences manifest themselves as phenotypic differences in positive emotionality? Davidson, Tomarken, and their colleagues have demonstrated that

happy individuals tend to show relatively greater resting activity in the left prefrontal cortex than in the right prefrontal area; conversely, dysphoric individuals display relatively greater right anterior activity. Unfortunately, it has proven difficult to isolate the specific effects of left versus right prefrontal activity in these studies. Based on recent evidence, however, it appears that positive affectivity primarily reflects the level of resting activity in the left prefrontal area, whereas negative affectivity is more strongly associated with right frontal activation (Davidson, 1992; Tomarken & Keener, 1998).

This left prefrontal activity, in turn, can be linked to the mesolimbic dopaminergic system, which has been strongly implicated in the operation of the behavioral facilitation system and in the subjective experience of positive mood. This dopaminergic system arises from cell groups located in the ventral tegmental area of the midbrain and has projections throughout the cortex (Depue & Collins, 1999; Depue, Luciana, Arbisi, Collins, & Leon, 1994). Consistent with the data reported by Davidson and Tomarken, these cortical projections tend to be concentrated in the left hemisphere, with a particularly strong asymmetry in the frontal region. The dopaminergic system mediates various approach-related behaviors, including heightened appetitive motivation and enhanced behavioral approach to incentive stimuli (Depue & Collins, 1999; Depue et al., 1994).

Taken together, these data strongly suggest that the dopaminergic system plays a key role in both left frontal activation and phenotypic differences in positive affectivity. Depue et al. (1994) examined this idea by administering biological agents known to stimulate dopaminergic activity, and then measuring the strength of the system's response. Consistent with their expectation, Depue et al. found that various measures of dopaminergic activity were strongly correlated with individual differences in positive affectivity but were unrelated to negative affectivity. It therefore appears that variations in the dopaminergic system may cause some individuals to have more of Meehl's (1975) "cerebral joy-juice."

Finally, some researchers have taken this analysis one step further and suggested that because of these neurobiological differences, individuals high in positive affectivity may be more responsive to—and better able to derive pleasure from—rewarding stimuli (Gross, Sutton, & Ketelaar, 1998; Rusting & Larsen, 1997; Tomarken & Keener, 1998). In support of this view, Extraversion scores predict increases in positive mood following a pleasant mood induction, but are unrelated to negative mood changes following an unpleasant mood induction (Gross et al., 1998; Rusting & Larsen, 1997).

Demographic and Environmental Correlates

An enormous literature has examined how numerous demographic variables—age, gender, marital status, ethnicity, income and socioeconomic status, and so on—are related to individual differences in happiness, life satisfaction, and trait affectivity (for reviews, see Argyle, 1987; Myers & Diener, 1995; Watson, 2000). From these studies, it is clear that objective demographic factors are relatively weak predictors of happiness and positive affectivity. For instance, as I discussed previously, positive affectivity scores are not systematically related to age. Along these same lines, variables such as annual income, level of educational attainment, and socioeconomic status are, at best, weakly related to happiness and well-being (Argyle, 1987; Lykken & Tellegen, 1996; Myers & Diener, 1995; Watson, 2000). Diener, Sandvik, Seidlitz, and Diener (1993), for example, found that income correlated only .13 with well-being in a sample of nearly 5,000 American adults; similarly, Lykken and Tellegen (1996) reported that income, educational attainment, and socioeconomic status each accounted for less than 2% of the variance in scores on the MPQ Well-Being scale. Thus, an individual's capacity for positive affectivity is not seriously limited by objective conditions such as age, wealth, and status.

Similarly, men and women report virtually identical levels of happiness and positive affectivity. For instance, in an analysis of 169,776 respondents across 16 nations, Inglehart (1990) found that 80% of men and 80% of women said that they were at least "fairly satisfied" with life. Watson and Clark (1994) compared men and women on the general Positive Affect scale of the PANAS-X in 10 large data sets (overall, these samples included 3,322 men and 4,709 women). A significant gender difference emerged in only 2 of these samples (with men reporting greater positive affectivity in one case, and women reporting high positive emotional-

ity in the other). Finally, Watson (2000) examined daily mood data collected from 144 male and 331 female college students. Each respondent completed the general Positive Affect scale of the PANAS-X on a daily basis for a minimum of 30 days; overall, these data represented 6,325 and 14,414 observations, respectively, from the male and female participants. Collapsed across all respondents, men and women produced mean daily Positive Affect scores of 28.38 and 28.39, respectively. Clearly, men and women do not systematically differ in their level of positive affectivity.

However, two variables consistently have emerged as significant predictors of positive affectivity. First, numerous studies have shown that positive affectivity—but not negative affectivity—is moderately correlated with various indicators of social behavior, including number of close friends, frequency of contact with friends and relatives, making new acquaintances, involvement in social organizations, and overall level of social activity (Argyle, 1987; Myers & Diener, 1995; Watson, 2000; Watson & Clark, 1997a). Relatedly, in analyses of large U.S. national samples, married people are significantly more likely to describe themselves as "very happy" than are those who have never married; moreover, contrary to popular belief, this "happiness gap" (Myers & Diener, 1995) is found in both men and women (Lee, Seccombe, & Shehan, 1991; Veroff, Douvan, & Kulka, 1981).

Thus, those who are high in positive affectivity tend to be extraverts who are socially active. As I have discussed in greater detail elsewhere, the underlying causality appears to be bidirectional, with social activity and positive affectivity mutually influencing each other (Watson, 2000; Watson & Clark, 1997a). On the one hand, it is well established that social interaction typically produces a transient elevation in positive emotionality; conversely, it also is true that feelings of cheerfulness, liveliness and enthusiasm are associated with an enhanced desire for affiliation and an increased preference for interpersonal contact. Thus, positive affectivity is both a cause and an effect of social behavior.

Second, people who describe themselves as "spiritual" or "religious" report higher levels of happiness than those who do not; this effect has been observed both in the United States and in Europe (Argyle, 1987; Myers & Diener, 1995; Inglehart, 1990; Watson, 2000). Well-being levels are particularly elevated among individuals who (a) report a strong, committed religious affiliation, (b) attend religious services regularly, and (c) espouse traditional religious beliefs. Moreover, my colleagues and I have found that religion and spirituality are positively related to positive affectivity but are unrelated to negative affectivity (Clark & Watson, 1999; Watson & Clark, 1993).

Why are spiritual and religious people happier? Two basic explanations have been offered (Argyle, 1987; Myers & Diener, 1995; Watson, 2000). First, religion may provide people with a profound sense of meaning and purpose in their lives, thereby supplying them with plausible answers to the basic existential questions of life (e.g., "Why am I here?" "What will happen to me after I die?") and delivering them from existential angst. Second, religious activity simply may represent a particular variety of social behavior. In other words, membership in a religious denomination allows people to congregate, espouse shared views, and form supportive relationships. Consistent with this explanation, people who are religious rate themselves as being less lonely than those who are not (Argyle, 1987).

Broader Significance of the Trait

Links to Psychopathology

Low levels of positive affectivity are associated with a number of clinical syndromes, including social phobia, agoraphobia, posttraumatic stress disorder, schizophrenia, eating disorder, and the substance disorders (Mineka, Watson, & Clark, 1998; Watson, 2000). However, low positive affectivity plays a particularly salient role in the mood disorders (Clark, Watson, & Mineka, 1994; Mineka et al., 1998; Watson, 2000; Watson et al., 1999). It is strongly linked to the melancholic subtype of major depression, which is characterized by either a "loss of pleasure in all, or almost all, activities" or a "lack of reactivity to usually pleasurable stimuli" (American Psychiatric Association, 1994, p. 384). It also is noteworthy that positive affectivity scores have predicted the subsequent development of depression in prospective data. These findings raise the intriguing possibility that lack of positive affectivity may be an important vulnerability factor for mood disorder (Clark et al., 1994).

This link with positive affectivity also may help to explain the cyclic course of the mood

disorders. This systematic temporal sequencing is an unusual component of the symptom picture, one that is not nearly as salient in most other disorders. For example, the intensity of phobic fear does not vary systematically as a function of the hour of the day or the season of the year. In sharp contrast, most of the mood disorders are characterized by well-defined cycles and episodes. This cyclicity is most apparent in the bipolar disorders, in which the individual fluctuates between well-defined episodes of mania (or hypomania) and depression. Similarly, major depression tends to occur in episodes that may spontaneously remit over time (American Psychiatric Association, 1994). Moreover, melancholic depression frequently shows a marked diurnal pattern in which the symptoms are worst in the morning and then lessen in strength over the course of the day. Finally, the mood disorders can show a marked seasonal pattern, as is exhibited in seasonal affective disorder, which is characterized by the onset of a prolonged depressive episode during the late fall or early winter.

It surely is not coincidental that these circadian and seasonal trends parallel those observed with positive mood. Indeed, melancholic depression and bipolar disorder appear to represent marked perturbations in positive affectivity and the Behavioral Facilitation System (Clark et al., 1994; Depue et al., 1987; Mineka et al., 1998; Watson et al., 1999). That is, manic episodes typically are associated with an extremely elevated positive mood (i.e., the individual feels elated and euphoric and has tremendous energy, confidence, and enthusiasm), whereas melancholic depression is characterized by a profound anhedonia and an almost total inability to experience pleasure. Furthermore, the mood disorders are associated with marked disturbances in the sleep-wake cycle (Watson, 2000; Watson et al., 1999; Wu & Bunney, 1990). For instance, sleep in individuals with melancholic depression tends to be relatively shallow, with increased Stage 1 and reduced amounts of slow-wave sleep. Moreover, the architecture of rapid eye movement (REM) sleep is seriously disturbed in many depressed individuals; specifically, REM episodes occur (a) unusually early in the NREM/REM cycle and (b) with unusual frequency during the early hours of sleep. Given that positive mood also varies as a function of the sleep-wake cycle (Watson et al., 1999), a reasonable conclusion is that positive affectivity, sleep, and the mood disorders all reflect common underlying mechanisms in which energy is expended and conserved in recurring cycles.

Job and Marital Satisfaction

Individuals who are high in positive affectivity feel good about themselves and their world. Consequently, they report greater satisfaction with important aspects of their lives. For instance, positive affectivity is a significant predictor of job satisfaction (Iverson, Olekalns, & Erwin, 1998; Watson, 2000; Watson & Slack, 1993). Agho, Price, and Mueller (1992), for example, reported a .44 correlation between positive affectivity and job satisfaction in a sample of 550 hospital employees. Watson and Slack (1993) used a prospective design in which employees initially completed a measure of positive affectivity (a short form of the MPQ Well-Being scale) and then rated their job satisfaction more than two years later (M interval = 27 months). Positive affectivity remained a significant, moderate predictor of various aspects of job satisfaction (with correlations ranging from .27 to .44), even when the measures were separated by a considerable time interval. Staw, Bell, and Clausen (1986) report even more striking evidence along these same lines. They found that a 17-item Affective Disposition scale (which appears to represent a combination of high positive affectivity/low negative affectivity)—assessed when the participants were adolescents—was a significant predictor of job satisfaction nearly 50 years later, even after controlling for objective differences in work conditions. On the basis of these data, one can conclude that trait affectivity plays an important etiological role in job satisfaction.

Positive affectivity also is significantly correlated with marital and relationship satisfaction. Watson, Hubbard and Wiese (in press) examined this issue in two different samples, one consisting of 74 married couples, and the other composed of 136 dating couples. Positive emotionality scores correlated .41 (women's satisfaction) and .48 (men's satisfaction) with satisfaction in the married couples, and .24 (women's satisfaction) and .40 (men's satisfaction) with satisfaction in the dating sample. These data are cross-sectional, so that it is unclear whether scores on this dimension can predict relationship satisfaction prospectively. There is considerable evidence, however, that negative affectivity scores obtained early in a relationship predict its subsequent course (Kar-

ney & Bradbury, 1995; Kelly & Conley, 1987). It therefore seems reasonable to conclude that trait affectivity plays a significant etiological role in relationship satisfaction.

Raising Positive Affectivity

Is Change Possible?

As I have shown, positive affectivity levels are not highly constrained by objective life conditions. People do not require all that much—in terms of material conditions, life circumstances, and so on—to feel cheerful, enthusiastic, and interested in life. Thus, one need not be young or wealthy or have a glamorous, high-paying job in order to be happy. This, in turn, suggests that virtually anyone is capable of experiencing substantial levels of positive affectivity (for a discussion, see Watson, 2000). Indeed, Diener and Diener (1996) demonstrated that most people—including the poor and the physically handicapped—describe themselves as experiencing at least moderate levels of positive emotionality.

Nevertheless, the fact remains that many of us are not as happy as we would like to be. Surely, few of us would object to feeling more cheerful, excited, and energetic than we currently are. This raises a crucial issue: Is true, long-term change really possible? In this regard, it is noteworthy that many contemporary models of happiness emphasize the importance of inertial forces that resist long-term change. For instance, various lines of evidence suggest that major life events exert a significant influence on well-being only in the short term and that people eventually adapt to them and gradually move back to their preexisting baseline or "set point" (Myers & Diener, 1995; Suh, Diener, & Fujita, 1996; Watson, 2000). Thus, it seems that we may be fated to remain on a "hedonic treadmill" (Eysenck, 1990)—no matter how dramatically our life changes, we always fall back to the same familiar level of positive affectivity.

Furthermore, as I discussed previously, positive affectivity levels clearly are strongly influenced by hereditary factors that influence the functioning of the central nervous system. These data strongly suggest that some people simply may be destined to be more cheerful and enthusiastic than others, regardless of major life events or any systematic attempts at change.

Consistent with an old "Wild West" maxim (quoted by Meehl, 1975, p. 298), it may be that "some men are just born three drinks behind."

One may easily exaggerate, however, the constraints imposed by genetic and biological factors. Behavior geneticists repeatedly have attacked the overly simplistic view that evidence of heritability necessarily implies that change is impossible. As Weinberg (1989) put it, "There is a myth that if a behavior or characteristic is genetic, it cannot be changed. Genes do not fix behavior. Rather, they establish a range of possible reactions to the range of possible experiences that environments can provide" (p. 101). In other words, inherited genotypes simply establish the maximum and minimum phenotypic values that are possible for a given individual; environmental factors then are free to determine exactly where the person falls within this range. Furthermore, unless a person already has reached his or her maximum phenotypic value (a condition that should occur rarely, if at all), it should be possible to increase positive affectivity significantly, regardless of whether one was born "three drinks behind" or "three drinks ahead."

Thus, change *is* possible. Indeed, people do show evidence of significant change in their lives. For instance, as discussed previously, long-term stability correlations in older adults generally fall in the .60 to .80 range; although these data establish that positive affectivity scores are quite stable over time, they also indicate that many respondents display substantial change. Along these same lines, Headey and Wearing (1991) reported that 31.1% of their participants had positive affectivity scores that shifted by more than one standard deviation over a 6-year period. Consequently, the genetic and biological data should not induce a fatalistic resignation; we still are free to increase our positive affectivity and to move closer toward our potential maximum.

Enhancing Positive Affectivity

How might a person raise his or her overall level of positive affectivity? Although a detailed discussion of this point is beyond the scope of this chapter, I will conclude by reviewing three general principles that emerge from research in this area. First, studies of short-term mood indicate that positive affect is more related to action than to thought, such that it is easier to induce a state of high positive affect through

doing than through *thinking* (Watson, 2000). In other words, high levels of positive mood are most likely when a person is focused outward and is actively engaging the environment. The data indicate, moreover, that two broad classes of activity are particularly conducive to elevated positive mood: (a) socializing and interpersonal behavior and (b) exercise and physical activity. Generally speaking, individuals who are high in positive affectivity tend to be physically, socially, and mentally active (Thayer, 1996; Watson, 2000; Watson & Clark, 1997a).

Second, contemporary researchers emphasize that it is the process of striving after goals—rather than goal attainment per se—that is crucial for happiness and positive affectivity (Watson, 2000). Myers and Diener (1995) express this point quite nicely, concluding that "happiness grows less from the passive experience of desirable circumstances than from involvement in valued activities and progress toward one's goals" (p. 17). Similarly, Csikszentmihalyi (1991) argued, "The best moments usually occur when a person's body or mind is stretched to its limits in a voluntary effort to accomplish something difficult and worthwhile" (p. 3). This is an interesting point because few of the events and experiences of our lives truly are important in any objective, absolute sense. Nevertheless, it is essential that we *perceive* these things to be important and as representing goals that are well worth pursuing. In other words, although little of what we do in life really is important, it is crucial that we do them, and that we *see* them as important.

Finally, attempts at change are most likely to be successful if they are based on a thorough understanding of these underlying mood systems. For instance, as I discussed previously, variability is an innate, preprogrammed feature of the Behavioral Facilitation System, such that periods of happiness and enthusiasm inevitably give way to feelings of lethargy and lassitude (Thayer, 1996; Watson, 2000; Watson et al., 1999). Because our society is not particularly sensitive to biological rhythms and cycles, many of us either try to ignore them or else mask them artificially through the use of stimulants such as caffeine. Those who attempt to perform complex tasks during these naturally occurring low points are likely to feel frustrated and incompetent because they lack the physical and mental resources to tackle them efficiently. Thus, by monitoring our moods and becoming more sensitive to these internal rhythms, we should be able to maximize feelings of efficacy and enjoyment, while minimizing stress and frustration.

On a related point, sleep researchers warn that a substantial percentage of the population is seriously sleep deprived (Dement & Vaughan, 1999). Because adequate amounts of sleep are essential to maintaining energy and alertness, this leads to reduced levels of positive affect in many individuals (Thayer, 1996). Once again, by understanding our mood systems and working with—not against—them, it should be possible for many of us to increase our positive affectivity significantly.

References

Agho, A. O., Price, J. L., & Mueller, C. W. (1992). Discriminant validity of measures of job satisfaction, positive affectivity and negative affectivity. *Journal of Occupational and Organizational Psychology, 65,* 185–196.

American Psychiatric Association. (1994). *Diagnostic and statistical manual of mental disorders* (4th ed.). Washington, DC: Author.

Argyle, M. (1987). *The psychology of happiness.* New York: Methuen.

Cannon, W. B. (1929). *Bodily changes in pain, hunger, fear and rage.* Boston: Branford.

Clark, L. A. (1993). *Schedule for Nonadaptive and Adaptive Personality (SNAP): Manual for administration, scoring, and interpretation.* Minneapolis: University of Minnesota Press.

Clark, L. A., & Watson, D. (1990). *The General Temperament Survey.* Unpublished manuscript, University of Iowa, Iowa City.

*Clark, L. A., & Watson, D. (1999). Temperament: A new paradigm for trait psychology. In L. A. Pervin & O. P. John (Eds.), *Handbook of personality* (2nd ed., pp. 399–423). New York: Guilford.

Clark, L. A., Watson, D., & Mineka, S. (1994). Temperament, personality, and the mood and anxiety disorders. *Journal of Abnormal Psychology, 103,* 103–116.

Costa, P. T., Jr., & McCrae, R. R. (1992a). *Revised NEO Personality Inventory (NEO-PI-R) and NEO Five-Factor Inventory (NEO-FFI) professional manual.* Odessa, FL: Psychological Assessment Resources.

Costa, P. T., Jr., & McCrae, R. R. (1992b). Trait psychology comes of age. In T. B. Sonderegger (Ed.), *Nebraska Symposium on Motivation: Psychology and aging* (pp. 169–204). Lincoln: University of Nebraska Press.

Costa, P. T., Jr., & McCrae, R. R. (1994). Stability and change in personality from adolescence through adulthood. In C. F. Halverson, G. A. Kohnstamm, & R. P. Martin (Eds.), *The developing structure of temperament and personality from infancy to adulthood* (pp. 139–150). Hillsdale, NJ: Erlbaum.

Csikszentmihalyi, M. (1991). *Flow: The psychology of optimal experience.* New York: Harper Perennial.

Davidson, R. J. (1992). Anterior asymmetry and the nature of emotion. *Brain and Cognition, 20,* 125–151.

Dement, W. C., & Vaughan, C. (1999). *The promise of sleep.* New York: Delacorte.

*Depue, R. A., & Collins, P. F. (1999). Neurobiology of the structure of personality: Dopamine, facilitation of incentive motivation, and extraversion. *Behavioral and Brain Sciences, 22,* 491–569.

Depue, R. A., Krauss, S., & Spoont, M. R. (1987). A two-dimensional threshold model of seasonal bipolar affective disorder. In D. Magnusson & A. Ohman (Eds.), *Psychopathology: An interactional perspective* (pp. 95–123). San Diego, CA: Academic Press.

Depue, R. A., Luciana, M., Arbisi, P., Collins, P., & Leon, A. (1994). Dopamine and the structure of personality: Relation of agonist-induced dopamine activity to positive emotionality. *Journal of Personality and Social Psychology, 67,* 485–498.

Diener, E., & Diener, C. (1996). Most people are happy. *Psychological Science, 7,* 181–185.

Diener, E., & Larsen, R. J. (1984). Temporal stability and cross-situational consistency of affective, behavioral, and cognitive responses. *Journal of Personality and Social Psychology, 47,* 871–883.

Diener, E., Sandvik, E., Seidlitz, L., & Diener, M. (1993). The relationship between income and subjective well-being: Relative or absolute? *Social Indicators Research, 28,* 195–223.

Digman, J. M. (1997). Higher-order factors of the Big Five. *Journal of Personality and Social Psychology, 73,* 1246–1256.

Eysenck, M. W. (1990). *Happiness: Facts and myths.* East Sussex, UK: Erlbaum.

Finkel, D., & McGue, M. (1997). Sex differences and nonadditivity in heritability of the Multidimensional Personality Questionnaire scales. *Journal of Personality and Social Psychology, 72,* 929–938.

Freud, S. (1936). *The problem of anxiety* (H. A. Bunker, Trans.). New York: Norton. (Original work published 1926)

Goldberg, L. R. (1993). The structure of phenotypic personality traits. *American Psychologist, 48,* 26–34.

Gough, H. G., & Heilbrun, A. B., Jr. (1983). *The Adjective Check List manual.* Palo Alto, CA: Consulting Psychologists Press.

Gross, J. J., Sutton, S. K., & Ketelaar, T. (1998). Relations between affect and personality: Support for the affect-level and affective-reactivity views. *Personality and Social Psychology Bulletin, 24,* 279–288.

Guilford, J. P., & Zimmerman, W. S. (1949). *The Guilford-Zimmerman Temperament Survey* [Manual]. Beverly Hills, CA: Sheridan Supply.

Headey, B., & Wearing, A. (1991). Subjective well-being: A stocks and flows framework. In F. Strack, M. Argyle, & N. Schwarz (Eds.), *Subjective well-being: An interdisciplinary perspective* (pp. 49–73). New York: Pergamon.

Helson, R., & Klohnen, E. C. (1998). Affective coloring of personality from young adulthood to midlife. *Personality and Social Psychology Bulletin, 24,* 241–252.

Inglehart, R. (1990). *Culture shift in advanced industrialized society.* Princeton, NJ: Princeton University Press.

Iverson, R. D., Olekalns, M., & Erwin, P. J. (1998). Affectivity, organizational stressors, and absenteeism: A causal model of burnout and its consequences. *Journal of Vocational Behavior, 52,* 1–23.

Izard, C. E., Libero, D. Z., Putnam, P., & Haynes, O. M. (1993). Stability of emotion experiences and their relations to traits of personality. *Journal of Personality and Social Psychology, 64,* 847–860.

Jang, K. L., McCrae, R. R., Angleitner, A., Riemann, R., & Livesley, W. J. (1998). Heritability of facet-level traits in a cross-cultural twin sample: Support for a hierarchical model of personality. *Journal of Personality and Social Psychology, 74,* 1556–1565.

John, O. P., Donahue, E. M., & Kentle, R. L. (1991). *The Big Five Inventory—Versions 4a and 54* (Technical Report). University of California, Institute of Personality and Social Research, Berkeley.

John, O. P., & Srivastava, S. (1999). The Big Five trait taxonomy: History, measurement, and theoretical perspectives. In L. A. Pervin & O. P. John (Eds.), *Handbook of personality* (2nd ed., pp. 102–138). New York: Guilford.

Joiner, T. E., Jr. (1996). A confirmatory factor-analytic investigation of the tripartite model of depression and anxiety in college students. *Cognitive Therapy and Research, 20,* 521–539.

Karney, B. R., & Bradbury, T. N. (1995). The longitudinal course of marital quality and stability: A review of theory, method, and research. *Psychological Bulletin, 118,* 3–34.

Kelly, E. L., & Conley, J. J. (1987). Personality and compatibility: A prospective analysis of marital stability and marital satisfaction. *Journal of Personality and Social Psychology, 52,* 27–40.

Larsen, R. J. (1987). The stability of mood variability: A spectral analytic approach to daily mood assessments. *Journal of Personality and Social Psychology, 52,* 1195–1204.

Lee, G. R., Seccombe, K., & Shehan, C. L. (1991). Marital status and personal happiness: An analysis of trend data. *Journal of Marriage and the Family, 53,* 839–844.

Lucas, R. E., Diener, E., & Suh, E. (1996). Discriminant validity of well-being measures. *Journal of Personality and Social Psychology, 71,* 616–628.

Lykken, D., & Tellegen, A. (1996). Happiness is a stochastic phenomenon. *Psychological Science, 7,* 186–189.

Mayer, J. D., & Gaschke, Y. N. (1988). The experience and meta-experience of mood. *Journal of Personality and Social Psychology, 55,* 102–111.

McCrae, R. R., & Costa, P. T., Jr. (1987). Validation of a five-factor model of personality across instruments and observers. *Journal of Personality and Social Psychology, 52,* 81–90.

McCrae, R. R., & Costa, P. T., Jr. (1997). Personality trait structure as a human universal. *American Psychologist, 52,* 509–516.

McGue, M., Bacon, S., & Lykken, D. T. (1993). Personality stability and change in early adulthood: A behavioral genetic analysis. *Developmental Psychology, 29,* 96–109.

McNair, D. M., Lorr, M., & Droppleman, L. F. (1971). *Manual: Profile of Mood States.* San Diego, CA: Educational and Industrial Testing Service.

*Meehl, P. E. (1975). Hedonic capacity: Some conjectures. *Bulletin of the Menninger Clinic, 39,* 295–307.

Mineka, S., Watson, D., & Clark, L. A. (1998). Comorbidity of anxiety and unipolar mood disorders. *Annual Review of Psychology, 49,* 377–412.

*Myers, D. G., & Diener, E. (1995). Who is happy? *Psychological Science, 6,* 10–19.

*Nesse, R. M. (1991, November/December). What good is feeling bad? The evolutionary benefits of psychic pain. *The Sciences,* 30–37.

Penner, L. A., Shiffman, S., Paty, J. A., & Fritzsche, B. A. (1994). Individual differences in intraperson variability in mood. *Journal of Personality and Social Psychology, 66,* 712–721.

Plomin, R., Corley, R., Caspi, A., Fulker, D. W., & DeFries, J. (1998). Adoption results for self-reported personality: Evidence for nonadditive genetic effects? *Journal of Personality and Social Psychology, 75,* 211–218.

Rusting, C. L., & Larsen, R. J. (1997). Extraversion, neuroticism, and susceptibility to positive and negative affect: A test of two theoretical models. *Personality and Individual Differences, 22,* 607–612.

Selye, H. (1936). A syndrome produced by diverse nocuous agents. *Nature, 138,* 32.

Staw, B., Bell, N. E., & Clausen, J. A. (1986). The dispositional approach to job attitudes: A lifetime longitudinal test. *Administrative Science Quarterly, 31,* 56–77.

Suh, E., Diener, E., & Fujita, F. (1996). Events and subjective well-being: Only recent events matter. *Journal of Personality and Social Psychology, 70,* 1091–1102.

Tellegen, A. (in press). *Multidimensional personality questionnaire.* Minneapolis: University of Minnesota Press.

Tellegen, A., Lykken, D. T., Bouchard, T. J., Jr., Wilcox, K. J., Segal, N. L., & Rich, S. (1988). Personality similarity in twins reared apart and together. *Journal of Personality and Social Psychology, 54,* 1031–1039.

*Thayer, R. E. (1996). *The origin of everyday moods.* New York: Oxford University Press.

Tomarken, A. J., & Keener, A. D. (1998). Frontal brain asymmetry and depression: A self-regulatory perspective. *Cognition and Emotion, 12,* 387–420.

Veroff, J., Douvan, E., & Kulka, R. A. (1981). *The inner American.* New York: Basic Books.

Watson, D. (1988). The vicissitudes of mood measurement: Effects of varying descriptors, time frames, and response formats on measures of positive and negative affect. *Journal of Personality and Social Psychology, 55,* 128–141.

*Watson, D. (2000). *Mood and temperament.* New York: Guilford.

Watson, D., & Clark, L. A. (1992a). Affects separable and inseparable: On the hierarchical arrangement of the negative affects. *Journal of Personality and Social Psychology, 62,* 489–505.

Watson, D., & Clark, L. A. (1992b). On traits and temperament: General and specific factors of emotional experience and their relation to the five-factor model. *Journal of Personality, 60,* 441–476.

Watson, D., & Clark, L. A. (1993). Behavioral disinhibition versus constraint: A dispositional perspective. In D. M. Wegner & J. W. Pennebaker (Eds.), *Handbook of mental control* (pp. 506–527). New York: Prentice-Hall.

Watson, D., & Clark, L. A. (1994). *The PANAS-X: Manual for the Positive and Negative Affect Schedule-Expanded Form.* Unpublished manuscript, University of Iowa, Iowa City.

*Watson, D., & Clark, L. A. (1997a). Extraversion and its positive emotional core. In R. Hogan, J. Johnson, & S. Briggs (Eds.), *Handbook of personality psychology* (pp. 767–793). San Diego, CA: Academic Press.

Watson, D., & Clark, L. A. (1997b). Measurement and mismeasurement of mood: Recurrent and emergent issues. *Journal of Personality Assessment, 68,* 267–296.

Watson, D., Hubbard, B., & Wiese, D. (2000). General traits of personality and affectivity as predictors of satisfaction in intimate relationships: Evidence from self- and partner-ratings. *Journal of Personality, 68,* 413–449.

Watson, D., & Slack, A. K. (1993). General factors of affective temperament and their relation to job satisfaction over time. *Organizational Behavior and Human Decision Processes, 54,* 181–202.

Watson, D., & Walker, L. M. (1996). The long-term stability and predictive validity of trait measures of affect. *Journal of Personality and Social Psychology, 70,* 567–577.

*Watson, D., Wiese, D., Vaidya, J., & Tellegen, A. (1999). The two general activation systems of affect: Structural findings, evolutionary considerations, and psychobiological evidence. *Journal of Personality and Social Psychology, 76,* 820–838.

Weinberg, R. A. (1989). Intelligence and IQ: Landmark issues and great debates. *American Psychologist, 44,* 98–104.

Wu, J. C., & Bunney, W. E. (1990). The biological basis of an antidepressant response to sleep deprivation and relapse: Review and hypothesis. *American Journal of Psychiatry, 147,* 14–21.

Zuckerman, M., & Lubin, B. (1985). *Manual for the MAACL-R: The Multiple Affect Adjective Check List Revised.* San Diego, CA: Educational and Industrial Testing Service.

9

Positive Emotions

Barbara L. Fredrickson

At first blush, it might appear that positive emotions are important to the field of positive psychology simply because they are markers of optimal well-being. Certainly moments in our lives characterized by experiences of positive emotions (such as joy, interest, contentment, love, and the like) are moments in which we are not plagued by negative emotions (such as anxiety, sadness, and anger). Consistent with this intuition, the overall balance of people's positive and negative emotions has been shown to contribute to their subjective well-being (Diener, Sandvik, & Pavot, 1991). In this sense, positive emotions *signal* optimal functioning. But this is far from their whole story. In this chapter, I argue that positive emotions also *produce* optimal functioning, not just within the present, pleasant moment but over the long term as well. The bottom-line message is that we should work to cultivate positive emotions in ourselves and in those around us not just as end states in themselves, but also as a means to achieving psychological growth and improved psychological and physical health over time.

History of Positive Emotions Research

My view represents a significant departure from traditional approaches to the study of positive emotions. In this section I provide a brief, selective review of the history of research on positive emotions.

Neglected Relative to Negative Emotions

Relative to the negative emotions, positive emotions have received little empirical attention. There are several, interrelated reasons for this. One, which has plagued psychology more generally (see Seligman, this volume), is the traditional focus on psychological problems alongside remedies for those problems. Negative emotions—when extreme, prolonged, or contextually inappropriate—produce many grave problems, ranging from phobias and anxiety disorders, aggression and violence, depression and suicide, eating disorders and sexual dysfunction, to a host of stress-related physical disorders. Although positive emotions do at times contribute to problems (e.g., mania, drug addiction), negative emotions, due in part to their association with health problems and dangers, have captured the majority of research attention.

Another reason positive emotions have been sidelined is the habit among emotion theorists of creating models of emotions *in general*. Such models are typically built to the specifications of those attention-grabbing negative emotions (e.g., fear and anger), with positive emotions squeezed in later, often seemingly as an afterthought. For instance, key to many theorists' models is the idea that emotions are, by definition, associated with *specific action tendencies* (Frijda, 1986; Frijda, Kuipers, & Schure, 1989; Lazarus, 1991; Levenson, 1994; Oatley & Jenkins, 1996; Tooby & Cosmides, 1990). Fear, for example, is linked with the urge to escape, anger with the urge to attack, disgust the urge to expel, and so on. No theorist argues that people invariably act out these urges when feeling particular emotions. Rather, people's ideas about possible courses of action narrow in on a specific set of behavioral options. A key idea in these models is that having a specific action tendency is what made an emotion evolutionarily adaptive. These were among the actions that worked best in getting our ancestors out of life-or-death situations. Another key idea is that specific action tendencies and physiological changes go hand in hand. So, for example, when you have an urge to escape when feeling fear, your body reacts by mobilizing appropriate autonomic support for the possibility of running.

Although specific action tendencies have been invoked to describe the form and function of positive emotions as well, these are notably vague and underspecified (Fredrickson & Levenson, 1998). Joy, for instance, is linked with aimless activation, interest with attending, and contentment with inactivity (Frijda, 1986). These tendencies, I have argued, are far too general to be called specific (Fredrickson, 1998). Although a few theorists previously had noted that fitting positive emotions into emotion-general models posed problems (Ekman, 1992; Lazarus, 1991), this acknowledgment was not accompanied by any new or revised models to better accommodate the positive emotions. Instead, the difficulties inherent in "shoehorning" the positive emotions into emotion-general models merely tended to marginalize them further. Many theorists, for instance, minimize challenges to their models by maintaining their focus on negative emotions, paying little or no attention to positive emotions.

Confused with Related Affective States

Perhaps because they have received less direct scrutiny, the distinctions among positive emotions and other closely related affective states such as sensory pleasure and positive mood often have been blurred instead of sharpened. Although working definitions of emotions vary somewhat across researchers, there is an emerging consensus that emotions (both positive and negative) are best conceptualized as multicomponent response tendencies that unfold over relatively short time spans. Typically, emotions begin with an individual's assessment of the personal meaning of some antecedent event—what Lazarus (1991) called the person-environment relationship, or adaptational encounter. Either conscious or unconscious, this appraisal process triggers a cascade of response tendencies manifested across loosely coupled component systems, such as subjective experience, facial expressions, and physiological changes.

Sometimes various forms of sensory pleasure (e.g., sexual gratification, satiation of hunger or thirst) are taken to be positive emotions because they share with positive emotions a pleasant subjective feel and include physiological changes, and because sensory pleasure and positive emotions often co-occur (e.g., sexual gratification within a loving relationship). Yet emotions differ from physical sensations in that emotions require cognitive appraisals or meaning assessments to be initiated. In contrast to positive emotions, pleasure can be caused simply by changing the immediate physical environment (e.g., eating or otherwise stimulating the body). Moreover, whereas pleasure depends heavily on bodily stimulation, positive emotions more often occur in the absence of external physical sensation (e.g., joy at receiving good news, or interest in a new idea). Pleasurable sensations, then, are best considered automatic responses to fulfilling bodily needs. In fact, Cabanac (1971) suggested that people experience sensory pleasure with any external stimulus that "corrects an internal trouble." A cool bath, for instance, is only pleasant to someone who is overheated (who thus needs to be cooled). Likewise, food is pleasant to the hungry person but becomes less pleasant—even unpleasant—as that person becomes satiated.

Positive emotions also are confused with positive moods. Yet emotions differ from moods in that emotions are *about* some personally meaningful circumstance (i.e., they have an object) and are typically short-lived and occupy the foreground of consciousness. In contrast, moods are typically free-floating or objectless, are more long-lasting, and occupy the background of consciousness (Oatley & Jenkins, 1996; Rosenberg, 1998). These distinctions between emotions and moods, however, are guarded more at theoretical than at empirical levels. In research practice, virtually identical techniques are used for inducing positive moods and positive emotions (e.g., giving gifts, viewing comedies).

Functions Linked to Urges to Approach or Continue

Most commonly, the function of all positive emotions has been identified as facilitating approach behavior (Cacioppo, Priester, & Berntson, 1993; Davidson, 1993; Frijda, 1994) or continued action (Carver & Scheier, 1990; Clore, 1994). From this perspective, experiences of positive emotions prompt individuals to engage with their environments and partake in activities, many of which are evolutionarily adaptive for the individual, its species, or both. This link between positive emotions and activity engagement provides an explanation for the often-documented positivity offset, or the tendency for individuals to experience mild positive affect frequently, even in neutral contexts (Diener & Diener, 1996; Ito & Cacioppo, 1999). Without such an offset, individuals most often would be unmotivated to engage with their environments. Yet with such an offset, individuals exhibit the adaptive bias to approach and explore novel objects, people, or situations.

Although positive emotions often do appear to function as internal signals to approach or continue, I argue that they share this function with other positive affective states as well. Sensory pleasure, for instance, motivates people to approach and continue consuming whatever stimulus is biologically useful for them at the moment (Cabanac, 1971). Likewise, free-floating positive moods motivate people to continue along any line of thinking or action that they have initiated (Clore, 1994). As such, functional accounts of positive emotions that emphasize tendencies to approach or continue may only capture the lowest common denominator across all affective states that share a pleasant subjective feel. This traditional approach, in my view, leaves uncharted the additional functions that are unique to positive emotions.

The Broaden-and-Build Theory of Positive Emotions

Traditional approaches to the study of emotions have tended to ignore positive emotions and squeeze them into purportedly emotion-general models, confuse them with closely related affective states, and describe their function in terms of generic tendencies to approach or continue. Sensing that these approaches did not do justice to positive emotions, I developed an alternative model that better captures their unique effects. I call this the broaden-and-build theory of positive emotions because positive emotions appear to *broaden* people's momentary thought-action repertoires and *build* their enduring personal resources (Fredrickson, 1998).

I contrast this new model to traditional models based on specific action tendencies. Specific action tendencies, in my view, work well to describe the form and function of negative emotions and thus should be retained for models of this subset of emotions. Without loss of theoretical nuance, a specific action tendency can be redescribed as the outcome of a psychological process that narrows a person's momentary thought-action repertoire by calling to mind an urge to act in a particular way (e.g., escape, attack, expel). In a life-threatening situation, a narrowed thought-action repertoire promotes quick, decisive action that carries direct and immediate benefit. Specific action tendencies called forth by negative emotions represent the sort of actions that worked best to save our ancestors' lives and limbs in similar situations.

Yet positive emotions seldom occur in life-threatening situations. As such, a psychological process that narrows a person's momentary thought-action repertoire to promote quick, decisive action may not be needed. Instead, I have argued that positive emotions have a complementary effect: They *broaden* people's momentary thought-action repertoires, widening the array of the thoughts and actions that come to mind. Joy, for instance, creates the urge to play, push the limits, and be creative, urges evident not only in social and physical behavior but also in intellectual and artistic behavior. Interest, a phenomenologically distinct positive emotion, creates the urge to explore, take in new information and experiences, and expand the self in the process. Contentment, a third distinct positive emotion, creates the urge to sit back and savor current life circumstances and integrate these circumstances into new views of self and of the world. And love—which I view as an amalgam of distinct positive emotions (e.g., joy, interest, and contentment) experienced within contexts of safe, close relationships—creates recurring cycles of urges to play with, explore, and savor our loved ones. These various thought-action tendencies—to play, to explore, or to savor and integrate—represent ways that positive emotions broaden habitual modes of thinking or acting.

In contrast to negative emotions, which carry direct and immediate adaptive benefits in situations that threaten survival, the broadened thought-action repertoires triggered by positive emotions are beneficial in other ways. Specifically, I have argued that these broadened mindsets carry indirect and long-term adaptive benefits because broadening *builds* enduring personal resources.

Take play as an example. Specific forms of chasing play evident in juveniles of a species—like running into a flexible sapling or branch and catapulting oneself in an unexpected direction—are reenacted in adults of that species exclusively during predator avoidance (Dolhinow, 1987). Such correspondences between juvenile play maneuvers and adult survival maneuvers suggest that juvenile play builds enduring physical resources (Boulton & Smith, 1992; Caro, 1988). Play also builds enduring social resources. Social play, with its shared amusement and smiles, builds lasting social bonds and attachments (Lee, 1983; Simons, McCluskey-Fawcett, & Papini, 1986), which can become the locus of subsequent social support. Childhood play also builds enduring intellectual resources by increasing levels of creativity (Sherrod & Singer, 1989) and fueling brain development (Panksepp, 1998). Similarly, the exploration prompted by the positive emotion of interest creates knowledge and intellectual complexity, and the savoring prompted by contentment produces self-insight and alters worldviews. So each of these phenomenologically distinct positive emotions shares the feature of augmenting individuals' personal resources, ranging from physical and social resources to intellectual and psychological resources (see Fredrickson, 1998, 2001; Fredrickson & Branigan, 2001, for more detailed reviews).

Importantly, the personal resources accrued during states of positive emotions are durable. They outlast the transient emotional states that led to their acquisition. By consequence, then, the often incidental effect of experiencing a positive emotion is an increase in one's personal resources. These resources can be drawn on in subsequent moments and in different emotional states. So, through experiences of positive emo-

tions people *transform* themselves, becoming more creative, knowledgeable, resilient, socially integrated, and healthy individuals. Figure 9.1 represents these three sequential effects of positive emotions (i.e., broadening, building, transforming) and also suggests that initial experiences of positive emotions produce upward spirals toward further experiences of positive emotions, a point I will return to in a subsequent section.

In short, the broaden-and-build theory describes the form of positive emotions in terms of broadened thought-action repertoires and describes their function in terms of building enduring personal resources. In doing so, the theory provides a new perspective on the evolved adaptive significance of positive emotions. Those of our ancestors who succumbed to the urges sparked by positive emotions—to play, explore, and so on—would have by consequence accrued more personal resources. When these same ancestors later faced inevitable threats to life and limb, their greater personal resources would have translated into greater odds of survival and, in turn, greater odds of living long enough to reproduce. To the extent that the capacity to experience positive emotions is genetically encoded, this capacity, through the process of natural selection, would have become part of our universal human nature.

Summary of Current Research Findings

The Broadening Hypothesis

The first central claim of the broaden-and-build theory is that experiences of positive emotions broaden a person's momentary thought-action repertoire. This is the broadening hypothesis. Indirect evidence consistent with this hypothesis can be drawn from a range of studies that have examined the cognitive and behavioral effects of positive affective traits and induced positive states. The manic states of individuals with bipolar disorder are, for instance, associated with expansive and over-inclusive thinking, characteristic of creativity (Derryberry & Tucker, 1994; Richards & Kinney, 1990). Moreover, patients on lithium treatment exhibit diminished mania as well as diminished creativity (Shaw, Mann, Stokes, & Manevitz, 1986). Broadened attention and cognition also are evident within normal ranges of positive affectivity. In laboratory studies that use global-local

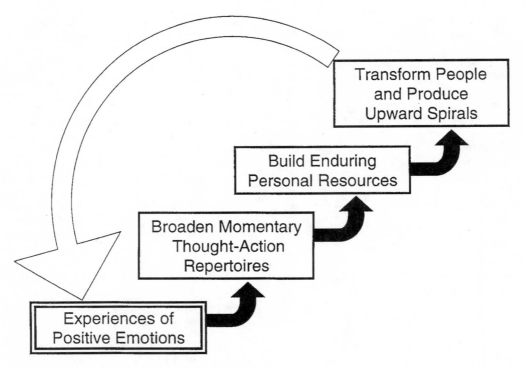

Figure 9.1 The broaden-and-build theory of positive emotions.

visual processing paradigms to assess biases in attentional focus, negative emotional traits like anxiety and depression predict a local bias consistent with a narrowed attentional focus, whereas positive emotional traits like subjective well-being and optimism predict a global bias consistent with a broadened attentional focus (Basso, Schefft, Ris, & Dember, 1996). Likewise, experimentally manipulated failure feedback produces a local bias, whereas success feedback produces a global bias (Brandt, Derryberry, & Reed, 1992, cited in Derryberry & Tucker, 1994). A critical ingredient missing from these studies, however, is a neutral comparison condition. Without one, it remains unclear whether the broadened scopes of attention associated with positive traits and success are in fact more expansive than is typical under normal (nonnegative) conditions. Work by Isen and colleagues is particularly valuable because induced positive states are compared with neutral states. Testing the effects of positive states on cognition, their experiments have shown that positive emotions produce patterns of thought that are notably unusual (Isen, Johnson, Mertz, & Robinson, 1985); flexible and inclusive (Isen & Daubman, 1984); creative (Isen, Daubman, & Nowicki, 1987); and receptive (Estrada, Isen,

& Young, 1997). Testing the effects of positive states on behavior, Isen and colleagues have shown that positive emotions produce more creative (Isen et al., 1987) and variable (Kahn & Isen, 1993) actions.

In general terms, then, positive emotions appear to "enlarge" the cognitive context (Isen, 1987), an effect recently linked to increases in brain dopamine levels (Ashby, Isen, & Turken, 1999). Such cognitive expansiveness is consistent with the hypothesis, drawn from the broaden-and-build theory, that positive emotions widen the array of thoughts and actions that come to mind. Even so, a direct test of the broadening hypothesis was necessary, one that compared the effects of multiple positive and negative emotions with a neutral condition, using a dependent measure that corresponds closely to the breadth of the momentary thought-action repertoire. The twin hypotheses are that, relative to neutral, nonemotional states, distinct types of positive emotions broaden people's thought-action repertoires, whereas distinct types of negative emotions narrow these same repertoires.

Together with Christine Branigan, I have tested these twin hypotheses in a straightforward laboratory experiment. We induced the specific emotions of joy, contentment, fear, and anger by showing research participants short, emotionally evocative film clips. We also used a nonemotional film clip as a neutral comparison condition. Immediately following each film clip, we measured the breadth of participants' thought-action repertoires. We did this by asking them to step away from the specifics of the film and take a moment to imagine themselves being in a situation in which similar feelings would arise. Given this feeling, we asked them to list all the things they would like to do right then. Participants were given 20 blank lines that began with the phrase "I would like to" in which to record their responses.

Tallying the potential actions each participant listed, we found support for the broadening hypothesis, which is illustrated in Figure 9.2. Participants in the two positive emotion conditions (joy and contentment) identified significantly more things that they would like to do right then relative to those in the two negative emotion conditions (fear and anger) and relative to those in the neutral control condition. Those in the two negative emotion conditions also named significantly fewer things than those in the neutral control condition (Fredrickson & Branigan, 2001).

These data provide initial direct evidence that two distinct types of positive emotion—a high-arousal state of joy, and a low-arousal state of contentment—produce a broader thought-action repertoire than does a neutral state. Likewise, two distinct types of negative emotion—fear and anger—produce a narrower thought-action repertoire than does a neutral state. This finding supports the first core proposition of the broaden-and-build theory: Positive emotions widen the array of thoughts and actions that come to mind. By contrast, negative emotions, as models based on specific action tendencies would suggest, shrink this same array.

The Building Hypothesis

The second central claim of the broaden-and-build theory is that experiences of positive emotions, through their broadening effects, build people's enduring personal resources. Indirect evidence consistent with this building hypothesis can be drawn from correlational and experimental studies of humans and animals that link positive traits and states and behaviors linked with positive states—such as play—to increases in physical, intellectual, and social resources. As previously indicated, ethologists who have observed nonhuman mammals have associated juvenile play with the development of specific survival maneuvers evident in both predator avoidance and aggressive fighting (Boulton & Smith, 1992; Caro, 1988), suggesting that play builds enduring physical resources. Reinforcing this claim, laboratory experiments that have deprived rats of juvenile social play have shown that, compared with nondeprived controls, deprived rats were slower to learn a complex motor task (Einon, Morgan, & Kibbler, 1978). Evidence suggesting that positive emotions build intellectual resources can be drawn from studies on individual differences in attachment styles. Securely attached children—those who experience the most consistent caregiver love

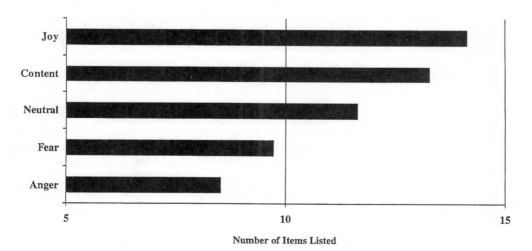

Figure 9.2 Breadth of the thought-action repertoire by emotion (Fredrickson & Branigan, 2001).

—are more persistent, flexible, and resource-ful problem solvers than their peers (Arend, Gove, & Sroufe, 1979; Matas, Arend, & Sroufe, 1978). They also engage in more independent exploration of novel places, and, by consequence, develop superior cognitive maps of those spaces (Hazen & Durrett, 1982). The intellectual resources associated with secure attachment also appear to last into adulthood. Securely attached adults are more curious and open to information than their insecurely attached peers (Mikulincer, 1997). Experiments with children ranging from preschool to high school reinforce the claim that positive emotions build intellectual resources by showing that induced positive states—in comparison to neutral and negative states—produce faster learning and improved intellectual performance (Bryan & Bryan, 1991; Bryan, Mathur, & Sullivan, 1996; Masters, Barden, & Ford, 1979). Finally, correlational studies with both humans and nonhuman mammals suggest that social play builds enduring social relationships (Boulton & Smith, 1992; Lee, 1983; Martineau, 1972). In times of need, these social relationships can become social resources.

In general terms, then, positive emotions can be linked to increases in physical, intellectual, and social resources. These findings provide indirect support for the hypothesis—drawn from the broaden-and-build theory—that positive emotions build enduring personal resources. Although a subset of this evidence is experimental and includes the critical comparison of positive to neutral states (e.g., Bryan et al., 1996; Masters et al., 1979), missing from this body of evidence are tests of the hypothesized role of broadening in the building process. The broaden-and-build theory makes the specific prediction that positive emotions—through their effects on broadened thought-action repertoires—build people's enduring personal resources.

Moreover, to the extent that positive emotions both broaden and build, over time they also should produce improved well-being. For example, if positive emotions broaden the scope of cognition and enable flexible and creative thinking, they also should facilitate coping with stress and adversity. Consistent with this view, studies have shown that people who experienced positive emotions during bereavement were more likely to develop long-term plans and goals. Together with positive emotions, plans and goals predicted greater psychological well-being 12 months after bereavement (Stein, Folkman, Trabasso, & Richards, 1997). Thus, the effects of positive emotions are hypothesized to accumulate and compound over time. By broadening people's modes of thinking and action, positive emotions should improve coping and thus build resilience. Increments in resilience should, in turn, predict future experiences of positive emotions.

The cognitive literature on depression already has documented a downward spiral in which depressed mood and the narrowed, pessimistic thinking it engenders influence one another reciprocally, leading to ever-worsening moods and even clinical levels of depression (Peterson & Seligman, 1984). In contrast, the broaden-and-build theory predicts a comparable upward spiral in which positive emotions and the broadened thinking they engender also influence one another reciprocally, leading to appreciable increases in well-being. In part, positive emotions may trigger these upward spirals by building resilience and influencing the ways people cope with adversity.

Together with Thomas Joiner, I have conducted an initial test of the hypothesis that, through cognitive broadening, positive emotions build psychological resilience and produce an upward spiral toward enhanced emotional well-being. We did this by assessing positive and negative emotions, as well as a concept we call *broad-minded coping*, at two time points, 5 weeks apart. For our measure of broad-minded coping, we drew items from Moos's (1988) Coping Responses Inventory that tap broadened thinking, such as "think of different ways to deal with the problem" and "try to step back from the situation and be more objective." Our aim was to predict changes in positive emotions and broad-minded coping over time.

Through a series of regression analyses and tests of mediation, our data revealed evidence for an upward spiral effect, represented in Figure 9.3. First, we found that, controlling for initial levels of broad-minded coping, initial levels of positive emotion predicted improvements in broad-minded coping from Time 1 to Time 2. These improvements in broad-minded coping in turn predicted subsequent increases in positive emotions (see dashed boxes in Figure 9.3). Next, we found evidence for the reciprocal relations. Controlling for initial levels of positive emotion, initial levels of broad-minded coping predicted improvements in positive emotions from Time 1 to Time 2. These improvements in pos-

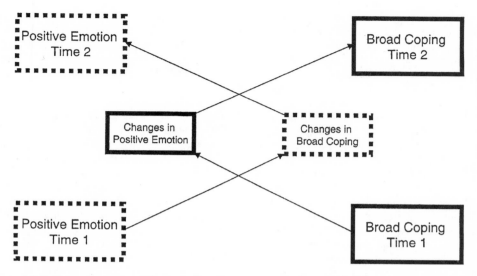

Figure 9.3 Evidence for an upward spiral effect for positive emotions (Fredrickson & Joiner, in press).

itive emotions in turn predicted subsequent increases in broad-minded coping (see solid boxes in Figure 9.3). Importantly, these effects were unique to positive emotions. Substituting negative emotions into the same regression equations yielded no significant relations whatsoever (Fredrickson & Joiner, in press).

These findings suggest that, over time, positive emotions and broad-minded coping mutually build on one another. Because broad-minded coping can be viewed as a form of psychological resilience, these data support the hypothesis, drawn from the broaden-and-build theory, that momentary experiences of positive emotion can build enduring psychological resources and trigger upward spirals toward emotional well-being. Thus, positive emotions not only make people feel good in the present moment but also—through their effects on broadened thinking—increase the likelihood that people will feel good in the future. The upward spiral effect is represented by the feedback loop in Figure 9.1.

Implications for Emotion Regulation: The Undoing Hypothesis

The broaden-and-build theory has implications for the strategies that people use to regulate their experiences of negative emotions. If negative emotions narrow the momentary thought-action repertoire, and positive emotions broaden this same repertoire, then positive emotions

ought to function as efficient antidotes for the lingering effects of negative emotions. In other words, positive emotions should "undo" the lingering aftereffects of negative emotions; this is the undoing hypothesis (Fredrickson & Levenson, 1998; Fredrickson, Mancuso, Branigan, & Tugade, 2000). The basic observation that positive and negative emotions (or key components of them) are somehow incompatible—or cannot fully and simultaneously coexist—is not new. This has been demonstrated in earlier work on anxiety disorders (e.g., systematic desensitization; Wolpe, 1958); motivation (e.g., opponent-process theory; Solomon & Corbit, 1974); and aggression (e.g., principle of incompatible responses; Baron, 1976). Even so, the mechanism ultimately responsible for this incompatibility has not been adequately identified. Broadening may turn out to be the mechanism. By broadening a person's momentary thought-action repertoire, a positive emotion may loosen the hold that a negative emotion has gained on that person's mind and body by dissipating or undoing preparation for specific action. In other words, negative and positive emotions may be fundamentally incompatible because a person's momentary thought-action repertoire cannot be simultaneously narrow and broad. One marker of the narrowed thought-action repertoire called forth by negative emotions is heightened cardiovascular activity. Invoking positive emotions following negative emotions, then, should speed recovery from this cardiovascular reactivity, returning the body to more midrange levels of activation. By accelerating cardiovascular recovery, positive emotions create the bodily context suitable for pursuing the wider array of thoughts and actions called forth.

My collaborators and I have tested this undoing hypothesis by first inducing a high-arousal negative emotion in all participants and then immediately, by random assignment, inducing mild joy, contentment, neutrality, or sadness by showing short, emotionally evocative film clips. The undoing hypothesis predicts that those who experience positive emotions on the heels of a high-arousal negative emotion will show the fastest cardiovascular recovery. We tested this by measuring the time elapsed from the start of the randomly assigned film until the cardiovascular reactions induced by the initial negative emotion returned to baseline levels. Figure 9.4 shows the results. Participants in the two positive emotion conditions (mild joy and contentment) exhibited faster cardiovascular recovery than those in the neutral control condition and faster than those in the sadness condition (Fredrickson et al., 2000, Study 1; see also Fredrickson & Levenson, 1998). Importantly, in another study (Fredrickson et al., 2000, Study 2), we found that the positive and neutral films used in this research, when viewed following a resting baseline, elicit virtually no cardiovascular reactivity whatsoever. So although the positive and neutral films do not differ in what they *do* to the cardiovascular system, they differ in what they can *undo* within this system. Two distinct types of positive emotions—mild joy and contentment—share the ability to undo the lingering cardiovascular aftereffects of negative emotions, a finding consistent with the idea that positive emotions broaden people's thought-action repertoires.

In subsequent work, we have discovered individual differences in people's abilities to harness this beneficial undoing effect of positive emotions. Specifically, we have found that people who score high on a self-report measure of psychological resilience (Block & Kremen, 1996) show faster cardiovascular recovery following negative emotional arousal than do those who score low on this measure. Moreover, this faster recovery is mediated by the positive emotions that highly resilient people bring to the situation. Resilient individuals experience more positive emotions than do their less resilient peers, both at ambient levels and in response to stressful circumstances. These positive emotions, in

turn, allow them to bounce back quickly from negative emotional arousal (Tugade & Fredrickson, 2001). In effect, then, resilient individuals are expert users of the undoing effect of positive emotions.

Intervention Programs to Increase the Prevalence of Positive Emotions

Although no intervention programs based directly on the broaden-and-build theory of positive emotions have yet been devised and tested, a handful of existing intervention techniques can be profitably reframed as techniques to increase the prevalence of positive emotions. To the extent that these existing techniques successfully elicit positive emotions, the broaden-and-build theory may explain their effectiveness (Fredrickson, 2000). In particular, I will discuss intervention strategies based on practicing relaxation and increasing pleasant activities. Notably, these two strategies emerged from psychology's era of behaviorism, which did not favor reference to emotional states. Reconsidering them now from an emotions perspective illuminates mechanisms through which they may have achieved their success, as well as pathways along which they may be further fine-tuned.

One lesson from contemporary emotions research is that, unfortunately, there is no fail-safe or direct way to elicit a given emotion reliably in all people. People cannot simply will themselves to feel a particular emotion, nor can clinicians or experimenters directly instill emotions in people. As such, all emotion induction techniques are by necessity indirect, often focusing on one component of the more complex, multicomponent emotion system. Because emotions typically unfold from individuals' appraisals of the personal meaning of particular circumstances, the most ecologically valid way to induce emotions is to shape people's appraisals of situations. Yet because meaning assessments are the products of unique personal histories and goals, they often are difficult to control. Instead, the focus often is placed on creating or recalling situations that, for most people, tend to elicit certain meanings, and therefore certain emotions. Other emotion induction techniques depart from ecological validity and aim to "jump-start" the emotion system by activating one or more downstream emotional responses: a facial or bodily muscle configuration, a phys-

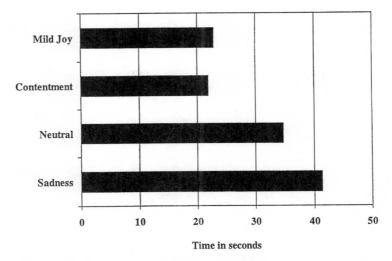

Figure 9.4 Speed of cardiovascular recovery by emotion (Fredrickson, Mancuso, Branigan, & Tugade, 2000).

iological state, or a mode of thinking. Laboratory experiments have shown that cultivating these downstream components of an emotion often (but not always) can initiate or jumpstart the entire, multicomponent emotion process (e.g., Levenson, Ekman, & Friesen, 1990; Schachter & Singer, 1962; Stepper & Strack, 1993; Velton, 1968). I use these perspectives on emotion induction to reexamine intervention strategies based on relaxation and increasing pleasant activities.

Practicing Relaxation

There is no single relaxation therapy or technique; rather, there are multiple, seemingly disparate relaxation practices. These range from traditional forms, like meditation and yoga, to more modern forms, like imagery exercises and progressive muscle relaxation. These various forms often are grouped together as a single class of treatments because each has been shown to produce relaxation and treat problems rooted in, or exacerbated by, negative emotions and stress. People use and prescribe relaxation techniques because they work. Even so, clear understanding of the mechanisms or active ingredients responsible for their effectiveness has remained elusive (Blumenthal, 1985).

I have argued that various relaxation practices work because, at one level or another, they cultivate or jump-start the positive emotion of contentment (Fredrickson, 2000). Contentment is a mindful emotion that elicits cognitive changes

more than outwardly visible physical changes. It calls forth the urge to savor the present moment and integrate those momentary experiences into an enriched appreciation of one's place in the world (Fredrickson, 1998, 2000). Relaxation practices induce one or more key components of contentment and, in doing so, create the conditions for experiencing this positive emotion. For instance, imagery exercises focus on situations, like nature scenes or personal successes, known to be frequent precursors to contentment. Similarly, progressive muscle relaxation creates a dynamic tension-release sequence that mimics intense laughter, which is known to give way to relaxed contentment. Finally, meditation exercises cultivate states of mindfulness, or full awareness of the present moment, that strongly resemble the modes of thinking characteristic of contentment. By cultivating key components of contentment (e.g., imagining situations or eliciting muscle configurations or mental states), various relaxation practices increase the probability that the full, multicomponent experience of contentment will emerge. As such, relaxation techniques may work to treat problems triggered by negative emotions because they capitalize on the undoing effects of positive emotions (Fredrickson, 2000). This prediction could be tested by assessing the degree of contentment elicited by relaxation techniques and examining whether experiences of contentment in fact mediate the positive association between relaxation practice and improved health and well-being. If relaxation techniques indeed reliably produce contentment, then the broaden-and-build theory would suggest that these techniques could be valuable not only for treating problems rooted in negative emotions but also for spurring psychological development and optimizing health and well-being.

Increasing Pleasant Activities

Interventions based on increasing pleasant events grew out of behavioral theories suggesting that depression results from a deficit in response-contingent positive reinforcement. Under this strategy, depressed individuals are encouraged to increase their rates of engagement in pleasant activities, such as socializing, being in nature, being creative, and being physically active. Although such interventions are successful in decreasing depression, as for relaxation therapies, a clear understanding of the mechanisms underlying their effectiveness has remained elusive (Lewinsohn & Gotlib, 1995).

Reflecting their roots in behaviorism, focus in these interventions was placed on pleasant activities and not on pleasant subjective experiences, like positive emotions. Although pleasant activities can produce positive emotions, an emotions perspective reminds us that whether and to what degree they do so depends on the personal meanings individuals construct for those activities. I have argued that consideration of personal meaning can account for and revitalize interventions based in increasing pleasant activities by connecting this work to the broadening and building effects of positive emotions (Fredrickson, 2000).

Positive emotions result from finding positive meaning. People find positive meaning within ordinary daily events and activities by reframing or infusing those events and activities with positive value (Folkman, 1997). A social activity, for instance, can be construed as feeling connected to others and cared about; a nature experience as having an opportunity to be distracted from everyday cares; a physical activity as a personal achievement, and so on. Finding positive meaning in these ways is likely to produce experiences of love, contentment, interest, joy, or other positive emotions. Recently, investigators have discovered that finding positive meaning also produces significant therapeutic effects, such as recovery from depressed mood and improvements in health and psychological well-being (Affleck & Tennen, 1996; Davis,

Nolen-Hoeksema, & Larson, 1998; Folkman, Chesney, Collette, Boccellari, & Cooke, 1996). I have argued that finding positive meaning produces these benefits because doing so generates positive emotions that broaden habitual modes of thinking and build enduring personal resources (Fredrickson, 2000). This prediction could be tested by assessing positive emotions and cognitive broadening, alongside positive meanings, and examining whether positive emotions and broadening mediate the positive relations between finding positive meaning and improved health and well-being. If such tests yield support for the broaden-and-build theory, intervention strategies focused on increasing pleasant events could be retooled to focus more directly on finding positive meaning and experiencing positive emotions.

Directions for Future Research

Despite the growing evidence in support of the broaden-and-build theory, the theory remains young, and additional tests are needed before it moves from a provocative proposal to a well-supported theory. In this section, I describe some critical directions for future research.

A first direction for research will be to further examine the broaden component of the broaden-and-build theory. Although the twin hypotheses (i.e., relative to neutral states, positive emotions broaden individuals' momentary thought-action repertoires, whereas negative emotions narrow these same repertoires) have received direct support in an initial experiment (Fredrickson & Branigan, 2001), many questions remain. For instance, are these effects replicable, and do they extend to other measures of the breadth of thought-action repertoires? If so, what changes in basic cognitive processes underlie changes in the scope of thoughts and actions called forth? Is the scope of attention enlarged during experiences of positive emotions, as suggested by a handful of inconclusive studies (Basso et al., 1996; Brandt et al., 1992, cited in Derryberry & Tucker, 1994)? Alternatively (or additionally), is the scope of working memory expanded during experiences of positive emotions? Finally, do emotion-related changes in the scopes of attention and cognition generate emotion-related differences in openness to information? In set-switching and creativity? In coping and interpersonal problem solving? My collaborators and I currently are undertaking a program of laboratory experiments to test these questions. We will induce positive, negative, and neutral states using both within-subjects and between-subjects designs and will assess the effects of distinct emotions on the scopes of action, attention, working memory, and measures of higher cognitive functioning, such as openness to information and problem solving.

Related questions for future research concern the neurological underpinnings of the broadening effects of positive emotions. Are these effects mediated by changing levels of circulating brain dopamine, as Ashby and colleagues (1999) have suggested? What brain structures, circuits, and processes are involved? These will be important questions for neuroscientists to address.

A second important direction for future research will be to assess the hypothesized link between the psychological and physiological effects of positive emotions. Specifically, does the psychological broadening effect track or mediate the physiological undoing effect? To test this hypothesis, repeated measures of cognitive broadening could be introduced into the cardiovascular undoing paradigm (Fredrickson et al., 2000), assessing the breadth of cognition at baseline, then immediately following negative emotion induction, and a third time following the experimental manipulation of positive, neutral, or negative states. The prediction would be that negative emotions simultaneously increase cardiovascular activation and narrow the scope of cognition, whereas positive emotions simultaneously undo cardiovascular activation and broaden the scope of cognition, and that changes in broadening mediate cardiovascular recovery. Confirmatory results from such a study would be necessary to support the claim that psychological broadening accounts for the cardiovascular undoing effect.

A third critical direction for future research will be to test the build component of the broaden-and-build theory. Although the evidence that positive emotions trigger an upward spiral toward enhanced emotional well-being (Fredrickson & Joiner, in press) provides initial support for the hypothesis that positive emotions build psychological resilience, the building hypothesis merits much additional testing. First, is this upward spiral effect replicable, and can it be demonstrated over more and more distal time points? Can experiences of positive emotions, over time, build other enduring personal resources (beyond broad-minded coping),

such as optimism, hopefulness, wisdom, and creativity? Can experiences of positive emotions, over time, build enduring social resources, such as empathy, altruism, intimacy motive, and relationship satisfaction? If so, are increments in these personal and social resources mediated by psychological broadening and followed by increases in emotional and physical well-being? These hypotheses could be tested with both clinical and nonclinical samples, in both longitudinal studies and field experiments. The field experiments could test the psychological, social, and physical outcomes of interventions aimed at cultivating positive emotions in daily life, through relaxation techniques or, perhaps more fruitfully, through finding positive meaning. Additional support for the twin hypotheses that positive emotions build enduring personal resources and trigger upward spirals would provide evidence that, over time, positive emotions not only alleviate disorders and illnesses rooted in negative emotions but also go beyond to build individual character, solidify social bonds, and optimize people's health and well-being.

In sum, the broaden-and-build theory underscores the ways in which positive emotions are essential elements of optimal functioning, and therefore an essential topic within positive psychology. The theory also carries an important bottom-line message. We should cultivate positive emotions in our own lives and in the lives of those around us not just because doing so makes us feel good in the moment but also because doing so will transform us to be better people, with better lives in the future.

Acknowledgment Fredrickson's research on positive emotions is supported by grants from the National Institute of Mental Health (MH53971 and MH59615), by a Rackham Faculty Grant and Fellowship from the University of Michigan, and by an award from the John Templeton Foundation and the American Psychological Association (2000 Templeton Positive Psychology Prize).

References

Affleck, G., & Tennen, H. (1996). Construing benefits from adversity: Adaptational significance and dispositional underpinnings. *Journal of Personality, 64,* 899–922.

Arend, R., Gove, F. L., & Sroufe, L. A. (1979). Continuity of individual adaptation from infancy to kindergarten: A predictive study of ego-resiliency and curiosity in preschoolers. *Child Development, 50,* 950–959.

*Ashby, F. G., Isen, A. M., & Turken, A. U. (1999). A neuropsychological theory of positive affect and its influence on cognition. *Psychological Review, 106,* 529–550.

Baron, R. A. (1976). The reduction of human aggression: A field study of the influence of incompatible reactions. *Journal of Applied Social Psychology, 6,* 260–274.

Basso, M. R., Schefft, B. K., Ris, M. D., & Dember, W. N. (1996). Mood and global-local visual processing. *Journal of the International Neuropsychological Society, 2,* 249–255.

Block, J., & Kremen, A. M. (1996). IQ and ego-resilience: Conceptual and empirical connections and separateness. *Journal of Personality and Social Psychology, 70,* 349–361.

Blumenthal, J. A. (1985). Relaxation therapy, biofeedback and behavioral medicine. *Psychotherapy, 22,* 516–530.

Boulton, M. J., & Smith, P. K. (1992). The social nature of play fighting and play chasing: Mechanisms and strategies underlying cooperation and compromise. In J. H. Barkow, L. Cosmides, & J. Tooby (Eds.), *The adapted mind: Evolutionary psychology and the generation of culture* (pp. 429–444). New York: Oxford University Press.

Bryan, T., & Bryan, J. (1991). Positive mood and math performance. *Journal of Learning Disabilities, 24,* 490–494.

Bryan, T., Mathur, S., & Sullivan, K. (1996). The impact of positive mood on learning. *Learning Disabilities Quarterly, 19,* 153–162.

Cabanac, M. (1971). Physiological role of pleasure. *Science, 173,* 1103–1107.

Cacioppo, J. T., Priester, J. R., & Berntson, G. G. (1993). Rudimentary determinants of attitudes: II. Arm flexion and extension have differential effects on attitudes. *Journal of Personality and Social Psychology, 65,* 5–17.

Caro, T. M. (1988). Adaptive significance of play: Are we getting closer? *Tree, 3,* 50–54.

Carver, C. S., & Scheier, M. F. (1990). Origins and functions of positive and negative affect: A control-process view. *Psychological Review, 97,* 19–35.

Clore, G. L. (1994). Why emotions are felt. In P. Ekman & R. Davidson (Eds.), *The nature of emotion: Fundamental questions* (pp. 103–111). New York: Oxford University Press.

Davidson, R. J. (1993). The neuropsychology of emotion and affective style. In M. Lewis & J. M. Haviland (Eds.), *Handbook of emotion* (pp. 143–154). New York: Guilford.

Davis, C. G., Nolen-Hoeksema, S., & Larson, J. (1998). Making sense of loss and benefiting from experience: Two construals of meaning. *Journal of Personality and Social Psychology, 75,* 561–574.

Derryberry, D., & Tucker, D. M. (1994). Motivating the focus of attention. In P. M. Neidenthal & S. Kitayama (Eds.), *The heart's eye: Emotional influences in perception and attention* (pp. 167–196). San Diego, CA: Academic Press.

Diener, E., & Diener, C. (1996). Most people are happy. *Psychological Science, 7,* 181–185.

Diener, E., Sandvik, E., & Pavot, W. (1991). Happiness is the frequency, not the intensity, of positive versus negative affect. In F. Strack (Ed.), *Subjective well-being: An interdisciplinary perspective* (pp. 119–139). Oxford: Pergamon.

Dolhinow, P. J. (1987). At play in the fields. In H. Topoff (Ed.), *The natural history reader in animal behavior* (pp. 229–237). New York: Columbia University Press.

Einon, D. F., Morgan, M. J., & Kibbler, C. C. (1978). Brief periods of socialization and later behavior in the rat. *Developmental Psychobiology, 11,* 213–225.

Ekman, P. (1992). An argument for basic emotions. *Cognition and Emotion, 6,* 169–200.

Estrada, C. A., Isen, A. M., & Young, M. J. (1997). Positive affect facilitates integration of information and decreases anchoring in reasoning among physicians. *Organizational Behavior and Human Decision Processes, 72,* 117–135.

*Folkman, S. (1997). Positive psychological states and coping with severe stress. *Social Science Medicine, 45,* 1207–1221.

Folkman, S., Chesney, M. A., Collette, L., Boccellari, A., & Cooke, M. (1996). Post-bereavement depressive mood and its pre-bereavement predictors in HIV+ and HIV− gay men. *Journal of Personality and Social Psychology, 70,* 336–348.

*Fredrickson, B. L. (1998). What good are positive emotions? *Review of General Psychology, 2,* 300–319.

*Fredrickson, B. L. (2000). Cultivating positive emotions to optimize health and well-being. *Prevention and Treatment, 3.* Available on the World Wide Web: http://journals.apa.org/prevention.

*Fredrickson, B. L. (2001). The role of positive emotions in positive psychology: The broaden-and-build theory of positive emotions. *American Psychologists, 56,* 218–226.

Fredrickson, B. L., & Branigan, C. (2001). *Positive emotions broaden the scope of attention and thought-action repertoires: Evidence for the broaden-and-build theory.* Manuscript under review.

Fredrickson, B. L., & Branigan, C. (2001). Positive emotions. In T. J. Mayne & G. A. Bonnano (Eds.), *Emotion: Current issues and future directions* (pp. 123–151). New York: Guilford.

Fredrickson, B. L., & Joiner, T. (in press). Positive emotions trigger upward spirals toward emotional well-being. *Psychological Science.*

Fredrickson, B. L., & Levenson, R. W. (1998). Positive emotions speed recovery from the cardiovascular sequelae of negative emotions. *Cognition and Emotion, 12,* 191–220.

Fredrickson, B. L., Mancuso, R. A., Branigan, C., & Tugade, M. (2000). The undoing effect of positive emotions. *Motivation and Emotion, 24,* 237–258.

Frijda, N. H. (1986). *The emotions.* Cambridge, England: Cambridge University Press.

Frijda, N. H. (1994). Emotions are functional, most of the time. In P. Ekman & R. Davidson (Eds.), *The nature of emotion: Fundamental questions* (pp. 112–122). New York: Oxford University Press.

Frijda, N. H., Kuipers, P., & Schure, E. (1989). Relations among emotion, appraisal, and emotional action readiness. *Journal of Personality and Social Psychology, 57,* 212–228.

Hazen, N. L., & Durrett, M. E. (1982). Relationship of security of attachment and cognitive mapping abilities in 2-year-olds. *Developmental Psychology, 18,* 751–759.

*Isen, A. M. (1987). Positive affect, cognitive processes, and social behavior. *Advances in Experimental Social Psychology, 20,* 203–253.

Isen, A. M., & Daubman, K. A. (1984). The influence of affect on categorization. *Journal of Personality and Social Psychology, 47,* 1206–1217.

Isen, A. M., Daubman, K. A., & Nowicki, G. P. (1987). Positive affect facilitates creative problem solving. *Journal of Personality and Social Psychology, 52,* 1122–1131.

Isen, A. M., Johnson, M. M. S., Mertz, E., & Robinson, G. F. (1985). The influence of positive affect on the unusualness of word associations. *Journal of Personality and Social Psychology, 48,* 1413–1426.

Ito, T. A., & Cacioppo, J. T. (1999). The psychophysiology of utility appraisals. In D. Kahneman, E. Diener, & N. Schwartz (Eds.) *Wellbeing: Foundations of hedonic psychology* (pp. 470–488). New York: Russell Sage Foundation.

Kahn, B. E., & Isen, A. M. (1993). The influence of positive affect on variety seeking among safe,

enjoyable products. *Journal of Consumer Research, 20,* 257–270.

Lazarus, R. S. (1991). *Emotion and adaptation.* New York: Oxford University Press.

Lee, P. C. (1983). Play as a means for developing relationships. In R. A. Hinde (Ed.), *Primate social relationships* (pp. 82–89). Oxford: Blackwell.

Levenson, R. W. (1994). Human emotions: A functional view. In P. Ekman & R. Davidson (Eds.), *The nature of emotion: Fundamental questions* (pp. 123–126). New York: Oxford University Press.

Levenson, R. W., Ekman, P., & Friesen, W. V. (1990). Voluntary facial action generates emotion-specific autonomic nervous system activity. *Psychophysiology, 27,* 363–384.

Lewinsohn, P. M., & Gotlib, I. H. (1995). Behavioral theory and treatment of depression. In E. E. Beckham & W. R. Leber (Eds.), *Handbook of depression* (2nd ed., pp. 352–375). New York: Guilford.

Martineau, W. H. (1972). A model of the social functions of humor. In J. H. Goldstein & P. E. McGee (Eds.), *The psychology of humor: Theoretical perspectives and empirical issues* (pp. 101–128). New York: Academic Press.

Masters, J. C., Barden, R. C., & Ford, M. E. (1979). Affective states, expressive behavior, and learning in children. *Journal of Personality and Social Psychology, 37,* 380–390.

Matas, L., Arend, R. A., & Sroufe, L. A. (1978). Continuity of adaptation in the second year: The relationship between quality of attachment and later competence. *Child Development, 49,* 547–556.

Mikulincer, M. (1997). Adult attachment style and information processing: Individual differences in curiosity and cognitive closure. *Journal of Personality and Social Psychology, 72,* 1217–1230.

Moos, R. H. (1988). *Coping responses inventory manual.* Palo Alto, CA: Stanford University and Department of Veterans Affairs Medical Centers.

Oatley, K., & Jenkins, J. M. (1996). *Understanding emotions.* Cambridge, MA: Blackwell.

Panksepp, J. (1998). Attention deficit hyperactivity disorders, psychostimulants, and intolerance of childhood playfulness: A tragedy in the making? *Current Directions in Psychological Science, 7,* 91–98.

Peterson, C., & Seligman, M. E. P. (1984). Causal explanations as a risk factor for depression: Theory and evidence. *Psychological Review, 91,* 347–374.

Richards, R., & Kinney, D. K. (1990). Mood swings and creativity. *Creativity Research Journal, 3,* 202–217.

*Rosenberg, E. L. (1998). Levels of analysis and the organization of affect. *Review of General Psychology, 2*, 247–270.

Schachter, S., & Singer, J. E. (1962). Cognitive, social, and physiological determinants of emotional state. *Psychological Review, 69*, 379–399.

Shaw, E. D., Mann, J. T., Stokes, P. E., & Manevitz, A. Z. (1986). Effects of lithium carbonate on associative productivity and idiosyncrasy in bipolar patients. *American Journal of Psychiatry, 143*, 1166–1169.

Sherrod, L. R., & Singer, J. L. (1989). The development of make-believe play. In J. Goldstein (Ed.), *Sports, games and play* (pp. 1–38). Hillsdale, NJ: Erlbaum.

Simons, C. J. R., McCluskey-Fawcett, K. A., & Papini, D. R. (1986). Theoretical and functional perspective on the development of humor during infancy, childhood, and adolescence. In L. Nahemow, K. A. McCluskey-Fawcett, & P. E. McGhee (Eds.), *Humor and aging* (pp. 53–77). San Diego, CA: Academic Press.

Solomon, R. L., & Corbit, J. D. (1974). An opponent-process theory of motivation: I. Temporal dynamics of affect. *Psychological Review, 81*, 119–145.

Stein, N. L., Folkman, S., Trabasso, T., & Richards, T. A. (1997). Appraisal and goal processes as predictors of psychological well-being in bereaved caregivers. *Journal of Personality and Social Psychology, 72*, 872–884.

Stepper, S., & Strack, F. (1993). Proprioceptive determinants of emotional and nonemotional feelings. *Journal of Personality and Social Psychology, 64*, 211–220.

Tooby, J., & Cosmides, L. (1990). The past explains the present: Emotional adaptations and the structure of ancestral environments. *Ethology and Sociobiology, 11*, 375–424.

Tugade, M., & Fredrickson, B. L. (2001). *Resilient individuals use positive emotions to bounce back from negative emotional arousal.* Manuscript under review.

Velton, E. (1968). A laboratory task for the induction of mood states. *Behavior Research and Therapy, 6*, 473–482.

Wolpe, J. (1958). *Psychotherapy by reciprocal inhibition.* Stanford, CA: Stanford University Press.

10

The Social Construction of Self-Esteem

John P. Hewitt

From the psychology of William James to the contemporary industry dedicated to its study and promotion, self-esteem has held a central place in the scholarly and popular understanding of the person in the United States. In this chapter, I will put self-esteem under a new microscope, focusing as much on its cultural resonance as its psychological essence. I will examine self-esteem as an element of a culture that nourishes a belief in the importance of the individual self even while making the self problematic; suggest reasons why the experience and discourse of self-esteem have been socially constructed; and show how this approach to self-esteem adds to our understanding of the individual in contemporary society.

The Conventional View

Self-esteem is generally (but imprecisely) defined as the evaluative dimension of the self-concept. It is viewed as a psychological state of self-evaluation on a scale that ranges from positive (or self-affirming) to negative (or self-denigrating). Although theoretically impoverished, this approach does foster straightforward measurement. Subjects reveal their level of self-esteem by agreeing or disagreeing with an array

of positive and negative self-referential statements. The classic measurement scales of Morris Rosenberg (1965) and Stanley Coopersmith (1967) take this approach. Self-esteem is operationalized by presenting the subject with statements such as "At times I think I am no good at all" or "On the whole I am satisfied with myself."

Investigators typically have been interested in both the antecedents and the consequences of self-esteem. They have examined the psychological processes and social conditions under which self-esteem is formed and sustained. What determines self-esteem, they have asked, and what accounts for stability and change in the self-concept? They also have been interested in the results of varying levels of self-esteem. Is low self-esteem the cause of socially undesirable or unproductive conduct? Does improving self-esteem lead to improvements in levels of individual achievement, happiness, or social adjustment?

Self-esteem researchers frequently emphasize its motivational import. The putative desire for a favorable self-concept is cited as an explanation for conduct ranging from socially conforming or prosocial behavior to deviant or antisocial behavior. People conform to social expectations in order to receive the approval of others, thereby enhancing self-esteem. They associate with others selectively, choosing those who will provide or confirm a positive self-evaluation. Therefore, people sometimes engage in deviant or antisocial conduct because it meets with the approval of one or another deviant reference group. They take on tasks and responsibilities at which they stand a chance of succeeding, thereby hoping to secure feelings of efficacy (Rosenberg, 1979, 1981). The quest for self-esteem also is said to motivate social perception: A self-serving bias guards self-esteem by allowing individuals to take credit for accomplishments and assign blame elsewhere for failure (Brown & Rogers, 1991; Miller & Ross, 1975; Snyder, Higgins, & Stucky, 1983).

The conventional approach to self-esteem has spawned a research literature of such magnitude and richness that it is impossible to summarize. The reader is referred to sources that can reveal far better than I the nuances of self-esteem (Gecas & Burke, 1995; Mecca, Smelser, & Vasconcellos, 1989; Wells & Marwell, 1976). In this chapter I attempt something more difficult but also potentially more rewarding. Rather than summarize the complex findings of this literature, I ask what the concept of self-esteem means in cultural terms. I take the position that psychological findings about self-esteem are not universal or essential facts but discoveries about the psychology of socially, culturally, and historically situated human beings.

My first task is therefore one of deconstruction. Suspending interest in self-esteem as a psychological variable opens the possibility of analyzing its cultural significance.

Deconstructing Self-Esteem

The contemporary psychological understanding of self-esteem is rooted in four ideas—acceptance, evaluation, comparison, and efficacy—that show strong and historically persistent resonance in American culture. Because a great deal of research has gone into identifying these elements and establishing their importance to self-esteem, it is tempting to accept them as "real." As theorists and researchers we understand that they are constructs and are not reality themselves, but they nonetheless seem to have the solidity of "facts." This is even more the case with popular audiences for psychological ideas, for whom self-esteem is an objectively real fact of human existence, one that

comes with the authority of science. Nonetheless, self-esteem is a social construction whose cultural roots can be uncovered.

To the contemporary mind, self-esteem seems anchored in unqualified acceptance of the child early in life, the receipt of positive evaluations from relevant others, favorable comparisons with others and with ideal versions of the self, and the capacity for efficacious action. Self-esteem is in the first instance thought to be dependent upon the child's acceptance within the social fold without regard to particular performances. It is built early on a foundation of security, trust, and unconditional love. Later, whatever standards of evaluation are employed, positive evaluations will enhance self-esteem and negative evaluations will damage it, other things being equal. Whether standards emphasize the accomplishment of challenging tasks or appropriate displays of "personality," positive is good, negative is bad. Likewise, self-esteem is enhanced when the person is able to make favorable comparisons with other people or with an ideal self, and it is enhanced when the person acts effectively in his or her physical or social environment (Damon, 1995; Gecas & Schwalbe, 1983; Owens, 1995; Rosenberg, 1979; Swann, 1996; Wills, 1981).

Membership in and acceptance by some group, the evaluation of persons along various dimensions, the propensity to make invidious comparisons, and the importance placed on individual action are deeply embedded in contemporary American culture. This culture fosters anxiety about the person's acceptance by others, emphasizing the individual's responsibility to create a social world or to carve out a place in an existing one where he or she can be warmly embraced. Likewise, American culture makes available numerous situations in which the individual is exposed to evaluation, imagines the evaluations others are making, or engages in self-evaluation. It provides numerous comparative occasions on which individuals reflect on how well or ill they fare in comparison with relevant others or with possible or desirable versions of themselves. And American culture emphasizes the capacity and responsibility of the individual to act independently and effectively (Bellah, Madsen, Sullivan, Swidler, & Tipton, 1985; Hewitt, 1998).

It is true, of course, that all human beings presumably need some minimal sense of belonging to a group. The propensity to evaluate is likewise inherent in the human condition.

Every individual or cooperative act has consequences for the welfare of the group as a whole, and some acts will have negative consequences and thus earn disapproval. Every role performance is a potential site for evaluation, and it is difficult to imagine a human society in which exceptionally fine or exceptionally bad performances do not receive special attention. Likewise, because human societies inevitably seem to hold up ideals to their members, comparisons with these ideals are an inevitable feature of group life. And the successful consummation of an act is intrinsically satisfying.

Acceptance, evaluation, comparison, and efficacy may be inherent features of the human condition, but particular cultures tend to magnify or diminish their importance and shape the ways in which they are problematic. A culture may make acceptance easily attainable or highly problematic, provide few or many evaluative and comparative occasions, and emphasize either individually efficacious actions or collective responsibility for success or failure. American culture makes the individual responsible for finding acceptance in a social world—for cultivating and making friends, establishing occupational or professional ties, or finding a mate. Likewise, it provides many evaluative and comparative occasions: Children are graded in school, rated on their athletic or musical prowess and accomplishments, and assigned to "popular" or "unpopular" peer groups. Adults are evaluated for their appearance and work performance. Social comparisons occur as parents compare their children with others, assess their own accomplishments relative to their aspirations, and strive to keep up with the social standing of their friends and neighbors. Furthermore, the individual rather than the group typically is held accountable and earns credit and satisfaction for actions performed.

Moreover, American culture does not present a single face with respect to acceptance, evaluation, comparison, and efficacy but rather seems in general to be highly conflicted about these and related matters (Erikson, 1976; Hewitt, 1989, 1998). The social world often is portrayed as an interpersonal oyster for the individual to crack and enjoy, but Americans also look wistfully for places where acceptance is guaranteed and "everybody knows your name." Schools do not apply evaluative criteria with equal rigor in all aspects of students' activities: Academic standards often are lax, and social promotion is expected, whereas only those with talent and a ca-

pacity for hard work make the varsity football team or the school orchestra. Powerful norms of social equality—especially with respect to the right of every child to feelings of self-worth—run counter to evaluation, comparison, and efficacy. Children are told to work hard and achieve but also that they have the right to feel good about themselves no matter how they do, that they should compete only with themselves, and that failure at a task does not mean they are not worthy human beings (Hewitt, 1998).

The cultural reality, then, is one of strong ambivalence about acceptance, evaluation, comparison, and efficacy. The individual's acceptance as a member of a group or community is thought to depend upon "personality" and a capacity for "networking" but also to be something to which all are entitled. Self-worth is held to depend upon adherence to standards but also to be an individual's right no matter how well he or she meets those standards. Social comparison is everywhere—in styles and levels of consumption, in the expression of values, in group membership—but it coexists with a powerful cultural ideology of equality. Individual efficacy is emphasized, yet there exists a vast vocabulary of excuses, apologies, justifications, and disclaimers that permit individuals to dismiss their failures. "Be all that you can be!" and "Accept yourself for who and what you are" both stand as compelling, albeit dissonant, messages for contemporary Americans.

Cultural Emphases and the Discourse of Self-Esteem

Self-esteem, both as an individual experience and as a topic of discourse, arises from a particular framework of cultural concerns. The question is why? That is, why do people experience a psychological reality that we have come to call self-esteem, and why do they engage in professional and popular discourse about it? I will begin by examining talk about self-esteem, for the character of this talk provides clues to the underlying nature of the reality that we have constructed and that we call self-esteem.

Acceptance, evaluation, comparison, and efficacy identify a core set of felt difficulties arising from the cultural polarities discussed earlier. Am I a person in good standing in my family, peer group, community, or profession? Am I a worthy person? How do I compare with others? Am I effective in my work or in my family life? To say that these terms identify felt difficulties is to say that American culture makes problematic what could be far less problematic. Acceptance is uncertain, personal worth is not assured, comparison of self with others is a more or less constant preoccupation, and efficacy is frequently in doubt. Moreover, it is the individual who experiences such difficulties and who must construct answers to such questions. Where do *I* belong? What am *I* worth? How do *I* compare with my peers? Have *I* accomplished what *I* should?

There is, to be sure, a powerful, countervailing collectivist impulse in the culture that mitigates its intense individualism. For some people under some conditions, self-worth is established by membership in a group and association with its members, social comparisons are between groups, and individuals take pride in group accomplishments. But the impulse to define the individual in relation to the collectivity—whether an ethnic, occupational, neighborhood, familial, or religious community—runs counter to a prime cultural emphasis on the individual. Americans' "first language" is that of individualism, and it is in relation to this language that the discourse of self-esteem has developed.

The discourse of self-esteem provides a "lingua franca"—a common language—Americans use to discuss felt difficulties with self-definition and self-validation, and in the same breath address cultural contradictions. *Self-esteem* is a word that cuts across lines of cultural division and, in doing so, provides a basis both for experiencing the culture and for resolving some of the difficulties it creates. This common language bridges competing definitions of success and happiness, providing for both competitive striving and self-acceptance, contentment in the present and excitement about the future. Moreover, it bridges individualism and collectivism, providing a central concept—self-esteem—on whose attainment all can agree even as they disagree on the proper means of attaining it. "Self-esteem" is a unifying object in a culture riven with contradictions and disagreements about the self. Self-esteem is a "real" experience, to be sure, and later I will attempt to delineate its psychological underpinnings. For the moment, however, I will concentrate on self-esteem as a term of discourse.

Americans take it for granted that it is good to have self-esteem—that the individual should ideally be able to experience and manifest feelings of worth, value, and positive self-feeling.

Those who lack self-esteem are wounded, and their capacity to act as cultural members is damaged. Beyond this surface consensus, however, their use of the word *self-esteem* conceals some fundamental disagreements about the sources, purpose, and effects of adequate or high self-esteem. In one view, self-esteem lies within the individual's control; he or she can learn to feel positively about self by engaging in a variety of techniques of verbal self-affirmation and positive thinking. In the contrasting view, self-esteem derives from the social world that surrounds the individual, and so the collectivity (the family, the peer group, the school) is obligated to treat its members in ways that will enhance their self-esteem. For some, the development of positive self-feelings is an end in itself, needing no justification because it is an individual entitlement. For others, self-esteem is valued primarily because it is a means to the attainment of individually or socially desirable ends—personal achievement in school or occupation, for example, or the avoidance of socially costly forms of behavior such as drug addiction, teen pregnancy, or delinquency. And while, for some, self-esteem is a right and therefore requires nothing of the individual other than self-affirmation, for others it is a privilege to be earned by appropriate conduct (Hewitt, 1998).

Currents of social disagreement swirl around the unifying object of self-esteem. The discourse of self-esteem persists because it contributes to the realization and reproduction of some fundamental divisions within the culture. That is, talk of self-esteem makes real and thus renews basic cultural fissures, even as it is used as a means of bridging them.

Americans are urged by their Declaration of Independence to feel entitled to the "pursuit of happiness" and by long tradition to believe each person deserves a chance at success. But the meanings of happiness and success have never been clear, and this ambiguity is a key to the psychology of Americans. Happiness is enjoined as a pursuit, which implies that its attainment is not guaranteed but depends on individual effort. Everyone deserves a chance at success, but some will grasp the brass ring and others will not. In this dominant version of cultural values, happiness and success are objects to strive for and to attain at some point in the future. But happiness and success also are seen as entitlements—conditions guaranteed to individuals as a matter of right and not something to be withheld from them or whose absence is tolerable (Hewitt, 1989).

These contrasting meanings of happiness and success mirror an American ambivalence about equality, specifically whether to emphasize equality of opportunity or equality of condition. The classic American tradition of equality emphasized a level playing field: Everybody should have a fair start at the game and play under the same rules. But the belief that Americans are entitled to equality of condition increasingly has gained adherents, and the scope of conditions that fall under "equal rights" has expanded. Happiness and success have to some degree become rights of citizenship (Marshall, 1964) rather than prizes to be sought and won.

Differing versions of self-esteem mirror these contrasting meanings of success, happiness, and equality. One cluster of meanings of self-esteem emphasizes that it is not a right but a privilege, to be achieved by individual effort and a willingness to develop appropriate attitudes and behavior. The other cluster emphasizes that self-esteem is an entitlement, that it requires no behavioral changes, and that the individual can bootstrap himself or herself to self-affirming feelings. Long-standing cultural disputes are thus expressed, and so also reproduced, in new terms as people debate the real nature of self-esteem and wonder on what basis they can feel "right" about themselves.

The language of self-esteem thus translates deeply rooted cultural issues into personal terms: Have I found a place where I belong and others like or respect me? Am I as happy or as successful as I could be? Am I entitled to think better of myself than I do? How can I feel better about me? What must I do to feel better? How can I justify the way I feel about myself? For those who are engaged in the *pursuit* of happiness and success and who feel themselves well on the way, "self-esteem" is a way of characterizing—and experiencing—their positive feelings about their lives. A view of self-esteem as something earned by virtue of effort and accomplishment validates their way of pursuing happiness and success. For those who feel themselves not far enough along on the path, talk of earning self-esteem is a motivational spur to further effort. It provides a way of imagining a future self and, in doing so, focusing present efforts on its attainment.

In contrast, those who espouse communitarian rather than individualist definitions of self, as well as those who have tried but failed in a future-oriented quest for success and happiness, also can find in the discourse of self-esteem the basis for comforting and reassuring self-perceptions. I am entitled to feel good about myself, one might say, because I am surrounded by friends and family who value me for virtues that transcend financial success. I am good and virtuous in their world. I am happy with who I am, another might say, for even though I have not gone far professionally or financially, I am content with my life and with those among whom I live.

The discourse of self-esteem thus provides a basis for experiencing and interpreting the very culture in which that discourse has arisen. Its vocabulary bridges cultural polarities, providing a common framework of understanding even in the midst of disagreement about what self-esteem means. In creating the concept of self-esteem and laying the basis for a popular discourse about it, social scientists thus have inadvertently done the culture an important service. In studying self-esteem professionally, they contribute to what Michel Foucault called "technologies of the self," creating the very terms and instruments whereby the self is experienced (Martin, Gutman, & Hutton, 1998). Their professional contribution has in turn fueled the efforts of legions of "conceptual entrepreneurs" who market the idea of self-esteem as well as techniques for its improvement.

The Experience of Self-Esteem

What is the *experience* of self-esteem in this culture? The approach I recommend here defines self-esteem as a socially constructed emotion. That is, self-esteem is a reflexive emotion that has developed over time in social processes of invention, that individuals learn to experience and to talk about, that arises in predictable social circumstances, and that is subject to social control (Smith-Lovin, 1995). Anchoring self-esteem within the realm of emotions gives a more precise theoretical formulation than its definition as the evaluative dimension of self-regard and better captures the reality of the experience from the individual's standpoint. Defining the emotion of self-esteem as a social construction permits consideration of cultural variations in self-esteem but at the same time allows one to examine its underlying visceral, physiological, and neurological correlates.

In this approach, emotions are named experiences, arising as individual responses to social life. Fear, anger, joy, and—in this analysis—self-esteem arise in individuals as they participate in everyday rounds of social activity as well as encounter frustrating, traumatic, exciting, or otherwise unusual circumstances. To say that these emotions are named is to say that experiencing an emotion requires that the individual interpret his or her response. Joy may be a spontaneous response to certain positive events, but to experience joy is to name the emotion and talk about it. Likewise, self-esteem may be a "natural" response for individuals in certain social circumstances, but its experience likewise requires naming and interpretation.

Emotions are associated with lines of activity. In the classic Jamesian formulation (James, 1890), we experience joy "because" we celebrate happy events. That is, the interpretive experience of joy occurs in connection with lines of activity associated with joy. These associations are as much conventional as natural, which is to say that they are more than simply animal responses to situations that inevitably provoke happiness. "We are joyful because we celebrate" means that we have learned to associate the emotion of joy with the activities in which we express joy and communicate its presence to others. The emotion of joy is a meaningful and not merely an automatic response to a situation and to particular lines of conduct within it.

Socially constructed emotions are, therefore, situated experiences and not merely constant or variable psychological states. That is, such emotions arise at predictable times and places under the influence of role requirements as well as status relationships, success or failure in the attainment of socially prescribed goals, and the actual or imagined evaluative judgments of others. This approach makes self-esteem more dependent upon the situation and its demands, opening the possibility that people manage self-esteem in the same ways they manage other emotions. That is, within limits, it proposes that people can lower or elevate self-esteem in response to role requirements, presenting a self with appropriate manifestations of self-esteem in much the same way they use the techniques of surface and deep acting to appear sad at funerals or happy at weddings (Hochschild, 1979).

Whether people feel proud or ashamed of their actions, are urged to think of themselves as inherently loathsome or angelic, or learn to interpret some feeling states as "self-esteem,"

affect is a central element of self-experience. The range of affect that may be directed toward the self is for all practical purposes the same as the range of affect of which humans are capable. That is, fear, anger, hatred, love, pride, satisfaction, anxiety, loathing, shame, guilt, embarrassment, and the like all figure in the experience of self in varying degrees and circumstances. These emotions may be aroused by one's thoughts and actions or by the words and deeds of others, and they apply as powerfully to the self as to any other object.

No one of these forms of self-directed affect is by itself the core of self-esteem. Yet what we—social scientists and lay people alike—understand as self-esteem is in one way or another tied to these emotional experiences. When we seek to develop items to measure self-attitudes, we readily turn to pride, shame, hatred, satisfaction, and other words in our cultural vocabulary of emotions as ways of communicating to subjects the kinds of self-reports we want from them. We may understand that self-esteem is none of these emotions in particular, but we sense it has something to do with some or all of them. People with low self-esteem are apt to say that they hate themselves, or that they are unhappy, or that they are anxious about how others view them. People with high self-esteem are apt to speak pridefully about themselves, to express satisfaction, to label themselves as self-confident.

The core of feeling to which a variety of other emotions become alloyed in the constructed emotion of self-esteem is best termed *mood*. Like other terms, mood carries considerable cultural baggage—there is no such thing as a culture-free world. However, mood offers a somewhat more primitive term, one that moves us closer to the affective reality that lies at the core of what we in the contemporary world know as self-esteem. Although difficult to define, even in culturally loaded terms, it offers a purchase on the linkage between affect, the self, and such higher order emotional constructs as self-esteem.

I use mood in its conventional sense of a generalized aroused or subdued disposition. At one extreme of mood lies euphoria—a pervasive good feeling that the individual might describe in a variety of culturally available terms: energized, happy, "psyched," self-confident, elated. At the other extreme lies dysphoria—a similarly pervasive feeling described in culturally opposite terms such as listless, sad, fearful, anxious, or depressed. In a state of mood closer to euphoria, the individual is aroused, organized, ready to act; in a state closer to dysphoria, the individual is more reserved, fearful, and reluctant to act. I posit that mood is a crucial animal experience; that it lies close to neurological, physiological, and visceral reality; that variations in mood are universal and can be explained in general terms; and that the words used to label mood are cultural constructs.

Self-esteem is not the only higher order construct applied to the universal human experience of mood. People tending toward euphoria may report that they are happy, excited, or self-confident, or that they feel good or are in a good mood. They may respond to self-esteem measures in ways that lead a social scientist to attribute high self-esteem to them. They may strike a clinician as healthy or, if too euphoric, as manic. And if they have access to the discourse of self-esteem, as nearly everyone nowadays does, they may say that they have high self-esteem. Variations in mood are describable by a variety of higher order cultural constructs, none of which provides the basis for an analysis of the nature of mood, its level, or of fluctuations in it.

Labels for mood have social and cultural origins. The contemporary individual afflicted with a mood disorder, for example, has access to the social machinery of psychiatry and its arsenal of therapies, medicines, and diagnostic categories. He or she will thus have the opportunity—and sometimes be under considerable social pressure—to accept a label of major depression and to take the steps recommended by psychologists, social workers, or psychiatrists. The 17th-century New England Puritan who had similar feelings of sadness, lack of self-worth, and morbid social sensitivity might well have been encouraged to look within. Believing in humankind's inherently sinful nature and uncertain of his or her own state of grace, such an individual would have found a different explanation for the same underlying feelings, and a different program of action would have been recommended.

The interpretation of underlying affective states, perhaps especially ones so generalized as mood, is thus shaped by the social processes that create and certify knowledge and assign its implementation to various experts. Interpretations also are shaped by the goals and values of particular cultures. Arguably the depressed Puritan found himself or herself culturally, if not personally, more at ease, for a dark mood could at least be assigned religious meaning and thus be accommodated by others. Contemporary Americans are enjoined to be happy and self-confident, and thus find in depression and low self-esteem painful personal experiences that their social world does not readily tolerate.

The Social Import of Mood

Mood, which has been extensively studied by psychologists, poses a complex challenge to social theory. Mood is both an unperceived background of everyday action and an object of attention in its own right. In other words, mood influences thoughts and actions, but it is also something people think about and act toward. It is influenced by events in the person's world but also by endogenous factors of which the individual has no knowledge. Hence, a good mood may result from the reality or appearance of something good happening, including events that result from individual actions. But a good mood also may arise or disappear independently of events as a result of malfunctioning neurotransmission (Morris, 1989).

Although the word *mood* sometimes is (Isen, 1984) used synonymously with "affect," Batson's (1990) distinction between *affect, mood,* and *emotion* is more helpful. *Affect* is the most general and primitive of the terms, and following Zajonc (1980), Batson argues that it serves to inform the organism about the more and less valued "states of affairs" it experiences. Changes toward more valued states of affairs produce positive affect, whereas changes toward less valued states produce negative affect. *Mood* is a more complex affective state, because it entails more or less well-formed *expectations* about the future experience of positive or negative affect. Mood is constituted by a change in expectation (together with the affective state evoked by the change), and thus refers to "the fine-tuning of one's perception of the general affective tone of what lies ahead" (Batson, 1990, p. 103). *Emotions* are present-oriented, focused on the person's relationship to a specific goal. Whereas the experience of a happy mood implies the expectation of more positive affect in the future, the emotion of joy arises in the present as goals are attained or attained more fully than imagined.

These ideas provide some support for a strong social determinism, in which affect, mood, and emotion are the key elements in the development and maintenance of ties between the individual and the social order. Culture supplements psychologically intrinsic satisfactions with its own menu of approved goals and definitions of positive affect. The social order governs access to the cognitive and material means of pursuing a socially approved goal—knowing what to do and how to do it, and having the resources needed to realize a desired end. Hence, the sources of positive affect, of changes in the expectation of positive affect, and of the person's capacity to act so as to create positive events lie in culture and society. External events shape affect, mood, and emotion, resulting in a tendency for people to do what others require, encourage, or make possible. Following socially approved courses of action to approved goals produces positive affect, inclines individuals to anticipate more such affect in the future, and rewards them with positive emotions in each succeeding present.

This strong social determinism is in several ways defective. First, it does not take sufficient account of the need to interpret mood or of the potential for interpretive variability. Morris (1989) suggests that mood is figure as well as ground. As Batson (1990) defines it, mood is a more or less well-defined set of *expectations* about the future. And as a sociologist in the symbolic interactionist tradition might put it, mood begins with an affective state but becomes mood only as the individual invokes a culturally supplied vocabulary and formulates those expectations in specific terms. Affective states demand interpretation, and it is in the process of interpretation that moods and emotions are created.

Moreover, interpretations of affective states vary, for there is no firm link between an affective state and the individual's perception of its origins or of the steps that might produce a more desired state. People make errors in attribution. Culture provides alternative goals and alternative vocabularies for experiencing mood and emotion. Hence, it is not necessarily obvious to the individual what actions will produce a more desirable affective result, and the link between social demands and individual lines of conduct is therefore not always a strong one.

Second, even though mood typically is linked to events, the linkage is not simple, and sometimes it breaks. Events do produce positive and negative affect and thus inform the organism of "states of affairs" that it does or does not value.

And such positive or negative affect may subsequently shape the expectation of future affective states. Thus, affective arousal influences mood, which in turn influences the person's approach to (or avoidance of) objects in the future. However, two psychological phenomena warn against strong social determinism. The "positivity offset" helps explain people's willingness sometimes to depart from established, socially patterned forms of conduct. Even without positive affective arousal there is a bias toward approaching an object even at great distance from it. How else, as Cacioppo and Gardner (1999) point out, could we expect the organism "to approach novel objects, stimuli, or contexts" (p. 191). Likewise, organisms react more strongly to negative stimuli than to positive ones. Presumably this negativity bias evolved to protect the organism against the untoward consequences of its own exploratory actions.

Moreover, endogenous factors—such as problems in neurotransmission—may govern mood on schedules independent of external events. Major depression, for example, may be precipitated by an external event that happens to the individual, but it also may arise spontaneously and for no reason apparent either to the observer or to the depressed person. Likewise, the rapid cycling that sometimes occurs in bipolar disorder puts those afflicted on a mood roller coaster over whose speed and direction they have no control. We refer to these conditions as *mood disorders* precisely because they subvert an orderly link between events and mood.

Third, mood shapes the person's perception of the social world and his or her experiences in it. The significance of events and of those who produce them is not given solely in the events themselves, for affect strongly influences what we see and how we make sense of it. Affect shapes attention and perception (Zajonc, 1998), memory (Phelps & Anderson, 1997), and altruism (Batson, 1990). Indeed, Isen (1984) argues that "affective states—even mild and even positive affective states—can influence thoughts, cognitive processing, and social behavior in some remarkable ways" (pp. 179–180). Thus, illustratively, people in a positive affective state seem to remember positive events better than negative ones (Isen, 1984). Positive moods increase helping behavior; more precisely, events that enhance mood make it more likely that those whose moods are enhanced will help others who were not responsible for the enhanced mood (Batson, 1990). And mood influences the way we think about other persons through a mood-congruent judgment effect. Improvements in mood are accompanied by more positive views of other people (Mayer & Hanson, 1995).

From the standpoint of a psychologically informed social theory, positive mood is most usefully seen as encouraging the perception of the social world in relatively benign and non-threatening terms. It fosters the perception of a self at ease with its others, one capable of taking actions they will find acceptable or at least understandable. It furthers the perception of a self accepted by friends and available for role-based interaction with strangers. In contrast, negative mood encourages the perception of a hostile social world and a self at risk in it. The dysphoric self is not a self at ease but an anxious self—anxious about what to do, about how others will respond, about the likelihood of taking successful action. It is a self located in a social world that may turn hostile at any moment, that may conceal its true attitudes, that may erect obstacles in the person's path. A euphoric person imagines a social world where it is easy to perceive opportunities, friendly and receptive others, and successful lines of conduct. A dysphoric person imagines a social world filled with obstacles, resistant or unfriendly others, and limited chances for success.

Mood, Self-Esteem, and Discourse

The time has come to draw together the lines of analysis developed here and to examine their significance for the positive psychology of the individual in the contemporary world. I begin by explaining why self-esteem is best analyzed as a socially constructed emotion grounded in mood.

Self-esteem has been constructed in an American cultural context that enjoins the pursuit of happiness and success. Although subject to conflicting definitions, these are nonetheless culturally important goals. When culture sets goals, people respond in two ways that are key to the analysis. First, they respond affectively to their pursuit and attainment of these goals. Success and failure generate positive and negative *affect* and produce changes in expectations of future affect, that is, *mood*. Mood is in part a product of how successfully the person has formed attachments to the social world and of

how well he or she has achieved its culturally enjoined goals. A sense of membership in the social world and of proper attainment of cultural ideals engenders elevated mood; failure in these respects engenders depressed mood.

Second, people respond to mood by interpreting it. Human beings are creatures who must name and interpret mood in order to link it to social and cultural reality. They engage in discourse that explores the meaning of cultural goals, of individuals' success or failure in attaining them, and of the resulting affective experiences. Individuals who are situated at particular times and places interpret their mood experiences by utilizing a language—a vocabulary and grammar of emotions—that is available to them as members of a social world and participants in its culture. To understand mood and its relationship to self-esteem, then, we must examine the linguistic opportunities that are available to individuals and the forces that constrain their selection.

Self-esteem is a relatively new linguistic opportunity for Americans. Although the word has been used professionally by psychologists and sociologists for over a hundred years, it gained popular currency only in the last third of the twentieth century. Its relative newness, therefore, may provide a clue to its contemporary appeal and significance. In particular, the construction of a language and an emotion of self-esteem has come about in response to the American cultural polarities discussed earlier. The polarities themselves are long-standing ones and they have been dealt with culturally in a variety of ways, most notably in the tradition of "positive thinking" (Meyer, 1988). It is the vocabulary of self-esteem that is relatively new.

The historically dominant pole of American culture emphasizes success as a result of individual achievement, happiness as a future state to be sought by individual effort, and equality of opportunity to seek success and happiness. In this version of the culture, the individual is a voluntary member of a social world and either succeeds or fails as an individual. Such cultural circumstances engender individual mood responses, for some will fail badly, others will succeed greatly, and most will fall somewhere in the middle. The interpretation of mood in this cultural moment, however, is unlikely to involve self-esteem. For even where the term and the experience of self-esteem exist, classic instrumental individualism (Bellah et al., 1985) has its own linguistic convention for interpreting the individual's experiences of success and failure, a convention in which the prominent terms are *pride* and *shame*.

It is difficult to imagine the enterprising farmers and mechanics who steadily populated the United States during the 19th century feeling or speaking of their "self-esteem" as enhanced by their success in wresting a living from the earth or creating new machines and industries. Rather, we today think of them—as they thought of themselves—as *proud* of their accomplishments and *ashamed* when they fell short in their own or their neighbors' eyes. Much the same was true of the industrialists of the late 19th century, and it remains true of individuals who subscribe to contemporary versions of instrumental individualism. They are proud when they succeed and ashamed when they fail. Pride is grounded in mood in much the same way as self-esteem is so anchored. But it is not the same emotion, for pride conveys images of self-respect and dignity, and the proud individual imagines an audience that applauds effort, hard work, achievement against the odds, and self-regard that is deserved because it has been earned.

Similarly, to fall short of one's own goals or the expectations of one's fellows engenders the emotion of shame. One who accepts an ethic of achievement is disappointed, downcast, depressed, and most of all ashamed when he or she fails. Like pride, shame interprets mood by emphasizing the individual's responsibility for a course of action and its outcome. The individual feels that he or she has failed and must therefore present a shameful face to the judging, evaluating world.

Self-esteem, in contrast, answers to the opposing pole of American culture, where the emphasis is more on expressive than instrumental individualism. Here, success and happiness are more likely to be viewed as entitlements, or at least to be subject to relaxed standards of evaluation. Thus, one is entitled to feel happy and successful regardless of one's station in life, or at the very least one can find validation of the right to feel contentment in lesser accomplishments. The social world is more likely to be seen as owing the individual both a respectable place and respect for occupying it. One's place in the social world ought to be assured. The watchword is equality of condition, not of opportunity.

It is this cultural configuration that fosters a language and emotion of self-esteem. There is

not room here to present the details of its creation over the last century. But it seems clear that this opposing moment of the culture has gradually found greater voice not only in the language of self-esteem but more broadly in humanistic psychology, in both secular and religious "positive thinking," and in assorted other popular psychologies and therapies that have proliferated in American life. Self-esteem has not driven out other words, nor has it trumped pride/shame as a principle motivating social emotion. Instrumental individualism is unlikely to disappear anytime soon. Indeed, that people nowadays debate the meaning of self-esteem (i.e., is it self-respect or self-liking?) is an indication that the sensibility of pride and shame persists even in the face of the new emotion of self-esteem.

Self-esteem does, however, support a different relationship between the individual and the social order. Pride and shame presume a relationship in which culture and society set goals for individuals and provide means for attaining them, and in which individuals readily accept cultural guidance. People feel proud and speak of pride when they achieve cultural ideals to which they feel positively attached. Self-esteem, in contrast, presumes a relatively more problematic, often oppositional relationship between the individual and the social world, one in which the individual feels at risk (cf. Turner, 1976). It is no accident that the self-esteem movement perceives an epidemic of low self-esteem and mounts a campaign to remedy the situation. In its frame of reference, self-esteem is an entitlement always at risk in a hostile, denigrating, judgmental social world.

What is the gain in transforming our view of self-esteem from a universal psychological trait and motivating force to a socially constructed emotion grounded in mood? Mainly, I think, it lies in a more precise understanding of the nature of the threat to the self posed by the social and cultural world in which we live, and of the ways human beings cope. To grasp how individuals function in that world, we must understand the emotional economy it creates for them and examine how they respond to it.

The emotion of self-esteem, the study of self-esteem, and a social movement that proposes to promote individual well-being and solve social problems by fostering self-esteem have arisen in a culture that puts the individual self on a shaky center stage. Acceptance, evaluation, comparison, and efficacy capture the main ways in which the experience of self is made precarious. The discourse and experience of self-esteem attempt to cope with this precarious existence by articulating a cultural vision of a satisfying personal life that runs explicitly counter to the dominant competitive, instrumental individualism. It proposes an alternative world in which the individual has a right to an assured place, evaluations are not the sole basis of positive self-feeling, social comparison is subdued, and all have the capacity for efficacious action and the right to positive self-regard. Where modern life depresses and enervates, those who emphasize self-esteem wish to elevate and energize.

Arguably, the discourse of self-esteem mounts a weak critique of American culture and a shaky program of action to counter it. The self-esteem movement and the discourse it employs often fail to recognize the tenacity of competitive individualism. Programs that seek to elevate individual self-esteem through positive thinking, "self-talk" (Helmstetter, 1987), and other forms of psychological bootstrapping merely pose a weaker expressive individualism against a dominant instrumental individualism. Such programs thus merely reproduce an existing set of cultural definitions rather than challenging them. They convey the illusion of action to solve personal and social problems, but in doing so accept the terms of the debate as it has been constructed by the dominant individualism. Most crucially for the present analysis, the discourse of self-esteem is apt to confuse a sign of well-being with its essence.

As a socially constructed and experienced emotion, self-esteem is more a sign of well-being than a condition that defines its essence. This is so in two senses. First, reasonably good self-esteem provides an indication that mood is working within optimal limits to motivate and caution human action. Self-esteem is a measure of the person's expectation of positive events and, accordingly, her or his willingness to approach objects and others. Second, and more broadly, good self-esteem is indicative of a positive and integral personal and social identity (cf. Hewitt, 1989)—that is, a sense that one is located securely in the social world, competent to meet its challenges, ready to participate in life with others, and able to balance social demands and personal desires (cf. Scheff, 1990).

Although self-esteem is a desirable state (or trait) because of what it signifies about personal well-being, it is not clear that the most effective way to achieve good self-esteem is through specific programs to promote it. The fundamental mistake of the self-esteem movement is not to emphasize its importance but to imagine that self-esteem is itself the goal to be pursued. Conditions that promote optimal human functioning also promote self-esteem, and these fundamental conditions are the ones worth pursuing: acceptance within a social fold, a sense of security, cultural competence, and the capacity to reconcile personal goals and social expectations.

Does the contemporary discourse and experience of self-esteem have any practical value, then, in fostering happier, more fully competent, creative human beings? Does it in any sense enhance life? The answer is emphatically yes. First, talk about self-esteem is itself to some degree healthful and restorative, given the particular burdens that American culture imposes by putting the individual person on a difficult center stage. Although the discourse of self-esteem provides a weak social critique and a blunted definition of individual human rights, it nonetheless carries the human banner haltingly forward. It asserts the right of all to "life, liberty, and the pursuit of happiness" in a society where too frequently only a few have enjoyed these conditions. Talk of human possibilities open to all may not enable people directly to realize these possibilities, but such talk does shape the conventional wisdom of what human beings may know, what they may hope, and what they should do (Snyder, Rand, & Sigmon, this volume).

Second, the experience of self-esteem, as opposed to discourse about it, has two notable features. As a sign of a positive and integral sense of self—of healthy personal and social identity—self-esteem is a culturally relevant measure of well-being. In a culture that so often poses individual and community against one another and provides conflicting criteria of success and happiness, self-esteem measures the success of individual efforts to come to grips with these cultural exigencies. To be able to hold oneself in solid and reasonably high regard is to have achieved something of value in a culture that makes the achievement of that goal both important and difficult.

Moreover, a positive and integral sense of identity—of which self-esteem is a key measure—is crucially important because it is fundamental to the capacity for empathic role taking, the capacity to see and to identify with the other's point of view. Positive and well-regulated mood, of which self-esteem is a key sign, is fundamental to the capacity to see virtue in others, good purposes in their action, and cooperative rather than competitive goals.

The American pragmatist philosopher George Herbert Mead (1934) thought that a defining attribute of human beings is our capacity to take the perspective of the other and thus to see things from the vantage point of a friend, a spouse, an enemy, the community of which one is a part, even the whole of humanity. By imaginatively "taking the role of the other," Mead said, the individual is able not only to govern his or her conduct so that it meshes with that of the other but also, and perhaps of greater significance, to empathize, to feel what the other is feeling and not only to think what the other is thinking. Mead was an optimist. He envisioned a world in which people would eventually learn to act in the interests of humanity as a whole, and in which individual creativity could live side by side with concern for the welfare of the community. The images of human nature favored by many contemporary social scientists are self-interest, conflict, and a propensity to exercise power over others whenever and however it is possible to do so. Even giving due credit to realism, this is a sad state of affairs for social science and for humanity.

I share Mead's fundamental optimism and believe it crucial to sustain it. More clearly than others he saw how self-interest and the good of the community might be reconciled. Individuals are products of their community but also its creators. We are, he saw, creatures with selves, who by their very nature are both separate from and joined to others. Although Mead emphasized the cognitive nature of the link between the individual and the community, his ideas provide a basis for understanding the equal or greater importance of affect in this relationship. My analysis of self-esteem in this chapter is grounded in these ideas. When people talk of self-esteem, they are expressing the importance of the affective link between themselves and others; when they experience self-esteem, they are living this connection. Discourse about self-esteem and the pursuit of it encounters many pitfalls and takes many wrong turns. Even so, the quest for a better social world and a better individual is advanced by a discourse that encourages people to explore the nature and importance of the social bond and by practices that seek to enhance it.

References

Batson, C. D. (1990). Affect and altruism. In B. S. Moore & A. M. Isen (Eds.), *Affect and social behavior* (pp. 89–125). Cambridge, England: Cambridge University Press.

Bellah, R. N., Madsen, R., Sullivan, W. M., Swidler, A., & Tipton, S. (1985). *Habits of the heart: Individualism and commitment in American life*. Berkeley: University of California Press.

Brown, J. D., & Rogers, R. J. (1991). Self-serving attributions: The role of physiological arousal. *Personality and Social Psychology Bulletin, 17,* 501–506.

Cacioppo, J. T., & Gardner, W. L. (1999). Emotion. In *Annual Review of Psychology*, 1999, Gale Group: WWW Version.

Coopersmith, S. (1967). *The antecedents of self-esteem*. San Francisco: Freeman.

*Damon, W. (1995). *Greater expectations: Overcoming the culture of indulgence in America's homes and schools*. New York: Free Press.

Erikson, K. T. (1976). *Everything in its path*. New York: Simon and Schuster.

*Gecas, V., & Burke, P. (1995). Self and identity. In K. Cook, G. A. Fine, & J. S. House (Eds.), *Sociological perspectives on social psychology* (pp. 41–67). Boston: Allyn and Bacon.

Gecas, V., & Schwalbe, M. (1983). Beyond the looking-glass self: Social structure and efficacy-based self-esteem. *Social Psychology Quarterly, 46,* 77–88.

Helmstetter, S. (1987). *The self-talk solution*. New York: Morrow.

*Hewitt, J. P. (1989). *Dilemmas of the American self*. Philadelphia: Temple University Press.

*Hewitt, J. P. (1998). *The myth of self-esteem: Finding happiness and solving problems in America*. New York: St. Martin's.

*Hochschild, A. R. (1979). Emotion work, feeling rules, and social structure. *American Sociological Review, 85,* 551–575.

Isen, A. M. (1984). Toward understanding the role of affect in cognition. In R. S. Wyer, Jr., & T. K. Srull (Eds.), *Handbook of social cognition* (Vol. 3, pp. 179–236). Hillsdale, NJ: Erlbaum.

James, W. (1890). *Principles of psychology*. New York: Holt.

Marshall, T. H. (1964). *Class, citizenship, and social development: Essays*. Garden City, NY: Doubleday.

Martin, L. H., Gutman, H., & Hutton, P. H. (Eds.). (1988). *Technologies of the self: A seminar with Michel Foucault*. Amherst: University of Massachusetts Press.

Mayer, J. D., & Hanson, E. (1995). Mood-congruent judgment over time. *Personality and Social Psychology Bulletin, 21,* 237–244.

*Mead, G. H. (1934). *Mind, self, and society*. Chicago: University of Chicago Press.

*Mecca, A. M., Smelser, N. J., & Vasconcellos, J.

(Eds.). (1989). *The social importance of self-esteem.* Berkeley: University of California Press.

Meyer, D. (1988). *The positive thinkers* (rev. ed.). Middletown, CT: Wesleyan University Press.

Miller, D. T., & Ross, M. (1975). Self-serving biases in attribution of causality: Fact or fiction? *Psychological Bulletin, 82,* 313–325.

Morris, W. N. (1989). *Mood: The frame of mind.* New York: Springer-Verlag.

Owens, K. (1995). *Raising your child's inner self-esteem: The authoritative guide from infancy through the teen years.* New York: Plenum.

Phelps, E. A., & Anderson, A. K. (1997). Emotional memory: What does the amygdala do? *Current Biology, 7,* 311–314.

Rosenberg, M. (1965). *Society and the adolescent self-image.* Princeton, NJ: Princeton University Press.

*Rosenberg, M. (1979). *Conceiving the self.* New York: Basic Books.

Rosenberg, M. (1981). The self-concept: Social product and social force. In M. Rosenberg & R. Turner (Eds.), *Social psychology: Sociological perspectives* (pp. 593–624). New York: Basic Books.

Scheff, T. J. (1990). *Microsociology: Discourse, emotion, and social structure.* Chicago: University of Chicago Press.

Smith-Lovin, L. (1995). The sociology of affect and emotion. In K. Cook, G. A. Fine, & J. S. House, (Eds.), *Sociological perspectives on social psychology* (pp. 118–148). Boston: Allyn and Bacon.

Snyder, C. R., Higgins, R. L., & Stucky, R. (1983). *Excuses: Masquerades in search of grace.* New York: Wiley Interscience.

*Swann, W. (1996). *Self-traps: The elusive quest for higher self-esteem.* New York: Freeman.

Turner, R. H. (1976). The real self: From institution to impulse. *American Journal of Sociology, 81,* 989–1016.

Wells, L. E., & Marwell, G. (1976). *Self-esteem.* Beverly Hills, CA: Sage.

Wills, T. A. (1981). Downward comparison principles in social psychology. *Psychological Bulletin, 90,* 245–271.

Zajonc, R. B. (1980). Feeling and thinking: Preferences need no inferences. *American Psychologist, 35,* 151–175.

Zajonc, R. B. (1998). Emotions. In D. T. Gilbert, S. T. Fiske, & L. Gardner (Eds.), *Handbook of social psychology* (pp. 591–634). New York: Oxford University Press.

11

The Adaptive Potential of Coping Through Emotional Approach

Annette L. Stanton, Anita Parsa, & Jennifer L. Austenfeld

I used to be pretty reserved, but since this breast cancer diagnosis, I've learned how important it is to express my emotions. I've started a journal, where I can say exactly how I feel. When I'm having a bad day with cancer, I make sure I write about it or talk about it. It's hard to face some of the feelings, but it just feels so much better than holding everything inside, like I used to.

Research participant

The words of this woman participating in our research on adjustment to breast cancer capture the focus of this chapter: an exploration of the adaptive potential of acknowledging, understanding, and expressing one's emotions under stressful conditions. Although some theorists have emphasized the destructive capacity of intense emotions, newer functionalist perspectives highlight their adaptive utility. We begin by attempting to reconcile findings in the empirical stress and coping literature suggesting that emotion-oriented coping is maladaptive with contrasting theoretical and empirical evidence from other domains indicating that processing and expressing emotion can be useful. We go on to outline the development and validation of our scales designed to measure coping through emotional approach, that is, coping through acknowledging, understanding, and expressing emotions. We then describe research revealing that emotional approach coping can yield psychological and health-related benefits and discuss likely moderators and mediators of the effects of coping through emotional approach. Finally, we provide examples of clinical interventions promoting these coping strategies and suggest directions for research.

History of the Construct and Its Measurement

Our interest in coping with adversity through actively processing and expressing emotions emerged from an attempt to make sense of several lines of theory and empirical inquiry on emotion. The first was a traditional view in psychology of the experience and expression of intense emotion as dysfunctional and in opposition to rationality (Averill, 1990). This view contrasts with a functionalist conceptualization of emotions as adaptive, organizing elements of human experience. Levenson (1994) provides a functionalist definition of emotion:

Emotions are short-lived psychological-physiological phenomena that represent efficient modes of adaptation. . . . Psychologically, emotions alter attention, shift certain behaviors upward in response hierarchies, and activate relevant associative networks in memory. Physiologically, emotions rapidly organize the responses of different biological systems . . . to produce a bodily milieu that is optimal for effective response. (p. 123)

Theorists and researchers in diverse areas have adopted a functionalist conceptualization of emotion, as illustrated in the developmental construct of emotional competence (e.g., Saarni, 1990); the personality construct of emotional intelligence (e.g., Salovey, Bedell, Detweiler, & Mayer, 1999); and clinical approaches such as process-experiential therapy (e.g., Greenberg & Paivio, 1997) and Mahoney's (1991) developmental constructivist approach. The work of Pennebaker and others has provided empirical support for the benefits of processing and expressing emotions through writing (for reviews, see Smyth, 1998; Smyth & Pennebaker, 1999), and experimental studies have demonstrated the costs of emotional suppression (e.g., Richards & Gross, 1999; Wegner, Schneider, Knutson, & McMahon, 1991).

In contrast to accumulating data from these lines of recent work that highlight the adaptive potential of emotions, findings from the empirical literature on stress and coping harken back to the traditional view of emotion as maladaptive. The theoretical grounding of this literature primarily lies in Lazarus and Folkman's (1984) influential conceptualization of coping, wherein coping is defined as "constantly changing cognitive and behavioral efforts to manage specific external and/or internal demands that are appraised as taxing or exceeding the resources of the person" (p. 141). In their framework, coping processes subsume both direct efforts to alter demands perceived as taxing one's resources (i.e., problem-focused coping) and attempts to regulate emotions surrounding the stressful encounter (i.e., emotion-focused coping). Problem-focused coping includes such strategies as defining the problem, generating and weighing alternative solutions, and following a plan of action. Emotion-focused coping includes processes such as avoidance, denial, seeking emotional support, and positive reappraisal. Lazarus and Folkman observed that people use both coping approaches in almost all difficult situations. They assumed that coping processes were neither inherently maladaptive nor adaptive and emphasized the importance of keeping coping efforts conceptually distinct from coping outcomes (e.g., psychological adjustment). In their view, the efficacy of coping efforts must be investigated within the situational context.

The dysfunctional outcomes associated with emotion-focused coping are not, therefore, embedded in the original construct. We argue that the empirical findings instead are accounted for largely by the way this construct has been operationalized in coping measures. To illustrate, we performed a review of the PsycInfo database for empirical articles in the 4-year period from 1995 through 1998 that included the key words *emotion* and *coping* and evaluated the relation between a measure or measures of emotion-focused coping and some indicator of adjustment in an adolescent or adult sample. We intended the review to be illustrative rather than exhaustive.

Of more than 100 articles located, the most frequently used coping instruments were the Ways of Coping Scale (WOC; Lazarus & Folkman, 1985), the COPE (Carver, Scheier, & Weintraub, 1989), and the Coping Inventory for Stressful Situations (CISS; Endler & Parker, 1990, 1994). The WOC was developed in 1980 and revised in 1985 as a measure of behavioral and cognitive strategies used to manage demands in specific stressful encounters. Factor analysis in an undergraduate sample (Lazarus & Folkman, 1985) yielded six emotion-focused subscales (i.e., wishful thinking, distancing, emphasizing the positive, self-blame, tension reduction, and self-isolation), one problem-focused scale, and one mixed-function scale assessing seeking social support. Subsequent studies yielded somewhat different factors (e.g., Folkman, Lazarus, Dunkel-Schetter, DeLongis, & Gruen, 1986), and some investigators conduct factor analyses on their own samples to derive subscales. Published in 1989, the COPE contains items based on the authors' theory of behavioral self-regulation, the Lazarus model of stress, and the empirical literature. In addition to five problem-focused coping scales, it contains five scales to assess emotion-focused coping (i.e., seeking of emotional support, positive reinterpretation, acceptance, denial, and turning to religion) and three scales to measure "coping responses that arguably are less useful" (p. 267; i.e., focus on and venting of emotions, behavioral disengagement, mental disengagement). The COPE is used in both dispositional and situational versions. The CISS was designed to assess dispositional coping styles and has three subscales, each containing 16 items: emotion-oriented coping, task-oriented coping, and avoidance-oriented coping. Emotion-oriented coping represents self-oriented efforts directed at reducing stress through emotional responses, self-preoccupation, and fantasizing.

Two conclusions emerged from a review of research including these measures. First, wide latitude is apparent in the operationalization of emotion-focused coping. For example, many studies using the COPE and the WOC did not use the originally derived subscales but rather used selected items or subscale composites to indicate emotion-focused coping. Unfortunately, conclusions reached by researchers often reference "emotion-focused coping" rather than the more circumscribed constructs assessed (e.g., avoidance). Second, when narrowed to an examination of scales most relevant to coping through processing and expressing emotion (i.e., CISS emotion-oriented coping scale and COPE Focus on and Venting of Emotion scale),[1] our review revealed a consistent association obtained between those scales and maladjustment. We located 1 longitudinal and 18 cross-sectional studies that examined the relation between the CISS emotion-oriented coping scale and adjustment indicators.[2] All 19 studies demonstrated an association of emotion-oriented coping with poorer adjustment, such as symptoms of depression and anxiety, neuroticism, low life satisfaction, and eating disturbance. Similarly, 7 of 8 cross-sectional studies using the relevant COPE subscale yielded significant relations with maladjustment, with the other study demonstrating an association of venting emotion with positive adjustment for females. Such findings have led reviewers of this literature to such conclusions as "Emotion-focused coping . . . has consistently proven to be associated with negative adaptation" (Kohn, 1996, p. 186). Thus, although Lazarus and Folkman (1984) cautioned against viewing coping strategies as invariably adaptive or maladaptive, some reviewers of the empirical literature have concluded otherwise.

Despite these empirical findings that emotion-focused coping is maladaptive, we contend that coping through emotional processing and expression is an important area of inquiry

for positive psychology. How can we reconcile these contrasting views and lines of research on emotion and coping? First, a functionalist perspective on emotion, which emphasizes its adaptive qualities, is not necessarily inconsistent with the view that, *under some conditions*, the experience and expression of emotion may bring negative consequences. Surely, any perspective that touts emotion as "all good" or "all bad" does not capture the complexity of emotional experience and expression in the real world. Likewise, coping through emotional approach might be said to carry adaptive *potential*, the realization of which may depend on an array of factors including the situational context, the interpersonal milieu, and attributes of the individual.

Second, the repeated finding of an association between emotion-focused coping and maladjustment may not reflect a valid association between emotional processing and expression and negative outcomes but rather result from problems with conceptualization and measurement of the emotion-focused coping construct. Stanton, Danoff-Burg, Cameron, and Ellis (1994) identified three problems with the operationalization of emotion-focused coping that help to account for its "bad reputation." First, many measures of emotion-focused coping strategies are contaminated with content reflecting psychological distress or self-deprecation, for example, "I get upset and let my emotions out" (Carver et al., 1989), "Become very tense" (Endler & Parker, 1990), and "Focus on my general inadequacies" (Endler & Parker, 1990). These confounded items result in measurement redundancy when emotion-focused coping measures are correlated with indices of distress or psychopathology. The observed correlations of emotion-focused coping and depression, pessimism, and neuroticism/negative affectivity are not surprising in light of the confounded nature of these coping items. A closely related second problem with commonly used coping measures is that they do not contain sufficient items that reflect unconfounded coping through attempting to acknowledge, understand, and express one's emotions surrounding a stressful encounter, that is, coping through emotional approach (Stanton et al., 1994). Third, measures of the construct include a diverse array of responses under the designation of emotion-focused coping. Some of the items reflect approach toward a stressor, whereas others indicate avoidance. Indeed, some emotion-focused coping subscales are correlated inversely (Scheier, Weintraub, & Carver, 1986). For example, the items "I let my feelings out" versus "I blame myself for becoming too emotional" and "I learn to live with it" versus "I say to myself, 'this isn't real' " all can be considered emotion-focused coping responses. When such diverse items are aggregated into single scales, it becomes difficult to interpret an association obtained between emotion-focused coping and dysfunctional outcomes.

Thus, although the stress and coping literature may on the surface suggest near-universally maladaptive consequences of emotion-focused coping, our closer look reveals that the case is far from closed. Let us now outline our approach to and examine research on the adaptive potential of coping through emotional processing and expression.

Processing and Expressing Emotion

We advocate two points of departure from the traditional emotion- and problem-focused conceptualization of coping. First, we recommend distinguishing, both conceptually and empirically, among emotion-focused strategies that involve active movement toward (e.g., active acceptance, emotional expression, positive reappraisal) versus away from (e.g., mental disengagement) a stressful encounter. This distinction is supported by hierarchical factor analyses revealing that the problem- and emotion-focused coping dimensions are subsumed by a more fundamental distinction between approach-oriented and avoidance-oriented processes (Tobin, Holroyd, Reynolds, & Wigal, 1989). Moreover, we advocate attention to distinct strategies within the realms of approach and avoidance. This suggestion counters the common practice of combining diverse coping strategies under the umbrella of emotion-focused coping. For example, expressing one's emotions surrounding a stressor and coming to reappraise it positively both may involve approaching the problem, but they may have distinct precursors and adaptive consequences. Here we focus on the approach-oriented coping strategies of processing and expressing emotion.

The second recommended point of departure from the extant coping literature concerns the operationalization of emotional approach coping and our focus on its adaptive potential. Stanton et al. (1994) demonstrated that many published

emotion-focused coping items are contaminated by psychological distress or self-deprecation, suggesting that at least part of the frequently cited association between emotion-focused coping and maladjustment results from overlap between putative coping items and items measuring distress. To measure coping through actively processing and expressing emotions, Stanton and colleagues (1994, 2000b) developed items that are unconfounded by distress, and it is these items or other unconfounded measures that we recommend for use in future research on coping through emotional approach.

In the remainder of this chapter, we focus on the operationalization and potentially adaptive function of coping through emotional processing and expression. This focus necessarily causes us to neglect a substantial literature related to other potentially adaptive approach-oriented coping mechanisms. For example, coping through active acceptance and use of humor were associated with lower distress in women with breast cancer (Carver et al., 1993). The interested reader can refer to other chapters in this volume for discussions of additional potentially positive coping strategies, such as benefit finding and reminding, humor, and spirituality.

Assessment and Current Research

Several self-report measures are available of dispositional constructs relevant to emotion that possess sound evidence of reliability and validity. These include, among others, the Berkeley Expressivity Questionnaire (Gross & John, 1995, 1997); the Affect Intensity Measure (Larsen, Diener, & Emmons, 1986); the Emotional Expressiveness Questionnaire (King & Emmons, 1990); the Ambivalence Over Emotional Expressiveness Questionnaire (King & Emmons, 1990); and the Family Expressiveness Questionnaire (Halberstadt, 1986). However, we were unable to locate measures of coping through emotional processing and expression that were directed specifically toward assessing emotion-oriented responses in stressful encounters and that did not contain distress-contaminated items. Hence, we sought to develop scales to assess these constructs (Stanton, Kirk, Cameron, & Danoff-Burg, 2000b).

Exploratory and confirmatory factor analyses of dispositional and situational coping item sets generated by our research team yielded two distinct emotional approach coping factors: emotional processing (i.e., active attempts to acknowledge and understand emotions) and emotional expression. Items for coping through emotional processing include "I realize that my feelings are valid and important," "I take time to figure out what I'm really feeling," "I delve into my feelings to get a thorough understanding of them," and "I acknowledge my emotions." Emotional expression coping items include "I feel free to express my emotions," "I take time to express my emotions," "I allow myself to express my emotions," and "I let my feelings come out freely." The two four-item scales, which yield high internal consistency and test-retest reliability, can be embedded in the COPE or other established coping measures. Distinct from other forms of coping, they are correlated moderately with other approach-oriented coping mechanisms (e.g., problem-focused coping, seeking social support), and coping through emotional expression is correlated moderately with measures of dispositional and family expressiveness (Study 1, Study 3). In a study of undergraduates and their parents (Study 2), the scales, and particularly the one tapping the more publicly observable coping through emotional expression, evidenced sound interjudge reliability. Furthermore, individuals with high scores on the scale assessing coping through emotional expression evidence more behavioral signs of sadness when asked to view a sad film, as rated by independent observers (Hamel & Stanton, 1999).

Findings with these new scales assessing coping through emotional approach suggest that, under particular conditions, emotional approach coping carries adaptive consequences. In cross-sectional analyses, emotional approach coping, and particularly coping through emotional processing, is associated with indicators of positive psychological adjustment, at least for young women. For example, coping through active attempts to acknowledge and understand emotions was related to greater hope (i.e., a sense of goal-directed agency and pathways to reach goals), instrumentality, and self-esteem and to lower neuroticism, trait anxiety, and depressive symptoms in samples of undergraduate women (Stanton et al., 2000b, Study 1, Study 3). Thus, when assessed with measures uncontaminated by distress-laden or self-deprecatory content, coping through emotional approach is associated with positive adjustment.

Longitudinal tests of the relations between emotional approach coping constructs and adap-

tive outcomes in stressful encounters allow for stronger causal inference. In analyses controlling for initial levels on the dependent variables, a preliminary, composite scale assessing emotional approach coping predicted enhanced adjustment in the form of increased life satisfaction and decreased depressive symptoms over time for young women coping with a self-nominated stressor and poorer adjustment for young men (Stanton et al., 1994). In a partial replication of this longitudinal study, Stanton et al. (2000b) found a significant interaction between coping through emotional processing and expression, such that greater coping through emotional processing and expression predicted enhanced adjustment over time when used alone, but their positive effects were not additive. The simultaneous use of low initial processing and expression or high initial processing and expression each predicted poorer adjustment across time. The interactions retained significance when neuroticism, depressive rumination, and coping through seeking social support were controlled statistically. A speculative interpretation is that emotional processing and expression might be most adaptive when used sequentially. Thus, expression might be most useful once individuals have come to understand their feelings (and thus report low processing).

Additional longitudinal work has been conducted with groups undergoing a specific stressor. Berghuis and Stanton (1994) found that emotional approach coping predicted lower depressive symptoms upon an unsuccessful insemination attempt in both members of heterosexual couples experiencing infertility, controlling for initial levels of depression. Moreover, when women were low on emotional approach coping, their partners' high emotional approach coping was beneficial in protecting the women from depressive symptoms. Although their emotional approach coping items included interpersonal content and thus also may reflect social support, Terry and Hynes (1998) also found that coping through emotional approach was related to more positive adjustment in women experiencing infertility. Infertility is experienced as a relatively uncontrollable stressor, in which partners typically rely on each other for support. Such stressful experiences may call for emotional approach coping.

Stanton et al. (2000a) went on to investigate the adaptive utility of emotional approach coping in women who recently had completed treatment for breast cancer. In a 3-month longitudinal study, they found that women who coped through expressing emotions surrounding cancer at study entry had fewer medical appointments for cancer-related morbidities (e.g., pain, lymphedema) during the subsequent 3 months, enhanced self-perceived physical health and vigor, and decreased distress relative to women low in coping through emotional expression. These relations held when participant age, other coping strategy scores (including seeking social support), and initial values on dependent variables were controlled statistically. Expressive coping also was related to improved quality of life for women who viewed their social contexts as highly receptive. Coping through emotional processing was associated only with one index reflecting greater distress over time. The strong and consistent findings for emotional expression relative to emotional processing in this study may reflect the lesser utility of emotional processing as a stressor persists. Because women on average had been diagnosed with cancer approximately 6 months prior to study entry, high scores on coping through emotional processing in part may have reflected rumination or an inability to come to a satisfactory understanding of their feelings surrounding cancer.

Additional analyses suggested that coping through emotional approach may serve as a successful vehicle for goal clarification and pursuit, as revealed by significant mediated and moderated relations of emotionally expressive coping with dispositional hope (Snyder et al., 1991). For example, through expressing her sense of loss of control engendered by a cancer diagnosis, a woman may begin to distinguish what she can and cannot control in her experience of cancer and her life more generally, to channel energy into attainable goals, and to work toward active acceptance of more uncontrollable aspects of her experience.

Experimental work also supports the validity of the emotional approach coping scales (Stanton et al., 2000b, Study 4). Undergraduates coping with a parent's psychological or physical disorder (e.g., cancer, alcoholism) were assigned randomly to talk about either their emotions regarding the parent's disorder or the facts relevant to the disorder across two sessions. Participants with high scores on emotionally expressive coping assessed in a prior screening session who then were induced to talk about their emotions evidenced reduced physiological arousal and negative affect compared with participants for whom preferred and induced coping were mismatched (e.g., highly expressive participants in the facts condition). Thus, one's preference for emotional approach coping may interact with environmental contingencies to determine the coping mechanisms' consequences.

Taken together, findings from research using the emotional approach coping scales suggest that coping through actively processing and expressing emotion can confer psychological and physical health advantages. But such coping is not uniformly beneficial. Under what conditions is emotional approach coping most likely to yield positive outcomes? The extant research provides several clues. As Lazarus and Folkman (1984) asserted, the utility of any coping strategy depends on situational contingencies. Thus, individuals who cope through processing and expressing emotions are likely to benefit to the extent that their interpersonal milieu welcomes emotional approach (Lepore, Silver, Wortman, & Wayment, 1996; Stanton et al., 2000a). Those who are isolated or who are punished for expressing emotions are less likely to benefit, unless they have satisfactory solitary outlets for emotional approach, such as journal writing (recall that emotional approach is associated with adjustment even when social support is controlled statistically; Stanton et al., 1994, 2000a, 2000b). The utility of emotional approach coping also might vary as a function of the nature of the stressful encounter. For example, emotional approach coping might be more useful for interpersonal than for achievement-related stressors (Stanton et al., 1994) and for situations perceived as relatively uncontrollable (Berghuis & Stanton, 1994; Terry & Hynes, 1998).

Other potential moderators of the effectiveness of emotional approach coping also require empirical attention. The utility of emotional approach may vary as a function of the specific emotion processed or expressed and the individual's comfort and skill in approaching such emotion. For example, some individuals may be able to use anger to motivate constructive action, whereas others who experience anger may lash out destructively or transform anger into persistent resentment. Individual difference characteristics such as gender, hope, and optimism may influence the utility of emotional approach coping. The timing of emotional approach coping efforts also may be important, with emotional processing most useful at the onset of the stressful encounter and emotional expression gaining maximal utility once one has come to understand one's feelings.

Given that emotional approach coping is beneficial under particular conditions, what are the mechanisms for its salutary effects? Coping through processing and expressing emotions may direct one's attention toward central concerns (Frijda, 1994) and result in identification of discrepancies between one's progress toward a goal and the expected rate of progress (Carver & Scheier, 1998). For example, acknowledging and attempting to understand one's anger may lead one to conclude that a central goal currently is blocked (e.g., maintaining a close relationship with one's partner), to identify contributors to the blockage (e.g., partners' differing styles of approaching conflict), and to generate ways of restoring progress toward the goal (e.g., accepting and reinterpreting the difference, expressing the anger constructively, seeking therapy). Thus, emotional approach coping may constitute a useful vehicle for defining goals and motivating action. Mediated relations of expressive coping with hope (Stanton et al., 2000a) and associations with problem-focused coping (Stanton et al., 2000b) support this interpretation.

Emotional approach coping also may aid in habituation to a stressor and its associated emotions (e.g., Foa & Kozak, 1986; Hunt, 1998), either simply through repeated exposure or through concomitant altered cognitive reappraisal of the stressor. For example, through processing and expressing emotions, one may conclude that the situation is not as dire as originally conceived, that painful emotions do indeed subside, and that some benefit can be gleaned from adversity (e.g., Davis, Nolen-Hoeksema, & Larson, 1998; Foa, Steketee, & Rothbaum, 1989). Analyzing six experiments on written emotional disclosure, Pennebaker, Mayne, and Francis (1997) found that use of words reflecting insightful and causal thinking was associated with improved health outcomes.

Finally, coping through expressing emotions may facilitate regulation of the social environment (e.g., Thompson, 1994). Letting a partner know of one's sadness can prompt comfort, for example. An understanding of one's inner emotional world also can allow individuals to select maximally satisfying emotional environments (Carstensen, 1998). We would suggest that the most interesting questions regarding emotional approach coping involve specifying for whom, under what conditions, and how coping through emotional processing and expression yields benefits, as well as how the resultant understanding can be translated into effective interventions for people confronting stressful experiences.

Clinical Interventions

It is clear from the foregoing that the experience and expression of emotion may be adaptive or maladaptive. In fact, most clients presenting for psychotherapy share the characteristic of some dysfunctional emotional patterns (Mahoney, 1991). Although some clinical approaches historically have touted pure expression as therapeutic, theorists now suggest that a central goal of psychotherapy and of successful human development is *balanced* emotional expression in which emotions are recognized, understood, and communicated appropriately in a way that eventually prompts a reduction in distress (Kennedy-Moore & Watson, 1999). Such therapies focus not just on unbridled expression of emotion but rather on emotional processing and expression that serve functions such as regulating arousal, fostering self-understanding, enhancing problem-solving, and improving interpersonal relationships.

One example of a therapy with such a goal is emotionally focused therapy (EFT; e.g., Greenberg & Paivio, 1997; Safran & Greenberg, 1991), which seeks to help clients achieve more adaptive functioning through evoking and exploring emotions and restructuring maladaptive emotional schemes. A recent meta-analysis of four randomized controlled trials of EFT for couples revealed that this approach clearly is effective in reducing marital distress (Johnson, Hunsley, Greenberg, & Schindler, 1999). Based on four studies of the mechanisms for change in EFT, Johnson et al. theorized that improvement is associated with expression of feelings and needs, and that this expression leads to positive shifts in relationship patterns.

Our review of the recent literature revealed other experimental studies designed to enhance emotional processing and/or expression that included a no-treatment control group. For example, Schut, Stroebe, van den Bout, and de Keijser (1997) offered seven sessions of problem- or emotion-focused counseling to men and women experiencing mildly complicated bereavement. Emotion-focused therapy was aimed at acceptance, exploration, and discharge of emotions related to the loss. Both interventions produced greater reduction in distress than a no-treatment control group, with the problem-focused intervention producing slightly better results than the emotion-focused intervention. Interestingly, problem-focused counseling was more effective in women, and emotion-focused counseling yielded better results for men. The effects of emotion-focused coping were observed only at follow-up, 7 months after the completion of treatment. In a study of women experiencing infertility, McQueeney, Stanton, and Sigmon (1997) assessed the efficacy of six sessions of problem- or emotion-focused counseling compared with a no-treatment control group. Both problem-focused and emotion-focused participants evidenced significantly reduced distress at treatment termination relative to controls. At a 1-month follow-up, only the emotion-focused group evidenced significantly better psychological adjustment than controls (i.e., lower depressive symptoms and greater infertility-specific well-being) and in fact showed continued gains from treatment termination through 1 month. At 18 months after treatment, a significant between-groups difference emerged on parental status. Eight of 10 problem-focused group members had become mothers (4 biological, 4 adoptive) versus 2 of 8 emotion-focused members and three of eight controls.

These studies provide support for the potential of interventions promoting emotional processing and expression, but they also suggest four important qualifiers. First, Schut et al. (1997) emphasized the importance of studying effects of coping skills interventions as a function of participant gender (also see Stanton et al., 1994). Interventions aimed at enhancing emotional approach coping may be more useful for some participants than others, and potential moderators require study. Second, the finding in both studies that emotional approach coping emerged as more beneficial at follow-up suggests that working with and expressing emotions may have a delayed impact as compared with problem-focused coping. It also highlights the need for longitudinal studies of the effects of emotional approach coping skills interventions. Third, although the mechanisms for change in these therapies presumably center on the facilitation of emotional processing and expression, specific mechanisms for change require identification. Finally, this research underlines Lazarus's (1999) cautions against di-

chotomizing emotion- and problem-focused coping. Both approaches may confer benefit, perhaps in different realms or at different points in the trajectory of the stressor, and integrated interventions may yield the most positive outcomes. Folkman and colleagues' (1991) Coping Effectiveness Training represents an intervention that combines training in emotion- and problem-focused skills. Effective in bolstering quality of life in HIV+ men, this approach includes (a) appraisal training to disaggregate global stressors into specific coping tasks and to differentiate between modifiable and immutable aspects of specific stressors; (b) coping training to tailor application of problem-focused and emotion-focused coping efforts to relevant stressors; and (c) social support training to increase effectiveness in selecting and maintaining supportive resources. Continued empirical exploration of emotionally evocative therapeutic frameworks is essential.

Directions for Research

Our investigation of coping through emotional approach has begun with self-report items that are brief and general in nature. Findings of initial studies have generated numerous, specific questions for research. Further specification of the functional and dysfunctional aspects of coping through emotional approach is of central importance. One important element of the emotional approach coping construct requiring closer scrutiny is the role of intentionality (Compas, Connor, Osowiecki, & Welch, 1997), that is, the conscious and purposive use of emotional processing and expression. This intentionality is embedded in the emotional approach items we have evaluated (e.g., "I take time to express my emotions") and may be intrinsic to the adaptiveness of emotional approach. When nonvolitional, emotional processing may become maladaptive rumination, and emotional expression may produce destructive outbursts. Continued examination of: (a) individual difference characteristics of the coper, such as hope, developmental attributes, and gender; (b) the nature of the stressor, such as its controllability, severity, and timing of emotional approach coping relative to stressor onset; (c) the specific emotions processed and expressed; and (d) aspects of the environmental context, including proximal social support and more distal cultural receptivity to emotional approach, also will facilitate the identification of for whom and under what conditions coping through emotional approach is effective. Further, developmental antecedents of emotional approach coping and mechanisms through which it produces effects warrant exploration. In addressing these research questions, the broader literatures on emotion regulation, developmental psychology, biological psychology, evolutionary psychology, and others will be useful in generating hypotheses and constructing methodologies.

Although the self-report measures of emotional approach coping we have described here have demonstrated evidence of interjudge reliability and correspondence with behavioral indicators of emotional expression, as well as predictive validity, our understanding of coping through emotional approach will be enhanced by the use of methods in addition to self-report questionnaires, including direct observation and thought sampling, experimental induction of emotional approach, and qualitative studies of coping processes. Longitudinal research designs that control for initial levels on dependent variables (e.g., psychological adjustment) also are essential to evaluate coping through emotional approach because benefits of these coping processes may emerge weeks or months after their initiation (Schut et al., 1997; McQueeny et al., 1997).

Findings to date demonstrate that, although correlated, emotional processing and expression can have differential relations with adaptive outcomes, suggesting that further investigation of their distinct qualities and consequences require study with these various methods. Clearly, the emotional approach coping constructs also should be distinguished from other presumably emotion-focused coping strategies, both conceptually and empirically. We suggest that researchers select coping assessments that are uncontaminated by psychological distress and clearly specify the coping processes assessed in their published reports (and abstracts) rather than use the "emotion-focused coping" umbrella term.

Intriguing research questions pertinent to clinical applications also are evident. For example, what are the implications for therapy process and outcome of discrepancies in emotional approach coping between partners in couples therapy? Does the extent of client-therapist congruence in emotional approach coping increase over the course of therapy and influence outcomes? How can we best design interventions to facilitate adaptive coping through emotional approach for clients with diverse attributes? Translation of coping theory and empirical findings into effective clinical interventions is under way in several domains (e.g., Folkman et al., 1991); integration of findings from research on coping through emotional approach may bolster the utility of such interventions for individuals confronting life's adversities.

Chapters in this volume illustrate the family of constructs and theories undergirding positive psychology. Functionalist theories of emotion and the empirical evidence presented here suggest that coping through emotional approach deserves inclusion in this diverse array of adaptive processes. To once again capture the potential of emotional approach, we close with eloquent words of a research participant, "My emotional life is rich now. Through facing my deepest fears, I realize my strength. Through expressing my sadness, I come to know my true companions. Once thought my enemy, my emotions are now my friends."

Notes

1. The relevant WOC items contain interpersonal content (e.g., "I talked to someone about how I was feeling") and thus often are included on a subscale reflecting seeking social support.

2. Space limitations prevent providing the citations for these studies. Please contact the first author for a complete list.

References

Averill, J. R. (1990). Inner feelings, works of the flesh, the beast within, diseases of the mind, driving force, and putting on a show: Six metaphors of emotion and their theoretical extensions. In D. E. Leary (Ed.), *Metaphors in the history of psychology* (pp. 104–132). New York: Cambridge University Press.

Berghuis, J. P., & Stanton, A. L. (August, 1994). Infertile couples' coping and adjustment across an artificial insemination attempt. In T. A. Revenson & N. P. Bolger (Chairs), *Stress, coping, and support processes in the context of marriage.* Symposium conducted at the annual meeting of the American Psychological Association, Los Angeles.

Carstensen, L. L. (1998). A life-span approach to social motivation. In J. Heckhausen & C. S.

Dweck (Eds.), *Motivation and self-regulation across the life span* (pp. 341–364). Cambridge, England: Cambridge University Press.

Carver, C. S., Pozo, C., Harris, S. D., Noriega, V., Scheier, M. F., Robinson, D. S., Ketcham, A. S., Moffat, F. L., & Clark, K. C. (1993). How coping mediates the effect of optimism on distress: A study of women with early stage breast cancer. *Journal of Personality and Social Psychology, 65*, 375–390.

Carver, C. S., & Scheier, M. F. (1998). *On the self-regulation of behavior*. New York: Cambridge University Press.

Carver, C. S., Scheier, M. F., & Weintraub, J. K. (1989). Assessing coping strategies: A theoretically based approach. *Journal of Personality and Social Psychology, 56*, 267–283.

Compas, B. E., Connor, J., Osowiecki, D., & Welch, A. (1997). Effortful and involuntary responses to stress: Implications for coping with chronic stress. In B. H. Gottlieb (Ed.), *Coping with chronic stress* (pp. 105–130). New York: Plenum.

Davis, C. G., Nolen-Hoeksema, S., & Larson, J. (1998). Making sense of loss and benefiting from the experience: Two construals of meaning. *Journal of Personality and Social Psychology, 75*, 561–574.

Endler, N. S., & Parker, J. D. A. (1990). *Coping Inventory for Stressful Situations (CISS): Manual*. Toronto: Multi-Health Systems.

Endler, N. S., & Parker, J. D. A. (1994). Assessment of multidimensional coping: Task, emotion, and avoidance strategies. *Psychological Assessment, 6*, 50–60.

Foa, E. B., & Kozak, M. J. (1986). Emotional processing of fear: Exposure to corrective information. *Psychological Bulletin, 99*, 20–35.

Foa, E. B., Steketee, G., & Rothbaum, B. O. (1989). Behavioral/cognitive conceptualizations of posttraumatic stress disorder. *Behavior Therapy, 20*, 155–176.

Folkman, S., Chesney, M., McKusick, L., Ironson, G., Johnson, D. S., & Coates, T. J. (1991). Translating coping theory into intervention. In J. Eckenrode (Ed.), *The social context of coping* (pp. 239–259). New York: Plenum.

Folkman, S., Lazarus, R. S., Dunkel-Schetter, C., DeLongis, A., & Gruen, R. (1986). The dynamics of a stressful encounter: Cognitive appraisal, coping, and encounter outcomes. *Journal of Personality and Social Psychology, 50*, 992–1003.

*Frijda, N. H. (1994). Emotions are functional, most of the time. In P. Ekman & R. J. Davidson (Eds.), *The nature of emotion: Fundamental questions* (pp. 112–122). New York: Oxford University Press.

*Greenberg, L. S., & Paivio, S. C. (1997). *Working with emotions in psychotherapy*. New York: Guilford.

Gross, J. J., & John, O. P. (1995). Facets of emotional expressivity: Three self-report factors and their correlates. *Personality and Individual Differences, 19*, 555–568.

Gross, J. J., & John, O. P. (1997). Revealing feelings: Facets of emotional expressivity in self-reports, peer ratings, and behavior. *Journal of Personality and Social Psychology, 72*, 435–448.

Halberstadt, A. G. (1986). Family socialization of emotional expression and nonverbal communication styles and skills. *Journal of Personality and Social Psychology, 51*, 827–836.

Hamel, B., & Stanton, A. L. (May, 1999). Effects of a sadness induction as a function of coping through emotional approach. Unpublished raw data, University of Kansas, Lawrence.

Hunt, M. G. (1998). The only way out is through: Emotional processing and recovery after a depressing life event. *Behaviour Research and Therapy, 36*, 361–384.

Johnson, S. M., Hunsley, J., Greenberg, L., & Schindler, D. (1999). Emotionally focused couples therapy: Status and challenges. *Clinical Psychology: Science and Practice, 6* (1), 67–79.

Kennedy-Moore, E., & Watson, J. C. (1999). *Expressing emotion*. New York: Guilford.

King, L. A., & Emmons, R. A. (1990). Conflict over emotional expression: Psychological and physical correlates. *Journal of Personality and Social Psychology, 58*, 864–877.

Kohn, P. M. (1996). On coping adaptively with daily hassles. In M. Zeidner & N. S. Endler (Eds.), *Handbook of coping: Theory, research, applications* (pp. 181–201). New York: Wiley.

Larsen, R. J., Diener, E., & Emmons, R. A. (1986). Affect intensity and reactions to daily life events. *Journal of Personality and Social Psychology, 51*, 803–814.

*Lazarus, R. S. (1999). *Stress and emotion: A new synthesis*. New York: Springer.

*Lazarus, R. S., & Folkman, S. (1984). *Stress, appraisal, and coping*. New York: Springer.

Lazarus, R. S., & Folkman, S. (1985). If it changes it must be a process: Study of emotion and coping during three stages of a college examination. *Journal of Personality and Social Psychology, 48*, 150–170.

Lepore, S. J., Silver, R. C., Wortman, C. B., & Wayment, H. A. (1996). Social constraints, intrusive thoughts, and depressive symptoms among bereaved mothers. *Journal of Personality and Social Psychology, 70*, 271–282.

*Levenson, R. W. (1994). Human emotion: A functional view. In P. Ekman & R. J. Davidson

(Eds.), *The nature of emotion: Fundamental questions* (pp. 123–126). New York: Oxford University Press.

*Mahoney, M. J. (1991). *Human change processes: The scientific foundations of psychotherapy.* New York: Basic Books.

McQueeney, D. A., Stanton, A. L., & Sigmon, S. (1997). Efficacy of emotion-focused and problem-focused group therapies for women with fertility problems. *Journal of Behavioral Medicine, 20,* 313–331.

Pennebaker, J. W., Mayne, T. J., & Francis, M. E. (1997). Linguistic predictors of adaptive bereavement. *Journal of Personality and Social Psychology, 72,* 863–871.

Richards, J. M., & Gross, J. J. (1999). Composure at any cost? The cognitive consequences of emotion suppression. *Personality and Social Psychology Bulletin, 25,* 1033–1044.

*Saarni, C. (1990). Emotional competence: How emotions and relationships become integrated. In R. Thompson (Ed.), *Nebraska symposium on motivation: Vol. 36. Socioemotional development* (pp. 115–182). Lincoln: University of Nebraska Press.

Safran, J. D., & Greenberg, L. S. (1991). *Emotion, psychotherapy, and change.* New York: Guilford.

*Salovey, P., Bedell, B. T., Detweiler, J. B., & Mayer, J. D. (1999). Coping intelligently: Emotional intelligence and the coping process. In C. R. Snyder (Ed.), *Coping: The psychology of what works* (pp. 141–164). New York: Oxford University Press.

Scheier, M. F., Weintraub, J. K., & Carver, C. S. (1986). Coping with stress: Divergent strategies of optimists and pessimists. *Journal of Personality and Social Psychology, 51,* 1257–1264.

Schut, H. A. W., Stroebe, M. S., van den Bout, J., & de Keijser, J. (1997). Intervention for the bereaved: Gender differences in the efficacy of two counselling programmes. *British Journal of Clinical Psychology, 36,* 63–72.

*Smyth, J. M. (1998). Written emotional expression: Effect sizes, outcome types, and moderating variables. *Journal of Consulting and Clinical Psychology, 66,* 174–184.

*Smyth, J. M., & Pennebaker, J. W. (1999). Sharing one's story: Translating emotional experiences into words as a coping tool. In C. R. Snyder (Ed.), *Coping: The psychology of what works* (pp. 70–89). New York: Oxford University Press.

Snyder, C. R., Harris, C., Anderson, J. R., Holleran, S. A., Irving, L. M., Sigmon, S. T., Yoshinobu, L., Gibb, J., Langelle, C., & Harney, P. (1991). The will and the ways: Development and validation of an individual-differences measure of hope. *Journal of Personality and Social Psychology, 60,* 570–585.

*Stanton, A. L., Danoff-Burg, S., Cameron, C. L., Bishop, M. M., Collins, C. A., Kirk, S. B., Sworowski, L. A., & Twillman, R. (2000a). Emotionally expressive coping predicts psychological and physical adjustment to breast cancer. *Journal of Consulting and Clinical Psychology, 68,* 875–882.

*Stanton, A. L., Danoff-Burg, S., Cameron, C. L., & Ellis, A. P. (1994). Coping through emotional approach: Problems of conceptualization and confounding. *Journal of Personality and Social Psychology, 66,* 350–362.

*Stanton, A. L., Kirk, S. B., Cameron, C. L., & Danoff-Burg, S. (2000b). Coping through emotional approach: Scale construction and validation. *Journal of Personality and Social Psychology, 78,* 1150–1169.

Terry, D. J., & Hynes, G. J. (1998). Adjustment to a low-control situation: Reexamining the role of coping responses. *Journal of Personality and Social Psychology, 74,* 1078–1092.

Thompson, R. A. (1994). Emotion regulation: A theme in search of definition. *Monographs of the Society for Research in Child Development, 59,* 25–52.

Tobin, D. L., Holroyd, K. A., Reynolds, R. V., & Wigal, J. K. (1989). The hierarchical factor structure of the Coping Strategies Inventory. *Cognitive Therapy and Research, 13,* 343–361.

Wegner, D. M., Schneider, D. J., Knutson, B., & McMahon, S. R. (1991). On polluting the stream of consciousness: The effect of thought suppression on the mind's environment. *Cognitive Therapy and Research, 15,* 141–152.

12

The Positive Psychology of Emotional Intelligence

Peter Salovey, John D. Mayer, & David Caruso

Out of the marriage of reason with affect there issues clarity with passion. Reason without affect would be impotent, affect without reason would be blind.

S. S. Tomkins, *Affect, Imagery, and Consciousness*

For psychologists, the 1990s were best known as the "Decade of the Brain." But there were moments during those 10 years when the popular press seemed ready to declare it the "Decade of the Heart," not so much for a popular interest in cardiovascular physiology but rather as a reflection on the growing interest in emotions and emotional intelligence, in particular. During the second half of the 1990s, emotional intelligence and EQ (we much prefer the former term to the latter) were featured as the cover story in at least two national magazines (Gibbs, 1995; Goleman, 1995b); received extensive coverage in the international press (e.g., Alcade, 1996; Miketta, Gottschling, Wagner-Roos, & Gibbs, 1995; Thomas, 1995); were named the most useful new words or phrases for 1995 by the American Dialect Society (1995, 1999; Brodie, 1996); and made appearances in syndicated

comic strips as diverse as *Zippy the Pinhead* and *Dilbert*.

What is this construct, and why has it been so appealing? Emotional intelligence represents the ability to perceive, appraise, and express emotion accurately and adaptively; the ability to understand emotion and emotional knowledge; the ability to access and/or generate feelings when they facilitate cognitive activities and adaptive action; and the ability to regulate emotions in oneself and others (Mayer & Salovey, 1997). In other words, emotional intelligence refers to the ability to process emotion-laden information competently and to use it to guide cognitive activities like problem solving and to focus energy on required behaviors. The term suggested to some that there might be other ways of being intelligent than those emphasized by standard IQ tests, that one might be able to develop these abilities, and that an emotional intelligence could be an important predictor of success in personal relationships, family functioning, and the workplace. The term is one that instills hope and suggests promise, at least as compared with traditional notions of crystallized intelligence. For these very reasons, emotional intelligence belongs in positive psychology. The purpose of this chapter is to review the history of and current research on emotional intelligence and to determine whether our positive assessments are appropriate or misplaced.

History of the Concept

Turning to the field of psychology, there are two references to emotional intelligence prior to our work on this concept. First, Mowrer (1960) famously concluded that "the emotions . . . do not at all deserve being put into opposition with 'intelligence' . . . they are, it seems, themselves a high order of intelligence" (pp. 307–308). Second, Payne (1983/1986) used the term in an unpublished dissertation. A framework for an emotional intelligence, a formal definition, and suggestions about its measurement were first described in two articles that we published in 1990 (Mayer, DiPaolo, & Salovey, 1990; Salovey & Mayer, 1990).

The tension between exclusively cognitive views of what it means to be intelligent and broader ones that include a positive role for the emotions can be traced back many centuries. For example, the Stoic philosophers of ancient Greece viewed emotion as too individualistic and self-absorbed to be a reliable guide for insight and wisdom. Later, the Romantic movement in late-18th-century and early-19th-century Europe stressed how emotion-rooted intuition and empathy could provide insights that were unavailable through logic alone.

The modern interest in emotional intelligence stems, perhaps, from a similar dialectic in the field of human abilities research. Although narrow, analytically focused definitions of intelligence predominated for much of this century, following Cronbach's (1960) often cited conclusion that a social intelligence was unlikely to be defined and had not been measured, cracks in the analytic intelligence edifice began to appear in the 1980s. For example, Sternberg (1985) challenged mental abilities researchers to pay more attention to creative and practical aspects of intelligence, and Gardner (1983/1993) even defined an intrapersonal intelligence that concerns access to one's feeling life, the capacity to represent feelings, and the ability to draw upon them as a means of understanding and a guide for behavior. Shortly thereafter, in their controversial book, *The Bell Curve*, Herrnstein and Murray (1994) revived debate about the genetic

basis for traditionally defined intelligence and the degree to which intelligence is affected by environmental circumstances. Paradoxically, instead of crystallizing support for the genetic intelligence position, the effect of *The Bell Curve* was to energize many educators, investigators, and journalists to question whether the traditional view of intelligence was conceptualized too narrowly and to embrace the notion that there might be other ways to be smart and succeed in the world.

It was in this context that we wrote our 1990 articles, introducing emotional intelligence as the ability to understand feelings in the self and others, and to use these feelings as informational guides for thinking and action (Salovey & Mayer, 1990). At that time, we described three core components of emotional intelligence—appraisal and expression, regulation, and utilization—based on our reading and organizing of the relevant literature rather than on empirical research. Since this original article, we have refined our conceptualization of emotional intelligence so that it now includes four dimensions (Mayer & Salovey, 1997), which we will discuss later in this chapter.

Our work was reinforced by neuroscientists' interest in showing that emotional responses were integral to "rational" decision making (e.g., Damasio, 1995). Through our theorizing, we also helped to stimulate the writing of the best-selling book *Emotional Intelligence*, in which Goleman (1995a) promised that emotional intelligence rather than analytical intelligence predicts success in school, work, and home. Despite the lack of data to support some of Goleman's claims, interest in emotional intelligence soared, with books appearing monthly in which the authors touted the value of emotional intelligence in education (Schilling, 1996), child rearing (Gottman & DeClaire, 1997; Shapiro, 1997), the workplace (Cooper & Sawaf, 1997; Goleman, 1998; Ryback, 1998; Simmons & Simmons, 1997; Weisinger, 1998), and personal growth (Epstein, 1998; Salerno, 1996; Segal, 1997; Steiner & Perry, 1997). Very little of this explosion of available resources on emotional intelligence represented empirically oriented scholarship.

In the past 5 years, there also has been great interest in the development of measures to assess the competencies involved in emotional intelligence. Not surprisingly, a plethora of supposed emotional intelligence scales and batteries of varying psychometric properties appeared (e.g., Bar-On, 1997; Cooper & Sawaf, 1996; Schutte et al., 1998). In reality, these instruments tapped self-reported personality constructs, and they were disappointing in terms of their discriminant and construct validities (Davies, Stankov, & Roberts, 1998). As an alternative, we have been arguing for the value of conceptualizing emotional intelligence as a set of abilities that should be measured as such (Mayer, Salovey & Caruso, 2000a, 2000b). We will describe this approach to measurement later in the chapter.

Current Model of Emotional Intelligence

What follows is a brief summary of our ability theory of emotional intelligence, displayed in Table 12.1; more detailed presentations can be found elsewhere (e.g., Mayer, Caruso, & Salovey, 1999; Mayer & Salovey, 1997; Salovey, Bedell, Detweiler, & Mayer, 2000; Salovey & Mayer, 1990). Although there is sometimes empirical utility in considering emotional intelligence as a unitary construct, most of our work suggests that it can be divided into four branches. The first of these branches, *emotional perception and expression*, involves recognizing and inputting verbal and nonverbal information from the emotion system. The second branch, *emotional facilitation of thought* (sometimes referred to as *using emotional intelligence*), refers to using emotions as part of cognitive processes such as creativity and problem solving. The third branch, *emotional understanding*, involves cognitive processing of emotion, that is, insight and knowledge brought to bear upon one's feelings or the feelings of others. Our fourth branch, *emotional management*, concerns the regulation of emotions in oneself and in other people.

The first branch of emotional intelligence begins with the capacity to perceive and to express feelings. Emotional intelligence is impossible without the competencies involved in this branch (see also Saarni, 1990, 1999). If each time unpleasant feelings emerged, people turned their attentions away, they would learn very little about feelings. Emotional perception involves registering, attending to, and deciphering emotional messages as they are expressed in facial expressions, voice tone, or cultural artifacts. A person who sees the fleeting expression of fear in the face of another understands much more about that person's emotions and

thoughts than someone who misses such a signal.

The second branch of emotional intelligence concerns emotional facilitation of cognitive activities. Emotions are complex organizations of the various psychological subsystems—physiological, experiential, cognitive, and motivational. Emotions enter the cognitive system both as cognized feelings, as is the case when someone thinks, "I am a little sad now," and as altered cognitions, as when a sad person thinks, "I am no good." The emotional facilitation of thought focuses on how emotion affects the cognitive system and, as such, can be harnessed for more effective problem solving, reasoning, decision making, and creative endeavors. Of course, cognition can be disrupted by emotions, such as anxiety and fear, but emotions also can prioritize the cognitive system to attend to what is important (Easterbrook, 1959; Mandler, 1975; Simon, 1982), and even to focus on what it does best in a given mood (e.g., Palfai & Salovey, 1993; Schwarz, 1990).

Emotions also change cognitions, making them positive when a person is happy and negative when a person is sad (e.g., Forgas, 1995; Mayer, Gaschke, Braverman, & Evans, 1992; Salovey & Birnbaum, 1989; Singer & Salovey, 1988). These changes force the cognitive system to view things from different perspectives, for example, alternating between skeptical and accepting. The advantage of such alterations to thought is fairly apparent. When one's point of view shifts between skeptical and accepting, the individual can appreciate multiple vantage points and, as a consequence, think about a problem more deeply and creatively (e.g., Mayer, 1986; Mayer & Hanson, 1995). It is just such an effect that may lead people with mood swings toward greater creativity (Goodwin & Jamison, 1990; see Simonton, this volume).

The third branch involves understanding emotion. Emotions form a rich and complexly interrelated symbol set. The most fundamental competency at this level concerns the ability to label emotions with words and to recognize the relationships among exemplars of the affective lexicon. The emotionally intelligent individual is able to recognize that the terms used to describe emotions are arranged into families and that groups of emotion terms form fuzzy sets (Ortony, Clore, & Collins, 1988). Perhaps more important, the relations among these terms are deduced—that annoyance and irritation can lead to rage if the provocative stimulus is not elim-

Table 12.1 The Four-Branch Model of Emotional Intelligence
(after Mayer & Salovey, 1997)

Emotional Perception and Expression

Ability to identify emotion in one's physical and psychological states
Ability to identify emotion in other people
Ability to express emotions accurately and to express needs related to them
Ability to discriminate between accurate/honest and inaccurate/dishonest feelings

Emotional Facilitation of Thought (Using Emotional Intelligence)

Ability to redirect and prioritize thinking on the basis of associated feelings
Ability to generate emotions to facilitate judgment and memory
Ability to capitalize on mood changes to appreciate multiple points of view
Ability to use emotional states to facilitate problem solving and creativity

Emotional Understanding

Ability to understand relationships among various emotions
Ability to perceive the causes and consequences of emotions
Ability to understand complex feelings, emotional blends, and contradictory states
Ability to understand transitions among emotions

Emotional Management

Ability to be open to feelings, both pleasant and unpleasant
Ability to monitor and reflect on emotions
Ability to engage, prolong, or detach from an emotional state
Ability to manage emotions in oneself
Ability to manage emotions in others

---

inated, or that envy often is experienced in contexts that also evoke jealousy (Salovey & Rodin, 1986, 1989). The person who is able to understand emotions—their meanings, how they blend together, how they progress over time—is truly blessed with the capacity to understand important aspects of human nature and interpersonal relationships.

Partly as a consequence of various popularizations, and partly as a consequence of societal pressures to regulate emotions, many people primarily identify emotional intelligence with its fourth branch, emotional management (sometimes referred to as emotional regulation). They hope emotional intelligence will be a way of getting rid of troublesome emotions or emotional leakages into human relations and rather, to control emotions. Although this is one possible outcome of the fourth branch, optimal levels of emotional regulation may be moderate ones; attempts to minimize or eliminate emotion completely may stifle emotional intelligence. Similarly, the regulation of emotion in other people is less likely to involve the suppressing of others' emotions but rather the har-

nessing of them, as when a persuasive speaker is said to "move" his or her audience.

Individuals use a broad range of techniques to regulate their moods. Thayer, Newman, and McClain (1994) believe that physical exercise is the single most effective strategy for changing a bad mood, among those under one's own control. Other commonly reported mood regulation strategies include listening to music, social interaction, and cognitive self-management (e.g., giving oneself a "pep talk"). Pleasant distractions (errands, hobbies, fun activities, shopping, reading, and writing) also are effective. Less effective (and, at times, counterproductive) strategies include passive mood management (e.g., television viewing, caffeine, food, and sleep), direct tension reduction (e.g., drugs, alcohol, and sex), spending time alone, and avoiding the person or thing that caused a bad mood. In general, the most successful regulation methods involve expenditure of energy; active mood management techniques that combine relaxation, stress management, cognitive effort, and exercise may be the most effective strategies for changing bad moods (reviewed by Thayer et al., 1994). Central to emotional self-regulation is the ability to reflect upon and manage one's emotions; emotional disclosure provides one means of doing so. Pennebaker (1989, 1993, 1997) has studied the effects of disclosure extensively and finds that the act of disclosing emotional experiences in writing improves individuals' subsequent physical and mental health (see Niederhoffer & Pennebaker, this volume).

Measuring Emotional Intelligence

We believe that the most valid approach for assessing emotional intelligence is the use of task-based, ability measures. Although self-report inventories assessing various aspects of emotional intelligence have proliferated in recent years (e.g., Bagby, Parker, & Taylor, 1993a, 1993b; Bar-On, 1997; Catanzaro & Mearns, 1990; EQ Japan, 1998; Giuliano & Swinkels, 1992; Salovey, Mayer, Goldman, Turvey, & Palfai, 1995; Schutte et al., 1998; Swinkels & Giuliano, 1995; Wang, Tett, Fisher, Griebler, & Martinez, 1997), these constructs are difficult to distinguish from already measured aspects of personality (Davies et al., 1998); moreover, whether emotional competency self-belief scores actually correlate systematically with those competencies per se has yet to be determined (Mayer et al., 1999). We ask the reader to imagine whether he or she would be convinced of the analytic intelligence of another person based on the respondent's answer to a question such as "Do you think you're smart?" We are not, and therefore since the beginning of our work on emotional intelligence, we have suggested that tasks that tap into the various competencies that underlie emotional intelligence are likely to have more validity than self-report measures (e.g., Mayer et al., 1990).

Task-based measures of emotional abilities developed on the basis of other theoretical frameworks may be useful in the assessment of emotional intelligence. For example, in the Levels of Emotional Awareness Scale (LEAS), respondents are asked to describe their feelings about various stimuli, and then these protocols are coded according to differentiations in the feeling language used (Lane, Quinlan, Schwartz, Walker, & Zeitlin, 1990). Another possibility is Averill and Nunley's (1992; see also Averill, 1999) test of emotional creativity, in which participants are asked to write about situations in which they experience three different emotions

simultaneously. Various measures of nonverbal emotional sending and receiving ability also have been explored over the years (e.g., Buck, 1976; Freedman, Prince, Riggio, & DiMatteo, 1980; Rosenthal, Hall, DiMatteo, Rogers, & Archer, 1979).

The first comprehensive, theory-based battery for assessing emotional intelligence as a set of abilities was the Multifactor Emotional Intelligence Scale (MEIS), which can be administered through interaction with a computer program or via pencil and paper (Mayer, Caruso, & Salovey, 1998, 1999). The MEIS comprises 12 ability measures that are divided into four branches, reflecting the model of emotional intelligence presented earlier: (a) perceiving and expressing emotions; (b) using emotions to facilitate thought and other cognitive activities; (c) understanding emotion; and (d) managing emotion in self and others (Mayer & Salovey, 1997). Branch 1 tasks measure emotional perception in Faces, Music, Designs, and Stories. Branch 2 measures Synesthesia Judgments (e.g., "How hot is anger?") and Feeling Biases (translating felt emotions into judgments about people). Branch 3's four tasks examine the understanding of emotion. Sample questions include "Optimism most closely combines which two emotions?" A participant should choose "pleasure and anticipation" over less specific alternatives such as "pleasure and joy." Branch 4's two tests measure Emotion Management in the Self and in Others. These tasks ask participants to read scenarios and then rate four reactions to them according to how effective they are as emotion management strategies focused on the self or on others.

An issue that comes up in task-based tests of emotional intelligence concerns what constitutes the correct answer. We have experimented with three different criteria for determining the "correct" answer to questions such as identifying the emotions in facial expressions or making suggestions about the most adaptive way to handle emotions in difficult situations. The first involves *target* criteria. Here we would ask the person whose facial expression is depicted on our test item what he or she was feeling. To the extent that the respondent's answer matches the target's, the answer would be scored as correct. A second approach is to use *expert* criteria. In this strategy, experts on emotion such as psychotherapists or emotion researchers would read test items and provide answers. To the extent that the respondent's answers match the experts', they would be scored as correct. Finally, the *consensus* criteria involve norming the test on a large, heterogeneous sample. The test-taker now receives credit for endorsing answers that match those of the larger group.

One might think that a consensus or a target criteria would not be an appropriate approach to scoring tasks measuring emotional competence. After all, aren't most people misguided about their true feelings? We were able to look at how the target, expert, and consensus criteria are interrelated across some of the MEIS ability tasks. The correlations were actually rather high; half were above $r = .52$ (Mayer et al., 1999). In general, the consensus approach correlated more highly with the target criteria than did the expert criteria. At the moment, we are recommending a consensus-based approach to scoring the MEIS for several reasons. Targets sometimes minimize their own negative feelings when asked to report on them (Mayer & Geher, 1996), but large normative samples, when responses are pooled, tend to be reliable judges (Legree, 1995).

Investigations using the MEIS are in rather preliminary stages, but there are a few findings to report (Mayer et al., 1999). In general, we found support for the theoretical model of emotional intelligence described earlier (Mayer & Salovey, 1997). In a sample of 503 adults, MEIS tasks were generally positively intercorrelated with one another, but not highly so (most were in the $r = .20$ to $.50$ range). As well, the test's factorial structure recommended two equally viable factorial models: (a) a three- to four-factor solution that separated out factors of emotional perception, understanding, management, and, at times, using emotions to facilitate cognitive activities; or (b) a hierarchical structure that first describes a general factor, g_{ei}. The internal consistency of the MEIS is reasonably high: Using consensus scoring, most of the 12 subscales had Cronbach alphas in the .70 to .94 range, though the Branch 3 tasks, which are the shortest subscales, tended to have lower internal consistency (although two of these tasks had alphas of .78 and .94, respectively; two others were .49 and .51). In an independent investigation, the Cronbach alpha reported for the MEIS as a whole was .90 (Ciarrochi, Chan, & Caputi, 2000).

The MEIS as a whole correlates positively with verbal intelligence (but only in the $r = .35$ to .45 range), self-reported empathy, and parental warmth and negatively with social anxiety and depression (Mayer et al., 1999). The MEIS

is not correlated with nonverbal measures of intelligence such as the Raven Progressive Matrices (Ciarrochi, Chan, & Caputi, 2000). Finally, and consistent with the idea that emotional intelligence is a set of abilities that are developed through learning and experience, scores on the MEIS improve with age (Mayer et al., 1999).

A refined and better normed successor to the MEIS, called the Mayer, Salovey, and Caruso Emotional Intelligence Scales (MSCEIT), presently is being prepared for distribution (Mayer, Salovey, & Caruso, in preparation). We recommend this set of tasks for assessing emotional intelligence as an ability. Structured much like the MEIS, the MSCEIT also is based on the four-branch model of emotional intelligence, but it allows for the assessment of emotional intelligence in less time than the MEIS. Poorly worded items have been eliminated, and extensive normative data will be available.

Current Research Findings

We have just started to publish research using ability-based measures of emotional intelligence, like the MEIS and the MSCEIT (see Salovey, Woolery, & Mayer, 2001, for a summary). However, there are some findings to report that are promising with respect to the prediction of important behavioral outcomes. We note that many of the findings described here are as of yet unpublished and unreviewed by other scientists, so they should be viewed as suggestive.

Mayer and his colleagues have been developing measures of individuals' life space—a description of a person's environment in terms of discrete, externally verifiable responses (e.g., How many pairs of shoes do you own? How many times have you attended the theater this year? see Mayer, Carlsmith, & Chabot, 1998). In these studies, higher scores on the MEIS are associated with lower self-reported, life-space measures of engagement in violent and antisocial behavior among college students; the correlations between the MEIS and these measures were in the $r = .40$ range. Other investigators also have reported that greater emotional intelligence is associated with lower levels of antisocial behavior. For example, Rubin (1999) found substantial negative correlations between a version of the MEIS developed for adolescents (the AMEIS) and peer ratings of their aggressiveness; prosocial behaviors rated by these schoolchildren's teachers were positively associated with emotional intelligence ($|r|s = .37$ to .49).

Research focused on adolescents' substance use has been conducted by Trinidad and Johnson (in press). They collected data from 205 culturally diverse seventh- and eighth-grade students using five subtests from the AMEIS. Those scoring high on overall emotional intelligence were significantly less likely to have ever tried smoking a cigarette or to have smoked recently. They were also less likely to report having had an alcoholic beverage in the past week. Emotional intelligence was positively correlated with endorsing the idea that doing well in school is important.

Emotional intelligence, as assessed with the MEIS, also appears to be important in workplace situations. In an intriguing study conducted with 164 employees of an insurance company assigned to 26 customer claim teams, Rice (1999) administered a shortened version of the MEIS, then asked a department manager to rate the effectiveness of these teams and their leaders. The MEIS scores were highly correlated with the manager's ratings of the team leaders' effectiveness ($r = .51$). The average MEIS scores of each of the teams—the team emotional intelligence—also was related to the manager's ratings of the team performance in customer service ($r = .46$). However, emotional intelligence was negatively associated with the team's speed in handling customer complaints ($r = -.40$). It appears that emotional intelligence may help team leaders and their teams to be better at satisfying customers but not necessarily to increase the efficiency with which they perform these behaviors. Perhaps dealing with customers' feelings in an adaptive way takes time.

Interventions to Improve Emotional Intelligence

Despite the paucity of predictive validity data on emotional intelligence, interventions are being developed aimed at raising emotional intelligence in a variety of contexts.

Interventions in Education

With the availability of materials suggesting how teachers can cultivate emotional intelligence in schoolchildren, there has been an in-creasing interest in the last decade in developing school-based programs focused on these abilities (Mayer & Cobb, 2000; Salovey & Sluyter, 1997). For example, in a guidebook for developing emotional intelligence curricula for elementary school students, Schilling (1996) recommends units on self-awareness, managing feelings, decision making, managing stress, personal responsibility, self-concept, empathy, communication, group dynamics, and conflict resolution. As should be obvious, the emotional intelligence rubric is being applied quite broadly to the development of a range of social-emotional skills. As a result, many of the school-based interventions designed to promote emotional intelligence are better classified under the more general label Social and Emotional Learning (SEL) programs (Cohen, 1999a; Elias et al., 1997).

There are over 300 curriculum-based programs in the United States purporting to teach Social and Emotional Learning (Cohen, 1999b). These range from programs based on very specific social problem-solving skills training (e.g., Elias & Tobias, 1996), to more general conflict resolution strategies (e.g., Lantieri & Patti, 1996), to very broad programs organized around themes like "character development" (Lickona, 1991). One of the oldest SEL programs that has a heavy dose of emotional intelligence development within it is the Social Development Curriculum in the New Haven, Connecticut, public schools (Shriver, Schwab-Stone, & DeFalco, 1999; Weissberg, Shriver, Bose, & DeFalco, 1997). The New Haven Social Development Program is a kindergarten through grade 12 curriculum that integrates the development of social and emotional skills in the context of various prevention programs (e.g., AIDS prevention, drug use prevention, teen pregnancy prevention; see also Durlak, 1995). The curriculum provides 25 to 50 hours of highly structured classroom instruction at each grade level. Included in the early years of this curriculum are units on self-monitoring, feelings awareness, perspective taking (empathy), understanding nonverbal communication, anger management, and many other topics, some of which are loosely consistent with our model of emotional intelligence. Although this program has not been evaluated in a randomized, controlled trial, a substantial survey administered every 2 years to New Haven schoolchildren has revealed positive trends since implementation of the program. For example, one change has been reduced school violence and feelings of hopelessness (Shriver et al., 1999).

Another well-known emotional intelligence curriculum is called Self Science, which was developed and field tested at the Nueva School in Hillsborough, California, in the first through eighth grades (Stone-McCown, Jensen, Freedman, & Rideout, 1998). This program begins with three assumptions: There is no thinking without feeling and no feeling without thinking; the more conscious one is of what one is experiencing, the more learning is possible; and self-knowledge is integral to learning. The Self Science curriculum is a flexible one, although it is organized around 54 lessons grouped into 10 goals. For example, Goal 3, called "Becoming More Aware of Multiple Feelings," includes lessons such as Naming Feelings, What Are Feelings? Reading Body Language, Emotional Symbolism, Evoking Emotions, Acting on Emotions, Sources of Feelings, and Responsibility for Feelings. This approach directly focuses on emotions in about half of the lessons. The goals of the Self Science curriculum include talking about feelings and needs; listening, sharing, and comforting others; learning to grow from conflict and adversity; prioritizing and setting goals; including others; making conscious decisions; and giving time and resources to the larger community (Stone-McCown et al., 1998).

Finally, many emotional intelligence interventions for schoolchildren take place within other more specific prevention programs. A good example is the Resolving Conflict Creatively Program (RCCP) that began in the New York City public schools (Lantieri & Patti, 1996). The program goals include increasing awareness of the different choices available to children for dealing with conflicts; developing skills for making these choices; encouraging children's respect for their own cultural background and the backgrounds of others; teaching children how to identify and stand against prejudice; and increasing children's awareness of their role in creating a more peaceful world. These goals are addressed in a 25-hour teacher's training program and in a program emphasizing peer mediation for children in grades 4 to 6. A follow-up program, Peace in the Family, trains parents in conflict resolution strategies. RCCP training programs emphasize identifying one's own feelings in conflict situations and taking the perspective of and empathizing with others' feelings. In an evaluation that included 5,000

children participating in the RCCP program in New York City, hostile attributions and teacher-reported aggressive behavior dropped as a function of the number of conflict resolution lessons the children had received, and academic achievement was highest among those children who received the most lessons (Aber, Brown, & Henrich, 1999; Aber, Jones, Brown, Chaudry, & Samples, 1998).

Although increasing numbers of Social and Emotional Learning programs are being evaluated formally (e.g., Elias, Gere, Schuyler, Branden-Muller, & Sayette, 1991; Greenberg, Kushe, Cook, & Quamma, 1995), many still have not been subjected to empirical scrutiny. There is virtually no reported research on whether these programs are effective by enhancing the kinds of skills delineated in our model of emotional intelligence.

Interventions in the Workplace

Possible interventions to increase emotional intelligence also can be found in the workplace (e.g., Caruso, Mayer, & Salovey, in press; Cherniss & Goleman, 1998; Goleman, 1998). These workplace programs, however, are at a much earlier stage of development than those designed for the classroom. Furthermore, many of these workplace "emotional intelligence" programs are really old and familiar training sessions on human relations, achievement motivation, stress management, and conflict resolution.

One promising approach to workplace emotional intelligence is the Weatherhead MBA Program at Case Western Reserve University, where training in social and emotional competency is incorporated into the curriculum for future business leaders (Boyatzis, Cowen, & Kolb, 1995). Although this program is not focused explicitly on emotions per se, these MBA students receive experiences designed to promote initiative, flexibility, achievement drive, empathy, self-confidence, persuasiveness, networking, self-control, and group management. Communication and emotion-related skills also are increasingly being incorporated into physician training (Kramer, Ber, & Moores, 1989).

Perhaps the workplace program that most explicitly addresses itself to emotional intelligence is the Emotional Competency Training Program at American Express Financial Advisors. The goal of the program is to assist managers in becoming "emotional coaches" for their employees. The training focuses on the role of emotion in the workplace and gaining an awareness of how one's own emotional reactions and the emotions of others affect management practices. Although systematic evaluation of this program has yet to be published, a higher business growth rate (money under management) has been found for the financial advisers whose managers had taken the training program as compared with those who had not (reported in Cherniss, 1999).

Directions for Future Research

Despite the rapid growth of interest in emotional intelligence, the measurement of emotional intelligence using ability-based indices is still in an early stage. Recently, as is inevitable for a new concept, emotional intelligence has received some criticism. In particular, using an array of available and, for the most part, poorly validated instruments as the basis for analysis, the construct validity of emotional intelligence has been questioned (Davies et al., 1998). It simply is premature to draw any such conclusions until investigators in our laboratory and other laboratories have completed and validated the appropriate ability-based measures of emotional intelligence.

The area of emotional intelligence is in need of energetic investigators interested in helping to refine the ability-based assessment of emotional intelligence and, subsequently, studying the predictive validity of emotional intelligence (over and above other constructs) in accounting for important outcomes in school, workplace, family, and social relationships. Given the present status of instrument development and validation, we would encourage investigators to focus their energies on the refinement of ability measures of emotional intelligence. Although we have been pleased with the MEIS and are confident that its successor, the MSCEIT, will be the measurement instrument of choice for assessing emotional intelligence as an ability, research needs to be conducted to measure emotional intelligence with even greater precision and with more easily administered and briefer tests. Further work also will be needed before we can confidently claim that one method of scoring—expert, target, or consensus—is clearly more valid than the others. And it will be necessary to investigate whether tests of emotional intelligence are culture-bound. The

fact is, we are in the early phase of research on emotional intelligence, in terms of both measuring it as an ability and showing that such measures predict significant outcomes.

After refining the measurement of emotional intelligence, we are hoping that many investigators will join us in exploring what this construct predicts, both as an overall ability and in terms of an individual's profile of strengths and weaknesses. The domains in which emotional intelligence may play an important part are limited only by the imagination of the investigators studying these abilities, and we are hoping to see an explosion of research in the near future establishing when emotional intelligence is important—perhaps more so than conventional intelligence—and, of course, when it is not.

Finally, and reflecting the theme of this volume, positive psychology, attention will need to be focused on how emotional intelligence can be developed through the life span. We suspect that work on the teaching and learning of emotion-related abilities might prove to be a useful counterpoint to the nihilistic conclusions of books like *The Bell Curve* and instead, may suggest all kinds of ways in which emotionally enriching experiences could be incorporated into one's life. We need to remind ourselves, however, that work on emotional intelligence is still in its infancy, and that what the field and general public need are more investigators treating it with serious empirical attention.

Acknowledgments Preparation of this chapter was facilitated by grants from the National Cancer Institute (R01-CA68427), the National Institute of Mental Health (P01-MH/DA56826), and the Donaghue Women's Health Investigator Program at Yale University to Peter Salovey.

References

Aber, J. L., Brown, J. L., & Henrich, C. C. (1999). *Teaching conflict resolution: An effective school-based approach to violence prevention.* New York: National Center for Children in Poverty, Joseph L. Mailman School of Public Health, Columbia University.

Aber, J. L., Jones, S. M., Brown, J. L., Chaudry, N., & Samples, F. (1998). Resolving conflict creatively: Evaluating the developmental effects of a school-based violence prevention program in neighborhood and classroom context. *Development and Psychopathology, 10,* 187–213.

Alcalde, J. (1996, December). Inteligencia emocional? *Muy Interesante,* 41–46.

American Dialect Society. (1995). American Dialect Society: e-mail from Allan Metcalf. http://www.americandialect.org/excite/collections/adsl/011272.shtml.

American Dialect Society. (1999). American Dialect Society: Words of the Year. http://www.americandialect.org/woty.

Averill, J. R. (1999). Individual differences in emotional creativity: Structure and correlates. *Journal of Personality, 67,* 331–371.

Averill, J. R., & Nunley, E. P. (1992). *Voyages of the heart: Living an emotionally creative life.* New York: Free Press.

Bagby, R. M., Parker, J. D. A., & Taylor, G. J. (1993a). The twenty-item Toronto Alexithymia Scale: I. Item selection and cross-validation of the factor structure. *Journal of Psychosomatic Research, 38,* 23–32.

Bagby, R. M., Parker, J. D. A., & Taylor, G. J. (1993b). The twenty-item Toronto Alexithymia Scale: II. Convergent, discriminant, and concurrent validity. *Journal of Psychosomatic Research, 38,* 33–40.

Bar-On, R. (1997). *Bar-On Emotional Quotient Inventory: A measure of emotional intelligence.* Toronto, Ontario: Multi-Health Systems.

Boyatzis, R. E., Cowen, S. S., & Kolb, D. A. (1995). *Innovation in professional education: Steps on a journey to learning.* San Francisco: Jossey-Bass.

Brodie, I. (1996, January 5). Neutron bomb fall-out changes slang. *The Times (Overseas News Section),* p. 26.

Buck, R. (1976). A test of nonverbal receiving ability: Preliminary studies. *Human Communication Research, 2,* 162–171.

Caruso, D. R., Mayer, J. D., & Salovey, P. (in press). Emotional intelligence and emotional leadership. In R. Riggio & S. Murphy (Eds.), *Multiple intelligences and leadership.* Mahwah, NJ: Erlbaum.

Catanzaro, S. J., & Mearns, J. (1990). Measuring generalized expectancies for negative mood regulation: Initial scale development and implications. *Journal of Personality Assessment, 54,* 546–563.

Cherniss, C. (1999). *Model program summaries.* Technical report issued by the Consortium for Research on Emotional Intelligence in Organizations (available at www.eiconsortium.org).

Cherniss, C., & Goleman, D. (1998). *Bringing emotional intelligence to the workplace.* Technical report issued by the Consortium for Research on Emotional Intelligence in Organizations (available at www.eiconsortium.org).

Ciarrochi, J. V., Chan, A. Y. C., & Caputi, P. (2000). A critical evaluation of the emotional intelligence construct. *Personality and Individual Differences, 3,* 539–561.

Cohen, J. (Ed.) (1999a). *Educating minds and hearts: Social emotional learning and the passage into adolescence.* New York: Teachers College Press.

Cohen, J. (1999b). Social and emotional learning past and present: A psychoeducational dialogue. In J. Cohen (Ed.), *Educating minds and hearts: Social emotional learning and the passage into adolescence* (pp. 2–23). New York: Teachers College Press.

Cooper, R. K., & Sawaf, A. (1997). *Executive EQ: Emotional intelligence in leadership and organizations.* New York: Grosset/Putnam.

Cronbach, L. J. (1960). *Essentials of psychological testing.* New York: Harper and Row.

Damasio, A. R. (1995). *Descartes' error: Emotion, reason, and the human brain.* New York: Avon.

Davies, M., Stankov, L., & Roberts, R. D. (1998). Emotional intelligence: In search of an elusive construct. *Journal of Personality and Social Psychology, 75,* 989–1015.

Durlak, J. A. (1995). *School-based prevention programs for children and adolescents.* Thousand Oaks, CA: Sage.

Easterbrook, J. A. (1959). The effects of emotion on cue utilization and the organization of behavior. *Psychological Review, 66,* 183–200.

Elias, M. J., Gere, M. A., Schuyler, T. F., Branden-Muller, L. R., & Sayette, M. A. (1991). The promotion of social competence: Longitudinal study of a preventive school-based program. *American Journal of Orthopsychiatry, 61,* 409–417.

Elias, M. J., & Tobias, S. E. (1996). *Social problem solving interventions in the schools.* New York: Guilford.

Elias, M. J., Zins, J. E., Weissberg, R. P., Frey, K. S., Greenberg, M. T., Haynes, N. M., Kessler, R., Schwab-Stone, M. E., & Shriver, T. P. (1997). *Promoting social and emotional learning: Guidelines for educators.* Alexandria, VA: Association for Supervision and Curriculum Development.

Epstein, S. (1998). *Constructive thinking: The key to emotional intelligence.* Westport, CT: Praeger.

EQ Japan, Inc. (1998). *Emotional Quotient Inventory.* Tokyo, Japan: Author.

Forgas, J. P. (1995). Mood and judgment: The affect infusion model (AIM). *Psychological Bulletin, 117,* 39–66.

Freedman, H. S., Prince, L. M., Riggio, R. E., & DiMatteo, M. R. (1980). Understanding and assessing nonverbal expressiveness: The Affective Communication Test. *Journal of Personality and Social Psychology, 39,* 333–351.

Gardner, H. (1983/1993). *Frames of mind: The theory of multiple intelligences* (10th anniversary edition). New York: Basic Books.

Gibbs, N. (1995, October 2). The EQ factor. *Time,* p. 60–68.

Giuliano, T., & Swinkels, A. (1992, August). *Development and validation of the Mood Awareness Scale.* Paper presented at the annual meeting of the American Psychological Association, Washington, DC.

*Goleman, D. (1995a). *Emotional intelligence.* New York: Bantam.

Goleman, D. (1995b, September 10). Why your emotional intelligence quotient can matter more than IQ. *USA Weekend,* pp. 4–8.

Goleman, D. (1998). *Working with emotional intelligence.* New York: Bantam.

Goodwin, F. K., & Jamison, K. R. (1990). *Manic-depressive illness.* New York: Oxford University Press.

Gottman, J., & DeClaire, J. (1997). *The heart of parenting: Raising an emotionally intelligent child.* New York: Simon and Schuster.

Greenberg, M. T., Kushe, C. A., Cook, E. T., & Quamma, J. P. (1995). Promoting emotional competence in school-aged children: The effects of the PATHS curriculum. *Development and Psychopathology, 7,* 117–136.

Herrnstein, R. J., & Murray, C. (1994). *The bell curve: Intelligence and class in American life.* New York: Free Press.

Kramer, D., Ber, R., & Moores, M. (1989). Increasing empathy among medical students. *Medical Education, 23,* 168–173.

Lane, R. D., Quinlan, D. M., Schwartz, G. E., Walker, P., & Zeitlin, S. B. (1990). The levels of emotional awareness scale: A cognitive-developmental measure of emotion. *Journal of Personality Assessment, 55,* 124–134.

Lantieri, L., & Patti, J. (1996). *Waging peace in our schools.* Boston: Beacon.

Legree, P. J. (1995). Evidence for an oblique social intelligence factor established with a Likert-based testing procedure. *Intelligence, 21,* 247–266.

Lickona, T. (1991). *Educating for character: How our schools can teach respect and responsibility.* New York: Bantam.

Mandler, G. (1975). *Mind and emotion.* New York: Wiley.

Mayer, J. D. (1986). How mood influences cognition. In N. E. Sharkey (Ed.), *Advances in cog-nitive science* (pp. 290–314). Chichester, West Sussex: Ellis Horwood.

Mayer, J. D., Carlsmith, K. M., & Chabot, H. F. (1998). Describing the person's external environment: Conceptualizing and measuring the life space. *Journal of Research in Personality, 32,* 253–296.

Mayer, J. D., Caruso, D. R., & Salovey, P. (1998). *Multifactor Emotional Intelligence Test (MEIS).* (Available from John D. Mayer, Department of Psychology, University of New Hampshire, Conant Hall, Durham, NH 03824.)

*Mayer, J. D., Caruso, D. R., & Salovey, P. (1999). Emotional intelligence meets standards for a traditional intelligence. *Intelligence, 27,* 267–298.

Mayer, J. D., & Cobb, C. D. (2000). Educational policy on emotional intelligence: Does it make sense? *Educational Psychology Review, 12,* 163–183.

Mayer, J. D., DiPaolo, M. T., & Salovey, P. (1990). Perceiving affective content in ambiguous visual stimuli: A component of emotional intelligence. *Journal of Personality Assessment, 54,* 772–781.

Mayer, J. D., Gaschke, Y., Braverman, D. L., & Evans, T. (1992). Mood-congruent judgment is a general effect. *Journal of Personality and Social Psychology, 63,* 119–132.

Mayer, J. D., & Geher, G. (1996). Emotional intelligence and the identification of emotion. *Intelligence, 22,* 89–113.

Mayer, J. D., & Hanson, E. (1995). Mood-congruent judgment over time. *Personality and Social Psychology Bulletin, 21,* 237–244.

*Mayer, J. D., & Salovey, P. (1997). What is emotional intelligence? In P. Salovey & D. Sluyter (Eds.), *Emotional development and emotional intelligence: Implications for educators* (pp. 3–31). New York: Basic Books.

*Mayer, J. D., Salovey, P., & Caruso, D. (2000a). Emotional intelligence as Zeitgeist, as personality, and as a mental ability. In R. Bar-On & J. D. A. Parker (Eds.), *The handbook of emotional intelligence* (pp. 92–117). New York: Jossey-Bass.

*Mayer, J. D., Salovey, P., & Caruso, D. (2000b). Models of emotional intelligence. In R. J. Sternberg (Ed.), *The handbook of intelligence* (2nd ed., pp. 396–420). New York: Cambridge University Press.

Mayer, J. D., Salovey, P., & Caruso, D. (in preparation). Mayer, Salovey, and Caruso Emotional Intelligence Test (MSCEIT). Toronto, Ontario: Multi-Health Systems.

Miketta, G., Gottschling, C., Wagner-Roos, L., & Gibbs, N. (1995, October 9). Die neue Erfolgs-formel: EQ. *Focus,* 194–202.

Mowrer, O. H. (1960). *Learning theory and behavior*. New York: Wiley.

Ortony, A., Clore, G. L., & Collins, A. (1988). *The cognitive structure of emotions*. Cambridge, England: Cambridge University Press.

Palfai, T. P., & Salovey, P. (1993). The influence of depressed and elated mood on deductive and inductive reasoning. *Imagination, Cognition, and Personality, 13*, 57–71.

Payne, W. L. (1983/1986). A study of emotion: Developing emotional intelligence; self-integration; relating to fear, pain and desire. *Dissertation Abstracts International, 47*, 203A. (University Microfilms No. AAC 8605928)

Pennebaker, J. W. (1989). Confession, inhibition, and disease. In L. Berkowitz (Ed.), *Advances in experimental social psychology* (Vol. 22, pp. 211–244). New York: Academic Press.

Pennebaker, J. W. (1993). Putting stress into words: Health, linguistic, and therapeutic implications. *Behavior Research and Therapy, 31*, 539–548.

Pennebaker, J. W. (1997). Writing about emotional experiences as a therapeutic process. *Psychological Science, 9*, 162–166.

Rice, C. L. (1999). *A quantitative study of emotional intelligence and its impact on team performance*. Unpublished master's thesis, Pepperdine University, Los Angeles.

Rosenthal, R., Hall, J. A., DiMatteo, M. R., Rogers, P., & Archer, D. (1979). *Sensitivity to nonverbal communication: A profile approach to the measurement of individual differences*. Baltimore: Johns Hopkins University Press.

Rubin, M. M. (1999). *Emotional intelligence and its role in mitigating aggression: A correlational study of the relationship between emotional intelligence and aggression in urban adolescents*. Unpublished manuscript, Immaculata College, Immaculata, PA.

Ryback, D. (1998). *Putting emotional intelligence to work: Successful leadership is more than IQ*. Boston: Butterworth-Heinemann.

Saarni, C. (1990). Emotional competence: How emotions and relationships become integrated. In R. A. Thompson (Ed.), *Socioemotional development: Nebraska symposium on motivation* (Vol. 36, pp. 115–182). Lincoln: University of Nebraska Press.

*Saarni, C. (1999). *Developing emotional competence*. New York: Guilford.

Salerno, J. G. (1996). *Emotional quotient (EQ): Are you ready for it?* Oakbank, Australia: Noble House of Australia.

*Salovey, P., Bedell, B. T., Detweiler, J. B., & Mayer, J. D. (1999). Coping intelligently: Emotional intelligence and the coping process. In C. R. Snyder (Ed.), *Coping: The psychology of what works* (pp. 141–164). New York: Oxford University Press.

*Salovey, P., Bedell, B. T., Detweiler, J. B., & Mayer, J. D. (2000). Current directions in emotional intelligence research. In M. Lewis & J. M. Haviland-Jones (Eds.), *Handbook of emotions* (2nd ed., pp. 504–520). New York: Guilford.

Salovey, P., & Birnbaum, D. (1989). The influence of mood on health-relevant cognitions. *Journal of Personality and Social Psychology, 57*, 539–551.

*Salovey, P., & Mayer, J. D. (1990). Emotional intelligence. *Imagination, Cognition, and Personality, 9*, 185–211.

Salovey, P., Mayer, J. D., Goldman, S. L., Turvey, C., & Palfai, T. P. (1995). Emotional attention, clarity, and repair: Exploring emotional intelligence using the Trait Meta-Mood Scale. In J. W. Pennebaker (Ed.), *Emotion, disclosure, and health* (pp. 125–154). Washington, DC: American Psychological Association.

Salovey, P., & Rodin, J. (1986). Differentiation of social-comparison jealousy and romantic jealousy. *Journal of Personality and Social Psychology, 50*, 1100–1112.

Salovey, P., & Rodin, J. (1989). Envy and jealousy in close relationships. *Review of Personality and Social Psychology, 10*, 221–246.

Salovey, P., & Sluyter, D. (Eds). (1997). *Emotional development and emotional intelligence: Implications for educators*. New York: Basic Books.

*Salovey, P., Woolery, A., & Mayer, J. D. (2001). Emotional intelligence: Conceptualization and measurement. In G. Fletcher & M. Clark (Eds.), *The Blackwell handbook of social psychology* (pp. 279–307). London: Blackwell.

Schilling, D. (1996). *Fifty activities for teaching emotional intelligence: Level I: Elementary*. Torrance, CA: Innerchoice Publishing.

Schutte, N. S., Malouff, J. M., Hall, L. E., Haggerty, D. J., Copper, J. T., Golden, C. J., & Dornheim, L. (1998). Development and validation of a measure of emotional intelligence. *Personality and Individual Differences, 25*, 167–177.

*Schwarz, N. (1990). Feelings as information: Informational and motivational functions of affective states. In E. T. Higgins & E. M. Sorrentino (Eds.), *Handbook of motivation and cognition* (Vol. 2, pp. 527–561). New York: Guilford.

Segal, J. (1997). *Raising your emotional intelligence: A practical guide*. New York: Holt.

Shapiro, L. E. (1997). *How to raise a child with a high EQ: A parents' guide to emotional intelligence*. New York: HarperCollins.

Shriver, T. P., Schwab-Stone, M., & DeFalco, K. (1999). Why SEL is the better way: The New

Haven Social Development Program. In J. Cohen (Ed.), *Educating minds and hearts: Social emotional learning and the passage into adolescence* (pp. 43–60). New York: Teachers College Press.

Simon, H. A. (1982). Comments. In M. S. Clark & S. T. Fiske (Eds.), *Affect and cognition* (pp. 333–342). Hillsdale, NJ: Erlbaum.

Simmons, S., & Simmons, J. C. (1997). *Measuring emotional intelligence*. Arlington, TX: Summit.

Singer, J. A., & Salovey, P. (1988). Mood and memory: Evaluating the Network Theory of Affect. *Clinical Psychology Review, 8*, 211–251.

Steiner, C., & Perry, P. (1997). *Achieving emotional literacy: A personal program to increase your emotional intelligence*. New York: Avon.

Sternberg, R. J. (1985). *The triarchic mind: A new theory of human intelligence*. New York: Penguin.

Stone-McCown, K., Jensen, A. L., Freedman, J. M., & Rideout, M. C. (1998). *Self-science: The emotional intelligence curriculum* (2nd ed.). San Mateo, CA: Six Seconds.

Swinkels, A., & Giuliano, T. A. (1995). The measurement and conceptualization of mood awareness: Monitoring and labeling one's mood states. *Personality and Social Psychology Bulletin, 21*, 934–939.

Thayer, R. E., Newman, J. R., & McClain, T. M. (1994). Self-regulation of mood: Strategies for changing a bad mood, raising energy, and reducing tension. *Journal of Personality and Social Psychology, 67*, 910–925.

Thomas, B. (1995, December 13). A la recherche du QE perdu. *Le Canard Enchaîné*, 5.

Tomkins, S. S. (1962). *Affect, imagery, and consciousness*: Vol. 1. *The positive affects*. New York: Springer.

Trinidad, D. R., & Johnson, C. A. (in press). The association between emotional intelligence and early adolescent tobacco and alcohol use. *Personality and Individual Differences*.

Wang, A. Y., Tett, R. P., Fisher, R., Griebler, J. G., & Martinez, A. M. (1997). *Testing a model of emotional intelligence*. Unpublished manuscript, University of Central Florida, Orlando, FL.

Weisinger, H. (1998). *Emotional intelligence at work: The untapped edge for success*. San Francisco: Jossey-Bass.

Weissberg, R. P., Shriver, T. P., Bose, S., & DeFalco, K. (1997). Creating a district wide social development project. *Educational Leadership, 54*, 37–39.

13

Emotional Creativity

Toward "Spiritualizing the Passions"

James R. Averill

The relation between emotions and creativity is complex and charged with ambivalence. In schools we try to encourage creativity, and in the arts and sciences, we reserve our greatest praise for its achievement. A person, it seems, cannot be too creative. By contrast, a person who is too prone to emotion risks being labeled as immature, uncouth, boorish, or worse. Even our language seems to disparage emotions: Most nonemotional words have a positive connotation; the opposite is true of emotional words, where those with a negative connotation outnumber those with a positive connotation by roughly 2 to 1 (Averill, 1980b).

The way creativity and emotions are evaluated in everyday affairs is reflected in our scientific theories. Psychologically, for example, creativity is classed among the "higher" thought processes, whereas emotions often are treated as noncognitive—a psychological euphemism for "lower" thought processes. Physiologically, creativity is considered a neocortical activity, whereas emotions are presumed to be a manifestation of paleocortical and subcortical regions of the brain. Finally, from a biological perspective, creativity is regarded as a late ev-olutionary development, whereas the emotions are treated as holdovers from our prehuman animal heritage.

Before we take such contrasts too seriously, it might be noted that the positive evaluation afforded creativity is, to put it bluntly, tautological. That is, only valued events and activities are labeled as creative. Moreover, the positive evaluation is typically made post hoc. Many innovations later judged as creative were condemned at the time of their occurrence, and their authors may even have been persecuted. The fate of Galileo is only the most familiar example of a distressingly common phenomenon.

Similar observations can be made with respect to the emotions, but in reverse; that is, emotions that are viewed negatively or condemned in the abstract often are encouraged in practice. For example, given an adequate provocation, the person who fails to respond with anger, grief, fear, or jealousy (as the case may be) is liable to be treated not as a morally superior human being but as shallow, at best, and perverted, at worst.

In short, our everyday conceptions of emotion and creativity can be misleading. This is particularly true when emotions and creativity are set in opposition to each other not only in evaluative terms but also in terms of underlying psychological processes. The primary purpose of this chapter is to present a contrary view, one in which emotions themselves are seen as creative products. A secondary purpose is reflected in the subtitle to the chapter, "spiritualizing the passions," which I adopt from Nietzsche (1889/1997, p. 25). I will not speculate about Nietzsche's meaning of this phrase; later, I offer my own interpretation. Suffice it to say that, as used in this chapter, spiritualization has no necessary ontological implications—a belief, for example, in a nonmaterial mode of existence. Acts of creation—or re-creation, as in aesthetic experiences (Averill, Stanat, & More, 1998; Richards, 1998)—provide the reference point for spiritualizing the passions as here conceived.[1]

In addition to presenting a model of emotion in which emotional creativity makes theoretical sense, I review briefly some empirical research on individual difference in emotional creativity, with special reference to alexithymia and mysticlike experiences—two conditions that represent low and high points along the continuum of emotional creativity. I also explore how neurotic syndromes can be interpreted as emotional creativity gone awry—a despiritualization of the passions, so to speak.

Historical Background in Brief

The idea of emotional creativity is a straightforward extension of a social-constructionist view of emotion (Averill, 1980a, 1984; Averill & Thomas-Knowles, 1991). It is not, however, limited to any one theoretical perspective, as the following brief sample of historical antecedents indicates. In his *Varieties of Religious Experience*, William James (1902/1961) observed, "When a person has an inborn genius for certain emotions, his life differs strangely from that of ordinary people" (p. 215). This observation epitomizes a view of emotion that bears little relation to the famous theory typically associated with James's name (together with that of the Danish physician Carl Lange). In the latter (James-Lange) theory, emotions are attributed to feedback from bodily responses; little allowance is made for the type of emotional genius described by James in the *Varieties*. I would only add the following caveat to James's

observation on emotional genius: Creativity in the emotional domain is not limited to a few individuals of exceptional talent any more than is creativity in the intellectual and artistic domains so limited.

Two other past theorists deserve brief mention. Otto Rank (1936/1978), an artist as well as a disciple of Freud, believed that many neurotic syndromes reflect creative impulses that are expressed in ways detrimental to the individual. In a similar vein, but at the other end of the neurotic-healthy spectrum, Abraham Maslow (1971) distinguished between primary and secondary creativity. Routine scientific research and artistic production, which depend more on technical competence and persistence than on original thought, exemplify the latter. Primary creativity, by contrast, is the ability to be inspired, to become totally immersed in the matter at hand, and to experience those "peak" moments that are "a diluted, more secular, more frequent version of the mystical experience" (p. 62). Again, a caveat is in order: Just as creativity is not limited to a few exceptional individuals (geniuses), neither are emotionally creative responses limited to a few extreme (peak or mystical) experiences.

To bring this brief historical review up to date, note should be made of a number of concepts that bear a family resemblance to emotional creativity, for example, emotional intelligence (Salovey, Mayer, & Caruso, this volume), emotional competence (Saarni, 1999), and emotional literacy (Steiner, 1996). Also worthy of mention are Gardner's (1993) intra- and interpersonal intelligences and Epstein's (1998) constructive thinking. There are important differences in the theoretical underpinnings to these concepts; what they have in common is an emphasis on the functional or adaptive aspects of emotional behavior.

A Model of Emotion

The theoretical model on which the present analysis is based is depicted in Figure 13.1. Because this model has been discussed in detail elsewhere (Averill, 1997, 1999a), I will outline it only briefly here. Although our emotions are conditioned by our evolutionary history, biological predispositions place only loose constraints on behavior. Beliefs and rules, the social analogue of genes, are of greater importance in organizing *emotional syndromes* and, ultimately, in the experience and expression of emotion.

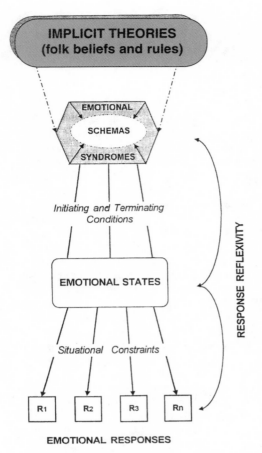

Figure 13.1 Emotional syndromes, schemas, states, and responses as related to one another and to implicit (folk) theories of emotion.

By emotional syndrome I mean those states of affairs recognized in ordinary language by such abstract nouns as *anger*, *grief*, and *love*. Emotional syndromes are not intrapsychic phenomena; rather, they are the folk equivalent of the theoretical constructs found in formal scientific theories. In medicine, for example, one can speak of smallpox as a syndrome, even though no one is actually afflicted with the disease. Succinctly put, the meaning of emotional syndromes depends on a matrix of culturally specific beliefs (implicit theories) about the nature of emotion, just as the meaning of disease syndromes depends on a matrix of beliefs (scientific theories) about microbes, immunity, homeostasis, and so on.

There are, of course, important differences between folk-theoretical concepts and the concepts of scientific theories. Among other things, scientific concepts are (relatively) value free,

whereas folk concepts about emotion are value laden. That is, emotional concepts presume not only beliefs about the nature of emotion per se but also beliefs about how a person *should* respond when emotional. The latter beliefs constitute the rules of emotion.

To the extent that emotional syndromes are constituted by rules, they are analogous to social roles (Averill, 1980a, 1990). Consider the following episode of grief manifested by a Kiowa woman at her brother's funeral: "She wept in a frenzy, tore her hair, scratched her cheeks, and even tried to jump into the grave" (LaBarre, 1947, p. 55). Within most modern, industrialized societies, this would appear to be an excessive reaction even to the loss of a dear brother. According to LaBarre, however, the deceased brother was not dear to the woman—but neither was her reaction excessive. "I happened to know," he writes, "that [the woman] had not seen her brother for some time, and there was no particular love lost between them: she was merely carrying on the way a decent woman should among the Kiowa. Away from the grave, she was immediately chatting vivaciously about some other topic. Weeping is used differently among the Kiowas" (p. 55).

Was the Kiowa woman merely playing the role of a grief-stricken sister? Not if we interpret "merely" to suggest that her performance was feigned. There is no reason to believe that the woman was insincere in her grief. Metaphorically speaking, grief *is* a role that societies create in order to facilitate transition following bereavement and that people may enact with greater or lesser involvement (Averill, 1979; Averill & Nunley, 1993). This is not to gainsay the importance of biology—the tendency to grieve at the loss of a loved one is part of what we are as a social species. However, biology only prompts; it does not write the script.

Returning now to the aspects of emotion depicted in Figure 13.1, before a person can respond emotionally (enter into an emotional role), the relevant beliefs and rules must be internalized to form *emotional schemas*. Because of individual differences in temperament, socialization, and position in society, people internalize with varying degrees of fidelity the beliefs and rules that help constitute emotional syndromes; hence, even within the same culture, no two individuals experience grief, or any other emotion, in exactly the same way.

An *emotional state* is a temporary (episodic) disposition to respond in a manner consistent with an emotional syndrome, as that syndrome is understood by the individual. In personality theory, the notion of a disposition is typically used to refer to enduring traits, such as extraversion. But dispositions can be temporary and reversible, in which case we speak of states rather than traits.

An emotional state is "switched on" when a relevant emotional schema is activated by conditions external (e.g., environmental events) or internal (e.g., physiological arousal) to the individual. In simple, oft-recurring situations, emotional schemas may exist preformed in the mind (or brain) of the individual. When the situation is unusual and the episode complex, however, emotional schemas are constructed "on-line," as an episode develops. In constructing a schema on-line, a person has recourse to a large database of experience stored in memory, as well as general guidelines (beliefs and rules) about the proper course of the emotion. Depending on the circumstances and the person's goals, only a subset of this stored information may be accessed in a given episode. Hence, even within the same individual, no two episodes of grief, or of any other emotion, will be experienced in exactly the same way.

Emotional responses are what a person does when in an emotional state. Instrumental acts (e.g., hitting, running), physiological changes (e.g., increased heart rate), and expressive reactions (e.g., smiling, frowning) are familiar examples of emotional responses. The cognitive appraisals or judgments that a person makes about events (e.g., that an event is dangerous in the case of fear) are also responses—a part of the emotional syndrome and not simply an antecedent condition (Solomon, 1993). In a similar vein, feelings—the subjective experience of emotion—can be considered responses a person makes. Like other subjective experiences (e.g., perceptual responses), emotional feelings can be veridical or illusory (Averill, 1993).

Emotions as Creative Products

A reflexive, or bidirectional, relation exists among emotional syndromes/schemas, states, and responses, as illustrated by the curved arrows at the right of Figure 13.1. As depicted in the figure, emotional creativity can start with a change in the beliefs and rules that help constitute emotional syndromes; or it can start from the bottom, with a change in behavior. In the latter case, alterations in beliefs and rules

may follow, first as a rationalization or post hoc legitimation for responses already made, and later as a basis for further action. Irrespective of how change is induced, whether from the top down or from the bottom up, creativity must ultimately be judged by its product.

In what ways can an emotion be a creative product? A brief detour into the realm of art will help us to address this question. The surrealists believed that any "found object" can be a work of art if appropriately selected and displayed; the object itself need undergo little or no change in the process. Marcel Duchamp's use of a porcelain urinal is a famous example. Of course, most artists (including Duchamp) are not content simply to use an object as it is, whether found in nature or ready-made. More commonly, a piece of wood or scrap metal, say, may be sculpted to give it representational form, for example, as a commemorative mask or statue. Going further, an artist may break with tradition and develop a new form of expression, one that may at first appear strange and even "unnatural" within the cultural context (e.g., as with dadaism and abstract expressionism, in their inception).

The division between ready-made, representational, and revolutionary art does not necessarily correspond to three levels of creativity. Ready-made art can be highly creative, whereas a representational painting or sculpture, although technically competent, may be unimaginative. And, needless to say, a radically new or untraditional form of expression need not be judged creative simply because it is different.

This threefold distinction also applies to emotions as creative products. First, corresponding to ready-made art, emotional creativity may involve the particularly effective application of a preexisting emotion, or combinations of emotions. Second, emotional creativity may involve the modification ("sculpting") of a standard emotion to better meet the needs of the individual or group. Third, emotional creativity may involve the development of new forms of expression, with fundamental changes in the beliefs and rules by which emotional syndromes are constituted.

Criteria for Judging an Object as Creative

Creativity is not an inherent feature of certain types of behavior but a judgment made about behavior. This is true, incidentally, of emotion as well as creativity. A perennial debate among theorists is whether emotions involve special processes (e.g., an affect system distinct from a cognitive system), or whether common processes underlie both emotional and cognitive behavior. Much depends, of course, on how "emotion" and "cognition" are defined (cf. Cacioppo & Berntson, 1999). The model of emotion presented earlier (Figure 13.1) presumes no special or uniquely emotional processes. Terms such as anger, fear, and love reflect judgments about behavior; they do refer to underlying mental or physiological mechanisms. This is a point worth emphasizing, for it helps break down the barrier so often erected between emotions and presumably "higher" thought processes, including creativity.

A similar special-versus common-process debate occurs with respect to creativity. There, too, a common-process perspective would seem adequate to account for known facts (Weisberg, 1986). But if not by reference to a special process, how do we recognize a response as creative? The criteria are threefold—novelty, effectiveness, and authenticity.

The criterion of novelty implies that something new is brought into being, something that did not exist before. Novelty is thus a relative concept; it presumes a standard of comparison (that which existed before). That standard may be a person's own past behavior, or it may be behavior of the group within which the person lives. The latter (group) comparison is more common in the assessment of creativity; however, it is important to keep in mind that all growth—to the extent that it is growth and not mere alternation or substitution—involves some novelty when compared with the individual's own past behavior.

A novel response may simply be bizarre. To be considered creative, the response must also be effective—for example, aesthetically (as in art), practically (as in technology), or interpersonally (as in leadership). Like novelty, effectiveness is a relative concept. Nothing can be effective in and of itself but only within a context. As the context changes, so, too, may effectiveness. Thus, a response that is effective in the short term may be ineffective in the long term, and vice versa. Similarly, a response that is effective for the individual may be ineffective for the group, and vice versa.

Finally, for a response to be considered creative, it should be an authentic expression of the person's own beliefs and values, and not a mere copy of others' expectations. This criterion has been particularly emphasized by Arnheim (1966, p. 298) with respect to works of art, but it applies equally well to the emotions. And, as will be discussed more fully in a later section, authenticity is especially important in spiritualizing the passions. For the moment, suffice it to note that an emotion that is not a true (authentic) reflection of a person's own beliefs and values cannot be considered fully creative, no matter how novel or effective.

Individual Differences in Emotional Creativity

In any given culture, some emotions are considered more basic than others. When viewed across cultures, however, considerable variation can be found among emotions, including the emotions considered most basic within Western cultures (e.g., anger, fear, grief). This fact is not in dispute, although its theoretical interpretation remains the topic of controversy (Ekman & Davidson, 1994). If we accept cultural variations as genuine, and not as mere patina on the *real* emotions, the question then becomes: How do such variations arise? The most parsimonious answer is: Through the accumulation and diffusion of typically small innovations made by countless individuals. In other words, cultural variations presume emotional creativity on the individual level.

Not everyone is equally creative in the emotional domain any more than in the intellectual or artistic domains. Years of preparation are typically required before creativity is achieved within the arts and sciences (Hayes, 1981; Weisberg, 1986). There is no reason to believe the situation to be different in the domain of emotion. Some people think about and try to understand their emotions, and they are sensitive to the emotions of others. Such people, we may presume, are on average better prepared emotionally than are their more indifferent—but not necessarily less reactive—counterparts.

To explore individual differences in the ability to be emotionally creative, a 30-item Emotional Creativity Inventory (ECI) has been constructed (Averill, 1999b). Seven of the items refer to emotional preparedness. The remaining items address the three criteria for creativity discussed earlier. Specifically, 14 items refer to the novelty of emotional experiences; 5 to effectiveness; and 4 to authenticity. Factor analysis indicates that the ECI can be broken down into three facets. The first facet comprises the *preparedness* items; the second facet, the *novelty* items; and the third facet, a combination of the *effectiveness and authenticity* items. Sample items from the three facets are presented in Table 13.1.

Scores on the ECI have been related to a variety of behavioral and personality variables, including peer ratings of emotional creativity, the ability to express emotions in words and pictures, and the "big five" personality traits (Averill, 1999b; Gutbezahl & Averill, 1996). I will limit the present discussion to two variables of particular relevance to this chapter, namely, alexithymia and mysticism. The relevant data are presented in Table 13.2.

Alexithymia and the Language of Emotion

Persons with alexithymia suffer from an impoverished fantasy life, a reduced ability to experience positive emotions, and poorly differentiated negative affect (Taylor, 1994). The Toronto Alexithymia Scale (TAS-20) is commonly used to measure the condition (Bagby, Parker, & Taylor, 1994). This scale consists of three factors: Factor 1 assesses a person's *difficulty identifying feelings* as distinct, say, from bodily sensations; Factor 2 reflects *difficulty describing feelings* or communicating feelings to others; and Factor 3 indicates a preference for *externally oriented thinking*, that is, a focus on situational details as opposed to one's own thoughts and feelings. The top half of Table

13.2 presents the correlations between the three facets of the ECI (Preparedness, Novelty, and Effectiveness/Authenticity) and the three dimensions of the TAS-20, based on a sample of 89 university students (see Averill, 1999b, Study 5, for details).

The data in Table 13.2 suggest that emotionally creative people differ from people with alexithymia in every respect save one, namely, both have difficulty identifying and describing their emotional experiences, as indicated by the positive association between the Novelty subscale of the ECI and the F1 and F2 factors of the TAS-20 ($r = .39$ and .18, respectively). However, the source of the difficulty is different for the two conditions. For people with alexithymia, the difficulty stems from an impoverished inner life; for emotionally creative persons, it stems from the complexity and originality of their experiences. As one of the items in the ECI reads, "I would have to be a poet or novelist to describe the kinds of emotions I sometimes feel, they are so unique."

When describing events that *lack* emotional content, people with alexithymia can be quite fluent, even poetic. This sometimes makes it difficult to distinguish alexithymia from emotional creativity. Consider the following stanzas from the poem *No Platonique Love*, by William Cartwright, a 17th-century Oxford don:

Tell me no more of minds embracing
  minds,
  And hearts exchang'd for hearts;
That Spirits Spirits meet, as Winds do
  Winds
  And mix their subt'lest parts;

Table 13.1 Sample Items from the Three Facets of the Emotional Creativity Inventory

Preparation (2 of 7 items)

When I have strong emotional reactions, I search for reasons for my feelings.
I pay attention to other people's emotions so that I can better understand my own.

Novelty (4 of 14 items)

My emotional reactions are different and unique.
I have felt combinations of emotions that other people probably have never experienced.
I sometimes experience feelings and emotions that cannot be easily described in ordinary language.
I like to imagine situations that call for unusual, uncommon, or unconventional emotional reactions.

Effectiveness/Authenticity (3 of 9 items)

My emotions help me achieve my goals in life.
The way I experience and express my emotions helps me in my relationships with others.
My outward emotional reactions accurately reflect my inner feelings.

Table 13.2 Correlations of the Emotional Creativity Inventory (ECI) with Alexithymia and Mysticism Scales

	Emotional Creativity Inventory			
Scale	Preparedness	Novelty	Effectiveness/ Authenticity	Total
Alexithymia (n = 89)				
F1: Difficulty identifying	−.01	.39***	−.45***	.02
F2: Difficulty describing	−.24*	.18	−.64***	−.25*
F3: Externally oriented	−.65***	−.46***	−.37***	−.61***
Mysticism (n = 91)				
F1: General	.26**	.46***	.09	.39***
F2: Religious	.40***	.40***	.25*	.46***

*$p < .05$, **$p < .01$, ***$p < .001$, two-tailed tests.

That two unbodi'd Essences may kiss,
And then like Angels, twist and feel one
    bliss.

I was that silly thing that once was wrought
   To practice this thin Love;
I climb'd from Sex to Soul, from Soul to
   Thought;
   But thinking there to move,
Headlong I roll'd from Thought to Soul,
   and then
From Soul I lighted at the Sex agen.[2]

Peréz-Rincón (1997) has used this poem to illustrate alexithymia, presumably on the basis of the poet's—Cartwright's—stated inability to appreciate love abstractly, in Thought, but only concretely, in Sex. Based on the poem alone, that is not an unreasonable interpretation. From the little we know of Cartwright's life, however, he was not at a loss for words in describing the emotions: "Those wild beasts (the Passions) being tuned and composed to tameness and order, by his sweet and harmonious language" (Lloyd, 1668, cited by Goffin, 1918, p. xvii). Cartwright's poem is like a reversible figure. When viewed from a different perspective, the image it presents changes from a picture of alexithymia to one of emotional creativity.

Love—even the thick, sexual love touted by Cartwright—does not just happen. It requires thought (preparation), and the quality of thought makes a difference in the novelty, effectiveness, and authenticity of subsequent behavior. Having "climb'd from Sex to Soul, from Soul to Thought," could Cartwright return to Sex again, unchanged? Only if he were suffering a complete disjunction between thought and

feeling, a condition more akin to psychopathy than alexithymia. More likely, Sex was transformed by Cartwright's Thought into something more than mere copulation; and, conversely, his Thought was transformed by Sex into something more than abstract contemplation.

Poetry, it has long been recognized, is closely allied to the emotions. In the words of Wordsworth (1805/1952), poetry is the "spontaneous overflow of powerful feelings . . . recollected in tranquility" (p. 84). Recollection, whether tranquil or not, is only part of the story. Poetry also is oriented toward the future: "Until a man has expressed his emotions, he does not yet know what emotion it is. The act of expressing it is therefore an exploration of his own emotions. He is trying to find out what these emotions are" (Collingwood, 1938/1967, p. 111).

Poetry is not the only means by which novel emotions may be given effective expression, but words possess a special power in determining the realities as well as our ideas of emotion (Parkinson, 1995). Like a tree, language sends its roots deep into the soil from which it draws sustenance, and the soil may be transformed in the process. Yet even at their poetic best, words are often insufficient to express some of our most profound and creative emotional experiences, including those that we might label mystical.

Spirituality: The Mysticism of Everyday Life

Full blown mystical experiences—the kind reported, say, by Meister Eckhart (translated by Blakney, 1941)—are as rare as they are difficult to describe. In more mild degree, however, mysticlike experiences are surprisingly common, if not often discussed (Greeley, 1974; Laski, 1968). The bottom half of Table 13.2 presents the correlations, based on a sample of 91 university students, between the ECI and a measure of self-reported mystical experiences (Hood, 1975). Hood's scale comprises two dimensions: Factor 1, *General Mysticism*, emphasizes the unity of experience, the transcendence of space and time, the loss of ego boundaries, and a sense that all things are alive; and F2, *Religious Interpretation*, emphasizes the holiness or sacredness of experience, as well as feelings of peace and joy. As Table 13.2 indicates, the ECI total score was associated ($r = .39$) with the General Mysticism subscale and ($r = .46$) with the Religious Interpretation subscale. All three facets of the ECI contributed to these relations, but particularly Preparedness and Novelty.[3]

To place these results in a broader context, let us return to Nietzsche's call for "spiritualizing the passions." From a psychological perspective, there are two ways of looking at spirituality. The first is as an emotional state per se, represented in extreme form by mystical experiences.[4] The second is as an attribute of other emotional states, to the extent that they have features in common with mystical experiences. Emotional creativity, I suggest, is associated not only with the tendency toward mystical experiences, as the data in Table 13.2 indicate, but also with the tendency to imbue other, more mundane emotions with mysticlike characteristics.

Three features are characteristic of mystical states and hence to a spiritualization of the passions. These are a sense of vitality, connectedness, and meaningfulness (Averill, 1999c). Each of these features can be approached from either a secular or a religious point of view, as illustrated in Figure 13.2.

Vitality

In one of its most common usages, spirituality implies a powerful force, especially one that has creative or life-giving properties. In animistic religions, spirits may dwell in any object—a volcano, say, or a tree or even a rock—from whence they venture forth to influence human affairs, for good or ill. However, we need not reify spiritual feelings into spiritual beings. From a secular perspective, spirituality (in the sense of vitality) implies a creative attitude. The person who is "free spirited" is adventurous and

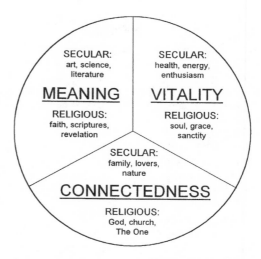

Figure 13.2 Three characteristics of spiritual experiences, as viewed from religious and secular perspectives.

open to new experiences. But vitality also can be manifested in more tranquil states; meditation, for example, provides opportunities for growth and inner exploration in the absence of high arousal.

Connectedness

One of the most ubiquitous features of mystical experiences is a feeling of union or harmony with another (Huxley, 1985). Sexual love and the love of a parent for a child are common metaphors for such a feeling. The "other" with which one unites need not be a person; it may be conceived broadly as an ethnic or cultural group, humanity as a whole, nature, or even the ground of all being (cf. the Buddhist concept of Brahman). And when the other is a person, that person need not be physically present—or even exist. For example, it is not uncommon to feel a strong connection to a deceased parent or child, or to a religious or political personage, real or mythic. But no matter how the other is conceived, feelings of connectedness bring a sense of completion or wholeness to the self; or, perhaps more accurately, connectedness brings a sense of self-transcendence, an identification with something beyond the self.

Meaningfulness

Spiritual experiences are deeply felt, even life-transforming. Like an encrypted message, the meaning of the experience may not be immediately apparent, but this only adds a sense of mystery and awe, which furthers the feeling of spirituality. From a religious perspective, revelation and scripture are typically used to help decipher the meaning of spiritual experiences, however opaquely. From a secular perspective, science, art, and literature serve similar functions.

It might be thought that most emotions automatically fulfill these three criteria for spirituality. A person devoid of emotion is considered "lifeless," unable to make human connections, and superficial. In science fiction, extraterrestrial beings (e.g., the "pods" in *Invasion of the Body Snatchers* or the automaton in *Terminator 2*) often are given the ability to think rationally but not to experience real emotions. Figuratively, they lack "soul" and hence never can be fully human.

As noted in the introduction to this chapter, however, emotions often are presented in a different, less flattering light—for example, as the animal in human nature, to be tamed and regulated by presumably "higher" (i.e., rational) thought processes. In everyday discourse, too, emotions often are depicted as alien to the self. For example, a common excuse for otherwise indefensible behavior is "I couldn't help it; I was overcome by emotion."

One way to get around this ambivalent, even self-contradictory, view of emotion is to distinguish between two kinds of emotional experiences—those that are considered true and those that are considered spurious. This distinction is epitomized by the hackneyed phrase "Get in touch with your true feelings." But what is a "true feeling," the kind of emotion that pods and automata cannot have? That question was addressed in a study by Morgan and Averill (1992), and the following is a greatly abbreviated answer: People judge as true those emotions that relate to their core beliefs and values, that help define who they are as individuals.

To be more specific, "true feelings" typically occur during periods of challenge or transition, when fundamental values and beliefs must either be amended or reaffirmed. The breakup of a love relationship is an example. The initial stage of an episode is typically marked by confusion, depression, and anxiety. These provide the affective context out of which true feelings emerge, as resolution is achieved. The feelings that are ultimately judged as true are difficult to describe; typically, they represent an amalgam of more specific emotions, such as love, anger, and pride. But regardless of the specific emotions involved, the true feelings, when they do emerge, are deeply and intensely felt; they reflect a state of clarification and resolve, an affirmation of values and self-worth.

In more colloquial terms, then, it might be said that "spiritualizing the passions" requires that one's emotions be rendered "true," that is, integrated with the beliefs and values that help constitute a person's evolving sense of self, both as an individual and in relation to others. This is a creative process—a creativity in the service of the self. But integration is not easily achieved, and when achieved, it is in need of constant repair. Emotional truths realized in one situation may lose their validity as circumstances change. Spiritualizing the passions must therefore be viewed as a process, not an end; moreover, it is a process fraught with difficulties. Saint John of the Cross (1618/1987) described the "dark nights" through which the soul must pass on its way to mystical union with God. Mystics the world over have described similar turmoil, albeit in terms appropriate to their own cultural context. In the more mundane world of everyday affairs, some strife and discord, both within the self and between the self and others, also can be expected when "spiritualizing the passions." This is a topic to which I will return in the conclusion to this chapter.[5]

Applications

If self-realization and expansion involve a spiritualization of the passions, neuroses of many types—not just alexithymia—might be characterized as a form of despiritualization. Neurotic syndromes not only are deficient in the features described earlier for spiritualization (vitality, connectedness, and meaningfulness) but also are contrary to the three criteria for emotional creativity discussed earlier (novelty, effectiveness, and authenticity). Neurotic behavior—for example, a hysterical conversion reaction—may be unique (abnormal) in terms of group norms; however, it ceases to be novel from the individual's perspective as it becomes uncontrollable and unyielding to change. Neurotic behavior also is ineffective, at least in the long term, and is not a true or authentic reflection of the individual's desires and values. It follows, then, that much of psychotherapy is an exercise in emotional creativity (Averill & Nunley, 1992;

Nunley & Averill, 1996). This suggests that some of the techniques used to foster creativity in other settings (Nickerson, 1999) might be fruitfully incorporated into psychotherapy. These techniques fall into four broad categories: (a) preparedness—gaining knowledge and expertise within a domain; (b) motivation—cultivating a desire to innovate on what is known, and a willingness to take risks; (c) imagination—learning to envision new approaches and realities; and (d) self-monitoring—guiding and assessing one's own efforts for effectiveness. But more than new techniques, emotional creativity suggests a different way of looking at the emotions and their disorders. Most therapies still treat the emotions (at least the "basic" emotions) as primitive reactions that may be regulated but not fundamentally altered. That belief can become a self-fulfilling prophecy.

The applications of emotional creativity are not limited to psychotherapy. To a certain extent, we are all emotional Luddites—we find it difficult to adjust to change. To illustrate, conduct the following thought experiment. What emotional adjustments would you have to make if you and others around you were to live to be 150 to 200 years old? Could you remain faithfully married to the same person for over 100 years, "until death do you part"? How long might you remain in a career before you were burned out or sought other challenges? Questions such as these could easily be multiplied, but there is no need. The point is simply that major accommodations would be required on both the individual and social levels. For example, "family values" would take on new meanings; the educational system would have to be reorganized to accommodate the return of (really) older students; current disputes over issues such as retirement and social security would pale by comparison (academics, in particular, would have to rethink tenure); and, if the reduction in the death rate were not matched by a corresponding reduction in the birth rate, overpopulation in the developed parts of the world would make present-day Bangladesh seem like a wilderness area.

Such a thought experiment is not mere fancy. Advances in genetic engineering and medicine may eventually double the human life span; much of the scientific knowledge is in place, and its feasibility has been demonstrated in lower (invertebrate) organisms. The extension to mammals and ultimately humans seems more a matter of when, not if (Kolata, 1999). Referring

to that eventuality, John Harris (2000), who holds the Sir David Alliance Chair of Bioethics at the University of Manchester, has advised that "we should start thinking now about how we can live decently and creatively with the prospect of such lives" (p. 59).

In some respects, the future is already upon us. In most industrialized countries, the elderly represent the fastest growing segment of the population. And with advanced age comes many challenges with which people must cope: retirement, failing health, loss of loved ones, to name but a few. Fortunately, the elderly may be more creative in meeting such challenges than popular stereotypes suggest.

The 19th-century French author George Sand (pseudonym of Aurore Dudevant) epitomizes successful aging. Shortly after her 67th birthday, Sand wrote to her friend and fellow author Gustave Flaubert: "On the day I decided to put youth behind me I immediately felt twenty years younger. You'll say the bark of the tree still has to bear the ravages of time. I don't mind that—the core is sound and the sap goes on doing its work, as in the old apple trees in my garden; the more gnarled they grow the more fruit they bear" (letter of 23 July 1871, in Steegmuller & Bray, 1993, p. 234). A few years later, Sand advised Flaubert (who was 17 years her junior): "Before long, you will gradually be entering upon the happiest and most propitious part of life: old age. It's then that art reveals itself in all its sweetness, in our youth it manifests itself in anguish" (letter of 12 January 1876, in Steegmuller & Bray, 1993, p. 384). Sand believed that when you are old, you love people and things for what they are, not for what they might contribute to your own future well-being.

Research by Carstensen and colleagues (e.g., Carstensen, Isaacowitz, & Charles, 1999) suggests that Sand was not unusual in her optimistic outlook toward old age. These investigators have found that older people tend to live more complex, more meaningful, and better regulated emotional lives than do their younger contemporaries, at least before the ravages of ill health and possible onset of senility take their toll. Particularly relevant to our present concerns, successful aging appears to be facilitated by a creative attitude toward life (Smith & van der Meer, 1997).[6]

Of course, not every person ages gracefully. Flaubert, for one, did not. "I have always lived my life from day to day, without plans for the future, pursuing my goal—my only goal—literature—looking neither to the left nor right!" he complained to Sand. "Everything that existed around me has disappeared, and I find myself in a desert" (letter of 10 May 1875, in Steegmuller & Bray, 1993, p. 367).

Creativity is not a unitary attribute that automatically infuses all aspects of a person's life. In the art of writing, Flaubert was more creative than Sand, but not in the art of living. In her younger years, Sand often scandalized her contemporaries with her unabashed affairs and unconventional behavior; when she grew older, she relished the company of her family and friends (without forgoing an occasional tryst). Flaubert, by contrast, led an eremitic existence, allowing himself few worldly pleasures. His creativity was almost entirely intellectual; he was a sensitive and astute spectator of life, but seldom an active participant.

The preceding observations on creativity and aging are illustrative of a larger issue. Increased life expectancy, with the attendant problems of old age, is only one change wrought by science and technology to which people will have to adjust in the coming decades and centuries. In a rapidly changing world, emotional creativity is more than an academic curiosity; it is indispensable to social and psychological well-being.

Conclusions

Psychology, with its emphasis on the causes and amelioration of human suffering, has been criticized for focusing on the negative; this handbook serves as a welcome counterbalance to that focus. Psychological well-being, however, is not simply the absence of suffering; rather, it involves an active engagement in the world, a sense of meaning or purpose in life, and connection to persons or objects beyond oneself. These characteristics help define the spiritual dimension of human experience; they also presume the ability to be creative—emotionally as well as intellectually.

Emotional creativity has potential drawbacks as well as benefits. "Every act of creation," Picasso observed, "is first of all an act of destruction" (quoted in May, 1975, p. 63). In the case of emotional creativity, familiar ways of responding may be disrupted, established personal relationships dissolved, and customary values discarded. This last is perhaps the most portentous act of destruction, for it threatens the fabric of society as well as the self.

Emotions embody the values of a society. If, for example, you strip all connotations of right and wrong, of good and bad, from concepts such as *love, anger, grief,* and *fear,* you also strip them of much of their meaning. Hence, any attempt to change an emotion in fundamental ways calls into question the values embodied by the emotion, and it will be met with resistance, even condemnation. This is true even when the change is lauded in the abstract, as might be expected with regard to spiritualizing the passions. Many mystics, for instance, have been condemned in their lifetimes as heretics. Mystical experiences tend to transcend ideological boundaries and hence pose a threat to accepted creeds. Claims to authenticity—a hallmark of spirituality as well as creativity—only exacerbate the apostasy. In such instances, recognition of the experience as effective may be long delayed—until there is a change in creed or the experience itself is given new meaning within established dogma.

Condemnation of emotional innovation is not limited to mystics and their inquisitors. Nietzsche's call for a spiritualization of the passions was not met with resounding approbation, even though his focus was on the more mundane emotions of everyday life. And, on a less philosophical plane, the emotional experimentation that marked the counterculture of the 1960s was roundly condemned at the time, even while the larger society was adopting some of its practices.

The resistance of society to changes in emotion, and hence in values, is not without warrant. Like genetic mutations, most emotional innovations may be harmful rather than beneficial. Some weeding out is necessary. What criteria should guide selection? This is not a question that is easily answered in advance. About all that can be said with certainty is that if selection is too lenient, anarchy will result; if too severe, stagnation. As history amply attests, a proper balance between anarchy and stagnation is difficult to attain.

An analogous difficulty exists on the individual level between inner chaos and inertia. But if the task seems difficult and the goal elusive, that is no reason for discouragement. Positive psychology promises challenge more than comfort; emotional creativity is part of that challenge.

Notes

1. Because of its religious connotations, psychologists have tended to avoid the term *spiritual*, preferring to call relevant phenomena by another name. For example, Viktor Frankl (1969/1988) used the terms *noological* or *noetic* to refer to the spiritual dimension of human experience, expressly because he wanted to avoid any religious implications (p. 17). Such technical terms may be apt for communicating among professionals; however, ordinary people are unlikely to describe their own experiences as noological. *Spiritual* may carry excess conceptual baggage, and hence the possibility for misunderstanding, but it is still a good term for the emotionally creative experiences discussed in this chapter.

2. From Goffin (1918), reprinted with the permission of Cambridge University Press.

3. Some of the items in Hood's original scale overlap in content with items from the Novelty subscale of ECI. A reanalysis suggested that these items could be eliminated without destroying the integrity or meaning of the F1 and F2 subscales. The data presented in Table 13.2 are for the emended subscales (see Averill, 1999b, Study 4, for details). The correlation between the *total* score on the ECI and the *total* score on the original mysticism scale was ($r = .46$, $p < .01$). In effect, elimination of overlapping items had little influence on the relation between the two scales.

4. According to the model presented earlier (see Figure 13.1), emotional states are determined, in part, by the cultural beliefs and rules (implicit theories) that help shape emotional syndromes. The model does not fit all emotions equally well. In particular, states of acute depression, anxiety, and mysticism lie on its periphery. I will discuss depression below (see note 5). With regard to mysticism, Rothberg (1990) points to the lengthy and rigorous training that typically precedes the attainment of a full mystical experience; we should entertain the possibility, he suggests, that such training is occasionally successful in transcending all cultural categories, including those that help define the self as an independent entity. Katz (1992), on the other hand, argues that a careful reading of mystical reports reveals a subtle but uneliminable influence of cultural beliefs and rules. This dispute pertains to the most extreme forms of mystical experience, where a breakdown or "deautomatization" (Deikman, 1969) of cognitive schemas at least approaches completion. Such occurrences are rare, if ever, and for the uninitiated person are more likely to produce anxiety than mystical bliss. Anxiety, at least some of its forms (cf. Kurt Goldstein's, 1939, "catastrophic reaction"), also involves a breakdown in the cognitive structures by which we impose meaning on the world, including our own selves (Averill, 1976).

5. Of all emotional states, episodes of endogenous depression might seem the least amenable to spiritualization. And that is generally the case. The depressed person feels empty, tends to withdraw from human contact, and experiences life as pointless. For want of a better explanation, in many cultures the condition is attributed to "soul loss" (Shweder, 1985). Even so, some people, especially those of unusual creative potential, can turn even depression into an animating and meaningful experience. Jamison (1993) provides many examples in her book on manic-depressive illness. The following observation by Herman Melville is representative: "The intensest light of reason and revelation combined, can not shed such blazonings upon the deeper truths in man, as will sometimes proceed from his own profoundest gloom. Utter darkness is then his light. . . . Wherefore is it, that not to know Gloom and Grief is not to know aught that an heroic man should learn" (quoted by Jamison, 1993, p. 216).

6. These findings by Carstensen et al. (1999) and Smith and van der Meer (1997) are consistent with Erikson's (1968) eighth and final stage of life, which, if properly negotiated, leads to a sense of integrity (vs. despair); and with integrity, according to Erikson, comes wisdom. However, Carstensen et al. do not restrict their findings of emotional refinement to old age. According to their "socioemotional selectivity theory," positive social interactions are encouraged, even if tinged with ambivalence, whenever temporal horizons are limited (e.g., by a terminal illness). Why be bothered (angered, worried, depressed) by people you don't expect to see again? Perhaps the best advice for persons of any age is the adage: Plan as though you will live to be 100, but live each day as though you will die tomorrow.

References

Arnheim, R. (1966). *Toward a psychology of art.* Berkeley: University of California Press.

Averill, J. R. (1976). Emotion and anxiety: Sociocultural, biological, and psychological determinants. In M. Zuckerman & C. D. Spielberger (Eds.), *Emotions and anxiety: New concepts, methods, and applications* (pp. 87–130). New York: LEA–John Wiley.

Averill, J. R. (1979). The functions of grief. In C. Izard (Ed.), *Emotions in personality and psychopathology* (pp. 339–368). New York: Plenum.

Averill, J. R. (1980a). A constructivist view of emotion. In R. Plutchik and H. Kellerman (Eds.), *Emotion: Theory, research and experience: Vol. 1. Theories of emotion* (pp. 305–339). New York: Academic Press.

Averill, J. R. (1980b). On the paucity of positive emotions. In K. R. Blankstein, P. Pliner, & J. Polivy (Eds.), *Assessment and modification of emotional behavior* (pp. 7–45). New York: Plenum.

Averill, J. R. (1984). The acquisition of emotions during adulthood. In C. Z. Malatesta & C. Izard (Eds.), *Affective processes in adult development* (pp. 23–43). Beverly Hills, CA: Sage.

Averill, J. R. (1990). Inner feelings, works of the flesh, the beast within, diseases of the mind, driving force, and putting on a show: Six metaphors of emotion and their theoretical extensions. In D. E. Leary (Ed.), *Metaphors in the history of psychology* (pp. 104–132). New York: Cambridge University Press.

Averill, J. R. (1993). Illusions of anger. In R. B. Felson & J. T. Tedeschi (Eds.), *Aggression and violence: Social interactionist perspectives* (pp. 171–192). Washington, DC: American Psychological Association.

Averill, J. R. (1997). The emotions: An integrative approach. In R. Hogan & J. A. Johnson (Eds.), *Handbook of personality psychology* (pp. 513–541). San Diego, CA: Academic Press.

Averill, J. R. (1999a). Creativity in the domain of emotion. In T. Dalgleish & M. Power (Eds.), *Handbook of cognition and emotion* (pp. 765–782). Chichester, England: Wiley.

Averill, J. R. (1999b). Individual differences in emotional creativity: Structure and correlates. *Journal of Personality, 67,* 331–371.

Averill, J. R. (1999c). Spirituality: From the mundane to the meaningful—and back. *Journal of Theoretical and Philosophical Psychology, 18,* 101–126.

*Averill, J. R., & Nunley, E. P. (1992). *Voyages of the heart: Living an emotionally creative life.* New York: Free Press.

Averill, J. R., & Nunley, E. P. (1993). Grief as an emotion and as a disease. In M. S. Stroebe, W. Stroebe, & R. O. Hansson (Eds.), *The handbook of bereavement* (pp. 77–90). New York: Cambridge University Press.

Averill, J. R., Stanat, P., & More, T. A. (1998). Aesthetics and the environment. *Review of General Psychology, 2,* 153–174.

Averill, J. R., & Thomas-Knowles, C. (1991). Emotional creativity. In K. T. Strongman (Ed.), *International review of studies on emotion* (Vol. 1, pp. 269–299). London: Wiley.

Bagby, R. M., Parker, J. D. A., & Taylor, G. J. (1994). The twenty-item Toronto Alexithymia Scale: I. Item selection and cross-validation of the factor structure. *Journal of Psychosomatic Research, 38,* 23–32.

Blakney, R. B. (1941). *Meister Eckhart: A modern translation.* New York: Harper and Row.

Cacioppo, J. T., & Berntson, G. G. (1999). The affect system: Architecture and operating characteristics. *Current Directions in Psychological Science, 8,* 133–137.

Carstensen, L. L., Isaacowitz, D. M., & Charles, S. T. (1999). Taking time seriously: A theory of socioemotional selectivity. *American Psychologist, 54,* 165–181.

Collingwood, R. G. (1938/1967). *The principles of art.* Oxford: Clarendon.

Deikman, A. J. (1969). Deautomatization and the mystic experience. In C. T. Tart (Ed.), *Altered states of consciousness* (pp. 23–43). New York: Wiley.

Ekman, P., & Davidson, R. J. (Eds.). (1994). *The nature of emotion: Fundamental questions. Question 1. Are there basic emotions?* New York: Oxford University Press.

Epstein, S. (1998). *Constructive thinking: The key to emotional intelligence.* Westport, CN: Praeger.

Erikson, E. H. (1968). *Identity, youth and crisis.* New York: Norton.

Frankl, V. E. (1969/1988). *The will to meaning: Foundations and applications of logotherapy.* New York: New American Library.

Gardner, H. (1993). *Frames of mind: The theory of multiple intelligences (tenth-anniversary edition).* New York: Basic Books.

Goffin, R. C. (1918). *The life and poems of William Cartwright.* Cambridge, England: Cambridge University Press.

Goldstein, K. (1939). *The organism: A holistic approach to biology.* New York: American Book Company.

*Greeley, A. M. (1974). *Ecstasy: A way of knowing.* Englewood Cliffs, NJ: Prentice-Hall.

Gutbezahl, J., & Averill, J. R. (1996). Individual differences in emotional creativity as manifested in words and pictures. *Creativity Research Journal, 9,* 327–337.

Harris, J. (2000, April 7). Intimations of immortality. *Science, 288,* 59.

Hayes, J. R. (1981). *The complete problem solver.* Philadelphia: Franklin Institute Press.

Hood, R. W., Jr. (1975). The construction and preliminary validation of a measure of reported mystical experience. *Journal for the Scientific Study of Religion, 14,* 29–41.

Huxley, A. (1985). *The perennial philosophy*. London: Triad Grafton.

*James, W. (1902/1961). *Varieties of religious experience*. New York: Collier.

Jamison, K. R. (1993). *Touched with fire*. New York: Free Press.

John of the Cross (1618/1987). The dark night. In K. Kavanaugh (Ed. and Trans.), *John of the Cross: Selected writings* (pp. 162–209). New York: Paulist Press.

*Katz, S. T. (Ed.). (1992). *Mysticism and language*. New York: Oxford University Press.

Kolata, G. (1999, March 9). Pushing the limits of the human life span. *New York Times*, pp. D1–D2.

LaBarre, W. (1947). The cultural basis of emotions and gestures. *Journal of Personality, 16*, 48–68.

Laski, M. (1968). *Ecstasy: A study of some secular and religious experiences*. New York: Greenwood.

Maslow, A. H. (1971). *The farther reaches of human nature*. New York: Viking.

May, R. (1975). *The courage to create*. New York: Norton.

Morgan, C., & Averill, J. R. (1992). True feelings, the self, and authenticity: A psychosocial perspective. In D. D. Franks & V. Gecas (Eds.), *Social perspectives on emotion* (Vol. 1, pp. 95–124). Greenwich, CT: JAI Press.

Nickerson, R. S. (1999). Enhancing creativity. In R. J. Sternberg (Ed.), *Handbook of creativity* (pp. 392–430). Cambridge, England: Cambridge University Press.

Nietzsche, F. (1889/1997). *Twilight of the idols. Morality as anti-nature* (R. Polt, Trans.). Indianapolis, IN: Hackett.

Nunley, E. P., & Averill, J. R. (1996). Emotional creativity: Theoretical and applied aspects. In K. T. Kuehlwein & H. Rosen (Eds.), *Constructing realities: Meaning-making perspectives for psychotherapists* (pp. 223–251). San Francisco: Jossey-Bass.

*Parkinson, B. (1995). *Ideas and realities of emotion*. London: Routledge.

Peréz-Rincón, H. (1997). Alexithymia considered as a survival of an archaic structure of language: Importance of Bruno Snell's theories. *New Trends in Experimental and Clinical Psychiatry, 13*, 159–160.

Rank, O. (1936/1978). *Truth and reality*. New York: Norton.

Richards, R. (1998). The subtle attraction: Beauty as a force in awareness, creativity, and survival. In S. W. Russ (Ed.), *Affect, creative experience, and psychological adjustment* (pp. 191–213). Philadelphia: Brunner Mazel.

Rothberg, D. (1990). Contemporary epistemology and the study of mysticism. In R. K. C. Forman (Ed.), *The problem of pure consciousness* (pp. 163–210). New York: Oxford University Press.

Saarni, C. (1999). *The development of emotional competence*. New York: Guilford.

Shweder, R. A. (1985). Menstrual pollution, soul loss, and the comparative study of emotions. In A. Kleinman & B. Good (Eds.), *Culture and depression: Studies in the anthropology and cross-cultural psychiatry of affect and disorder* (pp. 182–215). Berkeley: University of California Press.

Smith, G. J. W., & van der Meer, G. (1997). Creativity in old age. In M. A. Runco & R. Richards (Eds.), *Eminent creativity, everyday creativity, and health* (pp. 333–353). Greenwich, CT: Ablex.

*Solomon, R. C. (1993). *The passions*. Indianapolis, IN: Hackett.

Steegmuller, F., & Bray, B. (Trans.). (1993). *Flaubert–Sand: The correspondence*. New York: Knopf.

Steiner, C. M. (1996). Emotional literacy training: The application of transactional analysis to the study of emotions. *Transactional Analysis Journal, 26*, 31–39.

Taylor, G. J. (1994). The alexithymia construct: Conceptualization, validation, and relationship with basic dimensions of personality. *New Trends in Experimental and Clinical Psychiatry, 10* (2), 61–74.

*Weisberg, R. W. (1986). *Creativity: Genius and other myths*. New York: Freeman.

Wordsworth, W. (1805/1952). Preface to second edition of lyrical ballads. In B. Ghiselin (Ed.), *The creative process* (pp. 83–84). Berkeley: University of California Press.

IV

Cognitive-Focused Approaches

14

Creativity

Dean Keith Simonton

People are almost universal in their appreciation of creativity (Sternberg & Lubart, 1996). This is true in home and at school, and whether at work or at play. Rarely is creativity perceived as a negative quality for a person to possess. Likewise, people vary considerably in the magnitude of creativity that they can or usually do display. Whereas some students put together rather humdrum papers and projects, others fulfill the same course requirements with impressive imagination and wit. While some inventors may rest content with making minor improvements in already established technologies, others devise revolutionary inventions that dramatically transform our daily lives.

Creativity is so highly valued as a human resource that most modern societies have special means to encourage those of its citizens who exhibit creative behavior. At the most basic level, patent and copyright laws have been implemented so as to allow individuals to enjoy the fruits of their creative labors. At an even higher level of creative achievement, there are the honors and awards bestowed upon the most outstanding exemplars of creativity. Thus, the Nobel Prizes are awarded to the best creators in the sciences and literature, and each major literary tradition will have its own set of special prizes recognizing their best writers (Pulitzer,

Cervantes, Goethe, etc.). Likewise, the Academy Awards and Golden Globe Awards are granted to those who create the most notable films.

The worth of creative behavior may even continue to be recognized long after the creator has died. If the accomplishment is truly exceptional, the creator may "go down in history" as a "creative genius." These are people who have left a "name behind," such as Aristotle, Descartes, Shakespeare, Michelangelo, and Beethoven. Indeed, these names often are taken as indicative of the creative vitality of any given civilization at a particular point in time (Gray, 1966; Kroeber, 1944; Simonton, 1997b). When a culture is overflowing with eminent creators, it is said to exhibit a "golden age," whereas when examples of creative genius become few and far between, the culture is said to have entered a "dark age." Hence, creativity often is viewed as a human capacity that has both individual and sociocultural utility and value.

Given the foregoing considerations, it is impossible to imagine the emergence of a bona fide positive psychology that does not include creativity among its topics. I subsequently will examine what psychologists know about this crucial phenomenon. I begin by narrating the history of the concept, and then discuss how creativity can be measured. Next, I review some of the key empirical findings, as well as some of the central theoretical issues. After treating some of the practical applications, I close by suggesting the prospects for future work on the topic of creativity.

History of Creativity

To paraphrase what Ebbinghaus (1908, p. 3) once said of psychology, creativity has a long past but a short history, especially as a research topic in psychology. There is insufficient space to do any more than provide a sketch here, but fortunately more detailed narratives have been published elsewhere (e.g., Albert & Runco, 1999). I begin by discussing the history of creativity as a recognized human behavior and then trace the history of psychological research on the topic.

The Origins of Creativity as a Cultural Phenomenon

Given the manifest importance of creativity, it is rather surprising to learn that it is actually a somewhat recent concept. It is not listed among the classic human virtues, for example. The philosophers of ancient Greece listed prudence, temperance, fortitude, and justice, whereas the Christian theologians added faith, hope, and love—but creativity is overlooked entirely. Part of the reason for this neglect is that creativity originally was conceived as a defining characteristic of an omnipotent divine creator rather than an attribute of mere fragile mortals. In the biblical book of Genesis, for instance, God is portrayed as the Creator of the cosmos, the earth, and all life. Indeed, almost every culture possesses creation myths in which their gods have this very function and capacity.

Even when individual humans were seen as the locus of creative activity, the causal agents still sprung from a spiritual world. This linkage is apparent in the Greek doctrine of the Muses. There was a Muse for all major creative activities of classical times, including heroic or epic poetry, lyric and love poetry, sacred poetry, tragedy, comedy, music, dance, and even astronomy and history. The corresponding Muse was thought to provide a guiding spirit or source of inspiration for the mortal creator. This usage underlies several commonplace expressions, such as to say that one has lost one's muse when one has run out of creative ideas.

The Romans are responsible for a concept that is closely related to creativity—that of genius. According to Roman mythology, each individual was born with a guardian spirit who watched out for the person's fate and distinctive individuality. With time, the term was taken to indicate the person's special talents or aptitudes. Although in the beginning everybody could be said to "have a genius," at least in the sense of possessing a unique capacity, the term eventually began to be confined to those whose gifts set them well apart from the average. The expression "creative genius" thus unites two concepts with Greek and Roman roots pertaining to how the spiritual world permeates human affairs. Outstanding creativity was the gift of the gods or spirits, not a human act. Even during the Italian Renaissance, when European civilization was becoming secularized by the advent of humanism, rudiments of this ascription remain. In Vasari's classic (a. 1550/1968, p. 347) *Lives of the Painters, Sculptors, and Architects*, for example, we can read how "the great Ruler of Heaven looked down" and decided "to send to earth a genius universal in each art." This person would be endowed with such special qualities that his works would seem "rather divine than earthly." Vasari was speaking of Michelangelo.

With the increased secularization of European thought, however, the causal locus of creativity gradually moved away from the spiritual to the human world. Once this cultural shift took place, the phenomenon became the subject of psychological inquiry.

The Origins of Creativity as a Research Topic

In the early history of the field, psychologists occasionally would discuss creative thought and behavior. William James (1880), for example, described the creative process in terms of Darwinian theory (also see Campbell, 1960). In the 20th century, the Gestalt psychologists—most notably Wolfgang Köhler (1925) and Max Wertheimer (1945/1982)—displayed considerable interest in creative problem solving. Likewise, creativity sometimes would attract the attention of psychologists of differing theoretical persuasions, including the behaviorist B. F. Skinner (1972), the cognitive psychologist Herbert A. Simon (1986), the personality psychologist David C. McClelland (1962), and the humanistic psychologists Carl Rogers (1954),

Abraham Maslow (1959), and Rollo May (1975).

Although several psychologists touched upon this topic, the one who deserves more credit than any other for emphasizing creativity as a critical research topic is the psychometrician J. P. Guilford (1950). His address as president of the American Psychological Association, which was published in a 1950 issue of *American Psychologist*, is often considered a "call to arms" on behalf of this overlooked subject. More important, Guilford made many direct contributions to the research literature, most notably by devising widely used instruments for assessing individual differences in creativity (Guilford, 1967). In the latter half of the 20th century, the interest in creativity steadily grew and diversified such that researchers were covering a fairly wide range of subtopics (Feist & Runco, 1993). Following a minor lull in activity in the 1970s, creativity research has attained new heights in the 1980s and 1990s (Simonton, 1999a). This growth is demonstrated by (a) the advent of several creativity handbooks (e.g., Glover, Ronning, & Reynolds, 1989; Runco, 1997; Sternberg, 1999); (b) the appearance in 1988 of the *Creativity Research Journal*, which complemented the *Journal of Creative Behavior* founded previously in 1967; and (c) the 1999 publication of the two-volume *Encyclopedia of Creativity* (Runco & Pritzker, 1999). Indeed, creativity now can be considered as a legitimate topic for scientific inquiry in mainstream psychological research.

Measurement Approaches

Before a concept can be measured, it first must be defined. Fortunately, at least in the abstract, there is virtually universal agreement on what creativity is. In particular, creativity usually is said to entail the generation of ideas that fulfill the two following conditions:

1. Creativity must be *original*. These days, no one can be called "creative" who decides to "reinvent the wheel," nor can one earn that ascription for writing the lines "To be, or not to be." Creative ideas are novel, surprising, unexpected—sometimes even shocking. Originality is a necessary but not sufficient criterion for creativity, which brings us to the second condition.

2. Creativity must be *adaptive*. Someone who decides to make a blimp out of solid concrete can no doubt claim considerable originality, but whether this strange idea "can fly" is quite a different matter. Similarly, someone may propose a highly unusual advertising slogan like "The worst wurst in the West," but whether that phrase will convince potential consumers to buy more of that brand of sausage is highly unlikely.

Given the general definition of creativity as "adaptive originality," how can it be best measured? This turns out to be difficult. Creativity researchers have not agreed on the optimal instrument for assessing individual differences on this trait (Hocevar & Bachelor, 1989). The reason for this lack of consensus is that creativity can manifest itself in three distinct ways. First, creativity may be viewed as some kind of mental *process* that yields adaptive and original ideas (e.g., Sternberg & Davidson, 1995; Ward, Smith, & Vaid, 1997). Second, it can be seen as a type of *person* who exhibits creativity (e.g., Gardner, 1993; Wallace & Gruber, 1989). Third, creativity can be analyzed in terms of the concrete *products* that result from the workings of the creative process or person (e.g., Martindale, 1990; Simonton, 1980, 1998b). Each of these three manifestations suggests rather distinct measures, as will become apparent next.

The Creative Process

If the emphasis is on the thought processes that yield creative ideas, then the best assessment approach should be to tap individual differences in access to these processes. This was the approach adopted by Guilford (1967), who began by proposing a profound distinction between two kinds of thinking. *Convergent* thought involves the convergence on a single correct response, such as is characteristic of most aptitude tests, like those that assess intelligence. *Divergent* thought, in contrast, entails the capacity to generate many alternative responses, including ideas of considerable variety and originality. Guilford and others have devised a large number of tests purported to measure the capacity for divergent thinking (e.g., Torrance, 1988; Wallach & Kogan, 1965). Typical is the Alternate Uses test, in which the subject must come up with many different ways of using a common object, such as a paper clip or brick.

Another test that views the creative process in a manner similar to divergent thinking is the Remote Associates Test, or RAT, of Mednick (1962). This test was based on the premise that

creativity involves the ability to make rather remote associations between separate ideas.
Highly creative individuals were said to have a
flat hierarchy of associations in comparison to
the steep hierarchy of associations of those with
low creativity. A flat associative hierarchy
means that for any given stimulus, the creative
person has numerous associations available, all
with roughly equal probabilities of retrieval.
Because such an individual can generate many
associative variations, the odds are increased
that he or she will find that one association that
will make the necessary remote connection. The
RAT can therefore be said to operate according
to an implicit variation-selection model of the
creative process.

Many investigators have tried to validate
these divergent-thinking tests against other criteria of creative performance (see, e.g., Crammond, 1994). Although the researchers in these
validation studies have had some modicum of
success, it also has become clear that generalized
tests do not always have as much predictive validity as tests more specifically tailored to a particular domain of creativity (Baer, 1993, 1994;
for discussion, see Baer, 1998; Plucker, 1998).
Creativity in music, for example, is not going
to be very predictable on the basis of how many
uses one can imagine for a toothpick.

The Creative Person

To the extent that the content of the creative
process is domain specific, it would seem necessary to construct as many creativity instruments as there are creative domains. Fortunately, an alternative psychometric tactic exists
that is based on the assumption that the creative
individual is distinctively different in various
personal characteristics. Especially pertinent is
the evidence that creative people display personality profiles that depart from those of the
average person (Barron & Harrington, 1981;
Martindale, 1989; Sternberg & Lubart, 1995).
Creative personalities tend to possess those
characteristics that would most favor the production of both numerous and diverse ideas. In
particular, creative individuals tend to be independent, nonconformist, unconventional, even
bohemian; they also tend to have wide interests,
greater openness to new experiences, and a
more conspicuous behavioral and cognitive flexibility and boldness (see Simonton, 1999a). The
only major complication in this general picture
is that the personality profiles of artistic creators
tend to differ noticeably from those of scientific

creators (Feist, 1998). In a nutshell, the creative
scientists tend to fall somewhere between the
creative artists and noncreative personalities in
terms of their typical traits.

Not surprising given these results, several
measures of creativity are based on personality
scales, such as the 16 Personality Factor Questionnaire (e.g., Cattell & Butcher, 1968) or the
Adjective Check List (e.g., Gough, 1979). Yet
this is not the only person-based assessment
strategy. Presumably, the personality contrasts
between creative and noncreative individuals
may partially reflect significant differences in
their biographical characteristics, including family background, educational experiences, and career activities. As a consequence, some psy-
chometricians have designed instruments based
on biographical inventories (e.g., Schaefer &
Anastasi, 1968; Taylor & Ellison, 1967). For instance, creative persons often report having
much broader interests and a wider range of
hobbies than is the case for their less creative
colleagues.

The Creative Product

Because process- and person-based creativity
measures are relatively easy to design and administer, the bulk of the literature on creativity
has tended to use them. Yet one might argue
that the ultimate criterion of whether someone
can be considered creative is whether or not that
individual has successfully generated a product
that meets both requirements of creative behavior—originality and adaptiveness. This product-
based assessment is more direct and objective,
but it also has more than one operational definition. One approach is to simply ask individuals to identify what they would consider samples of their creative activities, such as poems,
paintings, and projects (e.g., Richards, Kinney,
Lunde, Benet, & Merzel, 1988a). Another approach is to have research participants generate
creative products under controlled laboratory
conditions and then have these products evaluated by independent judges (e.g., Amabile,
1982; Smith, Ward, & Finke, 1995; Sternberg &
Lubart, 1995). These two operational definitions
have the advantage that they are best designed
to assess individual differences in more everyday forms of the phenomenon.

Yet it is obvious that at higher levels of creative activity, the investigator can go beyond a
participant's self-report or a judge's subjective
evaluation. Inventors hold patents, scientists
publish journal articles, dramatists write plays,

directors create movies, and so forth. Hence, cross-sectional variation in creativity can be assessed in terms of individual differences in the output of such professionally or culturally acknowledged works (e.g., Simonton, 1991b, 1997a). Investigators may count total output (quantity), select output (quality), or output influence (impact). For example, researchers of scientific creativity may tabulate the total number of publications, just those publications that are actually cited in the literature, or the total number of citations those publications have received (e.g., Feist, 1993; Helmreich, Spence, Beane, Lucker, & Matthews, 1980). Happily, researchers have demonstrated quite conclusively that these three alternative measures correlate very highly among each other (e.g., Simonton, 1992b).

If creative persons have generated a substantial body of highly influential products, it is inevitable that they should attain eminence for their accomplishments (Simonton, 1991c). In fact, the single most powerful predictor of eminence in any creative domain is the number of works an individual has contributed (Simonton, 1977, 1991a, 1997a). Accordingly, sometimes cross-sectional variation in creativity will be assessed using some variety of eminence indicator (e.g., Cox, 1926; Feist, 1993; Simonton, 1976a). These may include expert ratings, the receipt of major honors, or having entries in biographical dictionaries and encyclopedias (e.g., Simonton, 1976b, 1998a).

Empirical Findings

Judging from the previous section, there seems to be an embarrassment of riches when it comes to the assessment of creativity. This superfluity, however, is only superficial. One of the most critical findings in the empirical research is that these alternative measures tend to display fairly respectable intercorrelations (Eysenck, 1995; Simonton, 1999b). In other words, creative products tend to emerge from creative persons who use the creative process in generating their output. The correlations are by no means perfect, but they do suggest that each instrument is gauging the same fundamental reality. Consequently, the various measures often yield the same general conclusions about the nature of human creativity. For example, a considerable literature exists on the relation between age and creativity (Simonton, 1988a). Despite some differences due to the creative domain and other

factors, pretty much the same developmental trends are observed for product- and process-based measures (see, e.g., Dennis, 1966; Lehman, 1953; McCrae, Arenberg, & Costa, 1987). That is, whether we are counting creative products or assessing the capacity for divergent thinking, longitudinal changes in creativity appear to be best described by a single-peaked curvilinear function. The only major discrepancy is that creativity according to the productivity definition can undergo a resurgence in the latter years of life that has no counterpart according to the psychometric definition (e.g., Simonton, 1989).

Because extensive reviews are readily available elsewhere (Simonton, 1999a), the best choice here is to discuss just two sets of empirical findings that have special relevance for a positive psychology of creativity. These concern early trauma and psychological disorder.

Early Trauma

According to the empirical literature, child prodigies and intellectually gifted children tend to have enjoyed rather happy childhoods (Feldman & Goldsmith, 1986; Terman, 1925). That is, their parents provided them with financially comfortable homes and ample intellectual and aesthetic stimulation; their parents had stable marriages, and the children were both physically healthy and educationally successful. Yet when researchers turn to highly creative individuals, a rather contrasting picture emerges (e.g., Goertzel & Goertzel, 1962; Goertzel, Goertzel, & Goertzel, 1978). The family may have experienced severe economic ups and downs, and the parents' marriage may have fallen far short of the ideal; the child may have been sickly or have endured some physical or cognitive disability (e.g., Roe, 1953). More remarkably, early development of the future creator may have been plagued with one or more traumatic experiences, such as the loss of one or both parents in childhood or adolescence (Eisenstadt, 1978; Roe, 1953). Yet what makes these findings all the more intriguing is that the same developmental events also are associated with negative life outcomes, such as juvenile delinquency or suicidal depression (Eisenstadt, 1978).

This peculiar paradox suggests that under the right conditions, exposure to traumatic or difficult experiences early in life can make a positive contribution to the development of creative potential (Simonton, 1994). Perhaps those who have the capacity to "rise to the challenge" will benefit, and creativity itself may be an adaptive response to such circumstances (Eisenstadt, 1978). Events that might have yielded a societal misfit instead produce an individual who can respond constructively with an adulthood of creative achievement rather than disappointment or alienation.

Psychological Disorder

One of the oldest debates in the study of creativity is the "mad-genius controversy" (Prentky, 1980). As far back as Aristotle, thinkers have speculated that outstanding creativity is associated with psychopathology. This view has persisted in more modern times, as is apparent in psychoanalytic psychobiographies of creative geniuses (i.e., "psychopathographies"). Not every psychologist agrees with this thesis, however. Humanistic psychologists, in particular, tend to see creativity as a symptom of mental health, not illness (e.g., Maslow, 1959; May, 1975). Based on the empirical research on this issue, it appears that there is some truth in both viewpoints (Eysenck, 1995).

On the one hand, the rates of apparent psychological disorder in samples of highly creative individuals do seem to be somewhat higher than in the general population (Eysenck, 1995; Richards, Kinney, Lunde, Benet, & Merzel, 1988b). The incidence rates are especially elevated for those who pursue artistic forms of creative expression (Jamison, 1993; Ludwig, 1995). Furthermore, there is a positive relation between the amount of psychopathological symptoms and the level of creative achievement attained (Barron, 1969; Eysenck, 1995; Ludwig, 1995). Finally, and perhaps most provocatively, family lines with disproportionate numbers of individuals with psychological disorders also are more likely to have highly creative individuals (Juda, 1949; Karlson, 1970; Richards et al., 1988b). As such, pathological and creative pedigrees tend to overlap to a degree that far exceeds chance expectation.

On the other hand, the empirical research also suggests that creativity and psychopathology are by no means equivalent (Rothenberg, 1990). For one thing, creative individuals often have character traits, such as high ego strength, which are not found in clinical populations (Barron, 1969; Eysenck, 1995). However bizarre their thoughts or behaviors may be, creators remain in self-command—even exploiting their

eccentricities for creative ends. In addition, their symptomatology is below pathological levels (Barron, 1969; Eysenck, 1995). Though their profiles do not fall in the normal range, they also do not reach truly pathological levels— they are at the borderline between the normal and the abnormal. Finally, psychopathology may be the consequence rather than the cause of a creative career (Simonton, 1994). That is, a life of creativity can have exceptional stresses related to the tremendous disappointments of failures and the unexpected distractions of fame (Schaller, 1997). It is telling that a standard measure of life stressors, the Social Readjustment Rating Questionnaire, assigns 28 points for any "outstanding personal achievement" (Holmes & Rahe, 1967). This is about the same weight granted to "change in responsibilities at work," a "son or daughter leaving home," or "in-law troubles." These 28 points probably understate the true magnitude of stress for the highest levels of creativity. After all, the weights assigned by this questionnaire were based on more everyday forms of achievement rather than creations on the level of the Sistine Chapel or *War and Peace*.

When one places these psychopathology findings alongside those for traumatic experiences, a significant lesson emerges: *Events and traits that might severely disable or retard personal development can sometimes be converted into forces for positive growth.* Or, if that is too strong an inference, one can safely infer the following optimistic alternative: *Such events and conditions need not prevent the development of exceptional creativity.* Indeed, people can be phenomenally robust, as they transform "liabilities" into assets.

Theoretical Issues

Despite the abundance of empirical findings, creativity researchers continue to wrestle with profound theoretical questions, two of which involve nature versus nurture and small-*c* versus big-*C* creativity. I explore these next.

The Nature-Nurture Issue

Is creativity born or made, or some combination of the two? Galton (1869) introduced this question in his book *Hereditary Genius*, and he later coined the terms *nature* and *nurture* in his book *English Men of Science: Their Nature and Nur-*

ture (1874). Subsequent researchers have suggested that creativity reflects a complex interaction of genetic and environmental factors (Eysenck, 1995; Simonton, 1999b). For example, genes may contribute to creativity according to a multiplicative (emergenic) rather than a simple additive model (Lykken, 1998; Simonton, 1999c). As a further complication, it may very well be that various environmental influences interact with genetic factors with equally complex functional relationships (Eysenck, 1995). To some extent, creative development requires a specific congruence between genetic inheritance and environmental stimulation. This intricate genetic-environmental determination helps to explain why creativity may display a highly skewed cross-sectional distribution in the general population (Simonton, 1999b). When optimal creative development requires a precise configuration of many different factors, it makes it more difficult for people to emerge who have the total package.

Small-c Versus Big-C Creativity

Small-*c* creativity enhances everyday life and work with superior problem-solving skills, whereas big-*C* creativity makes lasting contributions to culture and history. In the first case, we are speaking of the creative person, whereas in the latter case we are talking about the creative genius. The enigma is whether these two grades of creative behavior are qualitatively or quantitatively distinct. If everyday creativity is qualitatively different from genius-level creativity, then the personal attributes underlying the first may be different from those responsible for the second (e.g., any tendency toward psychopathology). If the two are only quantitatively different, however, then the factors that predict levels of small-*c* creativity would also predict levels of big-*C* creativity. The evidence to date supports the notion that these two grades represent regions on a continuous scale of creative activity (e.g., Eysenck, 1995; Helmreich et al., 1980; Rodgers & Maranto, 1989).

Practical Applications

If creativity truly is a highly desirable human characteristic, then it certainly would be valuable to know how to facilitate it. Consequently, it should come as no surprise that a considerable amount of research has focused on how people can become more creative. These creativity-enhancement methods have been aimed at childhood and adolescence, as well as adulthood.

Early Development

Children are naturally creative. Creativity appears in their fantasy play, for example. It often is thought that, were it not for the stultifying influences of home and school, this conspicuous creativity would persist into adulthood. Thus, the pressure to behave, grow up, and mature stifles creative capacities. As such, children get the message that their creative endeavors are childish in the eyes of adults. This view of creative development is consistent with creative adults' tendencies to exhibit childlike traits such as openness to experience, playfulness, and rich imagination (Feist, 1998). This view also suggests that if the goal is to enhance creativity, the place to begin would be the home and the place to continue such creativity lessons would be the school. In the former case, parents should encourage their children's creative activities, even if this means that the parents must relinquish considerable control over how their children spend their time (e.g., perhaps little attention to school homework). In the latter case, more attention would have to be given to the development of educational systems that nurture rather than inhibit creative classroom expressions and behaviors. There are many recommendations about implementing such changes (e.g., Colangelo & Davis, 1997), with the presumable benefit being a society replete with highly creative adults.

Researchers suggest, however, that the foregoing view is overly optimistic, even to an almost utopian degree. In the first place, it may not be accurate to assume that, without the external constraints imposed at home and school, childhood creativity would automatically transform into adulthood creativity. For instance, a similar developmental pattern is observed in the higher mammals (such as carnivores and primates)—where playful youth invariably converts into serious maturity. Hence, the longitudinal shift may reflect endogenous rather than exogenous factors (e.g., the positive impact of playful exploration on neurological development). In addition, it should be emphasized that many of the personal attributes contributing to adult creativity have respectable heritability coefficients, thereby signifying that environmental influences may play a minor role (at least for certain component traits; Simonton, 1999c). Closely related to this point is the existence of substantial individual differences in the characteristics that contribute to adulthood creativity. It may well be that only a relatively small proportion of the population enjoy the distinctive intellectual and dispositional profile that would enable them to manifest significant levels of creativity as adults. By adopting this perspective, the primary goal would be to identify those children with the most creative potential and then place them in special programs for the gifted and talented (Winner, 1996). Although this implication might seem elitist, it may be more practical than trying to make every child into a little creative genius.

The practical advantage of more select programs becomes especially apparent when we take into consideration the tremendous amount of investment required to convert the promise of youth to the accomplishments of maturity. Researchers have shown that it takes years of intense study and practice for someone to acquire the capacity to make creative contributions (Ericsson, 1996; Hayes, 1989; Simonton, 1991b). Moreover, this special training very often must depend on the attentive guidance of mentors, teachers, and coaches (Bloom, 1985; Simonton, 1992b). Thus, successful creative development typically necessitates an exceptional commitment of parental and school resources.

Adult Encouragement

Adults vary greatly in their creative potentials. Some may have very little capacity for generating new ideas, others may have enough to adapt well to everyday problems at home and work, whereas still others will attain levels worthy of the designation "creative genius." These individual differences do not operate in isolation, however, from various situational factors that enhance or inhibit the realization of creative potential. In this latter regard, many psychologists have investigated some of these situational influences. For example, a person's creativity is affected by extrinsic reward, evaluative supervision, and time pressure (Amabile, 1996). Such factors often operate in very complex ways to raise or lower creativity. For instance, rewards can harm creativity under some circumstances but enhance it under different conditions (Eisenberger & Cameron, 1996).

In the foregoing studies, the researchers focused on how various situations affect individual creativity. Yet in many applied settings—such as the research, development, or marketing teams in industry—creativity occurs as a group phenomenon (e.g., Dunbar, 1995). The question then becomes how to nurture the creative performance of the entire group, not just the individual group members. Indeed, the assumption is that group creativity often can achieve what cannot be accomplished by the various persons working separately. This assumption is the basis of various "brainstorming" techniques (Osborn, 1963). Researchers conclude that this approach to group creativity works well only under a specified set of circumstances (e.g., Diehl & Stroebe, 1987; Roy, Gauvin, & Limayem, 1996). Hence, creativity consultants in industrial and organizational settings must do their utmost to ensure that these particular conditions are met.

Creativity can take place in a variety of groups, including those that encompass whole domains, traditions, cultures, and civilizations (Csikszentmihaly, 1990; Harrington, 1990). For instance, particular creative activities in the arts or sciences may exhibit periods of florescence ("golden ages") alternating with periods of decadence or stagnation ("dark ages"; Simonton, 1975, 1988b). As noted earlier in this chapter, such fluctuations may coalesce to form grand "golden ages" separated by "dark ages." Hence, some researchers have concentrated on the political, economic, cultural, and social conditions that most favor the emergence and maintenance of eras in which creativity blossoms across many creative endeavors (Simonton, 1992a). For example, I (Simonton, 1975, 1976b) have shown how certain circumstances, such as military conflict and political anarchy, depress creative activity in most domains. Conversely, other conditions such as the infusion of cultural diversity—through immigration, political fragmentation, or nationalistic revolt—can revive creativity (Simonton, 1975, 1997b). Thus, to the degree that these events are under the control of a nation's leaders, countries can adopt policies that discourage or encourage creativity among their citizens.

Future Directions

Only half of a century has transpired since J. P. Guilford (1950) first strove to make creativity a mainstream research topic, and only a third of a century has elapsed since creativity could boast its own journal for the publication of research. As a consequence, creativity has an enormous potential for growth on three fronts.

First, many research questions remain that deserve far more attention. For example, there is a relative dearth of research on how creativity develops and manifests itself in various underrepresented populations, such as women and ethnic minorities (see, e.g., Helson, 1990; Simonton, 1992a). More work also is needed on the genetic basis of individual differences in creativity, using the latest theoretical and methodological advances in behavior genetics (e.g., Lykken, 1998; Waller, Bouchard, Lykken, Tellegen, & Blacker, 1993). Finally, the field would benefit from ambitious longitudinal studies, along the lines of Terman's (1925) classic inquiry, but with a specific focus on creative development from childhood through adulthood (cf. Csikszentmihalyi, Rathunde, & Whalen, 1993; Getzels & Csikszentmihalyi, 1976; Subotnik & Arnold, 1994). Indeed, it would be most advantageous to extend the span of such longitudinal analysis so as to determine the nature of creativity in the final years of life (cf. Csikszentmihalyi, 1997; Simonton, 1989).

Second, the psychological study of creativity would be greatly strengthened by a comprehensive and precise theoretical framework. It is not that the field lacks theoretical perspectives. On the contrary, there presently are many promising theories; perhaps, there are too many available theories. The proponents of psychoanalytic, Gestalt, behaviorist, and humanistic schools have offered their explanations for creativity, but no single theory has emerged as the consensual one in the field (see, e.g., Freud, 1908/1959; Rogers, 1954). Moreover, two alternative theoretical positions have emerged recently. These are the psychoeconomic theories that stress "investment in human capital" (Rubenson & Runco, 1992; Sternberg & Lubart, 1991) and the Darwinian theories that view creativity as a "variation-selection process" (Eysenck, 1995; Martindale, 1990; Simonton, 1999b). Both theoretical approaches aspire to integrate the myriad empirical findings in the literature, as well as to clarify the remaining theoretical issues. But as yet, neither approach has earned broad acceptance in the discipline. As such, creativity researchers lack theoretical coordination.

Third and last, practical new methods are needed for enhancing both personal and societal creativity. That is, to become full participants in the positive psychology movement, researchers ultimately must produce real improvements in both everyday and genius-grade manifestations of creativity. In part, this desideratum will be achieved automatically as our empirical and theoretical knowledge expands. Practical applications also may emerge, however, from advances outside of psychological research. Especially interesting possibilities on this latter point relate to the advent of the personal computer and the Internet linking virtually all the computers in the world. Tremendous advances already have been made in writing computer programs to successfully simulate the creative process (e.g., Boden, 1991; Johnson-Laird, 1993), and the communication networks between computers have provided the basis for electronic brainstorming (e.g., Roy et al., 1996). These innovations eventually may reach the point where linking each individual's brain with other thinking entities will magnify creativity both individually and collectively. These entities would be distributed throughout the world and would consist of both neurological and electronic units—both other human brains and sophisticated computer programs. The result could be a collective creative genius capable of producing a global golden age unlike any this earth has witnessed so far.

Thus, if psychological researchers can increase our understanding and use of creativity along the lines suggested in this chapter, not only will psychology become more positive, but the world should become more positive as well.

References

Albert, R. S., & Runco, M. A. (1999). A history of research on creativity. In R. J. Sternberg (Ed.), *Handbook of creativity* (pp. 16–31). New York: Cambridge University Press.

Amabile, T. M. (1982). Social psychology of creativity: A consensual assessment technique. *Journal of Personality and Social Psychology, 43,* 997–1013.

Amabile, T. M. (1996). *Creativity in context.* Boulder, CO: Westview.

Baer, J. (1993). *Creativity and divergent thinking.* Hillsdale, NJ: Erlbaum.

Baer, J. (1994). Divergent thinking is not a general trait: A multidomain training experiment. *Creativity Research Journal, 7,* 35–46.

Baer, J. (1998). The case for domain specificity of creativity. *Creativity Research Journal, 11,* 173–177.

Barron, F. X. (1969). *Creative person and creative process*. New York: Holt, Rinehart and Winston.

Barron, F. X., & Harrington, D. M. (1981). Creativity, intelligence, and personality. *Annual Review of Psychology, 32*, 439–476.

Bloom, B. S. (Ed.). (1985). *Developing talent in young people*. New York: Ballantine.

Boden, M. A. (1991). *The creative mind: Myths and mechanisms*. New York: Basic Books.

Campbell, D. T. (1960). Blind variation and selective retention in creative thought as in other knowledge processes. *Psychological Review, 67*, 380–400.

Cattell, R. B., & Butcher, H. J. (1968). *The prediction of achievement and creativity*. Indianapolis, IN: Bobbs-Merrill.

Colangelo, N., & Davis, G. A. (Eds.). (1997). *Handbook of gifted education*. Boston: Allyn and Bacon.

Cox, C. (1926). *The early mental traits of three hundred geniuses*. Stanford, CA: Stanford University Press.

Crammond, B. (1994). The Torrance Tests of Creative Thinking: From design through establishment of predictive validity. In R. F. Subotnik & K. D. Arnold (Eds.), *Beyond Terman: Contemporary longitudinal studies of giftedness and talent* (pp. 229–254). Norwood, NJ: Ablex.

Csikszentmihalyi, M. (1990). The domain of creativity. In M. A. Runco & R. S. Albert (Eds.), *Theories of creativity* (pp. 190–212). Newbury Park, CA: Sage.

Csikszentmihalyi, M. (1997). *Creativity: Flow and the psychology of discovery and invention*. New York: HarperCollins.

Csikszentmihalyi, M., Rathunde, K., & Whalen, S. (1993). *Talented teenagers: The roots of success and failure*. Cambridge, England: Cambridge University Press.

Dennis, W. (1966). Creative productivity between the ages of 20 and 80 years. *Journal of Gerontology, 21*, 1–8.

Diehl, M., & Stroebe, W. (1987). Productivity loss in brainstorming groups: Toward the solution of a riddle. *Journal of Personality and Social Psychology, 53*, 497–509.

Dunbar, K. (1995). How scientists really reason: Scientific reasoning in real-world laboratories. In R. J. Sternberg & J. E. Davidson (Eds.), *The nature of insight* (pp. 365–396). Cambridge, MA: MIT Press.

Ebbinghaus, H. (1908). *Psychology: An elementary text-book* (Max Meyer, Trans. & Ed.). Boston: Heath.

Eisenberger, R., & Cameron, J. (1996). Detrimental effects of reward: Reality or myth? *American Psychologist, 51*, 1153–1166.

Eisenstadt, J. M. (1978). Parental loss and genius. *American Psychologist, 33*, 211–223.

Ericsson, K. A. (Ed.). (1996). *The road to expert performance: Empirical evidence from the arts and sciences, sports, and games*. Mahwah, NJ: Erlbaum.

Eysenck, H. J. (1995). *Genius: The natural history of creativity*. Cambridge, England: Cambridge University Press.

Feist, G. J. (1993). A structural model of scientific eminence. *Psychological Science, 4*, 366–371.

Feist, G. J. (1998). A meta-analysis of personality in scientific and artistic creativity. *Personality and Social Psychology Review, 2*, 290–309.

Feist, G. J., & Runco, M. A. (1993). Trends in the creativity literature: An analysis of research in the *Journal of Creative Behavior* (1967–1989). *Creativity Research Journal, 6*, 271–286.

Feldman, D. H., with Goldsmith, L. T. (1986). *Nature's gambit: Child prodigies and the development of human potential*. New York: Basic Books.

Freud, S. (1959). Creative writers and daydreaming. In J. Strachey (Ed. and Trans.), *Standard edition of the complete psychological works of Sigmund Freud* (Vol. 9, pp. 141–153). London: Hogarth Press. (Original work published 1908)

Galton, F. (1869). *Hereditary genius: An inquiry into its laws and consequences*. London: Macmillan.

Galton, F. (1874). *English men of science: Their nature and nurture*. London: Macmillan.

Gardner, H. (1993). *Creating minds: An anatomy of creativity seen through the lives of Freud, Einstein, Picasso, Stravinsky, Eliot, Graham, and Gandhi*. New York: Basic Books.

Getzels, J. W., & Csikszentmihalyi, M. (1976). *The creative vision: A longitudinal study of problem finding in art*. New York: Wiley.

Glover, J. A., Ronning, R. R., & Reynolds, C. R. (Eds.). (1989). *Handbook of creativity*. New York: Plenum.

Goertzel, M. G., Goertzel, V., & Goertzel, T. G. (1978). *300 eminent personalities: A psychosocial analysis of the famous*. San Francisco: Jossey-Bass.

Goertzel, V., & Goertzel, M. G. (1962). *Cradles of eminence*. Boston: Little, Brown.

Gough, H. G. (1979). A Creative Personality Scale for the Adjective Check List. *Journal of Personality and Social Psychology, 37*, 1398–1405.

Gray, C. E. (1966). A measurement of creativity in Western civilization. *American Anthropologist, 68*, 1384–1417.

Guilford, J. P. (1950). Creativity. *American Psychologist, 5*, 444–454.

CHAPTER 14. CREATIVITY

Guilford, J. P. (1967). *The nature of human intelligence.* New York: McGraw-Hill.

Harrington, D. M. (1990). The ecology of human creativity: A psychological perspective. In M. A. Runco & R. S. Albert (Eds.), *Theories of creativity* (pp. 143–169). Newbury Park, CA: Sage.

Hayes, J. R. (1989). *The complete problem solver* (2nd ed.). Hillsdale, NJ: Erlbaum.

Helmreich, R. L., Spence, J. T., Beane, W. E., Lucker, G. W., & Matthews, K. A. (1980). Making it in academic psychology: Demographic and personality correlates of attainment. *Journal of Personality and Social Psychology, 39,* 896–908.

Helson, R. (1990). Creativity in women: Outer and inner views over time. In M. A. Runco & R. S. Albert (Eds.), *Theories of creativity* (pp. 46–58). Newbury Park, CA: Sage.

Hocevar, D., & Bachelor, P. (1989). A taxonomy and critique of measurements used in the study of creativity. In J. A. Glover, R. R. Ronning, & C. R. Reynolds (Eds.), *Handbook of creativity* (pp. 53–75). New York: Plenum.

Holmes, T. S., & Rahe, R. H. (1967). The social readjustment rating scale. *Journal of Psychosomatic Research, 11,* 213–218.

James, W. (1880, October). Great men, great thoughts, and the environment. *Atlantic Monthly, 46,* 441–459.

Jamison, K. R. (1993). *Touched with fire: Manic-depressive illness and the artistic temperament.* New York: Free Press.

Johnson-Laird, P. N. (1993). *Human and machine thinking.* Hillsdale, NJ: Erlbaum.

Juda, A. (1949). The relationship between highest mental capacity and psychic abnormalities. *American Journal of Psychiatry, 106,* 296–307.

Karlson, J. I. (1970). Genetic association of giftedness and creativity with schizophrenia. *Hereditas, 66,* 177–182.

Köhler, W. (1925). *The mentality of apes* (E. Winter, Trans.). New York: Harcourt, Brace.

Kroeber, A. L. (1944). *Configurations of culture growth.* Berkeley: University of California Press.

Lehman, H. C. (1953). *Age and achievement.* Princeton, NJ: Princeton University Press.

Ludwig, A. M. (1995). *The price of greatness: Resolving the creativity and madness controversy.* New York: Guilford.

Lykken, D. T. (1998). The genetics of genius. In A. Steptoe (Ed.), *Genius and the mind: Studies of creativity and temperament in the historical record* (pp. 15–37). New York: Oxford University Press.

Martindale, C. (1989). Personality, situation, and creativity. In J. A. Glover, R. R. Ronning, & C. R. Reynolds (Eds.), *Handbook of creativity* (pp. 211–232). New York: Plenum.

Martindale, C. (1990). *The clockwork muse: The predictability of artistic styles.* New York: Basic Books.

Maslow, A. H. (1959). Creativity in self-actualizing people. In H. H. Anderson (Ed.), *Creativity and its cultivation* (pp. 83–95). New York: Harper and Row.

May, R. (1975). *The courage to create.* New York: Norton.

McClelland, D. C. (1962). On the psychodynamics of creative physical scientists. In H. E. Gruber, G. Terrell, & M. Wertheimer (Eds.), *Contemporary approaches to creative thinking* (pp. 11–174). New York: Atherton Press.

McCrae, R. R., Arenberg, D., & Costa, P. T. (1987). Declines in divergent thinking with age: Cross-sectional, longitudinal, and cross-sequential analyses. *Psychology and Aging, 2,* 130–136.

Mednick, S. A. (1962). The associative basis of the creative process. *Psychological Review, 69,* 220–232.

Osborn, A. F. (1963). *Applied imagination: Principles and procedures of creative problem-solving* (3rd ed.). New York: Scribner.

Plucker, J. A. (1998). Beware of simple conclusions: The case for content generality of creativity. *Creativity Research Journal, 11,* 179–182.

Prentky, R. A. (1980). *Creativity and psychopathology: A neurocognitive perspective.* New York: Praeger.

Richards, R., Kinney, D. K., Lunde, I., Benet, M., & Merzel, A. P. C. (1988a). Assessing everyday creativity: Characteristics of the Lifetime Creativity Scales and validation with three large samples. *Journal of Personality and Social Psychology, 54,* 476–485.

Richards, R., Kinney, D. K., Lunde, I., Benet, M., & Merzel, A. P. C. (1988b). Creativity in manic-depressives, cyclothymes, their normal relatives, and control subjects. *Journal of Abnormal Psychology, 97,* 281–288.

Rodgers, R. C., & Maranto, C. L. (1989). Causal models of publishing productivity in psychology. *Journal of Applied Psychology, 74,* 636–649.

Roe, A. (1953). *The making of a scientist.* New York: Dodd, Mead.

Rogers, C. R. (1954). Toward a theory of creativity. *ETC: A Review of General Semantics, 11,* 249–260.

Rothenberg, A. (1990). *Creativity and madness: New findings and old stereotypes.* Baltimore: Johns Hopkins University Press.

Roy, M. C., Gauvin, S., & Limayem, M. (1996). Electronic group brainstorming: The role of feedback on productivity. *Small Group Research, 27,* 215–247.

Rubenson, D. L., & Runco, M. A. (1992). The psychoeconomic approach to creativity. *New Ideas in Psychology, 10,* 131–147.

*Runco, M. A. (1997). (Ed.). *The creativity research handbook.* Cresskill, NJ: Hampton Press.

*Runco, M. A., & Pritzker, S. (Eds.). (1999). *Encyclopedia of creativity.* San Diego, CA: Academic Press.

Schaefer, C. E., & Anastasi, A. (1968). A biographical inventory for identifying creativity in adolescent boys. *Journal of Applied Psychology, 58,* 42–48.

Schaller, M. (1997). The psychological consequences of fame: Three tests of the self-consciousness hypothesis. *Journal of Personality, 65,* 291–309.

Simon, H. A. (1986). What we know about the creative process. In R. L. Kuhn (Ed.), *Frontiers in creative and innovative management* (pp. 3–20). Cambridge, MA: Ballinger.

Simonton, D. K. (1975). Sociocultural context of individual creativity: A transhistorical time-series analysis. *Journal of Personality and Social Psychology, 32,* 1119–1133.

Simonton, D. K. (1976a). Biographical determinants of achieved eminence: A multivariate approach to the Cox data. *Journal of Personality and Social Psychology, 33,* 218–226.

Simonton, D. K. (1976b). Philosophical eminence, beliefs, and zeitgeist: An individual-generational analysis. *Journal of Personality and Social Psychology, 34,* 630–640.

Simonton, D. K. (1977). Eminence, creativity, and geographic marginality: A recursive structural equation model. *Journal of Personality and Social Psychology, 35,* 805–816.

Simonton, D. K. (1980). Thematic fame, melodic originality, and musical zeitgeist: A biographical and transhistorical content analysis. *Journal of Personality and Social Psychology, 38,* 972–983.

Simonton, D. K. (1988a). Age and outstanding achievement: What do we know after a century of research? *Psychological Bulletin, 104,* 251–267.

Simonton, D. K. (1988b). Galtonian genius, Kroeberian configurations, and emulation: A generational time-series analysis of Chinese civilization. *Journal of Personality and Social Psychology, 55,* 230–238.

Simonton, D. K. (1989). The swan-song phenomenon: Last-works effects for 172 classical composers. *Psychology and Aging, 4,* 42–47.

Simonton, D. K. (1991a). Career landmarks in science: Individual differences and interdisciplinary contrasts. *Developmental Psychology, 27,* 119–130.

Simonton, D. K. (1991b). Emergence and realization of genius: The lives and works of 120 classical composers. *Journal of Personality and Social Psychology, 61,* 829–840.

Simonton, D. K. (1991c). Latent-variable models of posthumous reputation: A quest for Galton's G. *Journal of Personality and Social Psychology, 60,* 607–619.

Simonton, D. K. (1992a). Gender and genius in Japan: Feminine eminence in masculine culture. *Sex Roles, 27,* 101–119.

Simonton, D. K. (1992b). Leaders of American psychology, 1879–1967: Career development, creative output, and professional achievement. *Journal of Personality and Social Psychology, 62,* 5–17.

Simonton, D. K. (1994). *Greatness: Who makes history and why.* New York: Guilford.

Simonton, D. K. (1997a). Creative productivity: A predictive and explanatory model of career trajectories and landmarks. *Psychological Review, 104,* 66–89.

Simonton, D. K. (1997b). Foreign influence and national achievement: The impact of open milieus on Japanese civilization. *Journal of Personality and Social Psychology, 72,* 86–94.

Simonton, D. K. (1998a). Achieved eminence in minority and majority cultures: Convergence versus divergence in the assessments of 294 African Americans. *Journal of Personality and Social Psychology, 74,* 804–817.

Simonton, D. K. (1998b). Fickle fashion versus immortal fame: Transhistorical assessments of creative products in the opera house. *Journal of Personality and Social Psychology, 75,* 198–210.

Simonton, D. K. (1999a). Creativity and genius. In L. Pervin & O. John (Eds.), *Handbook of personality theory and research* (2nd ed., pp. 629–652). New York: Guilford.

*Simonton, D. K. (1999b). *Origins of genius: Darwinian perspectives on creativity.* New York: Oxford University Press.

Simonton, D. K. (1999c). Talent and its development: An emergenic and epigenetic model. *Psychological Review, 106,* 435–457.

Skinner, B. F. (1972). *Cumulative record: A selection of papers* (3rd ed.). New York: Appleton-Century-Crofts.

Smith, S. M., Ward, T. B., & Finke, R. A. (Eds.). (1995). *The creative cognition approach.* Cambridge, MA: MIT Press.

*Sternberg, R. J. (Ed.). (1999). *Handbook of creativity.* New York: Cambridge University Press.

Sternberg, R. J., & Davidson, J. E. (Eds.). (1995). *The nature of insight.* Cambridge, MA: MIT Press.

Sternberg, R. J., & Lubart, T. I. (1991). An investment theory of creativity and its development. *Human Development, 34,* 1–31.

Sternberg, R. J., & Lubart, T. I. (1995). *Defying the crowd: Cultivating creativity in a culture of conformity.* New York: Free Press.

Sternberg, R. J., & Lubart, T. I. (1996). Investing in creativity. *American Psychologist, 51,* 677–688.

Subotnik, R. F., & Arnold, K. D. (Eds.). (1994). *Beyond Terman: Contemporary longitudinal studies of giftedness and talent.* Norwood, NJ: Ablex.

Taylor, C. W., & Ellison, R. L. (1967, March 3). Biographical predictors of scientific performance. *Science, 155,* 1075–1080.

Terman, L. M. (1925). *Mental and physical traits of a thousand gifted children.* Stanford, CA: Stanford University Press.

Torrance, E. P. (1988). The nature of creativity as manifest in its testing. In R. Sternberg (Ed.), *The nature of creativity: Contemporary psycholog-ical perspectives* (pp. 43–75). New York: Cambridge University Press.

Vasari, G. (1968). *Lives of the painters, sculptors, and architects* (A. B. Hinds, Trans.; W. Gaunt, Rev.; E. Fuller, Ed.). New York: Dell. (Original work published ca. 1550)

Wallace, D. B., & Gruber, H. E. (Eds.). (1989). *Creative people at work: Twelve cognitive case studies.* New York: Oxford University Press.

Wallach, M. A., & Kogan, N. (1965). *Modes of thinking in young children.* New York: Holt, Rinehart, and Winston.

Waller, N. G., Bouchard, T. J., Jr., Lykken, D. T., Tellegen, A., & Blacker, D. M. (1993). Creativity, heritability, familiality: Which word does not belong? *Psychological Inquiry, 4,* 235–237.

*Ward, T. B., Smith, S. M., & Vaid, J. (Eds.). (1997). *Creative thought: An investigation of conceptual structures and processes.* Washington, DC: American Psychological Association.

Wertheimer, M. (1982). *Productive thinking* (M. Wertheimer, Ed.). Chicago: University of Chicago Press. (Original work published 1945)

Winner, E. (1996). *Gifted children: Myths and realities.* New York: Basic Books.

15

The Role of Personal Control in Adaptive Functioning

Suzanne C. Thompson

The focus of positive psychology is on adaptive functioning, including the human capacity to maintain emotional well-being despite setback, major trauma, and the ups and downs of ordinary life. Perceived control is particularly relevant to this positive focus on the ability to find a meaningful life even in difficult circumstances. What is amazing about personal control is not just the adaptive function it serves but the incredible capacity many people have for keeping a sense of control in circumstances that appear to offer limited options. Examples of the ability to find a sense of control even in the most dire of situations abound. One particularly instructive example is described in Victor Frankl's (1963) autobiographical account of life as a prisoner in a Nazi concentration camp. Frankl relates how a sense of meaning and control in life was essential to survival. Prisoners had no control over most of their daily existence, yet some found personal control in their ability to control their attitude toward the circumstances in which they found themselves. Frankl reports that those who were able to keep this sense of self-effectiveness were more likely to survive the harsh prison environment.

This striking testament to the power of the human spirit to transform extreme circumstances into manageable conditions raises many questions. Why is personal control so important? How do people estimate their control, and how do some people manage to find empowerment even in very low control circumstances? Is it useful to have a sense of control in circumstances where so little real control is available? In this chapter, I first will cover the background of the perceived control concept in psychology and the mechanisms by which control has positive effects. Then I address the issues of how people estimate their control, how to measure control, and the adaptiveness of personal control beliefs when they seem to contradict reality. Finally, I examine individual differences in a sense of control, interventions to enhance control, and future directions for research.

Overview of Perceived Control Research and Theory

All animals strive to get what they need for life and to avoid undesirable outcomes. Humans stand out for their exceptional success not only at survival but also in learning how to control their environment and manipulate their surroundings to obtain the necessities for life, to protect themselves from misfortune, and to obtain desired levels of comfort and ease. A person's self-assessment of the ability to exert control is called *perceived control*—the judgment that one has the means to obtain desired outcomes and to avoid undesirable ones.

Perceived control has a long history as a central idea in psychological theory and research. In major theoretical approaches, scholars have attempted to explicate various aspects of perceived control, including why it is important (Miller, 1979; White, 1959), the variety of deficits associated with a lack of control (Seligman, 1975), and the role of control in coping with stressful life circumstances (Taylor, 1983).

Perhaps the most fundamental conceptualization of perceived control is Geary's (1998) evolutionary framework in which the desire for control serves as the basic motivation that guides all other motives, emotions, cognitions, and social behaviors. Through a process of evolutionary pressures, humans have been shaped to derive psychological benefits from a sense of control. Wanting to have control is adaptive because humans with this desire are more likely to obtain resources that are critical for survival and reproduction. Other theorists who do not specifically espouse an evolutionary framework also have claimed that a control drive is the central motivation guiding human behavior and development (Heckhausen & Schulz, 1995; White, 1959).

In keeping with the view that the control motive is basic to the human condition, researchers have demonstrated its many benefits. Perceptions of control are associated with better coping with stressful life circumstances (Glass, McKnight, & Valdimarsdottir, 1993; Litt, 1988; Thompson, Sobolew-Shubin, Galbraith, Schwankovsky, & Cruzen, 1993). Those with more perceived control are less anxious and depressed in the face of chronic illnesses (Griffin & Rabkin, 1998; Thompson, Nanni, & Levine, 1994) and less traumatized by victimization (Regehr, Cadell, & Jensen, 1999). In addition, those with a stronger sense of perceived control are more likely to take needed action to improve or protect their physical health (Peterson & Stunkard, 1989; Rodin, 1986) and generally have better physical health (England & Evans, 1992).

Perceived control also provides benefits in the workplace (Parkes, 1989), as well as in educa-

tional settings (Dicintio & Gee, 1999; Eccles et al., 1991). For example, children with a mastery orientation seek challenge in their tasks and persist even in the face of obstacles (Dweck, 1999). In almost every life arena, one's sense of personal control has positive implications for emotional well-being, for the likelihood that action will be taken, for physical health, and for general adaptive functioning.

Why Is a Sense of Control Beneficial?

The question of why a sense of control is important to psychological well-being does not have one simple answer. A number of advantages to perceived control have been identified, and, depending on the situation, one or more of these benefits may be critical.

According to the evolutionary perspective on perceived control, humans have been shaped through evolution to prefer a sense of control. Throughout human history, people who experienced positive emotions and a sense of well-being when they had control were more likely to work to have control and to manipulate the environment in ways that increased the chances that they and their offspring would survive. The innate association between personal control and emotional well-being had survival value, so it became widespread. In this view, well-being is dependent on perceived control because throughout the long history of humans in hunter-gatherer societies, those with a drive for control were more likely to survive and pass on their genes.

Perceptions of control also are advantageous because they may prompt individuals to take action and avoid stressful situations. More specifically, a sense of control activates problem solving and attention to solutions. Several researchers have produced support for this process. For example, Ross and Mirowsky (1989) report that individuals with a strong, rather than weak, sense of control are more likely to determine the cause of a problem and take action. Those with a low sense of control, on the other hand, tend to use the ineffective coping strategy of avoiding the problem. Another reason that personal control is beneficial is that a sense of control allows one to prepare for an upcoming stressor and ensure that the situation will not become intolerable (Miller, 1979). Thus the potentially negative event is not as stressful when it is accompanied by a belief in personal control.

Finally, a sense of uncontrollability has been associated with increased physiological reactivity to stress and depressed immune functioning (Brosschot et al., 1998; Dantzer, 1989). Thus, persons with a sense of control may protect themselves against the potentially health-compromising physiological effects of stress.

In summary, perceived control is beneficial because it is associated with positive emotions, leads to active problem solving, reduces anxiety in the face of stress, and buffers against negative physiological responses.

Estimating One's Own Control

Personal control is essentially a *perception* regarding one's ability to act on the environment to obtain desired goals. How do individuals decide on the control they have to get what they want? According to the proponents of the control heuristic approach, judgments of control are based on perceived intentionality and connection: If one intends an outcome and can see a connection between one's action and the outcome, then judgments of control will be high (Thompson, Armstrong, & Thomas, 1998). For example, a gambler who intends to throw a winning combination of dice and whose actions result in the desired dice throw is likely to feel a sense of control over what is, in fact, a random event. Even in situations such as gambling where the actual probabilities are quite clear, people greatly overestimate their control. Most of the time, however, the actual probabilities of exerting control are less obvious than the gambling example, thereby leaving even more leeway to overestimate control. For example, a woman who wants to avoid getting a respiratory infection might take an herbal remedy when she begins to feel symptoms coming on. Because she acts with the intention of avoiding an infection and can see a connection between her actions and health, she is likely to attribute a period of good health to her ability to exert control. Overall, therefore, the cognitive processes by which control is estimated appear to be biased toward control overestimation.

What People Do to Get a Sense of Control

In addition to the potential for overestimating control, there are many ways for people to en-

hance their control by accentuating intentionality and connections to outcomes. Thompson and Wierson (2000) suggest that people use at least three strategies to maintain control even in difficult circumstances, including changing to goals that are reachable in the current situation, creating new avenues for control, and accepting current circumstances.

First, making progress toward goals is an important source of perceived control and general well-being (see Snyder, 1996). When progress on an important goal is not possible, people who are flexible in identifying attainable alternate goals will be able to maintain a sense of control. Changing to reachable goals involves disengaging from goals that are no longer feasible in current life circumstances and finding satisfying, attainable alternatives. On this point, Brandtstaedter and Rothermund (1994) found that older adults maintain a strong sense of general control by de-emphasizing the importance of goals that have become difficult to achieve and focusing instead on more reachable goals. For example, persons with disabilities may switch to careers that are more attainable and possibly more satisfying (Krantz, 1995). Although it would not be adaptive to relinquish goals too readily, flexibility in the face of unreachable goals helps sustain perceptions of control.

Second, identifying and cultivating the areas of personal control that are still available is an effective way to maintain overall levels of control. For example, chronically ill individuals can influence the course of their illness by obtaining extensive medical information, getting good medical care, following the course of treatment, reducing stress in their lives, improving overall fitness through diet and exercise, and investigating alternate types of treatment. For some individuals, the active role may involve using alternative health care as a way of enhancing a sense of control. Because predictability enhances a sense of control (Thompson, 1981), just getting information on the causes and course of one's disease and treatment options can increase perceived control.

Some individuals may feel that the central cause of their stress is not amenable to control, but that they can exert some control over other areas in their lives by keeping a positive attitude or trying to reduce the stress for family members. Any activities that make salient the connection between one's own action and a desired outcome increase perceived control. As an example, one breast cancer survivor joined other women with breast cancer on a rowing team and reported that her involvement helped remind her of the effectiveness of her actions (Mitchell, 1997).

Third, there is the strategy of acceptance that is based on Rothbaum, Weisz, and Snyder's (1982) distinction between primary and secondary control. *Primary control* is the same as perceived control as it is defined in this chapter: the perception that one can get desired outcomes. *Secondary control* involves accepting one's life circumstances as they are, instead of working to change them. Acceptance can be achieved in a variety of ways, including finding benefits and meaning in the loss and in one's life situation. Even in an overall negative experience, many individuals are able to find some benefits or advantages in their situation (see Tennen & Affleck, this volume). For example, some stroke patients report that their stroke has helped them appreciate life and their spouse and that they have grown from the experience (Thompson, 1991). Acceptance increases a sense of control because it helps people feel less like helpless victims and reduces the discrepancy between desired and achieved outcomes.

Measuring Perceptions of Control

Many ways to measure perceived control are available, reflecting the complexity of the construct. Perceived control can refer to general perceptions such as overall control in one's life or to specific areas such as control in the academic arena or in the work setting. Generally, it is best to select measures that are geared to the context being addressed. For example, school-related perceived control (e.g., as measured by the Intellectual Achievement Responsibility Questionnaire; Crandall, Katkovsky, & Crandall, 1965) is likely to be a better predictor of academic achievement than is general control. However, if the research question is focused on overall levels of control (e.g., a study addressing decline in overall control associated with aging) or if comparisons are to be made across different domains, then a widely used general measure of control, the Pearlin and Schooler Mastery Scale (1978), is available.

Another distinction among control measures refers to the assessment of overall control versus the components of control judgments. Perceived control can be decomposed into two parts: (a) *locus of control,* which is the perception that most people's outcomes are influenced by personal action (internal) versus outside forces or other people (external), and (b) *self-efficacy,* which refers to the belief that one personally has the ability to enact the actions that are necessary to get desired outcomes. Perceived control is the combination of an internal locus (i.e., outcomes depend on personal action) and self-efficacy (i.e., I have the skills to take effective action). Some interesting questions can be addressed by measuring the components separately, but it is important to note that locus of control (also called *control ideology*) is not the same concept as perceived control. In addition, a number of studies that claim to measure perceived control have, in fact, assessed a different concept such as responsibility, self-blame, availability of a choice, or attempted problem solving. These are valid constructs to study, but they should not be confused with perceived control. For example, people can feel responsible without having a sense of control and can judge that they have control without blaming themselves for negative outcomes. Thus if the focus of the research is on perceptions of control, a measure that assesses the self-perception that one has the ability to get desired outcomes and avoid undesirable ones should be used.

Distinctions also are made between perceived control and desire for control. For example, some people may desire to have control in an area but not perceive themselves to currently have that capability. There are several measures of desire for control, such as the Desire for Control Scale (Burger & Cooper, 1979) and the Desired Control Scale (Reid & Ziegler, 1981). Researchers have found that desire for control can determine whether actual control is beneficial (e.g., Wallston et al., 1991). Thus the interactions between the level of desired control and the control afforded by a situation are important to investigate.

Realism and Illusion in the Effects of Personal Control

Having a sense of control is typical of those who handle stress well, so the construct fits well with the positive psychology focus of this handbook. However, the possibility that having a strong sense of control has a downside as well as being a mark of good functioning needs to be addressed. In particular, is it adaptive for people to *overestimate* their potential for influence? Or is perceived control useful only if it is an accurate reflection of one's capabilities? The reasoning goes like this: Although high control perceptions are beneficial, overestimations of control will be maladaptive because they can cause inappropriate and fruitless attempts to change a truly unchangeable situation and will lead to disappointment when expectations are disconfirmed.

This question of the effectiveness of perceived control in relation to its veridicality has been difficult to research because there is a lack of clarity in determining how much control people have in real-life situations. Nonetheless, we can turn to several sources to address this question. One involves laboratory studies of illusory control in which the actual level of control over a task is manipulated and participants are asked to estimate their control after completing the task (Alloy & Abramson, 1979). Illusory control consistently enhances adaptive functioning. For example, Alloy and Clements (1992) measured the degree to which college students exhibited the illusion of control on a laboratory task and then assessed students' immediate and long-term affective responses to both naturally occurring and experimentally generated negative stressors. Students who displayed greater illusions of control were *less* likely to (a) show immediate negative mood reactions after an induced failure, (b) become discouraged when they subsequently experienced negative life stressors, and (c) experience an increase in depressive symptoms a month later.

Correlational studies of coping with traumatic life events such as chronic illness also shed light on the adaptiveness of illusory control. Presumably, people with more serious loss or trauma have less real control, yet perceived control is just as beneficial for those who are facing more severely restrictive or adverse circumstances as it is for those in better circumstances (Helgeson, 1992; Reed, Taylor, & Kemeny, 1993; Thompson et al., 1993), indicating that control does not have to be realistic to be beneficial. Furthermore, in one study, breast cancer patients had high perceptions of control over their cancer despite the fact that these perceptions were most likely inaccurate (Taylor, Lichtman, & Wood, 1984). The control perceptions appeared to have benefits even when they were disconfirmed. Those who had a recurrence found another avenue for believing they had control (Taylor, 1983). Thus, despite the rea-

sonableness of the assumption that control needs to be realistic to be adaptive, the empirical results for coping with failure on laboratory tasks and with negative life events suggest otherwise.

That is not the whole story, however. Health-behavior deficits associated with illusory control were found by Thompson, Kent, Craig, and Vrungos (1999), who assessed the susceptibility of college students and gay men in the community to illusory control thinking in general, as well as their strategies for protecting themselves against HIV. Those who used more general illusory control also were more likely to use ineffective ways to protect against exposure to HIV. Furthermore, in another experiment, college research participants who received an intervention to undermine their illusions of control over protection from HIV and other sexually transmitted diseases reported more effective protection (e.g., condom use) in the 3-month period following the study than did those whose illusions were left intact (Thompson, Kyle, Vrungos, & Swan, 2000). In a study by Haaga and Stewart (1992), ex-smokers' self-efficacy for the recovery of abstinence from smoking after an initial lapse into smoking behavior was examined. Findings indicate that recent ex-smokers with a moderate level of self-efficacy sustained abstinence during the following year to a greater degree than did the more or less confident ex-smokers. These studies suggest that overestimations of control may be maladaptive in the context of health-related behaviors.

How might we explain the varying results regarding illusory control that have emerged from the coping and the health-behavior studies? First, in regard to the adaptiveness of overestimations of control, we turn to Shelley Taylor and her colleagues on this topic (Taylor, 1983; Taylor & Brown, 1988). In Taylor's view, illusions are an integral feature of normal cognitive functioning. Illusions are adaptive because they lead to persistence in meeting one's goals, which is associated with a higher probability of success (Taylor, 1983). Disconfirmation of one's control is not a major setback because high-control people are adept at finding substitute routes to getting their desired outcomes. In addition, most illusions are not wildly different from a realistic assessment, so people are not likely to act in ways that are greatly discrepant from their actual control (Taylor & Brown, 1988). Finally, many people may combine the best of both worlds by regularly overestimating their control but, at critical junctures, being more honest with themselves and making accurate assessments of their control (Taylor & Armor, 1996). These ideas explain why people who are coping with difficult life circumstances derive benefits from perceptions of control even if these judgments are overestimations of their actual control.

The difference in findings between the coping and the health-behavior studies may have to do with motivated thinking. Some people may be motivated to overestimate their control over health behaviors so as to avoid having to make difficult changes (e.g., use condoms 100% of the time). Illusory beliefs in the effectiveness of easier measures to avoid HIV, such as partner screening or serial monogamy, maintain a sense of protection without having to enact the more difficult strategies of consistent condom use or abstinence (Thompson et al., 1999). Thus, when the driving motive for overestimating control is to avoid an effective but difficult behavior, then the illusory control can be maladaptive. In contrast, when illusory control allows one to feel safe and experience less anxiety when undergoing a stressful experience (the situation being addressed in the studies of coping), overestimations of control can provide important benefits.

Individual Differences

People's control perceptions differ in at least two ways. First, there are differences in levels of perceived control, ranging from an extremely low level of control (helplessness) to very high personal mastery. Second, for some people, high levels of control are associated with good psychosocial outcomes; for others, there is a weak or no relationship between levels of control and psychosocial outcomes.

Control judgments follow a "realism principle," that is, they are generally responsive to the actual contingencies of the situation (Thompson, 1993). As a rule, people in circumstances with objectively more control have higher perceptions of control than do those in less responsive conditions. For instance, people in good health tend to have stronger control judgments than those who are ill (Thompson et al., 1993), and participants in laboratory studies where the actual control contingencies are manipulated have higher judgments of control

when the contingencies are objectively higher (Alloy & Abramson, 1979). Therefore, it appears that people with many available options and opportunities for control will have perceptions of high control.

There also are personality characteristics that relate to levels of perceived control. Depressive thinking is one dispositional characteristic that can affect judgments of control. Research on illusions of control in laboratory settings where the actual contingencies are manipulated has revealed that nondepressed individuals have higher estimates of control than their depressed counterparts (Alloy & Abramson, 1982; Martin, Abramson, & Alloy, 1984). Nondepressed individuals are more likely than depressed individuals to overestimate their control.

The relationship between demographic factors and perceived control also has been examined. Judgments of control tend to stay stable throughout the adult years, with declines coming only in the later years (Mirowsky, 1995; Nelson, 1993) or not at all (Lachman, 1991; Peng & Lachman, 1993). Perceived control is adaptive throughout the range of ages that have been studied (Andersson, 1992; Brandstadter & Rothermund, 1994). In fact, Rodin (1986) has suggested that a sense of control may have greater benefits for older than younger individuals.

Other studies have examined the effects of ethnicity and culture on control perceptions. Researchers have found that people in a variety of countries realize benefits from perceived control. Bobak, Pikhart, Hertzman, Rose, and Marmot (1998), for example, surveyed Russian adults and found that perceived control over their lives was strongly and positively related to better health and physical functioning. Grob, Little, Wanner, Wearing, and Euronet (1996) compared the beliefs of adolescents from Western European and Eastern European countries. Youth from Eastern European countries had higher perceptions of control, and for both groups, higher perceptions of control predicted better psychological well-being.

A somewhat different story emerges from Asian American and African American populations. For instance, Sastry and Ross (1998) found that both Asian Americans and Asians in Asia have lower levels of perceived control than do non-Asians in the United States. In addition, several studies find a relatively weak relationship between perceived control and psychological outcomes among Asian Americans and African Americans. Wong, Heiby, Kameoka, and Dubanoski (1999) surveyed both Asian American and White elder adults and found that more perceived control was associated with less depression only for the White elders. In the previously mentioned study by Sastry and Ross (1998), there were weaker relationships between perceived control and psychological distress for Asian Americans and Asians than for non-Asians. Thompson, Collins, Newcomb, and Hunt (1996) found a similar result for an African American sample: There were no differences in perceived control between African American and White prison inmates with HIV, but the relationship between control and adjustment differed for the two groups. More perceived control was strongly associated with better adjustment for White inmates, but no relationship emerged for the African Americans. It may be that people in less individualistic cultures derive less benefit from individual-level perceptions of control.

Interventions to Increase Control

An important research focus has been how to enhance the control perceptions of those who are in low control circumstances. The goal is to help people experience the positive psychological and physical health benefits often associated with having a sense of personal control. Intervention studies to enhance perceived control have explored a variety of techniques.

Comprehensive interventions that involve teaching stress-reduction and coping skills are one approach. The idea is that successful experience in reducing stress and handling problems will increase a sense of control. Along these lines, Cunningham, Lockwood, and Cunningham (1991) instructed cancer patients in a psychoeducational program with seven weekly 2-hour sessions that included learning coping skills, relaxation, positive mental imagery, stress control, cognitive restructuring, goal setting, and lifestyle change. After the program, participants had higher perceptions of self-efficacy, which, the authors suggest, led to their ability to exert control, improved mood, and improved relationships with others. Similarly, Telch and Telch (1986) found that group coping skills instruction improved self-efficacy for cancer patients. Slivinske and Fitch (1987) tested a comprehensive control-enhancing intervention for elderly individuals that focused on enhanced

responsibility, stress management, physical fitness, and spirituality. The group that received the intervention had a significant increase in perceived control and overall functioning. Parker et al. (1988) provided rheumatoid arthritis patients with cognitive behavioral therapy and training in coping, problem solving, distraction, and self-management. The group receiving this intervention reported less catastrophizing and stronger perceptions of control over pain. A cognitive behavioral treatment program for pain patients had the positive effect of reducing feelings of helplessness (Katz, Ritvo, Irvine, & Jackson, 1996), and a similar program for people with arthritis decreased pain, fatigue, and anxiety (Barlow, Turner, & Wright, 1998). These studies have found positive effects, but given the comprehensive nature of the interventions, we cannot deduce that it was the enhancement of control per se that produced the positive effects.

A second approach has been to use interventions that are more closely focused on specifically enhancing control. In several studies, people have been encouraged to participate more in their treatment or treatment decisions. For example, Johnston, Gilbert, Partridge, and Collins (1992) randomly assigned rehabilitation patients to a group that received a routine appointment letter with the message that their efforts would pay off or to a control group that did not get this message. The individuals who received the message had higher levels of perceived control and were more satisfied with information they received. In a study of patients with ulcer disease, participants were taught to read their own medical records and encouraged to ask questions of their medical care providers (Greenfield, Kaplan, & Ware, 1985). Other patients did not receive this intervention. Over time, those who received the instruction preferred a more active role in medical care and were more effective in obtaining information from their physicians. Langer and Rodin (1976) randomly assigned residents in a nursing home to experimental or control conditions in their study. Residents in the experimental condition were exhorted to take responsibility for themselves, offered choices to make, and given a houseplant to tend. Three weeks after the intervention, self-ratings and behavioral measures showed that members of the experimental group were more alert, participated more in residence activities, and had a higher sense of well-being than those in the control group.

A number of control interventions have been conducted in educational settings. For example, Bergin, Hudson, Chryst, and Resetar (1992) increased the perceived control of educationally disadvantaged young children, thereby improving their scores on standardized tests. In a study by Hazareesingh and Bielawski (1991), one group of student teachers received cognitive self-instruction training (positive self-talk) and saw models who took responsibility for their behavior. Compared with another group that did not get this training, the student teachers who received self-instruction and modeling perceived themselves as being in more control in classroom settings.

Although many researchers have found positive effects associated with interventions to increase perceptions of control, some studies have found mixed results. For example, in a study by England and Evans (1992), cardiac patients were invited to participate in a decision about their treatment. The invitation increased the perceived control of some patients but not others. This led the researchers to question whether encouraging patient participation is an effective control-enhancing strategy for all individuals. Along the same lines, the next three studies examined the circumstances under which control is or is not beneficial. Wallston et al. (1991) studied the interaction between cancer patients' desire for control and whether or not they were given a choice of antiemetic treatment for chemotherapy. Patients were randomly assigned to have or not have a choice of antiemetic drug. The choice had no effect for patients who were in the lower third or upper third in desire for control, but for those who had a moderate level of desired control, being given a choice seemed to reduce anxiety and lessen negative mood. Reich and Zautra (1991) used a comprehensive control-enhancement intervention with at-risk older adults (bereaved or disabled). The intervention involved cognitive and behavioral techniques to increase perceived control; for example, participants were helped to identify controllable and uncontrollable events in their lives. Older adults who were either physically disabled or bereaved were assigned to one of three levels of an intervention: control-enhanced, placebo-contact, or a no-contact group. The control enhancement increased mental health for individuals with a high internal locus of control, but the placebo-contact group worked best for those with a low internal locus. Those who were low in internality were

actually better off if they were encouraged to be dependent. Craig, Hancock, Chang, and Dickson (1998) found that a cognitive-behavioral therapy intervention for patients with spinal cord injuries increased feelings of control only for participants who initially had low feelings of control.

Overall, attempts to increase perceived control have shown some promise, especially if they increase general coping and stress-reduction skills. Interventions in which patients are given more control may need to be matched to their desired level of control and may be most effective for those who already are attuned to ways that they control outcomes.

Future Directions

The concept of perceived control has generated a great deal of research, and we now can reach some conclusions regarding its benefits and the circumstances under which it is adaptive. In general, perceptions of control help people maintain emotional well-being and deal effectively with life problems. Still, much remains to be discovered. Some suggestions for further research are discussed here.

Ethnic group differences in the adaptiveness of personal control need further explication. Based on the studies discussed earlier in this chapter, it seems that individuals from collectivist cultures do not derive as much benefit from a sense of personal control as do those from cultures with more individualistic orientations. Researchers need to establish the reliability of this effect and determine what underlies it. More studies of perceived control that include members of various minority groups also are essential. It may be the case that minority group members and those from collectivist cultures possess a sense of control that does not rely on individual empowerment, but rather rests on using group influence. Standard measures of personal control may not adequately detect these group-oriented perceptions of control.

The question of the adaptiveness of overly optimistic estimates of one's control also needs further exploration. One issue is whether people are psychologically shaken by an incident that clearly indicates they have less control than they had imagined. Based on results to date, there does not appear to be a downside to overestimating one's control when in low-control circumstances such as having a serious and debilitating chronic illness. In only a few studies, however, have researchers used the longitudinal designs that would be necessary to assess reactions before and after a disconfirmation of control. A second research issue involves testing the effects of motives on overestimations of control. It may be that when people make overly optimistic judgments of their control to avoid undertaking a more difficult, but effective, course of action, their illusory control may have negative effects. When motives to avoid action prevail, illusory control may discourage rather than encourage effective action. More research is needed on this topic, however, before this view can be validated.

Finally, researchers need to explore more ways to increase perceived control in everyday life. Although a variety of interventions for those who are chronically ill or receiving medical care have been tested, there has been little research on interventions to increase personal control in ordinary life circumstances. Many people are adept at finding a strong sense of personal control on their own, but for those who are not, control-enhancing programs could make the benefits of personal control more widely available. A central focus of positive psychology is to make beneficial ways of thinking and feeling available to the maximum number of people. Establishing environments where more people feel empowered to make positive changes in their lives is an important step in that direction.

References

Alloy, L. B., & Abramson, L. Y. (1979). Judgment of contingency in depressed and nondepressed students: Sadder but wiser? *Journal of Experimental Psychology: General, 108,* 441–483.

Alloy, L. B., & Abramson, L. Y. (1982). Learned helplessness, depression, and the illusion of control. *Journal of Personality and Social Psychology, 42,* 1114–1126.

Alloy, L. B., & Clements, C. M. (1992). Illusion of control: Invulnerability to negative affect and depressive symptoms after laboratory and natural stressors. *Journal of Abnormal Psychology, 101,* 234–245.

Andersson, L. (1992). Loneliness and perceived responsibility and control in elderly community residents. *Social Behavior and Personality, 7,* 431–443.

Barlow, J. H., Turner, A. P., & Wright, C. C. (1998). Sharing, caring, and learning to take control: Self-management training for people with arthritis. *Psychology, Health, & Medicine, 3,* 387–393.

Bergin, D. A., Hudson, L. M., Chryst, C. F., & Resetar, M. (1992). An afterschool intervention program for educationally disadvantaged young children. *Urban Review, 24,* 203–217.

Bobak, M., Pikhart, H., Hertzman, C., Rose, R., & Marmot, M. (1998). Socioeconomic factors, perceived control, and self-reported health in Russia: A cross-sectional survey. *Social Science and Medicine, 47,* 269–279.

Brandtstaedter, J., & Rothermund, K. (1994). Self-percepts of control in middle and later adulthood: Buffering losses by rescaling goals. *Psychology and Aging, 9,* 265–273.

Brosschot, J. F., Godaert, G. L. R., Benschop, R. J., Olff, M., Ballieux, R. E., & Heijnen, C. J. (1998). Experimental stress and immunological reactivity: A closer look at perceived controllability. *Psychosomatic Medicine, 60,* 359–361.

Burger, J. M., & Cooper, H. M. (1979). The desirability of control. *Motivation and Emotion, 3,* 381–393.

Craig, A., Hancock, K., Chang, E., & Dickson, H. (1998). The effectiveness of group psychological intervention in enhancing perceptions of control following spinal cord injury. *Australian and New Zealand Journal of Psychiatry, 32,* 112–118.

Crandall, V. C., Katkovsky, W., & Crandall, V. J. (1965). Children's beliefs in their own control of reinforcements in intellectual-academic achievement situations. *Child Development, 36,* 91–109.

Cunningham, A. J., Lockwood, G. A., & Cunningham, J. A. (1991). A relationship between perceived self-efficacy and quality of life in cancer patients. *Patient Education and Counseling, 17,* 71–78.

Dantzer, R. (1989). Neuroendocrine correlates of control and coping. In A. Steptoe & A. Appels (Eds.), *Stress, personal control and health* (pp. 277–294). New York: Wiley.

Dicintio, M. J., & Gee, S. (1999). Control is the key: Unlocking the motivation of at-risk students. *Psychology in the Schools, 36,* 231–237.

Dweck, C. S. (1999). *Self-theories: Their role in motivation, personality, and development.* Philadelphia: Psychology Press.

Eccles, J. S., Buchanan, C. M., Flanagan, C., Fuligni, A., Midgley, C., & Yee, C. (1991). Control versus autonomy during early adolescence. *Journal of Social Issues, 47*(4), 53–68.

England, S. L., & Evans, J. (1992). Patients' choices and perceptions after an invitation to participate in treatment decisions. *Social Science and Medicine, 34,* 1217–1225.

Frankl, V. E. (1963). *Man's search for meaning.* New York: Pocket Books.

Geary, D. C. (1998). *Male, female: The evolution of human sex differences.* Washington, DC: American Psychological Association.

Glass, D. C., McKnight, J. D., & Valdimarsdottir, H. (1993). Depression, burnout, and perceptions of control in hospital nurses. *Journal of Consulting and Clinical Psychology, 61,* 147–155.

Greenfield, S., Kaplan, S., & Ware, J. E. (1985). Expanding patient involvement in care. *Annals of Internal Medicine, 102,* 520–528.

Griffin, K. W., & Rabkin, J. G. (1998). Perceived control over illness, realistic acceptance, and psychological adjustment in people with AIDS. *Journal of Social and Clinical Psychology, 17,* 407–424.

Grob, A., Little, T. D., Wanner, B., Wearing, W., & Euronet. (1996). Adolescents' well-being and perceived control across 14 sociocultural contexts. *Journal of Personality and Social Psychology, 71,* 785–795.

Haaga, D. A. F., & Stewart, B. L. (1992). Self-efficacy for recovery from a lapse after smoking cessation. *Journal of Consulting and Clinical Psychology, 60,* 24–28.

Hazareesingh, N. A., & Bielawski, L. L. (1991). The effects of cognitive self-instruction on student teachers' perceptions of control. *Teaching and Teacher Education, 7,* 383–393.

*Heckhausen, J., & Schulz, R. (1995). A life-span theory of control. *Psychological Review, 102,* 284–304.

Helgeson, V. S. (1992). Moderators of the relation between perceived control and adjustment to chronic illness. *Journal of Personality and Social Psychology, 63,* 656–666.

Johnston, M., Gilbert, P., Partridge, C., & Collins, J. (1992). Changing perceived control in patients with physical disabilities: An intervention study with patients receiving rehabilitation. *British Journal of Clinical Psychology, 31,* 89–94.

Katz, J., Ritvo, P., Irvine, M. J., & Jackson, M. (1996). Coping with chronic pain. In M. Zeidner & N. S. Endler (Eds.), *Handbook of coping: Theory, research, and applications* (pp. 252–278). New York: Wiley.

Krantz, S. E. (1995). Chronic physical disability and secondary control: Appraisals of an undesirable situation. *Journal of Cognitive Psychotherapy: An International Quarterly, 9,* 229–248.

Lachman, M. E. (1991). Perceived control over memory aging: Developmental and intervention perspectives. *Journal of Social Issues, 47*(4), 159–175.

Langer, E. J., & Rodin, J. (1976). The effects of choice and enhanced personal responsibility: A field experiment in an institutional setting. *Journal of Personality and Social Psychology, 34,* 191–198.

Litt, M. D. (1988). Self-efficacy and perceived control: Cognitive mediators of pain tolerance. *Journal of Personality and Social Psychology, 4,* 149–160.

Martin, D. J., Abramson, L. Y., & Alloy, L. B. (1984). Illusion of control for self and others in depressed and nondepressed college students. *Journal of Personality and Social Psychology, 46,* 125–136.

Miller, S. M. (1979). Controllability and human stress: Method, evidence, and theory. *Behavior Research and Theory, 17,* 287–306.

Mirowsky, J. (1995). Age and the sense of control. *Social Psychology Quarterly, 58,* 31–43.

Mitchell, J. (May 28, 1997). Paddling toward life. *The Oregonian, Section D,* pp. 1, 3.

Nelson, E. A. (1993). Control beliefs of adults in three domains: A new assessment of perceived control. *Psychological Reports, 72,* 155–165.

Parker, J. C., Frank, R. G., Beck, N. C., Smarr, K. L., Buescher, K. L., Phillips, L. R., Smith, E. I., Anderson, S. K., & Walker, S. E. (1988). Pain management in rheumatoid arthritis patients: A cognitive-behavioral approach. *Arthritis and Rheumatism, 31,* 593–601.

Parkes, K. R. (1989). Personal control in an occupational context. In A. Steptoe & A. Appels (Eds.), *Stress, personal control, and health* (pp. 21–47). West Sussex, England: Wiley.

Pearlin, L., & Schooler, C. (1978). The structure of coping. *Journal of Health and Social Behavior, 19,* 2–21.

Peng, Y., & Lachman, M. E. (1993, August). *Primary and secondary control: Age and cultural differences.* Paper presented at the 101st Annual Convention of the American Psychological Association, Toronto, Canada.

Peterson, C., & Stunkard, A. J. (1989). Personal control and health promotion. *Social Science and Medicine, 28,* 819–828.

Reed, G. M., Taylor, S. E., & Kemeny, M. E. (1993). Perceived control and psychological adjustment in gay men with AIDS. *Journal of Applied Social Psychology, 23,* 791–824.

Regehr, C., Cadell, S., & Jensen, K. (1999). Perceptions of control and long-term recovery from rape. *American Journal of Orthopsychiatry, 69,* 110–115.

Reich, J. W., & Zautra, A. J. (1991). Experimental and measurement approaches to internal control in at-risk older adults. *Journal of Social Issues, 47*(4), 143–158.

Reid, D. W., & Ziegler, M. (1981). The Desired Control Measure and adjustment among the elderly. In H. M. Lefcourt (Ed.), *Research with the locus of control construct* (Vol. 1, pp. 127–157). New York: Academic Press.

*Rodin, J. (1986). Aging and health: Effects of the sense of control. *Science, 233*, 1271–1276.

Ross, C. E., & Mirowsky, J. (1989). Explaining the social patterns of depression: Control and problem solving—or support and talking? *Journal of Health and Social Behavior, 30*, 206–219.

Rothbaum, F., Weisz, J. R., & Snyder, S. S. (1982). Changing the world and changing the self: A two-process model of perceived control. *Journal of Personality and Social Psychology, 42*, 5–27.

Sastry, J., & Ross, C. E. (1998). Asian ethnicity and the sense of personal control. *Social Psychology Quarterly, 61*, 101–120.

Seligman, M. E. P. (1975). *Helplessness: On depression, development, and death.* San Francisco: Freeman.

Sieber, W. J., Rodin, R., Larson, L., Ortega, S., Cummings, N., Levy, S., Whiteside, T., & Herberman, R. (1992). Modulation of human natural killer cell activity by exposure to uncontrollable stress. *Brain, Behavior, and Immunity, 6*, 141–156.

Slivinske, L. R., & Fitch, V. L. (1987). The effect of control enhancing interventions on the well-being of elderly individuals living in retirement communities. *The Gerontologist, 27*, 176–181.

Snyder, C. R. (1996). To hope, to lose, and to hope again. *Journal of Personal and Interpersonal Loss, 1*, 1–16.

*Taylor, S. E. (1983). Adjustment to threatening events: A theory of cognitive adaptation. *American Psychologist, 38*, 1161–1173.

Taylor, S. E., & Armor, D. A. (1996). Positive illusions and coping with adversity. *Journal of Personality, 64*, 873–898.

Taylor, S. E., & Brown, J. D. (1988). Illusion and well-being: A social psychological perspective on mental health. *Psychological Bulletin, 103*, 193–210.

Taylor, S. E., Lichtman, R. R., & Wood, J. V. (1984). Attributions, beliefs about control, and adjustment to breast cancer. *Journal of Personality and Social Psychology, 46*, 489–502.

Telch, C. F., & Telch, M. J. (1986). Group coping skills instruction and supportive group therapy for cancer patients: A comparison of strategies.

Journal of Consulting and Clinical Psychology, 54, 802–808.

Thompson, S. C. (1981). Will it hurt less if I can control it? A complex answer to a simple question. *Psychological Bulletin, 90*, 89–101.

Thompson, S. C. (1991). The search for meaning following a stroke. *Basic and Applied Social Psychology, 12*, 81–96.

Thompson, S. C. (1993). Naturally occurring perceptions of control: A model of bounded flexibility. In G. Weary, F. Gleicher, & K. L. Marsh (Eds.), *Control motivation and social cognition* (pp. 74–93). New York: Springer-Verlag.

*Thompson, S. C., Armstrong, W., & Thomas, C. (1998). Illusions of control, underestimations, and accuracy: A control heuristic explanation. *Psychological Bulletin, 123*, 143–161.

Thompson, S. C., Collins, M. A., Newcomb, M. D., & Hunt, W. (1996). On fighting versus accepting stressful circumstances: Primary and secondary control among HIV-positive men in prison. *Journal of Personality and Social Psychology, 70*, 1307–1317.

Thompson, S. C., Kent, D. K., Thomas, C., & Vrungos, S. (1999). Real and illusory control over exposure to HIV in college students and gay men. *Journal of Applied Social Psychology, 29*, 1128–1150.

Thompson, S. C., Kyle, D., Vrungos, S., & Swan, J. (2001). *Condom intervention to reduce illusions of control.* Manuscript in preparation, Pomona College, Claremont, CA.

Thompson, S. C., Nanni, C., & Levine, A. (1994). Primary versus secondary and disease versus consequence-related control in HIV-positive men. *Journal of Personality and Social Psychology, 67*, 540–547.

Thompson, S. C., Sobolew-Shubin, A., Galbraith, M. E., Schwankovsky, L., & Cruzen, D. (1993). Maintaining perceptions of control: Finding perceived control in low-control circumstances. *Journal of Personality and Social Psychology, 64*, 293–304.

Thompson, S. C., & Wierson, M. (2000). Enhancing perceived control in psychotherapy. In C. R. Snyder & R. E. Ingram (Eds.), *Handbook of psychological change* (pp. 177–197). New York: Wiley.

Wallston, K. A., Smith, R. A. P., King, J. E., Smith, M. S., Rye, P., & Burish, T. G. (1991). Desire for control and choice of antiemetic treatment for cancer chemotherapy. *Western Journal of Nursing Research, 13*, 12–29.

White, R. W. (1959). Motivation reconsidered: The concept of competence. *Psychological Review, 66*, 297–333.

Wiedenfeld, S. A., O'Leary, A., Bandura, A., Brown, S., Levine, S., & Raska, K. (1991). Impact of perceived self-efficacy in coping with stressors on components of the immune system. *Journal of Personality and Social Psychology, 59,* 1082–1094.

Wong, S. S., Heiby, E. M., Kameoka, V. A., & Dubanoski, J. P. (1999). Perceived control, self-reinforcement, and depression among Asian American and Caucasian American elders. *Journal of Applied Gerontology, 18,* 46–62.

16

Well-Being

Mindfulness Versus Positive Evaluation

Ellen Langer

Life is a battle. On this point optimists and pessimists agree. Evil is insolent and strong; beauty enchanting but rare; goodness very apt to be weak; folly very apt to be defiant; wickedness to carry the day; imbeciles to be in very great places, people of sense in small, and mankind generally, unhappy. . . . In this there is mingled pain and delight, but over the mysterious mixture there hovers a visible rule, that bids us learn to will and seek to understand.

Henry James

Introducing Mindfulness

What is considered evil, beautiful, good, folly, and wickedness are products of our mind. It is surely easier to be happy living in a world full of beauty and goodness. Just as surely, it is easier to be happy if we think these things of ourselves. This chapter will consider the ways our mindless use of evaluation, be it positive or negative, leads to our unhappiness; the direct effects of mindfulness on happiness; and why teaching mindfulness may reap more benefits than try-

ing to teach people to be positive. Most will agree that pessimism is virtually synonymous with unhappiness. What might be worth considering is how positive evaluations may lead to the same result.

Before proceeding, however, it is important to take at least a brief look at what mindfulness is and is not: It is a flexible state of mind—an openness to novelty, a process of actively drawing novel distinctions. When we are mindful, we become sensitive to context and perspective; we are situated in the present. When we are mindless, we are trapped in rigid mind-sets, oblivious to context or perspective. When we are mindless, our behavior is governed by rule and routine. In contrast, when we are mindful, our behavior may be guided rather than governed by rules and routines. Mindfulness is not vigilance or attention when what is meant by those concepts is a stable focus on an object or idea. When mindful, we are actively varying the stimulus field. It is not controlled processing (e.g., 31×267), in that mindfulness requires or generates novelty. Mindlessness is not habit, although habit is mindless. Mindlessness need not arise as a function of repeated experience.

As demonstrated subsequently, mindlessness may come about on a single exposure to information.

For those of us who learned to drive many years ago, we were taught that if we needed to stop the car on a slippery surface, the safest way was to slowly, gently pump the brake. Today most new cars have antilock brakes. To stop on a slippery surface, now the safest thing to do is to step on the brake firmly and hold it down. Most of us caught on ice will still gently pump the brakes. What was once safe is now dangerous. The context has changed, but our behavior remains the same.

Much of the time we are mindless. Of course we are unaware when we are in that state of mind because we are "not there" to notice. To notice, we would have had to have been mindful. Yet over 25 years of research reveals that mindlessness may be very costly to us. In these studies we have found that an increase in mindfulness results in greater competence, health and longevity, positive affect, creativity, and charisma and reduced burnout, to name a few of the findings (see Langer, 1989, 1997).

Mindlessness comes about in two ways: either through repetition or on a single exposure to information. The first case is the more familiar. Most of us have had the experience, for example, of driving and then realizing, only because of the distance we have come, that we made part of the trip on "automatic pilot," as we sometimes call mindless behavior. Another example of mindlessness through repetition is when we learn something by practicing it so that it becomes like "second nature" to us. We try to learn the new skill so well that we do not have to think about it. The problem is that if we have been successful, it will not occur to us to think about it even when it would be to our advantage to do so.

Whether we become mindless over time or on initial exposure to information, we unwittingly lock ourselves into a single understanding of that information. For example, I learned that horses do not eat meat. I was at an equestrian event, and someone asked me to watch his horse while he went to get the horse a hot dog. I shared my fact with him. I learned the information in a context-free, absolute way and never thought to question when it might or might not be true. This is the way we learn most things. It is why we are frequently in error but rarely in doubt. He brought back the hot dog. The horse ate it.

When information is given by an authority, appears irrelevant, or is presented in absolute language, it typically does not occur to us to question it. We accept it and become trapped in the mind-set, oblivious to how it could be otherwise. Authorities are sometimes wrong or overstate their case, and what is irrelevant today may be relevant tomorrow. When do we want to close the future? Moreover, virtually all the information we are given is presented to us in absolute language. As such, we tend to mindlessly accept it. Too often we mindlessly learn what we should love, hate, fear, respect, and so forth. Our learned emotional responses to people, things, ideas, and even ourselves control our well-being. Yet many of these responses are taken at face value. It seems easier that way than to question the underlying values and premises on which our evaluations are built.

Mindfulness, Uncertainty, and Automatic Behavior

Most aspects of our culture currently lead us to try to reduce uncertainty: We learn so that we will know what things are. In this endeavor we confuse the stability of our mind-sets with the stability of the underlying phenomena. We hold things still purportedly to feel in control, yet because they are always changing, we give up the very control we seek. Instead of looking for invariance, perhaps we should consider exploiting the power of uncertainty so that we can learn what things can become rather than what they are. If we made a universal attribution for our uncertainty, rather than a personal attribution for incompetence, much of the stress and incompetence we experience would diminish. Mindfulness, characterized by novel distinction-drawing, leads us in this direction. It makes clear that things change and loosens the grip of our evaluative mind-sets so that these changes need not be feared.

A large body of experimental studies, including our own, make a cogent case for the automaticity of most human behavior (see Bargh & Chartrand, 1999). The costs of the unconsidered nature of most social behavior are either overlooked or weighed against presumed benefits. The argument given for these benefits can be broken up into a normative part and a descriptive part. Neither is unproblematic. The normative part of the argument is a classic "resource constraint" proposition. Because cognitive work is costly, as the argument goes, cognitive commitments to the values and perspectives that we will bring to bear on a particular predicament are efficient. It is a cognitive behavior that is well adapted to the circumstances of having to react to an environment that requires quick, decisive action. But for cognitive commitments, we would be "stuck," just like the ass in the medieval tale of Burridan, whose obsessive dithering between two stacks of hay leads him to starve to death. The alternative, a mindful engagement with the situation, is erroneously believed to lead to "analysis paralysis," which stifles decisive, purposive action.

This argument only works, however, if we accept that the environment is static and our understanding of it complete, or that we have discovered the "one best way" to deal with all possible eventualities. Both of these assumptions, however, are unrealistic. In our world, a world that is constantly changing in unpredictable ways, letting our beliefs die in our stead (Popper, 1973) is the hallmark of the successful individual. To be mindless is to close the future. At what point do we want to do this? Twentieth-century writing in epistemology teaches that scientific theories and models are regularly replaced by successors (Popper, 1959) whose premises are radically different from those of the incumbent theories. The succession of "paradigms" of scientific knowledge does not follow a path of "linear progress" toward more truthlike theories over time (Kuhn, 1981; Miller, 1994). Theories—or the models of the world or cognitive schemas that people use in order to choose between different courses of action— regularly change in fundamental ways, and the hallmark of rationality is not being able to salvage a theory from apparent refutation by the addition of fortifying hypotheses, but rather the ability to specify the conditions under which a theory will be abandoned (Lakatos, 1970).

Certainly it is no less important for the individual to question her theories than it is for science. When information is processed mindlessly, the potential for reconsideration is abandoned. This typically happens by default and not design, so that even if it were to the individual's advantage to question her theories, it will not occur to her to do so. Bargh and his colleagues focus on the fact that the environment often requires *prompt* action (Bargh & Chartrand, 1999). What they fail to consider is that *adaptive*, and therefore changing, actions also are required. Now, the emphasis is no longer on cognitive precommitments that aid actionability but rather on the ability to act while remaining open to the possibility that the theory on which the action is predicated may shortly be supplanted by a different theory. But if we are open to a potentially new theory, how can we take action? At this point, some are tempted to say analysis can paralyze us. Analysis paralysis, however, only follows if we assume that there is some level of analysis at which we may be able to identify a best theory. In this case we would keep searching for the "right" decision. Otherwise, there is no reason to be paralyzed by the process of reframing and reinterpreting the environment in terms of new models, because we know that all models are ultimately mistaken or can be significantly improved upon. We can take action in the face of uncertainty. Indeed, we do this all the time when we confuse the stability of our mind-set with the stability of the underlying problem. Even a seemingly unassailable theory like Newton's formulation of classical mechanics was abandoned by modern physicists in favor of the relativistic picture of space and time, in spite of the fact that Newton's theory may very well be salvaged from refutation by the addition of "fortifying" hypotheses (Lakatos, 1970).

The ability to refine one's theory—or to alter it dramatically in the face of new circumstances—seems to be critically dependent upon our ability to withhold judgment about the "best one." We never abandon a *theory* because it has been refuted but rather because we have a better theory that has been more severely tested and has withstood those tests more competently (Lakatos, 1970).

Studies of learning behavior suggest that keeping multiple perspectives of the same phenomenon "alive" at any given time is critical to the process of learning from "experience." As an example of this, Thomas Kuhn (1981) noted in his analysis of Piaget's studies of the ways in which children learn about the concept of "speed," being able to simultaneously hold the mental models of "speed as blurriness of moving object" and the mental model of "speed as minimum time of object to destination" is critical to the children's ability to make correct inferences about the rates of motion of moving objects. At the least, it is clear that learning is not likely to take place if we are closed to new information.

Our studies (e.g., Bodner, Waterfield, & Langer, 1995; Chanowitz & Langer, 1981;

Langer, Hatem, Joss, & Howell, 1989; Langer & Piper, 1987) showing that conditionalized presentation of information ("x can be seen as y") to students leads to better *performance* of the students on subsequent tests than does the unconditionalized presentation of information ("x is nothing but y," or "x is y") lend support to the notion that successful adaptive behavior depends on the *loosening* of the grip that our cognitive commitments have on our minds.

The argument for automatic behavior also relies on the questionable belief that automatic behavior is faster and somehow "easier" for people to engage. This deserves several comments. We might consider how often speed is really of the essence. To answer this, we may want to consider what the difference in speed is between mindless and mindful responses. We may produce the same response either mindfully or mindlessly. When we choose to do this, the difference in speed is likely to be trivial. On this point, my original work failed to make clear that while mindlessness closes us off to change, we also cannot be in a constant state of mindfully drawing distinctions about everything at once. To argue that mindlessness is rarely if ever beneficial means that we do not want to close ourselves off to possibility. Instead, we want to be either specifically mindful with respect to some particular content or "potentially" mindful. We may not want to notice the myriad ways each corn flake is different from the other, for example, but we do not want to be so automatic in what we do notice that we fail to see the metal nut that slipped into the bowl, either. A mindful breakfast, then, can take the same time as a mindless breakfast.

Furthermore, the need for exceptional speed, where milliseconds might matter, as in swerving the car to avoid hitting a child, may be avoided altogether by mindful behavior. When mindful, we often avert the danger not yet arisen.

In fact, mindfulness can increase, rather than decrease, one's performance. Consider states of "flow" (Csikszentmihalyi, 1990), which are characterized by a decrease in the effort required to process information and by an *enjoyment* of the experience of performance, *without* a loss of engagement or of the sense of being-in-the-present. It is difficult to argue that people who were found most likely to experience states of flow—such as surgeons and musicians—are also most likely to be automatic in their processing of the stimuli with which they interact.

Similarly, our studies on the prevention of mindlessness (see Langer, 1989, 1997) show that when people learned mindfully, they were more likely to enjoy the learning experience than were people presented with an unconditional version of the same information.

The error in the proposition that automaticity is "easier" to engage in than is a conscious awareness and engagement with the present is a faulty comparison, whereby "automatic" processing is contrasted with "controlled processing" of information (which by definition is effortful). Mindfulness is orthogonal to controlled processing (see Langer, 1992). For the former, one is actively engaged in drawing novel distinctions (e.g., when does $1 + 1 = 1$?— when adding one wad of gum to one wad of gum); for the latter, one relies on distinctions previously drawn (e.g., as when we multiply 237×36). Thus, mindfulness may seem effortful when it is confused with controlled processing. Similarly, it may seem effortful when it is confused with stressful thinking. Events appear stressful when we are certain that a particular occurrence will necessarily lead to an outcome that is negative for us. It is hard to think about negative things happening to us. It is the mindless presumption that it will be negative that is hard, not mindfulness. Perhaps the ease of mindfulness becomes apparent when we consider that when we are fully engaged in our work, just as when we are at play, we seek novelty rather than certainty. Indeed, humor itself relies on mindfulness (which is why a joke already heard and remembered, without being newly considered, is rarely funny). Mindfulness is not a cold cognitive process. We may be mindful when we simply notice our peaceful reactions to the world around us.

Most of us have the mind-set that practice makes perfect. We often take as a given that we should learn "the" basics of complex skills so well that we do not have to think about them again, so that we can go on to master the finer points of the task. In earlier work (Langer, 1997) I raised the question "Who decided what 'the' basics are?" To the extent that the learner differs from whoever that decision maker was, it may be advantageous to question "the" basics so that we can take advantage of our idiosyncratic strengths. Such questioning is ruled out when we are mindless. For example, it seems odd that a very small hand should hold a tennis racket the very same way a very large hand should and that in either case, the way should remain unchanged despite the weight of the racket. Does it make sense to freeze our understanding of a task at the point when we know the least about it? It is unlikely that experts do this; instead, they question basics. Our data (e.g., Langer & Imber, 1979) suggest that mindless practice leads to imperfect performance.

The costs of mindlessness go beyond performance decrements (see Langer, 1989, 1997). Even if our world (personal, interpersonal, and impersonal) were governed by certainty, it would be to our advantage to "be there" to experience it. In an uncertain world, mindlessness sets us up potentially to incur costs every time things change.

Uncertainty keeps us situated in the present. The perception of uncertainty leads to mindfulness, and mindfulness, in turn, leads to greater uncertainty. As such, mindfulness leads to engagement with the task at hand. Being situated in the present and involved in what we are doing are two ways mindfulness enables us to be content. Moreover, by drawing novel distinctions, we become sensitive to perspective, and in so doing, we come to see that evaluation is a function of our view rather than an inherent part of the stimulus. Our mindlessness regarding evaluation is perhaps the greatest cause of our unhappiness.

Mindlessness and Evaluation

We take for granted that evaluations exist independently of us. Each day we think and feel and act as if people, objects, and events were good or bad in themselves. For example, potholes, tax collectors, and divorce are bad, whereas caviar, philanthropists, and holidays are good. But we are essentially mindless to the fact that we have accepted value judgments that we have attached onto various events and objects and states of the world. We find something pleasing or displeasing because we choose to see it in a particular way. Such judgments are in our control, yet we too often are oblivious to this fact.

Things "out there" are not self-evidently good or bad. Sometimes we say this (e.g., "One man's passion is another man's poison"), yet our everyday experience signals otherwise. Potholes make cars slow down; a tax collector can be someone's beloved husband; divorce can be the best outcome for the child living in unspoken tension. When we are not locked into fixed evaluations, we have far more control than we

think over our well-being. We have control over the experience of the present. The prevalence of value judgments in our lives reveals nothing about the world, but much about our minds. We judge and evaluate in order to do the "good" thing, to have the "right" thing, or do the "right" thing. The resulting feelings we identify with happiness. We are rarely immediately conscious of the purpose of our evaluations. Evaluation is something we use to make ourselves happy. As we shall see, however, the use of the evaluative mind-set is self-defeating, for it brings us unhappiness instead.

Many of our thoughts are concerned with whether what we or others are doing or thinking is good or bad. Evaluation is central to the way we make sense of our world, yet in most cases, evaluation is mindless. We say that there are two sides to the proverbial coin. Although we acknowledge that everything has advantages and disadvantages, we tend to treat things as good or bad on the balance. A more mindful approach would entail understanding not only that there are advantages and disadvantages to anything we may consider but that each disadvantage is *simultaneously* an advantage from a different perspective (and vice versa). With this type of mindful approach, virtually every unpleasant aspect of our lives could change.

All behavior makes sense from the actor's perspective, or else the actor would not do it. This realization makes *all negative evaluations* of people suspect, and all action based on these predictions about people of questionable worth. If we are trying to predict what others will do in the future, and we believe the past is the best predictor, then it would behoove us to know better what the action meant to the actor.

A frog is put into a pot of water. The pot is slowly heated. The frog keeps adjusting and finally dies. Another frog is put into a pot of water. The heat is turned on very high. The frog notices the change and jumps out of the pot. When things "drastically" change for us, we notice a difference. Up until that time, we accommodate our experience into the extant frame we are using, and we seem to do this even when it is to our disadvantage. It does not occur to us to consider that the situation, our behavior, or the behavior of other people may be understood differently from the way we originally framed it. If we did, we could take advantage of cues that are less extreme to avoid the "heat."

Often negative evaluations lead us to give up. "Tomorrow will be better." "It's always darkest before the dawn." Implicit in these messages is the idea that we should give up the moment and accept that there are bad things.

Evaluation, positive or negative, is a state of mind. That does not mean that consequences are not real. It means that the number of consequences one could enumerate for any action are dependent on the individual's interest in noting them, and the evaluation of each of these consequences is dependent on the view taken of them. Events do not come with evaluations; we impose them on our experiences, and in so doing create our experience of the event. For pleasure, in winter Finns dip themselves in ice-cold water, and some Americans swim in the cold ocean; many watch horror movies and ride roller coasters for the purpose of becoming afraid.

Consider three different perspectives: (a) bad things are intolerable; (b) bad things happen, but if we just hold on, they will pass; and (c) bad things are context dependent—shift the context, and the evaluation changes. It is the third perspective that brings us most of what we currently value. Western culture currently teaches us only the second perspective. Even the saying "Every cloud has a silver lining" does not quite lead us to the third view. The implication here is that the bad thing will result in something good. Again we are expected to give up the moment and wait for it to pass, but now what will result is not just the passing of the bad but the arrival of something good. An optimist is said to be the one who, when surrounded by manure, knows there must be a pony in there somewhere. Again this is not what the third view is about. In this view there is an awareness that the very thing that is evaluated as negative is also positive. It is not that there may be 5 negative things and 5 positive—which surely is better than just seeing the negative—but that the 10 things are both negative and positive, depending on the context we impose on them.

The previously noted cultural expressions are encouragement to *hope*. Typically the encouragement to hope implicitly regards the present as necessarily bad. It is fine to want tomorrow to be good and to expect that it will be. When this is what we mean by encouraging hope, there is no problem. All too often, however, words of hope are expressed when people are feeling bad and they indirectly are led to accept that set of feelings. It is not fine to passively give up today. Such giving up follows from the view that is implicitly reinforced by the previous statements that events themselves are good or bad, rather than that our views make them good or bad.

Although the culture encourages us to be able to "delay gratification," waiting is mindless in that it suggests that there is no way to enjoy what is being done at the moment. Mindless hoping and learning to wait work against this concern. In one experiment aimed at testing these ideas, research participants were given cartoons to evaluate where the same task was defined as either work or play. When it was framed as work, it was found to be unpleasant, leading participants' minds to wander as they tried to just get through it. Although it was the same task, their response to it was very different as a function of the way they viewed it (Snow & Langer, 1997).

The downside of evaluation to intrapersonal processes is prodigious. We try to get through the "bad" times; we hesitate to decide because the "negative" consequences may be overwhelming. We try to feel better by comparing ourselves with those "worse off." We suffer guilt and regret because of the negative consequences we experience or have perpetrated on others. We lie because we see the negative aspects to our behavior and try to hide them from others. Each of these processes—social comparing, experiencing regret and guilt, and lying—implies that events are good or bad and that we must learn to accept them as they are and learn to deal with them, rather than to question our evaluation of them in the first place.

The implicit message given by the culture is that there is one yardstick by which to measure not just outcomes but ourselves and others. We look for new explanations only when all seems to fail. And, as with the frog, it may be too little too late. For evaluation to be meaningful, we need to use a common metric. The problem enters when we are oblivious to the fact that many other potential yardsticks can be used, with very different results. The prevailing view in the coping literature is to allow a period of grieving so that the person can thereafter reengage in life-goal pursuits. Indeed, the very worst thing that one can do to persons who have just undergone a tragedy or loss is to have them see the situation differently (see Snyder, 1996). After loss, people may need to go through a period of grief and depression, and then after a period of time, goal-directed hopeful thought can be useful (see Feldman & Snyder, 2000). People who have undergone traumas want to be heard and have others listen to their "pains" rather than trying to "see" those pains differently. In this latter regard, friends or helpers will lose credibility as listeners if they become too prescriptive (Tennen & Affleck, 1999).

This view is not incompatible with the position being argued here. If the event is already negatively evaluated, it should be treated respectfully. Nevertheless, many "tragedies" initially could have been understood as opportunities at best, or inconveniences at worst.

The Multiple Meanings of Behavior

When the stories we tell ourselves are compelling and so much information seems to fit our interpretation, it is hard to understand why the other person just doesn't get it. And so we become evaluative. Presently, for many of us to feel right, someone else must be wrong. This dichotomous reasoning is a cause and consequence of an implicit acceptance of a single perspective. Behavior makes sense from the actor's perspective, or else it would not have occurred. I am right, and so are you. The task of successful interpersonal relating, then, may be to search for the information to make this point clear to us or simply accept that the behavior in question must have made sense.

Psychologists (e.g., Jones & Nisbett, 1972) have long described differences that result from the differences in perspective depending on whether one is responsible for some action, the actor, or whether one is an observer of that action. The findings suggest that as observers, we are more likely to attribute other peoples' behavior to dispositions and our own to situations. Situational attributions help keep us in the present. Dispositional attributions hold things still, presumably to enable us to predict the future. Because of our tendencies to confirm our hypotheses (Langer & Abelson, 1974), they instead may become self-fulfilling prophecies, creating a world less pleasant than it otherwise would be. Negative dispositional attributions keep us at a distance from people and thus reduce the chance to see that the attribution was wrong.

Past researchers have pointed out that behavior engulfs the field of our observation. Thus, as observers we see most clearly the action taken, while the situational constraints effecting those actions are less visible. As actors those situational constraints are felt more keenly. As actors we often know why we had to do whatever we did. We also know that in other circumstances we have behaved differently. Observers usually do not have this information.

While the research on attribution theory has certainly yielded important findings, there is another factor that needs to be highlighted that has not yet been examined, one that may account for even more of the interpersonal misunderstanding and concomitant unhappiness that people experience. Not only do people see different information depending on their vantage points and motivation, but, as implied earlier, people often see the *same* information differently. All of the behavior is accounted for but with a different label that carries with it a very different evaluative tone. Consider, for example, serious versus grim, flexible versus unpredictable, spontaneous versus impulsive, private versus secretive, and so on. *All* behavior is vulnerable to labels connoting these different evaluative tones. If our behavior is mindlessly engaged so we are essentially oblivious to why we did whatever we did, however, even as actors we become vulnerable to negative dispositions.

We often think we know other people, and because of this assumption we don't ask, and because we don't ask, we don't learn that the "same" event may look very different to someone else.

Often we don't know how other people feel unless we ask; we don't ask because we think we know. We think we know because we know how we would feel in the same situation. That is, we overestimate how similar other people are to ourselves. Lee Ross and colleagues have called this the *false consensus effect* (Ross, Greene, & House, 1977). We presume that our behavior makes sense and that all well-adjusted people would do the same thing. If someone does something different, he or she must then be "that kind of a person." For example, people in various experiments were asked to predict the opinions and attitudes of others about topics as varied as defense spending, soup, and what constituted appropriate behavior in various situations. Time and again, people overestimated the proportion of other people who feel or would behave as they do. Again, if I assume that all of us feel the same and I find out that you feel differently, it is your strange behavior that calls for explanation.

It may not be so much that we overestimate how similar others are to ourselves. The mistake we may make is that when we look at ourselves as observers, we see ourselves the same way we see others (Storms, 1973). However, when we take action, we may do so as mindful actors and not observers. Often we see the *same* behavior from different vantage points, but we label it quite differently—different with respect, primarily, to its evaluative tone. "We" may be interested in getting along with others, for example, but he may be seen as conforming.

One major problem with our tendency toward false consensus occurs when we turn it on ourselves. When we look back at our own behavior, now from the observer's vantage point, we may see ourselves as having behaved like "one of them." Because, as Kierkegaard noted, we live our lives going forward but understand them looking back, it is important to consider what we do as observers of other people. When we look back, we, too, are the objects of our inquiries and may treat ourselves the way others might. Those who are less evaluative of others will be less evaluative of themselves. This is the hidden cost of making downward social comparisons. We may feel temporarily good at seeing ourselves as superior to someone else, but when we turn things around, we become "him," the observed.

Consider a person's decision: X is an unpleasant feeling for me. If I do Y, the unpleasantness goes away. It would, then, seem sensible to do Y. Let us briefly consider drinking in this light. Going forward in time, we may feel depressed and empty. We learn that drinking eases the pain. If we do not acknowledge that the behavior initially made sense and only attend to the negative consequences of "excessive" drinking, after the emptiness passes, we do ourselves and others an injustice. The negative feelings that result from the awareness of these consequences probably lead to more drinking, and the cycle continues (Snyder, Higgins, & Stucky, 1983).

From the observers' perspective, for example, "too much" drinking clearly creates unwanted problems for the drinker. The drinker does not say to him- or herself, "I have had enough, but I think I'll drink more." He drinks as much as is deemed necessary to accomplish whatever his goal may be. The behavior is not irrational. It is undertaken to achieve a state of mind, and it most often accomplishes this. On the other hand, when we become observers of our actions, we may become more aware of the negative consequences of those actions. Looking back as observers of ourselves, we may see that we have caused harm to our livers or hurt our loved ones. Typically we did not drink to bring about these ends. "Going forward" in time, the be-

havior was not driven by weakness. For most of us, it is easier to learn something new when we are feeling strong. At those times we feel up to the challenges that face us. It would seem, then, that learning how to manage stress or to understand alternative ways of dealing with emptiness, for example, if those are what prompted the drinking, would be easier if we felt good about ourselves. The point here is that we should feel better about ourselves if we see that in its own context, that is, from a going-forward mode, our behavior made sense. With that understanding, less costly alternatives for achieving our goal may be sought. In her doctoral research, Sharon Popp (personal communication, November 15, 1999) found that construction workers drank "excessively." Upon questioning, Popp found that when they were drinking, they opened up with each other and put their macho concerns aside. From these drinking interactions they discovered who they felt they could trust. Trust in their line of work is important. Should they drink or not? In more mundane circumstances, simply asking the question, How may this behavior be sensible? will quickly reveal reasonable understandings of our own behavior and that of other people. When we see behavior in a right and wrong frame, it is a question we do not think to ask.

Couples often come to feel that they see the same world, thus obviating the necessity for attention to actor-observer differences. Divorce statistics suggest otherwise.

Husband and wife are in two different rooms. Thinking it reasonable, she yells, " 'What are these?' She expects him to get up and go see what she is talking about, and usually she is not disappointed. But one friend once struck back at his wife. . . . When his wife returned home one day, and shouted to him in his study, 'Did they come?,' the husband, not knowing what she was talking about, nevertheless said, 'Yes!' The wife shouted to him again. 'Where did you put them?' He shouted back, 'With the others' " (Fairle, 1978, p. 43).

Usually couples do not get to see that they are seeing the same thing differently. *If we have the same frame of reference, we will respond in the same way.*

The power of most great literature and movies is that we come to see the sense of the actor's behavior when the actions are in some way deplorable to us. The tension between the two may be the power of the work. Consider *Lolita*. If we could just have disgust for Humbert, there would be no problem. After all, grown men are not supposed to become sexually aroused and active with adolescent girls. Nabokov's skill reveals itself in drawing us inside this character so that we cannot so easily dismiss him. Behavior makes sense from the actor's perspective. Hamlet did not just kill his father. That would not have been interesting. We come to see how we could have made the same awful mistake. We tend to enjoy literature and film when we can identify with the characters. Simply being observers barely justifies the price we have paid for the popcorn. But great pieces, perhaps, let us identify with the protagonist and take us places we thought we would never go.

If we have the same experience, we will respond similarly. When we respond differently, we would be wise to conclude that the experience was different. This suggests that individual differences may be more differences in experience than differences in individuals. You and I have our hand on a hot radiator. I have to remove my hand more quickly than you. Are you braver or more able to endure pain? No. If you felt what I felt, you would remove your hand when I removed mine.

I see 10 horses running toward us. I am pleased they are coming to say hello. There are six of us, and everyone else runs for protection. They say I'm in denial. I compare myself to others and wonder what is wrong with me. I see 10 horses running toward us. I am pleased they are coming to say hello. There are six of us, and all but one are equally pleased the horses are approaching. One of us runs away for protection. That person is seen as cowardly. In both cases the odd person makes an excuse for the difference in behavior. The rest do not get to learn that another perspective exists.

Interestingly, our culture provides us with norms that help us to misunderstand. If we or someone else commits an "error," we become contrite or indignant. Our response depends on whether, for example, we tell ourselves that "patience is a virtue" or "the early bird catches the worm." We may think we should have been satisfied with some outcome and not greedy if we think, "A bird in the hand is worth two in the bush" unless we think, "Nothing ventured nothing gained." We should not have been cowardly, "an eye for an eye," unless we think we should have "turned the other cheek." Even our most mundane behavior is hard to pin down: "Clothes make the man" versus "You can't

judge a book by its cover." We can always make sense out of our behavior, or we can take ourselves to task, and the culture provides some of our evidence for whichever we choose. The problem is that much of the time most of us do not realize that there is a choice to be made.

Often unaware of our motives, we tend to feel even more culpable or blaming when we call to mind any of these or similar refrains that suggest we should have known better. Just as each individual behavior has an individual perspective on it that lends reason to the action taken, so, too, does the opposite behavior.

Several seemingly mundane behaviors, both those taken as "bad" and some taken to be "good," look different when examined through this nonevaluative lens. Consider regret, making excuses, blame, and forgiveness in this new light.

Regrets

Regret happens under two conditions: when we are unhappy, and when we obscure the difference between our perspective at time one, when we took some action, and time two, when we evaluate the action we took. Regret is a prediction of our emotions: If we had chosen differently then, we would feel better now. If we feel fine now, the need for the prediction would not arise. When it does arise, it depends on the lack of awareness of the reasonableness of the action given the circumstances we faced at the time.

Much of the regret people experience concerns actions not taken. Perhaps the best way to feel bad is to see oneself as not having done anything when something could have been done. This is the most difficult case to deal with because any action taken can be used as at least some justification for not having taken some alternative action. "I couldn't get the phone because I was in the other room going through the mail, so I missed out on finding out about the trip in time to go" versus "I wasn't doing anything, and I missed the call and didn't find out in time to go." Are we ever really doing nothing?

To test whether future regrets could be prevented and "cured," we (Langer, Marcatonis, & Golub, 2000) conducted the following investigations. First, research participants showed up for a study on gambling in which they could win more than $100 and risk none of their own money. After the person showed up he or she was asked to wait until it was his or her turn, which would be indicated by a light above the waiting room door. Upon seeing the flashing light, the participant was to go to another floor in the building for the experiment. Participants were then randomly assigned to one of four conditions. We arranged it so that everyone missed an opportunity. Only those participants who were aware of spending their time well were expected to not feel regret.

Group 1: Participants in this group were simply told, "We do not need you to do anything at this time, so just wait until it is your turn."

Group 2: This was the same as Group 1, except that a Civil War documentary was playing on a VCR in the room.

Group 3: These subjects were invited to watch taped episodes of *Seinfeld* while they waited.

Group 4: These participants were asked to wait until it was their turn, but it was suggested that they spend the time thinking and feeling.

It was expected that Groups 1 and 2 would suffer the most regret; after all, to their minds, we reasoned, they were doing nothing and missed out on an opportunity. Although the mindful group, Group 4, was expected to feel the least regret, Group 3, based on popular ratings of the TV show, was expected to enjoy themselves and thus not regret the opportunity missed as much as the first two groups.

After waiting 20 minutes, the experimenter returned and informed the participants that they had missed their turn, and that two people who showed up won $200 and everyone else won at least $50. The experimenter checked the light above the door to show participants that it did indeed work.

Individuals in the Mindful condition (who were told to "be aware of what you are thinking and feeling" while they waited) (a) had a more positive experience as subjects; (b) found the experience of being a subject more beneficial; and (c) expressed less regret about the way they spent their time compared with individuals in the Civil War (CW) condition (who were allowed to watch a Civil War documentary) or those in the "Nothing" condition. Individuals in the Mindful condition were also more willing to

participate in future investigations than were those in the CW or Nothing conditions.

It may be unreasonable, given the world we currently live in, to be happy or mindful all the time. If we were, as this research suggests, we might never have to experience regret. This work suggests that if the regretted action cannot be undone, any engaging activity may remove the negative feelings. Rethinking why the regretted action or inaction occurred, however, has the clear advantage of preventing its return. But the best alternative, it would seem, is to start out with the assumption that their behavior made sense to them at the time given the circumstances as they saw them, or else they would have behaved differently. This research tells us that when we are aware of why we are doing what we are doing, there is little room for self-recrimination.

Counterfactual thinking is the generation of alternatives that run contrary to the facts of what happened (Roese, 1997). Typically the individual thinks that had he done otherwise, the outcome would have been better. Whereas upward comparisons, as in the social comparison literature, may initially result in feeling bad because of a realization of some positive alternative that might have been, over the long haul they may provide useful information and motivation for engaging in different behavior in the future: "If only I had taken her advice, this whole mess would have been avoided." Downward comparisons, in which we breathe a sigh of relief that we did not behave otherwise and thus avoided some negative outcome, result in positive feelings by contrast to what might have been: "Thank goodness I remembered to call, or else I, too, would have been fired."

It is true that if one imagines what else one might have done, there may be some experience of relief and the consideration of new information that may be of later use. Nevertheless, I would argue that there is a hidden downside to this kind of thinking. Surely if we proceed mindlessly, experience negative outcomes, and think about how we could have behaved differently, it is far better than believing we had no choice. But it is too easy for people to jump from "could have been," to "should have been" and then there arises the problem of how could we have been so stupid or incompetent not to have done it that way in the first place.

Counterfactual thinking occurs after the behavior has been engaged. Mindful thinking occurs before the activity has been engaged. This way people know why they did what they decided to do and why they did not do otherwise. The consideration of alternatives may still lead to information that may be useful in the future but without the self-recriminations.

Moreover, every time we say to ourselves that we "should have," we implicitly reinforce the illusion of certainty and the single-minded evaluation of consequences. For example, "If only I had gone on Thursday instead, all would have been right with the world." Many mishaps could have occurred on Thursday that probably went into the reasoning to go on Wednesday. We no more know all the consequences that could have arisen now than we could have known then. The difference is that if we thought about it then, we would be aware that we could not have foreseen everything. The consequences we did consider may have looked different to us at the time before the decision was made. Now, after the fact, we experience regret by freezing the evaluation of these consequences. Before: "I told him about your appointment because he was getting angry at you, and I thought that would upset you." After: "I'm sorry I violated your privacy by telling him about your appointment." If we are mindful of alternative courses of action and alternative views of the potential consequences, then we are more likely to see the uncertainty inherent in the situation. If we proceed mindlessly, we often take the current view as the only reasonable view. Our self-respect suffers because we then feel we should have known.

Counterfactual thinking is more likely to occur after the experience of negative outcomes than positive outcomes (e.g., Klauer & Migulla, 1996; Sanna & Turley, 1996). Anger, depression, boredom, or essentially any unhappiness can trigger thoughts of how we might have done things differently in the past. If we proceed more mindfully, our perspective is forward-looking, not backward-looking.

Counterfactual thinking or regret is also more likely to occur the closer the person is to the sought-after goal. This tendency is so great that we even do it in situations that we take to be largely chance-determined. For instance, if we choose a lottery number that misses by one number, we experience more regret than if we miss by many numbers. The reason for this is that the closer we are to the goal, the easier it is to see how we might have behaved differ-

ently. Missing a train by five minutes seems worse to most of us than missing it by half an hour. The more mutable the situation, the more regret we feel. But all the while, we ignore that our actions made some sense to us and that is why we so engaged in them, whether the distance to some other goal was great or small.

The more normative the "appropriate" behavior is taken to be, the more regret we experience for our behavior (Kahneman & Miller, 1986). But, again, this analysis is after the fact. It is important to realize that many norms can be brought to bear on any situation before the fact. If after the fact we learn that "everyone" went to the party, we will feel more regret than if going to the party was not as typical. Before the fact we may consider many different parties and conclude that there is no norm for attendance; people are as likely to go as to not go. Before the fact, there are many sources of reasonable information to consider in making our decisions, with many possible consequences. After the fact, there are fewer paths that make sense because consequences are now apparent. Regret denies the utility of our past experience to our present situation.

Excuses

Ask 10 people if making excuses is good or bad. Next, ask them why. Virtually all will answer that making excuses is bad, and most will offer a view that amounts to saying that the excuse-maker is not owning up to what she did. What does it mean to take responsibility for our actions? For which action should we be responsible?

Consider, again, that behavior always makes sense from the actor's perspective. If it did not, the actor would have done differently. People do not get up in the morning and say, "Today I'm going to be clumsy, inconsiderate, and hurtful." What were they intending when we experienced them that way? If we are not mindful of our intentions going forward, we become vulnerable to other people's characterization of our behavior looking back. The same behavior looks different from different perspectives. A negative view of our behavior necessitates an excuse.

What is the difference between an excuse and a reason? If I give an explanation that makes sense to us both, the explanation is taken as a reason for my action. When it is not accepted, a reason becomes an excuse. When it is not accepted, the actor's perspective is denied. The attribution of excuse-making allows the person to whom the excuse is made to feel superior, at least for the moment. The cost is loss of genuine interaction and understanding.

If our behavior made sense going forward in time and we were mindless to our intentions, we may offer a reason that is unacceptable to the blamer, and it will be taken as an excuse. If we respect ourselves enough to know that what we did must have made sense to us even if we cannot remember why we did it, we will reject the accusation. The alternative is that the behavior was the person's fault, engaged because he is bad. If he is not bad, then why did he do it? When people live in a world of absolute right and wrong without regard to perspective, any explanation different from their own is taken to be an excuse.

Our culture has confused reasons and excuses, with the result that the blamer has a ready reason not to listen. What does this mean when you think I am making excuses? Does it mean that I had no reason for what I did? I find myself saying, in such situations, "I know I care about you. Are you trying to persuade me that I don't?" "I know I'm a nice person. Are you trying to make me think I am not?"

The word *excuse* conveys an accusation on the part of the person to whom an explanation is given. It implies distrust regarding the speaker's motives and intentions. Our culture has become so tolerant of excuses that the difference between a reason and an excuse is not likely to be easily noticed. By obscuring the difference between the two, we unwittingly act as though our actions have no reasons, or that the only acceptable reason is one in which someone must look bad. As a result, self-respect suffers as others are given the final word over our intentions. If I paid attention to my actions before engaging in them, I would know why I did what I did after the action was completed. The cost of my mindlessness is that I am more likely now to accept your understanding of my behavior. What might have been a reason becomes an excuse.

If behavior makes sense from the actor's perspective, then we as actors become less vulnerable to other people's attributions of excuse-making. Moreover, the very idea of an "excuse" reinforces the view that consequences are inherently negative.

Blame and Forgiveness

"To err is human, to forgive divine." Or is it? Again, ask 10 people whether forgiveness is good or bad. All will probably tell you that it is good. Forgiveness is something to which we should aspire. The more wronged we have been, the more divine it is to be able to forgive. Now ask 10 people if blame is good or bad. All will probably tell you that blame is bad. And yet to forgive, we have to blame. If we do not blame in the first place, there is nothing to forgive.

But there is a step before blame and forgiveness that needs our consideration. Before we blame, we have to experience the outcome as negative. If your behavior resulted in something positive for me, blame would hardly make sense. Those who see more negativity in the world are then those more likely to blame.

The same behavior makes many different senses. If we do not appreciate that we may look at a situation and see different things or see the same things differently, then we will remain stuck in an evaluative mind-set. If we remain in this mind-set, then we will experience negative outcomes that could have been experienced as positive. If we experience negative outcomes, then we will be tempted to find someone to blame. If we blame, at least we can try to forgive. To be *forgiving* is "better" than to be *unforgiving*. Understanding that the action made sense to the actor obviates the necessity for forgiveness.

Discrimination Is Not Evaluation

We can be discriminating without being evaluative. Noticing new things is the essence of mindfulness. Unquestioningly accepting a single-minded evaluation of what is noticed is mindless. Our culture is replete with examples of mindless evaluation. Sadly, it is hard to conjure up examples of a more mindful stance. We take an evaluative component as an essential part of our beliefs. Without knowing if something is good or bad, after all, how would we know whether to approach or avoid ideas, people, places, and things? Yet accepting evaluation, rather than mindful discrimination, as essential, we set ourselves up for the experience of feeling inadequate. By mindlessly attaching this evaluative component to our beliefs, we become victims of our mind-sets. We experience this reactivity only when things go wrong. These are the times we try to change; yet these are the times we are least equipped to do so.

With the awareness that we are responsible for our evaluations, we are more likely to use them in a conditional way. As such, we can stay responsive to our circumstances rather than become reactive to them as absolute evaluations lead us to be.

When no news is bad news. If we give up evaluation, we give up the compliment but we are no longer vulnerable to the insult.

If someone compliments us, what is our reaction? If we are very pleased, it would suggest a certain amount of uncertainty about our level of skill. It also suggests a degree of vulnerability we would experience if we did not succeed. Imagine that somebody whose opinion you respected told you that you were great at spelling three-letter words. Chances are if you are over 10 years old, you would not be moved by this compliment. You know you can do it, so the feedback is essentially unimportant to you. Imagine the same respected person told you that the way that you pronounce vowels is extraordinary. Again, you would be unlikely to be very moved. This time you are not taken in by the compliment because the issue probably does not matter much to you. In both cases, when you were not testing yourself, the compliment was unimportant. Here, then, is a way to protect ourselves from negative remarks: *If we don't take the compliment, we are not vulnerable to the insult.*

The behaviorist literature tells us that there is positive and negative reinforcement. And there is positive and negative punishment. Positive reinforcement is the presentation of a positive stimulus—for example, a compliment. Negative reinforcement is the cessation of an aversive stimulus—for example, if someone is always insulting you, and now you do something and no insult follows, that behavior will be negatively reinforced. Reinforcement increases the response leading to it; whether it is positive or negative reinforcement, reinforcement feels good. Conversely, punishment is meant to stop the behavior leading to it. Positive punishment is the presentation of an aversive stimulus—for example, an insult. The interesting but less well known case is negative punishment: *the cessation of a positive stimulus*—time out from compliments. Because compliments feel so good, we are not inclined to look beyond them. Because compliments may help

control us, there is little motivation for others to see their costs to us. Compliments, like insults, generally concern what we do and not who we are. As such, they help keep us in an evaluative frame of mind. Evaluating the self takes one out of the experience; self becomes object rather than actor. Ironically, with less experience, there is less of a self to evaluate.

> If we give up evaluation, we give up downward social comparing.
> If you never assume importance
> You never lose it.
> (Lao Tse, The Way of Life)

The most frequent evaluation people make is to compare themselves with other people. When we want information about how to do a task better, we compare ourselves with others who are slightly better at the task. When we want to bolster our self-images, we compare ourselves with those who are less able then we are, that is, we make downward social comparisons.

A good deal of the work in psychology that deals with the "self" takes as a given that evaluation will occur and then proceeds to examine what information will be used and how it is used in making that evaluation. When evaluation does take place, it is carried out in the manner suggested by these researchers. The literature does not question whether or not there can be another way of being that is nonevaluative.

Leon Festinger (1954) went so far as to say that people have a drive to evaluate their opinions and abilities. When objective means for this comparison are not available, people make comparisons with others. People choose similar others for these comparisons. To feel good about themselves, people often make downward social comparisons. Regarding abilities, we make upward comparisons. I am more likely to compare my tennis skills with those of someone better than with those of someone I know cannot play as well. As Festinger was quick to note, of course in these upward comparisons I am not likely to compare myself with those far better than I am. I try, according to Festinger, to close the gap and become as similar to others as I can. There is also a tendency to reduce discrepancies regarding opinions. Both of these tendencies, regarding ability and opinion, implicitly reinforce the idea that there is a single view (a right and wrong), and that it is in our best interest to be like everyone else.

Is there any evidence that we can be completely nonevaluative? I do not know of any. Nevertheless, our own research suggests that this is the direction in which we might want to move. Johnny Welch, Judith White, and I (Langer, White, & Welch, 2000) conducted an investigation to look at the effect of being evaluative on negative emotions such as guilt, regret, stress, and the tendency to blame, keep secrets, and lie. First, we gave a questionnaire to people that simply asked them how often they compared themselves with other people, regardless of whether they saw themselves as better or worse. We then asked them to indicate how often they experienced the feelings or behaviors just noted (guilt, etc.). We divided the participants into two groups—those who answered that they frequently compared themselves with others and those who made these comparisons less often—and then looked at how often the two groups experienced the listed emotions and behaviors. The findings were clear. Those who were less evaluative experienced less guilt, regret, and so on. Moreover, in response to the question, "In general, how well do you like yourself?" the less evaluative group was found to like themselves more.

The next step in our research was an experiment in which we (Yariv & Langer, 2000) either encouraged or discouraged people to make evaluations and found that, as in the questionnaire study, those who were more evaluative also suffered more.

We may stay evaluative because positive evaluation helps us feel good in the short run. As soon as we agree to accept a positive evaluation as reason to feel good about ourselves, however, we open the door for the damaging consequences of perceived failure. Surely, depression, suicide, and just feeling bad all result in whole or part from an evaluative stance.

If one tries and does not succeed, one could feel like a failure. Alternatively, one could conclude that the chosen way was not effective (Dweck & Leggett, 1988; Langer, 1989; Langer & Dweck, 1973).

James Joyce's famous book *The Dubliners* was rejected by 22 publishers. Gertrude Stein submitted poems to editors for about 20 years before one was accepted. Fred Astaire and the Beatles were also initially turned down. The list goes on (Bandura, 1997).

We have much control over the valence of our experience. Research participants actively drew 0, 3, or 6 novel distinctions while engaged in disliked activities (listening to rap or classical music; watching football). We found that the more distinctions drawn, the more the activity was liked (Langer, 1997). That evaluations are malleable may also be seen in the classic research on the "mere exposure effect:" The more often you see something, the more you like it. We had hypothesized that this effect would obtain primarily if, on repetition, participants drew novel distinctions—that is, if they were mindful. In this research, exposure was held constant, but participants drew several or few distinctions. The mere exposure effect seems to rely on mindful distinction drawing and not on exposure alone (Fox, Langer, & Kulessa, 2000). In either case, however, we have control over the valence of our experience.

Consider how we look for change when we observe our children and thus constantly draw novel distinctions. Our affection for our children only grows. We look for stability when we observe our spouses or partners. Sadly, too often our affection diminishes for our spouses or partners. Positive affect, thus, seems to depend on our willingness to mindfully engage another person.

The Myth of Inaction

Let us return to the question of analysis paralysis. Would giving up evaluation lead to inaction? After all, if you cannot believe your action will be successful or that you will want the final outcome you have worked for, why engage in it at all? The short answer is, "Why not?"

Consider what many experience as a midlife crisis. At some point in life, many people come to realize that nothing has any intrinsic meaning. There are three possible responses to this. Those who do not successfully emerge from this belief stay depressed and cynical at the meaninglessness of it all. Some ignore this belief and proceed as if they never had it, although all the while it lurks in the background. Finally, there are those who accept that everything can be equally meaningless or meaningful. This last group is the most likely to stay situated in a self-constructed meaningful present.

Similarly, a person can take action falsely believing that the action will result in a singularly desirable end state and repeatedly suffer surprise and disappointment. Instead, the same person can come to see that the action may not lead to the outcome, and the outcome may not be desirable anyway, and thus decide not to take any action. But a third option also presents itself. The person may be freed to take action because feared negative consequences are just as unpredictable as desired positive consequences, and even if they do occur, they also have another side. It is more satisfying to do something than to do nothing. Action is the way we get to experience ourselves. And so we act not to bring about an outcome but to bring about ourselves. In fact, when asked if they would hesitate to act if assured that the outcome to their prediction would be positive, people overwhelmingly say no. The fear of inaction has hidden in it the evaluative belief that making the "wrong" decision may be costly. Recent research we have conducted (Langer, Lee, & Yariv, 2000), in fact, shows that people who are taught to reframe positive as negative, and vice versa, make their decisions more, not less, quickly. Giving up our evaluative tendencies does not seem to lead to inaction.

This is not to say that "inaction" is necessarily bad. Typically we see inaction as the absence of a particular action. That is, we do not make the phone call, buy the item, attend the event. We need not see ourselves as inactive, but rather actively pursuing another course. If we realized this, we might be less afraid of giving up the illusion of evaluative stability.

In our attempts to understand behavior, psychologists may have unwittingly contributed to the unhappiness we are now directly attempting to change. As researchers we have been in the perspective of observer, more often than not, oblivious ourselves to how the same behavior may have different meaning when understood from the actor's perspective in addition to our own.

Mindfulness Versus Positive Evaluation

Many years ago, we conducted an experimental investigation aimed at teaching people to be positive (Langer, Janis, & Wolfer, 1975). We looked at what the effects would be on preoperative stress of having a positive view of one's situation. We found that patients became less stressed, took fewer pain relievers and sedatives, and were able to leave the hospital sooner than comparison groups. Surely a single-mindedly positive view is likely to be more beneficial to health and well-being than a mindlessly negative view. But there are problems endemic to

teaching people to view things positively. First, in the way we normally use language, if things can be positive, other things would then seem to be inherently negative. Second, because evaluation is taken to be an inherent part of outcomes, changing one evaluation from negative to positive may suggest more that the person was originally mistaken than that all outcomes may be viewed in a positive way. As such, positivity training may be less likely to generalize to new situations. Third, it would seem to follow that to be positive would be to accept positive statements by others (i.e., compliments), but to do so sets us up for negative punishment. Fourth, if being positive means we should be grateful that we are not as badly off as others might be (i.e., make downward social comparisons), then such gratitude comes at a very high cost. Fifth, and most important, if we teach people to be positive, we may unintentionally teach them to keep evaluation tied to events, ideas, and people, and thus we promote mindlessness.

When mindful, we may find solutions to problems that made us feel incompetent. We may avert the danger not yet arisen. By becoming less judgmental, we are likely to come to value other people and ourselves. All told, it would seem that being mindful would lead us to be optimistic, obviating the necessity for learning how to be positive.

Conclusions

While well-being is more likely to be related to positive than negative evaluations, positive evaluation makes negative evaluations appear to be independent of us. "Positive" experiences like hoping and forgiving, regret over past actions, and delaying gratification for a future goal all implicitly suggest that there is still potential negativity that one may have to confront. Positive evaluations, then, may implicitly rob us of control. Similarly, downward social comparisons may work in the short run to alleviate negative affect, but they set the stage for upward comparisons in the future. By contrast, mindfulness keeps us engaged and situated in the present. The mindful individual comes to recognize that each outcome is potentially simultaneously positive and negative (as is each aspect of each outcome), and that choices can be made with respect to our affective experience. Thus, the mindful individual is likely to choose to be positive and will experience both the advantages of positivity and the advantages of perceived control for well-being.

References

Bandura, A. (1997). *Self-efficacy: The exercise of control*. New York: Freeman.

Bargh, J., & Chartrand, T. (1999). The unbearable automaticity of being. *American Psychologist, 54*, 462–479.

Bodner, T., Waterfield, R., & Langer, E. (2000). *Mindfulness in finance*. Manuscript in preparation, Harvard University, Cambridge, MA.

Chanowitz, B., & Langer, E. (1981). Premature cognitive commitment. *Journal of Personality and Social Psychology, 41*, 1051–1063.

Csikszentmihalyi, M. (1990). *Flow: The psychology of optimal experience*. New York: Harper and Row.

Dweck, C., & Leggett, E. (1988). A social-cognitive approach to motivation and personality. *Psychology Review, 95*, 256–273.

Fairle, H. (October, 1978). My favorite sociologist. *The New Republic, 7*, 43.

Feldman, D. B., & Snyder, C. R. (2000). *Hope, goals, and meaning in life: Shedding new light on an old problem*. Unpublished manuscript, University of Kansas, Lawrence.

Festinger, L. (1954). A theory of social comparison processes. *Human Relations, 7*, 117–140.

Fox, B., Langer, E., & Kulessa, G. (2000). *Mere exposure versus mindful exposure*. Unpublished manuscript, Harvard University.

Jones, E., & Nisbett, R. (1972). The actor and the observer: Divergent perceptions of the causes of behavior. In E. E. Jones, D. E. Kanouse, H. H. Kelley, R. E. Nisbett, S. Valins, & B. Weiner (Eds.), *Attribution: Perceiving the causes of behavior* (pp. 79–94). Morristown, NJ: General Learning Press.

Kahneman, D., & Miller, D. T. (1986). Norm theory: Comparing reality to its alternatives. *Psychological Review, 93*, 136–153.

Klauer, K. C., & Migulla, K. J. (1996). Spontaneous counterfactual processing. *Zeitschrift fur Sozialpsychologie, 26*, 34–42.

Kuhn, T. (1981). A function for thought experiments. In I. Hacking (Ed.), *Scientific revolutions* (pp. 6–27). New York: Oxford University Press.

Lakatos, I. (1970). Falsification and the methodology of scientific research programmes. In I. Lakatos & A. Musgrave (Eds.), *Criticism and the growth of knowledge* (pp. 91–196). New York: Cambridge University Press.

Langer, E. (1989). *Mindfulness*. Reading, MA: Addison-Wesley.

Langer, E. (1992). Interpersonal mindlessness and language. *Communication Monographs, 59*, 324–327.

Langer, E. (1997). *The power of mindful learning*. Reading, MA: Addison-Wesley.

Langer, E., & Abelson, R. (1974). A patient by any other name . . . : Clinician group differences in labeling bias. *Journal of Consulting and Clinical Psychology, 42*, 4–9.

Langer, E., & Dweck, C. (1973). *Personal politics*. Englewood Cliffs, NJ: Prentice-Hall.

Langer, E., Hatem, M., Joss, J., & Howell, M. (1989). Conditional teaching and mindful learning: The role of uncertainty in education. *Creativity Research Journal, 2*, 139–150.

Langer, E., & Imber, L. (1979). When practice makes imperfect. *Journal of Personality and Social Psychology, 37*, 2014–2025.

Langer, E., Janis, I., & Wolfer, J. (1975). Reduction of psychological stress in surgical patients. *Journal of Experimental Social Psychology, 11*, 155–165.

Langer, E., & Lee, Y. (2000). *The myth of analysis paralysis*. Manuscript in preparation, Harvard University, Cambridge, MA.

Langer, E., Marcatonis, E., & Golub, S. (2000). *No regrets: The ameliorative effect of mindfulness*. Manuscript in preparation, Harvard University, Cambridge, MA.

Langer, E., & Piper, A. (1987). The prevention of mindlessness. *Journal of Personality and Social Psychology, 53*, 280–287.

Langer, E., White, J., & Welch, J. (2000). *Negative effects of social comparison*. Unpublished manuscript, Harvard University, Cambridge, MA.

Lao Tse. (1962). *The way of life* (Witter Bynner, Trans.). New York: Capricorn Books.

Miller, D. (1994). *Critical rationalism*. Chicago: Open Court.

Popper, K. R. (1959). *The logic of scientific discovery*. London: Hutchinson.

Popper, K. R. (1973). *Objective knowledge*. London: Routledge.

Roese, N. J. (1997). Counterfactual thinking. *Psychological Bulletin, 121*, 133–148.

Ross, L., Greene, D., & House, P. (1977). The false consensus effort: An egocentric bias in social perception and attribution process. *Journal of Personality and Social Psychology, 13*, 279–301.

Sanna, L. J., & Turley, K. J. (1996). Antecedents to spontaneous counterfactual thinking: Effects of expectancy violation and outcome valence. *Personality and Social Psychology Bulletin, 22*, 906–919.

Snow, S., & Langer, E. (1997). Unpublished data. Reported in E. Langer, *The power of mindful learning*, Reading, MA: Addison-Wesley.

Snyder, C. R. (1996). To hope, to lose, and hope again. *Journal of Personal and Interpersonal Loss, 1*, 3–16.

Snyder, C. R., Higgins, R. L., & Stucky, R. (1983). *Excuses: Masquerades in search of grace*. New York: Wiley-Interscience.

Storms, M. (1973). Videotape and the attribution process: Reversing actors' and observers' points of view. *Journal of Personality and Social Psychology, 27*, 165–175.

Tennen, H., & Affleck, G. (1999). Finding benefits in adversity. In C. R. Snyder (Ed.), *Coping: The psychology of what works* (pp. 278–304). New York: Oxford University Press.

Yariv, L., & Langer, E. (2000). *Negative effects of social comparison*. Unpublished manuscript, Harvard University, Cambridge, MA.

17

Optimism

Charles S. Carver & Michael F. Scheier

Optimists are people who expect good things to happen to them; pessimists are people who expect bad things to happen to them. Folk wisdom has long held that this difference among people is important in many, if not all, aspects of living. Folk wisdom is not always accurate. However, this particular belief has received much support in contemporary research. As we describe in this chapter, optimists and pessimists differ in several ways that have a big impact on their lives. They differ in how they approach problems and challenges, and they differ in the manner—and the success—with which they cope with adversity.

Dictionary definitions of optimism and pessimism rest on people's expectations for the future. Scientific approaches to these constructs also rest on expectations for the future. This grounding in expectancies links the concepts of optimism and pessimism to a long tradition of expectancy-value models of motivation. The result of this is that the optimism construct, though having roots in folk wisdom, is also firmly grounded in decades of theory and research on human motives and how they are expressed in behavior.

Expectancy-Value Models of Motivation

We begin by briefly exploring the expectancy-value approach to motivation to show the dynamics we believe underlie the influence of optimism and pessimism. Expectancy-value theories begin with the assumption that behavior is organized around the pursuit of goals. Goals have been given a variety of labels by different theorists. They vary in important ways, but at this point we want to emphasize what goals have in common (for broader discussion, see Austin & Vancouver, 1996; Carver & Scheier, 1998).

Goals are states or actions that people view as either desirable or undesirable. People try to fit their behaviors—indeed, fit their very selves— to what they see as desirable, and they try to keep away from what they see as undesirable (you might think of the undesirable ones as "anti-goals"). The more important a goal is to someone, the greater is its *value* within the person's motivation. Without having a goal that matters, people have no reason to act.

The second conceptual element in expectancy-value theories is *expectancy*—a sense of confidence or doubt about the attainability of the goal value. If the person lacks confidence, again there will be no action. That's why a lack of confidence is sometimes referred to as "crippling doubt." Doubt can impair effort before the action begins or while it is ongoing. Only if people have enough confidence will they move into action and continue their efforts. When people are confident about an eventual outcome, effort will continue even in the face of great adversity.

Goals Vary in Breadth and Abstractness

Goals vary in specificity—from the very general, to those that pertain to a particular domain of life, to the very concrete and specific. This suggests that expectancies may have a comparable range of variation (Armor & Taylor, 1998; Carver & Scheier, 1998). That is, you can be confident or doubtful about having a fulfilling career, about making good impressions in social situations, about winning a particular golf game, about finding a nice place to have dinner, or about tying your shoes.

Which of these sorts of expectancies matter? Probably all of them. Expectancy-based theories generally suggest either explicitly or implicitly that behavior is predicted best when the level of the expectancy fits that of the behavior that is being predicted. Sometimes it is argued that prediction is best when you take into account several levels of specificity bearing on the behavior. Many outcomes in life, however, have multiple causes. People also often face situations they have never experienced, and situations that evolve over time. We have suggested that in such situations, generalized expectations are particularly useful in predicting people's behavior (Scheier & Carver, 1985).

The same principles that apply to a focused confidence also apply to the generalized sense of confidence that we think of as optimism. When we talk about optimism and pessimism, the sense of confidence is simply more diffuse and broader in scope. Thus, when confronting a challenge (and it really should not matter much what the challenge is), optimists should tend to take a posture of confidence and persistence (even if progress is difficult or slow). Pessimists should be doubtful and hesitant. This divergence may even be amplified under conditions of serious adversity. Optimists are likely to assume that the adversity can be handled successfully, in one fashion or another. Pessimists are likely to anticipate disaster (see also Peterson and Steen, this volume). These differences in how people approach adversity have important implications for the manner in which people cope with stress (Scheier & Carver, 1992).

Variations in Conception and Assessment

Expectancies are pivotal in theories of optimism, but there are at least two ways to think about expectancies and how to measure them (with two distinct literatures). One approach measures expectancies directly, asking people to indicate the extent to which they believe that their future outcomes will be good or bad. This is the approach we have taken (Scheier & Carver, 1992). Our approach thus adds no more conceptual complexity to what we have said so far. Expectancies that are generalized—expectancies that pertain more or less to the person's entire life space—are what we mean when we use the terms *optimism* and *pessimism*.

Some time ago, we developed a measure called the Life Orientation Test, or LOT (Scheier & Carver, 1985), to assess differences between people in optimism and pessimism. We now use a briefer form (six coded items), called the Life Orientation Test-Revised, or LOT-R (Scheier, Carver, & Bridges, 1994—see Appendix). The LOT-R has good internal consistency (Cronbach's alpha runs in the high .70s to low .80s) and is relatively stable over time. Because of the extensive item overlap between the original scale and the revised scale, correlations between the two scales are very high (Scheier et al., 1994). Both the LOT and the LOT-R provide continuous distributions of scores. Although we often refer to optimists and pessimists as though they were distinct groups, this is a matter of verbal convenience. People actually range from the very optimistic to the very pessimistic, with most falling somewhere in the middle.

Another approach to optimism relies on the assumption that people's expectancies for the future derive from their view of the causes of events in the past (Peterson & Seligman, 1984; Seligman, 1991). If explanations for past failures focus on causes that are stable, the person's expectancy for the future in the same domain will be for bad outcomes because the cause is seen as relatively permanent and thus likely to remain in force. If attributions for past failures focus on causes that are unstable, then the outlook for the future may be brighter because the cause may no longer be in force. If explanations for past failures are global (apply across aspects of life), the expectancy for the future across *many* domains will be for bad outcomes because the causal forces are at work everywhere. If the explanations are specific, the outlook for other areas of life may be brighter because the causes do not apply there.

Just as expectancies vary in breadth, so do attributions. Attributions can be to a particular area of action (e.g., skiing) or to a moderately broad domain (e.g., performance in sports), but they are usually assessed even more broadly. It is often assumed that people have "explanatory styles," which bear on the person's whole life space (see Peterson and Steen, this volume). The theory behind explanatory style holds that optimism and pessimism are defined by flexible versus rigid patterns of explanation (Peterson & Seligman, 1984; Seligman, 1991).

Although these two approaches to conceptualizing and measuring optimism have important differences, we focus here on what they share: the theme that expectations help determine people's actions and experiences. In both approaches optimism is the expectation of good outcomes; pessimism is the expectation of bad outcomes. The approaches differ in measuring variables prior to the expectancy (attributions) versus the expectancy itself.

These two approaches to optimism and pessimism have led to their own research literatures, each of which sheds light on the nature and function of optimism and pessimism (see also the literature on hope, another closely related member of this theoretical family discussed in the chapter by Snyder, Rand, & Sigmon, this volume). In what follows, however, we focus largely on optimism as we have operationalized it (Scheier & Carver, 1985, 1992; Scheier et al., 1994)—that is, in terms of self-reports of generalized expectancies.

As we said at the outset, optimism and pessimism are basic qualities of personality. They influence how people orient to events in their lives. They influence people's subjective experiences when confronting problems, and they influence the actions people engage in to try to deal with these problems. When we ask the question, Do optimists and pessimists differ in how they react to adversity? the answer has at least two parts. One part is whether they differ in their feelings of well-being versus distress. The other is whether they differ in how they act to deal with the adversity. These two themes are explored in the next two sections.

Optimism and Subjective Well-Being

When people confront adversity or difficulty, they experience a variety of emotions, ranging from excitement and eagerness to anger, anxiety, and depression. The balance among these feelings appears to relate to people's degree of optimism or pessimism. Optimists are people who expect to have positive outcomes, even when things are hard. This confidence should yield a mix of feelings that is relatively positive. Pessimists expect negative outcomes. This doubt should yield a greater tendency toward negative feelings—anxiety, guilt, anger, sadness, or despair (Carver & Scheier, 1998; Scheier & Carver, 1992; see also Snyder et al., 1996).

Relationships between optimism and distress have been examined in diverse groups of people facing difficulty or adversity. Included are the experiences of students entering college (Aspinwall & Taylor, 1992); employees of businesses (Long, 1993); survivors of missile attacks (Zeidner & Hammer, 1992); and people caring for cancer patients (Given et al., 1993) and Alzheimer's patients (Hooker, Monahan, Shifren, & Hutchinson, 1992; Shifren & Hooker, 1995). Research has also examined experiences of people dealing with childbirth (Carver & Gaines, 1987), abortion (Cozzarelli, 1993), coronary artery bypass surgery (Fitzgerald, Tennen, Affleck, & Pransky, 1993; Scheier et al., 1989), attempts at in vitro fertilization (Litt, Tennen, Affleck, & Klock, 1992), bone marrow transplantation (Curbow, Somerfield, Baker, Wingard, & Legro, 1993), the diagnosis of cancer (Carver et al., 1993; Friedman et al., 1992), and the progression of AIDS (Taylor et al., 1992). Thus, many of these studies focus on people who are undergoing truly serious crises rather than ordinary problems of daily life.

This group of studies varies in complexity, and thus in what inferences can be made from them. In many cases researchers examined responses to a difficult event but did so at only one time point. These studies show that pessimists experienced more distress after the event than did optimists. What they can *not* show is whether the pessimists had more distress beforehand. It is better to examine people repeatedly and see how their distress shifts over circumstances. Even if you cannot get people before the event, you can learn more about the process of adapting to it if you assess distress at several points. We focus here on studies in this literature in which people were assessed at multiple time points.

An early study of the effect of optimism on emotional well-being (Carver & Gaines, 1987) examined the development of depressed feelings after childbirth. Women completed the LOT and a depression scale in the last third of their pregnancy. They then completed the depression measure again 3 weeks after their babies were born. Optimism related to lower depression symptoms at the initial assessment. More important, optimism predicted lower levels of depressive symptoms postpartum, even when controlling for the initial levels. Thus optimism seemed to confer a resistance to the development of depressive symptoms after having a baby.

In another early study, Scheier and colleagues (1989) examined men undergoing and recovering from coronary artery bypass surgery. Patients completed questionnaires the day before surgery, a week after surgery, and 6 months after surgery. Before surgery, optimists reported less hostility and depression than pessimists. A week afterward, optimists reported more happiness and relief, more satisfaction with their medical care, and more satisfaction with emotional support from friends. Six months after surgery, optimists reported higher quality of life than pessimists. In a follow-up 5 years after surgery, optimists continued to experience greater subjective well-being and better quality of life compared with pessimists. All these differences remained significant when controlling for extent of surgery and other medical factors.

Later research on optimism and quality of life after coronary artery bypass surgery (Fitzgerald et al., 1993) assessed participants 1 month before surgery and 8 months afterward. Optimism related negatively to presurgical distress. Further, controlling for presurgical life satisfaction, optimism related positively to postsurgical life satisfaction. Further analysis revealed that the general sense of optimism appeared to operate on feelings of life satisfaction through a more focused sense of confidence about the surgery. That is, the general sense of optimism about life apparently was funneled into a specific optimism regarding the surgery, and from there to satisfaction with life.

Optimism also has been studied in the context of other kinds of health crises. One study examined adjustment to treatment for early-stage breast cancer (Carver et al., 1993). Diagnosis and treatment for breast cancer is a traumatic experience, in part because the disease is life-threatening. Because the prognosis for early-stage cancer is relatively good, however, there is enough ambiguity about the future to permit individual differences to be readily expressed. Patients in this study were interviewed at the time of diagnosis, the day before surgery, 7 to 10 days after surgery, and 3, 6, and 12 months later. Optimism inversely predicted distress over time, above and beyond the effect of medical variables and beyond the effects of earlier distress. That is, the prediction of distress at 3, 6, and 12 months after surgery was significant even when the immediately prior level of distress was controlled. Thus, optimism predicted not just lower initial distress but also resilience against distress during the year following surgery.

Another medical situation that has been studied with respect to optimism is infertility. A procedure called *in vitro fertilization* is one way to overcome fertility problems, but it does not always work. Litt and colleagues (1992) studied people whose attempts were unsuccessful. Approximately 8 weeks before the attempt, the researchers measured optimism, specific expectancies for fertilization success, coping strategies, distress levels, and the impact of the infertility on participants' lives. Two weeks after notification of a negative pregnancy test, distress was reassessed. Neither demographics, obstetric history, marital adjustment, nor the reported effect of infertility on participants' lives predicted Time 2 distress, but lower optimism did, even controlling for Time 1 distress.

Another recent study examined the influence of optimism on adjustment to abortion (Cozzarelli, 1993). One hour prior to an abortion, women completed measures of optimism, self-efficacy, emotional adjustment, and depression. Depression and adjustment were assessed 30 minutes after the abortion and again 3 weeks later. Optimists had less preabortion depression, better postabortion adjustment, and better 3-week adjustment than did pessimists. Cozzarelli concluded that optimism relates to psychological adjustment both directly and also indirectly through a sense of personal efficacy.

Optimism not only has a positive effect on the psychological well-being of people with medical problems but also influences well-being among caregivers. This conclusion was supported in a project that studied a group of cancer patients and their caregivers (Given et al.,

1993). Caregivers' optimism related to lower symptoms of depression, less impact of caregiving on physical health, and less impact on caregivers' daily schedules. Similar results have been found in research on caregiver spouses of Alzheimer's patients (Hooker et al., 1992; Shifren & Hooker, 1995). Optimism related to lower depression and higher levels of psychological well-being.

Although much of the evidence for the relationship between optimism and psychological well-being comes from samples encountering serious adversity, less extreme events have been examined in other studies. For example, the start of college is a difficult and stressful time, and researchers have examined students making their adjustment to their first semester of college (Aspinwall & Taylor, 1992). Optimism, self-esteem, and other variables were assessed when the students first arrived on campus. Measures of psychological and physical well-being were obtained at the end of the semester. Higher levels of optimism upon entering college predicted lower levels of psychological distress at the end of the semester. The relationship was independent of effects of self-esteem, locus of control, desire for control, and baseline mood.

Optimism, Pessimism, and Coping

Evidence reviewed in the previous section makes it clear that optimists experience less distress than pessimists when dealing with difficulties in their lives. Is this just because optimists are especially cheerful? Apparently not, because the differences often remain even when statistical controls are incorporated for previous levels of distress. There must be other explanations. Do optimists do anything in particular to cope that helps them adapt better than pessimists? In this section, we consider the strategies that optimists and pessimists tend to use, and the broader meaning of these strategies.

In many ways, this discussion is just a more detailed depiction of the broad behavioral tendencies we discussed earlier in the chapter in describing expectancy-value models of motivation. That is, people who are confident about the future exert continuing effort, even when dealing with serious adversity. People who are doubtful are more likely to try to push the adversity away as though they can somehow escape it by wishful thinking; they are more likely to do things that provide temporary distractions

but do not help solve the problem; and they sometimes even stop trying. Both effort and removal of effort can be expressed in a variety of ways. Those expressions—coping reactions and coping strategies—are the focus of this section.

Differences in coping methods used by optimists and pessimists have been found in a number of studies. In one early project Scheier, Weintraub, and Carver (1986) asked students to recall the most stressful event that had happened to them during the previous month and complete a checklist of coping responses with respect to that event. Optimism related to problem-focused coping, especially when the stressful situation was controllable. Optimism also related to the use of positive reframing and (when the situation was seen as uncontrollable) with the tendency to accept the situation's reality. In contrast, optimism related negatively to the use of denial and the attempt to distance oneself from the problem.

These findings provided the first indication that optimists use more problem-centered coping than pessimists. They also use a variety of emotion-focused coping techniques, including working to accept the reality of difficult situations and putting the situations in the best possible light. These findings hint that optimists may have a coping advantage over pessimists even in situations that cannot be changed.

Other researchers have examined differences in dispositional coping styles among optimists and pessimists (Carver, Scheier, & Weintraub, 1989; Fontaine, Manstead, & Wagner, 1993). As with situational coping, optimists reported a dispositional tendency to rely on active, problem-focused coping and being planful. Pessimism related to the tendency to disengage from the goals with which the stressor is interfering. While optimists reported a tendency to accept the reality of stressful events, they also reported trying to see the best in bad situations and to learn something from them. (They seem to try to find benefits in adversity, a process that Tennen and Affleck discuss in their chapter in this volume.) In contrast, pessimists reported tendencies toward overt denial and substance abuse, strategies that lessen their awareness of the problem. Thus, optimists appear generally to be approach copers, and pessimists appear to be avoidant copers.

Relationships between optimism and coping strategies have also been explored in more specific contexts. For example, in the workplace optimists use more problem-focused coping than do pessimists—self-control and directed problem solving (Strutton & Lumpkin, 1992). Pessimists use more emotion-focused coping, including escapism (such as sleeping, eating, and drinking), using social support, and also avoiding people. In a study of executive women, Fry (1995) found that optimists appraised daily hassles differently than did pessimists. Optimistic women expected gain or growth from such events. Their coping reflected acceptance, expressiveness, tension reduction, and use of social support rather than withdrawing, distancing, or engaging in self-blame.

Several studies described earlier in this chapter also indicate links between optimism and coping, and between coping and emotional well-being. In their early study of coronary artery bypass surgery, Scheier and colleagues (1989) assessed the use of attentional-cognitive strategies as ways of dealing with the experience. Before surgery, optimists more than pessimists reported they were making plans for their future and setting goals for their recovery. Optimists also tended to report being less focused on the negative aspects of their experience—their distress emotions and physical symptoms. As Stanton and her colleagues discuss in another chapter of this volume, focusing on emotions can have varying consequences, depending on how the person is focusing. In this case, however, the focusing was an enhanced awareness of the distress, which we doubt was adaptive. Indeed, the fact that pessimists focused on negative aspects of their experience raises the possibility that they are vulnerable to catastrophizing (see Peterson and Steen, this volume).

Once the surgery was past, optimists were more likely than pessimists to report seeking information about what their physician would require of them in the months ahead. Optimists also were less likely to say they were suppressing thoughts about their physical symptoms. There was also evidence that the positive impact of optimism on quality of life 6 months later occurred through the indirect effect of these differences in coping.

Coping also was examined in the study of failed in vitro fertilization described earlier (Litt et al., 1992). Pessimism related to escape as a coping strategy. Escape, in turn, related to greater distress after the fertilization failure. Optimists also were more likely than pessimists to report they had benefited somehow from the experience, for example, by becoming closer to their spouse.

Information regarding coping also comes from the study of AIDS patients described earlier (Taylor et al., 1992). In general, optimism related to active coping strategies. Optimism predicted positive attitudes and tendencies to plan for recovery, seek information, and reframe bad situations in terms of their most positive aspects. Optimists used less fatalism, self-blame, and escapism, and they did not focus on the negative aspects of the situation or try to suppress thoughts about their symptoms. Optimists also appeared to accept unchangeable situations rather than trying to escape them.

Relations between optimism and coping also have been the focus of several studies of cancer patients. Stanton and Snider (1993) recruited women scheduled for breast biopsy. Optimism, coping, and mood were assessed the day before biopsy and—among women who received a cancer diagnosis—24 hours before surgery and again 3 weeks after surgery. Women with a benign diagnosis completed a second assessment that corresponded to either the second or the third assessment of the cancer group. Pessimistic women in this study used more cognitive avoidance before the upcoming diagnostic procedure than did optimists. This avoidance contributed significantly to distress prior to biopsy. Indeed, cognitive avoidance proved to be a mediator of the association of pessimism with prebiopsy distress. Cognitive avoidance before the biopsy also predicted postbiopsy distress among women with positive diagnoses.

Another study of early-stage breast cancer patients, mentioned earlier in the chapter, examined how women coped during the first year after treatment (Carver et al., 1993). Optimism, coping, and mood were assessed the day before surgery. Coping and mood also were assessed 10 days after surgery and at three follow-up points during the next year. Both before and after surgery, optimism related to a pattern of coping responses that revolved around accepting the reality of the situation, placing as positive a light on the situation as possible, trying to relieve the situation with humor, and (at presurgery only) active coping. Pessimism related to denial and behavioral disengagement (giving up) at each time point.

The coping responses related to optimism and pessimism also related strongly to distress. Positive reframing, acceptance, and use of humor all related inversely to self-reports of distress before surgery and after. Denial and behavioral disengagement related positively to distress at all time points. At the 6-month point a new association emerged, such that distress related positively to another kind of avoidance coping: self-distraction. Further analyses revealed that the relation of optimism to distress was largely indirect—through coping—particularly at the postsurgery assessment.

The mediational role of coping in the relationship between optimism and psychological well-being also was examined in the college adaptation study described earlier (Aspinwall & Taylor, 1992). Optimistic students engaged in more active coping and less avoidance coping than did pessimistic students. Avoidance coping related to poorer adjustment; active coping related (separately) to better adjustment. As in the health studies, the beneficial effects of optimism in this context seemed to operate, at least in part, through the differences in coping.

Similarly, in a study described earlier on adjustment to pregnancy (Park, Moore, Turner, & Adler, 1997), optimistic women were more likely than pessimistic women to engage in constructive thinking (i.e., the tendency to think about and solve daily problems in an effective way). Furthermore, as did optimism, constructive thinking correlated negatively with subsequent anxiety and positively with positive states of mind. The association between optimism and each of these markers of psychological adjustment was mediated through the tendency of optimists to engage in constructive thinking.

In sum, it appears that optimists differ from pessimists both in their stable coping tendencies and in the kinds of coping responses they spontaneously generate when confronting stressful situations. Optimists also differ from pessimists in the way they cope with serious disease and concerns about specific health threats. In general, optimists tend to use more problem-focused coping strategies than do pessimists. When problem-focused coping is not a possibility, optimists turn to strategies such as acceptance, use of humor, and positive reframing. Pessimists tend to cope through overt denial and by mentally and behaviorally disengaging from the goals with which the stressor is interfering.

It is particularly noteworthy that optimists turn toward acceptance in uncontrollable situations, whereas pessimists turn more to the use of active attempts at denial. Although both tactics seem to reflect emotion-focused coping, there are important differences between them

that may, in turn, relate to different outcomes. More concretely, denial (the refusal to accept the reality of the situation) means attempting to hold onto a worldview that is no longer valid. In contrast, acceptance implies a restructuring of one's experience so as to come to grips with the reality of one's situation. Acceptance thus may involve a deeper set of processes, in which the person actively works through the experience, attempting to integrate it into an evolving worldview.

The active attempt to come to terms with the existence of problems may confer a special benefit to acceptance as a coping response. We should be clear, however, about the nature of this process. The acceptance we have in mind is a willingness to admit that a problem exists or that an event has happened—even an event that may irrevocably alter the fabric of the person's life. We are *not* talking, however, about a stoic resignation, a fatalistic acceptance of the negative consequences to which the problem or event might lead, no matter how likely those consequences might be. That response confers no benefit.

Consider, for example, the experience of a person diagnosed with terminal cancer. The ultimate outcome will be death. Yet, the person need not conclude, "I'm as good as dead." Such resignation may promote a kind of functional death, with the person prematurely disengaged from the opportunities of the life that remains. Consistent with this idea, people who react to diagnoses with stoic resignation or with passive acceptance of their own impending death actually die sooner than those who exhibit less of these qualities (Greer, Morris, & Pettingale, 1979; Greer, Morris, Pettingale, & Haybittle, 1990; Pettingale, Morris, & Greer, 1985; Reed, Kemeny, Taylor, Wang, & Visscher, 1994).

In contrast to this resignation, an acceptance of the diagnosis per se may have very different consequences. It may cause people to reprioritize their lives, to revise and cut back on long-term goals, and to use what time is left in constructive and optimal ways. Stated differently, by accepting the fact that life is compromised (but not over), people may develop a more adaptive set of parameters within which to live the time that remains. It is in this spirit that we have speculated that acceptance keeps the person goal-engaged, and indeed "life-engaged" (Carver & Scheier, 1998; Scheier & Carver, 2001).

Promoting Well-Being

In describing how optimists and pessimists cope, it also is worth noting some studies of proactive processes, processes that promote good health and well-being rather than just reacting to adversity. The reasoning behind the studies is that people who are optimistic may take active steps to ensure the positive quality of their future. This would be much the same as engaging in problem-focused coping, except there is no particular stressor threatening the person.

Looking at the possibility of individual differences in health promotion among a group of heart patients who were participating in a cardiac rehabilitation program, Shepperd, Maroto, and Pbert (1996) found optimism related to greater success in lowering levels of saturated fat, body fat, and an index of overall coronary risk. Optimism also related to increases in exercise across the rehabilitation period. Another study of the lifestyles of coronary artery bypass patients 5 years after their surgery found optimists more likely than pessimists to be taking vitamins, to be eating low-fat foods, and to be enrolled in a cardiac rehabilitation program (Scheier & Carver, 1992).

Heart disease is not the only aspect of health-related behavior that has been related to optimism. Another is HIV infection. By avoiding certain sexual practices (e.g., sex with unknown partners), people reduce their risk of infection. One study of HIV-negative gay men revealed that optimists reported having fewer anonymous sexual partners than pessimists (Taylor et al., 1992). This suggests that optimists were making efforts to reduce their risk, thereby safeguarding their health.

Optimism also has been studied with regard to the health-related habits of people with no particular salient health concerns. At least two such projects found that optimists reported more health-promoting behaviors than pessimists (Robbins, Spence, & Clark, 1991; Steptoe et al., 1994). Taken together, these various studies suggest that optimism is related to behaviors aimed at promoting health and reducing health risk.

Optimists are not simply people who stick their heads in the sand and ignore threats to their well-being. Indeed, they attend to risks, but selectively. They focus on risks that are applicable to them and also are related to potentially serious health problems (Aspinwall & Brunhart, 1996). If the potential health problem is minor, or if it is unlikely to bear on them, optimists do not show elevated vigilance. Only when the threat matters does vigilance emerge. Optimists appear to scan their surroundings for threats to well-being but save their behavioral responses for threats that are truly meaningful.

Pessimism and Health-Defeating Behaviors

We have characterized optimists throughout this discussion as persistent in trying to reach desired goals. This includes both efforts to deal with adversity and efforts to promote well-being apart from adversity. Theory suggests that pessimists are less likely to make efforts to ensure their well-being. There is, in fact, evidence that pessimists engage in behaviors that reflect a tendency to give up. Some of these behaviors have adverse consequences for well-being. Some even have deadly consequences.

Various forms of substance abuse can be seen as reflecting a giving-up tendency. Substance abuse in general, and excessive alcohol consumption in particular, often is seen as an escape from problems. If so, it follows that pessimists should be more vulnerable than optimists to engaging in this pattern of maladaptive behavior. At least three studies have produced findings that fit this picture.

One was a study of women with a family history of alcoholism. Pessimists in this group were more likely than optimists to report drinking problems (Ohannessian, Hesselbrock, Tennen, & Affleck, 1993). In another study of people who had been treated for alcohol abuse and were now entering an aftercare program, pessimists were more likely than optimists to drop out of the program and to return to drinking (Strack, Carver, & Blaney, 1987). Finally, Park et al. (1997) examined substance use among a group of pregnant women. Optimists were less likely than pessimists to engage in substance abuse during the course of their pregnancies.

Giving up can be manifested in many ways. Alcohol consumption dulls awareness of failures and problems. People can disregard their problems by distracting themselves. Even sleeping can help us escape from situations we do not want to face. Sometimes, though, giving up is more complete than this. Sometimes people give up not on specific goals but on all the goals that form their lives. Such extreme cases can prompt suicide (though Snyder, 1994, points out that successful suicide also requires effortful pursuit of one last goal). Some people are more vulnerable to suicide than others. It is commonly assumed that depression is the best indicator of suicide risk. But pessimism (as measured by the Hopelessness scale) is actually a stronger predictor of this act, the ultimate disengagement from life (Beck, Steer, Kovacs, & Garrison, 1985).

In sum, a sizable body of evidence indicates that pessimism can lead people into self-defeating patterns. The result can be less persistence, more avoidance coping, health-damaging behavior, and potentially even an impulse to escape from life altogether. With no confidence about the future, there may be nothing left to sustain life (Carver & Scheier, 1998).

Is Optimism Always Better Than Pessimism?

Throughout this chapter we have portrayed optimists as better off than pessimists. The evidence we have reviewed indicates that optimists are less distressed when times are tough, cope in ways that foster better outcomes, and are better at taking the steps necessary to ensure that their futures continue to be bright. Although there are certainly times and situations in which optimists are only slightly better off than pessimists, and probably cases where they have no advantage, there is remarkably little evidence that optimists are ever worse off than pessimists.

Several theorists have suggested the possibility that such situations do exist, that optimism may be potentially damaging (e.g., Tennen & Affleck, 1987; Schwarzer, 1994). And, indeed, there is logic behind this hypothesis. For example, too much optimism might lead people to ignore a threat until it is too late or might lead people to overestimate their ability to deal with an adverse situation, resulting in poorer coping.

Most of the data reviewed in the preceding sections indicate that this is generally not the case. On the other hand, two studies suggest the possibility that optimists may not always take action to enhance their future well-being. Goodman, Chesney, and Tipton (1995) studied the extent to which adolescent girls at risk for HIV infection sought out information about HIV testing and agreed to be tested. Those higher in optimism were less likely to expose themselves to the information and were less

likely to follow through with an actual test than those lower in optimism (see also Perkins, Leserman, Murphy, & Evans, 1993).

These findings seem to contradict the evidence reviewed earlier, and the basis of the inconsistency is not clear. Goodman et al. (1995) noted that the average level of optimism in their sample was much lower than typical; this may somehow have played a role in the results. Alternatively, perhaps the results do not really contradict previous findings at all. Perhaps it seems so only because of the absence of other data that would make the findings fit. For example, no information was gathered about the girls' knowledge of the serostatus of their sexual partners. Perhaps optimists had gone to greater lengths than pessimists to verify that their partners were HIV-negative. If so, they would have had less need to seek HIV-relevant information or have their HIV status tested. Obviously, more information is needed for these questions to be answered.

The idea that optimists may fail to protect themselves against threats is one way in which optimism might work against a person. Another possibility is that the optimist's worldview might be more vulnerable than that of a pessimist to the shattering impact of a traumatic event. After all, adversity confirms the pessimist's worldview. Given a diagnosis of metastatic cancer, the experience of a violent rape, or loss of one's home to fire or flood, will the optimist react more adversely than the pessimist? Will optimists be less able to rebuild the shattered assumptions of their lives? All of these possibilities are legitimate to raise. However, we know of no evidence that supports them.

Perhaps the lack of support for the idea that optimists respond worse to a shattering event reflects a more general lack of information about how personality predicts responses to trauma or to experiences such as terminal illness. There is not a great deal of information on these questions. However, at present we do not expect optimists to respond more adversely than pessimists. Rather, we expect them to reset their sights on their changed realities and to continue to make the best of the situations they are facing. Pessimists may find that their worldviews are confirmed by trauma or disaster, but we doubt that they will take much satisfaction in that. Rather, their experience will be the continuing anticipation of yet further adversity.

Can Pessimists Become Optimists?

Given the many ways in which the life of the optimist is better than that of the pessimist, there is good reason to want to be in the former category instead of the latter. There is at least a small problem, though, for those of us who are not already optimistic. Specifically, twin research suggests that optimism is subject to genetic influence (Plomin et al., 1992). There remains a question about whether optimism is *itself* heritable, or whether it displays heritability because of its relation to other aspects of temperament. Optimism relates both to neuroticism and to extraversion, and both are known to be genetically influenced. Although optimism is distinguishable from these temperaments (Scheier et al., 1994), it may be that the observed heritability of optimism reflects these associations.

Another potential influence on people's outlook on life is early childhood experience. For example, in discussing personality development, Erikson (1968) held that infants who experience the social world as predictable develop a sense of "basic trust," whereas those who experience the world as unpredictable develop a sense of "basic mistrust." These qualities are not all that different from the general sense of optimism and pessimism. Similarly, attachment theorists hold that some infants are securely attached in their relationships, and others are not (Ainsworth, Blehar, Waters, & Wall, 1978; Bowlby, 1988). This has also been extended to discussions of adult attachments (Hazan & Shaver, 1994). As it happens, insecurity of adult attachment is related to pessimism. This suggests that optimism may derive in part from the early childhood experience of secure attachment (see also Snyder, 1994). This is only one example, of course, of the many possible ways in which the environment can influence the development of optimism.

Whether one thinks of possible origins of optimism and pessimism in inheritance or in early childhood experience, these pathways to an optimistic or pessimistic outlook on life suggest that the quality is relatively pervasive and permanent. Genetically determined qualities are by definition part of your fundamental makeup and can be expected to exert a virtually unending influence on your behavior. Similarly, aspects of your worldview that are acquired early in life are the foundation from which you proceed to experience the *rest* of the events in your life. The more firmly shaped is that foundation, the more enduring is its influence.

If pessimism is that deeply embedded in a person's life, can it be changed? The answer seems to be a cautious yes, that change in an optimistic direction is possible. However, there remain questions about how large a change can be reasonably expected and how permanent the change will be. There also remain questions about whether an induced optimistic view on life will act in the same way—have the same beneficial effects—as does a naturally occurring optimistic view.

Of the many ways to try to turn a pessimist into an optimist, the most straightforward may be the group of techniques known collectively as cognitive-behavioral therapies. Indeed, trying to turn pessimists (either focused or generalized) into optimists seems an apt characterization of the main thrust of these therapies. Their earliest applications were to problems such as depression and anxiety (Beck, 1967). The logic behind them was that people with these problems make a variety of unduly negative distortions in their minds (e.g., "I can't do anything right"). The unrealistically negative thoughts cause negative affect (dysphoria, anxiety) and set people up to stop trying to reach their goals. In such cases, the distortions closely resemble what we would imagine to be the interior monologue of the pessimist.

If unduly negative cognitions and self-statements define the nature of the problem, the goal of the cognitive therapies is to change the cognitions, make them more positive, and thereby reduce distress and allow renewed effort. Many techniques exist for producing such changes. In general, this approach to therapy begins by having people pay close attention to their experience, to identify points where distress arises and also the thoughts associated with (or immediately preceding) these distress points. The idea is to make the person more aware of what are now automatic thoughts. In many cases, the thoughts in question turn out to be pessimistic beliefs. Once the beliefs have been isolated, they can be challenged and changed. (This attempt to deal with pessimistic beliefs by shifting them has an interesting resemblance to positive reframing, described earlier in the chapter as a useful coping strategy.)

Another method often used is personal efficacy training. The focus of such procedures is on increasing specific kinds of competence (e.g., by assertiveness training or social skill training). However, the techniques often address thoughts and behaviors that relate to a more general sense of pessimism. Training in problem solving, selecting and defining obtainable subgoals, and decision making improves the ways in which a person handles a wide range of everyday situations.

Although the development of positive expectations is an important goal of such therapies, it also is important to recognize that it can be counterproductive to try to substitute an unquestioning optimism for an existing doubt. Sometimes people are pessimistic because they have unrealistically high aspirations for themselves. They demand perfection, hardly ever see it, and develop resulting doubts about their adequacy. This tendency must be countered by establishing realistic goals and identifying which situations must be accepted rather than changed. The person must learn to relinquish unattainable goals and set alternative goals to replace those that cannot be attained (Carver & Scheier, 1998, 2000; Wrosch, Scheier, Carver, & Schulz, 2000).

Conclusions

It often is said that positive thinking is good and negative thinking is bad. The student preparing for an exam, the athlete heading into competition, and the patient facing a life-altering diagnosis is told to "think positive." Are there really benefits to thinking positive? The answer clearly is yes. A growing literature confirms that expectations for the future have an important impact on how people respond in times of adversity or challenge. Expectancies influence the way in which people confront these situations, and they influence the success with which people deal with them. We have yet to see clear evidence of a case in which having positive expectations for one's future is detrimental. Many questions remain unanswered: for example, about the precise mechanism by which optimism influences subjective well-being, and about potential pathways by which optimism may influence physical well-being. But we ourselves are optimistic about the future of work in this area, optimistic that research will continue to reveal the paths by which positive thinking works to people's benefit.

Acknowledgments Preparation of this chapter was facilitated by support from the National Cancer Institute (CA64710, CA64711, and CA78995).

APPENDIX

Items of the Life Orientation Test-Revised (Lot-R), a Measure of Optimism versus Pessimism.

---

1. In uncertain times, I usually expect the best.
2. It's easy for me to relax. (Filler)
3. If something can go wrong for me, it will.[a]
4. I'm always optimistic about my future.
5. I enjoy my friends a lot. (Filler)
6. It's important for me to keep busy. (Filler)
7. I hardly ever expect things to go my way.[a]
8. I don't get upset too easily. (Filler)
9. I rarely count on good things happening to me.[a]
10. Overall, I expect more good things to happen to me than bad.

Note: Respondents indicate the extent of their agreement with each item using a 5-point Likert scale ranging from "strongly disagree" to "strongly agree." After reverse coding the negatively worded items (those identified with the supercript *a*), the six nonfiller items are summed to produce an overall score.

From M. F. Scheier, C. S. Carver, & M. W. Bridges (1994), Distinguishing optimism from neuroticism (and trait anxiety, self-mastery, and self-esteem): A reevaluation of the Life Orientation Test, *Journal of Personality and Social Psychology, 67,* 1063–1078. Reproduced with the permission of the authors and the American Psychological Association.

References

Ainsworth, M. D. S., Blehar, M. C., Waters, E., & Wall, T. (1978). *Patterns of attachment.* Hillsdale, NJ: Erlbaum.

Armor, D. A., & Taylor, S. E. (1998). Situated optimism: Specific outcome expectancies and self-regulation. In M. Zanna (Ed.), *Advances in experimental social psychology* (Vol. 30, 309–379). San Diego, CA: Academic Press.

Aspinwall, L. G., & Brunhart, S. N. (1996). Distinguishing optimism from denial: Optimistic beliefs predict attention to health threats. *Personality and Social Psychology Bulletin, 22,* 993–1003.

Aspinwall, L. G., & Taylor, S. E. (1992). Modeling cognitive adaptation: A longitudinal investigation of the impact of individual differences and coping on college adjustment and performance.

Journal of Personality and Social Psychology, 61, 755–765.

Austin, J. T., & Vancouver, J. B. (1996). Goal constructs in psychology: Structure, process, and content. *Psychological Bulletin, 120,* 338–375.

Beck, A. T. (1967). *Depression: Clinical, experimental, and theoretical aspects.* New York: Harper and Row.

Beck, A. T., Steer, R. A., Kovacs, M., & Garrison, B. (1985). Hopelessness and eventual suicide: A 10-year prospective study of patients hospitalized with suicidal ideation. *American Journal of Psychiatry, 142,* 559–563.

Bowlby, J. (1988). *A secure base: Parent-child attachment and healthy human development.* New York: Basic Books.

Carver, C. S., & Gaines, J. G. (1987). Optimism, pessimism, and postpartum depression. *Cognitive Therapy and Research, 11,* 449–462.

*Carver, C. S., Pozo, C., Harris, S. D., Noriega, V., Scheier, M. F., Robinson, D. S., Ketcham, A. S., Moffat, F. L., & Clark, K. C. (1993). How coping mediates the effect of optimism on distress: A study of women with early stage breast cancer. *Journal of Personality and Social Psychology, 65,* 375–390.

*Carver, C. S., & Scheier, M. F. (1998). *On the self-regulation of behavior.* New York: Cambridge University Press.

Carver, C. S., & Scheier, M. F. (2000). Scaling back goals and recalibration of the affect system are processes in normal adaptive self-regulation: Understanding "response shift" phenomena. *Social Science and Medicine, 50,* 1715–1722.

Carver, C. S., Scheier, M. F., & Weintraub, J. K. (1989). Assessing coping strategies: A theoretically based approach. *Journal of Personality and Social Psychology, 56,* 267–283.

Cozzarelli, C. (1993). Personality and self-efficacy as predictors of coping with abortion. *Journal of Personality and Social Psychology, 65,* 1224–1236.

Curbow, B. Somerfield, M. R., Baker, F. Wingard, J. R., & Legro, M. W. (1993). Personal changes, dispositional optimism, and psychological adjustment to bone marrow transplantation. *Journal of Behavioral Medicine, 16,* 423–443.

Erikson, E. H. (1968). *Identity: Youth and crisis.* New York: Norton.

Fitzgerald, T. E., Tennen, H., Affleck, G., & Pransky, G. S. (1993). The relative importance of dispositional optimism and control appraisals in quality of life after coronary artery bypass surgery. *Journal of Behavioral Medicine, 16,* 25–43.

Fontaine, K. R., Manstead, A. S. R., & Wagner, H. (1993). Optimism, perceived control over stress, and coping. *European Journal of Personality, 7,* 267–281.

Friedman, L. C., Nelson, D. V., Baer, P. E., Lane, M., Smith, F. E., & Dworkin, R. J. (1992). The relationship of dispositional optimism, daily life stress, and domestic environment to coping methods used by cancer patients. *Journal of Behavioral Medicine, 15,* 127–141.

Fry, P. S. (1995). Perfectionism, humor, and optimism as moderators of health outcomes and determinants of coping styles of women executives. *Genetics, Social, and General Psychology Monographs, 121,* 211–245.

Given, C. W., Stommel, M., Given, B., Osuch, J., Kurtz, M. E., & Kurtz, J. C. (1993). The influence of cancer patients' symptoms and functional states on patients' depression and family caregivers' reaction and depression. *Health Psychology, 12,* 277–285.

Goodman, E., Chesney, M. A., & Tipton, A. C. (1995). Relationship of optimism, knowledge, attitudes, and beliefs to use of HIV antibody test by at-risk female adolescents. *Psychosomatic Medicine, 57,* 541–546.

Greer, S., Morris, T., & Pettingale, K. W. (1979). Psychological response to breast cancer: Effect on outcome. *Lancet, ii,* 785–787.

Greer, S., Morris, T., Pettingale, K. W., & Haybittle, J. L. (1990). Psychological response to breast cancer and 15-year outcome. *Lancet, i,* 49–50.

Hazan, C., & Shaver, P. R. (1994). Attachment as an organizational framework for research on close relationships. *Psychological Inquiry, 5,* 1–22.

Hooker, K., Monahan, D., Shifren, K., & Hutchinson, C. (1992). Mental and physical health of spouse caregivers: The role of personality. *Psychology and Aging, 7,* 367–375.

*Litt, M. D., Tennen, H., Affleck, G., & Klock, S. (1992). Coping and cognitive factors in adaptation to *in vitro* fertilization failure. *Journal of Behavioral Medicine, 15,* 171–187.

Long, B. C. (1993). Coping strategies of male managers: A prospective analysis of predictors of psychosomatic symptoms and job satisfaction. *Journal of Vocational Behavior, 42,* 184–199.

*Ohannessian, C. M., Hesselbrock, V. M., Tennen, H., & Affleck, G. (1993). Hassles and uplifts and generalized outcome expectancies as moderators on the relation between a family history of alcoholism and drinking behaviors. *Journal of Studies on Alcohol, 55,* 754–763.

Park, C. L., Moore, P. J., Turner, R. A., & Adler, N. E. (1997). The roles of constructive thinking and optimism in psychological and behavioral adjustment during pregnancy. *Journal of Personality and Social Psychology, 73,* 584–592.

Perkins, D. O., Leserman, J., Murphy, C., & Evans, D. L. (1993). Psychosocial predictors of high-risk sexual behavior among HIV-negative homosexual men. *AIDS Education and Prevention, 5,* 141–152.

Peterson, C., & Seligman, M. E. P. (1984). Causal explanations as a risk factor for depression: Theory and evidence. *Psychological Review, 91,* 347–374.

Pettingale, K. W., Morris, T., & Greer, S. (1985). Mental attitudes to cancer: An additional prognostic factor. *Lancet, i,* 750.

Plomin, R., Scheier, M. F., Bergeman, C. S., Pedersen, N. L., Nesselroade, J. R., & McClearn, G. E. (1992). Optimism, pessimism, and mental health: A twin/adoption analysis. *Personality and Individual Differences, 13,* 921–930.

Reed, G. M., Kemeny, M. E., Taylor, S. E., Wang, H-Y. J., & Visscher, B. R. (1994). Realistic acceptance as a predictor of decreased survival time in gay men with AIDS. *Health Psychology, 13,* 299–307.

Robbins, A. S., Spence, J. T., & Clark, H. (1991). Psychological determinants of health and performance: The tangled web of desirable and undesirable characteristics. *Journal of Personality and Social Psychology, 61,* 755–765.

Scheier, M. F., & Carver, C. S. (1985). Optimism, coping and health: Assessment and implications of generalized outcome expectancies. *Health Psychology, 4,* 219–247.

*Scheier, M. F., & Carver, C. S. (1992). Effects of optimism on psychological and physical well-being: Theoretical overview and empirical update. *Cognitive Therapy and Research, 16,* 201–228.

*Scheier, M. F., & Carver, C. S. (2001). Adapting to cancer: The importance of hope and purpose. In A. Baum & B. L. Andersen (Eds.), *Psychosocial interventions for cancer* (pp. 15–36). Washington, DC: American Psychological Association.

*Scheier, M. F., Carver, C. S., & Bridges, M. W. (1994). Distinguishing optimism from neuroticism (and trait anxiety, self-mastery, and self-esteem): A reevaluation of the Life Orientation Test. *Journal of Personality and Social Psychology, 67,* 1063–1078.

Scheier, M. F., Matthews, K. A., Owens, J. F., Magovern, G. J., Lefebvre, R. C., Abbott, R. A., & Carver, C. S. (1989). Dispositional optimism and recovery from coronary artery bypass surgery: The beneficial effects on physical and psychological well-being. *Journal of Personality and Social Psychology, 57,* 1024–1040.

Scheier, M. F., Weintraub, J. K., & Carver, C. S. (1986). Coping with stress: Divergent strategies of optimists and pessimists. *Journal of Personality and Social Psychology, 51,* 1257–1264.

Schwarzer, R. (1994). Optimism, vulnerability, and self-beliefs as health-related cognitions: A systematic overview. *Psychology and Health, 9,* 161–180.

Seligman, M. E. P. (1991). *Learned optimism.* New York: Knopf.

Shepperd, J. A., Maroto, J. J., & Pbert, L. A. (1996). Dispositional optimism as a predictor of health changes among cardiac patients. *Journal of Research in Personality, 30,* 517–534.

Shifren, K., & Hooker, K. (1995). Stability and change in optimism: A study among spouse caregivers. *Experimental Aging Research, 21,* 59–76.

Snyder, C. R. (1994). *The psychology of hope: You can get there from here.* New York: Free Press.

Snyder, C. R., Sympson, S. C., Ybasco, F. C., Borders, T. F., Babyak, M. A., & Higgins, R. L. (1996). Development and validation of the state hope scale. *Journal of Personality and Social Psychology, 70,* 321–335.

*Stanton, A. L., & Snider, P. R. (1993). Coping with breast cancer diagnosis: A prospective study. *Health Psychology, 12,* 16–23.

Steptoe, A., Wardle, J., Vinck, J., Tuomisto, M., Holte, A., & Wichstrøm, L. (1994). Personality and attitudinal correlates of healthy lifestyles in young adults. *Psychology and Health, 9,* 331–343.

Strack, S., Carver, C. S., & Blaney, P. H. (1987). Predicting successful completion of an aftercare program following treatment for alcoholism: The role of dispositional optimism. *Journal of Personality and Social Psychology, 53,* 579–584.

Strutton, D., & Lumpkin, J. (1992). Relationship between optimism and coping strategies in the work environment. *Psychology Reports, 71,* 1179–1186.

*Taylor, S. E., Kemeny, M. E., Aspinwall, L. G., Schneider, S. G., Rodriguez, R., & Herbert, M. (1992). Optimism, coping, psychological distress, and high-risk sexual behavior among men at risk for acquired immunodeficiency syndrome (AIDS). *Journal of Personality and Social Psychology, 63,* 460–473.

Tennen, H., & Affleck, G. (1987). The costs and benefits of optimistic explanations and dispositional optimism. *Journal of Personality, 55,* 377–393.

Wrosch, C., Scheier, M. F., Carver, C. S., & Schulz, R. (2000). *The importance of goal disengagement in a positive psychology.* Unpublished manuscript.

Zeidner, M., & Hammer, A. L. (1992). Coping with missile attack: Resources, strategies, and outcomes. *Journal of Personality, 60,* 709–746.

18

Optimistic Explanatory Style

Christopher Peterson & Tracy A. Steen

Optimism has a checkered reputation. Consider Voltaire's (1759) Dr. Pangloss, who blathered that this is the best of all possible worlds, or Porter's (1913) Pollyanna, who celebrated misfortunes befalling herself and others. Consider contemporary politicians who spin embarrassing news into something wonderful. So-called optimism has given thoughtful people pause because of connotations of naïveté and denial. In recent years, however, optimism has become a more respectable stance, even among the sophisticated. Optimism, conceptualized and assessed in a variety of ways, has been linked to positive mood and good morale, to perseverance and effective problem solving, to achievement in a variety of domains, to popularity, to good health, and even to long life and freedom from trauma.

Our purpose in this chapter is to review what is known about one cognate of optimism: *explanatory style*, how people habitually explain the causes of events that occur to them. We discuss studies on explanatory style, focusing on a relatively neglected question: What are the origins of explanatory style? We conclude by addressing issues that need to be considered by positive psychologists doing research on explanatory style.

History: From Learned Helplessness to Explanatory Style

Learned helplessness was first described by psychologists studying animal learning (Overmier & Seligman, 1967; Seligman & Maier, 1967). Researchers immobilized a dog and exposed it to a series of electric shocks that could be neither avoided nor escaped. Twenty-four hours later, the dog was placed in a situation in which electric shock could be terminated by a simple response. The dog did not make this response, however, and just sat, passively enduring the shock. This behavior was in marked contrast to that of dogs in a control group, which reacted vigorously to the shock and learned readily how to turn it off.

These investigators proposed that the dog had learned to be helpless: When originally exposed to uncontrollable shock, it learned that nothing it did mattered (Maier & Seligman, 1976). The shocks came and went independently of the dog's behaviors. Response-outcome independence was represented cognitively by the dogs as an expectation of future helplessness that was generalized to new situations to produce a variety of motivational, cognitive, and emotional deficits. The deficits that follow in the wake of uncontrollability have come to be known as the *learned helplessness phenomenon,* and the associated cognitive explanation as the *learned helplessness model.*

Much of the early interest in learned helplessness stemmed from its clash with traditional stimulus-response theories of learning (Peterson, Maier, & Seligman, 1993). Alternative accounts of learned helplessness were proposed by theorists who saw no need to invoke mentalistic constructs, and many of these alternatives emphasized an incompatible motor response learned when animals were first exposed to uncontrollable shock. This response was presumably generalized to the second situation, where it interfered with performance at the test task. For example, perhaps the dogs learned that holding still when shocked somehow decreased pain. If so, then they held still in the second situation as well, because this response was previously reinforced.

Steven Maier, Martin Seligman, and others conducted a series of studies testing the learned helplessness model and the incompatible motor response alternatives (Maier & Seligman, 1976). Several lines of research implied that expectations were operative. Perhaps the most compelling argument comes from the so-called *triadic design,* a three-group experimental design which shows that the uncontrollability of shocks is responsible for ensuing deficits. Animals in one group are exposed to shock that they are able to terminate by making some response. Animals in a second group are yoked to those in the first group and exposed to the identical shocks, with the only difference being that animals in the first group control their offset, whereas those in the second do not. Animals in a third group are exposed to no shock at all in the original situation. All animals are then given the same test task.

Animals with control over the initial shocks typically show no helplessness when subsequently tested. They act just like animals with no prior exposure to shock. Animals without control become helpless. Whether or not shocks are controllable is not a property of the shocks per se but rather of the relationship between the animal and the shocks. That animals are sensitive to the link between responses and outcomes implies that they must be able to detect and represent the relevant contingencies. A cognitive explanation of this ability is more parsimonious than one phrased in terms of incompatible motor responses.

Support for a cognitive interpretation of helplessness also appeared in studies showing that an animal can be immunized against the debilitating effects of uncontrollability by first exposing it to controllable events. Presumably, the animal learns during immunization that events can be controlled, and *this* expectation is sustained during exposure to uncontrollable events, precluding learned helplessness. In other studies, researchers showed that learned helplessness deficits can be undone by forcibly exposing a helpless animal to the contingency between behavior and outcome. So, the animal is compelled to make an appropriate response at the test task by pushing or pulling it into action. After several such trials, the animal notices that escape is possible and begins to respond on its own. Again, the presumed process at work is a cognitive one. The animal's expectation of response-outcome independence is challenged during the "therapy" experience, and hence learning occurs.

Human Helplessness

Psychologists interested in humans, and particularly human problems, were quick to see the parallels between learned helplessness as produced by uncontrollable events in the laboratory and maladaptive passivity as it exists in the real world. Thus, researchers began several lines of research on learned helplessness in people.

In one line of work, helplessness in people was produced in the laboratory much as it was in animals, by exposing them to uncontrollable events and observing the effects. Unsolvable problems usually were substituted for uncontrollable electric shocks, but the critical aspects of the phenomenon remained: Following uncontrollability, people show a variety of deficits (Mikulincer, 1994; Peterson et al., 1993). In other studies, researchers documented further similarities between the animal phenomenon and what was produced in the human laboratory. Uncontrollable bad events made anxiety and depression more likely. Previous exposure to controllable events immunized people against learned helplessness. Similarly, forcible exposure to contingencies reversed helplessness deficits.

Several aspects of human helplessness differ from animal helplessness, however, and these are worth emphasizing in the present context. What is most positive about the human condition may best be suggested by considering what is unique to people. First, uncontrollable bad events seem much more likely than uncontrollable good events to produce helplessness among human beings, probably because people are able to devise coherent (if not always veridical) accounts for why good things happen to them. Thus, the intriguing phenomenon of *appetitive helplessness* among animals probably has no reliable counterpart among people because they can readily create contingency interpretations.

More generally, people differ from animals in our sophistication of assigning meaning to events. As captured by the learned helplessness model, animals of course can learn that they do or do not have control over events. But people do so much more with respect to the making of meaning. People can construe events in ways that go far beyond their literal controllability. Indeed, Rothbaum, Weisz, and Snyder (1982) suggested that there are circumstances in which passivity, withdrawal, and submissiveness among people are not prima facie evidence of diminished personal control; rather, these reactions may represent alternative forms of control achieved by cognitively aligning oneself with powerful external forces. For example, religion provides a worldview that can blunt the effects of not being able to control events.

A second asymmetry is what can be termed *vicarious helplessness*. Problem-solving difficulties can be produced in people if they simply see someone else exposed to uncontrollability (Brown & Inouye, 1978). The significance of vicarious helplessness is that it greatly extends the potential ways in which helpless behavior can be produced in the natural world. The full parameters of this phenomenon have not been investigated, and questions arise as to whether we can immunize people against vicarious helplessness or undo its effects via therapy.

A third difference is that small groups of people can be made helpless by exposure to uncontrollable events. So, when a group works at an unsolvable problem, it later shows group problem-solving deficits relative to another group with no previous exposure to uncontrollability (Simkin, Lederer, & Seligman, 1983). On this point, group-level helplessness is not simply a function of individual helplessness produced among group members: When working alone, individual members of helpless groups show no deficits. Perhaps these results can be generalized to larger groups, including complex organizations or even entire cultures.

Again, the real-life implications of this phenomenon are intriguing, and future research into this phenomenon seems indicated.

In another line of work, researchers proposed various failures of adaptation as analogous to learned helplessness and investigated the similarity between these failures and learned helplessness. Peterson et al. (1993) proposed three formal criteria with which to judge the goodness of an application:

1. *Objective noncontingency.* The applied researcher must take into account the contingencies between a person's actions and the outcomes that he or she then experiences. Learned helplessness is present only when there is no contingency between actions and outcomes. In other words, learned helplessness must be distinguished from extinction (where active responses once leading to reinforcement no longer do so) and from learned passivity (where active responses are contingently punished and/or passive responses are contingently reinforced).
2. *Cognitive mediation.* Learned helplessness also involves a characteristic way of perceiving, explaining, and extrapolating contingencies. The helplessness model specifies cognitive processes that make helplessness more versus less likely following uncontrollable events. If measures of these processes are not sensibly related to ensuing passivity, then learned helplessness is not present.
3. *Cross-situational generality of passive behavior.* Finally, learned helplessness is shown by passivity in a situation different from the one in which uncontrollability was first encountered. Does the individual give up and fail to initiate actions that might allow him or her to control this situation? It is impossible to argue that learned helplessness is present without the demonstration of passivity in new situations. Other consequences also may accompany the behavioral deficits that define the learned helplessness phenomenon: cognitive retardation, low self-esteem, sadness, reduced aggression, immunosuppression, and physical illness.

Using these criteria, then, good applications include depression; academic, athletic, and vocational failure; worker burnout; deleterious psychological effects of crowding, unemployment, noise pollution, chronic pain, aging, mental retardation, and epilepsy; and passivity among ethnic minorities (see Peterson et al., 1993, Table 7-1). Other popular applications are unproven or simply wrong, usually because the particular examples of passivity are better viewed as instrumental. For example, victims of child abuse or domestic violence have been characterized as having "learned" to be helpless (Walker, 1977–1978). A more compelling argument is that they have learned to hold still. Such passivity is indeed problematic when generalized, but the underlying process is not the one described by the learned helplessness model.

As research ensued, it became clear that the original learned helplessness explanation was an oversimplification. The model failed to account for the range of reactions that people display in response to uncontrollable events. Some people show the hypothesized deficits across time and situation, whereas others do not. Furthermore, failures of adaptation that the learned helplessness model was supposed to explain, such as depression, are often characterized by a striking loss of self-esteem, about which the model is silent.

Attributional Reformulation and Explanatory Style

In an attempt to resolve these discrepancies, Lyn Abramson, Martin Seligman, and John Teasdale (1978) reformulated the helplessness model as it applied to people by melding it with attribution theory (Kelley, 1973; Weiner, 1974). Abramson et al. explained the contrary findings by proposing that people ask themselves why uncontrollable (bad) events happen. The nature of the person's answer then sets the parameters for the subsequent helplessness. If the causal attribution is stable ("it's going to last forever"), then induced helplessness is long-lasting; if unstable, then it is transient. If the causal attribution is global ("it's going to undermine everything"), then subsequent helplessness is manifest across a variety of situations; if specific, then it is correspondingly circumscribed. Finally, if the causal attribution is internal ("it's all my fault"), the person's self-esteem drops following uncontrollability; if external, self-esteem is left intact.

These hypotheses constitute the *attributional reformulation* of helplessness theory. This new theory left the original model in place, because uncontrollable events were still hypothesized to produce deficits when they gave rise to an expectation of response-outcome independence. The nature of these deficits, however, was now said to be influenced by the causal attribution offered by the individual.

In some cases, the situation itself provides the explanation made by the person, and the extensive social psychology literature on causal attributions documents many situational influences on the process (Shaver, 1975). In other cases, the person relies on his or her habitual way of making sense of events that occur, what is called one's *explanatory style*. People tend to offer similar explanations for disparate bad (or good) events. Explanatory style is therefore a distal, although important, influence on helplessness and the failures of adaptation that involve helplessness. An explanatory style characterized by internal, stable, and global explanations for bad events has been described as *pessimistic*, and the opposite style, characterized by external, unstable, and specific explanations for bad events, has been described as *optimistic* (Buchanan & Seligman, 1995).

According to the attributional reformulation, explanatory style is not a cause of problems but rather a dispositional risk factor. Given uncontrollable events and the lack of a clear situational demand on the proffered attribution for uncontrollability, explanatory style should influence how the person responds. Helplessness will *tend* to be long-lasting or transient, widespread or circumscribed, damaging to self-esteem or not, all in accordance with the individual's explanatory style.

In both the original and the reformulated version of the helplessness model, generalized expectations of response-outcome independence are the proximal cause of helplessness. Research in this tradition, however, has rarely looked at this mediating variable. Researchers instead measure explanatory style and correlate it with helplessness-related outcomes such as depression, illness, and failure. Invariably, those with an optimistic explanatory style fare better than those with a pessimistic explanatory style (Peterson & Park, 1998).

As explanatory style research has progressed and theory has been modified, the internality dimension has become of less interest (Abramson, Metalsky, & Alloy, 1989). It has more inconsistent correlates than stability or globality, it is less reliably assessed, and there are theoretical grounds for doubting that it has a direct impact on expectations per se (Peterson, 1991). Internality may well conflate self-blame and self-efficacy, which would explain why it fares poorly in empirical research.

Measures of Explanatory Style

Explanatory style typically is measured with a self-report questionnaire called the Attributional Style Questionnaire (ASQ). In the ASQ, respondents are presented with hypothetical events involving themselves and then are asked to provide "the one major cause" of each event if it were to happen (Peterson et al., 1982). Respondents then rate these provided causes along dimensions of internality, stability, and globality. Ratings are combined, keeping separate those for bad events and those for good events. Explanatory style based on bad events usually has more robust correlates than explanatory style based on good events, although correlations are typically in the opposite directions (Peterson, 1991).

A second way of measuring explanatory style is with a content analysis procedure called the CAVE (an acronym for Content Analysis of Verbatim Explanations), which allows written or spoken material to be scored for naturally occurring causal explanations (Peterson, Schulman, Castellon, & Seligman, 1992). Researchers identify explanations for bad or good events, extract them, and present them to judges, who then rate them along the scales of the ASQ. The CAVE technique makes possible longitudinal studies after the fact, so long as spoken or written material can be located from early in the lives of individuals for whom long-term outcomes of interest are known.

Origins of Explanatory Style

We know that cognitive therapy can change an individual's explanatory style from pessimistic to optimistic, reducing the extent of depressive symptoms in the process (Seligman et al., 1988). We also know that cognitive-behavioral interventions that impart problem-solving skills to schoolchildren make them more optimistic, preventing depression in the future (Gillham, Reivich, Jaycox, & Seligman, 1995). Explanatory style therefore is malleable.

But what initially sets explanatory style in place? Researchers have not attempted to an-

swer this question with a sustained line of research. What we find instead are isolated studies by various investigators that document diverse influences on explanatory style. In few of these studies has more than one influence at a time been investigated. Hence, we cannot say what are the more important versus less important influences on explanatory style. Nor can we say how different influences interact, although we doubt that they operate independently of one another.

Researchers have not studied explanatory style prior to age 8, when children are first able to respond to interview versions of the ASQ (Nolen-Hoeksema, 1986). We assume that explanatory style takes form at an earlier age, although we await appropriate assessment strategies to document this occurrence. This shortcoming aside, here is what is known about the natural history of explanatory style.

Genetics

Explanatory style is influenced by genetics. Schulman, Keith, and Seligman (1993) found that the explanatory styles of monozygotic twins were more highly correlated than the explanatory styles of dizygotic twins ($r = .48$ vs. $r = .00$). This finding does *not* mean that there is an optimism gene. As Schulman et al. noted, genes may be indirectly responsible for the concordance of explanatory style among monozygotic twins. For example, genes influence such attributes such as intelligence and physical attractiveness, which in turn lead to more positive (and fewer negative) outcomes in the environment, which in turn may encourage a more optimistic explanatory style.

Genetic influences aside, we presume that explanatory style is either acquired as a whole (e.g., when a child hears an explicit causal message from a parent or teacher) or abstracted from ongoing experience (e.g., when an individual ruminates on the meaning of failure or trauma and then draws a causal conclusion). We can identify the former mode of acquisition as direct and the latter as indirect, although these may blur together in actual instances. We next turn to how explanatory style is acquired from experiences.

Parents

Researchers have explored the relationship between the explanatory styles of parents and their offspring. Attributions by mothers and their children are usually the focus. The relevant data prove inconclusive, with some researchers finding convergence between the causal attributions of mothers and their children (Nolen-Hoeksema, 1986; Parsons, Adler, & Kaczala, 1982; Seligman et al., 1984), and others not (Holloway & Hess, 1982; Holloway, Kashiwagi, Hess, & Azuma, 1986; Kaslow, Rehm, Pollack, & Siegel, 1988; Turk & Bry, 1992; Yamauchi, 1989). Although there have been few studies where the focus was on the relationship between the explanatory styles of fathers and their children, Seligman and colleagues (1984) found that fathers' explanatory styles were *not* related to those of their children.

Perhaps the best way to make sense of these conflicting findings is to take them at face value and conclude that explanatory style is transmitted to children by some parents but not by others. Researchers therefore must do something more than calculate simple correlations between the explanatory styles of parents and children; they need to investigate plausible moderators of this possible link (cf. Snyder, 1994). How much time do parents and children spend together? About what do they talk? Do causal explanations figure in this discourse?

Attention to mechanisms is especially important when we look at optimistic explanatory style. Why are some children able to endorse an optimistic outlook despite external influences that would seem to undercut optimism? Why do some children transcend whatever genetic influences there might be on explanatory style?

We assume that the explanatory style of children can be affected by their parents through simple modeling. Children are most likely to imitate those whom they perceive as powerful and competent, and most parents, although not all, fit this description (Bandura, 1977). Children are attuned to the ways in which their parents interpret the world, and they therefore may be inclined to interpret their environments in a similar manner. If, for example, children repeatedly hear their parents give internal, stable, and global explanations for negative events, they are likely to adopt these pessimistic interpretations for themselves.

Another type of parental influence involves parents' interpretation of their children's behaviors. Criticisms implying pessimistic causes have a cumulative effect on how children view themselves (Peterson & Park, 1998; Seligman, 1990). For example, if a child says that she cannot find her house key, the parent may admonish her as being careless, thus providing an internal, stable, and global explanation of the child's behavior. Alternatively, a parent may respond by saying that the child needs to work on becoming more organized, thus providing an internal, unstable, and specific attribution. One response enforces a pessimistic view of a relatively minor event, whereas the other response allows a more optimistic view.

Related to this point, Vanden Belt and Peterson (1991) found that how parents explain events involving their children has implications for their children's achievement and adjustment in the classroom. In their study, children whose parents had a pessimistic explanatory style vis-à-vis events involving their children tended to work below their potential in the classroom—perhaps because they had internalized their parents' outlook.

Another type of parental influence is indirect but probably quite important: whether a safe and coherent world is provided for the young child. We know that children from happy and supportive homes are more likely as adults to have an optimistic explanatory style (Franz, McClelland, Weinberger, & Peterson, 1994). This finding follows from the fact that parental encouragement and support diminish fear of failure and enable children to take the risks necessary to find and pursue their real interests and talents. Success and confidence are generated, which in turn lead to expectations of further success (Peterson & Bossio, 1991). Thus, optimism is fostered and nurtured through a series of confidence-building experiences. Along these lines, Marks (1998) cautioned that children who are congenitally deaf and blind are at particular risk for developing a pessimistic explanatory style if their condition elicits too much coddling or results in too many experiences of failure. Parents and caregivers face the difficult task of providing appropriate challenges that allow these children to exercise control over the environment.

What happens to children whose parents are not consistently there to encourage a safe exploration of the world? Perez-Bouchard, Johnson, and Ahrens (1993) found that children (aged 8 to 14) of substance abusers were more likely to have a pessimistic explanatory style than children of parents without a history of substance abuse. One possible explanation of the link between parents' substance abuse and children's pessimism is that substance-abusing parents are less likely to be available to provide their children with the support and encouragement that facilitate successes. Furthermore, children of substance abusers may be forced to take on too many adult responsibilities that are beyond their developmental abilities, thus setting themselves up for failure rather than the success that fosters optimism. If children experience repeated failures at a critical age, they may learn that nothing they do makes a difference (Seligman, Reivich, Jaycox, & Gillham, 1995).

Teachers

As teachers administer feedback about children's performance, their comments may affect children's attributions about their successes and failures in the classroom. In a study by Heyman, Dweck, and Cain (1992), kindergarten students role-played scenarios in which one of their projects was criticized by a teacher. Thirty-nine percent of the students displayed a helpless response to the teacher's criticism: exhibiting negative affect, changing their original positive opinions of the project to more negative ones, and expressing disinclinations toward future involvements in that type of project. In addition, those children were more likely to make negative judgments about themselves that were internal, stable, and global.

Mueller and Dweck (1998) demonstrated that even praise can be detrimental to children when it is focused on a trait perceived to be fixed. In their study, children who were praised for their intelligence displayed more characteristics of helplessness in response to difficulty or failure than did children who were praised for their efforts. Whether providing positive or negative feedback, a teacher's habitual explanations for children's performances can be influential and may have a critical impact on their developing explanatory style (Dweck, 1999).

Media

Do the media play a role in producing explanatory style? Levine (1977) reported that CBS and NBC newscasts modeled helplessness 71% of the time, thereby offering ample opportunity for the vicarious acquisition of helplessness. Gerbner and Gross (1976) also examined television shows and found that televised violence, whether fictional or actual, resulted in intensified feelings of risk and insecurity that promote compliance with established authority. Explanatory style was not an explicit focus, but it seems plausible that a causal message was tucked into this form of influence. Even when television viewing produces ostensibly positive feelings, helplessness may result when viewers learn to expect outcomes unrelated to behaviors (Hearn, 1991).

Although people of all ages watch television, young people may be especially susceptible to its influence. According to a recent study, children under age 11 watched an average of 22 hours of television per week (Nielsen Media Research, 1998). Of particular concern is children's exposure to televised scenes of violence. From an explanatory style perspective, the issue is not televised violence per se but how its causes are portrayed.

Although to some extent television mirrors the world, its depictions of violence frequently become gratuitous. This is true not only of fictional portrayals but also of news reports. When violence erupts anywhere in the world, television cameras arrive to record every facet of misery with an intensity bordering on the obscene. Pictures of victims are displayed repeatedly; reporters review the sequence of events repeatedly; various professionals analyze the causes and effects repeatedly. Coverage is hourly, daily, lasting for weeks in some instances. In short, the medium ruminates on the violence, tacitly encouraging the viewer to do the same, and such rumination may take a toll, strengthening and cementing into place a pessimistic explanatory style (Nolen-Hoeksema, 1987).

Television's proclivity for ruminating in its news coverage compounds a tendency to magnify stories of violence in a self-serving way that may slant factual presentation (Levine, 1977). It is not in the interest of networks to place temporal or specific parameters on a story. Instead, they benefit from interpreting a story from a pessimistic vantage, specifying the stability and globality of its impact, and thereby enlarging the story's import. Unfortunately, the distortions in permanence and pervasiveness that serve the interest of the networks do not serve the best interests of young viewers who may adopt the pessimistic explanatory style to which they are repeatedly exposed.

Trauma

Trauma also influences the explanatory style of children. For example, Bunce, Larsen, and Peterson (1995) found that college students who reported experiencing a significant trauma (e.g., death of a parent, rape, incest) at some point in their childhood or adolescence currently had a more pessimistic explanatory style than those students who had never experienced trauma. Even more specifically, Gold (1986) found that women who had been sexually victimized during their childhood and adolescence were more likely to have a pessimistic explanatory style than were women who had not been sexually victimized. Furthermore, even the divorce of parents, common in our modern society, puts children at greater risk for developing a pessimistic explanatory style (Seligman, 1990).

Because isolated traumas have been shown to influence the development of a pessimistic explanatory style, it is not surprising to find evidence that chronic abuse has a similar effect. Cerezo and Frias (1994) found that children (aged 8 to 13) whose parents had physically and emotionally abused them for at least 2 years had a more pessimistic explanatory style than did children who were not abused. Because of the often arbitrary nature and seemingly random occurrence of the punishments, the abused children learned that there was no way to prevent them (Cerezo & Frias, 1994). In other words, they learned to be helpless. A study of the explanatory styles of prison inmates provides additional evidence that chronic uncontrollable events can influence explanatory style. Schill and Marcus (1998) found that inmates who had been incarcerated for 5 or more years had a more pessimistic explanatory style than did inmates who had been incarcerated for less than 1 year.

A great deal is known about the consequences of an optimistic versus pessimistic style of explaining the causes of events. Far less is known about the origins of explanatory style, however, and thus we have summarized the pertinent research. Unaddressed by any study looking at the development of explanatory style is a normative question: Is the typical person an optimist, a pessimist, or expectationally neutral? Said another way, does something unusual in the course of development need to occur in order to impart to someone an optimistic explanatory style? Is optimism simply the developmental default, deep-wired into human beings by evolution (Tiger, 1979)? Or is pessimism the default? Or perhaps the child is a blank slate, equally able to become an optimist or a pessimist, depending on the idiosyncratic influences to which he or she is exposed throughout life.

Certainly many researchers have been drawn to the study of factors that make people pessi-

mistic, although it is not clear if they are assuming that optimism needs no special explanation or instead that pessimism is a more pressing concern. Regardless, positive psychologists need to be concerned with how optimism *and* pessimism develop. To foreshadow a point we emphasize in the next section of this chapter, we can assume neither that optimism is the simple opposite of pessimism nor that the determinants of optimism can be gleaned from the study of the determinants of pessimism.

Directions for Future Research: Explanatory Style as Positive Psychology

The current stage in learned helplessness research began with the reframing of explanatory style by Seligman (1990) in his book *Learned Optimism*, where he described how his lifelong interest into what can go wrong with people had changed into an interest in what can go right (cf. Seligman, 1975). Research on helplessness began to take an interest in what Seligman called optimism, although it could have been called mastery, effectance, or control. The term *optimism* is justified by the central concern in helplessness theory with expectations. It is worth emphasizing again, however, that these expectations tend not to be explicitly studied and, further, that these expectations are not about the future likelihood of good events but rather about the future contingency between events good or bad and responses.

In any event, let us address why optimism in general and explanatory style in particular should be subsumed under positive psychology. Given the checkered reputation of optimism, it is not completely obvious that optimism fits as readily into a positive psychology as do other topics such as courage, wisdom, and happiness.

What do we understand positive psychology to be? In his role as the 1998 American Psychological Association president, Martin Seligman called for psychology to be as focused on strength as weakness, as interested in building the best things in life as in repairing the worst, and as concerned with fulfilling the lives of normal people as with healing the wounds of the distressed. He dubbed this new focus *positive psychology*, and representative topics are those addressed in this first handbook on the topic. The past concern of psychology with human problems is of course understandable and will not be abandoned anytime in the foreseeable future. Problems always will exist that demand psychological solutions, but psychologists interested in promoting human potential need to pose different questions from their predecessors who assumed a disease model of human nature.

What presumably distinguishes positive psychology from the humanistic psychology of the 1960s and 1970s and from the positive thinking movement is its reliance on empirical research to understand the human condition (Peterson & Seligman, 1999). Humanists were skeptical about the scientific method and what it could yield, and yet they were unable to offer an alternative other than the insight that people were good. In contrast, positive psychologists see both strength and weakness as authentic and as amenable to scientific understanding. By this test, then, optimistic explanatory style qualifies as an important topic in positive psychology. The *data* show that explanatory style is linked to various manifestations of health and happiness as well as to human ills.

Attention to Outcome Measures

More needs to be done. In most explanatory style research, the focus has remained on outcomes of interest to the helplessness model: depression, illness, and failure. These are authentic and important topics, to be sure, but one typical way of measuring these outcomes assigns zero points that correspond to *not* being depressed, *not* being ill, and *not* failing. This limitation can be glossed over by researchers describing what the data actually show. For example, if we find that pessimistic individuals are depressed and physically ill (e.g., Peterson & Seligman, 1984; Peterson, Seligman, & Vaillant, 1988), we may glibly render this result as showing that optimistic people are happy and healthy, even if our outcome measures did not allow people to manifest happiness or health (e.g., Peterson & Bossio, 1991).

There is more to perseverance than the absence of helplessness (Peterson, 1999). There is more to happiness than the absence of depression (Myers & Diener, 1995), and there is more to health than the absence of illness (Seeman, 1989). A familiar sports cliché cautions that "playing not to lose" differs from "playing to win." But somehow these obvious points can be ignored when optimism researchers interpret their findings. So long as outcome measures reflect only degrees of pathology, no conclusions can be drawn about well-being. This is an important lesson for positive psychologists of all

stripes. It is not enough to study positive predictors like optimism or generativity; one must also study positive outcomes or, even better, outcomes that range from negative to positive. Only with this strategy will we have a complete positive psychology.

To be sure, some studies in the explanatory style tradition have included outcome measures that tap the full range of functioning. Usually these have been studies of performance, in academic (Peterson & Barrett, 1987), athletic (Seligman, Nolen-Hoeksema, Thornton, & Thornton, 1990), and vocational (Seligman & Schulman, 1986) domains. Here the expected positive correlation between optimistic explanatory style and good performance is found. Unreported in such studies, though, is whether the correlation is best described as a literal straight line as opposed to one that merely meanders in an upward direction.

The distinction is important because it allows researchers to distinguish between the costs of pessimism versus the benefits of optimism (Robinson-Whelen, Kim, MacCallum, & Kiecolt-Glasser, 1997). Let us illustrate. We had available some data that included a composite measure of explanatory style for bad events and a measure of good mood (Peterson et al., 2000), specifically the vigor subscale of the Profile of Mood States (McNair, Lorr, & Droppleman, 1971). In the entire sample, we found the expected positive correlation between optimistic explanatory style and good mood.

But then we split the sample on our measure of explanatory style, creating groups of pessimists and optimists, and we recomputed the correlation between explanatory style and good mood within each group. The correlation remained significant among the optimists, but it became nonsignificant among the pessimists. Said another way, given that someone was a pessimist (by our rough classification), degree of pessimism had no link to mood. Given that someone was an optimist, greater optimism was associated with better mood. We believe that this sort of analysis can lead to some provocative results, and thus is a strategy that positive psychologists should routinely follow. Consider one of the implications of the tentative findings we have just reported: Interventions that target pessimism will have no discernible effect on good mood until a certain threshold has been passed.

As explanatory style researchers heed this call to study positive as well as negative outcomes, explanatory style based on good events might become more relevant than it has seemed in past research looking at negative outcomes. Abramson et al. (1989) suggested that the way people explain the causes of good events is related to how they savor their effects. Perhaps good moods are created and sustained by such savoring, and positive psychologists like Fredrickson (1998) have directed our attention to the diverse benefits of positive emotions. According to Fredrickson's analysis, positive emotions broaden people's cognitive and behavioral repertoires. Perhaps thriving is under the sway of a "good" explanatory style just as helplessness is influenced by a "bad" explanatory style.

Attention to Mechanisms

A valid criticism of explanatory style research to date is that it has looked much more at correlations between explanatory style and distant adaptational outcomes than at the mechanisms that lead from explanatory style to these outcomes. This imbalance is ironic given that learned helplessness research with animals has in recent years taken an ever closer look at the psychological and biological mechanisms that produce the helplessness phenomenon (Peterson et al., 1993). Explanatory style researchers, in contrast, have rapidly moved from one outcome measure to another to still another. This restlessness has doubtlessly kept alive interest in explanatory style, but it has precluded a full understanding of learned helplessness.

Especially as explanatory style researchers join the positive psychology movement, greater attention to mechanisms is needed. So long as a researcher's focus was on helplessness deficits and close cognates like depression, it was probably less necessary to explain just how these deficits were produced. After all, by definition the learned helplessness phenomenon is a set of deficits. When researchers start to show that an optimistic explanatory style is linked to positive outcomes, more of an explanation in terms of mechanisms is demanded.

Despite the ostensible simplicity of the learned helplessness model, we can expect that numerous mechanisms can lead from explanatory style to outcomes and further that the particular mix of mechanisms will depend on the outcome of interest (Peterson & Bossio, 1991). Complicating any specification of the process by which explanatory style produces effects is the fact that the same construct, for example, mood, may be a mechanism in one case but an outcome in another.

Likely mechanisms are to be found on a variety of levels, starting with biology. For example, Kamen-Siegel, Rodin, Seligman, and Dwyer (1991) showed that optimistic explanatory style is correlated with the vigor with which the immune system responds to an antigen challenge. Emotional mechanisms also deserve attention, given the extensive research literature showing an optimistic explanatory style to be incompatible with depression (Sweeney, Anderson, & Bailey, 1986).

There are probably several cognitive pathways that link explanatory style and outcomes. Someone's explanatory style is not an isolated belief but rather part of a complex knowledge system that can influence well-being in numerous ways. Dykema, Bergbower, and Peterson (1995), for example, showed that individuals with an optimistic explanatory style see the world as less filled with hassles than do their pessimistic counterparts; in turn, this tendency is linked to better health.

In another example, Peterson and de Avila (1995) found that an optimistic explanatory style is associated with the belief that good health can be controlled (i.e., maintained and promoted). Indeed, they reported that an optimistic explanatory style is positively correlated with what has been described as an optimistic bias in risk perception (i.e., the tendency of people to see themselves as below average in the likelihood of falling ill). This correlation was completely accounted for by the belief that one was able to do things to reduce risk, suggesting that the bias may not have been simply wishful thinking.

Another explanation of why optimistic thinking is related to outcomes entails a social pathway. People with a pessimistic explanatory style often are socially isolated (Anderson & Arnault, 1985), and social isolation predicts poor adaptation in a wide variety of realms (Cohen & Syme, 1985). Conversely, people with an optimistic explanatory style may reap the benefits of rich social networks and appropriate social support.

As we see it, the most typical and robust mechanism linking explanatory style and outcomes entails behavior. So, Peterson (1988) found that an optimistic explanatory style was associated with a variety of healthy practices, such as exercising, drinking in moderation, and avoiding fatty foods. Peterson, Colvin, and Lin

(1992) similarly found that people with optimistic as opposed to pessimistic explanatory styles were more likely to respond to colds with such appropriate actions as resting and consuming more of Mom's chicken noodle soup.

In one of our recent studies of optimistic explanatory style and physical well-being, we looked at more than 1,000 individuals over almost 50 years (Peterson, Seligman, Yurko, Martin, & Friedman, 1998). Pessimistic individuals had an increased likelihood of early death, and the large sample size made it possible to investigate associations between explanatory style and death from different causes. Although we expected that death by cancer and cardiovascular disease would be especially linked to pessimistic thinking, we found that pessimistic individuals were most likely to die accidental deaths. This effect was particularly pronounced for men.

Accidental deaths are not random. "Being in the wrong place at the wrong time" may be the result of an incautious and fatalistic lifestyle entwined not only with pessimism but also with the male gender role. In this study, we could not tell what our deceased research participants were doing when they died accidentally, but we strongly suspect that their behaviors were implicated, if only by affecting the settings they habitually entered or not (Peterson et al., 2000).

Switching our attention to positive outcomes, we speculate that optimistic individuals may be more likely than pessimists to enter settings in which good things can and do happen. The more general point is that positive psychologists should not look just within the person but also at the person's setting. Optimism may influence the settings that people choose as well as what they do in these settings. Just as important, settings differ in the degree to which they allow positive characteristics to develop and be deployed. Positive psychology should not decontextualize the strengths and abilities that make possible the good life; congratulating the winner should be no more a part of psychology than blaming the victim (cf. Ryan, 1978).

References

Abramson, L. Y., Metalsky, G. I., & Alloy, L. B. (1989). Hopelessness depression: A theory-based subtype of depression. *Psychological Review, 96,* 358–372.

*Abramson, L. Y., Seligman, M. E. P., & Teasdale, J. D. (1978). Learned helplessness in humans: Critique and reformulation. *Journal of Abnormal Psychology, 87,* 49–74.

Anderson, C. A., & Arnault, L. H. (1985). Attributional style and everyday problems in living: Depression, loneliness, and shyness. *Social Cognition, 3,* 16–35.

Bandura, A. (1977). *Social learning theory.* Englewood Cliffs, NJ: Prentice-Hall.

Brown, I., & Inouye, D. K. (1978). Learned helplessness through modeling: The role of perceived similarity in competence. *Journal of Personality and Social Psychology, 36,* 900–908.

*Buchanan, G. M., & Seligman, M. E. P. (Eds.). (1995). *Explanatory style.* Hillsdale, NJ: Erlbaum.

Bunce, S. C., Larsen, R. J., & Peterson, C. (1995). Life after trauma: Personality and daily life experiences of traumatized people. *Journal of Personality, 63,* 165–188.

Cerezo, M. A., & Frias, D. (1994). Emotional and cognitive adjustment in abused children. *Child Abuse and Neglect, 18,* 923–932.

Cohen, S., & Syme, S. L. (1985). *Social support and health.* Orlando, FL: Academic Press.

Dweck, C. S. (1999). *Self-theories: Their role in motivation, personality, and development.* Philadelphia: Psychology Press.

Dykema, J., Bergbower, K., & Peterson, C. (1995). Pessimistic explanatory style, stress, and illness. *Journal of Social and Clinical Psychology, 14,* 357–371.

Franz, C. E., McClelland, D. C., Weinberger, J., & Peterson, C. (1994). Parenting antecedents of adult adjustment: A longitudinal study. In C. Perris, W. A. Arrindell, & M. Eisemann (Eds.), *Parenting and psychopathology* (pp. 127–144). San Diego, CA: Academic Press.

Fredrickson, B. L. (1998). What good are positive emotions? *Review of General Psychology, 2,* 300–319.

Gerbner, G., & Gross, L. (1976). Living with television: The violence profile. *Journal of Communication, 26,* 173–199.

Gillham, J. E., Reivich, K. J., Jaycox, L. H., & Seligman, M. E. P. (1995). Prevention of depressive symptoms in schoolchildren: Two-year follow-up. *Psychological Science, 6,* 343–351.

Gold, E. R. (1986). Long-term effects of sexual victimization in childhood: An attributional approach. *Journal of Consulting and Clinical Psychology, 54,* 471–475.

Hearn, G. (1991). Entertainment manna: Does television viewing lead to appetitive helplessness? *Psychological Reports, 68,* 1179–1184.

Heyman, G. D., Dweck, C. S., & Cain, K. M. (1992). Young children's vulnerability to self-blame and helplessness: Relationship to beliefs about goodness. *Child Development, 63,* 401–415.

Holloway, S. D., & Hess, R. D. (1982). Causal explanations for school performance: Contrasts between mothers and children. *Journal of Applied Developmental Psychology, 3,* 319–327.

Holloway, S. D., Kashiwagi, K., Hess, R. D., & Azuma, H. (1986). Causal attributions by Japanese and American mothers and children about performance in mathematics. *International Journal of Psychology, 21,* 269–286.

Kamen-Siegel, L., Rodin, J., Seligman, M. E. P., & Dwyer, J. (1991). Explanatory style and cell-mediated immunity. *Health Psychology, 10,* 229–235.

Kaslow, N. J., Rehm, L. P., Pollack, S. L., & Siegel, A. W. (1988). Attributional style and self-control behavior in depressed and nondepressed children and their parents. *Journal of Abnormal Child Psychology, 16,* 163–175.

Kelley, H. H. (1973). The process of causal attribution. *American Psychologist, 28,* 107–128.

Levine, G. F. (1977). "Learned helplessness" and the evening news. *Journal of Communication, 27,* 100–105.

*Maier, S. F., & Seligman, M. E. P. (1976). Learned helplessness: Theory and evidence. *Journal of Experimental Psychology: General, 105,* 3–46.

Marks, S. B. (1998). Understanding and preventing learned helplessness in children who are congenitally deaf-blind. *Journal of Visual Impairment and Blindness, 92,* 200–211.

McNair, D., Lorr, M., & Droppleman, L. (1971). *Manual for the Profile of Mood States.* San Diego, CA: Educational and Industrial Testing Service.

Mikulincer, M. (1994). *Human learned helplessness: A coping perspective.* New York: Plenum.

Mueller, C. M., & Dweck, C. S. (1998). Praise for intelligence can undermine children's motivation and performance. *Journal of Personality and Social Psychology, 75,* 32–52.

Myers, D. G., & Diener, E. (1995). Who is happy? *Psychological Science, 6,* 10–19.

Nielsen Media Research. (1998). *1998 report on television.* New York: Nielsen Media Research.

Nolen-Hoeksema, S. (1986). *Developmental studies of explanatory style, and learned helplessness in children.* Unpublished doctoral dissertation, University of Pennsylvania, Philadelphia.

Nolen-Hoeksema, S. (1987). Sex differences in depression: Theory and evidence. *Psychological Bulletin, 101,* 259–282.

Overmier, J. B., & Seligman, M. E. P. (1967). Effects of inescapable shock upon subsequent escape and avoidance learning. *Journal of Comparative and Physiological Psychology, 63,* 23–33.

Parsons, J. E., Adler, T. F., & Kaczala, C. M. (1982). Socialization of achievement attitudes and beliefs: Parental influences. *Child Development, 53,* 310–321.

Perez-Bouchard, L., Johnson, J. L., & Ahrens, A. H. (1993). Attributional style in children of substance abusers. *American Journal of Drug and Alcohol Abuse, 19,* 475–489.

Peterson, C. (1988). Explanatory style as a risk factor for illness. *Cognitive Therapy and Research, 12,* 117–130.

*Peterson, C. (1991). Meaning and measurement of explanatory style. *Psychological Inquiry, 2,* 1–10.

Peterson, C. (1999). Personal control and well-being. In D. Kahneman, E. Diener, & N. Schwarz (Eds.), *Well-being: The foundations of hedonic psychology* (pp. 288–301). New York: Russell Sage.

Peterson, C., & Barrett, L. C. (1987). Explanatory style and academic performance among university freshmen. *Journal of Personality and Social Psychology, 53,* 603–607.

*Peterson, C., & Bossio, L. M. (1991). *Health and optimism.* New York: Free Press.

Peterson, C., Colvin, D., & Lin, E. H. (1992). Explanatory style and helplessness. *Social Behavior and Personality, 20,* 1–14.

Peterson, C., & de Avila, M. E. (1995). Optimistic explanatory style and the perception of health problems. *Journal of Clinical Psychology, 51,* 128–132.

*Peterson, C., Maier, S. F., & Seligman, M. E. P. (1993). *Learned helplessness: A theory for the age of personal control.* New York: Oxford University Press.

Peterson, C., Moon, C. H., Fletcher, C., Michaels, C. E., Bishop, M. P., Smith, J. A., & Michaels, A. J. (2000). *Explanatory style as a risk factor for traumatic mishaps.* Unpublished manuscript, University of Michigan, Ann Arbor.

Peterson, C., & Park, C. (1998). Learned helplessness and explanatory style. In D. F. Barone, M. Hersen, & V. B. Van Hasselt (Eds.), *Advanced personality* (pp. 287–310). New York: Plenum.

Peterson, C., Schulman, P., Castellon, C., & Seligman, M. E. P. (1992). CAVE: Content analysis of verbatim explanations. In C. P. Smith (Ed.), *Motivation and personality: Handbook of thematic content analysis* (pp. 383–392). New York: Cambridge University Press.

*Peterson, C., & Seligman, M. E. P. (1984). Causal explanations as a risk factor for depression: Theory and evidence. *Psychological Review, 91,* 347–374.

Peterson, C., & Seligman, M. E. P. (1999). Psychology. *Yearbook of science and the future 2000* (pp. 372–375). Chicago: Encyclopaedia Britannica.

Peterson, C., Seligman, M. E. P., & Vaillant, G. E. (1988). Pessimistic explanatory style is a risk factor for physical illness: A thirty-five-year longitudinal study. *Journal of Personality and Social Psychology, 55,* 23–27.

Peterson, C., Seligman, M. E. P., Yurko, K. H., Martin, L. R., & Friedman, H. S. (1998). Catastrophizing and untimely death. *Psychological Science, 9,* 49–52.

Peterson, C., Semmel, A., von Baeyer, C., Abramson, L. Y., Metalsky, G. I., & Seligman, M. E. P. (1982). The Attributional Style Questionnaire. *Cognitive Therapy and Research, 6,* 287–299.

Porter, E. H. (1913). *Pollyanna.* London: Harrap.

Rabkin, J. G., Remien, R., Katoff, L., & Williams, J. B. (1993). Resilience in adversity among long-term survivors of AIDS. *Hospital and Community Psychiatry, 44,* 162–167.

Robinson-Whelen, S., Kim, C., MacCallum, R. C., & Kiecolt-Glaser, J. K. (1997). Distinguishing optimism from pessimism in older adults: Is it important to be optimistic or not be pessimistic? *Journal of Personality and Social Psychology, 73,* 1345–1353.

Rothbaum, F., Weisz, J. R., & Snyder, S. S. (1982). Changing the world versus changing the self: A two-process theory of perceived control. *Journal of Personality and Social Psychology, 42,* 5–37.

Ryan, W. (1978). *Blaming the victim* (Rev. ed.). New York: Random House.

Schill, R. A., & Marcus, D. K. (1998). Incarceration and learned helplessness. *International Journal of Offender Therapy and Comparative Criminology, 42,* 224–232.

Schulman, P., Keith, D., & Seligman, M. E. P. (1993). Is optimism heritable? A study of twins. *Behaviour Research and Therapy, 31,* 569–574.

Seeman, J. (1989). Toward a model of positive health. *American Psychologist, 44,* 1099–1109.

*Seligman, M. E. P. (1975). *Helplessness: On depression, development, and death.* San Francisco: Freeman.

*Seligman, M. E. P. (1990). *Learned optimism.* New York: Knopf.

Seligman, M. E. P. (1998). Positive social science. *APA Monitor, 29* (4), 2, 5.

Seligman, M. E. P., Castellon, C., Cacciola, J., Schulman, P., Luborsky, L., Ollove, M., & Downing, R. (1988). Explanatory style change during cognitive therapy for unipolar depression. *Journal of Abnormal Psychology, 97,* 13–18.

Seligman, M. E. P., & Maier, S. F. (1967). Failure to escape traumatic shock. *Journal of Experimental Psychology, 74,* 1–9.

Seligman, M. E. P., Nolen-Hoeksema, S., Thornton, N., & Thornton, K. (1990). Explanatory style as a mechanism of disappointing athletic performance. *Psychological Science, 1,* 143–146.

Seligman, M. E. P., Peterson, C., Kaslow, N. J., Tanenbaum, R. L., Alloy, L. B., & Abramson, L. Y. (1984). Attributional style and depressive symptoms among children. *Journal of Abnormal Psychology, 93,* 235–238.

*Seligman, M. E. P., Reivich, K., Jaycox, L., & Gillham, J. (1995). *The optimistic child.* New York: Harper Perennial.

Seligman, M. E. P., & Schulman, P. (1986). Explanatory style as a predictor of productivity and quitting among life insurance sales agents. *Journal of Personality and Social Psychology, 50,* 832–838.

Shaver, K. G. (1975). *An introduction to attribution processes.* Cambridge, MA: Winthrop.

Simkin, D. K., Lederer, J. P., & Seligman, M. E. P. (1983). Learned helplessness in groups. *Behaviour Research and Therapy, 21,* 613–622.

Snyder, C. R. (1994). *The psychology of hope: You can get there from here.* New York: Free Press.

Sweeney, P. D., Anderson, K., & Bailey, S. (1986). Attributional style in depression: A meta-analytic review. *Journal of Personality and Social Psychology, 50,* 974–991.

Tiger, L. (1979). *Optimism: The biology of hope.* New York: Simon and Schuster.

Turk, E., & Bry, B. H. (1992). Adolescents' and parents' explanatory styles and parents' causal explanations about their adolescents. *Cognitive Therapy and Research, 16,* 349–357.

Vanden Belt, A., & Peterson, C. (1991). Parental explanatory style and its relationship to the classroom performance of disabled and nondisabled children. *Cognitive Therapy and Research, 15,* 331–341.

Voltaire, F. (1759). *Candide, ou L'Optimisme.* Geneva: Cramer.

Walker, L. E. (1977–1978). Battered women and learned helplessness. *Victimology, 2,* 525–534.

Weiner, B. (1974). *Achievement motivation and attribution theory.* Morristown, NJ: General Learning Press.

Yamauchi, H. (1989). Congruence of causal attributions for school performance given by children and mothers. *Psychological Reports, 64,* 359–363.

19

Hope Theory

A Member of the Positive Psychology Family

C. R. Snyder, Kevin L. Rand, & David R. Sigmon

An Introduction to Hope Theory

The Birth of a Theory

A new theory typically begins with the proponents offering a model that supposedly is more heuristic than the prevailing, older view. Our development of hope theory began in this manner. So, what was the accepted scholarly view of hope that we sought to alter? The perception that one's goals can be attained was a common thread in the scholarly work that defined hope in the 1950s through 1960s (Cantril, 1964; Farber, 1968; Frank, 1975; Frankl, 1992; Melges & Bowlby, 1969; Menninger, 1959; Schachtel, 1959). Our hypothesis was that this view, although shared by many previous scholars, did not fully capture that which is involved in hopeful goal-directed thought. At this beginning stage, we sought a definition of hope that was at once more inclusive and relatively parsimonious. Although we sensed that this new view of hope was possible and necessary, we were not sure what

that model would be. Our breakthrough came when we followed a suggestion made by a former colleague, Fritz Heider, that we ask people to talk about their goal-directed thoughts. After participating in informal interviews about their goal-directed thought processes, people repeatedly mentioned the pathways to reach their goals *and* their motivation to use those pathways. Recall the previous view of hope as "the perception that one can reach desired goals"; it was as if people were suggesting that this overall process involved two components of goal-directed thought—pathways and agency. With some listening on our part, a new theory was born. Simply put, hopeful thought reflects the belief that one can find pathways to desired goals and become motivated to use those pathways. We also proposed that hope, so defined, serves to drive the emotions and well-being of people. Having given this very brief history of that which has come to be called hope theory, in the remainder of this section we will describe the various aspects of this theory in detail.

Goals

We begin with the assumption that human actions are goal directed. Accordingly, goals are the targets of mental action sequences, and they provide the cognitive component that anchors hope theory (Snyder, 1994a, 1994c, 1998b; Snyder, Cheavens, & Sympson, 1997; Snyder, Sympson, Michael, & Cheavens, 2000; Stotland, 1969). Goals may be short- or long-term, but they need to be of sufficient value to occupy conscious thought. Likewise, goals must be attainable, but they also typically contain some degree of uncertainty. On this latter point, when people have been interviewed, they report that hope flourishes under probabilities of intermediate goal attainment (Averill, Catlin, & Chon, 1990).

Pathways Thinking

In order to reach their goals, people must view themselves as being capable of generating workable routes to those goals.[1] This process, which we call *pathways thinking*, signifies one's perceived capabilities at generating workable routes to desired goals. Likewise, we have found that this pathways thinking is typified by affirming internal messages that are similar to the appellation "I'll find a way to get this done!" (Snyder, Lapointe, Crowson, & Early, 1998).

Pathways thinking in any given instantiation involves thoughts of being able to generate at least one, and often more, usable route to a desired goal. The production of several pathways is important when encountering impediments, and high-hope persons perceive that they are facile at finding such alternate routes; moreover, high-hope people actually are very effective at producing alternative routes (Irving, Snyder, & Crowson, 1998; Snyder, Harris, et al., 1991).

Agency Thinking

The motivational component in hope theory is agency—the perceived capacity to use one's pathways so as to reach desired goals. Agentic thinking reflects the self-referential thoughts about both starting to move along a pathway and continuing to progress along that pathway. We have found that high-hope people embrace such self-talk agentic phrases as "I can do this" and "I am not going to be stopped" (Snyder et al., 1998). Agentic thinking is important in all

goal-directed thought, but it takes on special significance when people encounter impediments. During such instances of blockage, agency helps the person to apply the requisite motivation to the best alternate pathway (Snyder, 1994c).

Adding Pathways and Agentic Thinking

It is important to emphasize that hopeful thinking necessitates *both* the perceived capacity to envision workable routes *and* goal-directed energy. Thus, hope is "a positive motivational state that is based on an interactively derived sense of successful (1) agency (goal-directed energy) and (2) pathways (planning to meet goals)" (Snyder, Irving, & Anderson, 1991, p. 287). In the progression of hopeful thinking in the goal-pursuit sequence, we hypothesize that pathways thinking increases agency thinking, which, in turn, yields further pathways thinking, and so on. Overall, therefore, pathway and agency thoughts are iterative as well as additive over the course of a given sequence of goal-directed cognitions (see Snyder, Harris, et al., 1991).

Hope, Impediments, and Emotion

Although most other views have characterized hope as an emotion (Farina, Hearth, & Popovich, 1995), we have emphasized the thinking processes in hope theory. Specifically, we posit that positive emotions should flow from perceptions of successful goal pursuit. Perception of successful goal pursuit may result from unimpeded movement toward desired goals, or it may reflect instances in which the protagonist has effectively overcome any problems or blockages. Negative emotions, on the other hand, are the product of unsuccessful goal pursuits. The perceptions of unsuccessful goal pursuit can stem from insufficient agentic and/or pathway thinking or the inability to overcome a thwarting circumstance. We thus are proposing that *goal-pursuit cognitions cause emotions*.

Related to these points, through both correlational and causal methodologies, we have found that persons confronted with insurmountable goal blockages experience negative emotions, whereas successful, unimpeded goal pursuit or successful goal pursuit after overcoming impediments yields positive emotions (Snyder et al., 1996). These findings parallel those from other laboratories, where people who encounter severe difficulties in pursuit of important goals report lessened well-being (Diener, 1984; Emmons, 1986; Little, 1983; Omodei & Wearing, 1990; Palys & Little, 1983; Ruehlman & Wolchik, 1988). Furthermore, the growing consensus is that the perceived lack of progress toward major goals is the cause of reductions in well-being, rather than vice versa (Brunstein, 1993; Little, 1989).

Full Hope Model

Moving from left to right in Figure 19.1, one can see the proposed temporal order of the goal-directed thought sequence in hope theory. The etiology of the pathways and agency thoughts appears at the far left. Newborns undertake pathways thinking immediately after birth in order to obtain a sense of "what goes with what" (i.e., what events seem to be correlated in time with each other; Schulman, 1991). Over the course of childhood, these lessons eventually become refined so that the child understands the process of causation (i.e., events are not just related in time, but one event elicits another event). Additionally, at approximately 1 year of age, the baby realizes that she or he is separate from other entities (including the caregiver). This process, called *psychological birth*, portends another important insight for the very young child—that he or she can cause such chains of events to happen. That is to say, the self is perceived as a causal instigator. These psychological birth and instigator "lessons" contribute to a sense of personal agency.

In summary, the acquisition of goal-directed hopeful thought is absolutely crucial for the child's survival and thriving. As such, parents, caregivers, teachers, and members of society in general are invested in teaching this hopeful thinking. For the reader who is interested in detailed descriptions of the developmental antecedents of the hope process, we would suggest previous writings on this topic (e.g., McDermott & Snyder, 2000, pp. 5–18; Snyder,

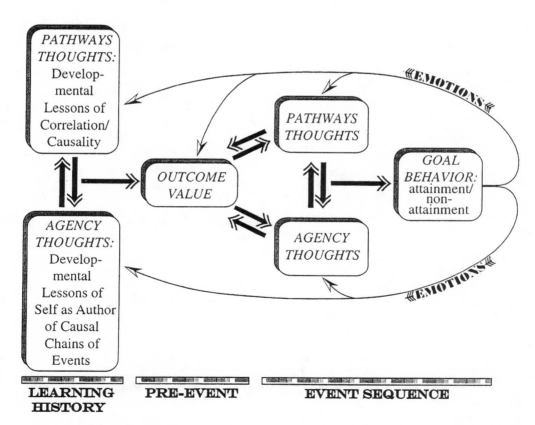

Figure 19.1 Schematic of Feed-forward and Feed-back Functions Involving Agency and Pathways Goal-Directed Thoughts in Hope Theory.

1994c, pp. 75–114; Snyder, 2000a, pp. 21–37; Snyder, McDermott, Cook, & Rapoff 1997, pp. 1–32).

As shown in Figure 19.1, "outcome value" becomes important in the pre-event analysis phase. If the imagined outcomes have sufficiently high importance so as to demand continued mental attention, then the person moves to the event sequence analysis phase wherein the pathways and agency thoughts iterate. Sometimes, however, the iterative process of pathways and agency thinking may cycle back in order to assure that the outcome remains of sufficient importance to warrant continued goal-directed processing. In turn, pathways and agency thoughts (as shown in the bidirectional arrows) continue to alternate and aggregate (summate) throughout the event sequence so as to influence the subsequent level of success in any given goal pursuit. The left-to-right broad-lined arrows of Figure 19.1 reflect the overall feed-*forward* flow of hopeful goal-directed thinking.

If a particular goal pursuit has been completed, the person's goal attainment (or nonattainment) thoughts and the resultant success-derived positive (or failure-derived negative) emotions should cycle back to influence subsequent perceived pathways and agentic capabilities in that situation and in general, as well as to impact the outcome value. As shown in the narrow-lined, right-to-left arrows in Figure 19.1, the feedback process is composed of the particular emotions that result from perceived successful or unsuccessful goal attainment. It is important to note, therefore, that hope theory involves an interrelated system of goal-directed thinking that is responsive to feedback at various points in the temporal sequence.

Individual-Differences Scales Derived From Hope Theory

One important step in the evolution of a new psychological theory is the development of individual-differences measures that accurately reflect the structure of the construct and are reliable and valid. Individual-differences measures allow for tests of a theory, and they facilitate the application of a given construct to research and applied settings. We report next on the development of three such instruments for measuring hope.[2]

Trait Hope Scale

The adult Trait Hope Scale (Snyder, Harris, et al., 1991) consists of four agency, four pathways, and four distracter items. In completing the items, respondents are asked to imagine themselves across time and situational contexts. This instrument demonstrates (a) both internal and temporal reliability, with two separate yet related agency and pathways factors, as well as an overarching hope factor (Babyak, Snyder, & Yoshinobu, 1993); and (b) extensive convergent and discriminant validational support (Cheavens, Gum, & Snyder, 2000; Snyder, Harris, et al., 1991). The Trait Hope Scale is shown in Appendix A.

State Hope Scale

The State Hope Scale (Snyder et al., 1996) has three agency and three pathways items in which respondents describe themselves in terms of how they are "right now." Numerous studies support the internal reliability and factor structure, as well as the convergent and discriminant validity of this scale (Feldman & Snyder, 2000; Snyder et al., 1996). The State Hope Scale is shown in Appendix B.

Children's Hope Scale

The Children's Hope Scale (for ages 8 to 16) (Snyder, Hoza, et al., 1997) comprises three agency and three pathways items. The internal and test-retest reliabilities of this scale have been documented, as has its two-factor structure. Relevant studies also support its convergent and discriminant validities (Moon & Snyder, 2000; Snyder, Hoza, et al., 1997). The Children's Hope Scale is shown in Appendix C.

Similarities Between Hope Theory and Other Positive Psychology Theories

We now turn to the relationships that hope theory has with five other related theories in the positive psychology family. Fortunately for the process of making comparison with hope theory, in addition to thorough theoretical expositions, each of these five other theories has an individual-differences scale. Our premise is that hope theory should manifest some relationship similarities to these other constructs so as to support its being part of the positive psychology group (i.e., convergent validity), and yet it should have sufficient differences so as not to be a proxy for an already existing theory (i.e., discriminant validity). We have prepared Table 19.1 to highlight the shared and not-shared components of the theories, as well as the relative emphases in each theory.[3]

Optimism: Seligman

Abramson, Seligman, and Teasdale (1978) emphasized attributions that people made for important negative life events in their reformulated helplessness model. In a subsequent evolution of those ideas, Seligman (1991) uses the attribution process as the basis for his theory of optimism (see Table 19.1). In this regard, the optimistic attributional style is the pattern of external, variable, and specific attributions for failures instead of internal, stable, and global attributes that were the focus in the earlier helplessness model.[4] Implicit in this theory is the importance placed on negative outcomes, and there is a goal-related quality in that optimistic people are attempting to distance themselves from negative outcomes. In hope theory, however, the focus is on reaching desired future positive goal-related outcomes, with explicit

emphases on the agency and pathways thoughts about the desired goal. In both theories, the outcome must be of high importance, although this is emphasized more in hope theory. Unlike the Seligman optimism theory, hope theory also explicitly addresses the etiology of positive and negative emotions.

Optimism: Scheier and Carver

Scheier and Carver (1985) emphasize generalized outcome expectancies in their theory and assume that optimism is a goal-based approach that occurs when an outcome has substantial value. In this optimism model, people perceive themselves as being able to move toward desirable goals and away from undesirable goals (antigoals; Carver & Scheier, 2000a). Although pathways-like thoughts and agency-involved thoughts are implicit in their model, the outcome expectancies (similar to agency) are seen as the prime elicitors of goal-directed behaviors (Scheier & Carver, 1985, 1987). Thus, Scheier and Carver emphasize agency-like thought, whereas equal and constantly iterative emphases are given to pathways and agent thoughts in hope theory (see Table 19.1).[5] Both hope theory and optimism theory are cognitive and explain behavior across situations (Snyder, 1995); moreover, measures of the two constructs cor-

Table 19.1 Implicit and Explicit Operative Processes and Their Respective Emphases in Hope Theory as Compared with Selected Positive Psychology Theories

Operative Process	Hope	Optimism: Seligman	Optimism: Scheier & Carver	Self-efficacy	Self-esteem	Problem-Solving
Attributions		+++				
Outcome Value	++	+	++	++	+	+
Goal-Related Thinking	+++	+	++	+++	+	+++
Perceived Capacities for Agency-Related Thinking	+++		+++	+++		
Perceived Capacities for Pathways-Related Thinking	+++		+	++		+++

+ Operative process is implicit part of model.
++ Operative process is explicit part of model.
+++ Operative process is explicit and emphasized in model.
Thus, interpret more plus signs (none to + to ++ to +++) as signifying greater emphasis attached to the given operative process within a particular theory.

relate in the .50 range (Snyder, Harris, et al., 1991). It should be noted, however, that hope has produced unique variance beyond optimism in the prediction of several variables, and that the factor structures of these two constructs differ (Magaletta & Oliver, 1999). Finally, these two theories differ in that hope theory describes the etiology of emotions (positive and negative), whereas Scheier and Carver are largely silent on this issue.

Self-Efficacy: Bandura

According to Bandura (1982, 1997), for self-efficacy to be activated, a goal-related outcome must be important enough to capture attention. This premise is similar to that held in hope theory. Although others have devised a trait measure of self-efficacy,[6] Bandura has steadfastly held that the cognitive processing in self-efficacy theory must focus on situation-specific goals. This goal emphasis parallels hope theory, but it differs in that for hope theory there may be enduring, cross-situational, and situational goal-directed thoughts. Within self-efficacy theory, the person is posited to analyze the relevant contingencies in a given goal attainment situation (called *outcome expectancies*, somewhat similar to pathways thought). Relative to the outcome expectancies wherein the focus is on the given contingencies, pathways thinking reflects the self-analysis of one's capabilities to produce initial routes to goals, as well as additional routes should the first become impeded. Thereafter, the person is hypothesized to evaluate her capacity to carry out the actions inherent in the outcome expectancies (called *efficacy expectancies*, with some similarity to agency thought). Whereas the efficacy expectancy emphasizes the personal perception about how a person *can* perform the requisite activities in a given situational context, hope theory emphasizes the person's self-referential belief that she or he will initiate (and continue) the requisite actions. A key difference is between the words *can* and *will*, with the former pertaining to the capacity to act and the latter tapping intentionality to act. Bandura posits that the situational self-efficacy (agency) thoughts are the last and most important cognitive step before initiating goal-directed action (see Table 19.1), whereas both agency and pathways thoughts are emphasized prior to and during the goal-pursuit sequence in hope theory. Ma-

galetta and Oliver (1999) report that hope provides unique variance independent of self-efficacy in predicting well-being, and that the factor structures of the two constructs vary. One final difference is worthy of note. Namely, Bandura's self-efficacy theory does not address the issue of emotions per se, whereas hope theory gives an explicit hypothesis about emotions being the result of goal-directed thoughts.

Self-Esteem

Hewitt (1998) concludes that self-esteem reflects the emotions flowing from persons' appraisals of their overall effectiveness in the conduct of their lives.[7] In the words of Coopersmith (1967), "Self-esteem is the personal judgment of worthiness" (p. 7). Additionally, self-esteem models are implicitly built on goal-directed thoughts (Hewitt, 1998; see Table 19.1), and they assume that an activity must be valued to implicate self-esteem. These latter two characteristics also apply in hope theory, but the emphasis in hope theory is on the analysis of the goal-pursuit process that elicits emotion or esteem. Self-esteem and hope correlate in the .45 range (Snyder, Harris, et al., 1991), but there is research support for the theoretical assumption that goal-pursuit thoughts (i.e., hope) influence esteem and not vice versa. It also has been reported that hope enhances the prediction of several positive outcomes beyond self-esteem (Curry, Snyder, Cook, Ruby, & Rehm, 1997; Snyder, Cheavens, & Michael, 1999).

Problem Solving

In problem-solving theory, the person's identification of a desired goal (a problem solution) is explicitly noted, and it is assumed implicitly that an important goal is involved (see Table 19.1; Heppner & Hillerbrand, 1991). Another major explicit emphasis, similar to that in hope theory, is on finding a pathway that is the basis for a problem-solving solution (D'Zurilla, 1986). Relative to problem-solving theories, the agentic thinking in hope theory is posited to provide the motivation to activate pathways thoughts (problem solving), and agency is thus explicit and emphasized. Significant positive correlations (rs of .40 to .50) have been found between hope and problem solving (Snyder, Harris, et al., 1991). Problem-solving theory does not touch upon the topic of emotions, whereas in hope theory the emotions are posited to result from the perceived success in goal pursuits.

Summary of Shared Processes in Theories

Although there are differences relative to hope theory to be discerned in our discussion of these five theories, one can see considerable overlap (with varying emphases) in the plus signs of hope theory and the plus signs of the other positive psychology constructs (see Table 19.1). Also, these theory-based similarities are buttressed by modest correlations between hope measures and the scales derived from each of the other theories. Finally, as a point that we believe is of considerable importance, hope and the other theories share in providing psychological and physical benefits to people, and they all are members of the positive psychology family.

Hope and Looking Through a Positive Psychology Lens

Elsewhere, we have written that the positive psychology lens "reflects the viewpoint that the most favorable of human functioning capabilities can be studied scientifically, and that . . . we should not be minuscule in our focus, but rather positive psychology should embrace many foci—a wide lens that is suitable for a big topic" (Snyder & McCullough, 2000, pp. 151–152). By adding hope theory, we have yet another research framework for understanding and enhancing adaptive ways of functioning that are the foci in positive psychology. In this section, we report on the various topics that have been looked at through the frame of hope theory.

Academics

Learning and performing well in educational settings are important avenues for thriving in American society. By applying hopeful thinking, students should enhance their perceived capabilities of finding multiple pathways to desired educational goals, along with the motivations to pursue those goals. Also, through hopeful thinking, students should be able to stay "on task" and not be blocked by interfering self-deprecatory thoughts and negative emotions (Snyder, 1999a).

Based on presently available research with grade school, high school, and college students, it appears that hope bears a substantial relationship with academic achievement (Snyder, Cheavens, & Michael, 1999). Hope relates to higher achievement test scores (grade school children; Snyder, Hoza, et al., 1997) and higher semester grade point averages (college students; Curry et al., 1997). In a 6-year longitudinal study, Hope Scale scores taken at the beginning of students' very first semester in college predicted higher cumulative grade point average[8] and graduation rate, as well as lower attrition (as tapped by dropout rate; Snyder, Wiklund, & Cheavens, 1999).[9] Imagine the negative ripples—lost opportunities, unfulfilled talents, and sense of failure—that may flow over a lifetime for some students who drop out of high school or college. Hope may offer a potential antidote.

Given the predictive power of the Hope Scale for academics, perhaps it also could be used to identify academically at-risk low-hope students who would especially profit by interventions to raise their hopeful thinking. Or such hope interventions may be targeted toward all students irrespective of their initial levels of hope. There are many opportunities to apply hope to the benefit of students. Indeed, interventions for schools already are being developed. For example, a college class aimed at teaching hopeful thinking could help students to improve their levels of hope and academic performances and, in turn, self-esteem. This is what has been found in an ongoing 6-year project at the University of Wyoming (Curry, Maniar, Sondag, & Sandstedt, 1999). Yet another approach that we are testing involves the beneficial effects of hope training for new college students during their first orientation week. Likewise, Lopez and his colleagues (Lopez, Bouwkamp, Edwards, & Teramoto Pedrotti, 2000) have had promising early results in a program for promoting hope in junior high students. Starting even earlier with students, perhaps we should explore how to maximize hopeful learning environments of children in grade schools.[10]

Athletics

Two athletes may have similar natural talents, and yet the more hopeful one should be more successful, especially during stressful points in their competitions (see Curry & Snyder, 2000). This follows because high-hope thinking enables an athlete to find the best routes to the goal in a given sport, as well as the motivation to use those routes. In support of these predictions, we (Curry, Snyder, et al., 1997) have found that Division I college track athletes with high as compared with low hope perform significantly better in their events (even when removing the variance related to natural athletic ability as rated by their coaches). In another study by Curry et al. (1997), athletes' trait and state hope together accounted for 56% of the variance related to their actual track performances.

Sports psychologists and coaches can use hope theory in working with individual athletes and teams. Actual courses to impart hope also should prove beneficial. In this regard, a college class titled "Principles of Optimal Performance" has been operating for several years, with resulting significant improvements in athletes' confidence in their performances (these benefits have been maintained at a 1-year follow-up; see Curry & Snyder, 2000).

Physical Health

In health psychology, the focus is on promoting and maintaining good health and preventing, detecting, and treating illness (Matarazzo, 1982). Based on our research, hope has been positively implicated in each of these areas (Irving et al., 1998; Snyder, 1996, 1998a; Snyder, Irving, & Anderson, 1991). Snyder, Feldman, Taylor, Schroeder, and Adams (2000) have described the powers of hope in terms of primary and secondary prevention. Primary prevention involves thoughts or actions that are intended to reduce or eliminate the chances that subsequent health problems (either physical [Kaplan, 2000] or psychological [Heller, Wyman, & Allen, 2000]) will occur in the future. Secondary prevention involves thoughts or actions that are directed at eliminating, reducing, or containing a problem once it has occurred (Snyder, Feldman, et al., 2000).

At the individual level, hope and the primary prevention of physical illness have begun to receive some attention. People with higher levels of hope seem to use information about physical illness to their advantage (Snyder, Feldman, et al., 2000). High-hope persons use information about the etiology of illness to do more of what helps and less of what hurts. Within the frame-

work of hope theory, knowledge is used as a pathway for prevention. Related to this point, women with higher as compared with lower hope have performed better on a cancer facts test, even when controlling for their academic performances and their contacts with other persons who have had cancer (Irving et al., 1998). In addition, higher hope women reported higher intentions to engage in cancer prevention activities than their lower hope counterparts. Additionally, people with high hope report engaging in more preventative behaviors (i.e., physical exercise) than those with low hope (Snyder, Harris, et al., 1991). Therefore, the scant available research does suggest that hopeful thinking is related to activities that help to prevent physical illness.

Beyond the individual level of primary prevention, hope theory can be applied at the societal level in order to prevent physical illness. Societal primary prevention involves thinking that reduces risks and inoculates entire segments of society against disease (Snyder, Feldman, et al., 2000). Societal primary prevention includes increasing desired behaviors and decreasing targeted bad behaviors through the use of advertisements, laws, and shared social values. Likewise, in the degree to which a society implements open and fair systems for obtaining the rewards, the negative repercussions of mass frustration should be quelled. For example, if established laws are perceived as fairly allowing all (or a maximal number of) people to pursue goal-directed activities, then citizens are less likely to become frustrated and act aggressively (Snyder, 1993, 1994b; Snyder & Feldman, 2000). This would result in fewer physical injuries in society. Related to this latter point, Krauss and Krauss (1968) found that the lack of profound goal blockages in countries across the world was associated subsequently with fewer deaths from suicide.

Once a physical illness develops, hope still plays an important role, but it does so in the context of secondary prevention. For example, hope should facilitate one's coping with the pain, disability, and other concomitant stressors of a physical illness. Consistent with this hypothesis, hope has been related to better adjustment in conditions involving chronic illness, severe injury, and handicaps. More specifically, higher hope has related to benefits in dealing with burn injuries (Barnum, Snyder, Rapoff, Mani, & Thompson, 1998), spinal cord injuries (Elliott, Witty, Herrick, & Hoffman, 1991), severe arthritis (Laird, 1992), fibromylagia (Affleck & Tennen, 1996; Tennen & Affleck, 1999), and blindness (Jackson, Taylor, Palmatier, Elliott, & Elliott, 1998).

Once ill, people with high versus low hope also appear to remain appropriately energized and focused on what they need to do in order to recuperate. This is in stark contrast to the counterproductive self-focus and self-pity (Hamilton & Ingram, 2001) that can overtake people with low hope. This self-focus in low-hope people increases anxiety and compromises the healing process. Furthermore, the higher anxiety in low-hope people may result in avoidance coping, which often can be quite unhealthy (Snyder & Pulvers, 2001).

An increasingly common problem involves people who are experiencing profound (and perhaps chronic) pain. Pain represents a difficult challenge for researchers and practitioners alike. We believe that persons with higher hope should be able to lessen their pain through enlisting more strategies (pathways) and having a higher likelihood of using those strategies (agency). Related to this point, in two studies using a cold pressor task (a pain tolerance measure), high-hope people experienced less pain and tolerated the pain almost twice as long as did the low-hope persons (Snyder, Odle, & Hackman, 1999).

Moving to the societal level, secondary prevention also may be influenced by hope. For example, successful television advertisements that are intended to promote health may work by giving people clear goals (e.g., "I definitely need to get help!") and pathways (e.g., referrals to local resources). These TV spots also influence agency by motivating people to get the help that they need. When people realize that their problem is not an isolated incident (i.e., it has high consensus), they tend to seek help. In support of this latter point, Snyder and Ingram (1983) found that people with targeted problems responded to high-consensus information so as to seek help. Overall, whether it is at the societal or the individual level, we foresee useful applications of hope theory in regard to prevention,[11] detection, and effective coping with illnesses.[12]

Psychological Adjustment

There are many ways in which we can use hope theory to foster better understanding of adjustment, as well as the best approaches for facilitating it. One way in which psychological adjustment is influenced by hope is through the belief in one's self, and this supposition is consistently supported in our research (e.g., Snyder, Hoza, et al., 1997). As posited earlier, hope should bear strong relationships with affectivity, and we have found that hope is related positively with positive affect and negatively with negative affect (correlations in .55 range). Moreover, manipulations to increase levels of hope have resulted in increases in positive affects and decreases in negative affects. Likewise, in tracking research participants over 28 days, higher hope was related to the report of more positive and fewer negative thoughts each day (Snyder et al., 1996). Furthermore, high-hope as compared with low-hope college students have reported feeling more inspired, energized, confident, and challenged by their goals (Snyder, Harris, et al., 1991), along with having elevated feelings of self-worth and low levels of depression (Snyder, Hoza, et al., 1997; Snyder et al., 1996).

In order to understand the stressor concept in the context of coping, we begin with a definition of coping. In this regard, coping is the ability to effectively respond to a stressor so as to reduce psychological (and physical) pain (Houston, 1988). Within hope theory, the stressor represents that which is interfering with one's normal ongoing goal of being happy. When confronting a stressor, therefore, one must find alternative paths to attain the "normalcy" goal, as well as become mobilized to use those paths. When confronted with a stressor, higher as compared with lower hope people produce more strategies for dealing with the stressor (pathways) and express a greater likelihood of using those strategies (agency; Snyder, 1994c, 2000d; Snyder, Harris, et al., 1991); moreover, higher hope persons are more likely to find benefits in their ongoing dealings with stressors (Affleck & Tennen, 1996; Tennen & Affleck, 1999). Relative to low-hope people, high-hope individuals also are less likely to use avoidance, a coping style that is linked to distress and decreased psychological adjustment when used over the long term (Suls & Fletcher, 1985).[13]

As is the case with physical health, hope also is crucial for psychological health. Hopeful thought entails assets such as the ability to establish clear goals, imagine workable pathways, and motivate oneself to work toward goals (Snyder, 2000a, 2000b, 2000c). For example, higher versus lower hope yields more successful goal pursuits in a variety of performance arenas (e.g., athletics, academics, coping; see, for review, Snyder, Cheavens, & Michael, 1999). Furthermore, this successful pursuit of goals is associated with elevated self-esteem and well-being (Snyder, Feldman, et al., 2000).

Psychological health is related to people's routine anticipation of their future well-being. In this regard, those with higher levels of hope should anticipate more positive levels of psychological health than persons with lower hope. These positive expectations also will yield higher confidence (Snyder, Feldman, et al., 2000), and high-hope people perceive that their hopeful thinking will protect them against future stressors (Snyder, 2000d). In addition, higher hope seems to moderate the relationship between unforeseen stressors and successful coping (see Snyder & Pulvers, 2001). Thus, in contrast to people with low levels of hope, who tend to catastrophize about the future, those with high levels of hope are able to think effectively about the future, with the knowledge that they, at times, will need to face major life stressors.

In a manner similar to that occurring for physical health, secondary prevention in psychological health involves thoughts or actions that eliminate, reduce, or contain a problem once it has appeared (Snyder, Feldman, et al., 2000). Hope also plays a role in this process. For example, when people with high hope encounter an immutable goal blockage, they are flexible enough to find alternative goals. In contrast, people with low hope tend to ruminate unproductively about being stuck (Michael, 2000; Snyder, 1999a, 1999b); moreover, their low-hope ruminations often involve fantasies about "magically" escaping their entrapments. This is tantamount to avoidance and disengaged coping behaviors, which generally have unhealthy consequences (Bolger, 1990; Carver et al., 1993; Litt, Tennen, Affleck, & Klock, 1992; Stanton & Snider, 1993). Furthermore, by coping through avoidance, the low-hope persons do not learn from past experiences (Snyder, Feldman, et al., 2000), and they become "passive pawns" in the game of life.

People with high hope also are likely to have friends with whom they share a strong sense of mutuality. In stressful circumstances, high-hope people can call on these friends for support (Crothers & Schraw, 1999; Sarason, Sarason, & Pierce, 1990). People with low hope, on the other hand, tend to be lonely and lack friends with whom they can talk. This seems to stem from their fear of interpersonal closeness (Crothers & Schraw, 1999). Likewise, even if low-hope people do have friends, those friends also are likely to have low hope (Cheavens, Taylor, Kahle, & Snyder, 2000). Unfortunately, a dyad of low-hope persons may be prone to "pity parties," in which the unending topic is how bad things are for them.

Human Connection

We have theorized that hope is inculcated in children through interactions with their caretakers, peers, and teachers (Snyder, Cheavens, & Sympson, 1997). As such, the goal of "connecting" with other people is fundamental, because the seeking of one's goals almost always occurs within the context of social commerce. Related to this point, it is the high-hope as compared with low-hope individuals who are especially invested in making contact with other people (Snyder, Hoza, et al., 1997). One measure of the motivation to be connected to others is the degree to which an individual is concerned with the perceptions that others form of him. In this vein, the increasing consensus is that a tendency to present oneself in a slightly positive light is an adaptive coping style (Taylor, 1989). Hope Scale scores have correlated slightly and positively with measures of social desirability and positive self-presentation (Snyder, Harris, et al., 1991; Snyder, Hoza, et al., 1997), suggesting an adaptive concern by high-hope people about impressions they make.

Researchers also have found that higher levels of hope are related to more perceived social support (Barnum et al., 1998), more social competence (Snyder, Hoza, et al., 1997), and less loneliness (Sympson, 1999). Furthermore, high-hope individuals have an enhanced ability to take the perspectives of others (Rieger, 1993). They appear to truly enjoy their interactions with others (Snyder, Hoza, et al., 1997), and they are interested in their goals and the goals of others around them (Snyder, 1994b, 1994c; Snyder, Cheavens, & Sympson, 1997).

Psychotherapy

From the 1960s through the 1980s, Jerome Frank (1968, 1973, 1975) pioneered a view that hope was a common process across differing psychotherapy approaches. We have continued his line of thought using hope theory as a framework for understanding the shared processes by which people are helped in psychotherapy (Snyder, Ilardi, Cheavens, et al., 2000; Snyder, Ilardi, Michael, & Cheavens, 2000; Snyder, Michael, & Cheavens, 1999; Snyder & Taylor, 2000). Whatever the particular system of psychotherapy, we believe that the beneficial changes occur because clients are learning more effective agentic and pathways goal-directed thinking. In particular, the agency component is reflected in the placebo effect (i.e., the natural mental energies for change that clients bring to psychotherapy). The particular psychotherapy approaches that are used to provide the client with a route or process for moving forward to attain positive therapeutic goals reflect the pathways component. By applying hope theory to several psychotherapies, a potential benefit would be increased cooperation among the proponents of varying camps (Snyder & Ingram, 2000).

Beyond the application of hope theory principles to psychotherapies in general, hope theory has been used to develop successful individual (Lopez, Floyd, Ulven, & Snyder, 2000; for related example, see Worthington et al., 1997) and group interventions (Klausner et al., 1998; Klausner, Snyder, & Cheavens, 2000). There also are two books (McDermott & Snyder, 2000; Snyder, McDermott, et al., 1997) and a chapter (McDermott & Hastings, 2000) in which hope theory has been applied specifically to aid parents and teachers in helping children, as well as a book based on hope theory that is targeted to benefit adults (McDermott & Snyder, 1999). Furthermore, a pretreatment therapy preparation program based on hope theory has yielded benefits for clients (Irving et al., 1997). In our estimation, however, we have only begun to explore the applications of hope theory for psychotherapies.

Meaning in Life

Viktor Frankl (1965, 1992) has provided an eloquent voice on the "What is the nature of meaning?" question. To answer this query, he advanced the concept of the "existential vacuum"—the perception that there is no meaning or purpose in the universe. The experience of this existential vacuum supposedly can be remedied to the extent that persons actualize "values." Frankl (1965, 1966) reasoned that meaning resulted from the choice to bring three major classes of values into one's life: (a) creative (instantiations include writing a paper, giving birth to a child, etc.); (b) experiential (seeing, touching, or any way of experiencing); and (c) attitudinal (the stances people take toward their plights of suffering). The Purpose in Life test (Crumbaugh & Maholick, 1964; Crumbaugh & Maholick, 1981) was developed to reflect Frankl's notion. There also are two other widely used measures of general life-meaning— the Life Regard Index (Battista & Almond, 1973) and the Sense of Coherence scale (Antonovsky & Sagy, 1986).

We posited that hope should relate strongly to meaning because it is through our self-reflections about the goals that one has selected and the perceived progress in the journey toward those goals that a person constructs meaning in his or her life (Snyder, 1994c). In support of this hypothesis, we (Feldman & Snyder, 1999) found that Hope Scale scores evidenced correlations in the .70 to .76 range with the aforementioned three meaning measures. Thus, we believe that hope theory offers a new angle for looking at the nature of meaning.

For Another Time and Place

In this section, we provide brief glimpses of additional arenas where hope may play an important role (for a review of various future applications of hope theory, see Snyder [2000e]). We have made a case for how hope theory can be used to understand depression (Snyder, 1994c; Cheavens, 2000) and have examined the inner hope-related self-talk of depressed persons (Snyder, Lapointe, et al., 1998).[14] Another topic is attentional focus, with the premise being that on-task rather than off-task focus is facilitated by hopeful thinking (Snyder, 1999a, 1999b). We also offer some insights into self-actualization by using hope theory. Although widely discussed, Maslow's (1970) hierarchy of needs has received little recent research attention. Perhaps by using hope theory, with its emphasis on goals, we could enhance our understanding of this hierarchy. The capstone of Maslow's hierarchy is self-actualization, and such an idea is very timely within the positive psychology perspective. On this point, the strongest correlation of any scale with the Hope Scale was obtained with a measure of self-actualization ($r = .79$; Sumerlin, 1997).

Using hope theory, we also may garner insights into major group differences. In this regard, in over 40 studies (with adults and children), there never has been a significant sex difference in hope. Why? We also need to expand our knowledge of how differing ethnic groups manifest hope (Lopez, Gariglietti, et al., 2000). Likewise, do older persons exhibit differing hope from younger persons, and if so, why (Cheavens & Gum, 2000)? Whether a relationship be of intimate partners, students and teachers, managers and employees, or physicians and patients, the effectiveness and satisfaction flowing from the interactions may be understood and improved via hope theory (Snyder, 1994c, chap. 7). We would emphasize that the topics in this section, as well as those described earlier, represent only a portion of the positive psychology issues that we can examine through the lens of hope theory.

Hope for the Many Rather Than the Few

Our last point, and one that is central to our view of positive psychology, is that the uses and benefits of hope should be made available to as many people as possible (Snyder & Feldman, 2000). Although we have remained at the level of individuals in making our various points in this chapter, we would hasten to add that hope theory also is applicable to people in the context of larger units. In this regard, hope theory could be applied to help build environments where people can work together to meet shared goals. Whether it is a business, city council, state legislature, or national or international organization, there is enormous potential in working together in the spirit of hope. Earlier in this chapter, we described hope theory as a lens for seeing the strengths in people. We would hasten to add, however, that hope is but one pane in the larger window of positive psychology. Through this window, looking across different lands and people, we envision a positive psychology for the many. This is a vision of hope.

APPENDIX A   The Trait Hope Scale

Directions: Read each item carefully. Using the scale shown below, please select the number that best describes YOU and put that number in the blank provided.

1   Definitely false
2   Mostly false
3   Somewhat false
4   Slightly false

5   Slightly true
6   Somewhat true
7   Mostly true
8   Definitely true

_____ 1. I can think of many ways to get out of a jam.
_____ 2. I energetically pursue my goals.
_____ 3. I feel tired most of the time.
_____ 4. There are lots of ways around any problem.
_____ 5. I am easily downed in an argument.
_____ 6. I can think of many ways to get the things in life that are important to me.
_____ 7. I worry about my health.
_____ 8. Even when others get discouraged, I know I can find a way to solve the problem.
_____ 9. My past experiences have prepared me well for my future.
_____ 10. I've been pretty successful in life.
_____ 11. I usually find myself worrying about something.
_____ 12. I meet the goals that I set for myself.

Notes: When administering the scale, it is called The Future Scale. The Agency subscale score is derived by summing items # 2, 9, 10, and 12; the Pathway subscale score is derived by adding items # 1, 4, 6, and 8. The total Hope Scale score is derived by summing the four Agency and the four Pathway items. From C. R. Snyder, C. Harris, et al., The will and the ways: Development and validation of an individual differences measure of hope, *Journal of Personality and Social Psychology* © (1991), Vol. 60, p. 585. Reprinted with the permission of the American Psychological Association and the senior author.

APPENDIX B   The State Hope Scale

Directions: Read each item carefully. Using the scale shown below, please select the number that best describes *how you think about yourself right now* and put that number in the blank before each sentence. Please take a few moments to focus on yourself and what is going on in *your life at this moment*. Once you have this "here and now" set, go ahead and answer each item according to the following scale:

1   Definitely false
2   Mostly false

3 Somewhat false
4 Slightly false
5 Slightly true
6 Somewhat true
7 Mostly true
8 Definitely true

_____ 1. If I should find myself in a jam, I could think of many ways to get out of it.

_____ 2. At the present time, I am energetically pursuing my goals.

_____ 3. There are lots of ways around any problem that I am facing now.

_____ 4. Right now, I see myself as being pretty successful.

_____ 5. I can think of many ways to reach my current goals.

_____ 6. At this time, I am meeting the goals that I have set for myself.

Notes: The Agency subscale score is derived by summing the three even-numbered items; the Pathways subscale score is derived by adding the three odd-numbered items. The total State Hope Scale score is derived by summing the three Agency and the three Pathways items. Scores can range from a low of 6 to a high of 48. When administering the State Hope Scale, it is labeled as the "Goals Scale for the Present." From C. R. Snyder, S. C. Sympson, et al., Development and validation of the State Hope Scale, *Journal of Personality and Social Psychology* © (1996), Vol. 70, p. 335. Reprinted with the permission of the American Psychological Association and the senior author.

APPENDIX C   The Children's Hope Scale

Directions: The six sentences below describe how children think about themselves and how they do things in general. Read each sentence carefully. For each sentence, please think about how you are in most situations. Place a check inside the circle that describes YOU the best. For example, place a check (√) in the circle (O) beside "None of the time," if this describes you. Or, if you are this way "All of the time," check this circle. Please answer every question by putting a check in one of the circles. There are no right or wrong answers.

1. I think I am doing pretty well.
   O *None of the time*
   O *A little of the time*
   O *Some of the time*
   O *A lot of the time*
   O *Most of the time*
   O *All of the time*

2. I can think of many ways to get the things in life that are most important to me.
   O *None of the time*
   O *A little of the time*
   O *Some of the time*
   O *A lot of the time*
   O *Most of the time*
   O *All of the time*

3. I am doing just as well as other kids my age.
   O *None of the time*
   O *A little of the time*
   O *Some of the time*
   O *A lot of the time*
   O *Most of the time*
   O *All of the time*

4. When I have a problem, I can come up with lots of ways to solve it.
   O *None of the time*
   O *A little of the time*
   O *Some of the time*
   O *A lot of the time*
   O *Most of the time*
   O *All of the time*

5. I think the things I have done in the past will help me in the future.
   O *None of the time*
   O *A little of the time*
   O *Some of the time*
   O *A lot of the time*
   O *Most of the time*
   O *All of the time*

6. Even when others want to quit, I know that I can find ways to solve the problem.
   O *None of the time*
   O *A little of the time*
   O *Some of the time*
   O *A lot of the time*
   O *Most of the time*
   O *All of the time*

Notes: When administered to children, this scale is not labeled "The Children's Hope Scale," but is called "Questions About Your Goals." To calculate the total Children's Hope Scale score, add the responses to all six items, with "None of the time" = 1; "A little of the time" = 2; "Some of the time" = 3; "A lot of the time" = 4; "Most of the time" = 5; and, "All of the time" = 6. The three odd-numbered items tap agency, and the three even-numbered items tap pathways. From C. R. Snyder, B. Hoza, et al., The development and validation of the Children's Hope Scale, *Journal of Pediatric Psychology* © (1997), Vol. 22(3), p. 421. Reprinted with the permission of the Journal and the senior author.

Notes

1. In Craig's (1943) *The Nature of Explanation*, which is a classic in the evolution of the cognitive psychology movement, he persuasively reasons that the purpose of the brain is to comprehend and anticipate causal sequences. Pinker (1997) makes a similar argument in his award-winning *How the Mind Works*. Additional volumes that were particularly helpful in forming our view about the importance of pathways thought in pursuing goals were Miller, Galanter, and Pribram's (1960) *Plans and the Structure of Behavior*, Newell and Simon's (1972) *Human Problem Solving*, and Anderson's (1983) *The Architecture of Cognition*.

2. We also have developed hope measures that are (a) for children aged 4 to 7; (b) aimed at tapping hope in particular life domains; (c) based on observing either children or adults; and (d) derived from written or spoken narratives. Contact the senior author for further information on these measures.

3. For the reader who is interested in more detailed comparisons of various other theories to hope theory, please refer to the following sources: Snyder (1994a); Snyder (1998b); Snyder (2000b, 2000d, 2000e); Snyder, Ilardi, Cheavens, et al. (2000); Snyder, Ilardi, Michael, and Cheavens (2000); Snyder, Irving, and Anderson (1991); and Snyder, Sympson, Michael, and Cheavens (2000).

4. The instrument used to measure attributional style in adults is called the Attributional Style Questionnaire (Peterson et al., 1982); the instrument used for children is called the Children's Attributional Style Questionnaire (Seligman et al., 1984).

5. There are indications, however, that optimists do use such planful thought (e.g., Carver & Scheier, 2000b; Scheier & Carver, 1985). For example, optimists have elevated problem-focused coping (Scheier, Weintraub, & Carver, 1986; Strutton & Lumpkin, 1992) and planfulness (Fontaine, Manstead, & Wagner, 1993; Friedman et al., 1992). Therefore, the positive goal-directed expectancies (in responses to the LOT and LOT-R)

implicitly may tap pathways-related thinking. Related to this issue, Magaletta and Oliver (1999) have found the pathways component of the Hope Scale to be orthogonal to items on the LOT in a factor analysis. The original instrument tapping optimism was called the Life Orientation Test (Scheier & Carver, 1985), and the revised instrument is called the Life Orientation Test-Revised (Scheier, Carver, & Bridges, 1994).

6. Nevertheless, a dispositional measure of self-efficacy has been developed by other researchers (see Sherer et al., 1982).

7. For related reviews, see Wells and Marwell (1976) and Wylie (1974, 1979).

8. The grade point averages of the high- and low-hope students were 2.85 and 2.43, respectively.

9. In the aforementioned studies, the predictive power of hope was not diminished when controlling for intelligence (children's studies), previous grades (cross-sectional college student studies), and entrance exam scores (longitudinal college study).

10. Such hope education also should be available to parents (McDermott & Snyder, 1999, 2000).

11. Based on prospective correlational research, using indices of hope other than the ones derived from hope theory, the absence of hope (i.e., hopelessness) appears to relate to morbidity and mortality. For example, Schmale and Iker (1966, 1971) found that hopelessness predicted later development of cervical cancer among healthy women at high risk for cervical cancer. More recently, Everson and colleagues (1996, 1997) found that hopelessness predicted later cardiovascular disease and cancer among middle-aged men (even beyond number of biological and behavioral risk factors). Although this is correlational research, these findings support the hypothesis that hope plays a role in the prevention of some life-threatening physical illnesses.

12. As an example of this latter point, the role of hope in maintaining adherence to a medicine regime in juvenile and adult diabetes patients is being examined in ongoing research in our laboratory. Results reveal that hope, particularly the agency component, predicts adherence, and that it does so beyond variances related to demographic or quality-of-life variables (Moon, 2000).

13. We refer the reader to the following sources for in-depth coverage of the role that hope plays in facilitating successful coping process: McDermott and Snyder, 1999; Snyder, 1994c; Snyder, Cheavens, and Michael, 1999; and Snyder, McDermott, et al., 1997.

14. Anxiety also can be understood within hope theory (Michael, 2000; Snyder, 1994c).

References

Abramson, L. Y., Seligman, M. E. P., & Teasdale, J. D. (1978). Learned helplessness in humans: Critique and reformulation. *Journal of Abnormal Psychology, 87,* 49–74.

Affleck, G., & Tennen, H. (1996). Construing benefits from adversity: Adaptational significance and dispositional underpinnings. *Journal of Personality, 64,* 899–922.

Anderson, J. R. (1983). *The architecture of cognition.* Cambridge, MA: Harvard University Press.

Antonovsky, H., & Sagy, S. (1986). The development of a sense of coherence and its impact on responses to stress situations. *Journal of Social Psychology, 126,* 213–225.

Averill, J. R., Catlin, G., & Chon, K. K. (1990). *Rules of hope.* New York: Springer-Verlag.

Babyak, M. A., Snyder, C. R., & Yashinobu, L. (1993). Psychometric properties of the Hope Scale: A confirmatory factor analysis. *Journal of Research in Personality, 27,* 154–169.

Bandura, A. (1982). Self-efficacy mechanism in human agency. *American Psychologist, 37,* 122–147.

Bandura, A. (1997). *Self-efficacy: The exercise of control.* New York: Freeman.

Barnum, D. D., Snyder, C. R., Rapoff, M. A., Mani, M. M., & Thompson, R. (1998). Hope and social support in the psychological adjustment of pediatric burn survivors and matched controls. *Children's Health Care, 27,* 15–30.

Battista, J., & Almond, R. (1973). The development of meaning in life. *Psychiatry, 36,* 409–427.

Bolger, N. (1990). Coping as a personality process: A prospective study. *Journal of Personality and Social Psychology, 59,* 525–537.

Brunstein, J. C. (1993). Personal goals and subjective well-being: A longitudinal study. *Journal of Personality and Social Psychology, 65,* 1061–1070.

Cantril, H. (1964). The human design. *Journal of Individual Psychology, 20,* 129–136.

Carver, C. S., Pozo, C., Harris, S. D., Noriega, V., Scheier, M. F., Robinson, D. S., Ketcham, A. S., Mofat, F. L., Jr., & Clark, K. C. (1993). How coping mediates the effect of optimism on distress: A study of women with early stage breast cancer. *Journal of Personality and Social Psychology, 65,* 375–390.

Carver, C. S., & Scheier, M. F. (2000a). Optimism, pessimism, and self-regulation. In E. C. Chang (Ed.), *Optimism and pessimism* (pp. 31–52). Washington, DC: American Psychological Association.

Carver, C. S., & Scheier, M. F. (2000b). Optimism. In C. R. Snyder (Ed.), *Coping: The psychology of what works* (pp. 182–204). New York: Oxford University Press.

Cheavens, J. (2000). Light through the shadows: Depression and hope. In C. R. Snyder (Ed.), *Handbook of hope: Theory, measures, and applications* (pp. 326–354). San Diego, CA: Academic Press.

Cheavens, J., & Gum, A. (2000). Gray Power: Hope for the ages. In C. R. Snyder (Ed.), *Handbook of hope: Theory, measures, and applications* (pp. 201–222). San Diego, CA: Academic Press.

Cheavens, J., Gum, A., & Snyder, C. R. (2000). The Hope Scale. In J. Maltby, C. A. Lewis, & A. Hill (Eds.), *A handbook of psychological tests* (pp. 248–258). Lampeter, Wales, UK: Edwin Mellen Press.

Cheavens, J., Taylor, J. D., Kahle, K., & Snyder, C. R. (2000). *Interactions of high- and low-hope individuals.* Unpublished manuscript, Psychology Department, University of Kansas, Lawrence.

Coopersmith, S. (1967). *The antecedents of self-esteem.* San Francisco: Freeman.

Craig, K. J. W. (1943). *The nature of explanation.* Cambridge, England: Cambridge University Press.

Crothers, M., & Schraw, G. (1999, August). *Validation of the Mutuality Assessment Questionnaire.* Presented at the annual meeting of the American Psychological Association, Boston.

Crumbaugh, J. C., & Maholick, L. T. (1964). An experimental study in existentialism: The psychometric approach to Frankl's concept of noogenic neurosis. *Journal of Clinical Psychology, 20,* 200–207.

Crumbaugh, J. C., & Maholick, L. T. (1981). *Manual of instructions for the Purpose in Life Test.* Murfeesboro, TN: Psychometric Affiliates.

Curry, L. A., Maniar, S. D., Sondag, K. A., & Sandstedt, S. (1999). *An optimal performance academic course for university students and student-athletes.* Unpublished manuscript, University of Montana, Missoula.

Curry, L. A., & Snyder, C. R. (2000). Hope takes the field: Mind matters in athletic performances. In C. R. Snyder (Ed.), *Handbook of hope: Theory, measures, and applications* (pp. 243–260). San Diego, CA: Academic Press.

Curry, L. A., Snyder, C. R., Cook, D. L., Ruby, B. C., & Rehm, M. (1997). The role of hope in student-athlete academic and sport achievement. *Journal of Personality and Social Psychology, 73,* 1257–1267.

Diener, E. (1984). Subjective well-being. *Psychological Bulletin, 95,* 542–575.

D'Zurilla, T. J. (1986). *Problem-solving therapy: A social competence approach to clinical intervention*. New York: Springer.

Elliott, T. R., Witty, T. E., Herrick, S., & Hoffman, J. T. (1991). Negotiating reality after physical loss: Hope, depression, and disability. *Journal of Personality and Social Psychology, 61*, 608–613.

Emmons, R. A. (1986). Personal strivings: An approach to personality and subjective well-being. *Journal of Personality and Social Psychology, 51*, 1058–1068.

Everson, S. A., Goldberg, D. E., Kaplan, G. A., Cohen, R. D., Pukkala, E., Tuomilehto, J., & Salonen, J. T. (1996). Hopelessness and risk of mortality and incidence of myocardial infarction and cancer. *Psychosomatic Medicine, 58*, 113–121.

Everson, S. A., Kaplan, G. A., Goldberg, D. E., Salonen, R., & Salonen, J. T. (1997). Hopelessness and 4-year progression of carotid artherosclerosis: The Kuopio ischemic heart disease risk factor study. *Arteriosclerosis Thrombosis Vascular Biology, 17*, 1490–1495.

Farber, M. L. (1968). *Theory of suicide*. New York: Funk and Wagnall's.

Farina, C. J., Hearth, A. K., & Popovich, J. M. (1995). *Hope and hopelessness: Critical clinical constructs*. Thousand Oaks, CA: Sage.

Feldman, D. B., & Snyder, C. R. (1999). *Natural companions: Hope and meaning*. Unpublished manuscript, University of Kansas, Lawrence.

Feldman, D. B., & Snyder, C. R. (2000). The State Hope Scale. In J. Maltby, C. A. Lewis, and A. Hill (Eds.), *A handbook of psychological tests* (pp. 240–245). Lampeter, Wales, UK: Edwin Mellen Press.

Fontaine, K. R., Manstead, A. S. R., & Wagner, H. (1993). Optimism, perceived control over stress, and coping. *European Journal of Personality, 7*, 267–281.

Frank, J. D. (1968). The role of hope in psychotherapy. *International Journal of Psychiatry, 5*, 383–395.

Frank, J. D. (1973). *Persuasion and healing* (Rev. ed.). Baltimore: Johns Hopkins University Press.

Frank, J. D. (1975). The faith that heals. *Johns Hopkins Medical Journal, 137*, 127–131.

Frankl, V. (1965). *The doctor and the soul: From psychotherapy to logotherapy* (R. Winston & C. Winston, Trans.). New York: Knopf.

Frankl, V. (1966). What is meant by meaning? *Journal of Existentialism, 7*, 21–28.

Frankl, V. (1992). *Man's search for meaning: An introduction to logotherapy* (I. Lasch, Trans.). Boston: Beacon.

Friedman, L. C., Nelson, D. V., Baer, P. E., Lane, M., Smith, F. E., & Dworkin, R. J. (1992). The relationship of dispositional optimism, daily life stress, and domestic environment to coping methods used by cancer patients. *Journal of Behavioral Medicine, 15*, 127–141.

Hamilton, N. A., & Ingram, R. E. (2001). Self-focused attention and coping: Attending to the right things. In C. R. Snyder (Ed.), *Coping with stress: Effective people and processes* (pp. 178–195). New York: Oxford University Press.

Heller, K., Wyman, M. F., & Allen, S. M. (2000). Future directions for prevention science: From research to adoption. In C. R. Snyder & R. E. Ingram (Eds.), *Handbook of psychological change: Psychotherapy process and practices for the 21st century* (pp. 660–680). New York: Wiley.

Heppner, P. P., & Hillerbrand, E. T. (1991). Problem-solving training implications for remedial and preventive training. In C. R. Snyder & D. R. Forsyth (Eds.), *Handbook of social and clinical psychology: The health perspective* (pp. 681–698). Elmsford, NY: Pergamon.

Hewitt, J. P. (1998). *The myth of self-esteem: Finding happiness and solving problems in America*. New York: St. Martin's Press.

Houston, B. K. (1988). Stress and coping. In C. R. Snyder & C. E. Ford (Eds.), *Coping with negative life events: Clinical and social psychological perspectives* (pp. 373–399). New York: Plenum.

Irving, L. M., Snyder, C. R., & Crowson, J. J. Jr. (1998). Hope and the negotiation of cancer facts by college women. *Journal of Personality, 66*, 195–214.

Irving, L., Snyder, C. R., Gravel, L., Hanke, J., Hilberg, P., & Nelson, N. (1997, April). *Hope and effectiveness of a pre-therapy orientation group for community mental health center clients*. Paper presented at the annual meeting of the Western Psychological Association Convention, Seattle, WA.

Jackson, W. T., Taylor, R. E., Palmatier, A. D., Elliott, T. R., & Elliott, J. L. (1998). Negotiating the reality of visual impairment: Hope, coping, and functional ability. *Journal of Clinical Psychology in Medical Settings, 5*, 173–185.

Kaplan, R. M. (2000). Two pathways to prevention. *American Psychologist, 55*, 382–396.

Klausner, E. J., Clarkin, J. F., Spielman, L., Pupo, C., Abrams, R., & Alexopoulas, G. S. (1998). Late-life depression and functional disability: The role of goal-focused group psychotherapy. *International Journal of Geriatric Psychiatry, 13*, 707–716.

Klausner, E. J., Snyder, C. R., & Cheavens, J. (2000). Teaching hope to a population of older, depressed adults. In G. Williamson (Ed.), *Advances in aging theory and research* (pp. 295–310). New York: Plenum.

Krauss, H. H., & Krauss, B. J. (1968). Cross-cultural study of the thwarting-disorientation theory of suicide. *Journal of Abnormal Psychology, 73,* 352–357.

Laird, S. (1992). *A preliminary investigation into prayer as a coping technique for adult patients with arthritis.* Unpublished doctoral dissertation, University of Kansas, Lawrence.

Litt, M. D., Tennen, H., Affleck, G., & Klock, S. (1992). Coping and cognitive factors in adaptation to in vitro fertilization failure. *Journal of Behavioral Medicine, 15,* 171–187.

Little, B. R. (1983). Personal projects: A rationale and method for investigation. *Environment and Behavior, 15,* 273–309.

Little, B. R. (1989). Personal projects analysis: Trivial pursuits, magnificent obsessions, and the search for coherence. In D. M. Buss & N. Cantor (Eds.), *Personality psychology: Recent trends and emerging directions* (pp. 15–31). New York: Springer-Verlag.

Lopez, S. J., Bouwkamp, J., Edwards, L. M., & Teramoto Pedrotti, J. (2000, October). *Making hope happen via brief interventions.* Paper presented at the second Positive Psychology Summit, Washington, DC.

Lopez, S. J., Floyd, R. K., Ulven, J. C., & Snyder, C. R. (2000). Hope therapy: Helping clients build a house of hope. In C. R. Snyder (Ed.), *Handbook of hope: Theory, measures, and applications* (pp. 123–150). San Diego, CA: Academic Press.

Lopez, S. J., Gariglietti, K. P., McDermott, D., Sherwin, E. D., Floyd, K. R., Rand, K., & Snyder, C. R. (2000). Hope for the evolution of diversity: On leveling the field of dreams. In C. R. Snyder (Ed.), *Handbook of hope: Theory, measures, and applications* (pp. 223–242). San Diego, CA: Academic Press.

Magaletta, P. R., & Oliver, J. M. (1999). The hope construct, will and ways: Their relative relations with self-efficacy, optimism, and general well-being. *Journal of Clinical Psychology, 55,* 539–551.

Maslow, A. H. (1970). *Motivation and personality* (2nd ed.). New York: Harper and Row.

Matarazzo, J. D. (1982). Behavioral health's challenge to academic, scientific, and professional psychology. *American Psychologist, 37,* 1–14.

McDermott, D., & Hastings, S. (2000). Children: Raising future hopes. In C. R. Snyder (Ed.), *Handbook of hope: Theory, measures, and applications* (pp. 185–199). San Diego, CA: Academic Press.

McDermott, D., & Snyder, C. R. (1999). *Making hope happen.* Oakland, CA: New Harbinger Publications.

McDermott, D., & Snyder, C. R. (2000). *The great big book of hope: Help your children achieve their dreams.* Oakland, CA: New Harbinger Publications.

Melges, R., & Bowlby, J. (1969). Types of hopelessness in psychopathological processes. *Archives of General Psychiatry, 20,* 690–699.

Menninger, K. (1959). The academic lecture on hope. *American Journal of Psychiatry, 109,* 481–491.

Michael, S. T. (2000). Hope conquers fear: Overcoming anxiety and panic attacks. In C. R. Snyder (Ed.), *Handbook of hope: Theory, measures, and applications* (pp. 355–378). San Diego, CA: Academic Press.

Miller, G. A., Galanter, E., & Pribram, K. H. (1960). *Plans and the structure of behavior.* New York: Holt, Rinehart, and Winston.

Moon, C. (2000). *The relationship of hope to children's asthma treatment adherence.* Unpublished master's thesis, University of Kansas, Lawrence.

Moon, C., & Snyder, C. R. (2000). Children's Hope Scale. In J. Maltby, C. A. Lewis, and A. Hill (Eds.), *A handbook of psychological tests* (pp. 160–166). Lampeter, Wales, UK: Edwin Mellen Press.

Newell, A., & Simon, H. A. (1972). *Human problem solving.* Englewood Cliffs, NJ: Prentice-Hall.

Omodei, M. M., & Wearing, A. J. (1990). Need satisfaction and involvement in personal projects: Toward an integrative model of subjective well-being. *Journal of Personality and Social Psychology, 59,* 762–769.

Palys, T. S., & Little, B. R. (1983). Perceived life satisfaction and organization of personal projects systems. *Journal of Personality and Social Psychology, 44,* 1221–1230.

Peterson, C., Semmel, A., von Baeyer, C., Abramson, L. Y., Metalsky, G. I., & Seligman, M. E. P. (1982). The Attributional Style Questionnaire. *Cognitive Therapy and Research, 6,* 287–299.

Pinker, S. (1997). *How the mind works.* New York: Norton.

Rieger, E. (1993). *Correlates of adult hope, including high- and low-hope adults' recollection of parents.* Unpublished psychology honors thesis, University of Kansas, Lawrence.

Ruehlman, L. S., & Wolchik, S. A. (1988). Personal goals and interpersonal support and hindrance as factors in psychological distress and well-being. *Journal of Personality and Social Psychology, 55,* 293–301.

Sarason, B. R., Sarason, I. G., & Pierce, G. R. (Eds.). (1990). *Social support: An interactional view.* New York: Wiley.

Schachtel, E. (1959). *Metamorphosis*. New York: Basic Books.

Scheier, M. F., & Carver, C. S. (1985). Optimism, coping, and health: Assessment and implications of generalized outcome expectancies. *Health Psychology, 4,* 219–247.

Scheier, M. F., & Carver, C. S. (1987). Dispositional optimism and physical well-being: The influence of generalized outcome expectancies on health. *Journal of Personality, 55,* 169–210.

Scheier, M. F., Carver, C. S., & Bridges, M. W. (1994). Distinguishing optimism from neuroticism (and trait anxiety, self mastery, and self-esteem): A reevaluation of the Life Orientation Test. *Journal of Personality and Social Psychology, 67,* 1063–1078.

Scheier, M. F., Weintraub, J. K., & Carver, C. S. (1986). Coping with stress: Divergent strategies of optimists and pessimists. *Journal of Personality and Social Psychology, 51,* 1257–1264.

Schmale, A. H., & Iker, H. (1966). The affect of hopelessness and the development of cancer: Identification of uterine cervical cancer in women with atypical cytology. *Psychosomatic Medicine, 28,* 714–721.

Schmale, A. H., & Iker, H. (1971). Hopelessness as a predictor of cervical cancer. *Social Science and Medicine, 5,* 95–100.

Schulman, M. (1991). *The passionate mind.* New York: Free Press.

Seligman, M. E. P. (1991). *Learned optimism.* New York: Knopf.

Seligman, M. E. P., Kaslow, N. J., Alloy, L. B., Peterson, C., Tanenbaum, R., & Abramson, L. Y. (1984). Attributional style and depressive symptoms among children. *Journal of Abnormal Psychology, 93,* 235–238.

Sherer, M., Maddux, J. E., Mercandante, B., Prentice-Dunn, S., Jacobs, B., & Rogers, R. (1982). The self-efficacy scale: Construction and validation. *Psychological Reports, 51,* 663–671.

Snyder, C. R. (1993). Hope for the journey. In A. P. Turnball, J. M. Patterson, S. K. Behr, D. L. Murphy, J. G. Marquis, & M. J. Blue-Banning (Eds.), *Cognitive coping, families and disability* (pp. 271–286). Baltimore: Brookes.

Snyder, C. R. (1994a). Hope and optimism. In V. S. Ramachandren (Ed.), *Encyclopedia of human behavior* (Vol. 2, pp. 535–542). San Diego, CA: Academic Press.

Snyder, C. R. (1994b, August). *Hope for the many vs. hope for the few.* Paper presented at the annual meeting of the American Psychological Association, Los Angeles.

Snyder, C. R. (1994c). *The psychology of hope: You can get there from here.* New York: Free Press.

Snyder, C. R. (1995). Conceptualizing, measuring, and nurturing hope. *Journal of Counseling and Development, 73,* 355–360.

Snyder, C. R. (1996). To hope, to lose, and hope again. *Journal of Personal and Interpersonal Loss, 1,* 3–16.

Snyder, C. R. (1998a). A case for hope in pain, loss, and suffering. In J. H. Harvey, J. Omarzu, & E. Miller (Eds.), *Perspectives on loss: A sourcebook* (pp. 63–79). Washington, DC: Taylor and Francis.

Snyder, C. R. (1998b). Hope. In H. S. Friedman (Ed.), *Encyclopedia of mental health* (pp. 421–431). San Diego, CA: Academic Press.

Snyder, C. R. (1999a). Hope, goal blocking thoughts, and test-related anxieties. *Psychological Reports, 84,* 206–208.

Snyder, C. R. (1999b, June). *A psychological look at people who do not reach their goals: The low-hope blues.* Paper presented at the annual meeting of the American Psychological Society, Denver, CO.

Snyder, C. R. (2000a). Genesis: Birth and growth of hope. In C. R. Snyder (Ed.), *Handbook of hope: Theory, measures, and applications* (pp. 25–57). San Diego, CA: Academic Press.

Snyder, C. R. (2000b, March). *Hope: The beneficent octopus.* Presentation at the annual meeting of the Eastern Psychological Association, Baltimore, MD.

Snyder, C. R. (2000c, August). *Hope theory: Pursuing positive ties that bind.* Paper presented at the meeting of the American Psychological Association, Washington, DC.

Snyder, C. R. (2000d). Hypothesis: There is hope. In C. R. Snyder (Ed.), *Handbook of hope: Theory, measures, and applications* (pp. 3–21). San Diego, CA: Academic Press.

Snyder, C. R. (2000e). The past and future of hope. *Journal of Social and Clinical Psychology, 19,* 11–28.

Snyder, C. R., Cheavens, J., & Michael, S. T. (1999). Hoping. In C. R. Snyder (Ed.), *Coping: The psychology of what works* (pp. 205–231). New York: Oxford University Press.

Snyder, C. R., Cheavens, J., & Sympson, S. C. (1997). Hope: An individual motive for social commerce. *Group Dynamics: Theory, Research, and Practice, 1,* 107–118.

Snyder, C. R., & Feldman, D. B. (2000). Hope for the many: An empowering social agenda. In C. R. Snyder (Ed.), *Handbook of hope: Theory, measures, and applications* (pp. 402–415). San Diego, CA: Academic Press.

Snyder, C. R., Feldman, D. B., Taylor, J. D., Schroeder, L. L., & Adams V., III. (2000). The roles of hopeful thinking in preventing problems and enhancing strengths. *Applied and Preventive Psychology, 15,* 262–295.

Snyder, C. R., Harris, C., Anderson, J. R., Holleran, S. A., Irving, L. M., Sigmon, S. T., Yoshinobu, L., Gibb, J., Langelle, C., & Harney, P. (1991). The will and the ways: Development and validation of an individual-differences measure of hope. *Journal of Personality and Social Psychology, 60,* 570–585.

Snyder, C. R., Hoza, B., Pelham, W. E., Rapoff, M., Ware, L., Danovsky, M., Highberger, L., Rubinstein, H., & Stahl, K. J. (1997). The development and validation of the Children's Hope Scale. *Journal of Pediatric Psychology, 22,* 399–421.

Snyder, C. R., Ilardi, S. S., Cheavens, J., Michael, S. T., Yamhure, L., & Sympson, S. (2000). The role of hope in cognitive behavior therapies. *Cognitive Therapy and Research, 24,* 747–762.

Snyder, C. R., Ilardi, S., Michael, S., & Cheavens, J. (2000). Hope theory: Updating a common process for psychological change. In C. R. Snyder & R. E. Ingram (Eds.), *Handbook of psychological change: Psychotherapy processes and practices for the 21st century* (pp. 128–153). New York: Wiley.

Snyder, C. R., & Ingram, R. E. (1983). The impact of consensus information on help-seeking for psychological problems. *Journal of Personality and Social Psychology, 45,* 1118–1126.

Snyder, C. R., & Ingram, R. E. (2000). Psychotherapy: Questions for an evolving field. In C. R. Snyder & R. E. Ingram (Eds.), *Handbook of psychological change: Psychotherapy processes and practices for the 21st century* (pp. 707–726). New York: Wiley.

Snyder, C. R., Irving, L., & Anderson, J. R. (1991). Hope and health: Measuring the will and the ways. In C. R. Snyder & D. R. Forsyth (Eds.), *Handbook of social and clinical psychology: The health perspective* (pp. 285–305). Elmsford, NY: Pergamon.

Snyder, C. R., Lapointe, A. B., Crowson, J. J., Jr., & Early, S. (1998). Preferences of high- and low-hope people for self-referential input. *Cognition and Emotion, 12,* 807–823.

Snyder, C. R., & McCullough, M. (2000). A positive psychology field of dreams: "If you build it, they will come. . . ." *Journal of Social and Clinical Psychology, 19,* 151–160.

Snyder, C. R., McDermott, D., Cook, W., & Rapoff, M. (1997). *Hope for the journey: Helping children through the good times and the bad.* Boulder, CO: Westview; San Francisco: HarperCollins.

Snyder, C. R., Michael, S., & Cheavens, J. (1999). Hope as a psychotherapeutic foundation for nonspecific factors, placebos, and expectancies.

In M. A. Huble, B. Duncan, & S. Miller (Eds.), *Heart and soul of change* (pp. 179–200). Washington, DC: American Psychological Association.

Snyder, C. R., Odle, C., & Hackman, J. (1999, August). *Hope as related to perceived severity and tolerance of physical pain.* Paper presented at the annual meeting of the American Psychological Association, Boston.

Snyder, C. R., & Pulvers, K. (2001). Dr. Seuss, the coping machine, and "Oh, the places you will go." In C. R. Snyder (Ed.), *Coping with stress: Effective people and processes* (pp. 3–19). New York: Oxford University Press.

Snyder, C. R., Sympson, S. C., Michael, S. T., & Cheavens, J. (2000). The optimism and hope constructs: Variants on a positive expectancy theme. In E. C. Chang (Ed.), *Optimism and pessimism* (pp. 103–124). Washington, DC: American Psychological Association.

Snyder, C. R., Sympson, S. C., Ybasco, F. C., Borders, T. F., Babyak, M. A., & Higgins, R. L. (1996). Development and validation of the State Hope Scale. *Journal of Personality and Social Psychology, 70,* 321–335.

Snyder, C. R., & Taylor, J. D. (2000). Hope as a common factor across psychotherapy approaches: A lesson from the Dodo's Verdict. In C. R. Snyder (Ed.), *Handbook of hope: Theory, measures, and applications* (pp. 89–108). San Diego, CA: Academic Press.

Snyder, C. R., Wiklund, C., & Cheavens, J. (1999, August). *Hope and success in college.* Paper presented at the annual meeting of the American Psychological Association, Boston.

Stanton, A. L., & Snider, P. R. (1993). Coping with a breast cancer diagnosis: A prospective study. *Health Psychology, 12,* 16–23.

Stotland, E. (1969). *The psychology of hope.* San Francisco: Jossey-Bass.

Strutton, D., & Lumpkin, J. (1992). Relationship between optimism and coping strategies in the work environment. *Psychological Reports, 71,* 1179–1186.

Suls, J., & Fletcher, B. (1985). The relative efficacy of avoidant and nonavoidant coping strategies: A meta-analysis. *Health Psychology, 4,* 249–288.

Sumerlin, J. (1997). Self-actualization and hope. *Journal of Social Behavior and Personality, 12,* 1101–1110.

Sympson, S. (1999). *Validation of the Domain Specific Hope Scale.* Unpublished doctoral dissertation, University of Kansas, Lawrence.

Taylor, S. E. (1989). *Positive illusions: Creative self-deception and the healthy mind.* New York: Basic Books.

Tennen, H., & Affleck, G. (1999). Finding benefits in adversity. In C. R. Snyder (Ed.), *Coping: The psychology of what works* (pp. 279–304). New York: Oxford University Press.

Wells, L. E., & Marwell, G. (1976). *Self-esteem: Its conceptualization and measurement.* Beverly Hills, CA: Sage.

Worthington, E. L., Jr., Hight, T. L., Ripley, J. S., Perrone, K. M., Kurusu, T. A., & Jones, D. R. (1997). Strategic hope-focused relation-ship-enrichment counseling with individuals. *Journal of Counseling Psychology, 44,* 381–389.

Wylie, R. C. (1974). *The self-concept: A review of methodological and measuring instruments* (Vol. 1, rev. ed.). Lincoln: University of Nebraska Press.

Wylie, R. C. (1979). *The self-concept: Theory and research on selected topics* (Vol. 2, rev. ed.). Lincoln: University of Nebraska Press.

20

Self-Efficacy

The Power of Believing You Can

James E. Maddux

The very little engine looked up and saw the tears in the dolls' eyes. And she thought of the good little boys and girls on the other side of the mountain who would not have any toys or good food unless she helped. Then she said, "I think I can. I think I can. I think I can."

The Little Engine That Could
(Watty Piper, 1930)

Some of the most powerful truths also are the simplest—so simple that a child can understand them. The concept of *self-efficacy* deals with one of these truths—one so simple it can be captured in a children's book of 37 pages (with illustrations), yet so powerful that fully describing its implications has filled thousands of pages in scientific journals and books over the past two decades. This truth is that believing that you can accomplish what you want to accomplish is one of the most important ingredients—perhaps *the* most important ingredient—in the recipe for success. Any child who has read *The Little Engine That Could* knows this is so. For over 20 years, hundreds

of researchers have been trying to tell us *why* this is so.

The basic premise of self-efficacy theory is that "people's beliefs in their capabilities to produce desired effects by their own actions" (Bandura, 1997, p. vii) are the most important determinants of the behaviors people choose to engage in and how much they persevere in their efforts in the face of obstacles and challenges. Self-efficacy theory also maintains that these efficacy beliefs play a crucial role in psychological adjustment, psychological problems, and physical health, as well as professionally guided and self-guided behavioral change strategies.

Since the publication of Albert Bandura's 1977 *Psychological Review* article titled "Self-Efficacy: Toward a Unifying Theory of Behavior Change," the term *self-efficacy* has become ubiquitous in psychology and related fields. Hundreds of articles on every imaginable aspect of self-efficacy have appeared in journals devoted to psychology, sociology, kinesiology, public health, medicine, nursing, and other fields. In this chapter, I attempt to summarize what we have learned from over two decades of research on self-efficacy. I will address three basic questions: What is self-efficacy? Where does it come from? Why is it important?

What Is Self-Efficacy?

A Very Brief History

English novelist and poet Thomas Hardy once said, "What are called advanced ideas are really in great part but the latest fashion in definition—a more accurate expression, by words in logy and ism, of sensations men and women have vaguely grasped for centuries" (1891/ 1998, p. 115). Such is true of self-efficacy. Although the term *self-efficacy* is of recent origin, interest in beliefs about personal control has a long history in philosophy and psychology. Spinoza, David Hume, John Locke, William James, and (more recently) Gilbert Ryle have all struggled with understanding the role of "volition" and "the will" in human behavior (Russell, 1945; Vessey, 1967). In this century, the theories of effectance motivation (White, 1959), achievement motivation (McClelland, Atkinson, Clark, & Lowell, 1953), social learning (Rotter, 1966), and helplessness (Abramson, Seligman, & Teasdale, 1978) are just a few of the many attempts to explore relationships between perceptions of personal competence and human behavior, as well as psychological well-being (see also Skinner, 1995). Bandura's 1977 article, however, both formalized the notion of perceived competence as *self-efficacy* and offered a theory of how it develops and how it influences human behavior. I believe that what has appealed to so many researchers and theorists from so many different fields is that Bandura offered a construct that had intuitive and commonsense appeal, yet he defined this commonsense notion clearly and embedded it in a comprehensive theory. The essential idea was not new; what was new and important was the empirical rigor with which this idea could now be examined.

Defining Self-Efficacy

One of the best ways to get a clear sense of how self-efficacy is defined and measured is to distinguish it from related concepts.

Self-efficacy is not perceived skill; *it is what I believe I can do with my skills under certain conditions*. It is concerned not with my beliefs about my ability to perform specific and trivial motor acts but with my beliefs about my ability to coordinate and orchestrate skills and abilities in changing and challenging situations.

Self-efficacy beliefs are not simply predictions about behavior. Self-efficacy is concerned not with what I believe I *will* do but with what I believe I *can* do.

Self-efficacy beliefs are not causal attributions. Causal attributions are explanations for events, including my own behavior and its consequences. Self-efficacy beliefs are my beliefs about what I am capable of doing.

Self-efficacy is not an intention to behave or an intention to attain a particular goal. An intention is what I say I will probably do; and research has shown that intentions are influenced by a number of factors, including, but not limited to, efficacy beliefs (Maddux, 1999b).

Self-efficacy is not self-esteem. Self-esteem is what I believe about myself, and how I feel about what I believe about myself. Efficacy beliefs in a given domain will contribute to my self-esteem only in direct proportion to the importance I place on that domain.

Self-efficacy is not a motive, drive, or need for control. I can have a strong need for control in a particular domain and still hold weak beliefs about my efficacy for that domain.

Self-efficacy beliefs are not *outcome expectancies* (Bandura, 1997) or *behavior-outcome expectancies* (Maddux, 1999b). A behavior-outcome expectancy is my belief that a specific behavior may lead to a specific outcome in a specific situation. A self-efficacy belief, simply put, is the belief that I can perform the behavior that produces the outcome.

Self-efficacy is not a personality trait. Most conceptions of competence and control—including self-esteem (Hewitt, this volume), locus of control (Rotter, 1966), optimism (Carver & Scheier, this volume), hope (Snyder, Rand, & Sigmon, volume), hardiness (Kobasa, 1979), and learned resourcefulness (Rosenbaum, 1990) —are conceived as traits or traitlike. Self-efficacy is defined and measured not as a trait but as beliefs about the ability to coordinate skills and abilities to attain desired goals in particular domains and circumstances. Measures of "general" self-efficacy have been developed (e.g., Sherer at al., 1982; Tipton & Worthington, 1984) and are used frequently in research, but they have not been as useful as more specific self-efficacy measures in predicting what people will do under more specific circumstances (Bandura, 1997; Maddux, 1995).

Where Does Self-Efficacy Come From?

As noted previously, self-efficacy is not a genetically endowed trait. Instead, self-efficacy beliefs develop over time and through experience. The development of such beliefs begins, we assume, in infancy and continues throughout life. Understanding how self-efficacy develops requires understanding a broader theoretical background. Self-efficacy is best understood in the context of *social cognitive theory*—an approach to understanding human cognition, action, motivation, and emotion that assumes that we are active shapers of rather than simply passive reactors to our environments (Bandura, 1986, 1997; Barone, Maddux, & Snyder, 1997). Social cognitive theory's four basic premises, shortened and simplified, are as follows:

1. We have powerful *cognitive* or *symbolizing* capabilities that allow for the creation of internal models of experience, the development of innovative courses of action, the hypothetical testing of such courses of action through the prediction of outcomes, and the communication of complex ideas and experiences to others. We also can engage in *self-observation* and can analyze and evaluate our own behavior, thoughts, and emotions. These self-reflective activities set the stage for *self-regulation*.
2. Environmental events, inner personal factors (cognition, emotion, and biological events), and behaviors are reciprocal influences. We respond cognitively, effectively, and behaviorally to environmental events. Also, through cognition we exercise control over our own behavior, which then influences not only the environment but also our cognitive, affective, and biological states.
3. Self and personality are socially embedded. These are perceptions (accurate or not) of our own and others' patterns of social cognition, emotion, and action as they occur in patterns of situations. Because they are socially embedded, personality and self are not simply what we *bring* to our interactions with others; they are *created* in these interactions, and they change through these interactions.
4. We are capable of *self-regulation*. We choose goals and regulate our behavior in the pursuit of these goals. At the heart of self-regulation is our ability to anticipate or develop expectancies—to use past knowledge and experience to form beliefs about future events and states and beliefs about our abilities and behavior.

These assumptions suggest that the early development of self-efficacy is influenced primarily by two interacting factors. First, it is influenced by the development of the capacity for symbolic thought, particularly the capacity for understanding cause-and-effect relationships and the capacity for self-observation and self-reflection. The development of a sense of personal agency begins in infancy and moves from the perception of the causal relationship between events, to an understanding that actions produce results, to the recognition that one can produce actions that cause results (Bandura, 1997). Children must learn that one event can cause another event; that they are separate from other things and people; and that, therefore, they can be the origin of actions that affect their environments. As children's understanding of language increases, so does their capacity for symbolic thought and, therefore, their capacity for self-awareness and a sense of personal agency (Bandura, 1997).

Second, the development of efficacy beliefs is influenced by the responsiveness of environments, especially social environments, to the infant's or child's attempts at manipulation and control. Environments that are responsive to the child's actions facilitate the development of efficacy beliefs, whereas nonresponsive environments retard this development. The development of efficacy beliefs encourages exploration, which in turn enhances the infant's sense of agency. The child's social environment (especially parents) is usually the most responsive part of his or her environment. Thus, children usually develop a sense of efficacy from engaging in actions that manipulate the people around them, which then generalizes to the nonsocial environment (Bandura, 1997). Parents can facilitate or hinder the development of this sense of agency not only by their responses to the infant's or child's actions, but also by encouraging and enabling the child to explore and master his or her environment.

Efficacy beliefs and a sense of agency continue to develop throughout the life span as we continually integrate information from five primary sources.

Performance Experiences

Our own attempts to control our environments are the most powerful source of self-efficacy information (Bandura, 1977, 1997). Successful attempts at control that I attribute to my own efforts will strengthen self-efficacy for that behavior or domain. Perceptions of failure at control attempts usually diminish self-efficacy.

Vicarious Experiences

Self-efficacy beliefs are influenced also by our observations of the behavior of others and the consequences of those behaviors. We use this information to form expectancies about our own behavior and its consequences, depending primarily on the extent to which we believe that we are similar to the person we are observing. Vicarious experiences generally have weaker effects on self-efficacy expectancy than do performance experiences (Bandura, 1997).

Imaginal Experiences

We can influence self-efficacy beliefs by imagining ourselves or others behaving effectively or ineffectively in hypothetical situations. Such images may be derived from actual or vicarious experiences with situations similar to the one anticipated, or they may be induced by verbal persuasion, as when a psychotherapist guides a client through imaginal interventions such as systematic desensitization and covert modeling (Williams, 1995). Simply imagining myself doing something well, however, is not likely to have as strong an influence on my self-efficacy as will an actual experience (Williams, 1995).

Verbal Persuasion

Efficacy beliefs are influenced by what others say to us about what they believe we can or cannot do. The potency of verbal persuasion as a source of self-efficacy expectancies will be influenced by such factors as the expertness, trustworthiness, and attractiveness of the source, as suggested by decades of research on verbal persuasion and attitude change (e.g., Eagly & Chaiken, 1993). Verbal persuasion is a less potent source of enduring change in self-efficacy expectancy than performance experiences and vicarious experiences.

Physiological and Emotional States

Physiological and emotional states influence self-efficacy when we learn to associate poor performance or perceived failure with aversive physiological arousal and success with pleasant feeling states. Thus, when I become aware of unpleasant physiological arousal, I am more likely to doubt my competence than if my physiological state were pleasant or neutral. Likewise, comfortable physiological sensations are likely to lead me to feel confident in my ability in the situation at hand. Physiological indicants of self-efficacy expectancy, however, extend beyond autonomic arousal. For example, in activities involving strength and stamina, such as exercise and athletic performances, perceived efficacy is influenced by such experiences as fatigue and pain (e.g., Bandura, 1986, 1997).

Why Is Self-Efficacy Important?

This is the most difficult question of all to answer because fully describing the many ways that self-efficacy beliefs are important would take hundreds of pages. I will focus on five areas: self-efficacy and psychological adjustment; self-efficacy and physical health; self-efficacy and self-regulation; self-efficacy and psychotherapy; and collective efficacy.

Self-Efficacy and Psychological Adjustment

Most philosophers and psychological theorists agree that a sense of control over our behavior, our environment, and our own thoughts and feelings is essential for happiness and a sense of well-being. When the world seems predictable and controllable, and when our behaviors, thoughts, and emotions seem within our control, we are better able to meet life's challenges, build healthy relationships, and achieve personal satisfaction and peace of mind. Feelings of loss of control are common among people who seek the help of psychotherapists and counselors.

Self-efficacy beliefs play a major role in a number of common psychological problems, as well as in successful interventions for these problems. Low self-efficacy expectancies are an important feature of depression (Bandura, 1997; Maddux & Meier, 1995). Depressed people usually believe they are less capable than other people of behaving effectively in many important areas of life. Dysfunctional anxiety and avoidant behavior are often the direct result of low self-efficacy expectancies for managing threatening situations (Bandura, 1997; Williams, 1995). People who have strong confidence in their abilities to perform and manage potentially difficult situations will approach those situations calmly and will not be unduly disrupted by difficulties. On the other hand, people who lack confidence in their abilities will approach such situations with apprehension, thereby reducing the probability that they will perform effectively. Those with low self-efficacy also will respond to difficulties with increased anxiety, which usually disrupts performance, thereby further lowering self-efficacy, and so on. Finally, self-efficacy plays a powerful role in attempts to overcome substance abuse problems and eating disorders (Bandura, 1997; DiClemente, Fairhurst, & Piotrowski, 1995). For each of these problems, enhancing self-efficacy for overcoming the problem and for implementing self-control strategies in specific challenging situations is essential to the success of therapeutic interventions (Bandura, 1997; Maddux, 1995).

Most of the research on self-efficacy and psychological adjustment has focused on traditional types of psychopathology. This limited focus, however, is a reflection of the orientations of researchers' interests, not the assumptions of self-efficacy theory. Self-efficacy theory and social cognitive theory are concerned less with understanding pathology and more with understanding the positive aspects of psychological functioning. They also are concerned less with risk factors and protective factors and more with *enablement factors*—the personal resources that allow people "to select and structure their environments in ways that set a successful course for their lives" (Bandura, 1997, p. 177).

Self-Efficacy and Physical Health

Health and medical care in our society gradually have been shifting from an exclusive emphasis on treating disease to an emphasis on preventing disease and promoting good health. Most strategies for preventing health problems, enhancing health, and hastening recovery from

illness and injury involve changing behavior. Research on self-efficacy has greatly enhanced our understanding of how and why people adopt healthy and unhealthy behaviors and of how to change behaviors that affect health (Bandura, 1997; Maddux, Brawley, & Boykin, 1995; O'Leary & Brown, 1995). Beliefs about self-efficacy influence health in two ways.

First, self-efficacy influences the adoption of healthy behaviors, the cessation of unhealthy behaviors, and the maintenance of behavioral changes in the face of challenge and difficulty. All the major theories of health behavior, such as protection motivation theory (Maddux & Rogers, 1983; Rogers & Prentice-Dunn, 1997), the health belief model (Strecher, Champion, & Rosenstock, 1997), and the theory or reasoned action/planned behavior (Ajzen, 1988; Fishbein & Ajzen, 1975; Maddux & DuCharme, 1997), include self-efficacy as a key component (see also Maddux, 1993; Weinstein, 1993). In addition, researchers have shown that enhancing self-efficacy beliefs is crucial to successful change and maintenance of virtually every behavior crucial to health, including exercise, diet, stress management, safe sex, smoking cessation, overcoming alcohol abuse, compliance with treatment and prevention regimens, and disease detection behaviors such as breast self-examinations (Bandura, 1997; Maddux et al., 1995).

Second, self-efficacy beliefs influence a number of biological processes that, in turn, influence health and disease (Bandura, 1997). Self-efficacy beliefs affect the body's physiological responses to stress, including the immune system (Bandura, 1997; O'Leary & Brown, 1995). Lack of perceived control over environmental demands can increase susceptibility to infections and hasten the progression of disease (Bandura, 1997). Self-efficacy beliefs also influence the activation of catecholamines, a family of neurotransmitters important to the management of stress and perceived threat, along with the endogenous painkillers referred to as *endorphins* (Bandura, 1997; O'Leary & Brown, 1995).

Self-Efficacy and Self-Regulation

Social cognitive theory and self-efficacy theory assume that we have the capacity for self-regulation and self-initiated change, and studies of people who have overcome difficult behavioral problems without professional help provide compelling evidence for this capacity (e.g.,

Prochaska, Norcross, & DiClemente, 1994). Research on self-efficacy has added greatly to our understanding of how we guide our own behavior in the pursuit of happiness. Self-regulation (simplified) depends on three interacting components (Bandura, 1986, 1997; Barone et al., 1997): goals or standards of performance, self-evaluative reactions to performance, and self-efficacy beliefs.

Goals are essential to self-regulation because we attempt to regulate our actions, thoughts, and emotions to achieve desired outcomes. The ability to envision desired future events and states allows us to create incentives that motivate and guide our actions. Through our goals, we adopt personal standards and evaluate our behavior against these standards. Thus, goals provide us with standards against which to monitor our progress and evaluate both our progress and our abilities (Snyder, Rand, & Sigmon, this volume).

Self-evaluative reactions are important in self-regulation because our beliefs about the progress we are making (or not making) toward our goals are major determinants of our emotional reactions during goal-directed activity. These emotional reactions, in turn, can enhance or disrupt self-regulation. The belief that I am inefficacious and making poor progress toward a goal produces distressing emotional states (e.g., anxiety, depression) that can lead to cognitive and behavioral ineffectiveness and self-regulatory failure. Strong self-efficacy beliefs and strong expectations for goal attainment, however, usually produce adaptive emotional states that, in turn, enhance self-regulation.

Self-efficacy beliefs influence self-regulation in several ways. First, self-efficacy influences the goals we set. The higher my self-efficacy in a specific achievement domain, the loftier will be the goals that I set for myself in that domain.

Second, self-efficacy beliefs influence our choices of goal-directed activities, expenditure of effort, persistence in the face of challenge and obstacles (Bandura, 1986; Locke & Latham, 1990), and reactions to perceived discrepancies between goals and current performance (Bandura, 1986). If I have strong efficacy beliefs, I will be relatively resistant to the disruptions in self-regulation that can result from difficulties and setbacks, and I will persevere. Perseverance usually produces desired results, and this success then increases my sense of efficacy (see Masten and Reed, this volume).

Third, self-efficacy for solving problems and making decisions influences the efficiency and effectiveness of problem solving and decision making (see Heppner & Lee, this volume). When faced with complex decisions, people who have confidence in their ability to solve problems use their cognitive resources more effectively than do those people who doubt their cognitive skills (e.g., Bandura, 1997). Such efficacy usually leads to better solutions and greater achievement. In the face of difficulty, if I have high self-efficacy, I am likely to remain *task-diagnostic* and continue to search for solutions to problems. If my self-efficacy is low, however, I am more likely to become *self-diagnostic* and reflect on my inadequacies, which detracts from my efforts to assess and solve the problem (Bandura, 1997).

Self-Efficacy and Psychotherapy

I use the term *psychotherapy* to refer to professionally guided interventions designed to enhance psychological well-being, while acknowledging that self-regulation plays an important role in all such interventions. In fact, most professionally guided interventions are designed to enhance self-regulation because they are concerned with helping individuals gain or regain a sense of efficacy over important aspects of their lives (Frank & Frank, 1991). Different interventions, or different components of an intervention, may be equally effective because they equally enhance self-efficacy for crucial behavioral and cognitive skills (Bandura, 1986, 1997; Maddux & Lewis, 1995).

Self-efficacy theory emphasizes the importance of arranging experiences designed to increase the person's sense of efficacy for specific behaviors in specific problematic and challenging situations. Self-efficacy theory suggests that formal interventions should not simply resolve specific problems but should provide people with the skills and sense of efficacy for solving problems themselves. Some basic strategies for enhancing self-efficacy are based on the four sources of self-efficacy previously noted.

Performance Experience

The phrase "seeing is believing" underscores the importance of providing people with tangible evidence of their success. When people actually can see themselves coping effectively with difficult situations, their sense of mastery is likely to be heightened. These experiences are likely to be most successful when both goals and strategies are specific. Goals that are concrete, specific, and proximal (short-range) provide greater incentive, motivation, and evidence of efficacy than goals that are abstract, vague, and set in the distant future (Snyder, Rand, & Sigmon, this volume). Specific goals allow people to identify the specific behaviors needed for successful achievement and to know when they have succeeded (Snyder, Rand, & Sigmon, this volume; Locke & Latham, 1990). For example, the most effective interventions for phobias and fears involve *guided mastery*—in vivo experience with the feared object or situation during therapy sessions, or between sessions as "homework" assignments (Williams, 1995). In cognitive treatments of depression, clients are provided structured guidance in arranging success experiences that will counteract low self-efficacy expectancies (Hollon & Beck, 1994).

Verbal Persuasion

Most formal psychological interventions rely strongly on verbal persuasion to enhance a client's self-efficacy and encouraging small risks that may lead to small successes. In cognitive and cognitive-behavioral therapies, the therapist engages the client in a discussion of the client's dysfunctional beliefs, attitudes, and expectancies and helps the client see the irrationality and self-defeating nature of such beliefs. The therapist encourages the client to adopt new, more adaptive beliefs and to act on these new beliefs and expectancies. As a result, the client experiences the successes that can lead to more enduring changes in self-efficacy beliefs and adaptive behavior (for reviews, see Hollon & Beck, 1994; Ingram, Kendall, & Chen, 1991). People also rely daily on verbal persuasion as a self-efficacy facilitator by seeking the support of other people when attempting to lose weight, quit smoking, maintain an exercise program, or summon up the courage to confront a difficult boss or loved one.

Vicarious Experience

Vicarious and imaginal means can be used to teach new skills and enhance self-efficacy for those skills. For example, modeling films and videotapes have been used successfully to encourage socially withdrawn children to interact with other children. The child viewing the film sees the model child, someone much like himself, experience success and comes to believe that he, too, can do the same thing (Conger & Keane, 1981). In vivo modeling has been used

successfully in the treatment of phobic individuals. This research has shown that changes in self-efficacy beliefs for approach behaviors mediate adaptive behavioral changes (Bandura, 1986; Williams 1995). Common everyday (nonprofessional) examples of the use of vicarious experiences to enhance self-efficacy include advertisements for weight-loss and smoking cessation programs that feature testimonials from successful people. The clear message from these testimonials is that the listener or reader also can accomplish this difficult task. Formal and informal "support groups"—people sharing their personal experiences in overcoming a common adversity such as addiction, obesity, or illness—also provide forums for the enhancement of self-efficacy.

Imaginal Experience

Live or filmed models may be difficult to obtain, but the imagination is an easily harnessed resource. Imagining ourselves engaging in feared behaviors or overcoming difficulties can be used to enhance self-efficacy. For example, cognitive therapy of anxiety and fear problems often involves modifying visual images of danger and anxiety, including images of coping effectively with the feared situation. Imaginal (covert) modeling has been used successfully in interventions to increase assertive behavior and self-efficacy for assertiveness (Kazdin, 1979). Systematic desensitization and implosion are traditional behavioral therapy techniques that rely on the ability to imagine coping effectively with a difficult situation (Emmelkamp, 1994). Because maladaptive distorted imagery is an important component of anxiety and depression, various techniques have been developed to help clients modify distortions and maladaptive assumptions contained in their visual images of danger and anxiety. A client can gain a sense of control over a situation by imagining a future self that can deal effectively with the situation.

Physiological and Emotional States

We usually feel more self-efficacious when we are calm than when we are aroused and distressed. Thus, strategies for controlling and reducing emotional arousal (specifically anxiety) while attempting new behaviors should increase self-efficacy and increase the likelihood of successful implementation. Hypnosis, biofeedback, relaxation training, meditation, and medication are the most common strategies for reducing the physiological arousal typically associated with low self-efficacy and poor performance.

Enhancing the Impact of Success

Success is subjective, and accomplishments that are judged "successful" by observers are not always judged so by the performer. Nor do such accomplishments automatically enhance efficacy beliefs. We often discount self-referential information that is inconsistent with our current self-views (Barone et al., 1997; Fiske & Taylor, 1991). Thus, when we feel distressed and believe we are incompetent and helpless, we are likely to ignore or discount information from therapists, family, friends, and our own behavioral successes that is inconsistent with our negative self-beliefs (Barone et al., 1997; Fiske & Taylor, 1991). Therefore, we need to make concerted efforts to increase success experiences, but we also must learn to interpret that success *as success* and as the result of our own efforts. We can interpret success experiences more effectively in three ways.

Viewing competence as incremental, not fixed: If we view competence as a set of skills to be performed in specific situations rather than as a trait, and as acquirable through effort and experience rather than as fixed, we are more likely to persist in the face of obstacles to success (Dweck, 2000). The perception that competence is incremental and can be increased by experience can be enhanced by comparing recent successful coping strategies with past ineffective behaviors. Therefore, we need to be continually vigilant for success experiences and actively retrieve past successes in times of challenge and doubt.

Changing causal attributions: Causal attributions are explanations we provide ourselves for our own behavior and the behavior of others. Causal attributions influence self-efficacy and vice versa (Maddux, 1999b). For this reason, we should attribute successes to our own effort and ability rather than to environmental circumstances or to the expertise and insights of others (Forsterling, 1986; Goldfried & Robins, 1982; Thompson, 1991).

Encouraging minor distortions: Beliefs about self and world need not always be accurate to be adaptive. Psychological adjustment is enhanced by minor distortions in the perception of control over important life events (e.g., Taylor & Brown, 1988). Strong beliefs of self-efficacy can be self-confirming because such beliefs encourage us to set challenging goals, persist in the face of obstacles, attend to efficacy-enhancing information, and select efficacy-enhancing environments. Encouraging discouraged people to believe that they are more competent than they think they are (based on their own observations) may prompt them into action and lead to efficacy-enhancing success.

Collective Efficacy

This chapter has focused so far on the efficacy beliefs of individuals about themselves as individuals. Positive psychology and social cognitive theory both emphasize the social embeddedness of the individual. For this reason I cannot leave the concept of efficacy locked inside of the person. Accomplishing important goals in groups, organizations, and societies always has depended on the ability of individuals to identify the abilities of other individuals and to harness these abilities to accomplish common goals. Thus, a concept of perceived mastery limited to individuals will have limited utility. Thus, in self-efficacy theory it is recognized that no man or woman is an island and that there are limits to what individuals can accomplish alone. This idea is captured in the notion of *collective efficacy*, a group's shared belief in its conjoint capabilities to organize and execute the courses of action required to produce given levels of attainments (Bandura, 1997, p. 477; also Zaccaro, Blair, Peterson, & Zazanis, 1995). Simply stated, collective efficacy is the extent to which we believe that we can work together effectively to accomplish our shared goals.

Despite a lack of consensus on its measurement (Bandura, 1997; Maddux, 1999a), collective efficacy has been found to be important to a number of "collectives." The more efficacious spouses feel about their shared ability to accomplish important shared goals, the more satisfied they are with their marriages (Kaplan & Maddux, in press). The collective efficacy of an athletic team can be raised or lowered by false feedback about ability and can subsequently influence its success in competitions (Hodges & Carron, 1992). The individual and collective efficacy of teachers for effective instruction seems to affect the academic achievement of schoolchildren (Bandura, 1993, 1997). The effectiveness of self-managing work teams (Little & Madigan, 1994) and group brainstorming (Prussia & Kinicki, 1996) also seems to be related to a collective sense of efficacy. Researchers also are beginning to understand the origins of collective efficacy for social and political change (Fernandez-Ballesteros, Diez-Nicolas, Caprara, Barbaranelli, & Bandura, 2000). Of course, personal efficacy and collective efficacy go hand in hand because a "collection of inveterate self-doubters is not easily forged into a collectively efficacious force" (Bandura, 1997, p. 480).

Conclusions

In this chapter, I was able to briefly discuss only a small number of basic issues concerning self-efficacy. I encourage the reader to consult the marked references with asterisks for additional information. We have learned much about the role of self-efficacy beliefs and psychological adjustment and maladjustment, physical health, and self-guided and professionally guided behavior change. There is, of course, much more to be learned. In keeping with the agenda of positive psychology (Seligman & Csikszentmihalyi, 2000), I suggest two broad avenues of future research.

First, positive psychology emphasizes the development of positive human qualities and the facilitation of psychological health and happiness over the mere prevention of or remediation of negative human qualities and human misery. It also embraces the notion that individuals can be self-initiating agents for change in their own lives and the lives of others. The emphasis of social cognitive theory and self-efficacy theory on the development of *enablement*—providing people with skills for selecting and attaining the life goals they desire—over prevention and risk reduction is consonant with both of these emphases. Self-efficacy research concerned with enhancing our understanding of self-regulation will enhance our understanding of how to provide people with these enablement skills.

Second, positive psychology emphasizes the social embeddedness of the individual and acknowledges that my individual success and happiness depends to a large degree on my ability to cooperate, collaborate, negotiate, and otherwise live in harmony with other people. In addition, the ability of businesses, organizations, communities, and governments (local, state, and national) to achieve their goals will increasingly depend on their ability to coordinate their efforts, particularly because these goals often conflict. For this reason, collective efficacy—including collective efficacy in organizations and

schools, and efficacy for social and political change—provides numerous important questions for future research. In a world in which communication across the globe often is faster than communication across the street, and in which cooperation and collaboration in commerce and government are becoming increasingly common and crucial, understanding collective efficacy will become even more important.

The simple yet powerful truth that children learn from *The Little Engine That Could* has been amply supported by over two decades of self-efficacy research—namely, that when equipped with an unshakable belief in one's ideas, goals, and capacity for achievement, there are few limits to what one can accomplish. As Bandura (1997) has stated, "People see the extraordinary feats of others but not the unwavering commitment and countless hours of perseverant effort that produced them" (p. 119). They then overestimate the role of "talent" in these accomplishments, while underestimating the role of self-regulation. The timeless message of research on self-efficacy is the simple, powerful truth that confidence, effort, and persistence are more potent than innate ability (Dweck, 2000). In this sense, self-efficacy is concerned with human potential and possibilities, not limitations, thus making it a truly *positive* psychology.

References

Abramson, L. Y., Seligman, M. E. P., & Teasdale, J. D. (1978). Learned helplessness in humans: Critique and reformulation. *Journal of Abnormal Psychology, 87,* 49–74.

Ajzen, I. (1988). *Attitudes, personality, and behavior.* Chicago: Dorsey.

*Bandura, A. (1977). Self-efficacy: Toward a unifying theory of behavioral change. *Psychological Review, 84,* 191–215.

*Bandura, A. (1986). *Social foundations of thought and action.* New York: Prentice-Hall.

Bandura, A. (1993). Perceived self-efficacy in cognitive development and functioning. *Educational Psychologist, 28,* 117–148.

*Bandura, A. (1997). *Self-efficacy: The exercise of control.* New York: Freeman.

*Barone, D., Maddux, J. E., & Snyder, C. R. (1997). *Social cognitive psychology: History and current domains.* New York: Plenum.

Conger, J. C., & Keane, S. P. (1981). Social skills intervention in the treatment of isolated or withdrawn children. *Psychological Bulletin, 90,* 478–495.

DiClemente, C. C., Fairhurst, S. K., & Piotrowski, N. A. (1995). Self-efficacy and addictive behaviors. In J. E. Maddux (Ed.), *Self-efficacy, adaptation, and adjustment: Theory, research, and application* (pp. 109–142). New York: Plenum.

*Dweck, C. S. (2000). *Self-theories: Their role in motivation, personality, and development.* Philadelphia: Taylor and Francis.

Eagly, A. H., & Chaiken, S. (1993). *The psychology of attitudes.* New York: Harcourt, Brace, Jovanovich.

Emmelkamp, P. M. G. (1994). Behavior therapy with adults. In A. E. Bergin & S. L. Garfield (Eds.), *Handbook of psychotherapy and behavior change* (4th ed., pp. 379–427). New York: Wiley.

Fernandez-Ballesteros, R., Diez-Nicolas, J., Caprara, G. V., Barbaranelli, C., & Bandura, A. (2000). *Determinants and structural relation of personal efficacy to collective efficacy.* Unpublished manuscript, Stanford University, Stanford, CA.

Fishbein, M., & Ajzen, I. (1975). *Belief, attitude, intention, and behavior: An introduction to theory and research.* Reading, MA: Addison-Wesley.

Fiske, S. T., & Taylor, S. E. (1991). *Social cognition* (2nd ed.). New York: McGraw-Hill.

Forsterling, F. (1986). Attributional conceptions in clinical psychology. *American Psychologist, 41,* 275–285.

Frank, J. D., & Frank, J. B. (1991). *Persuasion and healing: A comparative study of psychotherapy* (3rd ed.). Baltimore: Johns Hopkins University Press.

Goldfried, M. R., & Robins, C. (1982). On the facilitation of self-efficacy. *Cognitive Therapy and Research, 6,* 361–380.

Hardy, T. (1891/1998). *Tess of the d'Urbervilles.* New York: Barnes and Noble.

Hodges, L., & Carron, A. V. (1992). Collective efficacy and group performance. *International Journal of Sport Psychology, 23,* 48–59.

Hollon, S. D., & Beck, A. T. (1994). Cognitive and cognitive-behavioral therapies. In A. E. Bergin & S. L. Garfield (Eds.), *Handbook of psychotherapy and behavior change* (4th ed., pp. 428–466). New York: Wiley.

Ingram, R. E., Kendall, P. C., & Chen, A. H. (1991). Cognitive-behavioral interventions. In C. R. Snyder & D. R. Forsyth (Eds.), *Handbook of social and clinical psychology* (pp. 509–522). New York: Pergamon.

Kaplan, M., & Maddux, J. E. (in press). Goals and marital satisfaction: Perceived support for personal goals and collective efficacy for collective goals. *Journal of Social and Clinical Psychology.*

Kazdin, A. E. (1979). Imagery elaboration and self-efficacy in the covert modeling treatment of unassertive behavior. *Journal of Consulting and Clinical Psychology, 47,* 725–733.

Kobasa, S. C. (1979). Stressful life events and health: An inquiry into hardiness. *Journal of Personality and Social Psychology, 37,* 1–11.

Little, B. L., & Madigan, R. M. (1994, August). *Motivation in work teams: A test of the construct of collective efficacy.* Paper presented at the annual meeting of the Academy of Management, Houston, Texas.

Locke, E. A., & Latham, G. P. (1990). *A theory of goal setting and task performance.* Englewood Cliffs, NJ: Prentice-Hall.

Maddux, J. E. (1993). Social cognitive models of health and exercise behavior: An introduction and review of conceptual issues. *Journal of Applied Sport Psychology, 5,* 116–140.

*Maddux, J. E. (1995). Self-efficacy theory: An introduction. In J. E. Maddux (Ed.), *Self-efficacy, adaptation, and adjustment: Theory, research, and application* (pp. 3–36). New York: Plenum.

Maddux, J. E. (1999a). The collective construction of collective efficacy. *Group Dynamics: Theory, Research, and Practice, 3,* 1–4.

*Maddux, J. E. (1999b). Expectancies and the social-cognitive perspective: Basic principles, processes, and variables. In I. Kirsch (Ed.), *How expectancies shape behavior* (pp. 17–40). Washington, DC: American Psychological Association.

*Maddux, J. E., Brawley, L., & Boykin, A. (1995). Self-efficacy and healthy decision-making: Protection, promotion, and detection. In J. E. Maddux (Ed.), *Self-efficacy, adaptation, and adjustment: Theory, research, and application* (pp. 173–202). New York: Plenum.

Maddux, J. E., DuCharme, K. A. (1997). Behavioral intentions in theories of health behavior. In D. Gochman (Ed.), *Handbook of health behavior research I: Personal and social determinants* (pp. 133–152). New York: Plenum.

*Maddux, J. E., & Lewis, J. (1995). Self-efficacy and adjustment: Basic principles and issues. In J. E. Maddux (Ed.), *Self-efficacy, adaptation, and adjustment: Theory, research, and application* (pp. 37–68). New York: Plenum.

Maddux, J. E., & Meier, L. J. (1995). Self-efficacy and depression. In J. E. Maddux (Ed.), *Self-efficacy, adaptation, and adjustment: Theory, research, and application* (pp. 143–169). New York: Plenum.

Maddux, J. E., & Rogers, R. W. (1983). Protection motivation and self-efficacy: A revised theory of fear appeals and attitude change. *Journal of Experimental Social Psychology, 19,* 469–479.

McClelland, D. C., Atkinson, J. W., Clark, R. W., & Lowell, E. L. (1953). *The achievement motive.* New York: Appleton-Century-Crofts.

O'Leary, A., & Brown, S. (1995). Self-efficacy and the physiological stress response. In J. E. Maddux (Ed.), *Self-efficacy, adaptation, and adjustment: Theory, research, and application* (pp. 227–248). New York: Plenum.

Piper, W. (1989). *The little engine that could.* New York: Platt and Monk. (Original work published 1930)

Prochaska, J. O., Norcross, J. C., & DiClemente, C. C. (1994). *Changing for good.* New York: Morrow.

Prussia, G. E., & Kinicki, A. J. (1996). A motivational investigation of group effectiveness using social cognitive theory. *Journal of Applied Psychology, 81,* 187–198.

Rogers, R. W., & Prentice-Dunn, S. (1997). Protection motivation theory. In D. Gochman (Ed.), *Handbook of health behavior research 1: Personal and social determinants.* New York: Plenum.

Rosenbaum, M. (Ed.). (1990). *Learned resourcefulness: On coping skills, self-control, and adaptive behavior.* New York: Springer.

Rotter, J. B. (1966). Generalized expectancies for internal versus external control of reinforcement. *Psychological Monographs, 80* (1, Whole No. 609).

Russell, B. (1945). *A history of Western philosophy.* New York: Simon and Schuster.

Seligman, M. E. P., & Csikszentmihalyi, M. (2000). Positive psychology: An introduction. *American Psychologist, 55,* 5–14.

Sherer, M., Maddux, J. E., Mercandante, B., Prentice-Dunn, S., Jacobs, B., & Rogers, R. W. (1982). The self-efficacy scale: Construction and validation. *Psychological Reports, 51,* 633–671.

*Skinner, E. A. (1995). *Perceived control, motivation, and coping.* Thousand Oaks, CA: Sage.

Strecher, V. J., Champion, V. L., & Rosenstock, I. M. (1997). The health belief model and health behavior. In D. Gochman (Ed.). *Handbook of health behavior research I: Personal and social determinants* (pp. 71–92). New York: Plenum.

Taylor, S. E., & Brown, J. D. (1988). Illusion and well-being: A social psychological perspective on mental health. *Psychological Bulletin, 2,* 193–210.

Thompson, S. C. (1991). Intervening to enhance perceptions of control. In C. R. Snyder & D. R. Forsyth (Eds.), *Handbook of social and clinical psychology* (pp. 607–623). New York: Pergamon.

Tipton, R. M., & Worthington, E. L. (1984). The measurement of generalized self-efficacy: A study of construct validity. *Journal of Personality Assessment, 48,* 545–548.

Vessey, G. N. A. (1967). Volition. In P. Edwards (Ed.), *Encyclopedia of philosophy* (Vol. 8). New York: Macmillan.

Weinstein, N. D. (1993). Testing four competing theories of health-protective behavior. *Health Psychology, 12,* 324–333.

White, R. W. (1959). Motivation reconsidered: The concept of competence. *Psychological Review, 66,* 297–333.

Williams, S. L. (1995). Self-efficacy, anxiety, and phobic disorders. In J. E. Maddux (Ed.), *Self-efficacy, adaptation, and adjustment: Theory, research, and application* (pp. 69–107). New York: Plenum.

Zaccaro, S., Blair, V., Peterson, C., & Zazanis, M. (1995). Collective efficacy. In J. E. Maddux (Ed.), *Self-efficacy, adaptation, and adjustment: Theory, research, and application* (pp. 305–330). New York: Plenum.

21

Problem-Solving Appraisal and Psychological Adjustment

P. Paul Heppner & Dong-gwi Lee

Because we face a myriad of decisions, daily hassles, major life events, and ever-changing situations, people frequently are confronted with attention-demanding problems. How people typically respond to life's problems is of critical importance, particularly how they appraise their problem-solving skills and whether they generally approach or avoid the many problems of life. Problems are solved by moving ahead. Some people bring many skills and strengths in solving the multitude of problems in life, whereas others have significant problem-solving deficits. The research evidence in this chapter will clearly indicate that how people appraise their problem solving affects not only how they cope with problems, but also their psychological adjustment.

Consider the case of two female college students, each of whom recently broke up with her boyfriend. After a year of dating, Tanya decided to end the romantic relationship. Although there were many qualities in Michael that Tanya liked, there were also nagging differences in some of their long-term goals, values, and approach to life that would not go away. Although Tanya was feeling sad and "kind of down," after reflection she knew it was a good

decision. She knew in her heart the relationship would continue to pose difficulties as time passed, and she needed to end the relationship. Tanya also felt confident in her ability to meet and develop intimate relationships with other men. Even though Tanya was in a relationship that was not right for her, she was an effective problem solver and, most important, she appraised herself as an effective problem solver, both of which were important strengths that Tanya brought to coping with life's demands.

In contrast, Jennifer also recently broke up with her boyfriend. But a month later, Jennifer was quite depressed; when she tried to make up with her boyfriend, he refused. Jennifer felt she made a mistake and would never find a man like him again. She felt alone, anxious, and hopeless, had not studied much for the last 3 weeks, and was having a lot of difficulty sleeping. Jennifer lacked confidence in herself and felt herself slipping deeper into a dark hole; suicide had crossed her mind more than once in the last few weeks. Jennifer was not solving her problems very well, and she did not have a positive appraisal of her problem-solving ability.

These stories highlight how one's personal skills and resources affect responses to stressful life events. Positive psychology builds on people's strengths to enhance their well-being. A critical strength or resource for coping with life's demands is a person's appraisal of his or her problem-solving skills and style. This chapter focuses on how problem-solving appraisal has been empirically demonstrated to be an important asset in living and an important component of positive psychology. It begins with a brief history of applied problem solving, followed by an introduction to problem-solving appraisal, how it is measured, a summary of the problem-solving appraisal literature, a brief overview of problem-solving training interventions, and finally future research directions and conclusions.

Brief History of Applied Problem Solving

Because we are consistently confronted with attention-demanding problems, it is not surprising that psychologists have been exploring the problem-solving topic for years. Indeed, by the mid-1970s, the conceptions of problem solving included various learning (e.g., Skinner, 1974), Gestalt (e.g., Maier, 1970), and computer simulation approaches (e.g., Newell, Shaw, & Simon, 1963). In the bulk of this early research, the focus often has been on impersonal laboratory problems. In their landmark article, D'Zurilla and Goldfried (1971) reviewed applied problem-solving research with the goal of helping individuals become more effective applied problem solvers. Subsequently, more attention was given to how people grapple with and solve personal, ambiguous, ill-defined problems (e.g., Janis & Mann, 1977), as well as implications for persons in the helping professions (e.g., Heppner, 1978).

In the early applied problem-solving literature, problem solving was conceptualized as a constellation of relatively discrete, cognitive abilities or thought processes. For example, the pioneering work in the late 1960s and 1970s of Shure, Spivack, and their colleagues investigated interpersonal cognitive problem-solving skills such as problem sensitivity, means-ends thinking, alternative solution thinking, causal thinking, and consequential thinking (see Shure, 1982). In other early research, problem-solving skills were conceptualized within stage sequential models, with a notable exemplar being D'Zurilla and Goldfried's (1971) five-stage

model (general orientation, problem definition and formulation, generation of alternatives, decision making, and verification). This stage sequential model led to the development of problem-solving training interventions (see D'Zurilla, 1986; D'Zurilla & Nezu, 1982). Initially, the five stages also were used for conceptualizing psychotherapy activities (e.g., Heppner, 1978; Urban & Ford, 1971); later, with advances in our understanding of the complexities of information-processing, more sophisticated information processing theories were developed within problem-solving frameworks (e.g., Anderson, 1983). Subsequently, scholars proposed more comprehensive analyses of the problem-solving activities in the psychotherapy process (Heppner & Krauskopf, 1987). In the 1990s, there was yet further refinement of applied problem-solving models and training (e.g., D'Zurilla & Nezu, 1999).

Model Advocated in This Chapter: Problem-Solving Appraisal

Persistent difficulties in the applied literature have involved the conceptualization and measurement of actual problem-solving skills, effectiveness, or competence (e.g., Kendall & Fischler, 1984). Although this measurement remains problematic, in this chapter we will delve into a closely related construct—a person's appraisal of his or her problem-solving skills. Influenced by research on the importance of higher order or metacognitive variables in various cognitive processes, Butler and Meichenbaum (1981) suggested that a crucial target is not just with "the specific knowledge or processes that individuals may apply directly to the solution of problems but with higher order variables that affect how (and whether) they will solve problems" (p. 219; subsequently Bandura [1986] provided empirical support for this point). Butler and Meichenbaum also emphasized the centrality of an individual's self-appraisal in his or her problem-solving ability. Similarly, other writers in the coping literature suggested that appraisal of one's ability is related to coping with stress (e.g., Antonovsky, 1979). Consistent with this view, Heppner and Petersen (1982) developed the Problem Solving Inventory (PSI) in order to assess an individual's problem-solving appraisal. In this chapter, we will concentrate on the role of problem-solving appraisal in the psychological adjustment process.

Measuring Problem-Solving Appraisal

Measures of applied problem solving include (a) the Problem Solving Inventory (PSI; Heppner, 1988); (b) the Means-End Problem Solving Procedure (MEPS; Shure & Spivack, 1972); and (c) the Social Problem Solving Inventory (SPSI; D'Zurilla & Nezu, 1999). Only the PSI, however, is conceptualized as a global measure of problem-solving appraisal. As such, it is distinct from indices of problem-solving orientation and skills (e.g., the SPSI). In this section, we will briefly describe the PSI and its applications for counseling.

Problem Solving Inventory

The PSI has been one of the most widely used self-report inventories in applied problem solving (Nezu, Nezu, & Perri, 1989). In the PSI, perceptions of one's problem-solving ability, style, behavior, and attitudes are assessed (Heppner, 1988; Heppner & Baker, 1997). The PSI consists of 35 six-point Likert-type items (1 = "strongly agree" to 6 = "strongly disagree"), with a total score and three subscale scores (factors derived from a principle component factor analysis; Heppner & Petersen, 1982). The three subscales tap Problem-Solving Confidence (11 items), Approach-Avoidance Style (16 items), Personal Control (5 items), and 3 filler items. Problem-Solving Confidence is defined as an individual's self-assurance in a wide range of problem-solving activities, a belief and trust in one's problem-solving abilities (general problem-solving self-efficacy), and coping effectiveness. The Approach-Avoidance Style, as the label implies, refers to a general tendency to approach or avoid different problem-solving activities. Personal Control is defined as a belief in one's emotional and behavioral control (thereby reflecting emotional overreactivity and behavioral control; Heppner, 1988; Heppner & Baker, 1997). It should be noted that *higher scores on the PSI indicate a lack of problem-solving confidence, an avoidant problem-solving style, and an absence of personal control.*

The PSI appears to be internally consistent and temporally stable; for example, the estimates of internal consistency and temporal stability (test-retest) over a 2-week period for the total score and three factors are as follows: the total inventory, $\alpha = .90$, $r = .89$; Problem-Solving Confidence, $\alpha = .85$, $r = .85$; Approach-Avoidance Style, $\alpha = .84$, $r = .88$; and Personal Control, $\alpha = .72$, $r = .83$ (Heppner & Petersen, 1982). In addition, researchers have provided a wide range of data in support of the PSI's validity (see Heppner, 1988; Heppner & Baker, 1997). The PSI is easy to administer, typically requires 15 minutes for completion, and can be easily scored by hand or computer. The readability level is at the ninth grade (an adolescent version with fourth-grade reading level also is available).

With respect to counseling applications, the PSI can be used to quickly assess important information about the client's problem-solving style or appraisal that may facilitate or hinder his or her day-to-day functioning; moreover, the PSI can be used as a treatment outcome measure for problem-solving training interventions (aimed at client problems such as depression, anxiety, dysfunctional thoughts, and career indecision; see Heppner, 1988; Heppner & Baker, 1997).

Summary of the Problem-Solving Appraisal Literature

Problem-solving appraisal using the PSI has been the focus of over 100 empirical investigations. In this section, we briefly summarize the topics of psychological adjustment, physical health, coping, and educational and vocational issues. We have been selective because of space limitations, but we do provide references for more detailed reviews.

Psychological Adjustment

Early in the evolution of this topic, researchers claimed that problem solving was linked to psychological adjustment (D'Zurilla & Goldfried, 1971). In over 50 studies now, researchers have examined the link between problem-solving appraisal and psychological health. We will briefly discuss the literature specifically related to (a) general psychological adjustment, (b) depression, (c) hopelessness and suicidal behavior, (d) alcohol use/abuse, (e) personality variables, and (f) parental associations.

General Psychological Adjustment

Researchers have found in several studies conducted mostly with college student populations that perceived effective (as compared with ineffective) problem solvers report themselves to be *more* adjusted on (a) general measures such as the Minnesota Multiphasic Personality Inventory and Symptom Checklist-90 (e.g., Elliott, Herrick, & Witty, 1992); (b) specific measures of personality variables such as positive self-concepts (e.g., Heppner, Reeder, & Larson, 1983); and (c) personal problem inventories (e.g., Heppner, Hibel, Neal, Weinstein, & Rabinowitz, 1982). In addition, researchers have consistently found that a positive problem-solving appraisal as tapped by the PSI is related to good social skills as measured by self-report indices. For example, perceived effective (as compared with ineffective) problem solvers reported having (a) more social skills (e.g., Elliott, Godshall, Herrick, Witty, & Spruell, 1991), (b) less social uneasiness/distrust/distress (e.g., Larson, Allen, Imao, & Piersel, 1993), and (c) more social support (e.g., Wright & Heppner, 1991). Thus, there is a well-established association between positive problem-solving appraisal and better social and psychological adjustment.

Depression

There is extremely strong empirical support across a wide range of populations for a more positive problem-solving appraisal being associated with less depression. For example, in college student samples, these correlations typically range from .40 to .60 (e.g., Bonner & Rich, 1987). Additionally, similar statistically significant correlations have been found with persons who are in prison ($r = -.52$; Bonner & Rich, 1990); patients with chronic low back pain ($r = -.48$; Witty & Bernard, 1995); and adults with spinal cord injuries ($r = -.41$; Elliott, Herrick, & Witty, 1992). Similar associations also have been found in other cultures (e.g., Pretorius & Diedricks, 1994; Sahin, Sahin, & Heppner, 1993). Thus, the link between a more positive problem-solving appraisal and lower depression appears across populations and cultures.

Moreover, investigators have indirectly or directly examined the moderating role of problem-solving appraisal in predicting depression; these studies strongly suggest a positive

problem-solving appraisal moderates the relationship between stress and depression (e.g., Nezu, Nezu, Saraydarian, Kalmar, & Ronan, 1986). Moreover, in the investigations, problem-solving appraisals, negative life events, and their interactions accounted for 40% to 60% of the variance in depression scores. In one study, Nezu and Ronan (1988) used a longitudinal design and controlled for premorbid levels of depression. Impressively, appraisals, negative life events, and their interactions accounted for 87% of the variance in depression scores. Based on these results, it appears not only that perceived effective (as compared with ineffective) problem solvers report lower levels of depression, but also that perceived effective problem solvers under high levels of stress are particularly likely to exhibit lower depression. Thus, both positive problem-solving appraisal and its interaction with negative life events are important in predicting lower depression.

Hopelessness and Suicidal Behavior

Schotte and Clum's (1982, 1987) diathesis-stress-hopelessness model of suicidal behavior suggests when people who have strong problem-solving abilities are exposed to naturally occurring conditions of high negative life stress, they are cognitively more able to develop effective alternative solutions for adaptive coping as compared with those deficient in problem solving. Subsequently, those with effective (as opposed to ineffective) problem-solving skills, even under high stress, are less likely to experience hopelessness that put the individual at risk for suicidal behavior. Several studies have examined the relationship between problem-solving appraisal, hopelessness, and suicidal behavior to test Schotte and Clum's hypotheses and, in essence, provide strong support for their model (e.g., Bonner & Rich, 1992). These investigations indicate that diminished problem-solving appraisal is a consistent and stable predictor of hopelessness and suicidal ideation. On the contrary, increases in perceived effective problem solving were associated with lower levels of hopelessness (e.g., Witty & Bernard, 1995) and suicidal ideation (e.g., Rudd, Rajab, & Dahn, 1994) across a variety of populations (e.g., college students, correctional inmates, psychiatric patients, outpatient suicide ideators and attempters). Moreover, consistent with Schotte and Clum's theory, across all of the

studies that measured both hopelessness and suicidal ideation, there was a stronger association
between problem-solving appraisal and hopelessness (rs = .48 to .62) than between problem-
solving appraisal and suicidal ideation (rs = .11
to .43). Although there was a main effect for
problem-solving appraisal in predicting hopelessness and suicidal ideation across almost all
these studies, in some studies there also was an
interaction with stress (e.g., Bonner & Rich,
1992). More specifically, as predicted by Schotte
and Clum's model, perceived effective problem
solvers under high levels of stress were likely
to report low levels of hopelessness in three of
six studies. One investigation (Dixon, Heppner,
& Rudd, 1994) directly tested and found strong
support for the mediational role of hopelessness
between problem solving and suicidal ideation.
Consistent with Schotte and Clum's theory, the
study by Dixon et al. (1994) found that
problem-solving appraisal was related to suicide
ideation primarily through its impact on hopelessness, and accounted for 68% of the variance
in suicidal ideation.

Although it is unclear why people with a perceived effective problem-solving style under
high stress may be more able to ward off hopelessness and depression, one possible underlying mechanism may be the construct of hope,
particularly agency and pathways (planning to
meet goals; see Snyder, Cheavens, & Michael,
1999). Research has found that hope is a significant predictor of problem-focused coping
and is related to problem-solving appraisal (see
Snyder et al., 1999). Future research might
combine Snyder's hope theory with Schotte and
Clum's theory to develop a more comprehensive model of problem solving, hopelessness,
and suicidal behavior.

Alcohol Use/Abuse

The proponents of cognitive-social learning approaches propose that individuals who abuse
drugs and alcohol do so because they lack a
sense of self-efficacy for coping with stressful
situations. Thus, alcohol and drug consumption
may be their coping strategy for altering feelings of personal inadequacy. Related to this
thesis, support for this relationship between
problem-solving appraisal and alcohol/drug usage emerges in several studies. For example, two
studies (Heppner et al., 1982; Wright & Heppner, 1991) found a significant linear relationship between more positive problem-solving

appraisal and less alcohol use/abuse. In another
study, Larson and Heppner (1989) found that
nonclinical adults appraised their problem solving significantly more positively than individuals receiving inpatient treatment for alcohol
dependence. Moreover, in two studies (Larson
& Heppner, 1989; Williams & Kleinfelter,
1989), a more complex relationship between
problem-solving appraisal and alcohol use/abuse
emerged; there may be different drinking patterns associated with different components of
problem-solving appraisal. In short, although
there is some support for a significant linear relationship between a more positive problem-
solving appraisal and less alcohol use/abuse, a
more complex relationship may exist among
these variables.

Personality Variables

There is some evidence that problem-solving
appraisal is associated with other personality
variables. For example, researchers also have
found a consistent association between a more
positive problem-solving appraisal and lower
anxiety (e.g., Larson, Piersel, Imao, & Allen,
1990). Moreover, a more positive problem-
solving appraisal has been related to lower anger
and higher curiosity. In these associations,
stronger relationships appear with trait as opposed to state anxiety. Additionally, a more
positive problem-solving appraisal has been related to a stronger sense of instrumentality in
three studies (e.g., Heppner, Walther, & Good,
1995). Thus, it appears that problem-solving appraisal is associated more strongly with trait
versus state variables, particularly anxiety and
instrumentality.

Parental Associations

There is some evidence for a link between
mothers' problem-solving appraisal and children's behavior. For example, Walker and Johnson (1986) found that the more positively the
mothers appraised their own problem-solving
style, the more positive were their preschool
children's social and emotional development behaviors, such as more direct coping behaviors in
incest victims. Shorkey, McRoy, and Armendariz (1985) reported that a more positive
problem-solving appraisal by parents was associated with less reported use of parental
punishment in child-rearing situations. If we
are able to consistently find such links among

parental problem-solving appraisal, children's behavior, and parental punishment, problem-solving training with parents in remedial and preventive interventions may be a productive direction for future research.

Physical Health

Problem-solving appraisal has both theoretical and practical relevance to physical health. Positive problem-solving appraisal has been associated with positive health expectancies (e.g., Elliott & Marmarosh, 1994) and with fewer health complaints about premenstrual and menstrual pain, chronic pain, cardiovascular problems, and health problems in general (e.g., Elliott, 1992). These associations are stronger with clinical patients than with college students (Witty & Bernard, 1995).

Patients in medical settings are ideal for testing the validity of the PSI in predicting positive health outcomes. In this regard, more positive problem-solving appraisals have been found to be prospectively predictive of objective favorable behavioral health outcomes (e.g., Elliott, Pickelman, & Richeson, 1992). Thus, positive problem-solving appraisals appear to be implicated in effective coping behaviors and subsequent beneficial health outcomes.

Coping

Problem-solving appraisal has been conceptually linked with coping (Heppner & Krauskopf, 1987). In this section, we examine how problem-solving appraisal may be related to coping with stress across three different areas of research: hypothetical or laboratory problems, reported coping activities, and help seeking and use of helping resources.

Hypothetical or Laboratory Problems

One way that researchers have examined how people cope or solve problems is to present hypothetical or laboratory problems (e.g., water jar problems or anagram tasks; Wickelgren, 1974) and then study how subjects grapple with those problems. The results here are mixed—the expected relationship between a more positive problem-solving appraisal and effective coping was found in three of five studies (e.g., Nezu & Ronan, 1988). The complexity of the type of laboratory task might explain some of the discrepant results. In this regard, the significant re-

lationships were found in the three studies with more complex procedures and repeated trials. Therefore, future researchers might be well advised to use laboratory tasks that more closely approximate real-life personal problems entailing uncertainty and sufficient complexity with repeated problem-solving trials (see Larson, Potenza, Wennstedt, & Sailors, 1995).

Reports of Coping Activities

Several different researchers across nine studies that assessed various aspects of coping consistently found that a positive problem-solving appraisal was associated with reports of approaching and attempting to alter the cause of the stressful problem (e.g., MacNair & Elliott, 1992). Thus, a primary conclusion is that problem-solving appraisal is associated with the consistent report of actively focusing on the problem and attempting to resolve the cause of the problem (sometimes called problem-focused coping).

Why do people with a positive problem-solving appraisal tend to approach and engage in problem-focused coping? A possible explanation comes from a study by Baumgardner, Heppner, and Arkin (1986). Utilizing an experimental design in which they manipulated success or failure feedback to assess causal attributions, Baumgardner et al. found that the causal role of effort was a major distinguishing feature between the self-appraised effective and ineffective problem solvers; perceived effort was prominent for self-appraised effective problem solvers as a major cause of personal problems, as well as their allegedly "failed" laboratory performance in solving a problem. Thus, it appears that effective problem solvers assume responsibility for personal problems; moreover, their increased effort attributions for "failed" coping attempts underscore that their effort relates to the approach, rather than the avoidance of personal problems.

Help Seeking and Resource Utilization

The judicious use of one's environmental resources is important for coping with stressful events. Intuitively, effective problem solvers should be aware of their environment and efficiently use appropriate resources, whereas the opposite should be the case for ineffective problem solvers. In studies of college students, a more positive problem-solving appraisal has been found to be related to help-seeking variables—awareness, utilization, and satisfaction with campus resources (e.g., Neal & Heppner, 1986).

In sum, there clearly is a relationship between a more positive problem-solving appraisal and beneficial coping activities. Although the research that has examined the link between problem-solving appraisal and hypothetical problem solving is equivocal, in other research, problem-solving appraisal consistently is associated with reports of approaching and attempting to resolve problems, as well as the awareness, utilization, and satisfaction with helping resources. Thus, problem-solving appraisal is clearly associated with an array of coping activities.

Vocational Issues

A person's career decision-making processes may be construed as a specific instance of problem solving. Indeed, problem-solving appraisal and career planning and decision making have been found to be related in several studies (e.g., Larson, Heppner, Ham, & Dugan, 1988). Thus, how persons appraise their problem solving in general is related to how they approach a specific task, such as career decision making.

Problem-Solving Training Interventions

Problem-solving training (PST) has involved teaching (a) specific component skills (e.g., problem definition and formulation), (b) a general problem-solving model; and, (c) specific problem-solving skills in conjunction with other interventions (Heppner & Hillerbrand, 1991). In this section, we will briefly summarize the effectiveness of these three types of PST.

Teaching Specific Component Skills

In this line of PST, research typically has focused on teaching cognitive skills within a specific problem-solving stage; training is brief (e.g., 45 minutes), utilizing an experimental between-group design (a treatment group vs. a no-treatment control group; see D'Zurilla & Nezu, 1982). Those persons in the specific problem-solving skills training group typically have outperformed those in the control group, although long-term stability of the training is less clear. For example, Nezu and D'Zurilla

(1979) examined the effects of the decision-making skills training in three conditions: (a) specific training in decision making based on D'Zurilla and Goldfried's (1971) model; (b) teaching the general definition of decision making based on a utility approach; and (c) the control group with no instruction in decision making. Those in the first group were judged to be significantly more effective than persons in the other two groups.

Teaching a General Problem-Solving Model

In this approach, a general problem-solving model is used, such as the five-stage model of D'Zurilla and Goldfried (1971). The training usually includes didactics and practice in each of the stages over several training sessions, along with an applied integration step (Nezu, 1986). This approach is effective with many populations (e.g., psychiatric patients) and target goals (e.g., substance abuse and addictions, depression, stress, and anxiety; D'Zurilla & Nezu, 1999). The persons in the group receiving the general problem-solving training typically have outperformed the individuals in the control group (see D'Zurilla & Nezu, 1982, 1999). For example, Platt, Husband, Hermalin, Cater, and Metzger (1993) reported that individuals with drug abuse problems who participated in a PST group for 10 weeks, relative to those in a control group, were significantly more likely to be employed at posttreatment and at a 6-month follow-up (see D'Zurilla & Nezu, 1982, 1999; Heppner & Hillerbrand, 1991).

Teaching Specific Skills in Conjunction With Other Interventions

PST also has been used as part of a treatment package including other interventions such as anxiety management, communication skills, or study skills. This line of PST often consists of one or more problem-solving component skills. The PST has been effective in a wide range of populations (e.g., academic underachievers, psychiatric patients) and target goals (e.g., depression, phobias, marital and family problems, cigarette smoking, weight problems). For example, in order to enhance stress management skills for women with low incomes supported by public assistance, Tableman, Marciniak, Johnson, and Rodgers (1982) examined the effectiveness of PST in conjunction with other interventions such as stress reduction skills training, life planning, and goal-setting skills training. The participants in the combined training program manifested significant decreases in depression and anxiety.

In other research, problem-solving appraisal has been used as an outcome measure of PST. For example, in a PST group based on D'Zurilla and Nezu's (1982) general model, the participants reported a substantial increase in problem-solving appraisal, as well as a concurrent decrease in depression at posttreatment and at a 6-month follow-up (Nezu, 1986). Likewise, Heppner, Baumgardner, Larson, and Petty (1988) found that persons in an 8-week PST with a focus on self-management principles (e.g., self-analysis, self-reinforcement), as compared with those trained on specific problem-solving skills, showed posttreatment (and 1 year) improvements on the total PSI score and the Approach-Avoidance Style factor.

Future Research Directions and Conclusions

Clearly problem-solving appraisal has a significant role in positive psychology. How people appraise their problem-solving skills and style, as a psychological construct, is strongly linked to a wide range of indices of psychological adjustment. For example, a more positive (as opposed to negative) problem-solving appraisal has been associated with a positive self-concept, less depression and anxiety, and vocational adjustment. The PSI, as a measure of problem-solving appraisal, has a strong empirical base, and it portends to be of use to helping professionals.

Future research and theory development is needed to enhance our understanding of problem-solving appraisal and its role in coping and psychological adjustment. One promising direction may be to examine population issues such as biological sex, ethnicity, noncollege populations (e.g., adolescents, adults), as well as cultural issues, to distinguish between universal and culture-specific problem-solving appraisals. Moreover, little is known about problem solving within different cultural contexts (e.g., African American culture, Asian culture), which is an exciting arena. Another direction for future research is to examine the unique role of various components of problem-solving appraisal, as well as the combined effect of two or more

of the PSI factors in creating more complex coping styles (e.g., reporting being confident but avoiding problems). Most of the previous research has utilized the total PSI score, but exciting new theoretical developments might occur through the examination of the various PSI factors. Finally, the relationship between problem-solving appraisal and problem-solving performance remains unclear. Again, examining this complex issue may significantly facilitate our understanding of applied problem solving.

Most importantly, problem-solving appraisal is a learned assessment, based on thousands of interactions with one's environment. Thus, it is of utmost importance to examine how one's problem-solving appraisal is developed from childhood onward. It may be beneficial to examine to what extent parental modeling and training affect the early development of one's problem-solving appraisal. Likewise, to what extent does formal educational training play a later role in decreasing or enhancing a problem-solving appraisal in children and adolescents? Important and exciting new areas of research are available to determine the mechanisms that contribute to the development of individuals' problem-solving appraisal. In addition, it may be especially beneficial to examine how problem-solving appraisal may play a role in buffering people against effects of stressful life events.

Because problem-solving appraisal is learned, this implies that it is amenable to change, and the research literature indicates problem-solving training interventions are effective. It may be beneficial to examine the range of interventions that might affect changes in people's problem-solving appraisal. Most importantly, however, because problem-solving appraisal is amenable to change, this provides hope for millions of people to bring positive change to their lives through the integration of problem solving and positive psychology. There seem to be many exciting possibilities in future applied interventions to build on people's strengths in problem-solving appraisal to enhance life satisfaction and well-being.

References

Anderson, J. R. (1983). *The architecture of cognition*. Cambridge, MA: Harvard University Press.

Antonovsky, A. (1979). *Health, stress, and coping*. San Francisco: Jossey-Bass.

Bandura, A. (1986). *Social foundations of thought and action: A social cognitive theory.* Englewood Cliffs, NJ: Prentice-Hall.

Baumgardner, A. H., Heppner, P. P., & Arkin, R. M. (1986). Role of casual attribution in personal problem solving. *Journal of Personality and Social Psychology, 50,* 636–643.

Bonner, R. L., & Rich, A. R. (1987). Toward a predictive model of suicide ideation and behavior: Some preliminary data in college students. *Suicide and Life-Threatening Behavior, 17,* 50–63.

Bonner, R. L., & Rich, A. R. (1990). Psychosocial vulnerability, life stress, and suicide ideation in a jail population: A cross-validation study. *Suicide and Life-Threatening Behavior, 20,* 213–224.

Bonner, R. L., & Rich, A. R. (1992). Cognitive vulnerability and hopelessness among correctional inmates: A state of mind model. *Journal of Offender Rehabilitation, 17* (3–4), 113–122.

Butler, L., & Meichenbaum, D. (1981). The assessment of interpersonal problem-solving skills. In P. Kendall and S. D. Hollon (Eds.), *Assessment strategies for cognitive-behavioral interventions* (pp. 197–225). New York: Academic Press.

Dixon, W. A., Heppner, P. P., & Rudd, D. M. (1994). Problem-solving appraisal, hopelessness, and suicide ideation: Evidence for a mediational model. *Journal of Counseling Psychology, 41,* 91–98.

D'Zurilla, T. J. (1986). *Problem-solving therapy: A social competence approach to clinical intervention.* New York: Springer.

D'Zurilla, T. J., & Goldfried, M. R. (1971). Problem solving and behavior modification. *Journal of Abnormal Psychology, 78,* 107–126.

D'Zurilla, T. J., & Nezu, A. (1982). Social problem solving in adults. In P. C. Kendall (Ed.), *Advances in cognitive-behavioral research and therapy* (pp. 201–274). New York: Academic Press.

*D'Zurilla, T. J., & Nezu, A. (1999). *Problem-solving therapy: A social competence approach to clinical intervention* (2nd ed.). New York: Springer.

Elliott, T. R. (1992). Problem-solving appraisal, oral contraceptive use, and menstrual pain. *Journal of Applied Social Psychology, 22,* 286–297.

Elliott, T. R., Godshall, F. J., Herrick, J. M., Witty, T. E., & Spruell, M. (1991). Problem-solving appraisal and psychological adjustment following spinal cord injury. *Cognitive Therapy and Research, 15,* 387–398.

Elliott, T. R., Herrick, S. M., & Witty, T. E. (1992). Problem-solving appraisal and the effects of social support among college students and persons with physical disabilities. *Journal of Counseling Psychology, 39,* 219–226.

Elliott, T. R., & Marmarosh, C. (1994). Problem-solving appraisal, health complaints, and health-related expectancies. *Journal of Counseling and Development, 72,* 531–537.

Elliott, T. R., Pickelman, H., & Richeson, C. (1992). *Negative affectivity, problem-solving appraisal, and post-partum depression.* Paper presented at the annual meeting of the Society of Behavioral Medicine, New York.

Heppner, P. P. (1978). The effect of client perceived need and counselor role on clients' behaviors. *Journal of Counseling Psychology, 25,* 514–519.

*Heppner, P. P. (1988). *The Problem-Solving Inventory.* Palo Alto, CA: Consulting Psychologist Press.

*Heppner, P. P., & Baker, C. E. (1997). Applications of the problem solving inventory. *Measurement and Evaluation in Counseling and Development, 29,* 229–241.

*Heppner, P. P., Baumgardner, A. H., Larson, L. M., & Petty, R. E. (1988). The utility of problem-solving training that emphasizes self-management principles. *Counseling Psychology Quarterly, 1,* 129–143.

Heppner, P. P., Hibel, J., Neal, G. W., Weinstein, C. L., & Rabinowitz, F. E. (1982). Personal problem solving: A descriptive study of individual differences. *Journal of Counseling Psychology, 29,* 580–590.

*Heppner, P. P., & Hillerbrand, E. T. (1991). Problem-solving training: Implications for remedial and preventive training. In C. R. Snyder & D. R. Forsyth (Eds.), *Handbook of social and clinical psychology: The health perspective* (pp. 681–698). Elmsford, NY: Pergamon.

*Heppner, P. P., & Krauskopf, C. J. (1987). An information processing approach to personal problem solving. *The Counseling Psychologist, 15,* 371–447.

Heppner, P. P., & Petersen, C. H. (1982). The development and implications of a personal problem solving inventory. *Journal of Counseling Psychology, 29,* 66–75.

Heppner, P. P., Reeder, B. L., & Larson, L. M. (1983). Cognitive variables associated with personal problem-solving appraisal: Implications for counseling. *Journal of Counseling Psychology, 30,* 537–545.

Heppner, P. P., Walther, D. J., & Good, G. E. (1995). The differential role of instrumentality, expressivity, and social support in predicting problem-solving appraisal in men and women. *Sex Roles, 32,* 91–108.

Janis, I. L., & Mann, L. (1977). *Decision making: A psychological analysis of conflict, choice, and commitment.* New York: Free Press.

Kendall, P. C., & Fischler, G. L. (1984). Behavioral and adjustment correlates of problem solving: Validational analyses of interpersonal cognitive problem-solving measures. *Journal of Child Development, 55,* 227–243.

Larson, L. M., Allen, S. J., Imao, R. A. K., & Piersel, W. (1993). Self-perceived effective and ineffective problem solvers' differential view of their partners' problem-solving styles. *Journal of Counseling and Development, 71,* 528–532.

Larson, L. M., & Heppner, P. P. (1989). Problem-solving appraisal with male alcoholics. *Journal of Counseling Psychology, 36,* 73–78.

Larson, L. M., Heppner, P. P., Ham, T., & Dugan, K. (1988). Investigating multiple subtypes of career indecision through cluster analysis. *Journal of Counseling Psychology, 35,* 439–446.

*Larson, L. M., Piersel, W. C., Imao, R. A. K., & Allen, S. J. (1990). Significant predictors of problem-solving appraisal. *Journal of Counseling Psychology, 37,* 482–490.

Larson, L. M., Potenza, M. T., Wennstedt, L. W., & Sailors, P. J. (1995). Personal problem solving in a simulated setting: Do perceptions accurately reflect behavior? *Cognitive Therapy and Research, 19,* 241–257.

MacNair, R. R., & Elliott, T. R. (1992). Self-perceived problem-solving ability, stress appraisal, and coping over time. *Journal of Research in Personality, 26,* 150–164.

Maier, N. R. F. (1970). *Problem solving and creativity.* Belmont, CA: Brooks/Cole.

Neal, G. W., & Heppner, P. P. (1986). Problem-solving self-appraisal, awareness, and utilization of campus helping resources. *Journal of Counseling Psychology, 33,* 39–44.

Newell, A., Shaw, J. C., & Simon, H. A. (1963). GPS, a program that simulates human thought. In E. A. Feigenbaum & J. Feldman (Eds.), *Computers and thought* (pp. 39–70). New York: McGraw-Hill.

Nezu, A. M. (1986). Efficacy of a social problem solving therapy approach for unipolar depression. *Journal of Consulting and Clinical Psychology, 54,* 196–202.

Nezu, A., & D'Zurilla, T. J. (1979). An experimental evaluation of the decision-making process in social problem solving. *Cognitive Therapy and Research, 3,* 269–277.

Nezu, A. M., Nezu, C. M., & Perri, M. G. (1989). *Problem-solving therapy for depression: Therapy, research, and clinical guidelines.* New York: Wiley.

Nezu, A. M., Nezu, C. M., Saraydarian, L., Kalmar, K., & Ronan, G. F. (1986). Social problem solving as a moderating variable between negative life stress and depressive systems. *Cognitive Therapy and Research, 10,* 489–498.

*Nezu, A. M., & Ronan, G. F. (1988). Social problem solving as a moderator of stress-related depressive symptoms: A prospective analysis. *Journal of Counseling Psychology, 35,* 134–138.

Platt, J. J., Husband, S. D., Hermalin, J., Cater, J., & Metzger, D. (1993). A cognitive problem-solving employment readiness intervention for methadone clients. *Journal of Cognitive Psychotherapy: An International Quarterly, 7,* 21–33.

Pretorius, T. B., & Diedricks, M. (1994). Problem-solving appraisal, social support and stress-depression relationship. *South African Journal of Psychology, 24,* 86–90.

Rudd, M. D., Rajab, H., & Dahn, P. F. (1994). Problem-solving appraisal in suicide ideators and attempters. *American Journal of Orthopsychiatry, 64,* 136–149.

Sahin, N., Sahin, N. H., & Heppner, P. P. (1993). Psychometric properties of the Problem Solving Inventory (PSI) in a group of Turkish university students. *Cognitive Therapy and Research, 17,* 379–396.

Schotte, D., & Clum, G. A. (1982). Suicide ideation in a college population: A test of a model. *Journal of Consulting and Clinical Psychology, 50,* 690–696.

*Schotte, D., & Clum, G. A. (1987). Problem-solving skills in suicidal psychiatric patients. *Journal of Consulting and Clinical Psychology, 55,* 49–54.

Shorkey, C. T., McRoy, R. E., & Armendariz, J. (1985). Intensity of parental punishments and problem-solving attitudes and behaviors. *Psychological Reports, 56,* 283–286.

Shure, M. B. (1982). Interpersonal problem solving: A cog in the wheel of social cognition. In F. C. Serafica (Ed.), *Social-cognitive development in context* (pp. 132–166). New York: Guilford.

Shure, M. B., & Spivack, G. (1972). Means-ends thinking, adjustment and social class among elementary school-aged children. *Journal of Consulting and Clinical Psychology, 38,* 348–353.

Skinner, B. F. (1974). *About behaviorism.* New York: Knopf.

Snyder, C. R., Cheavens, J., & Michael, S. T. (1999). Hoping. In C. R. Snyder (Ed.), *Coping: The psychology of what works* (pp. 205–251). New York: Oxford University Press.

Snyder, C. R., Ilardi, S. S., Cheavens, J., Michael, S. T., Yamhure, L., & Sympson, S. (2000). The role of hope in cognitive behavior therapies. *Cognitive Therapy and Research, 24,* 747–762.

Tableman, B., Marciniak, D., Johnson, D., & Rodgers, R. (1982). Stress management for women on public assistance. *American Journal of Community Psychology, 10,* 357–367.

Urban, H., & Ford, H. (1971). Some historical and conceptual perspectives of psychotherapy and behavioral change. In A. Bergin & S. Garfield (Eds.), *Handbook of psychotherapy and behavior change* (pp. 3–35). New York: Wiley.

Walker, L. O., & Johnson, L. B. (1986). Preschool children's socio-emotional development: Endogenous and environmental antecedents in early infancy. *Final Report to the Hogg Foundation for Mental Health.*

Wickelgren, W. (1974). *How to solve problems.* San Francisco, CA: Freeman.

Williams, T. G., & Kleinfelter, K. T. (1989). Perceived problem-solving skills and drinking patterns among college students. *Psychological Reports, 65,* 1235–1244.

Witty, T. E., & Bernard, C. B. (1995, August). *Problem-solving appraisal and psychological adjustment of chronic low back pain patients.* Paper presented at the annual meeting of American Psychological Association, Los Angeles.

Wright, D. M., & Heppner, P. P. (1991). Coping among nonclinical college age children of alcoholics. *Journal of Counseling Psychology, 38,* 465–472.

22

Setting Goals for Life and Happiness

Edwin A. Locke

I begin with the egoistic premise that one's highest moral purpose is the achievement of one's own happiness. I am basing this on the philosophy of Ayn Rand (for an overview, see Gotthelf [2000]; for the validation, see Peikoff [1991]; Rand [1957, 1964]). In this chapter I will discuss some guidelines for achieving happiness, focusing primarily on psychological issues. I will assume a requisite political context of freedom. Totalitarian dictatorships and, to a considerable extent, "benevolent" dictatorships disallow the freedom to think and to act on the basis of one's thinking, and thus prevent the individual from acting to achieve the values that make happiness possible.

Thinking

To achieve happiness, individuals must understand their own natures, and especially their needs. "Life is a process of self-sustaining and self-generated action" (Rand, 1964, p. 16). On this latter point, Aristotle noted that self-generated action exists on three levels: (a) the vegetative level characteristic of plants and the internal organs of animals; (b) the sensory-perceptual level (which includes the vegetative), characteristic of the lower animals; and (c) the

intellectual or conceptual level (which includes the two lower levels), characteristic of man.*

Goal-directedness is the feature common to all levels of life. The goal inherent in the actions of living organisms is to sustain life. There are three attributes of goal-directed action (Binswanger, 1990): (a) First, there is self-generation, wherein action is fueled by internal energy sources; (b) second, there is value-significance in that the existence of living organisms is conditional upon certain courses of action; if an organism does not take action or takes the wrong action, it dies; (c) third, there is goal causation. Goal-directed action (at the molar level) is caused by a conscious idea of the goal in those organisms possessing consciousness and at the vegetative level is caused by the success of previously goal-directed action (e.g., the beating of the heart leads to future heartbeats).

Now consider what is unique to the intellectual or conceptual level of life. Man shares with the lower animals the possession of sense organs, a nervous system, and a brain. These provide man and animals with direct awareness of existence through sense perception. However, human beings have the power to go one, very large, step further—they can integrate the material provided by the senses into concepts; concepts are mental integrations of perceptual concretes (see Rand [1990] for a detailed analysis of the process of concept formation). Chimp sign language experiments notwithstanding (e.g., Terrace, 1979), this is a step that the lower animals cannot take. Consider that in over 4 million years on earth, chimps never have developed even the vestiges of a primitive culture.

Unlike the sensory-perceptual level of awareness, the conceptual level is both fallible and volitional. In contrast to sense perception, which gives us automatic knowledge of reality, conceptual thinking can be wrong. People may conclude incorrectly that $2 + 2 = 5$, that $e = mc^3$, and that disease is caused by evil spirits. Conceptual knowledge must be validated through observation and logic. The purpose of the branch of philosophy known as epistemology is to identify the means for gaining and validating conceptual knowledge (Rand, 1990).

Conceptual thinking is initiated and sustained by choice. In contrast to the lower animals, humans possess the power of cognitive self-regulation (Binswanger, 1991). The fundamental choice is the ability to switch on or switch off the rational faculty. Free will is the choice to think or not to think (Binswanger, 1991; Rand, 1964), that is, to raise one's awareness to the conceptual level or to let the mind drift at, or deliberately lower it to, the sensory-perceptual level. Thinking means focusing on reality, adherence to facts and logic, distinguishing knowledge from feelings, exerting mental effort, and doing one's own processing rather than relying passively on the thinking of others.

Needs

All living organisms have needs. A need is an objective requirement of a living organism's survival and well-being. A plant that does not get water and sunlight will not prosper. A conscious organism whose needs are frustrated or blocked will feel discomfort, pain, and/or unhappiness (see Snyder, Rand, & Sigmon, this volume). Severe need deprivation produces illness, and if the deprivation is too severe or prolonged, death is the result. Some need-satisfying action is automatic (e.g., a plant turning its leaves toward the sun; the beating of a heart), but at the human level automatic action alone is insufficient. People have to conceptually identify their needs and discover, through thinking and research, how to satisfy them.

I divide human needs into three categories:

1. Physical needs are the requirements of a healthy body—air, food, water, rest, tissue integrity, and the correct temperature. These needs are the province of the fields of medicine and nutrition.
2. Psychological needs are the requirements of a healthy consciousness—self-esteem (Locke, McClear & Knight, 1996; see also Hewitt, this volume), pleasure, love (see Hendrick and Hendrick, this volume), friendship, and art (for a discussion of art, see Rand [1966]). These needs are the province of psychology, psychiatry, and aesthetics.
3. Philosophical needs are the requirements of an integrated view of existence—including a moral code to guide one's choices and actions. (I view religion as a primitive form of philosophy.)

It is worth commenting on Maslow's (1970) theory of needs here because it is so frequently cited. Maslow argues that needs exist in a hierarchy with priority given in this order: physiological; safety; belongingness and love; esteem; and self-actualization. However, there is virtually no evidence that man is born with any built-in need hierarchy. Certain types of deprivation do result in death faster than other types; for example, oxygen deprivation causes irreversible brain damage within about 2 minutes, whereas people can live without water for several days and without food (if there is water) for several weeks. But this does not prevent people from risking their lives to save loved ones from drowning. Nor do physical needs automatically take priority over psychological needs. For example, a person with very low self-esteem may not eat or may commit suicide (Snyder, 1994).

There are additional problems with Maslow's theory. Although people discover their needs in part by the consequences of deprivation (e.g., they get hungry if they do not get food), there is no automatic drive to take the correct action because people do not automatically know what action to take. They may feel hungry but not know how to get food. They may feel worthless but not know how to develop self-esteem. Furthermore, people may anticipate their needs and take action before they even feel deprived.

As I noted previously, people discover their needs, how to satisfy them, and how to anticipate them through reason (thinking). Consider the need for food. A child "knows" reflexively how to swallow milk that is put in his mouth. But children do not know how to obtain the milk or even that (or why) it is good for them. It has taken millennia to learn how to grow, harvest, process, purify, preserve, store, and transport food well enough so that people can consistently avoid (at least in modern capitalist countries) starvation and malnutrition.

Values

It is now necessary to distinguish needs from values. Needs as such are inborn; they are part of an organism's nature. Values are acquired, that is, learned (Rokeach, 1972). Needs exist even if one is not aware of them; values exist in consciousness (or the subconscious). A value is "that which one acts to gain and/or keep" (Rand, 1964, p. 16). It is that which one regards, consciously or subconsciously, as conducive to one's welfare. People need food; they learn through experience to identify and to value such foods as rice, pizza, steak, and ice cream. People need self-esteem; they learn to value using their thinking powers in order to successfully manage their lives and thus earn their own self-respect (see Locke et al. [1996] for a discussion of various theories of self-esteem and for the identification of its proper roots).

Unlike the case of needs, people do need a value hierarchy because without one they would be unable to make choices. It is values that prioritize needs. If a person valued everything equally, at a given moment, all action would be paralyzed. Furthermore, a person with no value hierarchy would be unable to take any purposeful, long-range actions. If he did manage to act at a given moment, under the impetus of a temporary feeling of pain or pleasure, there would be no connection between that action and what he did at the next moment. They would be no more than what the behaviorists claimed: a series of disconnected chains of stimulus-response-reinforcement sequences or habits.

The most fundamental of all values are moral values—that which the individual considers good or right. A moral code is a code of values accepted by choice (Rand, 1964). Because people possess no instincts (i.e., inborn knowledge) and because they cannot survive guided solely by the pleasure-pain mechanism, they need a code of values to guide their choices and actions. An organism's survival depends on taking actions that further its own welfare (the good) as well as avoiding harmful actions (the bad). A code of morality tells him the difference between good and bad. The ultimate standard in morality according to Rand (1964), the standard of the good, is the organism's life. "It is only the concept of 'Life' which makes the concept of 'Value' possible" (Rand, 1964, p. 16). (See Peikoff [1991] and Rand [1964] for a validation of Ayn Rand's theory of ethics.)

Rational values are pro-life in that they are consonant with and help to fulfill the individual's objective needs. However, everyone's values are obviously not always rational. People sometimes take actions that frustrate rather than satisfy needs. There are three main reasons for this. First, people commit errors of knowledge. For example, they may eat foods that contain harmful bacteria because they do not know about the danger. Second, people may neglect to focus on what they are doing (e.g., driving without looking where they are going). Third, people may pursue things that give them short-range pleasure or short-range relief from pain or discomfort (e.g., large amounts of alcohol, illicit drugs, and cigarettes) but that harm them in the long run. The lower animals do not have the power to balance or prioritize short- and long-range pleasures, but people do. (For a discussion of self-defeating actions, see Baumeister & Scher [1988].)

Harmful or not, values are the key to individual differences in human motivation. Needs are the most basic concept in that they explain why people act at all; moreover, they explain why all cultures have some commonalities in terms of what people seek (e.g., food, shelter, friendship, love, art). Everyone has the same needs, but everyone, in part, is unique with respect to values. Almost everyone values food, but not the same foods and not to the same degree. No two people hold identical value hierarchies over the course of a lifetime. Aside from physical characteristics, values are what make people different. And they are more immediate determinants of human action than needs. Values function to prioritize needs, and they motivate people to gain what is required to satisfy needs. A hungry individual—one who needs food—may decide: Now is the time to eat, and I am choosing pizza.

Individuals' value hierarchies can and do change. For example, a serious college student will place getting an education at the top of his hierarchy. After college, this may be displaced by career concerns. Later, marriage and family, which were not emphasized earlier, may increase in importance. A working mother may shift priorities between work and family depending on the number and age of her children. A middle-aged couple may focus increasingly on financial planning for their later years. Retired elders may accentuate seeing grandchildren, health maintenance, and leisure activities.

I must emphasize here that a given action is not usually or necessarily motivated by just one value. For example, one's career efforts may be motivated by the desire to earn a living, the desire to achieve excellence ("need" for achievement), ambition (the desire to improve one's life), and the desire to achieve a personally significant, long-range purpose (e.g., be a fiction writer).

Furthermore, a given value may help to satisfy more than one need. Consider, for example, money. Most people value money, at least to some degree. It is not the case, however, as followers of Maslow seem to imply, that money is relevant only to the satisfaction of one's physical or safety needs. Because money has symbolic as well as material significance, it is implicated, directly or indirectly, in virtually all of one's needs. Consider self-esteem. It is true that you cannot buy self-esteem, but the ability to earn money, to the degree that it reflects one's ability to use one's mind productively, can contribute to self-esteem. What about friendship and love? Indeed, you cannot buy love, but having money may affect the types of people you will meet; and the ability to earn a living may affect the types of people who will show an interest in you. For example, women especially are usually not very attracted to men who are unable to manage their own professional and financial activities successfully. Furthermore, money affects the types of romantic activities that one can afford to engage in. It is much more romantic for most people to take a date or spouse to a fine restaurant than to McDonald's. Finally, consider self-actualization. If that vague abstraction has any meaning at all, it would be to fulfill your potential and achieve that which

you want most in life. If this involves a work achievement (e.g., starting a successful business), of course, you would make money in the process. But even if it does not, money would surely facilitate one's ability to fulfill one's potential.

Emotions

Emotions are the form in which people experience automatized, subconscious value judgments (Lazarus, 1991; Locke, 1969). Emotions reflect subconscious knowledge and also one's subconsciously held values and value hierarchy. Consider the example of a hiker who meets a grizzly bear on a wilderness trail. His emotional response will reflect his stored knowledge of grizzly bears, including their potential for aggression, his physical location in relation to the bear, and the (subconsciously) perceived relationship between this knowledge and his values. In the typical case, the value involved is the value the hiker places on his own life. If he perceives the bear to be a threat to his life and he values his life, he will experience the emotion of fear. Other emotional reactions are possible, however. If he has been searching for this grizzly bear in order to photograph it and does not see it as a threat, he will experience pleasure or satisfaction. If it is not the particular bear that he has been seeking to photograph, he will experience disappointment. If it strongly resembles his lost pet bear, he will experience hope or relief. If he is not sure what it will do or what he will do, he will experience anxiety.

Every emotion reflects a particular type of value appraisal. Fear is the response to physical threat, anxiety to an uncertain threat or a self-esteem threat, guilt to the breach of a moral value, satisfaction to value achievement, anger to another person doing something he should not have done, jealousy to another person having a value one wants for oneself, and so forth (Lazarus, 1991; Lazarus & Lazarus, 1994). The intensity of an emotion reflects the degree of subconsciously perceived value threat or value achievement, as well as the importance of the value in one's value hierarchy. More as opposed to less important values, when viewed subconsciously as relevant to a given circumstance, give rise to stronger emotions.

Complex emotions are those that reflect multiple value judgments. Complex emotions are especially prevalent when judging other people. Because people are multifaceted and frequently inconsistent, they can arouse in us many different and even contradictory emotions. Joe can like Susie for her sense of purpose, dislike her for her bossiness, love her for her beauty, fear her because of her occasional temper, admire her because of her honesty, envy her because of her intelligence, feel passionate because of her sensuous qualities, and feel angered by her tendency to belittle him.

Emotions may or may not reflect one's conscious estimates of value importance. Errors of introspection may lead people to profess value hierarchies that differ from their subconscious hierarchies. Consider a young man who professes to want a girlfriend who is intelligent, sensible, and dependable but who becomes infatuated by a girl who is seductive, wild, and irresponsible. Clearly his subconscious is weighting these latter traits much more highly than his conscious mind is weighting them.

Emotions contain built-in action tendencies (Arnold, 1960; Smith, 1991). There is a felt desire to approach and keep objects that are positively appraised (e.g., loved ones) and to avoid or destroy those that are negatively appraised (e.g., enemies). One is not forced or compelled to act on one's emotions, however, although one might think so after being exposed to modern culture, where it is considered perfectly normal and inevitable for people to act on every momentary whim. Through reason people have the power to identify their emotions, to understand the causes of these emotions, and to choose appropriate courses of action (including the choice of no action).

Goals

Goals and values are similar concepts, but I differentiate them with respect to level of generality. I view goals as the specific form of values; they are values applied to specific circumstances. Just as needs are fulfilled by pursuing values, values are achieved by pursuing goals. For example, if a person values education, the way to achieve it is to set and pursue specific educational goals—such as applying to college, signing up for courses, doing the assignments, getting the needed grades in each course, and accumulating the required number of credits to graduate. Similarly, if a person values good nutrition, the way to attain it is to set goals to eat specific types of foods in specific amounts at specific times of day.

Goals, by necessity, exist in a hierarchy just as do values. Due to context factors, however, goal hierarchies will change more frequently than value hierarchies. For example, the value of getting an education may stay constant for years. But on a given day, a student may have a variety of educational objectives (e.g., study for physics exam, go to the library to research a term paper in history, meet a professor to go over an English test, attend a makeup class in computer science) that are quite different from the educational goals on another day. Although a student's goals will change daily in response to exam schedules and assignments, for a purposeful student, each day's goals will facilitate the achievement of the value of getting an education.

To complicate matters yet further, people pursue multiple values and therefore multiple goals in life. Students want an education, but they also may want to eat, plan their finances, sleep, have fun with friends, get exercise, and so forth. Accordingly, they will pursue not just multiple goals but multiple goals tied to multiple values. It should be obvious from this discussion that *setting priorities in values and goals is critical to managing one's life, both in the short range and in the long range.*

The motivational sequence I have described previously is shown in Figure 22.1. To summarize, the sequence is as follows: Needs give rise to the necessity to choose and pursue values; value achievement necessitates the setting and pursuit of goals. From the other direction: Goals attain values, and values fulfill needs. The role of emotions is that of an impetus to action; they provide psychological and physical fuel. They serve (as does the pleasure-pain mechanism at the bodily or sensory level) as a reward for successful action and an inducement to avoid actions that cause pain or suffering. Without emotions, values would be experienced as dry, abstract, and intellectual. An individual who

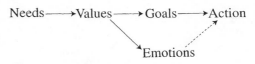

Figure 22.1 The motivation sequence.

could not experience emotions would think: "Yes, X is good, but so what? It has no personal meaning for me."

Cognition (thinking, knowledge) plays a role at every stage of the motivation sequence, from identifying needs, to choosing values, to understanding emotions, to setting goals, to discovering the means to achieve them. Because thinking is volitional, it is the active part of human psychology. Although emotions contain action tendencies, they are passive in that they occur automatically rather than volitionally. They are not willed by reason, although they can be changed (sometimes with great difficulty if the causes are deeply automatized) by reason, through changing the causal inputs. For example, consider a student I once had who was deeply depressed because of receiving a low test grade. He had concluded that his life was ruined because he was too dumb to do well in pre-med and therefore could never reach his childhood dream of becoming a doctor. I was able to explain that his automatized appraisal was mistaken. One test grade would not determine his course grade or his grade point average. Furthermore, doing badly on a test did not mean he was dumb; it might be due to the fact that he studied improperly for the test (which turned out to be the case). By helping him to modify his incorrect appraisals, I was able to help change the emotion. (This, of course, is the method used in cognitive therapy.)

To pursue long-range values requires a continual act of focus on:

- what one wants to achieve;
- the reasons one wants to achieve it;
- the goals to be set;
- the means to achieve them;
- how to prioritize conflicting demands;
- how to overcome obstacles and setbacks; and thus
- how to attain, at the end, the value that one envisioned.

One cannot attain happiness by living solely in a world of fantasy; one must act to bring one's vision into reality, into concrete, perceivable form. To quote Ayn Rand, "Happiness is that state of consciousness which proceeds from the achievement of one's values" (1964, p. 31). The achievement of values requires the achievement of the requisite goals. One's goals and values, however, must be consonant with one's needs, or they will result in self-destruction. There are many potential sources of pleasure in life (e.g., work, love, friendship, family and children, food and drink, art—novels, painting, sculpture, movies, TV, ballet, opera, concerts—sports and recreation, hobbies).

Happiness in Work and Love

In this chapter, I will focus on two sources of happiness: work and romantic love. I chose work because it fills the majority of most people's daily lives and because productive work is critical to one's survival (see Turner, Barling, & Zacharatos, this volume). There can be no consumption without production unless one becomes a parasite or a beggar. Work is the means by which one produces material values and thereby earns money, and money is a prerequisite for the fulfillment of many needs.

I chose romantic love, first, because it is a source of enormous pleasure. Love is a timeless theme in every sphere of art. Most people go through their lives longing for love, even though few find it in the form they desire. Second, love provides a useful contrast to business in one respect: In business the currency and the trade are material, whereas in romantic love the currency and the trade are spiritual, by which I mean pertaining to consciousness (i.e., thinking). I do not mean to imply here any mind-body dichotomy, for example, the conventional, Platonic idea that business success is based on some "lower" part of man's soul. I believe that the rational mind plays a critical role in the success of both business and love relationships (Rand, 1957). It is the nature of the exchange that differs in the two spheres: In business, it is my goods for your money; in love, it is my character for yours.

Goal-Setting Theory

Because goals are the means of achieving values and thereby fulfilling needs, I will begin by discussing what we know about goal setting. The best summaries of goal theory are found in Locke (1996) and Locke and Latham (1990). Goals determine the direction, intensity, and duration of action. They also affect cognitive processing and the use of task knowledge.

Difficulty

Assuming the requisite knowledge (skill) and commitment to the goal, the more difficult the goal, the greater the performance accomplishment. This finding, replicated in hundreds of studies with numerous types of tasks, goes against Atkinson's (1958) popular theory, which asserts that maximum motivation to perform occurs when task difficulty (probability of success) is moderate. We never have been able to replicate Atkinson's original finding; the key is not the difficulty per se of the task one is confronted with but rather what the individual is trying to accomplish. Given that people are committed to a goal, they exert effort in proportion to what the goal requires. So an easy goal stimulates low effort, a medium goal, moderate effort, and a difficult goal, high effort. Recent research in Germany reveals that the difficulty of the goal even affects the speed and efficiency of cognitive processing (Wegge, in press).

Specificity

Specific goals regulate action more reliably than do vague goals (see also McDermott & Snyder, 2000). Asking a person to "do his best" on a task does not lead him to do his best because such a vague goal leads people to define "best" in subjective terms. Asking someone to "increase sales" can be interpreted by one person as a 1% increase, by another as a 5% increase, and by another as a 15% increase. Compare this with asking everyone to achieve a 15% increase.

The highest task performance is attained when performance goals are both specific and difficult. Specificity usually requires an external, quantitative standard. This principle applies to employees working on clerical tasks, scientists doing research and development work, students working for grades, and even professors trying to get publications. People working toward specific, difficult goals reliably outperform those trying to do their best or those trying for specific, moderate or specific, easy goals.

Feedback

To keep track of goal progress, people need performance feedback (i.e., knowledge of results). When the feedback shows them to be on sched-

ule for goal success, they tend to sustain the same pace of work and the same strategy. When feedback shows them to be lagging, they tend to increase their efforts (if self-efficacy does not drop—see subsequent comment). They also may try new strategies; performance feedback may help reveal (indirectly) if the strategy they are using is effective. (Performance feedback must be distinguished from feedback about the correctness of one's actions [e.g., a poor backswing on a golf shot]; this type of feedback can have strictly cognitive benefits regardless of motivation as long as the person wants to do well.)

I should note that performance feedback (knowledge of results) in the absence of specific goals does not usually improve performance. Feedback is just information about performance. In order to evaluate their performances, people need standards against which to judge it; without such standards, they cannot distinguish good from poor performance and therefore have no motivation to change their direction or level of effort.

Commitment

For goals to be effective, people must be committed to them. This is especially critical when goals are difficult and thus require considerable thinking and effort. Action is the ultimate proof of commitment in that people can say they are committed and not really mean it. Two types of causal factors are critical in commitment: the belief that the goal is important and the belief that one can achieve or make progress toward it. For a goal to be important, it must be tied to an important value. This does not mean that the task or goal always has to be chosen by oneself. For example, one can be assigned a work task or goal by a leader and still accept it, because the company's mission is important and because one wants to do well on the job. There are many ways that a leader can foster commitment among subordinates such as by providing a compelling vision for the company's future (see Turner et al., volume). In work environments, participation in setting goals does not reliably lead to better commitment than being told what to do as long as a plausible rationale for the goal is given. The belief that one can achieve or make progress toward a goal is critical because it is hard to be motivated to try for something that is perceived as unattainable (see Brehm, Wright,

Soloman, Silka, & Greenberg [1983] for a similar view). This brings us to the concept of self-efficacy (see Maddux, this volume).

Self-Efficacy

This concept from social-cognitive theory (Bandura, 1986, 1997) refers to task-specific self-confidence. Bandura has shown that self-efficacy has important motivational effects in many domains of life, including work performance and career choice, education, physical and mental health, and sports. Self-efficacy plays an important role in goal setting. People with higher self-efficacy set more difficult goals for themselves, are more likely to be committed to difficult goals that are assigned, are more likely to sustain their efforts after negative feedback, and are more likely to discover successful task strategies than people with lower self-efficacy. Bandura notes that the main ways to build efficacy are through enactive mastery (training and practice), role modeling (observing others), and persuasion.

I must add that viewing a goal as important and believing one can attain it does not automatically lead to goal-directed action. There is a volitional element here: The person has to choose to keep his goals in mind at the time of action and not let alternative thoughts interfere with or block action.

Task Knowledge

Goals automatically arouse task knowledge and skills if they are perceived consciously or subconsciously as relevant to task or goal accomplishment. Goals increase the likelihood that people will use the knowledge they have, especially when the goals are difficult, because not using it may prevent goal achievement. When relevant task knowledge does not exist, goals stimulate the search for suitable task knowledge, although there is no guarantee that the right knowledge will be discovered. This depends on one's thinking. When a series of actions has to be consciously laid out, we call them plans. These, along with the use of already existing skills and knowledge, constitute the means to the goal. Acquiring the requisite knowledge to reach the end goal can be viewed as a subgoal.

Incentives and Personality

External incentive effects typically are mediated by self-set goals and self-efficacy. For example,

the effects of monetary incentives on performance and commitment are at least partly dependent on whether people set challenging goals and feel confident that they can attain the performance level needed to get the bonus (Lee, Locke, & Phan, 1997). It also has been found that goals and self-efficacy mediate the effects of personality traits on performance (Locke, 1997). In this respect, traits are like values; they are general and need to be applied to specific situations.

Affect

A goal is at once an object to aim for and a standard by which success is measured. These are not two separate functions but two sides of the same coin. A goal is that which you want to achieve and below which you do not want to achieve. Success then leads to satisfaction, and failure to dissatisfaction. As noted earlier, goal success fosters value achievement. It seems paradoxical that difficult goals, which motivate the highest performance, lead, necessarily, to the least degree of immediate satisfaction with performance (because they are less frequently attained). But this makes perfect sense if one understands what it means to set a difficult goal—it means not being satisfied with less. In the real world, of course, many benefits follow from achieving or partly achieving difficult goals, such as pride in self, better jobs, and better salaries.

Work

Some people truly resent the need to work. Resenting the responsibility of earning a living is tantamount to the resentment of reality, that is, one's own nature and needs as a living being. People who resent this responsibility will be hard-pressed to find happiness in work or anywhere else. Success in work, as in life, requires continual effort, including the consistent use of volition, that is, of one's capacity to think.

Let me now apply the previously described goal-setting principles to the case of those who do not resent working for a living. Ideally one wants to enjoy work and to make a good living at it. Generally, the more skills and credentials one has (assuming they are relevant to the market), the more options one has to choose from among the available jobs, and the more one will get paid when employed.

Thus, the first goal in preparation for work should be to acquire marketable skills, starting with a basic education. In most cases, the higher the level of education received the better job, especially as our economy becomes increasingly technological. This is not to say that everyone needs to go to college; there are many ways to acquire job skills, including on-the-job training. Gaining skills builds self-efficacy, and efficacy, as noted earlier, has many beneficial effects on performance.

Although basic intelligence is important in life, including in school and in work, it is no more, and perhaps less, important than effort. It is more beneficial to frame skills as acquirable rather than as innate and fixed (Bandura, 1997). For example, study effectiveness is strongly influenced by the methods one uses to study (Locke, 1998), and study skills are acquirable through practice. (After 33 years in academia, I continue to be shocked by how little many students know about proper study methods.) Even people with great natural ability need to work hard if they are to attain their full potential. We have found that the goals students set for grades have a substantial impact on their grade performances (Locke & Bryan, 1968).

The next goal should be to find a job that matches one's skills (and/or allows for skill development) and that matches one's values. It is particularly important to find a job that involves work that one enjoys. Research shows consistently that mental challenge—assuming one is willing to respond to the challenge—is a critical determinant of job satisfaction (Judge, 2000). Of course, one wants the right amount of challenge—not so much that one will feel overwhelmed and not so little that one will be bored. The ideal job is one where a person can say, "I can't believe they pay me to do something that is this much fun." Of course, not everyone can find such a job, but looking for it is usually well worth the effort. Someone people do not know what they like because they have not had enough work experience. So the goal should be to try different tasks, positions, and jobs until one finds something truly enjoyable.

The next goal should be to constantly increase one's knowledge and skill on the job. As one, very successful, person I know told me, "Every job I got, I set a goal to do it better than anyone else had done it before." (Although competition is not appropriate under all circumstances, it should be noted that competition itself is a form of goal setting—with the other's performance serving as the goal to beat.) If one fails to grow on the job, the job gradually becomes less enjoyable and also makes one more susceptible to being laid off. The loss of a job in a downturn due to lack of skills can mean long-term or permanent unemployment. Furthermore, the failure to grow will prevent one from moving ahead into more challenging, better paying jobs in an organization and reduces the options when looking for a better job elsewhere.

Skill development can no longer be left solely to one's employing organization. The organization may train people in the skills it needs at the moment, but there is no guarantee that these skills will have long-term market value or even value in other organizations. Many job skills are organization-specific, and even broader skills may become outdated in only a few years. Thus, people increasingly will have to take responsibility for acquiring new and upgraded job skills on their own.

People differ, of course, in their ability and in how much they value ambition. Everyone cannot be and should not try to be a CEO. But everyone is capable of improving his skills and knowledge. It is critical to consider one's own personal context when looking for a job, planning a career, and setting performance goals. For example, a useful way to hold one's personal context when setting performance goals is to try, at least, to improve over one's best previous performance.

If one does not receive regular feedback on job performance, it is important to seek feedback to learn both whether one is doing the right thing and whether one is doing it well. If there is negative feedback or failure on the job, this need not be a disaster if one learns from it. Asking a boss or colleagues for suggestions on how to improve skills can help change one's perspective from a failure frame to a learning frame. Failure should be viewed as diagnostic of one's current skill and effort level rather than as proof of one's fundamental inadequacy (Snyder, 1994). Self-efficacy can be kept high by focusing on the things one can do, including the steps that can be taken to acquire new skills or find a new job. It is important to set goals to take these various actions on a strict schedule to prevent wallowing in self-pity and self-doubt. Sometimes a failure experience can help one refocus one's career ideas and aspirations in a direction that is more compatible with one's values and abilities.

Romantic Love

Goals for Oneself

One myth about love is that it is a matter of "chemistry"—beyond reason and beyond understanding. This belief stems from the fact that love is an emotion and thus reflects subconscious value judgments. Because many people are not very good at introspection, they do not understand the causes of their romantic responses to others. They conclude, falsely, that the causes of love are simply too mysterious to identify. It may be true that "love at first sight" exists, but this "gut feel"—which is an immediate emotional response to the person—has causes consisting of subconscious inferences one makes about the other person based on that person's initial appearance and style.

Another myth is that love involves selfless sacrifice to the other party. Romantic love is not martyrdom but trade. As noted earlier, the currency in love is different than in business. The form of trade in business is material (my product or service for your money); the form of trade in love is spiritual (my character for yours). Again, I do not mean to imply any mind-body dichotomy. Business has a spiritual aspect—by spiritual I mean pertaining to consciousness. (I do not mean pertaining to religion.) Wealth is earned by the use of the rational mind; however, what is produced is material. Similarly, romantic love has physical aspects; if the relationship is purely platonic, then it is not romantic love. But a love relationship is sustained and driven by love for the other person's soul—a soul, admittedly, that is embodied.

If one's goal and value is to establish a successful romantic relationship, then the next goal should be to *make oneself lovable*. Making oneself lovable does not mean making oneself a selfless mirror of the other person's wants. To quote Howard Roark in *The Fountainhead*, "To say 'I love you' one must know first how to say the 'I' " (Rand, 1952, p. 376).

To have an "I" worth loving, one needs to acquire virtues. One cannot expect to be loved without cause. People can be attracted to superficial qualities in another person (e.g., charm, gaiety, and physique), but relationships based on so little usually do not last.

What virtues make one lovable? I would submit they are the same ones that make one fit to live successfully. Ayn Rand (1957) suggests the following:

- rationality: taking reality and reason seriously;
- independence: accepting the responsibility of using one's own judgment and earning one's own living;
- honesty: refusing to fake reality (see Locke & Woiceshyn, 1996);
- integrity: acting on one's rational convictions;
- productivity: producing the material values one's survival requires;
- justice: judging other people in accordance with the facts; and
- pride: seeking one's own moral perfection.

To this list one might add purpose: having a direction for one's life; passion: having strong values that are experienced emotionally (but not irrationally); maturity: being able to hold an adult context despite the emotions of the moment; and manners: respect for and politeness toward others.

I base the material that follows in this and the next section on my own clinical experience. To enhance lovability, it is advisable to take some reasonable actions to enhance and sustain one's physical attractiveness. (I am not advocating vanity.) Love is spiritual, but one does not fall in love with an actual disembodied spirit or a ghost. One falls in love with a physically real person. How one presents oneself physically not only affects one's attractiveness for aesthetic reasons but also reflects, in some measure, one's view of oneself. It is reasonable to look as attractive as possible within the context of one's raw material, income, and time. Totally ignoring one's appearance implies a split between mind and body—an unfortunate error.

Lovability can be affected by education (I include here self-education). Education projects knowledge, the ability to master the world, and some degree of ambition; it also may make one more interesting to talk to. The wider, dynamic issue involved here is cognitive growth. During the 15-year period that I worked part-time as a psychotherapist, the most frequent cause of marital breakups among my clients was partners growing, cognitively and emotionally, at different rates. This is also the single biggest factor causing breakups among people I know as friends and acquaintances. One's goal should be to grow constantly in one's knowledge across the range of a whole lifetime. Ideally, couples should grow together.

Lovability may be affected by mental health. People who are emotionally unstable (which may or may not be any fault of their own) tend to have more volatile romantic relationships. Thus one's goal here should be to become as mentally healthy as possible within the context of one's innate makeup (e.g., schizophrenia is partly controllable with drugs but not curable; depression can have chemical causes) and income (if therapy is needed). A factor that does much damage to romantic relationships is psychological "baggage" in the form of subconscious premises and conclusions based on earlier experiences that distort one's reactions to current situations. For example, someone who has been hurt a great deal in the past may withdraw in the face of a conflict, thus making the other party withdraw and become angry, thereby further undermining the relationship. A major goal of therapy in such cases should be to make people aware of their own subconscious premises and habits and to change them whenever possible. (A Nobel Prize should be given to the first psychologist to discover a method of fully deautomatizing deeply held, subconscious premises established in childhood.)

Lovability is affected by personality. We tend to think of personality as fixed, but it is not totally unchangeable. Two traits that are extremely damaging to romantic love are emotional repression and hostility. Repression is anathema to romance because romance requires emotional intimacy. I believe that emotional intimacy, not knowledge of sex films and exotic positions, is the essential factor in the enjoyment of sex. Emotional intimacy is only possible if each person is emotionally open, that is, willing to experience, acknowledge, and communicate emotions to the other. Obviously men typically have more difficulties in this realm than women because most men think they need to be tough and not show emotion. This may be true to an extent at work, but it is very damaging in romance. Openness is a trait that can be acquired if there is motivation to do so.

I differentiate hostility (the desire to hurt others) from anger (the response to goal frustration). I believe that hostility stems from childhood experiences of being humiliated and mistreated; the desire to hurt others, is in part,

a defense against being hurt. This defense is very destructive of oneself and others and makes a happy romantic relationship virtually impossible. The desire to hurt is the opposite of the desire to love. Emotional openness in this case does not help because it is the emotions themselves that are the problem. Becoming more intimate and less hostile will probably be achievable only if the person gets professional help—and even then not easily because the subconscious premises and habits involved may be pervasive and deep-seated. Hostility also may be associated with a lack of moral character (as in spousal abuse).

I would add one last factor here—I call it knowing how to value. Valuing another person means deeply and selfishly caring for them—because one regards that person as an important value. To love another person is to personally care deeply about that person's welfare. It is to value that person's self, character, values, goals and aspirations, ideas, feelings, looks. It is to find pleasure in the person's being and company, in the things you share and do together. Narcissists do not make good lovers because they simply cannot value anyone but themselves (and even that in a perverse way—narcissism, after all, is a psychological disorder).

Goals for the Partner

It is a truism that people are attracted to people like themselves (which does not mean that people want literal mirrors). Thus, to the degree that people possess traits that make them lovable, their goal usually will be to find these same qualities in their partners.

There are traits, aside from moral virtues, on which I believe a reasonable "match" is especially critical. These traits would include (a) self-esteem (Locke et al., 1996): if one party looks down on the other or feels inadequate to the other, a true partnership is impossible; of course, if both parties have low self-esteem there is trouble, so ideally both parties should have high self-esteem; (b) intelligence and education: people have to be able to communicate on the same wavelength; (c) age: there is some flexibility here, but enormous age differences are difficult because of differences in health, energy levels, and interests; (d) growth rate: as noted earlier, ideally couples will grow together at the same rate; and (e) philosophical (including religious) values: it is difficult for people with very different value systems and interests to live in harmony; it is not impossible, but it is critical in such cases to have a bond with respect to some core values that are strong enough to override any differences. It is crucial here for conscious and subconscious assessments of the other's values to be in harmony.

There is another category of goals that pertains to *personal preferences*. These do not necessarily have to match, but they should at least not be a cause of conflict. These will include such factors as looks (personal appearance), personality (other than the factors noted earlier), personal habits (e.g., smoking), tastes, lifestyle, interests, and attitude toward money. I am not saying that these preferences should not be taken seriously; rather, I mean that here there are no principles that apply to everyone.

I do not mean to imply from the foregoing that romance should originate with or be directed by a checklist. Personal relationships, as noted earlier, start with gut feel, that is, with first impressions that are largely emotional, for example, so and so turns me on, turns me off, leaves me cold. However, as one gets to know the other person better, one has the opportunity to learn more about that person and to identify the reasons for one's emotional responses (which may be complex). As one learns more about the person, one's emotional reactions may change. What is critical is that in the end there is harmony between one's characteristic emotional response and one's rational judgment. For example, if Ms. B concludes, "Mr. A is a dishonest rat, but I just cannot help swooning over him," more thinking is called for. For example, how long will the swooning last if Mr. A keeps lying? The goal should be to find a person who turns one on *and* who seems to be a good and suitable person.

Finally, let me address the issue of how to find people. Here it is important to set a goal to go places and do things where one has a chance of meeting the type of person one wants. Today, at least in the United States, people have the opportunity to connect with a much wider group of potential partners than in the past, not only because of the ease of travel but also because of modern technology such as the Internet. The Internet has sites where people can "meet" and look for at least some of the characteristics that they want in a partner before they ever meet in person. Although this approach is not without risks, especially for women, the potential of modern technology in this realm is astounding.

Blocks to Goal Achievement

It should be clear from the foregoing discussion that goal setting—which means fundamentally purposefulness—is necessary for living a successful, happy life. Most people, at some level, seem to know this. Why, then, are so many people unhappy? Three reasons, I think, are primary:

1. The most fundamental reason is irrationalism; this characteristically consists of putting one's wishes ahead of reality, for example, holding an image of a person that is based on what you want him to be, not on what he is.
2. A second reason is the unwillingness to put forth mental (and physical) effort—both in work and in love. Living successfully requires hard thinking followed by action, and many people do not want to bother. It is "easier" to live on the range of the moment by the principle of least effort. This is certainly encouraged by our schools, which teach that you can not know anything for certain and that how you feel is more important than how you think, and by movies and TV programs that show people "just doing it" based on their impulses at the moment.
3. The third reason is fear. The older I get, the more I come to realize how big a role fear plays in many people's lives: fear of change, fear of telling the truth, fear of being wrong, fear of being different, fear of thinking for oneself, fear of failure, fear of the subconscious and of knowing one's own motives, fear of disappointment, fear of disapproval, fear of being hurt, fear of being vulnerable, fear of the new, and fear of standing up for one's values. It is said that people live either by pursuing values or by avoiding loss. A famous radio psychologist once said that there are two kinds of people in the world: the vulnerable and the dead. Those who live only to avoid hurt are the living dead. The essence of life *is* goal-directed action, which entails a process of value choice, value pursuit, and value

achievement. When the striving for values stops, life indeed loses all meaning.

Conclusion

Goals are the means by which values and dreams are translated into reality. Happiness does not just happen. It has to be earned by thinking, planning, and the constant pursuit of values—both in work and in love—over the course of a lifetime. Goal-directed action is therefore critical to positive psychology.

Note

For literary convenience, I use the word *man* and the masculine pronoun in this chapter to refer to all human beings.

References

Arnold, M. (1960). *Emotion and personality: Psychological aspects* (Vol. 1). New York: Columbia University Press.

Atkinson, J. W. (1958). Towards experimental analysis of human motivation in terms of motives, expectancies, and incentives. In L. W. Atkinson (Ed.), *Motives in fantasy, actions and society* (pp. 288–305). Princeton, NJ: Van Nostrand.

Bandura, A. (1986). *Social foundations of thought and action: A social cognitive theory*. Englewood Cliffs, NJ: Prentice-Hall.

Bandura, A. (1997) *Self-efficacy: The exercise of control*. New York: Freeman.

Baumeister, R. F., & Scher, S. J. (1988). Self-defeating behavior patterns among normal individuals: Review and analysis of common self-destructive tendencies. *Psychological Bulletin, 104*, 3–22.

Binswanger, H. (1990). *The biological basis of teleological concepts*. Los Angeles: Ayn Rand Institute Press.

Binswanger, H. (1991). Volition as cognitive self-regulation. *Organizational Behavior and Human Decision Processes, 50*, 154–178.

Brehm, J. W., Wright, R. A., Soloman, S., Silka, L., & Greenberg, J. (1983). Perceived difficulty, energization, and the magnitude of goal valence. *Journal of Experimental Social Psychology, 19*, 21–48.

Gotthelf, A. (2000). *On Ayn Rand*. Belmont, CA: Wadsworth (Thomson Learning).

Judge, T. A. (2000). Promote job satisfaction through mental challenge. In E. A. Locke (Ed.), *Handbook of principles of organizational behavior* (pp. 75–89). Oxford, England: Blackwell.

Lazarus, R. (1991). *Emotion and adaptation*. New York: Oxford University Press.

Lazarus, R., & Lazarus, B. (1994). *Passion and reason*. New York: Oxford University Press.

Lee, T. W., Locke, E. A., & Phan, S. H. (1997). Explaining the assigned goal-incentive interaction: The role of self-efficacy and personal goals. *Journal of Management, 23*, 541–559.

Locke, E. A. (1969). What is job satisfaction? *Organizational Behavior and Human Performance, 4*, 309–336.

Locke, E. A. (1996). Motivation through conscious goal setting. *Applied and Preventive Psychology, 5*, 117–124.

Locke, E. A. (1997). The motivation to work: What we know. In P. Pintrich & M. Maehr (Eds.), *Advances in motivation and achievement* (Vol. 10, pp. 375–412). Stamford, CT: JAI Press.

Locke, E. A. (1998). *Study methods and motivation*. New Milford, CT: Second Renaissance Books.

Locke, E. A., & Bryan, J. F. (1968). Grade goals as determinants of academic achievement. *Journal of General Psychology, 79*, 217–228.

Locke, E. A., & Latham, G. P. (1990). *A theory of goal setting and task performance*. New York: Prentice-Hall.

Locke, E. A., McClear, K., & Knight, D. (1996). Self-esteem and work. In C. Cooper & I. Robertson (Eds.), *International review of industrial and organizational psychology* (Vol. 11, pp. 1–32). Chichester, England: Wiley.

Locke, E. A., & Woiceshyn, J. (1996). Why businessmen should be honest: The argument from rational egoism. *Journal of Organizational Behavior, 16*, 405–414.

Maslow, A. H. (1970). *Motivation and personality*. New York: Harper and Row.

McDermott, H. D., & Snyder, C. R. (2000). *The great big book of hope: Help your children achieve their dreams*. Oakland, CA: New Harbinger Press.

Peikoff, L. (1991). *Objectivism: The philosophy of Ayn Rand*. New York: Dutton.

Rand, A. (1952). *The fountainhead*. New York: Signet.

Rand, A. (1957). *Atlas shrugged*. New York: Signet.

Rand, A. (1964). *The virtue of selfishness*. New York: Signet.

Rand, A. (1966). *The romantic manifesto*. New York: Signet.

Rand, A. (1990). *Introduction to objectivist epistemology* (Expanded 2nd ed.). New York: NAL Books.

Rokeach, M. (1972). *Beliefs, attitudes and values: A theory of organization and change*. San Francisco: Jossey-Bass.

Smith, C. A. (1991). The self, appraisal and coping, In C. R. Snyder & D. R. Forsyth (Eds.), *Handbook of social and clinical psychology: The health perspective* (pp. 116–137). Elmsford, NY: Pergamon.

Snyder, C. R. (1994). *The psychology of hope: You can get there from here*. New York: Free Press.

Terrace, H. (1979). *Nim*. New York: Washington Square Press.

Wegge, J. (in press). Motivation, information processing and performance: Effects of goal setting on cognitive processes. In A. Efklides, J. Kuhl, & R. Sorrentino (Eds.), *Trends and prospects in motivation research*. Dordrecht, Netherlands: Kluwer.

23

The Passion to Know

A Developmental Perspective

Michael Schulman

According to *Discover Magazine* ("Armchair Astronauts," 2000), "the most heavily attended internet event ever" was not about a celebrity, sports, or sex. No, it was the on-line photo exhibit of Mars, transmitted back to earth by NASA's *Pathfinder* spacecraft. The *Pathfinder* home page received an incredible "566 million hits"!

To the average person this may not be surprising. People always have been fascinated by Mars, and now, finally, we could see it up close. But we psychologists should not be so nonchalant about those 566 million hits. Our theories have depicted humankind as drive-reducing organisms (Dollard & Miller, 1950; Freud, 1917/1949), stimulus-seeking organisms (Berlyne, 1960), arousal-optimizing organisms (Fiske & Maddi, 1961), competence-seeking organisms (Deci & Ryan, 1985), and computer-like information-processing organisms (Newell & Simon, 1972). But we have not paid sufficient attention to humans as pure knowledge-seeking or *information-seeking* organisms—despite the fact that human beings seeking knowledge are everywhere to behold, even on the Internet.

Indeed, our major theories have not generally recognized that much human behavior is motivated by an intrinsic desire to know more about this world we inhabit, to know things simply because they are interesting, not *necessarily* because they will help us reduce our drives or satisfy some supposedly more fundamental urges—to know things we do not *have to* know. My central thesis in this chapter is that, for humans, information seeking is both ubiquitous and fundamental, and starts at birth. Just as the newborn wildebeest is compelled to run, the newborn human is compelled to gain information. To borrow a contemporary phrase, some of us may have been "born to shop," but all of us are *born to know*.

A great deal of developmental research reveals that babies are surprisingly capable learners, as well as energetic and determined pursuers of information (Schulman, 1991). But what kind of information? Is there a useful way to conceptualize what babies want to know? In a television interview, a reporter asked the Nobel physicist Richard Feynman what he wanted to know about the world. Feynman thought for a moment, then exclaimed *"Everything!"* In a sense, all of us, includi͏ ͏s, have the same desire.

But, obviously, "everything" to most of us, and certainly to infants, is not the same as "everything" to a brilliant physicist studying the big bang or quarks. Yet in certain fundamental ways infants seek precisely the same kinds of information as Professor Feynman. Both want to know four basic things: *What's out there? What leads to what? What makes things happen?* and *What's controllable?* In other words, children in their explorations, scientists in their theorizing and experimenting, artists in their search for "truth," and the rest of us in our effort to make sense of the world and gain mastery over it seek to (a) identify and classify the phenomena we encounter, (b) discern temporal patterns between some of those phenomena, (c) determine causal relationships behind some of those temporal patterns, and (d) discover how to enter into the antecedent-consequent chain and become causal agents ourselves. The function of intelligence is to gain information in each of these domains.

Let us take a closer look at each of these areas from a developmental perspective, drawing upon a number of experimental and observational studies of children.

What's Out There? Discovering Categories and Concepts

The first task infants must master is to identify coherent patterns or "things" in their world, including faces, voices, milk, nipples, diapers, rattles, and so on. These all are located in the three-dimensional space surrounding and including the child. Their spatial existence is part of their identity. Mommy is not an abstract entity but appears there and then moves there. Mommy is not just a thing; she is also an event.

Beyond the identification of patterns, the key processes in learning what's out there are recognizing similarities (those things are dogs) and discriminating differences (those are collies, those are poodles). These similarities and differences then become the bases for a hierarchy of categories (dogs differ from cats but have similarities that make both animals, and other similarities that make them mammals). Knowing an object's category ("It's a cow") tells the child what to expect from that thing or how to use it ("It gives milk and moos").

Actually, some categorical learning is better described by the phrase *What's there* because we—child and adult—also learn to discern and label our private experiences, including our bodily sensations, ideations, and emotional states, none of which are experienced as "out" there.

Children perceive and distinguish patterns right from birth, recognizing the solidity and touchability of the objects they see; they cry when they cannot touch a nearby "object" created via an optical illusion (Bower, 1971). The patterns infants show the most interest in are the human face and voice. During their first week, newborns respond to faces as distinct entities and prefer looking at them over other patterns, even patterns consisting of facial features in unusual arrangements. One-day-olds will look longer at their mother than at another woman, indicating they can already distinguish between faces (Bushnell, Sai, & Mullin, 1989; Fantz, 1971; Salapatek, 1968). They can even distinguish different expressions on faces and will imitate some of the expressions they see (Meltzoff & Moore, 1977; Reissland, 1988).

Also, "within the first 3 days of postnatal development, newborns prefer the human voice, discriminate between speakers, and demonstrate a preference for their mothers' voices" (DeCasper & Fifer, 1980, p. 1176). By their second day, they can distinguish spoken words, will turn their face toward a speaker emitting a word, stop turning if the same word is repeated a few times, and turn again when the speaker emits a new word (Brody, Zelazo, & Chaika, 1984).

Infants, during their earliest days, will orient toward stimuli to bring them into sharper focus, indicating that despite their limited motor abilities they start out life actively exploring the world around them. They also use their mouths and hands to learn about objects, even handling soft, flexible objects differently from rigid ones (Rochat, 1987). That they learn to recognize objects from their mouthings is indicated by the fact that by 1 month they prefer looking at an object they have explored in their mouths but have never seen before rather than an unfamiliar object (Meltzoff & Borton, 1979).

By 12 months, children are learning what is out there by picking up cues from others, looking at things they see their parents look at or point to (Scaife & Bruner, 1975). They will even learn about the desirability or dangerousness of people and things through "social referencing," by observing their parents' reactions to them (Feinman & Lewis, 1983).

Learning Categories, Classes, and Concepts

During their first year, children begin to recognize and respond to classes of objects, understanding, for example, that robins and blue jays are both birds, despite their differences. When they respond to different birds the same way (say by flapping their arms) and to nonbirds differently (not flapping in the presence of dogs and cats), we would say they have acquired the concept "birds." Once they have a concept, new examples that meet the essential criteria (beaks, wings, skinny legs) will be given the same label (Sherman, 1985). Long before they can speak, when a parent says, "Look, birdies!" children know to look up (Roberts, 1988).

Beginning in the second year, with the rapid growth of language, concept acquisition accelerates, as do knowledge of concept hierarchies ("Frogs, giraffes, and ducks are all animals") and an understanding of allowed variations within concepts ("We both have families, but mine has more people").

Two-year-olds want to know the name of virtually everything they encounter. "Whazzat? Whazzat?" they will ask over and over. Three-year-olds are already quite adept at recognizing and naming common objects and concepts and will be heard to make surprisingly fine distinctions. When the father of a little girl (3 years 1 month) described to his wife how he had to *pull* their obdurate daughter down the street, the child corrected him, saying, "You didn't pull me. You *dragged* me" (Schulman, 1991, p. 39).

Tests of 4-year-olds show that they use concept knowledge to make reasonable inductive inferences about other objects (Gelman, 1988). They will recognize, for example, that what is true for a red apple (it contains pectin, they were told) is more likely to be true for a yellow apple than it is for a banana or stereo. Other research finds that even 18-month-olds can make such inductive inferences (Sugarman, 1983).

In the social realm, the 5-year-old's knowledge of what's out there can be surprisingly sophisticated. A 5½-year-old girl said of a classmate, "I love Nick. Well, I love his outside but not his inside. His outside is handsome but his inside is nasty" (Schulman, 1991, p. 39). Five-year-olds are already engaged in trying to understand the precise meaning of subtle moral concepts such as lying, tattling, and boasting, which can lead to questions like "If I tell my friend that I learned to float, is that boasting?" These kinds of questions reflect their awareness that there are not only actions out there but also intentions, and that when it comes to moral judgments, it is the intentions that count.

Other research shows that 3- and 4-year-olds appreciate the essential differences between human-made and living objects and will also accurately distinguish and describe different emotional and mental states (other people's as well as their own), correctly using terms like *sad, angry, hurt, know, understand, think, feel, forget,* and *dream* (Bretherton & Beeghly, 1982; Bretherton, Fritz, Zahn-Waxler, & Ridgeway, 1986; Wellman & Estes, 1987). The quest by children this age to understand what's out there can lead to surprisingly thoughtful questions. A child, 3 years 11 months, asked her father, "Is this real now? When I dream, I think it's real, but it's not. Is it real now? Or am I dreaming? Can I tell I'm awake?" (Schulman, 1991, p. 40).

The process of discovering patterns and sorting experiences into their valid and functional categories continues throughout life. In school an adolescent may learn that although French and Italian sound different, they are both Romance languages with common features that reflect their common derivation from Latin. For one person the quest to know more about what's out there may be expressed though an interest in learning the cuisines of different cultures ("Let's try that new Ethiopian restaurant"). For someone else, it might be learning whether life exists on other planets.

Using Logic, Metaphor, and Mathematics to Learn What's Out There

Various studies confirm that by their third or fourth year youngsters are using deductive logic to learn what's out there (Fabricius, Sophian, & Wellman, 1987; Hawkins, Pea, Glick, & Scribner, 1984). For example, they use logical inference to place events and objects in their proper categories: "That metal box has an electric wire. Mommy said things with electric wires are dangerous. Therefore, that must be dangerous"; "The street and the cars are wet. They only get wet when it rains. Therefore, it must have rained."

By their early grade-school years, children's conversations reveal their frequent use of logical inference. A girl (6 years 1 month), upon seeing her father eating a cheese sandwich, asked why cheese did not give him a bellyache. She knew that milk upset his stomach and that cheese was made from milk. Another child (5 years 6 months) speculated on why the dinosaurs became extinct: "Maybe all plant-eaters became extinct because the Tyrannosaurs ate them all, and then *they* became extinct because they had nothing left to eat" (Schulman, 1991, p. 41).

Preschoolers are also beginning to comprehend and use similes, metaphors, and analogies. Some delightful examples I have collected are "A turtle's home is its shell"; "My sore throat is like a street light that goes on and off and on and off"; and "My belly and my supper are having an argument." Metaphor and analogies help children learn what's out there by providing new perspectives on what they perceive, as in "A machine has to eat too" (Schulman, 1991, p. 41; see also Gentner, 1988; Vosniadou, 1987).

A *model* is a type of analogy (e.g., a black hole has been described as a kind of syrup that rotates, pulling things along with it). A child's first model is probably her use of fingers for counting. Ask a preschooler, "If you have two apples and I give you two more, how many will you have?" and she will probably use her fingers to find the answer. Her fingers are not apples, but she recognizes that they can serve as models for any counting problem regardless of content.

Counting and arithmetic are ways of learning about, and describing, what's out there. Other mathematical activities, such as geometry, trigonometry, algebra, and calculus, are also used to describe things and events, including their shapes, sizes, capacities, and changes over time, as well as how they compare and relate to other things and events. Mathematics, like logic, is used to deduce quantities and properties that are unknown—symbolized by the notorious x. There is evidence that even newborns respond to quantity (Antell & Keating, 1983), and it is not uncommon to find 2- and 3-year-olds who can count and use numbers as they gather and sort objects.

In sum, many processes are involved in learning what's out there, including pattern recognition, stimulus discrimination, classification, concept formation, social referencing, perceptual

learning, logical and numerical operations, and metaphor and analogy comprehension. Although these are often studied as distinct, unrelated cognitive skills, I am suggesting that they all serve the same basic function: they help us—child and adult—answer the question *What's out there?* By the age of 4, children are ordinarily able to use all of them.

It is abundantly clear from research that parents can foster their children's learning what's out there by introducing them to numerous stimuli and supporting their explorations (see Schulman, 1991, pp. 43–94 for an overview). The French writer Colette provided a lovely description of her mother, Sido, showing her the world:

> Sido's great word was "Look!" And it could signify "Look at the hairy caterpillar, it's like a little golden bear! Look at the first bean sprout that is raising up on its head a little hat of dried earth. . . . Look at the wasp, see how it cuts with its scissors mandibles a bit of raw meat." At sunset she would say, "Look at that red sky, it forecasts a high wind and storm." What matters the high wind of tomorrow, provided we admire that fiery furnace today? Or it would be, "Look, be quick, the bud of the purple iris is opening! Be quick, or it will open before you can see it." (Colette, 1966, p. 28)

What Leads to What? Discovering Sequences

Children also come into the world primed to discover temporal patterns—that some of the events out there happen in a regular sequence. For example, a toddler might recognize that right after his mom sniffs him and gets a certain look on her face, she proceeds to change his diaper. Or that after certain sounds ("ring . . . ring"), his parent will lift an object and say hello into it. An older child might see dark clouds and think he'd better wear his rain boots.

In other words, children learn that the world is made up of more than just isolated objects and events; some of the events are connected to each other through the regularity of their temporal relationship. The first event signals the later event (but does not necessarily cause it). One form of evidence for sequential knowledge in very young babies is their exhibiting "surprise" when the first event of a regular sequence occurs but the second one does not (Donahue & Berg, 1991).

Once children discern a sequence, they can forecast events and adjust their behavior accordingly. An early lie for many children is their response to the question "Is your diaper wet?" They know a "yes" will mean getting whisked off to the changing table. So, if they do not want their play interrupted, they may say "no," knowing full well that the diaper is sopping. My own daughter, when she was 2 years 3 months, provided an interesting example of a young child learning a temporal relationship. I was changing her diaper, and she asked me if I was angry. I was not (we had been having a lovely time together), but she had heard me sigh as I placed her on the table and was aware that I often sigh when I am angry.

Children start learning temporal associations and developing expectancies right from birth. If a tone is presented to a newborn just before she starts nursing, after a few such pairings she will start to suck as soon as the tone is sounded, without any nipple in her mouth (Marquis, 1931; Sameroff, 1971). Also, during her first few days an infant will learn to suck more on a nipple when she hears a sound ("pst" or "pat") that signals that sucking will be followed by her mother's (recorded) voice (Moon & Fifer, 1990).

Other researchers report that most 1-month-olds, crying to be fed, will calm down upon the approach of the parent, even before being picked up (Lamb & Malkin, 1986). They appear to anticipate being fed. By the time my daughter was 2 weeks old, her "I'm starving!" cry would subside shortly after she was picked up, as we walked from her bedroom toward the kitchen, where her milk was kept. But, if I changed direction, she would start to cry again.

Parents are well aware that during their first months, babies often become fussy when goodies (like milk) are delayed or routines (like diapering) are extended. In other words, along with learning sequences, infants also acquire an awareness of duration and develop expectations about how long recurring events ordinarily take (Richie & Brickhard, 1988).

Rhythms and melodies are also types of temporal patterns, and children can detect and distinguish these by their fourth month (Trehub, Thorp, & Morrongiello, 1987). Some studies re-

port that even during their first weeks infants can detect differences in temporal auditory and visual patterns made up of sequences of sounds and light. For example, the eye movements of month-old babies, after a brief training period, anticipated where a visual stimulus should show up next (Allen, Walker, Symonds, & Marcell, 1977; Canfield & Haith, 1991).

By about 18 months, babies are able to imitate a sequence of actions they have observed (putting a board on a wedge; then placing a toy frog on one end of the board; then hitting the other end to make the frog "jump"), indicating they have learned which actions follow which others (Bauer & Mandler, 1989). In studies of 2-year-olds' conversations with their parents, the children demonstrated a good grasp of the sequence of events in their normal routines, such as going to the market (e.g., you pay on the way out, not on the way in). Children this age also understand terms that refer to the past and future, such as "Remember when we *went* to the zoo?" and "Sit down, *we'll* go in a minute" (Carni & French, 1984; Pellegrini, Brody, & Stoneman, 1987).

Three-year-olds, as most parents know, learn the sequence of events in a story with considerable precision and have generally begun to understand and use the words *yesterday* and *tomorrow* (Harner, 1975). Nursery-school children routinely learn complex sequences in games, dances, and schedules (Friedman & Brudos, 1988).

As children mature, they continue to learn new sequences, schedules, and cycles and are able to connect events that are increasingly distant temporally. They will learn that a car's flashing tail light signals the direction it will turn, that a touchdown provides a chance to kick an extra point, that primaries precede elections, that certain skies precede certain kinds of weather, and that sun spots wax and wane in decade-long cycles. A number of studies have demonstrated that parents help children learn such temporal relationships by pointing out sequences and referencing the past and future in their daily discourses (Lucariello & Nelson, 1987; see also Schulman, 1991, pp. 98–107).

Along with the developmental research cited in this section, other formats that psychologists have used for studying the acquisition of what leads to what are sensory preconditioning, S-S learning, Pavlovian conditioning, probability learning, and observational learning.

What Makes Things Happen? Discovering Causes

During their earliest months, babies begin to detect that in some sequences, the first event appears to make the second event happen. The first is perceived as *causing* the second. For example, it does not take long for babies to realize that whenever dad or mom shakes the bed, the mobile attached to it tinkles and turns; or that whenever the light switch is flicked, the lights go on or off. And they also soon realize that different kinds of things have different kinds of causes.

Even during their earliest weeks, children appear to recognize a distinction between people and physical objects as both causes and effects. People initiate events, they *do* things, they pursue ends. Physical objects simply change in some way when they are impinged upon; they move when they get bumped into or they fall when they are not supported. Infants will smile, vocalize, and behave toward people in ways they don't toward objects; they will try to induce a person—but never a chair—to pick up something they want (Golinkoff, Harding, Carlson, & Sexton, 1984).

Young children are so attuned to causal relationships that 2- and 3-year-olds are already making sophisticated causal statements, using terms like *if* and *because*: for example, "I'm putting medicine on the lamb's leg cause he has a booboo"; "Don't ring the bell either. . . . Jenny will wake up"; "You can bring me my puzzle . . . very careful so pieces don't fall down"; "My other shirt is wet . . . cause I played in the water" (Bretherton & Beeghly, 1982; Byrnes & Duff, 1988; Hood & Bloom, 1979).

Children this age also ask endless causal questions ("Why you wrapping it around?") and answer causal questions (Adult: "Why are you taking your socks off?" Child: "Because it's not cold outside"). Moreover, their *why* questions reflect an awareness of the difference between people and inanimate objects as causal agents. When people (or animals) make things happen, they ask about intentions ("Why you doing that?"). When no living agents are involved, they ask about mechanisms ("Why that happen?"). By age 3, they will also have begun to ask "What if . . . ?" questions, trying to anticipate the outcomes of all manner of causal events ("What if the rain doesn't stop?").

Children's understanding of causal relationships typically starts out concrete (When I push the ball harder, it goes farther) and, with ex-perience, becomes increasingly more universal and abstract (The harder I push anything, the farther it goes). Ultimately, their understanding may take the form of a general principle (The greater the force, the greater the acceleration). By the time they are 6 or 7, children generally recognize and use causal principles (Bretherton et al., 1986). For example, after Annie (4 years 9 months) was praised for taking such good care of a visiting friend (who was new to Annie's other friends), the child replied, "You know Mommy, children's feelings can be hurt when their friend ignores them because they have another child to play with" (Schulman, 1991, p. 111).

As the following sections show, it is evident that young children recognize that causes fall into three distinct categories—that the causes of physical events (such as a doll falling over) are different from the causes of emotions and other psychological states (such as anger and hunger), and that both of these are different from the causes of actions (such as tossing a ball or running for office).

Discovering the Causes of Physical Events

Before children reach age 5 or 6, their causal judgments about physical events are based on the same four criteria that adults use: (a) causes always precede their effects; (b) causes are contiguous with and make some kind of physical contact with their effects; (c) the stronger the causal force acting on an object, the greater the effect; and (d) the more regular the temporal association between two events, the more likely that the first event is a cause—either sufficient or necessary—of the second.

For example, 3-year-olds consistently selected a *prior* event as the cause of something they observed that did not have a visible cause (a jack-in-the-box popping up); they never chose a subsequent event. Moreover, given a choice of two prior events, they consistently chose the one that appeared to make physical contact with the later event, indicating an implicit understanding of transfer of energy and mechanism. They also understood that a bump by a heavier object will move something farther than a bump by a lighter object (Bullock, Gelman, & Baillargeon, 1982).

Children this age are also adept at selecting the correct order when shown before and after pictures (e.g., an intact cup/a broken cup). And their explanations are properly "mechanistic";

they do not attribute intentions to inanimate objects (McCabe & Peterson, 1985). They will even spontaneously look for causes that are not evident (such as trying to find out why something moved all of a sudden), recognizing that things do not just happen for no reason (Shultz, 1982).

Other research shows that children between the ages of 3 and 5 use regularity as a criterion for making causal attributions (Shultz & Mendelson, 1975; Siegler, 1976). For example, they will attribute causality to a lever whose movement always coincides with a bulb lighting over one whose movement is less consistently associated with the light. By age 6, children can even use inductive inference to determine which of a number of potential causes (various foods eaten by different people) was consistently associated with an effect (sickness in some people; Long & Welch, 1941).

As children mature into adults, they will contemplate increasingly lengthy causal chains, eventually spanning even billions of years, such as the causal connection between the big bang and the ultimate fate of the universe.

Discovering the Causes of Emotions and Other Psychological States

Emotions arise as involuntary reactions to various stimulating circumstances. But emotional stimuli do not pass their energy on directly, as do the causes of physical events; the magnitude of a person's emotional reaction is not based on the energy that "bumped into" him or her. A whispered "I love you" can produce a far greater reaction than a shouted "Hello."

Children attend to and differentiate emotional expressions (e.g., smiles from frowns, changes in vocal quality) during their earliest months (Haviland & Lelwica, 1987; Ludermann & Nelson, 1988). And by age 2, their conversations reveal they have already learned a great deal about emotions and their causes (e.g., "I give a hug. Baby be happy"; "You sad, Mommy. What Daddy do?"; "It's dark. I'm scared"; "Maybe Gregg would laugh when he saw Beth do that"; Bretherton & Beeghly, 1982). In this last example the child is not merely describing an observed event but is predicting a specific emotional reaction to a particular arousing condition.

Young children can also infer causal principles about the antecedents of emotions. For example, a father reported that when he asked his 32-month-old daughter if she was still angry at him (he had removed her from the playground, and she screamed and cried all the way home), she replied, "Yes, because you weren't nice to me. If I stopped you from doing something you liked, you'd be angry too." This child understood not only what led to her own emotion but also that people *generally* get angry at those who interfere with their pleasure. Moreover, when children do not understand what led to an emotion, they will often ask for an explanation. One father reported that his 2½-year-old daughter asked him why her playing with food—a delightful activity to her—made him angry (Schulman, 1991, pp. 140–141).

During children's preschool years (from 3 to 5), their explanations of emotions become increasingly accurate and astute (Fabes, Eisenberg, McCormick, & Wilson, 1988): They begin to use subtle terms like *proud* correctly (Ridgeway, Waters, & Kuczaj, 1985); they also recognize that intended harmful acts arouse more emotions than unintended ones, and that different people have different emotional reactions to the same stimulus (Weiner & Handel, 1985). They are also becoming increasingly adept at purposely affecting another's emotions, such as by comforting someone in pain, giving gifts, and saying mean or kind things (McCoy & Masters, 1985).

By age 5 or 6, they recognize that some people are more prone to emotional reactions than others ("It's nothing you did; he's just a grouch") and that temporary factors can affect a person's emotionality ("Don't ask Mom now; she and Dad just had an argument"; Kelley, 1972).

Bretherton and Beeghly's (1982) recordings of 2-year-olds' conversations reveal that they understand many other psychological states besides emotions. The children's statements included "You better get shirt, so you won't freeze"; "Take bubblebath, Mom, to get warm"; "Me ski. Thirsty." By grade school, children's understanding of psychological states can be surprisingly refined. For example, a parent recorded her child (6 years 2 months) saying, "People are wrong when they say, 'If I were you, I'd do it different.' If they were really you, and felt what you felt, they'd do the same exact thing as you" (Schulman, 1991, p. 143).

Discovering the Causes of Actions

When we adults seek to explain someone's actions, we inquire about his or her *motivation*, which is a fundamentally different causal factor than those we use to explain physical events and emotional states. Motivation is a complex concept that includes knowing both the arousing stimuli (was the person angry, hungry, or in love?) and the specific intention or purpose of the act (to do harm, to obtain food, to contact the beloved). While psychologists and philosophers have long debated whether intentions are authentic causes of actions (see Schulman, 1991, pp. 147–150; Skinner, 1974), in our everyday explanations of normal actions an intention (conscious or unconscious) constitutes the last link in the causal chain producing the action.

Parents, in their earliest interactions with their infants, attempt to teach them about human intention or purpose. For example, a parent will move her hand slowly toward her baby's face and utter "Boop" as she touches the child's nose. In this and countless other instances of "play," the parent is seeking to communicate, "I'm doing this to you *on purpose.*"

Later, she might move her baby's hands about (again with coordinated vocalizations), looking for signs that the baby is *interacting* with her—moving with her or resisting and redirecting her movements in a manner that indicates he recognizes the purposefulness of her movements, anticipates their direction, and is asserting his own intention into the movement pattern. In other words, that he is *exchanging purpose* with her or, in everyday language, *playing* with her. Research shows that by 4 months, babies' vocal exchanges with their parents alternate in a give-and-take pattern that is similar to conversation, suggesting a recognition and exchange of purpose (Stevenson, Ver Hoeve, Roach, & Leavitt, 1986).

Two-year-olds will ask about intentions ("Why you do dat?") and explain their own behavior in terms of intentions ("I left it open because I wanna watch it [the TV]"). By age 3 (and probably much earlier), children distinguish between intended and accidental outcomes and will answer accusations by exclaiming, "Not on purpose!" They also recognize that some behaviors, such as reflexes, are not intended (Keasey, 1977). The 3-year-old will even use intentional attributions in making moral judgments, appraising some intentions as good and others as bad (Karniol, 1978; Nelson-LeGall, 1985).

Before they are age 2, children begin to use deception (e.g., lying about a wet diaper), indicating a keen awareness of intention. By age 3, they can use deception to try to get away with

a forbidden plan. For example, a young girl (3 years 2 months) told her surprised parents they could close her bedroom door when she went to sleep. With her door closed, she thought she could get away with turning on all four lamps in her room for the night (Schulman, 1991, p. 151).

Young children's statements about intentions reflect their awareness that the arousing stimuli behind an intention can vary in intensity, and that people are likely to use more extreme tactics to get things they want badly (Miller, 1985). For example, a child (3 years 11 months) replied to a playmate's assertion that she needed a broom with the correction, "You don't really need it. You just want it" (Schulman, 1991, p. 153).

As children grow, the intentions of others become an important consideration in evaluating relationships. For example, a girl (5 years 7 months) explained why she remained friends with a youngster who had tantrums when she didn't get her way: "Because she never tries to hurt my feelings. Kimmy or Bea don't have tantrums, but sometimes they do things to hurt my feelings" (Schulman, 1991, p. 153).

What's Controllable? Developing Mastery

The question, What's controllable? is an extension of the question, What makes things happen? But here the child's concern is "What can *I* make happen?" Newborns have many opportunities to discover causal relationships between their own actions and subsequent events—for instance, that screaming makes mommy come running and that kicking makes the bottle fall over. As parents and researchers have long noted, babies express delight in making things happen (Watson, 1972) and before long (at around 18 months) are insisting, "I want to do it myself!"

DeCasper and Fifer (1980) found that 2-day-olds could alter their sucking rate to produce a recording of their mother's voice, preferring her voice (after she had read to them on their first day) to another woman's. This extraordinary finding demonstrates that newborns can adjust their sucking rate—either faster or slower—to control outcomes that have nothing to do with the normal functions of sucking, such as nutrition and oral gratification. These babies appeared to be engaging in intentional behavior—

behavior designed to make things happen, as opposed to simple reflexive reactions to a nipple.

In another study, 1- and 2-day-olds learned to turn their heads to the side for sweet drinks; they even learned which of two sounds (tone or buzzer) signaled that the sweet drink was available, not turning when they heard the sound that signaled no drink (Lipsitt, 1979). In a more demanding task, 2-month-olds learned to roll their heads on a pillow to turn on a light or make a mobile move (Watson, 1972). Children this age also learn to shake a leg to move a mobile connected to it by a string, and even display an "aesthetic" preference for a red mobile over a white one (Rovee, Morrongiello, Aron, & Kupersmidt, 1978).

As their bodily control develops during their first year, babies become increasingly successful at making things happen, including grasping and manipulating objects and getting to desired places (Bower, 1989). If toddlers could tell you why they persist in trying to get to and into everything around them, they would probably offer the same answer Sir Edmund Hillary gave when asked why he climbed Mount Everest: "Because it's there!" By the end of their first year, babies will also begin to use "tools" to make things happen, such as pulling on a string or manipulating a stick to bring a toy closer (Bates, Carlson-Luden, & Bretherton, 1980; McCarty, Clifton, & Collard, 1999).

During their early months babies also begin adjusting their behavior to gain control over the people around them. They will vocalize more when vocalizing produces "social reinforcement," such as smiles, sounds, and touches by an adult (Rheingold, Gewirtz, & Ross, 1959). By 9 months, babies are dispatching all kinds of vocal and bodily signals to recruit their parents to help make things happen. Before their first birthday they will start to coordinate their behavior with an adult's to achieve some end; they will exchange objects, wait for the grown-up to get something for them, and alternate turns (Rogoff, Mistry, Radziszewska, & Germond, 1992). By age 3, children can make things happen *together*, engaging in cooperative tasks, such as building things and matching objects in games ("I need a big one. Do you have a big one?"; Cooper, 1980).

Children learn to make things happen through trial and error and also by observing and imitating others. One-year-olds who have seen someone stacking objects or opening a cabinet will try to do these same things, even after a delay of minutes or days (Kaye & Marcus, 1981; Meltzoff, 1988). Indeed, young children seem driven to do what they have observed others do. If they observe someone whistling, they will try to whistle; if they see someone hammering, they will insist on having a go at it; if they see another child on a tricycle, they will hop on at the first opportunity.

Self-control

Controlling people and objects requires knowing how they work or what motivates them. The same applies to learning to control oneself—and there is evidence that children begin engaging in self-control activities early in their first year. One can see them inhibiting impulses, redirecting behavior in midstream, and evaluating alternatives before acting. Such self-control requires anticipatory awareness of what one is inclined or about to do.

Evidence for self-control was found in a study of 3½-month-olds who learned to turn their heads to activate a sound and light show. A baby might "start to turn in the incorrect direction, hesitate, recheck the stimulus, and then change direction" (Caron & Caron, 1978, p. 291). Other studies confirm that children can engage in "effortful control" before they are a year old, and by age 2 can follow instructions to delay, modulate, or slow down an action (Kochanska, Murray, & Harlan, 2000).

In an interesting example of self-awareness and self-control, a 2½-year-old who had been getting cranky and bossy suddenly blurted out, "Put me in my crib. I'm not feeling friendly." Because she ordinarily protested placement in the crib and was confined there only when she misbehaved, the parent's impression was that she was anticipating her own misbehavior and wanted to avoid being controlled by someone else (Schulman, 1991, p. 168).

By age 3, children can even use formal principles to control their own behavior in frustrating circumstances, for example, by reminding themselves of the adage "If at first you don't succeed, try and try again."

Planning and Long-Term Goals

By age 2, toddlers can engage in a series of actions designed to produce a relatively remote outcome, like stacking nested cups or constructing an object in a stepwise fashion out of various parts. They will correct their mistakes in a manner that shows their awareness of the step-wise nature of the task, as well as their ability to formulate and follow a plan (Bauer, Schwade, Wewerka, & Delaney, 1999; DeLoache, Sugarman, & Brown, 1985). Three-year-olds can play games that require a number of steps and planning ahead, such as matching pairs of cards and deciding which cards to hold while waiting for a match.

Children this age also plan ahead in their everyday activities (Klahr, 1985; Wellman, Fabricius, & Sophian, 1985) and will say things like "Can I wear my blue dress when we visit Kirsten tomorrow; she has a blue dress too and it'll be fun if we match." Sometimes their plans involve negotiation ("If I eat *all* my broccoli, can I have *two* cookies?"), and sometimes they reveal surprising psychological insight ("If I pretend I don't want the toy, he'll give it to me"). By age 4, children are usually generating a lot of plans ("Let's make a wagon with a point in front so it looks like a rocket ship") and formulating hypotheses about the likely outcomes of various actions (Schuepfer & Gholson, 1983).

As children mature, their goals become increasingly distant (such as writing a script for the drama club or getting into a desirable college, or even getting into heaven), which requires breaking down plans into subplans and engaging in "thought experiments" in which courses of action are envisioned and evaluated mentally before actually being embarked upon. In addition, the successful pursuit of long-term goals requires prodigious quantities of self-control when faced with obstacles and setbacks. Psychologists have referred to those who manage to persist toward goals despite setbacks as having a high sense of "self-efficacy" (Bandura, 1977), an "internalized locus of control" (Rotter, 1966), a high level of "frustration tolerance" (Rosenzweig, 1938), a high "level of aspiration" or "generalized expectancy of success" (Zander, 1944), a high level of "optimism" (Seligman, 1990), and a high level of "hope" (Snyder, Cheavens, & Michael, 1999). A child, envisioning a certain little "engine that could," might call it having an "I think I can" attitude.

Problem Solving

As children age, their success at discovering what's out there, what leads to what, what makes things happen, and what's controllable will depend increasingly on their use of system-atic problem-solving strategies, from informal trial-and-error explorations to the scientific method. Moreover, different problem types require different strategies. In my book *The Passionate Mind* (Schulman, 1991, chap. 9), I identify and analyze six fundamental problem categories, referring to them as diagnostic, inductive, inventive, tactical, imaginative, and symbolic/mathematical problem types. Procedures that are useful for solving one kind of problem, such as inventing a lightbulb (inventive), may not be helpful for others, such as explaining electromagnetism (inductive), writing a symphony (imaginative), reviving a patient (diagnostic), outmaneuvering a chess opponent (tactical), or plotting the path of a spacecraft (symbolic/mathematical).

Various studies indicate that even preschoolers can learn formal problem-solving methods, like starting a 20-Questions-type inquiry with broad, encompassing questions (Courage, 1989) and reminding themselves to look carefully for similarities and differences in a matching task (Fjellstrom, Born, & Baer, 1988).

But keep in mind that problem solving is not something that we, children and adults, do only reluctantly, just when confronted with perplexing obstacles. On the contrary, humans *seek out* problems to be solved; solving problems is one of our great joys. We even organize many of our recreational activities around problems. We do crossword puzzles; play chess, charades, and trivia games; seek steeper mountains to climb and deeper waters to dive—and seek training to better meet the challenges. We take creative cooking courses and join wilderness groups; we fix old radios *for fun* and take *not*-for-credit courses after a long day's work—all in search of new problems to solve and new problem-solving skills.

Children come into the world on the alert to learn about it, and virtually everything they accomplish in life will be based on the information and skills they gather. But for some, unfortunately, on the way toward adulthood, their curiosity will diminish. This can happen if they get punished or mocked for their explorations and questions. It can also happen if, during their school years, they are asked to learn a mass of facts and operations that do not appear to answer any of the four basic questions that they are naturally inclined to explore: What's out there? What leads to what? What makes things happen? and What's controllable? Schools might do better at sustaining children's enthusiasm for learning by modifying lessons to highlight which of these four fundamental questions the information being taught is purporting to answer.

References

Allen, T. W., Walker, K., Symonds, L., & Marcell, M. (1977). Intrasensory and intersensory perception of temporal sequences during infancy. *Developmental Psychology, 13,* 225–229.

Antell, S. E., & Keating, D. P. (1983). Perception of numerical invariance in neonates. *Child Development, 54,* 695–701.

Armchair astronauts. (2000, January). *Discover Magazine,* 60.

Bandura, A. (1977). Self-efficacy: Toward a unifying theory of behavioral change. *Psychological Review, 84,* 191–215.

Bates, E., Carlson-Luden, V., & Bretherton, I. (1980). Perceptual aspects of tool using in infancy. *Infant Behavior and Development, 3,* 127–140.

Bauer, P. J., & Mandler, J. M. (1989). One thing follows another: Effects of temporal structure on 1- and 2-year olds' recall of events. *Developmental Psychology, 25,* 197–206.

Bauer, P. J., Schwade, J. A., Wewerka, S. S., & Delaney, K. (1999). Planning ahead: Goal-directed problem solving by 2-year-olds. *Developmental Psychology, 35,* 1321–1337.

Berlyne, D. E. (1960). *Conflict, arousal, and curiosity.* New York: McGraw-Hill.

Bower, T. G. R. (1971, Oct.). The object in the world of the infant. *Scientific American, 225,* 30–38.

Bower, T. G. R. (1989). *The rational infant.* New York: Freeman.

*Bretherton, I., & Beeghly, M. (1982). Talking about internal states: The acquisition of an explicit theory of mind. *Developmental Psychology, 18,* 906–921.

Bretherton, I., Fritz, J., Zahn-Waxler, C., & Ridgeway, D. (1986). Learning to talk about emotions: A functionalist perspective. *Child Development, 57,* 529–548.

Brody, L. R., Zelazo, P. R., & Chaika, H. (1984). Habituation-dishabituation to speech in the neonate. *Developmental Psychology, 20,* 114–119.

*Bullock, M., Gelman, R., & Baillargeon, R. (1982). The development of causal reasoning. In W. J. Friedman (Ed.), *The developmental psychology of time* (pp. 209–254). New York: Academic Press.

Bushnell, I. W. R., Sai, F., & Mullin, J. T. (1989). Neonatal recognition of the mother's face. *British Journal of Developmental Psychology, 7,* 3–15.

Byrnes, J. P., & Duff, M. A. (1988). Young children's comprehension and production of causal expressions. *Child Study Journal, 18,* 101–119.

Canfield, R. L., & Haith, M. M. (1991). Young infants: Visual expectations for symmetric and asymmetric stimulus sequences. *Developmental Psychology, 27,* 188–208.

Carni, E., & French, L. A. (1984). The acquisition of *before* and *after* reconsidered: What develops? *Journal of Experimental Child Psychology, 37,* 394–403.

Caron, R. F., & Caron, A. J. (1978). Effects of ecologically relevant manipulations on infant discrimination learning. *Infant Behavior and Development, 1,* 291–307.

Colette. (1966). *Earthly paradise: An autobiography drawn from her lifetime writings* (R. Phelps, Ed.). New York: Farrar, Straus and Giroux.

Cooper, C. R. (1980). Development of collaborative problem solving among preschool children. *Developmental Psychology, 16,* 433–440.

Courage, M. L. (1989). Children's inquiry strategies in referential communication and the game of Twenty Questions. *Child Development, 60,* 877–886.

DeCasper, A. J., & Fifer, W. P. (1980, June 6). Of human bonding: Newborns prefer their mothers' voices. *Science, 208,* 1174–1176.

*Deci, E. L., & Ryan, R. M. (1985). *Intrinsic motivation and self-determination in human behavior.* New York: Plenum.

DeLoache, J. S., Sugarman, S., & Brown, A. L. (1985). The development of error correction strategies in young children's manipulative play. *Child Development, 56,* 928–939.

Dollard, J., & Miller, N. E. (1950). *Personality and psychotherapy.* New York: McGraw-Hill.

Donahue, R. L., & Berg, W. K. (1991). Infant heart-rate responses to temporally predictable and unpredictable events. *Developmental Psychology, 27,* 59–66.

Fabes, R. A., Eisenberg, N., McCormick, S. E., & Wilson, M. S. (1988). Preschoolers' attributions of the situational determinants of others' naturally occurring emotions. *Developmental Psychology, 24,* 376–385.

Fabricius, W. V., Sophian, C., & Wellman, H. M. (1987). Young children's sensitivity to logical necessity in their inferential search behavior. *Child Development, 58,* 409–423.

Fantz, R. L. (1961, May). The origin of form perception. *Scientific American, 204,* 66–72.

Feinman, S., & Lewis, M. (1983). Social referencing at ten months: A second-order effect on infants' responses to strangers. *Child Development, 54,* 878–887.

Fiske, D. W., & Maddi, S. R. (1961). *Functions of varied experience.* Homewood, IL: Dorsey.

Fjellstrom, G. G., Born, D., & Baer, D. M. (1988). Some effects of telling preschool children to self-question in a matching task. *Journal of Experimental Child Psychology, 46,* 419–437.

Freud, S. (1949). *A general introduction to psychoanalysis* (J. Riviere, Trans.) New York: Permabooks. (Original work published 1917)

Friedman, W. J., & Brudos, S. L. (1988). On routes and routines: The early development of spatial and temporal representations. *Cognitive Development, 3,* 167–182.

Gelman, S. (1988). The development of induction within natural kind and artifact categories. *Cognitive Psychology, 20,* 65–95.

Gentner, D. (1988). Metaphor as structure mapping: The relational shift. *Child Development, 59,* 47–89.

Golinkoff, R. M., Harding, C. G., Carlson, V., & Sexton, M. E. (1984). The infant's perception of causal events: The distinction between animate and inanimate objects. In L. P. Lipsitt & C. Rovee-Collier (Eds.), *Advances in infancy research* (Vol. 3, pp. 145–151). Norwood, NJ: Ablex.

Harner, L. (1975). Yesterday and tomorrow: Development of early understanding of the terms. *Developmental Psychology, 11,* 864–865.

Haviland, J. M., & Lelwica, M. (1987). The induced affect response: 10-week-old infants' responses to three emotion expressions. *Developmental Psychology, 23,* 97–104.

Hawkins, J., Pea, R. D., Glick, J., & Scribner, S. (1984). "Merds that laugh don't like mushrooms": Evidence for deductive reasoning by pre-schoolers. *Developmental Psychology, 20,* 584–594.

*Hood, L., & Bloom, L. (1979). What, when, and how about why: A longitudinal study of early expressions of causality. *Monographs of the Society for Research in Child Development, 44*(6, Serial No. 181).

Karniol, R. (1978). Children's use of intentional cues in evaluating behavior. *Psychological Bulletin, 85,* 76–85.

Kaye, K., & Marcus, J. (1981). Infant imitation: The sensory-motor agenda. *Developmental Psychology, 17,* 258–265.

Keasey, C. B. (1977). Children's developing awareness and usage of intentionality and motives. In H. E. Howe, Jr. (Ed.), *Nebraska Symposium on Motivation* (Vol. 26, pp. 219–260). Lincoln: University of Nebraska Press.

Kelley, H. H. (1972). Attribution in social interaction. In E. E. Jones, D. E. Kanouse, H. H. Kelley, R. E. Nisbett, S. Valins, & B. Weiner (Eds.), *Attribution: Perceiving the causes of behavior* (pp. 1–26). Morristown, NJ: General Learning Press.

Klahr, D. (1985). Solving problems with ambiguous subgoal ordering: Preschoolers' performance. *Child Development, 56,* 940–952.

*Kochanska, G., Murray, K. T., & Harlan, E. T. (2000). Effortful control in early childhood: Continuity and change, antecedents, and implications for social development. *Developmental Psychology, 36,* 220–232.

Lamb, M. E., & Malkin, C. M. (1986). The development of social expectations in distress-relief sequences: A longitudinal study. *International Journal of Behavioral Development, 9,* 235–249.

Lipsitt, L. P. (1979). Learning capacities of the human infant. In R. J. Robinson (Ed.), *Brain and early behavior: Development in the fetus and infant* (pp. 227–249). New York: Academic Press.

Long, L., & Welch, L. (1941). Reasoning ability in young children. *Journal of Psychology, 12,* 21–44.

Lucariello, J., & Nelson, K. (1987). Remembering and planning talk between mothers and children. *Discourse Processes, 10,* 219–235.

Ludermann, P. M., & Nelson, C. A. (1988). Categorical representation of facial expressions by 7-month-old infants. *Developmental Psychology, 24,* 492–501.

Marquis, D. P. (1931). Can conditioned responses be established in the newborn infant? *Journal of Genetic Psychology, 39,* 479–492.

McCabe, A., & Peterson, C. (1985). A naturalistic study of the production of causal connectives by children. *Journal of Child Language, 12,* 145–159.

McCarty, M. E., Clifton, R. K., & Collard, R. R. (1999). Problem solving in infancy: The emergence of an action plan. *Developmental Psychology, 35,* 1091–1101.

McCoy, C. L., & Masters, J. C. (1985). The development of children's strategies for the social control of emotion. *Child Development, 56,* 1214–1222.

Meltzoff, A. N. (1988). Infant imitation after a 1-week delay: Long-term memory for novel acts and multiple stimuli. *Developmental Psychology, 24,* 470–476.

Meltzoff, A. N., & Borton, R. W. (1979, Nov. 22). Intermodal matching in human neonates. *Nature, 282,* 403–404.

Meltzoff, A. N., & Moore, M. K. (1977, Oct. 7).

Imitation of facial and manual gestures by human neonates. *Science, 198,* 75–78.

Miller, P. H. (1985). Children's reasoning about the causes of human behavior. *Journal of Experimental Child Psychology, 39,* 343–362.

Moon, C., & Fifer, W. P. (1990). Syllables as signals for 2-day-old infants. *Infant Behavior and Development, 13,* 377–390.

Nelson-LeGall, S. A. (1985). Motive-outcome matching and outcome foreseeability: Effects on attribution of intentionality and moral judgments. *Developmental Psychology, 21,* 332–337.

Newell, A., & Simon, H. A. (1972). *Human information processing.* Englewood Cliffs, NJ: Prentice-Hall.

Pellegrini, A. D., Brody, G. H., & Stoneman, Z. (1987). Children's conversational competence with their parents. *Discourse Processes, 10,* 93–106.

Reissland, N. (1988). Neonatal imitation in the first hour of life: Observations in rural Nepal. *Developmental Psychology, 24,* 464–469.

Rheingold, H. L., Gewirtz, J. L., & Ross, H. W. (1959). Social conditioning of vocalization. *Journal of Abnormal and Social Psychology, 52,* 68–73.

Richie, D. M., & Brickhard, B. H. (1988). The ability to perceive duration: Its relation to the development of the logical concept of time. *Developmental Psychology, 24,* 318–323.

Ridgeway, D., Waters, E., & Kuczaj, S. A., II. (1985). Acquisition of emotion-descriptive language: Receptive and productive vocabulary norms for ages 18 months to 6 years. *Developmental Psychology, 21,* 901–908.

Roberts, K. (1988). Retrieval of a basic-level category in prelinguistic infants. *Developmental Psychology, 24,* 21–27.

Rochat, P. (1987). Mouthing and grasping in neonates: Evidence for the early detection of what hard or soft substances afford for action. *Infant Behavior and Development, 10,* 435–449.

Rogoff, B., Mistry, J., Radziszewska, B., & Germond, J. (1992). Infants' instrumental social interaction with adults. In S. Feinman (Ed.), *Social referencing and the social construction of reality in infancy* (pp. 323–348). New York: Plenum.

Rosenzweig, S. (1938). A general outline of frustration. *Character and Personality, 7,* 151–160.

Rotter, J. B. (1966). Generalized expectancies for internal versus external control of reinforcement. *Psychological Monographs, 80*(1, Whole No. 609).

Rovee, C. K., Morrongiello, B. A., Aron, M., & Kupersmidt, J. (1978). Topographical response

differentiation and reversal in 3-month-old infants. *Infant Behavior and Development, 1,* 323–333.

Salapatek, P. (1968). Visual scanning of geometric pattern by the human newborn. *Journal of Comparative and Physiological Psychology, 66,* 247–258.

Sameroff, A. J. (1971). Can conditioned responses be established in the newborn infant: 1971? *Developmental Psychology, 5,* 1–12.

Scaife, M., & Bruner, J. (1975). The capacity for joint visual attention in the infant. *Nature, 253,* 265–266.

Schuepfer, T., & Gholson, B. (1983). From response-set to prediction hypotheses: Rule acquisition among preschoolers and second graders. *Journal of Experimental Child Psychology, 36,* 18–31.

*Schulman, M. (1991). *The passionate mind.* New York: Free Press.

Seligman, M. (1990). *Learned optimism.* New York: Knopf.

Sherman, T. (1985). Categorization skills in infants. *Child Development, 56,* 1561–1573.

*Shultz, T. R. (1982). Rules of causal attribution. *Monographs of the Society for Research in Child Development, 47*(1, Serial No. 194).

Shultz, T. R., & Mendelson, R. (1975). The use of covariation as a principle of causal analysis. *Child Development, 46,* 394–399.

Siegler, R. S. (1976). The effects of simple necessity and sufficiency relationships on children's causal inferences. *Child Development, 47,* 1058–1063.

Skinner, B. F. (1974). *About behaviorism.* New York: Knopf.

Snyder, C. R., Cheavens, J., & Michael, S. T. (1999). Hoping. In C. R. Snyder (Ed.), *Coping: The psychology of what works* (pp. 205–229). New York: Oxford University Press.

Stevenson, M. B., Ver Hoeve, J. N., Roach, M. A., & Leavitt, L. A. (1986). The beginning of conversation: Early patterns of mother-infant vocal responsiveness. *Infant Behavior and Development, 9,* 423–440.

Sugarman, S. (1983). The development of inductive strategy in children's early thought and language. *Quarterly Newsletter of the Laboratory of Comparative Human Cognition, 5,* 34–40.

Trehub, S. E., Thorpe, L. A., & Morrongiello, B. A. (1987). Organizational processes in infant's perception of auditory patterns. *Child Development, 59,* 741–749.

Vosniadou, S. (1987). Children and metaphor. *Child Development, 58,* 870–885.

*Watson, J. (1972). Smiling, cooing and "The Game." *Merrill-Palmer Quarterly, 18,* 323–339.

Weiner, B., & Handel, S. J. (1985). A cognition-emotion-action sequence: Anticipated emotional consequences of causal attributions and reported communication strategy. *Developmental Psychology, 21,* 102–107.

Wellman, H. M., & Estes, D. (1987). Children's early use of mental verbs and what they mean. *Discourse Processes, 10,* 141–156.

Wellman, H. M., Fabricius, W. V., & Sophian, C. (1985). The early development of planning. In H. M. Wellman (Ed.), *Children's searching* (pp. 123–149). Hillsdale, NJ: Erlbaum.

Zander, A. F. (1944). A study of experimental frustration. *Psychological Monographs, 54*(3, Whole No. 256).

24

Wisdom

Its Structure and Function in Regulating Successful Life Span Development

Paul B. Baltes, Judith Glück, & Ute Kunzmann

Toward a Positive Psychology of Optimal Development

In the history of the humanities and the social sciences, questions of perfection and optimality in human behavior and human development always have been part of the intellectual agenda. Fueled by philosophers and theologians, many proponents participated in the search for truth criteria of perfection and optimality (Brandt-städter & Schneewind, 1977; Lerner, 1986; Tetens, 1777). Since the times of secularization and subsequently the advent of evolutionary biology, however, the answers to questions of perfection and optimality became more and more relative and uncertain.

Perfection and Optimality: A Dilemma for Psychology

Aside from analytical philosophy and scholarship on ethics (e.g., Kekes, 1995), it is now uncommon for behavioral scientists and scholars to argue the case of absolute perfection or sin-

gular optimality. With a growing interest in promoting a tolerant conception of human rights and also the recognition of contextual variations in form and function, as well as culturally based differences in criteria of adaptive fitness, behavioral and social scientists have developed a preference for emphasizing particularities and the importance of flexibility in making decisions about what is right and wrong (Shweder, 1991). There are exceptions to this reluctance in the psychological research community to specify the foundation of optimality. Note, for instance, the theoretical orientation of some scholars in moral development and human motivation, such as Kohlberg (1971) or Maslow (1970). In this work, strong a priori assumptions are made regarding the structure and hierarchy of values and motivational dispositions. We will return to this line of scholarship later and outline some of its connections with our work on wisdom.

Our main point, however, is that such value- and morality-oriented work in psychology is the exception and often is evaluated as being of doubtful significance. Indeed, one can conclude that psychologists have proceeded to focus their studies on "secondary" virtues rather than on "primary" virtues. With secondary virtues we mean attributes or processes that are relevant for any goal attainment (e.g., traits like persistence, conscientiousness, or agreeableness measured by personality questionnaires) without evaluating these in terms of moral or ethical principles. Primary virtues, on the other hand, are cognitive and motivational dispositions that in themselves designate not only adaptive fitness for individuals' achievements but also the idea of convergence of individual goal achievements with becoming and being a good person from a communal and social-ethical point of view. Such a communal goods view of primary virtues would suggest, for instance, that individuals consider only those goals and means as ways of self-development that do not violate the rights of others and, in addition, coproduce resources for others to develop.

On Positive Psychology

For psychology to be an empirical science, abstinence regarding the question of a priori definitions of values and goals is understandable. However, this relative abstinence has its costs (see also Kendler, 1999), and therefore the recently growing search for a positive psychology has its well-founded raison d'être (Seligman & Csikszentmihalyi, 2000). The argument of proponents of positive psychology is that the primary focus of 20th-century psychology was too much on treating the dysfunctional and that this emphasis resulted in a neglect of the search for optimality and the conditions of excellence, individually and collectively.

The call for changes in emphases of psychological inquiry has a long tradition, and when those changes are propagated with force and seemingly missionary zeal, it is typically worthwhile to explore ways to modulate the radicality of the position taken. This is true for the present situation as well. Therefore, and to prevent a possible misunderstanding of our intellectual perspective on this topic, we first offer some modulating observations.

On the one hand, we suggest that the interpretation by Seligman and Csikszentmihalyi (2000) of 20th-century psychology as largely void of a spirit of positive psychology is overstated, if not misleading. In its radicality, it ig-

nores, for instance, the fundamental positivity associated with several fields of psychology—including developmental psychology, the one in which much of our own work is cast. By the very nature of the concept of development (growth), this field considers itself as a proponent of positivity (Harris, 1957; Lerner, 1998) and "perfection-oriented intervention" (Tetens, 1777) in psychological functioning. In recent psychology, there are also other lines of serious and cogent inquiry that highlight positivity. Consider, as a further example, the positivity emphasis of one of the most powerful theories of modern psychology, that is, self-efficacy theory (Bandura, 1986, 1995; see also Maddux, this volume). Bandura's work, while perhaps emanating from questions of dysfunctionality, is inherently oriented toward improvement and optimal functioning. The radical conclusion by proponents of positive psychology about the lack of positivity in past psychological work, therefore, surely is an overstatement, and it seems primarily informed by past research in that branch of psychology that is explicitly devoted to the regulation of the dysfunctional, that is, clinical psychology.

On the other hand, taking a radical position on the need for a positive psychology, as Seligman and Csikszentmihalyi (2000) do, can be defended if one treats it as a contribution to strengthening lines of scholarship whose primary interest is in improving our understanding of three contributors to a good life: positive subjective experiences, desirable individual traits, and civic virtues. Such a view on psychology as theory- and practice-oriented enterprise toward the betterment of human behavior is well-grounded in the history of sciences in general and psychology in particular.

Positive Psychology and the Study of Wisdom

Indeed, the emergence of our work on wisdom during the recent decades fits well with the continuous dynamic between understanding the positive and efforts to compensate for a dominance of concerns for understanding and repairing deficits in human behavior. Our interest in the concept of wisdom emerged because of a one-sided focus on the negative in gerontological research in the 1960s and 1970s (Baltes & Smith, 1990; Baltes & Staudinger, 2000). The dominant focus of aging research during that period was on counting "the wrinkles and failures" of humans as they grow older. There were very few instances in which aging was examined in its potentially positive manifestations. Perhaps the best known exception was Erik Erikson's (1968) theoretical work focused on generativity and wisdom as central tasks of adult life (see also M. Baltes & Baltes, 1977; Baltes & Labouvie-Vief, 1973; Clayton & Birren, 1980; Labouvie-Vief, 1982; McAdams & de St. Aubin, 1998; Perlmutter, 1990; Ryff, 1987, 1995).

A major reason for our efforts to articulate a psychological theory of wisdom, therefore, was the explicit commitment to understand what might be positive in adult development and aging. There were not many domains on which we could orient our microscope. One was wisdom. In research on subjective beliefs about aging, wisdom turned out to be one of the very few characteristics for which people expect a positive trajectory in late adulthood (Heckhausen, Dixon, & Baltes, 1989).

Actually, our first exploration into the positivity of old age involved cognitive training studies to understand the role of practice deficits and the latent learning potential of the older population in the sense of plasticity (Baltes & Lindenberger, 1988; Baltes & Willis, 1982; Willis & Baltes, 1980). In this research, we demonstrated that at least up to age 80 or so, many older adults possess more cognitive reserves (plasticity or learning potential) than we typically expect, although we need to acknowledge that we also observed definite losses in plasticity with advancing old age. Greatly influenced by the work of Vivian Clayton (Clayton & Birren, 1980), the concept of wisdom became the rallying point for our subsequent search for the hidden treasure of old age (Baltes, Dittmann-Kohli, & Dixon, 1984; Baltes, Smith, & Staudinger, 1992; Dixon & Baltes, 1986).

Meanwhile, our work on wisdom is not only informed by the study of positive aspects of human aging. On the contrary, we presently conceptualize wisdom as an instantiation of a construct that, for all phases and contexts of life, offers the potential for defining the means and ends toward a good or even optimal life. Based primarily on philosophical work, our challenge has been to extract statements about the means and goals of life that imply a value position (Kekes, 1995). From such extrapsychological

analyses, we specified a psychological theory of wisdom. Accordingly, it is the intermarriage of philosophical and psychological perspectives around the concept of wisdom that permits us to revisit the century-old question of optimal human development.

Wisdom as a Topic of Scientific Discourse About the Good Life

Wisdom has been discussed and studied in philosophy and religion for thousands of years (for an overview, see Assmann, 1994; Kekes, 1995; Rice, 1958). More recently, scholars from other disciplines such as cultural anthropology, political science, education, and psychology also have shown interest in wisdom. Indeed, one can argue that wisdom is becoming a center of transdisciplinary discourse (e.g., Agazzi, 1991; Arlin, 1990; Assmann, 1994; Baltes, 1993; Lehrer, Lum, Slichta, & Smith, 1996; Maxwell, 1984; Nichols, 1996; Nozick, 1993; Oelmüller, 1989; Smith & Baltes, 1990; Staudinger & Baltes, 1996b; Sternberg, 1990; Welsch, 1995).

In defining and studying wisdom from a psychological point of view, we attempt to pay careful attention to what philosophers offer regarding the nature of the structure and function of wisdom. Without such attention, we would lose the special strength that the concept of wisdom holds for specifying the content and form of the primary virtues and behaviors that individuals aspire to as they attempt to regulate their lives toward an "universal canon of a good life."

To prevent a possible misunderstanding, we acknowledge the scientific limits of our work on wisdom. Specifically, any empirical manifestation of wisdom falls short of the theoretical aspiration. In this spirit, we do not maintain that a psychological theory will ever capture wisdom in its full-blown cultural complexity. Our hope, however, is that this intermarriage of philosophy and psychology results in lines of psychological inquiry where virtues, values, and the mind can meet in a new and productive collaboration. We believe that this may be possible because, at a high level of analysis, the concept of wisdom appears to be culturally universal. To illustrate, Table 24.1 summarizes characteristics that in our historical studies of wisdom we have found in Asian, African, and Western traditions (Baltes, 1993; Baltes & Smith, 1990; Baltes & Staudinger, 2000).

Table 24.1 General Criteria Derived from an Analysis of Cultural-Historical and Philosophical Accounts of Wisdom

---

Wisdom addresses important and difficult questions and strategies about the conduct and meaning of life.

Wisdom includes knowledge about the limits of knowledge and the uncertainties of the world.

Wisdom represents a truly superior level of knowledge, judgment, and advice.

Wisdom constitutes knowledge with extraordinary scope, depth, measure, and balance.

Wisdom involves a perfect synergy of mind and character, that is, an orchestration of knowledge and virtues.

Wisdom represents knowledge used for the good or well-being of oneself and that of others.

Wisdom, though difficult to achieve and to specify, is easily recognized when manifested.

Psychological Theories of Wisdom: From Implicit to Explicit Theories

Because of its enormous cultural and historical heritage, a psychological definition and operationalization of wisdom is extremely difficult. This could be why many wisdom researchers have restricted their research efforts to laypersons' implicit theories of wisdom and wise persons (Clayton & Birren, 1980; Holliday & Chandler, 1986; Kramer, 2000; Sowarka, 1989; Staudinger, Sowarka, Maciel, & Baltes, 1997; Sternberg, 1985, 1990). Empirical research based on explicit theories of wisdom-related behavior is relatively rare.

Implicit Theories

With implicit theories, we mean the beliefs or mental representations that people have about wisdom and the characteristics of wise persons. In studies on implicit beliefs about wisdom and wise persons, one finds quite a high degree of overlap in the core aspects of wisdom, even though authors have focused on slightly different aspects and named their components differently.

All conceptions include cognitive as well as social, motivational, and emotional components (e.g., Birren & Fisher, 1990; Kramer, 2000). The cognitive components usually include strong intellectual abilities, rich knowledge and experience in matters of the human condition, and an ability to apply one's theoretical knowledge practically. A second basic component refers to reflective judgment that is based on knowledge about the world and the self, an openness for new experiences, and the ability to learn from mistakes. Socioemotional components generally include good social skills, such as sensitivity and concern for others and the ability to give good advice. A fourth motivational component refers to the good intentions that usually are associated with wisdom. That is, wisdom aims at solutions that optimize the benefit of others and oneself.

Sternberg's (1998) effort at specifying a comprehensive theory of wisdom is in the tradition of these implicit lines of inquiry. In his theory, consisting so far of a coordinated set of characterizations rather than empirical work, Sternberg emphasizes the role of "balance." Specifically, wisdom is conceptualized as the application of tacit knowledge toward the achievement of a common good achieved through a balance among multiple interests, including one's own interests and those of others.

A factor-analytic study conducted by Staudinger, Sowarka, et al. (1997) illustrates the implicit theories tradition of wisdom. One hundred and two participants rated 131 attributes regarding the degree to which each represents the notion of an ideally wise person. The attributes were selected from past work on implicit theories and work generated by the Berlin Wisdom Paradigm (see subsequently). As shown in Table 24.2 a four-dimensional structure of an ideally wise person was obtained. Consistent with past research, these dimensions refer to (a) exceptional knowledge concerning the acquisition of wisdom; (b) exceptional knowledge concerning its application; (c) exceptional knowledge about contextual and temporal variations of life; and (d) person-related competencies.

Explicit Theories

The second cluster of wisdom theories represents explicit psychological theories (Baltes & Smith, 1990; Baltes & Staudinger, 1993; Pasupathi & Baltes, in press; Sternberg, 1990). They

Table 24.2 Implicit Beliefs about Wise People: Four Dimensions

Factor 1	Exceptional knowledge about wisdom acquisition • comprehends the nature of human existence • tries to learn from his or her own mistakes
Factor 2	Exceptional knowledge about use of wisdom • knows when to give/withhold advice • is a person whose advice one would solicit for life problems
Factor 3	Exceptional knowledge about context of life • knows that life priorities may change during the life course • knows about possible conflicts among different life domains
Factor 4	Exceptional personality and social functioning • is a good listener • is a very humane person

are meant to focus on cognitive and behavioral expressions of wisdom and the processes involved in the joining of cognition with behavior. One main objective of such theories is to develop theoretical models of wisdom that allow for empirical inquiry—by means of quantitative operationalization of wisdom-related thought and behavior—as well as for the derivation of hypotheses that can be tested empirically (e.g., about predictors of behavioral expressions of wisdom).

To date, the theoretical and empirical work on explicit psychological conceptions of wisdom can be divided roughly into three groups: (a) the conceptualization of wisdom as a personal characteristic or a personality disposition (e.g., Erikson, 1959; McAdams & de St. Aubin, 1998); (b) the conceptualization of wisdom in the neo-Piagetian tradition of postformal and dialectical thinking (e.g., Alexander & Langer, 1990; Kramer, 1986, 2000; Labouvie-Vief, 1990; Peng & Nisbett, 1999); and (c) the conceptualization of wisdom as an expert system dealing with the meaning and conduct of life, as advocated in the Berlin Wisdom Paradigm (e.g., Baltes & Smith, 1990; Dittmann-Kohli & Baltes, 1990; Staudinger & Baltes, 1994). The latter is the focus of the remainder of this chapter.

The Berlin Wisdom Project: Wisdom as Expertise in the Fundamental Pragmatics of Life

In this section, we shall describe the conception of wisdom upon which the Berlin Wisdom Project is based. Thereafter, we will discuss some general considerations concerning the development of wisdom across the life span.

The Content Domain of Wisdom

Proceeding from the notion that wisdom involves some form of excellence (see Table 24.1), the Berlin Wisdom Project conceptualizes wisdom as an expertise in the meaning and conduct of life. Our conceptualization of wisdom as expertise signals that we expect most people not to be wise. What we expect, however, is that the behavioral expressions we observe in individuals can be ordered on a "wisdom scale." In general, wisdom is foremost a cultural product deposited in books of wisdom rather than in individuals.

The contents to which this expertise of wisdom refers are the "fundamental pragmatics of life," that is, knowledge about the essence of the human condition and the ways and means of planning, managing, and understanding a good life (cf. Baltes & Smith, 1990; Baltes & Staudinger, 1993, 2000). Examples of the fundamental pragmatics of life include knowledge and skills about the conditions, variability, ontogenetic changes, and historicity of human development; insight into obligations and goals in life; knowledge and skills about the social and situational influences on human life; as well as knowledge and skills about the finitude of life and the inherent limits of human knowledge.

As these examples reveal, the contents to which wisdom refers are markedly different from those of other domains that have been reported in the traditional expertise literature (Ericsson & Smith, 1991). Most research on expertise has focused on domains where well-defined problems can be used to systematically study experts' and laypersons' knowledge systems (e.g., physics or chess). In the domain of the fundamental pragmatics of life, contrariwise, problems are almost by definition ill-defined, and no clear-cut "optimal" solutions exist (see also Arlin, 1990). Nevertheless, we assume that wisdom has a clear conceptual core and that its manifestations can be evaluated. As our empirical studies show, most people, after some training, are able to reach high levels of consensus in their evaluation of wisdom-related products.

Antecedents of Wisdom

Our concept of wisdom as expertise and the linkage of this concept to life span theory (Baltes, 1987, 1997) suggest an ensemble of three broad domains of antecedents or determining factors—each comprising internal and external factors and processes—to be influential in the development of wisdom at the level of individuals. Before describing these three domains in detail, we need to discuss five more general considerations concerning the ontogenesis of wisdom.

First, as is typical for the development of expertise, we assume that wisdom is acquired through an extended and intense process of learning and practice. This clearly requires a high degree of motivation to strive for excellence, as well as a social-cultural and personal environment that is supportive of the search for wisdom. Second, wisdom is a complex and multifaceted phenomenon; therefore, for wisdom to emerge, a variety of experiential factors and processes on micro- and macro-levels are required to interact and collaborate. Third, given that wisdom involves the orchestration of cognitive, personal, social, interpersonal, and spiritual factors, its antecedents are diverse in nature. Fourth, because developmental tasks and adaptive challenges change across life, and the human condition is inherently a life-course phenomenon, we expect wisdom to reach its peak relatively late in adult life. Fifth, we believe that, as with other fields of expertise, the guidance of mentors, as well as the experience and mastery of critical life experiences, are conducive to individual manifestations of wisdom.

We now turn to the three domains of ontogenetic conditions and processes that influence the development of wisdom, namely, facilitative experiential contexts, expertise-relevant factors, and person-related factors (for a graphical representation of our developmental model, see Baltes & Staudinger, 2000, Figure 1, p. 121). In our developmental model, *facilitative experiential contexts* for the development of wisdom include chronological age, education, parenthood, professions that require individuals to strengthen their skills in social-emotional intelligence, familiarity with books such as autobiographical novels, or the historical period, which varies along dimensions of salience and facilitation in matters of the human condition. A second domain that is central to the development of wisdom refers to *expertise-relevant factors* such as experience in life matters, organized tutelage, the availability of mentorship in dealing with life problems, and motivational factors such as a general interest in aspects of human life or a motivation to strive for excellence. Finally, we consider *person-related factors* such as basic cognitive processes, aspects of intelligence, creativity, flexible cognitive styles, and personality dispositions such as openness to experience or ego strength.

These three domains of ontogenetic influences are interrelated, and we believe that, in the sense of equifinality (Kruglanski, 1996), different combinations of the domains may lead to similar outcomes. Thus, there is no single "optimal" pathway, but rather several different ways to acquire wisdom. Nevertheless, it is assumed that there is a productive collaboration among the relevant factors. For example, external factors like the presence of mentors or the experience and mastery of critical life experiences are certainly conducive to the development of wisdom. For these factors to be influential, however, preconditions such as being highly motivated to live in a "good" way and a requisite level of cognitive efficacy probably are necessary. The notion that wisdom requires the presence of several intra- and interindividual factors that need to interact in certain ways underlines that wisdom refers to qualities that can be acquired only by very few people.

The Berlin Wisdom Paradigm

Our paradigm for assessing wisdom comprises the following three core features: (a) Study participants are confronted with difficult life problems of fictitious people under standardized conditions. Specifically, they are asked to read short vignettes about problems of life management, planning, and review. (b) Participants are then instructed to think aloud about those life problems, and their responses are tape-recorded and transcribed. (c) A selected panel of trained judges then rates the protocols according to five criteria (see subsequent criteria) that were developed based on the general theoretical framework outlined. As an illustration, two responses that would be scored as either high or low on wisdom are presented in Table 24.3.

A Family of Five Criteria for the Evaluation of Wisdom-Related Material

In the context of our empirical work, we have developed five qualitative criteria that can be used for evaluating wisdom in any kind of material. The development of these five criteria was guided by several lines of research, including research on expertise, life-span psychology of cognition and personality, the neo-Piagetian tradition of cognitive development in adulthood, and our cultural-historical analyses of wisdom (see also Table 24.1).

The first two criteria derive logically from our view of wisdom as an expert system. They are *rich factual (declarative) knowledge about the fundamental pragmatics of life* and *rich procedural knowledge about the fundamental pragmatics of life*. Factual knowledge related to wisdom includes topics like human nature, lifelong development, interpersonal relations, social norms, and individual differences in development and outcomes. Procedural knowledge comprises strategies and heuristics for dealing with life problems, for example, heuristics for the structuring and weighing of life goals, ways to handle conflicts, or alternative backup strategies. We view these two knowledge criteria as basic criteria—they are necessary but not sufficient for achieving wisdom.

The three other criteria we refer to as metacriteria. *Life span contextualism* refers to knowledge about the many different themes and contexts of human life (education, family, work, friends, etc.), their interrelations, and cultural variations. This criterion includes a life span perspective, for example, regarding changes in the relevance of different domains and in motivational priorities during ontogeny from birth into old age.

Value relativism and tolerance refers to the acknowledgment of individual and cultural differences in values. Note, however, that wisdom does not mean tolerance of any possible value or priority system. On the contrary, wisdom includes an explicit interest in achieving a balance between individual and collective interests and a focus on human virtues. Aside from this fundamental constraint, however, wisdom encompasses a high level of tolerance and sensitivity for different opinions and values.

Recognition and management of uncertainty refers to knowledge about the limitations of human information processing and about the low predictability of occurrences and consequences in human life. Wisdom-related knowledge involves knowledge about such uncertainties, but also about ways to deal with such uncertainty.

Table 24.3 Examples of High-Level and Low-Level Responses

A 15-year-old girl wants to get married right away. What should one/she consider and do?

Low Wisdom-Related Score

A 15-year-old girl wants to get married? No, no way, marrying at age 15 would be utterly wrong. One has to tell the girl that marriage is not possible. It would be irresponsible to support such an idea. No, this is just a crazy idea.

High Wisdom-Related Score

Well, on the surface, this seems like an easy problem. On average, marriage for a 15-year-old girls is not a good thing. But there are situations where the average case does not fit. Perhaps in this instance, special life circumstances are involved, such that the girl has a terminal illness. Or the girl has just lost her parents. And also, this girl may be living in another culture or historical period. Perhaps she was raised with a value system different from ours. In addition, one has to think about adequate ways of talking with the girl and to consider her emotional state.

For the purpose of evaluating the protocols according to the five criteria, a select panel of raters has been extensively trained in the application of the criteria. A protocol is classified as approaching "wise" only if it has received high ratings on all five criteria. Raters are trained on the basis of a manual (Staudinger, Smith, & Baltes, 1994). Reliability and stability of the rating procedure have been shown to be very satisfactory.

Selected Findings From the Berlin Wisdom Project

In the following, we will discuss results regarding the relationship between age and wisdom-related performance, the influence of professional experience on wisdom-related performance, the performance of persons nominated as wise, the main variables that predict wisdom-related performance, and the activation of wisdom-related knowledge in the context of intervention or optimization research.

Age and Wisdom-Related Performance

Guided by the search for positive aspects of human aging, age-comparative studies of wisdom-related performance have been one of our central foci (Baltes & Staudinger, 2000; Pasupathi, Staudinger, & Baltes, 2000; Smith & Baltes, 1990; Staudinger, 1999). Figure 24.1 summa-

rizes the findings of several studies based on heterogeneous samples in terms of educational and socioeconomic backgrounds and representing the life span from adolescence to old age. Note that these data are cross-sectional rather than longitudinal and therefore are contaminated with cohort-related sampling and historical change (cohort) factors.

Our findings suggest that wisdom-related performance, as measured by the Berlin Wisdom Paradigm, increases sharply during adolescence and young adulthood (i.e., between 15 and 25 years) but, on average, remains relatively stable during middle adulthood and young old age (i.e., between 25 and 75 years). Peak performances, however, seem to be more likely in the 50s and 60s (Baltes, Staudinger, Maercker, & Smith, 1995). Tentatively, our data also suggest that wisdom-related performance may decline in very old age, beginning in current cohorts, at the average age of 75.

At first sight, it is surprising that wisdom seems to remain relatively stable during adulthood and old age, at least up to age 75. This empirical finding is inconsistent with the notion that wisdom may be a positive aspect of the aging process. In interpreting the empirical evidence, however, it is important to consider the dramatically different results from age-comparative studies on the fluid mechanics of cognitive functioning. These studies suggest that basic elementary cognitive functions such as speed of information processing begin to lose

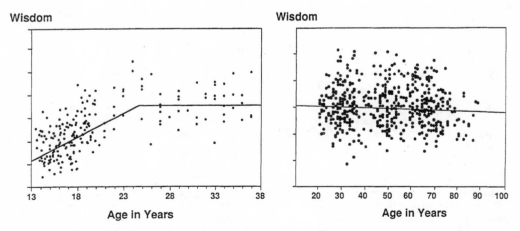

Figure 24.1 Cross-sectional age gradients and scatterplots for wisdom-related performance. The left panel shows data from Pasupathi, Staudinger, and Baltes (2000), including outcomes of a spline analysis. The right panel summarizes results from several studies with adult samples (see also Baltes & Staudinger, 2000; Staudinger, 1999).

efficiency much earlier in the life span than wisdom-related knowledge and judgment (Baltes, Staudinger, & Lindenberger, 1999; Salthouse, 1996; Schaie, 1996). Seen in this light, the stability of wisdom may represent the best possible outcome old age and aging can bring about, that is, maintaining one's level of wisdom-related performance despite deteriorating basic cognitive functions. Beyond age 75, however, the general decrease in basic cognitive functioning most likely limits higher level performance even in culture-rich domains such as wisdom.

The stability of wisdom during most of adulthood and old age is also consistent with the notion that age per se is a necessary rather than a sufficient condition for wisdom-related performance to improve. As we have outlined in our developmental model of wisdom (see above), several internal and external factors and processes need to interact and collaborate as an ensemble to ensure age-related improvement in wisdom. Moreover, to highlight the specific strengths in old age, it may be necessary to identify tasks and contexts of life that are more specific to old age than the tasks used so far.

The Role of Professional Experience

Given our definition and assessment of wisdom, it is clear that most adults are not wise; only some people have access to and acquire knowledge about the conduct and meaning of life that comes close to wisdom. In our past research, we were interested in identifying groups of people with constellations of life experiences and external conditions that facilitate the acquisition of wisdom-related knowledge.

As a first step, we investigated the members of a profession whose training and professional practice both involve continued and varied experience with difficult life problems, namely, clinical psychologists (Smith, Staudinger, & Baltes, 1994; Staudinger, Smith, & Baltes, 1992). These clinical psychologists were compared with professionals from fields in which training and everyday job tasks were not specifically dedicated to dealing with difficult problems concerning life meaning and conduct. As predicted, clinical psychologists showed higher levels of wisdom-related performance than the members of other professions. However, the clinical psychologists did not reach expert levels of performance in our theory-based measurement: On the 7-point scale used in our ratings

for the wisdom criteria, the clinical psychologists' mean was 3.8.

In interpreting this result, it is important to consider that the relatively higher level of wisdom-related performance displayed by clinical psychologists may not only be due to training and profession-related experiences. Rather, members of a profession may represent a selective group of people in terms of personality, motivation, and intellectual abilities. However, a communality analysis with professional specialization and multiple intellectual and personality dispositions as independent variables revealed professional specialization as the strongest unique predictor, accounting for 15% of the variance in wisdom-related performance (Staudinger, Maciel, Smith, & Baltes, 1998). Thus, professional training and experience in the field of clinical psychology seem to facilitate the acquisition of wisdom-related knowledge.

The Performance of Persons Nominated as Wise

But could it be that clinical psychologists showed superior performance because they were working on wisdom tasks that were developed by people having the same profession? To investigate whether our assessment procedure might be biased in this direction, we conducted a study in which we compared the performance of clinical psychologists with that of people who had been nominated as wise, independently of our definition of wisdom (Baltes et al., 1995). The 21 wisdom nominees of this study were persons of public distinction selected by a panel of nonpsychologists based on an intensive Delphi-like nomination process. Although the nominees were heterogeneous in terms of age (ranging from 41 to 79 years), most of the nominees were older adults (on average age 64).

Overall, the wisdom nominees performed at least as well as the clinical psychologists. Wisdom nominees even excelled in the task of existential life management and the criterion of value relativism. If there is a psychological bias to our conception of wisdom, this does not prevent nonpsychologists from being among the top performers.

Predictors of Wisdom-Related Performance

One of our central assumptions is that wisdom requires and reflects the orchestration of several domains of human functioning. On the level of person-related factors, this includes an integration of intellectual abilities, personality dispositions, and characteristics representing the interface between intelligence and personality. Staudinger, Lopez, and Baltes (1997) investigated the joint and unique effects of these three broad domains of person-related factors on wisdom-related performance. Overall, 33 psychometric indicators from 14 different tests covering psychometric intelligence (4 indicators), personality measures (12 indicators), and the personality-intelligence interface (17 indicators) were assessed. The three key findings of this study are summarized in Figure 24.2. First, at least 10 of the 33 indicators turned out to be significant predictors of wisdom-related performance. Overall, these 10 predictors accounted for 40% of the variance in wisdom-related performance. None of the indicators alone explained more than 18%, however.

Second, consistent with the orchestration idea of wisdom, there was a significant overlap between the three predictor domains: All three domains shared 9% of the predicted variance. Intelligence and personality each contributed only a small amount of unique variance (2% each), whereas the intelligence-personality interface variables explained 15% of unique variance. Among the interface variables, cognitive styles (Sternberg, 1996) and creativity showed the strongest correlations to wisdom-related performance. Judicial style (i.e., a preference for evaluating and comparing) and progressive style (i.e., willingness to move beyond existing rules and tolerance for ambiguity) turned out to be the cognitive styles most predictive of wisdom.

Third, after introducing all of the 33 predictors into the regression analysis, parallel measures (tasks) of wisdom accounted for an additional 19% of the otherwise unexplained variance. This finding indicates that our wisdom-related measures share a relatively high amount of unique variance: Wisdom is different from a combination of adaptive abilities and characteristics related to standard measures of personality, intelligence and their interface.

Optimization Research: Activating Wisdom-Related Knowledge

Positive psychology highlights the importance of optimizing human functioning and employing designs of facilitative interventions. In the following, we will discuss two studies to illustrate the potential of theory-based interventions.

Interactive Minds: The Social-Collaborative Aspect of Wisdom

One of our central ideas is that wisdom requires and results from social collaboration. As mentioned, we argue that individuals by themselves are only "weak" carriers of wisdom (Baltes & Smith, 1990; Staudinger, 1996). To examine the

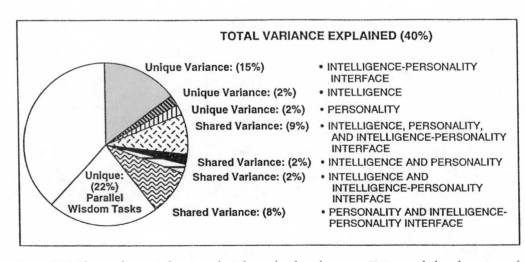

Figure 24.2 The psychometric location of wisdom-related performance: Unique and shared portions of predictive variance of measures of intelligence, personality, and the personality-intelligence interface (Staudinger, Lopez, & Baltes, 1997).

role of social interaction in wisdom-related performance, Staudinger and Baltes (1996a) conducted a study in which participants responded to wisdom-related tasks under different conditions of collaboration and social support. Participants in the first group discussed the problem with a significant other person before giving their responses individually; those in a second group engaged in an inner dialogue with a person of their choice about the problem before responding; and those in a third group were just given some free time to think about the problem by themselves prior to responding. In addition, some participants in the interactive-minds conditions received additional appraisal time after the interaction to reflect about the dialogue and the problem on their own.

The findings clearly suggest that social interaction, real or imaginary, can facilitate wisdom-related performance. Specifically, two interactive-minds conditions, namely, external dialogue plus appraisal time and internal dialogue, produced a substantial increase in performance amounting to almost one standard deviation. An interesting additional result was that older adults profited more from the actual-interaction condition than did the young adults.

Intervention Research: Activating Mental Scripts Associated With Wisdom by Means of a Memory Technique

In her dissertation, Böhmig-Krumhaar (1998) explored whether using a specific memory technique improved wisdom-related performance. Specifically, the goal was to improve performance on two of the five wisdom criteria—value relativism and life span contextualism—by teaching participants to use a cognitive strategy derived from the Method of Loci, a mnemonic used in past studies on memory plasticity (e.g., Baltes & Kliegl, 1992; Kliegl, Smith, & Baltes, 1990). Participants were first instructed to imagine traveling around the world on a cloud, visiting four places in four different cultures: Germany, Italy, Egypt, and China. Using visual illustrations and a list of object stimuli, participants were told to imagine life in those cultures and to construct some mental images related to the four places. To attain a certain level of automaticity and generalization, participants subsequently were presented with two practice wisdom tasks.

After this training phase, participants took a posttest in which they were told to use the "cloud journey" while working on new wisdom tasks. As predicted, the intervention led to significant increases in the two targeted wisdom criteria: value relativism and life span contextualism. This study illustrates how relatively permanently stored and practiced mental scripts, such as a worldwide journey on clouds, can activate and co-organize bodies of knowledge that are available in principle but typically would not be used as a guiding strategy. Such a strategy of orchestrated activation is in line with our view (see subsequently) that bodies of wisdom-related knowledge are available but generally not bound together until mental representations or mental scripts such as the wisdom concept are used as a coordinating cue (see also Stich, 1990).

Wisdom as a Metaheuristic to Orchestrate Behavior Toward Excellence in Mind and Virtue

Recently, we have proposed an additional aspect in our developing theory of wisdom (Baltes & Staudinger, 2000; Glück & Baltes, 2000). We have argued that wisdom can be viewed as a metaheuristic that activates and organizes knowledge about the fundamental pragmatics of life in the service of optimizing an integration between mind and virtue.

A heuristic usually is defined as a highly automatized and organized strategy for directing search processes or for organizing and using information in a certain class of situations (Dawes, 1988; Gigerenzer, Todd, & The ABC Group, 1999; Kahneman, Slovic, & Tversky, 1982; Nisbett & Ross, 1980). The function of heuristics in judgment and decision making is to reach solutions under conditions of limited resources. Thus, if it is impossible to use the full information—and this is typical of most real-world situations—heuristics guide which and how much information is taken into account in making a decision.

We believe that wisdom-related problems represent a class of situations that calls for the use of heuristics. In other words, what Simon (1983) defined as bounded rationality (i.e., using realistic amounts of time, information, and cognitive resources in making decisions) and efficient use of the critical information about ways and ends of a good life seem to be operative when dealing with wisdom tasks. Note in this context that we use the term *heuristic* in the same positive sense as Gestalt psychologists such as Wertheimer and Duncker (e.g., Duncker, 1945), Herbert Simon (e.g., Simon, 1956), and Gigerenzer and his colleagues (Gigerenzer et al., 1999). Wisdom experts may have more elaborate, flexible, and efficient systems of heuristics available than people with low levels of wisdom-related knowledge. As a consequence, wisdom experts may achieve high levels of performance when working on problems concerning the fundamental pragmatics of life faster and with fewer cues (cf. Hatano, 1988).

We consider wisdom a metaheuristic rather than a simple and task-specific heuristic. Given the wide range of wisdom as a body of knowledge about the fundamental pragmatics of life and the human condition, its applicability can be expected to be wide and operative at a high level of aggregation (see also Baltes & Staudinger, 2000). As a metaheuristic, wisdom guides the strategies that a person selects with respect to a large number of problems in the fundamental pragmatics of life (see also Glück & Baltes, 2000).

The search and judgment processes activated by wisdom could, for example, include translations of the three metacriteria for the evaluation of wisdom-related materials from the Berlin Wisdom Paradigm. Thus, the meta-criterion of value relativism and tolerance could be translated into heuristics such as considering others' opinions, trying not to be influenced by affect (Bodenhausen, 1993; Bodenhausen, Sheppard, & Kramer, 1994), or strategies of perspective change (Hirt & Markman, 1995). Life span contextualism could be translated into processes of search and judgment, such as always collecting information on a person's life context or assuming people to be situation-dependent rather than stable in their personality and behavior (Ross & Nisbett, 1991). Recognition and management of uncertainty could be translated into subheuristics such as postponing a decision in doubt or not basing judgments on too small samples of behavior (Kosonen & Winne, 1995; Nisbett, Krantz, Jepson, & Kunda, 1983; Nisbett, Fong, Lehman, & Cheng, 1987). Note that within this framework, a wise decision does not necessarily have to be based on more information or more careful planning; it also can be reached by using few, but optimal cues drawn from a high level of knowledge and experience.

Table 24.4 gives some quotations from a pilot study in which we asked participants to try to give wise responses to the tasks of the Berlin Wisdom Paradigm and then asked them how they had gone about this task. The responses listed in Table 24.4 illustrate the kind of candidate subheuristics named previously.

Another term that is useful to understand the orchestrating function of wisdom as a metaheuristic is that of *binding* (Ashby, Prinzmetal, Ivry, & Maddox, 1996; Singer, 1993, 2000; Stich, 1990). On a cognitive-mental-representational level, the objective of binding can be understood as an operation or a set of operations by which networks are achieved whose primary function is to link distinct bodies of knowledge—in this instance, otherwise unrelated bodies of knowledge about the means

Table 24.4 Sample Data from a Pilot Study Using a Wisdom Instruction

"How Did You Translate the Instruction to Give a Wise Response in Your Responses?"

"Keeping it as general as possible and not falling back upon personal experiences. . . . Seeing it in a totally neutral way, only from the content of the task."

"Well, being tolerant toward this young girl, not calling her totally crazy, but just looking at where the problem is situated."

"Taking the reasons of such a young person into account, . . . not being prejudiced. . . . So that I think that wise, in quotes, is when one thinks about it, approaches it from several aspects, from several sides, not just judging a priori but looking at different sides."

"I think wise is for me in a way if one views one's own situation relative to that of others and simply puts it into a larger context."

"Projecting oneself into someone else, to look how this person would act, to get off this impulsive level, this level of personal involvement a little bit. I think that's what is important, plus taking one's time."

"Taking oneself back and looking at this respective person and the circumstances and thinking about how could one be helpful to the person with what one says."

and ends of living a good life. Thus, the specific focus of this wisdom-generated binding process would be the interrelating of mind and virtue toward excellence (see also Baltes & Freund, in press).

Our general theoretical orientation—as well as research on subjective beliefs about wisdom and wise persons—would provide the initial information about the territory that is bound together by the wisdom heuristic. As noted previously, the activation of such a metaheuristic likely is associated with an ensemble of subheuristics. Thus, even though wisdom comprises a number of different, interrelated facets from different domains of human functioning, including pragmatic knowledge (e.g., knowledge acquired during the experiences of a long life), procedural knowledge (e.g., heuristics and strategies, including the ability to think and reason logically), emotional maturity (e.g., a balance in general emotional status), and self- as well as other-regarding motivation (e.g., the focus on virtues vs. vices), their activation in the context of wisdom coordinates (binds) these into an ensemble. Such a binding coordination would be the unique quality of wisdom.

Let us return to the opening of this chapter, that is, the discussion of positivity in human behavior: We argue that wisdom is a concept that identifies positive means and ends of a good life (Baltes & Staudinger, 2000; Kekes, 1995). From a metaheuristic perspective, a wise person has available an elaborate, effective, flexible, and orchestrated system of subheuristics in the domain of the fundamental pragmatics of life and uses this system as a repertoire to reach positive and avoid negative outcomes.

Linking Wisdom to Psychological Theories of Motivation and Values

Research on wisdom has a tradition of being treated as a separate arena. Therefore, in this concluding section, we attempt to embed work on wisdom in other lines of scholarship and illustrate its fertility. To this end, we consider the interface between the scholarship on wisdom and the psychological study of motivation and values.

Note at the outset that our position is that past psychological work refrained from a specification of the "truth value" of values and goals because psychology is not a normative-prescriptive science. Therefore, only indirect evidence such as subjective beliefs about norms or the social desirability of psychological properties could be relied on—leaving the scientific study of values without an explicit criterion of evaluation.

On a metalevel of analysis, our argument is that the philosophy-based treatment of the structure and function of wisdom provides an alternative. This alternative allocates to the philosophy of wisdom the frame of reference within which the general means and ends of a good life can be defined. Subsequently, psychologists can proceed to explicate how people consider such wisdom-based general criteria when pursuing their individual goals.

Thus, we attempt to open the door into interdisciplinarity and ask whether such an approach assists in the organization of personal values and motivational dispositions that psychologists have studied. To this end, we briefly describe several theoretical schemes of values, desirable motivational dispositions, and self-directed strengths as developed in psychological research. Subsequently, we specify their potential linkages to the wisdom construct. Our expectation is that this effort will open up not only new lines of inquiry but also thoughts about the cultural selection process associated with human development. In other words, the evolution of a conception of wisdom is one source of culture-based selection from the energizing system that biological-genetic evolution has evolved as the motivational nature of Homo sapiens. The concept of wisdom may function as a selector for enhancement and reduction of the emotions, values, and motives involved in becoming a "good" human being.

Psychological Theories of Values

A first example: Numerous value researchers have relied on the value theory developed by Milton Rokeach (1973). This theory is based on the following definition of values: "A value is an enduring belief that a specific mode of conduct or end-state of existence is personally or socially preferable to an opposite or converse mode of conduct or end-state of existence" (Rokeach, 1973, p. 5). As indicated by this definition, Rokeach distinguished two types of values. Values about modes of conduct, which he also called *instrumental values*, refer to beliefs about which means (e.g., being honest, courageous, or modest) lead to certain desirable outcomes. In contrast, values about end states of existence, also called *terminal values*, refer to desirable life outcomes themselves (e.g., salvation, a world at peace).

Although Rokeach has concentrated his attention on the distinction between instrumental and terminal values, he considered that instrumental and terminal values can be broken down further according to whether they refer to individual well-being or to other people's well-being. Instrumental values with self-focus were called *competence values* (e.g., being ambitious, intellectual, independent); those with a focus on other people's well-being were called *moral values* (e.g., being helpful, forgiving, polite). Similarly, terminal values with self-focus were called "personal values" (e.g., self-respect, a comfortable life, freedom), and those with an other-focus were labeled "social values" (e.g., equality, national security, a world at peace).

Rokeach's ideas about the origins and development of values suggest—as the wisdom concept would imply—that the distinction between self- and other-centered values may be of fundamental importance. He assumed: "Values are the joint results of sociological as well as psychological forces acting upon the individual—sociological because society and its institutions socialize the individual for the common good to internalize shared conceptions of the desirable; psychological because individual motivations require cognitive expression, justification, and indeed exhortation in socially desirable terms" (Rokeach, 1973, p. 29). In this view, values represent personally and socially desirable versions of individual needs and social demands.

More recently, Schwartz and his colleagues (Schwartz, 1992; Schwartz & Bilsky, 1987, 1990) developed a theory of personal values that is based on a similar idea about the origins of human values. Specifically, the authors assume that the multitude of values are represented by 10 value types (e.g., power, achievement, hedonism, stimulation, and self-direction), which in turn arise from three requirements for survival: biological needs of the individual, requisites of coordinated social interaction, and the survival and welfare needs of groups. Schwartz and his colleagues have proposed that the 10 value types can be investigated on a more general level because they are indicators of two bipolar value dimensions, "openness to change versus conservation" and "self-enhancement versus self-transcendence."

However, most of this research group's empirical work on individual and cultural differences in values and the consequences of values for social behaviors has focused on the 10 value types (Schwartz, 1990).

Interestingly, although both Rokeach and Schwartz consider individual needs and social demands as driving forces in the development of personal values, their theories and empirical work have not focused on the central importance of balancing self-serving and other-serving values for living a good life. As mentioned, on the most abstract level of description, Rokeach emphasized the difference between instrumental and terminal goals. Schwartz and his colleagues primarily have investigated people's value systems on the level of 10 value types.

As we will elaborate subsequently, a philosophy-based treatment of wisdom strongly suggests that the coordinated and balanced pursuit of self-serving and other-serving values is a central contributor to positive development and a good life (see also Sternberg, 1998). Thus, in contrast to past approaches on personal values, a wisdom-informed classification would consider the differentiation between self-serving and other-serving values as most fundamental.

Another research area that is directly relevant is work on moral competence. This line of inquiry, beginning with Piaget (1932) and Kohlberg (1969), has been concerned with the cognitive and behavioral manifestations of what we have called other-serving values (see also Turiel, 1998). Notably, proponents of research on moral competence have made explicit what they consider as developmental ideals from a theoretical and a priori basis. For example, Kohlberg formulated in his theory of moral competence six stages of development, each being closer to an ideal style of moral reasoning based on universal ethical principles such as equality and respect for individual dignity (e.g., Kohlberg, 1969, 1971).

To add a third area of interest, consider research developed in the context of humanistic psychology, which traditionally has focused on concepts related to the self (e.g., Bühler, 1959; Maslow, 1970; Rogers, 1961). Maslow, for instance, proposed in his theory on human motivation that individuals have five basic needs (physiological, safety, love, self-esteem, and self-actualization needs) that can be arranged in a hierarchy on the basis of the principle of relative potency (Maslow, 1970). According to Maslow, these five needs indicate levels of psychological adjustment ranging from poorly to well adjusted.

As interesting as these approaches toward a classification of personal values may be, from the perspective of the concept of wisdom, they are limited in that they have little to say about the interplay of self-serving versus other-serving values. While research on moral competence has been one-sided in that its focus lies on the manifestations of other-serving values, theories on human motivation—and this is true for most contemporary psychological research, at least in the Western tradition—have concerned themselves primarily with the development of self-serving goals and dispositions. It is here that the philosophy-based treatment of wisdom comes into play and may give us, on a metalevel of analysis, some indication of how self- and other-serving values may be orchestrated in the service of optimal functioning and a good life. In other words, the concept of wisdom provides a metaperspective on the organization of personal values that integrates more limited approaches advanced in past psychological research on morality and human motivation. Notably, Rokeach's and Schwartz's theoretical work comes closest to what we as wisdom researchers have in mind.

Views From Wisdom on Personal Values and Positive Life Span Development

In the following, to illustrate our general line of argument, we shall discuss two of the seven core features of wisdom (see Table 24.1) in more detail: (a) an orientation toward the common good involving the well-being of oneself and others, and (b) a balanced, holistic, and integrated view of the world of human affairs. We believe that both characteristics have important implications for a theoretical classification of personal values and their orchestration toward a positive development and a good life (see also Sternberg, 1998).

Wisdom Is an Orientation Toward the Common Good

Wisdom inherently is an intra- *and* interpersonal concept. On the one hand, wisdom entails knowledge about how we can lead a personally meaningful and satisfying life. Consistent with this idea, Garrett (1996) proposes the following

definition of wisdom: "Wisdom is that understanding which is essential to living the best life" (p. 221). Ryan (1996) suggests a similar definition of a wise person: "S is wise if (1) S is a free agent, (2) S knows how to live well, (3) S lives well, and (4) S's living well is caused by S's knowledge about how to live well" (p. 241). To cite a third philosopher, Kekes (1983) made the same general point: "Wisdom is a character-trait intimately connected with self-direction. The more wisdom a person has the more likely it is he will succeed in living a good life" (p. 277). "Wisdom is to arrange one's life so as to aim to satisfy those wants that accord with his ideals" (p. 285). "Growth in wisdom and self-direction go hand in hand" (p. 286). Notably, this line of thinking concerning the link between knowledge and behavior aimed at individual growth and self-realization in wisdom, is not new. It can be found in the treatments of wisdom of the classical Greek philosophers such as Socrates, Plato, and Aristotle (for an overview, see Baltes & Staudinger, in press).

On the other hand, and perhaps contrary to Maslow's and Ryan's primary focus on the self, from a philosophical point of view, a concern with interpersonal issues is equally part of the core of wisdom. Wisdom is not knowledge used for individual well-being alone; it also is used for the well-being of others (e.g., Kekes, 1995). In this spirit, philosophical-historical accounts of wisdom have focused on the property of a well-meaning counselor giving good advice to someone in a difficult situation and not of someone whose advice serves his or her own needs (for an overview, see Baltes & Staudinger, in press). Notably, this interpersonal orientation also is reflected in dictionary definitions of wisdom, which consistently regard good advice in difficult and uncertain matters of life as one central facet (e.g., *Oxford Dictionary of the English Language*, 1933, p. 191).

Taking these considerations together, philosophical approaches to defining wisdom, as diverse as they may be on more concrete levels of analyses, converge regarding the idea that wisdom includes the availability and application of knowledge about successful development of oneself *and* others. In this vein, wisdom considers the ancient idea of a good life, in which conceptions of individual and collective well-being are tied together, and it involves the insight that one cannot exist without the other.

Wisdom Is Integrative, Holistic, and Balanced Knowledge

There is a second central characteristic of wisdom that is equally important for questions concerning the potential of wisdom to function as a guide for leading a good life. That is, wisdom is integrative; it focuses on the whole and the weighing and moderation of its parts. Balance, in particular, is at the core of wisdom (see also Sternberg, 1998). The preceding discussion on values already has hinted at this problem. The concept of wisdom would suggest that psychological research needs to be designed to address the collaborative relationships among individuals' multiple values and motives.

Notably, this "modulated-balance" line of philosophical-based thinking is also central to several psychological theories of wisdom. In particular, dialectical approaches in the neo-Piagetian tradition of postformal thought also have emphasized the importance of balance in wisdom. These theories have focused on integration of various kinds of thinking (Labouvie-Vief, 1990), multiple self-systems such as cognitive, conative, and affective (Kramer, 1990, 2000), and various points of view (Kitchener & Brenner, 1990). As mentioned earlier, Sternberg (1998) has proposed a theory of wisdom that also emphasizes the notion of balance. Expanding on earlier theories, his theory emphasizes that wisdom involves not only a balance among multiple internal systems of functioning but also a balance between a person and his or her context.

To return to our central question: Can the philosophy-based concept of wisdom give us some indication about the organization and orchestration of personal values underlying the good life? Our answer to this question is positive. On a metalevel of analysis, wisdom would suggest that holding and pursuing personal values oriented toward one's own development *and* other people's well-being is a key facet in positive development and a good life. Importantly, it is the balanced and coordinated pursuit that indicates wisdom rather than the one-sided focus on developing either one's own potential or others' potential.

Suggestions for Future Research

To our best knowledge, there has not been much research on the connections among wisdom and personal values. Does wisdom-related knowledge make a difference in a person's system of self- and other-serving values, as we would predict? How many and which self- and other-serving values do wise persons have? It also remains to be seen whether people with different degrees of wisdom-related knowledge differ in specific types of self- and other-serving values. Wisdom may make a difference particularly in terms of what researchers of morality and human motivation may call more highly developed self- and other-regarding values (e.g., other-serving values that reflect more abstract moral principles or self-serving values that refer to an individual's self-actualization).

It is not only interesting to empirically investigate how many and what types of personal values people who approach wisdomlike qualities may hold. Equally important is the question of whether wiser people are particularly efficient in applying and pursuing their self- and other-serving values. For example, does wisdom make a difference in the behavioral manifestations of other-serving values? Is there an association between wisdom-related knowledge and what Rossi (in press) has called social productivity and responsibility? Are wise people who give high priority to self-serving values related to self-actualization particularly likely to have actualized their individual potentials?

Finally, and as we have mentioned already, especially the orchestration of self-and other-serving values may call for the knowledge and expertise typical of wisdom—given that, in many situations, it may not be possible to pursue both kinds of values. In a particular situation, for example, is it better to seek personal success or to remain honest, to act obediently or independently, to seek self-respect or social recognition? It would be interesting to know how wisdom-related knowledge influences people's decisions, behaviors, and emotional reactions when they are faced with those situations involving conflicts among self- and other-serving values.

A philosophy-based conception of wisdom would predict that a wise person does not prefer and pursue self-serving values at the expense of other-serving values and vice versa (for a similar view, see Snyder, Rand, & Sigmon, this volume). Thus, in contrast to research on moral development, this approach would not consider self-interests as less important than someone else's interest. Similarly, pursuing self-interests at the expense of other people's interests rarely can be considered as wise. Rather, the optimal solution to problems involving conflicting self-serving and other-serving values would be one in which the self both gains and gives.

With such observations, we have returned to the opening of this chapter, that is, the search for a construct that on an interdisciplinary plane of analysis permits the joining of philosophical and psychological conceptions of positivity in human behavior and human development. The puzzle has not been solved yet. We hope, however, that this courtship has contributed to a better understanding of why the concept of wisdom is being revisited and holds much promise.

References

Agazzi, E. (Ed.). (1991). *Science et sagesse: Entretiens de l'Académie Internationale de Philosophie des Sciences, 1990.* Freiburg, Germany: Universitätsverlag Freiburg.

Alexander, C. N., & Langer, E. J. (Eds.). (1990). *Higher stages of human development.* New York: Oxford University Press.

Arlin, P. K. (1990). Wisdom: The art of problem finding. In R. J. Sternberg (Ed.), *Wisdom: Its nature, origins, and development* (pp. 230–243). New York: Cambridge University Press.

Ashby, F. G., Prinzmetal, W., Ivry, R., & Maddox, W. T. (1996). A formal theory of feature binding in objective perception. *Psychological Review, 103,* 165–192.

Assmann, A. (1994). Wholesome knowledge: Concepts of wisdom in a historical and cross-cultural perspective. In D. L. Featherman, R. M. Lerner, & M. Perlmutter (Eds.), *Life-span development and behavior* (Vol. 12, pp. 187–224). Hillsdale, NJ: Erlbaum.

Baltes, M. M., & Baltes, P. B. (1977). The ecopsychological relativity and plasticity of psychological aging: Convergent perspectives of cohort effects and operant psychology. *Zeitschrift für experimentelle und angewandte Psychologie, 24,* 179–197.

Baltes, P. B. (1987). Theoretical propositions of life-span developmental psychology: On the dynamics between growth and decline. *Developmental Psychology, 23,* 611–626.

Baltes, P. B. (1993). The aging mind: Potential and limits. *Gerontologist, 33,* 580–594.

*Baltes, P. B. (1997). On the incomplete architecture of human ontogeny: Selection, optimization, and compensation as foundation of developmental theory. *American Psychologist, 52,* 366–380.

Baltes, P. B., Dittmann-Kohli, F., & Dixon, R. A. (1984). New perspectives on the development of intelligence in adulthood: Toward a dual-process conception and a model of selective optimization with compensation. In P. B. Baltes & O. G. Brim, Jr. (Eds.), *Life-span development and behavior* (Vol. 6, pp. 33–76). New York: Academic Press.

Baltes, P. B., & Freund, A. M. F. (in press). The intermarriage of wisdom and selective optimization with compensation (SOC): Two metaheuristics guiding the conduct of life. In C. L. M. Keyes & J. Haidt (Eds.), *Flourishing: The positive person and the good life.* Washington, DC: American Psychological Association.

Baltes, P. B., & Kliegl, R. (1992). Further testing of limits of cognitive plasticity: Negative age differences in a mnemonic skill are robust. *Developmental Psychology, 28,* 121–125.

Baltes, P. B., & Labouvie-Vief, G. (1973). Adult development of intellectual performance: Description, explanation, modification. In C. Eisdorfer & M. P. Lawton (Eds.), *The psychology of adult development and aging* (pp. 157–219). Washington, DC: American Psychological Association.

Baltes, P. B., & Lindenberger, U. (1988). On the range of cognitive plasticity in old age as a function of experience: 15 years of intervention research. *Behavior Therapy, 19,* 283–300.

Baltes, P. B., & Smith, J. (1990). The psychology of wisdom and its ontogenesis. In R. J. Sternberg (Ed.), *Wisdom: Its nature, origins, and development* (pp. 87–120). New York: Cambridge University Press.

Baltes, P. B., Smith, J., & Staudinger, U. M. (1992). Wisdom and successful aging. In T. Sonderegger (Ed.), *Nebraska symposium on motivation,* (Vol. 39, pp. 123–167). Lincoln: University of Nebraska Press.

Baltes, P. B., & Staudinger, U. M. (1993). The search for a psychology of wisdom. *Current Directions in Psychological Science, 2,* 75–80.

*Baltes, P. B., & Staudinger, U. M. (2000). Wisdom: A metaheuristic (pragmatic) to orchestrate mind and virtue toward excellence. *American Psychologist, 55,* 122–136.

Baltes, P. B., & Staudinger, U. M. (in press). *Wisdom: The orchestration of mind and character.* Boston: Blackwell.

Baltes, P. B., Staudinger, U. M., & Lindenberger, U. (1999). Lifespan psychology: Theory and application to intellectual functioning. *Annual Review of Psychology, 50,* 471–507.

Baltes, P. B., Staudinger, U. M., Maercker, A., & Smith, J. (1995). People nominated as wise: A comparative study of wisdom-related knowledge. *Psychology and Aging, 10,* 155–166.

Baltes, P. B., & Willis, S. L. (1982). Plasticity and enhancement of intellectual functioning in old age: Penn State's Adult Development and Enrichment Project ADEPT. In F. I. M. Craik & S. E. Trehub (Eds.), *Aging and cognitive processes* (pp. 353–389). New York: Plenum.

Bandura, A. (1986). *Social foundations of thought and action: A social cognitive theory.* Englewood Cliffs, NJ: Prentice-Hall.

Bandura, A. (1995). *Self-efficacy in a changing society.* New York: Cambridge University Press.

Birren, J. E., & Fisher, L. M. (1990). The elements of wisdom: Overview and integration. In R. J. Sternberg (Ed.), *Wisdom: Its nature, origins, and development* (pp. 317–332). New York: Cambridge University Press.

Bodenhausen, G. V. (1993). Emotions, arousal, and stereotypic judgments: A heuristic model of affect and stereotyping. In D. M. Mackie & D. L. Hamilton (Eds.), *Affect, cognition, and stereotyping: Interactive processes in group perception* (pp. 13–37). San Diego, CA: Academic Press.

Bodenhausen, G. V., Sheppard, L. A., & Kramer, G. P. (1994). Negative affect and social judgment: The differential impact of anger and sadness. *European Journal of Social Psychology, 24,* 45–62.

Böhmig-Krumhaar, S. (1998). *Leistungspotentiale wert-relativierenden Denkens* [Performance potentials of value-relativistic thinking]. Berlin, Germany: Max Planck Institute for Human Development.

Brandtstädter, J., & Schneewind, K. A. (1977). Optimal human development: Some implications for psychology. *Human Development, 20,* 48–64.

Bühler, C. (1959). *Der menschliche Lebenslauf als psychologisches Problem* [The human life course as a topic of psychological inquiry]. Göttingen, Germany: Verlag für Psychologie.

*Clayton, V. P., & Birren, J. E. (1980). The development of wisdom across the life span: A reexamination of an ancient topic. In P. B. Baltes & J. O. G. Brim (Eds.), *Life-span development and behavior* (Vol. 3, pp. 103–135). New York: Academic Press.

Dawes, R. M. (1988). *Rational choice in an uncertain world.* Orlando, FL: Harcourt Brace Jovanovich.

Dittmann-Kohli, F., & Baltes, P. B. (1990). Toward a neofunctionalist conception of adult intellectual development: Wisdom as a prototypical case of intellectual growth. In C. Alexander & E. Langer (Eds.), *Higher stages of human development: Perspectives on adult growth* (pp. 54–78). New York: Oxford University Press.

Dixon, R. A., & Baltes, P. B. (1986). Toward life-span research on the functions and pragmatics of intelligence. In R. J. Sternberg & R. K. Wagner (Eds.), *Practical intelligence: Nature and origins of competence in the everyday world* (pp. 203–234). New York: Cambridge University Press.

Duncker, K. (1945). On problem solving (L. S. Lees, Trans.). *Psychological Monographs, 58.* (Original work published 1935)

Ericsson, K. A., & Smith, J. (Eds.). (1991). *Towards a general theory of expertise: Prospects and limits.* New York: Cambridge University Press.

Erikson, E. H. (1959). *Identity and the life cycle.* New York: International University Press.

Erikson, E. H. (1968). *Identity, youth and crisis.* New York: Norton.

Garrett, R. (1996). Three definitions of wisdom. In K. Lehrer, B. J. Lum, B. A. Slichta, & N. D. Smith (Eds.), *Knowledge, teaching and wisdom,* (pp. 221–232). Dordrecht, Netherlands: Kluwer.

Gigerenzer, G., Todd, P. M., & The ABC Group. (1999). *Simple heuristics that make us smart.* New York: Oxford University Press.

Glück, J., & Baltes, P. B. (2000). *Wisdom as a meta-heuristic.* Unpublished manuscript, Max Planck Institute for Human Development, Berlin, Germany.

Harris, D. B. (Ed.). (1957). *The concept of development.* Minneapolis: University of Minnesota Press.

Hatano, G. (1988). Social and motivational bases for mathematical understanding. *New Directions for Child Development, 41,* 55–70.

Heckhausen, J., Dixon, R. A., & Baltes, P. B. (1989). Gains and losses in development throughout adulthood as perceived by different adult age groups. *Developmental Psychology, 25,* 109–121.

Hirt, E. R., & Markman, K. D. (1995). Multiple explanation: A consider-an-alternative strategy for debiasing judgments. *Journal of Personality and Social Psychology, 69,* 1069–1086.

Holliday, S. G., & Chandler, M. J. (1986). Wisdom: Explorations in adult competence. In J. A. Meacham (Ed.), *Contributions to human development* (Vol. 17, pp. 1–96). Basel, Switzerland: Karger.

Kahneman, D., Slovic, P., & Tversky, A. (Eds.). (1982). *Judgment under uncertainty: Heuristics and biases.* Cambridge, MA: Cambridge University Press.

Kekes, J. (1983). Wisdom. *American Philosophical Quarterly, 20,* 277–286.

*Kekes, J. (1995). *Moral wisdom and good lives.* Ithaca, NY: Cornell University Press.

Kendler, H. H. (1999). The role of value in the world of psychology. *American Psychologist, 54,* 828–835.

Kitchener, K. S., & Brenner, H. G. (1990). Wisdom and reflective judgment: Knowing in the face of uncertainty. In R. J. Sternberg (Ed.), *Wisdom: Its nature, origins, and development.* New York: Cambridge University Press.

Kliegl, R., Smith, J., & Baltes, P. B. (1990). On the locus and process of magnification of age differences during mnemonic training. *Developmental Psychology, 26,* 894–904.

Kohlberg, L. (1969). Stage and sequence: The cognitive-developmental approach to socialization. In D. A. Goslin (Ed.), *Handbook of socialization theory and research* (pp. 347–480). Chicago: Rand McNally.

Kohlberg, L. (1971). From is to ought: How to commit the naturalistic fallacy and get away with it in the study of moral development. In T. Mischel (Ed.), *Psychology and genetic epistemology* (pp. 151–235). New York: Academic Press.

Kosonen, P., & Winne, P. H. (1995). Effects of teaching statistical laws on reasoning about everyday problems. *Journal of Educational Psychology, 87,* 33–46.

Kramer, D. A. (1986). Relativistic and dialectical thought in three adult age-groups. *Human Development, 29,* 280–290.

Kramer, D. A. (1990). Conceptualizing wisdom: The primacy of affect-cognition relations. In R. J. Sternberg (Ed.), *Wisdom: Its nature, origins, and development* (pp. 121–141). New York: Cambridge University Press.

Kramer, D. A. (2000). Wisdom as a classical source of human strength: Conceptualization and empirical inquiry. *Journal of Social and Clinical Psychology, 19,* 83–101.

Kruglanski, A. W. (1996). Goals as knowledge structures. In P. M. Gollwitzer (Ed.), *The psychology of action: Linking cognition and motivation to behavior* (pp. 599–618). New York: Guilford.

Labouvie-Vief, G. (1982). Dynamic development and mature autonomy: A theoretical prologue. *Human Development, 25,* 161–191.

Labouvie-Vief, G. (1990). Wisdom as integrated thought: Historical and developmental perspectives. In R. J. Sternberg (Ed.), *Wisdom: Its nature, origins, and development* (pp. 52–83). New York: Cambridge University Press.

Lehrer, K., Lum, B. J., Slichta, B. A., & Smith, N. D. (Eds.). (1996). *Knowledge, teaching and wisdom.* Dordrecht, Netherlands: Kluwer.

Lerner, R. M. (1986). *Concepts and theories of human development* (2nd ed.). New York: Random House.

Lerner, R. M. (Ed.). (1998). *The handbook of child psychology: Vol. 1. Theoretical models of human development* (5th ed.). New York: Wiley.

Maslow, A. H. (1970). *Motivation and personality.* New York: Harper and Row.

Maxwell, N. (1984). *From knowledge to wisdom.* New York: Basil Blackwell.

McAdams, D. P., & de St. Aubin, E. (Eds.). (1998). *Generativity and adult development: How and why we care for the next generation.* Washington, DC: American Psychological Association.

Nichols, R. (1996). Maxims, "practical wisdom," and the language of action. *Political Theory, 24,* 687–705.

Nisbett, R. E., Fong, G. T., Lehman, D. R., & Cheng, P. W. (1987). Teaching reasoning. *Science, 238,* 625–631.

Nisbett, R. E., Krantz, D. H., Jepson, C., & Kunda, Z. (1983). The use of statistical heuristics in everyday inductive reasoning. *Psychological Review, 90,* 339–363.

Nisbett, R. E., & Ross, L. (1980). *Human inference: Strategies and shortcomings of social judgment.* Englewood Cliffs, NJ: Prentice-Hall.

Nozick, R. (1993). *The nature of rationality.* Princeton, NJ: Princeton University Press.

Oelmüller, W. (1989). *Philosophie und Weisheit.* Paderborn: Schöningh.

Oxford Dictionary of the English Language. (1933). Vol. XII. Oxford, England: Clarendon.

Pasupathi, M., & Baltes, P. B. (in press). Wisdom. In A. E. Kazdin (Ed.), *Encyclopedia of psychology.* New York: Oxford University Press.

Pasupathi, M., Staudinger, U. M., & Baltes, P. B. (2000). *Seeds of wisdom: Adolescents' knowledge and judgment about difficult life problems.* Unpublished manuscript, Max Planck Institute for Human Development, Berlin.

Peng, K., & Nisbett, R. E. (1999). Are there cultural differences in the way people reason about contradiction? *American Psychologist, 54,* 741–754.

Perlmutter, M. (1990). *Late-life potential.* Washington, DC: Gerontological Society of America.

Piaget, J. (1932). *The moral judgment of the child.* London: Routledge and Kegan Paul.

Rice, E. F., Jr. (1958). *The renaissance idea of wisdom.* Cambridge, MA: Harvard University Press.

Rogers, C. R. (1961). *On becoming a person.* Boston: Houghton Mifflin.

Rokeach, M. (1973). *The nature of human values.* New York: Free Press.

Ross, L., & Nisbett, R. E. (1991). *The person and the situation: Perspectives of social psychology.* New York: McGraw-Hill.

Rossi, A. S. (in press). *Caring and doing for others: Social responsibility in the domains of family, work, and community.* Chicago: University of Chicago Press.

Ryan, S. (1996). Wisdom. In K. Lehrer, B. J. Lum, B. A. Slichta, & N. D. Smith (Eds.), *Knowledge, teaching and wisdom* (pp. 233–242). Dordrecht, Netherlands: Kluwer.

Ryff, C. D. (1987). The place of personality and social structure research in social psychology. *Journal of Personality and Social Psychology, 53,* 1192–1202.

Ryff, C. D. (1995). Psychological well-being in adult life. *Current Directions in Psychological Science, 4,* 99–104.

Salthouse, T. A. (1996). The processing-speed theory of adult age differences in cognition. *Psychological Review, 103,* 403–428.

Schaie, K. W. (1996). *Adult intellectual development: The Seattle Longitudinal Study.* New York: Cambridge University Press.

Schwartz, S. H. (1990). Individualism-collectivism: Critique and proposed refinements. *Journal of Cross-Cultural Psychology, 21,* 139–157.

Schwartz, S. H. (1992). Universals in the content and structure of values: Theoretical advances and empirical tests in 20 countries. In M. P. Zanna (Ed.), *Advances in Experimental Social Psychology* (Vol. 25, pp. 1–65). San Diego, CA: Academic Press.

Schwartz, S. H., & Bilsky, W. (1987). Toward a universal psychological structure of human values. *Journal of Personality and Social Psychology, 53,* 550–562.

Schwartz, S. H., & Bilsky, W. (1990). Toward a theory of the universal content and structure of values: Extensions and cross-cultural replications. *Journal of Personality and Social Psychology, 56,* 878–891.

Seligman, M. E. P., & Csikszentmihalyi, M. (2000). Positive psychology: An introduction. *American Psychologist, 55,* 5–14.

Shweder, R. A. (1991). *Thinking through cultures.* Cambridge, MA: Harvard University Press.

Simon, H. A. (1956). Rational choice and the structure of the environment. *Psychological Review, 63,* 129–138.

Simon, H. A. (1983). *Reason in human affairs.* Stanford, CA: Stanford University Press.

Singer, W. (1993). Synchronization of cortical activity and its putative role in information processing and learning. *Annual Review of Physiology, 55,* 349–374.

Singer, W. (2000). Response synchronization: A universal coding strategy for the definition of relations. In M. S. Gazzaniga (Ed.), *The new cognitive neurosciences* (2nd ed., pp. 325–338). Cambridge, MA: MIT Press.

Smith, J., & Baltes, P. B. (1990). A study of wisdom-related knowledge: Age/cohort differences in responses to life planning problems. *Developmental Psychology, 26,* 494–505.

Smith, J., Staudinger, U. M., & Baltes, P. B. (1994). Occupational settings facilitating wisdom-related knowledge: The sample case of clinical psychologists. *Journal of Consulting and Clinical Psychology, 62,* 989–999.

Sowarka, D. (1989). Weisheit und weise Personen: Common-Sense-Konzepte älterer Menschen [Wisdom and wise persons: Commonsense views from elderly people]. *Zeitschrift für Entwicklungspsychologie und Pädagogische Psychologie, 21,* 87–109.

Staudinger, U. M. (1996). Wisdom and the social-interactive foundation of the mind. In P. B. Baltes & U. M. Staudinger (Eds.), *Interactive minds: Life-span perspectives on the social foundation of cognition* (pp. 276–318). New York: Cambridge University Press.

Staudinger, U. M. (1999). Older and wiser? Integrating results from a psychological approach to the study of wisdom. *International Journal of Behavioral Development, 23,* 641–664.

Staudinger, U. M., & Baltes, P. B. (1994). Psychology of wisdom. In R. J. Sternberg (Ed.), *Encyclopedia of human intelligence* (Vol. 2, pp. 143–152). New York: Macmillan.

Staudinger, U. M., & Baltes, P. B. (1996a). Interactive minds: A facilitative setting for wisdom-related performance? *Journal of Personality and Social Psychology, 71,* 746–762.

Staudinger, U. M., & Baltes, P. B. (1996b). Weisheit als Gegenstand psychologischer Forschung. *Psychologische Rundschau, 47,* 57–77.

Staudinger, U. M., Lopez, D., & Baltes, P. B. (1997). The psychometric location of wisdom-related performance: Intelligence, personality, and more? *Personality and Social Psychology Bulletin, 23,* 1200–1214.

Staudinger, U. M., Maciel, A. G., Smith, J., & Baltes, P. B. (1998). What predicts wisdom-related performance? A first look at personality, intelligence, and facilitative experiential contexts. *European Journal of Personality, 12,* 1–17.

Staudinger, U. M., Smith, J., & Baltes, P. B. (1992). Wisdom-related knowledge in a life review task: Age differences and the role of professional specialization. *Psychology and Aging, 7,* 271–281.

Staudinger, U. M., Smith, J., & Baltes, P. B. (1994). *Manual for the assessment of wisdom-related knowledge.* Berlin: Max-Planck-Institut für Bildungsforschung.

Staudinger, U. M., Sowarka, D., Maciel, A. G., & Baltes, P. B. (1997). *Subjective theories of wisdom and the Berlin Wisdom Theory.* Unpublished manuscript, Max Planck Institute for Human Development, Berlin, Germany.

Sternberg, R. J. (1985). Implicit theories of intelligence, creativity, and wisdom. *Journal of Personality and Social Psychology, 49,* 607–627.

Sternberg, R. J. (Ed.). (1990). *Wisdom: Its nature, origins, and development.* New York: Cambridge University Press.

Sternberg, R. J. (1996). Styles of thinking. In P. B. Baltes & U. M. Staudinger (Eds.), *Interactive minds: Life-span perspectives on the social foundation of cognition* (pp. 347–365). New York: Cambridge University Press.

*Sternberg, R. J. (1998). A balance theory of wisdom. *Review of General Psychology, 2,* 347–365.

Stich, S. P. (1990). *The fragmentation of reason: Preface to a pragmatic theory of cognitive evaluation.* Cambridge, MA: MIT Press.

Tetens, J. N. (1777). *Philosophische Versuche über die menschliche Natur und ihre Entwicklung.* Leipzig, Germany: Weidmanns Erben und Reich.

Turiel, E. (1998). The development of morality. In W. Damon & N. Eisenberg (Eds.), *Handbook of child psychology: Vol. 3. Social, emotional, and personality development* (5th ed., pp. 863–932). New York: Wiley.

Welsch, W. (1995). *Vernunft: Die zeitgenössische Vernunftkritik und das Konzept der transversalen Vernunft.* Frankfurt am Main, Germany: Suhrkamp.

Willis, S. L., & Baltes, P. B. (1980). Intelligence in adulthood and aging: Contemporary issues. In L. W. Poon (Ed.), *Aging in the 1980's: Psychological issues* (pp. 260–272). Washington, DC: American Psychological Association.

V

Self-Based Approaches

25

Reality Negotiation

Raymond L. Higgins

This chapter presents an overview of the development and status of the reality negotiation construct. It relates the construct to a variety of coping processes, including contemporary models of psychotherapeutic change and the maintenance of social support systems. Following definitional, historical, and measurement sections, an overview of reality negotiation strategies precedes illustrations of the dynamically interactive nature of reality negotiation, with examples relating to coping with adversity, the individual's effects on larger social groups, and the maintenance of social support. The chapter concludes with a brief discussion of the accountability challenges faced by contemporary constructivist approaches to psychotherapy, followed by some speculations about how a culture and psychology committed to a positive view of people might facilitate peoples' movement toward self-realization.

Reality Negotiation Defined

Snyder and Higgins (1988a, 1988b) first introduced the reality negotiation construct in discussions of how excuses lessen the self-image threats associated with negative outcomes. The central focus was on how people interpret negative self-relevant events in order to preserve their positive self-theories. More recent discussions have been expanded to include reality negotiation processes that preserve or enhance *negative* self-theories in the face of positively self-discrepant information (Barone, Maddux, & Snyder, 1997; Snyder & Higgins, 1997).

The reality negotiation construct proposes that people continually appraise the extent to which they are causally linked to the results of actions and the extent to which those outcomes are positively or negatively valenced (Higgins & Leibowitz, 1999; Higgins & Snyder, 1991). This linkage-valence framework may be represented as a two-dimensional matrix wherein "linkage to outcome" (ranging from none to total) forms the x-axis and "valence of outcome" (ranging from positive to negative) forms the y-axis. As Figure 25.1 illustrates, a person's self-theory may be mapped onto this matrix according to the extent to which the self is seen as being causally linked to outcomes. Figure 25.1 illustrates an individual with a positive self-theory who tends to associate the self with positive outcomes and to disassociate the self from negative outcomes. Figure 25.2, in contrast, depicts an individual with a negative self-theory who preferentially associates the self with negative outcomes.

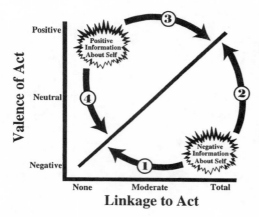

Figure 25.1 Positive-self theory on valence-of-act and linkage-to-act dimensions and the associated reality negotiation processes.

Reality negotiation *processes* sustain (or manage the rate of change in) one's self-theory by manipulating the perceived negativity or positivity of outcomes, the individual's perceived causal linkage to outcomes, or both. People with positive self-theories who are causally linked to negative acts may attempt to decrease their perceived linkage to them (see arrow 1 on Figure 25.1), to reduce the perceived negativity of those acts (see arrow 2 on Figure 25.1), or both. Similarly, people with negative self-theories who are confronted with having done something laudable may try to undercut the extent to which they are seen as causal (see arrow 1 on Figure 25.2), to lessen the perceived posi-

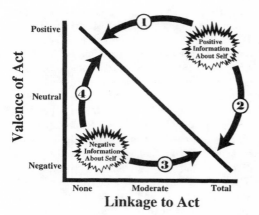

Figure 25.2 Negative-self theory on valence-of-act and linkage-to-act dimensions and the associated reality negotiation processes.

tivity of the act (see arrow 2 on Figure 25.2), or both.

Theoretically, people with positive self-theories also might want to enhance their positive status by working to increase their perceived causality for desirable outcomes (arrow 3 on Figure 25.1), or even to decrease the perceived positivity of outcomes they did not cause (arrow 4 on Figure 25.1). In a parallel fashion, people with negative self-theories may work to increase their perceived causal linkage to negative outcomes to which they are only weakly connected (see arrow 3 on Figure 25.2), or to increase the positivity of outcomes they have not authored (see arrow 4 on Figure 25.2). I will not elaborate further on reality negotiations in the service of negative self-theories in this chapter, however, because of the present emphasis on positive processes (for such discussions, see Barone et al., 1997; Snyder & Higgins, 1997).

Reality Negotiation in Context

The reality negotiation construct is part of the social constructivist tradition (Barone et al., 1997) that dates back to philosophers such as Kant (1781/1965), Hegel (1807/1967), and Vaihinger (1925). Moreover, the idea that people's social interactions are aimed at securing views of reality that preserve their "self-theories" clearly implies that the "self," itself, is a social construct. This notion, too, borrows from early expressions of self-constructive perspectives (Cooley, 1902; Mead, 1934; Piaget, 1936/1963). The roots of the reality negotiation construct also extend into those early psychotherapeutic traditions that incorporated perspectivistic and phenomenological orientations into their view of self-(re)constructive processes (e.g., Adler, 1912; Rogers, 1951).

The proximal impetus for the reality negotiation construct, however, grew out of work on the effectiveness of excuses (Higgins & Snyder, 1989; Snyder, Higgins, & Stucky, 1983). A central assumption was that excuses preserve one's positive sense of self and one's sense of being in control by reducing the perceived negativity of acts and/or by weakening the individual's perceived responsibility for them (Snyder, Higgins, & Stucky, 1983). As such, the work on excuses was based on that of earlier authors who had stressed the importance of self-esteem maintenance as a fundamental human motive (Epstein, 1973; Maslow, 1968; Rogers, 1951), as well as the scholars who had demonstrated the self-serving nature of causal attributions for positive and negative outcomes (Arkin, Cooper, & Kolditz, 1980; Miller, 1976; Zuckerman, 1979).

The negotiation aspect of the reality negotiation construct reflected the fact that excuse attributions for negative acts can be effective only when both the excuse maker *and* the target audience accept the attributions as plausible (Higgins & Snyder, 1989; Snyder & Higgins, 1988a, 1988b). The requisite "give-and-take" between the protagonist and his or her audience constitutes the negotiation. Even within solitary contexts, effective excuses require negotiation between the person and his or her *mental representations* of the judgments of important others. Epstein (1980), for example, has argued that the self "develops out of the desire of the child to gain approval and avoid disapproval" (p. 86). A sense of personal causal agency and an ability to judge the valence of one's actions in the eyes of others are fundamental not only for the individual's ability to stay on the positive side of the approval-disapproval continuum but also for the consolidation of such self-related schemata as "self-theories" (Barone et al., 1997; Higgins & Snyder, 1991; Snyder & Higgins, 1997). The term *revolving self-images* (Snyder, Higgins, & Stucky, 1983, p. 38) was coined to acknowledge that people's self-image concerns necessarily reflect the values of their role models and caregivers and that, therefore, even internal appraisal processes involve a fusion of internal and external audience concerns.

Given its focus on excuses, early thinking about reality negotiation emphasized shifting causal attributions for *negative* outcomes from "sources that are relatively more central to the person's sense of self to sources that are relatively less central" (Snyder & Higgins, 1988b, p. 23). This definition explicitly incorporated only a (causal) linkage dimension. The valence dimension was first introduced when Snyder (1989) presented the construct of "hoping." Whereas excuses weaken causal linkages to negative outcomes or decrease their perceived negativity, hoping was conceived as a process of increasing causal linkages to *positive* outcomes. The valence-linkage matrix, therefore, contrasted the excusing and hoping processes, and the reality negotiation construct became one that emphasized self-esteem enhancement as well as self-esteem maintenance.

Individual Differences in Reality Negotiation

Any measure that references standards of performance, values, causal attributions, or perceived control potentially relates to individual differences in reality negotiation. A few measures, however, have been directly associated with reality negotiation tendencies. The Self-Handicapping Scale (Jones & Rhodewalt, 1982; Strube, 1985), a measure of anticipatory excuse making, for example, stands out as an index that is related directly to the preferential use of linkage-weakening reality negotiation tactics (see Rhodewalt, 1990, for review).

Measures of self-esteem also have been related to differences in reality negotiation. Varying levels of self-esteem have been shown to relate to the use of downward social comparison (a valence-shifting tactic; Aspinwall & Taylor, 1993); to differences in the use of self-enhancement (linkage-shifting) strategies (Baumeister, Tice, & Hutton, 1989); and to differences in excuse-making behavior (Tice & Baumeister, 1984). Differences in self-handicapping also have been shown to vary as a function of high versus low uncertainty about one's self-esteem (Harris & Snyder, 1986).

Measures of depression also appear to be related to reality negotiation. Individuals who score high on measures of depression, for example, are prone to making internalizing (linkage-increasing) rather than externalizing (linkage-weakening) attributions for negative events (for review, see Burns & Seligman, 1991). Relatedly, there is evidence that dispositional (linkage-increasing) attributions for failure are more typical of depression than are attributions to personal behaviors (Anderson, Miller, Riger, Dill, & Sedikides, 1994). Both dispositional and behavioral attributions are to "internal" sources, but dispositions are more likely than specific behaviors to lie close to one's "core" sense of self (see also Janoff-Bulman, 1979).

To date, only four individual differences measures have been developed specifically to tap reality negotiation tendencies. Previously, I pointed out that Snyder's (1989) article introducing his concept of "hope" also introduced a valence dimension into the linkage-valence matrix. Subsequently, both trait (Snyder, Harris et al., 1991), and state (Snyder et al., 1996) versions of the Hope Scale have been developed. These scales tap individuals' motivation and perceived ability to achieve desired goals and show modest positive correlations with a wide array of indices related to self-presentation, coping, and health (for reviews, see Barone et al., 1997, pp. 266–268; Snyder, 1994; Snyder, Cheavens, & Michael, 1999; Snyder, Irving, & Anderson, 1991). Hope also has been posited to underlie the capacity for positive psychological change (Snyder, Ilardi, Michael, & Cheavens, 2000). The items from these adult-oriented scales also have been adapted for use with children. The Children's Hope Scale (Snyder et al., 1997) has been shown to have robust psychometric properties, as well as both convergent and discriminant validity.

The fourth and only theory-derived measure specifically designed to assess reality negotiation proclivities is the Linkage Into Valenced Elements Scale (LIVE; Snyder & Samuelson, 1998). The LIVE items sample from eight life arenas (i.e., appearance, health, intelligence, school, job, leisure, personality, and relationships) and refer to both positive characteristics (e.g., "superior intellectual abilities") and negative characteristics (e.g., "very poor academic performance"). Respondents use 9-point rating scales (1 = "not at all" to 9 = "totally") to indicate the extent to which they view themselves as causally linked to the outcomes represented in the items. At present, there are no published data relating to the validity or psychometric properties of the LIVE Scale. Samuelson (1996), however, tested an earlier, 80-item version of the scale with college students and found support for its construct validity, including a positive correlation with the trait version of the Hope Scale.

Reality Negotiation: An Overview

This section will survey those reality negotiation strategies that assist the individual in maintaining a positive sense of self in the face of negatively discrepant information.

Reality Negotiation as an Automatic Process

Reality negotiation processes are often automatic and "unconscious" in the sense that the individual may be unaware of the self-serving nature of his or her appraisals (Higgins & Snyder, 1989). Particular contexts activate correspondingly relevant self-schemas and render certain kinds of information more expected and

more easily recognized (Bargh & Pratto, 1986; Markus & Wurf, 1987), as well as more readily recalled (Higgins, King, & Mavin, 1982). Assuming the individual detects no significant discrepancy with his or her self-schema, incoming information is likely to simply confirm expectations (Higgins, 1989; Jones, 1990) and is unlikely to stimulate effortful, conscious processing.

Actively conscious processing, for purposes of comprehension and responding, becomes more likely as self-relevant information becomes increasingly unexpected or schema-discrepant (Hastie, 1984; Pyszczynski & Greenberg, 1981). The need to deal with external witnesses to schema-discrepant information also may push the individual's reality negotiation into awareness (Higgins & Snyder, 1989; Snyder & Higgins, 1988a, 1988b).

Linkage-Focused Reality Negotiation

As noted previously, excuses are strategies for preserving positive self-theories either by decreasing the perceived negativity of outcomes or by shifting causal attributions away from the individual's core sense of self (e.g., his or her sense of being a "good" or competent person). Effective excuses, then, weaken linkages to negative outcomes (see arrow 1 in Figure 25.1). Some excuses (e.g., denial) attempt to completely sever causal linkages. Most excuses, however, aim to *shift* causal attributions from one internal source to another, less central, internal source rather than to completely externalize and sever them. Many of these excuses can be understood from the perspective provided by Kelley's (1967, 1971) theory of attribution.

Consistency-lowering excuses, for example, may frustrate disposition-based causal attributions by implicating lack of effort (Miller, 1976), lack of intention (Rotenberg, 1980), or unforeseeable consequences. Other linkage-shifting tactics such as *consensus-raising* excuses also deflect dispositional attributions by elevating the importance of situational causes (e.g., task difficulty, bad luck) over personal causes (e.g., ability) in determining outcomes. Both consistency-lowering and consensus-raising excuses weaken but do not sever the individual's causal linkage to the outcomes (Miller, 1976; Zuckerman, 1979).

Kelley's attribution principles also apply to anticipatory excuses. For example, a person may set up a consistency-lowering excuse by failing to prepare for an evaluation. Similarly, an individual might contrive a consensus-raising excuse by pronouncing an upcoming task too difficult and, therefore, unfair (Smith, Snyder, & Handelsman, 1982). Such "self-handicapping" strategies (Berglas & Jones, 1978; Jones & Berglas, 1978) capitalize on Kelley's (1971) *discounting* principle. Namely, when outcomes are associated with more than one possible cause, the resulting confusion both obfuscates and weakens the attribution of causality to any one cause. If a person is evaluated while intoxicated, for example, it is difficult to clearly ascribe a subsequent failure to incompetence. Theoretically, self-handicaps also may capitalize on Kelley's (1971) principle of *augmentation*. In other words, when an individual succeeds despite being handicapped, attributions to ability may actually be enhanced (for more on self-handicapping, see Higgins, Snyder, & Berglas, 1990).

Many potential self-handicaps are temporary (e.g., intoxication, fatigue). Others, such as test anxiety (Smith et al., 1982), hypochondriasis (Smith, Snyder, & Perkins, 1983), or shyness (Snyder, Smith, Augelli, & Ingram, 1983), to name but a few, may constitute enduring characteristics of the individual. Although focusing causal attributions on one's negative dispositional characteristics would seem incompatible with preserving one's positive self-theories, doing so may actually be quite effective—if the dispositional characteristic is less central to the individual's core sense of self than is the threatened self-attribute. Threats to one's basic sense of competence, for example, may be thwarted by claiming to suffer from some relevant form of performance anxiety. See, however, Higgins and Snyder (1989) and Snyder and Higgins (1988c) for discussions of the potential drawbacks of such "incorporated" excuses.

Valence-Focused Reality Negotiation

In contrast to reality negotiation strategies that target causality, valence-shifting strategies aim to yield more positive (or, at least, less negative) views of threatening outcomes (see arrow 2 in Figure 25.1). One valence-shifting strategy, for example, is to discredit the source of threatening information (Aronson & Worchel, 1966; Clair & Snyder, 1979). Blaming victims (e.g., "She got what she deserved") or invoking exonerative moral reasoning (e.g., "It was for her own good"; "It would have been even more hurtful to tell the truth") also may soften the

perceived negativity of an act (Lerner, 1980). Similarly, direct attempts to minimize the negativity of outcomes (e.g., "It's not as bad as it looks"; Snyder, Irving, Sigmon, & Holleran, 1992) or to redefine them (e.g., "lies" become "white lies," emotional abuse or neglect becomes "tough love") also may be effective in negotiating more benign views of image-threatening outcomes.

Yet another valence-shifting tactic is to find meaning in an adverse outcome. An illness or disability, for instance, may wreak havoc with an individual's sense of being a "good and in-control" person. Finding the silver lining in the dark cloud, as in finding hidden benefits or "meaning" in one's malady, however, may help restore individuals' positive sense of themselves (see Tennen & Affleck, this volume; Nolen-Hoeksema & Davis, this volume).

Reality Negotiation as Coping

The view that reality negotiation enables people to sustain their self-theories in the face of disconfirming information suggests that, to some extent, adaptive or healthy self-theories are *illusional*. A major coping function associated with reality negotiation, then, is sustaining those adaptive advantages associated with positive self-illusions (see, for reviews, Brown, 1991; Taylor & Brown, 1988). Such advantages include the positive effects of perceived control on affect (Dunn & Wilson, 1990), health (Schulz, 1976), task persistence (Bandura, 1989), performance (Dweck & Leggett, 1988), and psychological well-being (Alloy & Abramson, 1988).

Although it seems counterintuitive, reality negotiation mechanisms that support *negative* self-illusions also may be adaptive at times. Brown and McGill (1989), for example, found that ostensibly desirable life changes were associated with increased illness among individuals with low self-esteem but with decreased illness among individuals with high self-esteem. Presumably, positive changes were stressful for the low-esteem individuals because they resulted in some degree of identity disruption. In fact, the idea that the stressfulness of an event is more related to the degree to which it demands personal redefinition than to its objective negativity finds support in studies reported by Swann (Swann, Hixon, & De La Ronde, 1992; Swann, Wenzlaff, Krull, & Pelham, 1992) and Hammen, Marks, Mayol, and DeMayo (1985), all of which point to the importance of self-consistency or self-verification in people's efforts to maintain a sense of predictability and control (see Swann & Pelham, this volume).

Although the preceding remarks emphasize reality negotiation's role in promoting self-theory stability, it would be erroneous to conclude that the essential aim of the process is stasis. Rather, it is to manage the pace and flow of self-theory change. Indeed, it is this rate-limiting aspect that renders reality negotiation fundamental to our efforts to cope with the implications of growth-promoting change as well as with adversity. As stated by Higgins and Leibowitz (1999), reality negotiation "aids in coping, *not because the resulting products are inherently self-enhancing or self-verifying, but rather because the individual experiences a degree of control over the self-definitional implications of the person-data transaction*" (p. 30). People must change and adapt as they traverse their lives. In doing so, however, it is important that they maintain a continuous and integrated sense of self. It is the self-constructive process of negotiating reality that makes it possible to unfold our lives in an orderly manner.

Reality Negotiation: Who Controls the Process?

Earlier discussions of reality negotiation acknowledged the role of external audiences in the process but focused primarily on the individual's image maintenance aims. Recently, however, a more dynamically interactive vision of reality negotiation has emerged (Higgins & Leibowitz, 1999; Snyder & Higgins, 1997). Snyder and Higgins (1997), for example, proposed that social groups, primarily through such socialization agents as parents, encourage individuals to adopt and sustain self-theories that complement and support the larger social interests. Higgins and Leibowitz (1999) extended this analysis to include the idea that, through their control of material and social support resources, social groups or agents reward and shape the individual's interpretations of reality so as to advance *the social agents'* image maintenance goals. A social agent's standing as a "good parent," for example, is related to the extent to which his or her children embody culturally favored values. Also, a school system's stature in the community is proportional to the extent to which its students embrace the virtues of scholarship and studiousness. Naturally, such perspectives raise interesting questions about who ultimately controls the direction and outcome of the reality negotiation process. Is it the individual, or is it the social group with which the individual identifies and traffics?

The answer is both. Through their roles as socializing agents, and through their control over material rewards and social support resources, representatives of society at large, as well as more narrowly focused interest groups, encourage individuals to affiliate with group-approved goal and value structures. Moreover, to the extent that the individual's sense of self is constructed from the reflected appraisals of important others (e.g., Markus & Cross, 1990), societal agents shape the very content of individuals' self-theories along with the parameters of those things they experience as self-theory discrepant. Relatedly, group memberships provide frames of reference from which to evaluate "reality," not to mention standards of performance with which to assess the "goodness" or "badness" of outcomes. Social groups also influence the reality negotiation process through their role as audiences or judges of the acceptability of an individual's interpretation of events. Through their mere presence, for example, audiences may foreclose on an individual's ability to engage in automatic, unconscious processing of outcomes and, in doing so, necessitate a more overt, conscious, and occasionally conflictual negotiation of the meanings that are to be attached to those outcomes. In keeping with the perspective that reality negotiation is dynamically interactive, however, it is important to recognize that the individual also influences society's participation in the enterprise. Among other things, it often happens that an individual's actions have implications for an audience's image or collective "self-theory." Consequently, audiences frequently have a direct interest in shaping how an individual's actions are construed.

Through either their own or others' initiative, individuals affiliate with groups or individuals whom they perceive as serving their self-definitional interests. Once established, these identifications endow such groups with vested interests in the individual's outcomes, and vice versa. This easily can be seen in close or intimate relationships (e.g., marriages), where one individual's outcomes, in essence, become community property. In such instances, partners may have strong needs to promote similar views of reality. Each partner has individual image concerns, but those concerns may converge in a group identity. For example, one child-abusing spouse's acts of brutality may be defined by both spouses as "tough love" in order to affirm (or not threaten) the nonabusing spouse's self-theory of being a loving and protective parent. Group investment in the definition of individual outcomes, however, extends well beyond the arena of intimate relationships. The currently converging issues of gun control and school violence provide a timely example.

There have been many instances in recent years in which seemingly senseless acts of violence by deranged or disenfranchised individuals have so threatened the images of particular interest groups that massive lobbying and public relations campaigns have been launched to promote self-serving views of those events. For example, the violent acts of adolescent or even preadolescent children have provoked the National Rifle Association (NRA) to point the finger of causation away from the problem of proliferating gun availability. Instead of guns, they blame the government's lax enforcement of existing gun laws, the specter of creeping moral decay within society, the lack of state-sanctioned prayer in public schools, and the U.S. Supreme Court's refusal to allow the Ten Commandments to be posted in school hallways. In fact, anything that serves to shift causal attributions away from gun availability or ownership is fair game. In a remarkable March 12, 2000, television interview, NRA spokesperson, Wayne LaPierre, accused the president of the United States of covertly wishing for and encouraging schoolyard gun mayhem because it served his antigun policy ends. This episode is remarkable not only because LaPierre's accusation attempted to shift the blame to an evil, scheming president but also because it tried to recast the NRA as the *victim* of the very gun violence others accused it of abetting. Such linkage-shifting tactics differ only in scope from those used by individuals to put the best face on a personal dilemma. Moreover, the tactics are not restricted to linkage-shifting.

The NRA and related groups also embrace valence-shifting strategies. Nobody, of course, argues that the victims of high school or grade school shootings "had it coming." Rather, the sanctity of the Second Amendment to the Constitution of the United States is invoked to counter any suggestions that widespread gun availability is problematic. According to this logic, gun availability is both good and, as a founding principle of the Bill of Rights, an essential guarantor of our civil freedoms. Similarly, when Wayne LaPierre's accusation of President Clinton was labeled as extremist and irresponsible, other NRA supporters countered that, in view of Clinton's ethical shortcomings (e.g., the Monica Lewinsky affair), such Machiavellian scheming would not be out of character for him (i.e., they proffered a dispositional attribution). Far from accepting the premise that gun availability is a problem, a few gun advocates have even argued that the real problem with schoolyard violence is that *there are not enough guns.* They reasoned that gun-wielding, grade school miscreants would think twice about opening fire if they thought that their teachers and principals also might be "packing heat" and prepared to shoot back. This particular valence-shifting tactic, however, met with such widespread incredulity that it has largely disappeared from public negotiations over how gun violence in the schools is to be viewed.

Such instances of reality negotiation aimed at alleviating threats to group image clearly illustrate the interplay between individual and group identities. Another arena, that of coping with serious health problems, also can be used to illustrate the workings of reality negotiation between protagonists and their audiences. For the present purposes, the specific focus will be on the dynamics of sustaining social support resources when faced with health problems.

Reality Negotiation and Social Support

When people are faced with illness or disability, they commonly respond by searching for the cause or causes of their suffering (Taylor, 1983). Often, the causes that are identified appear to further coping by preserving the individual's sense of being in control (Higgins & Snyder, 1991). Investigators, for example, have found *self-blame* to be associated with better adjustment to such health threats as spinal cord injury (Bulman & Wortman, 1977), breast cancer (Timko & Janoff-Bulman, 1985), and renal failure (Witenberg et al., 1983). It also appears, however, that the causes that individuals identify may help them maintain their relationships with important people in their social environments (Higgins & Leibowitz, 1999).

Because of their dependence on others for both material and emotional support, the victims of illness or disability need to sustain their social networks. They may be especially dependent on others for both material and emotional support. Consequently, in negotiating a consensual view of their health dilemmas, such individuals must accommodate their audiences' emotional needs to distance themselves from similar fates. When faced with people who have experienced health calamities, for example, external audiences often experience vicarious threat (Silver, Wortman, & Crofton, 1990) and engage in defensive attributional distortions (e.g., the victim deserved what he or she got) in order to preserve their beliefs that they can avoid similar fates (Shaver, 1970). In such contexts, individuals who blame themselves for their suffering not only may bolster their own sense of control but they also honor their fellow travelers' need to feel in control of *their* own destinies.

According to the literature on social reactions to victimization, however, self-blame sometimes may disrupt rather than sustain ties to important social support resources. Compared with those who are not seen as responsible, sufferers who are seen as responsible for their conditions may experience more negative social reactions (Herbert & Dunkel-Schetter, 1992). Indeed, this double-edged quality of self-blame may partially account for the inconsistent relationship that has sometimes been observed between self-blame and adaptation (Bulman & Wortman, 1977). It also may help explain why attributions regarding initial causation appear to fade in relevance to sufferers as other factors such as friends and material resources increase in importance over time (Schulz & Decker, 1985). In effect, it appears that people shift from negotiating a relationship with an initial trauma (or diagnosis) to negotiating a relationship with ongoing demands of living that require the individual to sustain or strengthen ties to the community. This, in turn, requires sufferers to negotiate meanings (valences) related to their disorders that acknowledge the needs of those important others in the social environment.

The idea that finding positive meaning in suffering may have long-term emotional or coping benefits is not new. The Greek philosopher Epictetus (ca. A.D. 60–120), for example, wrote that people are less disturbed by things than by their views of those things. More recently, benefit finding has been shown to aid in coping with such problems as myocardial infarction (Affleck, Tennen, Croog, & Levine, 1987), amputation (Dunn, 1996), breast cancer (Taylor, Lichtman, & Wood, 1984), and rheumatoid arthritis (Tennen, Affleck, Urrows, Higgins, & Mendola,

1992; also see Tennen & Affleck, this volume; Nolen-Hoeksema & Davis, this volume.) Higgins and Leibowitz (1999) speculate that such benefit finding (valence negotiation) may aid coping by securing the sufferer's access to social support resources.

Economic models of social support are based on the equitable exchange of resources. Ill or disabled individuals often are likely to be involved in objectively inequitable exchanges, and yet they frequently continue to elicit social support (Antonucci & Jackson, 1990). Higgins and Leibowitz (1999) argued that a reality negotiation perspective may help explain such findings by implicating ways in which the ill or disabled *are* positioned to contribute to relationships. These authors suggested "that those (ostensibly *individual*) coping strategies that aid adaptation via maintaining access to social support resources are those that also address the needs of the support providers and, therefore, form a sort of currency of exchange" (p. 36). One need of social support providers, of course, is to be perceived as being helpful or supportive. Accordingly, Silver et al. (1990) observed that helpers who are not rewarded by improvement in those they are helping react negatively and withdraw. Among physically ill or disabled individuals, it is those who negotiate a view of their helper's efforts as "helpful" who are likely to receive continuing support.

Yet another need of social support providers is to have their own personal illusions of control affirmed. A sufferer's self-blame, for example, may bolster the audience's sense of being in control of its own fate. Similarly, through finding such benefits as meaning, spiritual enlightenment, or renewed purpose in their suffering, ill or disabled individuals may detoxify the audience's assessment of the patients' condition. Thus, the social audience's anxieties about its own vulnerability are alleviated. In effect, the reality negotiation perspective suggests that sufferers preserve their access to social support resources by engaging in a series of transactions that lead to a more positive (or more benign) view of the sufferer's reality.

There are, of course, limits on the extent to which a sufferer may benefit through striking such "bargains." Those limits illustrate the sometimes delicate balance being sought in negotiating a consensual view of reality. Sufferers who convey either too little or too much distress are likely to lose social support. Schreurs and de Ridder (1997), for example, argued that both "good" and "bad" copers experience reduced support. For good copers, the reduction stems from insufficient communication of need. For bad copers, the reduction stems from the support providers' overwhelming experience of vicarious threat and feelings of helplessness at being unable to alleviate the target's suffering. Optimal levels of social support, in this view of things, are bestowed upon "balanced" copers.

It is noteworthy that such social support dynamics also are played out in professional helping relationships. In a discussion of reality negotiation within nursing settings, for example, Ersek (1992) addressed problems that arise when seriously ill patients hold unrealistically hopeful beliefs about their conditions. In essence, Ersek described a process of professional nurses becoming alienated from their patients when the patients are unwilling to adopt a "realistic" (from the nurses' perspective) outlook on their illnesses. In fact, Ersek argues that, in order to maintain nurses' ability to continue providing effective and professional services in such cases, it may be critical for health care institutions to step in and endorse the nurses' view of their patients' reality. The institutions, in such instances, serve as surrogates for the patients in the negotiation of a reality that enables the nurses to maintain their equilibrium in a helping role.

Reality Negotiation and Professional Accountability

Ersek's comments about professional nurses do more than simply illustrate the social forces that rein in intemperate views and the social disruptions that attend failures to achieve an accommodation of perspectives. They also raise issues at the growing edge of the reality negotiation construct. Are there limits, other than those imposed by the physical laws of nature, on the extent to which "reality" can or should be socially constructed? (The reader is encouraged to see Baumeister [1989] for some thoughtful observations concerning a related question.) A second question, and the one of primary interest here, is what is the proper role of health professionals in guiding or constraining their clients' construing? Health care providers may be uniquely positioned to promote integration, growth, and maturation through self-theory changes in their clients. Conversely, they may be uniquely positioned to promote harmful

changes. In view of the thesis that social audiences are influential protagonists in reality negotiations, it follows that professional helpers operate under powerful ethical and moral imperatives. The focus of the present section will be on presenting a reality negotiation perspective on professional accountability within those uniquely formal yet intimate relationships in which the objective is for one individual to help another to change.

A logical place to focus a discussion of professional accountability in reality negotiation is on those psychotherapy approaches that are rooted in constructivist philosophy. All psychotherapeutic relationships involve reality negotiation, and constructivist therapies have been practiced since early in the 20th century (Adler, 1912). The past two decades, however, have seen a particularly active development of approaches that are direct outgrowths of constructivist perspectives. Neimeyer and Stewart (2000), in their overview of such therapies, define psychotherapy, from a constructivist perspective, "as the variegated and subtle interchange and *negotiation* of (inter)personal meanings in the service of articulating, elaborating, and revising those constructions that the client uses to organize her or his experience and actions" (p. 341, emphasis added). One can easily interpolate into this definition the machinations of the linkage-valence matrix wherein the individual works to recast his or her relationship to elements that lie both within and without the self.

None of the various "schools" of psychotherapy is immune to unethical or incompetent practitioners. To a considerable extent, however, each school may be said to be uniquely vulnerable precisely in those areas it defines as critical to its expert execution. Approaches that rely on therapists' interpretative divination would appear to be especially vulnerable to diviners of unreliable or invalid interpretations. Approaches that cast the therapist as a "medical" practitioner whose principal task is to diagnose "mental illnesses" and apply appropriate medical treatments to them are vulnerable to both unskilled diagnosticians and the inadequacies of our current nosology of mental disorders (see Maddux, this volume). Approaches that purport to assist others in negotiating new and more liberating constructions of themselves and their worlds are especially vulnerable to the conscious and unconscious biases of their practitioners. They also are subject to criticisms that their effectiveness is difficult to establish using scientific methods because the outcomes of their treatments are so idiosyncratic.

One does not have to search far to find evidence that subtle therapist bias and suggestion can profoundly influence clients' sense of self, as well as their view of external reality. Nicholas Spanos, for example, within the context of hypnotic regression research, found that simple statements that reincarnation was scientifically defensible led participants to believe more strongly in the past-life identities they subsequently enacted than did participants who were told that past-life identities were merely interesting fantasies (Spanos, Menary, Gabora, DuBreuil, & Dewhirst, 1991). Spanos also demonstrated that subtle suggestions embedded within simulated "hypnotic" interviews routinely resulted in the emergence of alter identities similar to those associated with multiple personality disorder (MPD; Spanos, Weekes, Menary, & Bertrand, 1986). Kohlenberg (1973) demonstrated that personality alters in a clinical case of MPD waxed and waned depending on the amount of attention they were given. Add to this documented cases of iatrogenic MPD (e.g., Belluck, 1997) and the well-known problem of false memories associated with therapeutic suggestion (Loftus & Ketcham, 1994), and there is ample reason for constructivist or "narrative" therapists to carefully monitor their role in the (co)authorship of their clients' realities.

Although negotiated "realities" that purport to explain physical or emotional symptoms by invoking satanic ritual abuse or unresolved difficulties from previous existences are dramatic and, thankfully, relatively uncommon, they do occur. Moreover, from a constructivist perspective, it must be acknowledged that these, as well as the vast array of more mundane and commonplace therapeutic resolutions, are but a sampling of the available possibilities. According to Neimeyer and Stewart (2000), fruitful therapeutic encounters must entail the development of a shared epistemology that is unique to the relationship and "is irreducible to the individual systems of either partner in the therapeutic relationship" (p. 342). This posture bespeaks an absence of external guidelines for judging the success of psychotherapy and poses a daunting challenge for constructivist therapists to establish *standards* of accountability within their relativistic framework.

New Directions

Throughout this chapter, the emphasis has been on expanding the scope of the reality negotiation construct beyond the intrapersonal level to include interpersonal and intergroup vantage points. In keeping with this expansive motif, this discussion of new directions will highlight societal and cultural perspectives. This seems a natural progression, given the current volume's commitment to articulating a positive vision of psychology to contrast with the more traditional deficit, weakness, or illness models that so often dominate the psychological and, especially, psychiatric landscapes (see Maddux, this volume). The central question to be raised in this final section is this: Would the evolution of our culture into one committed to the principles of secular humanism, and the corresponding evolution of the science of psychology into one committed to the positive pursuit of human potential (see Seligman, this volume) bring fundamental changes to the dynamics of reality negotiations between individuals and the agents of society?

Freudianism, with its emphasis on unconscious, antisocial instincts, and Judeo-Christian theology, with its emphasis on the inherent (original) sinfulness of humanity, have been dominant influences in shaping American culture and Western thinking about human nature. Despite the fundamental antipathy of these two traditions on some levels, they share an underlying pessimism about the ability of people to transcend their (presumed) base nature. For one, "salvation" entails coming to terms with the onerous truth. For the other, it comes only through divine forgiveness. Biological psychiatry, another major player in the American cultural scene, also has located the source of human difficulties within the individual in the form of illnesses or disorders. Here, too, the individual is essentially helpless to rise above his or her (biomechanical) essence, and salvation comes in the form of "medical" interventions (e.g., drugs).

Together, these (and related) traditions have promulgated a Western worldview that largely explains social and emotional difficulties by emphasizing the flaws or deficits *within* people. Stated in terms that are consonant with the aims of this chapter, these traditions have negotiated a view of reality that locates the causes of social and personal ills within the most negatively affected individuals. Higgins and Snyder (1989) discussed the seductive pull such a worldview has on individuals who are confronted with chronic failure or difficulty in measuring up to accepted standards of performance. Acquiescing to the illness model of their problem, for example, absolves them of any *intentional* shortcoming and largely avoids attributions to basic competence. On the other hand, it may entail accepting enduring psychiatric labels and, possibly, some loss of freedom. *A related consequence is that society is largely excused from any need to reform.*

Framed within the terms associated with the linkage-valence matrix described previously, as long as the dominant worldview identifies the source of social or personal disruptions as defects or flaws within people, the emphasis will be on individuals' attempting to distance (unlink) themselves from negative outcomes, with "society" passing judgment on their efforts. The question posed at the beginning of this section, however, was whether a culture and a science of psychology committed to the principles of secular humanism would bring fundamental changes to the dynamics of reality negotiations between individuals and the agents of society.

Logic would suggest that a view of people as inherently positive and capable of self-realization would necessarily alter the dynamics of reality negotiations. Negotiations around how social disruptions or individual failings were to be viewed, for example, would tend not to focus primarily on troublesome dispositional elements within human nature. Rather, the negotiations would most likely begin with the underlying assumption that there are elements within culture, society, specific situations, or the individuals' learning histories that constrained them from effectively or adequately manifesting their positive natures. It should be noted that these are the very views of reality that individuals operating within the existing worldview typically seek to negotiate when confronted with their authorship of negative outcomes. In this latter context, they are the sought-after end points of reality negotiations aimed at excusing flaws. Within the former context of a worldview dominated by a positive view of people, however, such understandings would form the foundation for reality negotiations that aim at identifying strengths and building upon assets.

In language that is grounded in the reality negotiation linkage-valence matrix, a culture and psychology committed to a positive view of people and to a belief in their capacity for self-realization would tilt the reality negotiation process more in the direction of "hoping" and away from excusing. In other words, the focus would shift away from unlinking people from negative outcomes toward linking them to positive goals (see Snyder, Rand, & Sigmon, this volume). The "balance of power" between society and individuals would not change in the sense that both would remain fundamental to the process of generating a consensual view of events and of the world. People would, however, largely be freed from efforts to maintain their integrity in the face of challenges to their being "good and in-control," and *a need for societal as opposed to individual reforms would be more likely to emerge from the negotiations.* Certainly, an underlying belief in the positive nature of people would facilitate the likelihood of their self-realization. The positive psychology movement is a helpful force in advancing the negotiations in this direction.

References

Adler, A. (1912). *The neurotic constitution: Outline of a comparative individualistic psychology and psychotherapy.* New York: Moffat.

Affleck, G., Tennen, H., Croog, S., & Levine, S. (1987). Causal attribution, perceived benefits, and morbidity after a heart attack: An 8-year study. *Journal of Consulting and Clinical Psychology, 55,* 29–35.

Alloy, L. B., & Abramson, L. Y. (1988). Depressive realism: Four theoretical perspectives. In L. B. Alloy (Ed.), *Cognitive processes in depression* (pp. 223–265). New York: Guilford.

Anderson, C. A., Miller, R. S., Riger, A. L., Dill, J. C., & Sedikides, C. (1994). Behavioral and characterological attributional styles as predictors of depression and loneliness: Review, refinement, and test. *Journal of Personality and Social Psychology, 66,* 549–558.

Antonucci, T. C., & Jackson, J. S. (1990). The role of reciprocity in social support. In B. R. Sarason, I. G. Sarason, & G. R. Pierce (Eds.), *Social support: An interactional view* (pp. 173–189). New York: Wiley.

Arkin, R. M., Cooper, H., & Kolditz, T. (1980). A statistical review of the literature concerning the self-serving attribution bias in interpersonal influence situations. *Journal of Personality, 48,* 435–448.

Aronson, E., & Worchel, P. (1966). Similarity vs. liking as determinants of interpersonal attractiveness. *Psychonomic Science, 5,* 157–158.

Aspinwall, L. G., & Taylor, S. E. (1993). Effects of social comparison direction, threat, and self-esteem on affect, self-evaluation, and expected success. *Journal of Personality and Social Psychology, 64,* 708–722.

Bandura, A. (1989). Self-regulation of motivation and action through internal standards and goal systems. In L. Pervin (Ed.), *Goal concepts in personality and social psychology* (pp. 19–86). Hillsdale, NJ: Erlbaum.

Bargh, J. A., & Pratto, F. (1986). Individual construct accessibility and perceptual selection. *Journal of Experimental Social Psychology, 22,* 293–311.

Barone, D. F., Maddux, J. E., & Snyder, C. R. (1997). *Social cognitive psychology: History and current domains.* New York: Plenum.

Baumeister, R. F. (1989). The optimal margin of illusion. *Journal of Social and Clinical Psychology, 8,* 176–189.

Baumeister, R. F., Tice, D. M., & Hutton, D. G. (1989). Self-presentational motivations and personality differences in self-esteem. *Journal of Personality, 57,* 547–579.

Belluck, P. (1997, November 6). "Memory" therapy leads to a lawsuit and big settlement. *New York Times,* section A, pp. A1, A10.

Berglas, S., & Jones, E. E. (1978). Drug choice as a self-handicapping strategy in response to non-contingent success. *Journal of Personality and Social Psychology, 36,* 405–417.

Brown, J. D. (1991). Accuracy and bias in self-knowledge. In C. R. Snyder & D. R. Forsyth (Eds.), *Handbook of social and clinical psychology: The health perspective* (pp. 158–178). New York: Pergamon.

Brown, J. D., & McGill, K. L. (1989). The cost of good fortune: When positive life events produce negative health consequences. *Journal of Personality and Social Psychology, 57,* 1103–1110.

Bulman, R. J., & Wortman, C. B. (1977). Attributions of blame and coping in the "real world": Severe accident victims react to their lot. *Journal of Personality and Social Psychology, 35,* 351–363.

Burns, M. O., & Seligman, M. E. P. (1991). Explanatory style, helplessness, and depression. In C. R. Snyder & D. R. Forsyth (Eds.), *Handbook of social and clinical psychology: The health perspective* (pp. 267–284). New York: Pergamon.

Clair, M. S., & Snyder, C. R. (1979). Effects of instructor-delivered sequential evaluative feedback upon students' subsequent classroom-related performance and instructor ratings. *Journal of Educational Psychology, 71,* 50–57.

Cooley, C. H. (1902). *Human nature and the social order.* New York: Scribner.

Dunn, D. S. (1996). Well-being following amputation: Salutary effects of positive meaning, optimism, and control. *Rehabilitation Psychology, 41,* 285–302.

Dunn, D. S., & Wilson, T. D. (1990). When the stakes are high: A limit to the illusion-of-control effect. *Social Cognition, 8,* 305–323.

Dweck, C. S., & Leggett, E. L. (1988). A social-cognitive approach to personality and motivation. *Psychological Review, 95,* 256–273.

Epstein, S. (1973). The self-concept revisited: Or a theory of a theory. *American Psychologist, 28,* 404–416.

Epstein, S. (1980). The self-concept: A review and the proposal of an integrated theory of personality. In E. Staub (Ed.), *Personality: Basic issues and current research* (pp. 82–132). Englewood Cliffs, NJ: Prentice-Hall.

Ersek, M. (1992). Examining the process and dilemmas of reality negotiation. *IMAGE: Journal of Nursing Scholarship, 24,* 19–25.

Hammen, C. L., Marks, T., Mayol, A., & DeMayo, A. R. (1985). Depressive self-schemas, life stress, and vulnerability to depression. *Journal of Abnormal Psychology, 94,* 308–319.

Harris, R. N., & Snyder, C. R. (1986). The role of uncertain self-esteem in self-handicapping. *Journal of Personality and Social Psychology, 51,* 451–458.

Hastie, R. (1984). Causes and effects of causal attribution. *Journal of Personality and Social Psychology, 46,* 44–56.

Hegel, G. W. (1967). *The phenomenology of mind* (J. B. Baillie, Trans.). New York: Harper and Row. (Original work published 1807)

Herbert, T. B., & Dunkel-Schetter, C. (1992). Negative social reactions to victims: An overview of responses and their determinants. In L. Montada, S-H. Filipp, & M. J. Lerner (Eds.), *Life crises and experiences of loss in adulthood* (pp. 497–518). Hillsdale, NJ: Erlbaum.

Higgins, E. T. (1989). Knowledge accessibility and activation: Subjectivity and suffering from unconscious sources. In J. S. Uleman & J. A. Bargh (Eds.), *Unintended thought: Limits of awareness, intention, and control* (pp. 75–123). New York: Guilford.

Higgins, E. T., King, G. A., & Mavin, G. H. (1982). Individual construct accessibility and subjective impressions and recall. *Journal of Personality and Social Psychology, 43,* 35–47.

*Higgins, R. L., & Leibowitz, R. Q. (1999). Reality negotiation and coping: The social construction of adaptive outcomes. In C. R. Snyder (Ed.), *Coping: The psychology of what works* (pp. 20–49). New York: Oxford University Press.

*Higgins, R. L., & Snyder, C. R. (1989). Excuses gone awry: An analysis of self-defeating excuses. In R. C. Curtis (Ed.), *Self-defeating behaviors: Experimental research, clinical impressions, and practical implications* (pp. 99–130). New York: Plenum.

*Higgins, R. L., & Snyder, C. R. (1991). Reality negotiation and excuse-making. In C. R. Snyder & D. R. Forsyth (Eds.), *Handbook of social and clinical psychology: The health perspective* (pp. 79–95). Elmsford, NY: Pergamon.

*Higgins, R. L., Snyder, C. R., & Berglas, S. (1990). *Self-handicapping: The paradox that isn't*. New York: Plenum.

Janoff-Bulman, R. (1979). Characterological versus behavioral self-blame: Inquiries into depression and rape. *Journal of Personality and Social Psychology, 37,* 1798–1809.

Jones, E. E., & Berglas, S. (1978). Control attributions about the self through self-handicapping strategies: The appeal of alcohol and the role of underachievement. *Personality and Social Psychology Bulletin, 4,* 200–206.

Jones, E. E., & Rhodewalt, F. (1982). *The Self-Handicapping Scale.* (Available from F. Rhodewalt, Department of Psychology, University of Utah)

Jones, R. A. (1990). Expectations and delay in seeking medical care. *Journal of Social Issues, 46,* 81–95.

Kant, I. (1965). *Critique of pure reason* (unabridged ed.; N. K. Smith, Trans.). New York: St. Martin's Press. (Original work published 1781)

Kelley, H. H. (1967). Attribution theory in social psychology. In D. Levine (Ed.), *Nebraska Symposium on Motivation* (Vol. 15, pp. 192–238). Lincoln: University of Nebraska Press.

Kelley, H. H. (1971). *Attribution in social interaction.* New York: General Learning Press.

Kohlenberg, R. J. (1973). Behavioristic approach to multiple personality: A case study. *Behavior Therapy, 4,* 137–140.

Lerner, M. J. (1980). *The belief in a just world: A fundamental delusion.* New York: Plenum.

Loftus, E., & Ketcham, K. (1994). *The myth of repressed memory: False memories and allegations of sexual abuse.* New York: St. Martin's Press.

Markus, H. M., & Cross, S. (1990). The interpersonal self. In L. A. Pervin (Ed.), *Handbook of personality: Theory and research* (pp. 576–608). New York: Guilford.

Markus, H. M., & Wurf, E. (1987). The dynamic self-concept: A social psychological perspective. *Annual Review of Psychology, 38,* 299–337.

Maslow, A. (1968). *Toward a psychology of being* (2nd ed.). New York: Van Nostrand.

Mead, G. H. (1934). *Mind, self, and society.* Chicago: University of Chicago Press.

Miller, D. T. (1976). Ego involvement and attribution for success and failure. *Journal of Personality and Social Psychology, 34,* 901–906.

Neimeyer, R. A., & Stewart, A. E. (2000). Constructivist and narrative psychotherapies. In C. R. Snyder & R. E. Ingram (Eds.), *Handbook of psychological change: Psychotherapy processes and practices for the 21st Century* (pp. 337–357). New York: Wiley.

Piaget, J. (1963). *The origins of intelligence in children* (M. Cook, Trans.). New York: Norton. (Original work published in 1936)

Pyszczynski, T. A., & Greenberg, J. (1981). Role of disconfirmed expectancies in the instigation of attributional processing. *Journal of Personality and Social Psychology, 40,* 31–38.

Rhodewalt, F. (1990). Self-handicappers: Individual differences in the preference for anticipatory self-protective acts. In R. L. Higgins, C. R. Snyder, & S. Berglas, *Self-handicapping: The paradox that isn't* (pp. 69–106). New York: Plenum.

Rogers, C. R. (1951). *Client-centered therapy: Its current practice, implications, and theory.* Boston: Houghton Mifflin.

Rotenberg, K. (1980). Children's use of intentionality in judgments of character and disposition. *Child Development, 51,* 282–284.

Samuelson, B. E. A. (1996). *Measuring linkage into valenced elements: The LIVE scale.* Unpublished master's thesis, University of Kansas, Lawrence.

Schreurs, K. M. G., & de Ridder, D. T. D. (1997). Integration of coping and social support perspectives: Implications for the study of adaptation to chronic diseases. *Clinical Psychology Review, 17,* 89–112.

Schulz, R. (1976). Effects of control and predictability on the physical and psychological well-being of the institutionalized aged. *Journal of Personality and Social Psychology, 33,* 563–573.

Schulz, R., & Decker, S. (1985). Long-term adjustment to physical disability: The role of social support, perceived control and self-blame. *Journal of Personality and Social Psychology, 48,* 1162–1172.

Shaver, K. G. (1970). Defensive attribution: Effects of severity and relevance on the responsibility assigned for an accident. *Journal of Personality and Social Psychology, 14,* 101–113.

Silver, R. C., Wortman, C. B., & Crofton, C. (1990). The role of coping in support provision: The self-representational dilemma of victims of life crises. In B. R. Sarason, I. G. Sarason, & G. R. Pierce (Eds.), *Social support: An interactional view* (pp. 397–426). New York: Wiley.

Smith, T. W., Snyder, C. R., & Handelsman, M. M. (1982). On the self-serving function of an academic wooden leg: Test anxiety as a self-handicapping strategy. *Journal of Personality and Social Psychology, 42*, 314–321.

Smith, T. W., Snyder, C. R., & Perkins, S. C. (1983). The self-serving function of hypochondriacal complaints: Physical symptoms as self-handicapping strategies. *Journal of Personality and Social Psychology, 44*, 787–797.

*Snyder, C. R. (1989). Reality negotiation: From excuses to hope and beyond. *Journal of Social and Clinical Psychology, 8*, 130–157.

*Snyder, C. R. (1994). *The psychology of hope: You can get there from here.* New York: Free Press.

Snyder, C. R., Cheavens, J., & Michael, S. T. (1999). Hoping. In C. R. Snyder (Ed.), *Coping: The psychology of what works* (pp. 205–229). New York: Oxford University Press.

Snyder, C. R., Harris, C., Anderson, J. R., Holleran, S. A., Irving, L. M., Sigmon, S. T., Yoshinobu, L., Gibb, J., Langelle, C., & Harney, P. (1991). The will and the ways: Development and validation of an individual-differences measure of hope. *Journal of Personality and Social Psychology, 60*, 570–585.

Snyder, C. R., & Higgins, R. L. (1988a). Excuse attributions: Do they work? In S. L. Zelen (Ed.), *Self-representation: The second attribution-personality theory conference* (pp. 50–122). New York: Springer-Verlag.

*Snyder, C. R., & Higgins, R. L. (1988b). Excuses: Their effective role in the negotiation of reality. *Psychological Bulletin, 104*, 23–35.

Snyder, C. R., & Higgins, R. L. (1988c). From making to being the excuse: An analysis of deception and verbal/nonverbal issues. *Journal of Nonverbal Behavior, 12*, 237–252.

*Snyder, C. R., & Higgins, R. L. (1997). Reality negotiation: Governing one's self and being governed by others. *General Psychology Review, 1*, 336–350.

*Snyder, C. R., Higgins, R. L., & Stucky, R. J. (1983). *Excuses: Masquerades in search of grace.* New York: Wiley-Interscience.

Snyder, C. R., Hoza, B., Pelham, W. E., Rapoff, M., Ware, L., Danovsky, M., Highberger, L., Rubinstein, H., & Stahl, K. J. (1997). The development and validation of the Children's Hope Scale. *Journal of Pediatric Psychology, 22*, 399–421.

Snyder, C. R., Ilardi, S., Michael, S. T., & Cheavens, J. (2000). Hope theory: Updating a common process for psychological change. In C. R. Snyder, & R. E. Ingram (Eds.), *Handbook of psychological change: Psychotherapy processes and practices for the 21st century* (pp. 128–150). New York: Wiley.

Snyder, C. R., Irving, L. R., & Anderson, J. R. (1991). Hope and health. In C. R. Snyder & D. R. Forsyth (Eds.), *Handbook of social and clinical psychology: The health perspective* (pp. 285–305). New York: Pergamon.

Snyder, C. R., Irving, L. R., Sigmon, S. T., & Holleran, S. (1992). Reality negotiation and valence/linkage self theories: Psychic showdown at the "I'm OK" corral and beyond. In L. Montrada, S-H. Filipp, & M. J. Lerner (Eds.), *Life crises and experiences of loss in adulthood* (pp. 275–297). Hillsdale, NJ: Erlbaum.

Snyder, C. R., & Samuelson, B. E. A. (1998). *Development and validation of the LIVE Scale: Linkage into valenced elements.* Unpublished manuscript. University of Kansas, Lawrence.

Snyder, C. R., Smith, T. W., Augelli, R. W., & Ingram, R. E. (1983). On the self-serving function of social anxiety: Shyness as a self-handicapping strategy. *Journal of Personality and Social Psychology, 48*, 970–980.

Snyder, C. R., Sympson, S. C., Ybasco, F. C., Borders, T. F., Babyak, M. A., & Higgins, R. L. (1996). Development and validation of the State Hope Scale. *Journal of Personality and Social Psychology, 70*, 321–335.

Spanos, N. P., Menary, E., Gabora, N. J., DuBreuil, S. C., & Dewhirst, B. (1991). Secondary identity enactments during hypnotic past-life regression: A socio-cognitive perspective. *Journal of Personality and Social Psychology, 61*, 308–320.

Spanos, N. P., Weekes, J. R., Menary, E., & Bertrand, L. D. (1986). Hypnotic interview and age regression procedures in the elicitation of multiple personality symptoms: A simulation study. *Psychiatry, 49*, 298–311.

Strube, M. J. (1985). An analysis of the Self-Handicapping Scale. *Basic and Applied Social Psychology, 7*, 211–224.

Swann, W. B., Jr., Hixon, J. G., & De La Ronde, C. (1992). Embracing the bitter "truth": Negative self-concepts and marital commitment. *Psychological Science, 3*, 118–121.

Swann, W. B., Jr., Wenzlaff, R. M., Krull, D. S., & Pelham, B. W. (1992). Allure of negative feedback: Self-verification strivings among depressed persons. *Journal of Abnormal Psychology, 101*, 293–306.

Taylor, S. E. (1983). Adjustment to threatening events: A theory of cognitive adaptation. *American Psychologist, 38,* 1161–1173.

Taylor, S. E., & Brown, J. (1988). Illusion and well-being: A social psychological perspective on mental health. *Psychological Bulletin, 103,* 193–210.

Taylor, S. E., Lichtman, R. R., & Wood, J. V. (1984). Attributions, beliefs about control, and adjustment to breast cancer. *Journal of Personality and Social Psychology, 46,* 489–502.

Tennen, H., Affleck, G., Urrows, S., Higgins, P., & Mendola, R. (1992). Perceiving control, construing benefits, and daily processes in rheumatoid arthritis. *Canadian Journal of Behavioral Science, 24,* 186–203.

Tice, D. M., & Baumeister, R. F. (1984, May). *Self-handicapping, self-esteem, and self-presentation.* Paper presented at the meeting of the Midwestern Psychological Association, Chicago.

Timko, C., & Janoff-Bulman, R. (1985). Attributions, vulnerability and psychological adjustment: The case of breast cancer. *Health Psychology, 4,* 521–546.

Vaihinger, H. (1925). *The philosophy of "as if"* (C. K. Ogden, Trans.). New York: Harcourt Brace.

Witenberg, S. H., Blanchard, E. B., Suls, J., Tennen, H., McCoy, G., & McGoldrick, M. D. (1983). Perceptions of control and causality as predictors of compliance and coping in hemodialysis. *Basic and Applied Social Psychology, 4,* 319–336.

Zuckerman, M. (1979). Attribution of success and failure revisited: or The motivational bias is alive and well in attribution theory. *Journal of Personality, 47,* 245–287.

26

The Truth About Illusions

Authenticity and Positivity in Social Relationships

William B. Swann & Brett W. Pelham

We must select the illusion which appeals to our temperament, and embrace it with passion, if we want to be happy.
> C. Connolly, *The Unquiet Grave: A Word Cycle* (1945, p. 124)

Rather than love, than money, than fame, give me truth.
> Thoreau, *Walden* (1854, p. 23)

In the centuries-old struggle between advocates of truth and illusion, the illusionists seem to have gained the upper hand of late. In fact, illusion has emerged as the darling of the age, the source of a wide array of benefits including success, creativity, and even longevity. Truth, in contrast, has fallen into disfavor, the alleged origin of failure, rigidity, and even morbidity (e.g., Peterson & Seligman, 1987; Taylor & Brown, 1988).

Curiously, some of the most ardent advocates of illusion and wishful thinking have been behavioral scientists—the same group who championed truth and realism only a few decades ago. Proponents of positive thinking have buttressed their claims with mountains of empirical support. Some, for example, have pointed to evidence that optimism—particularly optimism about the self—seems to be a pervasive characteristic of psychological functioning. They also have cited evidence that people not only maintain flattering conceptions of self but also work to embellish such self-views by selectively attending to and recalling positive feedback. Indeed, people seem to engage in a wide array of mental gymnastics designed to accentuate the positive and minimize the negative, including strategies of self-presentation (Baumeister, 1982; Jones & Pittman, 1982; Schlenker, 1980); self-attribution (e.g., Greenwald, 1980; Snyder & Higgins, 1988); self-prediction (e.g., Alloy & Abramson, 1988; Kunda, 1987; Taylor & Brown, 1988; Weinstein, 1980); social comparison (e.g., Tesser, 1988; Wills, 1981); and even attitude change (e.g., Steele, 1988). The ubiquity of such processes has been taken as evidence of the potency of self-enhancement or positivity strivings (e.g., Greenwald, 1980; Jones, 1973; Schlenker, 1980).[1]

Others have asked how optimism influences

motivation and psychological well-being. Bandura (1986), for example, found that optimism fosters task persistence. In a similar vein, Mischel (1979) suggested, "To feel good about ourselves we may have to judge ourselves more kindly than we are judged. Self-enhancing processing and biased self-encoding may be both a requirement for positive affect and the price for achieving it" (p. 752). Thus, Mischel, like Alloy and Abramson (1988), argued that optimism tends to counteract depression.

Still others have examined the impact of self-enhancing biases on physical health. Several authors (e.g., Peterson & Seligman, 1987; Seligman, 1986) have suggested that people who make self-serving attributions live longer for so doing. Taylor and Brown (1988) summarized this work by suggesting that people engage in three distinct optimistic biases. First, people tend to overestimate their degree of personal control over their outcomes. Second, people believe they are more capable than they actually are. Third, people entertain unrealistically rosy views of the future. Taylor and Brown further argued that each of these biases has salutary physical, motivational, and interpersonal consequences.

Such testimonials to the power of positivity notwithstanding, we suggest that characterizing people exclusively in these terms offers an incomplete understanding of human nature. After all, evidence for positivity strivings comes almost exclusively from laboratory studies in which people receive evaluations from strangers with whom they never expect to have a real relationship (for exceptions, see Murray, Holmes, & Griffin, 1993, 2000). This is a significant limitation, because when people are unacquainted with others, they have little or no motivation to be known and understood by such persons. For this reason, although people in naturally occurring settings might benefit from modest amounts of optimism and illusion, significant illusions may foster epistemic anxiety and cause people to enter life situations for which they are unsuited (Baumeister, 1989; Colvin & Block, 1994). We propose that this rarely happens because a desire for coherence and predictability (e.g., Heider, 1958; Kelly, 1955; Lecky, 1945) counters the positivity bias and holds it in check. Specifically, we propose that coherence strivings motivate people to seek feedback that verifies rather than enhances their self-views. Self-verification theory explains why this is so.

The Why of Self-Verification Strivings

Behavioral scientists have long argued that interpersonal relationships are a source of self-verification. Sociologists, for example, noted that relationships serve as "opportunity structures" that encourage people to be the persons they believe themselves to be (e.g., Berger & Luckman, 1967; Gecas, 1991; McCall & Simmons, 1966). Similarly, existential philosophers argued cogently that people's relationship partners validate their self-conceptions and thereby bolster their perceptions of *authenticity* (see Harter, this volume). Buber (1951) carefully distinguished this desire for validation from positivity strivings: "The true turning of [a] person to another includes this confirmation, this acceptance. Of course, *such a confirmation does not mean approval;* but no matter in what I am against the other, by accepting him as my partner I have affirmed him as a person" (p. 112, emphasis added).

Self-verification theory (Swann, 1983, 1990, 1999) takes this argument a step further by suggesting that people actively work to acquire self-confirmatory feedback. The intellectual seeds of the theory were sown by Gestalt theorists and cultivated by self-consistency theorists (e.g., Aronson, 1968; Lecky, 1945; Festinger, 1957; Secord & Backman, 1965). Dissonance theorists, for example, originally proposed that people strive for cognitive symmetry. Soon, however, researchers recognized that a pristine desire for symmetry was too weak to have much impact on most social behavior. They accordingly "warmed up" the desire for cognitive balance by alloying it with positivity strivings. As a result, in their research they confronted participants with a very special type of inconsistency, an inconsistency between their own behavior and their belief that they were good and decent persons (e.g., Abelson, 1983; Aronson, 1968; Greenwald & Ronnis, 1978; Snyder, Higgins, & Stucky, 1983). Although such manipulations proved to be powerful, they also were problematic theoretically because they made it impossible to discern whether participants were sustaining their feelings of consistency or were struggling to feel good about themselves.[2] Not surprisingly, then, many contemporary theorists have either subsumed self-consistency strivings within a positivity perspective (e.g., Sedikides & Strube, 1997; Steele, 1988) or ignored them altogether.

The self-verification formulation departs from consistency theories by abandoning the notion that people are interested in consistency for its own sake (see also Epstein, 1985; Lecky, 1945; Secord & Backman, 1965). Instead, self-verification theory assumes that people work to confirm their self-conceptions out of a desire for coherence (e.g., Heider, 1958; Kelly, 1955; Lecky, 1945). The desire for coherence is so fundamental to mental life that its rudiments are present at birth. Karl Popper (1963), for example, noted that

> One of the most important of [the] expectations [that children are born with] is the expectation of finding a regularity. It is connected with an inborn propensity to look for regularities, or with *a need to find* regularities. . . . This "instinctive" expectation of finding regularities . . . is logically a priori to all observational experience, for it is prior to any recognition of similarities . . . and all observation involves the recognition of similarities (or dissimilarities). (pp. 47–48)

From very early in life, both human beings and animals appear to prefer familiar as opposed to unfamiliar experiences. Consider an example from Harlow's (1958) research on monkeys reared by surrogate mothers. One set of surrogate mothers consisted of soft terry cloth bodies and wooden heads with painted faces. Young monkeys frequently ran to these surrogate mothers for comfort in times of distress. By accident, however, one monkey was reared for its first 180 days by a mother without a face. When the researchers replaced the head on the defective mother with a standard head (featuring a painted face), the young monkey repeatedly screwed the new mother's head around so as to restore the beloved blank (for a summary, see Brown, 1965, pp. 39–40). Apparently, a familiar appearance is an important part of the magic of motherhood.

It seems safe to say that by adulthood, the preference for confirmatory experiences is well established. Studies of concept formation and concept utilization, for example, suggest that people are more compelled by positive instances of concepts than by negative ones (e.g., Hovland & Weiss, 1953). Similarly, people perceive evidence that confirms their hypotheses and beliefs to be more trustworthy, diagnostic, and easy to process than disconfirmatory evidence (e.g.,

Bruner, Goodnow, & Austin, 1956; Klayman & Ha, 1987). Finally, when people test the validity of their propositions and beliefs, they are especially likely to seek hypothesis-confirmatory evidence (e.g., Snyder & Swann, 1978; Wason & Johnson-Laird, 1972).

Even if there were no such thing as a general preference for expectancy-consistent information, people might still seek information that confirms their chronic self-views. After all, people's self-views presumably occupy the center of their psychological universes, providing the basis for all other knowledge. Stable self-views thus provide people with a crucial source of coherence, an invaluable means of defining their existence, organizing experience, predicting future events, and guiding social interaction (cf. Cooley, 1902; Lecky, 1945; Mead, 1934; Secord & Backman, 1965). In addition, by stabilizing behavior, self-views make people more predictable to *others* (Goffman, 1959). That is, when people behave in predictable ways, other people learn how to treat them. In this way, stable self-views foster a coherent social environment that further stabilizes people's original self-views.[3]

In short, people may seek self-verification either because verifying evaluations bolster people's perceptions that the world is coherent and predictable ("epistemic" concerns) or because verifying evaluations ensure that people's interactions proceed smoothly ("pragmatic" concerns). When these epistemic and pragmatic concerns are strong enough, self-verification strivings will override positivity strivings. This makes sense. Just as stable self-views anchor people's knowledge systems, self-discrepant evaluations rock people's epistemic boats. Self-discrepant evaluations may even undermine people's confidence that they can discriminate truly favorable evaluations from favorable but deceptive ones. Simply put, if people cannot be sure that their perceptions of reality are correct, they cannot use these perceptions to regulate their behavior.

Therefore, just as being perceived in a self-congruent manner may bolster feelings of existential security and grease the wheels of social interaction, being perceived in an incongruent manner may produce the epistemic and pragmatic equivalents of a train wreck.[4] To avoid such disasters, people engineer social worlds that confirm their self-views—even if so doing sometimes frustrates their desire for positivity.

The How of Self-Verification Strivings

There are two specific classes of activities through which people seek self-verifying feedback (Swann, 1983, 1990). As shown in Figure 26.1, the first such class of activities is behavioral. Specifically, people work to create self-confirmatory social environments, which is to say environments that reinforce their self-views (e.g., McCall & Simmons, 1966).

The second class of self-verification activities is cognitive. People's existing self-conceptions systematically distort their perceptions of social reality. In particular, people misperceive and misremember social experiences in ways that are compatible with their existing self-views. We first consider behavioral mechanisms of self-verification.

Developing a Self-Confirmatory Social Environment

Biologists and ecologists have noted that all living organisms inhabit "niches" that routinely satisfy their basic needs (e.g., Clark, 1954). Human beings are no exception. Out of a concern for self-verification, people attempt (consciously or not) to construct social environments that provide them with a steady diet of self-confirmatory feedback (McCall & Simmons, 1966).

In their efforts to construct self-verifying social environments, people engage in three distinct activities: They strategically choose interaction partners and social settings; they display identity cues; and they adopt interaction strategies that evoke self-confirmatory responses (Swann, 1983, 1987). We consider each of these strategies in turn.

Selective Interaction

The notion that people seek social contexts that provide them with self-confirmatory feedback has been around for several decades (e.g., Secord & Backman, 1965; Wachtel, 1977). Until recently, however, much of the evidence for this hypothesis has been correlational. Pervin and Rubin (1967), for example, found that students tended to drop out of school if they wound up in colleges that were incompatible with their self-views (see also Backman & Secord, 1962; Broxton, 1963; Newcomb, 1956).

Recent laboratory investigations have complemented earlier evidence by showing that people with negative self-views prefer interaction partners who appraise them unfavorably over those who appraise them favorably. Swann, Pelham, and Krull (1989), for example, told some participants (targets) that two others (perceivers) had evaluated them on performance dimensions that targets had previously identified as their "worst" attribute (e.g., athletic ability, physical appearance). One perceiver offered an unfavorable evaluation, and the other offered a favorable evaluation. Targets chose to interact with the unfavorable, self-verifying perceiver rather than with the favorable, nonverifying one.

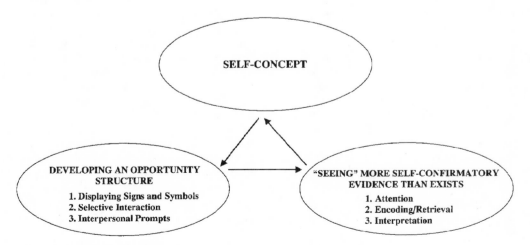

Figure 26.1 Self-verification processes.

In a similar vein, Swann, Stein-Seroussi, and Giesler (1992) asked people with positive and negative self-views whether they would prefer to interact with evaluators who had favorable or unfavorable impressions of them. They discovered that people with positive self-views preferred favorable partners, and people with negative self-views preferred unfavorable partners.

More than a dozen replications of this effect using diverse methodologies have confirmed that people with negative self-views seek unfavorable feedback and partners (e.g., Hixon & Swann, 1993; Robinson & Smith-Lovin, 1992; Swann, Hixon, Stein-Seroussi, & Gilbert, 1990; Swann et al., 1989; Swann, Wenzlaff, Krull, & Pelham, 1992). Both men and women display this propensity whether the self-views are, or are not, easily changed and whether the self-views are associated with specific qualities (intelligence, sociability, dominance) or global self-worth (self-esteem, depression). Similarly, people prefer to interact with self-verifying partners even if presented with the alternative of participating in a different experiment (Swann, Wenzlaff, & Tafarodi, 1992). Finally, people are particularly likely to seek self-verifying evaluations if their self-views are confidently held (e.g., Pelham & Swann, 1994; Swann & Ely, 1984; Swann, Pelham, & Chidester, 1988), important (Swann & Pelham, 1999), or extreme (Giesler, Josephs, & Swann, 1996).

The self-verification strivings of people with low self-esteem and depression are not masochistic, for such people do not savor unfavorable evaluations. Rather, people with negative self-conceptions feel ambivalent about such evaluations. In choosing a negative evaluator, one person with low esteem noted: "I like the [favorable] evaluation but I am not sure that it is, ah, correct, maybe. It *sounds* good, but [the unfavorable evaluator] . . . seems to know more about me. So, I'll choose [the unfavorable evaluator]" (Swann, Stein-Seroussi, & Giesler, 1992). The thoughts that give rise to such ambivalence emerge sequentially. Upon receiving positive feedback, even people with negative self-views are immediately drawn to it. When such persons are able to access their self-views and compare these self-views with the feedback, however, a preference for negative feedback emerges (e.g., Hixon & Swann, 1993; Swann et al., 1990). And often people *are* able to access their self-views. This explains why people tend to withdraw from incongruent relationships. For example, if people wind up in marriages in which their spouses perceive them more (or less) favorably than they perceive themselves, they become less intimate with those spouses (De La Ronde & Swann, 1998; Katz, Beach, & Anderson, 1996; Ritts & Stein, 1995; Schafer, Wickram, & Keith, 1996; Swann, De La Ronde, & Hixon, 1994).

Could the self-verification strivings of people with negative self-views reflect attempts to attain *positive feedback*? Apparently not. First, people with negative self-views seek negative feedback when they have no prospect of receiving additional feedback in the future (e.g., Bosson & Swann, 1999; Giesler et al., 1996; Hixon & Swann, 1993; Pelham & Swann, 1994; Robinson & Smith-Lovin, 1992; Swann et al., 1990; Swann et al., 1989; Swann, Wenzlaff, Krull, & Pelham, 1992). In addition, in two independent studies of the think-aloud protocols of people choosing interaction partners (Swann, Stein-Seroussi, & Giesler, 1992; Swann, Bosson, & Pelham, 2001), participants with negative self-views who self-verified specifically mentioned a desire for self-confirming reactions but mentioned nothing about a desire for positivity. Finally, among Swann and colleagues' (1994) married couples, there was no evidence that people with negative self-views were more intimate with spouses who thought poorly of them because they wanted to improve themselves, or as a means of obtaining negative specific appraisals coupled with global acceptance, nor did they embrace negative spouses because they believed that people who perceived them positively must be dull-witted.

Taken together, these data offer clear evidence that people gravitate toward relationships that provide them with self-confirmatory feedback. An important characteristic of such selective interaction strategies is that once people enter particular social relationships, legal contracts and social pressures tend to keep them there. The power of such contractual arrangements is obvious in the case of marriage, but a great deal of inertia also exists in friendships, collaborations, and dating relationships. Thus, selective interaction strategies often channel people into interpersonal feedback systems that are self-sustaining as well as self-verifying.

Displaying Identity Cues

Another way in which people can succeed in laying claim to a particular identity is by "looking the part." To be effective, identity cues must meet two criteria: They must be under the person's control, and they must predictably evoke desired responses from others.

Physical appearances represent a particularly salient class of identity cues. The clothes one wears, for example, can be used to advertise one's political leanings, income level, sexual preference, and so forth. Even body posture and demeanor communicate identities to others. Take, for example, the teenager who radiates anomie, the "punk" who projects danger, or the new father who exudes naïveté in the hope of avoiding responsibility (e.g., Stone, 1962). Similarly, Serpe and Stryker (1987) reported that college freshmen decorated their dorm rooms as they had their rooms at home, presumably in an effort to communicate their self-views to visitors.

Some people may actually modify their body structure to convey various identities to others. Self-perceived athletes, for example, may diet and lift weights to keep their muscles bulging. Others may resort to cosmetic surgery, whether it involve implants, transplants, lifts, or liposuction. Those who wish to avoid the surgeon's knife may rely on titles or material possessions to convey their identities to others. The cars people drive, the homes they live in, and the trophies they display in their dens may all be used to tell others who they are and how they expect to be treated (Goffman, 1959; Schlenker, 1980).

Advocates of positivity strivings may have noticed that virtually all of the identity cues that were mentioned in the foregoing examples happened to involve *positive* identities. Because most people possess relatively positive self-views (e.g., Swann, 1987; Taylor & Brown, 1988), this should come as no surprise. Nonetheless, it raises the question of whether people ever display signs and symbols of *negative* identities. We think so. The lowly bumper sticker provides some salient examples. As the popularity of the "My child is an honor student" bumper sticker has grown over the past few years, less self-congratulatory bumper stickers have appeared in its wake: "My kid beat up your honor kid" and "My kid is inmate of the month at the county jail." And if the humorous intent of bumper stickers ambiguates the goals of those who display them, Bettleheim's (1943) analysis of Jewish prisoners in Nazi concentration camps offers examples of people who advertise negative identities that are much more difficult to dismiss. The prisoners

initially resisted their oppressors' claims that they were inferior. After years of physical and psychological abuse, however, some of the prisoners became openly anti-Semitic and even wore discarded bits of the guards' clothing to symbolize their conversion. Allport (1954) commented on such findings by noting that the actions of "slaves . . . and concentration camp prisoners show that group oppression may destroy the integrity of the ego entirely, and reverse its normal pride, and create a groveling self-image" (p. 152; see also Jost & Banaji, 1994).

Interpersonal Prompts

Even if people fail to gain self-confirmatory feedback through selective interaction, they still may acquire such feedback. Swann, Wenzlaff, Krull, and Pelham (1990), for example, found that mildly depressed college students were more likely to solicit unfavorable feedback from their roommates than were nondepressed students. Moreover, students' efforts to acquire unfavorable feedback seem to have borne fruit: The more unfavorable feedback they solicited in the middle of the semester, the more their roommates derogated them and planned to find another roommate at the semester's end (see also Coyne, 1976; Coyne et al., 1987).

If people are motivated to bring others to verify their self-conceptions, they should *intensify* their efforts to elicit self-confirmatory reactions when they suspect that they are misconstrued. Swann and Read (1981, Study 2) tested this idea by informing people who perceived themselves as either likable or dislikable that they would be interacting with perceivers who had already formed impressions of them. Some people learned that the perceiver found them likable; others learned that the perceiver found them dislikable; still others learned nothing of the perceivers' evaluation.

Targets tended to elicit reactions that confirmed their self-views (see also Curtis & Miller, 1986). More important, this tendency was especially pronounced when targets suspected that perceivers' appraisals might *disconfirm* their self-conceptions. Targets who thought of themselves as likable elicited particularly favorable reactions when they thought perceivers disliked them, and targets who thought of themselves as dislikable elicited particularly unfavorable reactions when they suspected that perceivers liked them. In short, targets showed increased interest in self-verification when they suspected that perceivers' appraisals challenged their self-views.

Swann and Hill (1982) obtained similar findings using a different procedure and a different dimension of the self-concept (dominance). Targets began by playing a game (with a confederate) in which each player alternately assumed the dominant "leader" role or the submissive "assistant" role. During a break in the game, the experimenter asked the players to decide who should be the leader for the next set of games. This was the confederate's cue to give participants self-relevant feedback. In some conditions, the confederate said the participant seemed dominant; in others, the confederate said the participant seemed submissive. If the feedback confirmed targets' self-conceptions, they passively accepted the confederate's appraisal. If the feedback *dis*confirmed their self-conceptions, however, targets vehemently resisted it and sought to demonstrate that they were not the persons the confederate made them out to be. Thus, for example, self-conceived submissives labeled as dominant asked to play the submissive role (in fact, they insisted on it!).

An interesting feature of this study was that some people resisted the discrepant feedback more than others. Swann and Ely (1984) speculated that such differences in resistance might be due to differences in the extent to which people were certain of their self-conceptions. Specifically, they reasoned that heightened self-concept certainty would be associated with heightened interest in self-verification, and thus heightened resistance in the face of disconfirmation. To test this hypothesis, Swann and Ely (1984) had perceivers interview targets who were either certain or uncertain of their self-conceived extraversion. They led perceivers to develop an expectancy about targets that was always discrepant with the targets' self-conceptions. This situation created a potential "battle of wills," with perceivers' experimentally manipulated beliefs vying against targets' self-views.

Consistent with earlier research (Snyder & Swann, 1978; Swann & Giuliano, 1987), perceivers acted on their expectancies by soliciting responses designed to confirm their own expectancies but *disconfirm* targets' self-conceptions. For example, perceivers with extravert expectancies asked questions such as "What would you do to liven things up at a dull party?"

When perceivers were highly certain of their expectancies, targets who were low in self-certainty generally answered in ways that confirmed perceivers' expectancies (but disconfirmed their own self-conceptions). In contrast, targets who were high in self-certainty actively resisted the questions—regardless of the perceivers' level of certainty. Thus, as long as targets were high in self-certainty, self-verification overpowered behavioral confirmation.

The tendency for self-verification to triumph over behavioral confirmation seems to generalize to naturally occurring situations. For example, McNulty and Swann (1994) found that college students brought their roommates to see them as they saw themselves over the course of a semester. Furthermore, this tendency was stronger than the tendency for students to bring their roommates' self-views into harmony with their initial impression of them. Similarly, in an investigation of MBA students in study groups, Swann, Milton, and Polzer (1999) found that individual members of each group tended to bring the appraisals of other group members into agreement with their self-views; the countervailing tendency for the group members to shape the self-views of individuals in the group also appeared but was much weaker.

Together, these findings suggest that targets work to bring perceivers to see them as they see themselves. As effective as such behavioral efforts may often be, however, people sometimes fail to create fully self-confirmatory opportunity structures. When this happens, the survival of people's self-views may hinge on the effectiveness of the three *cognitive* self-verification strategies described next.

Seeing More Self-Confirmatory Evidence Than Actually Exists

Researchers have shown that expectancies (including self-conceptions) exert a powerful channeling influence on information processing (e.g., Higgins & Bargh, 1987). This suggests that self-conceptions may guide the processing of social feedback so as to promote their own survival (Shrauger & Shoeneman, 1979).

Selective Attention

To the extent that people are motivated to acquire self-confirmatory feedback, they should be especially attentive to it. Swann and Read (1981, Study 1) tested this hypothesis. Targets who perceived themselves as either likable or dislikable were led to suspect that a perceiver had a favorable or an unfavorable impression of them. All targets were then given an opportunity to examine some remarks that the perceiver had ostensibly made about them, remarks that were sufficiently vague as to apply to anyone.

The results showed that targets spent a longer time scrutinizing evaluations when they anticipated that the evaluations would confirm their self-conceptions. That is, just as self-perceived likables spent the most time looking when they expected the remarks would be favorable, self-perceived dislikables spent the most time looking when they expected the remarks would be unfavorable. In short, people are more attentive to social feedback when they suspect that it will confirm their chronic self-views.

Selective Encoding and Retrieval

Just as people may selectively attend to self-confirmatory feedback, they also may selectively remember it. Crary (1966) and Silverman (1964), for example, reported that people recalled more incidental information about experimental tasks in which they received self-confirmatory rather than self-discrepant feedback. Moreover, other research suggests that self-conceptions channel the *type* as well as the *amount* of feedback people recall. For example, Swann and Read (1981, Study 3) had targets who saw themselves as likable or dislikable listen to a perceiver make a series of positive and negative statements about them. Some targets expected that the statements would be generally positive; others expected that the statements would be generally negative. After a brief delay, targets attempted to recall as many of the statements as possible. Targets who perceived themselves as likable remembered more positive than negative statements, and those who perceived themselves as dislikable remembered more negative than positive statements. In addition, this tendency to recall self-confirmatory statements was greatest when targets had anticipated that the perceivers' statements would confirm their self-conceptions.

Selective Interpretation

Upon being evaluated, people may ask, "Is the source of feedback trustworthy? Does the feedback tell me anything informative about my-self?" Research suggests that people answer these questions in ways that promote the survival of their self-views.

Researchers have reported clear evidence that people endorse the validity of feedback only if it fits with their self-conceptions (Crary, 1966; Markus, 1977). Similarly, Shrauger and Lund (1975) reported that people expressed greater confidence in the perceptiveness of an evaluator when his impression confirmed their self-conceptions. Swann, Griffin, Predmore, and Gaines (1987) replicated this effect and also found that people tended to attribute self-confirmatory feedback to characteristics of themselves and self-disconfirmatory feedback to the source of the feedback.

Together, the attentional, encoding, retrieval, and interpretational processes described in this section may prove formidable adversaries for self-discrepant feedback. This may be one reason why people's self-conceptions sometimes conflict with the actual appraisals of others and, more specifically, why people overestimate the extent to which the appraisals of their friends and acquaintances confirm their self-conceptions (Shrauger & Shoeneman, 1979). Yet there is another reason why people's self-views sometimes conflict with the appraisals of others: People do not always self-verify. In the next section, we consider the factors that determine when people strive for positivity rather than self-verification.

Moderators of the Interplay Between Positivity and Self-Verification Strivings

Accessibility of the Self-View

For people to act on a self-view, they must have available the mental resources to access that self-view. In support of this idea, Swann et al. (1990) showed that participants' self-views had no impact on their choice of interaction partners when they were deprived of cognitive resources but did influence their choices when cognitive resources were available. In one study, resource-deprived participants had to rush through their choice of interaction partner. Participants with negative self-views who were rushed displayed a strong preference for the favorable evaluator—presumably because they had no time to perform the operations underlying self-verification. In contrast, participants who were not rushed self-verified, presumably because they possessed the requisite cognitive resources to do so. Hixon and Swann (1993, Experiment 1) extended this argument by showing that people with negative self-views endorsed the accuracy of positive evaluations when (but only when) they were cognitively taxed.

Research on the accessibility of attitudes suggests that individual differences in the accessibility of people's self-views might also play a role in self-verification. Specifically, Fazio and colleagues argued that people differ in the chronic accessibility of their attitudes (Fazio & Powell, 1997) and that more accessible attitudes are better predictors of behavior than are less accessible attitudes (Fazio, Powell, & Williams, 1989). Insofar as people's self-views operate in the same fashion as attitudes, people whose self-views are highly accessible should be more likely to verify these self-views. Consistent with this viewpoint, Pelham and Carrillo (1999) recently found that participants whose self-views had been made more temporarily accessible expressed a greater interest in receiving self-verifying appraisals from a dating partner.

Relevance of the Response to the Self-View

Responses vary in the extent to which they require respondents to access their self-views. For example, when provided with an evaluation and asked to indicate how self-descriptive it is, conscientious respondents should compare the evaluation with relevant self-views and respond accordingly. In light of this, it is not surprising that researchers have repeatedly found evidence of self-verification when they have studied "cognitive responses" such as the self-descriptiveness of feedback (e.g., McFarlin & Blascovich, 1981; Moreland & Sweeney, 1984; Swann et al., 1987). In contrast, when people receive an evaluation and are then asked how they feel, they may access their self-views only if the feedback promises to have implications for the nature of their identity. Because the identity implications of feedback will be low if it is from a stranger who does not know them, such feedback should not invoke people's self-views. In contrast, the identity implications of feedback from a credible evaluator will be much higher and should thus invoke their self-views. In support of this reasoning, Pinel and Swann (1999) found that when feedback was low in credibility, participants' self-views had no impact on their reactions to it: The more positive the feedback,

the better they felt. On the other hand, when the feedback was high in credibility, participants with positive self-views felt better upon receiving the positive feedback. However, participants with negative self-views grew anxious upon receiving such feedback (see also Shrauger, 1975).

Strength of the Self-View: Self-Certainty and Importance

To the extent that self-views are firmly held, people will be more inclined to rely on them in organizing their perceptions of the world and their social relationships. As a result, people should be more inclined to access highly certain, important self-views when deciding how to behave. Support for this proposition comes from evidence that people are most inclined to act on self-views that are high in certainty (e.g., Pelham, 1991; Pelham & Swann, 1994; Swann & Ely, 1984; Swann et al., 1988).[5] Similarly, people are more inclined to remain in relationships with roommates who support their important as compared with their unimportant self-views, even if those self-views are negative (e.g., Swann & Pelham, 1999).

People's purposes and goals may determine the nature of the feedback they seek. For example, the type of relationship people have with another person may determine whether people place a premium on positivity or self-verification. Consider dating partners. When dating, people are acutely aware of the fact that they must recruit the affections of their partner if the relationship is to survive: no positivity, no partner. When courtship culminates in marriage, however, the commitment is made. Convinced that they are in the relationship for the "long haul" and that it will be both epistemically and pragmatically advantageous to be understood, marriage partners work to bring their spouses to recognize their actual selves.

This reasoning led Swann and colleagues (1994) to hypothesize that people in dating relationships would prefer positive feedback and that people in marital relationships would prefer self-verifying feedback. In support of this hypothesis, they discovered that dating persons were more intimate when their partners viewed them favorably and married persons were more intimate when their partners saw them as they saw themselves, even when their self-views were negative.

What are dating couples thinking about when they express preferences for overly favorable appraisals from their partners? Swann, Bosson, and Pelham (2000) addressed this question. They found that rather than wanting uniformly positive evaluations from their dating partners, people preferred positive evaluations primarily on qualities that were most crucial to the survival of dating relationships (e.g., physical attractiveness) but preferred self-verifying feedback on other dimensions. Interestingly, participants intended to see to it that the highly positive feedback they sought on relationship-relevant dimensions would be self-verifying. That is, within the confines of particular relationships, they intended to "become" persons who deserved the stellar evaluations they sought to attain on goal-relevant dimensions (see also Schlenker, 1980). Moreover, they did it: participants actually received evaluations on relationship-relevant dimensions that were roughly as positive as their desired appraisals.

At first blush, the tendency of people with negative self-views to prefer evaluations that greatly exceeded their self-views may seem to confirm research and theory on positive illusions in relationships (e.g., Murray et al., 1993). After all, Murray and her colleagues have suggested that one of the primary means through which people seek happiness is by gravitating toward partners who see them more positively than they see themselves. Although we agree that the goal of maintaining stable romantic relationships may activate positivity strivings, we would stop short of suggesting that people strive to create positive *illusions* (Taylor & Brown, 1988; but cf. Colvin & Block, 1994) because from our participants' subjective, circumscribed perspectives, their highly positive preferred appraisals were quite accurate (Swann, 1984).

This evidence that people seek and obtain exceptionally positive evaluations on relationship-relevant dimensions may also seem discordant with previous research indicating that people who receive overly positive evaluations psychologically withdraw from the relationship (e.g., De La Ronde & Swann, 1998; Ritts & Stein, 1995; Swann et al., 1994; Swann & Pelham, 1999). Note, however, that previous workers examined how people with negative self-views react to positive reactions *on several dimensions*, only some of which were relationship-relevant. This is critical because findings by Swann et al. indicate that people do *not* present themselves in a highly positive manner on traits that are low in relationship relevance. Given

their modest self-presentations on low-relevance dimensions, they should conclude that highly positive evaluations on low-relevance dimensions are underserved. This means that if they did receive such evaluations, they would experience feelings of fraudulence that would encourage them to withdraw from the relationship (e.g., Lecky, 1945; Secord & Backman, 1965; Swann, 1983, 1999). This reasoning may also explain why Murray and her colleagues found that people with negative self-views embraced positive evaluations. An examination of the items in Murray et al.'s self-concept scale reveals an especially strong focus on qualities related to the success of the relationship (e.g., "emotional," "moody," "patient," "tolerant," "complaining," "open," "witty"). Conceivably, people desired positive evaluations on these goal-relevant domains because they had behaved in ways that they believed merited such evaluations. From this perspective, people may strive to keep their relationships alive by cultivating highly positive perceptions of themselves within relationship-relevant domains while seeking self-verification of their chronic self-views within domains that are important but not quite so critical to the survival of the relationship.

Implications of the Interplay of Self-Verification and Positivity Strivings for Clinical Interventions

For people who are depressed or have low self-esteem, one of their most important goals is to feel better about themselves. To this end, they may seek therapy. Yet self-verification strivings may often interfere with the therapeutic process.

Imagine a woman who seeks therapy in the hope of removing self-doubts that have plagued her since her youth. Although her therapist may succeed in bringing her to develop feelings of pride based on her strengths, she also may discover that these positive self-views are undone when she returns home to a contemptuous husband. Swann and Predmore (1985) investigated this process among dating couples in the laboratory. At one point the experimenter gave one member of the couple self-incongruent feedback while that person happened to be sitting with his or her intimate. Some of these intimates perceived their partner in a highly congruent fashion, and others viewed their partners less congruently. When the researchers measured how much people's self-views changed in response to the experimental feedback, they found that people were relatively impervious to incongruous feedback while sitting with an intimate who saw them congruently. This tendency for congruent relationship partners to insulate partners' against challenging feedback was equally true whether the partners' self-views were positive or negative.

Such evidence suggests an important addendum to Mark Twain's adage "A man cannot be comfortable without his own approval." To be comfortable with themselves, people must not only gain *their own* approval, they also must gain the approval and support of certain key interaction partners, including friends, coworkers, lovers, relatives, and so on. In this sense, people's self-views do not exist exclusively inside their own hearts and minds. Instead, they become a part of the social worlds that people construct around themselves. As a result, when people enter therapy, their therapists' efforts to convince them that they are lovable and competent may be undone when they return home to lovers or family members who think poorly of them. And if the therapists' efforts *are* effective, the patients' partners may respond by encouraging patients to revert to their former selves, withdraw from therapy, or both (e.g., Kerr, 1981; Wachtel & Wachtel, 1986).

But intimates who have unfavorable impressions of their partners may do more than stabilize their partners' negative self-views. Because intimates tend to assume that their partners' shortcomings reflect on *them*, they may be highly intolerant of such shortcomings and actively reject partners whom they perceive to suffer from such shortcomings (e.g., Swann et al., 1994). This means that when people with negative self-views choose intimates who see them as they see themselves, they increase the chances that their intimates will reject them. Such rejecting intimates may even go so far as to verbally and physically abuse them: Women with low self-esteem seem to be particularly apt to marry men who are high in negative instrumentality (i.e., who are hostile, egotistical, dictatorial, arrogant). Tragically, women involved with such men are especially apt to report being physically abused (Buckner & Swann, 1996).

The good news is that the therapeutic context may provide one way out of this dilemma. Therapists do not feel that the shortcomings of their patients reflect on them in the way that, for example, married people feel that their spouses reflect on them. The greater objectivity of therapists makes it more likely that they will be able to validate their patients' shortcomings (i.e., provide negative feedback) in a supportive and accepting context. When administered in such a context, negative feedback actually may be beneficial. Finn and Tonsager (1996), for example, established a warm and supportive relationship with patients and then gave them feedback that confirmed their self-views. Two weeks later, those who had received congruent feedback displayed improved psychological functioning and higher self-esteem relative to a no-feedback control group—despite the fact that the congruent feedback was sometimes decidedly negative (e.g., "you are depressed, thought disordered, angry, obsessional"). Patients seemed to benefit enormously from having someone else recognize and validate their shortcomings.

Why are confirming, negative evaluations beneficial? One reason is that congruent feedback delivered in a supportive context may increase people's perceptions that they are competent in at least one sphere: knowing themselves. This realization may foster a feeling of epistemological competence, a sense of mastery, predictability, and control, and these perceptions may reduce anxiety. In addition, being understood by a therapist may reduce feelings of alienation, for it tells patients that someone thought enough of them to attempt to understand them. For these and related reasons, negative but self-verifying feedback that comes from an emotionally supportive therapist may have beneficial effects.

Therapists also might utilize the self-verification strivings of patients in the service of changing their self-views. For instance, Swann and colleagues (1988) capitalized on the tendency for people to self-verify by resisting feedback that disconfirmed their self-views. They asked political conservatives questions that were *so* conservative (e.g., "Why do you think men always make better bosses than women?") that even staunch conservatives resisted the premises inherent in the questions. Upon observing themselves take a somewhat liberal position, these conservative participants adjusted their attitudes in a liberal direction. This effect is similar to "paradoxical" techniques in which therapists impute qualities to patients that are more extreme than patients' actual qualities (e.g., characterizing an unassertive person as a complete doormat) in the hope that they will behaviorally resist the innuendo (e.g., become more assertive) and adopt corresponding self-views (e.g., Watzlawick, Weakland, & Fisch, 1974).

There are, of course, additional strategies that may be utilized in attempting to change people's self-views. The more general point here, however, is that it is overly simplistic to assume that people are motivated to embrace positive evaluations and will thus cheerfully endorse positive affirmations ("I'm good enough, I'm smart enough, and darn it, people like me") and encouragement to "think positive." In reality, the situation that people in psychological distress confront is complicated by a desire for self-verification that may compel them to maintain their negative self-views by embracing confirming feedback, eschewing disconfirming feedback, and surrounding themselves with relationship partners who act as accomplices in maintaining their negative self-views. Research on the nature, underpinnings, and boundary conditions of such self-verification strivings may thus provide insight into the widely reported phenomenon of "resistance"—the tendency for patients in therapy to resist positive change. In so doing, it may pave the way for the development of intervention strategies that accommodate or exploit self-verification strivings rather than being sabotaged by them. Allowing people with negative self-views to slowly overcome their natural resistance to positivity may be, in the words of a recent filmmaker, "as good as it gets."

Acknowledgment This research was supported by a grant from the National Institutes of Mental Health MH57455-10A2 to William B. Swann Jr.

Notes

1. Hereafter we avoid the term *self-enhancement strivings* because past usages of it have rendered it ambiguous. For example, although the term itself (*self*-enhancement) implies that the processes to which it refers involve the self-concept, in reality the self-concept is *not* involved in many self-enhancement processes (e.g., strategic self-presentation, self-esteem maintenance). In addition, although the term *enhancement* means "to make greater, heighten," some prominent researchers (e.g., Tesser, 1988) have incorporated efforts to *maintain* high self-esteem into the self-enhancement family.

2. In principle, consistency strivings could have been disentangled from positivity strivings by demonstrating that they override positivity strivings in the case of people with negative self-views (Aronson, 1968). Unfortunately, early field studies were unpersuasive because the evidence was largely anecdotal (e.g., Newcomb, 1956). More systematic follow-ups were difficult to interpret due either to methodological and interpretative problems (e.g., Backman & Secord, 1962; Deutsch & Solomon, 1959) or to the inability of subsequent investigators to replicate their results consistently (Aronson & Carlsmith, 1962).

3. In a sense, the feeling of coherence produced by stable beliefs is nothing more than a sense of competence. Yet it is a very special form of competence. Whereas most competences are localized to particular tasks or domains (social, athletic, etc.), the sense of coherence grows out of people's ability to understand reality and themselves. Depriving people of this special form of competence is thus tantamount to taking away their sense of self. As a result, they will not merely feel incompetent; they will suffer the severe disorientation and psychological anarchy that people feel when their very existence is threatened.

4. To be sure, in some *ultimate* sense, people follow the dictates of these epistemic and pragmatic considerations for precisely the same reason that they strive for positivity—to maximize their outcomes. The fact that self-verification theory shares this hedonistic assumption with positivity theory does not mean that the two are indistinguishable, however. That is, *in the here and now*, positivity theory assumes that people strive for favorable feedback, and self-verification theory assumes that people strive for self-confirmatory feedback. Positivity theory therefore implies that people with negative self-views will strive to quench their desire for favorable feedback by seeking flattering appraisals, and self-verification theory assumes that people will work to satisfy their desire for authentic feedback by seeking *un*flattering appraisals. Although one could construct a version of positivity that stipulates that people work to acquire unfavorable feedback so that they will *later* feel good, expanding the theory in this way makes it nearly as elastic as the law of effect!

5. In principle, a person who is *extremely* high in self-certainty may simply dismiss discrepant feedback out of hand. Thus far, however, we have not encountered participants who are sufficiently certain of their self-views to do this.

References

Abelson, R. P. (1983). Whatever became of consistency theory? *Personality and Social Psychology Bulletin, 9,* 37–54.

Alloy, L. B., & Abramson, L. Y. (1988). Depressive realism: Four theoretical perspectives. In L. B. Alloy (Ed.), *Cognitive processes in depression* (pp. 223–265). New York: Guilford.

Allport, G. W. (1954). *The nature of prejudice.* New York: Addison-Wesley.

Aronson, E. (1968). A theory of cognitive dissonance: A current perspective. In L. Berkowitz (Ed.), *Advances in experimental social psychology* (Vol. 4, pp. 1–34). New York: Academic Press.

Aronson, E., & Carlsmith, J. M. (1962). Performance expectancy as a determinant of actual performance. *Journal of Abnormal and Social Psychology, 65,* 178–182.

Backman, C. W., & Secord, P. F. (1962). Liking, selective interaction, and misperception in congruent interpersonal relations. *Sociometry, 25,* 321–335.

Bandura, A. (1986). *Social foundations of thought and action: A social cognitive theory.* Englewood Cliffs, NJ: Prentice-Hall.

Baumeister, R. F. (1982). A self-presentational view of social phenomena. *Psychological Bulletin, 91,* 3–26.

Baumeister, R. F. (1989). The optimal margin of illusion. *Journal of Social and Clinical Psychology, 8,* 176–189.

Berger, P. L., & Luckman, T. (1967). *The social construction of reality.* Garden City, NY: Doubleday-Anchor.

Bettleheim, B. (1943). Individual and mass behavior in extreme situations. *Journal of Abnormal and Social Psychology, 38,* 417–452.

Bosson, J., & Swann, W. B., Jr. (1999). Self-liking, self-competence, and the quest for self-verification. *Personality and Social Psychology Bulletin, 25,* 1230–1241.

Brown, R. (1965). *Social psychology.* New York: Free Press.

Broxton, J. A. (1963). A test of interpersonal attraction predictions derived from balance theory. *Journal of Abnormal and Social Psychology, 66,* 394–397.

Bruner, J. S., Goodnow, J. J., & Austin, G. A. (1956). *A study of thinking.* New York: Wiley.

Buber, M. (1951). Distance and relation. *The Hibbert Journal: Quarterly Review of Religion, Theology and Philosophy, 49,* 105–113.

Buckner, C. E., & Swann, W. B., Jr. (1996, August). *Physical abuse in close relationships: The dynamic interplay of couple characteristics.* Paper presented at the annual meetings of the American Psychological Association, Washington, DC.

Clark, G. L. (1954). *Elements of ecology.* New York: Wiley.

Colvin, C. R., & Block, J. (1994). Do positive illusions foster mental health? An examination of the Taylor and Brown formulation. *Psychological Bulletin, 116,* 3–20.

Connolly, C. (1945). *The unquiet grave: A word cycle.* London: Hamish Hamilton.

Cooley, C. H. (1902). *Human nature and the social order.* New York: Scribner's.

Coyne, J. C. (1976). Toward an interactional description of depression. *Psychiatry, 39,* 28–40.

Coyne, J. C., Kessler, R. C., Tal, M., Turnbull, J., Wortman, C. B., & Greden, J. F. (1987). Living with a depressed person. *Journal of Consulting and Clinical Psychology, 55,* 347–352.

Crary, W. G. (1966). Reactions to incongruent self-experiences. *Journal of Consulting Psychology, 30,* 246–252.

Curtis, R. C., & Miller, K. (1986). Believing another likes or dislikes you: Behavior making the beliefs come true. *Journal of Personality and Social Psychology, 51,* 284–290.

De La Ronde, C., & Swann, W. B., Jr. (1998). Partner verification: Restoring shattered images of our intimates. *Journal of Personality and Social Psychology, 75,* 374–382.

Deutsch, M., & Solomon, L. (1959). Reactions to evaluations by others as influenced by self-evaluations. *Sociometry, 22,* 93–112.

Epstein, S. (1985). The implications of cognitive-experiential self-theory for research in social psychology and personality. *Journal for the Theory of Social Behavior, 15,* 282–309.

Fazio, R. H., & Powell, M. C. (1997). On the value of knowing one's likes and dislikes: Attitude accessibility, stress, and health in college. *Psychological Science, 8,* 430–436.

Fazio, R. H., Powell, M. C., & Williams, C. J. (1989). The role of attitude accessibility in the attitude-to-behavior process. *Journal of Consumer Research, 16,* 280–288.

Festinger, L. (1957). *A theory of cognitive dissonance,* Evanston, IL: Row, Peterson.

Finn, S. E., & Tonsager, M. E. (1996). Therapeutic impact of providing MMPI-2 feedback to college students awaiting therapy. *Journal of Psychological Assessment, 4,* 278–287.

Gecas, V. (1991). The self-concept as a basis for a theory of motivation. In J. A. Howard & L. P. Callero (Eds.), *The self-society dynamic: Cognition, emotion, and action* (pp. 171–187). New York: Cambridge University Press.

Giesler, R. B., Josephs, R. A., & Swann, W. B., Jr. (1996). Self-verification in clinical depression: The desire for negative evaluation. *Journal of Abnormal Psychology, 105,* 358–368.

Goffman, E. (1959). *The presentation of self in everyday life*. Garden City, NY: Doubleday-Anchor.

Greenwald, A. G. (1980). The totalitarian ego: Fabrication and revision of personal history. *American Psychologist, 35*, 603–618.

Greenwald, A. G., & Ronnis, D. L. (1978). Twenty years of cognitive dissonance: Case study of the evolution of a theory. *Psychological Review, 85*, 53–57.

Harlow, H. F. (1958). The nature of love. *American Psychologist, 13*, 673–685.

Heider, F. (1958). *The psychology of interpersonal relations*. New York: Wiley.

Higgins, E. T., & Bargh, J. A. (1987). Social cognition and social perception. In M. R. Rosenzweig & L. W. Porter (Eds.), *Annual review of psychology* (Vol. 38, pp. 369–425). Palo Alto, CA: Annual Reviews.

Hixon, J. G., & Swann, W. B., Jr. (1993). When does introspection bear fruit? Self-reflection, self-insight, and interpersonal choices. *Journal of Personality and Social Psychology, 64*, 35–43.

Hovland, C. I., & Weiss, W. (1953). Transmission of information concerning concepts through positive and negative instances. *Journal of Experimental Psychology, 45*, 175–182.

Jones, E. E., & Pittman, T. S. (1982). Toward a general theory of strategic self-presentation. In J. Suls (Ed.), *Psychological perspectives on the self* (pp. 231–262). Hillsdale, NJ: Erlbaum.

Jones, S. C. (1973). Self and interpersonal evaluations: Esteem theories versus consistency theories. *Psychological Bulletin, 79*, 185–199.

Jost, J. T., & Banaji, M. R. (1994). The role of stereotyping in system-justification and the production of false consciousness. *British Journal of Social Psychology, 33*, 1–27.

Katz, J., Beach, S. R. H., & Anderson, P. (1996). Self-enhancement versus self-verification: Does spousal support always help? *Cognitive Therapy and Research, 20*, 345–360.

Kelly, G. A. (1955). *The psychology of personal constructs*. New York: Norton.

Kerr, M. E. (1981). Family systems theory and therapy. In A. S. Gurman & D. P. Kiskern (Eds.), *Handbook of family therapy* (pp. 226–264). New York: Brunner/Mazel.

Klayman, J., & Ha, Y. W. (1987). Confirmation, disconfirmation, and information in hypothesis testing. *Psychological Review, 94*, 211–228.

Kunda, Z. (1987). Motivated inference: Self-serving generation and evaluation of causal theories. *Journal of Personality and Social Psychology, 53*, 636–647.

Lecky, P. (1945). *Self-consistency: A theory of personality*. New York: Island Press.

Markus, H. (1977). Self-schemas and processing information about the self. *Journal of Personality and Social Psychology, 35*, 63–78.

McCall, G. J., & Simmons, J. L. (1966). *Identities and interactions: An examination of human associations in everyday life*. New York: Free Press.

McFarlin, D. B., & Blascovich, J. (1981). Effects of self-esteem and performance on future affective preferences and cognitive expectations. *Journal of Personality and Social Psychology, 40*, 521–531.

McNulty, S. E., & Swann, W. B., Jr. (1994). Identity negotiation in roommate relationships: The self as architect and consequence of social reality. *Journal of Personality and Social Psychology, 67*, 1012–1023.

Mead, G. H. (1934). *Mind, self and society*. Chicago: University of Chicago Press.

Mischel, W. (1979). On the interface of cognition and personality: Beyond the person-situation debate. *American Psychologist, 34*, 740–754.

Moreland, R. L., & Sweeney, P. D. (1984). Self-expectancies and reaction to evaluations of personal performance. *Journal of Personality, 52*, 156–176.

Mori, D., Chaiken, S., & Pliner, P. (1987). "Eating lightly" and the self-presentation of feminity. *Journal of Personality and Social Psychology, 53*, 693–702.

Murray, S. L., Holmes, J. G., & Griffin, D. W. (1993). Seeing virtues in faults: Negativity and the transformation of interpersonal narratives in close relationships. *Journal of Personality and Social Psychology, 65*, 707–722.

Murray, S., Holmes, J. G., & Griffin, D. W. (1996). The benefits of positive illusions: Idealization and the construction of satisfaction in close relationships. *Journal of Personality and Social Psychology, 70*, 79–98.

Murray, S. L., Holmes, J. G., & Griffin, D. W. (2000). Self-esteem and the quest for felt security: How perceived regard regulates attachment processes. *Journal of Personality and Social Psychology, 78*, 478–498.

Newcomb, T. M. (1956). The prediction of interpersonal attraction. *American Psychologist, 11*, 575–586.

Pelham, B. W. (1991). On confidence and consequence: The certainty and importance of self-knowledge. *Journal of Personality and Social Psychology, 60*, 518–530.

Pelham, B. W., & Carrillo, M. A. (1999). [Accessibility of self-views and self-verification]. Unpublished raw data.

Pelham, B. W., & Swann, W. B., Jr. (1994). The juncture of intrapersonal and interpersonal knowledge: Self-certainty and interpersonal congruence. *Personality and Social Psychology Bulletin, 20,* 349–357.

Pervin, L. A., & Rubin, D. B. (1967). Student dissatisfaction with college and the college dropout: A transactional approach. *Journal of Social Psychology, 72,* 285–295.

Peterson, C., & Seligman, M. E. P. (1987). Explanatory style and illness. *Journal of Personality, 55,* 237–265.

Pinel, E. C., & Swann, W. B., Jr. (1999). *The cognitive-affective crossfire revisited: Affective reactions to self-discrepant evaluation.* Unpublished manuscript, University of Texas at Austin.

Popper, K. R. (1963). *Conjectures and refutations.* London: Routledge.

Ritts, V., & Stein, J. R. (1995). Verification and commitment in marital relationships: An exploration of self-verification theory in community college students. *Psychological Reports, 76,* 383–386.

Robinson, D. T., & Smith-Lovin, L. (1992). Selective interaction as a strategy for identity maintenance: An affect control model. *Social Psychology Quarterly, 55,* 12–28.

Schafer, R. B., Wickrama, K. A. S., & Keith, P. M. (1996). Self-concept disconfirmation, psychological distress, and marital happiness. *Journal of Marriage and the Family, 58,* 167–177.

Schlenker, B. R. (1980). *Impression management.* Monterey, CA: Brooks/Cole.

Secord, P. F., & Backman, C. W. (1965). An interpersonal approach to personality. In B. Maher (Ed.), *Progress in experimental personality research* (Vol. 2, pp. 91–125). New York: Academic Press.

Sedikides, C., & Strube, M. J. (1997). Self-evaluation: To thine own self be good, to thine own self be sure, to thine own self be true, and to thine own self be better. In M. P. Zanna (Ed.), *Advances in experimental social psychology* (Vol. 29, pp. 209–269). New York: Academic Press.

Seligman, M. E. P. (1986, August). *Explanatory style: Depression, Lyndon Baines Johnson and the Baseball Hall of Fame.* Paper presented at the 94th Annual Convention of the American Psychological Association, Washington, DC.

Serpe, R. T. & Stryker, S. (1987). The construction of self and reconstruction of social relationships. In E. Lawler & B. Markovsky (Eds.), *Advances in group processes* (pp. 41–66). Greenwich, CT: JAI.

Shrauger, J. S. (1975). Responses to evaluation as a function of initial self-perceptions. *Psychological Bulletin, 82,* 581–596.

Shrauger, J. S., & Lund, A. (1975). Self-evaluation and reactions to evaluations from others. *Journal of Personality, 43,* 94–108.

Shrauger, J. S., & Schoeneman, T. J. (1979). Symbolic interactionist view of self-concept: Through the looking glass darkly. *Psychological Bulletin, 86,* 549–573.

Silverman, I. (1964). Self-esteem and differential responsiveness to success and failure. *Journal of Social Psychology, 69,* 115–119.

Snyder, C. R., & Higgins, R. L. (1988). Excuses: Their effective role in the negotiation of social reality. *Psychological Bulletin, 104,* 23–35.

Snyder, C. R., Higgins, R. L., & Stucky, R. (1983). *Excuses: Masquerades in search of grace.* New York: Wiley.

Snyder, M., & Swann, W. B., Jr. (1978). Hypothesis testing processes in social interaction. *Journal of Personality and Social Psychology, 36,* 1202–1212.

Steele, C. M. (1988). The psychology of self-affirmation: Sustaining the integrity of the self. In L. Berkowitz (Ed.), *Advances in experimental social psychology* (Vol. 21, pp. 261–302). New York: Academic Press.

Stone, G. P. (1962). Appearance and the self. In A. Rose (Ed.), *Human behavior and social processes* (pp. 86–118). Boston: Houghton Mifflin.

*Swann, W. B., Jr. (1983). Self-verification: Bringing social reality into harmony with the self. In J. Suls & A. G. Greenwald (Eds.), *Psychological perspectives on the self* (Vol. 2, pp. 33–66). Hillsdale, NJ: Erlbaum.

Swann, W. B., Jr. (1984). The quest for accuracy in person perception: A matter of pragmatics. *Psychological Review, 91,* 457–477.

Swann, W. B., Jr. (1987). Identity negotiation: Where two roads meet. *Journal of Personality and Social Psychology, 53,* 1038–1051.

*Swann, W. B., Jr. (1990). To be adored or to be known: The interplay of self-enhancement and self-verification. In R. M. Sorrentino & E. T. Higgins (Eds.), *Handbook of motivation and cognition: Foundations of social behavior* (Vol. 2, pp. 408–448). New York: Guilford.

*Swann, W. B., Jr. (1999). *Resilient identities: Self, relationships, and the construction of social reality.* New York: Basic Books.

Swann, W. B., Bosson, J., & Pelham, B. W. (2001). Different partners, different selves: The versification of circumscribed identities. Unpublished manuscript, University of Texas at Austin.

*Swann, W. B., Jr., De La Ronde, C., & Hixon, J. G. (1994). Authenticity and positivity strivings in marriage and courtship. *Journal of*

Personality and Social Psychology, 66, 857–869.

Swann, W. B., Jr., & Ely, R. J. (1984). A battle of wills: Self-verification versus behavioral confirmation. *Journal of Personality and Social Psychology, 46*, 1287–1302

Swann, W. B., Jr., & Giuliano, T. (1987). Confirmatory search strategies in social interaction: When, how, why and with what consequences. *Journal of Clinical and Social Psychology, 5*, 511–524.

Swann, W. B., Jr., Griffin, J. J., Predmore, S., & Gaines, B. (1987). The cognitive-affective crossfire: When self-consistency confronts self-enhancement. *Journal of Personality and Social Psychology, 52*, 881–889.

Swann, W. B., Jr., & Hill, C. A. (1982). When our identities are mistaken: Reaffirming self-conceptions through social interaction. *Journal of Personality and Social Psychology, 43*, 59–66.

Swann, W. B., Jr., Hixon, J. G., Stein-Seroussi, A., & Gilbert, D. T. (1990). The fleeting gleam of praise: Behavioral reactions to self-relevant feedback. *Journal of Personality and Social Psychology, 59*, 17–26.

Swann, W. B., Jr., Milton, L., & Polzer, J. (1999). Creating a niche or falling in line: Identity negotiation and small group effectiveness. *Journal of Personality and Social Psychology*.

Swann, W. B., Jr., & Pelham, B. W. (1999). Who wants out when the going gets good? Psychological investment and preference for self-verifying college roommates. Unpublished manuscript, University of Texas at Austin.

Swann, W. B., Jr., Pelham, B. W., & Chidester, T. (1988). Change through paradox: Using self-verification to alter beliefs. *Journal of Personality and Social Psychology, 54*, 268–273.

Swann, W. B., Jr., Pelham, B. W., & Krull, D. S. (1989). Agreeable fancy or disagreeable truth? Reconciling self-enhancement and self-verification. *Journal of Personality and Social Psychology, 57*, 782–791.

*Swann, W. B., Jr., & Predmore, S. C. (1985). Intimates as agents of social support: Sources of consolation or despair? *Journal of Personality and Social Psychology, 49*, 1609–1617.

Swann, W. B., Jr., & Read, S. J. (1981). Self-verification processes: How we sustain our self-conceptions. *Journal of Experimental Social Psychology, 17*, 351–372.

*Swann, W. B., Jr., & Shroeder, D. G. (1995). The search for beauty and truth: A framework for understanding reactions to evaluative feedback. *Personality and Social Psychology Bulletin, 21*, 1307–1318.

Swann, W. B., Jr., Stein-Seroussi, A., & Giesler, B. (1992). Why people self-verify. *Journal of Personality and Social Psychology, 62*, 392–401.

Swann, W. B., Jr., Wenzlaff, R. M., Krull, D. S., & Pelham, B. W. (1992). The allure of negative feedback: Self-verification strivings among depressed persons. *Journal of Abnormal Psychology, 101*, 293–306.

Swann, W. B., Jr., Wenzlaff, R. M., & Tafarodi, R. W. (1992). Depression and the search for negative evaluations: More evidence of the role of self-verification strivings. *Journal of Abnormal Psychology, 101*, 314–371.

Taylor, S. E., & Brown, J. D. (1988). Illusion and well-being: Some social psychological contributions to a theory of mental health. *Psychological Bulletin, 103*, 193–210.

Tesser, A. (1988). Toward a self-evaluation maintenance model of social behavior. In L. Berkowitz (Ed.), *Advances in experimental social psychology* (Vol. 21, pp. 181–227). New York: Academic Press.

Thoreau, H. D. (1854). *Walden*. Boston: Ticknor and Fields.

Wachtel, E. F., & Wachtel, P. L. (1986). *Family dynamics in individual psychotherapy: A guide to clinical strategies*. New York: Guilford.

Wachtel, P. L. (1977). *Psychoanalysis and behavior therapy: Toward an integration*. New York: Basic Books.

Wason, P. C., & Johnson-Laird, P. N. (1972). *Psychology of reasoning: Structure and content*. London: D. T. Batsford.

Watzlawick, P., Weakland, J. H., & Fisch, R. (1974). *Change: Principles of problem formation and problem resolution*. New York: Norton.

Weinstein, N. D. (1980). Unrealistic optimism about future life events. *Journal of Personality and Social Psychology, 39*, 806–820.

Wills, T. A. (1981). Downward comparison principles in social psychology. *Psychological Bulletin, 90*, 245–271.

27

Authenticity

Susan Harter

Origins: "To Thine Own Self Be True"

The history of the concept of personal authenticity can be traced back to ancient Greek philosophy as revealed in injunctions such as "Know thyself" and "To thine own self be true." However, there is no single, coherent body of literature on authentic-self behavior, no bedrock of knowledge. Rather, there are unconnected islands that address different aspects of authenticity in rather piecemeal fashion, including historical analyses, clinical treatments, social-psychological perspectives, and developmental formulations.

Before exploring these islands of insight, it is important to define the construct of authenticity. In so doing, it can best be put in bold relief by considering its opposite, namely, lack of authenticity or false-self behavior. Consistent with the impetus for this volume, it should be noted that far more attention has been devoted to the *lack* of authentic-self behavior, within the clinical, social-psychological, and developmental literatures, where theorists and investigators have examined deceit of others, secrecy, imposter tendencies, self-monitoring, compliance, and self-deception. From a less scientific perspective, one can observe the vast vocabulary in the English language to describe deceit (Lerner, 1993),

suggesting its salience in our collective psyche. Verb forms make reference to fabricating, withholding, concealing, distorting, falsifying, pulling the wool over someone's eyes, posturing, charading, faking, and hiding behind a facade. Adjectives include elusive, evasive, wily, phony, artificial, two-faced, manipulative, calculating, pretentious, crafty, conniving, duplicitous, deceitful, and dishonest. Noun forms include hypocrite, charlatan, chameleon, impostor, phony, fake, and fraud.

At one level, authenticity involves *owning* one's personal experiences, be they thoughts, emotions, needs, wants, preferences, or beliefs, processes captured by the injunction to "know oneself." The exhortation "To thine own self be true" further implies that one *acts* in accord with the true self, expressing oneself in ways that are consistent with inner thoughts and feelings. When we have asked adolescents to define true-self behavior, descriptions include "the real me inside," "saying what you really think or believe," "expressing your honest opinion," and "telling someone how you really feel."

In contrast, false-self behavior is described as "being phony," "hiding your true thoughts and feelings," "saying what you think *others* want to hear, not what you really think." These definitions of false-self behavior imply that one is compromising the true self and acting in ways that are experienced as phony or artificial. It should be emphasized that acting differently in different relational contexts does not necessarily constitute false-self behavior (although it may appear chameleon-like to others). For example, role theories emphasize that people may legitimately behave differently across contexts, adjusting their behavior to be appropriate to each relationship (see Johnson & Boyd, 1995; Leary & Kowalski, 1990; Snyder, 1987). However, for the behavior to qualify as false-self behavior, the person must have the phenomenological experience that his or her actions and words lack authenticity. (Thus, self-report measures best assess the perception that one is behaving falsely or, alternatively, in accord with one's true nature.) Typically the false self is experienced as *socially implanted* against one's will, and as such it feels foreign. As a result, there may be psychological tension between the display of a false self and a person's sense of his or her true self. As such, there may be conscious concern over compromising who one really is.

Historically, these concerns became paramount in the 16th century (Baumeister, 1987; Trilling, 1971). Trilling describes the obsession with deceit and pretense that found its way into politics, philosophy, and literature (e.g., Shakespeare) in England. Baumeister observes that people were particularly worried that *others* may be concealing their true selves for manipulative purposes. With the 17th-century advent of Puritanism, people became more concerned over whether they were deceiving *themselves*, particularly with regard to those attributes (piety, faith, and virtue) considered essential to entering the kingdom of heaven. During the 19th century, emphasis on the hidden parts of the self was exacerbated by Victorian repressiveness; with heightened self-scrutiny, coupled with impossibly high moral standards, individuals gravitated to self-deception. Moreover, Freud's initial revelations concerning the prevalence of unconscious thought reinforced the view that parts of the true self may be inaccessible even to the person himself.

The Period of Modernism

In the 20th century, the period of modernism was ushered in by a variety of scientific and technological advances in the service of objectivity and truth-seeking (Gergen, 1991), many

with implications for the self. The machine became the metaphor for the self. In computer terminology, individuals were characterized as networks of associations, perceptual mechanisms, and cognitive structures, all with *rationality* as the essence of humanity. Proper socialization by family and by wider cultural forces would result in a "well-designed" person whose behavior would be self-directing, authentic, trustworthy, and consistent. As Gergen observes, "Modernist man is genuine rather than phony, principled, rather than craven, stable, rather than wavering" (p. 44).

The emphasis on rationality as the essence of human nature dramatically changed the nature of our psychological theories of self, particularly within the clinical community. The sources of psychological problems were no longer buried within the Freudian unconscious but rather were accessible through the realm of rational thought. In regard to pathology, in general, and false-self behavior, in particular, clinicians focused on the *barriers* to authenticity that could be observed in socialization practices and cultural constraints. Thus, the essence of the naturally good human being was corrupted by socioenvironmental conditions, sentiments that found their way into the works of Erich Fromm, Karen Horney, and Carl Rogers. Horney (1950) explicitly identified those social conditions that produced the person's alienation from the real self. She contended that the underlying cause of neurosis lay in the individual constructing images of what he or she *ought* to be. To the extent that these self-images were unrealistic, constructed primarily to garner the approval of others, people became alienated from their true selves.

The theme of alienation from one's true self can also be observed within the 20th century sociological and social psychological literatures, where lack of authenticity among adults, in particular, was considered to be motivated by attempts to present the self in a manner that would impress, or win the acceptance of, others. For example, Goffman (1959), in his treatment of the presentation of self in everyday life, described the manipulative motives that compete with our desire to be sincere. Various forms of "facework" communicate to others that we are competent, likable, moral, or worthy of respect, motives designed not only to protect and promote the self but also to curry favor, obtain social currency or power, and preserve critical relationships. Earlier in the same decade, Riesman

(1950), in *The Lonely Crowd*, distinguished between "inner-directed" individuals who were self-determining and, by definition, more true to themselves, and "outer-directed" individuals whose malleability, in the face of social demands, marked them as less authentic. The inner-directed individual was essentially the ideal image of the modernist man, as exemplified by Reisman's antipathy for the outer-directed individual, who is described as "superficial" and a "conformist," with an insatiable appetite for the approval of others.

A similar distinction has been offered by Snyder (1987) in identifying high versus low *self-monitors*. High self-monitors are very concerned about the situational and interpersonal appropriateness of their social behavior and are particularly sensitive to their self-presentation with others across situations, altering their behavior accordingly. Low self-monitors, in contrast, are less concerned about the appropriateness of their behavior and self-presentational skills; rather, they are more interested in being themselves with others. From one perspective, high self-monitors are presumed to suppress features of their true self in order to gain the approval of others. Thus, one could condemn the high self-monitor for superficiality if not deceit. In Snyder's (1987) subsequent treatment of the pros and cons of each orientation, however, he suggests that high self-monitoring can reflect the individual's flexibility in coping with the increasing diversity of social roles that one is expected to assume in contemporary life.

The Period of Postmodernism

The need to adapt to the diverse roles required in an increasingly complex society has become a reality in contemporary life, with potential perils. For example, Gergen develops a portrait of the "saturated" self, observing that easy access to air travel, electronic and express mail, fax machines, cellular phones, beepers, and answering machines has dramatically accelerated our social connectedness. For Gergen, these changes have profound implications for the self and its authenticity. The demands of multiple relationships split the individual into a multiplicity of self-investments, leading to a "cacophony of potential selves" across different relational contexts. Thus, if one is playing out many roles as a "social chameleon," adopting multiple roles for social gain, the individual may come to conclude that one is not being true

to oneself. Others (e.g., Lifton, 1993), as well as those who emphasize the adaptiveness of constructing "possible selves" that may vary from role to role (Markus & Nurius, 1986), are more sanguine about the likelihood that authenticity can be preserved in the face of the creation of multiple selves, a topic to which I shall return (see also Baumeister, Hutton, & Tice, 1989).

With these historical themes as a backdrop, I will deal with the following topics in this chapter. The issue of why authentic-self behavior and its converse become so salient during adolescence, when the search for the true self is of paramount concern, is first discussed. The need to create multiple selves across different relational contexts is a major developmental challenge that produces an interest in authentic-self behavior. I will then turn to those developmental factors in childhood and adolescence that foster true-self, versus false-self, behavior. I next shift to why we should care about authenticity. As will become apparent, there are a number of positive correlates and consequences of authentic-self behavior that have mental health implications. Many of these themes will be addressed in a section on authenticity within adult relationships. Thereafter, I return to the issue of whether authenticity can survive given the need to create multiple selves in adolescence and adulthood. The next question is whether one can be *too* authentic: Is honesty always the best policy? Finally, I will end the chapter with a treatment of several implications for interventions to promote greater authenticity and its associated psychological benefits.

The Developmental Emergence of an Interest in Authenticity During Adolescence

Although factors influencing authenticity begin in childhood, not until adolescence are individuals actively interested in, if not concerned about, whether their behavior reflects true-self or false-self behavior. One impetus for this preoccupation is the societal demand that the adolescent create *multiple selves* associated with different social roles or contexts. Not only do socialization pressures force the adolescent to behave differently in different contexts, but cognitive-developmental advances equip the adolescent with the ability to differentiate such selves (see Harter, 1999). Thus, one may be depressed with parents, cheerful with a group of friends, shy with a romantic other, open with a close friend, hardworking in school, responsible on a job, rowdy and less responsible with peers, and so forth (Harter, 1999). As a normative process, therefore, the adolescent comes to don different persona across relational contexts (see also Erikson, 1950; Hart, 1988; Harter & Monsour, 1992; Markus & Nurius, 1986; Smollar & Youniss, 1985).

With this proliferation of selves, there is a natural concern over which is "the real me," particularly when self-attributes in different roles (e.g., depressed with parents but cheerful with friends) appear to be contradictory. We observed this concern in administering our multiple-selves procedure, which requires that adolescents first spontaneously generate attributes across relevant relational contexts (see Harter, Bresnick, Bouchey, & Whitesell, 1997). They then are asked to indicate whether any pairs of attributes reflect "opposites" (e.g., outgoing with friends, shy on a date). Finally, they identify any pairs of opposites that are associated with internal "conflict," that is, that are experienced as clashing within their personality. All adolescents identify opposites in their self-portrait. However, the number of conflicts can vary from 1 to 15 or 20, depending on the developmental level and the gender of the adolescent. Conflict peaks in middle adolescence and is more prevalent for females than males at all developmental levels.

During our individually administered multiple-selves procedure, some teenagers have spontaneously agonized over which of these conflicting attributes represent true-self behavior, and which seemed false, suggesting the salience of this issue during adolescence. The following examples capture their concern:

- I really think I am a happy person, like with my friends, but then I get depressed around my family, and it bugs me because that's not what I want to be like, its not the real me.
- I hate the fact that I get so nervous on a date, I wish I wasn't so inhibited. The real me is talkative, I just want to be natural but I can't.
- I really think of myself as friendly and open to people, but the way the other girls act, they force me to become an introvert, even though I know that's not my true self.
- At work I am very responsible but then I go out with my friends and I get pretty crazy

and irresponsible. So which am I, responsible or irresponsible, which is the real me?

From a cognitive-developmental perspective (Fischer, 1980; Harter, 1999; Harter & Monsour, 1992), middle adolescence is the period during which teenagers wrestle most painfully with these issues because they have the cognitive ability to recognize contradictory attributes, one of which typically reflects their true self and one of which represents displays of false-self behavior; however, they do not yet have the ability to resolve such conflicts. Later in development, with the advent of the ability to create higher-order abstractions, the individual is more able to cognitively integrate apparent contradictions. For example, cheerfulness with peers and depression with parents can be viewed as two manifestations of an overarching trait, namely, flexibility or adaptiveness. In addition, adolescents come to *normalize* such seemingly opposing attributes, finding value in inconsistency, suggesting that it would unnatural to act similarly with everyone. Rather, they report that it is desirable and appropriate to be different in different relational contexts. One older teenager indicated, "You can be shy on a date, and then outgoing with friends because you are just different with different people; you can't always be the same person and probably shouldn't be." As another older adolescent put it, "There's a time you should listen and a time you should talk. You can do both." With the advent of emerging cognitive structures in later adolescence and early adulthood, coupled with expectations that a person should act differently in different relational contexts, normative adolescent conflict and concern over whether one is engaging in false-self behavior should abate.

By considering both cognitive-developmental factors and socialization pressures, we can enhance our understanding of the potential causes of adolescent preoccupation with authenticity. That is, normalizing such concerns allows for a more benevolent perspective on this period of development, helping to demystify the often strange and volatile conceptualizations that teenagers bring to bear upon the self. Moreover, the fact that many adolescents actively wrestle with whether they are being true to themselves versus engaging in false-self behavior suggests that behaving authentically is a *value*, a goal toward which they aspire. For example, adolescents report that they *like* their true-self attributes (which average around 80% of all attributes), whereas their ratings indicate that they do not admire their false-self attributes (averaging around 20%). Thus, our contemporary adolescents appear to value, and seem to be striving for, authenticity in the face of developmental constraints that may make their quest difficult.

Developmental Precursors of Authenticity and Its Opposite, in Childhood and Adolescence

Not until early adolescence do individuals consciously conceptualize their behavior as true versus false and seem preoccupied with this distinction. The foundations of authenticity, however, are laid down in early childhood. Although the emergence of *language* is critical to the development of authenticity, it is also a double-edged sword (Stern, 1985). On the positive side, the attainment of language is potent in the service of union and connectedness, because it provides a common symbol system, allowing for new levels of shared meaning. Verbal representation also provides a powerful vehicle through which the child can begin to construct a narrative of experiences, a "life story," preserved in autobiographical memory (see Fivush & Hudson, 1990; Nelson, 1989; Snow, 1990).

On the other hand, there are potential liabilities associated with language. Stern (1985), for example, argues that language can drive a wedge between two forms of interpersonal experience, as it is actually lived and as it is verbally represented. The very capacity for objectifying the self through language allows one to transcend, and therefore potentially distort, one's immediate experience (including how the self is portrayed). For example, emotional reactions as experienced by a child can be mislabeled by significant others (e.g., parents). According to Stein, Trabasso, and Liwag, 1994, the two most common mismatches occur when a mother reports that the child is mad whereas the child reported that he or she feels sad, and when a mother reports that the child is fearful whereas the child reports a different emotion. To the extent that children capitulate and accept the mother's interpretation of their emotions, in order to please them or avoid disapproval, they are distorting this true-self experiences. Alternatively, if parents accept children's accounts of their emotional reactions, such validation will promote their sense of authenticity

and reinforce their trust in the personal reality of their affective experiences.

Developmental psychologists (e.g., Fivush & Hudson, 1990; Nelson, 1989; Snow, 1990) who study autobiographical memory and the creation of a personal narrative similarly emphasize how parents heavily scaffold the content of these early narratives. That is, they are dictated by what the *parent* feels is important to codify in the construction of the child's autobiographical memory. Such a narrative may, in some families, represent a falsified version of the child's experience rather than an insistence on the experience that the child personally recalls. Alternatively, if parents encourage their children to construct a narrative based on their own memories of events, thereby validating the children's own experience, then the groundwork for authentic self-representations will be laid.

Within the child-clinical literature, theorists have also focused on the social-interactional precursors of false versus true-self behavior (Bleiberg, 1984; Winnicott, 1965). For Bleiberg, false-self behavior results from caregivers who do not validate the child's true self, leading him or her to become alienated from authentic self-experiences. For Winnicott, parents who are intrusively overinvolved with their young child foster the development of a false self based upon compliance. As such, personal representations of preferences, thoughts, wishes, needs, and emotions may be stifled to comply with parental demands. Contemporary theorists (e.g., Deci & Ryan, 1995) echo these themes, contending that a child's authentic self is fostered by caregivers who love the child for whom he or she is. In contrast, false-self behavior will emerge if caregivers make their approval contingent upon the child's living up to their particular standards, because the child must adopt a socially implanted self. This scenario is intensified for children who are victims of severe, chronic sexual abuse, where parental demands, coercion, enforced compliance, and secrecy pacts all force the true self to go underground (see Harter, 1999). (For a recent treatment of the negative psychological impact of secrecy, in general, see Kelly, 2001.) Throughout both developmental and clinical literatures, therefore, sincere parental validation of the child's own personal experiences and strengths represents the initial pathway to authenticity.

The importance of support and acceptance continues into later childhood and adolescence, where not only does parental validation of the child's true self remain critical but also peer validation becomes increasingly important. Central to this formulation is Rogers's concept of *unconditional positive regard* (1951). Although Rogers initially invoked this construct as a clinical tool whereby therapists are very accepting of patients' rendering of their experiences, parental and peer displays of positive regard for who one genuinely is also will promote authenticity. We examined this hypothesis directly in a study with middle school adolescents who were able to self-report on both their parents' and peers' behavior, as well as the extent to which they engaged in true-self versus false-self behavior (Harter, Marold, Whitesell, & Cobbs, 1996).

We first operationalized the latter construct as "acting in ways that reflect the real me or my true self" versus "acting in ways that are *not* the real me or my true self." Unconditional positive regard was tapped through items asking the extent to which parents and peers "accept me as I am," "like the kind of person I am," "really listen to what I have to say," and so forth. In contrast, conditionality was defined by items stating that parents or peers "will only accept me if I do exactly what *they* want me to do" or "will only care about me if I act just the way they want me to act." Bolstering our hypothesis about a critical pathway to authenticity, adolescents who reported the highest levels of true-self behavior were those who reported the most unconditional support from parents and peers; conversely, those who reported the highest levels of conditionality also reported the greatest degree of false-self behavior. When asked directly why they engaged in false-self behavior, many adolescents indicated that they did so because parents and peers did not like their true selves and therefore, by suppressing their true selves, they might garner approval or support. In the extreme, therefore, the demands of constructing a self to meet the standards and wishes of others can compromise one's authenticity.

The Ability to Voice Opinions as a Manifestation of Authenticity

When we have asked adolescents to define true-self and false-self behaviors, they indicate that a key factor is whether they can verbally express their thoughts, opinions, and feelings. Moreover, when we explicitly inquired about whether the failure to express oneself represented false-self behavior, the vast majority of adolescents reported that it did (Harter, Waters, & Whitesell, 1997). In our studies of the ability to voice one's thoughts, we have been particularly impressed by the vast individual differences in adolescents' self-reported ability to express their opinions. Whereas Gilligan and colleagues (Gilligan, Lyons, & Hanmer, 1989) have argued that girls in our culture lose their voices when they enter adolescence, we have not found such a decline. Mean voice levels (on a 4-point scale of low to high voice) hover around 3.0, well above the midpoint. Thus, the majority of adolescent girls report that they are perfectly capable of "saying what they think," "expressing their opinions," and "stating what is on their mind" across a range of relational contexts (e.g., with parents, teachers, male classmates, female classmates, and best friends). A smaller subset are much less able to voice their thoughts and opinions. Similarly, among male adolescents, there are those reporting high levels of voice and those who report that they have great difficulty expressing themselves. Thus, we sought to examine two potential determinants of authenticity as reflected in adolescents' ability to voice their thoughts and opinions to others, the role of support or validation, given our earlier findings, and gender orientation.

One very important form of validation is listening to what another has to say. Thus, we hypothesized that the level of *support* for voice from significant others should be associated with the adolescent's perceived *level* of voice. Accordingly, we created support-for-voice items that tapped the adolescent's perceptions of others' interest in what one had to say, respect for one's ideas even if there is disagreement, ability to listen to one's opinions and take them seriously, and attempts to understand one's point of view. In addition, we crafted items that allowed individuals to report their own level of voice, namely, their ability to state their opinions, express their thoughts and feelings, and so on, within each relational context. Both level of voice and support for voice were assessed on a 4-point scale (where 1 is low and 4 is high).

We have obtained dramatic results that are highly comparable for both genders and can be demonstrated across all relationships (Harter, Waters, & Whitesell, 1997). As can be seen in Figure 27.1, within every relationship, high school students (genders combined) who report the highest level of support for voice also reported the highest level of authenticity as in-

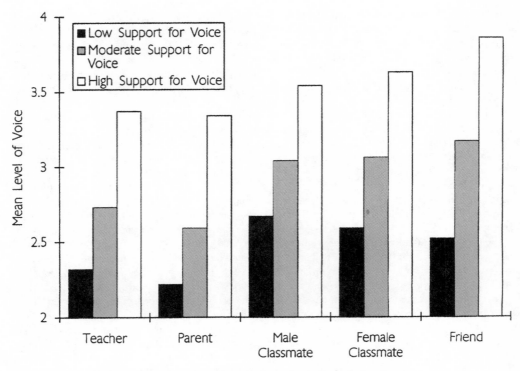

Figure 27.1 Level of voice as a function of support for voice in five relational contexts.

dexed by their own ability to voice their opinions. Those experiencing little support for voice reported the lowest levels of voice, whereas those reporting moderate levels of support for voice fell in between. Thus, validation in the form of genuinely listening and respecting adolescents' viewpoints is highly linked to authentic-self behavior.

As a second predictor among female adolescents, in particular, we examined the relationship between gender orientation, androgynous versus feminine, and level of voice. One of Gilligan et al.'s (1989) arguments is that adolescent girls observe and then emulate the cultural "good woman stereotype" of being more sensitive to others' needs and desires than to their own, the ethics of caring. Moreover, the "good woman" listens empathically to others and often does not speak her own mind. Yet what proportion of adolescent girls in the late 1990s actually accept this stereotype as their ideal?

Adapting existing sex-role inventories (Bem, 1985; Spence, Helmreich, & Stapp, 1975), we determined across several samples that between 60% and 70% of adolescent females endorsed an androgynous orientation, that is, they en-

dorsed both feminine attributes (e.g., sensitivity, warmth, empathy, expressions of affection) and masculine attributes (e.g., ability to make decisions, independence, risk-taking, confidence, athleticism, individualism). Only 25% to 30% endorsed the feminine items only. Thus, there would appear to be a cultural shift among female adolescents, with the majority now defining themselves in terms of both positive feminine characteristics and traditionally positive masculine attributes.

We hypothesized that an androgynous orientation would be associated with greater authenticity for female adolescents, whereas a feminine orientation would lead to compromised authenticity, as defined by level of voice. The findings revealed that femininity does represent a liability in *certain*, but not all, relational contexts (Harter, Waters, & Whitesell, 1997). In this regard, feminine girls reported significantly lower levels of voice than did androgynous girls in the more *public* context of school, with classmates and teachers. Indeed, it is in these more public social contexts that one might expect those highly feminine adolescent females to display behavior (e.g., suppression of voice) consistent with the "good-woman societal stereotype." (In contrast, there were no differences in voice between feminine and androgynous girls in the more *private* relational contexts, with close friends and parents, suggesting that femininity is not a liability within these relationships.) Thus, the arguments put forth by Gilligan et al. (1989) appear to be restricted to feminine girls who suppress their voices in more public arenas where stereotypical female behaviors (being nice, unassertive, quiet) are appropriate or demanded.

Pipher (1994), writing in the popular press, has advanced arguments similar to Gilligan's. She observes that "most girls choose to be socially accepted and split into two selves, one that is authentic and one that is culturally scripted. In public they become who they are supposed to be" (p. 38). However, our own findings reveal this does not necessarily represent the reality of "most" girls but applies to only a minority of girls who have publicly embraced the good-woman stereotype. In contrast, the majority of adolescent females who adopt an androgynous orientation report that they are capable of expressing their authenticity through voicing their opinions.

Why Should We Care About Authenticity? Correlates and Consequences

Adolescents' authenticity, as reflected in self-reported true-self behavior as well as in the ability to voice one's opinion, also is associated with a number of psychological benefits. Those adolescents reporting high levels of true-self behavior, coupled with the acknowledgment that they know or understand who they are as a person, report much higher *self-esteem*, more positive *affect*, and more *hope* for the future (Harter et al., 1996; see also Snyder, Rand, & Sigmon, this volume). Moreover, these adolescents are in the majority. In contrast, the minority of those who report high levels of false-self behavior likewise report low self-esteem, more depressed affect, and greater hopelessness about the future. A similar pattern emerges in our studies of voice. Those high in voice report greater levels of self-esteem and cheerfulness both at the global level and within each relational context. In addition, they report more cheerful affect. Conversely, the minority of adolescents with low levels of voice report low self-esteem as well as depressed affect.

Thus, authenticity is clearly a commodity that not only is enjoyed by the majority of adolescents but also is associated with adaptive psychological characteristics that mental health professionals, educators, and laypeople seek to foster.

The Authentic Self Within Adult Relationships

Similar processes can be observed in adult relationships in that validation, positive regard, and support for who one is as a person is associated with authenticity, which in turn is predictive of benefits such as self-esteem and cheerfulness. However, to fully understand the correlates of authenticity in adulthood, one needs to counter the dichotomy between autonomy and independence (typically associated with men) versus relational connectedness (typically associated with women). Historically, more value has been given to the former orientation. A number of contemporary theorists have argued that a healthy *combination* of autonomy with connectedness is most conducive to healthy outcomes, including authenticity. This emerging emphasis can be observed in literatures about the *infant* (Emde, 1994; Stern, 1985), *child* (Selman & Shultz, 1990), *adolescent* (Allen, Hauser, Bell, & O'Connor, 1994; Steinberg, 1990), and *adult* (Blatt, 1990; Jordan, 1991; Miller, 1986).

Jordan and Miller, from Wellsley's Stone Center, are perhaps most explicit on the point that the deepest sense of a true self is continuously formed in connection with others and is inextricably tied to growth within the relationship. Mutual empathy is the cornerstone of this perspective (see Batson, Ahmad, Lishner, & Tsang, this volume). Genuine empathic exchange and relatedness bring clarity and authenticity to the self (see also Lifton [1993], who views empathy as the path to self-awareness). These theorists attempt to counter the belief that a sense of self is lost given such empathically attuned connectedness. As Gergen (1991) also notes, "At a time when the evils of 'codependency' are so broadly assailed by mental-health professionals, a linguistic space is much needed for positive ways of viewing bonded relationships" (p. 248).

In our research on adult spousal or partner relationships (Harter et al., 1997), we have moved beyond the typical dichotomy (autonomy vs. connectedness) to espouse a framework in which we identify three relationship styles: self-focused autonomy, other-focused connectedness, and mutuality (a balance of healthy autonomy and connectedness). We hypothesized that there were liabilities associated with the two extreme styles. More specifically, we predicted that partners who reflected a combination of these two extreme styles would report less *validation* by their partner, which, in turn, would lead to more false-self behavior. Relationships between mutual individuals, in contrast, should result in the highest levels of validation and authentic-self behavior.

Our findings (from 2,500 adults who responded to a newspaper survey) revealed that the majority of individuals (70%) identified with the mutual relationship style, contradicting the common assumption that most men reflect self-focused autonomy and most women manifest other-focused connection. Partners who each viewed themselves as "mutual" reported the highest levels of validation and authentic-self behavior. Self-focused partners of both genders were perceived to be the least validating. Moreover, in terms of partner combinations, other-focused individuals (who compromise their own needs) with self-focused partners faired the worst in terms of perceived validation by their partner and their ability to be their authentic self within the relationship. As Miller (1986) cogently argues, subordination and authenticity are totally incompatible. Self-focused individuals with other focused partners fell in between the mutual-mutual combination and other-focused individuals with self-focused partners. Moreover, for the entire sample, we found support for a process model in which validation by one's partner predicts the extent to which one can exhibit authentic-self behavior within the relationship, which, in turn, predicts self-esteem and affect (cheerful to depressed). Thus, most individuals identified with the mutual style, which was also identified as the ideal style by approximately 80% of the sample. Mutual individuals provide more validation for their partners and report greater authenticity. Authenticity, in turn, is associated with the positive benefits of high self-esteem and cheerfulness.

Can Authenticity Survive Given the Need to Create Multiple Selves?

For some (e.g., Gergen, 1991), the creation of multiple selves to conform to particular rela-

tionship demands may compromise the sense that one has an obdurate core self that is authentic, thereby casting doubt on one's true identity. However, Gergen leaves the door open in suggesting that multiplicity may provide people with a sense of optimism and possibility as they navigate their interpersonal waters. Lifton (1993) also explores the implications of creating multiple selves in describing the "protean self," derived from the name of the Greek sea god Proteus, who displayed many forms. For Lifton, the protean self emerges from the confusion of contemporary life, in which we feel buffeted about by unmanageable historical, economic, political, and social uncertainties. The protean self, therefore, requires tactical flexibility that could well be experienced as lack of authenticity. However, Lifton emphasizes the resilience of the human condition, as well. Cultural crises may force the self to evolve in numerous directions, creating opportunities for personal expansion and growth. Protean flexibility can enable individuals to strive for connectedness to others (rather than rigid separateness), with more fluid boundaries between their multiple selves that do not compromise a sense of authenticity. Lifton observes that people can only be alienated from themselves if there is something within them from which to be alienated and that something is "authenticity, with meanings that, over the course of a life, one experiences as genuine. The protean quest, however flawed, enhances that authenticity" (p. 232).

Miller (1974), acknowledging the new polytheism that has come to define the postmodern era, also registers a note of optimism. He has described a pattern that was "the radical experience of equally real, but mutually exclusive aspects of the self. Personal identity cannot seem to be fixed. . . . The person experiences himself as many selves, each of which is felt to have a life of its own, coming and going without regard to the centered will of a single ego" (p. 193). Miller contends that such an orientation, far from being pathological, is extremely liberating.

Thus, although earlier theorists (e.g., Allport, 1961; Epstein, 1973; Lecky, 1945; Maslow, 1954; Rogers, 1951) emphasized the integrated and unified self, the pendulum appears to have swung back to an emphasis on multiplicity, as initially highlighted by William James (1892). There is now increasing zeal for models depicting how the self naturally varies across situations (see review in Harter, 1999). One solution for resolving potential contradictions within such a multifaceted self-portrait can be found in the role of autobiographical narratives (see McAdams, 1997). In developing a self-narrative, the individual creates a sense of continuity over time, as well as coherent connections among self-relevant life events, each of which can be experienced as authentic. Consistent with Lifton's (1993) analysis, such a narrative provides meaning and a sense of future direction. Moreover, narrative construction is a continuous process as we not only craft but also revise the story of our lives, creating new blueprints that facilitate further architectural development of the self. In so doing, one's life story can also emerge as a *true* story.

Can One Be Too Authentic?

Based on the arguments thus far, authenticity appears to be a valuable psychological commodity to be touted and encouraged. However, might there be liabilities associated with too much authenticity, with being "brutally honest"? Arguing from her position as a therapist, Lerner (1993) suggests that truth-telling is the foundation of "authenticity, self-regard, intimacy, integrity, and joy" (p. 15). Honesty, she feels, is essential in close relationships, whereas lying erodes trust. She observes, however, that "in the name of 'truth,' we may hurt friends and family members, escalate anxiety nonproductively, disregard the different reality of the other person, and generally move the situation from bad to worse" (p. 15). She concludes that much of what parades as truth-telling can actually involve "an unproductive effort to change, convince, or convert another person, rather than an attempt to clarify our own selves" (p. 115). As such, often we express our voices in ways that cannot realistically be heard, venting negative emotions rather than considering how best to communicate our feelings so as to preserve, rather than threaten, the relationship. Lerner further distinguishes between *honesty*, which can sometimes represent the uncensored expression of negative thoughts and feelings, and *truth*, which requires thought, timing, tact, and empathy for the other person's position. It is quite possible, therefore, to move beyond the boundaries of acceptable authenticity in our relationships. Honesty, therefore, is often *not* the best policy if it does not contain the elements of truth-telling that will facilitate, rather than jeopardize, relationships. From a cognitive-developmental perspective, it is interesting that it is not until later adolescence that individuals can appreciate the fact that the concepts of truth and kindness can logically co-occur (Fischer, 1980). Among older children and young adolescents, these concepts are viewed as mutually exclusive. With the emerging ability to construct higher order abstractions, older adolescents come to appreciate that one can be constructively critical, similar to Lerner's (1993) concept of truth-telling, in which one tactfully expresses oneself in a manner that can truly be heard.

Implications for Intervention

Our understanding of the developmental precursors of authenticity during childhood and adolescence implies several strategies for fostering true-self behavior. Encouraging parent figures to verbalize their *children's* reality, rather than their adult agenda, is one such pathway. Actively valuing or respecting the child's experience for what it is represents another critical socialization practice. Allowing children to play a central role in the construction of their own narratives, permitting them to be instrumental authors of their own true life stories, is also an essential ingredient. Moreover, children and adolescents need to be actively validated for who they are as a person; they need to be told that they are valued for their personal strengths. In addition, approval must be communicated so that the child comes to internalize or actively *own* the positive attributes rather than remain dependent on the external feedback of socializing agents. For example, when a child or adolescent engages in a commendable behavior, telling him or her that "you must be very proud of yourself for what you did" will be more likely to foster internalization than will a comment to the effect that as a parent you are glad that the child did what you wanted.

As the literature and our own findings reveal, providing unconditional positive regard for who the child is as a person, validating his or her intrinsic worth, will also foster authenticity. This does not mean, however, that a parent has to tolerate unacceptable behavior. Clearly, effective child-rearing practices require that parents clarify standards, provide expectations, and specify the consequences of misbehavior. However, if these practices are exercised within an atmosphere of nurturance, genuine concern for the child, and respect for who the child is as a person, not only will there be more compliance but the child will come to value the behaviors that parents would like to instill. To the extent that these values are internalized, they will eventually come to be perceived as true-self behavior.

Listening also is a powerful form of validation. By listening, one communicates that a child's thoughts, opinions, and feelings are respected. In turn, children and adolescents come to express themselves authentically, as our findings on the effects of support for "voice" have revealed. Parents may also serve as role models for the expression of voice (see Harter, 1999). Parents can model truth-telling, expressing their thoughts and feelings (employing tact and empathy) so as to be heard by their child or adolescent. This, in turn, should allow the child or adolescent to adopt a similar form of effective communication.

Although false-self behavior typically is regarded as the antithesis of true-self behavior, it is possible therapeutically to embrace a "false"-self attribute so as to have it gradually enter the repertoire of authentic-self characteristics. For example, consider individuals who (a) desire to become less anxious in social situations, or (b) want to become more relational than autonomous, or (c) desperately want to become more cheerful and optimistic than depressed and hopeless, or (d) desire to be more in touch with their innermost feelings than closed off emotionally. In practicing these behaviors, they may initially feel rather phony, because they do not feel genuine or authentic. However, as Lerner points out, "Sometimes pretending is a form of experimentation or imitation that widens our experience and sense of possibility; it reflects a wish to find ourselves in order to *be* ourselves" (p. 16). Thus, over time, the practice of desirable false-self behaviors becomes more natural, and, through repetition, these novel thoughts and behaviors become more embedded in the person's new life narrative as genuine-self attributes. In time, such authenticity becomes part of what Snyder and Higgins (1997) have described as a person's negotiated reality.

Finally, there are implications for those on antidepression medications. People with physiologically induced symptoms of depression may need to be counseled that their more cheerful self *on* the drug is their true self that the drug is allowing them to manifest. That is, one would want to prevent them from berating themselves for chemical dependence on a drug that is simply masking who they really are. A similar approach may be useful with hyperactive children on drugs such as Ritalin, conveying the message that their more controlled self on the drug represents their true self that has been obscured due to some chemical imbalances or neurological factors beyond their conscious control.

The suggestions in this section are speculative. Although they have been drawn from literature and clinical case material, they have not been examined empirically. Thus, there are ample hypotheses for future research. Indeed, understanding and fostering authenticity and its associated benefits are important agenda items for the unfolding field of positive psychology.

References

Allen, J. P., Hauser, S. T., Bell, K. L., & O'Connor, T. G. (1994). Longitudinal assessment of autonomy and relatedness in adolescent-family interactions as predictors of adolescent ego development and self-esteem. *Child Development, 64,* 179–194.

Allport, G. W. (1961). *Pattern and growth in personality.* New York: Holt, Rinehart and Winston.

*Baumeister, R. (1987). How the self became a problem: A psychological review of historical research. *Journal of Personality and Social Psychology, 52,* 163–176.

Baumeister, R. F., Hutton, D. G., & Tice, D. M. (1989). Cognitive processes during deliberate self-presentation: How self-presenters alter and misinterpret the behavior of their interaction partners. *Journal of Experimental Social Psychology, 25,* 59–78.

Bem, S. (1985). Androgyny and gender schema theory. In T. B. Sonderegger (Ed.), *Nebraska Symposium on Motivation* (Vol. 32, pp. 180–236). Lincoln: University of Nebraska Press.

Blatt, S. J. (1995). Representational structures in psychopathology. In D. Cicchetti & S. Toth (Eds.), *Rochester Symposium on Developmental Psychopathology: Emotion, cognition, and representation* (Vol. 6, pp. 1–34). Rochester, NY: University of Rochester Press.

Bleiberg, E. (1984). Narcissistic disorders in children. *Bulletin of the Menninger Clinic, 48,* 501–517.

*Deci, E. L., & Ryan, R. M. (1995). Human autonomy: The basis for true self-esteem. In M. H. Kernis (Ed.), *Efficacy, agency, and self-esteem* (pp. 31–46). New York: Plenum.

Emde, R. N. (1994). Individuality, context, and the search for meaning. *Child Development, 65,* 719–737.

Epstein, S. (1973). The self-concept revisited or a theory of a theory. *American Psychologist, 28,* 405–416.

Erikson, E. H. (1950). *Childhood and society* (2nd ed.). New York: Norton.

Fischer, K. W. (1980). A theory of cognitive development: The control and construction of hierarchies of skills. *Psychological Review, 87,* 437–531.

Fivush, R., & Hudson, J. A. (Eds.). (1990). *Knowing and remembering in young children.* New York: Cambridge University Press.

*Gergen, K. J. (1991). *The saturated self.* New York: Basic Books.

Gilligan, C., Lyons, N., & Hanmer, T. J. (1989). *Making connections.* Cambridge, MA: Harvard University Press.

Goffman, E. (1959). *The presentation of self in everyday life.* Garden City, NY: Doubleday.

Hart, D. (1988). The adolescent self-concept in social context. In D. K. Lapsley & F. C. Power (Eds.), *Self, ego, and identity* (pp. 71–90). New York: Springer-Verlag.

*Harter, S. (1999). *The construction of the self: A developmental perspective.* New York: Guilford.

*Harter, S., Bresnick, S., Bouchey, H., & Whitesell, N. R. (1997). The development of multiple role-related selves during adolescence. *Development and Psychopathology, 9,* 835–854.

Harter, S., Marold, D. B., Whitesell, N. R., & Cobbs, G. (1996). A model of the effects of parent and peer support on adolescent false self behavior. *Child Development, 67,* 360–374.

Harter, S., & Monsour, A. (1992). Developmental analysis of conflict caused by opposing attributes in the adolescent self-portrait. *Developmental Psychology, 28,* 251–260.

*Harter, S., Waters, P., Pettitt, L., Whitesell, N., Kofkin, J., & Jordan, J. (1997). Autonomy and connectedness as dimensions of relationship styles in adult men and women. *Journal of Social and Personal Relationships, 14,* 147–164.

Harter, S., Waters, P., & Whitesell, N. R. (1997). False self behavior and lack of voice among adolescent males and females. *Educational Psychology, 32,* 153–173.

Horney, K. (1950). *Neurosis and human growth.* New York: Norton.

James, W. (1892). *Psychology: The briefer course.* New York: Henry Holt.

Johnson, J. T., & Boyd, K. R. (1995). Dispositional traits versus the content of experience: Actor/ observer differences in judgments of the "authentic self." *Personality and Social Psychology Bulletin, 21,* 375–383.

Jordan, J. V. (1991). The relational self: A new perspective for understanding women's development. In J. Stauss & G. Goethals (Eds.), *The self: Interdisciplinary approaches* (pp. 136–149). New York: Springer-Verlag.

Kelly, A. E. (2001). Dealing with secrets. In C. R. Snyder (Ed.), *Coping and copers: Adaptive processes and people* (pp. 196–221). New York: Oxford University Press.

Leary, M. R., & Kowalski, R. M. (1990). Impression management: A literature review. *Psychological Bulletin, 107,* 34–47.

Lecky, P. (1945). *Self-consistency: A theory of personality.* New York: Island Press.

*Lerner, H. G. (1993). *The dance of deception.* New York: HarperCollins.

Lifton, R. J. (1993). *The protean self.* New York: Basic Books.

Markus, H., & Nurius, P. (1986). Possible selves. *American Psychologist, 41,* 954–969.

Maslow, A. H. (1954). *Motivation and personality.* New York: Harper and Row.

McAdams, D. (1997). The unity of identity. In R. D. Ashmore & L. Jussim (Eds.), *Self and identity: Fundamental issues* (pp. 46–80). New York: Oxford University Press.

Miller, D. (1974). *The new polytheism.* New York: Harper and Row.

Miller, J. B. (1986). *Toward a new psychology of women* (2nd ed.). Boston: Beacon.

Nelson, K. (1989). *Narratives from the crib.* Cambridge, MA: Harvard University Press.

Pipher, M. (1994). *Reviving Ophelia.* New York: Ballantine.

Riesman, D. (1950). *The lonely crowd.* New Haven, CT: Yale University Press.

Rogers, C. (1951). *Client-centered therapy.* Boston: Houghton Mifflin.

Selman, R. L., & Schultz, L. H. (1990). *Making a friend in youth.* Chicago: University of Chicago Press.

Smollar, J., & Youniss, J. (1985). Adolescent self-concept development. In R. L. Leahy (Ed.), *The development of self* (pp. 247–266). New York: Academic Press.

Snow, K. (1990). Building memories: The ontogeny of autobiography. In D. Cicchetti & M. Beegley (Eds.), *The self in transition: Infancy to childhood* (pp. 213–242). Chicago: University of Chicago Press.

*Snyder, C. R., & Higgins, R. L. (1997). Reality negotiation: Governing one's self and being governed by others. *Review of General Psychology, 4,* 336–350.

Snyder, M. (1987). *Public appearances, private realities: The psychology of self-monitoring.* New York: Freeman.

Spence, J. T., Helmreich, R., & Stapp, J. (1975). The Personal Attributes Questionnaire. *JSAS Catalog of Selected Documents in Psychology, 4,* 43–44.

Stein, N. L., Trabasso, T., & Liwag, M. D. (1994). The Rashomon phenomenon: Personal frames and future-oriented appraisals in memory for emotional events. In M. M. Haith, J. B. Benson, R. J. Roberts, & B. F. Pennington (Eds.), *The development of future-oriented processes,* (pp. 409–436). Chicago: University of Chicago Press.

Steinberg, L. (1990). Interdependency in the family: Autonomy, conflict, and harmony in the parent-adolescent relationship. In S. Feldman & G. Elliot (Eds.), *At the threshold: The developing adolescent* (pp. 255–276). Cambridge, MA: Harvard University Press.

Stern, D. (1985). *The interpersonal world of the infant.* New York: Basic Books.

Sullivan, H. S. (1953). *The interpersonal theory of psychiatry.* New York: Norton.

*Trilling, L. (1971). *Sincerity and authenticity.* Cambridge, MA: Harvard University Press.

Winnicott, D. W. (1965). *The maturational processes and the facilitating environment.* New York: International Universities Press.

28

Uniqueness Seeking

Michael Lynn & C. R. Snyder

I will not choose what many men desire,
Because I will not jump with common spirits
And rank me with the barbarous multitudes.

Shakespeare,
The Merchant of Venice

Similar to the character in Shakespeare's play whose lines open this chapter, people have a need to be distinctive and special. Interpersonal difference, or uniqueness, contributes to self-identity, attracts attention, and enhances self-esteem and social status (see Codol, 1984; Maslach, 1974; Tesser, 1988). On the other hand, people also have a need for similarity. Interpersonal similarity begets affiliation, belief validation, emotional security, empathy, helping, liking, and social influence (see Brock, 1965; Byrne, 1971; Schachter, 1959). These needs for distinctiveness and similarity oppose one another in the sense that the satisfaction of one enhances the potency of the other. Accordingly, people find a compromise position of intermediate levels of self-distinctiveness more satisfying than either extreme similarity or extreme dissimilarity relative to other persons (Brewer, 1991; Fromkin, 1968, 1970; Snyder & Fromkin, 1980).

Snyder and Fromkin (1980) formalized the preceding ideas in a theory of uniqueness seek-

ing. In this chapter, we review their theory and the related research. The review is divided into four major sections. First, evidence that people seek moderate levels of self-distinctiveness as predicted by uniqueness theory is presented. Second, individual differences in the need for uniqueness are discussed, with special attention given to the measurement and the origins of these differences. Third, research on the ways that individuals differentiate themselves from others is considered, and general principles that guide the direction of uniqueness-seeking efforts are identified. Finally, the societal benefits of uniqueness seeking are described, along with a call for greater social acceptance of human differences.

Uniqueness Theory

In uniqueness theory, Snyder and Fromkin (1980) addressed people's emotional, cognitive, and behavioral responses to information about their similarity to others. Specifically, Snyder and Fromkin posited that people seek to establish and maintain a sense of moderate self-distinctiveness, because perceptions of either extreme similarity or extreme dissimilarity to others are experienced as being unpleasant.

These predictions and the related research are discussed next.

Emotional Reactions to Similarity Information

According to uniqueness theory, the perception that the self is either highly similar or highly dissimilar to others arouses negative emotions. Thus, people should be happiest when perceiving that they are moderately different relative to others. In a test of this prediction, Fromkin (1972) gave students false feedback about how similar their responses on a lifestyle survey were to those of other respondents and then asked them to report their moods. As predicted, the students who were told that they were moderately similar to other respondents reported more positive moods than did those students who were told that they were either highly similar or highly dissimilar to other respondents. Other researchers have conceptually replicated this finding in studies in which changes in self-esteem (Ganster, McCuddy, & Fromkin, 1977), physical proximity to another (Snyder & Endelman, 1980), and the valence of word associations (Markus & Kunda, 1986) were used as indicators of emotional reactions to similarity feedback.

Cognitive and Behavioral Reactions to Similarity Information

According to uniqueness theory, the unpleasant affect associated with perceptions of extreme similarity motivates people to reestablish moderate levels of perceived self-distinctiveness. This means that as people perceive more similarity between themselves and others, they become increasingly motivated to reaffirm their distinctiveness. One way people can protect their perceptions of self-uniqueness is by discounting threatening information and recalling (or focusing on) available uniqueness-affirming information. Consistent with the existence of such a cognitive bias, people have rated themselves as being less similar to others under conditions of increased external threats to their perceived self-uniqueness (Fromkin, Brandt, Dipboye, & Pyle, 1974; Ganster et al., 1977). Additionally, Snyder and Batson (1974) discovered that threats to uniqueness elicited distinctive self-descriptions from people, with the strength of this uniqueness seeking abating over

time as the people seemingly fulfilled their uniqueness needs. Furthermore, Markus and Kunda (1986) found that individuals made to believe that they were extremely similar to others were quicker to endorse uniqueness-related words as being self-descriptive (and slower to endorse similarity-related words as self-descriptive) than were individuals made to believe that they were dissimilar to others.

Another way that people can reaffirm a threatened sense of self-distinctiveness is by increasing the distinctiveness of their attitudes and behaviors. Several researchers have found support for such tendencies. Specifically, they found that, in comparison with control subjects, people who were led to believe they were highly similar to many others (a) conformed less in a judgment task (Duval, 1972); (b) expressed less popular attitudes (Weir, 1971); (c) generated more unusual uses for common objects (Fromkin, 1968); and (d) placed more value on scarce experiences and messages (Fromkin, 1970; Powell, 1974).

Individual Differences in the Need for Uniqueness

The central tenet in uniqueness theory is that everyone has a need (or desire) to be moderately dissimilar to others. However, Snyder and Fromkin (1977, 1980) also argued that there should be individual differences in the strength of this need (see also Snyder, 1992). In the following, we review research on the measurement of this disposition and explore several ideas about the origin of these individual differences.

Measures of Individual Differences in Uniqueness Motivation

Snyder and Fromkin (1977) developed and validated the first individual differences measure of need for uniqueness. They began by generating a pool of 300 potential scale items and using judges' ratings of each item's face validity to narrow the pool to 117 items. Then they examined the correlations of these 117 items with individual difference measures of autonomy and succorance. The 32 items that correlated positively with autonomy and negatively with succorance were selected for inclusion in their final scale (see Appendix A). Scores on the scale were positively related to (a) unusual word associations, (b) memberships in gay and women's liberation groups, (c) signature sizes, (d) self-rated uniqueness, and (e) the appropriate responsiveness of participants' self-esteem to similarity feedback (i.e., when given situational similarity feedback that matched trait need for uniqueness, the esteem was high, whereas when given similarity feedback that did not match trait need for uniqueness, the esteem was low; Snyder & Fromkin, 1977, 1980).

Although a number of studies support the construct validity of Snyder and Fromkin's (1977, 1980) need for uniqueness (NU) scale, it has been criticized for placing too much emphasis on public and socially risky displays of uniqueness (Lynn & Harris, 1997a, 1997b; Tepper, 1996a, 1996b). Items on the scale load on three factors, which Snyder and Fromkin (1977) labeled as (a) lack of concern for the reactions of others, (b) desire to not always follow rules, and (c) willingness to publicly defend one's beliefs (also see Tepper & Hoyle, 1996). Although these three factors do tap ways of being unique, they also reflect behaviors that may anger and alienate other people. People also pursue uniqueness in more private and socially acceptable ways, such as by acquiring rare and inconspicuous possessions. In fact, Snyder and Fromkin (1980) state that people probably prefer socially acceptable ways of being unique over socially risky ones. Thus, their NU scale does not tap some important manifestations of uniqueness motives. In support of this criticism, Tepper, Bearden, and Hunter (in press) have noted that NU scale scores predicted consumer's selections of public but not private products, and that the NU scale scores predicted consumer's home decorating decisions only when those decisions involved high social risks.

In an attempt to provide an alternative measure that does not emphasize the public and risky displays of uniqueness that are tapped by the NU scale, Lynn and Harris (1997b) developed a four-item measure, which they called the self-attributed need for uniqueness (SANU) scale (see Appendix B). In the SANU scale, respondents are asked to indicate how different they want to be, how important being distinctive is to them, how often they intentionally try to differentiate themselves from others, and how strongly they need to be unique. Relative to scores on the NU scale, the scores on this SANU scale have been found to be more strongly related to a measure of the desire for

scarce products, a measure of the desire for customized products, and a latent variable reflecting the tendency to pursue uniqueness through consumption (Lynn & Harris, 1997b). Thus, the SANU scale appears to be a valid measure of uniqueness motives. Moreover, it taps the tendency to pursue uniqueness in socially acceptable ways and does so more than is the case for the NU scale.

Origins of Individual Differences in Uniqueness Motivation

Snyder and Fromkin (1980) speculated about the origins of a universal need for uniqueness. Although not formulated as such, their ideas suggest three potential explanations for individual differences in the strength of uniqueness motivation. Each of these explanations is considered next.

First, Snyder and Fromkin (1980) reasoned that the need for uniqueness arises because people are (in fact) moderately different from one another and have learned to perceive themselves accordingly. This self-image takes on motivational properties because people need a stable self-concept. This line of reasoning is consistent with research demonstrating that people actively resist challenges to their self-concepts (Swann, 1983; Swann & Pelham, this volume). It also provides a potential explanation for individual differences in uniqueness motivation. Some individuals may possess salient personal attributes that are more unusual than those of others and, therefore, may come to see themselves as more distinctive than others. Those self-perceptions, in turn, may influence the levels of self-distinctiveness that individuals find most desirable. Consistent with this possibility, researchers have found an especially strong need for uniqueness among people whose name or family circumstances are likely to make them experience a sense of specialness. Specifically, evidence of a higher than usual need for uniqueness has been found among (a) women with unusual first names (Zweigenhaft, 1981); (b) women whose nearest sibling is male rather than female (Chrenka, 1983); (c) students who are firstborn or only children versus latter born (Fromkin, Williams, & Dipboye, 1973); and (d) children of interfaith marriages (Grossman, 1990). The positive relationships between the need for uniqueness and all of these nonvoluntary sources of self-distinctiveness provide converging support for the idea that chronic self-perceptions affect the level of people's dispositional need for uniqueness.

Second, Snyder and Fromkin (1980) hypothesized that people learn to value a sense of uniqueness in environments that encourage freedom and reward independence. Thus, individual and group differences in the need for uniqueness may reflect different environmental backgrounds and reinforcement histories. For example, because independence is openly encouraged in Western cultures, whereas subjugation of the individual to the family and group is emphasized in Eastern cultures, one would expect that high uniqueness needs would be especially manifested in Western societies. Consistent with this latter supposition, the need for uniqueness has been found to be greater among European Americans than among Asians and Asian Americans in several studies (Burns & Brady, 1992; Kim & Markus, 1999; also see Maslach, Stapp, & Santee, 1985).

Third, Snyder and Fromkin (1980) suggested that people prefer a moderate level of self-distinctiveness because they have needs for social acceptance, approval, and validation, as well as a need for uniqueness. The former set of needs makes extreme dissimilarity unpleasant, whereas the latter need makes extreme similarity unpleasant (see also Brewer, 1991). Based on this line of thought, people with little as compared to great concern for social acceptance, approval, and validation should desire higher levels of uniqueness. Consistent with this hypothesis, studies have found that scores on the NU scale are negatively related to public self-consciousness, neuroticism, social anxiety, shyness, susceptibility to normative influence, and related traits (Case, 1974; Lynn & Harris, 1997b; Schroeder, 1990; Schroeder & Dugal, 1995; Snyder & Fromkin, 1977; Tepper, 1994; Tepper et al., in press; Tepper & Hoyle, 1996). It should be noted, however, that these predicted relationships were found with the NU scale, which emphasizes public and socially risky displays of uniqueness. Thus, additional research is needed to ascertain whether the need for *private* self-uniqueness also is related to these traits.

Domains of Self-Uniqueness

The self is a complex entity with many facets. For example, researchers who have asked people to describe their "selves" have found that they mention their abilities, appearances, beliefs, behaviors, families, friends, hobbies, personalities, pets, and possessions, among other attributes (Burns, 1979). Thus, there are many dimensions on which people can pursue self-uniqueness. Indeed, researchers have found evidence that attitudes (Weir, 1971), creative abilities (Fromkin, 1968), personality traits (Snyder & Shenkel, 1976), judgments (Duval, 1972), experiences (Fromkin, 1970), group memberships (Snyder & Fromkin, 1977), consumer products (Fromkin, Williams & Dipboye, 1974), and signatures (Omens, 1977) all serve as bases for feelings of self-uniqueness. However, two sources of a sense of uniqueness—group identifications and consumer products and experiences—have received the most research attention. We will explore these latter two bodies of research next. Then we will give our views about the general principles that underlie people's choices of domains in which to pursue uniqueness.

Group Identification as a Source of Uniqueness

Snyder and Fromkin (1980) suggested that people could find a sense of uniqueness through membership in groups that differ from the population at large. Building on this idea, Brewer (1991) argued that people's identification with social groups simultaneously serves their needs for similarity (through within-group comparisons) and uniqueness (through between-group comparisons). Furthermore, she theorized that people tend to identify with those groups that provide them with the optimal compromise between these competing needs. This theory, known as *optimal distinctiveness theory*, implies that people who are made to believe that they are highly similar to others will reassert their uniqueness by identifying with small, exclusive, and distinctive groups more than with large, inclusive, and indistinctive ones. The opposite will be true when people are made to believe that they are highly dissimilar to others. Several researchers have produced evidence in support of such speculation.

First, Jetten, Spears, and Manstead (1998) found that people evaluated their own group more favorably than another group, and that this bias was greatest when the two groups were moderately different from one another. When the two groups were highly similar or highly dissimilar, little in-group bias was evident. Although people's ratings of their own similarity to fellow group members did not display a similar pattern, the in-group bias in Jetten et al.'s studies may reflect an emotional identification with the in-group. If so, then the results support optimal distinctiveness theory by suggesting that people identify with those groups that provide a compromise between the needs for uniqueness and similarity.

Second, researchers have discovered that people perceive the members of their own groups, but not the members of other groups, as being more similar to one another when the groups are small than when they are large (Brewer, 1993). People also see themselves as being more stereotypical of their groups when the groups are small than when the groups are large (Brewer & Weber, 1994; Simon & Hamilton, 1994). These findings are consistent with the optimal distinctive theory predictions that membership in a group will confer greater specialness relative to nonmembers as group size and inclusiveness decline, and that this will increase the need or tendency to perceive similarity with (and among) fellow group members.

Third, Brewer and her colleagues found that making people feel similar to others caused them to evaluate their own groups more favorably than other groups when the groups were small but not when the groups were large (Brewer, Manzi, & Shaw, 1993; also see Hornsey & Hogg, 2000). In a separate study, making people feel similar to others also increased the importance they attached to membership in small groups but not the importance they attached to membership in large groups (Brewer & Pickett, 1999).

In summary, based on recent findings involving group identification, we can infer that (a) emotional identification is greatest for moderately distinctive groups; (b) membership in small groups satisfies uniqueness needs and heightens similarity seeking through within-group comparisons; and (c) heightening people's need for uniqueness increases their identification with small, exclusive groups. Thus, people seek moderate levels of self-distinctiveness through their identification with various social groups.

Consumer Products and Experiences as a Source of Uniqueness

Building on James's (1890) concept of the "material self," Snyder and Fromkin (1980) argued

that material possessions often are extensions of the self and that one source of self-uniqueness is the possession of consumer goods that are available to only a few others. This idea has given rise to one of the most active areas of research on uniqueness seeking. Consumer researchers have examined the role of uniqueness motives in the desire for, and acquisition of, products that are scarce, innovative, customized, and unpopular. In addition, they have examined the role of uniqueness motives in consumers' choices of shopping venues and in consumers' responses to marketing influence tactics. Finally, they have developed two new scales to measure individual differences in uniqueness seeking through consumption. Each of these areas of research is discussed in the paragraphs that follow.

Desire for Scarce Products

Fewer people can possess scarce products than can possess nonscarce ones. Thus, one way that consumers can satisfy their needs for uniqueness is by owning rare or difficult-to-obtain items (Brock, 1968; Lynn, 1991; Snyder & Fromkin, 1980). Consistent with this possibility, Fromkin et al. (1973) and Lynn (1987) found that people with a high dispositional need for uniqueness preferred scarce products over common ones, whereas people with a low dispositional need for uniqueness did not. This effect has not been replicated in other studies (Atlas & Snyder, 1978; Dutcher, 1975; Lynn, 1987, 1989; also see Okamoto, 1983), but several of these null results may be attributable to the use of the NU scale that is not sensitive to the private need for uniqueness. Consistent with this speculation, Lynn and Harris (1997b) found that the NU scale was less strongly related to the desire for scarce products than was their SANU scale.

Consumer Innovativeness

New products rarely gain immediate and widespread acceptance. Usually they are first adopted by a small number of consumer innovators, who then influence later adopters (Robertson, 1971; Rogers, 1983). Thus, adopting new products before others do is one way to satisfy the need for uniqueness (Burns & Krampf, 1992; Fromkin, 1970). Burns (1987, 1989; Burns & Rayman, 1991) has tested this hypothesis by looking at the relationship between the need for uniqueness and passage through different stages in the adoption of innovations. The results of these studies are mixed at best. However, Burns's measures of consumer innovation were tied to a relatively small number of specific products. He developed a list of 20 new consumer products and measured subjects' awareness, interest, consideration, trial, rejection, and adoption of these products. Given that literally thousands of new consumer products are introduced into the market each year, it should not be surprising that uniqueness motives were only weakly and inconsistently related to any specific and small sample of these innovations. A stronger relationship would be expected with a more general measure of consumer innovativeness. Consistent with this expectation, Lynn and Harris (1997b) found that both the NU scale and the SANU scale were significantly and positively related to a general, dispositional measure of consumer innovativeness.

Customization of Products

Customization of a product makes it different from the standard model that is available to most people. Thus, customizing products is another way that people can differentiate themselves from others. Evidence that people use customized products as a source of uniqueness is provided by Lynn and Harris (1997b), who found that individuals scoring high on the SANU scale reported a stronger desire to customize and personalize products than did people with lower SANU scores. Tepper et al. (in press) provide additional evidence in a study that gave research participants the opportunity to design their own lamps using components available from an on-line furniture company. Persons with strong needs for uniqueness (as reflected in NU scores) selected a larger number of unique lamp shade shapes, colors, and materials than did research participants with weaker needs for uniqueness.

Less Popular Products

Some brands, designs, and products are more common or popular. This fact gives people an opportunity to assert their uniqueness by resisting conformity pressures and selecting less popular offerings. Evidence that people do make less popular consumption choices in the service of uniqueness motives comes from three studies reported by Tepper et al. (in press). In one study

involving a hypothetical shopping scenario, these researchers found that people with high NU scores were more likely than people with low NU scores to say they would select the less popular of two backpacks. In a second study, they found that people with high NU scores were more likely than people with low NU scores to choose less popular brands, product colors, product materials, and product categories over more popular options. However, this effect was observed only for publicly visible products; people's NU scores were unrelated to their choices regarding less visible products. In a third study, Tepper et al. found that people with high NU scores selected less common paint and wallpaper colors to decorate a room than did people with low NU scores, but this occurred only when people thought others would evaluate their choices for "good taste." These findings suggest that less popular consumption choices do serve people's needs for public uniqueness but not their needs for private uniqueness. Consistent with the latter supposition, Lynn and Harris (1997b) found that a measure of the tendency to make conforming product choices was unrelated to their SANU scale and to a latent variable reflecting the tendency to pursue uniqueness through consumption (see also Lynn and Harris, 1997a).

Shopping Venue

Retail outlets differ in popularity and in the distinctiveness of their merchandise. This suggests that people may satisfy their needs for uniqueness by shopping at small, less popular outlets that carry uncommon merchandise. Several researchers have reported results consistent with this possibility. For example, Darley and Lim (1993) found that consumers who patronize thrift stores were more likely than others (not using such stores) to agree that these stores offer "the best selection of unique merchandise." Guttman and Mills (1982) reported that consumers who see themselves as different and standing out in a crowd regarding fashion shopped at specialty and upscale department stores more, and at mass-merchandise stores less, than did other consumers who did not see themselves as being different. Burns and Warren (1995) found that NU scores were positively (though weakly) related to the tendency to shop at regional shopping malls other than the ones closest to the subjects' homes. Lynn and Harris (1997b) reported that scores on both the NU scale and the SANU scale were positively related to a multi-item measure of the preference for unique shopping venues. Finally, Tepper and McKenzie (2001) found that people with strong needs to be unique consumers were more likely to have obtained their five favorite possessions from unconventional retail outlets (e.g., antique stores, consignment shops, and garage sales) than were people with weaker needs to be unique consumers. Clearly, uniqueness motives affect peoples' choices of shopping venues.

Response to Influence Tactics

Marketers use a variety of tactics, such as price reductions and puffed-up advertising claims, to increase the demand for their products. To the extent that these tactics are perceived as broadly effective in influencing consumer choice, some consumers can make themselves feel unique by resisting the tactics' influence. Consistent with this possibility, Simonson and Nowlis (2000) found that examples of sales promotions and of advertising "puffery" had smaller effects on the brand choices of people who scored high, as compared with those who scored low, on the NU scale. However, these and other need-for-uniqueness effects were observed only when the people were instructed to give reasons for their choices. Providing reasons emphasizes conscious and cognitive as opposed to unconscious or emotional bases for choice (see Wilson & Schooler, 1991). Thus, the fact that the need-for-uniqueness effects in these studies depended on subjects explaining their choices suggests the need for uniqueness may affect consumers' conscious, cognitive reactions to choice alternatives more than it does their unconscious and/or emotional reactions. This possibility deserves more investigation.

The Pursuit of Uniqueness Through Consumption

Lynn and Harris (1997b) suggested that people probably have characteristic, preferred ways of differentiating themselves from others. More specifically, they hypothesized that some people seek uniqueness through consumption, whereas others seek uniqueness in alternative ways. Thus, they argued that the effects of individual differences in the need for uniqueness on various consumer behaviors and dispositions would be mediated by a latent variable reflecting individual differences in the tendency to pursue uniqueness through consumption.

To test their hypothesis, Lynn and Harris (1997b) asked research participants to complete measures of (a) the self-attributed need for uniqueness; (b) the desire for scarce products; (c) consumer innovativeness; (d) consumer susceptibility to normative influence; (e) the preference for unique shopping venues; and (f) the desire for customized products. In a statistical path analysis of these data, the desire for scarce products, consumer innovativeness, the preference for unique shopping venues, and the desire for customized products (but not consumer susceptibility to normative influence) all loaded strongly on a latent variable that mediated their relationships with the self-attributed need for uniqueness. Moreover, this structural model fit the data very well (AGFI = .95), and it was a significant improvement over a model depicting the self-attributed need for uniqueness as a direct cause of the other measured consumer dispositions. These results support Lynn and Harris's (1997b) hypothesis that people differ not just in the general need for uniqueness but also in the tendency to pursue uniqueness through consumption.

Two groups of consumer researchers have independently set out to develop an individual difference measure of the tendency to pursue uniqueness through consumption (see Lynn & Harris, 1997a; Tepper et al., in press; Tepper & McKenzie, 2001). Lynn and Harris (1997a) developed an 8-item unidimensional measure, which they call the desire for unique consumer products (DUCP) scale (see Appendix C). Tepper et al. (1999) developed a 31-item measure with three underlying factors (labeled "creative choice counter-conformity," "unpopular choice counter-conformity," and "avoiding similarity"), which they call the consumer need for uniqueness (CNFU) scale. Both scales have adequate internal consistency and test-retest reliability. In addition, the factor structures of both scales generalize across student and nonstudent samples. Furthermore, both scales correlate as predicted with the NU scale and other personality measures. Finally, both scales predict unique consumption decisions. Thus, there appear to be two reliable and valid measures of the tendency to pursue uniqueness *through consumption*. These scales can be used as independent variables to provide stronger predictions of unique consumer preferences and behaviors than is possible via the use of the more general NU and SANU scales. In addition, these scales can be used as dependent measures in research examining the factors that direct the pursuit of uniqueness to the consumer domain rather than to other domains.

Principles Directing the Pursuit of Uniqueness

The plethora of attributes on which people can differentiate themselves from others raises a question about why people choose one attribute over another. Snyder and Fromkin (1980) proposed two answers to this question. They suggested that people prefer to be unique on attributes that are highly relevant to their self-concepts and that do not lead to social rejection. Building on these ideas, we identify three general principles that direct the pursuit of uniqueness. Specifically, we suggest that people are more likely to pursue uniqueness on attributes that are already self-defining, on attributes whose rarity is difficult to falsify, and on attributes whose rarity satisfies more than uniqueness needs. In the subsequent paragraphs, each of these general principles is discussed and used to generate more specific hypotheses about the paths that people will take to acquiring a sense of uniqueness.

Self-Relevance

The need for uniqueness is a secondary need derived in large part from the needs for identity and self-validation (see our introductory comments). Thus, people should be particularly prone to seek uniqueness on those attributes (and in those domains) that are central to their self-concepts (Snyder & Fromkin, 1980). Consistent with this hypothesis, Campbell (1986) found that people underestimated the number of others who shared their positive abilities and that this "false uniqueness" effect was stronger for those abilities that they rated as being more important to the self. In addition, Kernis (1984) reported that thinking about performing a behavior polarized estimates of the behavior's commonness in opposite directions for people high and low in need for uniqueness. Such thought increased the perceived commonness of the behavior among low-NU individuals and decreased it among high-NU individuals. Moreover, this thought by NU interaction was moderated by the self-relevance of the behavior—it occurred only when the behavior reflected a

trait that was an important part of the individuals' self-schemas.

Based on the aforementioned research findings, it does appear that people are more strongly motivated to seek uniqueness on dimensions important to their self-concepts than on less self-relevant dimensions. Interestingly, a slight twist on this idea also appears to be true, namely, people view their unique traits as more central and self-defining than their common traits (Miller, Turnbull, & McFarland, 1988). These two tendencies can be self-reinforcing in that increasing feelings of uniqueness in one domain of life increases the self-relevance of that domain, which further increases the pursuit of uniqueness in the domain. This suggests that an individual's uniqueness seeking may be concentrated in just a few domains of life where this self-reinforcing process has been started by some personal interest or source of distinctiveness. Lynn and Harris (1997b) have found individual differences in the tendency to pursue uniqueness through consumption that are consistent with such reasoning. Identifying other domain-specific individual differences in uniqueness seeking would be a fruitful direction for future research.

Falsifiability

Peoples' pursuit of uniqueness is constrained by reality. While the need for uniqueness can bias peoples' perceptions of themselves and others, those perceptions can deviate from reality only so much before the discrepancies become obvious and the perceptions are no longer sustainable in the context of interpersonal commerce. However, not all self-perceptions are equally constrained. Beliefs about one's distinctiveness on ambiguous traits are more difficult to falsify than are similar beliefs about well-defined traits because ambiguous traits can be more easily redefined in ways that minimize the relevance of challenging information. In addition, beliefs about one's distinctiveness on internal traits are more difficult to falsify than are similar beliefs about external traits because people generally have less information about others' internal workings. This suggests that people may be more likely to base their perceptions of self-uniqueness on the former than on the latter types of traits. Consistent with this possibility, researchers have found that peoples' tendency to perceive themselves as "better than average" is stronger for ambiguous traits than for well-defined traits (Dunning, Meyerowitz, & Holzberg, 1989) and stronger for internal than external traits (Miller & McFarland, 1987). In addition, Fromkin and Demming (1967) found that students perceived their attitudes, beliefs, and values (which are abstract, internal traits) as more distinctive than their behaviors (which are concrete, external traits).

Relevance to Other Needs

The need for uniqueness is but one of many different needs that drive human behavior. These other needs may play a role in directing people's uniqueness-seeking behaviors. Snyder and Fromkin (1980) acknowledged this possibility when they theorized that people tend to seek uniqueness in ways that are socially acceptable. Generalizing this idea, we suggest that people prefer to seek uniqueness on attributes whose rarity satisfies their other motives, and that they prefer to avoid uniqueness on attributes whose rarity threatens the satisfaction of their other motives. Using this principle, we suggest that people will prefer being distinctive on positive rather than negative traits, on abilities rather than opinions, and on normative rather than counternormative behaviors.

First, people should find being distinctive on positive traits preferable to being distinctive on negative traits. Having a positive trait is more *self-enhancing* when the trait is rare, but having a negative trait is more *self-demeaning* when the trait is rare. Thus, the need for self-esteem should lead people to prefer having unique positive traits and to prefer having common negative traits. Consistent with this reasoning, Ditto and Jemmott (1989) found that people were happier to learn that they had a positive medical condition (i.e., one that reduced their risks of illness) and were more upset to learn that they had a negative medical condition when the conditions were described as rare. In addition, Ditto and Griffin (1993) found that people with high as compared with low self-esteem perceived their most liked characteristics as more rare and their least liked characteristics as more common.

Second, people should prefer having distinctive abilities over distinctive opinions. Having rare positive abilities is self-enhancing and socially rewarding. In contrast, having rare opinions often leads to self-doubt and social rejection. This suggests that people will be more inclined to seek uniqueness on abilities than on opinions. Consistent with this expectation, Campbell (1986) found that people underestimated the prevalence of their positive abilities and overestimated the prevalence of their opinions.

Finally, people should prefer to distinguish themselves through normative rather than counternormative behaviors because acting in a manner consistent with social norms is generally rewarded, whereas acting in a counternormative way is not. Consistent with this reasoning, researchers have found that people tend to compete with others on socially defined criteria when they have a reasonable chance of winning, but that they try to compete on idiosyncratic criteria when they are disadvantaged in one arena (see Lemaine, 1974). For example, sibling competition for parental resources usually takes the form of firstborn children adopting conservative strategies that respect the status quo, and of latter-born children (who are at a disadvantage in competitions with their older siblings) adopting more radical strategies that challenge the status quo (see Sulloway, 1996). This research on competition can be interpreted as demonstrating that people prefer to distinguish themselves through superior normative performance and that they turn to counternormative behaviors only when the first option is unavailable to them. Additional support for this idea is provided by Codol (1975), who reviewed a series of studies finding that people present themselves as superior to others on whatever social norms happen to be salient. He attributed this tendency to the desire to simultaneously satisfy needs for distinctiveness and social acceptance.

Benefits of Uniqueness Seeking

When the NU scale article was first submitted to the *Journal of Abnormal Psychology* for editorial consideration in 1975, the senior author's (Snyder) purpose was to provide a positive view of human difference—along with an individual differences measure that was built on that model. This positive view of interpersonal differences had some precedence in the writings of early clinicians like Fromm (1941). It was also shared by a few contemporaneous social psychologists like Codol (1975), Fromkin (1970, 1972), and Maslach (1974). However, at the time, the *prevailing* view of interpersonal differences was decidedly negative. The message from social psychology was that similarity leads to social acceptance, liking, and influence, whereas difference leads to social rejection (see Brock, 1965; Byrne, 1971, Schachter, 1959). In clinical psychology, it was heresy to suggest that "abnormal" could be anything other than bad—pathology tainted the prevailing, accepted views of this term. Even sociologists focused on the notion of "deviance," which they used as a lens to understand how society creates and treats pariahs (see Becker, 1963). For the most part, social scientists seemed oblivious to the possibility that uniqueness brings personal and social benefits. Into this milieu, uniqueness theory (Snyder & Fromkin, 1980) was introduced as a means of casting a more favorable light upon the concept of interpersonal difference.

The establishment of a sense of uniqueness is emotionally satisfying to individuals. Moreover, it is necessary for our psychological welfare. In fact, one of the motives for seeking psychological help is the need for uniqueness (Snyder & Fromkin, 1980). Many (perhaps most) people who come for psychotherapy want to be listened to and treated as special. This may be why therapeutic interventions aimed at raising the clients' perceptions of their problems' prevalence have not worked (e.g., McCaul, 1978; Nisbett, Borgida, Crandall, & Reed, 1976). From the client's perspective, hearing that one's problem is common undermines any sense of uniqueness. Furthermore, a client may begin to doubt that she or he is being listened to and treated as an individual when the therapist implicitly or explicitly conveys the message "I have worked with many people with your same problem." Related to this latter point, researchers have consistently found that people are most likely to accept feedback that is particular to them and not for "people in general" (Snyder & Shenkel, 1976; Snyder, Shenkel, & Lowery, 1977).

In addition to promoting the psychological welfare of individuals, uniqueness seeking benefits society by promoting diversity. As people seek to differentiate themselves from others, they pursue different interests and goals. This diffusion of pursuits reduces competition and conflict over limited resources. It also creates entirely new arenas of success for people in general. To the extent that we increase the number of valued outcome arenas in our society—with high-need-for-uniqueness people helping to establish those new arenas—then more people will be able to succeed in the context of the society as a whole (Snyder, 1993, 1994; Snyder, Feldman, Taylor, Schroeder, & Adams, 2000).

As a result, uniqueness seeking should foster more societal hope (see Snyder & Feldman, 2000).

As people seek to differentiate themselves from others, they also develop different attitudes, beliefs, knowledge bases, and skills. This diversity of human resources is an asset of immense value. Across many domains of achievement, diversity of resources and efforts has increased the likelihood of success. For example, genetic and phenotypic diversity (achieved through sexual reproduction) enhances the likelihood of a species' survival because it increases the chances that some members of the species will be well adapted to changing and competitive environments (Geary, 1998). Similarly, diversity of scientific interests and pursuits increases the likelihood that a scientist will become eminent because it increases the chances that some of his or her ideas will fall on fertile ground (Sulloway, 1996). In addition, diversity of political systems increases the likelihood that advances in a geographic region's knowledge and technology will be preserved because it decreases the chances that regressive political leaders will rule the entire region (Diamond, 1999).

Diversity among people *can* help a society deal with problems because it increases the likelihood that the information, perspectives, and skills needed to solve those problems are available. However, the mere availability of these human resources is not sufficient to solve problems. The critical resources must be identified and applied if problems are to be solved. This requires that people publicly display their different beliefs, perspectives, and skills. A study by Simons, Pelled, and Smith (1999) illustrates and supports this point. Simons et al. found that companies with diverse top management teams experienced greater growth in sales and profits than did companies with more homogeneous top management teams, but only if the management teams routinely aired their different perspectives in vigorous debate. This kind of open airing of differences requires a social environment that encourages diversity and disagreement. As long as people fear that their differences will bring social rejection and isolation, many will be unwilling to publicly share their unique beliefs, perspectives, and skills (see Janis, 1982). Thus, to fully benefit from the diversity produced by the human pursuit of uniqueness, society must foster a greater appreciation and tolerance of individual differences. As individuals we all pursue some degree of distinctiveness. This human pursuit of difference is not something to be feared or squelched. Rather, as a society and as individuals, we need to celebrate and encourage it.

APPENDIX A   The Need for Uniqueness (NU) Scale

Respondents indicate the strength of their agreement or disagreement with each of the following items on a 5-point scale (1 = Strongest Disagreement; to 5 = Strongest Agreement).

1. When I am in a group of strangers, I am not reluctant to express my opinion publicly.
2. I find that criticism affects my self-esteem.
3. I sometimes hesitate to use my own ideas for fear that they might be impractical.
4. I think society should let reason lead it to new customs and throw aside old habits or mere traditions.
5. People frequently succeed in changing my mind.
6. I find it sometimes amusing to upset the dignity of teachers, judges, and "cultured" people.
7. I like wearing a uniform because it makes me proud to be a member of the organization it represents.
8. People have sometimes called me "stuck-up."
9. Others' disagreements make me uncomfortable.
10. I do not always need to live by the rules and standards of society.
11. I am unable to express my feelings if they result in undesirable consequences.
12. Being a success in one's career means making a contribution that no one else has made.
13. It bothers me if people think I am being too unconventional.
14. I always try to follow rules.
15. If I disagree with a superior on his or her views, I usually do not keep it to myself.
16. I speak up in meetings in order to oppose those whom I feel are wrong.
17. Feeling "different" in a crowd of people makes me feel uncomfortable.
18. If I must die, let it be an unusual death rather than an ordinary death in bed.
19. I would rather be just like everyone else than be called a "freak."
20. I must admit I find it hard to work under strict rules and regulations.
21. I would rather be known for always trying new ideas than for employing well-trusted methods.
22. It is better to agree with the opinions of others than to be considered a disagreeable person.
23. I do not like to say unusual things to people.
24. I tend to express my opinions publicly, regardless of what others say.
25. As a rule, I strongly defend my own opinions.
26. I do not like to go my own way.
27. When I am with a group of people, I agree with their ideas so that no arguments will arise.
28. I tend to keep quiet in the presence of persons of higher ranks, experience, etc.
29. I have been quite independent and free from family rule.
30. Whenever I take part in group activities, I am somewhat of a nonconformist.
31. In most things in life, I believe in playing it safe rather than taking a gamble.
32. It is better to break rules than always to conform with an impersonal society.

Reverse each of the scores on items 2, 3, 5, 7, 9, 11, 13, 14, 17, 19, 22, 23, 26, 27, 28, and 31. That is, on these items only, perform the following reversals: 1→ 5; 2→ 4; 3→ 3; 4→ 2; 5→ 1. Then add the scores on all 32 items, using the reversed scores for the aforementioned items. Higher scores reflect a higher need for uniqueness.

Source: From C. R. Snyder and H. L. Fromkin. (1977). Abnormality as a positive characteristic: The development and validation of scale measuring need for uniqueness. *Journal of Abnormal Psychology, 86*, 518–527. Reprinted with permission of the author and the American Psychological Association.

APPENDIX B   The Self Attributed Need for Uniqueness (SANU) Scale

Respondents complete the following sentences with the alternative that best describes them:

1. I prefer being ____ different from other people.
   (a) no,
   (b) slightly,
   (c) moderately,

(d) very,
(e) extremely

2. Being distinctive is ____ important to me.
   (a) not at all,
   (b) slightly,
   (c) moderately,
   (d) very,
   (e) extremely

3. I ____ intentionally do things to make myself different from those around me.
   (a) never,
   (b) seldom,
   (c) sometimes,
   (d) often,
   (e) always

4. I have a ____ need for uniqueness.
   (a) weak,
   (b) slight,
   (c) moderate,
   (d) strong,
   (e) very strong

For scoring, a = 1, b = 2, c = 3, d = 4, and e = 5. The total score reflects the sum of the responses to the four items. Higher scores reflect a higher need for uniqueness.

Source: From M. Lynn & J. Harris. (1997b). Individual differences in the pursuit of self-uniqueness through consumption. *Journal of Applied Social Psychology, 27,* 1861–1883. Reprinted with permission of the author and the journal.

APPENDIX C   The Desire for Unique Consumer Products (DUCP) Scale

Respondents indicate the strength of their agreement or disagreement with each of the following items on a 5-point scale (1 = Strongest Disagreement; to 5 = Strongest Agreement).

1. I am very attracted to rare objects.
2. I tend to be a fashion leader rather than a fashion follower.
3. I am more likely to buy a product if it is scarce.
4. I would prefer to have things custom-made than to have them ready-made.
5. I enjoy having things that others do not.
6. I rarely pass up the opportunity to order custom features on the products I buy.

7. I like to try new products and services before others do.
8. I enjoy shopping at stores that carry merchandise which is different and unusual.

Total scores are obtained by summing the responses to the eight items. Higher scores reflect a higher need for uniqueness.

Source: From M. Lynn & J. Harris. (1997a). The desire for unique consumer products: A new individual differences scale. *Psychology and Marketing, 14,* 601–616. Reprinted with permission of the author and the journal.

References

Atlas, M. S., & Snyder, C. R. (1978). *The effects of need for uniqueness upon valuation of scarce and nonscarce objects.* Unpublished honors thesis, University of Kansas, Lawrence.

Becker, H. S. (1963). *Outsiders.* New York: Free Press.

*Brewer, M. B. (1991). The social self: On being the same and different at the same time. *Personality and Social Psychology Bulletin, 17,* 475–482.

Brewer, M. B. (1993). Social identity, distinctiveness, and in-group homogeneity. *Social Cognition, 11,* 150–164.

Brewer, M. B., Manzi, J. M., & Shaw, J. S. (1993). In-group identification as a function of depersonalization, distinctiveness, and status. *Psychological Science, 4,* 88–92.

Brewer, M. B., & Pickett, C. L. (1999). Distinctiveness motives as a source of the social self. In T. R. Tyler and R. M. Kramer (Eds.), *The psychology of the social self* (pp. 71–87). Mahwah, NJ: Erlbaum.

Brewer, M. B., & Weber, J. G. (1994). Self-evaluation effects of interpersonal versus intergroup social comparison. *Journal of Personality and Social Psychology, 66,* 268–275.

Brock, T. (1965). Communicator-recipient similarity and decision-change. *Journal of Personality and Social Psychology, 1,* 650–654.

Brock, T. C. (1968). Implications of commodity theory for value change. In A. G. Greenwald, T. C. Brock, & T. M. Ostrom (Eds.), *Psychological foundations of attitudes* (pp. 243–275). New York: Academic Press.

Burns, D. J. (1987). *The effects of uniqueness seeking and sensation seeking upon innovative behavior and the adoption process.* Unpublished doctoral dissertation, Kent State University, Kent, OH.

Burns, D. J. (1989). The need for uniqueness and the adoption process. *Journal of Midwest Marketing, 4,* 28–37.

Burns, D. J., & Brady, J. (1992). A cross-cultural comparison of the need for uniqueness in Malaysia and the United States. *Journal of Social Psychology, 132,* 487–495.

Burns, D. J., & Krampf, R. F. (1992). Explaining innovative behavior: Uniqueness-seeking and sensation-seeking. *International Journal of Advertising, 11,* 227–237.

Burns, D. J., & Rayman, D. M. (1991). Need for uniqueness and the adoption process. In E. A. Tune & J. N. D. Gupta (Eds.), *Proceedings* (pp. 182–184). Indianapolis, IN: Decision Sciences Institute.

Burns, D. J., & Warren, H. B. (1995). Need for uniqueness: Shopping mall preference and choice activity. *International Journal of Retail and Distribution Management, 23,* 4–13.

Burns, R. B. (1979). *The self concept.* London: Longman.

Byrne, D. (1971). *The attraction paradigm.* New York: Academic Press.

*Campbell, J. D. (1986). Similarity and uniqueness: The effects of attribute type, relevance, and individual differences in self-esteem and depression. *Journal of Personality and Social Psychology, 50,* 281–294.

Case, T. L. (1974). *The effects of uniqueness-relevant feedback on individual opinion shifts, behaviors during group discussion, information recall, and perceptions of peers and self.* Unpublished doctoral dissertation, University of Georgia, Athens.

Chrenka, R. A. (1983). *Family structure and self-definition: Effects of birth order and sibling gender on sense of uniqueness.* Unpublished doctoral dissertation, University of Michigan, Ann Arbor.

Codol, J.-P. (1975). On the so-called "superior conformity of the self" behavior: Twenty experimental investigations. *European Journal of Social Psychology, 5,* 457–501.

*Codol, J.-P. (1984). Social differentiation and non-differentiation. In H. Tajfel (Ed.), *The social dimension.* Cambridge: Cambridge University Press.

Darley, W. K., & Lim, J. (1993). Store-choice behavior for pre-owned merchandise. *Journal of Business Research, 27,* 17–31.

Diamond, J. (1999). *Guns, germs and steel: The fates of human societies.* New York: Norton.

Ditto, P. H., & Griffin, J. (1993). The value of uniqueness: Self-evaluation and the perceived prevalence of valenced characteristics. *Journal of Social Behavior and Personality, 8,* 221–240.

Ditto, P. H., & Jemmott, J. B. (1989). From rarity to evaluative extremity: Effects of prevalence information on evaluations of positive and negative characteristics. *Journal of Personality and Social Psychology, 57,* 16–26.

Dunning, D., Meyerowitz, J. A., & Holzberg, A. D. (1989). Ambiguity and self-evaluation: The role of idiosyncratic trait definitions in self-serving assessments of ability. *Journal of Personality and Social Psychology, 57,* 1082–1090.

Dutcher, L. W. (1975). *Scarcity and erotica: An examination of commodity theory dynamics.* Unpublished doctoral dissertation, Southern Illinois University at Carbondale.

Duval, S. (1972). *Conformity on a visual task as a function of personal novelty on attitudinal dimensions and being reminded of the object status of the self.* Unpublished doctoral dissertation, University of Texas at Austin.

Fromkin, H. L. (1968). *Affective and valuational consequences of self-perceived uniqueness deprivation.* Unpublished doctoral dissertation, Ohio State University, Columbus.

Fromkin, H. L. (1970). Effects of experimentally aroused feelings of undistinctiveness upon valuation of scarce and novel experiences. *Journal of Personality and Social Psychology, 16,* 521–529.

*Fromkin, H. L. (1972). Feelings of interpersonal undistinctiveness: An unpleasant affective state. *Journal of Experimental Research in Personality, 6,* 178–182.

Fromkin, H. L., Brandt, J., Dipboye, R. L., & Pyle, M. (1974). *Number of similar strangers and feelings of undistinctiveness as boundary conditions for the similarity attraction relationship: A bridge between "different sandboxes"* (Paper No. 478). Lafayette, IN: Purdue University, Institute for Research in the Behavioral, Economic and Management Sciences.

Fromkin, H. L., & Demming, B. (1967). *A survey of retrospective reports of feelings of uniqueness.* Unpublished manuscript, Ohio State University, Columbus.

Fromkin, H. L., Williams, J. J., & Dipboye, R. L. (1973). Birth-order, responses to need-for-uniqueness scale items and valuation of scarce commodities. Cited in H. L. Fromkin, *The psychology of uniqueness: Avoidance of similarity and seeking of differences* (Paper No. 438). Lafayette, IN: Purdue University, Institute for Research in the Behavioral, Economic and Management Sciences.

Fromm, E. (1941). *Escape from freedom.* New York: Avon.

Ganster, D., McCuddy, M., & Fromkin, H. L. (1977). *Similarity and undistinctiveness as de-*

terminants of favorable and unfavorable changes in self-esteem. Paper presented at the meeting of the Midwestern Psychological Association, Chicago.

Geary, D. G. (1998). *Male, female*. Washington, DC: American Psychological Association.

Grossman, B. L. (1991). Children of interfaith marriage. *Dissertation Abstracts International, 51* (5-B), 2621.

Guttman, J., & Mills, M. K. (1982). Fashion life style, self-concept, shopping orientation, and store patronage: An integrative analysis. *Journal of Retailing, 58,* 64–86.

Hornsey, M. J., & Hogg, M. A. (2000). Subgroup relations: A comparison of mutual intergroup differentiation and common ingroup identity models of prejudice reduction. *Personality and Social Psychology Bulletin, 26,* 242–256.

James, W. (1890). *The principles of psychology* (Vol. 1). New York: Henry Holt.

Janis, I. L. (1982). *Groupthink* (2nd ed.). Boston: Houghton Mifflin.

Jetten, J., Spears, R., & Manstead, A. S. R. (1998). Defining dimensions of distinctiveness: Group variability makes a difference to differentiation. *Journal of Personality and Social Psychology, 74,* 1481–1492.

Kernis, M. H. (1984). Need for uniqueness, self-schemas, and thoughts as moderators of the false-consensus effect. *Journal of Experimental Social Psychology, 20,* 350–362.

Kim, H., & Markus, H. R. (1999). Deviance or uniqueness, harmony or conformity? A cultural analysis. *Journal of Personality and Social Psychology, 77,* 785–800.

Lemaine, G. (1974). Social differentiation and social originality. *European Journal of Social Psychology, 4,* 17–52.

Lynn, M. (1987). *The effects of scarcity on perceived value: Investigations of commodity theory*. Unpublished doctoral dissertation, Ohio State University, Columbus.

Lynn, M. (1989). Scarcity effects on value: Mediated by assumed expensiveness? *Journal of Economic Psychology, 10,* 257–274.

Lynn, M. (1991). Scarcity effects on value: A quantitative review of the commodity theory literature. *Psychology and Marketing, 8,* 43–57.

*Lynn, M., & Harris, J. (1997a). The desire for unique consumer products: A new individual differences scale. *Psychology and Marketing, 14,* 601–616.

*Lynn, M., & Harris, J. (1997b). Individual differences in the pursuit of self-uniqueness through consumption. *Journal of Applied Social Psychology, 27,* 1861–1883.

Markus, H., & Kunda, Z. (1986). Stability and malleability of the self-concept. *Journal of Personality and Social Psychology, 51,* 858–866.

Maslach, C. (1974). Social and personal bases of individuation. *Journal of Personality and Social Psychology, 29,* 411–425.

Maslach, C., Stapp, J., & Santee, R. T. (1985). Individuation: Conceptual analysis and assessment. *Journal of Personality and Social Psychology, 49,* 729–738.

McCaul, K. D. (1978). *Symptom information consensus and emotional responses to stress*. Unpublished doctoral dissertation, University of Kansas, Lawrence.

Miller, D. T., & McFarland, C. (1987). Pluralistic ignorance: When similarity is interpreted as dissimilarity. *Journal of Personality and Social Psychology, 53,* 298–305.

Miller, D. T., Turnbull, W., & McFarland, C. (1988). Particularistic and universalistic evaluation in the social comparison process. *Journal of Personality and Social Psychology, 55,* 908–917.

Nisbett, R. E., Borgida, E., Crandall, R., & Reed, H. (1976). Popular induction: Information is not always informative. In J. S. Carroll & J. W. Payne (Eds.), *Cognition and social behavior* (pp. 113–134). Hillsdale, NJ: Erlbaum.

Okamoto, K. (1983). Effects of excessive similarity feedback on subsequent mood, pursuit of difference, and preference for novelty or scarcity. *Japanese Psychological Research, 25,* 69–77.

Omens, A. E. (1977). *The presentation of uniqueness behaviors as a function of need for uniqueness, audience, and sex*. Unpublished doctoral dissertation, University of Kansas, Lawrence.

Powell, F. A. (1974). The perception of self-uniqueness as a determinant of message choice and valuation. *Speech Monographs, 41,* 163–168.

Robertson, T. S. (1971). *Innovative behavior and communication*. New York: Holt, Rinehart and Winston.

Rogers, E. M. (1983). *Diffusion of innovations* (3rd ed.). New York: Free Press.

Schachter, S. (1959). *The psychology of affiliation*. Stanford, CA: Stanford University Press.

Schroeder, J. E. (1990). *Psychological foundations of consumer preferences: The role of affiliation, conformity, individuation, and uniqueness*. Unpublished doctoral dissertation, University of California at Berkeley.

Schroeder, J. E., & Dugal, S. S. (1995). Psychological correlates of the materialism construct. *Journal of Social Behavior and Personality, 10,* 243–253.

Simmel, G. (1957). Fashion. *American Journal of Sociology, 62*, 541–558. (Original work published 1904)

Simon, B., & Hamilton, D. L. (1994). Self-stereotyping and social context: The effects of relative in-group size and in-group status. *Journal of Personality and Social Psychology, 66*, 699–711.

Simons, T., Pelled, L. H., & Smith, K. A. (1999). Making use of difference: Diversity, debate and decision comprehensiveness in top management teams. *Academy of Management Journal, 42*, 662–673.

Simonson, I., & Nowlis, S. M. (2000). The role of explanations and need for uniqueness in consumer decision making: Unconventional choices based on reasons. *Journal of Consumer Research, 27*, 49–68.

Snyder, C. R. (1992). Product scarcity by need for uniqueness interaction: A consumer catch-22 carousel? *Basic and Applied Social Psychology, 13*, 9–24.

Snyder, C. R. (1993). Hope for the journey. In A. Turnbull, J. M. Patterson, S. K. Behr, D. L. Murphy, J. G. Marquis, & M. J. Blue-Banning (Eds.), *Cognitive coping, families, and disability: Participatory research in action* (pp. 271–286). Baltimore: Brookes.

Snyder, C. R. (1994). *The psychology of hope: You can get there from here.* New York: Free Press.

Snyder, C. R., & Batson, C. D. (1974). *The balanced interpersonal perception of differences and similarities: A model of psychological distance.* Paper presented at the meeting of the Western Psychological Association, San Francisco.

Snyder, C. R., & Endelman, J. R. (1980). Effects of degree of interpersonal similarity on physical distance and self-reported attraction: A comparison of uniqueness and reinforcement theory predictions. *Journal of Personality, 47*, 492–505.

Snyder, C. R., & Feldman, D. B. (2000). Hope for the many: An empowering social agenda. In C. R. Snyder (Ed.), *Handbook of hope: Theory, measures, and applications* (pp. 389–409). San Diego, CA: Academic Press.

Snyder, C. R., Feldman, D. B., Taylor, D. B., Schroeder, L. L., & Adams, III. V. (2000). The roles of hopeful thinking in preventing problems and promoting strengths. *Applied and Preventive Psychology, 15*, 262–295.

*Snyder, C. R., & Fromkin, H. L. (1977). Abnormality as a positive characteristic: The development and validation of a scale measuring need for uniqueness. *Journal of Abnormal Psychology, 86*, 518–527.

*Snyder, C. R., & Fromkin, H. L. (1980). *Uniqueness: The human pursuit of difference.* New York: Plenum.

Snyder, C. R., & Shenkel, R. J. (1976). Effects of "favorability," modality, and relevance upon acceptance of general personality interpretations prior to and after receiving diagnostic feedback. *Journal of Consulting and Clinical Psychology, 32*, 258–265.

Snyder, C. R., Shenkel, R. J., & Lowery, C. R. (1977). Acceptance of personality interpretations: The "Barnum Effect" and beyond. *Journal of Consulting and Clinical Psychology, 45*, 104–114.

Sulloway, F. J. (1996). *Born to rebel.* New York: Pantheon.

Swann, W. B. (1983). Self-verification: Bringing social reality into harmony with the self. In J. Suls & A. G. Greenwald (Eds.), *Psychological perspectives on the self* (Vol. 2, pp. 33–66). Hillsdale, NJ: Erlbaum.

Tepper, K. (1994). Need for uniqueness: An individual difference factor affecting nonconformity in consumer response. In C. W. Park & D. C. Smith (Eds.), *Marketing theory and applications: Proceedings of the 1994 AMA Winter Educators' Conference.* Chicago: American Marketing Association.

Tepper, K. (1996a). Estimating model fit when data are not multivariate normal: An assessment of the generalizability of the consumers' need for uniqueness scale. In C. Droge & R. Calantone (Eds.), *AMA Educators' Proceedings* (Vol. 7, pp. 29–36). Chicago: American Marketing Association.

Tepper, K. (1996b). Understanding consumers' counterconformity behavior: A critical appraisal of trait measures employed in nonconformity research. In C. Droge & R. Calantone (Eds.), *AMA Educators' Proceedings* (Vol. 7, pp. 252–257). Chicago: American Marketing Association.

Tepper, K., Bearden, W. O., & Hunter, G. (in press). Consumers' need for uniqueness: Scale development and validation. *Journal of Consumer Research*, Lexington.

Tepper, K., & Hoyle, R. H. (1996). Latent variable models of need for uniqueness. *Multivariate Behavioral Research, 31*, 467–494.

Tepper, K., & McKenzie, K. (2001). The long-term predictive validity of the consumers' need for uniqueness scale. *Journal of Consumer Psychology, 10*, 171–193.

Tesser, A. (1988). Toward a self-evaluation maintenance model of social behavior. In L. Berkowitz (Ed.), *Advances in experimental social psychology* (Vol. 21, pp. 181–227). San Diego, CA: Academic Press

Weir, H. B. (1971). *Deprivation of the need for uniqueness and some variables moderating its effects*. Unpublished doctoral dissertation, University of Georgia, Athens.

Wilson, T. D., & Schooler, J. W. (1991). Thinking too much: Introspection can reduce the quality of preferences and decisions. *Journal of Personality and Social Psychology, 60*, 181–192.

Zweigenhaft, R. L. (1981). Unusual names and uniqueness. *Journal of Social Psychology, 114*, 297–298.

29

Humility

June Price Tangney

Although humility is commonly equated with a sense of unworthiness and low self-regard, true humility is a rich, multifaceted construct that is characterized by an accurate assessment of one's characteristics, an ability to acknowledge limitations, and a "forgetting of the self." In this chapter, I describe current conceptions of humility, discuss the challenges in its measurement, and review the scant empirical work addressing it directly and indirectly. I also will discuss briefly interventions for enhancing humility.

History of the Psychology of Humility: Still at the Point of Humble Beginnings

Scientific study of humility is still in its infancy. A review of the empirical literature from the last 20 years yields only a handful of research studies with any consideration of this long-revered construct. Furthermore, in virtually every case where humility is addressed, it has been tangential to the main research focus.

Why has humility been neglected so long? Two factors come readily to mind. First, the concept of humility is linked to values and religion in many people's minds. As a field, for many years, mainstream psychology steered clear of such value-laden topics as religion, virtue, and (with the exception of Kohlberg's work on *forms* of moral *thinking*) morality. In their zeal to establish psychology as a bona fide *science*, psychological scientists embraced notions of objectivity and fact. Indeed, it is worth noting that the virtues *as a group* have been relatively neglected in psychology. Until very recently, wisdom, gratitude, and forgiveness, for example, all represented "black holes" in the literature based on a century of psychological science.

A second factor undoubtedly contributing to the neglect of humility is the lack of a well-established measure of this construct. If you can't measure it, you can't study it. Psychology and the sciences in general are chock full of examples of how an advance in measurement can lead to a dramatic expansion in empirical research. For example, after years of neglect, the scientific study of shame virtually exploded in the early 1990s—shortly after the development of several psychometrically sound, easily administered measures of individual differences in proneness to shame (Harder & Lewis, 1987; Hoblitzelle, 1987; Tangney, 1990). As discussed in greater detail later, measurement remains a significant challenge in the area of humility.

Contrasting Conceptions of Humility

Another challenge facing psychological scientists interested in humility centers on the varying definitions of the construct. For many, humility simply means holding oneself in low regard. For example, in the *Oxford English Dictionary* (1998), humility is defined as "the quality of being humble or having a lowly opinion of oneself; meekness, lowliness, humbleness: the opposite of *pride* or *haughtiness*." In other dictionaries, humility is defined largely as a state of being "humble," which in turn is defined, for example, by *Funk & Wagnalls Standard College Dictionary* (1963) as "lowly in kind, state, condition, etc.; of little worth; unimportant; common. . . . Lowly in feeling; lacking self-esteem; having a sense of insignificance, unworthiness, dependence, or sinfulness; meek; penitent" (p. 653). From this "low self-esteem" perspective, humility certainly does not stand out as one of the more attractive virtues. For example, most of us would have difficulty appreciating a friend's efforts to strengthen our character by "humbling" us (e.g., making us lower in state or condition, reducing possessions or esteem, abasing us).

The "low self-esteem" conception of humility is prevalent not only in dictionaries but also in the psychological literature (e.g., Klein, 1992; Knight & Nadel, 1986; Langston & Cantor, 1988; Weiss & Knight, 1980), as well as in common parlance. Nonetheless, it is clear that when "experts" (e.g., philosophers, theologians, sociologists, psychologists, and other "wise" persons) delve into the broader significance of humility, they have a different—and much richer—notion of this construct.

Emmons (1998) clearly articulated this alternative view of humility by stating:

> Although humility is often equated in people's minds with low self-regard and tends to activate images of a stooped-shouldered, self-deprecating, weak-willed soul only too willing to yield to the wishes of others, in reality humility is the antithesis of this caricature. To be humble is not to have a low opinion of oneself, it is to have an accurate opinion of oneself. It is the ability to keep one's talents and accomplishments in perspective (Richards, 1992), to have a sense of self-acceptance, an understanding of one's imperfections, and to be free from arrogance and low self-esteem (Clark, 1992) (p. 33).

Templeton (1997) presents a similar conceptualization of humility:

> Humility is not self-deprecation. To believe that you have no worth, or were created somehow flawed or incompetent, can be foolish. Humility represents wisdom. It is knowing you were created with special talents and abilities to share with the world; but it can also be an understanding that you are one of many souls created by God, and each has an important role to play in life. Humility is knowing you are smart, but not *all-knowing*. It is accepting that you have personal power, but are not omnipotent. . . . Inherent in humility resides an open and receptive mind. . . . it leaves us more open to learn from others and refrains from seeing issues and people only in blacks and whites. The opposite of humility is arrogance—the belief that we are wiser or better than others. Arrogance promotes separation rather than community. It looms like a brick wall between us and those from whom we could learn. (pp. 162–163)

For many, there is a religious dimension to humility—the recognition that "God infinitely exceeds anything anyone has ever said of Him, and that He is infinitely beyond human comprehension and understanding" (Templeton, 1997, p. 30; see also Schimmel, 1997). Here, too, the emphasis is not on human sinfulness, unworthiness, and inadequacy but rather on the notion of a higher, greater power and the implication that, although we may have considerable wisdom and knowledge, there always are limits to our perspective. Humility carries with it an open-mindedness, a willingness to admit mistakes and seek advice, and a desire to learn (Hwang, 1982; Templeton, 1997).

Also inherent in the state of humility is a relative lack of self-focus or self-preoccupation. Templeton (1997) refers to a process of becoming "unselved," which goes hand in hand with the recognition of one's place in the world. A person who has gained a sense of humility is no longer phenomenologically at the center of his or her world. The focus is on the larger community, of which he or she is one part. From this perspective, the excessively self-deprecating person can be seen, in some important respects, as *lacking* humility. Consider the person who repeatedly protests, "Oh, I'm not really very good in art. I never did very well in art class at school. Oh, *this* little painting that *I* did really is nothing. *I* just whipped it together last night. It (*my* painting) is really nothing." Such apparently humble protests betray a marked self-focus. The person remains at the center of attention, with the self as the focus of consideration and evaluation.

In relinquishing the very human tendency toward an egocentric focus, persons with humility become ever more open to recognizing the abilities, potential, worth, and importance of others. One important consequence of becoming "unselved" is that we no longer have the need to enhance and defend an all-important self at the expense of our evaluation of others (Halling, Kunz, & Rowe, 1994). Our attention shifts outward, and our eyes are opened to the beauty and potential in those around us. As Means, Wilson, Sturm, Biron, and Bach (1990) observed, humility "is an increase in the valuation of others and not a decrease in the valuation of oneself" (p. 214). Myers (1979) effectively captured these latter two elements of humility, stating:

> The true end of humility is not self-contempt. . . . To paraphrase C. S. Lewis, humility does not consist in handsome people trying to believe they are ugly, and clever people trying to believe they are fools. . . . True humility is more like self-forgetfulness. . . . It leaves people free to esteem their special talents and, with the same honesty, to esteem their neighbor's. Both the neighbor's talents and one's own are recognized as gifts and, like one's height, are not fit subjects for either inordinate pride or self-deprecation. (p. 38)

In the theological, philosophical, and psychological literatures, therefore, humility is portrayed as a rich, multifaceted construct, in sharp contrast to dictionary definitions that emphasize a sense of unworthiness and low self-regard. Specifically, the key elements of humility seem to include:

- an accurate assessment of one's abilities and achievements (*not* low self-esteem, self-deprecation)
- an ability to acknowledge one's mistakes, imperfections, gaps in knowledge, and limitations (often vis-à-vis a "higher power")
- openness to new ideas, contradictory information, and advice

- keeping one's abilities and accomplishments—one's place in the world—in perspective (e.g., seeing oneself as just one person in the larger scheme of things)
- a relatively low self-focus, a "forgetting of the self," while recognizing that one is but part of the larger universe
- an appreciation of the value of all things, as well as the many different ways that people and things can contribute to our world

What Humility Is Not

Humility is a rich psychological construct that is related to, but conceptually distinct from, familiar constructs such as narcissism, modesty, and self-esteem. Clearly, from the foregoing discussion, humility is *not* low self-esteem (Ryan, 1983), nor is it an underestimation of one's abilities, accomplishments, or worth. Furthermore, as explained subsequently, humility is related to, but distinct from, modesty and narcissism.

The concept of modesty focuses primarily on a moderate estimate of personal merits or achievements. As such, *modesty* does not capture other key aspects of humility such as a "forgetting of the self" and an appreciation of the variety of ways in which others can be "worthy." Rather, use of the term "modesty" often extends into issues of propriety in behavior and dress, where the notion of humility is less relevant. Thus, modesty is both too narrow, missing fundamental components of humility, and too broad, relating also to bodily exposure and other dimensions of propriety. One might view modesty—in the sense of an accurate, unexaggerated estimation of one's strengths—as a component of humility. But it does not tell the whole story.

The construct of narcissism is perhaps most closely related to humility. People who are narcissistic clearly lack humility. It is not clear, however, that an *absence* of narcissism can be equated with the *presence* of humility. In conceptualizing narcissism, social psychologists tend to focus on grandiosity, an exaggerated sense of self-importance, and an overestimation of one's abilities. But there's much more to the clinical conceptions of narcissism. Clinical theorists, drawing on a long history of "object relations," typically use the term *narcissism* to refer to a distinctly pathological form of self-focus and fluctuating self-regard, which stems from fundamental defects in the self system (e.g., Kohut, 1971). When clinicians refer to a person with narcissism, they generally have in mind a seriously disturbed individual who exhibits pervasive adjustment difficulties that go hand in hand with a *DSM-IV* (American Psychiatric Association, 1994) diagnosis of personality disorder. This is not simply an overconfident, conceited dolt, but rather someone with a damaged sense of self. Attempts to shore up the self with unrealistic fantasies of grandiosity inevitably alternate with a grinding sense of emptiness and self-loathing. Other hallmarks of narcissism include a pervasive self-focus and a corresponding inability to focus on and empathize with others.

Narcissistic individuals clearly lack many of the essential components of humility. But it is not clear that people who score low on a measure of narcissism necessarily embody humility. People low on narcissism may or may not make accurate assessments of their abilities and achievements. For example, low-self-esteem, self-deprecating individuals are neither narcissistic nor paragons of humility. Similarly, people without narcissistic tendencies may or may not have the wisdom to keep their places in the world in perspective (e.g., seeing themselves as one person in the larger scheme of things). They may or may not have a deep appreciation for the unique gifts and talents of others.

In defining complex constructs such as humility, as well as in developing measurement instruments, it is important to specify how the focal construct differs from other related but distinct concepts. As underscored by Campbell and Fiske (1959), *discriminant validity* is a critical component of measurement validation. It is important to know not only that a measure correlates well (positively or negatively) with (measures of) other relevant constructs in a theoretically meaningful way. It is also important to demonstrate that the measure *does not* correlate too highly with (or behave identically to) established measures of some other construct.

Measures that are "confounded" by items tapping other nonfocal constructs not only present conceptual ambiguity but also impede science by blurring the boundaries between constructs, inadvertently precluding the possibility of studying functional relations *among* them. For example, in the case of forgiveness, it is impossible to examine meaningfully the functional relationship between empathy and forgiveness if one uses a forgiveness measure that includes items tapping empathy. In short, it is important to decide where to draw the conceptual line.

Measurement of Humility: Two Levels of Measurement, Two Levels of Questions

Halling et al. (1994) observed that doing research on humility is humbling. Quite possibly, the quest for a reliable and valid measure of humility is the most humbling aspect of research on this topic. By its very nature, the construct of humility poses some special challenges in the area of measurement. As a consequence, psychological scientists have yet to develop a well-validated tool for assessing humility. This is a glaring gap in the literature, because without a solid assessment method, the science pretty much comes to a halt. It is also worth noting that psychologists are most likely to develop strong, meaningful measures when those measures are informed by theory. Although we have some clear definitions of humility, comprehensive theories or models need to be developed and refined, which in turn would form a solid foundation for assessment.

Theoretically, humility could be assessed at two distinct levels—at the level of *states* and at the level of *dispositions*. A *dispositional* assessment would focus on stable, individual differences in humility. In this context, humility would be viewed as a component of one's personality, as a relatively enduring disposition that a person brings to many different kinds of situations. In contrast, a *state* measure would focus on feelings or experiences of humility "in the moment." Personality and individual differences aside, most of us have humility in some situations but not in others.

Regarding dispositional humility, a few options presently are available to researchers, but each has significant drawbacks. In several earlier studies, humility has been operationalized as low self-esteem (e.g., Weiss & Knight, 1980), but this clearly is inconsistent with broader conceptualizations of humility. In fact, theoretically, scores on self-esteem measures such as the Rosenberg (1965) and Janis and Fields (1956) scales should be positively correlated with (although not identical to) individual differences in humility. Consider the types of items included on the Rosenberg Self-Esteem Scale (rated on a scale of 1 to 5, from "always false" to "always true"): "I feel that I'm a person of worth, at least on an equal plane with others" and "I feel I have a number of good qualities." The person with a true sense of humility would be expected to endorse such items positively, not negatively.

Taking a different approach, Farh, Dobbins, and Cheng (1991) and Yu and Murphy (1993) operationalized workers' "modesty" by comparing self-ratings to ratings made of them by knowledgeable others (e.g., supervisors and co-workers). Those who rated themselves lower than their supervisors were viewed as showing a "modesty bias." Here, too, there are some conceptual ambiguities with such "self versus knowledgeable other" comparisons. Given that humility theoretically entails an *accurate* assessment of one's abilities, one could argue that high humility should be indexed by high levels of *agreement* between self and other, not self-deprecating discrepancies.

Emmons (personal communication, December 4, 1998) attempted to develop a self-report measure of humility. Using a forced-choice format to circumvent social desirability biases, Emmons developed an array of theoretically derived items tapping the diverse components of humility described previously. The measure is well crafted in design and content. Unfortunately, Emmons's initial analyses of the measure's internal reliability were disappointing, and he is now rather skeptical that this construct can be adequately assessed via self-report.

With regard to experiences of humility "in the moment," currently there is no established self-report measure of state humility. But Exline, Bushman, Faber, and Phillips (2000) recently developed a technique for experimentally inducing a sense of humility by asking people to write about "a time when they felt humble or experienced a sense of humility" versus "a time when they felt important or had a sense of importance." Based on results from an initial study, some complications arise in using this technique to prime humility. Specifically, people receiving humility instructions wrote two very different types of narratives. The majority of persons described instances in which they felt *bad about themselves* for doing something stupid or wrong. For this group, the instructions seemed to prime a sense of humiliation or shame rather than a sense of humility. A smaller subset of respondents described events that seemed more directly to the experience of humility—for example, situations that evoked a

"forgetting of the self" or that caused respondents to see themselves in a broader context. Thus, in using the Exline et al. (2000) priming technique, it is important to distinguish between stories involving humiliation versus humility themes. In addition, some modifications to the instructions may be necessary in order to more consistently elicit stories of "true" humility rather than shaming experiences.

No doubt, psychologists will continue efforts to develop psychometrically sound measures of both state and dispositional humility in the years to come. It is worth noting that researchers generally rely on self-report methods for assessing personality traits. In the case of humility, however, there is a potentially serious catch. To the degree that a key component of humility is a "forgetting of the self," self-reflection and self-report of one's level of humility may be oxymoronic. What do we make of a person who views him- or herself as someone with "unusually high humility"? As Halling et al. (1994) point out, "One can reflect on one's own experience of fear, isolation, or self-rejection, but the attention during the experience of humility is directed toward others" (p. 121). Similarly, Singh (1967) observed that "true humility is freedom from all consciousness of self, which includes freedom from the consciousness of humility. The truly humble man never knows that he is humble" (p. 4).

There are good reasons for psychologists' preference for self-report measures of personality traits. Traits such as humility are not easily inferred from quick observation. Also, systematic behavioral observational methods are cumbersome and time-consuming. So there is a strong preference for paper-and-pencil questionnaires that require little time and training to administer and score. But humility may represent a rare personality construct that is simply unamenable to direct self-report methods. Thus, the present bottom line is that the measurement of humility remains an unsolved challenge in psychology.

Psychological and Social Implications of Humility: Relevant Empirical Research

Researchers have yet to directly address the psychology of humility and develop a theory-based, reliable, and valid measure. Some insights can be gleaned, however, from related areas of psychological research. In this section, I provide a brief review of relevant findings from related literatures.

Basic research on the self and its operations suggests that humility may be a relatively rare human characteristic. The pervasiveness of "self-enhancement biases" is underscored in the social psychological literature (Baumeister, 1998; Greenwald, 1980). From this literature, we learn that the self is remarkably resourceful at accentuating the positive and deflecting the negative. For example, research consistently shows that people are inclined to take credit for "their" successes but blame other factors for "their" failures and transgressions (Baumeister, Stillwell, & Wotman, 1990; Snyder, Higgins, & Stucky, 1983; Zuckerman, 1979). As another example, people are more likely to notice, think about, and remember positive information about themselves, with negative information being "lost in the shuffle" (Mischel, Ebbesen, & Zeiss, 1976). Indeed based on this self-enhancement literature, one might infer that humility is quite antithetical with human nature.

Nonetheless, people apparently can control the degree to which they self-enhance in response to situational demands. On this point, Tice, Butler, Muraven, and Stillwell (1995) demonstrated that people adjust their self-enhancement according to the nature of the social setting, showing more modesty in the company of friends than strangers.

Whether with friends or strangers, some degree of humility may be beneficial. The benefits of modesty—especially "moderate" modesty—have been underscored in numerous studies (Baumeister & Ilko, 1995; Bond, Leung, & Wan, 1982; Forsyth, Berger, & Mitchell, 1981; Jones & Wortman, 1973; Robinson, Johnson, & Shields, 1995). People *like* and feel less threatened by others who are modest about their achievements, whereas boastful, arrogant behavior often results in social disapproval. The benefits of modesty seem to extend beyond positive evaluation in purely social contexts. In answer to the objection that "you can't get ahead without tooting your own horn," Wosinka, Dabul, Whetstone-Dion, and Cialdini (1996) have provided some evidence that modesty can be attractive in work contexts, as well.

Likewise, tendencies toward self-enhancement, grandiosity, and narcissism bode poorly for long-term adjustment, especially in the interpersonal realm (Ehrenberg, Hunter, & Elterman, 1996; Means et al., 1990). Although much has been written about the benefits of various "positive illusions" (Brown, 1993; Taylor & Brown, 1988, 1994), researchers also have shown repeatedly that tendencies toward self-enhancement are problematic. Specifically, psychological *mal*adjustment is associated with the degree to which people rate themselves more favorably than others rate them (Asendorpf & Ostendorf, 1998; Colvin, Block, & Funder, 1995). Joiner and Perez (2000) also found that people who are immodest (relative to how others rate them) are more inclined toward physical aggression than are their more modest peers. Along the same lines, researchers have shown that narcissistic individuals are sensitive to interpersonal slights, quick to anger, and less inclined to forgive others (Exline & Baumeister, 2000; Exline, Campbell, Baumeister, Joiner, & Krueger, in press; Sandage, Worthington, Hight, & Berry, 1999; Tangney, Boone, Fee, & Reinsmith, 1999). From these findings, one might infer that a sense of humility inhibits anger and aggression and fosters forgiveness.

In one of the few studies to explicitly address the psychology of humility, Exline et al. (2000) found results suggestive of a link between humility and forgiveness. People who were successfully primed to experience humility (e.g., who wrote personal accounts of a non-self-deprecating humility experience) were slower to retaliate in response to provocation on a laboratory task. In contrast, individuals primed to feel morally superior judged another person's transgression more harshly and as less forgivable.

Humility not only implies an accurate assessment of oneself (neither unduly favorable nor unfavorable) but also entails a "forgetting of the self," an outwardly directed orientation toward a world in which one is "just one part." This process of becoming "unselved" may have significant psychological and physical benefits. Clinicians have long noted the links between excessive self-focus and a broad range of psychological symptoms, including anxiety, depression, social phobias, and so on. As Baumeister (1991) argues, there are many advantages to "escaping the self," not the least of which is a relief from the burden of self-preoccupation (Halling et. al., 1994) and the "Western" imperative to defend the vulnerable self. Even in the area of physical health, researchers suggest that excessive self-focus is a risk factor for coronary heart disease (Fontana, Rosenberg, Burg, Kerns, & Colonese, 1990; Scherwitz & Canick, 1988).

Interventions to Enhance Humility?

Psychologists have not developed interventions aimed specifically at promoting humility, although many therapies include components that may do so. A focus on "humility promotion" is most likely to be observed in the treatment of narcissistic personality disorder. For example, cognitive-behavioral therapy of the disorder may include efforts to reduce the client's egocentric bias—correcting "cognitive distortions" regarding the centrality and importance of the self relative to others, reducing self-serving biases, and so forth. Beyond the treatment of narcissism per se, many psychotherapies inevitably touch on philosophical and existential issues centrally relevant to a sense of humility. Insight-oriented, humanistic, and existential therapies are especially likely to include examination and exploration of one's place in the world. Finally, a common goal in virtually all "talk" therapies is to help clients develop a realistic assessment and acceptance of both their strengths and their weaknesses.

Outside of the therapist's office, parents, teachers, heroes, and community leaders all play a role in modeling (or not modeling) a sense of humility for the subsequent generation. Throughout their early years, children learn important lessons about themselves, the world, and their place in the world. As they mature, a sense of humility may be further fostered by exposure to different peoples and cultures, by life-changing events (a life-threatening illness, a serious accident, birth of a child, dissolution of a marriage), by religious beliefs, or via other types of "transcendental" experiences.

Future Directions

As one of the classic "virtues," humility has a well-deserved place in positive psychology. Although little research has directly examined causes and consequences of humility, psychological science provides a good deal of indirect evidence supporting its presumed virtues. Consistent with age-old wisdom, a sense of humility appears beneficial for both the individual and his or her social group. But this is nearly virgin territory, and many intriguing questions remain. In what specific domains is a sense of humility adaptive? And via what mechanisms? Are there circumstances in which humility is a liability? Are there important gender and/or cultural differences in the meaning and implications of humility? How can parents, teachers, and therapists foster an adaptive sense of humility? Certainly at the top of the research agenda is the need for continued efforts to develop a well-articulated theoretical framework and associated psychological measures of both state and dispositional humility. Armed with a solid conceptual and measurement base, scientists will no doubt develop a clearer picture of this long-neglected source of human strength.

Acknowledgments Many thanks to members of our "humility" reading group—Luis ClaviJo, Rosangela Di Manto, Andy Drake, Ronda Fee, Ramineh Kangarloo, Jean No, and Justin Reznick—for their invaluable insights, and to Bob Emmons for his wisdom and advice. Preparation of this chapter was supported in part by a grant from the John Templeton Foundation. Portions were adapted from Tangney (2000).

References

American Psychiatric Association. (1994). *Diagnostic and statistical manual of mental disorders* (4th ed.). Washington, DC: Author.

Asendorpf, J. B., & Ostendorf, F. (1998). Is self-enhancement healthy? Conceptual, psychometric, and empirical analysis. *Journal of Personality and Social Psychology, 74,* 955–966.

Baumeister, R. F. (1991). *Escaping the self: Alcoholism, spirituality, masochism, and other flights from the burden of selfhood.* New York: Basic Books.

Baumeister, R. F. (1998). The self. In D. T. Gilbert, S. T. Fiske, & G. Lindzey (Eds.), *The handbook of social psychology* (4th ed., pp. 680–740). New York: McGraw-Hill.

Baumeister, R. F., & Ilko, S. A. (1995). Shallow gratitude: Public and private acknowledgement of external help in accounts of success. *Basic and Applied Social Psychology, 16,* 191–209.

Baumeister, R. F., Stillwell, A., & Wotman, S. R. (1990). Victim and perpetrator accounts of interpersonal conflict: Autobiographical narratives about anger. *Journal of Personality and Social Psychology, 59,* 994–1005.

Bond, M. H., Leung, K., & Wan, K. C. (1982). The social impact of self-effacing attributions: The Chinese case. *Journal of Social Psychology, 118,* 157–166.

Brown, J. D. (1993). Coping with stress: The beneficial role of positive illusions. In A. P. Turnbull, J. M. Patterson, S. K. Behr, D. L. Murphy, J. G. Marquis, & M. J. Blue-Banning (Eds.), *Cognitive coping, families, and disability* (pp. 123–137). Baltimore: Paul H. Brookes.

Campbell, D. T., & Fiske, D. W. (1959). Convergent and discriminant validation by the multitrait-multimethod matrix. *Psychological Bulletin, 56,* 81–105.

Clark, A. T. (1992). Humility. In D. H. Ludlow (Ed.), *Encyclopedia of Mormonism* (pp. 663–664). New York: Macmillan.

Colvin, C. R., Block, J., & Funder, D. C. (1995). Overly positive self-evaluations and personality: Negative implications for mental health. *Journal of Personality and Social Psychology, 68,* 1152–1162.

Ehrenberg, M. F., Hunter, M. A., & Elterman, M. F. (1996). Shared parenting agreements after marital separation: The roles of empathy and narcissism. *Journal of Consulting and Clinical Psychology, 64,* 808–818.

Emmons, R. A. (1998). *The psychology of ultimate concern: Personality, spirituality, and intelligence.* Unpublished manuscript, University of California at Davis.

Exline, J. J., & Baumeister, R. F. (2000.). [Narcissism, grudges, and forgiveness]. Unpublished raw data, Case Western Reserve University.

Exline, J. J., Bushman, B., Faber, J., & Phillips, C. (2000, February). Pride gets in the way: Self-protection works against forgiveness. In J. J. Exline (Chair), *Ouch! Who said forgiveness was easy?* Symposium conducted at the annual meeting of the Society for Personality and Social Psychology, Nashville, TN.

Exline, J. J., Campbell, K. W., Baumeister, R. F., Joiner, T. E., & Krueger, J. (in press). Bringing ourselves down to size: Toward a positive psychology of humility. *American Psychologist.*

Farh, J. L., Dobbins, G. H., & Cheng, B. S. (1991). Cultural relativity in action: A comparison of self-ratings made by Chinese and U.S. workers. *Personnel Psychology, 44,* 129–147.

Fontana, A. F., Rosenberg, R. L., Burg, M. M., Kerns, R. D., & Colonese, K. L. (1990). Type A behavior and self-referencing: Interactive risk factors? *Journal of Social Behavior and Personality, 5,* 215–232.

Forsyth, D. R., Berger, R. E., & Mitchell, T. (1981). The effect of self-serving versus other-serving claims of responsibility on attraction and attributions in groups. *Social Psychology Quarterly, 44,* 59–64.

Funk & Wagnalls. (1963). *Standard College Dictionary.* New York: Harcourt, Brace and World.

Greenwald, A. G. (1980). The totalitarian ego: Fabrication and revision of personal history. *American Psychologist, 35,* 603–618.

Halling, S., Kunz, G., & Rowe, J. O. (1994). The contributions of dialogal psychology to phenomenological research. *Journal of Humanistic Psychology, 34,* 109–131.

Harder, D. W., & Lewis, S. J. (1987). The assessment of shame and guilt. In J. N. Butcher & C. D. Spielberger (Eds.), *Advances in personality assessment* (Vol. 6, pp. 89–114). Hillsdale, NJ: Erlbaum.

Hoblitzelle, W. (1987). Attempts to measure and differentiate shame and guilt: The relation between shame and depression. In H. B. Lewis (Ed.), *The role of shame in symptom formation* (pp. 207–235). Hillsdale, NJ: Erlbaum.

Hwang, C. (1982). Studies in Chinese personality: A critical review. *Bulletin of Educational Psychology, 15,* 227–242.

Janis, I. L., & Fields, P. B. (1956). A behavioral assessment of persuasibility: Consistency of individual differences. *Sociometry, 19,* 241–259.

Joiner, T. E., & Perez, M. (2000). *Threatened egotism and self-reported physical aggression among undergraduates and their roommates.* Manuscript submitted for publication.

Jones, E. E., & Wortman, C. (1973). *Ingratiation: An attributional approach.* Morristown, NJ: General Learning Press.

Klein, D. C. (1992). Managing humiliation. *Journal of Primary Prevention, 12,* 255–268.

Knight, P. A., & Nadel, J. I. (1986). Humility revisited: Self-esteem, information search, and policy consistency. *Organizational Behavior and Human Decision Processes, 38,* 196–206.

Kohut, H. (1971). *The analysis of the self.* New York: International Universities Press.

Langston, C. A., & Cantor, N. (1988). Social anxiety and social constraint: When making friends is hard. *Journal of Personality and Social Psychology, 56,* 649–661.

Means, J. R., Wilson, G. L., Sturm, C., Biron, J. E., & Bach, P. J. (1990). Theory and practice: Humility as a psychotherapeutic formulation. *Counseling Psychology Quarterly, 3,* 211–215.

Mischel, W., Ebbesen, E. B., & Zeiss, A. R. (1976). Determinants of selective memory about the self. *Journal of Consulting and Clinical Psychology, 44,* 92–103.

Myers, D. G. (1979). *The inflated self: Human illusions and the biblical call to hope.* New York: Seabury.

Oxford English Dictionary. (1998). [On-line]. Available: http://etext.virginia.edu/etcbin/oed-bin/oed-id?id=191647477

Richards, N. (1992). *Humility.* Philadelphia: Temple University Press.

Robinson, M. D., Johnson, J. T., & Shields, S. A. (1995). On the advantages of modesty: The benefits of a balanced self-presentation. *Communication Research, 22,* 575–591.

Rosenberg, M. (1965). *Society and the adolescent self-image.* Princeton, NJ: Princeton University Press.

Ryan, D. S. (1983). Self-esteem: An operational definition and ethical analysis. *Journal of Psychology and Theology, 11,* 295–302.

Sandage, S. J., Worthington, E. L., Jr., Hight, T. L., & Berry, J. W. (2000). Seeking forgiveness: Theoretical context and an initial empirical study. *Journal of Psychology and Theology, 28,* 21–35.

Scherwitz, L., & Canick, J. C. (1988). Self-reference and coronary heart disease risk. In B. K. Houston & C. R. Snyder (Eds.), *Type A behavior pattern: Research, theory, and intervention* (pp. 146–167). New York: Wiley.

Schimmel, S. (1997). *The seven deadly sins.* New York: Oxford University Press.

Singh, S. K. (1967). *Untitled* [On-line]. Available: www.humboldt1.com/~jiva/humility.html

Snyder, C. R., Higgins, R. L., & Stucky, R. (1983). *Excuses: Masquerades in search of grace.* New York: Wiley-Interscience.

Tangney, J. P. (1990). Assessing individual differences in proneness to shame and guilt: Development of the self-conscious affect and attribution inventory. *Journal of Personality and Social Psychology, 59,* 102–111.

Tangney, J. P. (2000). Humility: Theoretical perspectives, empirical findings, and directions for future research. *Journal of Social and Clinical Psychology, 19,* 70–82.

Tangney, J. P., Boone, A. L., Fee, R., & Reinsmith, C. (1999). *Individual differences in the propensity to forgive: Measurement and implications for psychological and social adjustment.* Fairfax, VA: George Mason University.

Taylor, S. E., & Brown, J. D. (1988). Illusion and well-being: A social psychological perspective on mental health. *Psychological Bulletin, 103,* 193–210.

Taylor, S. E., & Brown, J. D. (1994). Positive illusions and well-being revisited: Separating fact from fiction. *Psychological Bulletin, 116,* 21–27.

Templeton, J. M. (1997). *Worldwide laws of life.* Philadelphia: Templeton Foundation Press.

Tice, D. M., Butler, J. L., Muraven, M. B., & Stillwell, A. M. (1995). When modesty prevails: Differential favorability of self-presentation to friends and strangers. *Journal of Personality and Social Psychology, 69,* 1120–1138.

Weiss, H. M., & Knight, P. A. (1980). The utility of humility: Self-esteem, information search, and problem-solving efficiency. *Organizational Behavior and Human Performance, 25,* 216–223.

Wosinska, W., Dabul, A. J., Whetstone-Dion, R., & Cialdini, R. B. (1996). Self-presentational responses to success in the organization: The costs and benefits of modesty. *Basic and Applied Social Psychology, 18,* 229–242.

Yu, J., & Murphy, K. R. (1993). Modesty bias in self-ratings of performance: A test of the cultural relativity hypothesis. *Personnel Psychology, 46,* 357–363.

Zuckerman, M. (1979). Attribution of success and failure revisited: or The motivational bias is alive and well in attribution theory. *Journal of Personality, 47,* 245–287.

VI

Interpersonal Approaches

30

Relationship Connection

The Role of Minding in the Enhancement of Closeness

John H. Harvey, Brian G. Pauwels, & Susan Zickmund

Relationship is a pervading and changing mystery ... brutal or lovely, the mystery waits for people wherever they go, whatever extreme they run to.

Eudora Welty,
The Quotable Woman

History of "Minding" as Relationship Connection

Our purpose in this chapter is to articulate the concept of relationship connection and to propose that it is a vital part of positive psychology. What is relationship connection? In the present chapter, this term will refer to ways in which people can enhance their closeness with others with whom they have romantic relationships. How can romantic couples maintain and enhance closeness? By closeness, we mean mutual satisfaction and behavior that contributes to one another's goals and hopes in life. While our ideas have been developed in the context of close, romantic relationships, they also have relevance to friendships and family relationships.

Kelley et al. (1983) defined close relationship as "one of strong, frequent, and diverse interdependence [between two people] that lasts over a considerable period of time" (p. 38). Interdependence was operationalized as the extent to which two people's lives are closely intertwined, in terms of their behavior toward one another and thoughts and feelings about one another. They also viewed the time factor as involving months or years rather than days. The conception of relationship connection to be articulated in this chapter views interdependence as being pivotal.

Another vital feature of this connection is that of the dialectic in close relationships. Welwood (1990) defines a close relationship as "rather than being just a form of togetherness, a ceaseless flowing back and forth between joining and separating" (p. 117). The "pulling" part frequently represents one partner's or both partners' work at autonomy. Similarly, Baxter and Montgomery (1996) more explicitly address the dialectical nature of relationships (e.g., our co-occurring needs for autonomy and dependency). Thus, the yin and yang of a close relationship are how to achieve balance between the couple's need for being united on many critical dimensions and the autonomy needs of each partner.

We will discuss our (Harvey & Omarzu, 1997, 1999) theory, referred to as "minding the close relationship," of how couples can maintain and enhance their close romantic relationships. In this theory, we give considerable attention to how people focus and give thought to their relationships. *Minding* is an interactive combination of thought and behavior patterns that we propose as promoting stability and feelings of closeness. More specifically, we define minding as *a reciprocal knowing process involving the nonstop, interrelated thoughts, feelings, and behaviors of persons in a relationship*. There are five specific components of minding, which are described subsequently.

Minding Model

Knowing and Being Known

The first component of minding refers to behaviors aimed at having partners know each other. These include questioning your partner about his thoughts, feelings, and past experiences, as well as disclosing appropriately about yourself (Altman & Taylor, 1973). Through this search to know a partner, intuition can develop. Partners often learn so much about each other that it is relatively easy to discern nonverbal cues, and to "read between the lines" about motivations, emotions, and experiences that may be troubling the other.

In *well-minded* relationships, each partner will recognize that people change in many ways over time. These changes can involve ever so subtle aspects of their physical bodies and their psychological compositions. Minding partners also will recognize that continuous change increases the challenge in knowing each other. It takes time and energy for both partners to find the right forums to discuss certain issues and to feel comfortable in being very open and expressive.

Most important, the focus in minding is on *wanting to know* about one's partner. There is great motivation to know about the other's background, hopes, fears, uncertainties, and so on. "Good communication" in a relationship must constantly be nurtured, and built on the premise that one can express feelings often and

fully. In minding theory, accurate and frequent communication is important, but the emphasis is on *actively seeking the other's self-expression or information, rather than pursuing self-expression*. It is this overt desire to really know another person that, we believe, creates an atmosphere that allows more open disclosure and "good communication" about "we" over "me" perspectives.

This search to know and understand the other also should be undertaken amid a continuing stream of explicit *behaviors* aimed at facilitating the relationship. Everything from doing an errand to smiling at one's partner falls under this rubric. If the errand is one you know your partner dreads doing herself, or if the smile is given across the room as an acknowledgment of a private joke, these facilitative acts are based on knowledge that partners have shared. Buying your partner flowers is an affectionate act, but it is much more meaningful when you choose a particular variety because you know it is your partner's favorite. It is a loving gesture regardless, but the latter has the extra impact of minding the relationship—moving the partners toward a closer bond.

Attribution

The second component is the attributions that individuals make about their partners' behavior. Attributions refer to the interpretations or explanations that people make for events in their lives. Attribution has been a central concept in the close relationship field for decades (Harvey, 1987). Fritz Heider (1958, 1976), who pioneered the description of human attributional patterns, suggested that attribution was a broad, pervasive type of activity that occurred almost anytime persons interacted with or encountered events in their environment. One of his examples was an occasion when he heard the back door of his home slam shut and immediately hypothesized (i.e., formed the attributional hunch) that his wife, Grace, had returned from the grocery store. The slamming of the door created the need for an explanation, which in Fritz's thinking was his wife's return. In Heider's view, we continually create these attributional explanations for each incident in our daily lives.

One of the most common types of attributional patterns that Heider identified is how we explain others' behaviors in terms of either the situation or their personalities. In relationships, the critical attributions pertain to the dispositional explanations (Jones & Davis, 1965) that people make when they observe their partner act in certain ways. For example, a wife comes home and begins screaming that she wants to be left alone, then goes into the bedroom and says that she does not want to talk about how she feels. The husband compares this act with her typical behavior after returning home from the office. If this type of behavior is rare, he may conclude that a unique external event must have occurred, perhaps at work, and caused his wife's negative behavior. If, however, she often acts in this way, he likely will attribute the behavior more to her grouchy and unhappy disposition than to some particular incident that she encountered.

Just as Heider asserted that attribution occurs constantly in everyday life, we reassert that attributions always are occurring in close relationships. Attributional activity is a central way in which we develop a sense of meaning about our relationships. As such, attributional activity reflects our trust and belief in our partners. When we attribute our partners' negative behaviors, such as rudeness or insensitivity, to outside causes, we are essentially telling ourselves that they are *not* really insensitive; it's the situation. We believe better of them. If we attribute our partners' positive, caring acts to outside events or to self-interest, however, we are doubting their love and sincerity.

Relationship-enhancing attributions tend to be those that attribute positive behaviors to dispositional causes: He came home early to spend time with me. She called me at work because she cares about me. Negative behaviors, on the other hand, are attributed more often to external causes: She yelled at me because she is stressed at work. He is late for our date because his car broke down. Attribution theorists such as Heider recognized that people's attributions of causality and responsibility often are mixtures of internal and external attribution. For example, the husband in the previous example may emphasize his wife's stress at work but also attribute part of her temper display to her susceptibility to such stresses. In well-minded relationships, these attributional activities will be carefully carried out, which includes working to develop fair mixtures of internal and external attributions. Partners will recognize how easy it is to be mistaken about one another's behavior, feelings, intentions, and motivations, and how important it is to feel firm about attributions regarding their partner's behavior in different situations.

Flexibility and willingness to reexamine attributions about one's partner and the relationship characterize well-minded relationships. Partners who are minding well can use the knowledge they have gained about each other to help ensure that they do not automatically attribute all good, or all bad, to their partners. Parts of the minding process build on each other. The knowledge and attribution components work together to help couples build trust and positive beliefs that are based in real knowledge and about which they can feel confident.

Acceptance and Respect

Acceptance and respect are high on the list of the prototypical features of love (Fehr, 1988). Through the minding process, one finds out a great deal of information about a partner, sharing innermost thoughts and feelings and revealing the past. We need to accept what we come to know about our close other through this process and to respect the other based on this knowledge. If we have doubts or cannot accept major parts of who our partners are, then minding is much more difficult to implement. Empathy and empathic accuracy (Ickes, 1996) are at the center of acceptance and respect in close relationships (see Batson, Ahmad, Lishner, & Tsang, this volume).

Researchers (e.g., Gottman, 1994, 1995) who follow couples over time and study their interactions have found that those who display positive types of social behavior together are more satisfied with their relationships. These positive behaviors include listening respectfully to the other's opinions, working out compromises that accept the other's needs, paying attention to the other during conflicts, and accepting the other's responses. All these behaviors are illustrative of respect for the other and acceptance of the other's feelings and thoughts. Less happy couples, on the other hand, tend to display less respectful behavior toward each other, such as verbal attacks, withdrawal, or criticism of the other's ideas.

Gottman (1994, 1995) has done extensive work with couples, observing their interactions and conflicts in a controlled experimental setting. He has followed many couples over time, some for several years. Based on his observations, he has argued that couples who stay happily married for long periods of time are good at repairing conversations when they become corrosive and negative. They do not let negativity become habitual or a common reaction to stress. They are good at soothing and neutralizing tensions and anger. At the core of this behavior is respectful negotiation. They are, essentially, rewarding one another much more often than they are punishing one another.

Gottman has described what he refers to as the "Four Horsemen of the Apocalypse," factors he perceives to be the signs of a relationship headed for failure: pervasive criticism, contempt, stonewalling, and defensiveness. He argues that discussion of complaints and disagreements in a relationship can be a healthy, good thing. Criticism, on the other hand, is not. He distinguishes between criticism and complaint by identifying criticism as an attack on the other's personality or character. Whereas a legitimate complaint involves a description of behavior, "doing" something negative, destructive criticism blames a partner for "being" a certain way. He also maintains that while healthy complaints focus on a specific instance of behavior, criticism is more global and therefore more difficult for the criticized partner to handle. For instance, if one member of a couple neglects the other by working nights and weekends, the abandoned partner may *complain* to the other, "You've been working so much recently. I didn't see you at all this weekend." *Criticism*, on the other hand, might sound more like, "You are so selfish. All you care about is money and your job. You never think about me at all."

When contempt (read lack of respect) creeps into a relationship, it signals a level of unhappiness and dissatisfaction that, Gottman's (1994) research indicates, often results in the dissolution of the relationship. In the Gottman hierarchy of relationship problems, contempt is stronger than criticism because it involves the intent to "insult [or] psychologically abuse your partner" (p. 79). He lists four common methods of expressing contempt: insults and name-calling; hostile humor directed at each other; mockery of the other; and disrespectful or disgusted body language. Contempt boils down to a lack of respect or admiration for the partner and can lead to a third destructive factor.

Avoidance or defensive behavior contribute to relationship breakdown through what Gottman terms *stonewalling*. Stonewalling is virtually avoiding communication with a partner, either by physically distancing oneself so that communication is impossible or by emotionally withdrawing until it seems futile for the other partner to try. To withdraw or avoid contact with a partner in this way also signals a lack of respect for the partner's desire to engage in discussion or social interaction. It is tantamount to ignoring one's partner, which is an effective silent way of conveying disapproval or lack of acceptance.

Gottman's (1994, 1995) program of research into close relationships makes clear that almost all couples display negative patterns of interaction at one time or another. One way of avoiding destructive effects is to concentrate on keeping negative interactions specific and complaint-oriented (i.e., focused on behaviors). In other words, it can be healthy for couples to argue or to disagree. It is not healthy to let arguments degenerate into the lack of respect typified by criticism, contempt, and avoidance.

The second key to handling negative interactions, Gottman says, is to consistently express more positive than negative communications toward each other. Some couples who appear to argue a great deal of the time may thus remain stable and satisfied together if they are simply a highly emotional pair whose positive interactions *still* outnumber their negative ones (Gottman, 1994, 1995).

Minding emphasizes the positive forms of interaction by specifically incorporating respect and acceptance into its principles. Couples who are minding their relationship well will be alert to the potential corrosion of a continued period of negativity in communication, feelings, and family atmosphere. They will be aware of the destructive power of criticism, contempt, and avoidance. They will recognize that each partner needs to have a voice and feel affirmed in the behavior and decisions that characterize the relationship (Rusbult, Zembrodt, & Gunn, 1982).

Recently, attention has been focused on a new type of marital therapy that also emphasizes acceptance and respect (Schrof, 1998). In this method, termed *acceptance therapy*, couples learn how to change their ways of thinking about partners. Rather than setting up a program of behavioral changes, as has been traditional in marital therapy, in acceptance therapy tolerance of previously annoying behaviors and personality characteristics is highlighted. Ultimately, the goal is to learn to not only tolerate but also appreciate a partner's differences, and perhaps even to develop affection for these differences. Jacobson and Christensen (1996) explored the effectiveness of this type of therapy and have reported that it seems to be especially successful with couples who have not been helped by other kinds of traditional marriage counseling. Acceptance therapy's successes make sense from the perspective of minding theory. It is not change in outward behavior that produce satisfaction in marriages but change in thinking. Specifically, it is an increased ability to accept and respect another's unique past and personality.

The search for knowledge about a potential partner begins quickly, and problems may be uncovered before serious commitments are made. This allows partners time to reflect on whether they are capable of accepting the implications of such negative information. It allows them to search for enhancing attributions and to build those attributions into their overall cognitive schemas about the partner and the relationship. It also allows partners to disengage from a relationship early on, before too much time and emotion have been invested. This knowledge search requires that partners open up to each other, disclose personal backgrounds, and share experiences.

Acceptance is important, even early in a relationship, to ensure that adequate disclosure occurs. There are inherent risks involved in revealing information about oneself to another that may prevent individuals from disclosing important information about themselves to others. Communication scholars Baxter and Montgomery (1996) have identified four possible risks of disclosing: rejection by the listener, reduction of one's autonomy and personal integrity, loss of control or self-efficacy, and the possibility of hurting or embarrassing the listener. All of these risks affect willingness to open up to a new partner; an atmosphere of respect and acceptance reduces these risks.

A climate of acceptance not only increases disclosure but also reduces fears of overall rejection in partners. Fearing or perceiving rejection by a partner can lead to feelings of insecurity and unhappiness in a relationship. People who are more sensitive to rejection seem to have less committed relationships and to feel less secure and satisfied with their relationships. They also appear to undermine their relationships by displaying more hostility, jealousy, and controlling behavior (Downey & Feldman,

1996). While these findings pertain to people who are more generally sensitive to rejection, it can be inferred that anyone who feels rejected may respond in this destructive way. When a relationship does not contain acceptance, both partners may suffer from these rejection fears, and their interactions may deteriorate rapidly into defensiveness and control attempts.

Acceptance also implies trustworthiness and discretion. We begin by attributing positive qualities such as sincerity to our partners, and we check their behavior over time to verify whether such dispositional traits apply to them. Of course, our partners make the same type of checks about our dispositional traits. We may come to different conclusions regarding a partner's trustworthiness. If, for example, a person belies this trust by making public the contents of intimate knowledge so as to embarrass or denigrate a partner, this is an act of bad faith that is not in keeping with the minding of a relationship.

One of the key benefits of minding is that the emphasis on seeking knowledge about a partner helps to uncover negative information early, before commitment is made. Nevertheless, sometimes secrets may come out late in relationships. It is conceivable that a partner might have originally withheld the information because it was embarrassing or because it did not seem relevant to the current relationship. Or perhaps a couple's relationship was not well minded in the past but the couple is seeking to improve, and it is through the new minding behaviors that such information finally comes out. For example, what if, after having been married 5 years, you discover that your husband had committed a felony? What are the limits of acceptance in such a case?

Such a revelation in a well-established relationship may lead to some serious discussion about why the information was withheld, and possibly to some reevaluation of the attributions previously made about the partner. But it need not be "fatal" to the relationship because of the restorative value of such discussion and the acceptance and respect both accorded and attributed by the partners to one another. Continuance of the relationship will be facilitated if there is a history of trust and positive attributions developed through the minding process.

Are there realistic limits to acceptance, or is it all-encompassing? How, in minding theory, for example, should we deal with negative information about a partner or a potential partner? Obviously, acceptance is not intended to be absolute. It is built into minding that as much as possible is discovered as early as possible so that potentially disastrous relationships can be avoided altogether. But even after a commitment has been made, some behaviors will be unacceptable. Certainly a partner who causes physical or emotional harm to the other and refuses to desist in such behavior cannot be accepted. Refusing to participate equally in a relationship or in the spirit of the minding process of relating may be a choice that is too destructive for another partner to accept. Overt dishonesty about past events that have direct impact on a current relationship also may cause insurmountable changes in partners' thoughts and feelings about each other. But problems from the past, personality quirks, or differences of opinion that cause no direct damage to the other or to the relationship are aspects of a partner that most likely can be accepted and respected, even when learned about years later.

The ability to accept and respect each other is crucial to the success of the complete minding process. Over time, minding leads to feelings of deep intimacy as each person recognizes the large amount of sincerity, effort, and care being exhibited by both partners. Acceptance is necessary for this feeling of closeness and intimacy to be created.

Reciprocity in Minding

Minding cannot long involve just one member of a couple engaged in the requisite behavioral patterns that we have outlined. There needs to be a sense of equity in relationships, such that each partner receives benefits from the relationship roughly equal to the amount he or she contributes to the relationship. When a person gives more than is received, this could lead to a sense of being underappreciated or "used." Conversely, someone who gives little to a relationship but receives much from the other may conceivably develop equally uncomfortable feelings of guilt or obligation. An inequitable relationship situation can thus affect long-term relationship stability and satisfaction.

There are challenges to this view. Communal relationship theorists (Mills & Clark, 1982) hypothesize that in some kinds of relationships, people are willing to give and contribute freely without requiring any "return" on their investment or effort. The ability of individuals to give communally is believed to be adaptive for families, when parents, for example, give unconditionally to children. Communal relationship theory may indeed be applicable to relationships in which the participants differ greatly in terms of power or resources, and where these differences are dictated by outside circumstances (age, serious illness, etc.). Most romantic relationships involve people who are at least possible equals.

Some studies have documented that, at least for American couples, a sense of equality is connected to higher relationship satisfaction. People who feel either "underbenefited" or "overbenefited" in their relationships express less satisfaction than those who believe they are equitably treated by their partners (Van Yperen & Buunk, 1991).

This idea of equity is translated in minding theory into the idea of reciprocity: each partner's active participation and involvement in relationship-enhancing thoughts and behaviors. One partner may stimulate, or trigger, the other partner's involvement, but that reciprocity must not be long delayed, lest the more constructively active partner feel betrayed and lose interest in preserving the relationship. Both partners will be involved in the process, even if part of the time their representative behaviors are carried out in a scripted manner (Schank & Abelson, 1977).

Scripts are preplanned "programs" for behavior that are carried out on a routine basis. Scripts can save people time and cognitive energy because they can be relied on and acted on with little thought or discussion. Couples often rely on scripts in their daily lives to simplify necessary decisions that must be made on a continuing basis. For example, a couple may decide just once who picks up the kids after school or who buys groceries, and then that person continues to follow that "script" regularly without further daily discussion.

Scripts can help people cope with time and energy pressures. If they help to divide work in a reciprocal fashion or assist in the couple's achievement of relationship goals, they are not incompatible with minding. But both partners must be wary about the potential power of scripts to replace the process that produced the comfort of closeness. It can be easy to fall back on scripts, even when they are no longer satisfactory, and allow communication and connection in a relationship to stagnate. Minding a relationship permits scripts to be included in a couple's life, but only if they have been created based on the knowledge, enhancing attribution, and mutual respect that minding has helped a couple to achieve.

Is one gender at a disadvantage when considering the reciprocal element of minding? Acitelli and colleagues (e.g., Acitelli & Holmberg, 1993) have found that women generally are more aware of relationship patterns than men. While we do not necessarily posit that this gender difference is found overall in minding activity, we do believe that minding requires a high level of relationship awareness and communication about troubling matters on the part of both partners.

Berscheid (1994) suggests that women may possess more highly developed relationship schemas because they appear to spend more time in social interaction and in talking about relationships than do men. We would suggest that men who have learned well their lessons of relating will be responsive to the "We need to talk" requests sometimes made by women (Tannen, 1990). If they are not, they risk the development of possible secondary issues, including women's attributions that they do not have the motivation or ability to engage in dialogue about relationship problems. Women, in turn, may become more attuned to a male partner's nonverbal expressions of relationship commitment through use of the minding process. Minding does not insist that men become aware of relationships in the same way as are women, but it does insist that partners in an individual relationship strive for equal awareness of each other and each other's needs.

In part, what people are doing in minding is learning about the other's attributions regarding relationship patterns and making adjustments according to what they learn. The adjustments may involve challenges of these attributions or accepting and taking these attributions into account. Berley and Jacobson (1984) describe such a procedure for using attributions in relationship therapy on minding and counseling couples. Reciprocity and mutuality are features of minding that cannot end if the relationship is to be close and satisfying.

Continuity and Minding

Continuity pertains to a criterion for closeness articulated by Kelley and colleagues in a 1983

book: "The close relationship is one of strong, frequent, and diverse interdependence that lasts over a considerable period of time" (p. 38). Because people and situations change, the knowledge gained about a partner through minding cannot remain static. This is a point that Kelley (1967) also made about attributions mirroring the data appropriately, accurately reflecting the behavior or situation. Each and every person represents an intricate set of experiences, personal qualities, dispositions, hopes, plans, and potential reactions to environmental stimuli. Being and staying close to any person over an extended period requires personal planning and action aimed at acquiring and updating knowledge on a regular basis.

We agree that the amount of time a couple has been together does not necessarily correlate to how well that couple is minding. One couple may be minding well after knowing each other a few weeks, while another couple may fail to achieve a high state of minding after 30 years. Because of the complex nature of relationships, however, a relatively complex process is necessary to understand and describe them. Minding is such a process and will take some time to fully mature in a relationship. We also emphasize that minding is a *process* that leads to closeness and satisfaction, not an ultimate destination: Process implies time and continuity, which is a principle that cannot be overlooked by the couple that wishes to be close (Aron & Aron, 1986).

This line of reasoning is consistent with the classic treatment of mind and the structure of behavior by Miller, Galanter, and Pribram (1960). These theorists discussed the interaction of plans with behaviors designed to test those plans. Such sequences take time to unfold. Miller and colleagues proposed sequences of "tests—operations—tests—exits" in which plans are checked out against real-world circumstances. This type of sequence can be followed in the minding process as well.

People develop plans to become closer to others. As has been suggested in the minding sequence, people thus come to know and be known by, to attribute qualities to, and to accept and respect their partner over some period of time. Throughout this process, individuals are constantly "testing" their thoughts and beliefs about their partners, as well as their overall level of closeness and satisfaction with their relationships. When the tests detect a problem or discrepancy, a new "minding operation" can be directed at correcting it. All of this involves the checking of the "plan to be close" with which each partner starts.

We do not believe that our focus on time is trivial. As implied by Miller and colleagues (1960), the planning and testing parts of the process of minding and the structure of behavior for highly intricate social behavior are learned over lengthy spans of our lives. We need experience. We need to do a lot of observing and checking to obtain that experience. Knowledge also is imperative to plans to stay close and execute related forms of behavior. But knowledge, too, is acquired over considerable time, and time is required to fully integrate that knowledge into a repertoire of behaviors and attributions regarding a partner or a relationship.

Given the complexity of each person, the minding process will require an extensive period of time to become well established. How long? That probably varies across people and couples. Skill at the minding process develops along with care and thoughtfulness regarding how one carries out one's life as it intersects with the life of another person with whom one aspires to having a long and close bond.

Table 30.1 presents adaptive and nonadaptive steps for developing close relationships based on minding theory. It can be seen in Table 30.1 that the process moves from knowing and being known through acceptance and respect, with reciprocity, motivation to continue the process, and actual continuity as ongoing throughout. Nonadaptive steps may occur at any or all points in this process.

Directions for Further Work

Are certain people better minders of their close relationships than others? Harvey and Omarzu (1997, 1999) have speculated that minding is a skill that can be taught. It should be a skill reflected in individual differences that can be measured, similar to intimacy motivation in general (McAdams, 1989). Minding is a combination of cognitive, emotional, motivational, and behavioral skill. Ongoing research (Omarzu, Whalen, & Harvey, in press) is aimed at developing a minding scale that would differentiate persons who mind well versus those who do not. A preliminary version of this scale is presented in Table 30.2.

Other work is directed at differentiating minding theory from general intimacy theory of close relationships (Prager, 1995; Reis & Patrick, 1996), and from major contemporary conceptions of how people achieve and maintain closeness. For example, minding is similar to the detailed cognitive-behavioral logic presented by Beck (1988) in his influential book *Love Is Never Enough*. Minding also resonates with the arguments of Schwartz (1994) in articulating the conditions of "peer marriage" (that is prem-

Table 30.1 Minding Theory: Adaptive and Nonadaptive Steps

Adaptive	Nonadaptive
Via an in-depth knowing process, both partners in step in seeking to know and be known by the other	One or both partners out of step in seeking to know and be known by the other
Both partners use the knowledge gained in enhancing relationship	Knowledge gained in knowing process is not used, or not used well (may be used to hurt other)
Both partners accept what they learn and respect the other for the person they learn about	Acceptance of what is learned is low, as is respect for the other person
Both partners motivated to continue this process and do so indefinitely, such that synchrony and synergy of thought, feeling, and action emerge	One or both partners are not motivated to engage in the overall minding process, or do so sporadically; little synchrony and synergy emerge
Both partners in time develop a sense of being special and appreciated in the relationship	One or both partners fail to develop a sense of being special and appreciated in the relationship

Table 30.2 The Minding Scale

Items should be rated on a scale of 1 to 6 (1 = Strongly Agree; 6 = Strongly Disagree).

1. Successful romantic partners have the same opinions about things.
2. You should avoid telling a loved one too much personal detail about your past.
3. It is irritating when people ask you to do favors.
4. Partners should be as much alike as possible.
5. People will take advantage of you if they can.
6. There is no reason to discuss your past relationships with a new love.
7. Partners who have different opinions will have a poor relationship.
8. It is difficult to be close to someone whose past is different from your own.
9. Partners should spend lots of time talking together.*
10. People mainly look out for their own welfare, even in close relationships.
11. You should find out as much as you can about a new love.*
12. Even when people love you, they think mainly about themselves.
13. It is important to keep some mystery about yourself in a relationship.
14. Romantic partners should agree about all things.
15. The people that we love are really strangers to us.
16. Partners should give each other the benefit of the doubt, no matter what.*
17. People who do nice things for you usually want something from you in return.
18. Close partners often have different friends and interests.*

*Reverse score these items.
(Optional item assessing reciprocity in existing relationships)
A. On a scale of 0–100%, how much time and effort do you put into your relationship? ____
B. On a scale of 0–100%, how much time and effort does your partner put into your relationship? ____
(To score, find the absolute value of Response A − Response B.)

ised on friendship) and Wallerstein and Blakeslee (1995) in formulating what constitutes a "good marriage." To the extent that these theories are process-oriented and emphasize a never-ending diligence in addressing central aspects of a close relationship, they bear considerable overlap with minding theory. Minding theory, however, can be readily differentiated from other prominent positions on relationship closeness, such as the emphasis on the value of positive illusions (e.g., Murray, Holmes, & Griffin, 1996). As suggested in the earlier discussion of attribution, minding embraces a strong reality orientation and dialogue about faults that one or both partner might wish not to address. In minding theory, we contend that people need to recognize their faults in relationships and, as best they can, work to redress those faults, or not let them interfere with their attainment of closeness. Thus, from the position of minding theory, positive illusions would be problematic to the extent the relationship is primarily based on them versus realistic assessments of the relationship.

Harold Kelley (1979) concluded his analysis of the structures and processes of personal relationships with the following eloquent observation about the difficult quest each human faces in trying to connect intimately with another mind:

> The unavoidable consequence of human social life is a realization of the essentially private and subjective nature of our experience of the world, coupled with a strong wish to break out of that privacy and establish contact with another mind. Personal relationships hold out to their members the possibility, though perhaps rarely realized in full, of establishing such contact. (1979, p. 169)

We believe that the process we have called minding offers us the best means by which we can attempt to break out of our private, subjective experience and connect intimately with another human mind and life. Minding makes people feel special. Nothing else does it better. Minding makes our relationships meaningful. Minding helps us solve problems and plan. Minding bonds and over time creates and sustains a sense of connection between two minds and lives.

References

Acitelli, L. K., & Holmberg, D. (1993). Reflecting on relationships: The role of thoughts and memories. In D. Perlman & W. H. Jones (Eds.), *Personal relationships* (Vol. 4, pp. 71–100). London: Kingsley.

Altman, I., & Taylor, D. (1973). *Social penetration: The development of interpersonal relationships.* New York: Holt, Rinehart and Winston.

Aron, A., & Aron, E. N. (1986). *Love as the expansion of self: Understanding attraction and satisfaction.* New York: Hemisphere.

Baxter, L. A., & Montgomery, B. M. (1996). *Relating: Dialogues and dialectics.* New York: Guilford.

*Beck, A. (1988). *Love is never enough.* New York: Harper and Row.

Berley, R. A., & Jacobson, N. S. (1984). Causal attributions in intimate relationships: Toward a model of cognitive-behavioral marital therapy. *Advances in Cognitive-Behavioral Research and Therapy, 3,* 1–35.

Berscheid, E. (1994). Interpersonal relationships. *Annual Review of Psychology, 45,* 79–129.

Downey, G., & Feldman, S. I. (1996). Implications of rejection sensitivity for intimate relationships. *Journal of Personality and Social Psychology, 70,* 1327–1343.

Fehr, R. (1988). Prototype analysis of the concepts of love and commitment. *Journal of Personality and Social Psychology, 55,* 557–579.

Gottman, J. (1994). *What predicts divorce? The relationship between marital processes and marital outcomes.* Hillsdale, NJ: Erlbaum.

*Gottman, J. (1995). *Why marriages succeed or fail.* New York: Fireside.

Harvey, J. H. (1987). Attributions in close relationships: Research and theoretical developments. *Journal of Social and Clinical Psychology, 5,* 8–20.

Harvey, J. H., & Omarzu, J. (1997). Minding the close relationship. *Personality and Social Psychology Review, 1,* 223–239.

*Harvey, J. H., & Omarzu, J. (1999). *Minding the close relationship: A theory of relationship enhancement.* New York: Cambridge University Press.

Heider, F. (1958). *The psychology of interpersonal relationships.* New York: Wiley.

Heider, F. (1976). A conversation with Fritz Heider. In J. H. Harvey, W. J. Ickes, & R. F. Kidd (Eds.), *New directions in attribution research* (Vol. 1, pp. 1–10). Hillsdale, NJ: Erlbaum.

Ickes, W. (Ed.). (1996). *Empathic accuracy.* New York: Guilford.

Jacobson, N. S., & Christensen, A. (1996). *Integrative couple therapy: Promoting acceptance and change.* New York: Norton.

Jones, E. E., & Davis, K. E. (1965). From acts to dispositions: The attribution process in person perception. In L. Berkowitz (Ed.), *Advances in experimental social psychology* (Vol. 2, pp. 219–266). New York: Academic Press.

Kelley, H. H. (1967). Attribution theory in social psychology. In D. Levine (Ed.), *Nebraska Symposium on Motivation* (Vol. 15, pp. 192–240). Lincoln: University of Nebraska Press.

Kelley, H. H. (1979). *Personal relationships: Their structures and processes.* Hillsdale, NJ: Erlbaum.

Kelley, H. H., Berscheid, E., Christensen, A., Harvey, J. H., Huston, T., Levinger, G., McClintock, E., Peplau, A., & Peterson, D. (1983). *Close relationships.* San Francisco: Freeman.

McAdams, D. P. (1989). *Intimacy: The need to be close.* New York: Doubleday.

Miller, G. A., Galanter, E., & Pribram, K. H. (1960). *Plans and the structure of behavior.* New York: Holt, Rinehart and Winston.

Mills, J., & Clark, M. S. (1982). Exchange and communal relationships. *Review of Personality and Social Psychology, 3,* 121–144.

Murray, S. L., Holmes, J. G., & Griffin, D. W. (1996). The benefits of positive illusions: Idealization and the construction of satisfaction in close relationships. *Journal of Personality and Social Psychology, 1,* 79–98.

Omarzu, J., Whalen, J. K., & Harvey, J. H. (in press). Assessing how people mind their close relationships. In J. H. Harvey & A. Wenzel (Eds.), *Close, romantic relationships: Maintenance and enhancement.* Mahwah, NJ: Erlbaum.

Prager, K. J. (1995). *The psychology of intimacy.* New York: Guilford.

Reis, H. T., & Patrick, B. C. (1996). Attachment and intimacy: Component processes. In E. T. Higgins & A. Kruglanski (Eds.), *Social psychology: Handbook of basic principles* (pp. 523–563). New York: Guilford.

Rusbult, C. E., Zembrodt, I. M., & Gunn, L. K. (1982). Exit, voice, loyalty, and neglect: Responses to dissatisfaction in romantic involvements. *Journal of Personality and Social Psychology, 43,* 1230–1242.

Schank, R. C., & Abelson, R. P. (1977). *Scripts, plans, goals, and understanding.* Hillsdale, NJ: Erlbaum.

Schrof, J. M. (1998, January 19). Married . . . with problems. *U.S. News and World Report*, 56–57.

*Schwartz, P. (1994). *Peer marriage*. New York: Free Press.

Tannen, D. (1990). *You just don't understand: Women and men in conversation*. New York: Morrow.

Van Yperen, N. W., & Buunk, B. P. (1991). Equity theory and exchange and communal orientation from a cross-national perspective. *Journal of Social Psychology, 131*, 5–20.

*Wallerstein, J., & Blakeslee, S. (1995). *The good marriage*. New York: Warner.

Welwood, J. (1990). *Journey of the heart*. New York: HarperCollins.

31

Compassion

Eric J. Cassell

Philoktetes has been given a magical bow by the demigod Herakles. On the way to the war against Troy, in the company of Odysseus and his crew, a sacred serpent bites Philoktetes. The divinely inflicted wound is unbearably painful and foul smelling. Because his cries of agony and the smell are intolerable, the crew stops at the island of Lemnos and casts Philoktetes away. Discovering after 10 years of war that Troy cannot be beaten without Philoktetes and his bow, Odysseus returns to get him. Philoktetes has suffered alone on the barren island in the intervening years when the crew searches him out near the mouth of his cave. The chorus speaks:

> I pity him for all his woes,
> For his distress, for his loneliness,
> With no countryman at his side;
> He is accursed, always alone,
> Brought down by bitter illness;
> He wanders, distraught,
> Thrown off balance by simple needs.
> How can he withstand such ceaseless misfortune?
>
> (Sophokles, 1986, p. 17)

The chorus seems to be describing the same feeling that has been evoked by so many scenes of the last century: the crying baby sitting alone on the railroad tracks in 1930s Manchuria surrounded by the destruction of war; dead or living dead victims of the Holocaust; the killing fields of Cambodia; starving children in Africa; wounded or dead children being carried from the wreckage of the Oklahoma bombing; the dead at Columbine High School and the terrified parents waiting to find out if their child is alive; the benumbed parents of the killers; and on and on it goes. Our hearts go out, we say, to the victims of these horrors. We feel compassion, pity, and sadness for them, sympathy for their terrible state, or indignation at the injustice of their fate. On a more personal level, people decry the coldness of modern technological medicine and look for physicians, seemingly rare, who have both scientific knowledge and the capacity to empathize with their patients. When they are sick and when they are well, people search for compassionate partners, caregivers, psychologists, therapists, physicians, and others who can meet their need for succorance.

What actually is compassion, and where does it come from? Is it an emotion similar to grief, sadness, or joy? Is it a duty, or a virtue, a personality characteristic, or simply a feeling common to humankind (and even some animals), or is it all four? It appears to be an emotion that is specifically social or communal, in the same family, perhaps, with the feeling of patriotism or group-specific feeling (communitas, team spirit). Because of this complexity, it has been the subject of debate from the beginnings of Western culture, and it has played a part in major Eastern religions. Compassion has figured in the disputes about reason versus the passions and in controversies about the proper role of medicine and the behavior of physicians.

Basic Requirements for Compassion

As in so many other aspects of human nature, it is useful to start with Aristotle. *Compassion* is the word most often used in connection with the emotion evoked by the sufferings of others. Aristotle (1984, 1385b 15–18), however, used the word *pity* to stand for "a feeling of pain at an apparent evil, destructive or painful, which befalls one who doesn't deserve it, and which we might expect to befall ourselves or some friend of ours, and moreover befall us soon." Reading these words today, most might say that Aristotle was speaking of compassion. Which word is used is less important than recognizing that such feelings exist and have been commented on since antiquity. (It is possible, however, that the emotions marked by the different words—e.g., compassion, pity, sympathy—might be somewhat different.) Whereas we have feelings of compassion for suffering strangers, for those closest to us the feelings are different. Again, Aristotle (1984, 1386a 19–22): "The people we pity are those whom we know, if only they are not very closely related to us. For this reason Amasis did not weep, they say, at the sight of his son being led to death, but did weep when he saw his friend begging; the latter sight was pitiful, the former terrible and the terrible, is different than the pitiful."

Since Aristotle it has been generally accepted that there are three requirements for compassion: First, we must feel that the troubles that evoke our feelings are serious; second, we require that the sufferers' troubles not be self-inflicted—that they be the result of an unjust fate; finally, it is believed that for compassion to be evoked, we must be able to picture ourselves in the same predicament.

If only serious troubles evoke our compassion, who is to judge the seriousness? Compassion is our feeling, not that of the persons who evoke it. As long as the suffering arises from war, murder, mayhem, rape, or nature's random destruction, little question arises because both onlookers and victims know that awful things have happened. What of the children, however, who have grown up amid war and know no different, or families denied opportunity or education because of oppression? They, too, may make us cry in compassion although they do not know themselves to be suffering. In like manner, the plight of a person with dementia who has no awareness of difficulty may evoke compassion even from strangers. To make the point more strongly that compassion is a unilateral emotion, remember that it is most commonly brought forth in settings in which the sufferer(s) have no awareness of the feelings they are evoking in others. They are usually not proximate in space and perhaps not even in time so that, for example, reading about the sufferings of people in the past may bring sadness at their difficulty.

The requirement that the suffering not be self-inflicted demands that the objects of compassion be seen as victims. Michel Foucault's (1979) book on the history of punishment opens with a graphic description of a man who was convicted of regicide being drawn and quartered. The ghastly spectacle went on for a whole day and seems to have been—like the famous executions by guillotine after the French Revolution—an occasion for public entertainment rather than for compassion. The man and the beheaded royalty were seen as having brought their punishment on themselves, and thus not due sympathy or compassion. Another example here is a description by a New York City subway motorman of his reaction to people being run over by his train. In describing the first two times in which a person was killed by a train he was operating (1987 and 1988), Mr. Anthanio, the motorman, seemed more irritated than disturbed: "It was their own fault, you might even say foolishness, that landed them on the tracks in the first place. One man was drunk. The other fellow turned out to have been on drugs." But when a third accident occurred (1989), the motorman did not see the repairmen on the tracks until it was too late. His reactions were very different than in the first two accidents. In his words, "The look on their faces; it was like looking into a mask of horror" (*New York Times*, 2000, p. B1). Indeed, it took Mr. Anthanio almost two years to get over this last accident.

The final requirement for compassion and its cognate feelings is said to be identification with the sufferer. Aristotle (1984, 1386a 25–28) again: "Also we pity those who are like us in age, character, disposition, social standing, or birth; for in all these cases it appears more likely that the same misfortune may befall us also. Here too we have to remember the general principle that what we fear for ourselves excites our pity when it happens to others." This comes closer to the social nature of compassion and at the same time to the inescapably social nature of being human. The paradox of compassion, like that of love, is that it is private, born of personal subjectivity, and social. To understand compassion, then, requires a better understanding of identification: how we know that someone is like us.

Compassion's Core: Connecting and Identifying with Others

At its core, compassion is a process of connecting by identifying with another person. The roots of this identification process can be found in more than one place. First, research with infants has shown that even in the first days of their lives they begin to mirror the facial expressions and simple bodily movements of the mother. They are seeing themselves in the other and the other in themselves. This, of course, shows the newborn infant to be more responsive to its caregivers and its environment than previously had been believed and places the onset of identification at the earliest age (Meltzoff, 1985; Meltzoff & Kuhl, 1989; Meltzoff & Moore, 1977; Stern, 1985; Trevarthen, 1988). For George Herbert Mead (1934), in fact, the "self" arises and is developed through the social experience of others; there is no self or self-definition without others. There is reason to believe that the child also is able to mirror, to absorb through feelings, the emotional state of the parent, so that identification continues into the domain of feelings.

We see the same attempts at synonymy in older children and teenagers as they dress alike and adopt new styles of clothing, language, or behavior in a neighborhood or nation almost simultaneously. Often the new fashion copies a popular athlete or entertainer. In adults this apparently general desire to identify with others (especially those who are admired) is promoted by and is the basis of the fashion industry. In the

18th century it was considered essential, if you wanted to understand human behavior, to know about four human characteristics: self-esteem, the desired to be approved of, emulativeness (the desire to equal or surpass), and the desire to be like those one admires (Lovejoy, 1961). These features, it would seem, are as much in evidence today. For example, uniqueness seeking (the modern expression of emulativeness) has been well described and supported (see Lynn & Snyder, this volume; Snyder & Fromkin, 1980). It is clear from this work that the desire to be unique sits in tension with the other social needs, with its place on the spectrum determined by era, culture, and personality.

What I am describing now is the identification with others that occurs below the level where uniqueness seeking or its congeners are determined. Consider, for example, the sometimes profound physical as well as psychological effects of abandonment. As we look more closely, we see that virtually all aspects of everyday life—how life is conducted in a specific environment and among others generally unknown to us—is firmly governed by a dense set of "rules," with a closely written script of whose presence we are mostly unaware. These strictures are not merely what is called etiquette, the conventional rules of personal behavior observed in the intercourse of polite society; they cover virtually every facet of existence—how clothing is worn, the rules of speech, walking on the street and other responses to gravity, facial expression, posture in relation to others (e.g., sitting in a classroom), telephone calls, love letters, the expressions of emotion, eating in all its dimensions, and maintenance of personal hygiene, among countless others. Because we believe in, indeed are proud of, our right to choose, how can such a lack of freedom be suggested? Unquestionably, there is considerable freedom of choice, but it is virtually always choice at a higher level of behavior, and even there within relatively narrow limits and at times more apparent than real. The social nature of the self and the identification with others is quite compatible with individuality (Mead, 1934). The fact of choice that we cherish, and which we defend with vigor, occurs largely within consciousness (although also in the domain of the unconscious), which, like consciousness itself, as Alfred North Whitehead once pointed out, is a mere flickering on the surface. The level of identification I am describing is virtually invisible.

One of the many consequences of the ubiquity of social regulation that is of special importance to understanding compassion is that individuals from widely diverse circumstances share an essentially and recognizably similar humanity with each other. This accounts for the fact that identification is possible even with people from different nations and disparate cultures. A connection thus exists between almost all; the pain of compassion can be brought about by the sufferings of any of the earth's inhabitants. John Donne (1624/1994) expressed this in his well-known meditation, "No man is an island entire of itself; every man is a piece of the continent, a part of the main; if a clod be washed away by the sea, Europe is the less as well as if a premonitory were, as well as if a manor of thy friends or thine own were; any man's death diminishes me, because I am involved in mankind" (p. 441).

Another possible source of identification has been labeled spirit. Events sometimes reinforce the belief that the connection that underlies compassion cannot be accounted for solely by universal identification borne of the social forces described earlier. For example, in the same period in the late 1960s in which social upheaval attributed to the Vietnam War was occurring in the United States, student uprisings and general agitation also were taking place in France and Germany, where the war was perceived as being relatively unimportant because it involved the United States. Similarly, a turn to religious fundamentalism occurred simultaneously in very different cultures throughout the world in the late 1970s. For the 19th-century German philosopher G. W. F. Hegel (1977), such events would be examples of the fact that all humans are bound together through the universal category of spirit. Each human both shares and is a part, and this spirit, despite its immense complexities and attendant philosophical disputes, provides a way to explain how all of us (unknowingly) actively participate in a universal humanity that has concrete existence (Olson, 1992). Earlier in Meditation XVII, Donne (1624/1994) writes, "The Church is catholic, universal, and so are all her actions. When she baptizes a child, that action concerns me; for that child is thereby connected to that Head which is my Head too, and engrafted into that Body, whereof I am a member. All mankind is of one Author" (p. 441). This a religious statement of Hegel's secularized concept. Whether through spirit or through the shared experience of living,

we know others to be as we are, so that when something happens to them, whether in Oklahoma City or Eritrea, we can identify with their sufferings. When it seems that there might be, at first sight, little conscious basis for identification with sufferers, then the pure bodily source of the suffering pulls compassion from us because everyone has a similar body. The sight of people whose limbs have been hacked off has sad meaning to all. Similarly, when children are involved, identification with the helplessness of a child or parental loss is universal.

Our body of knowledge about others provides a further basis for identification. Martha Nussbaum (1996), in a rich examination of compassion as classical authors discuss it, points out that the identification with others reveals one's own weaknesses and potential for injury. Nussbaum quotes Rousseau's Emile:

> Why are kings without pity for their subjects? Because they count on never being human beings. Why are the rich so hard toward the poor? Because they have no fear of being poor. Why does a noble have such contempt for a peasant? It is because he will never be a peasant. Do not, therefore, accustom your pupil to regard the sufferings of the unfortunate and the labors of the poor from the height of his glory; and do not hope to teach him pity if he considers them alien to him. Make him understand well that the fate of these unhappy people can be his, that all of their ills are there in the ground beneath his feet, that countless unforeseen and inevitable events can plunge him into them from one moment to the next. Teach him to count on neither birth nor health nor riches. Show him all the vicissitudes of fortune. (Rousseau, 1996, p. 224)

This suggests that the third route to identification with others is through knowledge of the human condition. In Buddhism, the statement that Buddha has infinite knowledge and compassion links the two: "Wisdom is the bliss of seeing through the delusion of self-preoccupation to reveal the underlying dimension of freedom. Compassion is the expression of such bliss to others. Compassion is the sensitivity to others' suffering. It sees them imprisoned in self-involvement, and reaches out to show them the way to freedom" (Thurman, 1997, p. 17).

The more one knows about others, the less quickly one will assign blame to those others for their misfortunes. The frailties and failings of people can be seen in anyone so that when people suffer from what appear to be their own actions, their fate nevertheless may have been beyond their conscious control. Thus, experienced health professionals are less likely to condemn or censure and more likely to feel compassion because they have seen and known how fraught with difficulties are people's lives. So also the clergy may pity and forgive where others would censure. In the episode of torture described by Foucault (1979), only the priest extends his kindness to the suffering man.

It is common experience that people differ in the depth or intensity of their compassion. What brings tears to the eyes of one is a matter of indifference to another. The differences appear to be explained by the varying degree of experienced identification with the suffering other. For Arthur Schopenhauer (who was greatly influenced by Buddhism), such identification required transcending preoccupation with the centrality of the self (the *principium individionis*). The suffering he sees in others touches him almost as much as does his own. He therefore tries to strike a balance between the two, denies himself pleasures, and undergoes privations in order to alleviate another's suffering. He perceives that the distinction between himself and others, which "to the wicked man is so great a gulf, belongs only to fleeting, deceptive phenomenon" (Schopenhauer, 1969, p. 372). Compassion, empathy, pity, and charity all require the ability to identify with another, to see in the plight of another what might cause distress in oneself. For compassion, because often it is felt toward strangers, even aliens, the act of identification requires bridging the gap between the self and another, when there is no direct connection with the other—or, put another way, when the connection to the other is merely conceptual.

Disconnecting: When Compassion Is Absent

"History tells us that it is by no means a matter of course for the spectacle of misery to move men to pity; even during the long centuries when the Christian religion of mercy determined moral standards of Western civilization, compassion operated outside the political realm and frequently outside the established hierarchy of the Church" (Arendt, 1963, p. 65).

In the same manner that identification is required to understand compassion, its complete absence may require disidentification—undoing or veiling the identification with individuals or groups so as to make them alien. It is well known that in many traditional and non-Western societies the category of person was extended only to members of the tribe or social group, and that those outside this category were considered alien—not of one's own. In some tribal languages, a person is someone who is a member of the tribe; others are not persons and are not due the recognition due humans—an idea that may be exemplified in contemporary African intertribal brutalities (Mauss, 1985). Compassion may not be extended to aliens. The horrors and brutality perpetrated against the Indians by America's settlers and against the settlers by the Indians falls in this category. From the behavior of soldiers killing in battle to those who commit atrocities, an essential step seems to be to define the object of murder or brutality as "not being us." The repeated instances of brutality so common in the 20th century appear to have demonstrated this truth. An important element of Nazism was defining Germans by use of the term *Aryan*, with its 19th-century connotations of nationalism, that permitted the Nazis to define Jews as alien, despicable, beyond the pale, and outside the boundaries of human. (All of which makes more remarkable, considering its time, the Old Testament injunction to compassion in Leviticus 19:34: "The stranger who sojourns among you shall be to you as one born among you and you shall love him as yourself; for you were strangers in the land of Egypt: I am the Lord your God.")

The sometimes awful actions of people lacking compassion and a sense of identification with others raise the idea, associated with Thomas Hobbes, that the life of humans in a state of nature (the absence of society) is solitary, poor, nasty, brutish, and short. Hobbes (1651/1962) believed that this facet of human nature, that humankind is brutal, was held in check by self-interest and humankind's universal fear of death. Schopenhauer (1969), two centuries later, agreed on the importance of self-interest as one of the three basic motives of human behavior. He also identified gratuitous malice as one of the basic human traits. For humans are the only animals to cause pain to others without any further purpose than just to cause it. Other animals never do this except to satisfy their hunger or in the rage of combat. The appalling record of human life, of human suffering and infliction of pain by humans is relieved only when the third motive, sympathy or compassion, appears. As Alisdair MacIntyre (1966) points out in his discussion of Schopenhauer:

> To feel compassion is to put oneself imaginatively in the place of the sufferer and to alter one's actions appropriately either by desisting from what would have caused pain or by devoting oneself to its relief. But the exhibiting of compassion has yet a further significance. In a moment of compassion we extinguish self-will. We cease to strive for our own existence; we are relieved from the burden of individuality and we cease to be the playthings of Will. (p. 22)

Compassion as Evidence for the Nature of Humankind

Why is it necessary in a discussion of compassion to raise these philosophical issues? Because if compassion is a social emotion having to do with the relationships of people to each other, then it must raise philosophical, political, and ideological questions. Because the existence of compassion goes to the heart of what it means to be human, its significance has been argued over the centuries. What a particular speaker says about compassion stands a good chance of being influenced by where that person stands on the political spectrum. Hobbes's (1651) pessimistic position about human nature was influenced by belief in original sin and the corrupt state of humankind after the Fall. This view was held throughout the many centuries of the Middle Ages in which Scholasticism and the profound influence of the Church prevailed. The rise of humanism in the late 16th century, easily seen in the works of Montaigne and Shakespeare, began to build a kinder, more "liberal" view. By the latter part of the 17th century and certainly in the 18th century, as manifested by the Enlightenment, interest in the innate "moral sense" and indications of the essential goodness of humankind began to be widespread. It is easily seen why the evidence produced by the emotion of compassion was important to these theorists. Here, for example, is Adam Smith (1759/1976) in his 18th-century *Theory of Moral Sentiments*:

> How selfish soever man may be supposed, there are evidently some principles in his nature, which interest him in the fortunes of others, and render their happiness necessary to him, though he derives nothing from it except the pleasure of seeing it. Of this kind is pity or compassion, the emotion we feel for the misery of others when we see it, or are made to conceive it in a very lively manner. (p. 9)

Well into the 19th century, debate continued as to whether democracy and capitalism, where the market economy reigned, would decrease the impact of compassion because of the importance of self-interest in such an environment or increase it because of the sheer number of people with which one might identify. Alexis de Tocqueville (1955), in his famous study of young America, noted that compassion seemed to be characteristic of a democratic society. Considering the political struggles of the 20th century, it is not surprising that the controversy continues (Arons, 1993; Sznaider, 1998). In the contemporary world, communities and individuals mark themselves on the evidence of their compassion. Appeals for philanthropy frequently are couched in such terms. On the other hand, in a study of attitudes toward public assistance for victims of severe floods, the political ideology (self-defined) of the respondents was related to their answers to questions about the appropriateness of monetary help. Even in the context of a natural disaster, respondents sought out information about the victims' personal responsibility (e.g., whether they had purchased flood insurance). Liberals were more likely to provide humanitarian aid to the "irresponsible" than were conservatives. Conservatives consistently held individuals more responsible for their plight and for resolving it. The reactions of each group to the needs of flood-damaged communities were generally in line with their responses to needy individuals (Skitka, 1999).

The place of compassion as a motivation for individual or societal behavior, and as one of the foundations for civil society, is a continual topic of debate (Brown, 1996). The debate continues (since Kant) as to whether compassion is a passion and thus in opposition to reason, or whether it is an emotion, albeit an inherently rational one (Nussbaum, 1996). Some physicians, psychologists, and scientists may become impatient with these discussions, viewing them as philosophical time wasting. This is a pity, however, because such discussions would not go on for centuries if they were trivial. Furthermore, the thinking of philosophers often determines the attitude of the rest of society. Witness the long-lasting impact, not gone to this day (sadly), of René Descartes's 17th-century notions of duality of mind and body.

Compassion and the Nature of Suffering

Emotions and feelings are similar to adjectives that spontaneously comment on and modify the facts of experience as they flow by. In this regard, compassion is more complex than other emotions. It demands knowledge of the suffering of others and moves the compassionate person to action (see Batson, Ahmad, Lishner, & Tsang, this volume). Previously, I noted that compassion requires knowing that others are suffering, identification with the sufferer, and, especially where compassion is felt, knowledge of what the sufferer is experiencing. How is such knowledge acquired, and how does one know that someone suffers?

It is necessary to pause and look at the nature of suffering (Cassell, 1982). It is common to identify suffering with pain or other physical symptoms. They certainly may start the chain of events leading to suffering, but the more proximate and crucial sources of suffering are what the person believes the symptoms mean and what is expected will happen (in the future) if the symptom continues. Bodies may have physical symptoms, but they do not have a sense of the future and are not concerned with the meaning of things. Bodies do not suffer; only persons do. Suffering is above all highly personal, an affliction of persons. It occurs when persons perceive their impending destruction or loss of integrity as persons, and it continues until the threat of disintegration is passed or until the integrity of the person can be restored in some other manner. Most generally, then, suffering can be defined as the state of severe distress associated with events that threaten the intactness of person. Suffering is not only psychological, or social, or physical; it denies the utility of thinking only in such categories if it is to be understood, because suffering involves all aspects of the person.

Let's consider the word "person." We all know ourselves to be persons, but as definitions are attempted, the word's complexity becomes apparent. Persons, for example, think of themselves as more than merely individuals, even though that is a common synonym. One reason it is difficult to define what someone means when he or she says "I am a person" is that the meaning has changed through history. For example, the idea that persons are individual and unique did not enter Western civilization until about the 11th century, and only in the 20th century were persons widely acknowledged to have a rich interior and unconscious life. Persons, then, are not only minds, not only selves, not just bodies, and are not simply boundaried like other objects of science. Persons are the entire complex trajectory through time and space of the wholes that are made up of their pasts and believed-in futures, their family and their family's past, their body and their relationships with their body, relationships with others, day-to-day behaviors and activities, roles, inculcated culture and society, their political dimension, their secret life (the conscious hopes, aspirations, fantasies, and secret relationships that are wished for or actual, and much more, as in the movie *The Secret Life of Walter Mitty*), their unconscious, and their spiritual dimension. Suffering may occur in relation to any aspect of the person. For example, sickness, war, or poverty may disrupt persons' relationships to significant others or to the roles or works of a lifetime, thus destroying the persons they know themselves to be. Because everyone is different and distinct from others, suffering always is individual and unique. Suffering also is marked by self-conflict, profound loss of or change in central purpose, and resistance to the loss of personal intactness. Suffering can occur as much from psychological and social insults as from physical ones, and it appears as often in acute as in chronic illness (Cassell, 1991).

Knowing That Others Are Suffering

The challenge of knowing that someone else is suffering (and why) is particularly difficult because the quintessential fact about suffering is that it is lonely. The loneliness, which further adds to the suffering, results from its highly personal and individual nature. The most underutilized method of discovering that people are suffering is to ask them. Sufferers themselves may not know that they suffer, however, and may point instead to their diseases or other external circumstances rather than to their disintegrations as people. The early stages of their suffering may be mute and unutterable. Later, the sufferers may become expressive, lamenting what is happening and repeatedly telling the story of their disease or victimization as though looking for someone to help in their search for a new story in which they once again become complete (Reich, 1987). Or one might know the sufferer so well as an individual that the roots of his or her suffering are laid bare. This seems improbable, however, in that we rarely even know ourselves this well.

We often claim to know of another's suffering because of the compassion we have in identifying with that sufferer. What has happened to that (or those) person(s) is so terrible that if it happened to me I certainly would suffer. Such sickness, loss, or injury is so awful that I never would be able to stand it. How can the victims of so much disease, destruction, and death not be suffering? My heart goes out to them. There can be no other way of knowing suffering when groups are involved, or when those persons experiencing compassion are separated in time or space from the victims. This "blind" compassion has two difficulties. It may not appreciate that others suffer even if the onlookers do not believe the cause is great enough, or onlookers may believe suffering is present when, in fact, victims have risen above the injury—have grown through their experience and thus are no longer suffering (see Tennen & Affleck, this volume; Nolen-Hoeksema & Davis, this volume). Or the compassionate onlooker may not realize that the victims see the injuries as an opportunity to identify with a larger cause, thus relieving their suffering by giving it meaning just as the saints identified with the suffering of Christ.

On an individual level, the compassionate can be aware of the sights and sounds of the sufferer, and they can feel the pain, sadness, anxiety, and anger through the direct transfer of feelings. More intimately, the compassionate share the same universe with the sufferer—dark and light, air, gravity, noise, and quiet. Also shared are worlds of common values, ideas, beliefs, and aesthetics. We know each other through proximity. Our knowledge of others is a central and constantly expanding feature of life. In other words we share community—a "we-ness" where all are joined—and from which the absence of the sufferer who is withdrawn into the suffering can be recognized. Thus, compassion is realized through all these

methods—identification; knowledge of behaviors; the sights and sounds of suffering; the transfer of feelings; awareness of the change in goals and purposes of sufferers; the sense of absence of the sufferer from the group—and through their mutual reinforcement.

Compassion and Medicine

Compassion is called for by Item 1 of the American Medical Association's Principles of Medical Ethics (1981): "A physician shall be dedicated to providing competent medical services with compassion and respect for human dignity." Some still debate whether it is more important to have a competent or a compassionate physician, as though the two qualities are in conflict, mirroring the dispute over the (supposed) opposition between reason and emotion. Most believe, however, that compassion should be an inherent part of medicine and that physicians should be compassionate (Barber, 1976).

It is possible now to tease apart the question raised initially: Is compassion a human emotion, a personality characteristic (different persons have it in varying degrees), a duty, or a virtue? Compassion is the feeling aroused by an acknowledged awareness that others are suffering. The feeling depends on the ability inherent in humans (and some animals) to make a connection with others so as to be aware of their suffering. Compassion necessitates identification with the sufferer(s), and it allows for an evaluation of the magnitude of the suffering. Absent such identification, the sufferer can be considered alien, and no connection will be formed. (In its absence brutality may become permissible.) The ability to connect and identify with others is of varying degrees, with the feeling of compassion varying in intensity with the nature of the person and the circumstance. Compassion is an emotion, and its magnitude is a function of personality characteristics (among other things).

Generally, felt compassion evokes the desire to do something to relieve the sufferer(s). The wish to be helpful is not compassion itself, but it suggests that compassion, similar to other emotions (anger, for example), may motivate behaviors that reduce the tension brought on by the emotion. There can be no objection to someone feeling compassion, but there may be problems associated with the action that might follow. This is why it has been said that unfettered compassion may be as dangerous as an untrained scalpel.

I noted previously that the words *pity* and *sympathy* (and even *empathy*) often are used synonymously with *compassion*, especially in discussions from antiquity. Understanding of emotion has evolved greatly in Western history, especially in the last two centuries. (For example, presently I do not believe many would agree with Aristotle [1370b 15] when he said, "We feel comparatively little anger or none at all, with those who are much our superiors in power.") Whereas both sympathy and pity require some sense of connection to the victim, sympathy acknowledges fellow feelings for an equal, but pity (similar to mercy) has come to connote an emotion directed downward. The victim may play no active part in the onset of these social emotions; moreover, recipients may resent the expression of compassion, "not want your sympathy," or resent the status connotations of pity. Part of the difficulty in understanding emotion is failing to make the distinctions between an emotion, its state of being, and its associated behavior. This is the difference, for example, between a flash of anger, being angry, and acting angrily. Hearing that some children were killed in a school bus accident, I may feel a surge of compassion for their parents. Seeing very sick patients struggling to maintain their dignity despite their impairments may fill my being with compassion so that I am in a state of compassion. In that state, I may act compassionately, my actions guided not only by my technical knowledge but also by my awareness through identification with the patients and my knowledge of sickness in general, so that in my actions I enhance the patients' feelings of self-worth and adult humanity. It follows that a person may feel compassion but neither become compassionate nor act compassionately.

These distinctions help clarify whether one can say that a universal human emotion that is, in part, a personality characteristic also can be a virtue and required as a duty. One cannot demand that someone feel a surge of compassion as a consequence of something that befalls another individual or group. It might be possible to change things by showing people why the victims deserve their compassion, pity, or sympathy, but evocation of the emotion itself is beyond conscious control. But maintaining oneself in an emotional state can be learned. It can be

shown that the discomforts of compassion, for example, the feeling of an uncomfortable urgency to do something when that is not possible, are tolerable as is the emotion itself. In fact, one can help a student discover that the sustained emotion can be an uplifting experience. The state of compassion is a virtuous one, and it can lead to virtuous action. It is, in general, a virtue we should like the citizens of a democratic nation to exhibit as they show appropriate compassion to their fellows from any part of the country (or the globe, for that matter).

Compassion should be desirable in all helpers—whatever their profession. Because I am a physician, I would like to share observations about my field. Compassion is a virtue that has come to be expected of physicians involved in patient care because it is directly related to the recognition and treatment of suffering. Physicians concerned only with the manifestations of disease or the exercise of their technologies may fail to address the suffering that always has its locus in the person rather than only in the body. In not being aware of or dealing with suffering, the physician has failed his or her duties.

The central duties of physicians are the fiduciary responsibility to put the patient's interests first, including the duty not to harm, to deliver proper care, and to maintain confidentiality. Compassion figures in each of these duties because it heightens awareness of the patients' interests; increases the probability that care will be tuned to this patient's needs (and that physicians will maintain their knowledge and skills); and promotes the intimacy of knowledge about each patient that physicians require (Dougherty & Purtillo, 1995).

Compassion and Love

One of the routes to compassion noted previously was knowledge of humankind, a knowledge that also seemed to be the basis of the Buddhist association of wisdom and compassion. Yet the important place of compassion in the healing professions and our belief that it is both a virtue and a duty for caregivers raise the possibility that compassion is not merely a result of knowledge of the suffering of patients, but that it is a basis for that knowledge, and not simply, as Loewy (1998) suggests, because curiosity causes caregivers to discover things about another that then arouse compassion. As

I hear my patient recount the story of his illness and all its pain and sadness and see the sickness speaking from his features, my compassion is aroused. I become connected to the patient; we have begun to fuse. I am no longer in an ordinary social interaction where the "distance" between the participants is maintained and where attempts to get closer than the particular culture allows may be perceived as a breach of social convention. When that happens, I begin to listen, look, and intuit with greater intensity, and more information flows toward me. If I make myself conscious of what is happening, I can begin to feel the patient's emotions, and even my hand palpating the abdomen appears to receive more information than it otherwise would. Despite our closeness, and despite the fact that the patient's experience has begun to be part of my experience, we are doctor and patient, not friends (no matter how friendly we may be). If the patient dies, my experience of loss will be real but limited and brief. Armed with the information my compassion has facilitated, my actions will be more appropriate to the needs of my patient for skilled medical care.

Where else does such closeness exist? Even dear friends are rarely so intimate, although the possibility exists. In love? Relationships of love are marked by the closeness of the connection between the loving parties. Here, too, one may experience the feelings of the beloved, know what he or she is thinking. Is this the love (agape) of God for humankind, all-accepting and all-forgiving? No. Nor is it personal love that seeks enduring and intensifying connection and attachment with its object, through which each will become more than she or he was without this love. It is a kind of love whose desire is to help, to do things for its object, and to obtain the knowledge and information necessary for right action. But it is love nonetheless. In a phrase coined by Pope Gregory the Great in the sixth century, "amor ipse notitia est" (love itself is a form of knowledge). "All love (caritas) is compassion or sympathy," said Schopenhauer (1969, p. 374).

Compassion, whose existence testifies to the inherent closeness possible between individuals, is a social emotion with a wide spectrum. At one end is the emotion evoked by the suffering of strangers with whom some identification is possible, and at the other end is the feeling whose effects make it cognate with personal love. Little wonder that it has been the subject of so much discussion and debate in such diverse circles over the last 25 centuries.

A Physician's Compassion and Positive Psychology

For most of the history of Western medicine, the effectiveness of physicians has been identified with their knowledge of medical science, so much so that in the last 50 years it has come to seem as though the knowledge itself makes patients better. Currently, even though people sometimes know a great deal about medications, technology and medical care, when they are really sick, they need doctors. They require doctors for more than just their technical skills, because it is physicians themselves who are the instruments of care. Their knowledge of patients and the therapeutic relationship are the conduit through which the appropriate science and technology are applied. Compassion is the emotion that starts the process of bringing physicians close to their patients, causes them to make the healing connection, and drives their desire to help. What do physicians actually know (if, in fact, they do), and where in them is this knowledge? At their best, they understand the effect of sickness on normal human behavior; they know that the land of the sick is different than that of the well (Cassell, 1985). They know how to find the path to healing that the therapeutic relationship makes possible, to relieve suffering even when pain or other symptoms will not yield to treatment, and to help rebuild the relationships of the sick and their significant others. They understand the importance and the method of restoring hope and returning the ability to act to the sick when hopelessness and helplessness threaten destruction (Snyder, 2000).

Even when physicians know these things, unfortunately, their knowledge is usually untaught, unvoiced, and wordless, learned by experience and intuition over many years. This body of information is too vital to the proper care of the sick to remain the tacit (and spotty) possession of only some physicians. It should be part of medical education. Who knows enough to teach it, however, even if a place were to be made in the medical curriculum? The kind of knowledge of human behavior, of which I have mentioned only a few examples, is in the domain of positive psychology—the subject of this volume. It must continue to be studied scientifically and taught systematically. It is crucial to medicine's progress.

References

American Medical Association. (1981). *Principles of medical ethics*. Chicago: Author.

Arendt, H. (1963). *On revolution*. New York: Viking.

Aristotle. (1984). *Rhetoric. Complete works* (Vol. 2, J. Barnes, Ed.). Princeton, NJ: Princeton University Press.

Arons, M. (1993). Philosophy, psychology, and the moral crisis: Reflections on compassion "between tradition and another beginning." *Humanistic Psychologist, 21*, 296–324.

Barber, B. (1976). Compassion in medicine: Toward new definitions and new institutions. *New England Journal of Medicine, 295*, 939–943.

Brown, L. M. (1996). Compassion and societal well-being. *Pacific Philosophical Quarterly, 77*, 216–224.

Cassell, E. J. (1982). The nature of suffering and the goals of medicine. *New England Journal of Medicine, 306*, 639–645.

Cassell, E. J. (1985a). *The healers art*. Cambridge, MA: MIT Press.

Cassell, E. J. (1985b). *The nature of suffering*. New York: Oxford University Press.

Donne, J. (1994). *Devotions upon emergent occasions: The complete poetry and selected prose of John Donne*. New York: Modern Library. (Original work published 1624)

Dougherty, C. J., & Purtillo, R. (1995). Physicians' duty of compassion. *Cambridge Quarterly of Healthcare Ethics, 4*, 426–433.

Foucault, M. (1979). *Discipline and punish* (A. Sheridan, Trans.). New York: Vintage.

Hegel, G. W. F. (1977). *Phenomenology of spirit* (A. V. Miller, Trans.). New York: Oxford University Press.

Hobbes, T. (1651/1962). *Leviathan* (T. Oakeshott, Ed.). New York: Oxford University Press.

Loewy, E. H. (1998). Curiosity, imagination, compassion, science, and ethics: Do curiosity and imagination serve a central function? *Health Care Analysis, 6*, 286–294.

Lovejoy, A. (1961). *Reflections on human nature*. Baltimore: Johns Hopkins University Press.

MacIntyre, A. (1966). *A short history of ethics*. New York: Macmillan.

Mauss, M. (1985). A category of the human mind: The notion of person; The notion of self. In M. Carrithers, S. Collins, & S. Lukes (Eds.), *The category of the person: Anthropology, philosophy, history* (W. D. Halls, Trans., pp. 1–25) New York: Cambridge University Press.

Mead, G. H. (1934). *Mind, self, and society: From the standpoint of a social behaviorist*. Chicago: University of Chicago Press.

Meltzoff, A. (1985). The roots of social and cognitive development: Models of man's original nature. In T. M. Field & N. A. Fox (Eds.), *Social perception in infants* (pp. 1–30). Norwood, NJ: Ablex.

Meltzoff, A., & Kuhl, P. K. (1989). Infant perception of faces and speech sound: Challenges to developmental theory. In P. R. Zelazo and R. G. Barr (Eds.), *Challenges to developmental paradigms* (pp. 67–91). Hillsdale, NJ: Erlbaum.

Meltzoff, A., & Moore, M. K. (1977). Imitation of facial and manual gestures by human neonates. *Science, 198*, 75–78.

New York Times. (2000, June 13), p. B1.

Nussbaum, M. (1996). Compassion: The basic social emotion. *Social Philosophy and Policy, 13*, 27–58.

Olson, A. M. (1992). *Hegel and the spirit*. Princeton, NJ: Princeton University Press.

Reich, W. (1987). Models of point suffering: Foundations for an ethic compassion. *Acta Neurochirurgica* (Suppl. 38), 117–122.

Rousseau, J. J. (1976). *Emile* (A. Bloom, Trans.). New York: Basic Books.

Schopenhauer, A. (1969). *The world as will and representation* (Vol. 1, E. F. J. Payne, Trans.). New York: Dover.

Skitka, L. J. (1999). Ideological and attributional boundaries on public compassion: Reactions to individuals and communities affected by a natural disaster. *Personality and Social Psychology Bulletin, 25*, 793–808.

Smith, A. (1976). *The theory of moral sentiments*. Indianapolis, IN: Liberty Classics. (Original work published 1759)

Snyder, C. R. (Ed.). (2000). *The handbook of hope: Theory, measures, and applications*. New York: Academic Press.

Snyder, C. R., & Fromkin, H. L. (1980). *Uniqueness: The human pursuit of difference*. New York: Plenum.

Sophokles. (1986). *Philoktetes* (G. McNamee, Trans.) Port Townsend, WA: Copper Canyon Press.

Stern, D. N. (1985). *The interpersonal world of the infant*. New York: Basic Books.

Sznaider, N. (1998). The sociology of compassion: A study in the sociology of morals. *Cultural Values, 2*, 117–119.

Thurman, R. A. F. (1997). Wisdom and compassion: The heart of Tibetan culture. In M. M.

Rhie & R. A. F. Thurman (Eds.), *Wisdom and compassion: The sacred art of Tibet* (pp. 17–19). New York: Tibet House.

Tocqueville, A. de. (1955). *Democracy in America* (H. Reeve, Trans.). London: Oxford University Press.

Trevarthen, C. (1988). Universal cooperative motives: How infants begin to know the language and culture of their parents. In G. Jahoda & I. M. Lewis (Eds.), *Acquiring culture: Cross cultural studies in child development* (pp. 37–90). London: Croom Helm.

32

The Psychology of Forgiveness

Michael E. McCullough & Charlotte vanOyen Witvliet

It would give us some comfort if we could only forget a past that we cannot change. If we could only choose to forget the cruelest moments, we could, as time goes on, free ourselves from their pain. But the wrong sticks like a nettle in our memory. The only way to remove the nettle is with a surgical procedure called forgiveness.

Smedes, *The Art of Forgiving*

Without being forgiven, released from the consequences of what we have done, our capacity to act would . . . be confined to a single deed from which we could never recover; we would remain the victims of its consequences forever.

Arendt, *The Human Condition*

Human beings appear to have an innate proclivity to reciprocate negative interpersonal behavior with more negative behavior. When insulted by a friend, forsaken by a lover, or attacked by an enemy, most people are motivated at some level to *avoid* or to *seek revenge against* the transgressor. Although both of these two post-transgression motivations can be destructive, revenge is usually the more potent and almost always the more glamorous of the two. Seeking revenge also is so basic that Reiss and Havercamp (1998) recently posited it to be one of 15 fundamental human motivations (also see Newberg, d'Aquili, Newberg, & deMarici, 2000).

The tendency to retaliate or seek retribution after being insulted or victimized is deeply ingrained in the biological, psychological, and cultural levels of human nature. Primatologists have documented that certain species of old-world primates (including chimpanzees and macaques) coordinate retaliatory responses after being victimized by another animal, sometimes even after considerable time has passed (Aureli, Cozzolino, Cordischi, & Scucchi, 1992; de Waal, 1996; Silk, 1992). Psychologically, the human proclivity for revenge is also codified in the norm of reciprocity (Gouldner, 1960): People are motivated to respond to injuries and transgressions by committing further injuries and transgressions equivalent to those they have suffered. However, revenge rarely is perceived as being equitable. Victims tend to view transgressions as more painful and harmful than do perpetrators. Moreover, when a victim exacts revenge, the original perpetrator often perceives the revenge as greater than the original offense and may retaliate to settle the score, thereby perpetuating a vicious cycle of vengeance (see Baumeister, Exline, & Sommer, 1998).

The motivation to return harm for harm has long been a part of human culture and is one of the most rudimentary approaches to dealing with perceived injustice (Black, 1998). Nearly all cultures have attempted to codify the *lex talionis* (i.e., the law of retaliation) so that revenge could be taken out of the hands of individuals and placed in the hand of a dispassionate third party (such as the society itself). Indeed, the formation of stable political life has been virtually dependent on the regulation of the revenge response (Shriver, 1995).

Forgiveness in Psychology

People have devised a variety of potential solutions to the corrosive effects of interpersonal transgressions (Fry & Björkqvist, 1997). One mechanism that can interrupt the cyclical nature of avoidance and vengeance is forgiveness, an approach whereby people quell their natural negative responses to transgressors and become increasingly motivated to enact positive ones instead. Many of the world's religions have articulated the concept of forgiveness for millennia (McCullough & Worthington, 1999; Rye et al., 2000). Indeed, the proposition that people have been forgiven by God and, as a result, should forgive their own transgressors is common to all three great monotheistic traditions (McCullough & Worthington, 1999).

Despite the importance of forgiveness within many religious traditions, social theorists and social scientists basically have ignored forgiveness for the last three centuries. Forgiveness fails to warrant even a footnote in 300 years of post-Enlightenment thought. In the final two decades of the 20th century, however, social scientists began to study forgiveness (McCullough, Pargament, & Thoresen, 2000b). They progressed in defining and measuring it, and in exploring its developmental, personality, and social substrates. They also made progress in assessing its value for individual and social well-being, and in designing interventions to promote forgiveness. Evidence of scientific progress can be found in the growing number of empirical journal articles, the convening of several national conferences, and the production of several edited collections devoted to forgiveness (e.g., Enright & North, 1998; McCullough, Pargament, & Thoresen, 2000a; Worthington, 1998). Moreover, in 1998 the John Templeton Foundation and other philanthropic foundations began a campaign to provide $10 million in funding for scientific research on forgiveness (Holden, 1999). With national interest in the topic, strong financial support, and scores of research teams, we may be entering a golden era of forgiveness research (McCullough, 2001).

In the present chapter, we first define the term *forgiveness* and differentiate three senses in which it can be applied as a psychological construct. Then we review the existing research on the psychology of forgiveness.

What Is Forgiveness?

Theorists and researchers generally concur with Enright and Coyle's (1998) assertion that forgiveness is different from pardoning (which is, strictly speaking, a legal concept); condoning (which involves justifying the offense); excusing (which implies that a transgression was committed because of extenuating circumstances); forgetting (which implies that the memory of a transgression has decayed or slipped out of conscious awareness); and denial (which implies an unwillingness or inability to perceive the harmful injuries that one has incurred). Most scholars also agree that forgiveness is distinct from *reconciliation*, a term that implies the restoration of a fractured relationship (Freedman, 1998). To go further in defining forgiveness, however, we must differentiate among three senses in which the term can be used. Forgiveness may be defined according to its properties as a response, as a personality disposition, and as a characteristic of social units.

As a response, forgiveness may be understood as a prosocial change in a victim's thoughts, emotions, and/or behaviors toward a blameworthy transgressor. A variety of conceptualizations of forgiveness as a response can be found in the published literature (McCullough & Worthington, 1994; Scobie & Scobie, 1998). All of these definitions, however, are built on one core feature: When people forgive, their responses (i.e., what they feel and think about, what they want to do, or how they actually behave) toward people who have offended or injured them become less negative and more positive—or prosocial—over time (McCullough, Pargament, & Thoresen, 2000b).

As a personality disposition, forgiveness may be understood as a propensity to forgive others across a wide variety of interpersonal circumstances. In this sense, people can be scaled along a forgiving-unforgiving continuum, with most people (by definition) falling somewhere toward mean of the population. The disposition to forgive might itself have several aspects (Mullet, Houdbine, Laumonier, & Girard, 1998).

As a quality of social units, forgiveness may be understood as an attribute that is similar to intimacy, trust, or commitment. Some social structures (e.g., some marriages, families, or communities) are characterized by a high degree of forgiveness (e.g., marriages, families, or communities in which participants are forgiven readily for their transgressions), whereas other social structures are characterized by less forgiveness (e.g., social institutions that hasten to ostracize or retaliate against members who commit transgressions).

Measures of Forgiveness

A variety of measures have been developed to operationalize the three understandings of forgiveness described here. Several psychometric studies have focused on developing self-report measures that operationalize forgiveness as a response (McCullough, Hoyt, & Rachal, 2000). Instruments that assess how much a person has forgiven another person for a specific offense are widely available (e.g., McCullough et al., 1998; Subkoviak et al., 1995; Trainer, 1981; Wade, 1989). For example, Enright and colleagues (e.g., Subkoviak et al., 1995) developed the 60-item Enright Forgiveness Inventory (EFI), which consists of six subscales that assess the extent to which the victim experiences positive and negative affects, cognitions, and behaviors/behavioral intentions regarding a transgressor. Recently, McCullough et al. (1998) refined a set of items from Wade's (1989) Forgiveness Scale into a 12-item measure called the Transgression-Related Interpersonal Motivations (TRIM) Inventory. The TRIM Inventory consists of two subscales: one for assessing the extent to which an offended person is motivated to avoid a transgressor (Avoidance) and one for assessing the harm done to the transgressor (Revenge). The TRIM Inventory, which appears as an appendix at the end of this chapter, has good internal consistency, good convergent and discriminant validity, and the theoretically specified two-factor structure (McCullough et al., 1998; McCullough & Hoyt, 1999).

Many measures for assessing the disposition to forgive and other forgiveness-like personality constructs are available or are under development (for review see McCullough, Hoyt, & Rachal, 2000). For example, Enright and colleagues (e.g., Enright, Santos, & Al-Mabuk, 1989) developed an interview measure for assessing the moral-cognitive development of reasoning about forgiveness. In addition, several paper-and-pencil measures have been developed to assess people's attitudes and behaviors related to revenge or forgiveness (e.g., Ashton, Paunonen, Helmes, & Jackson, 1998; Caprara, 1986; Emmons, 1992; Mauger et al., 1992; Mullet et al., 1998; Schratter, Iyer, Jones, Lawler, & Jones, 2000; Snyder & Yamhure, 2000; Stuckless & Goranson, 1992). Also, at least four scenario-based measures of the propensity to forgive are currently under development (Berry, Worthington, Parrot, O'Connor, & Wade, 2000; in press; Rye et al., 1999; Tangney, Fee, Reinsmith, Boone, & Lee, 1999). In Berry et al.'s (in press) Transgression Narrative Test of Forgivingness (TNTF), respondents rate how likely they would be to forgive offenders (e.g., a classmate, friend, or cousin) described in 5 paragraph-long scenarios. The TNTF has good test-retest reliability. Berry et al. (2000) have also developed the Trait Forgivingness Scale, in which respondents rate how much they agree or disagree with 10 statements related to forgiveness. This scale has adequate reliability and validity. The Forgiveness Likelihood Scale (Rye et al., 1999) assesses how likely respondents would be to forgive in 15 scenarios described in one or two sentences (e.g., a family member humiliates the respondent, a stranger breaks in and steals money, a significant other betrays the respondent). The Forgiveness Likelihood Scale shows good internal consistency and good test-retest reliability, and it is positively correlated with the Enright Forgiveness Inventory. Tangney et al.'s (1999) Multidimensional Forgiveness Inventory presents 16 one- to two-sentence scenarios in which the respondent alternates between taking the perspective of the perpetrator or the victim. The instrument measures how likely respondents are to ask for forgiveness and to forgive themselves when they are in the perpetrator role, and how likely they are to forgive their offenders when in the victim role. The Multidimensional Forgiveness Inventory also has good internal consistencies.

We are aware of only one measure that could be used to assess forgiveness as an attribute of social units or relationships (Hargrave & Sells, 1997). This measure can be used to assess the extent to which people experience forgiveness for another person within a specific relationship, typically a family member with whom one has a long-standing history of relational transgression. Clearly, more psychometric work should be devoted to developing instruments for assessing the nature and extent of forgiveness within dyads, families, communities, and other social units.

Summary of Current Research Findings

Using measures such as those we have described, researchers have begun to shed light on several dimensions of forgiveness. In particular, they have explored: (a) how the propensity to forgive develops across the life span; (b) the personality traits that are linked to forgiveness; (c) the social-psychological factors that influence forgiveness; and (d) the links of forgiveness to health and well-being.

Development of the Disposition to Forgive

Darby and Schlenker (1982) were the first researchers to notice age-related trends in forgiveness. Consistent with Darby and Schlenker's (1982) original findings, other researchers have found that people appear generally to become more forgiving as they age (Enright et al., 1989; Girard & Mullet, 1997; Mullet & Girard, 2000; Mullet et al., 1998; Park & Enright, 1997; Subkoviak et al., 1995). For example, Enright et al. (1989) found that chronological age and reasoning about forgiveness were correlated strongly in a sample of American children, adolescents, and adults. Girard and Mullet (1997) also reported age differences in willingness to forgive among a sample of 236 French adolescents, adults, and older adults (age range, 15–96). They found that older adults reported significantly higher likelihoods of forgiving in a variety of transgression scenarios than did the adolescents and adults. Furthermore, the adults were more forgiving than were the adolescents. Mullet et al. (1998) also found that older adults scored considerably higher than did young adults on measures of the disposition to forgive (but cf. Mauger et al., 1992).

It is reasonable to ask whether these age-related trends in forgiveness are linked to age-related trends in general cognitive or moral development. Enright and colleagues (e.g., Enright et al., 1989; Enright & Human Development Study Group, 1994) hypothesized that reasoning about forgiveness develops along the same trajectory as does Kohlbergian moral reasoning (Kohlberg, 1976). Correspondingly, they proposed that people at the earliest stages of moral reasoning about forgiveness—the stages of *revengeful forgiveness* and *restitutional forgiveness*—reason that forgiveness is only appropriate after the victim has obtained revenge and/or the transgressor has made restitution. People at the intermediate stages—*expectational forgiveness* and *lawful expectational forgiveness*—reason that forgiveness is appropriate because social, moral, or religious pressures compel them to forgive. People at the high stages—*forgiveness as social harmony* and *forgiveness as love*—reason that forgiveness is appropriate because it promotes a harmonious society and is an expression of unconditional love. In support of this hypothesis, Enright et al. (1989) found in two studies that Kohlbergian moral reasoning, as assessed with standard interview measures, was positively correlated with people's stage of reasoning about forgiveness.

Personality and Forgiveness

Forgiving people differ from less-forgiving people on many personality attributes. For example, forgiving people report less negative affect such as anxiety, depression, and hostility (Mauger, Saxon, Hamill, & Pannell, 1996). Forgiving people are also less ruminative (Metts & Cupach, 1998), less narcissistic (Davidson, 1993), less exploitative, and more empathic (Tangney et al., 1999) than their less-forgiving counterparts. Forgivers also tend to endorse socially desirable attitudes and behavior (Mauger et al., 1992). Moreover, self-ratings of the disposition to forgive correlate negatively with scores on hostility and anger (Tangney et al., 1999), as well as with clinicians' ratings of hostility, passive-aggressive behavior, and neuroticism (Mauger et al., 1996).

What can we deduce from this array of correlates? To some extent, they probably convey redundant information because many personality traits can be reduced to a handful of higher order personality dimensions. Within the Big Five personality taxonomy (e.g., John & Srivastava, 1999), for example, the disposition to forgive appears to be related most strongly to agreeableness and neuroticism (McCullough & Hoyt, 1999). Adjectives such as *vengeful* and *forgiving* tend to be excellent markers for the Agreeableness dimension of the Big Five taxonomy, and other research confirms the link between agreeableness and forgiveness (Ashton et al., 1998; Mauger et al., 1996). Researchers have found also that forgiveness is related inversely to measures of neuroticism (Ashton et al., 1998; McCullough & Hoyt, 1999). Thus, the forgiving person appears to be someone who is relatively high in agreeableness and relatively low in neuroticism/negative emotionality.

Social Factors Influencing Forgiveness

Forgiveness is influenced also by the characteristics of transgressions and the contexts in which they occur. Generally, people have more difficulty forgiving offenses that seem more intentional and severe and that have more negative consequences (Boon & Sulsky, 1997; Girard & Mullet, 1997).

The extent to which an offender apologizes and seeks forgiveness for a transgression also influences victims' likelihood of forgiving (Darby & Schlenker, 1982; Girard & Mullet, 1997; McCullough, Worthington, & Rachal, 1997; McCullough et al., 1998; Weiner, Graham, Peter, & Zmuidinas, 1991). Why do apologies facilitate forgiveness? By and large, the effects of apologies appear to be indirect. They appear to cause reductions in victims' negative affect toward their transgressors (Ohbuchi, Kameda, & Agarie, 1989) and increases in empathy for their transgressors (McCullough et al., 1997; McCullough et al., 1998). Victims also form more generous impressions of apologetic transgressors (Ohbuchi et al., 1989). Perhaps apologies and expressions of remorse allow the victim to distinguish the personhood of the transgressor from his or her negative behaviors, thereby restoring a more favorable impression and reducing negative interpersonal motivations. In this way, apologies may represent an effective form of reality negotiation (Snyder, Higgins, & Stucky, 1983). Indeed, Snyder's theory of reality negotiation explains why many of transgressors' posttransgression actions (including cancellation of the consequences of the offense; Girard & Mullet, 1997) influence the extent to which victims forgive. Other general theories of social conduct (e.g., Weiner, 1995) lead to similar predictions.

Interpersonal Correlates of Forgiveness

Forgiveness may be influenced also by characteristics of the interpersonal relationship in which an offense takes place. In several studies (Nelson, 1993; Rackley, 1993; Roloff & Janiszewski, 1989; Woodman, 1991), researchers have found that people are more willing to forgive in relationships in which they feel satisfied, close, and committed.

McCullough et al. (1998) surveyed both partners in over 100 romantic relationships to examine more closely the association of relational variables to acts of forgiveness. Both partners rated their satisfaction with and commitment to their romantic partner. Partners also used the Transgression-Related Interpersonal Motivations (TRIM) Inventory to indicate the extent to which they had forgiven their partner for two transgressions—the worst transgression their partner ever committed against them, and the most recent serious transgression their partner committed against them. Partners' forgiveness scores were correlated both with their own relational satisfaction and commitment and with their partners' relational satisfaction and commitment. McCullough et al. (1998) also found evidence consistent with the idea not only that relationship closeness facilitates forgiveness but also that forgiveness facilitates the reestablishment of closeness following transgressions.

The proposition that forgiveness is related to relationship factors such as satisfaction, commitment, and closeness raises the question of whether the dynamics of forgiveness could vary for different types of relationships. We would not expect people to forgive perfect strangers in the same way they forgive their most intimate relationship partners, for example. However, currently we know little about the unique dynamics of forgiveness within specific types of relationships (Fincham, 2000).

Forgiveness, Health, and Well-Being

Empirical research on the links between forgiveness and mental health had a humble beginning in the 1960s. In the first known study of forgiveness and well-being, Emerson (1964) used a Q-sort method and found what he perceived as a link between emotional adjustment and forgiveness. Following Emerson's work, however, researchers did not consider the links between forgiveness, health, and well-being again until the 1990s.

Correlational Studies on Forgiveness, Mental Health, and Well-Being

In general, self-report measures of the propensity to forgive (and, conversely, the propensity toward vengeance) are correlated positively (or, conversely, negatively) with measures of mental health and well-being. In developing the Forgiveness of Others Scale and the Forgiveness of Self Scale, Mauger et al. (1992) correlated both measures with the clinical scales from the Minnesota Multiphasic Personality Inventory (MMPI; Hathaway & McKinley, 1943). Interestingly, low scores on the Forgiveness of *Self* Scale were more strongly related to depression, anger, anxiety, and low self-esteem than were scores on the Forgiveness of *Others* Scale, suggesting that people who had a propensity toward feeling forgiven were less prone to experience such psychological difficulties.

In validating the scenario-based Multidimensional Forgiveness Inventory, Tangney et al. (1999) found that the tendency to forgive others was related to lower depression, hostility-anger, paranoid ideation, and interpersonal sensitivity (i.e., inadequacy or inferiority). Similarly, the propensity to forgive oneself was inversely related to depression, paranoid ideation, interpersonal sensitivity, and psychoticism.

Other researchers have examined whether measures of forgiveness for specific real-life transgressions could be related to mental health and well-being (Hargrave & Sells, 1997; Mc-Cullough, Bellah, Kilpatrick, & Johnson, 2001; Subkoviak et al., 1995), and the results have not been impressive. Typically, researchers have found modest and/or statistically nonsignificant correlations between measures of forgiveness and self-report measures of negative affect or psychological symptoms. Furthermore, Mc-Cullough et al. (2001) found that although forgiveness of a particular transgressor and satisfaction with life were correlated cross-sectionally, there was no evidence that forgiving led to improvements in people's satisfaction with their lives over an 8-week follow-up period.

Whereas most of the literature on forgiveness has focused on interpersonal forgiving, Exline, Yali, and Lobel (1999) found that the experience of forgiving God was related to mental health variables. In a group of 200 undergraduates, difficulty forgiving God independently predicted anxious and depressed mood. In contrast, forgiving God for a particular negative life experience was related to fewer depressive and anxious symptoms.

Much of the research on forgiveness, mental health, and well-being to date has had a major methodological weakness: To the extent that forgiveness is measured in terms of people's experiences of negative and/or positive affect toward a transgressor (as in many of the existing measures) and mental health is measured in terms of self-reported negative affect (e.g., depressive or anxious feelings), the observed correlations between measures of forgiveness and measures of affect or symptomatology may be due to their semantic overlap rather than substantive relationships between the concepts. Thus, in the future, researchers interested in the links between forgiveness and mental health should exert greater care to incorporate multimethod assessments that can circumvent such potential methodological confounds.

Forgiveness, Mental Health, and Well-Being in Small Groups and Structured Interventions

Could participation in small groups that help people forgive enhance mental health and well-being? Many members of such groups seem to think so. Wuthnow (2000) gathered survey data on 1,379 Americans' participation in small religious groups, along with their experiences with forgiveness, addictions, and well-being. Sixty-one percent of the respondents reported that their group had helped them forgive. Furthermore, membership in a group that explicitly fostered forgiveness was related significantly to self-reported attempts and successes in overcoming addiction, overcoming guilt, and perceiving encouragement when feeling discouraged.

Other data on the links between forgiveness, health, and well-being come from several experimental studies. In the first of these studies, Hebl and Enright (1993) tested the efficacy of a forgiveness intervention. Twenty-four elderly women who felt hurt by a particular interpersonal experience were randomly assigned to either an 8-week forgiveness intervention group or a discussion-based control group. Women in the forgiveness group scored higher on measures of forgiveness and willingness to forgive, although anxiety and depression scores improved in *both* groups. Nevertheless, when data from all participants were analyzed, higher levels of forgiveness were associated with higher levels of self-esteem and lower levels of anxiety and depression at posttest.

Building on Hebl and Enright's work, Al-Mabuk, Enright, and Cardis (1995) conducted two studies on the effects of a group intervention designed to help adolescents forgive their parents for perceived love deprivation. In their first study, Al-Mabuk et al. compared the efficacy of a human relations group and a group designed to foster adolescents' commitment to forgive. Adolescents in the four-session, 2-week forgiveness group showed more hope and willingness to forgive, even though their forgiveness scores were not greater than those of the controls. In a second study Al-Mabuk et al. compared the efficacy of a human relations group and a group designed to help participants actually grant forgiveness. In this study, adolescents in the six-session, 6-week program showed significant improvements in forgiveness, hope, trait-anxiety, and attitudes toward their parents. They also showed higher self-esteem but did not differ on measures of depression or state-anxiety compared with people who participated in the human relations group. Analyses of the data from all participants across both studies revealed that forgiving one's parents was associated with higher self-esteem, better attitudes toward fathers and mothers, lower anxiety, lower depression, and higher hope.

Freedman and Enright (1996) conducted a forgiveness intervention with 12 female survivors of physical contact incest by a male relative 2 or more years prior. Pairs of women were matched on demographic and abuse history variables. One woman from each pair was randomly assigned to the one-on-one forgiveness treatment, and the other to a wait-list control group. Women in the forgiveness treatment group showed improvements in forgiveness, hope, anxiety, and depression in comparison to women in the control group. These improvements remained at a 1-year follow-up. Once the women in the control condition completed the forgiveness intervention, they also showed improvements on mental health and self-esteem measures, thereby reinforcing the conclusion that this intervention was more effective than a no-treatment control condition.

More recently, Coyle and Enright (1997) used a similar forgiveness intervention with 10 men who identified themselves as feeling hurt by their partners' decisions to have abortions.

They were randomly assigned to a 12-week one-on-one forgiveness intervention or a wait-list control group. Those men receiving the forgiveness intervention reported significant increases in forgiveness and significant decreases in grief, anger, and anxiety after treatment. They maintained these gains at a 3-month follow-up. Furthermore, once the wait-listed men completed treatment, they, too, showed significant improvements in forgiveness, anxiety, and grief.

Forgiveness and Physical Health

There is a growing interest in the possibility that forgiveness may be related to physical health (Kaplan, 1992; Thoresen, Harris, & Luskin, 2000). At present, however, researchers have only just begun to conduct studies on forgiveness and physical health, so the majority of relevant research has been focused on the physical costs of unforgiving responses rather than the potential physical benefits of forgiving responses.

Forgiveness-related studies of physical health have focused primarily on reducing the adverse cardiovascular effects of one type of unforgiving response: hostility (see Friedman & Rosenman, 1974). Most studies using the widely accepted measures of hostility have revealed that hostility has negative effects on physical health (Miller, Smith, Turner, Guijarro, & Hallet, 1996; Williams & Williams, 1993). Given these data, it stands to reason that reducing hostility ought to reduce coronary problems. Friedman et al. (1986) randomly assigned Type A patients who were at risk for recurring heart attacks to a behavioral modification program or standard treatment from a cardiologist. Those in the behavioral modification intervention program showed a greater reduction in hostile behavior and in heart problems than those who received standard care only. According to Kaplan (1992), forgiveness was an important antidote to hostility in this efficacious intervention. In a post-intervention assessment, patients indicated that learning how to cultivate the forgiving outlook (p. 6) was one of the keys to reducing their hostility. Kaplan's description provides some impetus for more formal investigations into how forgiveness might promote coronary health by reducing the adverse physical effects of sustained anger and hostility.

The results of psychophysiological research complement Kaplan's (1992) description (Witvliet, Ludwig, & Vander Laan, 2001). Using a within-subjects repeated measures design, Witvliet and colleagues tested the physiological responses of undergraduates as they imagined responding to their real-life offenders in both unforgiving ways (mentally rehearsing the hurtful offense, nursing a grudge) and forgiving ways (empathizing with the humanity of the offender, granting forgiveness). Across multiple counterbalanced imagery trials, participants showed significantly greater reactivity in cardiovascular measures (heart rate, blood pressure) and sympathetic nervous system measures (skin conductance levels) during the unforgiving imagery trials compared with the forgiving imagery trials. Participants also reported significantly higher levels of negative emotion (e.g., anger, sadness) and lower levels of perceived control during the unforgiving imagery trials. In contrast, during the forgiving imagery conditions, participants experienced less physiological stress, lower levels of negative emotion, higher levels of positive emotion, and greater perceived control. These results suggest that when people adopt unforgiving responses to their offenders, they may incur emotional and physiological costs. In contrast, when they adopt forgiving responses, they may accrue psychophysiological benefits, at least in the short term.

Interventions to Promote Forgiveness

As described previously in this chapter, several research groups have developed and tested interventions for promoting forgiveness. Many of these interventions are designed for delivery to groups rather than to individuals. Several of the forgiveness intervention studies were based on the work of Enright (e.g., Al-Mabuk et al., 1995; Hebl & Enright, 1993), and others were based on the theoretical work of McCullough and colleagues (e.g., McCullough & Worthington, 1995; McCullough et al., 1997). Some of these intervention programs have focused on clinical populations, whereas others have had a more preventive or psychoeducational focus. Other researchers also are launching evaluations of intervention programs.

To summarize the effects of such interventions, Worthington, Sandage, and Berry (2000) conducted a meta-analysis of data from 12 group intervention studies. They reported that these group interventions were generally effective, improving group members' forgiveness

scores by 43% of a standard deviation (Cohen's $d = .43$). Among the 8 intervention studies that involved 6 hours or more of client contact, group members' forgiveness scores were 76% of a standard deviation higher than the scores of control group members (Cohen's $d = .76$). In contrast, the 4 intervention studies that involved less than 6 hours of client contact were substantially less efficacious (Cohen's $d = .24$). Thus, participation in short-term interventions (particularly those involving at least 6 hours of client contact) appears to be moderately effective in helping people to forgive specific individuals who have harmed them. As reviewed earlier, individual psychotherapy protocols that include forgiveness as a treatment goal also appear to be more efficacious than no-treatment control conditions (Coyle & Enright, 1997; Freedman & Enright, 1996).

Directions for Future Research

Research is beginning to illuminate several facets of forgiveness, but many more remain. We highlight a number of questions that still need to be addressed.

How does forgiveness unfold in specific relational contexts? As noted previously, one valuable research approach would be to explore how the dynamics of forgiveness unfold in specific relational contexts (McCullough, 2000; Fincham, 2000). Most likely, the conditions that foster and inhibit forgiveness among partners in long-standing, stable marriages are different from those that would foster and inhibit forgiveness among victims of violent trauma. Similarly, the *effects* of forgiveness might differ across relational contexts. Forgiving a friend for a minor transgression probably has few or no consequences for health and well-being, whereas forgiving an abusive spouse might have important psychological sequelae (indeed, these consequences could be negative; see Katz, Street, & Arias, 1997).

What are the precursors, processes, and outcomes associated with seeking and receiving forgiveness? With but a few noteworthy exceptions (e.g., Gassin, 1998; Tangney et al., 1999), forgiveness researchers typically have explored how people *grant* forgiveness to their transgressors. As a result, *seeking* and *receiving* forgiveness have been largely ignored. How do people go about asking for forgiveness? How do seeking and receiving forgiveness relate to confession and to moral emotions such as guilt and shame? What are the effects of feeling truly forgiven? These and other questions are important in addressing the many psychological contours of forgiveness.

Is forgiveness really related to mental and physical health? Many clinicians are claiming that forgiveness is beneficial for preventing and ameliorating physical and mental health problems. However, empirical research is still in its early stages. As our understanding of forgiveness and health develops, we may discover that its story line has many subplots. Rather than a simple theme, such as "forgiveness is good for health," the plot may have twists and turns. For example, people who are more prone to feel wounded by a given transgression (that others shrug off) may suffer more health costs, even if they eventually forgive their transgressors. As another example, it is possible that in some cases, low-forgivers may function better than high-forgivers particularly when the offenses endured by the high-forgivers are severe or traumatic. Another scenario may be that some people derive significant satisfaction (and even some type of health benefit) from seeking revenge. In still other situations, victims may be surrounded by strong social support networks that encourage begrudging and hostile responses toward offenders in ways that make the victim feel justified, comforted, and satisfied with their unforgiving stance. With sufficient social support for unforgiving responses, victims may not experience any negative emotional or physical consequences. In contrast, people who feel coerced to "forgive and forget" may find their post-offense distress exacerbated in comparison to those given time to grieve the loss they experienced. As these scenarios suggest, the forgiveness-health connection is likely to have numerous nuances that qualify seemingly simple relationships.

How can methodological quality be improved? Regardless of the substantive directions that researchers take, the field would benefit greatly from additional experimental research. It is generally both ethical and feasible to manipulate experimentally many of the variables that might influence forgiveness (e.g., McCullough et al., 1997; Sandage & Worthington, 1999). It is possible also to manipulate (or at least simulate) forgiveness in laboratory settings (Witvliet et al., 2001) and clinical settings (e.g., Coyle & Enright, 1997; McCullough &

Worthington, 1995; McCullough et al., 1997) so that the possible effects of forgiveness can be studied experimentally. When experimental research is not ethical or feasible, researchers should consider utilizing longitudinal designs to strengthen their ability to make causal inferences.

In investigating such questions, regardless of the research design, we recommend that researchers move away from an exclusive reliance on self-report measures (McCullough, Hoyt, & Rachal, 2000). With but a few exceptions (e.g., Malcom & Greenberg, 2000; Trainer, 1981; Witvliet et al., 2001), researchers have relied exclusively on self-report measures of forgiveness. As forgiveness research progresses, monomethod bias will loom as a threat to the validity of the entire body of research unless alternative assessment methods are developed (McCullough, Hoyt, & Rachal, 2000). Multimethod assessments that include, for example, peer and partner ratings, physiological measures, and behavioral measures—such as "forgiveness" responses in the Prisoner's Dilemma Game (see, e.g., Wu & Axelrod, 1995)—also would sharpen our understanding of forgiveness and its relevance to human experience.

Conclusions

Forgiveness is an important corrective to the proclivities toward avoidance and revenge—people's typical negative responses to interpersonal transgressions, which seem to be etched deeply into the human template. For millennia, the world's great religious traditions have commended forgiveness as: (a) a response with redemptive consequences for transgressors and their victims; (b) a human virtue worth cultivating; and (c) a form of social capital that helps social units such as marriages, families, and communities to operate more harmoniously.

Psychologists are beginning to grapple empirically with the diverse dimensions of forgiveness. They have developed methods for assessing forgiveness, adducing data that point to the substrates of forgiveness in development, personality, and social interaction. They have begun to explore the potential links of forgiveness to health and well-being. Finally, they have investigated the promising efficacy of clinical and psychoeducational interventions to promote forgiveness.

We believe research on forgiveness is likely to flourish in the years to come for at least three reasons. First, many of the most important and interesting questions remain to be addressed. Second, many researchers and institutions are highly committed to advancing knowledge in this area. Finally, as interdependent people, we simply have too much at stake to ignore the promise of forgiveness as a balm for some of our species' destructive propensities.

APPENDIX Transgression-Related Interpersonal Motivations Scale—12-Item Form (TRIM-12)

For the following questions, please indicate your current thoughts and feelings about the person who hurt you. Use the following scale to indicate your agreement with each of the questions.

1 = Strongly Disagree
2 = Disagree
3 = Neutral
4 = Agree
5 = Strongly Agree
_____ 1. I'll make him/her pay.
_____ 2. I keep as much distance between us as possible.
_____ 3. I wish that something bad would happen to him/her.
_____ 4. I live as if he/she doesn't exist, isn't around.
_____ 5. I don't trust him/her.
_____ 6. I want him/her to get what he/she deserves.
_____ 7. I find it difficult to act warmly toward him/her.
_____ 8. I avoid him/her.
_____ 9. I'm going to get even.
_____10. I cut off the relationship with him/her.
_____11. I want to see him/her hurt and miserable.
_____12. I withdraw from him/her.

Scoring Instructions

Avoidance Motivations: Add up the scores for items 2, 4, 5, 7, 8, 10, and 12.

Revenge Motivations: Add up the scores for items 1, 3, 6, 9, and 11.

Source: McCullough et al. (1998).

References

Al-Mabuk, R. H., Enright, R. D., & Cardis, P. A. (1995). Forgiveness education with parentally love-deprived late adolescents. *Journal of Moral Education, 24,* 427–444.

Arendt, H. (1958). *The human condition.* Chicago: University of Chicago Press.

Ashton, M. C., Paunonen, S. V., Helmes, E., & Jackson, D. N. (1998). Kin altruism, reciprocal altruism, and the Big Five personality factors. *Evolution and Human Behavior, 19,* 243–255.

Aureli, F., Cozzolino, R., Cordischi, C., & Scucchi, S. (1992). Kin-oriented redirection among Japanese macaques: An expression of a revenge system? *Animal Behaviour, 44,* 283–291.

Baumeister, R. F., Exline, J. J., & Sommer, K. L. (1998). The victim role, grudge theory, and two dimensions of forgiveness. In E. L. Worthington Jr. (Ed.), *Dimensions of forgiveness: Psychological research and theological perspectives* (pp. 79–104). Philadelphia: Templeton Foundation Press.

Berry, J. W., Worthington, E. L., Jr., Parrott, L., III, O'Connor, L. E., & Wade, N. G. (in press). Dispositional forgivingness: Construct validity and development of the Transgression Narrative Test of Forgivingness (TNTF). *Personality and Social Psychology Bulletin.*

Berry, J. W., Worthington, E. L., Jr., Parrott, L. III, O'Connor, L. E., & Wade, N. G. (2000). *The measurement of trait forgivingness.* Manuscript submitted for publication.

Black, D. (1998). *The social structure of right and wrong.* San Diego, CA: Academic Press.

Boon, S. D., & Sulsky, L. M. (1997). Attributions of blame and forgiveness in romantic relationships: A policy-capturing study. *Journal of Social Behavior and Personality, 12,* 19–44.

Caprara, G. V. (1986). Indicators of aggression: The Dissipation-Rumination Scale. *Personality and Individual Differences, 17,* 23–31.

Coyle, C. T., & Enright, R. D. (1997). Forgiveness intervention with postabortion men. *Journal of Consulting and Clinical Psychology, 65,* 1042–1046.

Darby, B. W., & Schlenker, B. R. (1982). Children's reactions to apologies. *Journal of Personality and Social Psychology, 43,* 742–753.

Davidson, D. L. (1993). Forgiveness and narcissism: Consistency in experience across real and hypothetical hurt situations. *Dissertation Abstracts International, 54,* 2746.

de Waal, F. (1996). *Good natured: The origins of right and wrong in humans and other animals.* Cambridge, MA: Harvard University Press.

Emerson, J. G. (1964). *The dynamics of forgiveness*. Philadelphia: Westminster Press.

Emmons, R. A. (1992, August). *Revenge: Individual differences and correlates*. Paper presented at the 100th annual meeting of the American Psychological Association, Washington, DC.

Enright, R. D., & Coyle, C. T. (1998). Researching the process model of forgiveness within psychological interventions. In E. L. Worthington Jr. (Ed.), *Dimensions of forgiveness: Psychological research and theological perspectives* (pp. 139–161). Philadelphia: Templeton Foundation Press.

*Enright, R. D., & Human Development Study Group. (1994). Piaget on the moral development of forgiveness: Identity or reciprocity? *Journal of Moral Education, 21,* 63–80.

*Enright, R. D., & North, J. (Eds.). (1998). *Exploring forgiveness*. Madison: University of Wisconsin Press.

*Enright, R. D., Santos, M. J. D., & Al-Mabuk, R. (1989). The adolescent as forgiver. *Journal of Adolescence, 12,* 99–110.

Exline, J., Yali, A. M., & Lobel, M. (1999). When God disappoints: Difficulty forgiving God and its role in negative emotion. *Journal of Health Psychology, 4,* 365–379.

Fincham, F. D. (2000). The kiss of the porcupines: From attributing responsibility to forgiving. *Personal Relationships, 7,* 1–23.

Freedman, S. (1998). Forgiveness and reconciliation: The importance of understanding how they differ. *Counseling and Values, 42,* 200–216.

*Freedman, S. R., & Enright, R. D. (1996). Forgiveness as an intervention goal with incest survivors. *Journal of Consulting and Clinical Psychology, 64,* 983–992.

Friedman, M., & Rosenman, R. H. (1974). *Type A behavior and your heart*. New York: Knopf.

Friedman, M., Thoresen, C. E., Gill, J., Ulmer, D., Powell, L. H., Price, V. A., Brown, B., Thompson, L., Rabin, D. D., Breall, W. S., Bourg, W., Levy, R., & Dixon, T. (1986). Alteration of Type A behavior and its effect on cardiac recurrences in post-myocardial infarction patients: Summary results of the Recurrent Coronary Prevention Project. *American Heart Journal, 112,* 653–665.

Fry, D. P., & Björkqvist, K. (Eds.). (1997). *Cultural variation in conflict resolution: Alternatives to violence*. Mahwah, NJ: Erlbaum.

Gassin, E. A. (1998). Receiving forgiveness as moral education: A theoretical analysis and initial empirical investigation. *Journal of Moral Education, 27,* 71–87.

*Girard, M., & Mullet, É. (1997). Propensity to forgive in adolescents, young adults, older adults, and elderly people. *Journal of Adult Development, 4,* 209–220.

Gouldner, A. W. (1960). The norm of reciprocity: A preliminary statement. *American Sociological Review, 25,* 161–178.

Hargrave, T. D., & Sells, J. N. (1997). The development of a forgiveness scale. *Journal of Marital and Family Therapy, 23,* 41–62.

Hathaway, S. R., & McKinley, J. C. (1943). *The Minnesota Multiphasic Personality Inventory* (Rev. ed.). Minneapolis: University of Minnesota Press.

Hebl, J. H., & Enright, R. D. (1993). Forgiveness as a psychotherapeutic goal with elderly females. *Psychotherapy, 30,* 658–667.

Heider, F. (1958). *The psychology of interpersonal relations*. New York: Wiley.

Holden, C. (1999, May 21). Subjecting belief to the scientific method. *Science, 284,* 1257–1259.

John, O. P., & Srivastava, S. (1999). The Big Five trait taxonomy: History, measurement, and theoretical perspectives. In L. A. Pervin and O. P. John (Eds.), *Handbook of personality: Theory and research* (pp. 102–138). New York: Guilford.

Kaplan, B. H. (1992). Social health and the forgiving heart: The Type B story. *Journal of Behavioral Medicine, 15,* 3–14.

Katz, J., Street, A., & Arias, I. (1997). Individual differences in self-appraisals and responses to dating violence scenarios. *Violence and Victims, 12,* 256–276.

Kohlberg, L. (1976). Moral stages and moralization: The cognitive-developmental approach. In T. Lickona (Ed.), *Moral development and behavior* (pp. 31–53). New York: Holt.

Malcom, W. M., & Greenberg, L. S. (2000). Forgiveness as a process of change in individual psychotherapy. In M. E. McCullough, K. I. Pargament, & C. E. Thoresen (Eds.), *Forgiveness: Theory, research, and practice* (pp. 179–202). New York: Guilford.

Mauger, P. A., Perry, J. E., Freeman, T., Grove, D. C., McBride, A. G., & McKinney, K. E. (1992). The measurement of forgiveness: Preliminary research. *Journal of Psychology and Christianity, 11,* 170–180.

Mauger, P. A., Saxon, A., Hamill, C., & Pannell, M. (1996, March). *The relationship of forgiveness to interpersonal behavior*. Paper presented at the annual convention of the Southeastern Psychological Association, Norfolk, VA.

*McCullough, M. E. (2000). Forgiveness as human strength: Conceptualization, measurement, and links to well-being. *Journal of Social and Clinical Psychology, 19,* 43–55.

McCullough, M. E. (2001). Forgiving. In C. R. Snyder (Ed.), *Coping with stress: Effective people and processes* (pp. 93–113). New York: Oxford University Press.

McCullough, M. E., Bellah, C. G., Kilpatrick, S. D., & Johnson, J. L. (2001). Vengefulness: Relationships with forgiveness, rumination, well-being, and the Big Five. *Personality and Social Psychology Bulletin, 27,* 601–610.

McCullough, M. E., & Hoyt, W. T. (1999, August). *Recovering the person from interpersonal forgiving.* Paper presented at the 107th annual convention of the American Psychological Association, Boston.

McCullough, M. E., Hoyt, W. T., & Rachal, K. C. (2000). What we know (and need to know) about assessing forgiveness constructs. In M. E. McCullough, K. I. Pargament, & C. E. Thoresen (Eds.), *Forgiveness: Theory, research, and practice* (pp. 65–88). New York: Guilford.

*McCullough, M. E., Pargament, K. I., & Thoresen, C. T. (Eds.). (2000a). *Forgiveness: Theory, research, and practice.* New York: Guilford.

McCullough, M. E., Pargament, K. I., & Thoresen, C. T. (2000b). The psychology of forgiveness: History, conceptual issues, and overview. In M. E. McCullough, K. I. Pargament, & C. E. Thoresen (Eds.), *Forgiveness: Theory, research, and practice* (pp. 1–14). New York: Guilford.

*McCullough, M. E., Rachal, K. C., Sandage, S. J., Worthington, E. L., Jr., Brown, S. W., & Hight, T. L. (1998). Interpersonal forgiving in close relationships. II. Theoretical elaboration and measurement. *Journal of Personality and Social Psychology, 75,* 1586–1603.

McCullough, M. E., & Worthington, E. L., Jr. (1994). Models of interpersonal forgiveness and their applications to counseling: Review and critique. *Counseling and Values, 39,* 2–14.

McCullough, M. E., & Worthington, E. L., Jr. (1995). Promoting forgiveness: A comparison of two brief psychoeducational group interventions with a waiting-list control. *Counseling and Values, 40,* 55–68.

McCullough, M. E., & Worthington, E. L., Jr. (1999). Religion and the forgiving personality. *Journal of Personality, 67,* 1141–1164.

*McCullough, M. E., Worthington, E. L., Jr., & Rachal, K. C. (1997). Interpersonal forgiving in close relationships. *Journal of Personality and Social Psychology, 73,* 321–336.

Metts, S., & Cupach, W. R. (1998, June). *Predictors of forgiveness following a relational transgression.* Paper presented at the Ninth International Conference on Personal Relationships, Saratoga Springs, NY.

Miller, T. Q., Smith, T. W., Turner, C. W., Guijarro, M. L., & Hallet, A. J. (1996). A meta-analytic review of research on hostility and physical health. *Psychological Bulletin, 119,* 322–348.

Mullet, É., & Girard, M. (2000). Developmental and cognitive points of view on forgiveness. In M. E. McCullough, K. I. Pargament, & C. E. Thoresen (Eds.), *Forgiveness: Theory, research, and practice* (pp. 111–132). New York: Guilford.

Mullet, É., Houdbine, A., Laumonier, S., & Girard, M. (1998). "Forgivingness": Factor structure in a sample of young, middle-aged, and elderly adults. *European Psychologist, 3,* 289–297.

Nelson, M. K. (1993). *A new theory of forgiveness.* Unpublished doctoral dissertation, Purdue University, West Lafayette, IN.

Newberg, A. B., d'Aquili, E. G., Newberg, S. K., & deMarici, V. (2000). The neuropsychological correlates of forgiveness. In M. E. McCullough, K. I. Pargament, & C. E. Thoresen (Eds.), *Forgiveness: Theory, research, and practice* (pp. 91–110). New York: Guilford.

Ohbuchi, K., Kameda, M., & Agarie, N. (1989). Apology as aggression control: Its role in mediating appraisal of and response to harm. *Journal of Personality and Social Psychology, 56,* 219–227.

Park, Y. O., & Enright, R. D. (1997). The development of forgiveness in the context of adolescent friendship conflict in Korea. *Journal of Adolescence, 20,* 393–402.

Rackley, J. V. (1993). *The relationships of marital satisfaction, forgiveness, and religiosity.* Unpublished doctoral dissertation, Virginia Polytechnic Institute and State University, Blacksburg, VA.

Reiss, S., & Havercamp, S. M. (1998). Toward a comprehensive assessment of fundamental motivation: Factor structure of the Reiss profiles. *Psychological Assessment, 10,* 97–106.

Roloff, M. E., & Janiszewski, C. A. (1989). Overcoming obstacles to interpersonal compliance: A principle of message construction. *Human Communication Research, 16,* 33–61.

Rye, M. S., Loiacono, D., Kmett, C., Folck, C., Hovanscek, A., Olszewski, B., Martin, J., Madia, B., Danko, S., Heim, T., & Ryan, C. (1999, August). *Evaluation of the psychometric properties of two forgiveness scales.* Poster presented at the 107th annual meeting of the American Psychological Association, Boston.

Rye, M. S., Pargament, K. I., Ali, M. A., Beck, G. L., Dorff, E. N., Hallisey, C., Narayanan, V., & Williams, J. G. (2000). Religious perspectives on forgiveness. In M. E. McCullough, K. I. Pargament, & C. E. Thoresen (Eds.), *Forgiveness: Theory, research, and practice* (pp. 17–40). New York: Guilford.

Sandage, S. J., & Worthington, E. L., Jr. (1999, August). *An ego-humility model of forgiveness: An empirical test of group interventions.* Poster presented at the 107th annual meeting of the American Psychological Association, Boston.

Schratter, A. K., Iyer, V. C., Jones, W. H., Lawler, K. A., & Jones, J. E. (2000, February). *Personality and interpersonal correlates of forgiveness.* Paper presented at the annual meeting of the Society for Personality and Social Psychology, Nashville, TN.

Scobie, E. D., & Scobie, G. E. W. (1998). Damaging events: The perceived need for forgiveness. *Journal for the Theory of Social Behaviour, 28,* 373–401.

Shriver, D. (1995). *An ethic for enemies.* New York: Oxford University Press.

Silk, J. B. (1992). The patterning of intervention among male bonnet macaques: Reciprocity, revenge, and loyalty. *Current Anthropology, 33,* 318–324.

Smedes, L. B. (1996). *The art of forgiving: When you need to forgive and don't know how.* Nashville, TN: Moorings.

Snyder, C. R., Higgins, R. L., & Stucky, R. (1983). *Excuses: Masquerades in search of grace.* New York: Wiley-Interscience.

Snyder, C. R., & Yamhure, L. C. (2000). *Heartland Forgiveness Scale.* Unpublished manuscript, University of Kansas, Lawrence.

Stuckless, N., & Goranson, R. (1992). The Vengeance Scale: Development of a measure of attitudes toward revenge. *Journal of Social Behavior and Personality, 7,* 25–42.

Subkoviak, M. J., Enright, R. D., Wu, C., Gassin, E. A., Freedman, S., Olson, L. M., & Sarinopoulos, I. (1995). Measuring interpersonal forgiveness in late adolescence and middle adulthood. *Journal of Adolescence, 18,* 641–655.

Tangney, J. P., Fee, R., Reinsmith, C., Boone, A. L., & Lee, N. (1999, August). *Assessing individual differences in the propensity to forgive.* Paper presented at the annual meeting of the American Psychological Association, Boston.

Thoresen, C. E., Harris, A. H. S., & Luskin, F. (2000). Forgiveness and health: An unanswered question. In M. E. McCullough, K. I. Pargament,

& C. E. Thoresen (Eds.), *Forgiveness: Theory, research, and practice* (pp. 254–280). New York: Guilford.

Trainer, M. F. (1981). *Forgiveness: Intrinsic, role-expected, expedient, in the context of divorce.* Unpublished doctoral dissertation, Boston University, Boston.

Wade, S. H. (1989). *The development of a scale to measure forgiveness.* Unpublished doctoral dissertation, Fuller Graduate School of Psychology, Pasadena, CA.

Weiner, B. (1995). *Judgments of responsibility: A foundation for a theory of social conduct.* New York: Guilford.

Weiner, B., Graham, S., Peter, O., & Zmuidinas, M. (1991). Public confession and forgiveness. *Journal of Personality, 59,* 281–312.

Williams, R., & Williams, V. (1993). *Anger kills.* New York: Random House.

*Witvliet, C. V. O., Ludwig, T., & Vander Laan, K. (2001). Granting forgiveness or harboring grudges: Implications for emotion, physiology, and health. *Psychological Science, 121,* 117–123.

Woodman, T. (1991). *The role of forgiveness in marital adjustment.* Unpublished doctoral dissertation, Fuller Graduate School of Psychology, Pasadena, CA.

*Worthington, E. L., Jr. (1998). *Dimensions of forgiveness: Psychological research and theological perspectives.* Philadelphia: Templeton Foundation Press.

Worthington, E. L., Jr., Sandage, S. J., & Berry, J. W. (2000). Group interventions to promote forgiveness: What researchers and clinicians ought to know. In M. E. McCullough, K. I. Pargament, & C. E. Thoresen (Eds.), *Forgiveness: Theory, research, and practice* (pp. 228–253). New York: Guilford.

Wu, J., & Axelrod, R. (1995). How to cope with noise in the iterated Prisoner's Dilemma. *Journal of Conflict Resolution, 39*(1), 183–189.

Wuthnow, R. (2000). How religious groups promote forgiving: A national study. *Journal for the Scientific Study of Religion, 36,* 124–137.

33

Gratitude and the Science of Positive Psychology

Robert A. Emmons & Charles M. Shelton

The concept of gratitude recently has attracted considerable interest in the popular culture. The prevalence of books targeted to general audiences on the topic (Breathnach, 1996; Hay, 1996; Miller, 1995; Ryan, 1999; Steindl-Rast, 1984; Turner, 1998; Van Kaam & Muto, 1993) testify to the broad appeal of this timeless concept. Following a similar format, these popular books generally consist of reflections on the value of gratefulness, along with strategies for cultivating an attitude of gratitude. The essential message of these volumes is that a life oriented around gratefulness is *the* panacea for insatiable yearnings and life's ills. Grateful responses to life can lead to peace of mind, happiness, physical health, and deeper, more satisfying personal relationships.

Surprisingly, despite the public's fascination with gratitude, this emotion has received relatively little sustained attention in scientific psychology. Although intuitively compelling, many of the general claims in popular books concerning the power of a grateful lifestyle are speculative or empirically untestable. In one popular book on gratitude, for instance, the author asserts, "Gratitude is the most passionate transformative force in the cosmos" (Breath-

nach, 1996, p. 1). All in all, the contribution of gratitude to health, well-being, and overall positive functioning remains speculative and without rigorous empirical confirmation.

Popular writings are not the only sources on the topic of gratitude. Classical writers who focused on the good life emphasized the cultivation and expression of gratitude for the health and vitality of both citizenry and society. Across cultures and time spans, experiences and expressions of gratitude have been treated as both basic and desirable aspects of human personality and social life. For example, gratitude is a highly prized human disposition in Jewish, Christian, Muslim, Buddhist, and Hindu thought. Cicero (*Pro Plancio*) held that "gratitude is not only the greatest of virtues, but the parent of all the others." The Buddha suggested that thankfulness is a core aspect of the noble person. Christian devotional writers such as Thomas à Kempis, Thomas Aquinas, and Bernard of Clairvaux expounded on the virtues of gratitude and the sinfulness of ingratitude. Indeed, the consensus among the world's religious and ethical writers is that people are obligated to feel and express gratitude in response to received benefits. Moreover, on the basis of these quotations, one can infer that the response of grateful people benefit not only themselves but also the wider community.

In recognition of the importance of gratitude, members of the United Nations General Assembly declared 2000 as the International Year of Thanksgiving. Although around the world people experience and express gratitude in diverse ways (Streng, 1989), they typically feel grateful emotions (i.e., thankful, appreciative) and have developed linguistic and cultural conventions for expressing such gratitude. For example, in Japanese culture the conventional expression of apology—*sumimasen*—is also used to express the feeling of thanks. Gratitude may in fact be a positive, universal characteristic that transcends historical and cultural periods. Therefore, illuminating the nature of gratitude and its functioning in both individual and societal contexts might help to elucidate crosscultural similarities and differences in emotional experience and expression, and, consequently, advance psychology's mission in identifying a taxonomy of human strengths (McCullough & Snyder, 2000).

Gratitude as an Emotional Response to Life

Gratitude is derived from the Latin *gratia*, meaning grace, graciousness, or gratefulness. All derivatives from this Latin root "have to do with kindness, generousness, gifts, the beauty of giving and receiving, or getting something for nothing" (Pruyser, 1976, p. 69). As a psychological state, gratitude is a felt sense of wonder, thankfulness, and appreciation for life. It can be expressed toward others, as well as toward impersonal (nature) or nonhuman sources (God, animals). Some of the most profound reported experiences of gratitude can be religiously based or associated with reverent wonder toward an acknowledgment of the universe (Goodenough, 1998). The roots of gratitude can be seen in many of the world's religious traditions. In the great monotheistic religions of the world, the concept of gratitude permeates texts, prayers, and teachings. Worship with gratitude to God for his many gifts and mercies is a common theme, and believers are urged to develop this quality. As such, gratitude is one of the most common emotions that religions seek to provoke and sustain in believers. Thus, for many people, gratitude is at the core of spiritual and religious experience. The spiritual quality of gratitude is aptly conveyed by Streng (1989): "In this attitude people recognize that they are connected to each other in a mysterious and miraculous way that is not fully determined by physical forces, but is part of a wider, or transcendent context" (p. 5). Emmons and Crumpler (2000) discuss the theological foundations of gratitude in Judaism, Christianity, and Islam.

In addition to its association with religious traditions, the sense of wonder and appreciation for life was one of the core characteristics of self-actualizing individuals studied by Maslow (1970). Self-actualizers, according to Maslow, had the capacity to "appreciate again and again, freshly and naively, the basic goods of life with awe, pleasure, wonder, and even ecstasy, however stale these experiences may have become to others" (p. 136). This ability to freshly appreciate everyday experience enabled self-actualizers to derive a sense of pleasure, inspiration, and strength from even mundane happenings. Toward the end of his life, Maslow regarded the ability both to experience and to express gratitude as essential for emotional health and lamented the paucity of research on this noble and vital topic (Lowry, 1982). Maslow believed that life could be "vastly improved if we could count our blessings as self-actualizing people do" (p. 137), and he suggested some specific experiential techniques for enhancing gratitude (Hoffman, 1996). Sadly, as he surveyed the human condition, he became convinced that taking one's blessings for granted was a primary cause of suffering and misery.

In addition to its merit as an intrinsically rewarding state, gratitude may lead to other positive subjective experiences. Chesterton contended that "gratitude produced the most purely joyful moments that have been known to man" (1924, p. 114). Empirically, gratitude is a pleasant state and is linked with positive emotions, including contentment (Walker & Pitts, 1998), happiness, pride, and hope (Overwalle, Mervielde, & De Schuyter, 1995). In a recent Gallup (1998) survey of American teens and adults, over 90% of respondents indicated that expressing gratitude helped them to feel "extremely happy" or "somewhat happy." Also, Emmons and Crumpler (2000) have reported that a conscious focus on gratitude makes life more fulfilling, meaningful, and productive.

Although a variety of life experiences can elicit feelings of gratitude, prototypically gratitude stems from the perception of a positive personal outcome that is due to the actions of another person. Social psychologist Fritz Heider (1958) provided a commonsense view that people feel grateful when receiving a benefit that intentionally resulted from another's action. As a consequence, the Heiderian perspective sharpened the focus on the perceived intentionality of the sender as a critical element in shaping the recipient's sense of gratitude. Building on his viewpoint, in order to have gratitude, two elements are required. The first is an interpersonal context, for gratitude is an interpersonal emotion, which precludes it from being directed toward oneself. Second, implicit in the experience of gratitude is the recipient's theory of mind from which he or she infers another's well-meaning intention, resulting in one's feeling loved and esteemed (see Shelton, 1990). That is to say, we can logically infer that a person feeling grateful might be more inclined to feel loved and cared for by others (Shelton, 1990). From this more expansive perspective, gratitude is fundamentally a moral affect with empathy at its foundation: In order to acknowledge the cost of the gift, the recipient must identify with the psychological state of the one who has provided it. The benefactor's giving is interpreted by the recipient as freely offered, and with that comes the acknowledgment that such offering might prove costly to or incur hardship for the benefactor. Such an understanding blends fittingly with some object relations formulations of gratitude, where it is seen as a major derivative of the capacity for love (Klein, 1957). Klein summarizes this entire discussion nicely when she observes that gratitude "underlies the appreciation of goodness in others and in oneself" (1957, p. 187).

Gratitude in Emotion Theory

Given that gratitude is a commonly occurring affect, it is remarkable that psychologists specializing in the study of emotion have, by and large, failed to explore its contours. The term *gratitude* rarely appears in the emotion lexicon (Shaver, Schwarz, Kirson, & O'Connor, 1987). *Gratitude* appears nowhere in the index of the *Handbook of Emotions* (Lewis & Haviland-Jones, 2000), only once in the wide-ranging *Handbook of Cognition and Emotion* (Dalgleish & Power, 1999), and not at all in the presumably comprehensive *Encyclopedia of Human Emotions* (Levinson, Ponzetti, & Jorgensen,

1999). Widespread ambiguity and uncertainty concerning its status as an emotion account for its scant attention. For example, although Lazarus and Lazarus (1994) discuss the concept at some length, in his earlier comprehensive monograph, Lazarus (1991) remarked, "I have ignored gratitude—though with some misgiving, because in some instances, it may be a strong emotional state" (p. 265). In his structural theory of the emotions, de Rivera (1977) neglected gratitude, yet in a later chapter (de Rivera, 1984) he included gratitude as one of 80 common emotion terms. Yet another emotion theorist displaying this "gratitudinal ambivalence" is Keith Oatley, who omits gratitude from his scholarly treatise (1992) but groups it with the social emotions in a later work (Oatley & Jenkins, 1996). In his social-interactional theory of the emotions, Kemper (1978) locates gratitude within the overarching coordinates of status and power.

Appraisal theorists, on the other hand, are more inclined to include gratitude within their framework of emotion. Weiner's (1985) attributional model emphasizes causal appraisals about events as the main determinants of emotional responses. Underlying properties or dimensions of causal attribution, in combination with event valence, influence the direction and magnitude of the felt emotion. There are two sets of emotions: outcome-dependent and attribution-dependent. General affective reactions of happiness and unhappiness are outcome dependent, whereas secondary emotional reactions of, say, pride, anger, or gratitude follow specific patterns of causal attribution. In this framework, attribution to another for a pleasant outcome elicits gratitude. In a recent study using sophisticated causal modeling techniques, the researchers lent support to Weiner's attributional model (Overwalle et al., 1995).

Ortony, Clore, and Collins (1988) introduced a goal-based model of appraisal, where the consequences of events are appraised for their relevance to one's ongoing goal pursuits. Representational systems consisting of goals, standards (consisting of "oughts"), and attitudes (a dispositional liking or disliking of objects) mediate between objective events and the attendant emotional reactions. In their framework, gratitude is a compound of admiration and joy: It consists of approving of someone else's praiseworthy actions and feeling joy for the desirability of the outcome. The variables that affect the intensity of gratitude are (a) the degree of judged praiseworthiness, (b) the deviation of the agent's action from role-based expectations, and (c) the desirability of the event. The main contribution of this model is that it specifies conditions under which gratitude is and is not likely to occur and calls attention to nuances that might remain undetected in other emotion-based frameworks. For example, felt gratitude may reflect the potential desirability of an event independent of the event's outcome, such as when someone aids in the unsuccessful search for a lost child.

Lazarus and Lazarus (1994) place gratitude in the class of empathic emotions because, along with compassion, it depends on the capacity to empathize with others. Each emotion is associated with a distinctive dramatic plot, defining what is happening to the person and its significance for the person's well-being (what he also has referred to as the emotion's "core relational theme"). The dramatic plot for gratitude is the appreciation of an altruistic gift. Both giving and receiving of the gift involve empathy because one must sense the donor's positive intention, and the donor must sense the need of the recipient. Lazarus and Lazarus describe the "many faces of gratitude" (p. 118) and suggest that within an interpersonal transaction, the personal meanings people attach to giving and receiving influence their experience of gratitude. More recently, Lazarus (1999) described several of the subtleties involved in gift exchanges and called attention to ways in which gratitude may be shaped by the dynamics between donor and recipient. Working within Lazarus's cognitive-motivational theory, Smith (1992) identified the appraisal components of gratitude as (a) a motivationally relevant outcome that is (b) motivationally congruent or desirable for the person and (c) credited to the efforts of another. Functionally, gratitude motivates the person to reward the other's prosocial behavior.

Gratitude as Virtue: Insights From Moral Philosophy

In contrast to psychology's view of gratitude as an emotional state, moral philosophy and theology portrays gratitude as a virtue. Whether one considers the classical Hebrew, Christian, or Graeco-Roman writings, gratitude is viewed as a highly prized human disposition, or virtue. Virtues, in essence, are good habits that connote

excellence in personal character. Thus, the natural outcome of living a virtuous life is a greater attainment of or movement toward completeness and wholeness (Zagzebski, 1996). Virtues have been defined as "character traits that a human being needs to flourish or to live well" (Hursthouse, 1991, p. 224), as "a quality which expresses the highest potentials of human nature" (Jeffries, 1998, p. 153). For Thomas Aquinas, gratitude was understood as a secondary virtue associated with the primary virtue of justice (Aquinas, 1981). The Thomistic notion of justice entails rendering to others their right or due, and in accord with some measure of basic equality. Gratitude is a motivator of altruistic action, according to Aquinas, because it entails thanking one's benefactors and generating a fitting and appropriate response.

As a virtue, gratitude is expressed as an enduring thankfulness that is sustained across situations and over time. Gratitude represents "an attitude toward the giver, and an attitude toward the gift, a determination to use it well, to employ it imaginatively and inventively in accordance with the giver's intention" (Harned, 1997, p. 175). A grateful person recognizes the receipt of someone else's generosity. Perhaps the core element of gratitude is that it is a response to perceived, intentional benevolence. Furthermore, one is willing to be indebted to the benefactor. In contrast, a gift that is resented or perceived as an obligation or whose reception incurs an obligation precludes even the possibility of gratefulness. On the other hand, sheer dislike of the gift is irrelevant; one can be grateful for the intentions of the benefactor (e.g., "it's the thought that counts").

There is an intriguing aspect to gratitude, overlooked by psychologists, to which writers in the domain of moral philosophy have called attention. To be genuinely grateful is to feel indebted in a way that defies repayment. Given this reality, the very attempt to repay is an authentic grateful expression. Roberts (1991) soberly points out that no amount or form of repayment can compensate for sacrificial gifts. Even so, gifts obligate the recipient to recognize the gift and express appropriate gratitude. Gratitude is both a duty (Berger, 1975) and an obligation (Meilaender, 1984). Schimmel (1997) also writes about gratitude as a moral obligation, as something that we "owe" to others on whom we are profoundly dependent for our well-being. Echoing Maslow's sentiments voiced earlier, Schimmel writes: "Gratitude as a moral virtue is not emphasized in our culture" (p. 208).

Ingratitude as Vice

Ingratitude is the failure to acknowledge the beneficence of others. Throughout recorded history, the ungrateful person has been the recipient of harsh criticism.

- Tiruvalluvar: "There is salvation to those guilty of any wicked deed; but there is no life for those who are ungrateful."
- Cicero: "Men detest one forgetful of a benefit."
- Kant: "Ingratitude . . . is the essence of vileness."
- Seneca: "Ingratitude . . . is an abomination."

Reflecting on classical views of ingratitude, Amato (1982) declared, "Ingratitude is a universally powerful accusation" (p. 27). From these quotations, we can infer that people who cannot or will not acknowledge benefits that others have conferred upon them are widely scorned. The ungrateful person regularly responds to others' beneficence with resentment, hostility, or indifference. In this regard, Gabriel (1998) classifies ingratitude as a type of insult, equivalent to stereotyping, scapegoating, rudeness, and other interpersonally destructive defects. Because gratitude serves to sustain people's sense of personal goodness while linking them to a moral horizon toward which they might strive, it cultivates an individual's sense of interconnectedness and personal growth. By way of contrast, ingratitude leads ineluctably to a confining, restricting, and "shrinking" sense of self.

From a clinical viewpoint, ingratitude can be viewed as a characterological defect. For example, utilizing a psychodynamic perspective, Bergler (1945) described the psychopathology of ingratitude and speculated on the conscious and unconscious reasons for its occurrence (e.g., impugning the generous motives of their benefactor). In case material, Heilbrunn (1972) illustrates various negative emotional sequelae (such as rejection, depression, anger, anxiety, and guilt) that people suffered following the failure to acknowledge gifts received.

Above all, the ungrateful person is best characterized by a personality structure crippled by narcissistic dynamics. The prominent features of narcissism include excessive self-importance, overt or covert arrogance, vanity, insatiable hunger for admiration, and interpersonal entitlement (Stone, 1998). People with narcissistic tendencies erroneously believe they are deserving of special rights and privileges. Along with being demanding and selfish, they exhibit an exaggerated sense of self-importance, which leads them to expect special favors without assuming reciprocal responsibilities. Further, they will express surprise and anger ("narcissistic rage") when others fail to conform to their wishes. The sense of entitlement, combined with insensitivity to the needs of others engenders, whether consciously or unconsciously intended, interpersonal exploitation. In short, if one is entitled to everything, then one is thankful for nothing.

Based on clinical observations, McWilliams and Lependorf (1990; see also Pruyser, 1976) noted that narcissistic people are incapable of experiencing and expressing sincere gratitude. A core issue for narcissistic people is their slavish adherence to self-sufficiency. Expressions of gratitude are acknowledgments that one is dependent on other people for one's well-being, and therefore not self-sufficient. Given this reality, such individuals find expressions of gratitude to be highly unpleasant. Furthermore, because narcissistic individuals possess a distorted sense of their own superiority, they might be reluctant to express gratitude in response to benefactors whose generosity or kindness they summarily dismiss as little more than an attempt to curry favor. In support of these conjectures, Farwell and Wohlwend-Lloyd (1998) found that in the context of a laboratory-based interdependence game, narcissism was inversely related to the extent to which participants experienced liking and gratitude for their partners.

Beyond the Self: Interpersonal Consequences of Gratitude

While this chapter has conceptualized gratitude as primarily an internal psychological characteristic, gratitude has important implications both for societal functioning and for collective well-being. In this regard, gratitude can be conceived of as a vital civic virtue. Positing a theory that conceptualizes gratitude as a moral affect, McCullough, Kilpatrick, Emmons, and Larson

(2001) hypothesize that by experiencing gratitude, a person is motivated to carry out prosocial behavior, energized to sustain moral behaviors, and inhibited from committing destructive interpersonal behaviors. By referring to gratitude as a moral affect, they are not proposing that the emotion and expression of gratitude itself are moral but that gratitude typically results from and stimulates moral behavior, that is, behavior that is motivated out of concern for another person. Because of gratitude's specialized functions in the moral domain, they liken it to empathy, sympathy, guilt, and shame. Like empathy, sympathy, guilt, and shame, gratitude has a special place in the grammar of moral life. Whereas empathy and sympathy operate when people have the opportunity to respond to the plight of another person, and guilt and shame operate when people have failed to meet moral standards or obligations, gratitude operates typically when people acknowledge that they are the recipients of prosocial behavior. In particular, McCullough et al. posited that gratitude has three specific moral functions: It functions as a *moral barometer* (an affective readout that is sensitive to a particular type of change in one's social relationships, the provision of a benefit by another moral agent that enhances one's well-being); as a *moral motive* (prompting grateful people to behave prosocially themselves); and, when people express their grateful emotions in words or actions, as a *moral reinforcer* that increases the likelihood of future benevolent actions. McCullough et al. review the empirical evidence for each of the three hypothesized functions of gratitude as a moral affect and conclude that there is considerable evidence for the moral barometer and moral reinforcer hypotheses but insufficient research to judge the veracity of the moral motive hypothesis.

In line with gratitude-as-moral-affect theory, some have compellingly argued that the cohesiveness of society would be seriously torn asunder were it not for experiences and expressions of gratefulness among its citizens. Sociologist Georg Simmel (1950), for example, referred to gratitude as "the moral memory of mankind. . . . if every grateful action . . . were suddenly eliminated, society (at least as we know it) would break apart" (p. 388).

In all likelihood, the first influential theoretical treatment of gratitude from this broader communal perspective arose from the political economist Adam Smith (1790/1976) in his volume *The Theory of Moral Sentiments*. Deeply influenced by both Christian writers and the Roman Stoics, Smith held the view that human nature is guided by intelligent design, and that even in the moral realm, human passions provide individuals with guidance for moral judgment and behavior. In this context, Smith proposed gratitude as an essential social emotion— on a par with emotions such as resentment and affection. Gratitude is, according to Smith, one of the primary motivators of benevolent behavior toward a benefactor. To this point, Smith wrote, "The sentiment which most immediately and directly prompts us to reward, is gratitude" (p. 68). When a benefactor has brought good fortune upon a beneficiary, gratitude prompts the beneficiary to find ways to acknowledge the gift. Until the beneficiary has been instrumental in promoting the well-being of someone perceived to have conferred a benefit, the beneficiary will continue to feel a sense of gratitude toward the benefactor.

Smith observed that society can function purely on utilitarian grounds or on the basis of gratitude, but he clearly believed that societies of gratitude were more attractive in large part because they provide an important emotional resource for promoting social stability. Similarly, Oatley and Jenkins (1996) more recently stated that "gratitude is the prototype of exchanges that are universal in human societies, perhaps the basis for modern economic relations" (p. 90). Likewise, Camenisch (1981) stated that a grateful outlook can even dominate the life of an entire culture, as when individuals in certain Eastern cultures view themselves as recipients of endless ancestrally bestowed blessings.

Following the line of thought initiated by Smith, Simmel (1950) argued that gratitude was a cognitive-emotional supplement to sustain one's reciprocal obligations. Because formal social structures such as the law and social contracts are insufficient to regulate and ensure reciprocity in human interaction, people are socialized to have gratitude, which then serves to remind them of their need to reciprocate. Thus, during exchange of benefits, gratitude prompts one person (a beneficiary) to be bound to another (a benefactor) during exchange of benefits, thereby reminding beneficiaries of their reciprocity obligations.

Moreover, Simmel expanded the sociological and psychological nature of gratitude far beyond isolated benefactor-beneficiary dyads. He argued persuasively that gratitude linked people to wider societal networks, functioning, and concerns. People often experience gratitude for people whose roles (e.g., artists, politicians, or poets) have proven beneficial to them. As such, prosocial sentiments and attitudes are intertwined within a vast, interlocking social network. Simmel also enlarges the notion of gratitude-like "benefits" to include intangible goods of a psychological nature (e.g., love, support, and inspiration). He also addresses the obligatory nature of gratitude and notes that some people are disinclined to receive gifts or resources because of both the moral reciprocity imperative and the uncomfortable feeling of indebtedness. Gratitude might even be a response to the recognition that some gifts (e.g., the gift of life) cannot be returned, in which case, the only possible moral response, in Simmel's view, is a call to permanent faithfulness and obligation.

Intervention: Cultivating Gratitude

Can gratefulness be nurtured? On this point, a grateful outlook does not require a life full of material comforts but rather an interior attitude of thankfulness regardless of life circumstances. A number of questions might be posed concerning gratitude-centered interventions. Could a depressed individual profit from learning thankfulness? Can the individual use gratitude to alleviate distress, as well as to enhance positive well-being? It is known that rumination prolongs and intensifies depressive mood (Nolen-Hoeksema, 1998). What if we redirected ruminative thoughts from self-inadequacy to ones of undeserved merit? Might these serve as a buffer for people at risk for depression? Similarly, by experiencing gratitude, perhaps a person could control anger or other interpersonally destructive emotions? Consider envy. In her classic work cited earlier, Klein (1957) argued that the person experiencing gratitude is protected from the destructive impulses of envy and greed. Conversely, envy is a breeding ground for ingratitude. The practice of gratitude as a spiritual discipline (a "thank-you therapy") has been suggested as a cure to excessive materialism and its attendant negative emotions of envy, resentment, disappointment, and bitterness (Clapp, 1998; Csikszentmihalyi, 1999; Schimmel, 1997). The core problem with envy is a nonawareness of the blessings that one is consistently surrounded by (Bonder, 1997).

Schwarz (1971) writes: "The ungrateful, envious, complaining man . . . cripples himself. He is focused on what he has not, particularly on that which somebody else has or seems to have, and by that he tends to poison his world" (p. 184).

At least two specific programs have been suggested for nurturing skills that allow for a greater awareness of gratitude in one's life. Miller (1995) offers a simple, four-step, behavioral-cognitive approach for learning gratitude: (a) Identify nongrateful thoughts, (b) formulate gratitude-supporting thoughts, (c) substitute the gratitude-supporting thoughts for the nongrateful thoughts, and (d) translate the inner feeling into outward action. By following these four steps, a person is able to live with greater contentment.

Shelton (2000) has framed gratitude as one of four key ingredients that make up a daily moral inventory which individuals can use to foster moral growth. According to Shelton, developing a healthy moral life involves, first of all, self-awareness that one is a moral being. Self-talk ("I am a moral person" or "I have a conscience") is a critical first step down the path toward moral growth. The theme of gratitude occupies the second step in his model. We will discuss the benefits of gratitude in a roundabout way by initially briefly sketching the final two steps. The third step is a self-examination of one's day, and the fourth step encourages the moral resolve to initiate at least some minimal behavioral change with an eye toward increasing, over the long run, one's moral maturity. It is the carrying out of a self-examination in an authentic and meaningful way that brings us to gratitude's key role. Assuming that one engages in a daily moral inventory with the genuine intention to foster personal moral growth, then experiencing gratitude and the positive feeling states associated with it (e.g., humility and empathy toward others) more than likely inclines one to enter any moral examination of one's life with greater sincerity and resolve. In this regard, gratitude might be conceived of as serving a "buffering" role that allays embarrassment, shame, or other negative emotions that might undermine self-honesty.

Moreover, though experienced for the most part as a pleasant affective state, a felt sense of gratitude can require, at times, considerable effort. Events, people, or situations that are apt to evoke gratitude can easily be taken for granted or shunted aside as one contends with life's daily hassles and struggles to regulate intense negative feelings (e.g., anger, shame, resentment). Nonetheless, making the personal commitment to invest psychic energy in developing a personal schema, outlook, or worldview of one's life as a "gift" or one's very self as being "gifted" holds considerable sway from the standpoint of positive psychology. Indeed, numerous groups have absorbed this insight. For example, many religiously oriented events such as reflection days or scheduled weeklong retreats have as a recurring theme the idea of "gift" (e.g., those influenced by Jesuit spirituality), as do many self-help groups and organizations (e.g., Alcoholics Anonymous). All in all, setting aside time on a daily basis to recall moments of gratitude associated with even mundane or ordinary events, personal attributes one has, or valued people one encounters has the potential to interweave and thread together a sustainable life theme of highly cherished personal meaning just as it nourishes a fundamental life stance whose thrust is decidedly positive.

Research on Gratefulness in Everyday Life

Can an intentional, grateful focus such as that described in the preceding section, affect health and well-being? Many writers have commented on the happiness-bestowing properties of gratitude. Chesterton (1924) claimed that gratitude was the key to happiness. Recently conducted research (reviewed in Emmons & Crumpler, 2000) provides an empirical test of these assertions. Undergraduate students enrolled in a health psychology class were asked, for 10 weeks, to complete a weekly log of their emotions, physical symptoms, health behaviors (exercise, alcohol consumption, and aspirin usage), and predominant coping behaviors. They rated the extent to which they felt each of 30 different mood states and noted their experience of physical symptoms (headaches, runny nose, sore throat, etc.). Six items assessed their approach/avoidance coping tendencies with the most serious problem encountered during each week. If subjects received social support for help with this problem, they were asked to rate their feelings toward the support provider on eight adjectives (including *grateful, angry, embarrassed,* and *understood*). The weekly log also included two global judgments where participants were asked to evaluate their life as a

whole during the past week along with their expectations for the upcoming week.

In addition, one-third of the research participants were asked to record up to five major events or circumstances that most affected them during the week, another third were asked to write down five hassles or minor stressors that occurred in the past week, and the final third were asked to write down five things for which they were grateful or thankful. Was there an effect of these different attentional manipulations on emotional and physical well-being? Results indicated significant differences between the three groups. Relative to the hassles and events group, participants in the gratitude condition felt better about their lives as a whole and were more optimistic regarding their expectations for the upcoming week. In other words, the focus on blessings appeared to influence both concurrent well-being and anticipated affect. Looking at physical symptomatology, a similar pattern emerged. The thankful group reported fewer physical complaints overall than the hassles group, although it did not differ from the neutral condition. The largest difference on the outcome measures between the groups also was one of the most interesting: Subjects in the gratitude condition spent significantly more time exercising than did subjects in the other two groups. Specifically, they spent 4.38 hours in exercise compared with 3.01 hours for the hassles group. Although in need of replication, when combined with the differences seen in physical symptom reporting, this finding suggests that the emotional and mental benefits of thankfulness may extend to the somatic realm. Somewhat surprisingly, we did not find that the practice of gratitude buffered individuals from the experience of unpleasant emotions. In fact, persons in the thankful group reported higher levels of the agitation-related emotions (irritability, nervousness, anger) than did people in the other two conditions. Gratefulness does not appear to be equivalent to a Pollyannish state where suffering and adversity are selectively ignored, but it might induce the requisite psychological resources to successfully weather unpleasant emotional states.

We recently replicated the mental health benefits associated with the grateful focus in a daily study in which gratitude journals were kept over 21 consecutive days. In this study, participants who kept gratitude logs scored higher on measures of psychological well-being and were also more likely to report having helped someone with a personal problem or offered emotional support to another, suggesting prosocial motivation as a consequence of the gratitude induction. Additionally, scores on an individual differences measure of gratitude were positively associated with frequency of engaging in prosocial activities (volunteering, tutoring, donating time or resources, and the like).

Grateful in All Circumstances?

Cynics may argue that gratitude in the midst of abundance is easy. But what about in the midst of deprivation? One potential and perhaps surprising place to look for expressions of gratitude is in the aftermath of trauma. How common is it for people to be grateful in unpleasant life circumstances, and to what extent are these a significant context for gratitude-generating experiences? Is the biblical injunction to "be thankful in all circumstances" (1 Thess. 5:18, RSV) realistic, even for religious persons? In this regard, the examination of gratitude in the lives of people coping with major adversities might be illuminating. An attitude of gratitude may be one means by which tragedies are transformed into opportunities for growth, being thankful not so much for the circumstance but rather for the skills that will come from dealing with it. The ability to discern blessings in the face of tragedy is a magnificent human strength. In fact, gratitude may require a degree of contrast or deprivation. One greatly appreciates a mild spring after a harsh winter, a gourmet meal following a fast, and sexual intimacy after a period of abstinence. Contrast effects have major influence on judgments of well-being (Schwarz & Strack, 1999); they may be equally potent in influencing one's felt gratitude.

Moreover, reminding oneself to "be grateful" or to maintain a grateful attitude might also be a common way of coping with particularly stressful life circumstances. In *The Hiding Place*, Corrie TenBoom (1970) gave thanks for the fleas in her World War II concentration camp barracks, for the fleas kept the guards at bay. There is actually some empirical research on gratitude in the face of adverse conditions. Coffman (1996) conducted intensive qualitative interviews with 13 parents who lived in the area of south Florida damaged during Hurricane Andrew in 1992. After conducting 90-minute in-

terviews, Coffman analyzed transcripts to identify the essence of the experience of persons' coping, as well as any additional descriptive themes that were frequently cited by parents. Parents reported an overwhelming sense of gratitude for what they had *not* lost during the hurricane. Although five of the families' homes had been so damaged that relocation had been necessary, *none of them had lost a loved one*. Because they were spared the loss of what was truly important to them, they experienced profound gratitude in the midst of life-changing disaster.

In their study of new parents, Ventura and Boss (1983) also found that "reminding oneself of things for which to be grateful" was rated among the most helpful coping behaviors (after "doing things with the child," "being a parent to the baby," "and trusting in one's partner"). "Reminding oneself to feel grateful" appears to be a commonly used coping strategy for many people, and one that potentially could be legitimately helpful to people undergoing significant life events. Reminding oneself to be grateful might be similar to the benefit-finding and benefit-reminding processes described by Affleck and Tennen (1996). A greater sense of appreciation for life appears to be one of the common positive reactions to major medical problems.

Two additional lines of research also prove illuminating. Colby and Damon (1992) reported that their moral exemplars were often overwhelmingly grateful for the opportunity to serve other, less fortunate individuals. What was especially remarkable about these extraordinary people was that their sacrifices and service to others were often met with *ingratitude*. In contrast to the normative responses to ingratitude described earlier, these moral exemplars responded with even greater love and compassion for the people they were serving. Although in general displays of ingratitude tend to be scorned, in this instance those helping were grateful for the opportunity afforded by those in need seemingly regardless of the beneficiary's reactions.

In their study of life narratives, McAdams, Reynolds, Lewis, and Bowman (in press) identified "redemption sequences" as one of two distinct narrative styles that people use when telling their life stories. In a redemptive sequence, there is a transformation from an unpleasant circumstance to a positive outcome. For instance, alcoholism might be followed by sobriety, job failure by promotion, or devastating failure by a confidence-building success. Notably present in the redemptive sequences generated in these interviews were feelings of thankfulness and appreciation. One sequence was that of an unwanted pregnancy and painful birth resulting in thankfulness and happiness for the pregnancy. Another was of a serious motorcycle injury resulting in a greater appreciation for life and a renewed commitment to life goals. One can draw a significant conclusion from these studies, in our estimation, in that grateful individuals are not naively optimistic, nor are they under some illusion that suffering and pain are nonexistent. Rather, these persons have consciously taken control by choosing to extract benefits from adversity, with one of the major benefits being the perception of life as a gift. Grateful people may have more psychic maneuverability than the ungrateful, enabling them to be less defensive and more open to life. As such, they are likely to express agreement with John Calvin (1559/1984), who wrote: "In short, we are well-nigh overwhelmed by so great and so plenteous an outpouring of benefactions, by so many and mighty miracles discerned wherever one looks, that we never lack reason for praise and thanksgiving" (p. 63).

Developmental Issues: The Emergence of Gratitude

Based on the evidence reviewed in this chapter, it appears that one of several positive attributes that parents might encourage in their children is a sense of thankfulness. As an emotion or as a characterological disposition, gratitude does not emerge spontaneously in newborns. Recall that virtues are acquired excellences. They are acquired only through sustained focus and effort. To be sure, we cannot claim originality for these ideas. The authors of children's books (Hallinan, 1981; Swamp, 1997) and articles in parenting magazines (Fisher, 1999; Kirkpatrick, 1999; Taffel, 1999) regularly encourage the cultivation of gratitude and thankfulness in children and offer strategies for parental inculcation. For example, Baumgartner-Tramer (1938) suggested that parents emphasize the sense of community created or strengthened through gratefulness and diminished or destroyed through ingratitude, rather than appeal to its politeness function or its obligatory nature. The

author contends that the latter two are more likely to elicit negative reactions.

From a developmental perspective, psychological research has shown that children's comprehension of gratitude is a process played out over several years (Baumgartner-Tramer, 1938; Graham, 1988; Harris, Olthof, Meerum Terwogt, & Hardman, 1987; Russell & Paris, 1994). More specifically, gratitude does not appear to occur regularly in response to receiving benefits until middle childhood. Gleason and Weintraub (1976), for example, found that few children (i.e., 21%) younger than 6 years of age expressed thanks to adults who gave them candy, whereas most children (e.g., more than 80%) of 10 years of age or older expressed gratitude in the same situation. Based on these data, it appears that the link between attributions of responsibility for positive outcomes, the experience of gratitude, and the desire to do good to one's benefactor probably is solidified between the ages of 7 and 10 (see also Weiner & Graham, 1988, for a review). Despite these studies, relatively little research has been conducted on the emergence of gratitude in children. In this regard, programmatic, developmental research stands out as a critical priority. Only a sustained research commitment would enable parents and educators to guide more effectively their children's passage into responsible and grateful adulthood.

Conclusions

Although social scientists have been slow to recognize it, the importance of gratitude is undeniable. With the emergence of the positive psychology movement, now is the time for a renewed focus on gratitude as a valued subjective experience, a source of human strength, and an integral element promoting the civility requisite for the flourishing of families and communities. A world without gratitude, one writer wrote, would be "unendurable" (Schwarz, 1971, p. 168). Gratitude is—at the same time—private and public, just as it is personal and communal. Its utility extends beyond a social convention. Gratitude provides life meaning, by encapsulating life itself as a gift. Within such a framework, it can come to dominate one's entire life outlook, seemingly even when sources of gratitude are absent. Moreover, in the context of material prosperity, by maintaining a grateful focus a person may avoid disillusionment (Csikszentmihalyi, 1999). A grateful focus can also enable an individual to confront and overcome obstacles by means of thanksgiving for the newly acknowledged strengths that result from such challenging confrontations.

Although some inroads have been made, the social scientific study of gratitude is in its infancy. By drawing upon classical sources of wisdom in combination with contemporary theory and rigorous methodologies, future researchers will enhance our appreciation and respect for this timeless concept.

Acknowledgment   Preparation of this chapter was supported by a generous grant from the John Templeton Foundation.

References

Affleck, G., & Tennen, H. (1996). Construing benefits from adversity: Adaptational significance and dispositional underpinnings. *Journal of Personality. 64,* 899–922.

Amato, J. A., II. (1982). *Guilt and gratitude: A study of the origins of contemporary conscience.* Westport, CT: Greenwood.

Aquinas, T. (1981). *Summa theologica.* Westminster, MD: Christian Classics.

Baumgartner-Tramer, F. (1938). "Gratefulness" in children and young people. *Journal of Genetic Psychology, 53,* 53–66.

Becker, J. A., & Smenner, P. C. (1986). The spontaneous use of *thank you* by preschoolers as a function of sex, socioeconomic status, and listener status. *Language in Society, 15,* 537–546.

Berger, F. R. (1975). Gratitude. *Ethics, 85,* 298–309.

Bergler, E. (1945). Psychopathology of ingratitude. *Diseases of the Nervous System, 6,* 226–229.

Bonder, N. (1997). *The kabbalah of envy: Transforming hatred, anger, and other negative emotions.* Boston: Shambhala.

Breathnach, S. B. (1996). *The simple abundance journal of gratitude.* New York: Warner.

Calvin, J. (1984). *The Christian life* (J. H. Leith, Ed.). San Francisco: Harper and Row. (Original work published 1559)

Camenisch, P. F. (1981). Gift and gratitude in ethics. *Journal of Religious Ethics, 9,* 1–34.

Chesterton, G. K. (1924). *St. Francis of Assisi.* New York: George Doran.

Clapp, R. (Ed.). (1998). *The consuming passion: Christianity and the consumer culture.* Downers Grove, IL: InterVarsity Press.

Coffman, S. (1996). Parents' struggles to rebuild family life after Hurricane Andrew. *Issues in Mental Health Nursing, 17,* 353–367.

Colby, A., & Damon, W. (1992). *Some do care: Contemporary lives of moral commitment.* New York: Free Press.

Csikszentmihalyi, M. (1999). If we are so rich, why aren't we happy? *American Psychologist, 54,* 821–827.

Dalgleish, T., & Power, M. J. (Eds.). (1999). *Handbook of cognition and emotion.* New York: Wiley.

de Rivera, J. (1977). *A structural theory of the emotions.* New York: International Universities Press.

de Rivera, J. (1984). Development and the full range of emotional experience. In C. Z. Malatesta & C. E. Izard (Eds.), *Emotion in adult life* (pp. 45–63). Beverly Hills, CA: Sage.

Emmons, R. A. (2000). *An experimental study of gratitude and its effects on psychological and physical well-being.* Unpublished manuscript, University of California, Davis.

Emmons, R. A., & Crumpler, C. A. (2000). Gratitude as human strength: Appraising the evidence. *Journal of Social and Clinical Psychology, 19,* 56–69.

Farwell, L., & Wohlwend-Lloyd, R. (1998). Narcissistic processes: Optimistic expectations, favorable self-evaluations, and self-enhancing attributions. *Journal of Personality, 66,* 65–83.

Fisher, S. W. (1999, January/February). Raising thankful kids: How to develop the virtue of gratefulness. *Christian Parenting Today, 12,* 19–21.

Gabriel, Y. (1998). An introduction to the social psychology of insults in organizations. *Human Relations, 51,* 1329–1354.

Gallup, G. H. Jr. (1998). *Thankfulness: America's saving grace.* Paper presented at the National Day of Prayer Breakfast, Thanks-Giving Square, Dallas.

Gallup survey results on gratitude, adults and teenagers. *Emerging Trends, 20,* 9.

Gleason, J. B., & Weintraub, S. (1976). The acquisition of routines in child language. *Language in Society, 5,* 129–136.

Goodenough, U. (1998). *The sacred depths of nature.* New York: Oxford University Press.

Graham, S. (1988). Children's developing understanding of the motivational role of affect: An attributional analysis. *Cognitive Development, 3,* 71–88.

Hallinan, P. K. (1981). *I'm thankful each day.* Nashville, TN: Hambleton-Hill Publishing.

Harned, D. B. (1997). *Patience: How we wait upon the world.* Cambridge, MA: Cowley.

Harris, P. L., Olthof, T., Meerum Terwogt, M., & Hardman, C. E. (1987). Children's knowledge of the situations that provoke emotion. *International Journal of Behavioral Development, 10,* 319–344.

Hay, L. L. (1996). *Gratitude: A way of life.* Carlsbad, CA: Hay House.

Heider, F. (1958). *The psychology of interpersonal relations.* New York: Wiley

Heilbrunn, G. (1972). "Thank you." *Journal of the American Psychoanalytic Association, 20,* 512–516.

Hoffman, E. (Ed.). (1996). *Future visions: The unpublished papers of Abraham Maslow.* Thousand Oaks, CA: Sage.

Hursthouse, R. (1991). Virtue theory and abortion. *Philosophy and Public Affairs, 20,* 223–246.

Jeffries, V. (1998). Virtue and the altruistic personality. *Sociological Perspectives, 41,* 151–167.

Kemper, T. D. (1978). *A social-interactional theory of emotion.* New York: Wiley.

Kirkpatrick, L. (1999, November/December). Giving thanks: Thirteen creative ways to encourage gratefulness this Thanksgiving. *Christian Parenting Today, 12,* 54.

Klein, M. (1957). *Envy and gratitude: A study of unconscious sources.* New York: Basic Books.

Lazarus, R. S. (1991). *Emotion and adaptation.* New York: Oxford University Press.

Lazarus, R. S. (1999). *Stress and emotion: A new synthesis.* New York: Springer.

Lazarus, R. S., & Lazarus, B. N. (1994). *Passion and reason: Making sense of our emotions.* New York: Oxford University Press.

Levinson, D., Ponzetti, J. J., Jr., & Jorgensen, P. F. (Eds.). (1999). *Encyclopedia of human emotions.* New York: Macmillan.

Lewis, M., & Haviland-Jones, J. M. (Eds.). (2000). *Handbook of emotions* (2nd ed.). New York: Guilford.

Lowry, R. J. (Ed.). (1982). *The journals of Abraham Maslow.* Lexington, MA: Lewis Publishing Company.

Maslow, A. H. (1970). *Motivation and personality* (3rd ed.). New York: Harper and Row.

McAdams, D. P., Reynolds, J., Lewis, M., & Bowman, P. (in press). When bad things turn good and good things turn bad: Sequences of redemption and contamination in life narrative and their relation to psychosocial adaptation in adulthood. *Personality and Social Psychology Bulletin.*

McCullough, M. E., Kilpatrick, S., Emmons, R. A., & Larson, D. (2001). Gratitude as moral affect. *Psychological Bulletin.*

McCullough, M. E., & Snyder, C. R. (2000). Classical sources of human strength: Revisiting an old home and building a new one. *Journal of Social and Clinical Psychology, 19,* 1–10.

McWilliams, N., & Lependorf, S. (1990). Narcissistic pathology of everyday life: The denial of remorse and gratitude. *Contemporary Psychoanalysis, 26,* 430–451.

Meilaender, G. C. (1984). *The theory and practice of virtue.* Notre Dame, IN: University of Notre Dame Press.

Miller, T. (1995). *How to want what you have.* New York: Avon.

Moore, D. W. (1996). *Americans most thankful for family and health: Young also thankful for career/job.* Report on 1996 Gallup Survey.

Nolen-Hoeksema, S. (1998). Ruminative coping with depression. In J. Heckhausen & C. S. Dweck (Eds.), *Motivation and self-regulation across the life span* (pp. 237–256). New York: Cambridge University Press.

Oatley, K. (1992). *Best laid schemes.* New York: Cambridge University Press.

Oatley, K., & Jenkins, J. M. (1996). *Understanding emotions.* Cambridge, MA: Blackwell.

Ortony, A., Clore, G. L., & Collins, A. (1988). *The cognitive structure of emotions.* New York: Cambridge University Press.

Overwalle, F. V., Mervielde, I., & De Schuyter, J. (1995). Structural modeling of the relationships between attributional dimensions, emotions, and performance of college freshmen. *Cognition and Emotion, 9,* 59–85.

Prager, M. (1998). The spiritual practice of blessing. *Tikkun, 13,* 35–36.

Pruyser, P. W. (1976). *The minister as diagnostician: Personal problems in pastoral perspective.* Philadelphia: Westminster Press.

Roberts, R. C. (1991). Virtues and rules. *Philosophy and Phenomenological Research, 51,* 325–343.

Russell, J. A., & Paris, F. A. (1994). Do children acquire concepts for complex emotions abruptly? *International Journal of Behavioral Development, 17,* 349–365.

*Ryan, M. J. (1999). *Attitudes of gratitude: How to give and receive joy every day of your life.* Berkeley, CA: Conari Press.

Schimmel, S. (1997). *The seven deadly sins: Jewish, Christian, and classical reflections on human nature.* New York: Free Press.

Schwarz, B. V. (1971). Some reflections on gratitude. In B. V. Schwarz (Ed.), *The human person and the world of values: A tribute to Dietrich von Hildebrand by his friends in philosophy* (pp. 168–191). Westport, CT: Greenwood.

Schwarz, N. N., & Strack, F. (1999). Reports of subjective well-being: Judgmental processes and their methodological implications. In D. Kahneman, E. Diener, & N. Schwarz (Eds.), *Wellbeing: Foundations of hedonic psychology* (pp. 61–84). New York: Russell Sage.

Shaver, P. R., Schwarz, J., Kirson, D., & O'Connor, C. (1987). Emotion knowledge: Further exploration of a prototype approach. *Journal of Personality and Social Psychology, 52,* 1061–1086.

Shelton, C. M. (1990). *Morality of the heart: A psychology for the Christian moral life.* New York: Crossroad.

Shelton, C. M. (2000). *Achieving moral health.* New York: Crossroad.

*Simmel, G. (1950). *The sociology of Georg Simmel.* Glencoe, IL: Free Press.

*Smith, A. (1976). *The theory of moral sentiments* (6th ed.). Oxford: Clarendon. (Original work published 1790)

Smith, C. A. (1991). The self, appraisal, and coping. In C. R. Snyder & D. R. Forsyth (Eds.), *Handbook of social and clinical psychology* (pp. 116–137). Elmsford, NY: Pergamon.

*Steindl-Rast, D. (1984). *Gratefulness, the heart of prayer.* New York: Paulist.

Stone, M. H. (1998). Normal narcissism. In E. F. Ronningstam (Ed.), *Disorders of narcissism: Diagnostic, clinical, and empirical implications* (pp. 7–28). Washington, DC: American Psychiatric Press.

*Streng, F. J. (1989). Introduction: Thanksgiving as a worldwide response to life. In J. B. Carman & F. J. Streng (Eds.), *Spoken and unspoken thanks: Some comparative soundings* (pp. 1–9). Dallas, TX: Center for World Thanksgiving.

Swamp, J. (1997). *Giving thanks: A Native American good morning message.* New York: Lee and Low.

Taffel, R. (1999, November). Thanks, mommy: Teaching kids to be grateful. *Parents,* 138–147.

TenBoom, C. (1970). *The hiding place.* Washington Depot, CT: Chosen Books.

Turner, D. (1998). *Grateful living.* Homewood, IL: High Tide Press.

Van Kaam, A., & Muto, S. (1993). *The power of appreciation: A new approach to personal and relational healing.* New York: Crossroad.

Ventura, J. N., & Boss, P. G. (1983). The family coping inventory applied to parents with new babies. *Journal of Marriage and the Family, 45,* 867–875.

Walker, L. J., & Pitts, R. C. (1998). Naturalistic conceptions of moral maturity. *Developmental Psychology, 34,* 403–419.

Weiner, B. (1985). An attributional theory of achievement motivation and emotion. *Psychological Review, 92,* 548–573.

Weiner, B., & Graham, S. (1988). Understanding the motivational role of affect: Life-span research from an attributional perspective. *Cognition and Emotion, 3,* 401–419.

Zagzebski, L. T. (1996). *Virtues of the mind.* New York: Cambridge University Press.

34

Love

Susan Hendrick & Clyde Hendrick

Romantic love may not be essential to life, but it may be essential to joy. Life without love would be for many people like a black-and-white movie—full of events and activities but without the color that gives it vibrancy and provides a sense of celebration.
        S. Hendrick & Hendrick, 1992, p. 117

In this quotation from the end of our book, *Romantic Love*, we construe love as one of the most important defining qualities of life. In that volume, we focused on romantic love, but the quotation could be extended to other types of love—the love of parents (and grandparents) for a newborn child, the love of siblings, the love of best friends, and so on. What is more important than love for a *happy* human life? Our answer is "nothing is more important," and in this response we advocate love as being a centerpiece of a positive psychology.

In this chapter, we review briefly the progress of the study of love over the past three decades. Only recently has love been a topic of study in psychological research. Like the evening news, psychology historically has been more concerned with the bad and the ugly of human life than with the good and the beautiful. Traditionally, a respectable hard-nosed psychologist simply would not study a "soft" topic such as love. Thus, the creation of a research discipline for the study of love was not easy. It took courage for Berscheid and Walster (1969, 1978) to introduce romantic love into the study of "interpersonal attraction," for Rubin (1970) to distinguish loving from liking, and for Harlow (1974) to extend the study of love to nonhuman species.

These and other research pioneers in the study of love paved the way for today's flourishing research on love within the larger discipline of relationship science (Berscheid, 2000). Our goal is to convey some of the interest and drama of this new discipline, which has been developed by "scholars who have been attentive and responsive to societal concerns while attempting, at the same time, to develop a unified and cohesive science in which an understanding of process is awarded as much importance as are structure and outcomes" (Berscheid, 2000, p. xix). We begin with a historical overview of the meaning of love. We then consider current scientific meanings (theories and models) and methods for measuring love. We provide a sample of current research findings and suggest some possible applications of this research. We conclude with some suggestions regarding future research.

History of Romantic Love

A comprehensive history of love was written by Irving Singer in three large volumes (1984a, 1984b, 1987). *The Nature of Love* is a philosophical history of love from antiquity to the modern era. Very early, conceptual thought about love was largely linked to abstract virtues (e.g., "the good") or to gods. Singer discerned four broad conceptual traditions: *Eros* (desire for the good or the beautiful); *Philia* (friendship love); *Nomos* (submission to a god's will; in human terms, obedience to the desires of a loved one); and *Agape* (a divine bestowal of love upon creation). Over the centuries, various writers worked with these disparate conceptions, attempting to synthesize and translate them into human terms.

Some have questioned whether romantic/passionate love even existed before the last two or three centuries; however, Hatfield (1988; Hatfield & Rapson, 1996) proposed that passionate love, as an intense attraction, has existed in all cultures and all historical periods and is essentially a "human universal." Passionate love *and* marriage to the same person, however, is a relatively recent cultural invention. Throughout much of human history, marriage for love was unknown. As it developed during the Middle Ages, courtly love involved a highly stylized ritual and, as such, may have been a historical harbinger of change. Courtly love idealized the love felt toward another person, a love of intense passion between a man and a woman who generally were not married to each other (Singer, 1984b).

Slowly, this notion of passionate love between man and woman, within a courtship context, led to "love marriages," often to the consternation of those who held to traditional norms. The growth of love marriages spread widely in the Western world in the 18th century. Detailed histories are available in many sources (e.g., Gadlin, 1977; Murstein, 1974). The perceived link between love and marriage still is undergoing dynamic change. Simpson, Campbell, and Berscheid (1986) examined college students' perceptions of the importance of love as a basis for marriage, in data collected over a 30-year period. Students over time reported romantic love as being an increasingly important basis for marriage. Students also viewed remaining in love as necessary for continuing the marriage. Given this change in beliefs, the increased divorce rate may be driven by the view that when the passions die, so, too, do the marriages or intimate relationships. If the passion aspect of love is not sufficient to bond partners in a relationship, perhaps the addition of other love components such as friendship would strengthen the bond. If one could also be good friends, perhaps even best friends, with one's passionate lover, then perhaps the *relationship* could survive the turbulent comings and goings of passion.

There is some evidence that the aforementioned cultural change is under way. The old adage that "you can't be friends with the one you love" is no longer true. In fact, many young couples now seek actively partners who are good companions as well as good lovers. Related to this point, in a study by S. Hendrick and Hendrick (1993), college students wrote essays about their romantic relationships or about their closest friendship. Not only was friendship the dominant theme in describing romantic relationships but almost half of the participants spontaneously named their romantic partner as their closest friend. Consistent with these findings, Sprecher and Regan (1998) found that *both* companionate love and passionate love were related to commitment and relationship satisfaction. Friendship, along with passion, is thus an important ingredient of love.

Sexuality and marriage have typically been connected, but we believe that love, sex, marriage (or cohabitation), and friendship are increasingly being linked in romantic relationships. This cohesion is a powerful "bundling" of four of the most positive facets of life. Today, people generally should find more joy in their romantic relationships than was possible in previous centuries. There is a price, however, in that the expectations of these relationships are also much higher.

Models for Explaining Love

There are many perspectives on the study of love. We provide a sketch of the most popular approaches, with a sample of research findings to follow in later sections. Theories of love are disparate and difficult to classify. Nevertheless, they may be grouped under two broad headings: naturalistic/biological and psychological/social. Naturalistic approaches are rooted in the body, in emotion, and in our evolutionary heritage—especially as evolution relates to sexuality. In the psychological/social approach, there are concepts such as cognition (e.g., prototypes), social motives, interaction and communication, and various classifications of love.

Naturalistic/Biological Approaches

Approaches to passionate and companionate love, attachment processes, and the evolution of love provide an overview of the naturalistic/biological classification.

Passionate and Companionate Love

Berscheid and Walster (1978) defined passionate love as a state of total absorption of two lovers, with mood swings between ecstacy and anguish. Companionate love is the affection felt by two people whose lives are deeply intertwined. Thus, love begins in the heat of passion but eventually cools into the quiet glow of companionship. This contrast of passion versus companionship received its fullest development from Walster and Walster (1978). More recently, Hatfield (1988) viewed the two types of love as coexisting in a relationship rather than as being sequential. Hatfield also noted that people appear to want both passion and companionship in their love relationships. This theme of including both passion and companionship or friendship within the love bond was noted earlier and has been echoed by other scholars (e.g., Noller, 1996; Sprecher & Regan, 1998).

Attachment Approaches

This approach was developed out of the work of Bowlby (1969), who studied the types of relationships (e.g., secure, anxious, avoidant) that infants form with their caregivers. These early attachments are posited to be causally related to subsequent relationships. For example, Hazan and Shaver (1987) applied attachment theory to adult love relationships, noting that it provides an explanation for both the joys and the sorrows manifested in adult love. It should be noted, however, that the evidence regarding this proposed relationship between childhood and adult attachment styles is mixed, with questions of attachment "stability" awaiting further research (Feeney & Noller, 1996).

Evolution of Love

Mellen (1981) argued that the survival of the human species necessitated an emotional bond between breeding pairs of partners so that both partners would attend to their helpless infants. Lacking intensive caregiving from both adults, pairs without such bonds lost the evolutionary race through higher infant mortality. Such primitive emotional bonding was hypothesized to be the beginning of love. Related themes have been developed further by evolutionary psychologists. For example, Buss (1988) defined love as consisting of behaviors enacted by both females and males that strengthen the bonding function and ultimately serve to perpetuate the human species. Building on Trivers's (1972) differential parental investment model, in which males seek to mate with many females, whereas females mate more selectively and nurture their few offspring, evolutionary psychologists have hypothesized selected gender differences in courtship and mating strategies. There is some supportive research for this evolutionary approach to interpersonal behaviors (e.g., Buss & Kenrick, 1998; C. Hendrick & Hendrick, 1991), although there also are vigorous counterarguments (Eagly & Wood, 1999).

Psychological/Social Approaches

Because of space constraints, we will discuss only a sample of these approaches. They are diverse, ranging from a cognitive psychological to a sociological perspective.

Prototypes of Love

Fehr (e.g., 1993, 1994) construed love as a prototype or "best example," defined by its best or most representative set of features. Focusing on love in general, Fehr discovered that respondents rated companionate love as most typical of love, with maternal love, parental love, and friendship as the best examples. Passionate and sexual love received lower prototypicality ratings. Regan, Kocan, and Whitlock (1998), in a prototype study of romantic love in which participants rated the central features of romantic love, found that passion was among the list of central features, but it still ranked below several companionate features (e.g., honesty, trust). Within this research paradigm, it appears that the most general concept of love is that of companionship. Romantic love is conceived as companionate love plus passion.

Self-Expansion

Aron and Aron (1986, 1996), based on Eastern traditions (e.g., Hinduism) concerning the concept of self, proposed that humans have a basic motive for self-expansion. This growth of self may incorporate physical possessions, as well as power and influence. Falling in love creates a rapid expansion of self-boundaries and therefore is pleasurable. When two people are falling in love, they can mutually incorporate one another into the expansion process. In this way, "you and me" becomes "us."

Love Triangles

In his Triangular Theory of Love, Sternberg (1986) proposed that love is a mix of intimacy, passion, and commitment. A given relationship may be high or low on each concept, with eight types of love being possible. For example, the presence of all three components is named "consummate love," the absence of all three is "nonlove," and so on.

More recently, Sternberg has focused on love as a social construction, varying across time and cultures (e.g., Beall & Sternberg, 1995). Consistent with this view, Sternberg (1998) has proposed that love is also a very personal form of social construction, a story that each individual creates by living it.

Love Styles

In developing a typology of the different ways that people love each other, Lee (1973) used the metaphor of a color wheel on which to place his many "colors" of love. As with color, there were primary love styles and secondary, and even tertiary, mixes. Considerable research on love styles has built on Lee's theory (e.g., C. Hendrick & Hendrick, 1986). Attention has focused on six relatively independent types (styles) of love. In brief, the six styles cover the gamut. *Eros* is passionate love, where the lover idealizes the partner, has definite preferences for physical characteristics in a partner, and pursues love with intensity. A faint hint of Platonic eros lingers in the definition of this style. *Ludus* is love played as a game, for mutual enjoyment, without the intensity of Eros. Ludus is short on commitment, and the "game of love" can occur with multiple partners simultaneously. This love style is reminiscent of medieval courtly love. *Storge* is friendship love and is analogous to companionate love, discussed previously. *Pragma* is practical love; it involves "shopping" for a mate with a list of desired qualities in hand (e.g., computer matching). In Pragma, a mate is selected on the basis of an "appraisal" (discussed

later in the measurement section). *Mania* is "manic" love. A manic lover desperately wants love but often finds that it is painful. Thus, "stormy passion" is an apt descriptor, and a cycle of jealousy, dramatic breakups, and equally dramatic reconciliations characterizes this love style. *Agape* is selfless and giving love where the person is fully concerned with the partner's welfare. Some degree of agapic altruism bolsters a love relationship; *total* agapic love is reserved typically for the heavenly, not the human, realm.

These six love styles capture the multidimensionality of love as experienced by people. We have conducted research on these love styles and will discuss such research in the following sections.

Measurement of Love

Singer (1984a) made a basic distinction between *appraisal* and *bestowal*. People constantly appraise objects and other people on both physical and psychological attributes. Appraisal of value is a human judgment process that lends itself readily to measurement. But is high appraisal of another person on a particular set of attributes the same as love? Singer is ambivalent on this question, believing that love requires something more—a bestowal. What is bestowal? According to Singer, the bestowal of love, although initially based on appraisal, ultimately becomes independent of appraisal and constitutes an unqualified, unencumbered emotional valuing of the other. Love is offered to the partner simply as a gift (not unlike aspects of Agape, discussed earlier).

An idea such as bestowal creates measurement problems. How do we measure something that is as essential and yet as ethereal as bestowal? Yet we should not dismiss a concept just because we do not currently know how to measure it. Concepts such as bestowal seem important for the development of a positive psychology:

> The concept of bestowal as a human process that becomes independent of appraisal is intriguing because it provides a means for new creation within the world. Bestowal as gift is an aptly chosen metaphor. Love as bestowal creates what did not exist before, a new value. In this sense love can be unconditional. It is its own value. This notion also suggests why people are so preoccupied with

love. On one view, love may be nothing but a bonding glue for creatures who evolved as group animals; but from the inside, from the human viewpoint, love, as bestowal, is the very act of creation that allows humans to be god-like. Only in bestowing love is something truly new created, and people return to that magic potion again and again. It sustains life—and the species. (S. Hendrick & Hendrick, 1992, p. 34)

In the future, perhaps disparate concepts such as appraisal and bestowal can be joined within one theoretical framework through the use of nonlinear dynamics (e.g., Kaplan & Glass, 1995). Nonlinear dynamics involves the use of a set of mathematical approaches in which one searches for order in what may appear to be complex random events. For example, nonlinear equations may show that a phenomenon in State A was in fact deterministically transformed into State B, even though raw observation might suggest only random variation from A to B. In this sense, some future theory of love might transform appraisal in an orderly way into the ostensibly very different state of bestowal via nonlinear dynamics (see Eiser, 1994; Guastello, 1997).

For now, however, we have the various paper-and-pencil questionnaires that purport to measure one or more types of love. Some of the more popular of these measures include Rubin's (1970) scales that assess loving and liking; Hatfield and Sprecher's (1986) Passionate Love Scale; a variety of instruments to measure attachment based on Hazan and Shaver's (1987) seminal study; Fehr's (1993) various prototype measures of love; Davis and Todd's (1985) Relationship Rating Form; and Sternberg's (1986) Triangular Theory of Love Scale.

Our own measure of love, the Love Attitudes Scale (LAS), is based on Lee's (1973) typological approach to love. We construed the six types of love as six variables and, based on work by Lasswell and Lasswell (1976), developed an initial set of six subscales (C. Hendrick & Hendrick, 1986). The subscales of the LAS have good psychometric properties (e.g., factor structure and loadings, alphas, test-retest reliabilities) and are relatively independent of each other. The LAS offers a promising approach to the quantitative measurement of a qualitative typology (see research reported in a later section). Refinements of the LAS include a relationship-specific version (C. Hendrick &

Hendrick, 1990) and a rigorously validated short form with four items per subscale (see this short form of the LAS in the appendix; C. Hendrick, Hendrick, & Dicke, 1998).

Current Research on Love

The theories about love discussed in the preceding section have led to considerable empirical research in recent decades. In this section, we explore current love research, including the topics of how people communicate love, love styles, love across cultures, love's links with sexuality, and love's relationship to happiness.

Communicating Love

Researchers in communications are particularly interested in how people communicate love to one another. Marston, Hecht, and Robers (1987), who examined how love was both experienced and communicated in intimate relationships, used qualitative analyses of interview information to derive categories of communication "toward" a partner and "from" a partner. People reported communicating love to a partner and having love communicated to them from a partner by saying "I love you," being understanding and supportive, touching, spending time together, communicating emotion, and giving eye contact (Marston et al., 1987). Extending this research, Hecht, Marston, and Larkey (1994) developed a typology of "love ways," which included both verbal and nonverbal methods of showing love to a partner. They identified five different ways (or styles) of love (active/collaborative, committed, intuitive, secure, traditional), each of which used somewhat different methods of communicating. As we have discussed elsewhere, "Although this research was interesting in a number of ways, perhaps its most significant contribution was the recognition of love as multifaceted and as subjective and to some degree, unique within each person's experience" (S. Hendrick & Hendrick, 2000b, p. 209).

Love and other aspects of relationships are communicated in complex ways, of course. For example, research on the "positive illusions" that love partners hold about each other and their relationship (Murray & Holmes, 1997; Murray, Holmes, & Griffin, 1996) suggests that such illusions may actually influence relationship outcomes positively: "A willingness to make a leap of faith—to see relationships in the best possible light—is a critical feature of satisfying, stable relationships" (Murray & Holmes, 1997, p. 600).

In related research, Meeks, Hendrick, and Hendrick (1998), assessed both love variables and communication variables for college student dating couples. They found that both love variables and communication variables, including the ability to handle conflict constructively, were predictive of relationship satisfaction. Consistent with the research of Murray and her colleagues (1996, 1997), perceptions of some partner variables such as self-disclosure were more predictive of participants' relationship satisfaction than were partners' actual levels of disclosure.

Love Styles

As noted earlier, the love styles approach also captures the multidimensional aspects of love. These six different love attitudes or styles have been used to explore many aspects of love, including gender differences, relationship satisfaction, and love and friendship.

Gender differences in love styles have occurred in most research studies, with men typically appearing to report more game-playing (ludic) love and women more friendship-oriented (storgic), practical (pragmatic), and possessive (manic) love (C. Hendrick & Hendrick, 1986). These findings are relatively stable. But these gender differences may have little to do with whether or not love is experienced positively. For example, men disagree less than women with ludic love. But they still disagree! Game-playing love has been shown to be negatively related to relationship satisfaction (S. Hendrick, Hendrick, & Adler, 1988). Women may be more friendship-oriented, practical, and possessive than men, but these love styles are not related strongly to satisfaction. On the other hand, women and men differ little on passionate love, which *is* related strongly to satisfaction (S. Hendrick et al., 1988). In fact, passion is very predictive of satisfaction across both ages and cultures (Contreras, Hendrick, & Hendrick, 1996).

Love Across Cultures

Although some scholars note that the rich texture and subtle nuances of love need to be understood within a cultural context (Dion &

Dion, 1996), others believe that most fundamental aspects of love transcend place and time. Cho and Cross (1995) found that the themes of passionate love, obsessive love, casual love, devoted love, and free choice of a mate were present in Chinese literature dating back thousands of years. Thus these phenomena are not new. These authors used the Love Attitudes Scale (C. Hendrick & Hendrick, 1986) to ascertain the current love attitudes of Taiwanese students living in the United States (average time spent in the United States was 31 months). Specifically, they examined whether the themes expressed in ancient Chinese literature were still present and whether they would map onto the six love styles or attitudes. The authors found many similarities between the Taiwanese students and American participants, though the six love styles did not match perfectly across cultures. For example, Agape (altruistic) and Pragma (practical) love combined and became "Obligatory love" for the Taiwanese.

In other research, European American, Japanese American, and Pacific Islander residents of Hawaii were compared on several aspects of love and relationships (Doherty, Hatfield, Thompson, & Choo, 1994). All the groups were similar in both companionate and passionate love. Sprecher et al. (1994) found similar love attitudes and experiences when they studied American, Japanese, and Russian approaches to love. Though there certainly were cultural differences—Japanese respondents identified less with certain romantic beliefs, and Russians were less likely to require love as a prerequisite for marriage—similarities abounded. Similarities between ethnic groups also were identified by Contreras et al. (1996), who studied Mexican American and Anglo married couples. They found only modest love and sex attitude differences among the groups. In addition, Hispanic-oriented, bicultural, and Anglo groups were similar in passionate, altruistic, and friendship-oriented love, as well as in their relationship satisfaction. Commenting on the findings in this area, Hatfield and Rapson (1996) concluded that "throughout the modern world, people turn out to be surprisingly similar in the way they experience passionate love" (p. 88). We are indeed more the same than we are different.

In addition to learning more about cultural similarities and differences in love and relationships, attention is finally being paid to phenomena that have important implications for persons' well-being: love and sex.

Love and Sexuality

Scholars of relationships typically have either separated the study of love from that of sexuality (with some people studying one topic, and different people studying the other topic), or they have tried to subsume one by the other. Aron and Aron (1991) visualized scholarship on the topics as a continuum, with "sex is really love" at one end and "love is really sex" at the other end. Some scholars view the two aspects of human experience as linked, however, with both sex and love having important and related roles in intimate, partnered relationships. Regan (1998; Regan & Berscheid, 1999), for example, noted that sexual desire is a fundamental component of romantic love. In our work, we have found positive relationships between love (as measured by the LAS; C. Hendrick & Hendrick, 1986) and sex (as measured by the Sexual Attitudes Scale; S. Hendrick & Hendrick, 1987). For example, greater erotic (Eros) and altruistic (Agape) love are related to more idealistic sexuality (the Communion subscale of the Sexual Attitudes Scale), whereas game-playing love (Ludus) is related positively to casual and biologically oriented sexuality (Permissiveness and Instrumentality subscales).

More recently, we (S. Hendrick & Hendrick, 2000a) have assumed that people link love and sex (broadly construed as more than just intercourse) in their relationships and have asked people to describe these links. Several themes emerged, including love being the most important thing in the relationship and coming before sex in both significance and sequencing. Another significant theme is that sex is viewed as a profoundly important way of demonstrating love.

In a major large-scale study of sexual behavior in the United States, Laumann, Gagnon, Michael, and Michaels (1994) found that respondents who expressed the greatest physical pleasure and emotional satisfaction in their relationships were those in partnered, monogamous relationships. Although love is not discussed directly, it surely is implied. Researchers may have been slow to link sex with love, but based on our personal, observational, and clinical experience, we know the two are related. While it is possible to experience love without sexual/physical immediacy (as in long-distance relationships where partners are separated for extended periods), or to experience sex without love (presumably the case in most encounters between prostitutes and clients), for most of us, most of the time, love and sex are linked.

Love and Happiness

Love clearly is important to the human condition, as is being in a relationship. Baumeister and Leary (1995) have argued persuasively that humans are a group species and thus have a "need to belong." Consistent with this thesis, Myers and Diener (1995), in discussing happiness, noted, "Throughout the Western world, married people of both sexes report more happiness than those never married, divorced, or separated" (p. 15). Still other research results confirm this finding. In a series of studies exploring people's perceptions of the links between love and sex (S. Hendrick & Hendrick, 2000a), we also examined the links between happiness and several relationship variables. In one sample of 348 college students, people who were in love were significantly happier than people not in love, as measured by a question concerning happiness. In addition, people who were in a relationship were happier than those not in a relationship. In addition, for this same sample, happiness scores were correlated positively with passionate love ($r = .33$, $p < .001$), friendship love ($r = .13$, $p < .05$), and relationship satisfaction scores ($r = .35$, $p < .001$). Findings were quite similar for another sample of 274 college-age participants. Given the correlational nature of these data, it may be that people who are satisfied with their romantic/partnered relationships are happier, or people who are happier are more satisfied with their relationships. Though the correlation between passionate love and happiness was more modest (only .18 in our second study), it nevertheless indicated some link between happiness and love.

The findings discussed so far in this chapter lead to a significant question. If we wish to foster positive conditions in the human community, and if love, satisfaction, and happiness are all related to one another to some degree, how might we augment people's experiencing of these phenomena?

Interventions to Increase Love and Satisfaction

We have discussed elsewhere some ways of "teaching" love (C. Hendrick & Hendrick, 2000;

S. Hendrick & Hendrick, 2000b) and of conducting couple therapy so as to repair or enrich love (S. Hendrick, 1995; S. Hendrick & Hendrick, 1992). In the following section, we offer additional suggestions.

Teaching About Love as Well as Teaching Love

Courses dealing with sexuality, close relationships, courtship and marriage, interpersonal skills, and so on are relatively popular offerings on college campuses in many countries. Such courses provide opportunities for students to learn about themselves and their romantic, family, and friendship relationships through understanding theories and concepts, as well as by examining their own attitudes and values. For example, students might be asked to fill out the Love Attitudes Scale for a current or previous romantic relationship and then to ask their best friend to fill out the scale. They might be asked to discuss their answers with their friend and to compare their similarities and differences. They then could use class time to discuss the experience of learning about their own and their friends' love styles and talking together about them. Such an exercise would teach the students not only about love but also about friendship, self-disclosure, and how aspects of close relationships fit with each other. Any other love measures or relationship measures could be employed in a similar fashion.

Although teaching "about" love is important and potentially useful, a much more profoundly difficult yet important undertaking is "teaching love." Where should we look for our models of this? Some of our major social institutions, organized religions, for example, might posit that they teach love in the context of teaching religion. To the extent that such groups profess tolerance, openness, a valuing of diversity, and extension of oneself in service of another, they do indeed teach love. Voluntary organizations such as the Red Cross or the Salvation Army teach love in large measure by showing love. Love also can be ably "taught" by recovery organizations, most notably Alcoholics Anonymous.

Ideally, we teach love in our families, by enjoying each other, protecting each other, and offering social support to each other. Selfless giving (i.e., bestowal) is nowhere more evident than in parents caring for a new baby. Or, at the other end of the life span continuum, love is evident in the care of an elderly parent by a middle-aged adult child.

It is easy to offer examples of love and say that we "teach" it by modeling, but if we were to teach a course on love, we might do more. We would draw readings from religion, philosophy, literature, and other areas and discuss them in depth. We would ask student participants to spend time with a parent or other family member, specifically telling that person how much he or she is appreciated. At another time, students would be asked to spend time with their best friend, simply engaging in a favored activity. Another "assignment" would involve spending time with a small child—walking in the park, feeding ducks, reading stories. Still more time would be spent quietly, in a place they considered "holy," remembering all the people who had loved them. Admittedly, these tasks would be easier for some people than others, for those who have been well loved as opposed to less loved. But all would surely profit from a focus on the cup as half full (or one quarter full or three quarters full) rather than half empty, as well as a serious contemplation on acts of loving and being loved. And *acts* is an operative word. Teaching love means teaching acts, as well as teaching words. Yet increasing love does not necessarily imply adding things to one's life; it can also mean subtracting things.

Removing Barriers to Love

Although removing barriers to love could mean something like removing racial and religious intolerance, we are referring here to the strategies a therapist might employ in helping long-term partners achieve a more satisfying love relationship. When couples seek relationship counseling, the presenting problem or problems may be related to a range of stressors, including money, sex, children, in-laws, gender role conflicts, and the like. A therapist's tendency may be to "prescribe" activities such as time set aside every evening for talking and sharing the events of the day, or a "date" every weekend, for which the children, cares, and problems ostensibly are left at home. But such a message may simply suggest to couples that they have to add something else to their already too busy schedules.

What therapists may need to do is advise their clients to dispense with some of what they are already doing before they add something

new, even something positive. They might selectively dispense with having a clean house,
nice meals, and ironed clothes and settle for a
house cleaned once a month, meals that are
sometimes just soup and sandwiches, and
clothes worn straight from the dryer. Some of
kids' lessons and activities, for families affluent
enough to afford them, might be dropped also,
leaving more time for family activities and for
unstructured time in which kids can be kids. Although it can be anxiety-provoking to "simplify," it can also be anxiety-relieving. The gift
of time is one of the most loving gifts there is.

If therapists tried to help couples make more
"space" in their lives before prescribing any
tasks to address other issues, much, or in some
cases all, of the presenting problem would take
care of itself. Sometimes less is more, and sometimes less busy-ness means more love.

Future Directions

The study of love needs to become a priority
for researchers and funding agencies in *the near
future*. One need only look around to understand that love already is a priority for much of
humanity. Scientists have begun once again to
view humans as whole persons, not as disconnected minds and bodies. Along with this newfound regard for the interplay of mind and
body—nowhere more evident than in the
current volume—must come an awareness that
people's intimate relationships, most particularly their love relationships, are an essential
aspect of this interplay.

One aspect of this recognition of the inter-
weaving of mind and body is an appreciation for
the (often) shared context of love and sexuality.
As noted previously, rather than trying to subsume sex within love or love within sex, we
prefer to view the two as coequals in partnered
intimate relationships. And sex needs to be *very
broadly* defined in future research to include all
forms of physical affection rather than only
sexual intercourse.

In our own research linking love and sex, we
try to make it explicit to respondents that "sex"
can mean many types of physical involvement.
Kissing, caressing, and other such affectionate
touching can potentially be more important
than intercourse. Humans may be hardwired
for intercourse, but they are even more fundamentally hardwired for physical touch. Babies

require touching. Premature infants who are
touched gain weight more rapidly (Field, 1998).
People with pets (whom they presumably
touch) show health benefits (Vormbrock &
Grossberg, 1988). Massage therapists are being
frequented by more and more people. All these
manifestations of the need to touch and be
touched speak to the importance of physical
contact, enacted in romantic love relationships
by sexual touching and sexual interaction (including but not limited to intercourse) as well
as more affectional touching.

In addition to linking love with sex and construing sexuality more broadly, in future research we should more fully engage the issue
of sexuality in aging. The aging of the United
States population, the lengthening life span, and
the Viagra phenomenon have not so much
changed sexuality in later life as made it more
visible. Both academic writing (Levy, 1994) and
a series of popular articles in American Association of Retired Persons' *Modern Maturity*
make clear that later-life sexuality is physically
and emotionally satisfying, limited less by age
than by the availability of a suitable partner.
And for the aged, as for the young, "Sexual intercourse isn't everything. Just being together
is an essential part of intimacy" (Mathias-
Riegel, 1999, p. 48). Yet "society stubbornly
hangs on to stereotypes about older sex"
(Mathias-Riegel, 1999, p. 47), so research that
enriches our knowledge about love, sex, and aging should be popularized and disseminated
widely. Love and sex span all of life (Latham,
1997; Pickett, 1995).

Love and sex at any age are affected negatively by stress, one of positive psychology's
worst enemies. " 'Less stress' and 'more free
time' are the top things 45–59-year-olds say
would most improve their sex life" (Jacoby,
1999, p. 43). And Herbert Benson (1996) noted
that "the vast majority of the medical complaints brought to doctors' offices are stress-
and belief-related" (p. 292). The "less is more"
philosophy we espoused earlier has stress reduction as its proximal purpose. If we can help
people to simplify their lives, thus reducing
their stress levels, it is very likely that peoples'
relationships (including love and sex) would be
enriched greatly. Moreover, the positive aspects
of their lives would be enriched accordingly.

In our introduction, we noted that love, sex,
friendship, and marriage are increasingly linked
in romantic relationships. We also have argued

for the integrated study of love and sexuality throughout the life span. We wish to close by generalizing our argument: Love should be studied as a central concept with links to many other positive psychological concepts. In this way, a systematic approach to a positive psychology can be developed.

Perhaps an example will make our vision more specific. Aron and Aron (1996) noted that their self-expansion approach to love could serve as a metatheory, linking broad sets of empirical findings. If self-expansion is intrinsically desirable, and love promotes self-expansion, then being in love should be related to many other positive attributes. Being in love should result in higher self-esteem and stronger self-affirmation, as well as more other-affirmation. Positive emotional states such as happiness and an optimistic outlook should correlate positively with love. Hope for the future should be abundant. Along with such hope should go a heightened sense of self-efficacy and the ability to cope with one's world.

If Singer (1984a) is correct that love becomes bestowal and thereby creates new value in the world, then love should create new meaning in the world, meaning that is rich in surplus attributes. One such attribute might be an enhanced empathy and altruism, not only for the loved one but perhaps toward the world at large. Along with the heightened sense of self-efficacy, an enlightened altruism, perhaps combined with an enlivened sense of creativity, could fuel the generation of great works. Thus, we view love as a central concept within a linked, dynamic structure of other positive concepts. The concepts are fundamentally related, their relational nature mirroring the relational nature of the human community. With this view, a much broader, more fully integrated understanding of the human condition is possible, one that will allow a complete positive psychology to emerge.

APPENDIX   Love Attitudes Scale— Short Form

Eros 1. My partner and I have the right physical "chemistry" between us.
2. I feel that my partner and I were meant for each other.
3. My partner and I really understand each other.

4. My partner fits my ideal standards of physical beauty/handsomeness.

Ludus 5. I believe that what my partner doesn't know about me won't hurt him/her.
6. I have sometimes had to keep my partner from finding out about other partners.
7. My partner would get upset if he/she knew of some of the things I've done with other people.
8. I enjoy playing the "game of love" with my partner and a number of other partners.

Storge 9. Our love is the best kind because it grew out of a long friendship.
10. Our friendship merged gradually into love over time.
11. Our love is really a deep friendship, not a mysterious, mystical emotion.
12. Our love relationship is the most satisfying because it developed from a good friendship.

Pragma 13. A main consideration in choosing my partner was how he/she would reflect on my family.
14. An important factor in choosing my partner was whether or not he/she would be a good parent.
15. One consideration in choosing my partner was how he/she would reflect on my career.
16. Before getting very involved with my partner, I tried to figure out how compatible his/her hereditary background would be with mine in case we ever had children.

Mania 17. When my partner doesn't pay attention to me, I feel sick all over.
18. Since I've been in love with my partner, I've had trouble concentrating on anything else.
19. I cannot relax if I suspect that my partner is with someone else.
20. If my partner ignores me for a while, I sometimes do stupid things to try to get his/her attention back.

Agape 21. I would rather suffer myself than let my partner suffer.
22. I cannot be happy unless I place my partner's happiness before my own.
23. I am usually willing to sacrifice my own wishes to let my partner achieve his/hers.
24. I would endure all things for the sake of my partner.

Note: Each item is rated on a five-point basis, ranging from strongly agree to strongly disagree with the statement. Adapted from C. Hendrick, S. S. Hendrick, & A. Dicke. 1998. "The Love Attitudes Scale: Short Form."*Journal of Social and Personal Relationships, 15,* 147–159. Adapted with permission of the authors.

References

Aron, A., & Aron, E. N. (1986). *Love and the expansion of self: Understanding attraction and satisfaction.* New York: Hemisphere.

Aron, A., & Aron, E. N. (1991). Love and sexuality. In K. McKinney & S. Sprecher (Eds.), *Sexuality in close relationships* (pp. 25–48). Hillsdale, NJ: Erlbaum.

Aron, E. N., & Aron, A. (1996). Love and expansion of the self: The state of the model. *Personal Relationships, 3,* 45–58.

Baumeister, R. F., & Leary, M. R. (1995). The need to belong: Desire for interpersonal attachments as a fundamental human motivation. *Psychological Bulletin, 117,* 497–529.

Beall, A. E., & Sternberg, R. J. (1995). The social construction of love. *Journal of Social and Personal Relationships, 12,* 417–438.

Benson, H. (1996). *Timeless healing: The power and biology of belief.* New York: Scribner's.

Berscheid, E. (2000). Foreword: Back to the future and forward to the past. In C. Hendrick & S. S. Hendrick (Eds.), *Close relationships: A sourcebook* (pp. ix–xxi). Thousand Oaks, CA: Sage.

Berscheid, E., & Walster, E. (1969). *Interpersonal attraction.* Reading, MA: Addison-Wesley.

Berscheid, E., & Walster, E. (1978). *Interpersonal attraction* (2nd ed.). Reading, MA: Addison-Wesley.

Bowlby, J. (1969). *Attachment and loss: Vol. 1. Attachment.* New York: Basic Books.

Buss, D. M. (1988). Love acts: The evolutionary biology of love. In R. J. Sternberg & M. L. Barnes (Eds.), *The psychology of love* (pp. 100–117). New Haven, CT: Yale University Press.

Buss, D. M., & Kenrick, D. T. (1998). Evolutionary social psychology. In D. T. Gilbert, S. T. Fiske, & G. Lindzey (Eds.), *The handbook of social psychology* (Vol. 2, 4th ed., pp. 982–1026). Boston: McGraw-Hill.

Cho, W., & Cross, S. E. (1995). Taiwanese love styles and their association with self-esteem and relationship quality. *Genetic, Social, and General Psychology Monographs, 121,* 283–309.

Contreras, R., Hendrick, S. S., & Hendrick, C. (1996). Perspectives on marital love and satisfaction in Mexican American and Anglo couples. *Journal of Counseling and Development, 74,* 408–415.

Davis, K. E., & Todd, M. J. (1985). Assessing friendship: Prototypes, paradigm cases and relationship description. In S. Duck & D. Perlman (Eds.), *Understanding personal relationships: An interdisciplinary approach* (pp. 17–38). London: Sage.

Dion, K. K., & Dion, K. L. (1996). Cultural perspectives on romantic love. *Personal Relationships, 3,* 5–17.

Doherty, R. W., Hatfield, E., Thompson, K., & Choo, P. (1994). Cultural and ethnic influences on love and attachment. *Personal Relationships, 1,* 391–398.

Eagly, A. H., & Wood, W. (1999). The origins of sex differences in human behavior. *American Psychologist, 54,* 408–423.

Eiser, J. R. (1994). *Attitudes, chaos and the connectionist mind.* Cambridge, MA: Blackwell.

Feeney, J., & Noller, P. (1996). *Adult attachment.* Thousand Oaks, CA: Sage.

Fehr, B. (1993). How do I love thee? Let me consult my prototype. In S. Duck (Ed.), *Individuals in relationships* (pp. 87–120). Newbury Park, CA: Sage.

Fehr, B. (1994). Prototype-based assessment of laypeople's views of love. *Personal Relationships, 1,* 309–331.

Field, T. M. (1998). Touch therapies. In R. R. Hoffman, M. F. Sherrick, & J. S. Warm (Eds.), *Viewing psychology as a whole* (pp. 603–624). Washington, DC: American Psychological Association.

Gadlin, H. (1977). Private lives and public order: A critical view of the history of intimate relations in the United States. In G. Levinger & H. L. Raush (Eds.), *Close relationships: Perspectives on the meaning of intimacy* (pp. 33–72). Amherst: University of Massachusetts Press.

Guastello, S. J. (1997). Science evolves: An introduction to nonlinear dynamics, psychology, and life sciences. *Nonlinear Dynamics, Psychology, and Life Sciences, 1,* 1–6.

Harlow, H. F. (1974). *Learning to love*. New York: Jason Aronson.

Hatfield, E. (1988). Passionate and companionate love. In R. J. Sternberg & M. L. Barnes (Eds.), *The psychology of love* (pp. 191–217). New Haven, CT: Yale University Press.

Hatfield, E., & Rapson, R. L. (1996). *Love and sex: Cross-cultural perspectives*. Boston: Allyn and Bacon.

Hatfield, E., & Sprecher, S. (1986). Measuring passionate love in intimate relations. *Journal of Adolescence, 9,* 383–410.

Hazan, C., & Shaver, P. (1987). Romantic love conceptualized as an attachment process. *Journal of Personality and Social Psychology, 52,* 511–524.

Hecht, M. L., Marston, P. J., & Larkey, L. K. (1994). Love ways and relationship quality. *Journal of Social and Personal Relationships, 11,* 25–43.

Hendrick, C., & Hendrick, S. S. (1986). A theory and method of love. *Journal of Personality and Social Psychology, 50,* 392–402.

Hendrick, C., & Hendrick, S. S. (1990). A relationship-specific version of the Love Attitudes Scale. *Journal of Social Behavior and Personality, 5,* 230–254.

Hendrick, C., & Hendrick, S. S. (1991). Dimensions of love: A sociobiological interpretation. *Journal of Social and Clinical Psychology, 10,* 206–230.

*Hendrick, C., & Hendrick, S. S. (Eds.). (2000). *Close relationships: A sourcebook*. Thousand Oaks, CA: Sage.

Hendrick, C., Hendrick, S. S., & Dicke, A. (1998). The Love Attitudes Scale: Short Form. *Journal of Social and Personal Relationships, 15,* 147–159.

Hendrick, S. S. (1995). *Close relationships: What couple therapists can learn*. Pacific Grove, CA: Brooks/Cole.

Hendrick, S. S., & Hendrick, C. (1987). Multidimensionality of sexual attitudes. *Journal of Sex Research, 23,* 502–526.

*Hendrick, S. S., & Hendrick, C. (1992). *Romantic love*. Thousand Oaks, CA: Sage.

Hendrick, S. S., & Hendrick, C. (1993). Lovers as friends. *Journal of Social and Personal Relationships, 10,* 459–466.

Hendrick, S. S., & Hendrick, C. (2000a). *Linking romantic love and sex*. Manuscript in preparation, Texas Tech University, Lubbock.

Hendrick, S. S., & Hendrick, C. (2000b). Romantic love. In C. Hendrick & S. S. Hendrick (Eds.), *Close relationships: A sourcebook* (pp. 203–215). Thousand Oaks, CA: Sage.

Hendrick, S. S., Hendrick, C., & Adler, N. L. (1988). Romantic relationships: Love, satisfaction, and staying together. *Journal of Personality and Social Psychology, 54,* 980–988.

Jacoby, S. (1999, September–October). Great sex: What's age got to do with it? *Modern Maturity, 42w,* 41–45, 91.

Kaplan, D., & Glass, L. (1995). *Understanding nonlinear dynamics*. New York: Springer.

Lasswell, T. E., & Lasswell, M. E. (1976). I love you but I'm not in love with you. *Journal of Marriage and Family Counseling, 38,* 211–224.

*Latham, A. (1997). *The ballad of Gussie and Clyde: A true story of true love*. New York: Villard.

Laumann, E. O., Gagnon, J. H., Michael, R. T., & Michaels, S. (1994). *The social organization of sexuality: Sexual practices in the United States*. Chicago: University of Chicago Press.

Lee, J. A. (1973). *The colors of love: An exploration of the ways of loving*. Don Mills, Ontario: New Press.

Levy, J. A. (1994). Sex and sexuality in later life stages. In A. S. Rossi (Ed.), *Sexuality across the life course* (pp. 287–309). Chicago: University of Chicago Press.

Marston, P. J., Hecht, M. L., & Robers, T. (1987). "True love ways": The subjective experience and communication of romantic love. *Journal of Social and Personal Relationships, 4,* 387–407.

Mathias-Riegel, B. (1999, September–October). Intimacy 101: A refresher course in the language of love. *Modern Maturity, 42w,* 46–49, 84.

Meeks, B. S., Hendrick, S. S., & Hendrick, C. (1998). Communication, love, and relationship satisfaction. *Journal of Social and Personal Relationships, 15,* 755–773.

Mellen, S. L. W. (1981). *The evolution of love*. San Francisco: Freeman.

Murray, S. L., & Holmes, J. G. (1997). A leap of faith? Positive illusions in romantic relationships. *Personality and Social Psychology Bulletin, 23,* 586–604.

Murray, S. L., Holmes, J. G., & Griffin, D. W. (1996). The self-fulfilling nature of positive illusions in romantic relationships: Love is not blind but prescient. *Journal of Personality and Social Psychology, 71,* 1155–1180.

Murstein, B. I. (1974). *Love, sex, and marriage through the ages*. New York: Springer.

Myers, D. G., & Diener, E. (1995). Who is happy? *Psychological Science, 6,* 10–19.

Noller, P. (1996). What is this thing called love? Defining the love that supports marriage and family. *Personal Relationships, 3,* 97–115.

*Pickett, K. (1995). *Love in the 90s: B.B. & Jo: The story of a lifelong love*. New York: Warner.

Regan, P. C. (1998). Romantic love and sexual desire. In V. C. deMunck (Ed.), *Romantic love* and sexual behavior: Perspectives from the social sciences (pp. 91–112). Westport, CT: Praeger.

*Regan, P. C., & Berscheid, E. (1999). Lust: What we know about human sexual desire. Thousand Oaks, CA: Sage.

Regan, P. C., Kocan, E. R., & Whitlock, T. (1998). Ain't love grand! A prototype analysis of the concept of romantic love. Journal of Social and Personal Relationships, 15, 411–420.

Rubin, Z. (1970). Measurement of romantic love. Journal of Personality and Social Psychology, 16, 265–273.

Simpson, J. A., Campbell, B., & Berscheid, E. (1986). The association between romantic love and marriage: Kephart (1967) twice revisited. Personality and Social Psychology Bulletin, 12, 363–372.

Singer, I. (1984a). The nature of love: Vol. 1. Plato to Luther (2nd ed.). Chicago: University of Chicago Press.

Singer, I. (1984b). The nature of love: Vol. 2. Courtly and romantic. Chicago: University of Chicago Press.

Singer, I. (1987). The nature of love: Vol. 3. The modern world. Chicago: University of Chicago Press.

Sprecher, S., Aron, A., Hatfield, E., Cortese, A., Potapova, E., & Levitskaya, A. (1994). Love: American style, Russian style, and Japanese style. Personal Relationships, 1, 349–369.

Sprecher, S., & Regan, P. C. (1998). Passionate and companionate love in courting and young married couples. Sociological Inquiry, 68, 163–185.

Sternberg, R. J. (1986). A triangular theory of love. Psychological Review, 93, 119–135.

*Sternberg, R. J. (1998). Love is a story. New York: Oxford University Press.

Trivers, R. L. (1972). Parental investment and sexual selection. In B. Campbell (Ed.), Sexual selection and the descent of man (pp. 136–179). Chicago: Aldine.

Vormbrock, J. K., & Grossberg, J. M. (1988). Cardiovascular effects of human–pet dog interactions. Journal of Behavioral Medicine, 11, 509–517.

Walster, E., & Walster, G. W. (1978). A new look at love. Reading, MA: Addison-Wesley.

35

Empathy and Altruism

C. Daniel Batson, Nadia Ahmad, David A. Lishner,
& Jo-Ann Tsang

Altruism refers to a specific form of motivation for one organism, usually human, benefiting another. Although some biologists and psychologists speak of altruistic behavior, meaning behavior that benefits another, we do not recommend this use. Such use fails to consider the motivation for the behavior, and motivation is the central issue in discussions of altruism. If one's ultimate goal in benefiting another is to increase the other's welfare, then the motivation is altruistic. If the ultimate goal is to increase one's own welfare, then the motivation is egoistic. We shall use the term *altruism* to refer to this specific form of motivation and the term *helping* to refer to behavior that benefits another.

A Basic Question: Is Altruism Part of Human Nature?

Clearly, we humans devote much time and energy to helping others. We send money to rescue famine victims halfway around the world—or to save whales. We stay up all night to comfort a friend who has just suffered a broken relationship. We stop on a busy high-

way to help a stranded motorist change a flat tire.

Why do we humans help? Often, of course, the answer is easy. We help because we have no choice, because it is expected, or because it is in our own best interest. We may do a friend a favor because we do not want to lose the friendship or because we expect to see the favor reciprocated. But it is not for such easy answers that we ask ourselves why we help; it is to press the limits of these answers. We want to know whether our helping is always and exclusively motivated by the prospect of some benefit for ourselves, however subtle. We want to know whether anyone ever, in any degree, transcends the bounds of self-interest and helps out of genuine concern for the welfare of another. We want to know whether altruism is within the human repertoire.

Proponents of universal egoism claim that everything we do, no matter how noble and beneficial to others, is really directed toward the ultimate goal of self-benefit. Proponents of altruism do not deny that the motivation for much of what we do, including much that we do for others, is egoistic. But they claim more. They claim that at least some of us, to some degree, under some circumstances, are capable of a qualitatively different form of motivation, motivation with an ultimate goal of benefiting someone else.

Those arguing for universal egoism have elegance and parsimony on their side in this debate. It is simpler to explain all human behavior in terms of self-benefit than to postulate a motivational pluralism in which both self-benefit and another's benefit can serve as ultimate goals. Elegance and parsimony are important criteria in developing scientific explanations, yet they are not the most important criterion. The most important task is to explain adequately and accurately the phenomena in question. We need to know if altruistic motivation exists, even if this knowledge plays havoc with our assumptions about human nature. If altruistic motivation is within the human repertoire, then both who we are as a species and what we are capable of doing are quite different than if it is not. Altruism, if it exists, provides an important cornerstone for positive psychology.

Whether altruism exists is not a new question. This question has been central in Western thought for centuries, from Aristotle (384–322 B.C.) and St. Thomas Aquinas (1225–1274), through Thomas Hobbes (1588–1679), the Duke de la Rochefoucauld (1613–1680), David Hume (1711–1776), Adam Smith (1723–1790), and Jeremy Bentham (1748–1832), to Friedrich Nietzsche (1844–1900) and Sigmund Freud (1856–1939). The majority view among Renaissance and post-Renaissance philosophers, and more recently among biologists and psychologists, is that we are, at heart, purely egoistic—we care for others only to the extent that their welfare affects ours (see Mansbridge, 1990, and Wallach & Wallach, 1983, for reviews).

The many forms of self-benefit that can be derived from helping make the case for universal egoism seem very persuasive. Some forms of self-benefit are obvious, as when we get material rewards and public praise or when we escape public censure. But even when we help in the absence of external rewards, we still may benefit. Seeing someone in distress may cause us to feel distress, and we may act to relieve that person's distress as an instrumental means to relieve our own. Alternatively, we may gain self-benefit by feeling good about ourselves for being kind and caring, or by escaping the guilt and shame we might feel if we did not help.

Even heroes and martyrs can benefit from their acts of apparent selflessness. Consider the soldier who saves his comrades by diving on a grenade or the man who dies after relinquishing his place in a rescue craft. These persons may have acted to escape anticipated guilt and shame for letting others die. They may have acted to gain the admiration and praise of those left behind—or benefits in an afterlife. Perhaps they simply misjudged the situation, not thinking that their actions would cost them their lives. To suggest that heroes' noble acts could be motivated by self-benefit may seem cynical, but the possibility must be faced if we are to responsibly address the question of whether altruism exists.

Empathic Emotion: A Possible Source of Altruistic Motivation

In both earlier philosophical writings and more recent psychological works, the most frequently mentioned possible source of altruistic motivation is an other-oriented emotional reaction to seeing another person in need. This reaction has variously been called "empathy" (Batson, 1987; Krebs, 1975; Stotland, 1969); "sympathy" (Eisenberg & Strayer, 1987; Heider, 1958; Wispé, 1986, 1991); "sympathetic distress" (Hoffman, 1981); "tenderness" (McDougall, 1908); and "pity" or "compassion" (Hume, 1740/1896; Smith, 1759/1853). We shall call this other-oriented emotion *empathy*. Empathy has been named as a source—if not *the* source—of altruism by philosophers ranging from Aquinas to Rousseau to Hume to Adam Smith, and by psychologists ranging from William McDougall to contemporary researchers such as Hoffman (1981), Krebs (1975), and Batson (1987).

Formally, we define empathy as *an other-oriented emotional response elicited by and congruent with the perceived welfare of someone else*. If the other is perceived to be in need, then empathic emotions include sympathy, compassion, softheartedness, tenderness, and the like. It is important to distinguish this other-oriented emotional response from a number of related psychological phenomena, each of which also has at one time or another been called empathy. We have identified seven related concepts from which empathic emotion should be distinguished.

Seven Related Concepts

(1) *Knowing another person's internal state, including thoughts and feelings.* Some clinicians

and researchers have called knowing another person's internal state "empathy" (e.g., Brothers, 1989; de Waal, 1996; Dymond, 1950; Kohler, 1929; Wispé, 1986). Others have called this knowledge "being empathic" (Rogers, 1975), "accurate empathy" (Truax & Carkuff, 1967), or "empathic accuracy" (Ickes, 1993). Still others speak of "understanding" (Becker, 1931) or "perceiving accurately" (Levenson & Ruef, 1992). It might appear that such knowledge is a necessary condition for the other-oriented emotional response claimed to evoke altruistic motivation, but it is not. Empathic emotion requires that one *think* one knows the other's state because empathic emotion is based on a perception of the other's welfare. It does not, however, require that this perception be accurate, or even that it match the other's perception, which is often the standard used to define empathic accuracy (Ickes, 1993). An attempt to help motivated by empathic feeling is, of course, more likely to be beneficial if the feeling is based on an accurate perception of the other's needs. Thus, it is not surprising that clinicians, whose primary concern is to help the client, tend to emphasize accurate perception of the client's feelings more than feeling for the client.

(2) *Assuming the posture of an observed other.* Assuming the physical posture or attitude of an observed other is a definition of empathy in many dictionaries. Among psychologists, however, assuming another's posture is more likely to be called "motor mimicry" (Bavelas, Black, Lemeray, & Mullett, 1987; Hoffman, 1981; Murphy, 1947; Dimberg, Thunberg, & Elmehed, 2000); "physiological sympathy" (Ribot, 1911); or "imitation" (Becker, 1931; Lipps, 1903; Titchener, 1909). Feeling empathic emotion may be facilitated by assuming another's posture, but assuming the other's posture is neither necessary nor sufficient to produce empathy as we are using the term.

(3) *Coming to feel as another person feels.* Feeling the same emotion that another person feels also is a common dictionary definition of empathy, and it is a definition used by some psychologists (Berger, 1962; Eisenberg & Strayer, 1987; Englis, Vaughan, & Lanzetta, 1982; Freud, 1922; Stotland, 1969). Among philosophers, coming to feel as the other feels is more likely to be called "sympathy" (Hume, 1740/1896; Smith, 1759/1853). Scientists—including psychologists—who have been influenced by philosophy also typically refer to this state as "sympathy" (Allport, 1924; Cooley,

1902; Darwin, 1871; McDougall, 1908; Mead, 1934; Spencer, 1870; Wundt, 1897). Feeling the same emotion as another also has been called "fellow feeling" (Hume, 1740/1896; Smith, 1759/1853); "emotional identification" (Freud, 1922), "emotional contagion" (Becker, 1931; de Waal, 1996; Hatfield, Cacioppo, & Rapson, 1992; Heider, 1958); "affective reverberation" (Davis, 1985), and "empathic distress" (Hoffman, 1981). Although feeling as the other feels may be an important stepping-stone to the other-oriented feeling that has been claimed to be a source of altruism, it is neither a necessary nor a sufficient precondition (Batson, Early, & Salvarani, 1997). Feeling as the other feels may actually inhibit feeling for the other if it leads one to become focused on one's own emotional state. For example, sensing the nervousness of other passengers on an airplane in rough weather, one may become nervous, too, and focused on one's own nervousness.

(4) *Intuiting or projecting oneself into another's situation.* Projecting oneself into another's situation is the psychological state referred to by Lipps (1903) as *Einfülung* and for which Titchener (1909) originally coined the term "empathy." This state also has been called "projective empathy" (Becker, 1931). Originally, these terms were intended to describe an artist's act of imagining what it would be like to be some person or, more often, some inanimate object—such as a gnarled, dead tree on a windswept hillside. This original definition of empathy as aesthetic projection often appears in dictionaries, but it is rarely what is meant by the term in contemporary psychology (although Wispé, 1968, has called this state "aesthetic" empathy).

(5) *Imagining how another is feeling.* Wispé (1968) called imagining how another is feeling "psychological" empathy in order to differentiate it from the aesthetic empathy just described. Stotland (1969) spoke of this as a particular form of perspective taking—an "imagine him" (or, more generally, an "imagine other") perspective. Experimental instructions to adopt this imagine-other perspective often have been used to induce empathic emotion in participants in laboratory research (see Batson, 1991, and Davis, 1994, for reviews).

(6) *Imagining how one would think and feel in the other's place.* Adam Smith (1759/1853) prosaically referred to this act of imagination as "changing places in fancy." Mead (1934) sometimes called it "role taking" and sometimes

"empathy"; Becker (1931) coined the term "mimpathizing." In the Piagetian tradition, imagining how one would think in the other's place has been called either "perspective taking" or "decentering" (Piaget, 1932/1965; Steins & Wicklund, 1996). Stotland (1969) called this an "imagine-self" perspective, distinguishing it from the imagine-other perspective described previously. These imagine-self and imagine-other forms of perspective taking often have been confused or equated in spite of research evidence suggesting that they should not. When attending to another person in distress, an imagine-other perspective stimulates the other-oriented emotional response that we are calling empathy, whereas an imagine-self perspective may stimulate empathy but is also likely to elicit more self-oriented feelings of personal distress (Batson, Early, & Salvarani, 1997).

(7) *Being upset by another person's suffering.* The state of personal distress evoked by seeing another in distress to which we just referred has been given a variety of names. It has been called "sympathetic pain" (McDougall, 1908); "promotive tension" (Hornstein, 1982); "unpleasant arousal occasioned by observation" (Piliavin, Dovidio, Gaertner, & Clark, 1981); and "empathy" (Krebs, 1975). Here, one does not feel distressed *for* the other nor distressed *as* the other but feels distressed *by* the state of the other.

We have listed these seven other empathy concepts for three reasons. First, we wish to point out the range of psychological states to which the term empathy has been applied, hoping both to reduce confusion and to discourage imperialist attempts to identify it with only one of these phenomena. Second, we wish to distinguish each of the seven other empathy concepts from the other-oriented emotional response that has been claimed to be a source of altruistic motivation. Third, we wish to suggest how each of the other seven concepts relates to this empathic emotional response. Most of the other empathy concepts describe cognitive or perceptual states that are potential precursors to and facilitators of empathic emotion (Concepts 1, 2, 4, 5, and 6). Two describe alternative emotional states: feeling as the other feels (Concept 3) and feeling personal distress (upset) as a result of witnessing the other's suffering (Concept 7). Feeling as the other feels may serve as a stepping-stone to empathic feelings and, hence, to altruistic motivation, but it also may lead to self-focused attention and inhibit other-oriented

feelings. Feeling personal distress is not likely to be a stepping-stone to altruism. Instead, it is likely to evoke an egoistic motive to relieve one's own distress (Batson, Fultz, & Schoenrade, 1987; Piliavin et al., 1981).

Although distinctions among the eight concepts in the empathy cluster are sometimes subtle, there seems little doubt that each of these states exists. Indeed, most are familiar experiences. Their familiarity, however, should not lead us to ignore their psychological significance. The processes whereby one person can sense another's cares and wishes are truly remarkable, as are the range of emotions that these processes can arouse. Some great thinkers (e.g., David Hume) have suggested that these processes are the basis for all social perception and interaction. They are certainly key—and underappreciated—elements of our social nature.

Empathic Emotion as Situational, Not Dispositional

Note that all eight of the empathy concepts we have considered are situation specific. None refers to a general disposition or personality trait. There may well be individual differences in the ability and inclination to experience these various states (see Davis, 1994, for a suggestive discussion), but attempts to measure these differences by standard retrospective self-report questionnaires seem suspect at best. Such questionnaires are more likely to reveal the degree of desire to see oneself and to be seen by others as empathic rather than to provide a valid measure of one's proclivity to be empathic.

Testing the Empathy-Altruism Hypothesis

The claim that feeling empathic emotion for someone in need evokes altruistic motivation to relieve that need has been called the *empathy-altruism hypothesis* (Batson, 1987, 1991). According to this hypothesis, the greater the empathic emotion, the greater the altruistic motivation.

Considerable evidence supports the idea that feeling empathy for a person in need leads to increased helping of that person (Coke, Batson, & McDavis, 1978; Dovidio, Allen, & Schroeder, 1990; Krebs, 1975; see Batson, 1991, and Eisenberg & Miller, 1987, for reviews). To observe an empathy-helping relationship, however, tells us nothing about the nature of the motivation that underlies this relationship. Increasing the other person's welfare could be an ultimate goal, an instrumental goal sought as a means to the ultimate goal of gaining one or more self-benefits, or both. That is, the motivation could be altruistic, egoistic, or both.

Three general classes of self-benefits can result from helping a person for whom one feels empathy. Helping enables one to (a) reduce one's empathic arousal, which may be experienced as aversive; (b) avoid possible social and self-punishments for failing to help; and (c) gain social and self-rewards for doing what is good and right. The empathy-altruism hypothesis does not deny that these self-benefits of empathy-induced helping exist. It claims, however, that with regard to the motivation evoked by empathy, these self-benefits are unintended consequences of reaching the ultimate goal of reducing the other's need. Advocates of egoistic alternatives to the empathy-altruism hypothesis disagree; they claim that one or more of these self-benefits is the ultimate goal of empathy-induced helping. In the past two decades, more than 25 experiments have tested these three egoistic alternatives to the empathy-altruism hypothesis.

Aversive-Arousal Reduction

The most frequently proposed egoistic explanation of the empathy-helping relationship is aversive-arousal reduction. According to this explanation, feeling empathy for someone who is suffering is unpleasant, and empathically aroused individuals help in order to eliminate their empathic feelings. Benefiting the person for whom empathy is felt is simply a means to this self-serving end.

Researchers have tested the aversive-arousal reduction explanation against the empathy-altruism hypothesis by varying the ease of escape from further exposure to a person in need without helping. Because empathic arousal is a result of witnessing the person's suffering, either terminating this suffering by helping or terminating exposure to it by escaping should reduce one's own aversive arousal. Escape does not, however, enable one to reach the altruistic goal of relieving the other's distress. Therefore, the aversive-arousal explanation predicts elimination of the empathy-helping relationship when escape is easy; the empathy-altruism hy-

pothesis does not. Results of experiments testing these competing predictions have consistently supported the empathy-altruism hypothesis, not the aversive-arousal reduction explanation. These results cast serious doubt on this popular egoistic explanation (see Batson, 1991, for a review of these experiments).

Empathy-Specific Punishment

A second egoistic explanation claims that people learn through socialization that additional obligation to help, and so additional shame and guilt for failure to help, is attendant on feeling empathy for someone in need. As a result, when people feel empathy, they are faced with impending social or self-censure beyond any general punishment associated with not helping. They say to themselves, "What will others think—or what will I think of myself—if I don't help when I feel like this?" and then they help out of an egoistic desire to avoid these empathy-specific punishments. Once again, experiments designed to test this explanation have consistently failed to support it; instead, results have consistently supported the empathy-altruism hypothesis (again, see Batson, 1991).

Empathy-Specific Reward

The third major egoistic explanation claims that people learn through socialization that special rewards in the form of praise, honor, and pride are attendant on helping a person for whom they feel empathy. As a result, when people feel empathy, they think of these rewards and help out of an egoistic desire to gain them.

The general form of this explanation has been tested in several experiments and received no support (Batson et al., 1988, Studies 1 and 5; Batson & Weeks, 1996), but two variations have been proposed for which at least some support has been claimed. Best known is the negative-state relief explanation proposed by Cialdini et al. (1987), who suggested that the empathy experienced when witnessing another person's suffering is a negative affective state—a state of temporary sadness or sorrow—and the person feeling empathy helps in order to relieve this negative state.

At first glance, this negative-state relief explanation may appear to be the same as the aversive-arousal reduction explanation. In fact, it is not. Although both explanations begin with the proposition that feeling empathy for someone in need involves a negative affective state, from this common starting point they diverge. The aversive-arousal reduction explanation claims that the goal of helping is to eliminate the negative state; the negative-state relief explanation claims that the goal of helping is to gain mood-enhancing self-rewards that one has learned are associated with helping.

Although the negative-state relief explanation received some initial support (Cialdini et al., 1987; Schaller & Cialdini, 1988), subsequent researchers have found that this support was likely due to procedural artifacts. Experiments avoiding these artifacts have consistently supported the empathy-altruism hypothesis (Batson et al., 1989; Dovidio et al., 1990; Schroeder, Dovidio, Sibicky, Matthews, & Allen, 1988). It now seems clear, therefore, that the motivation to help evoked by empathy is not directed toward the egoistic goal of negative-state relief.

A second variation on an empathy-specific reward explanation was proposed by Smith, Keating, and Stotland (1989). They proposed that, rather than helping to gain the rewards of seeing oneself or being seen by others as a helpful person, empathically aroused individuals help in order to feel joy at the needy individual's relief: "It is proposed that the prospect of empathic joy, conveyed by feedback from the help recipient, is essential to the special tendency of empathic witnesses to help.... The empathically concerned witness ... helps in order to be happy" (Smith et al., 1989, p. 641).

Some early self-report data were supportive, but more rigorous experimental evidence has failed to support this empathic-joy hypothesis. Instead, experimental results consistently have supported the empathy-altruism hypothesis (Batson et al., 1991; Smith et al., 1989). The empathic-joy hypothesis, like other versions of the empathy-specific reward explanation, seems unable to account for the empathy-helping relationship.

A Tentative Conclusion

Reviewing the empathy-altruism research, as well as recent literature in sociology, economics, political science, and biology, Piliavin and Charng (1990) observed:

> There appears to be a "paradigm shift" away from the earlier position that behavior that appears to be altruistic must, under closer scrutiny, be revealed as reflecting egoistic motives. Rather, theory and data

now being advanced are more compatible with the view that true altruism—acting with the goal of benefiting another—does exist and is a part of human nature. (p. 27)

Pending new evidence or a plausible new egoistic explanation of the existing evidence, this observation seems correct. It appears that the empathy-altruism hypothesis should—tentatively—be accepted as true.

Other Possible Sources of Altruistic Motivation

Might there be sources of altruistic motivation other than empathic emotion? Several have been proposed, including an "altruistic personality" (Oliner & Oliner, 1988), principled moral reasoning (Kohlberg, 1976), and internalized prosocial values (Staub, 1974). There is some evidence that each of these potential sources is associated with increased motivation to help, but as yet it is not clear that this motivation is altruistic. It may be, or it may be an instrumental means to the egoistic ultimate goals of maintaining one's positive self-concept or avoiding guilt (Batson, 1991; Batson, Bolen, Cross, & Neuringer-Benefiel, 1986; Carlo, Eisenberg, Troyer, Switzer, & Speer, 1991; Eisenberg et al., 1989). More and better research exploring these possibilities is needed.

Two Other Possible Prosocial Motives

Thinking more broadly, beyond the egoism-altruism debate that has been a focus of attention and contention for the past two decades, might there be other forms of prosocial motivation, forms in which the ultimate goal is neither to benefit self nor to benefit another individual? Two seem worthy of consideration, collectivism and principlism.

Collectivism

Collectivism is motivation to benefit a particular group as a whole. The ultimate goal is not to increase one's own welfare or the welfare of the specific others who are benefited; the ultimate goal is to increase the welfare of the group. Robyn Dawes and his colleagues put it succinctly: "Not me or thee but we" (Dawes, van de Kragt, & Orbell, 1988). They suggested that collectivist motivation is a product of group identity (Tajfel, 1981; Turner, 1987).

As with altruism, what looks like collectivism may actually be a subtle form of egoism. Perhaps attention to group welfare is simply an expression of enlightened self-interest. After all, if one recognizes that ignoring group needs and the public good in headlong pursuit of self-benefit will lead to less self-benefit in the long run, then one may decide to benefit the group as a means to maximize overall self-benefit. Certainly, appeals to enlightened self-interest are commonly used by politicians and social activists to encourage response to societal needs: They warn of the long-term consequences for oneself and one's children of pollution and squandering natural resources; they remind that if the plight of the poor becomes too severe, the well-off may face revolution. Such appeals seem to assume that collectivism is simply a form of egoism.

The most direct evidence that collectivism is independent of egoism comes from research by Dawes, van de Kragt, and Orbell (1990). They examined the responses of individuals who had been given a choice between allocating money to themselves or to a group. Allocation to oneself maximized individual but not group profit; allocation to the group maximized collective but not individual profit. Dawes et al. found that if individuals faced with this dilemma made their allocation after discussing it with other members of the group, they gave more to the group than if they had no prior discussion. Moreover, this effect was specific to the in-group with whom the discussion occurred; allocation to an out-group was not enhanced. Based on this research, Dawes et al. (1990) claimed evidence for collectivist motivation independent of egoism, arguing that their procedure ruled out the two most plausible egoistic explanations—enlightened self-interest and socially instilled conscience. There is reason to doubt, however, that their procedure effectively ruled out self-rewards and self-punishments associated with conscience. We may have a standard or norm that says "share with your buddies" rather than one that simply says "share." So, although this research is important and suggestive, more and better evidence is needed to justify the conclusion that collectivist motivation is not reducible to egoism.

Principlism

Most moral philosophers argue for the importance of a prosocial motive other than egoism. Most since Kant (1724–1804) shun altruism and collectivism as well. Philosophers reject appeals to altruism, especially empathy-induced altruism, because feelings of empathy, sympathy, and compassion are judged to be too fickle and too circumscribed. Empathy is not felt for everyone in need, at least not in the same degree. They reject appeals to collectivism because group interest is bounded by the limits of the group. Collectivism not only permits but may even encourage doing harm to those outside the group. Given these problems with altruism and collectivism, moral philosophers typically advocate prosocial motivation with an ultimate goal of upholding a universal and impartial moral principle, such as justice (Rawls, 1971). This moral motivation has been called *principlism* (Batson, 1994).

Is acting with an ultimate goal of upholding a moral principle really possible? When Kant (1785/1898, pp. 23–24) briefly shifted from his analysis of what ought to be to what is, he admitted that concern we show for others that appears to be prompted by duty to principle may actually be prompted by self-love. The goal of upholding a moral principle may only be an instrumental means to reach the ultimate goal of self-benefit. If this is true, then principle-based motivation is actually egoistic.

The self-benefits of upholding a moral principle are conspicuous. One can gain the social and self-rewards of being seen and seeing oneself as a good person. One also can avoid the social and self-punishments of shame and guilt for failing to do the right thing. As Freud (1930) suggested, society may inculcate such principles in the young in order to bridle their antisocial impulses by making it in their best personal interest to act morally (also see Campbell, 1975). Alternatively, through internalization (Staub, 1989) or development of moral reasoning (Kohlberg, 1976; Gilligan, 1982), principles may come to be valued in their own right and not simply as instrumental means to self-serving ends.

The issue here is the same one faced with altruism and collectivism. Once again, we need to know the nature of a prosocial motive. Is the desire to uphold justice (or some other moral principle) an instrumental goal on the way to the ultimate goal of self-benefit? If so, then this desire is a subtle and sophisticated form of egoism. Alternatively, is upholding the principle an ultimate goal, with the ensuing self-benefits unintended consequences? If so, then principlism is a fourth type of prosocial motivation, independent of egoism, altruism, and collectivism.

Results of recent research suggest that people often act so as to appear moral while, if possible, avoiding the cost of actually being moral; this sham morality has been called *moral hypocrisy* (Batson, Kobrynowicz, Dinnerstein, Kampf, & Wilson, 1997; Batson, Thompson, Seuferling, Whitney, & Strongman, 1999). Results of this research also suggest that if moral motivation exists, it is easily overpowered by self-interest. Many of us are, it seems, quite adept at moral rationalization. We are good at justifying to ourselves—if not to others—why a situation that benefits us or those we care about does not violate our moral principles: why, for example, storing our nuclear waste in someone else's backyard is fair; why terrorist attacks by our side are regrettable but necessary evils, whereas terrorist attacks by the other side are atrocities; why we must obey orders, even if it means killing innocent people. The abstractness of most moral principles, and their multiplicity, makes such rationalization easy.

But this may be only part of the story. Perhaps upholding a moral principle *can* serve as an ultimate goal, defining a form of motivation independent of egoism. If so, then perhaps these principles can provide a rational basis for responding to the needs of others that transcends reliance on self-interest or on vested interest in and feeling for the welfare of certain other individuals or groups. This is quite an "if," but it seems well worth conducting research to find out.

Toward a General Model of Prosocial Motivation

Staub (1989) and Schwartz (1992) have for many years emphasized the importance of values as determinants of prosocial behavior. Batson (1994) has proposed a general model that links prosocial values and motives: The value underlying egoism is enhanced personal welfare; the value underlying altruism is the enhanced welfare of one or more individuals as individuals; the value underlying collectivism is enhanced group welfare; and the value underlying principlism is upholding a moral principle. Four experiments have provided evidence for the predicted link between empathic emotion—a source of altruistic motivation—and valuing another individual's welfare (Batson, Turk, Shaw, & Klein, 1995); the other value-motive links await test.

Prosocial values usually are assumed to be mutually supportive and cooperative; concern for the welfare of others and concern for the welfare of the society are assumed to be moral (Hoffman, 1989; Staub, 1989). If, however, the different values evoke different ultimate goals and therefore different motives, they may at times conflict rather than cooperate. For example, concern for the welfare of a specific other person (altruism) may conflict not only with self-interest but also with concern for the welfare of the group as a whole (collectivism) or concern to uphold a moral principle (principlism). Evidence of such conflicts has been found (Batson, Ahmad, et al., 1999; Batson, Batson, et al., 1995; Batson, Klein, Highberger, & Shaw, 1995).

To entertain the possibility of multiple prosocial motives (egoism, altruism, collectivism, and principlism) based on multiple prosocial values (self, other, group, principle) begs for a better understanding of cognitive representation of the self-other relationship. Several representations have been proposed. Concern for another's welfare may be a product of: (a) a sense of we-ness based on cognitive unit formation or identification with the other's situation (Hornstein, 1982; Lerner, 1982); (b) the self expanding to incorporate the other (Aron & Aron, 1986); (c) empathic feeling for the other, who remains distinct from self (Batson & Shaw, 1991; Jarymowicz, 1992); (d) the self being redefined at a group level, where me and thee become interchangeable parts of a self that is we (Dawes et al., 1988; Turner, 1987); or (e) the self dissolving in devotion to something outside itself, whether another person, a group, or a principle (James, 1910/1982).

Most of these proposals seem plausible, some even profound. Yet not all can be true, at least not at the same time. Based on research to date, it appears that empathic feelings are not a product of self-other merging (Batson, Sager, et al., 1997; Cialdini, Brown, Lewis, Luce, & Neuberg, 1997), but the effect on one's self-concept of caring for people, groups, and principles is not, as yet, well understood.

Theoretical Implications of the Empathy-Altruism Relationship

Returning to the empathy-altruism relationship, it is clear that this relationship has broad theoretical implications. Universal egoism—the assumption that all human behavior is ultimately directed toward self-benefit—has long dominated not only psychology but also other social and behavioral sciences (Campbell, 1975; Mansbridge, 1990; Wallach & Wallach, 1983). If individuals feeling empathy act, at least in part, with an ultimate goal of increasing the welfare of another, then the assumption of universal egoism must be replaced by a more complex view of motivation that allows for altruism as well as egoism. Such a shift in our view of motivation requires, in turn, a revision of our underlying assumptions about human nature and human potential. It implies that we humans may be more social than we have thought: Other people can be more to us than sources of information, stimulation, and reward as we each seek our own welfare. We have the potential to care about their welfare as well.

The empathy-altruism relationship forces us to face the question of why empathic feelings exist. What evolutionary function do they serve? Admittedly speculative, the most plausible answer relates empathic feelings to parenting among higher mammals, in which offspring live for some time in a very vulnerable state (de Waal, 1996; Hoffman, 1981; McDougall, 1908; Zahn-Waxler & Radke-Yarrow, 1990). Were parents not intensely interested in the welfare of their progeny, these species would quickly die out. Empathic feelings for offspring—and the resulting altruistic motivation—may promote one's reproductive potential not by increasing the number of offspring but by increasing the chance of their survival.

Of course, empathic feelings extend well beyond one's own children. People can feel empathy for a wide range of targets (including nonhumans), as long as there is no preexisting antipathy (Batson, 1991; Krebs, 1975; Shelton & Rogers, 1981). From an evolutionary perspective, this extension is usually attributed to cognitive generalization whereby one "adopts" others, making it possible to evoke the primitive and fundamental impulse to care for progeny when these adopted others are in need (Batson, 1987; Hoffman, 1981; MacLean, 1973). Such cognitive generalization may be facilitated by human cognitive capacity, including symbolic thought, and the lack of evolutionary advantage for sharp discrimination of empathic feelings in early human small hunter-gatherer bands. In these bands, those in need were often one's children or close kin, and one's own welfare was

tightly tied to the welfare even of those who were not close kin (Hoffman, 1981).

William McDougall (1908) long ago described these links in his depiction of the "parental instinct." As with all of McDougall's theorized instincts, the parental instinct involved cognitive, affective, and conative (motivational) components: Cues of distress from one's offspring, including cognitively adopted offspring (e.g., a pet), evoke what McDougall called "the tender emotion" (our "empathy"), which in turn produces altruistic motivation. Although few psychologists would wish to return to McDougall's emphasis on instincts, his attempt to integrate (a) valuing based on cognitive generalization of the perception of offspring in distress, (b) empathic (sympathetic, compassionate, tender) emotional response, and (c) goal-directed altruistic motivation seems at least as much a blueprint for the future as a curio from the past.

Practical Implications of the Empathy-Altruism Relationship

The empathy-altruism relationship also has broad practical implications. Given the power of empathic feelings to evoke altruistic motivation, people may sometimes suppress or avoid these feelings. Loss of the capacity to feel empathy for clients may be a factor, possibly a central one, in the experience of burnout among case workers in the helping professions (Maslach, 1982). Aware of the extreme effort involved in helping or the impossibility of helping effectively, these case workers—or nurses caring for terminal patients, or even pedestrians confronted by the homeless—may try to avoid feeling empathy in order to avoid the resulting altruistic motivation (Shaw, Batson, & Todd, 1994; Stotland, Mathews, Sherman, Hansson, & Richardson, 1978).

More positively, the empathy-altruism relationship suggests the use of empathy-based socialization practices to enhance prosocial behavior, practices that are very different from the currently dominant practices involving inhibition of egoistic impulses through shaping, modeling, and internalized guilt (see Batson, 1991, for some suggestions). Further, therapeutic programs built around facilitating altruistic impulses by encouraging perspective taking and empathic feelings might enable individuals to develop more satisfactory interpersonal relations, especially those that are long term. There may be personal health benefits as well (Luks, 1988; Williams, 1989).

At a societal level, experiments have indicated that empathy-induced altruism can be used to improve attitudes toward stigmatized out-groups. Empathy inductions have been used to improve racial attitudes, as well as attitudes toward people with AIDS, the homeless, and even convicted murderers (Batson, Polycarpou, et al., 1997; Dovidio, Gaertner, & Johnson, 1999). Empathy-induced altruism also has been found to increase cooperation in a competitive situation (a Prisoner's Dilemma)—even when one knows that the person for whom one feels empathy has acted competitively (Batson & Ahmad, 2001; Batson & Moran, 1999).

Conclusions

Why do people help others, even at considerable cost to themselves? What does this behavior tell us about the human capacity to care, about the degree of interconnectedness among us, about how social an animal we humans really are? These classic philosophical questions have resurfaced in the behavioral and social sciences in the past several decades. Psychological research has focused on the claim that empathic emotion evokes altruistic motivation—motivation with the ultimate goal of increasing another's welfare. To understand this research, it is important to distinguish empathic emotion—an emotional state congruent with the perceived welfare of another person—from a number of other empathy concepts. We identified seven other empathy concepts: knowing another person's internal state; assuming the physical posture of an observed other; coming to feel as another person feels; projecting oneself into another's situation; imagining how another is feeling; imagining how one would think and feel in another's place; and being upset by another person's suffering.

The empathy-altruism hypothesis states that empathic emotion evokes altruistic motivation. Results of the over 25 experiments designed to test this hypothesis against various egoistic alternatives have proven remarkably supportive, leading to the tentative conclusion that feeling empathy for a person in need does indeed evoke altruistic motivation to help that person. Sources of altruistic motivation other than empathy also have been proposed, but as yet there

is no compelling research evidence to support these proposals.

Thinking beyond the egoism-altruism debate, two additional forms of prosocial motivation seem especially worthy of consideration: collectivism and principlism. Collectivism—motivation with the ultimate goal of benefiting some group or collective as a whole—has been claimed to result from group identity. Principlism—motivation with the ultimate goal of upholding some moral principle—has long been advocated by religious teachers and moral philosophers. Whether either is a separate form of motivation, independent of and irreducible to egoism, is not yet clear. Research done to test the independent status of empathy-induced altruism may serve as a useful model for future research assessing the independent status of collectivism and principlism.

We know more now than we did a few years ago about why people help. As a result, we know more about human motivation, and even about human nature. These are substantial gains. Still, many questions remain about the emotional and motivational resources that could be tapped to build a more caring, humane society. Providing answers to these questions is, we believe, an important agenda item for positive psychology.

References

Allport, F. H. (1924). *Social psychology*. Boston: Houghton Mifflin.

Aron, A., & Aron, E. N. (1986). *Love and the expansion of self: Understanding attraction and satisfaction*. Washington, DC: Hemisphere.

Batson, C. D. (1987). Prosocial motivation: Is it ever truly altruistic? In L. Berkowitz (Ed.), *Advances in experimental social psychology* (Vol. 20, pp. 65–122). New York: Academic Press.

*Batson, C. D. (1991). *The altruism question: Toward a social-psychological answer*. Hillsdale, NJ: Erlbaum.

Batson, C. D. (1994). Why act for the public good? Four answers. *Personality and Social Psychology Bulletin, 20,* 603–610.

Batson, C. D., & Ahmad, N. (2001). Empathy-induced altruism in a Prisoner's Dilemma II: What if the target of empathy has defected? *European Journal of Social Psychology, 31,* 25–36.

Batson, C. D., Ahmad, N., Yin, J., Bedell, S. J., Johnson, J. W., Templin, C. M., & Whiteside, A. (1999). Two threats to the common good: Self-interested egoism and empathy-induced altruism. *Personality and Social Psychology Bulletin,* 25, 3–16.

Batson, C. D., Batson, J. G., Griffitt, C. A., Barrientos, S., Brandt, J. R., Sprengelmeyer, P., & Bayly, M. J. (1989). Negative-state relief and the empathy-altruism hypothesis. *Journal of Personality and Social Psychology, 56,* 922–933.

Batson, C. D., Batson, J. G., Slingsby, J. K., Harrell, K. L., Peekna, H. M., & Todd, R. M. (1991). Empathic joy and the empathy-altruism hypothesis. *Journal of Personality and Social Psychology, 61,* 413–426.

Batson, C. D., Batson, J. G., Todd, R. M., Brummett, B. H., Shaw, L. L., & Aldeguer, C. M. R. (1995). Empathy and the collective good: Caring for one of the others in a social dilemma. *Journal of Personality and Social Psychology, 68,* 619–631.

Batson, C. D., Bolen, M. H., Cross, J. A., & Neuringer-Benefiel, H. E. (1986). Where is the altruism in the altruistic personality? *Journal of Personality and Social Psychology, 50,* 212–220.

Batson, C. D., Dyck, J. L., Brandt, J. R., Batson, J. G., Powell, A. L., McMaster, M. R., & Griffitt, C. (1988). Five studies testing two new egoistic alternatives to the empathy-altruism hypothesis. *Journal of Personality and Social Psychology, 55,* 52–77.

Batson, C. D., Early, S., & Salvarani, G. (1997). Perspective taking: Imagining how another feels versus imagining how you would feel. *Personality and Social Psychology Bulletin, 23,* 751–758.

Batson, C. D., Fultz, J. N., & Schoenrade, P. A. (1987). Distress and empathy: Two qualitatively distinct vicarious emotions with different motivational consequences. *Journal of Personality, 55,* 19–40.

Batson, C. D., Klein, T. R., Highberger, L., & Shaw, L. L. (1995). Immorality from empathy-induced altruism: When compassion and justice conflict. *Journal of Personality and Social Psychology, 68,* 1042–1054.

Batson, C. D., Kobrynowicz, D., Dinnerstein, J. L., Kampf, H. C., & Wilson, A. D. (1997). In a very different voice: Unmasking moral hypocrisy. *Journal of Personality and Social Psychology, 72,* 1335–1348.

Batson, C. D., & Moran, T. (1999). Empathy-induced altruism in a Prisoner's Dilemma. *European Journal of Social Psychology, 29,* 909–924.

Batson, C. D., Polycarpou, M. P., Harmon-Jones, E., Imhoff, H. J., Mitchener, E. C., Bednar, L. L., Klein, T. R., & Highberger, L. (1997). Empathy and attitudes: Can feeling for a member of a stigmatized group improve feelings toward the group? *Journal of Personality and Social Psychology, 72,* 105–118.

Batson, C. D., Sager, K., Garst, E., Kang, M., Rubchinsky, K., & Dawson, K. (1997). Is empathy-induced helping due to self-other merging? *Journal of Personality and Social Psychology, 73,* 495–509.

Batson, C. D., & Shaw, L. L. (1991). Evidence for altruism: Toward a pluralism of prosocial motives. *Psychological Inquiry, 2,* 107–122.

Batson, C. D., Thompson, E. R., Seuferling, G., Whitney, H., & Strongman, J. (1999). Moral hypocrisy: Appearing moral to oneself without being so. *Journal of Personality and Social Psychology, 77,* 525–537.

Batson, C. D., Turk, C. L., Shaw, L. L., & Klein, T. R. (1995). Information function of empathic emotion: Learning that we value the other's welfare. *Journal of Personality and Social Psychology, 68,* 300–313.

Batson, C. D., & Weeks, J. L. (1996). Mood effects of unsuccessful helping: Another test of the empathy-altruism hypothesis. *Personality and Social Psychology Bulletin, 22,* 148–157.

Bavelas, J. B., Black, A., Lemeray, C. R., & Mullett, J. (1987). Motor mimicry as primative empathy. In N. Eisenberg & J. Strayer (Eds.), *Empathy and its development* (pp. 317–338). New York: Cambridge University Press.

Becker, H. (1931). Some forms of sympathy: A phenomenological analysis. *Journal of Abnormal and Social Psychology, 26,* 58–68.

Berger, S. (1962). Conditioning through vicarious instigation. *Psychological Review, 69,* 450–466.

Brothers, L. (1989). A biological perspective on empathy. *American Journal of Psychiatry, 146,* 10–19.

Campbell, D. T. (1975). On the conflicts between biological and social evolution and between psychology and moral tradition. *American Psychologist, 30,* 1103–1126.

Carlo, G., Eisenberg, N., Troyer, D., Switzer, G., & Speer, A. L. (1991). The altruistic personality: In what contexts is it apparent? *Journal of Personality and Social Psychology, 61,* 450–458.

Cialdini, R. B., Brown, S. L., Lewis, B. P., Luce, C., & Neuberg, S. L. (1997). Reinterpreting the empathy-altruism relationship: When one into one equals oneness. *Journal of Personality and Social Psychology, 73,* 481–494.

Cialdini, R. B., Schaller, M., Houlihan, D., Arps, K., Fultz, J., & Beaman, A. L. (1987). Empathy-based helping: Is it selflessly or selfishly motivated? *Journal of Personality and Social Psychology, 52,* 749–758.

Coke, J. S., Batson, C. D., & McDavis, K. (1978). Empathic mediation of helping: A two-stage model. *Journal of Personality and Social Psychology, 36*, 752–766.

Cooley, C. H. (1902). *Human nature and the social order.* New York: Scribner's.

Darwin, C. (1871). *The descent of man and selection in relation to sex.* New York: Appleton.

Davis, M. H. (1994). *Empathy: A social psychological approach.* Madison, WI: Brown and Benchmark.

Davis, M. R. (1985). Perceptual and affective reverberation components. In A. P. Goldstein & G. Y. Michaels (Eds.), *Empathy: Development, training, and consequences* (pp. 62–108). Hillsdale, NJ: Erlbaum.

Dawes, R., van de Kragt, A. J. C., & Orbell, J. M. (1988). Not me or thee but we: The importance of group identity in eliciting cooperation in dilemma situations: Experimental manipulations. *Acta Psychologica, 68*, 83–97.

Dawes, R., van de Kragt, A. J. C., & Orbell, J. M. (1990). Cooperation for the benefit of us—not me, or my conscience. In J. J. Mansbridge (Ed.), *Beyond self-interest* (pp. 97–110). Chicago: University of Chicago Press.

*de Waal, F. B. M. (1996). *Good natured: The origins of right and wrong in humans and other animals.* Cambridge, MA: Harvard University Press.

Dimberg, U., Thunberg, M., & Elmehed, K. (2000). Unconscious facial reactions to emotional facial expressions. *Psychological Science, 11*, 86–89.

Dovidio, J. F., Allen, J. L., & Schroeder, D. A. (1990). The specificity of empathy-induced helping: Evidence for altruistic motivation. *Journal of Personality and Social Psychology, 59*, 249–260.

Dovidio, J. F., Gaertner, S. L., & Johnson, J. D. (1999, October). *New directions in prejudice and prejudice reduction: The role of cognitive representations and affect.* Paper presented at the annual meeting of the Society of Experimental Social Psychology, St. Louis, MO.

Dymond, R. F. (1950). Personality and empathy. *Journal of Consulting Psychology, 14*, 343–350.

Eisenberg, N., & Miller, P. (1987). Empathy and prosocial behavior. *Psychological Bulletin, 101*, 91–119.

Eisenberg, N., Miller, P. A., Schaller, M., Fabes, R. A., Fultz, J., Shell, R., & Shea, C. L. (1989). The role of sympathy and altruistic personality traits in helping: A re-examination. *Journal of Personality, 57*, 41–67.

Eisenberg, N., & Strayer, J. (Eds.). (1987). *Empathy and its development.* New York: Cambridge University Press.

Englis, B. G., Vaughan, K. B., & Lanzetta, J. T. (1982). Conditioning of counter-empathetic emotional responses. *Journal of Experimental Social Psychology, 18*, 375–391.

Freud, S. (1922). *Group psychology and the analysis of the ego.* London: International Psycho-Analytic Press.

Freud, S. (1930). *Civilization and its discontents* (J. Riviere, Trans.). London: Hogarth.

Gilligan, C. (1982). *In a different voice: Psychological theory and women's development.* Cambridge, MA: Harvard University Press.

Hatfield, E., Cacioppo, J. T., & Rapson, R. L. (1992). Primitive emotional contagion. In M. S. Clark (Ed.), *Emotion and social behavior* (pp. 151–177). Newbury Park, CA: Sage.

Heider, F. (1958). *The psychology of interpersonal relations.* New York: Wiley.

*Hoffman, M. L. (1981). Is altruism part of human nature? *Journal of Personality and Social Psychology, 40*, 121–137.

Hoffman, M. L. (1989). Empathic emotions and justice in society. *Social Justice Research, 3*, 283–311.

Hornstein, H. A. (1982). Promotive tension: Theory and research. In V. Derlega & J. Grzelak (Eds.), *Cooperation and helping behavior: Theories and research* (pp. 229–248). New York: Academic Press.

Hume, D. (1896). *A treatise of human nature* (L. A. Selby-Bigge, Ed.). Oxford: Oxford University Press. (Original work published 1740)

Ickes, W. (1993). Empathic accuracy. *Journal of Personality, 61*, 587–610.

James, W. (1910/1982). The moral equivalent of war. In *The works of William James: Essays in religion and morality* (pp. 162–173). Cambridge, MA: Harvard University Press.

Jarymowicz, M. (1992). Self, we, and other(s): Schemata, distinctiveness, and altruism. In P. M. Oliner, S. P. Oliner, L. Baron, L. A. Blum, D. L. Krebs, & M. Z. Smolenska (Eds.), *Embracing the other: Philosophical, psychological, and historical perspectives on altruism* (pp. 194–212). New York: New York University Press.

Kant, I. (1898). *Kant's Critique of Practical Reason and other works on the theory of ethics* (4th ed., T. K. Abbott, Trans.). New York: Longmans, Green. (Original work published 1785)

Kohlberg, L. (1976). Moral stages and moralization: The cognitive-developmental approach. In T. Lickona (Ed.), *Moral development and behavior: Theory, research, and social issues* (pp. 31–53). New York: Holt, Rinehart and Winston.

Kohler, W. (1929). *Gestalt psychology.* New York: Liveright.

Krebs, D. L. (1975). Empathy and altruism. *Journal of Personality and Social Psychology, 32*, 1134–1146.

Lerner, M. J. (1982). The justice motive in human relations and the economic model of man: A radical analysis of facts and fictions. In V. J. Derlega & J. Grzelak (Eds.), *Cooperation and helping behavior: Theories and research* (pp. 249–278). New York: Academic Press.

Levenson, R. W., & Ruef, A. M. (1992). Empathy: A physiological substrate. *Journal of Personality and Social Psychology, 63,* 234–246.

Lipps, T. (1903). *Grundlegung der Aesthetek: I.* Leipzig, Germany: Voss.

Luks, A. (1988). Helper's high. *Psychology Today, 22* (10), 39–42.

MacLean, P. D. (1973). *A triune concept of the brain and behavior.* Toronto: University of Toronto Press.

*Mansbridge, J. J. (Ed.). (1990). *Beyond self-interest.* Chicago: University of Chicago Press.

Maslach, C. (1982). *Burnout: The cost of caring.* Englewood Cliffs, NJ: Prentice-Hall.

McDougall, W. (1908). *An introduction to social psychology.* London: Methuen.

Mead, G. H. (1934). *Mind, self, and society.* Chicago: University of Chicago Press.

Murphy, G. (1947). *Personality: A biological approach to origins and structure.* New York: Harper.

*Oliner, S. P., & Oliner, P. M. (1988). *The altruistic personality: Rescuers of Jews in Nazi Europe.* New York: Free Press.

Piaget, J. (1965). *The moral judgment of the child.* New York: Free Press. (Original work published 1932)

Piliavin, J. A., & Charng, H.-W. (1990). Altruism: A review of recent theory and research. *American Sociological Review, 16,* 27–65.

*Piliavin, J. A., Dovidio, J. F., Gaertner, S. L., & Clark, R. D., III (1981). *Emergency intervention.* New York: Academic Press.

Rawls, J. (1971). *A theory of justice.* Cambridge, MA: Harvard University Press.

Ribot, T. (1911). *The psychology of the emotions* (2nd ed.). New York: Scribner's.

Rogers, C. R. (1975). Empathic: An unappreciated way of being. *The Counseling Psychologist, 5,* 2–10.

Schaller, M., & Cialdini, R. B. (1988). The economics of empathic helping: Support for a mood-management motive. *Journal of Experimental Social Psychology, 24,* 163–181.

Schroeder, D. A., Dovidio, J. F., Sibicky, M. E., Matthews, L. L., & Allen, J. L. (1988). Empathy and helping behavior: Egoism or altruism? *Journal of Experimental Social Psychology, 24,* 333–353.

Schwartz, S. H. (1992). Universals in the content and structure of values: Theoretical advances and empirical tests in 20 countries. In M. P. Zanna (Ed.), *Advances in experimental social psychology* (Vol. 25, pp. 1–65). San Diego, CA: Academic Press.

Shaw, L. L., Batson, C. D., & Todd, R. M. (1994). Empathy avoidance: Forestalling feeling for another in order to escape the motivational consequences. *Journal of Personality and Social Psychology, 67,* 879–887.

Shelton, M. L., & Rogers, R. W. (1981). Fear-arousing and empathy-arousing appeals to help: The pathos of persuasion. *Journal of Applied Social Psychology, 11,* 366–378.

Smith, A. (1853). *The theory of moral sentiments.* London: Alex Murray. (Original work published 1759)

Smith, K. D., Keating, J. P., & Stotland, E. (1989). Altruism reconsidered: The effect of denying feedback on a victim's status to empathic witnesses. *Journal of Personality and Social Psychology, 57,* 641–650.

Spencer, H. (1870). *The principles of psychology* (Vol. 1, 2nd ed.). London: Williams and Norgate.

Staub, E. (1974). Helping a person in distress: Social, personality, and stimulus determinants. In L. Berkowitz (Ed.), *Advances in experimental social psychology* (Vol. 7, pp. 293–341). New York: Academic Press.

Staub, E. (1989). Individual and societal (group) values in a motivational perspective and their role in benevolence and harmdoing. In N. Eisenberg, J. Reykowski, & E. Staub (Eds.), *Social and moral values: Individual and societal perspectives* (pp. 45–61). Hillsdale, NJ: Erlbaum.

Steins, G., & Wicklund, R. A. (1996). Perspective-taking, conflict, and press: Drawing an *E* on your forehead. *Basic and Applied Social Psychology, 18,* 319–346.

*Stotland, E. (1969). Exploratory investigations of empathy. In L. Berkowitz (Ed.), *Advances in experimental social psychology* (Vol. 4, pp. 271–313). New York: Academic Press.

Stotland, E., Mathews, K. E., Sherman, S. E., Hansson, R. O., & Richardson, B. Z. (1978). *Empathy, fantasy, and helping.* Beverly Hills, CA: Sage.

Tajfel, H. (1981). *Human groups and social categories: Studies in social psychology.* Cambridge, England: Cambridge University Press.

Titchener, E. B. (1909). *Lectures on the experimental psychology of the thought processes.* New York: Macmillan.

Truax, C. B., & Carkuff, R. R. (1967). *Toward effective counseling and psychotherapy.* Chicago: Aldine.

Turner, J. C. (1987). *Rediscovering the social group: A self-categorization theory*. London: Basil Blackwell.

*Wallach, M. A., & Wallach, L. (1983). *Psychology's sanction for selfishness: The error of egoism in theory and therapy*. San Francisco: Freeman.

Williams, R. (1989). *The trusting heart: Great news about Type A behavior*. New York: Random House.

Wispé, L. (1968). Sympathy and empathy. In D. L. Sills (Ed.), *International encyclopedia of the social sciences* (Vol. 15, pp. 441–447). New York: Free Press.

Wispé, L. (1986). The distinction between sympathy and empathy: To call forth a concept a word is needed. *Journal of Personality and Social Psychology, 50*, 314–321.

*Wispé, L. (1991). *The psychology of sympathy*. New York: Plenum.

Wundt, W. (1897). *Ethics: An investigation of the laws of the moral life* (Vol. 1). New York: Macmillan.

Zahn-Waxler, C., & Radke-Yarrow, M. (1990). The origins of empathic concern. *Motivation and Emotion, 14*, 107–130.

36

How We Become Moral

The Sources of Moral Motivation

Michael Schulman

The front-page stories in our newspapers provide us, almost daily, with horrific descriptions of murders, assaults, rapes, and tyrannies. Yet there are other stories—usually deeper in the pages of the paper, with smaller headlines—that recount extraordinary acts of moral courage, kindness, and self-sacrifice.

In trying to explain the good and bad of our species, we psychologists (like newspaper editors) have also paid much more attention to our malevolence than our morality. In classical psychoanalytic theory, for example, aggression and acquisitiveness are viewed as fundamental to our natures, whereas our moral motives emerge only after an arduous process of socialization (primarily through the supposed resolution of the Oedipus complex, at about age 7, according to Freud, 1921/1960). Similarly, in prominent behavioral theories, concern for others is based on learned, or *secondary*, reinforcers that are derived from more egocentric primary reinforcers (e.g., Hull, 1952; Skinner, 1971).

Such motivational theories explain behavior in terms of some benefit or reinforcement to the individual doing the behaving. But morality is about *getting reinforced by some benefit to an-* *other*. Therefore, a theory of moral motivation has to account for the sources of this capacity to be reinforced by beneficial outcomes to others—an unusual challenge.

Correspondingly, a theory of moral education has to figure out how to strengthen this capacity so that individuals become truly concerned about the well-being of others, rather than behaving well merely to acquire external rewards such as money or praise, or to avoid punishers such as a spanking or ostracism. This, too, is challenging because traditional motivational research has been focused much more on how already-established reinforcers (like food, money, and praise) strengthen behavior than on how to go about strengthening reinforcers (Schulman, 1990, 1996).

Unfortunately, even the "moral development" theories of Piaget (1965) and Kohlberg (1969) offer little insight into moral motivation. These theorists paid little attention to the *sources of* and *individual differences in* our moral motives. Instead, they looked for universals (or "stages") in children's *conceptions* of justice and propriety as they age (conceptions which, by the way, rarely have been found to correlate with measures of moral action such as helping or honesty; see Schulman and Mekler, 1994, pp. 16–17).

My goal in this chapter is to show that our moral motives are as primary, powerful, and emotionally intense as our aggressive and acquisitive ones; that concern for others emerges *spontaneously* in very young children (unconnected to any developmental stages and long before the Oedipus complex is supposedly resolved); and that morality is so crucial to our survival as a species that it has evolved in *three* separate forms, producing significant individual differences in "moral styles."

Murder and mayhem may grab the headlines, but if kindness, or at least civility, were not more common, then the human race would likely have gone the way of the dinosaurs. Indeed, various studies show that children perform far more helpful and cooperative interactions than hostile ones (Hay & Rheingold, 1984; Walters, Pearce, & Dahms, 1957), although the hostile ones tend to get noticed more.

A Theory of Moral Motivation

Mark Twain (1967), contemplating the sources of morality, reckoned that "there are several good protections against temptations but the surest is cowardice" (p. 4). Obviously, fear of punishment does keep some people from yielding to temptations and doing harm—at least some of the time. But we do not ordinarily think of fear of punishment as a moral motive. On the contrary, the moral person resists temptation and treats others well out of "internal" motives, doing so even when he or she can get away with doing otherwise.

So what is the source of our moral motives? Actually, one can distinguish at least three independent sources—empathy, principles, and moral affiliations—suggesting that nature has been engaging in what engineers call "redundant" design. Engineers build in *redundancy* so that vital mechanisms have backup systems in case they fail. Nature often uses the same strategy, which is presumably why many of our vital organs and senses come in pairs, such as our kidneys, ovaries, eyes, and ears.

If moral motivation does derive from three independent sources (indicating redundant design), it suggests that consciences, like kidneys, are critical to our survival. We, like all social animals, flourish as our group flourishes, and our group flourishes best when there is harmony and helpfulness among members. But harmony and helpfulness are not automatic for us. No, we are eminently capable of harming each other and are frequently roused to do so. Nor, like some social animals, do we have instinctive mechanisms to help us resolve conflicts (e.g., we do not automatically terminate an attack against an opponent who signals submission by baring his neck). Instead, what we humans do have, or are capable of having, are powerful consciences that move us to care about others and aspire toward high moral ideals.

What Does "Moral" Mean?

Philosophers, theologians, talk show hosts, and countless others have argued endlessly about the meaning of *moral*. Some of the confusion arises from the fact that in common discourse the word has more than one meaning. As used in this chapter, *moral* refers only to *acts intended to produce kind and/or fair outcomes*. This is a core meaning of the term in all major ethical and religious traditions and probably is its most common usage.

Thus, according to this definition, when we call an act moral, it is not because of some physical aspect of the behavior or even because some good was achieved; rather, it is because we have inferred that some *good intention* lay behind the act, that the actor's true goal was to produce a kind outcome to benefit one or more others, or a fair outcome to provide each relevant party with the benefit he or she deserves (typically based on considerations of equity or equality). In other words, we have inferred that the true reinforcer for the act was benefit to one or more others, and that the act was not undertaken out of coercion or obligation or to induce reciprocity. (When we refer to *people* as moral, and not just their acts, it is because we believe their actions *generally* spring from such benevolent intentions.)

But the intention to produce kind and fair outcomes is not the only meaning of moral. For example, *sexual morality* generally refers to refraining from sex except in approved ways under authorized circumstances, and its motive sources (such as religious and community traditions, sexual rivalries, taboos, and aversions) are very different from those motivating the inclination to treat others kindly and fairly. Indeed, many of us know "good" (that is, *kind*) people who do not adhere to traditional sexual codes, as well as "bad" (that is, *mean*) people who do. Sexual behavior that might be censured in certain sexuality-based moralities (such as premarital or gay sex) might not even enter into considerations of character in a morality based on kindness and fairness. (In this regard, because we as a society are less inclined than earlier generations to base judgments of character on sexual behavior, when religious leaders and mental health professionals call for a return to traditional sexual mores, they frequently justify their position more in terms of claims about physical and psychological health than virtue; e.g., Lickona, 1991, p. 357.)

In another different conception of morality, moral status is contingent on obedience to authorities, such as to parents or religious or political leaders. Here, too, the motivational sources are not the same as those that prompt kindness and fairness. Indeed, there are many instances when the morality of obedience and the morality of kindness and fairness pull in opposite directions (which is why, in this day and age, few would accept "I was just following orders" as a tenable moral defense).

The Three Moral Systems

A comprehensive understanding of moral motivation must take into account three separate and independent sources: (a) the arousal of empathy; (b) moral affiliations (or identifications with moral models); and (c) the commitment to principles or personal standards of right and wrong. In more experiential terms, one might say we become moral because we are: (a) moved by people's feelings (especially their suffering); (b) moved by the goodness of moral models; and (c) moved by ideas of the "good," such as noble principles and ideals.

Empathy

Empathy refers to that remarkable capacity we humans have to experience what other people are feeling, to imagine ourselves in another's *psychological* place and feel his or her joys and sorrows as if they were our own. Like many psychological attributes, the capacity for empathy may be a normally distributed characteristic, and, as Martin Hoffman (1977) and others have demonstrated, children often begin to exhibit signs of empathy, spontaneously, by their 18th month. For example, children of this age

will show concern and sadness when a parent or sibling appears sad and also offer help, say, by offering to share their "comforter" blanket (Young, Fox, & Zahn-Waxler, 1999). Empathy, thus, becomes a source of moral motivation by inducing altruistic acts to make someone else feel better.

Empathic responses are akin to reflexes in the sense that they are unlearned reactions to the emotional states of others. And they can be extraordinarily intense. Anyone who has been unable to ease the pain of someone he or she has *felt for*—a parent with a hurt or sick child, for instance—knows how intense the psychological discomfort of an empathic response can be. But children and adults do not feel empathy for everyone; someone perceived as an enemy or even a competitor is not likely to arouse empathy (see Cassell, this volume). The more similar we believe others are to us, the more likely we will be to empathize with them and treat them well (Eisenberg, 1983).

A growing body of research by C. Daniel Batson (1990; see also Batson, Ahmad, Lishner, & Tsang, this volume), among others, has demonstrated a direct relationship between empathy and altruism: We tend to help and protect those with whom we empathize and are less likely to do them harm (Feshbach & Feshbach, 1969; Roberts & Strayer, 1996; Toi & Batson, 1982). Conversely, low empathy scores are associated with a higher propensity for antisocial behavior and delinquency (Cohen & Strayer, 1996).

The recent research into *William's syndrome*, a genetically based disorder, which (like *Down's syndrome*) has physiognomic, physiological, and behavioral manifestations, may help uncover the genetic roots of empathy. Among the characteristics of those born with this syndrome are unusually strong empathic responses to others (Bower, 2000).

Moral Affiliations

Moral affiliations, our second source of moral motivation, produce morality through identification with "good" others such as a parent, a mentor, a political or religious figure, or even a fictional character. It is common for children to love goodness in others, spontaneously and without instruction or prompting. This may be why so many children are enthralled by Mr. Rogers, Barney, and other caring characters. No one has to teach them this response or force them to watch these TV shows. Children do not turn on *Mr. Rogers* or *Barney* for adventure or laughs; no, they watch—avidly and ardently—because they are naturally attracted to exemplars of goodness.

Through such identifications with moral exemplars, children learn what to say to themselves and what they *should* do when faced with temptations, their own nasty impulses, or others in need. They want to live up to the standards of the admired models, to be like them, feel one with them, and be worthy of their admiration in turn. The words and images of the model then become guides for behavior (Sears, Maccoby, & Levin, 1957).

As children enter the grade school years, their moral models may become less genteel models of virtue than Mr. Rogers and Barney. For boys, they are often action heroes who, for the sake of justice and decency, zap the "bad guys" into oblivion. Heroines for girls are frequently caring figures with spunk and determination who can take charge when someone needs help. In their games and fantasies, children commonly take on the personas of their heroes, identifying with them quite literally—sometimes even wearing their costumes—and internalizing their values. (Unfortunately, some youngsters identify more readily with destructive figures, particularly if they appear powerful, perhaps because these children are enticed more by images of domination and force than by images of love.)

Many of us have had moral models—some real, some fictional—that have stayed in our thoughts throughout our lives, guiding and inspiring us to express our best selves. It might be a religious figure like Christ or the Rebbe, a loving grandparent, a fictional character like Atticus Finch in *To Kill a Mockingbird,* or the stirring presence of Martin Luther King Jr.; for Martin Luther King Jr., it was Gandhi.

Our communions with our moral models are frequently intense (even if they are fictional characters or people we have only read about), and our desire to honor and feel one with them gives them substantial influence over us, even leading to confessions of transgressions in order to reestablish our sense of belonging in the community of the good (Sears et al., 1957). Emulating such good figures and taking on their values as our own makes us, like them, worthy beings. And often, through them, we feel embedded in a moral community (e.g., our family, church, lodge, country) that provides us with a source of pride.

Through internalization, children begin to judge their behavior as "right" and "wrong," and not just as effective or ineffective in getting them what they want. Like empathy, affiliation-based morality starts very early, as young as age 2, and may also be a normally distributed characteristic. Given the centrality of love in the internalization process, it is not surprising that internalization of parental rules is most evident in children whose parents treat them with warmth and sensitivity, explain their rules clearly, give firm correctives, but do not rely on physical punishment (Grusec, 1966; Hart, DeWolf, Wozniak, & Burts, 1992; Londerville & Main, 1981; Stayton, Hogan, & Salter-Ainsworth, 1971; Zahn-Waxler, Radke-Yarrow, & King, 1979).

Principles

The third foundation stone of moral motivation is the formation of principles or personal standards of right and wrong. These are rules of conduct that we believe we ought to live up to regardless of the approval or disapproval of parents or any authority, and even when we do not feel empathy for those with whom we interact. Our moral standards are sustained by our imaginations—because we can foresee that living up to them will bring about a more ideal world.

Once such standards are established, we try to make our actions consistent with them and pay a price in self-esteem when we fall short (Greenstein, 1976; Rokeach, 1973). Personal standards, then, are the rules of conduct we espouse for the sake of our ideals. A single precept, such as "Do unto others as you would have them do unto you," if adopted as a personal standard and invoked at moral choice points, can affect one's behavior in a great range of circumstances.

Like the development of empathy and moral affiliations, children appear to develop principles of right and wrong spontaneously by the age of 3. For example, young children seem to recognize with little or no instruction that harming is bad and helping is good. Even children who do not always do or prefer the good recognize that one should help and should not harm. Ask a 3-year-old in a nursery school if it is okay to eat on one side of the room. If there is a rule against it, he will say no. Then ask him, "What if teacher says it's okay?" He'll answer, "Yes, then it's okay." Next ask him if it is okay to push Johnny off the chair if you want to sit in it. Again he will say no (even if he sometimes pushes). Then ask again, "What if teacher says it's okay?" He will reply, "No, teacher shouldn't say that."

On their own, children seem to recognize that there should be rules against harming, rules that are not based on authorities. In a series of studies, Elliot Turiel (1983) and his colleagues have repeatedly demonstrated this seemingly intrinsic recognition of the significance of moral rules (rules about behavior that impacts on feelings) in comparison to other kinds of rules (such as conventional rules about where one is supposed to eat). Moreover, children are much more accepting of their parents' enforcement of moral rules (such as a rule against stealing) than conventional rules (such as rules about chores).

Along with this intrinsic sensitivity to harming and helping, personal moral standards may also derive from the child's intrinsic "mastery motive." Psychologists have long recognized that children have a natural desire to gain mastery over the environment and excel (MacTurk, McCarthy, Vietze, & Yarrow, 1987; White, 1959). The mastery goals of babies are biologically determined, but as children get older, their notions of what is worth mastering come increasingly under the influence of the culture they grow up in, particularly by what their parents and significant others extol as the highest human achievements.

When the adults in their lives define excellence in terms of moral striving, and not just as achievement in sports or school or business, children become more apt to strive to live up to moral values. As Martin Hoffman (1975) found, parents who openly espouse "altruistic" values such as "showing consideration of other people's feelings" and "going out of one's way to help other people" were more likely to have children who "care about how other kids feel and try not to hurt their feelings" and who "stick up for some kid that the other kids are making fun of or calling names."

The evaluative categories "good" and "bad" are already very important for 3-year-olds, who readily apply them to their own actions (DiVesta & Stauber, 1971; Masters, Furman, & Barden, 1977). When children rank themselves high on the good/bad scale, they are laying the foundation for the development of a positive *moral identity*, seeing themselves as moral agents who judge their actions according to whether they meet moral criteria. They then begin to define themselves in terms of their general moral goals (e.g., "I want to be a good person") and their moral affiliations and positions on moral issues (e.g., "I am a good Christian"; "I'm for civil rights"; "I'm against the death penalty"). Once a positive moral identity is established and one thinks of oneself as a person who "stands for the good," one's self-esteem depends on behaving in a manner that is consistent with that identity (Hart & Fegley, 1995).

We adopt moral standards as our own for the same reason that we adopt any behavioral standards: because we believe they will lead to desirable outcomes. Children come to believe that living up to moral standards will produce desirable outcomes through personal experience and observation (they find that sharing toys leads to more fun with playmates), as well as through their imaginations (they foresee the kinds of behavior that will lead to a better world).

Their beliefs are also affected by inspirational and persuasive messages from the adults and peers with whom they interact. Of all the creatures on earth, only human beings can be inspired toward higher ideals; indeed, one might say that we are the inspirable species. Adolescents seem particularly susceptible to inspirational messages that convey a vision of a better world that is within reach (Bronfenbrenner, 1962).

Young children are also responsive to persuasive arguments about moral rules. June Tapp (Tapp & Kohlberg, 1971) coined the lovely phrase "persuasion to virtue" based on her research finding that children as young as 5 could understand the connection between moral rules and the reasons given to support them. Moreover, she found that children this age believe that rules and laws can be changed if they are more harmful than good. In other research, children were more likely to adopt parental standards as their own when they were persuaded that their parents' rules were fair. Youngsters who participated in formulating the rules they were asked to follow were particularly committed to those standards (Elder, 1963; Pikas, 1961).

Additionally, Eva Fogelman (1994), in her research on Christian rescuers of Jews during the Holocaust, has isolated the same three motivational sources that I have just described. Some rescued Jews, risking their own lives and those of family members, out of empathy, saying they were moved by the suffering they witnessed and could not turn their backs on those who were victimized. Others rescued more out of principle than empathy, explaining that they saw evil and could not live with themselves if they did not take a stand against it. These people talked in terms of injustice rather than an emotional connection to suffering individuals. Still others rescued because of their connection to a moral leader or moral community, such as their family or church.

In sum, looking at our three sources of moral motivation, one might say that morality is based on the *head* (on principles or cognitively based standards of right and wrong and the recognition of oneself as a moral agent), on the *heart* (on empathic reactions to another's feelings), and on the *moral community* (on identification with moral exemplars such as parents, heroes, and moral groups).

Moral Emotions

Associated with each moral motivational process are positive and negative feeling states that influence the kinds of actions we take toward others. The negative feelings are *guilt* (connected to empathy), *shame* (connected to moral affiliations), and *self-loathing* (connected to principles). When we are empathically "inside" the feelings of another, any pain we inflict on him or her boomerangs back to us in the form of guilt. There is some evidence for guilt in toddlers (Zahn-Waxler et al., 1979), but it becomes more common as children approach their fourth or fifth year.

When we violate the standards of admired and internalized moral models, we feel unworthy of their love and ashamed to face them. When we violate our own moral principles, we experience self-loathing, a feeling of being ashamed of oneself, of not being able to live with oneself.

On the positive emotional side, we experience empathic good feelings when making someone with whom we empathize feel good; we feel proud and worthy of our moral model's love when we live up to his or her standards; and we feel proud of ourselves and have a sense of personal integrity or wholeness (and no cognitive dissonance) when living up to our own moral standards.

These emotional states, both the positive and the negative, are powerful motivators. For example, when people describe their experience of guilt, they often use words like *agonizing* and *overwhelming* to convey the intensity of their suffering. The negative moral emotions are strong enough to lead some to thoughts of suicide. On the positive side, some people are brought to tears of reverence in the presence of their moral heroes or when they read the speeches of Abraham Lincoln or the Bill of Rights or other tracts that embody humankind's highest ideals and noblest sentiments.

Moral Styles

As any parent with more than one child knows, from early childhood, individuals appear to differ in their relative endowments of empathy, their affinity for moral principles, and their connections with moral exemplars. Some children seem to be naturally more empathic than others, whereas others seem more prone to articulate personal standards or principles for themselves; still others get attached more readily to moral exemplars and express their morality through their affiliations with caring individuals and organizations.

Here is where redundancy comes in: A child who is low on empathy may turn out to be a person of high principle, or vice versa. Parents may worry because their child does not seem to have a "good heart," in the sense that he does not spontaneously put himself in another's place or feel deeply for others. But this child may turn out to be a person of honor and moral courage, someone with high ideals and a high capacity for self-loathing when he fails to live up to those ideals.

Recognizing these three sources of moral motivation and the moral styles they generate can be useful for a therapist, educator, or parent, especially when dealing with children who are having social problems. By assessing the relative strengths of these three sources of moral motivation in a child, one can ascertain whether empathic appeals (such as "Think how you would feel") are more or less likely to be effective than appeals in terms of ideals (such as "What kind of world would it be if everyone did that?") or affiliations (such as "Is that the way a Scout is supposed to behave?").

Also, if one recognizes serious deficiencies in any of the three areas, such as a child who experiences little empathy for others or only for very few others, one can set up a program to bolster that area, say, by talking more about feelings with the child and by widening his or her notion of who should be thought of as "us" and therefore worthy of empathy.

Parents may not put it into words, but they usually recognize these differences in their children. As one father told me after I discussed these moral styles in a lecture, "You've just described my three daughters. Each is moral, but each in her own way." I am currently developing an assessment instrument to evaluate children's relative strengths and weaknesses in these three moral domains.

Fostering Morality in Children

There is ample evidence that children's capacities for the development of empathy, moral affiliations, and principles emerge between the second and fourth years of life, beginning shortly after children start to toddle about and maneuver independently in their social worlds (Burleson, 1982). There is also ample evidence that how these capacities unfold can be affected by the social environments in which children develop, including the ways they are treated and instructed by parents, peers, and significant others. In other words, during their early years, children spontaneously develop what might be called *susceptibilities* to moral influence and instruction. These susceptibilities can be partitioned into our three domains.

Thus, when a parent says, "Think how you would feel if someone did that to you," she is tapping into the child's empathic capacities. When she invokes the Golden Rule or explains that "everyone here deserves to be treated equally," she is engaging his capacity to develop principles. And when she frowns and tells him, "It disappoints me when you treat someone that way" or "That's not how members of our family behave," she is engaging his capacity for moral affiliation.

Theorists have long debated whether morality is "taught" or "caught," with some arguing that morality needs to be instilled through explicit demands and declarations about right and wrong (Bennett, 1993), and others contending that morality is best instilled by bringing up children in an atmosphere where adults express moral concerns and provide moral models (Bryan & Walbek, 1970). According to the "moral motivation" framework presented here,

both approaches have value, and both have a place in each of the three moral domains.

Fostering Morality Through Empathy

Studies of how parents foster empathy find that an important technique is direct instruction to children to put themselves in another's place (Barnett, Howard, King, & Dino, 1980; Hughes, Tingle, & Sawin, 1981; Krevans & Gibbs, 1996). Children need to learn the impact of their behavior on others, and often this can be accomplished with simple reminders such as "Think how you would feel" or "Remember when you were treated that way."

When such reminders are not sufficient, one can intensify the empathy-arousing stimuli by giving the child more detailed information about the other person, especially about his or her strivings and struggles, or by having him imagine or even role-play aspects of the other person's experience (Chandler, 1973; Iannotti, 1978).

Empathy starts from an awareness of another's feelings, and one way parents can educate their children about feelings is by including discussions of emotions and their causes in everyday conversations with their children, including accounts of the parents' own emotional experiences (Feshbach, 1983). Various studies show that helping children focus on the feelings of others and recognize the similarities between themselves and others will increase the likelihood of empathic responses to them (Houston, 1990; Krebs, 1975). It is also helpful when parents acknowledge and commend the child's tenderhearted feelings, point out and praise compassionate people in the community, and speak about their own tenderhearted impulses. Stories about compassionate fictional and real-life heroes, famous and unsung, will also help convey the message that empathic concern for others is both good and natural (see Schulman & Mekler, 1994, chap. 3).

Empathy leads to a desire to be helpful or ease someone's pain. But frequently children are too confused about how to help, or too shy or insecure to actually offer help or comfort. Prompts and instructions from parents and other caregivers on when and how to help can go a long way toward providing children with the know-how and courage to take that crucial step from *feeling for* someone to actually doing something on his or her behalf (Staub, 1971).

Fostering Morality Through Affiliations

Research teams led by Grazyna Kochanska (Kochanska, Aksan, & Koenig, 1995), Susan Londerville (Londerville & Main, 1981), and Donelda Stayton (Stayton et al., 1971) found that parents who were sensitive, accepting, and cooperative with their children and who handled them in a warm and affectionate manner had the most cooperative children. Even before they were 2 years old, children of such parents were showing signs of internalized controls, reminding themselves of parental injunctions.

Children apparently take far more seriously a rule or a reprimand from a parent who is ordinarily encouraging and accepting—one who they know is fundamentally on their side—than from one who is routinely restrictive and harsh. The goal of moral training is not an obedient child but a cooperative one, and the best way to produce a cooperative child turns out to be being a cooperative parent. Moral instruction often involves asking children to give up or postpone doing or getting things they want, which is not always easy for them. But it is much easier if they believe their parents truly want to help them achieve their goals (at least those goals that are not harmful to others or themselves).

Parents also foster internalization by giving children clearly and forcefully stated rules, and good reasons for following them (Clark et al., 1977; Sanders & Dadds, 1982). "Take turns playing with the toy" is easier for a child to understand than the simple command "Share!" When parents give reasons for their rules, such as "Everyone should have an equal chance to have fun," they teach a child about the purpose behind a rule and that being "good" means striving for certain openly stated values and not merely following parental orders blindly and mechanically. Only by understanding the reasons behind rules can a child carry moral lessons into new situations and also be better prepared to resist the inducements of *immoral* authority figures.

The studies conducted by Zahn-Waxler et al. (1979) affirm that punishment by parents was *not* associated with high altruism in children, and simply giving a child "prohibitions without explanations" worked *against* the development of altruism. On the other hand, increased internalization was associated with emotionally toned disapprovals and expressions of disap-

pointment over moral infractions (Radke-Yarrow & Zahn-Waxler, 1984).

Because internalization involves talking to oneself, parents and caregivers can teach children in very direct ways what to say to themselves in ordinarily troublesome situations. For example, if parents find that their youngster is likely to pick on a classmate after a bad day on the ball field, they can actually help him work out what he might tell himself when such occasions arise (such as, "It's not right to try to make myself feel better by making someone else feel bad"). Indeed, parents can provide specific instructions on many moral skills, such as conflict resolution, sportsmanship, constructive criticism, and welcoming.

Other useful techniques include *good behavior assignments* (called "mitzvahs" in traditional Jewish practice), in which a youngster must choose and perform a good deed that benefits someone, and *positive attributions*, in which a child who does something good (such as sharing, helping, or defending) is told that he has a "good heart" or that he is a kind person (Jensen & Moore, 1977; Toner, Moore, & Emmons, 1980). Most parenting manuals advise parents, probably wisely, to criticize the act, not the child, when their child misbehaves. With regard to prosocial behavior, research suggests that when a youngster is kind and fair, it is effective to praise the act *and* the child (see Schulman & Mekler, 1994, chap. 2).

Fostering Morality Through Principles

One can help a child develop personal standards through both *inspirational* and *practical* discourse. For example, moral ideals can be inspired by giving children a vision of a more humane and just world and teaching them that their actions as individuals count toward bringing those ideals into being (or toward subverting them). Most children want goodness to prevail and are readily inspired by visions of a better family, a better community, and a better world.

Practical messages are designed to get children to focus on the long-term effects of their actions, that is, on whether or not what they do will, in the long run, lead to worthy ends—for example, that giving everyone an equal chance and an equal say yields better outcomes than hogging and shoving and shouting each other down (Levitt, Weber, Clark, & McDonnell, 1985). Similarly, reminding them of occasions when they felt good after helping others should increase the probability that they will adopt a standard like "One should help others in need."

A technique that embraces both the inspirational and the practical taps into youngsters' natural eagerness to piece together their own visions of "the good." As Socrates and other moral philosophers have long established, questions like *What is a good life?* and *What is worth dying for?* have an almost magical allure for youth. The quest for answers, whether through dialogue, reading, or private reflection, can turn out to be transformative, stimulating youngsters to reason their way toward moral commitments and an articulated moral identity.

Discussions can also include the parents' own moral confusions ("I'm not sure if I'm harming or helping the homeless people on the street when I give them money"), as well as a sympathetic examination of the child's moral dilemmas (such as trying to satisfy opposing demands by friends).

While reasoning can help one ascertain what one truly values and whether one's actions are consistent with those values and an effective means to fulfill them, morality is never ultimately based on reason. One can never *prove* that the moral life is the best choice. As moral philosophers have pointed out, one cannot reason one's way from an "is" (a statement about the way things are) to an "ought" (a statement about the way things should be).

Actually, a moral inclination is more like a taste or an aesthetic response than it is a product of inference and deduction. A child does not reason her way to hating cruelty or loving goodness, or feeling empathy for someone's suffering, or being moved by noble ideals, just as she does not reason her way to hating spinach and loving ice cream; they all derive from her biological predispositions and personal history. One might say that the goal of moral education is to make kindness and fairness "taste good."

Whether moral education is based on empathy, affiliations, or principles, caregivers need to remember that moral growth is an ongoing process, and that morality is not a quality that one either does or does not possess in some universal and everlasting way (Hartshorne & May, 1930). Although there is longitudinal evidence for consistency in "prosocial dispositions" from early childhood into adulthood (Eisenberg et al., 1999), few of us, children or adults, always do the right thing, and most of us do better in

some areas than others (such as the person who will cheat on a spouse but not an employer). Moreover, new temptations and moral quandaries always arise, which makes it critically important to help the child develop his or her identity as a moral agent, as someone who *wants to* be moral and who, after moral lapses, resolves to do better the next time.

A positive moral identity is easier to sustain when there is sufficient optimism and hope that things can be made better. Children develop optimism and hope in various ways (Seligman, 1995; Snyder, 2000). One way they can be fostered in the moral sphere is by apprising youngsters of the successes of good people, especially when they band together. Stories about people making the world a better place are especially important nowadays because, in our "information age," even young children hear so much about cruelty and injustice that it easy for cynicism and hopelessness to set in at an early age (see Schulman & Mekler, 1994, chap. 4).

Schools can also make a contribution to the development of ideals. For example, they can highlight and take pride in their lofty mission, which is to pass on to students the best of human civilization in an atmosphere that is a true moral community, one in which everyone (students, teachers, secretaries, bus drivers, etc.) can expect kind and fair treatment. Schools can also include more moral content of various kinds in their curricula. For example, history not only can be taught as a series of momentous events carried out by important people or as the playing out of economic dialectics, but it also can include an analysis of the moral issues inherent in those momentous events and how those important people dealt with them (see Schulman, 1995, for a comprehensive school-based moral education program).

Religion and Morality

All religions draw from all three moral domains (empathy, affiliation, and principles), but different religions, or sects within religions, emphasize one domain more than another. Judaism, for example, stresses personal standards or principles, and much labor is devoted to figuring out how to apply them in everyday life. The Torah furnishes the principles, whereas the Talmud provides fervently reasoned disputations on how they should be lived.

Christianity emphasizes the affiliative domain: Morality stems primarily from one's relationship to Christ. Christ is always present, and one's commitment to others is mediated by his presence. One is good *for* Christ.

Hinduism stresses empathic bonds, as exemplified by the following quotation from the Hitopadesa, a sacred text: "As one's life is dear to oneself, so also are those of all beings. The good show compassion towards all living beings because of their resemblance to themselves."

Religions also motivate good behavior by threatening believers with God's wrath and eternal damnation. But doing good to avoid punishment is about concern for oneself, not others. Therefore, such actions would not be considered morally motivated behavior as the term has been defined here.

Religion has been a major source of moral inspiration in virtually every culture. It has also been a source of cruelty and strife. Gandhi was inspired by his religious beliefs. But so was the man who killed him. Religions teach the importance of kindness and justice, but sometimes only for fellow believers; sometimes they teach that there is virtue in torturing and exterminating non-believers. History provides many examples of atrocities committed in the name of a fervent and sincere morality. Are there lessons to be learned from these events?

Moral Pitfalls

There is certainly truth in the maxim "The road to hell is paved with good intentions." Considerable bad has been done by people who thought they were doing good. There are at least three reasons: yielding moral responsibility to others, thinking of others as inherently undesirable, and suppressing "bad" thoughts.

Yielding Moral Responsibility to Others

We yield our moral judgments to others because we believe they have special knowledge about right and wrong, say, because God is believed to have spoken to them or because their position gives them exclusive jurisdiction over the interpretation of God's words. They then become, in effect, the gatekeepers to heaven, and we can feel virtuous following their commands, even when they tell us to slaughter thousands (as happened in the Crusades and many other holy wars, before and since).

Similar abdications of moral responsibility occur in civil institutions, particularly when "obedience to authority" is taught as a preeminent virtue. Soldiers are commonly taught "Yours is not to reason why," which then allows them to justify unspeakable atrocities with the rejoinder "I was just following orders."

Thinking of Others as Inherently Undesirable

When others are considered inherently inferior or undesirable, one can feel righteous by isolating or enslaving them, or even wiping them out entirely. The moral rules of our group do not apply to the inherently undesirable. Jews, Gypsies, dark-skinned people, and homosexuals have been among the most frequent victims of such moral exclusion, but most peoples (races, religions, nationalities, castes, ethnic groups, classes, etc.) have, at some time in their history, known similar vilification and persecution.

The solution, of course, is to bring up children to believe that there are no *non*people, none who are inherently inferior or undesirable, none who are so unlike *us* that they fall beyond the moral boundary.

Suppressing "Bad" Thoughts

So-called bad thoughts, like those accompanying anger and envy, are common and natural. But people brought up to believe that "a bad thought is as bad as a bad deed" will often mislabel and deny such unwanted thoughts in order to maintain their positive self-concepts (a psychologically minded observer might then call their anger "unconscious"). This can lead to serious problems in self-regulation. For example, anger, whether acknowledged or not, generates an appetite for aggression. But before we can institute self-regulation strategies to sever the anger-aggression link, we must first recognize that we are experiencing anger. Only then can we tell ourselves, "I'm angry now and must take care not to strike out at this person." Such mislabeling is less likely to occur when we learn to judge our morality by what we do, not what we think.

Moral Versus Antisocial Motivations

Over the years, theorists have implicated an array of constructs to explain antisocial behavior, including aggressive instincts and drives; neuronal, genetic, and hormonal aberrations; disturbed personalities and weak superegos; dysfunctional families; abusive childhood experiences; negative peer pressure; cultural and media influences (such as violent films, books, and games); and various forms of social injustice, such as poverty and racism.

As with moral motivation, no single construct will explain all forms of antisocial impulses. The motive behind the violence of the cool, calculating mugger is very different from the wrath of the spurned lover, as it is from the premeditated cruelty of a sadist, an assassination by a zealous nationalist, a drive-by shooting to impress fellow gang members, or a response to inner voices that say "kill." Depending on the motive behind any given act of violence, it might be seen as a product of rationality or psychosis, as consistent with long-standing personality patterns or as an anomaly, emerging from exceptional passions or drastic circumstances; some might even see it as moral if its goal is to right some wrong or protect the innocent.

Efforts to reduce violence can focus either on decreasing the strength of people's antisocial motives or on strengthening the moral motives—or on both. Strategies that focus only on reducing antisocial motives contain the implicit assumption that aggression and avarice are predominantly products of social or psychological pathology, such as poverty, racism, alienation, repressed impulses, or arrested superego development. Presumably one does not have to promote morality; one merely has to clear up the pathology that is supposedly keeping people from being nice to each other (Schulman, 1990).

The position espoused here is quite different, contending that base behavior is frequently as much a product of *moral motivation deficits* (such as too little empathy, inadequate attachments to moral exemplars and a moral community, and a dearth of moral principles) as it is of unchecked antisocial impulses (see Hastings, Zahn-Waxler, Robinson, Usher, & Bridges, 2000). An implication of this moral motivation deficits position is that parents, teachers, and others who work with children need to take active steps to boost their charges' moral motivation. Children need to hear from adults that they are expected to treat others kindly and fairly, even when they would rather not. Unfortunately, many children nowadays

grow up without ever having heard this message clearly and forcefully.

Sometimes parents are afraid that their child will become *too* kind and sensitive to others and therefore too easily taken advantage of. Research does not support this worry. Children and adults who are kind out of empathy or principle (in contrast to insecure individuals who try to please others to gain attention and friendship) tend to be perceptive and resilient, and are generally respected by peers (Carlson, Lahey, & Neeper, 1984; Kurdek & Krile, 1982).

On an optimistic note, most children do turn out to have consciences, and most of us probably encounter a lot more kindness than unkindness in our daily lives. It is curious and heartening that kindness moves us and does not seem unnatural, that when we learn about extreme acts of kindness or self-sacrifice (say, a soldier risking his life for a buddy or someone jumping into a river to rescue a stranger), we are not ordinarily shocked, as if the behavior were bizarre and alien. Such acts fall in a range considered normal, and we can comprehend and identify with the motives behind the acts (there is no *DSM-IV* category for extreme kindness).

In contrast, extreme cruelty often baffles us; we wonder how anyone could be so heartless. We may find evil fascinating, but most also find it repellent and confusing. And children usually cannot understand it at all. They cannot fathom why the wicked witch wants to kill the children, or why people murder total strangers or their own babies, or why Hitler murdered so many millions.

And we adults cannot give them good explanations; we do not understand it either. When we learn about extreme acts of violence, like someone randomly shooting classmates in a school, none of the many proposed explanations feels satisfying. It is as if some people have an appetite for violence that is so far beyond normal that their motivations remain incomprehensible.

That extreme goodness feels more normal to us than extreme badness is worth remembering as we, scientists and laypersons, try to piece together an understanding of human nature. Somehow, we have been ushered down a unique evolutionary path where, unlike any other biological system, we have come to care about goodness. This interest in, and responsiveness to, morality has played a major role in the development of human civilization and has contributed enormously to the survival and flourishing of our species.

References

Barnett, M. A., Howard, J. A., King, L. M., & Dino, G. A. (1980). Antecedents of empathy: Retrospective accounts of early socialization. *Personality and Social Psychology Bulletin, 6,* 361–365.

*Batson, C. D. (1990). How social an animal? The human capacity for caring. *American Psychologist, 45,* 336–346.

Bennett, W. J. (1993). *The book of virtues.* New York: Simon and Schuster.

Bower, B. (2000, Feb. 26). Genes to grow on. *Science News, 157,* 142–143.

Bronfenbrenner, U. (1962). Soviet methods of character education: Some implications for research. *American Psychologist, 17,* 550–564.

Bryan, J. H., & Walbek, N. H. (1970). The impact of words and deeds concerning altruism on children. *Child Development, 41,* 747–757.

Burleson, B. R. (1982). The development of comforting communication skills in childhood and adolescence. *Child Development, 53,* 1578–1588.

Carlson, C. L., Lahey, B. B., & Neeper, R. (1984). Peer assessment of the social behavior of accepted, rejected, and neglected children. *Journal of Abnormal Child Psychology, 12,* 189–198.

Chandler, M. (1973). Egocentrism and antisocial behavior: The assessment and training of social perspective-taking skills. *Developmental Psychology, 9,* 326–332.

Clark, H. B., Greene, B. F., MacRae, J. W., McNees, M. P., Davis, J. L., & Risely, T. R. (1977). A parent advice package for family shopping trips: Development and evaluation. *Journal of Applied Behavior Analysis, 10,* 605–624.

Cohen, D., & Strayer, J. (1996). Empathy in conduct-disordered and comparison youth. *Developmental Psychology, 32,* 988–998.

DiVesta, F. J., & Stauber, K. A. (1971). Identification of verbal concepts by preschool children. *Developmental Psychology, 5,* 81–85.

Eisenberg, N. (1983). Children's differentiations among potential recipients of aid. *Child Development, 54,* 594–602.

Eisenberg, N., Guthrie, I. K., Murphy, B. C., Shepard, S. A., Cumberland, A., & Carlo, G. (1999). Consistency and development of prosocial dispositions: A longitudinal study. *Child Development, 70,* 1360–1372.

Elder, G. (1963). Parental power legitimation and the effect on the adolescent. *Sociometry, 26,* 50–65.

Feshbach, N. D. (1983). Learning to care: A positive approach to child training. *Journal of Clinical Child Psychology, 12,* 266–271.

Feshbach, N. D., & Feshbach, S. (1969). The relationship between empathy and aggression in two age groups. *Developmental Psychology, 1,* 102–107.

Fogelman, E. (1994). *Conscience and courage: Rescuers of Jews during the Holocaust.* New York: Anchor.

Freud, S. (1960). *Group psychology and the analysis of the ego.* New York: Bantam. (Original work published 1921)

Greenstein, T. (1976). Behavior change through value self-confrontation: A field experiment. *Journal of Personality and Social Psychology, 34,* 254–262.

Grusec, J. (1966). The antecedents of self-criticism. *Journal of Personality and Social Psychology, 4,* 244–252.

Grusec, J. E., & Redler, E. (1980). Attribution, reinforcement, and altruism: A developmental analysis. *Developmental Psychology, 16,* 525–534.

Hart, C. H., DeWolf, D. M., Wozniak, P., & Burts, D. C. (1992). Maternal and paternal disciplinary styles: Relations with preschoolers' playground behavioral orientations and peer status. *Child Development, 63,* 879–892.

Hart, D., & Fegley, S. (1995). Prosocial behavior and caring in adolescence: Relations to self-understanding and social judgment. *Child Development, 66,* 1346–1359.

Hartshorne, H., & May, M. S. (1930). *Studies in the nature of character* (Vol 3). New York: Macmillan.

Hastings, P. D., Zahn-Waxler, C., Robinson, J., Usher, B., & Bridges, D. (2000). The development of concern for others in children with behavior problems. *Developmental Psychology, 36,* 531–546.

Hay, D. F., & Rheingold, H. L. (1984). The early appearance of some valued social behaviors. In D. L. Bridgeman (Ed.), *The nature of prosocial development: Interdisciplinary theories and strategies* (pp. 73–94). New York: Academic Press.

Hoffman, M. L. (1975). Altruistic behavior and the parent-child relationship. *Journal of Personality and Social Psychology, 31,* 937–943.

*Hoffman, M. L. (1977). Empathy, its development and prosocial implications. In C. B. Keasey (Ed.), *Nebraska Symposium on Motivation* (Vol. 25), pp. 169–218. Lincoln: University of Nebraska Press.

Houston, D. A. (1990). Empathy and the self: Cognitive and emotional influences on the evaluation of negative effects in others. *Journal of Personality and Social Psychology, 59,* 859–868.

Hughes, R., Jr., Tingle, B. A., & Sawin, D. B. (1981). Development of empathic understanding in children. *Child Development, 52,* 122–128.

Hull, C. L. (1952). *A behavior system.* New York: Wiley.

Iannotti, R. J. (1978). Effect of role-taking experiences on role-taking, empathy, altruism, and aggression. *Developmental Psychology, 14,* 119–124.

Jensen, A. M., & Moore, S. G. (1977). The effect of attribute statements on cooperativeness and competitiveness in school-age boys. *Child Development, 48,* 305–307.

Kochanska, G., Aksan, N., & Koenig, A. (1995). A longitudinal study of the roots of preschoolers' conscience: Committed compliance and emerging internalization. *Child Development, 66,* 1752–1769.

Kohlberg, L. (1969). Stage and sequence: The cognitive-developmental approach to socialization. In D. A. Goslin (Ed.), *Handbook of socialization theory and research* (pp. 343–480). Chicago: Rand McNally.

Krebs, D. L. (1975). Empathy and altruism. *Journal of Personality and Social Psychology, 32,* 1134–1146.

Krevans, J., & Gibbs, J. C. (1996). Parents' use of inductive discipline: Relations to children's empathy and prosocial behavior. *Child Development, 67,* 3263–3277.

Kurdek, L. A., & Krile, D. (1982). A developmental analysis of the relation between peer acceptance and both interpersonal understanding and perceived social self-competence. *Child Development, 53,* 1485–1491.

Levitt, M. J., Weber, R. A., Clark, M. C., & McDonnell, P. (1985). Reciprocity of exchange in toddler sharing behavior. *Developmental Psychology, 21,* 122–123.

Lickona, T. (1991). *Educating for character.* New York: Bantam.

Londerville, S., & Main, M. (1981). Security of attachment, compliance, and maternal training methods in the second year of life. *Developmental Psychology, 17,* 289–299.

MacTurk, R. H., McCarthy, M. E., Vietze, P. M., & Yarrow, L. J. (1987). Sequential analysis of mastery behavior in 6- and 12-month-old infants. *Developmental Psychology, 23,* 199–203.

Masters, J. C., Furman, W., & Barden, R. C. (1977). Effects of achievement standards, tangible rewards, and self-dispensed achievement evaluations on children's task mastery. *Child Development, 48,* 217–224.

Piaget. J. (1965). *The moral judgment of the child.* New York: Free Press.

Pikas, A. (1961). Children's attitudes toward rational versus inhibiting parental authority. *Journal of Abnormal and Social Psychology, 62,* 315–321.

*Radke-Yarrow, M., & Zahn-Waxler, C. (1984). Roots, motives, and patterns in children's prosocial behavior. In J. Reykowski, J. Karylowski, D. Bar-Tal, & E. Staub (Eds.), *The development and maintenance of prosocial behavior: International perspectives* (pp. 155–176). New York: Plenum.

Roberts, W., & Strayer, J. (1996). Empathy, emotional expressiveness, and prosocial behavior. *Child Development, 67,* 449–470.

Rokeach, M. (1973). *The nature of human values.* New York: Free Press.

Sanders, M. R., & Dadds, M. R. (1982). The effects of planned activities and child management procedures in parent training: An analysis of setting generality. *Behavior Therapy, 13,* 452–461.

Schulman, M. (1990). The prevention of antisocial behavior through moral motivation training (or Why isn't there more street crime?). In R. P. Lorion (Ed.), *Protecting the children: Strategies for optimizing emotional and behavioral development* (pp. 255–275). New York: Haworth Press.

*Schulman, M. (1995). *Schools as moral communities: A framework and guide for school administrators, principals, and teachers.* New York: Anti-Defamation League.

Schulman, M. (1996). The Caring Profile: A values modification program for adolescents in residential facilities. *Residential Treatment for Children and Youth, 14,* 9–23.

*Schulman, M., & Mekler, E. (1994). *Bringing up a moral child: A new approach for teaching your child to be kind, just, and responsible.* New York: Doubleday.

Sears, R. R., Maccoby, E. E., & Levin, H. (1957). *Patterns of child rearing.* New York: Row, Peterson.

Seligman, M. E. P., Reivich, K., Jaycox, L., & Gillham, J. (1995). *The optimistic child.* New York: Houghton Mifflin.

Skinner, B. F. (1971). *Beyond freedom and dignity.* New York: Knopf.

Snyder, C. R. (2000). Genesis: The birth and growth of hope. In C. R. Snyder (Ed.), *Handbook of hope: Theory, measures, and applications* (pp. 25–38). San Diego, CA: Academic Press.

Staub, E. (1971). A child in distress: The influence of nurturance and modeling on children's attempts to help. *Developmental Psychology, 5,* 124–132.

Stayton, D., Hogan, R., & Salter-Ainsworth, M. (1971). Infant obedience and maternal behavior: The origins of socialization reconsidered. *Child Development, 42,* 1057–1069.

Tapp, J. L., & Kohlberg, L. (1971). Developing senses of law and legal justice. *Journal of Social Issues, 27* (2), 65–91.

Toi, M., & Batson, C. D. (1982). More evidence that empathy is a source of altruistic motivation. *Journal of Personality and Social Psychology, 43,* 281–292.

Toner, I. J., Moore, L. P., & Emmons, B. A. (1980). The effect of being labeled on subsequent self-control in children. *Child Development, 51,* 618–621.

*Turiel, E. (1983). *The development of social knowledge.* New York: Cambridge University Press.

Twain, M. (1967). *A treasury of Mark Twain.* Kansas City, MO: Hallmark.

Walters, J., Pearce, D., & Dahms, L. (1957). Affectional and aggressive behavior of preschool children. *Child Development, 28,* 15–26.

White, R. W. (1959). Motivation reconsidered: The concept of competence. *Psychological Review, 66,* 297–333.

Young, S. K., Fox, N. A., & Zahn-Waxler, C. (1999). The relations between temperament and empathy in 2-year-olds. *Developmental Psychology, 35,* 1189–1197.

Zahn-Waxler, C., Radke-Yarrow, M., & King, R. (1979). Child-rearing and children's prosocial initiations toward victims in distress. *Child Development, 50,* 319–330.

VII

Biological Approaches

37

Toughness

Richard A. Dienstbier & Lisa M. Pytlik Zillig

The ancient Greeks had it right; mind and body are integrally connected. In modern psychology, we are catching up. We have begun to explore the mind-body connection, but we have typically approached it by emphasizing the mind's influence on the body—how our emotions and thoughts influence health and physical well-being through processes that range from immune function to neuroendocrine availability. Toughness emphasizes the reciprocal path— how body influences mind. Because the evidence for toughness comes largely from experimental studies in which the researchers have demonstrated positive impacts on mind from manipulations that change the body, in toughness theory we propose that lifestyle choices enhance psychological well-being through observable neuroendocrine mediation.

At an abstract level, toughness is about the harmony between physiological systems and ultimately, about the correspondences of physiological systems with psychological ones. The anthropologist Gregory Bateson (1979) observed that when a changed environment forces an organ system to adapt so much that the system nears the limits of its genetic potential, not only is that system strained, but other organ systems with which that system interacts are similarly strained. As an example of cascading negative impacts, consider the downstream impacts of a lifetime of smoking on reducing respiratory efficiency. By leading to reduced physical activity, respiratory insufficiency may ultimately lead to muscular weakness, and then to a higher ratio of fat to lean tissues. Those changes may in turn lead to bone decalcification and perhaps to insulin insensitivity, sugar intolerance, circulatory breakdown, infection, and so on. Based on Bateson's observations, we suggest several principles that underlie toughness theory. The first is that all major physiological systems within an organism interact, so that the state of one system (e.g., the major muscles) will influence most others (e.g., the endocrine and neural systems). The second is that in order to maintain general health, physical systems should be stimulated and used in ways that maintain them near the midpoints of their genetically determined operating potentials. The third principle follows from the first two—similar to most systems, for best results the body must be exposed to environments it was designed to experience, and in general ways the organism must behave in ways that correspond with the ways it was designed to behave.

More specifically, in toughness theory we emphasize that balances within the neuroendocrine systems are modifiable by lifestyles but also by aging. Those modifications in neuroendocrine systems that result from activities that toughen (i.e., usually increased capacities, responsivity, and sensitivities to hormones, neural modulators, and transmitters), in turn, positively influence a variety of performance, personality, and health outcomes.

In this chapter we begin with a brief review of the theoretical perspective concerning toughness. We have sequenced the initial section according to the order that various literatures contributed to the toughness concept as it was initially discussed by the first author (Dienstbier, 1989). Subsequently we will explore research areas that we have not previously related to toughness (e.g., possible impacts of toughening on serotonin levels and the apparent toughening effects of antidepressants). As will be quickly evident, the toughness concept consists of a series of inferences about apparent interrelationships between research and theory from fields ranging from social and clinical psychology to immunology and pharmacology. We are not experts in most of those areas, and we therefore invite suggestions about possible omissions.

Definitions and Physiological Systems

While our thinking about stress has been influenced by Lazarus and colleagues (e.g., Folkman & Lazarus, 1985), the concept of toughness requires a firm distinction between challenges, on the one hand, and stressors, including threat and harm/loss, on the other. Challenges are potentially taxing situations appraised as likely to lead to positive outcomes and positive emotions. Threatening situations are similarly taxing, but threats are appraised more pessimistically. Toughness is less relevant to situations experienced as harm/loss, where negative outcomes already have occurred, and where instrumental coping is thought to be useless. As will become evident in our subsequent discussion of the toughness concept, there is a mutually causal relationship between appraisals of challenge versus threat and physiological toughness.

Because the physiological concepts that we will use in this chapter are not complex, we can describe them quite briefly. Reference to central nervous system (CNS) monoamines includes serotonin and the catecholamines noradrenaline, adrenaline, and dopamine. Reference to peripheral catecholamines suggests adrenaline and noradrenaline, associated with arousal of the sympathetic nervous system (SNS); dopamine is not included as a peripheral catecholamine because it is found largely in conjugated or inactive forms in the body (Bove, Dewey, & Tyce, 1984). Arousal of the SNS stimulates various arousal-generating systems in the body including the adrenal medulla, which then secretes adrenaline; this arousal complex is referred to as the *SNS-adrenal medullary system*, here accorded the friendly acronym *SAM*. Adrenaline contributes to arousal in a variety of ways, especially stimulating the release of glucose into the blood and facilitating the subsequent utilization of glucose and other fuels for energy. SAM arousal occurs in contexts of both positive and negative emotion-evoking circumstances and when physical activity or mental effort is required. It is a system that may cease to provide arousal quickly after the circumstances requiring arousal have passed because the half-life of the catecholamines in the periphery is less than 2 minutes in humans.

Arousal of the pituitary-adrenal-cortical (PAC) system begins with a hypothalamic hormone (CRH) that stimulates a pituitary hormone (ACTH) that leads to the adrenal cortex secreting the corticosteroids, of which cortisol is primarily important in humans. The stimulation of this system occurs in novel situations and following attributions of threat; the experiences of harm/loss, social tension, helplessness, and lingering depression also are associated with elevated cortisol levels. Like the SAM system, cortisol stimulates energy. However, its contribution to energy comes at some costs, such as immune system suppression. And when distressing circumstances end, the arousal fostered by the PAC system is not as easily discontinued as is SAM arousal because the half-life of cortisol in humans is around 90 minutes.

Elements of the Toughness Model

Toughness theory begins with the recognition that there is a "training effect" for neuroendocrine systems. That is, certain manipulations lead to specific neuroendocrine system modifications that, in turn, mediate specific impacts on personality, performance, and health. While a great deal of experimental animal research supports this model, those causal relationships are supported by research with human participants that is largely, but not exclusively, correlational.

Manipulations That Toughen

At the most general and abstract level, lifestyles, training programs, or laboratory manipulations that lead to the physiological changes called toughness include repeated episodes of challenge/threat followed by recovery periods (hereafter "intermittent challenge/threat"). A single episode of an effective toughening manipulation should tax or stimulate an organism sufficiently to result in noticeable neuroendocrine expenditures or even in short-term neuroendocrine depletion. For animal subjects, toughening manipulations typically include swimming in cold water, running in an exercise wheel, being handled or shocked, or even having neuroendocrines depleted by pharmacological interventions. For humans, well-established toughening manipulations include aerobic exercise and working in cold environments. Less well established but likely toughening activities for humans range from intellectual stimulation through games, socializing, and challenging occupations to humor. Whether an activity leads to toughening depends on the original state of toughness. Thus one who is bedridden may achieve toughness with regular exposure to humor, whereas far more substantial activities may be required to increase toughness in a young and active 20-year-old. As illustrated by the research reviewed subsequently, a wide variety of intermittently repeated stimuli and activities have been shown to toughen.

The number of repetitions of taxing activity and recovery that lead to toughening undoubtedly depends on the nature of the manipulations and the associated coping activities. However, most effective laboratory programs with animal subjects span periods of at least 2 to 4 weeks and use 24-hour rhythms of stimulation and rest (e.g., DeBoer, Koopmans, Slangen, & Van der Gugten, 1990). Comparable training programs with humans span longer periods but also typically depend on 24-hour stimulation and rest sequences (e.g., Winder, Hagberg, Hickson, Ehsani, & McLane, 1978).

Some toughening "manipulations" such as living in cold environments may appear to be continuous, but behaviorally adapting organisms may experience them as intermittent (e.g., by periodically retreating to nests or to warm homes). Therefore, such "manipulations" should foster the development of toughness. On the other hand, some situations such as social stressors that appear to be intermittent may be experienced as continuous stressors if individuals ruminate about them. If they are experienced as continuous, such "manipulations" may weaken the organism. Finally, aging is associated with decreasing neuroendocrine capacities. Therefore, unfortunately, aging past young adulthood has weakening effects (Dienstbier, 1992).

Neuroendocrine Mediators

The reason that some manipulations toughen is because repeating taxing (but manageable) episodes with intermittent rest periods leads eventually to the development of compensatory physiological capacities, with greater protection against future neuroendocrine depletion. Thus the neuroendocrine training effects introduced previously refer to changes in the CNS and in the SAM and PAC systems. That is, toughening manipulations enhance the capacity for various tissues in the CNS to generate the monoamines, especially noradrenaline and serotonin, and enhance the capacity of the body other than CNS (hereafter "periphery") to generate noradrenaline and adrenaline. The increased CNS monoamine capacities result in resistance to depletion of CNS noradrenaline (and probably serotonin) in episodes of extended stress. Increased peripheral catecholamine capacity results in high rates of catecholamine release for extended time periods in the context of long and especially taxing challenge/stress episodes. On the other hand, in shorter and less taxing episodes, decreased neuroendocrine responses are likely because of the increased physiological efficiency of the tough individual.

That increased physiological efficiency in the toughened individual results largely from increases in physiological sensitivity and responsivity to important neuroendocrine systems. For example, the sensitivities to catecholamines of the alpha-receptors and beta-receptors in the CNS are modified, and the physiological responsivity of some peripheral tissue is increased. As an example of peripheral effects, in the toughened individual there is a greater release of glucose by the liver per "dose" of circulating catecholamine (LeBlanc et al., 1977). In turn, to keep arousal from increasing when it is not needed, the increased tissue sensitivity necessitates a reduction in base rates of neuroendocrine secretion, as indicated by reduced *base rates* of peripheral catecholamine secretion, as measured with urinary assays. Those reductions in base rate levels of neuroendocrines often result, in turn, in a net reduction in base rates of some other physical indicators, such as heart rate.

In taxing situations, not all neuroendocrine responses are increased in the toughened individual. For example, much (but not all) research indicates that the increased capacity of the body to secrete catecholamines and the increased responsivity of the body to those neuroendocrines then leads to delay and/or suppression of PAC responses in challenge/threat episodes. And, once coping is no longer required, tough individuals show faster recovery to base rate levels in most indicators of arousal (e.g., as reviewed by Linden, Earle, Gerin, & Christenfeld, 1997). That faster recovery from arousal is evidenced particularly when organisms are subjected to a series of related challenge/stress episodes. Both animal and human research suggests that toughened individuals return to (particularly PAC) base rate levels after fewer episodes than is the case for weaker individuals (e.g., Baade, Ellertsen, Johnsen, & Ursin, 1978).

Personality, Performance, and Health

Our approach to toughness suggests that the physiological mediators listed earlier cause a syndrome of positive changes in personality and performance. However, the causal paths from those neuroendocrine mediators to personality and performance are less well established, because these observations depend less on causal research and more on correlational research with human participants. Nevertheless, sufficient research exists to conclude that the pattern of physiological changes (i.e., toughness) corresponds positively with performance in challenging tasks, enhanced learning abilities, emotional stability, resistance to depression in humans (and resistance to "learned helplessness" or behavioral suppression in animals), and positive physical health.

As social-personality psychologists, we are interested mainly in understanding how the physiological pattern of toughness leads to the personality, performance, and health consequences described here; but some speculation embellishes our ideas about those links. To avoid mixing research-based levels of analyses with those that are less so, we will first sketch some of the support for the existence of the nomological network of toughness and will deal with the softer explanations of why and how later. (Readers wishing to see the more complete nomological net and extensive references should contact the first author.)

A Brief History of Toughness

In this section we describe the paths that led toward this model as it was initially formulated by Dienstbier (1989). Each of the following paragraphs presents a separate literature; together they lead to the major tenets of toughness. We begin with the four-decades-old observation, based on the research of Seymour Levine (1960) and others, that emotional stability in adult animals (usually rats or mice) followed from their exposure as pups to intermittent stimulation, ranging from daily shocking to handling. The adult calmness of those early-stimulated animals seemed especially curious following the most stressful manipulations (i.e., the shocking). Similarly, the observation that those calm animals had *larger* adrenal glands and thus apparently greater arousal capacity fit poorly with classical stress theories and with the finding that such animals tended to be calm and to have reduced stressor-induced PAC responses (Hennessy & Levine, 1979).

While that research on the early experience of animals suggested that increased capacity for arousal was associated with a calm temperament, other literatures of that era suggested the opposite relationship. For example, an examination of the literature on autonomic nervous system balance in humans would lead one to infer that "SNS types" (i.e., those with greater arousal reactivity) would be anxious and neurotic. But "SNS types" should be tolerant of cold temperatures because cold tolerance is associated with the body's ability to stimulate energy through SAM arousal (i.e., through the increased generation of and sensitivity to adrenaline and noradrenaline; e.g., LeBlanc, Dulac, Cote, & Girard, 1975). Following that reasoning, one could predict that cold tolerance and the associated strong and responsive SAM arousal capacity should correspond to anxiety and neuroticism. But in our research the results demonstrated the opposite relationship: that cold tolerance and hence a strong and responsive SAM arousal capacity corresponded to emotional stability (Dienstbier, LaGuardia, & Wilcox, 1987).

Working with only human participants, researchers at the Karolinska Institute (and elsewhere in Europe) similarly concluded that greater arousal capabilities predicted both positive personality and positive task performance on a variety of tests and tasks both inside and outside of laboratories. Frankenhaeuser and her colleagues (e.g., Frankenhaeuser, 1979) had shown that better performance in even very complex tasks was associated with greater adrenergic responsivity in humans (assaying urinary catecholamines at the end of the task and comparing those with base rates). Furthermore, individuals who showed increased adrenergic responsivity in the context of many tests and tasks were more emotionally stable than were less responsive individuals. However, these more stable individuals also tended to have lower catecholamine base rates.

With several colleagues, the first author explored the growing but often flawed literature on the impact of exercise on temperament. Imperfect or not, a consistent finding in the research was that like early-stimulated animals, people who undertook programs of aerobic training were subsequently more energetic and more emotionally stable (for a review, see Dienstbier, 1984). It followed that an interesting link would be forged with the literatures discussed earlier if we could show that aerobic exercise changed neuroendocrine responses. That link would be particularly strong if those neuroendocrine changes were evident in mentally challenging situations and if they were like those shown by the Scandinavian researchers to characterize their emotionally stable and high-performing participants. Clearly, this hypothesis, that aerobic training would lead to increased catecholamine capacities, ran counter to most physiologically oriented research with humans, especially research on the "Type A" personality. Researchers in that tradition typically hypothesized that following conditioning with regular exercise, positive personality changes and performance enhancement would follow from *reduced* arousal intensity in response to a variety of situations (e.g., Blumenthal et al., 1990). However, it was clear that episodes of exercise elicited high SNS arousal and catecholamine generation, suggesting that repeated cycles of use/depletion followed by recovery

would stimulate an increased ability to generate such arousal. In short, we hypothesized a neuroendocrine "training effect." Other researchers already had shown that when aerobically trained participants were tested under physically exhausting conditions, they produced higher catecholamine levels (Hull, Young, & Ziegler, 1984). But our focus was on the relevance of toughness to situations requiring mental coping. In a series of three studies, we found that, when tested on a nonexercise day after a program of aerobic training, our participants responded to an extended mental challenge/threat condition with increased adrenergic arousal (over base rates, in contrast to themselves before training and in contrast to untrained control groups; Dienstbier, LaGuardia, Barnes, Tharp, & Schmidt, 1987). In a study without control participants, Cleroux, Peronnet, and de Champlain (1985) found similar increases in adrenaline in challenge contexts for eight men following aerobic training; moreover, others have noted faster recovery to base rate levels for aerobically conditioned participants following laboratory challenges (as discussed by Linden et al., 1997).

Even before the era of exercise research described previously, researchers working with animals had advanced and confirmed similar hypotheses regarding CNS adrenergic capacities. In a series of elegant studies, Weiss and colleagues had noted that "learned helplessness" in animals was associated with CNS catecholamine depletion in certain brain regions. To induce resistance to such helplessness, those researchers "toughened up" their animals (a term first applied by Miller, 1980). Long-term increases in CNS catecholamine capacity resulted from manipulations ranging from daily shocking (e.g., Weiss, Glazer, Pohorecky, Brick, & Miller, 1975) and exercise (e.g., Brown et al., 1979) to systematic CNS catecholamine depletion through chemical means (e.g., Glazer, Weiss, Pohorecky, & Miller, 1975). In addition to showing that those manipulations that decreased CNS catecholamines in the short term increased those neuroendocrine capacities in the long term, in some of the studies in that tradition the increased neuroendocrine capacities were shown to be the mediators of the manipulation-induced increases in stress tolerance (i.e., resistance to behavioral suppression; Weiss et al., 1975).

Because of this pattern of compatible findings in research with both animals and human participants and supportive research from other areas, "toughening up" was expanded to the current toughness concept. In the initial discussion of toughness by Dienstbier (1989), the research review showed that each of the toughening manipulations (active and passive intermittent challenges/stressors for young and mature organisms) led to the entire complex of physiological changes (with CNS and peripheral catecholamine enhancement effects and cortisol suppression), and that those physiological mediators were in turn associated with each of the personality/performance variables listed previously in the section on personality, performance, and health.

Limitations of the Model

When and Where Toughness Will Be Evident

Physiological toughening does not lead to identical or equal toughness in all tissues. For example, in the heart both base rates *and* rates in response to physical and psychological challenge/threats often decline after toughening; and there is evidence that even under maximal workloads, noradrenaline production and turnover in heart tissue are reduced. On the other hand, as with most organs studied, noradrenaline turnover in the livers of toughened animals is greatly enhanced (Mazzeo, 1991). Thus, in those "Type A" studies where it was shown that physical conditioning leads to reduced heart rates in response to physical and psychological challenges and threats, focus was on an aspect of arousal that, although very important, is the exception rather than the prototype.

Demonstrations of increased neuroendocrine capacities from toughness also depend on the researcher's choice of training and testing tasks. This issue is illustrated by Konarska and colleagues in research where blood samples from live animals were used to assess catecholamines. After a few weeks of daily exposure to an intermittent stressor, rats subsequently generated a reduced SAM response in response to the same stressor (reduced blood adrenaline and noradrenaline; Konarska, Stewart, & McCarty, 1989a), whereas they showed increased peripheral catecholamine responses to unfamiliar stressors (Konarska, Stewart, & McCarty, 1989b). While their interpretation was that "sensitization" to unfamiliar stressors results from exposure to intermittent stressors, our in-

terpretation of their findings is closer to the suggestion originally made by Kvetnansky (1980), namely, that toughness training induces physiological adaptation with increased neuroendocrine capacities, but those capacity increases also are accompanied by psychological habituation to now-familiar stressors. Those increased catecholamine capacities in toughened organisms will be evident only when energy demands are unusual, as a result of prolonged extreme stressors or novel ones where responses are inefficient or where searching for solutions occurs.

This interpretation seems particularly applicable to the data of Konarska et al. (1989b) from animals forced at final test to swim (or sink). When tested in very cold water, where extreme energy output is required, toughened animals show higher and much more long-lasting increases in catecholamines than do untoughened animals, whereas in temperate water absolute catecholamine levels were much lower and between-group differences smaller (Konarska, Stewart, & McCarty, 1990). Happily, the toughened animals swam longer, too.

When this interpretation is applied to research with humans, a similar logic holds and can be used to explain apparently inconsistent findings concerning SAM responses to tests following aerobic training or other toughening manipulations. That is, in most aerobic training studies with humans, dependent measures are typically very short-term mental tasks (e.g., 15 minutes or less). In such test circumstances, trained individuals showed reduced indicators of arousal, including reduced catecholamines (using blood assays; e.g., Blumenthal et al., 1990). As discussed more extensively elsewhere (Dienstbier, 1991), in order to observe the increased catecholamine capacities of toughened humans, it is necessary to use taxing tests that are longer in duration (45 minutes is probably minimal) and to employ urinary rather than blood assays because the urinary measures provide a more appropriate and accurate measure of long-term neuroendocrine use and turnover (Steptoe, 1987; recall that because the half-life of the catecholamines in humans is less than 2 minutes, blood measures are of limited usefulness in assessing SAM arousal across longer intervals).

Training That Will Not Toughen

Just as the increased capacities and responsivities that result from toughening are not evident in all test situations, toughening is not accomplished in all programs of intermittent challenges or stressors. For example, it is possible to overwhelm organisms with training that is too intense, extended, or unexpected; even a single episode of a traumatic stressor can be overwhelming.

In the first instance of programs of intermittent stressors that weaken, it has been observed that several weeks of 2 hours daily of restraint stress (as standardized by Kvetnansky) seems to have detrimental impacts on later stress tolerance of rats, sometimes leading to increased catecholamine base rates (McCarty, Horwatt, & Konarska, 1988). Similarly, a combination of unpredictability with great severity may overwhelm the capacity of organisms to recover, leading to weakness rather than toughness (Rodriguez Echandia, Gonzalez, Cabrera, & Fracchia, 1988). Apparent parallels in human research are noted with stress levels that are overwhelming or not truly intermittent, as may be the case with stressors (such as combat) that lead to posttraumatic stress disorders. Similarly, repeated workouts that are too intense to allow complete recovery may cause endurance athletes to experience "staleness," a syndrome that is characterized by increased psychological symptoms of anxiety with increased SNS, catecholamine, and cortisol base rates (e.g., Morgan, Brown, Raglin, O'Connor, & Ellickson, 1987).

Paralleling the observation that animals may be weakened by single episodes of overwhelming stressors, people who were exposed to single early traumatic episodes may display exaggerated PAC responses to acute stressors (Levine & Levine, 1989). For example, maternal death during an individual's childhood has been related to reduced stress resistance in adulthood, resulting in depression (Brown, 1988); similarly, the conditions that lead to posttraumatic stress disorders often result in effects opposite to toughening (e.g., Barlow, Chorpita, & Turovsky, 1996).

Extensions of Toughness Relationships

In this section we expand the toughness model beyond its original formulations (in Dienstbier, 1989, 1991). Specifically, based on our review of relevant literatures, we suggest that regimes of antidepressant medication and electroconvulsive shock (ECS) should be included with our list of "manipulations" that toughen. Those manipu-

lations, in turn, lead to CNS serotonin availability; thus, we add serotonin availability to the list of physiological mediators. In addition, learning enhancement should be added to the performance-personality column, because learning improves with several of the physiological changes that constitute toughness.

Antidepressant Medication, ECS, Serotonin, and Receptor Sensitivities

There are many changes induced in the CNS by the manipulations discussed in this section, and there is little certainty about which of these changes are the critical ones for the personality/performance effects noted. Tranquilizers (e.g., chlorpromazine) that prevent episodes of acute stress from depleting neuroendocrines prevent toughening, even in the context of long-term manipulation programs (Adell, Garcia-Marquez, Armario, & Gelpi, 1989). Antidepressant medication and ECS (Weiner, 1984) regimes, however, have toughening impacts on the CNS that are similar to the effects of intermittent stressors. That is, ECS, tricyclic antidepressants such as imipramine, and intermittent stressors all initially stimulate CNS monoamine release, in the long term increasing the availability of catecholamines and serotonin in many brain areas (e.g., increases in adrenaline and noradrenaline in the hypothalamus; Roth, Mefford, & Barchas, 1982). Increased availability leads to resistance to depletion of CNS monoamines during subsequent prolonged stress and apparently stimulates secondary changes in receptor sensitivities, such as the down-regulation (decreased sensitivity) of CNS beta-receptors (as reflected in reduced cyclic AMP responses; Adell et al., 1989; Anisman & Zacharko; 1982; Stone, McEwen, Herrera, & Carr, 1987). All these physiological responses coincide with the positive personality/performance changes that are fostered by these therapeutic regimes (and by other toughening manipulations).

The noradrenaline-activated neurons of the locus ceruleus (LC) that form a major relay area for neural responses during stress also are altered by the neuroendocrine processes induced by toughening. That is, LC discharge rates are reduced both by increased CNS adrenaline and by decreased CNS levels of CRH (the hypothalamic hormone responsible for activation of PAC arousal; Butler, Weiss, Stout, & Nemeroff, 1990). This circle of relationships is completed by noting that CNS adrenaline and noradrenaline both inhibit the release of CRH (Kvetnansky, 1980). (This facilitating impact of CRH on LC firing may be one of the means by which CRH infusion induces anxiety [Bakke, Bogsnes, & Murison, 1990].)

A remaining controversial issue is whether the toughening-induced down-regulation of brain monoamine receptors ultimately leads to reduced neural activity (Stone, 1983). Reduced beta-receptor sensitivity is associated with increased monoamine capacities and therefore potentially with increased transmitter discharge and neural responsivity under certain conditions. Another avenue for sustained or increased neural responsivity despite beta-receptor down-regulation is suggested by the down-regulation of the alpha-2-receptors (that inhibit noradrenaline discharge from neurons); those changes also result from the antidepressant regimes and probably from other toughening manipulations as well (Siever, 1983; Smith & Zelnik, 1983). Inferential evidence of increased neural responsivity despite receptor down-regulation is seen in the functioning of peripheral organs, where intermittent stress or prolonged catecholamine administration is known to decrease beta-adrenergic-receptor densities and/or cyclic AMP responsivity in heart, brown fat, white fat, and salivary glands with no decrease in function, but rather an increase in organ output in response to catecholamines (Stone, 1983).

Toughening Links to Learning Enhancement

While most of the research on learning enhancement has been done with animal subjects, there are supportive findings from research on learning in older humans. Peripheral catecholamine arousal (McGaugh, 1990) and/or glucose elevations (Gold, 1986) during or immediately following a learning opportunity lead to vastly improved retention in animals, whereas processes that reduce catecholamines and/or glucose have opposite effects. Because chronic or severe acute stress depletes both the catecholamines and blood glucose, it follows (and is observed) that memory consolidation is disrupted for tasks that follow extreme stress in untoughened animals (Foy, Foy, Levine, & Thompson, 1990). On the other hand, memory facilitation effects follow sugar ingestion in animals (Messier & Destrade, 1988) and in older humans (Manning, Hall, & Gold, 1990). There are four observations that we would make in regard to

the relationship of those memory processes to toughness. First, as discussed earlier, toughening increases the storage and synthesis of the neuroendocrines (primarily catecholamines) that stimulate glucose release. Thus, toughening manipulations may impact learning by indirectly changing glucose availability. Remember that glucose is the only source of energy that is used by the CNS, and glucose uptake in the brain is related to localized brain function, differing between brain areas depending on the nature of the learning required (Starter, Bodewitz, & Steckler, 1989). (Glucose also may regulate CNS function through direct impact on cholinergic functions [Stone, Cottrill, Walker, & Gold, 1988].) Second, as suggested by McGaugh (1990), it is likely that peripheral adrenaline directly stimulates peripheral receptors that, in turn, elicit noradrenaline release within the amygdala, thereby facilitating memory consolidation. Third, there is experimental evidence that aerobic exercise programs with elderly humans lead to enhanced mental performance in a variety of complex tasks (though such improvement could result from factors other than a more responsive catecholamine-glucose axis; Chodzko-Zajko, 1991). Fourth, and finally, there are neurotoxic effects from glucocorticoids acting on the hippocampus. The hippocampus (vital in memory consolidation) becomes damaged in normal animals as they age as a result of the normal activation of the PAC system. A program of toughening from early handling of rodents, however, results in adult animals that sustain lower base rates of PAC arousal and are better able to suppress stress-induced PAC arousal. As they age, those toughened animals show less age- and stress-related hippocampal damage, and they are superior to control animals in resisting aging-related spatial memory impairments (Meaney, Aitken, Viau, Sharma, & Sarrieau, 1989).

How Toughness Leads to Improved Coping and Emotional Stability

Before we elaborate this sequence of relationships, consider a basic model of interaction of mind and body. Cognitions and perceptions often elicit neuroendocrine changes that, in turn, cause end-organ physiological changes that then influence emotional or motivational states. Those state changes, in turn, modify (usually by sensitizing) readiness to perceive or generate relevant perceptions and cognitions. Any one of the elements of this circle may be the beginning of the interacting sequence. The influence of situation-induced physiological changes on the experience of panic discussed by Barlow et al. (1996) fits this model; interactions between mind and body in sequences of sexual arousal similarly fit; and, similarly, food perception or preoccupations that lead to insulin-induced blood-glucose decline, and to subsequent increased hunger, may increase readiness to perceive and engage food cues. Our foci involve how perceptions of challenge/threat situations lead to arousal in the physiological systems of concern in this thesis, and how those changes in turn impact the personality/performance variables introduced previously.

The two most important relationships in the following sequence are that perceptions of challenge versus threat differentially impact arousal quality, and that physiological toughness similarly impacts both the quality and quantity of arousal. The Karolinska researchers (e.g., Frankenhaeuser, 1979) and others (e.g., Tomaka, Blascovich, Kibler, & Ernst, 1997, Study 1) show that one's interpretation of a situation as challenging leads to arousal of the SAM system, whereas perceptions of threat lead to a combination of PAC and SAM arousal. Recent research suggests that negative appraisals leading to PAC arousal occur more reliably for men than for women (e.g., Earle, Linden, & Weinberg, 1999). Even with nonhuman subjects, when active coping behaviors are permitted, leading to the experience of control and the possibility of successful coping, arousal of the PAC system is reduced (Hennessy & Foy, 1989; Levine & Levine, 1989). (Activation of the PAC system therefore seems relevant to Gray's [1981] behavioral inhibition system, and arousal of the SAM system, with its stimulation of energy, relates to Gray's behavioral activation system.)

Another key point in our argument is that with SAM arousal, energy will be stimulated by increased catecholamine availability (particularly by adrenaline, acting to stimulate glucagon and the breakdown of glycogen to glucose [glycogenolysis]). In combination with coping skills, if that energy is appraised as sufficient to successfully meet demands (a secondary appraisal, in the Lazarus system), then the (primary) appraisal of a potentially positive outcome is supported. Activities that previously have toughened the organism enhance this effect by

increasing the liver's generation and utilization of the catecholamines with increasing glycogenolysis and thus the experience of energy (Mazzeo, 1991; U'Prichard & Kvetnansky, 1980).

On the other hand, consider the negative appraisal that stimulates the PAC system. While that system contributes to the processes of energy generation by increasing tissue sensitivity to the catecholamines (and by other more costly impacts such as facilitating the conversion of lean tissue to energy) that energization comes at some expense. That is, PAC arousal may contribute to the experience of anxiety, particularly via CRH effects in the brain (Butler et al., 1990), and to depression, particularly from cortisol and other corticosteroids (Barnes, 1986). Once those negative mood states have begun, self-focused attention rather than effective coping may result, with the subsequent reinforcement of the original negative appraisal and continued reactivation of PAC arousal. (Activation of that system also is associated with suppression of the immune system [O'Leary, 1990] and with some CNS neural damage [Meaney et al., 1989].)

Stripped of embellishments and references for simplicity, the following summarizes the foregoing:

1. Some of the elements of toughness (e.g., having a greater capacity for arousal and energy when needed, and being resistant to depression) lead to successful experiences rather than to failures.
2. Such a history of successes leads to optimistic appraisals in future situations where either challenge or threat could be perceived (i.e., one of the most common social-psychological manipulations to encourage optimistic predictions is to provide a history of past success).
3. Both optimistic appraisals and physiological toughness lead to activation of SAM-based arousal and associated feelings of energy, with minimal tension due to delayed activation of the PAC system.
4. Feeling energy rather than tension reinforces the optimistic secondary appraisal that coping will be successful, allowing one to focus on instrumental coping.
5. Attention to instrumental coping leads to frequent successes more reliably than does the self-focused attention and emotion-focused coping that tension frequently stimulates.

6. Successful coping leads to acceptance rather than avoidance of future challenges.
7. Acceptance of challenges over the long term leads to toughness.

Another feature of physiological toughness is the reduction in base rates of arousal in both the SAM and PAC systems. Apparently *sustained* arousal induced by either or both systems is eventually experienced as tension. Thus, it is commonplace to use arousal elevation as an indicator of strain (though researchers often are imprecise as to whether it is base rates or situation-induced arousal that they assess). It is these high base rates rather than increased situationally induced SAM responsivity that are associated with the psychosomatic problems often misattributed to responsivity (e.g., Matthews, 1986; Rauste–von Wright, von Wright, & Frankenhaeuser, 1981). Returns to base rates are studied infrequently but are undoubtedly centrally important in determining whether physiological damage results.

Finally, other modern additions to the previous observations from Tomaka, Blascovich, and colleagues (e.g., Tomaka et al., 1997) suggest that challenge appraisals lead to highly increased cardiac output with decreased total peripheral vascular resistance (the kind of arousal also associated with physical exercise). In contrast, threat appraisals are associated with only moderate cardiac output increases but with increased peripheral vascular resistance, suggesting physiological desynchronization with the possibility of long-term cardiovascular damage.

Recently, following Epel, McEwen, and Ickovics (1998), we have added "thriving" to the toughness concept. In these researchers' conceptualization of "thriving," neuroendocrine processes are divided into the traditional anabolic (growth and conservation of energy) versus catabolic (arousal and tissue-degrading) processes. Their emphasis is primarily on the catabolic and dysregulating effects of chronically elevated cortisol levels on PAC system balance, and insensitivities that then develop to both insulin and growth hormone.

On the other hand, Epel et al. suggested parallels to the toughness model by emphasizing anabolic "counterregulatory responses" that promote growth and toughening when organisms generate the catabolic responses that result from the experience of manageable challenges and stressors in the rhythms of intermittent ex-

posure described here. In an empirical study, women who showed consistently elevated cortisol to lab stressors that were experienced across several days had lower psychological adjustment on a variety of indices (e.g., spiritual growth and appreciation for life).

Conclusions

Psychologists have traditionally focused on deficit conditions such as helplessness and depression. Those conditions tend to be self-sustaining. That is, the pessimism associated with depression leads to an avoidance of challenges and a corresponding lack of experiences that could have led to growth and an emergence from depression. The lack of energy that depression fosters similarly stimulates the avoidance of potentially restorative physical activity.

On the other hand, our emphasis on the positive psychology of toughness suggests that positive cycles can be similarly self-sustaining. Thus, once an individual becomes tough and thereby experiences the sustained energy (with minimal tension) necessary for successful coping, that person is likely to experience a greater variety of situations as challenging rather than threatening. That combination of optimism and energy should lead to the successes that stimulate further optimism and the acceptance of even more challenges. Toughness will increase with such a rhythm.

References

Adell, A., Garcia-Marquez, C., Armario, A., & Gelpi, E. (1989). Chronic administration of clomipramine prevents the increase in serotonin and noradrenaline induced by chronic stress. *Psychopharmacology, 99,* 22–26.

Anisman, H., & Zacharko, R. M. (1982). Depression: The predisposing influence of stress. *Behavioral and Brain Sciences, 5,* 89–137.

Baade, E., Ellertsen, B., Johnsen, T. B., & Ursin, H. (1978). Physiology, psychology, and performance. In H. Ursin, E. Baade, & S. Levine (Eds.), *Psychobiology of stress: A study of coping men* (pp. 163–182). New York: Academic Press.

Bakke, H. K., Bogsnes, A., & Murison R. (1990). Studies on the interaction between ICV effects of CRF and CNS noradrenaline depletion. *Physiology and Behavior, 47,* 1253–1260.

Barlow, D. H., Chorpita, B. F., & Turovsky, J. (1996). Fear, panic, anxiety and disorders of emotion. In D. A. Hope (Ed.), *Nebraska Symposium on Motivation: Perspectives on anxiety, panic, and fear* (Vol. 43, pp. 251–328). Lincoln: University of Nebraska Press.

Barnes, D. M. (1986). Steroids may influence changes in mood. *Science, 232,* 1344–1345.

Bateson, G. (1979). *Mind and nature: A necessary unity.* London: Fontana Paperbacks.

Blumenthal, J. A., Fredrikson, M., Kuhn, C. M., Ulmer, R. L., Walsh-Riddle, M., & Appelbaum, M. (1990). Aerobic exercise reduces levels of cardiovascular and sympathoadrenal responses to mental stress in subjects without prior evidence of myocardial ischemia. *American Journal of Cardiology, 65,* 93–98.

Bove, A. A., Dewey, J. D., & Tyce, G. M. (1984). Increased conjugated dopamine in plasma after exercise training. *Journal of Laboratory and Clinical Medicine, 104,* 77–85.

Brown, B. S., Payne, T., Kim, C., Moore, G., Krebs, P., & Martin, W. (1979). Chronic response of rat brain norepinephrine and serotonin levels to endurance training. *Journal of Applied Physiology: Respiration, Environmental and Exercise Physiology, 46,* 19–23.

Brown, G. W. (1988). Early loss of parent and depression in adult life. In S. Fisher & J. Reason (Eds.), *Handbook of life stress, cognition and health* (pp. 441–466). Chichester, England: Wiley.

Butler, P. D., Weiss, J. M., Stout, J. C., & Nemeroff, C. B. (1990). Corticotropin-releasing factor produces fear-enhancing and behavioral activating effects following infusion into the locus ceruleus. *Journal of Neuroscience, 10,* 176–183.

Chodzko-Zajko, W. J. (1991). Physical fitness, cognitive performance, and aging. *Medicine and Science in Sports and Exercise, 23,* 868–872.

Cleroux, J., Peronnet, F., & de Champlain, J. (1985). Sympathetic indices during psychological and physical stimuli before and after training. *Physiology and Behavior, 35,* 271–275.

DeBoer, S. F., Koopmans, S. J., Slangen, J. L., & Van der Gugten, J. (1990). Plasma catecholamine, corticosterone and glucose responses to repeated stress in rats: Effect of interstressor interval length. *Physiology and Behavior, 47,* 1117–1124.

Dienstbier, R. A. (1984). The effect of exercise on personality. In M. L. Sachs & G. B. Buffone (Eds.), *Running as therapy: An integrated approach.* Lincoln: University of Nebraska Press.

*Dienstbier, R. A. (1989). Arousal and physiological toughness: Implications for mental and physical health. *Psychological Review, 96,* 84–100.

*Dienstbier, R. A. (1991). Behavioral correlates of sympathoadrenal reactivity: The toughness model. *Medicine and Science in Sports and Exercise, 22,* 846–852.

Dienstbier, R. A. (1992). Mutual impacts of toughening on crises and losses. In L. Montada, S.-H. Filipp, & M. J. Lerner (Eds.), *Life crises and experiences of loss in adulthood* (pp. 367–384). Hillsdale, NJ: Erlbaum.

Dienstbier, R. A., LaGuardia, R. L., Barnes, M., Tharp, G., & Schmidt, R. (1987). Catecholamine training effects from exercise programs: A bridge to exercise-temperament relationships. *Motivation and Emotion, 11,* 297–318.

*Dienstbier, R. A., LaGuardia, R. L., & Wilcox, N. S. (1987). The relationship of temperament to tolerance of cold and heat: Beyond "cold hands—warm heart." *Motivation and Emotion, 11,* 269–295.

Earle, T. L., Linden, W., & Weinberg, J. (1999). Differential effects of harassment on cardiovascular and salivary cortisol stress reactivity and recovery in women and men. *Journal of Psychosomatic Research, 46,* 125–141.

Epel, E. S., McEwen, B. S., & Ickovics, J. R. (1998). Embodying psychological thriving: Physical thriving in response to stress. *Journal of Social Issues, 54,* 301–322.

Folkman, S., & Lazarus, R. S. (1985). If it changes it must be a process: Study of emotion and coping during three stages of a college examination. *Journal of Personality and Social Psychology, 48,* 150–170.

Foy, M. R., Foy J. G., Levine, S., & Thompson, R. F. (1990). Manipulation of pituitary-adrenal activity affects neural plasticity in rodent hippocampus. *Psychological Science, 1,* 201–204.

*Frankenhaeuser, M. (1979). Psychoneuroendocrine approaches to the study of emotion as related to stress and coping. In H. E. Howe Jr. & R. A. Dienstbier (Eds.), *Nebraska Symposium on Motivation, 1978: Human emotion* (Vol. 26, pp. 123–161). Lincoln: University of Nebraska Press.

Glazer, H. I., Weiss, J. M., Pohorecky, L. A., & Miller, N. E. (1975). Monoamines as mediators of avoidance-escape behavior. *Psychosomatic Medicine, 37,* 535–543.

Gold, P. E. (1986). Glucose modulation of memory storage processing. *Behavioral and Neural Biology, 45,* 342–349.

Gray, J. A. (1981). *The physiopsychology of anxiety.* Oxford: Oxford University Press.

Hennessy, J. W., & Levine, S. (1979). Stress, arousal, and the pituitary-adrenal system: A psychoendocrine hypothesis. In J. M. Sprague & A. N. Epstein (Eds.), *Progress in psychobiology and physiological psychology* (Vol. 8, pp. 33–67). New York: Academic Press.

Hennessy, M. B., & Foy, T. (1989). Nonedible material elicits chewing and reduces the plasma corticosterone response during novelty exposure in mice. *Behavioral Neuroscience, 101,* 237–245.

Hull, E., Young, S., & Ziegler, M. (1984). Aerobic fitness affects cardiovascular and catecholamine responses to stressors. *Psychophysiology, 21,* 253–260.

Konarska, M., Stewart, R. E., & McCarty, R. (1989a). Habituation of sympathetic-adrenal medullary responses following exposure to chronic intermittent stress. *Physiology and Behavior, 45,* 255–261.

Konarska, M., Stewart, R. E., & McCarty, R. (1989b). Sensitization of sympathetic-adrenal medullary responses to a novel stressor in chronically stressed laboratory rats. *Physiology and Behavior, 46,* 129–135.

*Konarska, M., Stewart, R. E., & McCarty, R. (1990). Habituation and sensitization of plasma catecholamine responses to chronic intermittent stress: Effects of stressor intensity. *Physiology and Behavior, 47,* 647–652.

Kvetnansky, R. (1980). Recent progress in catecholamines under stress. In E. Usdin, R. Kvetnansky, & I. J. Kopin (Eds.), *Catecholamines and stress: Recent advances* (pp. 1–7). New York: Elsevier North Holland.

LeBlanc, J., Boulay, M., Dulac, S., Jobin, M., Labrie, A., & Rousseau-Migneron, S. (1977). Metabolic and cardiovascular responses to norepinephrine in trained and nontrained human subjects. *Journal of Applied Physiology, 42,* 166–173.

LeBlanc, J., Dulac, S., Cote, J., & Girard, B. (1975). Autonomic nervous system and adaptation to cold in man. *Journal of Applied Physiology, 39,* 181–186.

Levine, R., & Levine S. (1989). Role of the pituitary-adrenal hormones in the acquisition of schedule-induced polydipsia. *Behavioral Neuroscience, 103,* 621–637.

Levine, S. (1960). Stimulation in infancy. *Scientific American, 202,* 80–86.

Linden, W., Earle, T. L., Gerin, W., & Christenfeld, N. (1997). Physiological stress reactivity and recovery: Conceptual siblings separated at birth? *Journal of Psychosomatic Research, 42,* 117–135.

Manning, C. A., Hall, J. L., & Gold, P. E. (1990). Glucose effects on memory and other neuropsychological tests in elderly humans. *Psychological Science, 5,* 307–311.

Matthews, K. A. (1986). Summary, conclusions, and implications. In K. A. Matthews, S. M.

Weiss, T. Detre, T. M. Dembroski, B. Falkner, S. B. Manuck, & R. B. Williams Jr. (Eds.), *Handbook of stress, reactivity, and cardiovascular disease* (pp. 461–473). New York: Wiley.

Mazzeo, R. S. (1991). Catecholamine responses to acute and chronic exercise. *Medicine and Science in Sports and Exercise, 23,* 839–845.

McCarty, R., Horwatt, K., & Konarska, M. (1988). Chronic stress and sympathetic-adrenal medullary responsiveness. *Social Science and Medicine, 26,* 333–341.

*McGaugh, J. L. (1990). Significance and remembrance: The role of neuromodulatory systems. *Psychological Science, 1,* 15–25.

*Meaney, M. J., Aitken, D. H., Viau, V., Sharma, S., & Sarrieau, A. (1989). Neonatal handling alters adrenocortical negative feedback sensitivity and hippocampal Type II glucocorticoid receptor binding in the rat. *Neuroendocrinology, 50,* 597–604.

Messier, C., & Destrade, C. (1988). Improvement of memory for an operant response by posttraining glucose in mice. *Behavioral Brain Research, 31,* 185–191.

Miller, N. E. (1980). A perspective on the effects of stress and coping on disease and health. In S. Levine & H. Ursin (Eds.), *Coping and health* (pp. 323–354). New York: Plenum.

Morgan, W. P., Brown, D. R., Raglin, J. S., O'Connor, P. J., & Ellickson, K. A. (1987). Psychological monitoring of overtraining and staleness. *British Journal of Sports Medicine, 27,* 107–114.

O'Leary, A. (1990). Stress, emotion, and human immune function. *Psychological Bulletin, 108,* 363–382.

Rauste–von Wright, M., von Wright, J., & Frankenhaeuser, M. (1981). Relationships between sex-related psychological characteristics during adolescence and catecholamine excretion during achievement stress. *Psychophysiology, 18,* 362–370.

Rodriguez Echandia, E. L., Gonzalez, A. S., Cabrera, R., & Fracchia, L. N. (1988). A further analysis of behavioral and endocrine effects of unpredictable chronic stress. *Physiology and Behavior, 43,* 789–795.

Roth, K. A., Mefford, I. M., & Barchas, J. D. (1982). Epinephrine, norepinephrine, dopamine and serotonin: Differential effects of acute and chronic stress on regional brain amines. *Brain Research, 239,* 417–424.

Siever, L. J. (1983). Mode of action of antidepressant agents: Increased output or increased efficiency? *Behavioral and Brain Sciences, 6,* 558.

Smith, C. B., & Zelnik, T. C. (1983). Alpha-2 adrenergic receptors and the mechanism of action of antidepressants. *Behavioral and Brain Sciences, 6,* 559.

Starter, M., Bodewitz, G., & Steckler, T. (1989). 2-[3H] Deoxyglucose uptake patterns in rats exploring a six-arm radial tunnel maze: Differences between experienced and nonexperienced rats. *Behavioral Neuroscience, 103,* 1217–1225.

Steptoe, A. (1987). Invited Review: The assessment of sympathetic nervous function in human stress research. *Journal of Psychosomatic Research, 31,* 141–152.

Stone, E. A. (1983). Problems with current catecholamine hypotheses of antidepressant agents: Speculations leading to a new hypothesis. *Behavioral and Brain Sciences, 6,* 535–547.

Stone, E. A., McEwen, B. S., Herrera, A. S., & Carr, K. D. (1987). Regulation of alpha and beta components of noradrenergic cyclic AMP response in cortical slices. *European Journal of Pharmacology, 141,* 347–356.

Stone, W. S., Cottrill, K. L., Walker, D. L., & Gold, P. E. (1988). Blood glucose and brain function: Interactions with CNS cholinergic systems. *Behavioral and Neural Biology, 59,* 325–334.

Tomaka, J., Blascovich, J., Kibler, J., & Ernst, J. M. (1997). Cognitive and physiological antecedents of threat and challenge appraisal. *Journal of Personality and Social Psychology, 73,* 63–72.

U'Prichard, D. C., & Kvetnansky, R. (1980). Central and peripheral adrenergic receptors in acute and repeated immobilization stress. In E. Usdin, R. Kvetnansky & I. J. Kopin (Eds.), *Catecholamines and stress: Recent advances* (pp. 299–308). New York: Elsevier North Holland.

Weiner, R. D. (1984). Does electroconvulsive therapy cause brain damage? *Behavioral and Brain Sciences, 7,* 1–53.

*Weiss, J. M., Glazer, H. I., Pohorecky, L. A., Brick, J., & Miller, N. E. (1975). Effects of chronic exposure to stressors on avoidance-escape behavior and on brain norepinephrine. *Psychosomatic Medicine, 37,* 522–534.

Winder, W. W., Hagberg, J. M., Hickson, R. C., Ehsani, A. A., & McLane, J. A. (1978). Time course of sympathoadrenal adaptation to endurance exercise training in man. *Journal of Applied Physiology, 45,* 370–376.

38

A Role for Neuropsychology in Understanding the Facilitating Influence of Positive Affect on Social Behavior and Cognitive Processes

Alice M. Isen

A growing body of research indicates that mild positive affect (happy feelings), induced in subtle, common ways that can occur frequently in everyday life, facilitates a broad range of important social behaviors and thought processes. For example, work from approximately the past decade shows that positive affect leads to greater creativity (e.g., Isen, Daubman, & Nowicki, 1987; see Isen, 1999a, for review); improved negotiation processes and outcomes (Carnevale & Isen, 1986); and more thorough, open-minded, flexible thinking and problem solving (e.g., Estrada, Isen, & Young, 1997; Isen, Rosenzweig, & Young, 1991). And this is in addition to earlier work showing that positive affect promotes generosity and social responsibility in interpersonal interactions (see, e.g., Isen, 1987, for review). The literature indicates that, under most circumstances, people who are feeling happy are more likely to do what they want to do, want to do what is socially responsible and helpful and what needs to be done, enjoy what they are doing more, are more motivated to accomplish their goals, and are more open to information and think more clearly. Although people experiencing positive affect sometimes appear not to perform as well as controls, this seems to occur only in limited circumstances, such as when a task is neither interesting nor important (e.g., Isen, Christianson, & Labroo, 2001 Melton, 1995; see Isen, 2000, for discussion). Significantly, recent research now clearly has countered the previously widely held view that positive affect, by its nature, typically leads to oversimplification or superficial cognitive processing and thus impairs systematic processing (for statements of the previously held view, see, e.g., Bless, Bohner, Schwarz, & Strack, 1990; Mackie & Worth, 1991; Schwarz & Bless, 1991; for examples of studies countering that view, see, e.g., Bless et al., 1996; Estrada et al., 1997; Isen, 1993; Isen et al., 1991; Lee & Sternthal, 1999).

The purpose of this chapter is to focus attention on the effects that positive affect has on thinking, problem solving, and social behavior and to explore a possible role for neuropsychology in understanding this influence. Thus, I will summarize these and related findings briefly and then consider what, neurobiologically, may underlie these effects. That is, noting that positive affect promotes cognitive flexibility, for example, one may ask what in the neurobiology of the organism enables cognitive flexibility, and what relation might such neurobiological processes have to positive affect? The reasoning is that, if positive affect causes creativity, and creativity involves a certain neuropsychological process, then positive affect also may involve that neurological process.

From this reasoning alone, it would not be possible to say whether positive affect caused the neurological process directly, whether something else that regularly accompanies positive affect (e.g., certain cognitive aspects or consequences of the affective state) caused the neurological process, whether the neurological process caused the positive affect, or whether the affect and the neurological process simply occurred together. However, adopting this approach would provide a starting point for exploring a potential neuropsychological link because it would be possible to say at least that positive affect is not incompatible with this neurological process.

Thus, this approach would increase our understanding of positive affect by identifying neuropsychological processes that are compatible with positive affect but also by adding whatever else may be known about those neurological processes. For example, if the neurological process that underlies cognitive flexibility also mediates other cognitive functions, then we might expect positive affect to be compatible with those functions also. If, in addition, that neurological process can be related specifically to positive affect in a fundamental way, then our understanding of what else positive affect may be expected to do, and how positive affect may have its effects, could be expanded even further. Let us begin, then, by briefly summarizing some effects of positive affect that are known.

Positive Affect Promotes Improved Functioning

Social Behavior

Considerable research over the past three decades documents the impact of positive affect on social interaction such as helping and generosity

(see, e.g., Isen, 1987, for review). All else being equal, people in whom mild positive affect has been induced are more helpful and generous to others (e.g., Aderman, 1972; Cunningham, 1979; Cunningham, Steinberg, & Grev, 1980; Isen, 1970; Isen & Levin, 1972); more sociable and friendly (e.g., Veitch & Griffitt, 1976); and more socially responsible (e.g., Berkowitz, 1972; Berkowitz & Daniels, 1964). For example, in one series of studies, people who were told they had succeeded on a task, or who were offered a cookie, or who found change in the coin return of a public telephone donated more to a charity collection can, were more helpful to a stranger who needed help carrying several books and papers, and were more willing to help a passerby who dropped a folder of papers (Isen, 1970; Isen & Levin, 1972). Similarly, positive-affect-inducing conditions have been found to reduce interpersonal conflict (e.g., Baron, 1984; Isen & Baron, 1991) and to facilitate face-to-face negotiations (Carnevale & Isen, 1986).

In the negotiation study by Carnevale and Isen (1986), positive affect induced by a small gift (a pad of paper) and a few cartoons significantly increased the tendency of bargainers who were face-to-face to reach agreement and to obtain the optimal outcome possible for both parties in the negotiation. In contrast, negotiators in the control condition (no affect induced) bargaining face-to-face most often broke off negotiation without reaching any agreement. Their sessions also were characterized by open hostility and conflict, and the parties reported not enjoying the process. This contrasts markedly with the experiences of those in the positive-affect condition, whose sessions were reported to be pleasant and enjoyable. Although some might assume that the improved outcomes for those in the positive-affect condition were attributable to social factors, there is reason to believe that cognitive factors also are implicated in the process. This latter issue is explored next.

Flexibility in Thinking

A substantial literature supports the conclusion that positive affect promotes flexible thinking. This includes flexible categorization of neutral material (e.g., Isen, 1987, p. 234; Isen & Daubman, 1984; Isen, Niedenthal, & Cantor, 1992; Kahn & Isen, 1993; Murray, Sujan, Hirt, & Sujan, 1990); broader product consideration sets and more diverse and less typical word associations to neutral stimuli (e.g., Isen, Johnson, Mertz, & Robinson, 1985; Kahn & Isen, 1993); and openness to ideas (e.g., Estrada et al., 1997). In addition, extensive research carried out in a variety of settings and assessing the responses of diverse populations (from young adolescents to practicing physicians and managers in organizations) shows that this flexibility translates into increases in actual creativity and in more successful problem solving (e.g., Estrada, Isen, & Young, 1994; Estrada et al., 1997; Greene & Noice, 1988; Hirt, Melton, McDonald, & Harackiewicz, 1996; Isen et al., 1987; Staw & Barsade, 1993; see Isen, 1999a, for review and discussion). For example, in one series of studies, medical students and practicing physicians in whom positive affect had been induced showed increased creativity as measured by Remote-Associates-Test items (Estrada et al., 1994), improved performance on tasks related to medical diagnosis, and more open, flexible consideration of diagnostic alternatives (Estrada et al., 1997; Isen et al., 1991).

Other studies reveal that the decision-making processes of people in whom positive affect has been induced, as compared with those of persons in control conditions, are both more efficient and, simultaneously, more thorough (e.g., Isen & Means, 1983; Isen et al., 1991). For example, in one protocol-analysis study, people choosing a fictitious car for purchase made their choices earlier (although their choices did not differ, on average, from those of the control group) and made the choice more efficiently by exhibiting, for example, less redundancy in their search processes (Isen & Means, 1983). When this same choice problem was recast as a disease identification task and given to medical-student subjects, results again showed that people in the positive-affect condition, in contrast with controls, solved the assigned problem earlier (in this case by identifying the correct patient earlier in their protocols). In this instance, however, the positive-affect group did not stop working on the materials once the assigned task was completed but instead, significantly more than controls, went beyond the assigned task (doing things such as diagnosing the other patients or suggesting treatments), integrated the material more, and showed less confusion in their decision making (Isen et al., 1991).

Most recently, a protocol-analysis study examining the influence of positive affect on physicians' diagnostic processes showed that doctors in the positive-affect condition, as compared with a control condition, correctly identified the domain of the illness they were attempting to diagnose significantly earlier in their protocols and showed significantly less "anchoring" to an initial hypothesis. That is, they were more open to information—even information that countered what they were currently thinking—as shown by their significantly lower likelihood, compared with doctors in the control condition, to distort or ignore information that did not fit with their existing hypothesis (Estrada et al., 1997). It also was observed, as would be compatible with such a finding, that they were not likely to jump to conclusions, to show premature closure, or to display any evidence of superficial or faulty processing.

Flexibility Facilitates Interpersonal Problem Solving as Well as Nonsocial Problem Solving

The two-person negotiation situation described previously is an example of one kind of interpersonal problem-solving situation in which positive affect may contribute to improved outcomes (and processes). It is important to note that this interpersonal effect of positive affect, in which happy feelings facilitated the bargaining process and outcome, may have occurred not only because of an effect on friendliness or pro-social inclination but at least in part because of the cognitive effects of positive feelings—particularly positive affect's influence on cognitive flexibility. This is because success on the bargaining task required reasoning integratively about possibilities and making trade-offs between alternatives. In addition, the task was one in which simple yielding would not lead to a satisfactory outcome (see Pruitt, 1983, for discussion of the task). It also should be noted that people in the positive-affect condition were better able to describe the other party's payoff matrix—a fact not disclosed during the session— when asked about it after the session. This suggests that they had been better able than controls to take the other party's perspective during the session.

Flexibility May Facilitate Pro-Social Interaction More Directly

Flexibility in perspective-taking also may underlie the helping findings that have been observed. This follows because such flexibility may allow a person to see another person's perspective as well as his or her own view. This broadening of focus, or possible reduction in self-focus, may play a role in the increased generosity and helpfulness that result from positive affect. For example, in one of the earliest demonstrations of the link between positive affect and helping, Isen (1970) reported a narrowing of the range of attention among participants who had failed, relative to those who had succeeded. The relatively broader range of attention among people in whom positive affect had been induced actually may represent more flexibility in their focus of attention—that is, more ability to switch back and forth between attention to their own needs and those of others, or to consider both views simultaneously. Increased flexibility in thinking also may explain why people who are experiencing positive affect do not stop attending to their own welfare at the same time that they broaden their foci to include the welfare of others (e.g., Isen & Simmonds, 1978).

Similarly, another finding that integrates the impact of positive affect on cognitive flexibility with its influence on pro-social interaction is one reported by Dovidio, Gaertner, Isen, and Lowrance (1995). This study found that people in a positive-affect condition were more likely than controls to form an inclusive group representation that linked their own group and another group. This resulted in better evaluations of the out-group members, more acceptance and liking of the other group, and lower levels of intergroup bias; moreover, a path analysis confirmed the crucial roles of positive affect and of group representation (categorization of the groups) in producing such effects.

Most recently, this effect was explored further by Urada and Miller (2000), who reported results of four studies investigating the influence of positive affect on crossed categorization. (Crossed categorization refers to situations in which out-group members share some qualities with in-group members but differ from them on others.) Their results indicate that positive affect changed the representation and improved the evaluation of out-group (crossed) members when they shared an important quality with the in-group but not when they shared only an unimportant quality. Thus, positive affect results in more flexible, broadened consideration of social concepts, as well as of nonsocial concepts. Current research is expanding the exploration of this broadening effect of positive affect and its constructive influence on both cognitive and

social processes (e.g., Dovidio, Gaertner, Isen, Rust, & Guerra, 1998; Fredrickson, 1998; Fredrickson, Mancuso, Branigan, & Tugade, 2000; Isen, 1990; Kahn & Isen, 1993; Urada & Miller, 2000).

Flexibility Enables More Detailed and Responsive Consideration of Situations and Possible Outcomes

Throughout the literature on positive affect, study results indicate that positive affect does not act via any simple biasing or distortion of perception or decision making. For example, the experience of positive affect does not lead to general biasing in a positive direction or in a simplifying direction—two hypotheses that were suggested early in the work on positive affect and cognition. Rather, accumulating evidence indicates that positive affect leads people to consider many aspects of situations simultaneously and to make evaluations and choose behaviors that are responsive to the situation and task demands. Thus, the operative process is the product of thought rather than of simple bias.

For example, studies have shown that positive affect leads to improved evaluation of neutral or ambiguous material but not of clearly positive or negative material (e.g., Isen & Shalker, 1982; Schiffenbauer, 1974). Similarly, a study on the influence of positive affect on word associations showed that positive affect resulted in more extensive and diverse word associations to neutral words but not to negative or even positive words (Isen et al., 1985). In addition, a study investigating categorization of people into person-type categories found that positive affect influenced perception (classification) of marginal category representatives into positive person categories (such as "bartender" into the category "nurturant people"), but not of marginal category representatives into negative person categories (such as "genius" into the category "unstable people"; Isen et al., 1992).

Similarly, in the studies by Urada and Miller (2000), positive affect influenced the group representation and acceptance of out-group members who shared an important, but not an unimportant, characteristic with the in-group. This, too, indicates that positive affect's influence on thought processes and cognitive organization does not just reflect a global bias, or simplistic or superficial processing, but rather stems from broadened, integrated categorization and a detailed, integrated consideration of the relevant materials to be thought about in the situation. In yet another example, a study set in an organizational context showed that positive affect influenced task perceptions and satisfaction for an enriched task but not for an unenriched task (Kraiger, Billings, & Isen, 1989). In the organizational behavior literature, an *enriched task* is one that allows employees an opportunity for some autonomy, diversity of activity, and sense of control and meaningfulness, whereas an *unenriched task* is one that requires only relatively routine, scripted activity and/or allows little sense of control or meaningfulness. *An important point here is that positive affect cues positive material about items for which positive thoughts exist in the person's mind and does not simply result in a global perceptual or response bias, as if the person were viewing everything through "rose-colored glasses" or responding thoughtlessly.* Even more important, positive affect appears to promote detailed consideration of situations and stimuli, including their relative importance or relevance, and flexible responding to situations based on that integrated consideration of factors and possible outcomes.

Positive Affect Enables Improved Coping

A growing body of work in the coping literature indicates that positive affect may help people to cope with problematic situations (see Aspinwall & Taylor, 1997; Taylor & Aspinwall, 1996, for reviews), and this may result, at least in part, from the flexibility engendered by positive affect. Similarly, people in positive affect have been found to be less defensive (Aspinwall, 1998; Reed & Aspinwall, 1998; Trope & Netter, 1994; Trope & Pomerantz, 1998) and less likely to distort or ignore information that does not fit their preconceptions (Estrada et al., 1997), and to show superior coping skills and styles (Aspinwall & Taylor, 1997; Showers & Cantor, 1985; Taylor & Aspinwall, 1996). In a related finding, people relatively high in optimism and hope are known to persist more at tasks and show better management of stress than those low in optimism (see Armor & Taylor, 1998; Scheier & Carver, 1992; Snyder, 1994; Taylor & Aspinwall, 1996, for reviews). It should be noted, however, that positive affect leads people to disengage more rapidly from unsolvable tasks if there are solvable tasks to be done, and to perform better on the solvable tasks (e.g., Aspinwall & Richter, 1999). This is yet another

way in which positive affect fosters improved flexibility and coping.

Positive Affect Reduces Dangerous Risk Taking

The significant interactions between positive affect and other aspects of situations also suggest that affect's role is not simply to influence decisions in a positive direction regardless of the dangers or other factors that may be present. This reflects another way in which positive affect may contribute to adaptive functioning; it leads or enables people to use good judgment and be especially cautious of dangerous risks. In illustration, several studies, to be described next, have shown that positive affect's influence on risk preference, or behavior in risky situations, is characterized by significant interactions between affective state and the amount of potential unpleasantness or danger of the outcome under consideration. This indicates that positive affect's influence on such behavior is complex, the product of thought, rather than simple or impulsive.

Subjective Probability of Winning or Losing and Utility of Possible Gains or Losses

This work suggests that the effects of positive affect on risk preference and behavior result from differential effects of positive affect on the subjective probability of losing and the perceived utility (actually the disutility) of the potential loss. More specifically, although positive affect decreases the subjective probability of losing, it increases the negative utility of the potential loss (e.g., Isen, Nygren, & Ashby, 1988; Johnson & Tversky, 1983; Nygren, Isen, Taylor, & Dulin, 1996). That is, although the probability of losing may seem smaller for those who are feeling happy as compared with control persons, the bad feeling that would result from the potential loss seems greater to the positive-affect group. Thus, perhaps seeking to maintain their positive state, such persons are more likely than controls to refrain from taking a large and consequential risk (e.g., Isen & Geva, 1987; Isen & Patrick, 1983).

Risk Preference

Studies on the influence of positive affect on risk preference or choices among gambles having alternative odds and win-loss structures show that, although positive affect may appear to increase risk taking in a low-risk or hypothetical situation, it actually leads to risk avoidance or decreased risk preference in situations of high, real risk or possible genuine, meaningful loss (e.g., Isen & Geva, 1987; Isen & Patrick, 1983). This significant interaction, like those described previously, indicates that positive affect influences thinking in a complex manner that involves elaboration and evaluation of outcomes, rather than just by biasing responding in a positive direction. This suggests that positive affect fosters thinking about whatever needs to be thought about in the situation and does not lead people to downplay, ignore, or distort potential negative information. In fact, in one study, where a high risk of a genuine loss was involved, people in the positive-affect condition, relative to controls, had significantly more thoughts about the potential loss (as reflected in a thought-listing task following the risk measure; Isen & Geva, 1987). This finding in particular is also compatible with the previously described findings of improved coping and reduced defensiveness because it indicates that people in positive affect can deploy their cognitive resources flexibly and attend to the crucial factors in the situation that serve their long-term best interest. Thus, even though, all else being equal, people experiencing positive affect seem to prefer not to lose their happy feelings, they are not limited to immediate affect maintenance as a goal.

Variety Seeking

A series of potentially related studies has shown that people in positive-affect conditions prefer to experience variety, if the options involved are safe and enjoyable. For example, in three studies looking at consumers' choices among snack foods, Kahn and Isen (1993) found that, as long as the products promised to be enjoyable, positive affect led to increased preference for variety (as measured by number of alterations between products [higher], diversity in the set of items considered [larger], and market share of the most preferred item [smaller]). (*Market share* refers to the percentage of the total number selected that is captured by one alternative; market share of the most preferred item would be the percentage of choices that goes to the most preferred item; and variety seeking, or preference for variety, would be reflected by the

most preferred brand/item's receiving a smaller market share or percentage of the total number of choices.) This was not true, however, when the items were unfamiliar and the description of them (e.g., low salt) suggested that they might taste bad. In that circumstance, the positive-affect and control groups did not differ in their degrees of variety seeking. This suggests that the increase in preference for variety that results from positive affect arises because of greater anticipated enjoyment, but that, as found in other contexts, this assessment is quite responsive to the details of the situation.

To summarize, then, extensive research using varied affect inductions and/or measures of optimism and self-esteem, and varied measures of creativity and flexibility, supports the conclusion that positive affect fosters cognitive flexibility, creativity, and innovation, and at the same time careful adaptive thinking and reasonable responses. As noted, people in whom positive affect has been induced show more unusual (but still reasonable and sensible) word associations to neutral words, more liking for unusual, nontypical products, and more flexible categorization of neutral words into topic categories, and of products into product classes; and they show greater preference for variety among safe, enjoyable alternatives (Isen et al., 1985; Isen & Daubman, 1984; Kahn & Isen, 1993; Murray et al., 1990; Showers & Cantor, 1985). As described, this effect also applies to people's classification of person-types into positive categories (but not into negative categories) and other-group members into in-groups (Dovidio et al., 1995; Isen et al., 1992; Urada & Miller, 2000). Relative to control groups, people in positive-affect conditions have better negotiation outcomes and enjoy the task more, where the bargaining situation requires a problem-solving approach and they can take the other person's perspective (Carnevale & Isen, 1986); thus, it seems that the influence of positive affect on flexibility also may play some role in positive affect's improvement of interpersonal interaction (see, e.g., Isen, 1999b, for discussion).

Neuropsychological Underpinnings

As noted earlier, this chapter also explores some neurological processes that may enable, or (to put it more neutrally) be associated with, these effects of positive affect. One reason for considering this question is to extend our understanding of affect by adding another level of analysis to our inquiry. However, the neurological analysis is not intended to replace the cognitive and behavioral levels of analysis but rather to supplement them. That is, asking about the neuropsychological concomitants of positive affect should not be taken to imply that other levels of analysis are less important or less informative. Rather, it seeks to discover what can be added to our understanding by investigating the neurological processes associated with positive affect or with the processes that have been found to result from positive affect. For example, neuropsychological analyses may suggest new dimensions or variables that are important for understanding the impact of affect on cognition or behavior, or they may suggest additional influences of affect at the behavioral or cognitive level that are not yet recognized.

To address the question of the neurological processes that may be involved in positive affect's influence on cognition and behavior, one first can describe certain effects of positive affect that have been observed and then consider what neurological processes are known to enable or be involved in those cognitive processes. One may begin by making the simple point that such neurological processes also must be present during positive affect. As a first step, all that may be said is that that neurological process is not incompatible with positive affect or that positive affect is not incompatible with that neurological process. Nonetheless, this consideration can provide important information because it suggests that positive affect does not interfere with certain neurological processes, and that positive affect may even cause or facilitate those processes. Then additional questions can be asked about the effects or processes activated by that neurological system. This, in turn, can extend our understanding of affect and enable us to generate new predictions about expected neurological, cognitive, and behavioral effects of affect.

The Dopamine Hypothesis

In the case of positive affect, as has been described in this chapter, one of the most clear, and most distinctive, cognitive effects observed is increased flexibility and creativity. Thus, initially, one question that may be asked is about the neuropsychological substrate of flexible thinking. Of course, to be relevant to positive affect, it would be most clear if any neuropsychological process identified also were related not only to flexibility but also to positive affect. Thus, beginning with this question of what neurological processes enable or are associated with cognitive flexibility, we also asked whether any such identified processes also are associated with positive affect. Because dopamine in frontal regions of the brain is associated with both cognitive flexibility and reward (which may potentially be related to positive affect), it seemed especially promising to explore the potential role of the dopamine system in the impact of positive affect on thinking (see Ashby, Isen, & Turken, 1999).

A large body of literature on the neuropsychology of reward suggests the importance of dopamine in the mediation of reward and particularly in the process of learning from reward (see Ashby et al., 1999, for review). We assume that positive-affect conditions and the experiencing of reward may share some elements. In addition, the literature indicates that dopamine in the anterior cingulate region of the brain enables cognitive perspective-taking or set-switching (e.g., Owen et al., 1993; see Ashby et al., 1999). Thus, the neuropsychological work shows, in animal studies, that dopamine is released in the brain in response to reward; and, in both animal and human studies, that dopamine is associated with cognitive flexibility. In addition, reductions in dopamine (e.g., as occur in Parkinson's disease) are associated with humans' diminished performance on tasks requiring them to switch "set." Thus, my colleagues and I have proposed that the influence of positive affect on cognitive processes may be mediated by release of the neurotransmitter dopamine. Direct evidence is yet to be obtained for this hypothesis; however, based on the data just reviewed, this suggestion seems plausible.

Additional predictions follow from the dopamine hypothesis. For example, because there are dopamine projections into frontal brain regions responsible for processes such as thinking, working memory, and the like (as illustrated in Figure 38.1), this hypothesis suggests that positive affect should enhance working memory and processes related to thinking, through activation of these brain regions. In contrast, since the visual and auditory areas of the brain are not rich in dopamine receptors, this hypothesis would not predict that positive affect should influence visual or auditory perception (see Ashby et al., 1999, for discussion).

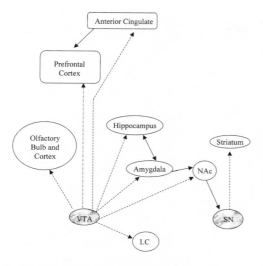

Figure 38.1 Some dopamine projections in the human brain. Dopamine-producing areas are shaded, and dopamine projections are illustrated by the dashed lines. Nac = nucleus accumbens: VTA = ventral tegmental area; SN = substantia nigra; LC = locus ceruleus. From Ashby, Isen, & Turken (1999).

In this regard, the suggestion that the dopamine system is involved in positive affect also has been advanced by Depue and colleagues, although they adopt a somewhat different perspective (e.g., Depue & Collins, 1999; Depue, Luciana, Arbisi, Collins, & Leon, 1994). Their work takes an individual-difference approach and characterizes people in terms of their relatively stable levels of positive emotionality (e.g., as reflected by the personality trait of extraversion). Depue and his colleagues have reported increased levels of brain dopamine activity among people who score relatively high in characteristics such as extraversion. Also consistent with the argument being put forth here, other work has found that people scoring relatively high in measures of dispositional "positivity" (as measured by instruments such as the Positive Affectivity Negative Affectivity Scale [PANAS]; e.g., Watson & Tellegen, 1985) also show increases in problem-solving performance (e.g., George & Brief, 1996; Staw & Barsade, 1993).

One might wonder how a trait approach could be compatible with my present suggestion that mildly induced positive affective states can influence the dopamine system or have their impact on cognition through release of dopamine in the brain. This may seem especially problematic in light of Depue and colleagues' proposition that the dopamine system itself is different in people who are high, rather than low, in the personality characteristic of "extraversion" (e.g., Depue & Collins, 1999). Those authors relate "extraversion" to positive incentive motivation and maintain that some individuals ("extraverts") have a ventral tegmental area dopamine system (VTA-DA) that functions to increase their positive incentive motivation or approach behavior. According to Depue and colleagues, the characteristic VTA dopamine system that sets extraverts apart can come about in any of three ways: through genetic endowment, through "experience-expectant" processes, or through "experience-dependent" processes. Their view holds, however, that regardless of how this development occurs, the requisite VTA dopamine system becomes a stable characteristic by adulthood. Thus, in consideration of Depue's view, it might seem difficult to argue that induced positive affect has its impact through activation of the dopamine system.

There are several potential ways of integrating these two dopamine-related positions. First, it may be that effects of positive-affect inductions may differ for people with differently developed dopamine systems, or for those who are very high or very low in certain dispositional tendencies. However, because the experimental findings show effects of induced affect when people have been randomly assigned to conditions, this cannot be the primary way to integrate these lines of research.

Second, then, it is noteworthy that other authors have taken issue with aspects of Depue's position in ways that make it possible to integrate Depue's findings with the suggestion that induced positive affect can influence the dopamine system. For example, Cabib and Puglisi-Allegra (1999) point out that the functioning of the VTA dopamine system may not be immutable even in adulthood, noting that, at least in animal studies, the dopamine system continues to be very responsive to environmental conditions even in mature organisms. In addition, other authors suggest that the direction of influence between the VTA and behavior/cognition in humans is not necessarily only from dopamine to behavior. For example, Isom and Heller (1999) and Miller (1996) reason, and provide many examples in support of their logic, that cognitive-behavioral interventions can influence neurobiology. This means that the causal arrow can go in either direction, or in both directions. Thus, even if there are individual differences in people's dopamine systems, it is still possible that these systems remain malleable, and that affective experiences may continue to influence both the dopamine system and the cognitive and behavioral effects that are produced. Consequently, it remains plausible that the neurological system is responsive even among adults, that induced positive affect in humans may have its effects through the VTA dopamine system, and that these effects can be powerful, even for adults. This position does not deny that the dopamine system or the cognitive and social patterns associated with its functioning may be built up over time, as held by Depue and colleagues, but it does suggest a more flexible, malleable, bidirectional process than is usually assumed.

Additional neuropsychological work, although focusing primarily on other factors, also has yielded results that fit with the suggestion that brain dopamine may play a role in the effects of positive affect on cognition that have been observed. Davidson (1993, 1999), for example, investigating lateralization of brain function, and using PET and fMRI techniques to observe which brain areas are active at the time of processing of different types of materials or stimuli, hypothesized that positive affect is processed in the left frontal and right posterior areas of the brain. Although the suggestion that positive affect is mediated by the dopamine system does not focus specifically on hemispheric lateralization of brain function, it is worth noting that these regions postulated by Davidson to be active in positive affect, especially the left frontal region, are rich in dopamine receptors.

Conclusions

As revealed throughout this chapter, positive affect is a source of human strength. Contrary to some of the earlier misconceptions, the experience of positive affect does not generally result in superficial or flawed thought processes, even where careful thinking about serious matters is required. Many studies on cognitive processes such as memory, decision making, and problem solving have shown that positive affect is generally facilitating. For example, it enables flexible thinking and creative problem solving on tasks that otherwise are very difficult, and it

promotes thinking that is not only efficient but also careful, open-minded, and thorough. Furthermore, the experience of positive affect is known to promote social interaction, helpfulness, generosity, and social responsibility—and it does so without undermining attention to a person's own long-term welfare.

Although some earlier papers suggested that positive affect impaired systematic processing either because of draining limited cognitive capacity or interfering with motivation to process carefully (e.g., Bless et al., 1990; Mackie & Worth, 1989), many authors did not find results compatible with that suggestion (e.g., Isen et al., 1991; Smith & Shaffer, 1991; Staw & Barsade, 1993), and still other investigators reported findings pertaining to deployment of attention that would lead to an opposite conclusion (e.g., Derryberry, 1993). More recently, several studies have found that the previously reported impairing effects of positive affect primarily occurred when the task was dull or unpleasant *and* unimportant or not to be taken seriously by people (e.g., Isen et al., 2001; also see Isen, 1993, 2000, for discussion).

As noted earlier, it has been proposed that at least some of the effects of positive affect may depend on the neurotransmitter dopamine (e.g., Ashby et al., 1999; Depue et al., 1994; Depue & Collins, 1999). This hypothesis carries the implication that positive affect may especially influence tasks that are controlled by brain regions containing dopamine receptors. Consequently, this suggestion may lead us to more specific ways of defining the kinds of tasks that may or may not be facilitated by positive affect. This may help us to avoid the use of vague terms, such as *heuristic* versus *systematic* processing, which have sometimes fostered confusion in understanding the impact of affect on cognitive processing (see Isen, 1993, 2000, for discussion).

Most likely, the full picture will be more complex than seems implied at first. For example, the effects of combinations of different neurotransmitters will have to be considered, and their interactions can be quite complex. There already have been propositions put forth, for example, about the effects of dopamine in the presence of serotonin (where it is thought to result in intelligent switching between responsive engagement and long-term planning) versus where serotonin is blocked (e.g., Katz, 1999). Similarly, even though dopamine may be the primary neurotransmitter associated with extraversion, the presence or absence of serotonin may play an important role in which aspect of extraversion (e.g., sociability vs. impulsiveness) is salient (e.g., Heller, 1997). The work linking affect (especially positive affect) and brain function is only just beginning, and certainly it will take some time to develop and refine this information.

As this development is pursued, however, the purposive nature of people's thinking and behavior will need to be integrated into our understanding of the effects of various neurotransmitters, singly or in concert. That is, the fact that people's goals influence their interpretations of situations and their behaviors in those situations is supported by so much evidence that such processes cannot be ignored in subsequent neurological analyses. This means that simple reductionism will not be appropriate; rather, insights from the cognitive, behavioral, and neuropsychological levels of analysis will have to be integrated and recognized as being mutually informative. To illustrate this point, consider the dopamine hypothesis of the mediation of the effects of positive affect on cognition. This hypothesis arose from the observation, at the behavioral and cognitive levels, that positive affect fosters cognitive flexibility and the ability to switch perspectives (together with the understanding that dopamine in the anterior cingulate region of the brain enables flexible perspective-taking or set-switching). (See also Isom & Heller, 1999, and Miller, 1996, for discussion of the bidirectionality of neurological, cognitive, and social or behavioral influence.)

Finally, it should be emphasized that all of the aforementioned effects of positive affect have resulted from mild, everyday affect inductions, experiences that can occur frequently in daily life. Furthermore, these effects have been observed when people were randomly assigned to experimental conditions. This indicates that these effects, many of which are beneficial and highly sought after (e.g., creative problem solving, helpfulness, improved conflict resolution), can be fostered readily in virtually everyone. Although there may be individual differences among people in abilities and skills underlying these processes, and perhaps even variability in genetic propensity toward them, those are not sufficient to negate the substantial power of simply induced, mild, happy feelings to enhance performance. For this reason, the currently pop-

ular foci involving genetic endowment, early-childhood experience, or individual differences developed over many years should not obscure the fact that people respond to their surroundings and that a small positive event can have powerful effects on many important processes. As current brain research is showing, even brain development itself responds to environmental stimuli throughout the life span. Thus, happy feelings not only are a source of important strength for people but also constitute one that is potentially available to all of us and those in our charge.

References

Aderman, D. (1972). Elation, depression and helping behavior. *Journal of Personality and Social Psychology, 24,* 91–101.

Armor, D. A., & Taylor, S. E. (1998). Situated optimism: Specific outcome expectancies and self-regulation. *Advances in Experimental Social Psychology, 30,* 309–379.

Ashby, F. G., Isen, A. M., & Turken, A. (1999). A neuropsychological theory of positive affect and its influence on cognition. *Psychological Review, 106,* 529–550.

Aspinwall, L. G. (1998). Rethinking the role of positive affect and self-regulation. *Motivation and Emotion, 23,* 1–32.

Aspinwall, L. G., & Richter, L. (1999). Optimism and self-mastery predict more rapid disengagement from unsolvable tasks in the presence of alternatives. *Motivation and Emotion, 23,* 221–245.

Aspinwall, L. G., & Taylor, S. E. (1997). A stitch in time: Self-regulation and proactive coping. *Psychological Bulletin, 121,* 417–436.

Baron, R. A. (1984). Reducing organizational conflict: An incompatible response approach. *Journal of Applied Psychology, 69,* 272–279.

Berkowitz, L. (1972). Social norms, feelings, and other factors affecting helping and altruism. In L. Berkowtiz (Ed.), *Advances in experimental social psychology* (Vol. 6, pp. 63–108). New York: Academic Press.

Berkowitz, L., & Daniels, L. (1964). Affecting the salience of the social responsibility norm: Effect of past help on response to dependency relationships. *Journal of Abnormal and Social Psychology, 67,* 275–281.

Bless, H., Bohner, G., Schwarz, N., & Strack, F. (1990). Mood and persuasion: A cognitive response analysis. *Personality and Social Psychology Bulletin, 16,* 331–345.

Bless, H., Clore, G. L., Schwarz, N., Golisano, V., Rabe, C., & Wolk, M. (1996). Mood and the use of scripts: Does a happy mood really lead to mindlessness? *Journal of Personality and Social Psychology, 71,* 665–679.

Cabib, S., & Puglisi-Allegra, S. (1999). Of genes, environment, and destiny. *Behavioral and Brain Sciences, 22,* 519.

Carnevale, P. J. D., & Isen, A. M. (1986). The influence of positive affect and visual access on the discovery of integrative solutions in bilateral negotiation. *Organizational Behavior and Human Decision Processes, 37,* 1–13.

Cunningham, M. R. (1979). Weather, mood, and helping behavior: Quasi-experiments in the sunshine Samaritan. *Journal of Personality and Social Psychology, 37,* 1947–1956.

Cunningham, M. R., Steinberg, J., & Grev, R. (1980). Wanting to and having to help: Separate motivations for positive mood and guilt-induced helping. *Journal of Personality and Social Psychology, 38,* 181–192.

Davidson, R. J. (1992). Emotion and affective style: Hemispheric substrates. *Psychological Science, 3,* 39–43.

Davidson, R. J. (1993). The neuropsychology of emotion and affective style. In M. Lewis & J. Haviland (Eds.), *Handbook of emotions* (pp. 143–154). New York: Guilford.

Davidson, R. J. (1999). Neuropsychological perspectives on affective styles and their cognitive consequences. In T. Dalgleish & M. Power (Eds.), *The handbook of cognition and emotion* (pp. 103–123). Sussex, England: Wiley.

Depue, R. A., & Collins, P. F. (1999). Neurobiology of the structure of personality: Dopamine, facilitation of incentive motivation, and extraversion. *Behavioral and Brain Sciences, 22,* 491–569.

Depue, R. A., Luciana, M., Arbisi, P., Collins, P., & Leon, A. (1994). Dopamine and the structure of personality: Relation of agonist-induced dopamine activity to positive emotionality. *Journal of Personality and Social Psychology, 67,* 485–498.

Derryberry, D. (1993). Attentional consequences of outcome-related motivational states: Congruent, incongruent, and focusing effects. *Motivation and Emotion, 17,* 65–90.

Dovidio, J. F., Gaertner, S. L., Isen, A. M., & Lowrance, R. (1995). Group representations and intergroup bias: Positive affect, similarity, and group size. *Personality and Social Psychology Bulletin, 21,* 856–865.

Dovidio, J. F., Gaertner, S. L., Isen, A. M., Rust, M., & Guerra, P. (1998). Positive affect, cognition, and the reduction of intergroup bias. In C. Sedikides, J. Schopler, & C. A. Insko (Eds.), *Intergroup cognition and intergroup behavior* (pp. 337–366). Mahwah, NJ: Erlbaum.

Estrada, C. A., Isen, A. M., & Young, M. J. (1994). Positive affect influences creative problem solving and reported source of practice satisfaction in physicians. *Motivation and Emotion, 18,* 285–299.

Estrada, C. A., Isen, A. M., & Young, M. J. (1997). Positive affect facilitates integration of information and decreases anchoring in reasoning among physicians. *Organizational Behavior and Human Decision Processes, 72,* 117–135.

Fredrickson, B. L. (1998). What good are positive emotions? *Review of General Psychology, 2,* 300–319.

Fredrickson, B. L., Mancuso, R. A., Branigan, C., & Tugade, M. M. (2000). The undoing effect of positive emotions. *Motivation and Emotion, 24,* 237–258.

George, J. M., & Brief, A. P. (1996). Motivational agendas in the workplace: The effects of feelings on focus of attention and work motivation. In L. L. Cummings & B. M. Staw (Eds.), *Research in organizational behavior, 18,* (pp. 75–109). Greenwich, CT: JAI Press.

Greene, T. R., & Noice, H. (1988). Influence of positive affect upon creative thinking and problem solving in children. *Psychological Reports, 63,* 895–898.

Heller, W. (1997). Emotion. In M. Banich (Ed.), *Neuropsychology: The neural bases of mental function,* Boston: Houghton Mifflin.

Hirt, E. R., Melton, R. J., McDonald, H. E., & Harackiewicz, J. M. (1996). Processing goals, task interest, and the mood-performance relationship: A mediational analysis. *Journal of Personality and Social Psychology, 71,* 245–261.

Isen, A. M. (1970). Success, failure, attention and reactions to others: The warm glow of success. *Journal of Personality and Social Psychology, 17,* 107–112

Isen, A. M. (1987). Positive affect, cognitive processes and social behavior. In L. Berkowitz (Ed.), *Advances in experimental social psychology* (pp. 203–253). New York: Academic Press.

Isen, A. M. (1990). The influence of positive and negative affect on cognitive organization: Implications for development. In N. Stein, B. Leventhal & T. Trabasso (Eds.), *Psychological and biological processes in the development of emotion* (pp. 75–94). Hillsdale, NJ: Erlbaum.

Isen, A. M. (1993). Positive affect and decision making. In M. Lewis & J. Haviland (Eds.), *Handbook of emotions* (pp. 261–277). New York: Guilford.

Isen, A. M. (1999a). On the relationship between affect and creative problem solving. In S. Russ (Ed.), *Affect, creative experience, and psychological adjustment* (pp. 3–17). Philadelphia: Taylor and Francis.

Isen, A. M. (1999b). Positive affect. In T. Dalgleish & M. Power (Eds.), *The handbook of cognition and emotion* (pp. 521–539). Sussex, England: Wiley.

Isen, A. M. (2000). Positive affect and decision making. In M. Lewis & J. Haviland-Jones (Eds.), *Handbook of emotions* (2nd ed., pp. 417–435). New York: Guilford.

Isen, A. M., & Baron, R. A. (1991). Positive affect in organizations. In L. Cummings & B. Staw (Eds.), *Research in organizational behavior, 13,* 1–52. Greenwich, CT: JAI Press.

Isen, A. M., Christianson, M., & Labroo, A. (2001). *The nature of the task influences whether positive affect facilitates task performance.* Unpublished manuscript, Cornell University, Ithaca, NY.

Isen, A. M., & Daubman, K. A. (1984). The influence of affect on categorization. *Journal of Personality and Social Psychology, 47,* 1206–1217.

Isen, A. M., Daubman, K. A., & Nowicki, G. P. (1987). Positive affect facilitates creative problem solving. *Journal of Personality and Social Psychology, 52,* 1122–1131.

Isen, A. M., & Geva, N. (1987). The influence of positive affect on acceptable level of risk: The person with a large canoe has a large worry. *Organizational Behavior and Human Decision Processes, 39,* 145–154.

Isen, A. M., Johnson, M. M. S., Mertz, E., & Robinson, F. G. (1985). The influence of positive affect on the unusualness of word association. *Journal of Personality and Social Psychology, 48,* 1413–1426.

Isen, A. M., & Levin, P. F. (1972). The effect of feeling good on helping: Cookies and kindness. *Journal of Personality and Social Psychology, 21,* 384–388.

Isen, A. M., & Means, B. (1983). The influence of positive affect on decision-making strategy. *Social Cognition, 2,* 18–31.

Isen, A. M., Niedenthal, P., & Cantor, N. (1992). The influence of positive affect on social categorization. *Motivation and Emotion, 16,* 65–78.

Isen, A. M., Nygren, T. E., & Ashby, F. G. (1988). The influence of positive affect on the perceived utility of gains and losses. *Journal of Personality and Social Psychology, 55,* 710–717.

Isen, A. M., & Patrick, R. (1983). The influence of positive feelings on risk taking: When the chips are down. *Organizational Behavior and Human Performance, 31,* 194–202.

Isen, A. M., Rosenzweig, A. S., & Young, M. J. (1991). The influence of positive affect on clinical problem solving. *Medical Decision Making, 11,* 221–227.

Isen, A. M., & Shalker, T. E. (1982). Do you "accentuate the positive, eliminate the negative" when you are in a good mood? *Social Psychology Quarterly, 45,* 58–63.

Isen, A. M., Shalker, T. E., Clark, M., & Karp, L. (1978). Affect, accessibility of material in memory and behavior: A cognitive loop? *Journal of Personality and Social Psychology, 36,* 1–12.

Isen, A. M., & Simmonds, S. F. (1978). The effect of feeling good on a helping task that is incompatible with good mood. *Social Psychology Quarterly, 41,* 345–349.

Isom, J., & Heller, W. (1999). Neurobiology of extraversion: Pieces of the puzzle still missing. *Behavioral and Brain Sciences, 22,* 524.

Johnson, E., & Tversky, A. (1983). Affect, generalization, and the perception of risk. *Journal of Personality and Social Psychology, 45,* 20–31.

Kahn, B., & Isen, A. M. (1993). The influence of positive affect on variety-seeking among safe, enjoyable products. *Journal of Consumer Research, 20,* 257–270.

Katz, L. D. (1999). Dopamine and serotonin: Integrating current affective engagement with longer-term goals. *Behavioral and Brain Sciences, 22,* 527.

Kraiger, K., Billings, R. S., and Isen, A. M. (1989). The influence of positive affective states on task perceptions and satisfaction. *Organizational Behavior and Human Decision Processes, 44,* 12–25.

Lee, A., & Sternthal, B. (1999). The effects of positive mood on memory. *Journal of Consumer Research, 26,* 115–127.

Mackie, D. M., & Worth, L. T. (1989). Cognitive deficits and the mediation of positive affect in persuasion. *Journal of Personality and Social Psychology, 57,* 27–40.

Mackie, D. M., & Worth, L. (1991). Feeling good but not thinking straight: The impact of positive mood on persuasion. In J. P. Forgas (Ed.), *Emotion and social judgment* (pp. 201–220). Oxford, England: Pergamon.

Melton, R. J. (1995). The role of positive affect in syllogism performance. *Personality and Social Psychology Bulletin, 21,* 788–794.

Miller, G. A. (1996). How we think about cognition, emotion, and biology in psychopathology. *Psychophysiology, 33,* 615–628.

Murray, N., Sujan, H., Hirt, E. R., & Sujan, M. (1990). The influence of mood on categorization: A cognitive flexibility interpretation. *Journal of Personality and Social Psychology, 59,* 411–425.

Nygren, T. E., Isen, A. M., Taylor, P. J., & Dulin, J. (1996). The influence of positive affect on the decision rule in risk situations: Focus on outcome (and especially avoidance of loss) rather than probability. *Organizational Behavior and Human Decision Processes, 66,* 59–72.

Owen, A. M., Roberts, A. C., Hodges, J. R., Summers, B. A., Polkey, C. E., & Robbins, T. W. (1993). Contrasting mechanisms of impaired attentional set-shifting in patients with frontal lobe damage or Parkinson's disease. *Brain, 116,* 1159–1175.

Pruitt, D. G. (1983). Strategic choice in negotiation. *American Behavioral Scientist, 27,* 167–194.

Reed, M. B., & Aspinwall, L. G. (1998). Self-affirmation reduces biased processing of health-risk information. *Motivation and Emotion, 22,* 99–132.

Scheier, M. F., & Carver, C. S. (1992). Effects of optimism on psychological well-being: Theoretical overview and empirical update. *Cognitive Therapy and Research, 16,* 201–228.

Schiffenbauer, A. (1974). Effects of observer's emotional state on judgments of the emotional state of others. *Journal of Personality and Social Psychology, 30,* 31–36.

Schwarz, N., & Bless, H. (1991). Happy and mindless, but sad and smart? The impact of affective states on analytic reasoning. In J. P. Forgas (Ed.), *Emotion and social judgment* (pp. 55–71). Oxford, England: Pergamon.

Showers, C., & Cantor, N. (1985). Social cognition: A look at motivated strategies. *Annual Review of Psychology, 36,* 275–305.

Smith, S. M., & Shaffer, D. R. (1991). The effects of good moods on systematic processing: "Willing but not able, or able but not willing?" *Motivation and Emotion, 15,* 243–279.

Snyder, C. R. (1994). *The psychology of hope: You can get there from here.* New York: Free Press.

Staw, B. M., & Barsade, S. G. (1993). Affect and managerial performance: A test of the sadder-but-wiser vs. happier-and-smarter hypotheses. *Administrative Science Quarterly, 38,* 304–331.

Taylor, S. E., & Aspinwall, L. G. (1996). Mediating and moderating processes in psychosocial stress: Appraisal, coping, resistance and vulnerability. In H. B. Kaplan (Ed.), *Psychosocial stress: Perspectives on structure, theory, life-course, and methods* (pp. 71–110). San Diego, CA: Academic Press.

Trope, Y., & Netter, E. (1994). Reconciling competing motives in self-evaluation: The role of self-control in feedback seeking. *Journal of Personality and Social Psychology, 66,* 646–657.

Trope, Y., & Pomerantz, E. M. (1998). Resolving conflicts among self-evaluative motives: Positive experiences as a resource for overcoming defensiveness. *Motivation and Emotion, 22,* 53–72.

Urada, M., & Miller, N. (2000). The impact of positive mood and category importance on crossed categorization effects. *Journal of Personality and Social Psychology, 78,* 417–433.

Veitch, R., & Griffitt, W. (1976). Good news–bad news: Affective and interpersonal effects. *Journal of Applied Social Psychology, 6,* 69–75.

Watson, D. A., & Tellegen, A. (1985). Toward a consensual structure of mood. *Psychological Bulletin, 98,* 219–235.

39

From Social Structure to Biology

Integrative Science in Pursuit of Human Health and Well-Being

Carol D. Ryff & Burton Singer

What does it mean to be psychologically well, and what are the factors that promote such well-being? These are the initial questions we will explore in this chapter. A multidimensional formulation of psychological well-being derived from numerous conceptual frameworks will be described, and we will use this framework to summarize findings on individual differences in positive psychological functioning. Variation associated with sociodemographic factors (i.e., age, gender, socioeconomic status) is of particular interest. Data from community and national samples (both cross-sectional and longitudinal) will be reviewed to illustrate how well-being is *contoured* by broad life course and social structural influences.

We then shift to different questions—namely, what are the physiological substrates of psychological well-being, and how do they influence physical health? We will describe a conception of positive human health that is fundamentally anchored in psychological and social well-being. Our approach contrasts with the prevailing formulations of health, which are de-fined primarily in negative terms (e.g., illness, disease, functional limitations, disability). Although the science of positive human health is in its infancy, we highlight beginning lines of inquiry that illustrate links between psychological and social well-being and health. The neurobiological mechanisms that might account for these outcomes also are considered.

The overarching objective of this chapter is to advance a perspective of human health and well-being that is deeply *integrative*. On the one hand, our research reaches *outward* to connect psychological well-being to macro-level, social structural forces; on the other hand, our agenda reaches *inward* to probe the biology of well-being and its role in extending both length and quality of life. In terms of integrative science, the approach we advocate is consistent with E. O. Wilson's (1998) challenge to scholars of the 21st century to embark on the task of *consilience*—that is, the linking of facts and theories across the scientific disciplines. We believe that understanding the nature of human well-being—what it is and how it comes about, as well as its implications for biology and health—illustrates a rich forum within which to pursue consilience. It also affords promising new directions for promoting positive health via interventions targeted at enhancing individuals' psychosocial well-being.

Psychological Well-Being: What Is It and Who Has It?

Portrayals of the Positive

The discipline of psychology has long been interested in what constitutes positive psychological functioning (for reviews see Ryff, 1985, 1989a; Ryff & Singer, 1998a, in press-a). William James (1902/1958), for example, articulated a vision of "healthy-mindedness"; Carl Jung (1933) wrote about processes of individuation, self-realization, and coming into selfhood; Abraham Maslow (1968) offered detailed descriptions of what it means to be self-actualized; Erik Erikson (1959) depicted the continuing challenges from infancy to old age for the developing ego; Gordon Allport (1961) put forth a conception of maturity; Carl Rogers (1961) characterized the fully functioning person; Karl and Charlotte Bühler (Bühler, 1935) wrote about basic life tendencies that work toward the fulfillment of life; and Marie Jahoda (1958) drew on many of these formulations to enumerate positive components of mental health, in contrast to the prevailing construals of mental health as the absence of the negative (e.g., depression, anxiety).

As a cursory review of contemporary texts in personality psychology would reveal, more players could be added to the list of "positive psychologists." The field of psychology thus has shown a persistent interest in healthy, adaptive sides of human functioning. Outside the discipline are yet other efforts to delineate optimal features of the human experience. Coan (1977) summarized visions of what constitutes the best in us via a sweeping historical portrayal that contrasted ideals of the early Greeks with views from the Middles Ages, the Renaissance and Romantic eras, and more recent philosophies (e.g., existentialism). In each period, unique qualities were upheld as the pinnacle of human potentiality (e.g., reason, close contact with the divine, creative self-expression). Coan also juxtaposed these Western varieties of ultimate capacities with Eastern perspectives that elevate other qualities (e.g., transcending the illusion of separateness, overcoming desire—the source of suffering, living mindfully). From the field of philosophy, Becker (1992) offers yet another view via different formulations of specific criteria that define the "good life."

Taken together, these accounts illustrate the abiding interest, in psychology and beyond, in depicting the highest levels of human functioning and the ideals toward which we, as mere mortals, strive in our life journeys. Viewed in this light, recent interest in positive psychology represents a return to core issues that have captivated the imagination of scholars and philosophers throughout time. To grapple with what constitutes optimal functioning is, at the most basic level, to broach ultimate questions of why we are here and how we should live. Contemporary social science has much to contribute, via its empirical findings, and to gain, via the science of human betterment, engagement with these questions.

Nonetheless, it is the case that empirically oriented realms of psychology have been slow to embark on scientific studies of the positive. Why is this so? A key factor undoubtedly reflects funding priorities—that is, it always has been easier to obtain grant support to study maladies of the human condition rather than human strengths. The latter often have been dismissed as low-priority luxuries vis-à-vis real social problems that must be given preference in allocating scarce resources. Fortunately, growing interest in health promotion and increasing evidence that prevention works are signaling shifts in funding climates toward support for research on the positive (Albee & Gullotta, 1997; Raczynski & DiClemente, 1999).

A further impediment to the science of well-being has been the paucity of reliable and valid assessment tools. Without instruments that operationalize the preceding characterizations of optimal functioning, it is impossible to probe their varieties, causes, or consequences. One response to the need for measurement tools has been a multidimensional model of positive psychological functioning that represents points of convergence in many of the previously described formulations (see Ryff, 1989a). Six key dimensions (see definitions in Table 39.1) provided conceptual starting points for developing assessment instruments (see Ryff, 1989b; Ryff & Keyes, 1995). Together, these dimensions encompass diverse features of what it means to be well, including having positive regard for one's self and one's past life, good-quality relationships with others, a sense that life is purposeful

Table 39.1 Definitions of Theory-Guided Dimensions of Well-Being

Self-Acceptance

High scorer: possesses a positive attitude toward the self; acknowledges and accepts multiple aspects of self, including good and bad qualities; feels positive about past life.

Low scorer: feels dissatisfied with self; is disappointed with what has occurred in past life; is troubled about certain personal qualities; wishes to be different than what he or she is.

Positive Relations with Others

High scorer: has warm, satisfying, trusting relationships with others; is concerned about the welfare of others; capable of strong empathy, affection, and intimacy; understands give-and-take of human relationships.

Low scorer: has few close, trusting relationships with others; finds it difficult to be warm, open, and concerned about others; is isolated and frustrated in interpersonal relationships; is not willing to make compromises to sustain important ties with others.

Autonomy

High scorer: is self-determining and independent; is able to resist social pressures to think and act in certain ways; regulates behavior from within; evaluates self by personal standards.

Low scorer: is concerned about the expectations and evaluations of others; relies on judgments of others to make important decisions; conforms to social pressures to think and act in certain ways.

Environmental Mastery

High scorer: has a sense of mastery and competence in managing the environment; controls complex array of external activities; makes effective use of surrounding opportunities; is able to choose or create contexts suitable to personal needs and values.

Low scorer: has difficulty managing everyday affairs; feels unable to change or improve surrounding context; is unaware of surrounding opportunities; lacks sense of control over external world.

Purpose in Life

High scorer: has goals in life and a sense of directedness; feels there is meaning to present and past life; hold beliefs that give life purpose; has aims and objectives for living.

Low scorer: lacks a sense of meaning in life; has few goals or aims; lacks sense of direction; does not see purpose in past life; has no outlooks or beliefs that give life meaning.

Personal Growth

High scorer: has a feeling of continued development; sees self as growing and expanding; is open to new experiences; has sense of realizing his or her potential; sees improvement in self and behavior over time; is changing in ways that reflect more self-knowledge and effectiveness.

Low scorer: has a sense of personal stagnation; lacks sense of improvement or expansion over time; feels bored and uninterested with life; feels unable to develop new attitudes or behaviors.

---

and meaningful, the capacity to effectively manage one's surrounding world, the ability to follow inner convictions, and a sense of continuing growth and self-realization. Other components undoubtedly could be added to this provisional model, which, whatever its limitations, has provided tools for empirical assessment of well-being.

Empirical Coordinates of Psychological Well-Being: Variations by Age, Gender, and Socioeconomic Status

In this section, we briefly summarize findings from multiple studies regarding variation in well-being by age, gender, and socioeconomic

status (indexed primarily by level of education). We target these variations because all three speak to how well-being is *contoured* by larger forces, be they biological (aging/maturational processes), or social structural influences (position in social hierarchies, access to resources and life opportunities). Our investigations also have linked well-being to other psychological variables (e.g., social comparison processes, attributions, coping strategies, personality traits), but for the present purposes we restrict our focus to sociodemographic variation.

With both local community samples and nationally representative samples, we have documented replicable patterns of *age differences* in well-being (Ryff, 1989b, 1991; Ryff & Keyes,

1995; Ryff & Singer, 1998c). Recent data from MIDUS, a national survey conducted by the MacArthur Midlife Research Network, illustrate these patterns (see Figure 39.1). What is apparent is the diversity of patterns by age—that is, some aspects of well-being show incremental profiles, others decremental, and still others, little variation with age. Environmental mastery and autonomy, for example, have repeatedly shown incremental patterns from

young adulthood through midlife to old age. Purpose in life and personal growth, in contrast, repeatedly show downward trajectories across these age periods. Self-acceptance, in turn, tends to show little age variation, as do positive relations with others (only for women). Such replicable patterns have been obtained with scales of different depth of measurement (e.g., 20-item, 14-item, 3-item; Ryff, 1989b, 1991; Ryff & Keyes, 1995).

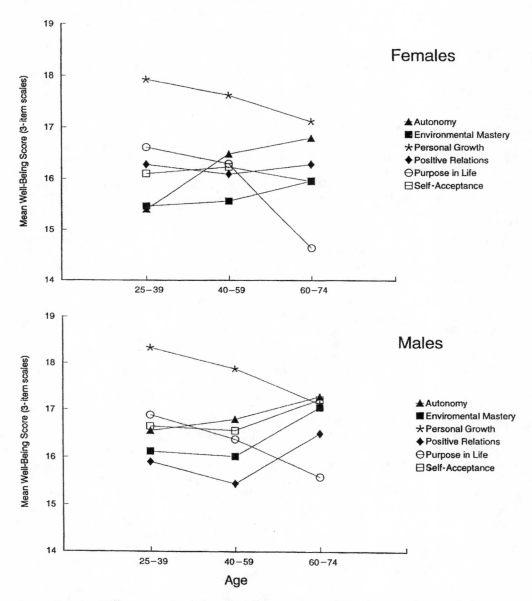

Figure 39.1 Age Differences in Psychological Well-Being. *Source:* MIDUS (MacArther National Survey)

Though cross-sectional data cannot clarify whether these patterns represent aging/maturational changes or cohort differences, other longitudinal findings have shown that change in well-being does occur with aging, particularly in the context of life transitions (Kling, Ryff, & Essex, 1997; Kling, Seltzer, & Ryff, 1997). The strong consistency (in both national and community samples) of the sharply lower scores on purpose in life and personal growth among older adults compared with young and midlife adults speaks, we believe, to important societal challenges regarding the growing aged population. More people are living ever longer, but relative to younger groups, they report diminished opportunities to keep their lives purposeful and engaged as well as limited venues for continued growth and development. These findings perhaps are related to what sociologists refer to as the *structural lag* problem—namely, that contemporary social institutions "lag behind" the added years of life that many now experience (Riley, Kahn, & Foner, 1994). As such, the research points to important societal challenges regarding the rapidly expanding aged population.

With regard to *gender differences* in well-being, our studies also have uncovered important new findings. Specifically, women have shown comparable or more positive profiles on well-being compared with men. For the interpersonal dimension of well-being—positive relations with others—women always score significantly higher than men. In fact, as shown in Figure 39.1, interpersonal well-being is the lowest rated dimension for men, although open-ended interviews have documented that men, like women, espouse relatedness as a key component of ideal functioning (see Ryff, 1989c). In several studies (including a Korean sample), women also have shown higher profiles on personal growth relative to men (Ryff & Singer, 1998c). These findings offer an important counterpoint to evidence that women are at greater risk for depression than men (Culbertson, 1997). Women's psychological strengths in the well-being realm do not challenge these gender differences in depression; rather, they enrich the picture by pointing out that psychological vulnerabilities may exist, side by side, with notable psychological strengths. Alternatively, for men, the data have underscored that their interpersonal well-being may be compromised (relative to women and relative to their own ideals). Multidimensional assessment of well-being thus has provided a more comprehensive understanding of gender differences in mental health.

Do psychological strengths accrue disproportionately to those possessing greater access to resources and opportunities in life? This is the question of *socioeconomic differences* in psychological well-being, which relates to the growing interest in social inequalities in health, both mental and physical (Adler, Marmot, McEwen, & Stewart, 1999). Prior studies have documented that the poor and disadvantaged are more likely to experience mental and physical illness, as well as greater life stress, than those with socioeconomic advantages (Adler et al., 1994; McLeod & Kessler, 1990). Are they also less likely to experience positive well-being? Figure 39.2 summarizes educational differences in psychological well-being among members of the Wisconsin Longitudinal Study (WLS), begun in 1957 with a random sample of high school seniors. The data, based on assessments of well-being at age 53 ($N = 6,306$), show higher profiles of well-being for those persons with more education, with the results being particularly strong for women. Even after controlling for other life history variables (e.g., high school IQ, parental education, income, occupational status), education remains a strong predictor of psychological well-being (see Ryff, Magee, Kling, & Wing, 1999).

Similar patterns are evident in the MIDUS national survey, where well-being and other indicators of health have been shown to be compromised among persons with less education (Marmot et al., 1998; Marmot, Ryff, Bumpass Shipley, & Marks, 1997). Another representative sample—the National Survey of Families and Households (based on 13,017 Americans)—revealed both age *and* educational differences on purpose in life (Bumpass & Aquilino, 1995). That is, the findings converged with prior results, showing that with age one is less likely to report high levels of purpose in life, but in addition clarified that one is less likely to have high purpose if one has less education. Figure 39.3 summarizes the results of age and education and the likelihood of being in the upper quartile on life purpose. Because positive psychological functioning may well constitute a protective resource in the face of challenge and life adversity (Ryff & Singer, 2000a; Ryff, Singer, Love, & Essex, 1998),

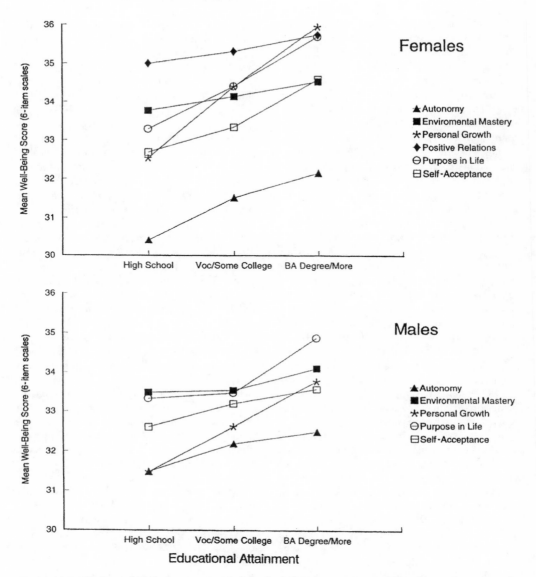

Figure 39.2 Educational Differences in Psychological Well-Being. *Source:* MIDUS (MacArther National Survey)

these findings draw attention to the diminished profile of such strengths among persons with less education.

Another finding that has emerged from the assessment of psychological well-being in nationally representative samples is illustrated in Figure 39.4. Arrayed in the figure are maximum and minimum values and 25th, 50th, and 75th percentiles of well-being (in this case, for purpose in life, although similar pat-

terns are evident for other dimensions). What can be seen is that variability in well-being *increases* as one moves down the educational hierarchy. That is, there is greater spread, particularly at the low end, among individuals with less education. These findings are important for two reasons. First, they underscore the importance of assessing psychological well-being in sociodemographically diverse samples. Such effects would be missed entirely with the

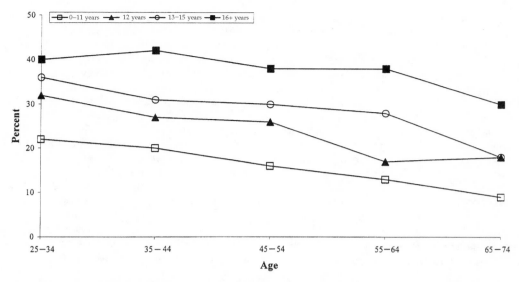

Figure 39.3 High Purpose in Life: Age and educational variation (percent in upper quartile of scale). *Source:* NSFH (National Survey of Families & Households)

college-sophomore subject pools, whose restricted range, in turn, will fundamentally limit efforts to connect well-being to other factors. Second, distributions such as the one illustrated in Figure 39.4 point to new directions in the study of psychological resilience, defined as having high well-being *despite educational disadvantage.* Inquiry along these lines can be instrumental in identifying the

sustaining strengths that enable some to experience well-being, despite life's inequities (see Markus, Ryff, & Barnett, in press; see also other chapters in this volume on topics of resilience, optimism, and hope).

This select summary of findings excludes the extensive work that has been conducted on how well-being is influenced by life experiences and life transitions (e.g., parenthood, caregiving, re-

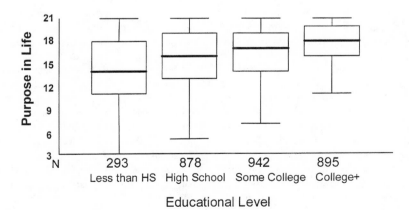

Figure 39.4 Variation in purpose in life by level of education (five-number summary).

location, marital status changes; e.g., Li, Seltzer, & Greenberg, 1999; Marks & Lambert, 1998; Ryff, Schmutte, & Lee, 1996; Smider, Essex, & Ryff, 1996), as well as by goals, social comparison processes, personality traits, and coping strategies (e.g., Heidrich & Ryff, 1993; Kling, Seltzer, & Ryff, 1997; McGregor & Little, 1998; Ryff & Singer, 1998d; Schmutte & Ryff, 1997). We chose to focus on sociodemographic variation to underscore the influence of social structural and life course factors on well-being, and thereby to broaden the disciplinary purview of how to think about individual differences in well-being.

Well-Being, Biology, and Health: Are the Criterial Goods Protective?

Positive Health and the Physiological Substrates of Flourishing

In 1948 the World Health Organization defined health as a "state of complete physical, mental, and social well-being and not merely the absence of disease or infirmity" (World Health Organization, 1948, p. 28). Unfortunately, this visionary conception did not guide subsequent studies of human health. Rather, the past half century shows a persistent focus on health defined in terms of illness, disease, dysfunction, and disability. We recently called for renewed emphasis on "positive health" (Ryff & Singer, 1998a, 1998b), albeit with a somewhat different slant. We argued that psychological and social well-being are, indeed, part of health; but, more important, we underscored the need to understand the neurobiology that underlies psychosocial flourishing. This is a call to embark on a new era of science on positive functioning conceived as a *biopsychosocial nexus*, that is, the salubrious joining of mind and body (Ryff & Singer, 2000a).

To explicate mechanisms that might account for how the "criterial goods" (e.g., quality relationships, purposeful engagement) might influence health, we put forth three promising research directions: examination of allostatic load, cerebral activation asymmetry, and immune competence. The first pertains to a measure of cumulative wear and tear on numerous physiological systems (cardiovascular, metabolic, hypothalamic-pituitary-adrenal [HPA] axis, sympathetic nervous system; Seeman, Singer, Rowe, Horwitz, & McEwen, 1997; Seeman,

McEwen, Rowe, & Singer, 2001). Longitudinal aging research has shown that high allostatic load predicts incident cardiovascular disease, cognitive impairment, declines in physical functioning, and mortality. The key question for positive health, however, is whether psychological and social strengths *decrease* the likelihood of high physiological wear and tear (i.e., decrease high allostatic load)? In other words, does well-being serve a protective function? In a subsequent section, we will offer preliminary evidence providing an affirmative answer.

The second venue, that of cerebral activation asymmetry, emerges from affective neuroscience and its elaboration of the neural circuitry of emotion (Davidson, 1995, 1998; Sutton & Davidson, 1997). This work has demonstrated that individuals showing greater left as compared with right prefrontal activation in response to emotional stimuli are more likely to show positive affect and are less vulnerable to depression. Viewed more broadly, the positive health question is whether psychological strengths (e.g., purposeful engagement, positive self-regard) are neurally instantiated in particular patterns of neural activation. Although affective neuroscience has actively pursued the brain mechanisms that are implicated in depression, it is also important to advance scientific agendas that probe the neural circuitry of human flourishing.

The third direction, immune competence, is derived from the growing literature on psychoneuroimmunology, which links psychosocial factors and immune function (Maier, Watkins, & Fleshner, 1994). Here, three decades of research has probed the psychological modulation of immunity, but the emphasis has been primarily on exposure to stressors (e.g., electric shocks, restraints, or maternal separation in animals; exams, divorce, caregiving, or loneliness in humans). The positive counterpoint that would link, for example, zestful engagement in living, or loving and nurturing social relationships to cellular and humoral immunity has received far less scientific attention. These are questions that go to the core of whether psychosocial strengths are protective.

Other mechanisms could be added as promising routes for elaborating the neurobiology of flourishing, such as via central neuropeptides (oxytocin and vasopressin), neurogenesis, anabolic systems and growth factors, and gene expression (for examples of each, see Ryff & Singer, 2000a, 2000b). Indeed, the scientific opportunities for connecting psychological and social flourishing to processes within the brain and the body are vast. In the following sections, we briefly describe select lines of inquiry that have begun to explore connections between different aspects of well-being and health. With regard to physiological substrates, our illustrative focus is on allostatic load.

Quality Relationships With Others and Health

Having good-quality relationships with others is universally endorsed as being central to optimal living (Ryff & Singer, 1998a). The relational world has received extensive attention by social scientists, as in studies of attachment, close personal relationships, marital quality, and family ties, although much of this literature has not been explicitly concerned with health (Ryff & Singer, 2000b). Alternatively, two decades of social epidemiology has provided repeated evidence that social isolation or lack of social support is related to increased risk of disease and reduced length of life (Berkman, 1995; House, Landis, & Umberson, 1988; Seeman, 1996).

In reviewing this prior literature and seeking to advance the positive health agenda, we have enumerated several targets for future research (Ryff & Singer, 2000b, in press-b; Ryff, Singer, Wing, & Love, 2001). One pertains to the need to capture more fully the *emotions of interpersonal flourishing*, particularly the delicate dance between positive and negative emotions that constitute quality ties to significant others. Rewarding relationships (phenomenologically and possibly physiologically) are not those in which negative affect and adverse experience are largely absent, but rather those in which adversity and difficult feelings are successfully negotiated. Thus, negative emotions are fundamental to social relationships, but how they are handled is likely what differentiates healthy from unhealthy ties. A second emphasis addresses the need to track social relationships through time so as to understand *cumulative profiles of relational well-being*. If loving (or tormenting) ties to others have a neurobiological signature, it is the chronic, recurring nature of such beneficial (or detrimental) connection that is likely to be consequential for health. And, as noted previously, understanding these consequences requires explication of underlying mechanisms.

To illustrate our efforts to implement these ideas, we briefly will describe recent findings from a biological subsample of members of the Wisconsin Longitudinal Study (WLS; Ryff et al., 2001; Singer & Ryff, 1999). The WLS was initiated in 1957 with a random sample of one-third of all high school seniors in the state of Wisconsin. A large majority of these individuals was followed over the ensuing decades, with detailed data collected on numerous aspects of their educational and occupational achievements, as well as work and family lives, health, and well-being. To pursue the kinds of research questions described previously, we collected neurobiological data on a subsample (106 individuals, 57 male and 49 female) of the WLS. Respondents were selected to be within geographic proximity to the UW-Madison campus (where biological data were collected). It should be noted, however, that this small subsample matched the full WLS sample on income, in both their families of origin and their own adult household incomes (see Singer & Ryff, 1999).

To pursue the idea of cumulative relationship pathways (positive and negative), we asked the respondents to complete two inventories. One (the Parental Bonding Scale) assessed the extent to which their parents (assessed separately for mothers and fathers) were caring, supportive, and affectionate when they were growing up. The other (PAIR Inventory) was designed to assess multiple dimensions of adult spousal intimacy (emotional, sexual, recreational, intellectual). Individuals were defined as being on the *positive relationship pathway* if they had at least one parent (mother or father) who was caring and affectionate (i.e., above the median on the Parental Bonding Scale) and they also had at least one of two forms of adult spousal intimacy (i.e., above the median emotional/sexual scales or intellectual/recreational scales). Individuals were defined as being on the *negative relationship pathway* if they had negative bonds with both parents and/or had negative interaction with a spouse on both combined aspects of intimacy described previously. The majority on the negative pathway (61% for women, 74% for men) fulfilled both criteria (for details see Ryff et al., 2001).

Our question was whether these cumulative relationship profiles would be related to the respondents' levels of allostatic load—specifically, would those on the positive pathway be less likely to have high allostatic load than those on the negative pathway? Allostatic load was mea-

sured with multiple components of physiological function (systolic and diastolic blood pressure, waist-hip ratio, cholesterol [HDL and ratio
of total cholesterol to HDL], glycosylated he-
moglobin, urinary cortisol, urinary epinephrine,
urinary norepinephrine, DHEA-S). Collectively,
these address the cardiovascular system, the
HPA axis, the metabolic system, and the sympathetic nervous system (for details see Seeman
et al., 1997; Singer & Ryff, 1999). Figure 39.5
shows the percentage of individuals having high
allostatic load (defined as being in the top quartile of risk for three or more of the preceding
indicators) as a function of whether they were
on the positive or negative relationship pathway. As predicted, those on the positive pathway were significantly less likely to have high
allostatic load than were those on the negative
pathway, although the effects were stronger for
men than for women.

These findings suggest possible protective influences associated with having persistently
positive, loving, caring, intimate relationships
with one's significant others. In further analyses, we juxtaposed these relational histories
with the respondents' economic histories
(Singer & Ryff, 1999). Following from our preceding emphasis on socioeconomic factors, we
expected that individuals who had lived with cumulative economic disadvantage (i.e., being below the median on household income in childhood and adulthood) would be more likely to
have high allostatic load than those having persistent economic advantage. We found this to
be the case: 50% of those on the negative economic pathway (n = 22) had high allostatic
load, compared with 36% on the positive economic pathway (n = 19). However, putting
these economic and relational pathways together, we learned something additionally important—namely, that positive relationship profiles could help *offset* the likelihood of
experiencing high allostatic load if one was on
the negative economic pathway. Specifically,
among those with persistent economic adversity, but positive relational profiles (n = 13),
only 22% had high allostatic load, compared
with 69% of those with the same economic profile but on the negative relational path (n = 9).

Given the limited sample size as well as the
retrospective nature of the relational assessments, these findings are preliminary. Nonetheless, they provide initial evidence of the possible physiological benefits associated with
having good-quality relations, particularly in

the contexts of disadvantage and adversity. The
latter illustrate a kind of biopsychosocial pathway of resilience, something we believe warrants further attention in future research (Ryff
et al., 1998).

Psychological Well-Being and Allostatic Load

Using data from the same biological subsample
of the WLS, we will conclude this section on
positive health with a brief summary of how
levels of allostatic load are distributed as a function of an individual's standing on each of the
six dimensions described in detail in preceding
sections. These analyses have the advantage of
providing a more differentiated perspective on
positive psychology vis-à-vis biology than the
prior relational analyses, but they lack the emphasis on *cumulative* well-being described in
the preceding relationship profiles. Nonetheless,
they are informative next steps in efforts to
probe the physiological substrates of numerous
dimensions of flourishing.

Figure 39.6 summarizes the data, presented
separately for men (n = 57) and women (n =
49). Using median-split procedures, each sample
is divided between those at or below the median
and those above the median on all six dimensions of well-being. On all aspects of well-being
except one (autonomy), men with higher well-
being were less likely to have high allostatic
load. Echoing our preceding analyses, however,
the strongest differences were evident on the
interpersonal dimension of well-being: 60% of
men with low scores on positive relations with
others had high allostatic load, compared with
about 36% of men with high scores on interpersonal well-being. The next most noticeable
differences were evident for the purpose in life
assessments, followed by personal growth, self-
acceptance, and environmental mastery. Only
the differences for positive relations were statistically significant (perhaps linked to the small
sample and hence limited statistical power).

What is first evident for women is that, overall, they have a lower likelihood of having high
allostatic load compared with men. This finding
may be informative considering the near 7-year
advantage in life expectancy that women have
relative to men. However, the direction of effects between women with high versus low
well-being is *opposite* to what we had predicted
for all outcomes. That is, women are more
likely to have high allostatic load if they have

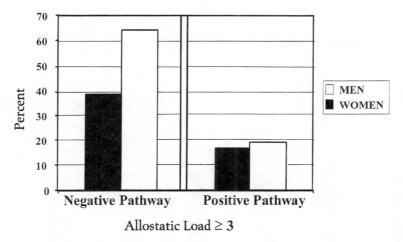

Figure 39.5 Relationship pathways and high allostatic load.

higher well-being, with the differences being most pronounced for women who report high levels of personal growth (statistically significant difference), followed by high environmental mastery (approached statistical significance) and purpose in life. What do these findings mean? We know from examining the underlying components of allostatic load that women are more likely than men to show high profiles on indicators from the HPA axis (cortisol, epinephrine, norepinephrine). Thus, the results suggest that women who are striving to realize their talents through continuing growth and are highly engaged in managing complex environments may have higher activation of stress hormones. Whether these elevated profiles translate to downstream differences in other physiological systems (i.e., is an elevated HPA axis a precursor to an elevated cardiovascular profile?) and/or functional health outcomes remains to be answered. And certainly, the small sample calls for more data collection cases as well as replication efforts.

That the outcomes for positive relations with others for women did not converge with the prior findings on relationship pathways is a conundrum, perhaps explained by the emphasis on significant primary relationships (i.e., parents, spouse) in the prior analyses as well as their cumulative features. Whatever the interpretation, these findings underscore the need for future inquiries linking psychological and social strengths to physiological systems, and point to possible gender differences therein. And, as we have described earlier, there are nu-

merous other bridges to be built between neurobiology and well-being (e.g., cerebral activation asymmetry, neurogenesis, immune function, gene expression). The present work serves as a preliminary illustration of a much larger agenda.

Interventive Significance: Can Well-Being Be Promoted?

A fundamental question in the study of positive psychology is what, if anything, can be done to promote greater levels of well-being for ever larger segments of the population? Can interventions be developed to enhance individuals' experience of the criterial goods in life? Although some may argue that propensities for well-being are inscribed in one's genes—that is, that some have more "joy juice" than others (Meehl, 1975)—a new line of intervention work suggests that even those who suffer from major depression can, in fact, benefit from efforts to improve their capacities to experience positive self-regard, quality ties to others, a sense of purpose and direction, continued growth, and so on. This is the work of Giovanni Fava (Fava, 1999; Fava, Rafanelli, Cazzaro, et al., 1998; Fava, Rafanelli, Grandi Conti, & Belluardo, 1998) that has addressed the problem of relapse among those who suffer from depression.

Fava and colleagues argue that in the residual phase of major depression, when debilitating symptoms have subsided but well-being is not fully regained, individuals are at high risk

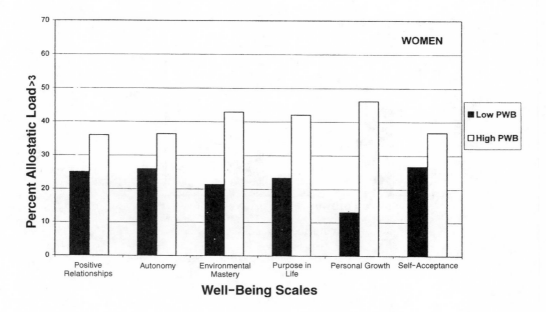

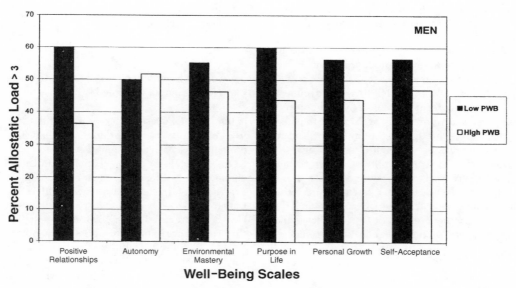

Figure 39.6 High versus low well-being and high allostatic load (for women and men).

for relapse. It is during this period that they particularly need therapy designed to help increase their share of joy juice. To help achieve this end, he implements "well-being therapy," in which clients, via the keeping of daily diaries, are instructed to write about their positive experiences, whatever these might be. When brought to therapy, these experiences are then used by the clinician to help enlarge the clients' understanding of various aspects of well-being (using the Ryff multidimensional model as a guide) and also to help them understand ways in which they may undermine or prematurely curtail their own experiences of the positive. Those participating in such therapy have shown improved remission profiles compared with those receiving standard clinical treatment (Fava, Rafanelli, Grandi, et al., 1998). Thus, it appears that even among those for whom well-being is most elusive, there may be hope (see Snyder, Rand, & Sigmon, this volume).

Conclusions

Our purpose in this chapter has been to summarize a program of research dealing with psychological well-being. We have argued that psychology, philosophy, and history have shown long-standing interest in what it means to function optimally. However, empirical research has lagged behind efforts to assess and understand human dysfunction and distress. A multidimensional formulation of well-being was presented as a provisional model for measuring positive functioning. We then showed individual differences on these various dimensions of well-being related to one's age, gender, and socioeconomic standing. Collectively, these studies have drawn attention to particular areas of vulnerability among the aged and to particular strengths among women, and they have underscored the diminished profiles of well-being among individuals with less education.

We followed these analyses with more recent efforts to link positive psychosocial strengths to health. A full understanding of human health encompasses not only physical well-being but also psychological and social flourishing. What is needed, however, are scientific strides that clarify the neurobiology associated with such flourishing and its role in promoting both length and quality of life. To illustrate the work that needs to be done to advance the positive health agenda, we summarized findings showing that individuals with more positive social relationship histories were less likely to show high allostatic load than those with more negative relational histories. We also described preliminary links between allostatic load to the six dimensions of well-being, with the findings highlighting gender differences in need of further clarification in future research.

Overall, our aim as been to take psychological well-being, a prototype of positive psychology, and link it outward to social structure and inward to biology. Traversing this wide territory demonstrates the multidisciplinary scope of research on positive functioning, both how it is contoured by macro-level societal forces and

what its consequences are for understanding health as the presence of wellness. As noted at the beginning of this chapter, this is a scientific agenda in the true spirit of consilience. Finally, that well-being can be promoted, even among those least likely to experience it (Fava's well-being therapy), underscores the interventive promise of this new area of inquiry.

Acknowledgments This research was supported by the John D. and Catherine T. MacArthur Foundation Research Networks on Successful Midlife Development and Socioeconomic Status and Health, as well as National Institute on Aging Grant R01-AG13613, National Institute of Mental Health Grant P50-MH61083, and a grant to the General Clinical Research Center of the University of Wisconsin–Madison (M01-RR03186).

References

Adler, N. E., Boyce, T., Chesney, M. A., Cohen, S., Folkman, S., Kahn, R. L., & Syme, L. (1994). Socioeconomic status and health: The challenge of the gradient. *American Psychologist, 49*, 15–24.

Adler, N. E., Marmot, M., McEwen, B. S., & Stewart, J. (Eds.). (1999). Socioeconomic status and health in industrialized nations: Social, psychological, and biological pathways. *Annals of the New York Academy of Sciences* (Vol. 896). New York: New York Academy of Sciences.

Albee, G. E., & Gullotta, T. P. (Eds.). (1997). *Primary prevention works.* Thousand Oaks, CA: Sage.

Allport, G. W. (1961). *Pattern and growth in personality.* New York: Holt, Rinehart and Winston.

Becker, L. C. (1992). Good lives: Prolegomena. *Social Philosophy and Policy, 9*, 15–37.

Berkman, L. F. (1995). The role of social relations in health promotion. *Psychosomatic Medicine, 57*, 245–254.

Bühler, C. (1935). The curve of life as studied in biographies. *Journal of Applied Psychology, 19*, 405–409.

Bumpass, L. L., & Aquilino, W. S. (1995). *A social map of midlife: Family and work over the middle life course.* Vero Beach, FL: John D. and Catherine T. MacArthur Foundation Research Network on Successful Midlife Development.

Coan, R. W. (1977). *Hero, artist, sage, or saint? A survey of what is variously called mental health, normality, maturity, self-actualization, and human fulfillment.* New York: Columbia University Press.

Culbertson, F. M. (1997). Depression and gender: An international review. *American Psychologist, 52,* 25–31.

Davidson, R. J. (1995). Cerebral asymmetry, emotion, and affective style. In R. J. Davidson & K. Hugdahl (Eds.), *Brain asymmetry* (pp. 361–387). Cambridge, MA: MIT Press.

Davidson, R. J. (1998). Affective style and affective disorders: Perspectives from affective neuroscience. *Cognition and Emotion, 12,* 307–330.

Erikson, E. (1959). Identity and the life cycle. *Psychological Issues, 1,* 18–164.

Fava, G. A. (1999). Well-being therapy: Conceptual and technical issues. *Psychotherapy and Psychosomatics, 68,* 171–179.

Fava, G. A., Rafanelli, C., Cazzaro, M., Conti, S., & Grandi, S. (1998). Well-being therapy: A novel psychotherapeutic approach for residual symptoms of affective disorders. *Psychological Medicine, 28,* 475–480.

Fava, G. A, Rafanelli, C., Grandi, S., Conti, S., & Belluardo, P. (1998). Prevention of recurrent depression with cognitive behavioral therapy. *Archives of General Psychiatry, 55,* 816–821.

Heidrich, S. M., & Ryff, C. D. (1993). The role of social comparison processes in the psychological adaptation of the elderly. *Journal of Gerontology, 48,* P127–P136.

House, J. S., Landis, K. R., & Umberson, D. (1988). Social relationships and health. *Science, 241,* 540–545.

Jahoda, M. (1958). *Current concepts of positive mental health.* New York: Basic Books.

James, W. (1958). *The varieties of religious experience.* New York: New American Library. (Original work published 1902)

Jung, C. G. (1933). *Modern man in search of a soul.* New York: Harcourt, Brace, and World.

Kling, K. C., Ryff, C. D., & Essex, M. J. (1997). Adaptive changes in the self-concept during a life transition. *Personality and Social Psychology Bulletin, 23,* 989–998.

Kling, K. D., Seltzer, M. M., & Ryff, C. D. (1997). Distinctive late life challenges: Implications for coping and well-being. *Psychology and Aging, 12,* 288–295.

Li, L. W., Seltzer, M. M., & Greenberg, J. S. (1999). Change in depressive symptoms among daughter caregivers: An 18-month longitudinal study. *Psychology and Aging, 14,* 206–219.

Maier, S. F., Watkins, L. R., & Fleshner, M. (1994). Psychoneuroimmunology: The interface between behavior, brain, and immunity. *American Psychologist, 49,* 1004–1017.

Marks, N. F., & Lambert, J. D. (1998). Marital status continuity and change among young and midlife adults: Longitudinal effects on psychological well-being. *Journal of Family Issues, 19,* 652–686.

Markus, H. R., Ryff, C. D., & Barnett, K. (in press). In their own words: Well-being among high school and college-educated adults. In O. G. Brim, C. D. Ryff, & R. C. Kessler (Eds.), *A portrait of midlife in the U.S.* Chicago: University of Chicago Press.

Marmot, M. G., Fuhrer, R., Ettner, S. L., Marks, N. F., Bumpass, L. L., & Ryff, C. D. (1998). Contributions of psychosocial factors to socioeconomic differences in health. *Milbank Quarterly, 76,* 403–448.

Marmot, M. G., Ryff, C. D., Bumpass, L. L., Shipley, M., & Marks, N. F. (1997). Social inequalities in health: Converging evidence and next questions. *Social Science and Medicine, 44,* 901–910.

Maslow, A. (1968). *Toward a psychology of being* (2nd ed). New York: Van Nostrand.

McGregor, I., & Little, B. R. (1998). Personal projects, happiness, and meaning: On doing well and being yourself. *Journal of Personality and Social Psychology, 74,* 494–512.

McLeod, J., & Kessler, R. (1990). Socioeconomic status differences in vulnerability to undesirable life events. *Journal of Health and Social Behavior, 31,* 162–172.

Meehl, P. E. (1975). Hedonic capacity: Some conjectures. *Bulletin of the Menninger Clinic, 39,* 295–307.

Raczynski, J. M., & DiClemente, R. J. (Eds.). (1999). *Handbook of health promotion and disease prevention.* New York: Kluwer Academic/Plenum.

Riley, M. W., Kahn, R. L., & Foner, A. (1994). *Age and structural lag.* New York: Wiley.

Rogers, C. D. (1961). *On becoming a person.* Boston: Houghton Mifflin.

Ryff, C. D. (1985). Adult personality development and the motivation for personal growth. In D. Kleiber & M. Maehr (Eds.), *Advances in motivation and achievement: Motivation and adulthood* (Vol. 4, pp. 55–92). Greenwich, CT: JAI Press.

Ryff, C. D. (1989a). Beyond Ponce de Leon and successful aging: New directions in quest of successful aging. *International Journal of Behavioral Development, 12,* 35–55.

Ryff, C. D. (1989b). Happiness is everything, or is it? Explorations on the meaning of psychological well-being. *Journal of Personality and Social Psychology, 57,* 1069–1081.

Ryff, C. D. (1989c). In the eye of the beholder: Views of psychological well-being among middle and old-aged adults. *Psychology and Aging,* 4, 195–210.

Ryff, C. D. (1991). Possible selves in adulthood and old age: A tale of shifting horizons. *Psychology and Aging, 6,* 286–295.

Ryff, C. D., & Keyes, C. L. M. (1995). The structure of psychological well-being revisited. *Journal of Personality and Social Psychology, 69,* 719–727.

Ryff, C. D., Lee, Y. H., Essex, M. J., & Schmutte, P. S. (1994). My children and me: Mid-life evaluations of grown children and of self. *Psychology and Aging, 9,* 195–205.

Ryff, C. D., Magee, W. J., Kling, K. C., & Wing, E. H. (1999). Forging macro-micro linkages in the study of psychological well-being. In C. D. Ryff & V. W. Marshall (Eds.), *The self and society in aging processes* (pp. 247–278). New York: Springer.

Ryff, C. D., Schmutte, P. S., & Lee, Y. H. (1996). How children turn out: Implications for parental self-evaluation. In C. D. Ryff & M. M. Seltzer (Eds.), *The parental experience in midlife* (pp. 3–25). Chicago: University of Chicago Press.

*Ryff, C. D., & Singer, B. (1998a). The contours of positive human health. *Psychological Inquiry, 9,* 1–28.

Ryff, C. D., & Singer, B. (1998b). Human health: New directions for the next millennium. *Psychological Inquiry, 9,* 69–85.

Ryff, C. D., & Singer, B. (1998c). Middle age and well-being. In H. S. Friedman (Ed.), *Encyclopedia of mental health* (pp. 707–719). San Diego, CA: Academic Press.

Ryff, C. D., & Singer, B. (1998d). The role of purpose in life and personal growth in positive human health. In P. T. P. Wong & P. S. Fry (Eds.), *The human quest for meaning: A handbook of psychological research and clinical applications* (pp. 213–235). Mahwah, NJ: Earlbaum.

Ryff, C. D., & Singer, B. (2000a). Biopsychosocial challenges of the new millennium. *Psychotherapy and Psychosomatic Medicine, 69,* 170–177.

*Ryff, C. D., & Singer, B. (2000b). Interpersonal flourishing: A positive health agenda for the new millennium. *Personality and Social Psychology Review, 4,* 30–44.

Ryff, C. D., & Singer, B. (in press-a). Ironies of the human condition: Health and well-being on the way to mortality. In L. G. Aspinwall & U. M. Staudinger (Eds.), *A psychology of human strengths: Perspectives on an emerging field.* Washington, DC: American Psychological Association.

Ryff, C. D., & Singer, B. (in press-b). The role of emotion on pathways to positive health. In R. J. Davidson, H. H. Goldsmith, & K. Scherer (Eds.), *Handbook of affective science.* New York: Oxford University Press.

Ryff, C. D., Singer, B., Love, G. D., & Essex, M. J. (1998). Resilience in adulthood and later life. In J. Lomranz (Ed.), *Handbook of aging and mental health* (pp. 69–94). New York: Plenum.

Ryff, C. D., Singer, B., Wing, E., & Love, G. D. (2001). Elective affinities and uninvited agonies: Mapping emotion with significant others onto health. In C. D. Ryff & B. Singer (Eds.), *Emotion, social relationships, and health* (pp. 133–175). New York: Oxford University Press.

Schmutte, P. S., & Ryff, C. D. (1997). Personality and well-being: What is the connection? *Journal of Personality and Social Psychology, 73,* 549–559.

Seeman, T. E. (1996). Social ties and health: The benefits of social integration. *Annals of Epidemiology, 6,* 442–451.

Seeman, T. E., Singer, B. H., Rowe, J. W., Horwitz, R. I., & McEwen, B. S. (1997). The price of adaptation: Allostatic load and its health consequences: MacArthur Studies of Successful Aging. *Archives of Internal Medicine, 157,* 2259–2268.

Seeman, T. E., McEwen, B. S., Rowe, J. W., & Singer, B. (2001). Allostatic load as a marker of cumulative biological risk: MacArthur studies of successful aging. *Proceedings of the National Academy of Sciences, 98,* 4770–4775.

Singer, B., & Ryff, C. D. (1999). Hierarchies of life histories and associated health risks. In N. E. Adler, B. S. McEwen, & M. Marmot (Eds.), *Socioeconomic status and health in industrialized countries. Annals of the New York Academy of Sciences, 896,* 96–115.

Singer, B., Ryff, C. D., Carr, D., & Magee, W. J. (1998). Life histories and mental health: A person-centered strategy. In A. Raftery (Ed.), *Sociological methodology, 1998* (pp. 1–51). Washington, DC: American Sociological Association.

Smider, N. A., Essex, M. J., & Ryff, C. D. (1996). Adaptation to community relocation: The interactive influence of psychological resources and contextual factors. *Psychology and Aging, 11,* 362–371.

Sutton, S. K., & Davidson, R. J. (1997). Prefrontal brain asymmetry: A biological substrate of the behavioral approach and inhibitor systems. *Psychological Sciences, 8,* 204–210.

Wilson, E. O. (1998). *Consilience: The unity of knowledge.* New York: Knopf.

World Health Organization. (1948). World Health Organization Constitution. In *Basic Documents.* Geneva, Switzerland: World Health Organization.

40

Toward a Biology of Social Support

Shelley E. Taylor, Sally S. Dickerson,
& Laura Cousino Klein

People are, by nature, social animals, and group living is thought to be one of the most significant evolutionary mechanisms by which human beings have survived and thrived (Caporael, 1997). Living in social groups has enabled people to avoid the ill effects of clear physical limitations relative to other species that are larger, have endogenous weapons such as teeth and claws, and have greater mobility and speed. Group living affords collective enterprises such as gathering, hunting, and defense that also facilitate survival.

Researchers in health psychology have discovered another significant and well-established benefit of group living—the health benefits of social contact and social support, particularly during times of stress. In prospective studies controlling for baseline health status, people with a higher quantity and quality of social relationships consistently are shown to be at lower risk of death (Seeman, 1996). In studies of both humans and animals, social isolation is a major risk factor for mortality (House, Landis, & Umberson, 1988). In more than 100 empirical investigations, social support has been tied to reduced health risks of all kinds, affecting both the likelihood of illness initially and the course of recovery among people who are already ill

(see Seeman, 1996, for a review). As yet, however, the biological mechanisms underlying the health benefits of social contact and social support are poorly understood, and by the end of this chapter, they will be only modestly clarified. A substantial orchestrated research enterprise will be required to clarify the tantalizing proposed hypotheses, many of which currently draw primarily or entirely on evidence from animal studies.

We begin our analysis with a discussion of early social relationships. Specifically, a close emotional and physical relationship with a caregiver during infancy is believed to be essential for both human and animal development. In addition to the psychological benefits of this relationship, there are important benefits for the development of stress-regulatory systems whose dysfunctions are implicated in many diseases and disorders. We focus on the physiological and neuroendocrine effects of the presence of attachment figures on offspring responses to stress and speculate about the mechanisms whereby these early relationships may permanently affect health across the life span. We then address early experiences of separation and separation distress in animals and humans and their physiological and neuroendocrine concomitants. We next examine the literature implicating neuroendocrine mechanisms, especially oxytocin and endogenous opioid peptides, as being potentially central to the psychological and physical benefits observed in the social support literature. We also address the possible roles of other neurohormones in these phenomena, for which information is less plentiful, including vasopressin, norepinephrine, and serotonin (Nelson & Panksepp, 1998). We end with hypotheses about the protective and health-compromising biobehavioral consequences of social relationships and their underlying mechanisms.

Attachment and Development

Early Development and Attachment Processes

Attachment refers to the tendency to seek closeness with particular others and to feel more secure in their presence. Initially, attachment processes were conceptualized in both animal and human studies as the need for infant closeness to the mother, although it is now believed that any sensitive, nurturant caregiver can provide these benefits. In early studies with monkeys, Harlow and Harlow (1962) found that close contact with a mother or caregiver is important to normal development. Monkeys raised with an artificial terry cloth mother and isolated from other monkeys during the first 6 months of life show disruptions in their subsequent adult social behavior. They fail to interact normally with other monkeys, their sexual responses are inappropriate, and they show either highly fearful or abnormally aggressive behaviors. They also are less likely to groom other monkeys, and the females that have children become poor mothers, at least with their firstborns.

Similar adversities are found in human offspring who are exposed to long separations from their primary caregivers. In early work with children separated from their mothers, Spitz and Wolf (1946) reported that these children showed high levels of emotional disturbance, especially severe depression. More recent findings regarding Romanian and other Eastern European abandoned infants confirm that without the affectionate attentions of caregivers, the infants fail to thrive, and many die (Carlson & Earls, 1997). Failure to thrive is a complex disorder characterized by a lack of growth and development, and it has both psychological and

biological correlates that often can lead to systemwide dysfunction. Failure to thrive has been characterized by a relative imbalance of catabolic (i.e., cortisol, catecholamines) to anabolic (growth hormone, insulin) hormones (Epel, McEwen & Ickovics, 1998; Verdery, 1995). This overabundance of catabolic hormones can lead not only to inhibition of growth hormone but also to malabsorption of nutrients during digestion, thereby further exacerbating growth problems (Sapolsky, 1998). The infants who do survive often have profound deficiencies in both physical growth and mental development, as well as marked dysregulation of the hypothalamic-pituitary-adrenocortical (HPA) axis, which is vital in biological responses to stress (Carlson & Earls, 1997).

Bowlby (1946), who developed attachment theory, reported that children who experienced early and protracted separations from their caregivers were at risk for a range of emotional and behavioral disturbances. The inability to form a secure attachment to one or more people in the early years, Bowlby argued, interferes with the ability to develop close relationships in adulthood (Bowlby, 1973). Attachment processes in human infants and young children have commonly been studied through a methodology known as the *separation paradigm*. Typically, a mother-infant pair is brought into the laboratory. After an initial period of adjustment to the novel situation, the mother leaves and eventually returns to the experimental room. During the caregiver's absence and again upon return, the infant is observed through a one-way mirror, and his or her activity level, play, crying and signs of distress, and attempts to gain the attention of the mother and willingness to interact with her upon her return are measured. On the basis of these behaviors, infants are categorized into one of three groups. A first group of securely attached infants (about 70%) shows moderate distress at the mother's departure and acknowledges her return. The remaining 30% of infants show one of three insecurely attached patterns. One group of insecurely attached/avoidant babies shows little distress upon the departure of the mother and little enthusiasm upon her return; these infants often ignore her or do not interact with her directly. A second group of insecurely attached/ambivalent infants both seeks and resists physical contact; these infants may cry to be picked up but squirm to get down, and they may cry passively on the mother's departure but fail to approach her when she returns. The third group of insecurely attached infants shows a disorganized attachment style (Main & Solomon, 1990); these infants appear disoriented, emotionless, and depressed during the separation procedure and, upon the mother's return, approach and then avoid her. Children who fail to thrive are disproportionately more likely to show this disorganized attachment style than normally growing children.

The main determinant of whether an infant develops a secure attachment is whether he or she is in the care of a sensitively responsive caregiver. For example, mothers of securely attached infants usually respond quickly when a baby cries and are affectionate as they pick up the baby. They meet the baby's needs quickly and use the baby's signals to determine when feeding should begin and end, in contrast to the mothers of insecurely attached infants, who typically respond to their own rather than their babies' needs. The mothers of children with the disorganized attachment pattern commonly show little maternal sensitivity (Ward, Kessler, & Altman, 1993). Maternal sensitivity is multidetermined and can be affected by a number of interconnected biological and social variables, including the stressfulness of the present environment, past experiences, and hormone levels (Fleming, O'Day, & Kraemer, 1999).

Attachment and the Development of Stress-Regulatory Systems

Attachment processes are important because they affect both future social relationships and the development of stress-regulatory systems. Specifically, attachment influences how infants and children respond in stressful situations by moderating physiological and neuroendocrine responses to stress. Stressful circumstances produce immediate changes in sympathetic nervous system activity, including elevations in heart rate and blood pressure. Alterations in HPA functioning also occur. Specifically, in response to stress, the hypothalamus releases corticotrophin-releasing hormone (CRH), which stimulates the pituitary gland to secrete adrenocorticotropic hormone (ACTH), which in turn stimulates the adrenal cortex to release corticosteroids (e.g., cortisol, corticosterone). This integrated pattern of HPA activation is a critical component of the stress response because it modulates a wide range of somatic functions needed for appropriate responses to stress

(e.g., energy release, immune activity, mental activity, growth, and reproductive function). Appropriate cortisol regulation (i.e., increased cortisol levels in response to stress followed by decreased cortisol, an indicator of HPA responses to stress) allows the body to respond to stress by preparing for short-term demands. There are costs associated with the stress response as well, and persistent activation of the HPA system (e.g., chronic elevated cortisol levels) may be associated with deleterious effects on the development of physical, cognitive, and emotional functioning (e.g., Gunnar, 1998; Liu et al., 1997; Meaney et al., 1996; Sapolsky, 1996). For example, Meaney and colleagues (e.g. Frances, Diorio, Liu, & Meaney, 1999; Liu et al., 1997; Liu et al., 2000) explicitly link caregiving to infant stress responses and demonstrate consequent effects on the development of stress-regulatory systems. In one of their paradigms, infant rats are removed from the nest, handled by a human experimenter, and then returned to the nest. The immediate response of the mother is intense licking and grooming and arched-back nursing, which provides the pup with nurturant and soothing immediate stimulation; over the long term, this maternal behavior results in better regulation of somatic growth and neural development, especially the enhancement of hippocampal synaptic development and consequent spatial learning and memory.

Early contact with a caregiver and concomitant attachment processes appear to be implicated in physiological and neuroendocrine stress responses in human infants and children, just as they are in animal studies. For example, Gunnar and her associates studied 15-month-old children receiving well-baby examinations and inoculations. Those infants who were securely attached were less likely to show elevated cortisol responses to these normal stressors (i.e., inoculations) than those who were insecurely attached (Gunnar, Brodersen, Kruger, & Rigatuso, 1996; Nachmias, Gunnar, Mangelsdorf, Parritz, & Buss, 1996). These protective effects of secure attachment were especially evident for socially fearful or inhibited children. Hart, Gunnar, and Cicchetti (1996) found that children who had been physically abused in their families had disturbances in normal cortisol rhythms (see also Hertsgaard, Gunnar, Erickson, & Nachmias, 1995). Likewise, in a study of 264 infants, children, and adolescents, Flinn and England (1997) found that a family environment characterized by few positive affectionate interactions and a high level of negative interactions, including irrational punishment and unavailable or erratic attention from parents, was associated with abnormal cortisol response profiles, diminished immunity, and frequent illnesses (see also Chorpita & Barlow, 1998).

Separation from the attachment figure has been associated with potentially permanent changes in stress reactivity. For example, extended daily maternal separation of rats during the first 2 weeks of life resulted in elevated ACTH and CRH reactivity to stressors in adulthood (Plotsky & Meaney, 1993), indicating a permanent change in the stress response as a result of early separation experiences. There is some evidence that separation can have long-lasting effects in humans as well. Luecken (1998) found that individuals who had lost a parent during childhood demonstrated altered patterns of stress reactivity as adults, specifically elevated cortisol responses to a laboratory speech task, compared with those who had not lost a parent. Separation from a parent does not uniformly lead to detrimental effects, however. In several studies with monkeys, the magnitude of the stress response when separated from a parent was dependent on the availability of a surrogate parent or another source of social support (Levine, 1993; Reite, Kaemingk, & Boccia, 1989). Gunnar, Larson, Hertsgaard, Harris, and Brodersen (1992) found a similar pattern in human infants: The stress response due to a brief separation period from the mother was virtually eliminated when the infant was left in the care of a responsive, warm, attentive caregiver.

Thus, on the basis of results from both animal and human studies, it appears that a strong and nurturant relationship with a primary caregiver is important for the development of an appropriate biological stress-regulatory system, especially appropriate HPA responses to acutely stressful circumstances. Importantly, however, the availability of an alternative attachment figure can buffer the stress response to separation from the primary attachment caregiver.

Social Support and Biobehavioral Responses to Stress

Adult Social Support

A growing literature indicates that social support processes buffer sympathetic and HPA responses to acute stress in adults as well. In a typical investigation, an individual is brought into the laboratory either alone, with a friend, or with a supportive stranger; asked to go through stressful tasks (such as mental arithmetic or giving a speech in front of an audience); and assessed as to sympathetic and neuroendocrine functioning initially, at peak stress, and again during a recovery period. The presence of a supportive person, whether friend or stranger, consistently has been shown to reduce sympathetic (SNS) and HPA responses to stress and facilitate recovery from the physiological effects of acute stress (e.g., Fontana, Diegnan, Villeneuve, & Lepore, 1999; Glynn, Christenfeld, & Gerin, 1999; Kirschbaum, Klauer, Filipp, & Hellhammer, 1995; Seeman and McEwen, 1996, for a review).

These findings are potentially of great importance in accounting for the beneficial health effects of social support. Chronic exposure to stressful environments taxes and may ultimately alter sympathetic activity in response to stress, laying the groundwork for chronic disorders such as coronary heart disease (CHD) and cardiovascular disease (Uchino, Cacioppo, & Kiecolt-Glaser, 1996). Allen, Matthews, and Sherman (1997), for example, found that cardiovascular reactivity to stress among boys as young as 8 to 10 years old was associated with increased left ventricular mass, a risk factor for CHD. Ballard, Cummings, and Larkin (1993) found that children of hypertensive parents showed heightened systolic blood pressure reactivity to angry exchanges between adults, responses that may be precursors of later difficulties in stress management and risk for hypertension. The adverse effects of stress on SNS and HPA functioning, in turn, may adversely affect immune functioning (Uchino, Uno, & Holt-Lunstad, 1999). Immune functioning is related both to infectious disease and to more chronic, life-threatening diseases such as cancer and HIV infection progression. For example, Cohen, Doyle, Skoner, Rabin, and Gwaltney (1997) found that individuals with more diverse social networks were less likely to develop respiratory infections following experimental exposure to a virus than were those persons with less diverse networks.

Sympathetic reactivity in response to stress also may reflect contributions from the parasympathetic nervous system. Like sympathetic activity, parasympathetic activity is responsive to cognitive and emotional states, and chronic negative emotions, such as anxiety and hostility, have been associated with lower heart rate variability, a marker of reduced parasympathetic response (Kawachi, Sparrow, Vokonas, & Weiss, 1994; Sloan et al., 1994). Lower heart rate variability, in turn, has been linked to increased health risks (Kristal-Boneh, Raifel, Froom, & Rivak, 1995). These findings suggest that chronic stress, unmitigated by social support, may lead to reductions in parasympathetic activity, which is an important counterregulatory break on sympathetic activity. Any such reductions would contribute to the greater overactivation of the sympathetic response to stress and lead to a propensity for chronic disorders, such as hypertension and CHD.

Chronic HPA activation can lead to permanent alterations in HPA reactivity, with potential long-term implications for immune-related disorders, as well as for cognitive and emotional functioning. In particular, persistent activation of the HPA system is associated with immune deficiencies, inhibited growth, delayed sexual maturity, damage to the hippocampus, cognitive impairment, and psychological problems such as depression (Sapolsky, 1998; Seeman & McEwen, 1996).

Whether the beneficial health effects of social support can be largely accounted for by the regulation of the sympathetic and HPA responses to stress is unknown at present. It seems likely, though, that such processes account for some of the observed beneficial health effects of social support (Cacioppo & Berntson, 1992; Uchino et al., 1999). The question we next address is whether there is evidence for other biological regulatory mechanisms being implicated in the processes by which social support yields beneficial health effects. For example, in addition to reducing the adverse effects of stress on biological regulatory systems, might social support restore, result in, or actively foster a physiological and neuroendocrine environment that is conducive to good health? In our discussion, we will focus specifically on the involvement of oxytocin and endogenous opioid peptides and their possible role in muting adverse physiological and neuroendocrine responses to stress.

Oxytocin, Social Support, and Responses to Stress

Oxytocin is a peptide released from the posterior pituitary in response to stress and touch and during breastfeeding. Oxytocin has been heavily studied concerning its role in milk ejec-tion during nursing and uterine contractions during labor, but only recently have its potential roles in the neurobiology of stress responses and in affiliative responses to stress been examined (Taylor et al., 2000). Several lines of evidence from animal and human studies suggest a potential role for oxytocin in the beneficial effects of social support on health: Oxytocin is implicated in the development of attachment relationships; oxytocin is secreted in response to stress; oxytocin stimulates pro-social contact; social contact leads to the secretion of oxytocin (at least in some species); and oxytocin is associated with down-regulation of sympathetic and HPA responses, with concomitant anxiety reduction.

Oxytocin is one of the earliest hormones to be released in response to at least some sources of stress (Sapolsky, 1996), and based on evidence from animal studies, it may be implicated in the down-regulation of sympathetic and HPA responses to stress. McCarthy (1995) maintains that, among animals in the natural environment that face a constant barrage of stress, oxytocin is associated with parasympathetic functioning, which, as just noted, plays a counterregulatory role in fear responses to stress (Dreiffus, Dubois-Dauphin, Widmer, & Raggenbass, 1992; Sawchenko & Swanson, 1982). In experimental studies with animals, oxytocin enhances sedation and relaxation, reduces behavioral indications of anxiety, and decreases sympathetic activity (Altemus et al., 1997). Exogenous administration of oxytocin in rats results in decreases in blood pressure, pain sensitivity, and corticosteroid levels, among other findings indicative of a reduced stress response (Uvnas-Moberg, 1997). Oxytocin also appears to inhibit the secretion of ACTH and cortisol in humans (Chiodera & Legros, 1981; Legros, Chiodera, & Demy-Ponsart, 1982).

Human studies also are suggestive as to a role for oxytocin in down-regulating responses to stress. Taylor, Klein, Greendale, and Seeman (2000) found that oxytocin release in response to stress was associated with reduced cortisol responses during stress and a more rapid return to baseline during recovery. Lower levels of sympathetic arousal and HPA responses to stress have been found in lactating versus nonlactating women (Adler, Cook, Davidson, West, & Bancroft, 1986; Altemus, Deuster, Galliven, Carter, & Gold, 1995; Wiesenfeld, Malatesta, Whitman, Grannose, & Vile, 1985). Thus, oxytocin may have beneficial effects on animals and humans, especially in stressful circumstances, by muting sympathetic and HPA responses to stress.

A growing literature also suggests that there are affiliative concomitants of oxytocin, thereby implicating this hormone in support seeking in response to stress. Studies of ewes have found that central nervous system (intracerebroventricular) administration of oxytocin stimulates maternal behavior (Kendrick, Keverne, & Baldwin, 1987). The resulting grooming and touching that occurs in mother-infant contact may help soothe infants under stressful conditions. These effects appear to be bidirectional inasmuch as oxytocin enhances affiliative and affectionate contact with offspring, which in turn enhances the flow of oxytocin. In studies with rats, administration of an oxytocin-blocking agent diminished the attractive qualities of conditioned maternal cues (Panksepp, Nelson, & Bekkedal, 1999). Social contact is enhanced and aggression is diminished following central oxytocin treatment in estrogen-treated prairie voles (Witt, Carter, & Walton, 1990), and in experimental studies with female rats, the administration of oxytocin causes an increase in social contact and in grooming (Argiolas & Gessa, 1991; Carter, DeVries, & Getz, 1995; Witt, Winslow, & Insel, 1992). Because social contact is protective against certain forms of stress (such as attack by predators), and because such protection may be especially helpful to females nurturing infants, oxytocin-facilitated affiliative responses to stress are thought to represent an adaptive response to stressful circumstances (Drago, Pederson, Caldwell, & Prange, 1986; Fahrbach, Morrell, & Pfaff, 1985; McCarthy, 1995). In summary, oxytocin, released in response to stress, appears to induce a state of mild sedation and relaxation, reduce anxiety, decrease sympathetic and HPA activity, and promote affiliative and pro-social behavior under stressful circumstances.

Oxytocin also may be implicated in many forms of human social attachment, including caregiver-infant attachments, adult pair bonds, and other forms of affiliative behavior such as friendship (Carter, 1998; Carter & Altemus, 1997). For example, Uvnas-Moberg (1996) found that women who were breastfeeding and, therefore, had very high levels of plasma oxytocin, perceived themselves as feeling calmer and rated themselves as more social than did age-matched women who were not breastfeeding or pregnant (i.e., who had lower amounts of plasma oxytocin). Moreover, the level of plasma oxytocin in these breastfeeding women correlated strongly with the level of calm reported, and oxytocin pulsatility (changes in oxytocin) was significantly correlated with self-reported sociability (Uvnas-Moberg, 1996). Oxytocin may be related either to enhanced perceptions of one's sociability and the positivity of one's social relationships or to behavioral tendencies that lead to more pro-social activity or both. Dunn and Richards (1977) reported higher levels of maternal behavior among lactating versus nonlactating new mothers. Keverne, Nevison, and Martel (1999) suggested that other bonding relationships may have piggybacked onto the evolutionary adaptation of maternal-infant bonding and the corresponding attachment processes. Consistent with this hypothesis, animals prefer to spend time with animals in whose presence they have experienced high brain oxytocin in the past, suggesting that friendships may be mediated at least in part by the same system that mediates maternal urges.

As is true for rats and primates, human responses to stress are often characterized by affiliation (see Taylor et al., 2000). The conclusion from reviews of the literature is that affiliative responses to stress may be more characteristic of women than men. The high investment of girls and women in the creation and maintenance of social networks, relative to boys and men, is one of the most robust gender differences in adult human behavior, and it is the primary gender difference in adult human behavioral responses to stress (Belle, 1987; Luckow, Reifman, & McIntosh, 1998). Across the entire life cycle, females are more likely to mobilize social support in times of stress, especially from other females. They seek it out more, they receive more support, and they are more satisfied with the support they receive (Belle, 1987; Copeland & Hess, 1995; McDonald & Korabik, 1991; Ogus, Greenglass, & Burke, 1990; Ptacek, Smith, & Zanas, 1992; Wethington, McLeod, & Kessler, 1997).

In the early studies on affiliation under conditions of stress, the primary focus was on females because the affiliative response to stress was reliable only in female participants (Schachter, 1959). A survey study (Veroff, Kulka, & Douvan, 1981) found that women were 30% more likely than men to have provided some type of support in response to network stressors. In their analysis of gender differences in coping, Luckow et al. (1998) found that the largest difference arose on "seeking and using social support," and the combined statistical significance of this effect was significant beyond the $p < .0000001$ level. Specifically, of the 26 studies that tested for gender differences, 1 study found no differences, and 25 studies favored women's greater seeking and use of social support; there were no reversals. Moreover, these findings have substantial cross-cultural generalizability. In a study of 6 cultures, Whiting and Whiting (1975) found that women and girls sought more help and gave more help to others than did men in stressful times, and Edwards (1993) found similar sex differences across 12 additional cultures.

Oxytocin may be at the core of these sex differences in affiliation, in that the effects of oxytocin may be more pronounced in females than in males. Animal studies show that (a) oxytocin release in response to stress appears to be greater in females than in males (Jezova, Jurankova, Mosnarova, Kriska, & Skultetyova, 1996); (b) there appears to be an inhibitory action of androgen on oxytocin release under conditions of stress, thereby potentially limiting its effects on males during stressful conditions (Jezova et al., 1996); and (c) the effects of oxytocin appear to be strongly modulated by estrogen such that estrogen enhances the anxiolytic (antianxiety) properties of oxytocin (McCarthy, 1995; Windle, Shanks, Lightman, & Ingram, 1997). Taylor and her associates (Taylor et al., 2000) found oxytocin release in response to stress to be greater in postmenopausal women who were on estrogen replacement therapy than in those who were not, suggesting a facilitating effect of estrogen on oxytocin in humans as well.

To summarize, oxytocin is secreted by mothers in many species immediately following the birth of offspring, and it may facilitate the behaviors that lead to the attachment processes typically seen between mother and offspring. Oxytocin is released in response to (at least some) stressors in both animals and humans; moreover, it is associated with reduced sympathetic and HPA responses, and with increases in pro-social behaviors under stress (e.g., as seeking the company of others in both animal and human studies). The particular tendency for women to seek and provide social support under stress, coupled with animal data suggesting that the concomitants of oxytocin may be true primarily for females (down-regulation of stress responses, increase in maternal and other affil-

iative behaviors), leads to potentially important inferences: Oxytocin may have a general role in underlying human affiliative responses to stress and a particular role for social responses to stress in women (Taylor et al., 2000).

How might oxytocin play a role in the health benefits of social support? Many illnesses including acute disorders such as colds and flus, as well as CHD, are thought to result from stress-related wear and tear on stress-regulatory systems, including the SNS and HPA responses just described. If oxytocin release in response to social contact mutes these responses, then it may reduce the wear and tear on these systems, thereby limiting vulnerability to disease initially and/or facilitating the likelihood of recovery. Other mechanisms also may be implicated in the beneficial effects of social support, however, and we now turn our attention to those.

Opioid Mechanisms, Social Support, and Stress

Based on evidence from animal studies, endogenous opioids also may be implicated in the beneficial effects of social relationships on health. As is true of oxytocin, the secretion of endogenous opioid peptides appears to occur in response to positive social contact, and as is also true for oxytocin, endogenous opioid secretion has been tied to down-regulation of sympathetic and HPA responses to stress.

Much of the work relating endogenous opioids to affiliative behavior has been conducted with animals in studies by Panksepp and associates (e.g., Nelson & Panksepp, 1998; Panksepp, 1998). These researchers' brain opioid theory of social attachment has several supportive lines of investigation, including the following points: (a) endogenous opioids are released during social contact; (b) endogenous opioid peptide release attenuates distress in response to social separation; (c) endogenous opioids are rewarding and can produce odor and place preferences; and (d) low levels of endogenous opioids can act as an incentive to seek social contact (Nelson & Panksepp, 1998).

As is true for oxytocin, endogenous opioid mechanisms are implicated in maternal attachment processes in animals. In a study with rhesus monkeys, administration of an endogenous opioid peptide-blocking agent, naloxone, was associated with less caregiving and protective behavior toward infants (Martel, Nevison, Rayment, Simpson, & Keverne, 1993). Similarly, administration of naltrexone, also an opioid antagonist, inhibits maternal behavior in sheep under experimental conditions (Kendrick & Keverne, 1989). In studies with rats, administration of opioid antagonists blocked behavioral indicators of infant-mother attachment (Panksepp, Nelson, & Bekkedal, 1999). As one would expect, then, the mother-infant separation paradigm, coupled with experimental manipulation of opioid agonists and antagonists, has been useful for examining the impact of endogenous opioids on distress indicators. Separation reliably produces behavioral indications of anxiety and distress vocalizations. Consistent with Panksepp's model, administration of opioid agonists reliably leads to reductions in distress vocalizations in a broad array of species; moreover, there is parallel evidence that opioid antagonists enhance such vocalizations (see Nelson & Panksepp, 1998, for a review).

Endogenous opioids also may modulate biological responses to stress. The opioid antagonist naloxone can increase basal levels of ACTH and cortisol, as well as alter stress reactivity (McCubbin, 1993). In a series of experiments, McCubbin and colleagues found that blocking opioid activity with an antagonist increases SNS and HPA responses to stress both in the laboratory (McCubbin, 1993) and in natural settings (McCubbin et al., 1998). Interestingly, they find that those people who demonstrated an elevated SNS response to stress under normal conditions do not show this increase in the stress response with opioid blockade. These findings may have implications for a mechanism of how opioids could reduce stress responses. People who respond to acute stress with high levels of sympathetic activity also have larger stress-related increases in HPA activity and larger changes in immune functioning (Sgoutas-Emch et al., 1994). Additionally, those who respond to acute stress with large increases in SNS activity are not affected by an opioid blockade; that is, they do not appear to have opioid-mediated inhibition of the stress response. Opioid mechanisms have been hypothesized to operate on CRF neurons in the hypothalamus (McCubbin et al., 1998), and CRH can then orchestrate the activation of the HPA and SNS systems. Thus, people with low levels of opioids could have a larger stress response due to larger increases in CRF that would ultimately lead to increases or changes in SNS, HPA, and immune activity. Opioids can also directly regulate heart rate and blood pressure (Verrier & Carr, 1991) and mod-

ulate certain aspects of immunity. Over time, this constant overactivation due to a faulty opioidergic mechanism could lead to chronic elevations in stress hormones, which, in turn, could increase vulnerability to a variety of health problems and diseases.

Endogenous opioids also may modulate affiliative and social responses to stress. The present evidence for this role of the peptides is clearer for females than for males. In both animal and human studies, higher levels of endogenous opioids are associated with higher levels of social interaction. For example, Martel and associates (1993) found that administration of naloxone in rhesus monkeys reduced females' social grooming of other females. In a study of college women, Jamner, Alberts, Leigh, and Klein (1998) found that administration of naltrexone increased the amount of time that women spent alone, reduced the amount of time they spent with their friends, and reduced the reported pleasantness of the women's social interactions, as compared with those of men. In addition, women given naltrexone rather than a placebo substance initiated fewer social interactions. Parallel effects were not obtained within men. Thus, endogenous opioids may play a role in regulating social interactions, especially for women. Inasmuch as the affiliative response to stress has been reliably documented only in women, these parallel sex differences in the affiliative concomitants of endogenous opioids are intriguing.

As is true of oxytocin, physical contact leads to central endogenous opioid release in a number of species, and such release has been observed in response to rough-and-tumble play, grooming, and holding. Correspondingly, social isolation has been associated with reduced basal endogenous opioid levels, and social contact restores opioid levels and produces a consequent state of euphoria. Through this action, Panksepp (1998; Nelson and Panksepp, 1998) suggests, a social addiction process may result, whereby the release of opioids in response to social stimuli leads to further seeking out of social stimuli. Support for this model, however, remains preliminary, and it is unclear whether it applies to humans.

To summarize the argument thus far, social support has reliable and beneficial effects on health that may be mediated in part or entirely by the down-regulation of sympathetic and HPA responses to stress. Yet the biological mechanisms underlying these effects have been largely unknown. Both oxytocin and endogenous opioid peptides are released in response to stress and have behavioral (pro-social) and biological (down-regulation of stress responses) consequences that may be implicated in these mechanisms. To date, however, the evidence for the role of these hormones in the propensity to seek and provide social support, as well as their role in down-regulating stress responses, is more plentiful for women than for men.

Additional Potential Biological Substrates of Human Social Behavior

The animal literature on affiliative responses to stress reveals other tantalizing clues for exploration in humans. Vasopressin, a posterior pituitary hormone that is similar in structure to oxytocin, may have a role in affiliation in young rats, especially contact with the mother. In the prairie vole, vasopressin is linked to paternal behavior and to males' guarding of mothers and infants during times of stress. Vasopressin may be implicated in male-female pair bonds at least in some species, and there is a modest literature linking vasopressin to memory for social stimuli (Englemann, Wotjak, Neumann, Ludwig, & Landgraf, 1996). The role that vasopressin may play in human affiliative responses, especially those exhibited under stress, as yet is unknown. Based on intriguing evidence from animal studies, vasopressin may play a particular role in males' social responses.

Norepinephrine, serotonin, and prolactin also may be involved in social responses to stress, although they have received less attention. Specifically, norepinephrine, a catecholamine also released during stress, has been implicated in olfactory learning related to social stimuli and to maternal behavior in animals (Nelson & Panksepp, 1998). In particular, norepinephrine projections to the olfactory bulb are believed to underlie maternal learning in some species, enabling mothers to identify and approach their own young. Norepinephrine also may be involved in social affect and social memory in primates (e.g., Kraemer, 1992). The role of norepinephrine in social behavior in humans is presently unknown. Serotonin also may be involved in animal and human social relationships. Alterations in serotonergic functioning are implicated in the frequency of rat pup separation distress calls, and serotonergic enhancers have been related to affiliative gestures, increased grooming, and a rise in the dominance hierarchy in some old-world monkey species (Insel & Winslow, 1998). In humans, serotonin is associated with social confidence and feelings of connectedness to others, and reduction in brain serotonin activity is a consequence of prolonged social isolation (Nelson & Panksepp, 1998). Prolactin also may be an important stress-related hormone. For example, increases in prolactin levels have been observed in bereaved women, and these levels correlated with grief and depression scores (Lane et al., 1987).

Conclusions

In summary, there is evidence that oxytocin, endogenous opioids, and perhaps vasopressin, norepinephrine, and serotonin may play significant roles in affiliation in a variety of mammalian species and potentially in humans as well. Indeed, Panksepp and associates (e.g., Nelson and Panksepp, 1998; Panksepp, 1999) have argued that they are part of a unitary brain process of affiliative circuitry that regulates mammalian affiliative behavior. First activated in the context of maternal-infant bonding (or, in the case of humans, caregiver-infant bonding), this system that results in attachment appears to underlie both biological responses to stress and the development of the biological stress-regulatory systems themselves. This system also may underlie a broad array of social relationships across the life span, as well as their beneficial effects on health; exactly how this works is unknown at present. In addition, the extent to which hormonal regulation is critical for extrafamilial relationships or adult relationships, especially in humans, remains unknown. The presence of a large neocortex, which facilitates the acquisition and learning of information, means that much human social behavior is freed from exclusive hormonal control, but whether there still may be some aspects of hormonal initiation or control of social behavior under stress is as yet unknown.

In the literature to date, it appears that there may be differences between men and women in the neuroendocrine underpinnings of seeking social support and in the neuroregulation of the benefits of social support as well. These divergences are somewhat surprising, inasmuch as both men and women show health benefits of social support. The pathways appear to be somewhat better charted in women than in men. Specifically, in females, oxytocin and endogenous opioid peptides are released in response to (at least some) stressors, prompting affiliative responses and leading to down-regulation of sympathetic and HPA responses to stress. In addition, both sexes also may profit from the appraisal benefits that appear to come from the availability of social support on sympathetic and HPA concomitants of stress, the routes by which the health benefits of social support have customarily been thought to occur (Seeman & McEwen, 1996; Uchino et al., 1996). Exactly how and if vasopressin, serotonin, and prolactin may be involved in these processes is unknown. The fact that social support has such clear health benefits, however, underscores both the likelihood and the importance of the role that biological mechanisms play in affiliative processes, including affiliation under stress.

Though long acknowledged, the psychologically and biologically protective aspects of social support are only beginning to be understood. Despite gaps in the evidence, it is clear that human beings' social relationships can contribute substantially to optimum functioning, constituting a significant resource. Such findings underscore a broader point, namely, that as researchers increasingly uncover the dimensions of the positive psychology of optimum functioning, charting the interplay of biology and behavior and the biobehavioral pathways by which such strengths exert protective effects on mental and physical health will be vital to this effort.

Acknowledgments   Preparation of this manuscript was supported by grants to the first author from the National Science Foundation (SBR 9905157) and the National Institute of Mental Health (MH 056880), by funds from the MacArthur Foundation's SES and Health Network, and by a National Science Foundation Graduate Fellowship to the second author.

References

Adler, E. M., Cook, A., Davidson, D., West, C., & Bancroft, J. (1986). Hormones, mood and sexuality in lactating women. *British Journal of Psychiatry, 148,* 74–79.

Allen, M. T., Matthews, K. A., & Sherman, F. S. (1997). Cardiovascular reactivity to stress and left ventricular mass in youth. *Hypertension, 30,* 782–787.

Altemus, M. P., Deuster, A., Galliven, E., Carter, C. S., & Gold, P. W. (1995). Suppression of hypothalamic-pituitary-adrenal axis response to stress in lactating women. *Journal of Clinical Endocrinology and Metabolism, 80,* 2954–2959.

Altemus, M., Redwine, L., Leong, Y. M., Yoshikawa, T., Yehuda, R., Detera-Wadleigh, S., & Murphy, D. L. (1997). Reduced sensitivity to glucocorticoid feedback and reduced glucocorticoid receptor mRNA expression in the luteal phase of the menstrual cycle. *Neuropsychopharmacology, 17,* 100–109.

Argiolas, A., & Gessa, G. L. (1991). Central functions of oxytocin. *Neuroscience and Biobehavioral Reviews, 15,* 217–231.

Ballard, M. E., Cummings, E. M., & Larkin, K. (1993). Emotional and cardiovascular responses to adults' angry behavior and to challenging tasks in children of hypertensive and normotensive parents. *Child Development, 64,* 500–515.

Belle, D. (1987). Gender differences in the social moderators of stress. In R. C. Barnett, L. Biener, & G. K. Baruch (Eds.), *Gender and stress* (pp. 257–277). New York: Free Press.

Bowlby, J. (1946). *Forty-four juvenile thieves.* London: Balliere, Tindell, and Cox.

Bowlby, J. (1973). *Attachment and loss.* New York: Basic Books.

Cacioppo, J. T., & Berntson, G. G. (1992). Social psychological contributions to the decade of the brain. Doctrine of multilevel analysis. *American Psychologist, 47,* 1019–1028.

Caporael, L. R. (1997). The evolution of truly social cognition: The Core Configurations Model. *Personality and Social Psychology Review, 1,* 276–298.

Carlson, M., & Earls, F. (1997). Psychological and neuroendocrinological sequelae of early social deprivation in institutionalized children in Romania. *Annals of the New York Academy of Sciences, 807,* 419–428.

Carter, C. S. (1998). *Neuroendocrine perspectives on social attachment and love.* Psychoneuroendocrinology, 23, 779–818.

Carter, C. S., & Altemus, M. (1997). Integrative functions of lactational hormones in social behavior and stress management. *Annals of the New York Academy of Sciences, 807,* 164–174.

Carter, C. S., DeVries, A. C., & Getz, L. L. (1995). Physiological substrates of mammalian monogamy: The prairie vole model. *Neuroscience and Biobehavioral Reviews, 19,* 303–314.

Chiodera, P., & Legros, J. J. (1981). L'injection intraveineuse d'osytocine entraine une diminution de la concentration plasmatique de cortisol chez l'homme normal. *Comptes Rendus des Séances de la Société de Biologie et de Ses Filiales (Paris), 175,* 546.

Chorpita, B. F., & Barlow, D. H. (1998). The development of anxiety: The role of control in the early environment. *Psychological Bulletin, 124,* 3–21.

Cohen, S., Doyle, W. J., Skoner, D. P., Rabin, B. S., & Gwaltney, J. M. (1997). Social susceptibility to the common cold. *Journal of the American Medical Association, 277,* 1940–1944.

Copeland, E. P., & Hess, R. S. (1995). Differences in young adolescents' coping strategies based on gender and ethnicity. *Journal of Early Adolescence, 15,* 203–219.

Drago, F., Pederson, C. A., Caldwell, J. D., & Prange, A. J., Jr. (1986). Oxytocin potently enhances novelty-induced grooming behavior in the rat. *Brain Research, 368,* 287–295.

Dreifuss, J. J., Dubois-Dauphin, M., Widmer, H., & Raggenbass, M. (1992). Electrophysiology of oxytocin actions on central neurons. *Annals of the New York Academy of Science, 652,* 46–57.

Dunn, J. B., & Richards, M. P. (1977). Observations on the developing relationship between mother and baby in the neonatal period. In H. R. Scaefer (Ed.), *Studies in mother-infant interaction* (pp. 427–455). New York: Academic Press.

Edwards, C. P. (1993). Behavioral sex differences in children of diverse cultures: The case of nurturance to infants. In M. E. Pereira & L. A. Fairbanks (Eds.), *Juvenile primates: Life history, development, and behavior* (pp. 327–338). New York: Oxford University Press.

Engelmann, M., Wotjak, C. T., Neumann, I., Ludwig, M., & Landgraf, R. (1996). Behavioral consequences of intracerebral vasopressin and oxytocin: Focus on learning and memory. *Neuroscience and Biobehavioral Reviews, 20,* 341–358.

Epel, E. S., McEwen, B. S., & Ickovics, J. R. (1998). Embodying psychological thriving: Physical thriving in response to stress. *Journal of Social Issues, 54,* 301–322.

Fahrbach, S. E., Morrell, J. I., & Pfaff, D. W. (1985). Possible role for endogenous oxytocin in estrogen-facilitated maternal behavior in rats. *Neuroendocrinology, 40,* 526–532.

Fleming, A. S., O'Day, D. H., & Kraemer, G. W. (1999). Neurobiology of mother-infant interactions: Experience and central nervous system plasticity across development and generations. *Neuroscience and Biobehavioral Reviews, 23,* 673–685.

Flinn, M. V., & England, B. G. (1997). Social economics of childhood gluticosteroid stress responses and health. *American Journal of Physical Anthropology, 102,* 33–53.

Fontana, A. M., Diegnan, T., Villeneuve, A., & Lepore, S. J. (1999). Nonevaluative social support reduces cardiovascular reactivity in young women during acutely stressful performance situations. *Journal of Behavioral Medicine, 22,* 75–91.

Francis, D., Diorio, J., Liu, D., & Meaney, M. J. (1999, November 5). Nongenomic transmission across generations of maternal behavior and stress responses in the rat. *Science, 286,* 1155–1158.

Glynn, L. M., Christenfeld, N., & Gerin, W. (1999). Gender, social support, and cardiovascular responses to stress. *Psychosomatic Medicine, 61,* 234–242.

Gunnar, M. R. (1998). Quality of early care and buffering of neuroendocrine stress reactions: Potential effects on the developing human brain. *Preventive Medicine, 27,* 208–211.

Gunnar, M. R., Brodersen, L., Kruger, K., & Rigatuso, J. (1996). Dampening of adrenocortical responses during infancy: Normative changes and individual differences. *Child Development, 67,* 877–889.

Gunnar, M. R., Larson, M. C., Hertsgaard, L., Harris, M. L., & Brodersen, L. (1992). The stressfulness of separation among nine-month-old infants: Effects of social context variables and infant temperament. *Child Development, 63,* 290–303.

Harlow, H. F., & Harlow, M. K. (1962). Social deprivation in monkeys. *Scientific American, 207* (5), 136–146.

Hart, J., Gunnar, M., & Cicchetti, D. (1996). Altered neuroendocrine activity in maltreated children related to symptoms of depression. *Development and Psychopathology, 8,* 201–214.

Hertsgaard, L. G., Gunnar, M. R., Erickson, M. R., & Nachmias, M. (1995). Adrenocortical responses to the strange situation in infants with disorganized/disoriented attachment relationships. *Child Development, 66,* 1100–1106.

House, J. S., Landis, K. R., & Umberson, D. (1988, July 29). Social relationships and health. *Science, 241,* 540–545.

Insel, T. R., & Winslow, J. T. (1998). Serotonin and neuropeptides in affiliative behaviors. *Biological Psychiatry, 44,* 207–219.

Jamner, L. D., Alberts, J., Leigh, H., & Klein, L. C. (1998, March). *Affiliative need and endogenous opioids.* Paper presented to the annual meetings of the Society of Behavioral Medicine, New Orleans, LA.

Jezova, D., Jurankova, E., Mosnarova, A., Kriska, M., & Skultetyova, I. (1996). Neuroendocrine response during stress with relation to gender differences. *Acta Neurobiologae Experimentalis, 56*, 779–785.

Kawachi, I., Sparrow, D., Vokonas, P. S., & Weiss, S. T. (1994). Symptoms of anxiety and risk of coronary heart disease: The Normative Aging Study. *Circulation, 90*, 2225–2229.

Kendrick, K. M., & Keverne, E. B. (1989). Effects of intracerebroventricular infusions of naltrexone and phentolamine on central and peripheral oxytocin release and on maternal behaviour induced by vaginocervical stimulation in the ewe. *Brain Research, 505*, 329–332.

Kendrick, K. M., Keverne, E. B., & Baldwin, B. A. (1987). Intracerebroventricular oxytocin stimulates maternal behaviour in the sheep. *Neuroendocrinology, 46*, 56–61.

Keverne, E. B., Nevison, C. M., & Martel, F. L. (1999). Early learning and the social bond. In C. S. Carter, I. I. Lederhendler, & B. Kirkpatrick (Eds.), *The integrative neurobiology of affiliation* (pp. 263–274). Cambridge, MA: MIT Press.

Kirschbaum, C., Klauer, T., Filipp, S., & Hellhammer, D. H. (1995). Sex-specific effects of social support on cortisol and subjective responses to acute psychological stress. *Psychosomatic Medicine, 57*, 23–31.

Kraemer, G. W. (1992). A psychobiological theory of attachment. *Behavior and Brain Science, 15*, 493–541.

Kristal-Boneh, E., Raifel, M., Froom, P., & Rivak, J. (1995). Heart rate variability in health and disease. *Scandinavian Journal of Work and Environmental Health, 21*, 85–95.

Lane, R. D., Jacobs, S. C., Mason, J. W., Wahby, V. S., Kasl, S. V., & Ostefeld, A. M. (1987). Sex differences in prolactin change during mourning. *Journal of Psychosomatic Research, 31*, 375–383.

Legros, J. J., Chiodera, P., & Demy-Ponsart, E. (1982). Inhibitory influence of exogenous oxytocin on adrenocorticotrophin secretion in normal human subjects. *Journal of Clinical Endocrinology and Metabolism, 55*, 1035–1039.

Levine, S. (1993). The psychoneuroendocrinology of stress. *Annals of the New York Academy of Sciences, 697*, 61–69.

Liu, D., Diorio, J., Day, J. C., Francis, D. D., Mar, A., & Meaney, M. J. (2000). Maternal care, hippocampal synaptogenesis and cognitive development in rats. *Nature Neuroscience, 3*, 799–806.

Liu, D., Diorio, J., Tannenbaum, B., Caldji, C., Francis, D., Freedman, A., Sharma, S., Pearson, D., Plotsky, P. M., & Meaney, M. J. (1997, September 12). Maternal care, hippocampal glucocorticoid receptors, and hypothalamic-pituitary-

adrenal responses to stress. *Science, 277*, 1659–1662.

Luckow, A., Reifman, A., & McIntosh, D. N. (1998, August). *Gender differences in coping: A meta-analysis.* Poster presented to the annual meetings of the American Psychological Association, San Francisco.

Luecken, L. J. (1998). Childhood attachment and loss experiences affect adult cardiovascular and cortisol function. *Psychosomatic Medicine, 60*, 765–772.

Main, M., & Solomon, J. (1990). Procedures for identifying infants as disorganized/disoriented during the Ainsworth strange situation. In M. T. Greenberg, D. Cicchetti, & E. M. Cummings (Eds.), *Attachment in the preschool years* (pp. 121–160). Chicago: University of Chicago Press.

Martel, F. L., Nevison, C. M., Rayment, F. D., Simpson, M. J. A., & Keverne, E. B. (1993). Opioid receptor blockade reduces maternal affect and social grooming in rhesus monkeys. *Psychoneuroimmunology, 18*, 307–321.

McCarthy, M. M. (1995). Estrogen modulation of oxytocin and its relation to behavior. In R. Ivell & J. Russell (Eds.), *Oxytocin: Cellular and molecular approaches in medicine and research* (pp. 235–242). New York: Plenum.

McCubbin, J. (1993). Stress and endogenous opioids: Behavioral and circulatory interactions. *Biological Psychology, 35*, 91–122.

McCubbin, J. A., Bruehl, S., Wilson, J. F., Sherman, J. J., Norton, J. A., & Colclough, G. (1998). Endogenous opioids inhibit ambulatory pressure during naturally occurring stress. *Psychosomatic Medicine, 60*, 227–231.

McDonald, L. M., & Korabik, K. (1991). Sources of stress and ways of coping among male and female managers. *Journal of Social Behavior and Personality, 6*, 185–198.

Meaney, M. J., Diorio, J., Francis, D., Widdowson, J., LaPlante, P., Caldji, C., Sharma, S., Seckl, J. R., & Plotsky, P. M. (1996). Early environmental regulation of forebrain glucocorticoid receptor gene expression: Implications for adrenocortical responses to stress. *Developmental Neuroscience, 18*, 49–72.

Nachmias, M., Gunnar, M., Mangelsdorf, S., Parritz, R. H., & Buss, K. (1996). Behavioral inhibition and stress reactivity: The moderating role of attachment security. *Child Development, 67*, 508–522.

Nelson, E. E., & Panksepp, J. (1998). Brain substrates of infant-mother attachment: Contributions of opioids, oxytocin, and norepinephrine. *Neuroscience and Biobehavioral Reviews, 22* (3), 437–452.

Ogus, E. D., Greenglass, E. R., & Burke, R. J. (1990). Gender-role differences, work stress and depersonalization. *Journal of Social Behavior and Personality, 5,* 387–398.

Panksepp, J. (1998). *Affective neuroscience.* London: Oxford University Press.

Panksepp, J., Nelson, E., & Bekkedal, M. (1999). Brain systems for the mediation of social separation distress and social-reward: Evolutionary antecedents and neuropeptide intermediaries. In C. S. Carter, I. I. Lederhendler, & B. Kirkpatrick (Eds.), *The integrative neurobiology of affiliation* (pp. 221–244). Cambridge, MA: MIT Press.

Plotsky, P. M., & Meaney, M. J. (1993). Early postnatal experience alters hypothalamic corticotropin-releasing factor (CRF) mRNA, median eminence CRF content and stress induced release in adult rats. *Molecular Brain Research, 18,* 195–200.

Ptacek, J. T., Smith, R. E., & Zanas, J. (1992). Gender, appraisal, and coping: A longitudinal analysis. *Journal of Personality, 60,* 747–770.

Reite, M., Kaemingk, K., & Boccia, M. L. (1989). Maternal separation in bonnet monkey infants: Altered attachment and social support. *Child Development, 60,* 473–480.

Sapolsky, R. M. (1996, August 9). Why stress is bad for your brain. *Science, 273,* 749–750.

Sapolsky, R. M. (1998). *Why zebras don't get ulcers.* New York: Freeman.

Sawchenko, P. E., & Swanson, L. W. (1982). Immunohistochemical identification of neurons in the paraventricular nucleus of the hypothalamus that project to the medulla or to the spinal cord in the rat. *Journal of Comparative Neurology, 205,* 260–272.

Schachter, S. (1959). *The psychology of affiliation.* Stanford, CA: Stanford University Press.

Seeman, T. E. (1996). Social ties and health: The benefits of social integration. *Annals of Epidemiology, 6,* 442–451.

Seeman, T. E., & McEwen, B. S. (1996). Impact of social environment characteristics on neuroendocrine regulation. *Psychosomatic Medicine, 58,* 459–471.

Sgoutas-Emch, S. A., Cacioppo, J. T., Uchino, B. N., Malarkey, W., Pearl, D., Kiecolt-Glaser, J. K., & Glaser, R. (1994). The effects of an acute psychological stressor on cardiovascular, endocrine and cellular immune response: A prospective study of individuals high and low in heart rate reactivity. *Psychophysiology, 31,* 264–271.

Sloan, R. P., Shapiro, P. A., Bigger, T., Jr., Bagiella, E., Steinman, R. C., & Gorman, J. M. (1994). Cardiac autonomic control and hostility in health subjects. *American Journal of Cardiology, 74,* 298–300.

Spitz, R. A., & Wolf, K. M. (1946). Anaclitic depression. *Psychoanalytic Study of the Child, 2,* 313–342.

Taylor, S. E., Klein, L. C., Greendale, G., & Seeman, T. E. (2001). *Oxytocin downregulates HPA responses to acute stress in women.* Manuscript under review.

Taylor, S. E., Klein, L. C., Lewis, B. P., Gruenewald, T. L., Gurung, A. R., & Updegraff, J. A. (2000). Biobehavioral responses to stress in females: Tend-and-befriend, not fight-or-flight. *Psychological Review, 107,* 411–429.

Uchino, B. N., Cacioppo, J. T., & Kiecolt-Glaser, K. G. (1996). The relationships between social support and physiological processes: A review with emphasis on underlying mechanisms and implications for health. *Psychological Bulletin, 119,* 488–531.

Uchino, B. N., Uno, D., & Holt-Lunstad, J. (1999). Social support, physiological processes, and health. *Current Directions in Psychological Science, 5,* 145–148.

Uvnas-Moberg, K. (1996). Neuroendocrinology of the mother-child interaction. *Trends in Endocrinology and Metabolism, 7,* 126–131.

Uvnas-Moberg, K. (1997). Oxytocin-linked antistress effects—the relaxation and growth response. *Acta Psychologica Scandinavica (Supplementum), 640,* 38–42.

Verdery, R. B. (1995). Failure to thrive in the elderly. *Clinics in Geriatric Medicine, 11,* 653–659.

Veroff, J., Kulka, R., & Douvan, E. (1981). *Mental health in America: Patterns of help-seeking from 1957 to 1976.* New York: Basic Books.

Verrier, R. L., & Carr, D. B. (1991). Stress, opioid peptides and cardiac arrhythmias. In J. A. McCubbin, P. G. Faufmann, & C. B. Nemeroff (Eds.), *Stress, neuropeptides, and systemic disease* (pp. 409–427). San Diego, CA: Academic Press.

Ward, M. J., Kessler, D. B., & Altman, S. C. (1993). Infant-mother attachment in children with failure to thrive. *Infant Mental Health Journal, 14,* 208–220.

Wethington, E., McLeod, J. D., & Kessler, R. C. (1997). The importance of life events for explaining sex differences in psychological distress. In R. C. Barnett, L. Biener, & G. K. Baruch (Eds.), *Gender and stress* (pp. 144–156). New York: Free Press.

Whiting, B., & Whiting, J. (1975). *Children of six cultures.* Cambridge, MA: Harvard University Press.

Wiesenfeld, A. R., Malatesta, C. Z., Whitman, P. B., Grannose, C., & Vile, R. (1985). Psychophysiological response of breast- and bottle-feeding mothers to their infants' signals. *Psychophysiology, 22,* 79–86.

Windle, R. J., Shanks, N., Lightman, S. L., & Ingram, C. D. (1997). Central oxytocin administration reduces stress-induced corticosterone release and anxiety behavior in rats. *Endocrinology, 138,* 2829–2834.

Witt, D. M., Carter, C. S., & Walton, D. (1990). Central and peripheral effects of oxytocin administration in prairie voles (*Microtus ochrogaster*). *Pharmacology, Biochemistry, and Behavior, 37,* 63–69.

Witt, D. M., Winslow, J. T., & Insel, T. R. (1992). Enhanced social interactions in rats following chronic, centrally infused oxytocin. *Pharmacology, Biochemistry, and Behavior, 43,* 855–886.

VIII

Specific Coping Approaches

41

Sharing One's Story

On the Benefits of Writing or Talking About Emotional Experience

Kate G. Niederhoffer & James W. Pennebaker

One approach to positive psychology is to document the psychological factors that promote physical and mental health. Consistent with this approach, in the past few years we have been exploring the psychological factors that operate when individuals cope with major emotional upheavals. We have been intrigued by the variety of processes that individuals endure following a traumatic event. For example, some individuals are able to shrug it off and move on; others may talk about the event in detail for several days or weeks before getting on with their lives. Only a minority—perhaps about 20% to 30%—continue to suffer from the trauma for months or years afterward (cf. Wortman & Silver, 1989). What distinguishes those who quickly move past a trauma from those who become mired down by it? More important, is there a way to use these naturally occurring processes to help individuals cope with a wide range of traumatic experiences?

Our interest in coping with emotional upheavals is rooted in people's apparent need to talk with others after a distressing event. It has long been argued that the self-disclosure of upsetting experiences serves as a basic human motive (Jourard, 1971). According to Rimé (1995), over 95% of emotional experiences are shared within the same day of occurrence, usually within a few hours. Although talking about traumatic events may be the norm, there are some experiences that people have great difficulty sharing—experiences such as rape, failure, or other secrets that many of us hold. Is it possible that not talking about emotional upheavals can have adverse effects? If so, would people who are encouraged to talk or write about these secrets improve in mental and physical health?

For almost two decades, researchers have been exploring the potential value of translating emotional experiences into words. One purpose of this chapter is to explore how and why constructing stories about important personal events is so beneficial. First, we will give a brief description of our paradigm and an overview of the research findings, followed by an examination of its historical antecedents. In the remainder of the chapter, we suggest some underlying processes that might explain the power of narrative. In this discussion, three recurring and overlapping processes are explored: those associated with emotional inhibition, cognitive processes, and linguistic processes that occur within the rubric of social dynamics. Specifically, not talking about important emotional events engages powerful, negative changes in each of these processes. However, by constructing stories through writing or talking, these dynamics can be reversed.

The Writing Paradigm: An Overview

The initial studies investigating the effect of putting emotional upheavals into words were founded on the hypothesis that giving people the opportunity to disinhibit or disclose their emotions would improve health. Students were brought into the laboratory and told they would be participating in an experiment to learn more about "writing and psychology." They were instructed to write about an assigned topic for 15 minutes daily, over four consecutive days. Participants were assured that their writing would be anonymous and that they would not receive any feedback. The only rule about the writing assignment was that once they began writing, they were to continue to do so without stopping, without regard to spelling, grammar, or sentence structure. Participants were then randomly assigned to either an experimental or a control group: One group was encouraged to delve into their emotions, and the other to describe objects and events dispassionately.

Those assigned to the experimental group were asked to spend each daily session writing about one or more traumatic experience in their lives. They were given the following instructions:

> For the next four days, I would like for you to write about your very deepest thoughts and feelings about the most traumatic experience of your life. In your writing, I'd like you to really let go and explore your very deepest emotions and thoughts. You might tie your topic to your relationships with others, including parents, lovers, friends, or relatives. You may also want to link your experience to your past, your present, or your future, or to who you have been, who you would like to be, or who you are now. You may write about the same general issues or experiences on all days of writing, or on different traumas each day. All of your writing will be completely confidential. (Pennebaker, 1989, p. 215)

Those in the control group were asked to write about nonemotional topics. Examples of their assigned writing topics included describing the laboratory room in which they were seated or their own living room.

The most profound result of these writing studies was people's seemingly intuitive drive to disclose. Participants in the experimental condition enjoyed the writing process and found it to be extremely "valuable and meaningful." Similarly, 98% of participants reported that they would participate in the study again if given the choice (Pennebaker, 1997). Most surprising were the painful array of tragic and depressing stories about which these predominantly upper-middle-class college students wrote. Rape, family violence, suicide attempts, drug problems, and other horrors were common topics.

While the narratives themselves were compelling, our primary interest was the influence of the writing on physical health. The long-term effects (beginning at least 2 weeks after the studies) were overwhelmingly salutary. Participants in the experimental condition had significantly reduced numbers of physician visits in the next year (in comparison to those in the control condition). Contrary to the long-term effects, however, the immediate effects of the writing were not overtly positive; many students reported crying or being deeply upset by the experience. Understandably, in the hours after writing, participants in the experimental condition felt distressed and unhappy as they reexperienced the negative emotions that were elicited by the traumatic topics about which they wrote.

In further studies, we found similarly beneficial health outcomes for participants in the writing-about-trauma condition as measured by basic biological processes related to immune functioning (Pennebaker, Kiecolt-Glaser, & Glaser, 1988; Petrie, Booth, & Pennebaker, 1998), and positive influences on behavior—including increases in job offers received by a group of engineers after a massive layoff and increases in grades for incoming college students. Positive health and behavioral effects also have been found with maximum-security prisoners, medical students, community-based samples of distressed crime victims, arthritis and chronic pain sufferers, and women who recently gave birth to their first child. Furthermore, these findings are consistent across a variety of groups of individuals, including all social classes and major racial and ethnic groups in the United States, as well as samples in Mexico City, French-speaking Belgium, the Netherlands, Spain, and Japan (for a more complete review, see Smyth, 1998).

Having demonstrated that the mere act of emotional disclosure through writing is a powerful therapeutic agent, we have since sought to more thoroughly investigate the possible mediators, moderators, and overall parameters of this relationship. We have explored the differential effects of writing versus talking about trauma, the topic of disclosure, time span of writing tasks, audience affects (via actual or implied feedback), individual differences in personality type and story-making abilities, and educational, linguistic, and cultural effects. Many of these variables will be considered in our discussion of individual differences.

History

Although the knowledge that disclosive writing can affect health and behavior has practical value, one of the more intriguing aspects of this research has been in trying to find the theories that best explain it. Because writing about emotional topics has been found to change biological processes, overt behaviors, and self-reports, we and others have adopted several theoretical approaches to try to capture these different levels of analysis. Our theoretical views, then, have evolved tremendously as the scope of the writing effects has broadened. As outlined here, the theoretical and research progression in this work began as a model of inhibition. Although the inhibition framework continues to provide valuable insights, a number of researchers began to emphasize the importance of cognitive processes. Most recently, we have begun to explore the role writing must have on the social dynamics of the people who write. Each of these theoretical positions is briefly discussed in the following sections.

The Role of Inhibition

Our original idea was that not talking about emotional upheavals was ultimately unhealthy. This was based on the significant, salutary bi-

ological changes we witnessed among participants who expressed emotion while talking or writing about traumatic events. During confession in the laboratory or immediately after disclosure, for example, participants demonstrated reductions in blood pressure, muscle tension, and skin conductance (Pennebaker, 1989). More specifically, this verified that holding back or inhibiting one's thoughts, emotions, or behaviors was a form of physiological work that had the power to exacerbate stress-related problems.

The original theory motivating our writing studies was based on the assumption that not talking about important psychological events—constraining thoughts, feelings, and behaviors linked to emotional upheaval—is a form of inhibition. This active inhibition, in turn, is a form of physiological work, reflected in autonomic and central nervous system activity. Inhibition acts as a general stressor that can cause or exacerbate psychosomatic processes and thereby lead to long-term health problems (Traue & Deighton, 1999). Reducing inhibition as a strategy to improve health has been demonstrated by studies showing that both informal confiding and confiding in professionals through psychotherapy subsequently reduced illness (Mumford, Schlesinger, Glass, Patrick, & Cuerdon, 1998).

There are, of course, some striking similarities between our ideas about inhibition and Freud and Joseph Breuer's talking cure. During their relatively brief collaboration, Freud and Breuer asserted that holding back pent-up feelings would result in the development of psychic tension, which in turn would result in neuroses. However, when people talked about the causes of their symptoms, they were cured of the symptoms. Freud went on to propose the "cathartic method" whereby talking about one's deepest feelings and thoughts, in a stream-of-consciousness manner, was thought to release pent-up emotions and cure people of their anxiety-related problems. Inhibition in Freud's world was ultimately linked to the deeper constructs of suppression and repression. The foundation of his theory was that the emotions associated with extreme stress must be deliberately and consciously "worked through," a concept we will return to in discussing the mechanisms by which writing brings about change (Freud, 1914/1958).

However, "letting go" of these thoughts as a way to reduce the stress of inhibition has not been sufficient in fully explaining the link of this process with better health outcomes. The method we now propose differs in its focus beyond the mere expression of pent-up emotions to an inclusion of the role of thought and insight. If merely expressing one's emotions was single-handedly effective, both verbal and nonverbal expression would bring about the same effects; however, recent studies have been unable to achieve similarly effective results using expressions such as art, music, and dance (Krantz & Pennebaker, 1997). We have come to realize that, in addition, there are two integral dimensions of disclosure beyond emotional disinhibition: cognitive and social.

The Role of Cognitive Processes

The cognitive roots of the paradigm are related to Gestalt psychologists' views on perception. When individuals experience trauma, they temporarily become disconnected from their core self or identity. This disconnection is exacerbated by the inhibition of the thoughts and feelings surrounding this emotional upheaval. Gestalt views explain our inherent need to integrate the many facets of a single event into a more coherent whole (Helson, 1925). An artifact of our ambiguous and unpredictable world is the anxiety of not attaining completion and not understanding a simple cause-and-effect explanation for traumatic disturbances. Alas, we naturally search for meaning and the completion of events; it gives us a sense of control and predictability over our lives.

In light of Bluma Zeigarnik's (1927/1938) finding that people have better memories for interrupted tasks than completed ones, it is easy to understand people's inherent need to obtain closure and resolve emotional upheaval. This, too, is related to Freud, who suggested that dreams were a symbolic way of completing unresolved tasks or wishes. Zeigarnik's, Freud's, and more recent research findings suggest that individuals tend to ruminate, talk, and dream about things that are not resolved in their minds, or about tasks that are not completed. Because we are motivated to complete our goal-related thoughts, these thoughts remain active when the task cannot be finished or resolved (Martin & Tesser, 1989). Furthermore, the more one tries to suppress these thoughts, paradoxically, the more frequently will they intrusively return to mind (cf. Wegner, 1994). The distressing nature of intrusive ruminations produces anxiety that can contribute to autonomic arousal.

Normally our drive to find meaning and obtain closure is helpful; once we understand why an event has occurred, we can put the thought out of mind forever—or at least better prepare for future occurrences. However, in the face of a major upheaval or overwhelming trauma, which by definition disrupts life goals or tasks, we are driven to find meaning in a situation that might not lend itself to a plausible explanation. Nevertheless, our brains are constructed and/or our minds trained to move toward completion; this results in an endless obsession or preoccupation to figure out why the event happened and perhaps how we can cope with it.

Research in narrative psychology suggests that we make sense of our lives by putting them into storylike format (Neimeyer & Stewart, 2000). Similarly, modern psychotherapy is founded on the principle that clients must confront their anxieties and problems by creating a story to explain and understand past and current life concerns. Constructing a story facilitates a sense of resolution that gives individuals a sense of predictability and control over their lives—allowing them to be "in synch" with their core selves (a connection disrupted by emotional upheaval).

Through language, individuals can give structure to their experiences. An individual can create a coherent narrative, which, once formed, can be summarized, stored, and ultimately forgotten or, as narrative psychologists would say, "put away" more efficiently. Language serves as the scaffolding for persons to organize their thoughts and feelings surrounding the traumatic event.

Innovative work in narrative psychology suggests that we use a "self-narrative" to account for the critical events in our lives (Gergen & Gergen, 1988; McAdams, 1996). Similar to a good story, these narratives include a guiding reason, or story goal with important events that are related in a sensible order to the goal. The beauty of the narrative is that it allows us to tie all the changes in our life together into a broad, comprehensive story. Indeed, we can create themes, plots, and subplots and arrange our multifaceted lives in an orderly, if not logical and hierarchical, fashion.

The Importance of Social Dynamics

The final component of not disclosing trauma involves the social repercussions. This phenomenon is described by Emile Durkheim (1951).

An inherent benefit of forming a narrative involves being able to translate one's life story into a language that is both understandable and communicable. Not being able or willing to tell anyone about significant emotional upheaval disconnects people from their social worlds. Whether it is embarrassment, shame, or fear of incrimination that prevents an individual from disclosing, keeping a secret detaches one from society (see Kelly, 2001, for exceptions).

Research on secrecy suggests that having a secret will encourage obsessive preoccupation and rumination about the event (Wegner, Lane, & Dimitri, 1994). Suppressing thoughts on a daily basis is a large cognitive load, making it difficult to organize thoughts about the event and to make sense of what happened. Thus, the keeper of the secret will be more guarded, and the surrounding people who will be unaware of the individual's thoughts and feelings cannot offer sympathy or help. As a result, the individual becomes more isolated or, as Durkheim explained, less socially integrated.

Varied bodies of literature have established that social integration is one of the keys to both psychological and physical health. Durkheim (1951) argued that the less socially integrated people were, the more likely they were to commit suicide. Others have demonstrated that feelings of loneliness and isolation are associated with more health problems. Similarly, based on literature pertaining to the role of social support in health and illness, it appears that supportive interactions are key to maintaining mental health and that benefits arise not from the number of friends one has but from the quality of the friendships (Holahan, Moos, Holahan, & Brennan, 1996). However, social integration remains a somewhat ambiguous concept in psychology. We are yet unable to precisely label or measure its causes and constituents. Commonly, social integration is conceptualized as a sense of belonging, cohesion, confidence, and security with others. Our definition of social integration also incorporates the sense of coherence that one obtains in creating a synchrony in behaviors, beliefs, and language both within individuals and with their social group.

In the remainder of this chapter, our aim is to explain further the value of writing about emotional topics as a mechanism toward overall health and, more specifically, an important dimension of mental health, social integration. We will present a summary of our research findings, as well as hypothesized mechanisms by which these findings came about.

The Search for Process

As described previously, the writing research has evolved from three different theoretical perspectives. Because of this odd ancestry, research has been conducted that both extends the writing phenomenon and, at the same time, explores different explanations. Using the different historical backgrounds—inhibition, cognition, and social processes—we will trace the separate routes that have been taken by researchers to explain the beneficial effects of writing about emotional topics.

Research on Inhibition and Disclosure

There are many reasons that prevent people from disclosing trauma. Unfortunately, people who do not confide have greater risk for both major and minor health problems. In our early research we found that out of approximately 24,000 respondents to a survey in a popular magazine, 22% of females and 11% of males reported that they had had a traumatic sexual experience prior to age 17. These people also were more likely to have been hospitalized in the last year, to have been diagnosed with cancer, and to have high blood pressure, ulcers, and the flu (for a summary of this work, see Pennebaker, 1997). The significance of the relationship between these reported sexual traumas and such poor health outcomes is clearly not attributable to the nature of the trauma per se. Sexual trauma, however, is a prime example of an experience that is not readily discussed. Furthermore, subsequent studies have established that regardless of the type of trauma experienced, whether or not the trauma has been discussed strongly impacts health.

As our research progressed, we investigated the mechanism of disinhibition as the link between the disclosing of traumas and improved health. To do this, we used the previously discussed writing paradigm in which participants wrote consistently for 15 minutes daily over 4 consecutive days. Recall that in the experimental condition, participants were instructed to write about emotional topics: their "deepest thoughts and feelings about [their] most traumatic experience." In the control condition, participants simply wrote about nonemotional topics, such as the description of the room in which they were seated.

Whereas writing about traumas produced increased health benefits as compared with controls, in a variety of more recent studies, researchers have shown that simply writing about one's thoughts and feelings about coming to college, or about the experience of getting laid off (in the case of the unemployed engineers), produced comparable salubrious health outcomes. Similarly, when students were asked to write about imaginary traumas as though they had lived through them, they evidenced similar health benefits as compared with individuals who wrote about their own trauma (Greenberg, Stone, & Wortman, 1996).

The venting of emotions per se appears insufficient in the absence of cognitive processing. Although such venting may bring about subjective improvements and self-reports of improved mental health, health gains appear to require the translating of one's experiences into language. This was demonstrated in a study in which participants were asked either to express a traumatic experience using bodily movement, to express an experience using movement and then write about it, or to exercise in a prescribed manner for 3 days, 10 minutes per day. Only the "movement plus writing" group evinced significant improvements in physical health and grade point average (Krantz & Pennebaker, 1997). It is clear from all the studies that exploring emotions and thoughts—regardless of the content—is critical for the elicitation of health benefits.

Based on his meta-analysis, Smyth (1998) concludes that emotional disclosure is a necessary but not sufficient factor to beget the benefits from writing about trauma. Recent research findings support a two-step, multidimensional approach to explain the effects of disclosure. First, confiding traumas (a) reduces the physiological arousal associated with inhibition and (b) increases one's ability to understand and integrate the experience (Salovey, Rothman, & Rodin, 1998). Furthermore, as we will explain subsequently, it appears that one specific style of emotional confrontation is more effective than the others.

Cognitive Processes

In speaking to participants in the experimental conditions of the original writing studies, it was clear that they were gaining more through the writing than simply disclosing would suggest. In listening to the words that participants used to recount their experiences—such as "realize," "understand," "come to terms," and "getting past"—we gleaned that the writing was fostering a better understanding of both themselves and the situations about which they wrote. On an intuitive level, it seemed that an individual's cognitive reorganization was crucial for the positive outcomes we had been witnessing.

In two more systematic examinations, this point was substantiated: first in a topical analysis of the writings and, second, in a computer program that analyzed the linguistic components in more detail. In the first analysis, independent raters assessed the writing samples of participants whose health improved after writing, as compared with those whose health remained unchanged. Writing samples of participants who improved were judged to be more self-reflective, emotionally open, and thoughtful.

To investigate further the specific language that led to these assessments, we then developed a computerized text analysis program that could detect emotional and cognitive categories of words. The computer program, Linguistic Analysis and Word Count (LIWC), allowed us to reanalyze previous writing studies and link word usage among individuals in the experimental conditions with various health and behavioral outcomes. LIWC detects 70 word categories, 4 of which are of primary relevance (Pennebaker & Francis, 1999). The emotion categories include negative-emotion words (*sad, angry*) and positive-emotion words (*happy, laugh*), and the cognitive categories include causal (*because, reason*) and insight words (*understand, realize*). The two cognitive categories were designed to capture the degree to which participants were actively thinking in their writing, attempting to put together causes and reasons for the events and emotions they were describing. LIWC, in turn, produces a probabilistic rating for each linguistic category.

Thus, we reanalyzed six studies: two in which college students wrote about traumas where blood immune measures were collected; two in which first-year college students wrote about their deepest thoughts and feelings about coming to college; one study of maximum-security prisoners in a state penitentiary; and one using professionals who unexpectedly had been laid off from their jobs after over 20 years of employment (Pennebaker, Mayne, & Francis,

1997). In these efforts, we uncovered two important findings. The more that people used positive-emotion words, the more their health improved. Individuals who used a moderate number of negative-emotion words in their writing about upsetting topics evidenced the greatest drops in physician visits in the months after the study. Those people who used a very high rate of negative-emotion words and those who used very few were the most likely to have continuing health problems after participating in the study.

From a statistical perspective, the cognitive categories accounted for the most variance in predicting improvements in health. Specifically, people whose health improved the most used an increasing amount of causal and insight words over the 3- to 5-day course of the experiment. It was clear that participants demonstrating this pattern of language were constructing, over time, a story that was replete with causal implications. Stories were built on the foundation of causal links surrounding participants' experiences and feelings. Constructing this narrative appeared critical in reaching an understanding and achieving better health. Indeed, those participants who began the study with a coherent story that explained some past event did not benefit from writing; merely having a story is not sufficient to assure good health. The *process* of constructing a story is crucial.

Similarly, Clark (1993) asserts in her work on conversation and language that in order to convey a story, the speech act must be coherent. Linguistic coherence subsumes several characteristics, including structure, use of causal explanation, repetition of themes, and an appreciation of the listener's perspective. Constructing a coherent story resembles what many psychologists in the coping literature refer to as "working through" a problem. As a result of working through loss, an individual is thought to achieve resolution by accepting the loss intellectually. Indeed, the increased use of causal and insight words detected in our linguistic analyses provides good support for this process.

An inherent benefit of forming a narrative involves being able to translate one's life story into a language that is both understandable and communicable. Once constructed, this story not only helps the beholder to better understand himself and the causes of his trauma but also allows him to communicate it to others. Not being able to tell anyone, or the unwillingness

to be open and honest about significant emotional upheaval disconnects a person from his social world. The sharing of one's story leads us to the third proposed mechanism by which these benefits come about: social communication.

Social Processes

Traumatic events are socially isolating. Implicit in this statement is that by talking to others (or writing) about traumatic experiences, traumatized individuals can establish richer social connections to their social networks. The importance of human communication in mental health is of primary importance. Social support has been associated with mental and physical health, with speedier recovery from illness, and with the likelihood of remaining healthy when stressors occur (cf. Holahan et al., 1996). Indeed, social relationships especially protect individuals from ill health under periods of high stress.

It is important to maintain social connections because social groups offer a venue for growth, social experimentation, and change. Sharing our story alerts our friends to our emotional and psychological state. In contrast, keeping a secret engenders a social chasm between the secret-keepers and their friends. Keeping a secret is a cognitively consuming load that prevents the secret-keeper from being a good listener and thereby exacerbates the social disconnection.

In a recent study of mutual support, both online and face-to-face, we found that social support groups are a significant way by which people change their health behavior (Davison, Pennebaker, & Dickerson, 2000). With the onset of an illness or a traumatic experience comes anxiety and uncertainty. The resulting intense emotions of an afflicted individual can be reduced through interpersonal exchange. Groups of others with similar concerns or conditions provide a standard of normalcy against which people can compare themselves, as well as to share their thoughts and feelings surrounding their conditions.

In our most recent studies, we are investigating whether writing could facilitate social integration, specifically, whether one of the health benefits of writing enables individuals to better connect with their social group. Do people begin to interact differently with others, or perhaps see themselves in a new light, after writing about an emotional topic? In order to explore these ideas, we have attempted to capture how people naturally talk and interact with others by developing an Electronically Activated Recorder (EAR)—a simple tape recorder with an attached computer chip that records for 30 seconds every 12 minutes. The EAR is lightweight and non-intrusive, worn by participants like a walkman for 2 consecutive days. A small external microphone allows us to hear pieces of conversations, as well as determine where participants are and what they are doing (Mehl, Pennebaker, Crow, & Dabbs, 2000).

In the first study, participants wore the EAR for 2 consecutive days, 2 weeks prior to participating in a routine writing study and again 2 weeks afterward. Transcriptions of the conversations yielded promising results in terms of participants' physical behaviors, as well as their language as analyzed by LIWC. As compared with participants in the control condition, who were asked to write about time management, trauma-writers began talking to their friends more, laughing more, and using significantly more positive emotions in their daily language. Trauma-writers also demonstrated significant drops in their resting levels of both diastolic and systolic blood pressure. Similarly, writing about emotion appears to have encouraged participants to use more present-tense words and fewer past-tense words. Interestingly, these effects were far stronger for men, who are naturally less socially integrated than women.

Currently we are investigating some of the likely linguistic components of social integration that we refer to as *synchrony*. Whereas other authors have conceptualized social integration from a self-report perspective, as a sense of belonging, cohesion, confidence, and security with others (Bille-Brahe, 1996), we are defining social integration as a *synchrony* in behaviors, beliefs, and language within a social group. From a subjective perspective, synchrony among members of a dyad may be perceived as a "click" or feeling "in synch": having a conversation that is comfortable and fluid. Linguistically, we expect that synchrony will be portrayed by similar patterns in the way people talk across LIWC word categories—for example, coordination in the number and types of words used within a dyad. Psychologists have demonstrated that synchrony (albeit among behaviors) communicates interest and approval (Kendon, 1970); thus, we are exploring whether a synchronized pattern of language can facilitate social integration.

Guiding our research is the idea that a linguistically synchronized interaction is an indicator of effective communication between members. Researchers examining interpersonal interactions have found that when people communicate, they will mimic one another's body language and synchronize the timing of their behaviors (Burgoon, Stern, & Dillman, 1995). In studies of emotional contagion, researchers have indicated that when people are in conversation, they automatically and continuously mimic and synchronize their movements with the facial expressions, voices, postures, movements, and instrumental behaviors of others (Hatfield, Cacioppo, & Rapson, 1994). In their pioneering work on synchrony, Condon and Ogston (1966) concluded that synchrony was a fundamental, universal characteristic of human communication.

We believe that synchrony in language may facilitate connections and social bonds between conversational members, thereby facilitating social integration. The flip side of the coin, an inability to have synchronized interactions, should dispose one to a life of seclusion: the antithesis of social integration. This idea is related to the inhibition paradigm, as described earlier, in that an inability to communicate with others engenders hidden parts of the self, possibly due to a fear of not being understood or accepted by others. As we see from the study by Davison et al. (2000), connection brings about beneficial health outcomes.

An important dimension to coping with stressors is the degree to which people discuss or confront traumas after their occurrence (Pennebaker, 1997). We propose that our paradigm facilitates confession by first enabling people to personally understand their trauma and ultimately to allow them to discuss it with others, thereby becoming socially integrated. In turn, social integration is an integral component of physical and psychological health. Although psychological health remains an ambiguous, sometimes illusory construct in psychology, our method of constructing and sharing one's story offers a way to reduce the physiological effects of a massive life stressor, as well as to gain control, find meaning, and facilitate social integration.

Individual Differences

Do some people benefit more from writing than others? In the first 15 years of the writing paradigm, no researcher was able to demonstrate consistently that one individual difference was linked to health. The problem may have been that health measures, such as physician visits, are notoriously variable. With such unstable dependent measures, it is exceptionally difficult to detect individual differences that are correlated with within-condition effects.

In recent years, some promising findings have begun to be reported. In Smyth's (1998) meta-analysis of 14 writing studies, men tended to benefit more from writing than did women. Christensen and Smith (1993) reported that individuals high in hostility evidenced greater immune response to writing than those persons who were low in hostility. Most recently, Paez, Velasco, and Gonzalez (1999) found that people who were high in the trait of alexithymia (a condition characterized by the inability to detect, interpret, or label emotions) benefited more from writing than did those low in the trait. The common thread of all these studies is that people who are *not* naturally emotionally open or likely to talk with others about feelings may be the very people who benefit most from writing about their internal states.

Recently individual differences in story making and narrative construction have been explored. Smyth, True, and Souto (2001) evaluated the role of narrative structuring by experimental manipulation and found that the self-reported health of people who wrote about a traumatic experience in a narrative fashion was better than for those who wrote about this topic in a disjointed, listlike way. Unfortunately, this may reflect the general task of writing more than a specific ability to write good stories. In a recent study, Graybeal, Seagal, and Pennebaker (in press) tried to evaluate if a person who was a good "story maker" in writing about traumas also was a good story maker in response to Thematic Apperception Test card or an inkblot test. There was virtually no relationship. Although the ability to construct a good narrative about one's own trauma apparently is beneficial, there does seem to be a group of very healthy story makers in the world who are accounting for all of our variance.

Conclusions

Emotional upheavals can have a variety of adverse effects on people's mental and physical health. They make us think differently about life, our friends, and ourselves. They also have the potential to profoundly disrupt our ongoing relationships with others. As many researchers have begun to discover, disclosure—through writing or talking—has a remarkable potential in alleviating these effects. Putting upsetting experiences into words allows people to stop inhibiting their thoughts and feelings, to begin to organize their thoughts and perhaps find meaning in their traumas, and to reintegrate into their social networks.

Writing is not a panacea. Not everyone benefits from writing. We suspect that it has the potential to disrupt people's lives. As an example, a recent writing participant told us that, after writing, she reevaluated her life and her marriage. She then divorced her husband of 8 years and was forced to move with her children to a much smaller apartment. Although she reports being happier and healthier because of the writing, some might argue that writing had some very negative side effects.

It is somewhat ironic that the writing paradigm is discussed as a feature of positive psychology. Although we have demonstrated that writing about traumatic experiences can have significant health benefits, in a sense, our paradigm encourages participants to dwell on the misery in their lives. We are essentially bringing inhibited or secret negative emotions to the forefront. This can be an anxiety-provoking experience; recall that many participants in the experimental condition cry and report feeling greater sadness, depression, frustration, and guilt in the short run (Pennebaker, 1989). In fact, emotional state after writing depends on how participants are feeling prior to writing such that the better they feel before, the worse they feel afterward.

Is this distress necessary for the positive outcomes we witness in participants' health? If the achievement of insight is truly responsible for the benefits we have demonstrated, is emotional expression—when it appears to be the exact opposite of uplifting—a necessary component? Intuitively, participants' reports of distress seem antithetical to their reports of the value and meaningfulness they ascribe to participating in our experiments. Instead, it appears that they acknowledge the importance of distress as a prelude to overcoming trauma.

We have presented the writing paradigm as a *process* toward achieving mental health. We emphasize the importance of process in order to prevent the notion that one can automatically achieve health benefits. Clearly, one might have to endure some negativity to be healthy. Society has an obsessive focus on strategies aimed toward reducing the awareness of unpleasant emotions. Focus on negative emotions, how-ever, may be necessary in order to genuinely overcome trauma and grow as a mentally healthy human being.

One cannot ascribe too much importance to positivity by neglecting what appears to be a necessary psychological cost. At the risk of sounding trite, we note that our research find-ings highlight the importance of being true to oneself—confronting negative thoughts and ac-knowledging negative emotions. The path to a satisfying and fulfilling life does not bypass dif-ficulties and negative thoughts and feelings. In-deed, one of the goals in positive psychology is to increase our understanding and abilities to transverse those impediments more effectively. Thus, by openly facing our traumas, we no longer end up in such psychological ditches. Rather, we can begin to build bridges to the considerable strengths that we all possess. As such, the psychological road that heretofore has been less traveled may become a main thor-oughfare of positive psychology.

Acknowledgment Preparation of this manu-script was aided by a grant from the National Institute of Mental Health (MH52391).

References

Bille-Brahe, U. (1996). Measuring social integra-tion and social support. *Nordic Journal of Psy-chiatry, 50,* 41–46.

Burgoon, J., Stern, L., & Dillman, L. (1995). *Inter-personal adaptation: Dyadic interaction pat-terns.* New York: Cambridge University Press.

Christensen, A. J., & Smith, T. W. (1993). Cynical hostility and cardiovascular reactivity during self-disclosure. *Psychosomatic Medicine, 55,* 193–202.

*Clark, L. F. (1993). Stress and the cognitive-conversational benefits of social interaction. *Journal of Social and Clinical Psychology, 12,* 25–55.

Condon, W. S., & Ogston, W. D. (1966). Sound film analysis of normal and pathological behav-ior patterns. *Journal of Nervous and Mental Disease, 143,* 338–347.

*Davison, K. P., Pennebaker, J. W., & Dickerson, S. S. (2000). Who talks? The social psychology of illness support groups. *American Psycholo-gist, 55,* 205–217.

Durkheim, E. (1951). *Suicide.* New York: Free Press.

Freud, S. (1958). Remembering, repeating and working through. In J. Strachey (Ed.), *The stan-dard edition of the complete works of Sigmund Freud* (Vol. 12). London: Hogarth. (Original work published 1914)

Gergen, K. J., & Gergen, M. M. (1988). Narrative and the self as relationship. In L. Berkowitz (Ed.), *Advances in experimental social psychol-ogy* (Vol. 21, pp. 17–56). New York: Academic Press.

Graybeal, A., Seagal, J., & Pennebaker, J. W. (in press). The role of story-making in benefit-ing from disclosure writing. *Psychology and Health.*

Greenberg, M. A., Stone, A. A., & Wortman, C. B. (1996). Health and psychological effects of emo-tional disclosure: A test of the inhibition-confrontation approach. *Journal of Personality and Social Psychology, 71,* 588–602.

Hatfield, E., Cacioppo, J. T., & Rapson, R. (1994). *Emotional contagion.* Cambridge, England: Cambridge University Press.

Helson, H. (1925). The psychology of Gestalt. *American Journal of Psychology, 36,* 494–526.

Holahan, C. J., Moos, R. H., Holahan, C. K., & Brennan, P. L. (1996). Social support, coping strategies, and psychosocial adjustment to car-diac illness: Implications for assessment and pre-vention. *Journal of Prevention and Intervention in the Community, 13,* 33–52.

Jourard, S. M. (1971). *Self-disclosure: An experi-mental analysis of the transparent self.* New York: Wiley-Interscience.

Kelly, A. E. (2001). Dealing with secrets. In C. R. Snyder (Ed.), *Coping with stress: Effective peo-ple and processes* (pp. 196–221). New York: Ox-ford University Press.

Kendon, A. (1970). Movement coordination in so-cial interaction: Some examples described. *Acta Psychologica, Amsterdam, 32*(2), 101–125.

Krantz, A., & Pennebaker, J. W. (1997). *Bodily versus written expression of traumatic experi-ence.* Unpublished manuscript.

Martin, L. L., & Tesser, A. (1989). Toward a mo-tivational and structural theory of ruminative thought. In J. S. Uleman, J. A. Bargh et al. (Eds.), *Unintended thought* (pp. 306–326). New York: Guilford.

*McAdams, D. P. (1996). Personality, modernity, and the storied self: A contemporary framework for studying persons. *Psychological Inquiry, 7,* 295–321.

*Mehl, M., Pennebaker, J. W., Crow, D. M., & Dabbs, J. (2000). *The Electronically-Activated Recorder (EAR): A device for sampling natu-ralistic daily activities and conversations.* Man-uscript submitted for publication.

Mumford, E., Schlesinger, H. J., Glass, G. V., Patrick, C., & Cuerdon, T. (1998). A new look at evidence about reduced cost of medical utilization following mental health treatment. *Journal of Psychotherapy Practice and Research, 7,* 68–86.

Neimeyer, R. A., & Stewart, A. E. (2000). Constructivist and narrative psychotherapies. In C. R. Snyder & R. E. Ingram (Eds.), *Handbook of psychological change: Psychotherapy processes and practices for the 21st century* (pp. 337–357). New York: Wiley.

Paez, D., Velasco, C., & Gonzalez, J. L. (1999). Expressive writing and the role of alexithymia as a dispositional deficit in self-disclosure and psychological health. *Journal of Personality and Social Psychology, 77,* 630–641.

*Pennebaker, J. W. (1989). Confession, inhibition, and disease. In L. Berkowitz (Ed.), *Advances in experimental social psychology* (Vol. 22, pp. 211–244). New York: Academic Press.

*Pennebaker, J. W. (1997). *Opening up: The healing power of expressing emotions* (Rev. ed.). New York: Guilford.

Pennebaker, J. W., & Francis, M. E. (1999). *Linguistic Inquiry and Word Count (LIWC): A computer-based text analysis program.* Mahwah, NJ: Erlbaum.

Pennebaker, J. W., Kiecolt-Glaser, J., & Glaser, R. (1988). Disclosure of traumas and immune function: Health implications for psychotherapy. *Journal of Consulting and Clinical Psychology, 56,* 239–245.

*Pennebaker, J. W., Mayne, T. J., & Francis, M. E. (1997). Linguistic predictors of adaptive bereavement. *Journal of Personality and Social Psychology, 72,* 863–871.

Petrie, K. P., Booth, R. J., & Pennebaker, J. W. (1998). The immunological effects of thought suppression. *Journal of Personality and Social Psychology, 75,* 1264–1272.

Rimé, B. (1995). Mental rumination, social sharing, and the recovery from emotional exposure. In J. W. Pennebaker (Ed.), *Emotion, disclosure, and health* (pp. 271–291). Washington, DC: American Psychological Association.

Salovey, P., Rothman, A. J., & Rodin, J. (1998). Health behavior. In D. Gilbert, S. Fiske, & G. Lindzey (Eds.), *Handbook of social psychology* (Vol. 2, 4th ed., pp. 633–683). Boston: McGraw-Hill.

Smyth, J. M. (1998). Written emotional expression: Effect sizes, outcome types, and moderating variables. *Journal of Consulting and Clinical Psychology, 66,* 174–184.

*Smyth, J. M., True, N., & Souto, J. (2001). Effects of writing about traumatic experiences: The necessity for narrative structuring. *Journal of Social and Clinical Psychology, 20,* 161–172.

Traue, H. C., & Deighton, R. (1999). Inhibition, disclosure, and health: Don't simply slash the Gordian knot. *Advances in Mind-Body Medicine, 15,* 184–193.

Wegner, D. M. (1994). Ironic processes of mental control. *Psychological Review, 101,* 34–52.

Wegner, D. M., Lane, J. D., & Dimitri, S. (1994). The allure of secret relationships. *Journal of Personality and Social Psychology, 66,* 287–300.

Wortman, C. B., & Silver, R. C. (1989). The myths of coping with loss. *Journal of Consulting and Clinical Psychology, 57,* 349–357.

Zeigarnik, B. (1938). On finished and unfinished tasks. In W. D. Ellis (Ed.), *A source book of Gestalt psychology* (pp. 300–314). London: Routledge and Kegan Paul. (Original work published 1927)

42

Benefit-Finding and Benefit-Reminding

Howard Tennen & Glenn Affleck

Individuals facing adversity frequently report benefits in their negative experiences (Affleck & Tennen, 1996). Benefit-finding has been linked to psychological and physical health, and it plays a prominent role in theories of cognitive adaptation to threatening circumstances (Janoff-Bulman, 1992; Taylor, 1983), posttraumatic growth (Tedeschi & Calhoun, 1995), and psychological thriving (Epel, McEwen, & Ickovics, 1998). Snyder and McCullough (2000) refer to benefit-finding as a human strength, and they urge its inclusion in the emerging positive psychology paradigm. Yet the empirical literature in this area is a long way from fulfilling its promise. Problems include the tenuous conceptual status of benefit-finding, along with an excessive reliance on cross-sectional designs and measures of negative psychological states. Because of these difficulties, we believe that the potential of benefit-finding for the positive psychology movement has been compromised. In this chapter we summarize the prevalence of benefit-finding and describe what is known about the related emotional and health advantages. We then briefly examine key assumptions about benefit-finding and offer several yet-to-be-tested alternatives to the dominant conceptualization of benefit-finding as a form of cognitive adaptation. Finally, we propose directions

for future research and consider the implications of this area of inquiry for positive psychology. Readers interested in how benefit-finding is related to positive personality characteristics such as optimism, extraversion, and hope will find detailed treatments elsewhere (Affleck & Tennen, 1996; Tedeschi & Calhoun, 1995; Tennen & Affleck, 1999).

Cross-Sectional Studies of Benefit-Finding

Researchers on the topic of benefit-finding, similar to other investigators in the broader personality and social psychology fields, rely excessively on cross-sectional correlational designs. We examined 20 studies in which the concurrent association between benefit-finding and well-being was a focus. The majority of participants in these studies endorsed at least some benefit in diverse threatening circumstances, including invasive medical treatment, life-threatening illness, chronic disability, HIV infection, rape, sexual abuse, accident, and natural disaster. Fourteen of the 20 studies established that benefit-finding was associated with better adjustment, 1 study found that benefit-finding was associated with poorer adjustment, and 5 studies reported no reliable association. We found no clear differences in the populations studied, the sample size, or the measurement of benefits or adjustment that adequately explain the observed variation across studies. A major limitation of this body of work for investigators interested in positive psychology, however, is its primary focus on indicators of maladjustment and distress. But the focus on maladaptation also is conceptually limiting because benefit-finding is now considered a primary appraisal tied to positively toned emotions (Lazarus, 1999). And, of course, one cannot disentangle temporal precedence in these cross-sectional studies. It may be that those who are better adjusted find it easier to construe positive aspects of a negative experience. Thus, we turn our attention to longitudinal investigations.

Longitudinal Studies of Benefit-Finding

We located six longitudinal studies and two "microlongitudinal" (i.e., daily process) studies of the predictive significance of benefit-finding. Excluded are the few longitudinal studies with foci on the psychological benefits of more global constructs such as "positive reappraisal" (Leana, Feldman, & Tan, 1998); "finding meaning" (McIntosh, Silver, & Wortman, 1993) and "positive meaning" (Folkman, Chesney, Collette, Boccellari, & Cooke, 1996; Park & Folkman, 1997); and several intervention studies, which we will describe at the conclusion of this chapter. Because these eight studies provide our only window to the temporal dynamics of benefit-finding and adaptation, and provide a unique opportunity to examine whether benefit-finding anticipates psychological and health outcomes or is simply a correlate of emotional and physical well-being, we describe them in some detail.

Victims of Fire

In the first published longitudinal study of finding benefits in adversity, Thompson (1985) surveyed individuals whose apartments had been partially or completely destroyed by fire. Although the sample was small, and Thompson combined benefit-finding with cognitive adaptations such as imagining worse situations and making social comparisons, this study provided the first evidence that benefit-finding might predict later negative mood, pleasure in daily activities, and physical symptoms. Two thirds of

the sample reported finding some benefit in the experience, most commonly citing others' helpfulness and important life lessons. Although Thompson did not examine whether benefit-finding per se predicted changes in well-being, she found that the composite indicator of cognitive adaptation 1 to 2 weeks after the fire predicted well-being a year later. The long-term correlates unique to benefit-finding remained to be discovered. In several subsequent studies, the specific foci were the adaptational benefits of benefit-finding.

Bereaved Individuals

The loss of a loved one places an individual at increased risk for psychological and physical morbidity. Yet the variability in emotional and health outcomes makes bereavement a fertile arena in which to study how benefit-finding influences subsequent psychological adjustment. Davis, Nolen-Hoeksema, and Larson (1998) took advantage of this variability in a prospective study of individuals whose parent, spouse, partner, child, or sibling was in hospice care. As part of a structured interview 6 months following the loss, participants were asked if they had found anything positive in the experience of having lost a loved one. Seventy-three percent reported that they had found something positive in the experience, and their specific responses were consistent with those reported in previous cross-sectional studies of benefit-finding, including personal growth, new life perspective, strengthening family bonds, and support from others.

Davis et al. (1998) examined whether finding a benefit 6 months following the loss predicted distress 7 months later. Although this analysis did not control for distress at 6 months following the loss, it did control for distress prior to the loss, as well as the extent to which participants had made sense of the loss (i.e., found meaning) at the 6-month interview. Remarkably, Davis et al. found that benefit-finding uniquely predicted 13-month distress, even after controlling for the extent to which the loss "made sense." These investigators also found that it was not the number of benefits that held predictive value but rather whether *any* benefit was endorsed. Thus, whatever psychological function was served by finding benefits, it seemed to be served adequately once any benefit was found. This observation has implications for how we measure benefit-finding, whether multi-item scales are required, and whether we should expect indicators of benefit-finding to meet traditional psychometric criteria for internal consistency. We will return to these issues at the conclusion of this chapter.

Mothers of Acutely Ill Newborns

In their study of mothers whose infants were in a neonatal intensive care unit (NICU), Affleck, Tennen, and Rowe (1991) asked their participants whether they had found any benefits from their child's hazardous delivery and hospitalization. Seventy-five percent of these mothers cited at least one benefit, including improved relationships with family and friends, the importance of keeping life's problems in perspective, increased empathy, positive changes in their personality, and the certainty that their child was now even more precious to them. Mothers who cited benefits during their infant's hospitalization reported brighter mood and less distress 6 and 18 months later, even when their mood during the initial interview was statistically controlled. This ability of benefit-finding to predict later emotional well-being also was independent of an objective severity index of the child's medical problems. Thus, benefit-finding appears to anticipate emotional well-being and is not confounded by objective measures of the severity of the problem.

A unique result of this study was that benefit-finding predicted not only mothers' own well-being but also their child's developmental test scores 18 months later. The relationship remained significant even after controlling for mothers' predischarge mood, age, education, and parity and the severity of infants' perinatal medical problems. This discovery is critical because it extends the positive outcomes of benefit-finding beyond the realm of self-report and psychological well-being. Although it is tempting to speculate about the mechanisms through which perceived benefits during their infants' hospitalization were associated with later developmental outcomes, no clues as to the mediating processes are provided in the study.

Men Who Experienced a First Heart Attack

Another demonstration that objective health outcomes can be predicted from earlier benefit-finding comes from a long-term study of men who survived a first heart attack (Affleck, Tennen, Croog, & Levine, 1987). Seven weeks after

their initial heart attack, 58% of these men cited benefits, including anticipated changes in lifestyle, increased enjoyment, valued lessons about the importance of health behavior, and positive changes in their values and life philosophies. Eight years later (and controlling for age, socioeconomic status, and the severity of the initial attack), those men who had reported benefits were in better cardiac health and were less likely to have suffered another attack.

As in the aforementioned study of mothers of NICU infants, few clues in this investigation were provided regarding the processes through which benefit-finding buffered these men from the recurrence of a heart attack. It is tempting to argue that benefit-finding predicted morbidity because those who referred to anticipated lifestyle and health behavior changes actually made such changes, which in turn produced superior cardiac health (Affleck & Tennen, 1996; Tennen & Affleck, 1999). But as anyone who has worked in a cardiac rehabilitation service, or has tried to stop smoking or maintain a weight loss diet, will attest, the road from appreciating the benefits of health behavior to cardiac health 8 years later is fraught with motivational and interpersonal impediments. Moreover, Davis et al.'s (1998) discovery that one particular benefit is less consequential than finding any benefit (cf. Affleck et al., 1991) calls into question the notion that health behavior changes mediated the effect of benefit-finding on reinfarction or cardiac health. Although some evidence of physiological mediation is beginning to emerge (see Bower, Kemeny, Taylor, & Fahey, 1998), we remain a long way from understanding the mechanisms through which benefit-finding predicts health outcomes.

Disaster Victims

The three longitudinal studies described thus far involved men and women who had experienced the loss of a loved one, mothers who were dealing with their newborn infants' threatening medical situation, and men who were recovering from their first heart attacks. Although each of these contexts is unique, what they share is that either the respondents themselves (Affleck et al., 1987) or a close relative (Affleck et al., 1991; Davis et al., 1998) was facing a serious medical condition. McMillen, Smith, and Fisher (1997) extended this line of inquiry in their longitudinal study of people who had experienced one of three disasters involving extensive property damage and loss of life: a severe tornado; a plane crashing into a hotel lobby, or a mass shooting. Survivors of these three disasters were interviewed 4 to 6 weeks after the incident and again 3 years later. The interview included a question asking whether anything positive had come from the incident. As in other studies of benefit-finding, most participants' responses could be categorized as reflecting personal growth or increased closeness with others.

McMillen et al. (1997) also measured mental health status and characteristics of the disaster. Through a structured diagnostic interview, they assessed current and lifetime major depression, generalized anxiety disorder, alcohol abuse-dependence and posttraumatic stress disorder (PTSD). Because diagnostic incidence rates at the 3-year follow-up were not sufficiently high to serve as dependent variables, the investigators focused on the current diagnosis of PTSD and the change in number of diagnoses from the 4- to 6-week to the 3-year interview. Four characteristics of the disaster also were assessed in the initial interview: whether respondents thought they were going to die during the disaster; whether they were injured, whether they knew anyone who died during the disaster, and whether they saw or did anything they found disgusting during or immediately after the disaster. Scores on these four disaster characteristics were summed to create a severity of exposure index.

Although perceived benefits were reported by a majority of individuals across the three disasters, there was considerable variation across disaster sites. Fifty-five percent of those involved in the plane crash reported some kind of benefit, compared with 76% of those involved in the shooting and 90% of those who survived the tornado. As in the longitudinal studies of bereaved individuals, mothers of NICU infants, and heart attack victims, participants who reported benefits soon after experiencing one of these adverse events were less likely to evidence extreme distress (PTSD) 3 years later. Whether the benefit was *personal growth* or *increased closeness* had no bearing on subsequent diagnosis. This association between perceiving *no* benefits and a later PTSD diagnosis is particularly impressive because it controlled for injury during the disaster, gender, and the number of preincident diagnoses, each of which also made a unique contribution to the prediction of PTSD. Equally impressive is that perceived benefit moderated the effect of severity of exposure on mental health change.

Participants with high exposure who perceived some benefit had the greatest recovery (i.e., change in number of diagnoses), whereas those with high exposure who did not perceive benefit had the least recovery.

Bereaved HIV-Seropositive Men

In the four longitudinal studies described thus far, benefit-finding predicted subsequent psychological distress, psychiatric diagnoses, or one's own or a loved one's physical morbidity. Yet, as we mentioned in relation to Affleck et al.'s (1987) study of heart attack victims, these investigations were not designed to examine the mediators of these prospective relationships. In a recent study of AIDS-related mortality among bereaved HIV-seropositive men, Bower et al. (1998) examined both physiological and behavioral mediators. They conducted a semistructured interview on average 8 months after these seropositive participants had lost a close friend or partner to AIDS. Perhaps because Bower et al. (1998) were interested specifically in major shifts in values, priorities, or perspectives in response to the loss, they found a somewhat lower incidence of benefit-finding (40%) than was reported in other studies of benefit-finding. Yet respondents' specific interview responses paralleled those offered by participants in the studies described previously: greater appreciation for loved ones, a perception of life as precious, increased self-understanding, and enhanced interpersonal functioning.

Every 6 months participants were examined for signs and symptoms of AIDS and were interviewed regarding their health behaviors, including their use of AZT, recreational drugs, and alcohol in the past 6 months, and their sexual practices, exercise, and sleep patterns. At each 6-month visit, HIV progression was assessed via levels of CD4 T lymphocytes. AIDS-related mortality was determined through death certificates.

Bower et al. (1998) found that benefit-finding, which they referred to as "the discovery of meaning," anticipated CD4 T lymphocyte decline. This relationship was retained after controlling for the extent to which participants were engaged in deliberate, effortful, or long-lasting thinking about the death of their friend or partner. Moreover, benefit-finding was associated with a lower rate of AIDS-related mortality over the next 4 to 9 years. Neither of these associations was mediated by the health behaviors measured, but the prospective relationship between benefit-finding and mortality was fully mediated by CD4 slope, that is, the lower rate of AIDS-related mortality among those who had reported benefits was due to their less rapid decline in CD4 lymphocytes. Based on this pattern of findings, those individuals faced with a major loss who emphasize close relationships and personal growth appear to have physiological benefits and a lower rate of mortality. But whether benefit-finding produces better functioning in the everyday lives of chronically ill individuals, and whether they can derive such enhanced functioning from active efforts to construct benefits or gains remain unclear from longer term longitudinal studies. In our daily process studies of individuals with chronic pain, described subsequently, we examined the day-to-day benefits of benefit-finding and sharpened the distinction between *benefit-finding* and intentional *benefit-reminding* (Affleck & Tennen, 1996; Tennen & Affleck, 1999).

Rheumatoid Arthritis Patients

In a study of individuals experiencing chronic pain, we (Tennen, Affleck, Urrows, Higgins, & Mendola, 1992) assessed benefit-finding among rheumatoid arthritis (RA) patients before they completed a diary of daily pain, mood and pain-related activity limitations each evening for 75 days. Benefit-finding in this study was assessed with an internally consistent five-item scale in which participants rated potential benefits associated with RA (e.g., "Dealing with my pain has made me a stronger person"). We found that perceived benefits moderated the relationship between pain severity and activity limitations. That is, with increased levels of daily pain, individuals who had endorsed more benefits from their illness at the start of the study went on to report fewer days on which their activities were limited by their pain.

Benefit-Finding, Benefit-Reminding, and Everyday Life With Chronic Pain

In the findings described thus far, individuals who perceived personal benefits from the major loss, illness, or disaster they experienced were more likely to show long-term health benefits, decreased morbidity and mortality, and less

functional impairment day to day. Despite the intuitive appeal and consistency of these findings across situations and indicators of health and psychological well-being, we cannot make inferences about whether *deliberately* thinking about benefits or gains provided the psychological and health benefits. In our study of women with fibromyalgia (Affleck & Tennen, 1996; Tennen & Affleck, 1999), a chronic pain syndrome with unknown etiology, we examined the deliberate daily use of benefit cognitions, which we called *benefit-reminding,* and used a self-monitoring methodology to determine how benefit-reminding unfolds day to day.

The time-intensive self-monitoring methodology used in this study involved a combination of a nightly structured diary with a computer-assisted "real-time" assessment of pain intensity and mood several times each day. One item on the nightly questionnaire asked participants to describe how much that day they had reminded themselves of some of the benefits that have come from living with their chronic pain. The average respondent reported benefit-reminding on 24 of the 30 study days, although 33 of our 89 participants never reminded themselves of benefits. Some who had cited many benefits on an initial questionnaire never reminded themselves of these benefits during the subsequent month of daily recording. On the other hand, some who had cited only one benefit on the questionnaire also reported benefit-reminding on many days.

The design of our study enabled a within-person analysis of day-to-day differences in benefit-reminding with day-to-day variation in pain and mood. On this point, we discovered that days characterized by more benefit-reminding did not differ in pain intensity, but they were accompanied by improved mood— specifically, increased levels of pleasant, aroused, and aroused-pleasant (i.e., peppy, stimulated) mood. When all three of these mood dimension scores were examined together as correlates of benefit-reminding frequency, there remained a unique relation with pleasant mood. Thus, on days when these chronic pain sufferers made greater efforts to remind themselves of the benefits that have come from their illness, they were especially more likely to experience pleasurable mood, regardless of their pain intensity on these days.

The "Assumptive World" of Theory and Research on Benefit-Finding

From our overview of the literature, benefit-finding appears to be common among individuals facing a myriad of threatening events, and it predicts emotional and physical adaptation months and even years later. Yet much of what we have learned about the adaptational advantages of benefit-finding has been framed in the traditional language of psychological inquiry—emotional symptom reduction, fewer psychiatric syndromes, a reduced risk for adverse medical outcomes, and decreased mortality. With some exceptions (e.g., Affleck & Tennen, 1996; Davis et al., 1998), studies have not examined positive psychological functioning. Thus, investigators approaching the phenomenon of benefit-finding from a positive psychology perspective have much to offer.

It would be unfortunate, however, if proponents of positive psychology now entered the breach armed with countless new outcome indicators but absent guiding conceptual frameworks. More than anything else, benefit-finding needs a conceptual home. The original assumption among theorists was that victims' reports of benefits or gains were a form of denial or a maladaptive reality distortion. This assumption has been supplanted in current theoretical formulations by three other assumptions reflecting the view that benefit-finding (a) is a selective appraisal, (b) is a coping strategy, and (c) emerges only later in the process of adjusting to adversity. We now examine each of these suppositions, which like the "assumptive world" (Janoff-Bulman, 1992) of our research participants, has persisted in the absence of empirical support. Our goal is to provide a cautioning voice so as to avoid incorrectly reifying these assumptions in the lore of positive psychology should it continue to embrace the construct of benefit-finding.

Benefit-Finding Is a Selective Evaluation

Benefit-finding is typically viewed as a "selective evaluation" (Taylor, Wood, & Lichtman, 1983). According to Taylor et al. "Selective evaluation processes minimize victimization by focusing on . . . beneficial qualities of the situation" (p. 26). Other selective evaluations include finding a sense of order and purpose in the threatening experience, imagining "worse worlds," and making comparisons with less fortunate others. These selective appraisals are assumed to help individuals restore valued assumptions and cherished beliefs about themselves as worthy and relatively invulnerable and their world as orderly, predictable, meaningful, and benevolent or at least benign.

Implied in this constructivist interpretation of benefit-finding is that it is the *appraisal* of benefits that helps people adapt to victimization. Yet when individuals identify greater family harmony as an unexpected benefit of a crisis, might the adaptational benefits associated with this appraisal be due to their improved ability to obtain social support? Might someone who knows a disaster victim well agree with his or her appraisal of positive personality change? If so, the inferred cognitive adaptation may be an epiphenomenon, of interest only as a marker of an influential change that has occurred. We return to this possibility in our discussion of stress-related growth.

Benefit-Finding Is a Coping Strategy

Finding benefits in threatening circumstances also has been construed as a coping strategy by many investigators and theorists (cf. Tedeschi, Park, & Calhoun, 1998). Despite Lazarus and Folkman's (1984) care to focus on the effortful and strategic nature of coping, they included perceived benefits as an indicator of emotion-focused coping. The Ways of Coping Scale (Folkman & Lazarus, 1988), for example, includes the following items: *changed or grew as a person in a good way; came out of the experience better than when I went in; found new faith;* and *discovered what is important in life.* Yet coping theory distinguishes among adaptive behaviors that do not require effort, beliefs (which any of these questionnaire items may reflect), and coping strategies. Although not all investigators and theorists agree that "a hallmark of coping is conscious choice" (Haan, 1992, p. 268), we are persuaded by this point of view (Tennen, Affleck, Armeli, & Carney, 2000). From this perspective, searching for evidence of benefits is coping. Taking the time to remind oneself of these perceived benefits is also coping. But concluding that there have indeed been benefits associated with a negative life event and reporting this belief during an interview is *not* an example of coping. The adaptive value of this conclusion is irrelevant to whether it is a coping strategy (Lazarus & Folkman, 1984). Whereas only those who already have discovered benefits from their adversity can use this discovery to comfort themselves in difficult times, there is nothing about the admission of benefits per se which implies that benefit-related cognitions will be used as effortful coping strategies. The confusion between benefit-finding as a coping strategy and benefit-finding as a conclusion reflects a confusion in the broader coping literature that has only rarely been addressed (e.g., Aldwin & Revenson, 1987; Tennen & Affleck, 1997).

Benefit-Finding Emerges Later in the Adjustment Process

Current conceptualizations of how people adapt to negative events typically portray a gradual process. Constructs such as "working through" and moderated "dosing" of traumatic material into awareness (Horowitz, 1986) capture this sense of an unfolding process. Even more explicit is the idea that people rebuild shattered assumptions and pace their recovery over the course of coping and adjustment (Janoff-Bulman, 1992). Recently, these process-oriented models have been applied to benefit-finding. Park (1998), for example, has suggested that only over time do individuals come to alter the perceived value of a traumatic experience or derive benefits from the experience. Similarly, Tedeschi and Calhoun (1995) reserve benefits such as a sense of personal strength and perceived growth as emerging rather late in the process of adapting to adversity.

The recent distinction between "sense-making" (i.e., making sense of adversity within one's existing worldview) and benefit-finding (Davis et al., 1998; Janoff-Bulman & Frantz, 1997) also assumes that benefit-finding should emerge relatively late in the process of adapting to adversity. It has been argued that if sense-making is going to emerge from a negative event, it should do so within several months of the event (Wortman, Silver, & Kessler, 1993), and that individuals who adapt successfully to a threatening event first make sense of the event and only later find benefit from the experience (Janoff-Bulman & Frantz, 1997).

One way to test this assumption is through the association between the time since the event and benefit-finding. Based on cross-sectional studies in which there have been tests of this association, no support has emerged for the notion that benefit-finding emerges later during adjustment. Among these studies, a positive association between time since the negative event and benefit-finding was found in one (Ferrell, Dow, Leigh, Ly, & Gulasekaram, 1995), a negative association was reported in another (Fromm, Andrykowski, & Hunt, 1996), and no associations were reported in others (e.g., Park, Cohen, & Murch, 1996).

In the longitudinal studies that we summarized earlier, there also is no strong support for the assumption that benefit-finding emerges later in the adjustment process. Thompson (1985) found that victims of a fire showed *no* change in their perception of benefits over the course of a year. Although Davis et al. (1998) found support for Janoff-Bulman and Frantz's (1997) hypothesis that benefit-finding is more strongly related to positive adjustment over time, and they categorized slightly more of their bereaved participants as "benefit gainers" rather than "benefit losers" from 6 months postloss to 13 months postloss, the vast majority of participants reported no changes in benefit-finding. McMillen et al. (1997) found that tornado victims and survivors of a mass shooting showed comparably high levels of benefit-finding several weeks and 3 years after the event, whereas those involved in a plane crash reported a decline in perceived benefits over the same time frame. The 8 years during which Affleck et al. (1987) followed heart attack victims affords us the longest time in which to examine this issue regarding the temporal dynamics of benefit-finding. Yet they, too, reported remarkable stability from 7 weeks to 8 years after the first attack.

In sum, there is little empirical support for the three major assumptions guiding current theory and research on benefit-finding in the aftermath of a negative life event. Although finding benefits *may* for some individuals reflect a selective evaluation, there is no evidence that participants in the studies we reviewed were making selective evaluations. Similarly, while benefit-finding *can* be a coping strategy, rarely has it been measured in a way that would warrant such an inference. And when it has been measured as a coping strategy in the form of benefit-reminding, it shows only modest concordance to benefit-finding measured as a belief or conclusion (Affleck & Tennen, 1996). Finally, the assumption that benefit-finding emerges relatively late in the process of adapting to a major loss or threatening event is supported neither in cross-sectional nor in longitudinal studies. Rather, benefits appear to be found within weeks of the event and retained for many years.

Testable Alternatives

If benefit-finding as it has been examined in the psychological literature is neither a selective evaluation nor a coping strategy, and if it does not emerge over time as part of an effort to "work through" a painful encounter, how might we best understand this phenomenon? We now entertain five alternative views of benefit-finding, each of which we believe warrants empirical examination.

Benefit-Finding as a Personality Characteristic

McAdams (1993) has conjectured that trauma or crisis provides an opportunity for people to re-create their life narratives and to structure a life story with coherence and meaning. From this perspective, there are individuals who characteristically provide narratives in which misfortune or life tragedy contains a positive aspect or leads to a positive outcome. Those people with the greatest psychological resources may also be the ones who describe episodes in which adversity ultimately leads to some personal gain or benefit. If this is so, perhaps the positive qualities interpreted by investigators as adaptational consequences of benefit-finding are actually a characteristic of those individuals who are more likely to generate "redemptive sequences" in which personal benefit or gain is an integral part. We may gain important insights by exploring this explanation of the relationship between benefit-finding and adjustment.

Benefit-Finding as a Reflection of Growth or Change

An emerging literature on posttraumatic growth (Tedeschi & Calhoun, 1995) and thriving (Epel et al., 1998) approaches the claim of benefits not as a cognitive construction designed to protect threatened assumptions but as an indicator of genuine positive change. The distinction between benefit-finding as a selective appraisal and reported benefits as a veridical perception of change is critical to how we interpret research findings linking benefit-finding to adaptational outcomes. Consider the woman who has experienced a natural disaster and re-

sponds to an interviewer's query about benefits or gains by claiming that the disaster has made her see what is important in life. Along with her new perspective, she finds that she is less disturbed by everyday disappointments and that others are responding to her new outlook on life with both emotional and material support. How should the investigator interpret her scores on an indicator of well-being? Is her positive adaptation a product of a selective appraisal (i.e., benefit-finding), or is her appraisal an accurate representation of her positive adaptation? In the only study, to our knowledge, in which there has been an attempt to corroborate reports of personal growth derived from negative events, Park et al. (1996) found significant intrapair agreement between the reports of participants and those of close friends and relatives who served as informants. We believe that consensual validation of reports of personal growth presents a genuine challenge to a purely constructivist view of benefit-finding.

Benefit-Finding as an Explanation of One's Temperament

Some of the benefits reported by individuals facing adversity may represent a way in which they explain their characteristic hedonic level (Brickman, Coates, & Janoff-Bulman, 1978). The well-adjusted extrovert who feels relatively happy regardless of his circumstances may find himself feeling happy despite a recent life crisis. To make sense of his continued positive emotional state—which does not fit the stereotype of someone in the aftermath of crisis—he attributes it to what may seem like a newfound capacity to appreciate life's small pleasures or to feel grateful for past good fortune. When asked in a research interview if he has experienced any benefits or gains from his untoward experience, he is likely to offer his appreciation of the little things in life and sense of gratitude. In doing so, he may be providing a satisfying explanation for his temperament. McCrae (personal communication, May 1996) asserts that because distressing events are incompatible with high hedonic levels, the people who are most likely to experience benefits are those who already are functioning well. Individuals who are more chronically distressed have no need for cognitive reappraisal when they face adversity because their emotional state fits their circumstance. The notion that benefit-finding is motivated by a need to provide a satisfying explanation of one's temperament poses yet another challenge to current formulations of cognitive adaptation to adversity and underscores the need for prospective inquiry by proponents of positive psychology who are interested in benefit-finding. The idea inherent in this interpretation of benefit-finding, that people hold personal theories regarding how they should be responding to adversity, is central to yet another alternative explanation of benefit-finding to which we now turn.

Perceived Benefits and Implicit Theories of Consistency and Change

By its very nature, the report of some benefit in the aftermath of an untoward event requires an individual to compare her current status on a particular dimension with her status on the same dimension prior to the event. Thus, for an individual who is facing adversity to determine that her self-concept, relationships with others, or life priorities have changed in a positive way, she must compare her current standing on these dimensions with a recalled version of a former self.

Drawing on Tulving's (1972) distinction between episodic and semantic memory and wide-ranging investigations of the recall process, Ross (1989) argues convincingly that "people possess implicit theories of change, ideas about the conditions that are likely to foster alterations in themselves and others," and that "people's theories may lead them to overestimate the amount of change that has occurred" (p. 342).

Ross (1989) asserts that the recollection of personal attributes at a previous time involves two steps. First the individual notes his or her present status on the attribute. Using present status as a benchmark, he or she then uses an *implicit theory* of stability or change to guide a construction of the past. When pertinent information cannot be recalled, the individual uses his or her implicit theory and present status on the relevant attribute to create a plausible past (cf. Belleza & Bower, 1981). As Ross (1989) notes and as evidence indicates (e.g., Woodruff & Birren, 1972), people's theories may lead them to experience more change than has actually occurred.

A long and widely held premise in Western culture is that people gain wisdom, positive personality changes, more meaningful relations

with others, and more productive lives in the aftermath of threatening encounters (Collins, Taylor, & Skokan, 1990). Such changes are precisely those reported regularly by research participants in studies of adaptation to threatening events. These culturally anticipated benefits from adversity have been a central theme in Western literature, poetry, and widely read accounts of traumatic experiences. The notion of benefiting from adversity also appears in philosophical writings and has found its way into social commentaries, self-help manuals, and increasingly popular accounts of trauma.

Whereas in the current models of adaptation to adversity benefit-finding is interpreted as a *motivated construction of the present*, the implicit theory approach views benefit-finding as a by-product of the *"dispassionate" reconstruction of the past* (Ross, 1989). It predicts that exaggeration of positive change should occur when a person's theory of change leads him or her to anticipate such change when little or no change has actually occurred. Experimental findings (e.g., Conway & Ross, 1984; see also Singer & Salovey, 1993) provide evidence for this reconstruction process.

Yet not everyone who experiences adversity cites benefits. The implicit theories approach acknowledges individual differences in the perception of positive change, and Ross (1989) offers several situational factors that should produce a negative bias in the recollection of one's personal history, and thus the perception that the present is more positive than the past. First, the more widely a theory of change is embraced in a culture, the more likely it is that the majority of individuals will implicitly accept the theory. Second, the more time that has passed, the more people turn to implicit theories to fill the gaps. Third, whereas little or no actual change provides fertile ground for biasing one's recollection of the past, unequivocal negative change on a particular dimension makes it difficult for an individual to evaluate him- or herself as even more negative in the past. Together, these three situational parameters lead to the following predictions: (a) in view of pervasive cultural support for the implicit theory of benefits from adversity, many people should cite such benefits; (b) although people may perceive benefits at any time during a threatening encounter, such benefits are more likely to emerge later in the encounter; and (c) benefits are far less likely to be reported on a particular dimension among individuals who have experienced an obvious decline on that dimension. In the literature on benefit-finding, we see unambiguous support for the first prediction, no support for the second prediction, and virtual silence regarding the third prediction.

Unfortunately, because of the constructivist underpinnings in most current theories of benefit-finding, investigators have not been encouraged to examine whether participants have declined, remained the same, or actually made gains on the dimension for which benefits have been reported. For those who retain quaint notions of "reality" and gains "actually made," such data would be most helpful in direct comparisons of competing explanations. According to the implicit theories model, an individual who has actually declined in a particular life domain following a threatening event is unlikely to report benefits in that domain. Thus, people who have had notable declines in their self-concepts, relationships with social networks, and life priorities—the three most consistently reported domains in which benefits have been reported (Updegraff & Taylor, 2000)—are least likely to report benefits. Furthermore, to the extent that such declines are associated with demoralization, these individuals are also most likely to report high levels of negative affect, low levels of positive affect, and more distress than their counterparts. Therefore, the rather consistent association between benefit-finding and emotional well-being may be telling us how deteriorated functioning in the aftermath of adversity produces both emotional distress and the inhibition of perceived benefits.

More skeptical readers might argue that although the implicit theories model offers an alternative explanation for the association between benefit-finding and emotional well-being, it cannot explain how perceived benefits predict the health outcomes we described earlier, including a second heart attack and related morbidity (Affleck et al., 1987), an infant's developmental outcome (Affleck et al., 1991), and AIDS-related mortality (Bower et al., 1998). This is true, though there is converging evidence that positive emotions promote physical health (Taylor, Kemeny, Reed, Bower, & Gruenewald, 2000). More to the point, existing formulations of benefit-finding also are unable to explain why finding benefits anticipates decreased morbidity and mortality. Although there has been no shortage of speculation regarding the physiological mediators of such a relationship, including the possibility that benefit-finding buffers stress-related changes in the sympathetic nervous system and/or the hypothalamic-pituitary-adrenal axis (Bower et al., 1998), or that it facilitates cortisol habituation (Epel, et al., 1998), the devil, as always, is in the details. Moreover, even firm conceptual and empirical links between benefit-finding and health outcomes would favor no particular model regarding the *emergence* of perceived benefits among individuals facing adverse circumstances. We urge investigators approaching the phenomenon of benefit-finding from the positive psychology perspective to consider and test these competing formulations.

Benefit-Finding as a Temporal Comparison

Individuals experiencing serious illness and other major threats compare themselves with less fortunate others while affiliating with individuals who appear to be adapting well to a similar threat. Taylor and colleagues (e.g., Buunk, Collins, Taylor, Van Yperen, & Dakof, 1990) have documented how people facing a life-threatening illness turn to downward social comparisons to make their own situation seem less severe, and to upward comparisons to maintain hope. But serious illness also is likely to increase the salience of one's own past. As Klauer, Ferring, and Filipp (1998) note, a central tenet of temporal comparison theory (TCT; Albert, 1977) is that people are most likely to compare their current situation with the past during critical life events. TCT posits that although individuals are inclined to evaluate the self as stable, when efforts to reduce negative discrepancies between the past and the present are unsuccessful, they will then construct positive changes, including subjective evidence of maturation, progress, and growth (Klauer et al., 1998).

Although temporal comparisons have been examined occasionally in studies of adaptation to serious illness (Collins et al., 1990), we are unaware of any study in which there has been a direct comparison of perceived benefits and temporal comparisons. Yet Klauer et al. (1998) found that the most commonly endorsed temporal comparisons were related to beliefs about life and relationships with social networks. These perceived changes mirror those reported in the benefit-finding literature. In view of these similarities, we encourage positive psychology investigators to distinguish temporal comparisons from benefit-finding, and to determine if benefit-finding uniquely influences well-being.

Directions for Research and Intervention and Implications for Positive Psychology

We are confident that the phenomenon of benefit-finding has a great deal to offer the existing literature on adaptation to adversity and the emerging literature on positive psychology. The sense of wisdom, enhanced capacity for forgiveness and empathy, increased spirituality, and more positive relations with others often reported by individuals who have experienced adversity correspond to the characteristics that have fueled the recent surge of interest in positive psychology. But it would be unfortunate if investigators interested in positive psychological constructs turned to the same cross-sectional designs as their predecessors, or if they thought that relying almost exclusively on self-reports of positive emotional states was actually a major improvement over previous studies that have relied excessively on self-reports of negative states. If we could offer only one message for positive psychology, it would be to underscore the need for *prospective* studies of benefit-finding and benefit-reminding that include *objective* indicators of health and well-being.

Another problem that demands our attention is that little is actually known about how best to measure benefit-finding. On the one hand, multi-item questionnaires of stress-related growth (Park et al., 1996), posttraumatic growth (Tedeschi & Calhoun, 1995), and benefit-finding (Tennen et al., 1992) stand on the premise that finding more benefits in adversity yields a greater adaptational advantage than finding fewer benefits. Yet interview-based studies consistently find that any reported benefit provides adaptational advantages compared with no benefits, and that finding more than one benefit provides no additional gain.[1] In fact several authors (e.g., Lehman et al., 1993; Park, 1998) have suggested that a balance between perceptions of positive changes and the recognition of negative sequelae may best predict positive adjustment (but see King & Miner, 2000). But before rushing to improve the measurement of

benefit-finding, positive psychology would do well by focusing on its conceptualization. We suspect that superior measures of benefit-finding will emerge only after we are able to discern whether this phenomenon is best conceived as a selective evaluation, a coping strategy, a personality characteristic, a reflection of verifiable change or growth, an explanation of one's temperament, a manifestation of an implicit theory of change, or a temporal comparison. Such conceptual challenges may be even more daunting than the methodological challenges facing this area of investigation. But if positive psychology is to make genuine contributions to this field of inquiry, theorists and researchers must be ready to do much more than offer new indicators of positive adjustment.

The rather consistent connection between benefit-finding and both psychological and health outcomes has led to the understandable desire to directly influence these adaptational processes. Nothing in this chapter should be taken as evidence that deliberate attempts to influence the perception of benefits will be helpful. Yet three recent studies suggest that the perception of benefits may be influenced by carefully constructed interventions. King and Miner (2000) found that compared with control subjects, college students who wrote about the benefits they experienced from a negative life event had fewer health center visits over the next 5 months. Similarly, Stanton et al. (2000) reported that women who wrote about positive thoughts and feelings regarding their ongoing experience with breast cancer had fewer medical appointments for cancer-related morbidities than did women in a control group. But neither of these experimental interventions attempted to shape or influence the perception of benefits. Antoni et al. (2001) found that a cognitive-behavioral stress management intervention, which focused on emotional expression, discouraged avoidance coping, and encouraged a sense of confidence and positive reframing as a coping response, increased patients' reports of benefits from having had breast cancer. Their intervention, however, did not specifically attempt to get these women to acknowledge benefits. As we have mentioned elsewhere (Affleck et al., 1991; Tennen & Affleck, 1999), our research participants have mentioned repeatedly that they view even well-intentioned efforts to encourage benefit-finding as insensitive and inept. They are almost always interpreted as an unwelcome attempt to minimize the unique burdens and challenges that need to be overcome. The positive psychology movement can have its greatest influence on this area of investigation by pushing the envelope in theory, measurement, and study design. Interventions will then follow naturally.

Acknowledgment   The authors are grateful to Mark Saadehm for his contributions to this chapter.

Note

1. Schwarz and Strack (1999) demonstrate convincingly that how we pose questions to research participants can influence the association we obtain between a person's circumstances in the past and his or her current functioning.

References

*Affleck, G., & Tennen, H. (1996). Construing benefits from adversity: Adaptational significance and dispositional underpinnings. *Journal of Personality, 64,* 899–922.

Affleck, G., Tennen, H., Croog, S., & Levine, S. (1987). Causal attribution, perceived benefits, and morbidity following a heart attack: An eight-year study. *Journal of Consulting and Clinical Psychology, 55,* 29–35.

Affleck, G., Tennen, H., & Rowe, J. (1991). *Infants in crises: How parents cope with newborn intensive care and its aftermath.* New York: Springer-Verlag.

Albert, S. (1977). Temporal comparison theory. *Psychological Review, 84,* 485–503.

Aldwin, C. M., & Revenson, T. A. (1987). Does coping help? A reexamination of the relation between coping and mental health. *Journal of Personality and Social Psychology, 53,* 337–348.

Antoni, M. H., Lehman, J. M., Kilbourn, K. M., Boyers, A. E., Yount, S. E., Culver, J. L., Alferi, S. M., McGregor, B. A., Arena, P. L., Harris, S. D., Price, A. A., & Carver, C. S. (2001). Cognitive-behavioral stress management intervention decreases the prevalence of depression and enhances the sense of benefit among women under treatment for early-stage breast cancer. *Health Psychology, 20,* 20–32.

Belleza, F. S., & Bower, G. H. (1981). Person stereotypes and memory for people. *Journal of Personality and Social Psychology, 41,* 856–865.

*Bower, J. E., Kemeny, M. E., Taylor, S. E., & Fahey, J. L. (1998). Cognitive processing, discovery of meaning, CD4 decline, and AIDS-related mortality among bereaved HIV-seropositive men. *Journal of Consulting and Clinical Psychology, 66,* 979–986.

Brickman, P., Coates, T., & Janoff-Bulman, R. (1978). Lottery winners and accident victims: Is happiness relative? *Journal of Personality and Social Psychology, 36,* 917–927.

Buunk, B. P., Collins, R. L., Taylor, S. E., Van Yperen, N. W., & Dakof, G. A. (1990). The affective consequences of social comparison: Either direction has its ups and downs. *Journal of Personality and Social Psychology, 59,* 1238–1249.

Collins, R. L., Taylor, S. E., & Skokan, L. A. (1990). A better world or shattered vision? Changes in life perspectives following victimization. *Social Cognition, 8,* 263–285.

Conway, M., & Ross, M. (1984). Getting what you want by revising what you had. *Journal of Personality and Social Psychology, 47,* 738–748.

Davis, C. G., Nolen-Hoeksema, S., & Larson, J. (1998). Making sense of loss and benefiting from the experience: Two construals of meaning. *Journal of Personality and Social Psychology, 75,* 561–574.

Epel, E. S., McEwen, B. S., & Ickovics, J. R. (1998). Embodying psychological thriving: Physical thriving in response to stress. *Journal of Social Issues, 54,* 301–322.

Ferrell, B. R., Dow, K. H., Leigh, S., Ly, J., & Gulasekaram, P. (1995). Quality of life in long-term cancer survivors. *Oncology Nursing Forum, 22,* 915–922.

Folkman, S., Chesney, M., Collette, L., Boccellari, A., & Cooke, M. (1996). Postbereavement depressive mood and its prebereavement predictors in HIV+ and HIV− gay men. *Journal of Personality and Social Psychology, 70,* 336–348.

Folkman, S., & Lazarus, R. S. (1988). *The Ways of Coping Questionnaire.* Palo Alto, CA: Consulting Psychologists Press.

Fromm, K., Andrykowski, M. A., & Hunt, J. (1996). Positive and negative psychosocial sequelae of bone marrow transplantation: Implications for quality of life assessment. *Journal of Behavioral Medicine, 19,* 221–240.

Haan, N. (1992). The assessment of coping, defense, and stress. In L. Goldberger & S. Breznitz (Eds.), *Handbook of stress: Theoretical and clinical aspects* (2nd ed., pp. 258–273). New York: Free Press.

Horowitz, M. J. (1986). *Stress response syndromes.* Northvale, NJ: Aronson.

Janoff-Bulman, R. (1992). *Shattered assumptions: Towards a new psychology of trauma.* New York: Free Press.

*Janoff-Bulman, R., & Frantz, C. M. (1997). The impact of trauma on meaning: From meaningless world to meaningful life. In M. Power & C. R. Brewin (Eds.), *The transformation of meaning in psychological therapies* (pp. 91–106). New York: Wiley.

King, L. A., & Miner, K. N. (2000). Writing about the perceived benefits of traumatic events: Implications for physical health. *Personality and Social Psychology Bulletin, 26,* 220–230.

Klauer, T., Ferring, D., & Filipp, S. H. (1998). "Still stable after all this . . . ?": Temporal comparison in coping with severe and chronic disease. *International Journal of Behavioral Development, 22,* 339–355.

Lazarus, R. S. (1999). *Stress and emotion: A new synthesis.* New York: Springer.

Lazarus, R. S., & Folkman, S. (1984). *Stress, appraisal, and coping.* New York: Springer.

Leana, C. R., Feldman, D. C., & Tan G. Y. (1998). Predictors of coping behavior after a layoff. *Journal of Organizational Behavior, 19,* 85–97.

Lehman, D. R., Davis, C. G., DeLongis, A., Wortman, C. B., Bluck, S., Mandel, D. R., & Ellard, J. (1993). Positive and negative life changes after bereavement and their relations to adjustment. *Journal of Social and Clinical Psychology, 12,* 90–112.

McAdams, D. P. (1993). *The stories we live by: Personal myths and the making of the self.* New York: Morrow.

McIntosh, D. N., Silver, R. C., & Wortman, C. B. (1993). Religion's role in adjustment to a negative life event: Coping with the loss of a child. *Journal of Personality and Social Psychology, 65,* 812–821.

McMillen, J. C., Smith, E. M., & Fisher, R. H. (1997). Perceived benefit and mental health after three types of disaster. *Journal of Consulting and Clinical Psychology, 65,* 733–739.

Park, C. L. (1998). Implications of posttraumatic growth for individuals. In R. G. Tedeschi, C. L. Park, & L. G. Calhoun (Eds.), *Posttraumatic growth: Positive changes in the aftermath of crisis* (pp. 153–177). Mahwah, NJ: Erlbaum.

Park, C. L., Cohen, L. H., & Murch, R. L. (1996). Assessment and prediction of stress-related growth. *Journal of Personality, 64,* 71–105.

Park, C. L., & Folkman, S. (1997). Meaning in the context of stress and coping. *Review of General Psychology, 2,* 115–144.

*Ross, M. (1989). Relation of implicit theories to the construction of personal histories. *Psychological Review, 96,* 341–357.

Schwarz, N., & Strack, F. (1999). Reports of subjective well-being: Judgmental processes and their methodological implications. In D. Kahneman, E. Diener, & N. Schwarz (Eds.), *Well-being: The foundations of hedonic psychology* (pp. 61–84). New York: Russell Sage Foundation.

Singer, J. A., & Salovey, P. (1993). *The remembered self: Emotion and memory in personality.* New York: Free Press.

Snyder, C. R., & McCullough, M. E. (2001). A positive psychology field of dreams: "If you build it, they will come . . ." *Journal of Social and Clinical Psychology, 19,* 151–160.

Stanton, A. L., Danoff-Burg, S., Sworowski, L. A., Collins, C. A. (2001). Randomized, controlled study of written emotional disclosure and benefit finding in breast cancer patients. *Psychosomatic Medicine, 63,* 122.

Taylor, S. E. (1983). Adjustment to threatening events: A theory of cognitive adaptation. *American Psychologist, 38,* 1161–1173.

Taylor, S. E., Kemeny, M. E., Reed, G. M., Bower, J. E., & Gruenewald, T. L. (2000). Psychological resources, positive illusions, and health. *American Psychologist, 55,* 99–109.

Taylor, S. E., Wood, J. V., & Lichtman, R. R. (1983). It could be worse: Selective evaluation as a response to victimization. *Journal of Social Issues, 39,* 19–40.

Tedeschi, R. G., & Calhoun, L. G. (1995). *Trauma and transformation: Growing in the aftermath of suffering.* Thousand Oaks, CA: Sage.

*Tedeschi, R. G., Park, C. L., & Calhoun, L. G. (1998). Posttraumatic growth: Conceptual issues. In R. G. Tedeschi, C. L. Park, & L. G. Calhoun (Eds.), *Posttraumatic growth: Positive changes in the aftermath of crisis* (pp. 1–22). Mahwah, NJ: Erlbaum.

Tennen, H., & Affleck, G. (1997). Social comparison as a coping process. In B. Buunk & R. Gibbons (Eds.), *Health, coping and well-being* (pp. 263–298). Hillsdale, NJ: Erlbaum.

Tennen, H., & Affleck, G. (1999). Finding benefits in adversity. In C. R. Snyder (Ed.), *Coping: The psychology of what works* (pp. 279–304). New York: Oxford University Press.

Tennen, H., Affleck, G., Armeli, S., & Carney, M. A. (2000). A daily process approach to coping: Linking theory, research, and practice. *American Psychologist, 55,* 626–636.

Tennen, H., Affleck, G., Urrows, S., Higgins, P., & Mendola, R. (1992). Perceiving control, construing benefits, and daily processes in rheumatoid arthritis. *Canadian Journal of Behavioral Science, 24,* 186–203.

Thompson, S. (1985). Finding positive meaning in a stressful event and coping. *Basic and Applied Social Psychology, 6,* 279–295.

Tulving, E. (1972). Episodic and semantic memory. In E. Tulving & W. Donaldson (Eds.), *Organization of memory* (pp. 381–403). New York: Academic Press.

Updegraff, J. A., & Taylor, S. E. (2000). From vulnerability to growth: Positive and negative effects of stressful life events. In J. H. Harvey & E. D. Miller (Eds.), *Loss and trauma: General and close relationship perspectives* (pp. 3–28). Philadelphia: Brunner-Routledge.

Woodruff, D. S., & Birren, J. E. (1972). Age changes and cohort differences in personality. *Developmental Psychology, 6,* 252–259.

Wortman, C. B., Silver, R. C., & Kessler, R. C. (1993). The meaning of loss and adjustment to bereavement. In M. S. Strobe, W. Strobe, & R. O. Hansson (Eds.), *Bereavement: A sourcebook of research and intervention* (pp. 349–366). London: Cambridge University Press.

43

Positive Responses to Loss

Perceiving Benefits and Growth

Susan Nolen-Hoeksema & Christopher G. Davis

I tend to look at it generally as if all the things that happen in my life are a gift, for whatever reason, or however they happen. It doesn't necessarily have to be only pleasant gifts, but everything that happens . . . there's a meaning. I've had a lot of suffering in my life . . . and through that I've learned a great deal. While I wouldn't want to go back and relive that, I'm grateful for it because it makes me who I am. There's a lot of joys and sorrows, but they all enrich life.

(Alicia, quoted in Nolen-Hoeksema &
Larson, 1999, p. 143)

Alicia had recently lost someone she loved dearly to a long battle with cancer. Although the death of a loved one is a negative experience by any definition, Alicia's positive outlook on her loss is typical. In our research with recently bereaved people, we have found that 70% to 80% report finding some positive aspect in their experience with loss (Davis, Nolen-Hoeksema, & Larson, 1998; see also Calhoun & Tedeschi, 1990; Edmonds & Hooker, 1992; Lehman et al.,

1993; Tennen & Affleck, 1999; Yalom & Lieberman, 1991).

Such reports of positive life changes do not necessarily reflect or signify growth or positive transformation of the self. For example, such statements also might reflect defensiveness or self-esteem protection (see Davis, Lehman, & Wortman, 2000). Yet we suspect that at least for some individuals who have been through significant adversity, the positive life changes that they report may be part of a process of growth or positive transformation. The experience of loss can lead people to change how they see themselves, how they perceive the world around them, and where they are going with their lives. Loss events, especially those that are sudden or unexpected, often appear to initiate a personal evaluation or stocktaking of the meaning of one's life.

In this chapter, we review and integrate some empirical research on the processes by which people find meaning and growth within their loss experiences. We draw a distinction between two notions of meaning—making sense of a loss and finding benefit in the experience with loss—

and suggest that both may facilitate the process of growth or positive transformation. We examine the predictors of who is and is not able to find something positive in loss, as well as the mental health consequences of finding something positive. We end by discussing the implications of our work for interventions with the bereaved.

Historical Roots

An interest in the growth potential of humans has long been a tenet of humanistic and existential psychology. Viktor Frankl, a leading proponent of the existentialist movement in psychology, has argued that a fundamental, motivating force in people's behavior is a *will to meaning* (Frankl, 1955/1986; 1959/1962). According to this view, creating and sustaining meaning gives one's life a sense of authenticity (see Snyder, Rand, & Sigmon, this volume). Frankl argued that when meaning is lacking, people are motivated to restore or develop new life meanings to avoid the pain and angst of a meaningless existence.

Frankl (1959/1962) theorized that meaninglessness stems from despair over the perceived loss of goals, ambitions, and purpose in life. Thus, to the extent that loss and trauma events shatter goals, ambitions, and purpose in one's life, one is apt to experience such an existential crisis. How one responds to this crisis is critical, according to Frankl, and he challenged his clients to create new life meanings as a means of defeating the feelings of loss and suffering:

> Whenever one has to face a fate which cannot be changed, just then one is given a last chance to actualize the highest value, to fulfill the deepest meaning, the meaning of suffering. For what matters above all is the attitude we take toward suffering, the attitude in which we take our suffering upon ourselves. (Frankl, 1959/1962, p. 114)

From this perspective, growth represents a process of establishing and committing oneself to a new set of broad goals, ambitions, or purpose that gives one's life a general sense of direction (see also Snyder, 2000). As such, it is intimately tied to what McAdams (1996) has described as the deepest level of personality: one's sense of self or identity. In our view, then, growth or transformation represents a funda-

mental shifting of the life goals and purposes that significantly influence one's sense of identity.

But how do people create new or revised life meaning following an existential crisis brought on by loss? How does one transform the experience of loss into a positive, life-renewing experience? Empirically, there is little to guide us because we and others have struggled to adequately measure growth (as defined previously). But from our reading of the literature and the observations culled from the wisdom of our bereaved research participants, we suggest that two processes of meaning-making might facilitate the process of growth following personal loss: making sense of loss and perceiving benefits or positives in the experience of coping with that loss (Davis et al., 1998).

Making Sense of Loss Versus Finding Benefit in the Experience

The modern literature on meaning-making following a loss or trauma generally has not distinguished clearly between finding some meaning in a loss and finding some benefit in a loss experience (for detailed discussion of these issues, see Davis et al., 1998; Davis et al., 2000). Recent theorizing, however, has sharpened the distinction between these two processes (e.g., Affleck & Tennen, 1996; Janoff-Bulman & Frantz, 1997). Janoff-Bulman and Frantz (1997) have suggested that making sense of a trauma or loss involves understanding how the event fits with one's view of the world (in terms of beliefs about justice, fairness, predictability of one's social world). They refer to this type of meaning as *meaning-as-comprehensibility*. At least in Western cultures, people tend to believe that important events in their lives are controllable and understandable (e.g., Heider, 1958; Kelley, 1972). People believe that negative events are not distributed randomly, that people get what they deserve, and that justice will prevail (Janoff-Bulman, 1992; Lerner, 1980). Events such as the loss of a loved one can shatter these assumptions. This is particularly likely to be true when the loss is unexpected, due to tragic circumstances (such as a car accident), or "nonnormative," for example, when a young child dies.

In contrast to the notion of meaning as comprehensibility, Janoff-Bulman and Frantz (1997) suggest that benefit-finding represents an attempt to understand the value or worth of the loss for one's life, which they describe as *meaning-as-significance*. Perceiving some benefit to the loss, such as reporting a change in one's life perspective, can help to mitigate feelings of helplessness and grief and preserve the sense that one's own life has purpose, value, and worth. Janoff-Bulman and Frantz (1997) argue that successful adaptation involves turning a desire to make sense of the event into finding some value or benefit in the experience.

Our own work leads us to suggest that making sense of loss and finding benefit in the experience represent two distinct processes, with different predictors, different time courses, and different outcomes (Davis et al., 1998). This is not to say that the two proposed processes do not jointly influence the adjustment process. Elsewhere we have proposed that perceiving benefits may alleviate, and in some sense compensate for, a strong desire to comprehend a senseless death (Davis & Nolen-Hoeksema, 2001).

Our data come from the Stanford Bereavement Project, a large, multiwave bereavement study conducted in the San Francisco Bay area (Davis et al., 1998; Nolen-Hoeksema & Davis, 1999; Nolen-Hoeksema & Larson, 1999; Nolen-Hoeksema, Parker, & Larson, 1994). Potential participants were recruited through a number of hospices in the Bay area. At initial contact, all participants were losing a loved one through terminal illnesses. When possible, participants took part in structured, in-person interviews prior to the loss and then were followed for approximately 18 months after the loss, with structured, in-person interviews occurring at approximately 1, 6, 13, and 18 months following the loss.

When we were designing the interview for this study, there were already clues in the literature that making sense of a loss and finding benefits in it were two different issues. Thus, in open-ended questions at the end of the 6-, 13-, and 18-month postloss interviews, we asked participants two questions. One addressed whether respondents had been able to make sense of their loss: "Do you feel that you have been able to make sense of the death?" The other asked respondents whether they had found anything positive in their loss: "Sometimes people who lose a loved one find some positive aspect in the experience. For example, some people feel they learn something about themselves or others. Have you found anything

positive in this experience?" Responses to each of these questions were coded in two ways. First, three independent coders categorized each open-ended response as either "yes," "no," "ambiguous or partly," or "not interested in the issue." Second, the responses were coded for the particular type of meaning or benefit respondents said they had gained.

At all three interviews in which these two questions were asked (i.e., at 6, 13, and 18 months), the majority of respondents indicated that they had been able to make sense of the loss (68%, 68%, and 63%, respectively), and a majority reported that they had been able to find something positive in the loss (73%, 80%, and 77%, respectively). But, consistent with other research (Davis, Wortman, Lehman, & Silver, in press), there was very little overlap between the responses to the making-sense and finding-benefit questions. Among those respondents coded "yes" or "no" to both of the questions (i.e., excluding those coded "ambiguous/partly" or "not interested in the issue"), there was no association between being able to make sense of the loss and reporting benefits (Davis et al., 1998). In addition, there was little overlap in the particular ways respondents said they had made sense or had gained benefit. That is, statements of benefit or growth were rarely given in response to the make-sense question, and statements that explained how the respondent had made sense of the loss were rarely offered in response to the finding-benefit question.

Although both finding meaning and finding benefit in the loss were associated with better adjustment (see later discussion), the time course for the association between these variables and adjustment differed. The respondents who were unable to make sense of their loss within the first 6 months generally were unable to make sense of it later on. In addition, those who did make sense for the first time at the 13- or 18-month interviews gave explanations that differed in content and tone from those who were able to make sense 6 months after the loss. These late-arriving explanations tended to suggest that the world is not as ordered, just, or benevolent as they once thought it was. As one respondent put it,

> The sense of his death is that there is no sense. Those things just happen. . . . The sense of his death for me is "get ready to die." Don't be surprised when it happens. Don't think that somehow you're going to

be exempt from it. . . . There's no underlying sense of order in the sense that things progress in an expectable pattern. Well, the pattern is that you're born and you die.

This respondent ironically is making sense by adopting the philosophy that death makes no sense. The respondent seems to have come to the conclusion that the only way to make sense of the event is to change a benign worldview— that what happens in life is ordered and predictable—to one that is considerably less benign. In contrast, those who made sense by 6 months overwhelmingly suggested meanings or interpretations of the event that were largely consistent with worldviews that are more benign (e.g., perceiving the event as a natural part of the life cycle, or as part of God's plan). Moreover, whereas making sense in the first 6 months after the loss was significantly associated with decrements in emotional distress (from pre-loss to post-loss), making sense for the first time in later interviews was not significantly associated with changes in emotional distress (see Davis et al., 1998). Similar patterns of findings have appeared in other bereavement studies (Davis et al., 2000).

In contrast to the meaning responses, finding something positive in the loss was associated with better adjustment at all three interviews, even when respondents were finding something positive for the first time at the later interviews. In addition, the relationship between finding something positive and adjustment increased significantly over time. That is, the later in the grief process respondents found benefit in their loss, the more the finding benefit relieved their distress.

Thus, finding some benefit in a loss and finding some meaning in the loss appear to be distinct processes. First, they are uncorrelated with each other. Second, they unfold along different time courses. People who find meaning shortly after a loss appear to find more positive meanings and have better emotional adjustment than people who finding meaning long after a loss. In contrast, finding benefit in a loss is associated with positive adjustment regardless of when benefits are found.

We have focused on the predictors and implications of finding meaning in a loss in other publications (Davis & Nolen-Hoeksema, 2001; Davis et al., 2000). In this chapter, we focus on what it means to find something positive in a loss.

The Implications of Finding Benefit in a Loss

Theorists have disagreed on whether finding something positive in a trauma represents a way of *coping* with the trauma or a true *transformation* in the wake of a trauma (Affleck & Tennen, 1996; Tedeschi & Calhoun, 1996). Those theorists who view finding something positive as a way of coping note that learning about one's strength in the face of adversity, or gaining insight into the meaning of life or the importance of relationships, may help to mitigate the feelings of loss or helplessness at the passing of a loved one. Through these processes, a person preserves or restores the idea that life has purpose and worth, which may be critical to well-being (Antonovsky, 1987; Frankl, 1959/1962; Janoff-Bulman, 1992; Taylor, 1983; Thompson & Janigian, 1988). Taylor (1983, 1989; Taylor & Armor, 1996) has argued that threats to one's sense of self often are diminished by perceiving the event as a "wake-up call" suggesting that one's priorities and goals are not as they should be. The reordering of priorities and the revision of life goals are part of a reappraisal of the event as an opportunity for growth rather than only as a loss (Park, Cohen, & Murch, 1996), and this reappraisal may be a coping strategy that helps to bolster self-esteem (Affleck & Tennen, 1996; Taylor & Armor, 1996).

Other theorists have argued, however, that traumatic events such as loss can create true developmental change by confronting people with new situations and issues (Tedeschi & Calhoun, 1995; Thompson & Janigian, 1988). Major roles may change—a woman may perceive she is no longer her husband's wife or mother's daughter. People who lose their parents now may perceive themselves as the "head of the family" or "the last one left in my generation." Young widowhood may mean being thrust abruptly and involuntarily into single parenthood. These shifts in roles and in self-perceptions can lead to major developmental changes. Certainly, observing yourself doing things you never thought you could do also can lead to growth and change in self-perceptions.

Whatever the role of finding benefit in a trauma, the types of benefits that people tend to find show remarkable consistency over differing traumas (e.g., Collins, Taylor, & Skokan, 1990; Lehman et al., 1993; Park et al., 1996; Taylor, Kemeny, Reed, & Aspinwall, 1991; Tennen & Affleck, 1999). Three benefits commonly reported across studies are that the experience with the event led to a growth in character, a gain in perspective, and a strengthening of relationships. We will illustrate each of these benefits with material from our interviews with recently bereaved people.

The bereaved people in our research talked about a number of ways in which their personalities have changed for the better and about new skills they gained as a result of the loss experience (see also Calhoun & Tedeschi, 1990; Lund, Caserta, & Dimond, 1993). Sometimes the growth in character that they detected in themselves was in the form of an increased empathy for and understanding of others, as described by these two bereaved people, who lost their mothers to cancer:

I learned about compassion, I learned about suffering. Suffering leads to compassion. Compassion leads to beauty. It was an opportunity to look at myself and to be non-complacent. I was always very complacent before. I thought I had it made. I was stagnating. It opened my heart, my mind, and my spirit. I wish it had happened another way, but that's the way it happened.

I learned about love, and empathy. Not so much sympathy, because there was nothing to be sympathetic, but empathy. I can look at people now and have more feeling for their pain, for their feelings. I think I have learned more patience and tolerance for—I see real old people in wheelchairs, people who are having a struggle. I feel more for them than I did before taking care of my mother. (quoted in Nolen-Hoeksema & Larson, 1999, pp. 146–147)

Many of the participants in our study had been caregivers to their loved ones for weeks or months, while the loved ones were in the final stages of cancer or some other terminal disease. They described engaging in activities they never would have believed they could do, such as providing nursing care to the loved one, asserting their loved one's rights with physicians and insurance agencies, and managing conflicts in their families. Martha, who cared for her 83-year-old father as he died of cancer, said:

I saw myself acting in a role of competence where I had to pull on all my resources just

to get through sometimes. I would have to be directing the medical people about what I wanted to do. A person like me who hates showing anger and can't stand conflict. I would have to stand and demand care from the nursing home, and it was necessary and I did it. So I came away with a feeling of competence and strength and gratitude. The gratitude not for having to go through it, I would never have asked for it, but I can see how the experience was a real benefit to me. I was forced to grow. (quoted in Nolen-Hoeksema & Larson, 1999, p. 148)

Related to a growth in character is a shift in perspectives that many bereaved people report experiencing. The loss of their loved one makes them acutely aware of the fragility and shortness of life. As a result, they often reprioritize their goals and re-evaluate their lifestyles. Most commonly, they say that the loss of their loved one has caused them to focus more on the here and now rather than always focusing on the future, as Keith, who lost his wife to ovarian cancer, describes:

I probably take a lot shorter term view of what's going on. I think there's a lot more of *now* than there ever was before. I think we all tend to respond that way to things— you know, we've got plenty of time, and things will take care of themselves. I've said things to people, and asked people to do things that I'd no more done 6 months ago than fly. I came from a family, hell, everybody lived into their nineties. If there's anything I want to do, don't put if off, is the whole thing I'm saying. (quoted in Nolen-Hoeksema & Larson, 1999, pp. 145–146)

Finally, many bereaved people describe their relationships with family members and friends as being stronger and richer following their loss (see also Calhoun & Tedeschi, 1990; Malinak, Hoyt, & Patterson, 1979; Zemore & Shepel, 1989). Because they had a greater appreciation for the shortness of life, they were more willing to openly express their love for family members and to forgive old conflicts. They made more time for others and tried to be more constructive in their relationships with others, as Karen, whose partner died of cancer, explains:

I learned that when you love someone, the relationship is so important. It's enhanced my relationship with other people because I realize that time is so important, and you can waste so much effort on small, insignificant events or feelings. I feel that in my present relationship, I'm better able to be a real good friend, and I don't take things so personally. I don't feel that someone's got to fill me up. (quoted in Nolen-Hoeksema & Larson, 1999, p. 150)

Although the illness and loss of a family member can create conflict among the rest of the family, many of the bereaved people in our study reported that they and their family members had confronted and resolved long-standing conflicts. Often the conflicts had been with the dying family member, but the impending death had provided the motivation to overcome them. Will, whose 80-year-old mother died of pancreatic cancer after a long illness, explains:

During the last years of her life my mom stopped drinking, so I came to know her in a way that I was unable to when I was growing up. I learned a lot about the reasons why my parents did some of the things they did, felt some of the ways they felt, and acted some of the ways they acted. It did not exactly reconcile me to the situation, but it's sort of a balance. (quoted in Nolen-Hoeksema & Larson, 1999, p. 151)

Who Is Able to Find Something Positive?

The most consistent and strong predictor of finding benefit in a trauma, in our work and several other studies, is dispositional optimism (e.g., Affleck & Tennen, 1996; Davis et al., 1998; Park et al., 1996; Tedeschi & Calhoun, 1995; Tennen & Affleck, 1999). People who generally expect positive outcomes in their lives appear to actively look for opportunities to turn seemingly bad outcomes into good (see Carver and Scheier, this volume). Consistent with this interpretation, dispositional optimists were more likely to use reappraisal coping—purposely searching for positive reappraisal of events as a way of coping with their aftermath (Nolen-Hoeksema & Larson, 1999). In turn, the more reappraisal coping they used, the more likely they were to find something positive in their loss. These results bolster Frankl's (1959/1962)

claim that it is the attitude that one adopts to adversity that is critical for adjustment.

Other positive coping strategies that were associated with finding benefit in the loss in our bereavement study were engaging in active problem solving, seeking social support, and engaging in constructive expression of emotions (Nolen-Hoeksema & Larson, 1999). In contrast, finding something positive was not associated with the negative coping strategy known as avoidance coping. This suggests that seeking something positive following a loss is not simply a form of denial or defensiveness but is part of a package of positive and active coping strategies.

These results correspond to those of Snyder (1994; Snyder, Cheavens, & Michael, 1999; see also Tennen & Affleck, 1999), who found that people high on dispositional hope use positive reappraisal, problem solving, and positive distraction as coping strategies for a variety of stressors but do not use avoidance coping and denial. Dispositional hope is more than dispositional optimism in that hopeful people focus not only on future goals, as optimists do, but also on goals they believe they can attain. This suggests that people high on dispositional hope would be precisely those people who go searching for benefits in their losses (see Snyder, 2000).

Although it may seem that it is easier to find benefits in some types of loss than others, we found that the characteristics of the loss did not predict who was able to find something positive (Davis et al., 1998). For example, the age of the deceased at the time of death did not predict whether respondents were able to find something positive, suggesting that it is not more difficult to find something positive in less normative losses, such as the loss of a young person, than in more normative losses, such as the loss of an elderly person. Similarly, whether respondents had or had not been a caregiver to the deceased did not predict their ability to find something positive in their loss. This lack of association between the characteristics of the event and finding something positive is not just a feature of our study. As we noted earlier, the types of benefits people report finding (growth in character, change in life perspective, and strengthened relationships) are similar across many kinds of trauma, including natural and human-made disasters, personal loss, and the threat of death brought on by diagnosis of a terminal disease (e.g., McMillen, Smith, &

Fisher, 1997; Park et al., 1996; for reviews, see Schaefer & Moos, 1992; Tedeschi & Calhoun, 1995; and Updegraff & Taylor, in press). *This suggests that benefit-finding has more to do with characteristics of the individual than with characteristics of the event.*

In contrast to the benefit-finding results, the ability to make sense of the loss was associated with characteristics of the loss, particularly with the age of the deceased (Davis et al., 1998). Only 60% of respondents whose loved one was relatively young (under 57 years of age) were able to make sense of their loss by 6 months after the loss. In contrast, 87% of respondents whose loved one was over 72 years of age were able to make sense of their loss. Similarly, several bereavement researchers have suggested that losses of young adults and children are more likely to violate our assumptions about the natural order of life—that the old should die before the young (de Vries, Dalla Lana, & Falk, 1994). Indeed, one reason the loss of a child is perceived as more difficult to adjust to than any other type of loss is because it is so difficult to find any meaning in such losses (e.g., Craig, 1977; de Vries, Davis, Wortman, & Lehman, 1997; Miles & Crandall, 1983; Rubin, 1993; Sanders, 1980).

Religious beliefs appeared to help the respondents find some meaning or understanding of their loss (Davis et al., 1998; for similar results, see McIntosh, Silver, & Wortman, 1993). Most often, religious people made sense of their loss by saying that God had needed or wanted their family member or, more generally, that the family member's death was a part of God's plan. Religious beliefs did not help people find something positive in their loss, however (Davis et al., 1998). Thus, religious beliefs may provide an explanation or rationale for why the death happened, but they do not necessarily lead people to find some benefit in their loss.

The Psychological Consequences of Finding Something Positive

As we noted earlier, the bereaved people who were able to find something positive in their loss showed better adjustment on indicators of depressive symptoms, posttraumatic stress symptoms, and positive affect (Davis et al., 1998). The relationship between finding benefits and adjustment held up over time, and indeed became stronger as the time since the loss increased. When family members reported finding something positive in their loss, there was a positive change in their reported levels of adjustment, even when controlling for their prior levels of adjustment. Those family members who reported first finding benefits 13 months after their loss showed even steeper changes in emotional adjustment than those who were able to find benefits 6 months after the loss.

The particular benefit respondents found in their loss—whether it was through a gain in perspective, growth in their character, or a strengthening of relationships—did not influence their adjustment (Davis et al., 1998). Rather, it was finding a benefit of any kind that was associated with better adjustment.

It might be argued that finding something positive is related to better adjustment only because it is a proxy for dispositional optimism. Yet we found that the relationship between finding something positive and adjustment remained significant when we controlled for respondents' dispositional optimism (Davis et al., 1998). Indeed, finding something positive mediated the relationship between dispositional optimism and adjustment. This suggests that dispositional optimism is a distal influence on adjustment that operates through the proximal mechanism of finding something positive. In other words, one reason dispositional optimists are able to adjust better to a loss is because they are more likely to find something positive in the loss.

Not only do we see evidence that those citing benefits tend to report less distress over time, but they become somewhat more optimistic over time (as measured by Scheier & Carver's [1985] Life Orientation Test). The fact that these effects seem to grow stronger with time also suggests that, at least for some people, the changes that they are perceiving are beginning to take root. A year after the loss, some people are beginning to perceive themselves differently and to feel confident with these new perspectives. This seems to be what Alicia (quoted in this chapter's epigraph) and several others quoted throughout this chapter are trying to communicate.

Implications and Conclusions

It might seem that our results hold few clues as to how to intervene with and support grieving people. Suggesting to someone who has lost a close loved one that he or she should try to find something positive in the loss could easily be perceived as being unsupportive (see Tennen & Affleck, 1999). Indeed, some of the comments from family members and friends that bereaved people find most unhelpful are those that try to put a positive spin on the loss (Lehman, Ellard, & Wortman, 1986). This is illustrated by a comment made by Veronica, a woman in our study whose elderly mother died after a long illness:

> I got real angry when she died, but people would tell me to look at the other side—she had been just laying there, just wasting away. I got angry at that! (quoted in Nolen-Hoeksema & Larson, 1999, p. 88)

Based on the types of benefits that people do say that they gain following a loss, however, we can deduce some clues as to the supportive interventions that may be helpful for some bereaved people. First, many people say that the loss has caused them to grow in character and gain new skills. Supportive interventions could highlight this growth in an effort to enhance the bereaved person's self-esteem and sense of self-efficacy. For example, a friend might say to a bereaved person, "I know this loss has caused you tremendous pain. I have been really impressed at how hard you worked to make your mother's last days good ones. You did things I don't think I could have done!" Similarly, friends and others could point out how much the bereaved person seems to have grown—becoming very thoughtful, sensitive, and so on—as a result of the loss.

Second, many bereaved people say they have gained new perspectives on life as a result of their loss. Family members, friends, and therapists could ask bereaved people about changes in their perspective as a result of the loss. The answers they get will not always be positive—sometimes the change in perspective will be a negative one. But when the change is a positive one, this provides an opportunity for bolstering the bereaved person's self-esteem and self-efficacy for coping.

Third, many bereaved people say that the strengthening of relationships is an important benefit. This suggests that the level and type of support that family members and friends provide the bereaved person are crucial to the person's ability to find anything positive in the loss. Indeed, our study found people who had high-quality emotional and practical support from others were more likely to find something

positive in their loss (Nolen-Hoeksema & Larson, 1999). This is illustrated by a response to our question about finding benefit from Fran, a woman in our study whose cousin died of complications of AIDS:

> We had incredible support from family and friends, unbelievable from our church and our pastor. And even school friends. We anticipated some negative response to our caring for a person with AIDS, particularly with children in our home, and nothing negative was ever said to us during or since. That was quite amazing. He was very touched by the expressions of concern from friends of ours who would come in and visit him. It was a very close time for my family, that is, my husband, children, and my parents. My mother and I worked in tandem, and our relationship was altered as a result of this. We kind of emerged from this experience as peers. We're much closer. That has been absolutely wonderful. (quoted in Nolen-Hoeksema & Larson, 1999, p. 84)

The impact of any of the interventions we have suggested may be small at first. But they can sow seeds that later lead bereaved persons to be better able to internalize the growth-promoting experiences that they have noted following loss. All interventions with bereaved people, however, need to begin with nonjudgmental listening and appreciation for their pain, and an understanding that the process of grief takes different amounts of time for different people.

In conclusion, based on our research and several other studies, we conclude that the majority of people who face a major trauma such as the loss of a loved one are able to find some benefit in their experience, usually some way they have grown, have gained perspective, or have enhanced relationships with others. This suggests that a focus on recovery from a loss to a previous level of functioning misses the true process of change that many people experience following a loss. Rather than just expecting people to "get back to normal" in their functioning, we can begin to look for ways that traumas contribute to growth to new and higher levels of functioning.

Acknowledgments This work was supported by U.S. Public Health Grant 1 R01 MH43760.

We thank the following hospices and home health care agencies for recruiting participants whose experiences are represented in this manuscript: Hospice of Contra Costa, Hospice Caring Project of Santa Cruz County, Hospice of Marin, Hospice of the Valley, Lifesource of Larkspur and Mountain View, Mills-Peninsula Hospital, Mission Hospice, Vesper Hospice, Visiting Nurse Association of San Jose, and Visiting Nurses and Hospice of San Francisco. We also thank Dr. Judith Larson for running this study and contributing to its development.

References

Affleck, G., & Tennen, H. (1996). Construing benefits from adversity: Adaptational significance and dispositional underpinnings. *Journal of Personality, 64,* 899–922.

Antonovsky, A. (1987). *Unraveling the mystery of health.* San Francisco: Jossey-Bass.

Calhoun, L. G., & Tedeschi, R. G. (1990). Positive aspects of critical life problems: Recollections of grief. *Omega: Journal of Death and Dying, 20,* 265–272.

Collins, R. L., Taylor, S. E., & Skokan, L. A. (1990). A better world or a shattered vision? Changes in life perspective following victimization. *Social Cognition, 8,* 263–285.

Craig, Y. (1977). The bereavement of parents and their search for meaning. *British Journal of Social Work, 7,* 41–54.

Davis, C. G., Lehman, D. R., & Wortman, C. B. (2000). *Finding meaning in loss and trauma: Making sense of the literature.* Manuscript submitted for publication.

Davis, C. G., & Nolen-Hoeksema, S. (2001). Loss and meaning: How do people make sense of loss? *American Behavioral Scientist, 44,* 726–741.

*Davis, C. G., Nolen-Hoeksema, S., & Larson, J. (1998). Making sense of loss and benefiting from the experience: Two construals of meaning. *Journal of Personality and Social Psychology, 75,* 561–574.

Davis, C. G., Wortman, C. B., Lehman, D. R., & Silver, R. C. (2000). Searching for meaning in loss: Are clinical assumptions correct? *Death Studies, 24,* 497–540.

de Vries, B., Dalla Lana, R., & Falk, V. T. (1994). Parental bereavement over the life course: A theoretical intersection and empirical review. *Omega: Journal of Death and Dying, 29,* 47–69.

de Vries, B., Davis, C. G., Wortman, C. B., & Lehman, D. R. (1997). Long-term psychological and somatic consequences of later life parental bereavement. *Omega: Journal of Death and Dying, 35,* 97–117.

Edmonds, S., & Hooker, K. (1992). Perceived changes in life meaning following bereavement. *Omega: Journal of Death and Dying, 25,* 307–318.

Frankl, V. E. (1962). *Man's search for meaning: An introduction to logotherapy.* Boston: Beacon. (Original work published 1959)

Frankl, V. E. (1986). *The doctor and the soul: From psychotherapy to logotherapy* (3rd ed.). New York: Vintage. (Original work published 1955)

Heider, F. (1958). *The psychology of interpersonal relations.* New York: Wiley.

*Janoff-Bulman, R. (1992). *Shattered assumptions: Towards a new psychology of trauma.* New York: Free Press.

*Janoff-Bulman, R., & Frantz, C. M. (1997). The impact of trauma on meaning: From meaningless world to meaningful life. In M. Power & C. R. Brewin (Eds.), *The transformation of meaning in psychological therapies* (pp. 91–106). New York: Wiley.

Kelley, H. H. (1972). Attribution in social interaction. In E. E. Jones, D. E. Kanouse, H. H. Kelley, R. E. Nisbett, S. Valins, & B. Weiner (Eds.), *Attribution: Perceiving the causes of behavior* (pp. 1–26). Morristown, NJ: General Learning Press.

Lehman, D. R., Davis, C. G., DeLongis, A., Wortman, C. B., Bluck, S., Mandel, D. R., & Ellard, J. H. (1993). Positive and negative life changes following bereavement and their relations to adjustment. *Journal of Social and Clinical Psychology, 12,* 90–112.

Lehman, D. R., Ellard, J. H., & Wortman, C. B. (1986). Social support for the bereaved: Recipients' and providers' perspectives on what is helpful. *Journal of Consulting and Clinical Psychology, 54,* 438–446.

Lerner, M. J. (1980). *The belief in a just world.* New York: Plenum.

Lund, D. A., Caserta, M. S., & Dimond, M. F. (1993). The course of spousal bereavement in later life. In M. S. Stroebe, W. Stroebe, & R. O. Hansson (Eds.), *Handbook of bereavement: A sourcebook of research and intervention* (pp. 240–254). London: Cambridge University Press.

Malinak, D. P., Hoyt, M. F., & Patterson, V. (1979). Adults' reactions to the death of a parent: A preliminary study. *American Journal of Psychiatry, 136,* 1152–1156.

McAdams, D. P. (1996). Personality, modernity, and the storied self: A contemporary framework for studying persons. *Psychological Inquiry, 7,* 295–321.

McIntosh, D. N., Silver, R. C., & Wortman, C. B. (1993). Religion's role in adjustment to a negative life event: Coping with the loss of a child. *Journal of Personality and Social Psychology, 65,* 812–821.

McMillen, J. C., Smith, E. M., & Fisher, R. H. (1997). Perceived benefit and mental health after three types of disaster. *Journal of Consulting and Clinical Psychology, 65,* 733–739.

Miles, M. S., & Crandall, E. K. B. (1983). The search for meaning and its potential for affecting growth in bereaved parents. *Health Values, 7,* 19–23.

Nolen-Hoeksema, S., & Davis, C. G. (1999). Thanks for sharing that: Ruminators and their social support networks. *Journal of Personality and Social Psychology, 77,* 801–814.

Nolen-Hoeksema, S., & Larson, J. (1999). *Coping with loss.* Mahwah, NJ: Erlbaum.

Nolen-Hoeksema, S., Parker, L. E., & Larson, J. (1994). Ruminative coping with depressed mood following loss. *Journal of Personality and Social Psychology, 67,* 92–104.

*Park, C. L., Cohen, L. H., & Murch, R. L. (1996). Assessment and prediction of stress-related growth. *Journal of Personality, 64,* 71–105.

Rubin, S. S. (1993). The death of a child is forever: The life course impact of child loss. In M. S. Stroebe, W. Stroebe, & R. O. Hansson (Eds.), *Handbook of bereavement: A sourcebook of research and intervention* (pp. 285–299). London: Cambridge University Press.

Sanders, C. M. (1980). A comparison of adult bereavement in the death of a spouse, child, and parent. *Omega: Journal of Death and Dying, 10,* 303–322.

Schaefer, J. A., & Moos, R. H. (1992). Life crisis and personal growth. In B. N. Carpenter (Ed.), *Personal coping: Theory, research, and application* (pp. 149–170). Westport, CT: Praeger.

Scheier, M. F., & Carver, C. S. (1985). Optimism, coping, and health: Assessment and implications of generalized outcome expectancies. *Health Psychology, 4,* 219–247.

Snyder, C. R. (1994). *The psychology of hope: You can get there from here.* New York: Free Press.

Snyder, C. R. (2000). The hope mandala: Coping with the loss of a loved one. In J. Gillham (Ed.), *Optimism and hope* (pp. 124–148). Radnor, PA: Templeton Foundation.

Snyder, C. R., Cheavens, J., & Michael, S. T. (1999). Hoping. In C. R. Snyder (Ed.), *Coping: The psychology of what works* (pp. 205–227). New York: Oxford University Press.

*Taylor, S. E. (1983). Adjusting to threatening events: A theory of cognitive adaptation. *American Psychologist, 38,* 1161–1173.

Taylor, S. E. (1989). *Positive illusions: Creative self-deception and the healthy mind.* New York: Basic Books.

Taylor, S. E., & Armor, D. A. (1996). Positive illusions and coping with adversity. *Journal of Personality, 64,* 873–898.

Taylor, S. E., Kemeny, M. E., Reed, G. M., & Aspinwall, L. G. (1991). Assault on the self: Positive illusions and adjustment to threatening events. In J. Strauss & G. R. Goethals (Eds.), *The self: Interdisciplinary approaches* (pp. 239–254). New York: Springer-Verlag.

*Tedeschi, R. G., & Calhoun, L. G. (1995). *Trauma and transformation: Growing in the aftermath of suffering.* Thousand Oaks: Sage.

Tedeschi, R. G., & Calhoun, L. G. (1996). The Posttraumatic Growth Inventory: Measuring the positive legacy of trauma. *Journal of Traumatic Stress, 9,* 455–471.

*Tennen, H., & Affleck, G. (1999). Finding benefits in adversity. In C. R. Snyder (Ed.), *Coping: The psychology of what works* (pp. 279–304). New York: Oxford University Press.

Thompson, S. C., & Janigian, A. S. (1988). Life schemes: A framework for understanding the search for meaning. *Journal of Social and Clinical Psychology, 7,* 260–280.

Updegraff, J. A., & Taylor, S. E. (in press). From vulnerability to growth: Positive and negative effects of stressful life events. In J. Harvey and E. Miller (Eds.), *Handbook of loss and trauma.* New York: Bruner/Mazel.

Yalom, I. D., & Lieberman, M. A. (1991). Bereavement and heightened existential awareness, *Psychiatry, 54,* 334–345.

Zemore, R., & Shepel, L. F. (1989). Effects of cancer and mastectomy on emotional support and adjustment. *Social Science and Medicine, 28,* 19–27.

44

The Pursuit of Meaningfulness in Life

Roy F. Baumeister & Kathleen D. Vohs

Human beings begin life as animals and remain tied throughout life to natural cyles of birth and death, eating and sleeping, reproduction, danger and safety, and more. Yet to this natural dimension of human life must be added a cultural one. Humans use their thinking capacity to transcend their immediate environment and their natural urges and responses. Thinking usually involves meaning, as in the use of language, symbols, and connections between concepts. Whereas natural law depends on the principles of physics, chemistry, and biology, culture rests on language and meaning. Hence, an account of the human being that neglected meaning would miss much that is essential and, indeed, much that is distinctively human.

Psychologists gradually have begun to study meaning in life. Frankl's (1959/1976) early work emphasized the importance of finding value in life, and he is widely credited with being a pioneer in the study of meaning. His work constituted a courageous rebellion against the behaviorist and psychodynamic paradigms that dominated psychological theorizing at that time. Another important work in the history of the study of meaning was Klinger's (1977) book *Meaning and Void*, which emphasized the importance of purposes for conferring meaning on life. Still, these works were isolated intellectu-

ally from the main work of their time. In a more recent edited volume by Wong and Fry (1998), however, there are many different authors with broad and multifaceted interests in the human quest for meaning and its implications for psychological functioning. Clearly, there appears to be more attention given to meaning in psychological theorizing.

The Nature of Meaning

The essence of meaning is connection. Meaning can link two things even if they are physically separate entities, such as if they belong to the same category, are owned by the same person, or are both used for a common goal. The connection between the two is not part of their physical makeup and thus can only be appreciated by a human mind (or some other mind capable of processing meaning). Ultimately, therefore, meaning is a nonphysical reality. It is real in that it can have genuine causal consequences, and yet it cannot be reduced to physical principles.

Money provides one of the best illustrations of the nonphysical reality of meaning. A dollar bill certainly has a physical reality as a scrap of green paper with a certain molecular structure.

But no amount of analyzing that molecular structure will reveal what that dollar bill has in common with 10 dimes or 4 quarters. It is only in terms of meaning that this dollar bill is the same as the 10 dimes. Moreover, that meaning links the particular dollar bill to many other bills in far-off places, all of which are defined as having exactly the same value, even though the price of bread or gasoline may vary from place to place.

Furthermore, it should be noted that a great deal of money does not exist in physical form. If all the existing American bills and coins were accumulated in one pile, they would add up to less than a third of the total American monetary system. Much of America's money exists only in the form of abstract representations. For example, if you have a bank account, the bank theoretically holds some of your money. In fact, however, the bank does not stockpile a stack of bills and coins that constitutes your money (or the money of anyone, for that matter). In the old "bank runs," the rumor that a bank would run out of money would cause people to hurry to ask the bank to give them their savings in cash, and the bank did not have enough cash to satisfy that demand. As another example, many purchases are made by check or credit card, and no actual coins or bills are used. These transactions are not physical events that can be fully, adequately explained in terms of atomic, molecular, chemical, or biological processes.

In contrast, life is a biological process that can be fully explained in physical terms (except insofar as its course is changed by meaning—such as if someone moves to a new country in pursuit of religious freedom). Human life is bound by the rules of natural law, and, as such, the basic animal needs continue to exert a powerful influence on human activity.

A seeming paradox in the concept of a meaning of life is that meaning is stable whereas life is malleable. Because meaning must be shared by many people, language is only usable in society if the meanings of words remain largely constant over time. If half the people in your town started saying "no" when they meant "yes," whereas the others continued to use "yes" to mean "yes," chaos would ensue. Likewise, your address, social security number, membership in a family, and other meanings that define you are inherently stable, except for well-established procedures for changing them (such as when you sell your house and move to another). The way that people understand highly abstract concepts such as justice or patriotism can evolve slowly in periods of social change, but even then some continuity is usually necessary, and most of the meanings in the language will remain stable.

Life, in contrast, is characterized by ongoing change. Growth, decline, ingesting food, eliminating waste, reproducing, and other natural parts of life all involve change. Your physical being is constantly in flux, even if your meaningful identity as defined by society remains essentially the same.

A meaning of life is therefore an imposition of a stable conception onto a changing biological process. This may seem quixotic, as if one were trying to pin a stable definition onto a moving target. Yet there probably is a deeper reason for the contrast between the stability of meaning and the flux of life. Although life is marked by constant change, living things strive for stability. Change is not welcome to most living things, and almost anyone who has lived with animals can attest to their pronounced preference for stable, predictable routines and environments. Rick Snyder, the senior editor of this volume, told us a relevant story about his 25-year-old parrot named Norman, who recently was moved to a new and much nicer cage. When Norman was let out of his new cage for the first time, he went into a shrieking tantrum and destroyed a nearby cloth chair.

Thus, meaning can be regarded as one of humanity's tools for imposing stability on life. The human organism is exposed to change but desires stability, and it turns to meaning to help create that stability. For example, sexual attraction and emotional intimacy wax and wane, and long-term relationships are a process of ongoing adaptation and mutual evolution. Yet this seeming instability is counteracted by imposing a stable meaning, namely, marriage. The act of marriage is not a physical event in the sense that the atoms and molecules of someone's body undergo a change, but the wedding does establish certain lasting meanings (such as who has the right to have sexual relations with whom), and these provide a stable framework for defining how two people are connected to each other. Thus, the marital link promotes a more stable relationship even in the context of changing emotions and sexual desires.

Another important aspect of meaning is that it has multiple levels, and indeed most events can be described at multiple levels. Drawing on works pertaining to the philosophy of action,

Vallacher and Wegner (1985, 1987) explicated how people's behaviors and experiences are altered by shifting among different levels of meaning. Low levels involve concrete, immediate, and specific meanings, whereas high levels invoke long time spans and broad concepts. For example, the activity of walking to school can be described in low-level terms as a sequence of leg movements and other physical events. It can be described at medium levels of meaning such as going to school. At high levels of meaning, it can be described as part of the process of getting an education and advancing one's life. Each of these meanings is equally correct.

As shown in the research studies by Vallacher and Wegner (1985, 1987), the different levels have different consequences and implications. People who are aware of their activities at low levels of meaning are quite amenable to influence and change. In contrast, people who are aware of their activities at high levels of meaning are able to guide them by intelligent reference to values and principles. Low levels of meaning focus on specifics and details, whereas high levels of meaning make connections across time and to broad goals. When people encounter difficulties or problems, they "shift down" because these lower levels of meaning seem to facilitate solving problems and making changes. When things are going well, they shift to higher levels. The very shift upward to a higher level of meaning is typically experienced as a very positive event that brings satisfaction and pleasure. This last point—the increase in satisfaction that comes from moving to high levels of meaning—is especially relevant to positive psychology. Increases in level of meaning do more than help one escape from suffering: They also enhance positive satisfaction and the sense of fulfillment.

Four Needs for Meaning

After reviewing evidence from several scholarly fields, Baumeister (1991) concluded that the quest for a meaningful life can be understood in terms of four main needs for meaning. These constitute four patterns of motivation that guide how people try to make sense of their lives. People who have satisfied all four of these needs are likely to report finding their lives as being very meaningful. In contrast, people who cannot satisfy one or more of these needs are likely to report insufficient meaningfulness in their lives.

The first need is for purpose. The essence of this need is that present events draw meaning from their connection with future events. The future events lend direction to the present so that the present is seen as leading toward those eventual purposes. Purposes can be sorted into two main types. One is simply goals: an objective outcome or state that is desired but not yet real, and so the person's present activities take meaning as a way of translating the current situation into the desired (future) one. The other form is fulfillments, which are subjective rather than objective. Life can be oriented toward some anticipated state of future fulfillment, such as living happily ever after, being in love, or going to heaven.

The second need is for values, which can lend a sense of goodness or positivity to life and can justify certain courses of action. Values enable people to decide whether certain acts are right or wrong, and, if people shape their actions by these values, they can remain secure in the belief that they have done the right things, thereby minimizing guilt, anxiety, regret, and other forms of moral distress. Frankl's (1959/1976) influential discussion of life's meaning emphasized value as the main form of meaning that people needed. Values are hierarchical, and each question about whether something is good or bad is typically answered by appealing to a broader level of abstraction and a principle about what is good. Ultimately, of course, there must be some things that are good in and of themselves, without needing further justification. These can be called *value bases* (Baumeister, 1991). For example, many religious people believe that God's will is a value base, insofar as they regard it as supremely right and good and do not hold that God serves some yet higher purpose.

The third need is for a sense of efficacy. This amounts to a belief that one can make a difference. A life that had purposes and values but no efficacy would be tragic: The person might know what was desirable but could not do anything with that knowledge. It is relatively clear that people seek control over their environments (and over themselves; see Baumeister, 1998), and a deep lack of control can provoke a serious personal crisis that can have a negative impact on physical and mental health.

The fourth and last need is for a basis for self-worth. Most people seek reasons for believing that they are good, worthy persons. Self-worth can be pursued individually, such as by finding ways of regarding oneself as superior to others (see Wood, 1989). It also can be pursued collectively, such as when people draw meaningful self-esteem from belonging to some group or category of people that they regard as worthy (Turner, 1975).

It is popularly believed that people can find a single source that will satisfy all their needs for meaning. Indeed, the colloquial question about life's meaning is usually phrased as if the answer were singular: What is the meaning of life? Empirically, however, people's lives usually draw meaning from multiple sources, including family and love, work, religion, and various personal projects (Emmons, 1997).

Having multiple sources of meaning in life protects the individual against meaninglessness. Even if family life turns bad and leads to divorce and the dissolution of the family, for instance, the person may still have work and religion to furnish meaning. Another benefit of having multiple sources of meaning is that there is less pressure for each of the sources to satisfy all four sources of meaning. For example, modern work may offer many goals and a powerful sense of efficacy but not much in the way of value. A person therefore may find that the career is quite satisfying in some respects but fails to yield a firm sense of what is right and wrong. Family life, however, may provide that very sense of value (e.g., doing what is best for the children is typically regarded as an important good) that is not found in workplace activities.

The Value Gap and the Self

The four needs for meaning can be used to assess not only the meaning of individual lives but even the meaningfulness throughout a society. Applying these four needs throughout a society necessarily glosses over many important variations among individuals. Nevertheless, Baumeister (1991) was able to draw some general conclusions about how people succeed and fail at finding meaning in modern life.

Modern Western society seems reasonably adept at satisfying three of the four needs for meaning. Of course, this is not to suggest that all individuals are able to satisfy these needs. In general, however, the culture does offer adequate and varied means of satisfying needs for meaning.

First, there are abundant purposes, especially in the form of goals. Throughout most of human history, most people have been farmers and homemakers, which entailed doing work that remained essentially the same year after year. In the 20th century, however, the nature of work changed so that more and more people had careers, in the sense that their work lives progressed through a series of different jobs with different responsibilities, tasks, and rewards (see Bellah, Madsen, Sullivan, Swidler, & Tipton, 1985; Rodgers, 1978). The shift in the nature of work into being careers means that people find a seemingly endless hierarchy or sequence of goals that can structure their work.

Fulfillments, the other form of purpose, also are offered in modern society, but there are some recurring problems in the nature of fulfillment that always have plagued secular ideals of fulfillment. For example, the idea of fulfillment is that it will mark a permanent improvement in life—"living happily ever after"—whereas in reality most fulfillment states are relatively short-lived. Still, the pursuit of fulfillment does form a central aspect of the meaning of many lives, and it can continually provide meaning across the life span.

In regard to the need for a sense of efficacy, there are several available routes in society today. People can exert control in many ways and on many levels. Work, family, hobbies, volunteer work, and other pursuits typically offer abundant means of satisfying the quest for efficacy.

Modern society also furnishes an appealing assortment of ways to establish self-worth. Both group and individual criteria for self-worth are available, and the diversity of pursuits and spheres means that nearly everyone probably can find some way to be better than other people. In contrast to the abundant options for satisfying the three needs for purpose, efficacy, and self-worth, modern society does not seem to succeed as well at offering people a reliable and convincing set of values. Moral discourse has lost its bearings and foundations (Bellah et al., 1985), and Baumeister's (1991) appraisal emphasized the "value gap" as the most widespread difficulty that people today have in finding meaning in life.

One reason for this difficulty is the loss of consensus about values. The very diversity and multiplicity of endeavors in modern society seems to frustrate the quest for solid values, even while it may facilitate the effort to satisfy other needs for meaning. In order to tolerate diversity, it is sometimes necessary to accept that other people's values can be different than one's own, and this seems to make one's own values seem arbitrary or replaceable, which undermines the assumptions on which values are based (see Berger, 1967, on plausibility structures).

Another reason for the value gap is that the transition to a modern society replaces traditional values with bureaucratic rationality. The strong values that guided our ancestors, such as tradition and religion, have been weakened during the modernization of society, and no firm values have replaced them. The transition to modern society is perhaps inherently destructive of certain value bases, and once a value base is lost, it is difficult to revive or replace (Habermas, 1973).

The relative lack of firm, consensually recognized values—the value gap—is thus the most common and socially pervasive problem in the modern quest for a meaningful life. The other needs for meaning can be problematic for many individuals, but at least society does offer ample means of satisfying them. Values in particular are the area in which society is least helpful. Indeed, the positive psychology movement may be able to make a substantial contribution to modern well-being and meaningfulness if it can help people with the process of finding ways to see their lives as having value.

The rising emphasis on self and identity in the modern world can be viewed as a response to the value gap. Modern culture has elevated the self to the status of serving as a basic value. People feel a moral obligation and an entitlement to seek self-knowledge, to cultivate their talents and fulfill their potentialities, and to do what is best for their personal growth and happiness. This is a remarkable change from the traditional moral system, which usually arrayed moral injunctions against anything that was self-serving. Indeed, the restraint of selfish pursuits is arguably the essential core of previous morality and the reason that morals emerged in the first place. Shifting the cultivation of self from the enemy of moral values to one of the staunchest bases of moral values is a fundamental and far-reaching realignment.

Happiness and Suffering

A happy life and a meaningful life are not the same thing. For example, a terrorist or revolutionary fighter may have an extremely meaningful life, but it is not likely to be a very happy one. Baumeister (1991) reviewed extensive evidence showing that having children reduces the happiness and life satisfaction of parents, but that this loss of happiness may be compensated by an increase in meaningfulness (i.e., parenthood can help satisfy all four needs for meaning).

It would be excessive to conclude from such examples, however, that happiness and meaningfulness are opposites or even that they are negatively correlated. In the majority of cases, more meaningful lives will be happier ones, and the existential despair that accompanies a profound sense of meaninglessness is likely to be incompatible with lasting happiness.

Probably the best way to reconcile these conflicting signs with the weight of human experience is to propose that meaning is necessary but not sufficient for happiness. People who cannot find meaning in life (i.e., who cannot satisfy the needs for meaning), and whose lives therefore are experienced as severely lacking in meaning, are probably unable to achieve happiness. But meaningfulness is probably not enough to ensure happiness. Meaning is a prerequisite for happiness, but there also are other necessary ingredients.

Turning to the topic of suffering, it appears to stimulate the needs for meaning (see Baumeister, 1991). When people suffer some misfortune, they often cope with it by finding some form of meaning. Giving meaning to the negative life event may constitute a form of control, even if it has no practical value (e.g., Rothbaum, Weisz, & Snyder, 1982). For example, people who suffer from chronic pain report feeling better if they are able to put a label on the pain so as to define and explain it, even if that diagnosis entails that nothing can be done about it (Hilbert, 1984). Simply having a label is comforting and eases stress; in turn, this allows the person to move on (see Snyder & Pulvers, 2001).

In her influential paper on how people cope with misfortune, Taylor (1983) demonstrated the power of suffering to stimulate the needs for meaning. In her account, people cope with suffering and misfortune by means of three general strategies: finding purpose in it, rebuilding a sense of mastery or control, and bolstering their self-worth. These correspond to three of the four needs for meaning (i.e., purpose, efficacy, and self-worth). The fourth, for value, probably deserves to be included as well, because when people believe that their suffering serves some positive value, they can bear it more easily. Indeed, part of the long-standing appeal of Christian religion is that it confers value on suffering for its own sake, insofar as the sufferer is imitating Christ. The symbolic link between one's own misfortune and the suffering of the divine figure ("we all have our crosses to bear," in the revealing cliche) transforms one's suffering by conferring value and thereby facilitating coping.

Making Meaning

The term *meaning-making* refers to an active process through which people revise or reappraise an event or series or events (e.g., Taylor, 1983). This reappraisal often involves finding some positive aspect (such as the proverbial silver lining) in a negative event. The transformation process from adversity to prosperity has been referred to as the *benefit-finding* aspect of meaning-making (Davis, Nolen-Hoeksema, & Larson, 1998). A second aspect of meaning-making involves looking for attributions (e.g., that God intended for the event to occur) in an effort to understand the event. This aspect has been referred to as the *sense-making* function of meaning-making (Davis et al., 1998). Meaning-making also has been defined as the search for significance (Park & Folkman, 1997). Park and Folkman (1997) distinguished between the global and situational levels of meaning-making. *Global meaning-making* refers to the establishment of a basic orientation, long-term belief system, or set of valued goals. *Situation-specific meaning-making* refers to finding meaning in a particular context or situation that is congruent with one's global meaning structure.

It is tempting to imagine that all aspects of human life evolved because they serve a purpose and are part of a grand evolutionary plan. Evolutionary psychologists (Buss, Haselton, Shackelford, Bleske, & Wakefield, 1998) and neuroscientists, however, maintain that not all human psychological and behavioral outcomes are purposeful from an evolutionary perspective. Nevertheless, the ability to create higher order meaning from seemingly unrelated stimuli or events does seem to have been hardwired into human brains. Gazzaniga (e.g., 1993, 1997) has proposed that part of the human brain is designed specifically to interpret incoming information. This so-called left brain interpreter was first discovered in patients who had split-brain surgery in which the bundle of fibers connecting the brain's two hemispheres was sev-

ered; thus, each hemisphere no longer could relate information to the opposite hemisphere. Gazzaniga noticed that these patients' verbal accounts of an event were supplemented with contextual information that aided in making sense of an event that only half of the brain knew about. In a famous example, Patient P.S. was shown different pictures to each half of her brain and then asked to respond in various ways. After her left hemisphere was flashed a picture of a chicken claw and her right hemisphere was flashed a picture of a snow scene, P.S. was asked to choose from an array of pictures in front of her which object was related to what she saw. After (correctly) choosing the picture of the chicken with her right hand and the picture of the snow shovel with her left hand, she was asked why she selected those items. She responded by saying, "The chicken claw goes with the chicken, and you need a shovel to clean out the chicken shed" (Gazzaniga, 1993, p. 253). The left hemisphere had observed the left hand's selection and had interpreted it with the contextual knowledge it had, which did not include the knowledge that the right hemisphere had seen a snow scene. In subsequent investigations, there has been support for the theory that the left brain is hardwired to produce a narrative reflection of the brain's inputs.

The seemingly universal development of meaningful interpretation also suggests that human beings are hardwired to seek meaning. Kagan (1981) observed how voraciously children seem to learn language, including the toddler habits of naming everything and narrating one's own actions. He concluded that human beings are innately predisposed to acquire and use meaningful thought. After all, children do not need to be forced or pressured to learn language—on the contrary, they generally pick it up rapidly and eagerly, regardless of whether parents encourage, discourage, or ignore the process (see also Snyder, 1994).

Research Methods for Studying Meaning-Making

Meaning-making has been explored through several methodologies. In general, these methods share the basic assumption that meaning-making is idiosyncratic. Often researchers study meaning-making with interview methods (e.g., Davis et al., 1998). The interviews are conducted by trained professionals and may take place in the context of a therapeutic session (e.g., Clarke, 1996). Interviews are advantageous because they allow research participation by people who are not able to convey information in written form (e.g., after a physically limiting accident). Additionally, interviews are open-ended and can touch on a variety of topics, thereby allowing for more depth and breadth of information.

Researchers who study meaning-making through writing have used a number of approaches. Some researchers ask participants to write a story or narrative on a specific topic, whereas others ask participants to write their life stories with no direction to content (e.g., Heatherton & Nichols, 1994; McAdams, Diamond, de St. Aubin, & Mansfield, 1997; Pennebaker, 1993). The narrative method typically involves asking people to write an account of an event or period in their lives, such as a traumatic experience (Pennebaker, 1993) or successful or failed attempts at life change (Heatherton & Nichols, 1994). Life stories (e.g., McAdams, 1985) are in-depth descriptions of a person's whole life. In research conducted by McAdams and colleagues (e.g., McAdams, 1993; McAdams et al., 1997), people are asked to look at their life as a book with a title, chapters (significant periods in life), and plot summaries. The advantage of written meaning-making communications is that they usually are constructed in a linear fashion, allowing for a more cohesive body of knowledge.

Beyond the precaution that these methods may restrict the demographics of participants, it does appear that simply putting thoughts and emotions into language facilitates one's ability to construct meaning (see Esterling, L'Abate, Murray, & Pennebaker, 1999; see Niederhoffer and Pennebaker, this volume).

Benefits of Making-Meaning

There is abundant evidence that engaging in meaning-making has positive effects. Benefits to the self can occur because meaning-making allows a person to establish his or her identity and affirm self-worth (Baumeister & Wilson, 1996; McAdams, 1996). In addition, there are physical and psychological health benefits to finding meaning in life. A consistent theme throughout meaning-making research is that the people who achieve the greatest benefits are those who transform their perceptions of circumstances from being unfortunate to fortunate. For example, transforming a bad event or undesirable set of circumstances into a positive outcome is the central theme of generative people—those who are concerned for and committed to the well-being of future generations (McAdams et al., 1997).

McAdams (1996) noted that a life story can be used to create, transform, solidify, or highlight important aspects of life. Indeed, he proposed that personal identity can be established through the task of asking people to write a life story with one central theme. This task provides an opportunity to reflect on one's purpose in life, which, in turn, may guide future life choices. Because accomplishments and goals achieved can be featured as central events, creating a life story can also boost one's self-worth. Thus, creating a life story provides an opportunity to bask in one's accomplishments and also to create a personal ideology.

Researchers examining the mental and physical health effects of meaning-making consistently report that meaning-making is associated with positive health outcomes. Pennebaker's research on traumatic events indicates that even short writing sessions over 3 days can have wide-ranging effects. This research has shown that writing about emotional upheavals is related to heightened immune system functioning (Pennebaker, Kiecolt-Glaser, & Glaser, 1988), fewer physical illnesses and physician visits (Pennebaker & Beall, 1986), and improved liver enzyme functioning (Francis & Pennebaker, 1992). There is also evidence that this type of writing is related to improved academic performance (Pennebaker, Colder, & Sharp, 1990) and resumed employment after being unemployed (Spera, Buhrfeind, & Pennebaker, 1994).

Indeed, the very meaning of Pennebaker's findings has shifted toward a greater emphasis on making meaning. His early explanations for the benefits of writing about traumatic events were based on the hunch that people wanted to communicate about their problems but actively inhibited these impulses, and the inhibition itself was considered to be a source of harm to the body. Subsequently, however, he has begun to emphasize that writing or speaking about the trauma was beneficial because it helped people make sense of what they had suffered (Esterling et al., 1999).

A powerful example of the effect of meaning-making on physical health is illustrated in research on HIV-positive men who recently had experienced the loss of a close friend or lover to AIDS (Bower, Kemeny, Taylor, & Fahey, 1998). Interviews and physical health indices show that between 2 and 3 years after the death, the bereaved people who engaged meaning-making about their loss showed a less rapid decline in CD4 T lymphocyte cells, a key immunological marker of HIV progression.

Mental health also is positively affected by meaning-making. People coping with the loss of a family member show better adjustment if they engage in meaning-making (Davis et al., 1998). Specifically, Davis et al. found that two aspects of meaning-making—making sense of the loss and finding something positive in the experience—differentially predicted psychological adjustment. Up to 12 months after the loss, making sense of the event predicted decreased distress (i.e., psychological adjustment), whereas at 13 to 18 months after the loss, finding something positive predicted decreased psychological distress (see Nolen-Hoeksema and Davis, this volume).

Meaning-making has been studied in the contexts of psychotherapy and career burnout. Clarke (1996) and others reported that meaning-making in the process of psychotherapy was associated with more successful outcomes. In fact, some therapists explicitly use a story or narrative metaphor to represent what occurs in the therapy hour (see Neimeyer & Stewart, 2000). This method has advantages for both the therapist and the client, in that the story metaphor provides a script to follow.

Research on attitudes toward one's career has shown that attempts to find meanings in life are related to career burnout (Pines, 1993). Pines argued that, in American culture, career often takes the place of religion in people's lives, which then compels people to find significance in their work. Because work does not easily lend itself to existential significance, however, relying on career for meaning in life is associated with career burnout.

Meaning-making—or the lack thereof—has been linked to a variety of cognitive and emotional states. For instance, an impoverishment of meaning is associated with feeling emotional dejection (e.g., sadness) but not agitation (van Selm & Dittman-Kohli, 1998). Interestingly, writing about a traumatic event, which is a form of meaning-making that is strongly associated with positive outcomes, leads to a surge in negative affect and a decrease in positive affect immediately after writing about the event (see Es-

terling et al., 1999). After a period of several weeks, however, people have experienced significantly less negative affect and more positive affect as a result of writing about the event.

In addition to emotional changes, cognitions and perceptions change as a result of meaning-making. People attempting to find meaning often undergo a period of rumination. Rumination has been conceptualized as a way to revise the script of an event so as to acquire a new understanding of the experience (Silver, Boon, & Stones, 1983; Tedeschi, 1999). In support of this theorization, King and Pennebaker (1996) found that, for a person facing a loss, rumination may aid in resolving the loss (King & Pennebaker, 1996). Indeed, some theorists maintain that cognitive changes are central to meaning-making (Esterling et al., 1999).

How Meaning Is Made

We now review the possible mechanisms through which meaning-making produces its effects. Researchers have found that writing (and to some extent talking) about an event forces structure onto thoughts and feelings that previously had not been clearly organized (Esterling et al., 1999; King & Pennebaker, 1996). Language provides an opportunity to develop new insights and coping strategies. Content analyses of written traumatic accounts revealed that a growth in insight from the start of the writing period to its end is most predictive of later positive outcomes. Similarly, a greater number of causal links and revelations of understanding during the writing process also predict psychological and physical benefits (Pennebaker & Francis, 1996).

In telling a story, both the background and the ordering of events are important. Similarly, a story about one's life includes not only the objective facts but also the context in which the events occurred. Thus, the person is able to place the story in a setting appropriate to its outcome or purpose (e.g., Heatherton & Nichols, 1994). In addition, McAdams (e.g., McAdams et al., 1997) has found that generative people tend to write their stories in a particular order, such that the story begins with a bad event or burden, which ultimately is transformed into a positive outcome. In this way, the protagonist triumphs over adversity, thereby creating a main character (self) who is strong, moral, and good.

Although the empirical knowledge about the process of making meaning is still in a very early state of development, it seems reasonable to speculate that the main way that meaning-making achieves benefits involves imposing a coherent structure on events and in particular imposing a structure that is characterized by movement from negative to positive.

Importance for Positive Psychology

The study of making meaning began by focusing on how meaning can help people cope with misfortune, trauma, and other bad events. In that respect, it conforms to the focus on the negative that has been deplored by the proponents of positive psychology. Perhaps that pattern and sequence were understandable. On this point, Baumeister, Vohs, Bratslavsky, and Finkenauer (2000) have proposed that one general principle of psychology is that bad is stronger than good, and so it is hardly surprising that early psychologists have focused on the bad rather than the good (simply because they wanted to begin work with the strongest effects).

In this chapter, however, we have contended that meaning is powerful both for remedying the bad and for enhancing the good. True, meaning is most urgently sought by victims and sufferers, because the need to reduce suffering takes precedence over most other human motivations. But that is only one side to the story of meaning.

Happiness, fulfillment, generativity, and other forms of positive well-being are the essential focus of positive psychology, and meaning is integral to all of them. Moreover, a meaningful life is itself a highly positive outcome. As Ryff and Singer (1998) wrote, "Purpose in life and personal growth are not contributors to, but in fact defining features of positive mental health" (p. 216). The essential contribution of positive psychology is to emphasize that the desirability of a meaningful life goes beyond the fact that meaningfulness reduces suffering. Even in the absence of suffering, trauma, pathology, or misfortune, human life will fall far short of its best potential if it lacks meaning. By understanding how people seek and find meaning in their lives, positive psychology can enhance the human experience immensely.

References

Baumeister, R. F. (1991). *Meanings of life.* New York: Guilford.

Baumeister, R. F. (1998). The self. In D. T. Gilbert, S. T. Fiske, & G. Lindzey (Eds.), *The handbook of social psychology* (4th ed., pp. 680–740). Boston: McGraw-Hill.

Baumeister, R. F., Vohs, K. D., Bratslavsky, E., & Finkenauer, C. (2000). *Bad is stronger than good.* Manuscript submitted for publication.

Baumeister, R. F., & Wilson, B. (1996). Life stories and the four needs for meaning. *Psychological Inquiry, 7,* 322–325.

Bellah, R. N., Madsen, R., Sullivan, W. M., Swidler, A., & Tipton, S. M. (1985). *Habits of the heart: Individualism and commitment in American life.* Berkeley: University of California Press.

Berger, P. L. (1967). *The sacred canopy: Elements of a sociological theory of religion.* Garden City, NY: Doubleday Anchor.

Bower, J. E., Kemeny, M. E., Taylor, S. E., & Fahey, J. L. (1998). Cognitive processing, discovery of meaning, CD4 decline, and AIDS-related mortality among bereaved HIV-seropositive men. *Journal of Consulting and Clinical Psychology, 66,* 979–986.

Buss, D. M., Haselton, M. G., Shackelford, T. K., Bleske, A. L., & Wakefield, J. C. (1998). Adaptations, exaptations, and spandrels. *American Psychologist, 53,* 533–548.

Clarke, K. M. (1996). Change processes in a creation of meaning event. *Journal of Consulting and Clinical Psychology, 64,* 465–470.

Davis, C. G., Nolen-Hoeksema, S., & Larson, J. (1998). Making sense of loss and benefiting from the experience: Two construals of meaning. *Journal of Personality and Social Psychology, 75,* 561–574.

Emmons, R. A. (1997). Motives and goals. In R. Hogan, & J. A. Johnson (Eds.), *Handbook of personality psychology* (p. 485–512). San Diego, CA: Academic Press.

Esterling, B. A., L'Abate, L., Murray, E. J., & Pennebaker, J. W. (1999). Empirical foundations for writing in prevention and psychotherapy: Mental and physical health outcomes. *Clinical Psychology Review, 19,* 79–96.

Francis, M. E., & Pennebaker, J. W. (1992). Putting stress into words: The impact of writing on physiological, absentee, and self-reported emotional well-being measures. *American Journal of Health Promotion, 6,* 280–287.

Frankl, V. E. (1976). *Man's search for meaning.* New York: Pocket. (Original work published 1959)

Gazzaniga, M. S. (1993). Brain mechanisms and conscious experience. In *Experimental and theoretical studies of consciousness: Ciba Foundation Symposium* (pp. 247–262). Chichester, England: Wiley.

Gazzaniga, M. S. (1997). Why can't I control my brain? In M. Ito & Y. Miyashita (Eds.), *Cognition, computation, and consciousness* (pp. 69–79). Oxford, England: Oxford University Press.

Habermas, J. (1973). *Legitimation crisis.* (T. McCarthy, Trans.). Boston: Beacon.

Heatherton, T. F., & Nichols, P. A. (1994). Personal accounts of successful versus failed attempts at life change. *Personality and Social Psychology Bulletin, 20,* 664–675.

Hilbert, R. A. (1984). The accultural dimensions of chronic pain: Flawed reality construction and the problem of meaning. *Social Problems, 31,* 365–378.

Kagan, J. (1981). *The second year: The emergence of self awareness.* Cambridge, MA: Harvard University Press.

King, L. A., & Pennebaker, J. W. (1996). Thinking about goals, glue, and the meaning of life. In R. S. Wyer (Ed.), *Advances in social cognition* (Vol. 9, pp. 97–106). Mahwah, NJ: Erlbaum.

Klinger, E. (1977). *Meaning and void: Inner experience and the incentives in people's lives.* Minneapolis: University of Minnesota Press.

McAdams, D. P. (1985). *Power, intimacy, and the life story: Personological inquiries into identity.* New York: Guilford.

McAdams, D. P. (1993). *The stories we live by: Personal myths and the making of the self.* New York: Morrow.

McAdams, D. P. (1996). Personality, modernity, and the storied self: A contemporary framework for studying persons. *Psychological Inquiry, 7,* 295–321.

McAdams, D. P., Diamond, A., de St. Aubin, E., & Mansfield, E. (1997). Stories of commitment: The psychosocial construction of generative lives. *Journal of Personality and Social Psychology, 72,* 678–694.

Neimeyer, R. A., & Stewart, A. E. (2000). Constructivist and narrative psychotherapies. In C. R. Snyder & R. E. Ingram (Eds.), *Handbook of psychological change* (pp. 337–357). New York: Wiley.

Park, C. L., & Folkman, S. (1997). Meaning in the context of stress and coping. *Review of General Psychology, 1,* 115–144.

Pennebaker, J. W. (1993). Putting stress into words: Health, linguistic, and therapeutic implications. *Behavioral Research and Therapy, 31,* 539–548.

Pennebaker, J. W., & Beall, S. K. (1986). Confronting a traumatic event: Toward an understanding of inhibition and disease. *Journal of Abnormal Psychology, 95,* 274–281.

Pennebaker, J. W., Colder, M., & Sharp, L. K. (1990). Accelerating the coping process. *Journal of Personality and Social Psychology, 58,* 528–537.

Pennebaker, J. W., & Francis, M. E. (1996). Cognitive, emotional, and language processes in disclosure. *Cognition and Emotion, 10,* 601–626.

Pennebaker, J. W., Kiecolt-Glaser, J., & Glaser, R. (1988). Disclosure of traumas and immune function: Health implications for psychotherapy. *Journal of Consulting and Clinical Psychology, 56,* 239–245.

Pines, A. M. (1993). Burnout: An existential perspective. In W. B. Schaufeli & C. Maslach (Eds.), *Professional burnout: Recent developments in theory and research* (pp. 33–51). Washington, DC: Taylor and Francis.

Rodgers, D. T. (1978). *The work ethic in industrial America 1850–1920.* Chicago: University of Chicago Press.

Rothbaum, F., Weisz, J. R., & Snyder, S. S. (1982). Changing the world and changing the self: A two-process model of perceived control. *Journal of Personality and Social Psychology, 42,* 5–37.

Ryff, C. D., & Singer, B. (1998). The role of purpose in life and personal growth in positive human health. In P. Wong & P. Fry (Eds.), *The human quest for meaning* (pp. 213–236). Mahwah, NJ: Erlbaum.

Silver, R. L., Boon, C., & Stones, M. H. (1983). Searching for meaning in misfortune: Making sense of incest. *Journal of Social Issues, 39,* 81–102.

Snyder, C. R. (1994). *The psychology of hope: You can get there from here.* New York: Free Press.

Snyder, C. R., & Pulvers, K. M. (2001). Dr. Seuss, the coping machine, and "Oh, the places you will go." In C. R. Snyder (Ed.), *Coping and copers: Adaptive processes and people* (pp. 3–29). New York: Oxford University Press.

Spera, S., Buhrfeind, E., & Pennebaker, J. W. (1994). Expressive writing and job loss. *Academy of Management Journal, 37,* 722–733.

Taylor, S. E. (1983). Adjustment to threatening events: A theory of cognitive adaptation. *American Psychologist, 38,* 1161–1173.

Tedeschi, R. G. (1999). Violence transformed: Posttraumatic growth in survivors and their societies. *Aggression and Violent Behavior, 4,* 319–341.

Turner, J. C. (1975). Social comparison and social identity: Some prospects for intergroup behaviour. *European Journal of Social Psychology, 5,* 5–34.

Vallacher, R. R., & Wegner, D. M. (1985). *A theory of action identification*. Hillsdale, NJ: Erlbaum.

Vallacher, R. R., & Wegner, D. M. (1987). What do people think they're doing: Action identification and human behavior. *Psychological Review, 94*, 3–15.

van Selm, M., & Dittman-Kohli, F. (1998). Meaninglessness in the second half of life: The development of a construct. *International Journal of Aging and Human Development, 47*, 81–104.

Wong, P. T. P., & Fry, P. S. (1998). *The human quest for meaning*. Mahwah, NJ: Erlbaum.

Wood, J. V. (1989). Theory and research concerning social comparisons of personal attributes. *Psychological Bulletin, 106*, 231–248.

45

Humor

Herbert M. Lefcourt

Early Responses to the Phenomenon of Humor

Although a sense of humor often is regarded as an asset today, this has not always been the case. In the early writings of Plato (in *Philebus*), Aristotle (in *Poetics*), Hobbes (in *Leviathan*), and Rousseau (in *Lettre à M. d'Alembert*), humor was characterized as a form of hostility. For these philosophers, the derisive qualities of laughter, most often directed at ugliness and deformities in others, made humor seem undesirable and cruel. Laughter was said to reflect the more unattractive aggressive qualities of humans that resulted in the victimization of others. Aristotle suggested that "comedy aims at representing man as worse, tragedy as better than in actual life," and "the ludicrous is merely a subdivision of the ugly" (Piddington, 1963). It is instructive to recall that until the end of the 19th century, for example, it was routine for the fashionable set to visit mental institutions to enjoy a good laugh at the expense of pitifully disheveled inmates who were often shackled to their cages. The films *The Elephant Man* and *The Wild Child* (based on J. Itard's famous case study, *The Wild Boy of Aveyron*) provide good reminders of how people would visit fairgrounds to gawk and laugh at deformed and diseased persons.

Lengthy debates about whether humor can be regarded as a blessing or a curse have been proffered in the writings of Robertson Davies and Umberto Eco. In the third book of Davies's (1975) classic *Deptford Trilogy*, titled *World of Wonders*, for example, there is a prolonged discussion among the protagonists about whether humor and joking are not the province of the devil rather than a gift from God. They argue that joking about the past is a way of diminishing its importance and "veiling its horror." This "veiling of horror" is said to simply prepare people to accept yet further horrors and is held responsible for human failure to learn how to avoid the circumstances that produce misery. Humor, in these terms, is essentially evil because it prevents people from learning what they would need to know if they are to survive without further duress. As one of Davies's characters notes, "Only the Devil could devise such a subtle agency and persuade mankind to value it" (p. 92). Interestingly, this "veiling of horror," which is viewed so negatively by the protagonists in Davies's novel, comprises what psychological humor theorists mean when they speak of humor positively as an emotion-focused coping strategy, a means by which emotional responses may be muted.

A disputation about humor also is contained in Umberto Eco's novel *The Name of the Rose* (1980), where it plays a more central role in the story than it does in Davies's work. Two monks, who become the main antagonists in this wonderfully engaging mystery, enter into an intense dialogue about the nature of humor shortly before one or both of them are likely to be killed by the other. The malevolent monk reveals his hatred and dread of humor in arguing that it is essentially blasphemous and that it has the potential to destroy faith and the "order of the universe." His contention is that if humor were allowed to undo the fear of God, humans would inevitably come to revere the profane, "the dark powers of corporal matter." Humor is seen as a nullifier of obedience and a tool for insurrection. The second monk, who is the mentor of the assumed writer of this memoirlike novel, counters this position, arguing, much as modern-day humor advocates might, that puritanism is the very hell that threatens to make life an agony in the here and now. He asserts that the use of fear and terror (and murder of would-be insubordinates in this case), while supporting order, reflects the devil's "arrogance of the spirit, faith without smile, truth that is never seized by doubt" (p. 477).

Whereas philosophers have argued about the value of humor, physicians seem to have held humor, or at least laughter, in positive regard for some time. In a delightful article titled "A Laugh a Day: Can Mirth Keep Disease at Bay?," Jeffrey Goldstein (1982) has cited contributions of physicians and philosophers from the 13th through 19th centuries, presenting a series of priceless testimonials for and against the value of humor for health. Among them is one by Gottlieb Hufeland, a 19th-century professor who is quoted as saying:

> Laughter is one of the most important helps to digestion with which we are acquainted; the custom in vogue among our ancestors, of exciting it by jesters and buffoons, was founded on true medical principles. Cheerful and joyous companions are invaluable at meals. Obtain such, if possible, for the nourishment received amid mirth and jollity is productive of light and healthy blood. (Goldstein, 1982, p. 22)

In the 13th century, a surgeon named Henri de Mondeville suggested that laughter could be used as an aid in the recovery from surgery: "The surgeon must forbid anger, hatred, and sadness in the patient, and remind him that the body grows fat from joy and thin from sadness" (Goldstein, 1982, p. 22).

In the 16th century, Joubert (1579) claimed that laughter produces an excessive blood flow that helps to create healthy-looking complexions and vitality in facial features. Laughter was, therefore, said to be aligned with recuperative forces that contribute to a patient's wellness.

Another testimonial from a 16th-century physician was offered by Richard Mulcaster, who believed that laughter could be thought of as a physical exercise promoting health: "He wrote that laughter could help those who have cold hands and cold chests and are troubled by melancholia, since it moveth much aire in the breast, and sendeth the warmer spirites outward" (Goldstein, 1982, p. 22).

In the early years of the 20th century, a medical professor at Fordham University named Walsh wrote the book *Laughter and Health* (1928), in which he states:

> The best formula for the health of the individual is contained in the mathematical expression: health varies as the amount of laughter. . . . This favorable effect on the mind influences various functions of the body and makes them healthier than would otherwise be the case. (p. 143)

It would seem, then, that where many philosophers and theologians, and those concerned with morality and religion from earlier centuries, excoriated humor and laughter as being derived from malicious delight at the failings and misfortunes of others, physicians were more observant of the health benefits of laughter and humor. This latter orientation has received strong support in recent decades in the writings of Norman Cousins. In *Anatomy of an Illness*, Cousins (1979) described the important therapeutic role of humor as he struggled with a life-threatening disease. In Cousins's case, the use of humor may have helped to change the course of his disease, a point he came to emphasize in two subsequent books concerned with healing processes during encounters with different diseases (Cousins, 1983, 1989).

Among the earliest psychological contributions depicting the positive effects of humor was that of William McDougall (1903, 1922), who suggested that laughter could reduce the impact of social forces that otherwise might undermine rational behavior. Laughter was described as a device for avoiding excessive sympathy and for saving us from depression, grief, and other potentially destructive emotions. This position parallels recent writings about humor as a means of alleviating distress (emotional arousal). McDougall (1922) wrote:

> The possession of this peculiar disposition (laughter) shields us from the depressing influence which the many minor mishaps and shortcomings of our fellows would exert upon us if we did not possess it, and which they do exert upon those unfortunate persons in whom the disposition seem to be abnormally weak or altogether lacking. It not only prevents our minds from dwelling upon these depressing objects, but it actually converts these objects into stimulants that promote our well-being, both bodily and mentally, instead of depressing us through sympathetic pain or distress. And now we see how the acquirement of laughter was worth while to the human species; laughter is primarily and fundamentally the antidote of sympathetic pain. (p. 299)

Similarly, Freud, in his book *Jokes and Their Relation to the Unconscious* (1905), described laughter as a release of defensive tension that had been aroused by circumstances preliminary to the laugh. Tension was said to be elicited by anything that could provoke feelings or thoughts associated with anger and sexuality in situations where their expression would be inappropriate. When ego defenses that inhibit such emotional expression proved to be unnecessary, as when a joker provides a punch line to his story and thereby relieves the listener of possible emotional responses, the energy exerted in inhibiting emotional responses was said to be released in laughter. In Freud's writings, similar to McDougall's, he hinted at the beneficial effects of humor in reducing the impact of emotional duress.

Freud also wrote a brief paper titled "Humor" (1928), wherein he presented a view of "humor" that differentiated it from "wit" and the "comic." Humor was said to represent the internalization of parental forgiveness that enables an individual to gain perspective and relief from the emotions attendant upon disappointments and failures. Humor involved the rein-

terpretation of failures as being of lesser importance or seriousness than had initially been believed, thereby transforming such failures into "mere child's play." In this way, humor becomes a means of coming to terms with disappointments and averting episodic anxiety and depression. It is this form of humor, described by Freud and hinted at by McDougall, that characterizes much of contemporary research on humor as an alleviator of emotional distress.

A Current Model of Humor as a Positive Asset

Norman Dixon (1980) has proposed that humor may have evolved as an alternative to feelings of anger, which became less adaptive when humans began living in less nomadic and more populous groups. As Jared Diamond (1997) has noted, anger and violence become less acceptable means for resolving conflicts when people have to live in close proximity to each other in stable societies. As long as people were nomadic, following herds of animals or continually seeking new places with more clement weather and edible plants, violence could be of a hit-and-run nature. Nomadic perpetrators of violence did not often remain in proximity to camps or neighborhoods where friends and relatives of a murdered family member might come seeking vengeance as would be the case in a stable food-producing society. As Dixon has argued, the expression of anger and aggression would have become maladaptive in settings where populations were stable. Here, humor may have evolved as an alternative response to the annoyances and irritations that could otherwise escalate into violence and murder. The contemporary epidemic of "road rage" is an example of anger-driven aggressive responses to interference by strangers that may have characterized nomadic societies. Crowded urban settings provide similar opportunities for violence as did nomadic societies. Urban metropolises are places where the paths of strangers rarely cross a second time, and violent offenders may retreat from their misdeeds without being recognized. For survival purposes and feelings of security in the urban milieu, road rage seems to be the very sort of emotional expression that will have to become subdued, if not by humor then, at least, by law.

If humor helps to avert the likelihood of violence between people, it also can enhance interactions within social groups. As Bonanno and Keltner (1997) have found, bereaved persons who can smile and laugh as they speak about their deceased spouses are judged to be more attractive and appealing to their interviewers than are those who remain solemn. If people can laugh about what had been a difficult or even dreaded experience, they become more approachable. Laughter, smiling, and humor signify that mourners are ready to return to social interaction, making it easier for others to approach them. To this end, Keltner and Bonanno (1997) assert that laughter gives evidence that the bereaved person is becoming more involved in current ongoing social experiences and is in the process of retreating from a life of reminiscence and relationships with deceased persons. These developments enhance the likelihood that people will become reinvolved in their social groupings, which, in turn, may protect them from the effects of ongoing stresses.

Could these contentions about the positive roles of humor and laughter in facilitating social interaction be the very same phenomena that early philosophers held up to such ridicule? Obviously, humor comes in many forms, and laughter can be derisive on some occasions and supportive on others, though some theorists insist that humor is always derisive, with laughter signifying victory over others (e.g., Gruner, 1997).

In his longitudinal study of Harvard men titled *Adaptation to Life*, Vaillant (1977) described humor as a "mature defense mechanism" and differentiated between "self-deprecating" humor and wit, which often is perceived as tendentious humor. The former was described as adaptive because laughing at ourselves while undergoing stress can lessen the emotional impact of those stressful events. Wit or hostile humor, on the other hand, was thought to be an aggressive means for controlling others and, therefore, less likely to afford relief when a person is on the receiving end of stressful experiences. There is no acceptance of the inevitable, no relief from taking oneself too seriously in humor that is characterized by competition and aggression. Only in self-directed humor, whereby people laugh at their own disappointments and failings, was relief to be expected. Vaillant (1977) described humor that could reduce the seriousness with which failure is regarded as being among the most mature of ego defenses.

In recent research, Janes and Olson (2000) offer support for the differentiation between self-deprecating and hostile humor. Disparaging humor was found to be intimidating to those who observed it even if they were not its target. In the presence of hostile joking, people became more conforming, fearful, and sensitive to rejection than did those who observed self-deprecating humor. Unlike disparaging humor, self-deprecating humor evidently does not have dampening effects on the well-being of observers. The former may result in social isolation of the comic even if the expression of dislike for his ridiculing humor is not made obvious by "fearful" observers. On the other hand, self-deprecating comics may continue to enjoy the pleasure of social engagement because their humor does not arouse the fear of rejection among observers.

Currently, self-directed as opposed to disparagement or hostile humor is regarded as an asset. If Dixon's (1980) assertion that humor evolved as an alternative to the experience and expression of anger is correct, it obviously would be the nonhostile form of humor that would prove most adaptive and arousal reducing, the sort that Freud presciently labeled "humor" in that brief but seminal paper desciibing humor as an emotion-focused coping strategy.

Individual Differences in Humor

The assessment of humor always has been problematic because of social desirability. Few persons readily admit to having an inadequate sense of humor. Gordon Allport (1961) found that 94% of people questioned reported that their sense of humor was either average or above average. In early measures of humor, however, the issue of self-promotion was skirted by simply assessing preferences for one kind of humor or another (sexual, aggressive, nonsense, etc.). Typical of the approach was Tollefson and Cattell's *IPAT Humor Test of Personality* (1963), wherein respondents judged the funniness of 100 different jokes. The resulting scores reflected their appreciation of each of five humor factors, which, assumedly, reflected certain underlying personality characteristics. O'Connell (1960) and Eysenck (1942, 1943) developed similar measures in which the appreciation of jokes and cartoons constituted the subject matter. In a review of these early measures, however, Babad (1974) concluded that such preferences for types of jokes or cartoons were not related to important criteria such as peer ratings of the respondents' senses of humor. As a consequence, when Rod Martin and I began our research into humor, we decided to use different approaches to investigate humor as a personality characteristic.

In our early studies we adopted the aforementioned Freudian view of "humor"—that people with a good rather than poor sense of humor could take themselves and their experiences less seriously. To pursue our investigations, we constructed two scalar measures of humor, the Situational Humor Response Questionnaire (SHRQ; Martin & Lefcourt, 1984) and the Coping Humor Scale (CHS; Martin & Lefcourt, 1983), both of which were then deployed in studies examining the stress-moderating effects of humor.

In the SHRQ respondents are asked to describe how often and to what degree they are apt to respond with mirth in situations that could be as irritating as they might be amusing. Reactions could range from not being amused at all to laughing out loud. In hindsight, this measure seems to be assessing a readiness to experience humor in lieu of annoyance or anger; accordingly, the SHRQ can be thought of as an index of emotion-focused coping whereby unsettling emotions are circumvented or short-circuited by laughter. In the CHS, however, respondents are queried as to their deliberate use of humor to alter difficult circumstances. This differs from the SHRQ in that the focus is upon actively changing the stressful nature of a situation rather than undoing its negative emotional effects. Thus the SHRQ is more intrapersonal and the CHS is more interpersonal in focus. These two instruments overlap one another and yet are dissimilar, as is evident by typical correlations of approximately .25 (rarely exceeding .50). Both scales manifest acceptable internal consistencies and temporal stabilities, encouraging their widespread use. Martin (1996) has documented the reliability and validity data for the SHRQ and CHS based on a decade of research. Martin (1998) has more recently reviewed findings obtained with most of the scalar measures that have been used in humor research. (Copies of the SHRQ and CHS scales, along with their norms and up-to-date research references, are available from this author [also see Lefcourt, 2001]).

In a series of validity studies, the CHS and SHRQ along with subscales from the Sense of Humor Questionnaire (SHQ; Svebak, 1974), have been found to be associated in the predicted directions with a number of criteria, including the following: laughter during an interview; peer ratings of humor; positive moods; self-esteem; mirth expressed during failure experiences; witty remarks and funniness while creating impromptu comedy routines; humorous content of narratives produced while watching stressful films; and funny comments produced spontaneously during tests of creativity. Thus, the results have been quite supportive. One consistent finding, however, needs to be highlighted. The SHRQ seems to be more predictive of male humor, whereas the CHS is more predictive of female behavior. These sex-specific findings also have emerged in subsequent research and have led to discussions about the different meanings and manifestations of humor for males and females (for discussions, see Lefcourt, 2001; Lefcourt & Thomas, 1998). (I will further explore sex differences in humor later in this chapter.)

Current Research Findings

The results from our first studies evaluating the power of humor as a stress moderator lent support for the hypothesized "emotion-focused coping" role that had been advanced previously by Freud, McDougall, and Cousins. Significant moderating effects were found for Svebak's (1974) and our scalar measures of sense of humor and for tasks that we created which required the active production of humor. Specifically, with higher scores on each of the various humor measures, we found fewer mood disturbances as people dealt with potentially stressful life circumstances. Higher scores on the various measures of humor related to less depression and irritability regardless of the frequency and intensity of the life stressors.

Several investigators attempted to replicate and expand upon our findings. The two initial follow-up investigations offered conflicting support. In the first study, which yielded disconfirming results, Porterfield (1987) used both the CHS and the SHRQ to predict emotional responses to life stressors. Elevated humor was related directly to lower depression, but no interactions emerged between humor and stress in the prediction of depression. Thus, humor seemed to be a simple correlate and not a potential moderator of moods displayed in stressful circumstances. It may be that differences in sample characteristics between Porterfield's and our investigation account for the different findings. Although Porterfield had secured a large sample ($N = 220$) of undergraduates, they exhibited substantially higher than normative depression scores (more than one standard deviation higher than the normative means for this measure). A common problem in depression research is that among persons with elevated scores, it is often difficult to produce any beneficial effects. This may have contributed to Porterfield's not finding any moderator effects for humor.

In the following year Nezu, Nezu, and Blissett (1988) reported a study with strong confirmatory findings. In this investigation, both the CHS and the SHRQ were evaluated for their moderator effects on the relationships between life stress, depression, and anxiety. Two parallel data sets were collected. One was cross-sectional, in which stress and dysphoria were measured at the same time, and the other was prospective, with dysphoria measured subsequent to the stressful experiences. Nezu et al. found significant main effects and interactions between stress and humor in the prediction of depression, at both times of testing. In the prospective analysis, where earlier measures of depression and anxiety were entered as covariates in predicting the later measures of same, the analyses were even stronger than at the first cross-sectional prediction of depression. In both the cross-sectional and the prospective data sets, however, depression scores increased with stress primarily among subjects with low scores on either the CHS or the SHRQ measure of humor. Those persons who scored high on humor varied little with changing levels of stress and were always less depressed than their low-scoring counterparts. On the other hand, the results obtained when anxiety was the dependent variable were unrelated to humor.

In summarizing these early findings, we could conclude that in certain circumstances humor has been found to alter the emotional consequences of stressful events. In others, however, humor has been found to be a negative correlate of dysphoria regardless of the levels of stress that subjects had undergone. The latter findings suggest that humor could be regarded as similar to traits such as well-being, optimism, or cheerfulness.

In the ensuing years a number of studies have been reported with further varied results. I have summarized and discussed these elsewhere (see Lefcourt, 2001; Lefcourt & Thomas,

1998). In brief, humor has most often been found to be associated with lessened dysphoric affects. The role of humor as a stress moderator, however, has not been clearly resolved. Nevertheless, a number of investigations attesting to the beneficial roles that humor may play in concert with other psychological characteristics known to reduce the impact of stress encourage us to maintain our original hypotheses about humor as a stress moderator.

Humor as a Positive Asset in Recovery From Illness

Carver et al. (1993) have reported on the ways in which a sample of women coped with surgery at an early stage in the development of breast cancer. While these investigators' primary interests were in the effects of optimism as a moderator of the illness-distress relationship, they also explored the effects of other coping mechanisms, including the women's use of humor during this period. In each of five assessments at presurgery, postsurgery, and then at 3-, 6-, and 12-month follow-ups, use of humor, being able to joke and laugh about breast cancer itself, was found to be positively correlated with optimism. In turn, optimism and the use of humor were found to be negatively associated with distress at all five time periods. Because the distress involved in coming to terms with life-threatening illnesses like cancer may leave a person more vulnerable to the ravages of that illness through immunosuppression (Kiecolt-Glaser et al., 1987), optimism and humor can be said to be positive assets in the struggle against serious illness. Given the nature of the very real stressful circumstances explored in this study, the positive effects for optimism and humor are compelling.

In another study examining patients' responses to hospitalization for orthopedic procedures, Rotton and Shats (1996) found humor to have some utility as a pain reducer following orthopedic surgery. For example, requests for "minor analgesics" (aspirin, tranquilizers) in the days following surgery were significantly fewer among patients who were given the opportunity to view comic films during the recovery period than among those who viewed serious films. Also, among those who viewed comedies, dosage levels of "major analgesics" (Demerol, Dilaudid, and Percodan) were lowest for patients who were allowed to choose which comedy films they were to watch compared with those for whom the films had been "assigned." Given the idiosyncratic preferences people have for particular forms of humor, these results are not especially surprising.

In general, the findings from these two studies indicate that humor can be a positive asset in the survival and recovery from illness, as had been suggested by physicians in earlier centuries. Humor seems to help us withstand the debilitating effects of pain and fear that are associated with medically threatening circumstances.

Humor as a Positive Asset for Dealing With Mortality

In another approach to the study of stress moderation, my students and I have examined the affective responses of people who have been led to contemplate their own mortality. The assumption underlying this research was that many of the questions that constitute life event measures of stress contain intimations about the death of loved ones and of the respondents themselves. In one study (Lefcourt et al., 1995), students were led to think about their own deaths through the completion of a series of tasks: completing a death certificate in which students had to guess at the cause and time of their future deaths; composing a eulogy that they would like to have delivered at their funerals; and constructing a will disposing of the worldly goods they anticipated having at the time of their deaths. Scores indicative of mood disturbance had been assessed prior to and following these "death exercises." As was predicted, most persons exhibited an increase in mood disturbance, reporting more depression, tension, anger, and confusion following completion of the death exercises. The only exceptions to this trend were among those persons who had scored high on a measure assessing "perspective-taking humor." These persons showed little or no change in their moods following completion of the death exercises. The perspective-taking humor measure consisted of an index reflecting appreciation and comprehension of a set of Gary Larson's *Far Side* cartoons (Larson, 1988), which had been especially selected for their "perspective-taking" character. Each of the cartoons required "distancing" in order to be appreciated and understood. That is, respondents had to be capable of perceiving the nonsense in everyday human activity to comprehend and enjoy the humor inherent in these cartoons. Perspective-taking humor, the ability to assume a humorously distant position from everyday life, seems to have provided some protection from the dysphoria that commonly results from the contemplation of our mortality.

In a second study concerned with humor and mortality (Lefcourt & Shepherd, 1995), humor was used to predict the willingness to become an organ donor. We reasoned that the very act of signing an organ donation form required, if only for a moment, recognition of the possibility of sudden and accidental death. This recognition of that possibility, however brief, would be aversive enough that most people would never get around to signing an organ donation form. To confirm that belief, we first found that organ-donation signing was related to behaviors indicating acceptance as opposed to dread of death. For example, willingness to visit a mortally ill friend and readiness to discuss death with one's parents and relatives were positively associated with the signing of organ donation forms. This led us to assert that persons who had signed their organ donation forms were generally less phobic about death-related thoughts and behaviors. In turn, when organ-donation signing was examined for its relationship to humor, it was found to be positively associated with both the SHRQ and our cartoon measure of perspective-taking humor. These data were interpreted as indicating that humor reveals a tendency to not regard oneself too seriously. Not being overly serious about oneself allows one to acknowledge feelings and thoughts about mortality without succumbing to morbid affects.

In a previously mentioned set of studies, humor, observed during interviews conducted 6 months after the loss of a spouse, was used to predict how well persons would eventually come to terms with the loss of their loved ones (Bonanno & Keltner, 1997; Keltner & Bonanno, 1997). These investigators found that adjustment favored survivors who could laugh while they were speaking about their former partners. Those who could laugh during interviews reported that they felt less anger and were enjoying their lives more than they had in the period immediately following their spouse's death. Like humor, laughter could be said to reflect a distancing from the grief attendant upon death, allowing the person to recover and enjoy current life more fully.

In these studies, humor and laughter seem to provide a degree of protection from morbid affects, enabling people to cope with thoughts and feelings about death. Because considering death can arouse anxiety and dread (Becker, 1973; Solomon, Greenberg, & Pyszczynski, 1991), humor may be thought of as a positive asset that allows us to continue our daily activities despite surrounding perils that always serve to remind us of the ephemerality of our lives.

Coping Styles Associated With Humor

Investigations concerned with the effects of stress often direct their attention to coping styles that facilitate or obstruct optimal functioning under threatening conditions. It is often asserted that coping methods that involve avoidance or denial of impending stressful experiences leave persons more vulnerable to those stressors than coping styles that involve awareness and active dealing with stressors (Lazarus, 1966; Janis, 1958). In a series of studies, humor has been found to be associated with more active and confrontative coping styles and negatively related to avoidance and denial.

In the previously mentioned investigation by Carver et al. (1993), use of humor and optimism were found to be positively correlated, and both were associated with less distress in response to breast cancer. Optimism and humor were also associated with positive reframing and were negatively related to denial and behavioral disengagement. Other investigators have found similar patterns of coping styles associated with humor. Rim (1988) found humor to be associated with positive reframing but negatively related to suppression, the tendencies to seek succorance and to blame others, and substitution, the latter being examples of avoidance coping responses made to stressful events.

Humor has also been found to be associated with "approach" coping styles by Kuiper, Martin, and Olinger (1993) in their study of students' responses to academic examinations. These authors found the CHS to be positively associated with the degree to which students appraised exams as challenging rather than threatening. As well, the CHS was found to be positively related to distancing and confrontive coping, subscales from the Ways of Coping Scale (Lazarus & Folkman, 1984). These latter findings suggest that persons who use humor as a coping mechanism are apt to engage in problem-focused coping with minimal emotional responses during their encounters with stress. In support of this contention, these au-

thors also found that the CHS was negatively correlated with trait measures of Perceived Stress (Cohen, Kamarck, & Mermelstein, 1983) and Dysfunctional Attitudes (Cane, Olinger, Gotlib, & Kuiper, 1986), the latter of which assesses dysfunctional self-evaluative standards that are associated with vulnerability to dysphoria.

Studies that have examined the relationship between humor and coping styles lend support to earlier research investigations suggesting that humor can play a role as a moderator of stressful experiences. The coping styles associated with humor seem to be the kind that augur active confrontation with stressful experiences, helping to reduce distress, if not immediately, then after sufficient time has elapsed to allow for a change in perspective.

Humor and Immune System Functioning

Another means of assessing whether psychological characteristics are positive or not inheres in their relationships with physiological processes with known benefits or detriments. Immune system functioning that is essential for health is strongly affected by psychological experience. Stressful events can result in immunosuppression which leaves an organism more vulnerable to a range of illnesses (Kiecolt-Glaser et al., 1987; Pennebaker, Kiecolt-Glaser, & Glaser, 1988). Dillon, Minchoff, and Baker (1985) hypothesized that if stress and negative affect can eventuate in immunosuppression, humor, a positive emotional state, may be an "antidote," or a potential immune system enhancer. Dillon et al. (1985) found that laughter induced by a humorous videotape led to a significant increase in concentrations of salivary immunoglobulin A (S-IgA), which is often descibed as the first line of defense against upper respiratory infection (URI). In addition, these investigators had their subjects complete the CHS and found that the CHS and S-IgA concentrations were positively and highly correlated (average $r = .75$, $p < .02$ across four measurements of S-IgA). To obtain such high-magnitude relationships between biochemical changes and a paper-and-pencil measure, albeit with a small sample, is not a common event and could not be ignored.

Dillon and Totten (1989) replicated and expanded upon their own findings. With a small sample of mothers who were breastfeeding their infants, these investigators again found strong relationships between CHS and S-IgA ($r = .61$)

and also between CHS and URI ($r = -.58$). Even more interesting, mothers' CHS scores and their infants' URI were related ($r = -.58$) as well.

Other investigators have replicated these compelling findings. Martin and Dobbin (1988) found that the relationship between a daily hassles measure of stress and changes in S-IgA concentrations obtained a month and a half later were moderated by scores on the CHS, SHRQ, and a subscale of the SHQ. In each interaction, they found that low-humor subjects exhibited the greatest decline in S-IgA concentrations from baseline levels when they had experienced many hassles. High-humor subjects, on the other hand, showed minimal change in S-IgA levels as a function of their daily hassles.

Further linkage between humor and immune system functioning was established by Lefcourt, Davidson, and Kueneman (1990), who found that the presentation of humorous material resulted in increased concentrations of S-IgA. When the humorous material was universally rated as being highly funny ("Bill Cosby Live"), S-IgA concentrations of most subjects increased. However, when the humorous material produced variation in funniness ratings (Mel Brooks and Carl Reiner's 2000-Year-Old Man), larger increases were found only among those who scored high on the CHS measure of humor in one sample and on the SHRQ in another.

Berk and colleagues (1988) have reported that mirthful laugher elicited during a humorous film was associated with increased spontaneous lymphocyte blastogenesis and natural killer cell activity. Evidently, changes in immune system activity with laughter are not restricted to immunoglobulin A concentrations.

In each of these studies, then, humor was found to be associated with positive changes in immune system functioning. Because immunosuppression commonly occurs in stressful circumstances when negative affect is elicited, these findings suggest that humor may reduce negative affect and/or increase positive affect, which, in turn, disinhibits potential activity of the immune system.

Humor and Other Stress-Related Physiological Processes

In addition to linkage between humor and immune system functioning, humor has also been found to be linked with physiological responses associated with stress. For example, Berk et al.

(1989) examined the effects of humor on neuroendocrine hormones that are involved in classical stress responses. Experimental subjects watched a 60-minute humorous videotape during which blood samples were taken every 10 minutes. Control-group subjects were provided with an equivalent "quiet time" during which they were exposed to neutral stimuli. Blood samples were later assayed for corticotropin (ACTH), cortisol, beta-endorphin, dopac, epinephrine, norepinephrine, growth hormone, and prolactin, all of which usually change during stressful experiences. Of these eight neuroendocrine hormones, five were found to have notably decreased among experimental subjects while remaining stable among control subjects. Berk et al. (1989) concluded that mirthful laughter modifies or attenuates some of the neuroendocrine and hormone levels that are associated with stress.

Newman and Stone (1996) found that the act of creating a humorous monologue to accompany a stressful film (the industrial accident film used in lab studies of stress; Lazarus, 1966) had a marked effect on heart rate, skin conductance, and skin temperature. In contrast to subjects who were asked to create a serious monologue to accompany the film, those creating a humorous monologue evinced lower heart rates and skin conductance levels and higher skin temperatures than their "serious" counterparts. Therefore, active humor creation seemed to have had an anxiety-reducing effect during the presentation of this stressful film. That the film had been stressful was evident in that heart rate and skin conductance had both increased as the film progressed while skin temperature declined, all three returning gradually to baselines several minutes after the film ended.

Finally, we (Lefcourt, Davidson, Prkachin, & Mills, 1997) have found evidence with regard to humor as a stress moderator that may shed some light on the occasional variability of results and conclusions notable in this literature. Subjects in our study engaged in five stressful tasks during each of which blood pressure was monitored at regular intervals. In general, systolic blood pressures increased above resting levels, reaching a peak toward the end of each stressful task, and then receded toward resting levels after a further 5 minutes had lapsed. When humor scores were examined opposite blood pressure, similar patterns were found during the performance of each task. Women who scored high on the CHS measure of humor invariably exhibited lower mean blood pressure levels than women who scored low on the CHS and men, regardless of their humor scores. However, men who scored high on the CHS exhibited higher mean systolic blood pressures than men who scored low on the CHS, and this obtained throughout the testing sessions, even during rest periods. Although the results were not as consistent as they were with the CHS, men who scored high on the SHRQ often manifested lower systolic blood pressures than men who had scored low on that scale. Among women the results with the SHRQ were less evident. The SHRQ, then, seemed particularly predictive of male blood pressures, whereas the CHS was more predictive of female blood pressures.

These contrasting findings suggest that some of the variations in previous results in the study of humor as a stress moderator may be attributable to the inappropriate aggregation of data from males and females. Discussion of these findings is available elsewhere (Lefcourt, 2001; Lefcourt & Thomas, 1998). With regard to humor as a positive asset, research with immune system activity and stress-related physiological processes indicates that humor is a correlate of optimal physiological processes.

Based on evidence derived from the early stress-moderator studies, from research concerning the resistance to dysphoria while thinking about mortality, from investigations linking humor with active, approach coping styles, and from studies connecting humor with immune system activity and healthful physiological processes, we can see that humor is a positive asset, a "wired-in" response that enhances our well-being and protects us against the ravages brought on by stress.

Interventions for Improving Sense of Humor

Although there is evidence and much anecdotal lore about the beneficial effects of humor for health and well-being, there is a surprising dearth of literature concerning how people can improve their sense of humor. Several programs have been designed to encourage the development of humor (Goodman, 1983; McGhee, 1994; Salameh, 1987; Ziv, 1988). With the exception of McGhee's efforts, however, there has been little attempt to subject these programs to

any form of rigorous evaluation or empirical testing. Even in this one instance where there was an assessment of change, it consisted only of a self-report follow-up questionnaire to measure change in humor. Given the social desirability issues in the assessment of humor, it would seem highly problematic to obtain validity data in this fashion.

There has been some attention given to reviewing the use of humor within various psychotherapeutic enterprises (Fry & Salameh, 1987, 1993), but these efforts have largely consisted of descriptive accounts of humor use rather than focusing on the improvement of humor itself. Recently, Nevo, Aharonson, and Klingman (1998) described a more systematically designed program to increase the use of humor among a sample of Israeli schoolteachers. In failing to find definitive results, this study revealed more about how difficult it was to conduct suitable outcome research than about the substance of the results. Good-naturedly, the researchers admitted to several flaws in their investigations. Nevertheless, they did present a useful model for programs designed to improve sense of humor. Their program was based on Ziv's (1981) distinctions between the appreciation, production, and disposition toward humor. Nevo et al. (1998) expanded the dispositional element to include motivational, emotional, social, and behavioral components of humor that became targets for instruction in their program. In essence, they sought to alter their subjects' desire to improve their humor and to enhance the cognitive skills associated with humor such as rapid shifting of cognitions, tolerance of childishness, playfulness, and the like. Ultimately, they sought to alter their subjects' abilities to produce and appreciate humor but failed to demonstrate such changes. Aside from basic sampling problems, the measures of outcomes—ratings by peers or completion of cartoons or creativity tasks—were difficult and unlikely to change within the 20-hour period during which the programs were completed. Nevertheless, the authors' description of their plans of operation could provide a good starting point for anyone wishing to conduct such research.

If one did little else, the encouragement of flexible thinking, of learning to generate multiple responses to singular stimuli, and lessening the fear of rejection for attempts at being comical or provoking laughter could be good starting points for those investigators wishing to enhance the humorous capacity of their subjects.

Directions of Future Research

It should be evident that research into the effects and concomitants of humor is at a youthful stage of development even if the convergence of previous findings is compelling. A potentially fruitful direction for future positive psychology research would involve the ways in which various forms of humor can promote the well-being of individuals. Raconteurs such as Jean Shepherd, Garrison Keillor, Bill Cosby, and Stuart McLean typify the "genuinely funny comic" who is capable of rendering sympathetic accounts of life's tribulations. They provide warm feelings toward others through their gentle form of self-effacing humor. There is no edge or hostility in their humorous tales. Their stories are largely about persons who are surrogates for ourselves. In essence, we become the potential targets of the humor being described, and we can do so without taking offense. In my book *Humor: The Psychology of Living Buoyantly* (Lefcourt, 2001), I have explored the different impacts that could result from self-deprecating as opposed to hostile humor. The former, as suggested in the Janes and Olson (2000) research study, may encourage a sense of cohesion with others, whereas the latter may yield sullen conformity and diminished cognitive functioning. One major area of research that I advocate, therefore, pertains to the power of humor to bond people to one another. As such, humor warrants research exploration as an antidote to feelings of being isolated and forgotten. As is evident in the biological and psychological literatures (Sapolsky, 1994; Sarason & Sarason, 1985), social support and social embeddedness play large roles in the sustenance and health of individuals.

A second area of importance for future research attention concerns the different roles that humor plays for males and females. We have some evidence that men and women use humor differently. Among males, humor often is derisive and divisive, whereas among females, it often promotes social cohesion. An example of earlier research into sex differences in humor can be found in a paper by Zillmann and Stocking (1976). These sex difference findings illuminate the social functions of humor

and help to explain some of the early controversies about whether humor is a virtue or a vice.

Finally, the assessment of humor needs refining. To that end, Thomas (2001) has attempted to develop a measure that clearly differentiates between hostile and self-directed humor; moreover, Ruch (1996) has developed extensive measures of what he refers to as "humorous temperament." Both have conducted substantial psychometric research with their instruments, providing useful tools for the assessment of individual differences in humor. Hopefully, these devices will encourage further research into humor that will prove stimulating for those who are interested in positive psychology. That humor is pertinent to positive psychology would seem to be self-evident. Its relevance is well supported by the extant empirical demonstrations of linkage between humor and the positive ways in which humans cope with stress in their daily lives.

References

Allport, G. (1961). *Pattern and growth in personality*. New York: Holt, Rinehart and Winston.

Babad, E. Y. (1974). A multi-method approach to the assessment of humor. *Journal of Personality, 42*, 618–631.

Becker, E. (1973). *The denial of death*. New York: Free Press.

Berk, L. S., Tan, S. A., Fry, W. F., Napier, B. J., Lee, J. W., Hubbard, R. W., Lewis, J. E., & Eby, W. C. (1989). Neuroendocrine and stress hormone changes during mirthful laughter. *American Journal of the Medical Sciences, 298*, 390–396.

Berk, L. S., Tan, S. A., Nehlsen-Cannarella, S., Napier, B. J., Lewis, J. E., Lee, J. W., & Eby, W. C. (1988). Humor associated laughter decreases cortisol and increases spontaneous lymphocyte blastogenesis. *Clinical Research, 36*, 435A.

Bonanno, G. A., & Keltner, D. (1997). Facial expressions of emotion and the course of conjugal bereavement. *Journal of Abnormal Psychology, 106*(1), 126–137.

Cane, D. B., Olinger, L. J., Gotlib, I. H., & Kuiper, N. A. (1986). Factor structure of the Dysfunctional Attitude Scale in a student population. *Journal of Clinical Psychology, 42*, 307–309.

Carver, C. S., Pozo, C., Harris, S. D., Noriega, V., Scheier, M. F., Robinson, D. S., Ketcham, A. S., Moffat, F. L., & Clark, K. C. (1993). How coping mediates the effect of optimism on distress: A study of women with early stage breast cancer. *Journal of Personality and Social Psychology,* 63(2), 375–390.

Cohen, S., Kamarck, T., & Mermelstein, R. (1983). A global measure of perceived stress. *Journal of Health and Social Behavior, 24,* 385–396.

Cousins, N. (1979). *Anatomy of an illness.* New York: Norton.

Cousins, N. (1983). *The healing heart.* New York: Norton.

Cousins, N. (1989). *Head first: The biology of hope.* New York: Dutton.

Davies, R. (1975). *World of wonders.* Toronto: Macmillan.

Diamond, J. (1997). *Guns, germs, and steel: The fates of human societies.* New York: Norton.

Dillon, K. M., Minchoff, B., & Baker, K. H. (1985). Positive emotional states and enhancement of the immune system. *International Journal of Psychiatry in Medicine, 15,* 13–17.

Dillon, K. M., & Totten, M. C. (1989). Psychological factors, immunocompetence, and health of breast-feeding mothers and their infants. *Journal of Genetic Psychology, 150*(2), 155–162.

Dixon, N. F. (1980). Humor: A cognitive alternative to stress? In I. G. Sarason & C. D. Spielberger (Eds.), *Stress and anxiety,* Vol. 7 (pp. 281–289). Washington, DC: Hemisphere.

Eco, U. (1980). *The name of the rose.* New York: Harcourt Brace Jovanovich.

Eysenck, H. J. (1942). The appreciation of humor: An experimental and theoretical study. *British Journal of Psychology, 32,* 295–309.

Eysenck, H. J. (1943). An experimental analysis of five tests of "appreciation of humor." *Educational and Psychological Measurement, 3,* 191–214.

Freud, S. (1905). *Jokes and their relation to the unconscious.* Leipzig, Germany: Deuticke.

Freud, S. (1928). Humor. *International Journal of Psychoanalysis, 9,* 1–6.

Fry, W. F., & Salameh, W. A. (1987). *Handbook of humor and psychotherapy: Advances in the clinical use of humor.* Sarasota, FL: Professional Resource Exchange.

Fry, W. F., & Salameh, W. A. (1993). *Advances in humor and psychotherapy.* Sarasota, FL: Professional Resource Exchange.

Goldstein, J. (1982). A laugh a day. *The Sciences, 22,* 21–25.

Goodman, J. (1983). How to get more smileage out of your life: Making sense of humor, then serving it. In P. E. McGhee & J. H. Goldstein (Eds.), *Handbook of humor research* (Vol. 2, pp. 1–21). New York: Springer-Verlag.

Gruner, C. R. (1997). *The game of humor: A comprehensive theory of why we laugh.* New Brunswick, NJ: Transaction.

Janes, L. M., & Olson, J. M. (2000). Jeer pressures: The behavioral effects of observing ridicule of others. *Personality and Social Psychology Bulletin, 26*(4), 474–485.

Janis, I. L. (1958). *Psychological stress.* New York: Wiley.

Joubert, L. (1579). *Treatise on laughter.* Paris: Chez Nicolas Chesneav.

Keltner, D., & Bonanno, G. A. (1997). A study of laughter and dissociation: Distinct correlates of laughter and smiling during bereavement. *Journal of Personality and Social Psychology, 73,* 687–702.

Kiecolt-Glaser, J. K., Fisher, L., Ogrocki, P., Stout, J. C., Speicher, C. E., & Glaser, R. (1987). Marital quality, marital disruption, and immune function. *Psychosomatic Medicine, 49,* 13–34.

Kuiper, N. A., Martin, R. A., & Olinger, L. J. (1993). Coping, humor, stress, and cognitive appraisals. *Canadian Journal of Behavioural Science, 25*(1), 81–96.

Larson, G. (1988). *The Far Side gallery 3.* Kansas City, MO: Andrews and McMeel.

Lazarus, R. S. (1966). *Psychological stress and the coping process.* New York: McGraw-Hill.

Lazarus, R. S., & Folkman, S. (1984). *Stress, appraisal, and coping.* New York: Springer.

*Lefcourt, H. M. (2001) *Humor: The psychology of living buoyantly.* New York: Plenum.

Lefcourt, H. M., Davidson, K., & Kueneman, K. (1990). Humor and immune system functioning. *Humor—International Journal of Humor Research, 3,* 305–321.

Lefcourt, H. M., Davidson, K., Prkachin, K. M., & Mills, D. E. (1997). Humor as a stress moderator in the prediction of blood pressure obtained during five stressful tasks. *Journal of Research in Personality, 31,* 523–542.

Lefcourt, H. M., Davidson, K., Shepherd, R. S., Phillips, M., Prkachin, K. M., & Mills, D. E. (1995). Perspective-taking humor: Accounting for stress moderation. *Journal of Social and Clinical Psychology, 14,* 373–391.

Lefcourt, H. M., & Shepherd, R. (1995). Organ donation, authoritarianism and perspective-taking humor. *Journal of Research in Personality, 29,* 121–138.

*Lefcourt, H. M., & Thomas, S. (1998). Humor and stress revisited. In W. Ruch (Ed.), *The sense of humor* (pp. 179–202). New York: Mouton de Gruyter.

Martin, R. A. (1996). The Situational Humor Response Questionnaire (SHRQ and the Coping

Humor Scale (CHS): A decade of research findings. *Humor—International Journal of Humor Research, 9,* 251–272.

Martin, R. A. (1998). Approaches to the sense of humor: A historical review. In W. Ruch (Ed.), *The sense of humor* (pp. 15–62). New York: Mouton de Gruyter.

Martin, R. A., & Dobbin, J. P. (1988). Sense of humor, hassles and immunoglobulin A: Evidence for a stress-moderating effect of humor. *International Journal of Psychiatry in Medicine, 18,* 93–105.

Martin, R. A., & Lefcourt, H. M. (1983). Sense of humor as a moderator of the relation between stressors and mood. *Journal of Personality and Social Psychology, 45,* 1313–1324.

Martin, R. A., & Lefcourt, H. M. (1984). The Situational Humor Response Questionnaire: A quantitative measure of the sense of humor. *Journal of Personality and Social Psychology, 47,* 145–155.

McDougall, W. (1903). The nature of laughter. *Nature, 67,* 318–319.

McDougall, W. (1922). A new theory of laughter. *Psyche, 2,* 292–303.

McGhee, P. E. (1994). *How to develop your sense of humor.* Dubuque, IA: Kendal and Hunt.

Nevo, O., Aharonson, H., & Klingman, A. (1998). The development and evaluation of a systematic program for improving sense of humor. In W. Ruch (Ed.), *The sense of humor* (pp. 385–404). New York: Mouton de Gruyter.

Newman, M. G., & Stone, A. A. (1996). Does humor moderate the effects of experimentally-induced stress? *Annals of Behavioral Medicine, 18,* 101–109.

Nezu, A. M., Nezu, C. M., & Blissett, S. E. (1988). Sense of humor as a moderator of the relation between stressful events and psychological distress: A prospective analysis. *Journal of Personality and Social Psychology, 54,* 520–525.

O'Connell, W. E. (1960). The adaptive functions of wit and humor. *Journal of Abnormal and Social Psychology, 61,* 263–270.

Pennebaker, J. W., Kiecolt-Glaser, J. K., & Glaser, R. (1988). Disclosure of traumas and immune function: Health implications for psychotherapy. *Journal of Consulting and Clinical Psychology, 56,* 239–245.

Piddington, R. (1963). *The psychology of laughter: A study in social adaptation.* New York: Gamut Press.

Porterfield, A. L. (1987). Does sense of humor moderate the impact of life stress on psychological and physical well-being? *Journal of Research in Personality, 21,* 306–317.

Rim, Y. (1988). Sense of humor and coping styles. *Personality and Individual Differences, 9,* 559–564.

Rotton, J., & Shats, M. (1996). Effects of state humor, expectancies and choice on post-surgical mood and self-medication: A field experiment. *Journal of Applied Social Psychology, 26,* 1775–1794.

Ruch, W. (1996). Assessing the "humorous temperament": Construction of the facet and standard trait forms of the State-Trait-Cheerfulness-Inventory-STCI. *Humor—International Journal of Humor Research, 9,* 303–339.

Salameh, W. A. (1987). Humor in integrative short-term psychotherapy. In W. F. Fry & W. A. Salameh (Eds.), *Handbook of humor and psychotherapy: Advances in the clinical use of humor* (pp. 195–240). Sarasota, FL: Professional Resource Exchange.

Sapolsky, R. M. (1994). *Why zebras don't get ulcers: A guide to stress, stress-related diseases, and coping.* New York: Freeman.

Sarason, I. G., & Sarason, B. R. (1985). *Social support: Theory, research and applications.* Boston: Martinus Nijhoff.

Solomon, S., Greenberg, J., & Pyszczynski, T. (1991). Terror management theory of self-esteem. In C. R. Snyder & D. R. Forsyth (Eds.), *Handbook of Social and Clinical Psychology* (pp. 21–40). New York: Pergamon.

Svebak, S. (1974). Revised questionnaire on the sense of humor. *Scandinavian Journal of Psychology, 15,* 328–331.

Thomas, S. (2001). *An investigation into the use of humor for coping with stress.* Unpublished doctoral dissertation. University of Waterloo, Waterloo, Ontario, Canada.

Tollefson, D. L., & Cattell, R. B. (1963). *Handbook for the IPAT Humor Test of Personality.* Champaign, IL: Institute for Personality and Ability Testing.

Vaillant, G. E. (1977). *Adaptation to life.* Toronto: Little, Brown.

Walsh, J. J. (1928). *Laughter and health.* New York: Appleton.

Zillmann, D., & Stocking, S. H. (1976). Putdown humor. *Journal of Communication. 26,* 154–163.

Ziv, A. (1981). *Psychology of humor.* Tel Aviv: Yachdav.

Ziv, A. (1988). Teaching and learning with humor: Experiment and replication. *Journal of Experimental Education, 57,* 5–15.

46

Meditation and Positive Psychology

Shauna L. Shapiro, Gary E. R. Schwartz, & Craig Santerre

Mental health, similar to physical health, has been defined in terms of absence of illness (Ryff & Singer, 1998). In the 1960s, interest shifted toward exploring positive mental health (e.g., Allport, 1961; Maslow 1968). This led to an exploration of other traditions, such as the Eastern, where thousands of years of effort have been devoted toward developing an expanded vision of human potential (Shapiro, 1980).

One result was the introduction of the Eastern practice of meditation into Western scientific study. The scientific study of meditation began in earnest in the 1970s and has since increased exponentially. This transplantation of meditation occurred within a traditional behavioral framework, however, in which the emphasis was symptom reduction and alleviation, with little attention given to development, enhancement, growth, and cultivation of positive psychological qualities and experiences. As a result, one of the main goals of meditation, to uncover the positive and to catalyze our internal potential for healing and development, has been largely ignored (Alexander, Druker, & Langer, 1990; Shapiro & Walsh, 1984). We focus on the positive aspects of meditation in this chapter.

History of Concept

Toward a Definition of Meditation

Meditation originally was conceived within the religious and philosophical context of Eastern spiritual disciplines. Meditation has been an essential element in nearly all contemplative religious and spiritual traditions, however, including Judaism, Christianity, and Islam (Goleman, 1988). Various methods whose background and techniques are quite different (e.g., transcendental meditation [TM], Zen meditation, Vipassana meditation) are placed collectively under the umbrella term of *meditation*. To enhance clarity and avoid misunderstanding in this chapter, we will use the following definition: "Meditation refers to a family of techniques which have in common a conscious attempt to focus attention in a non-analytical way, and an attempt not to dwell on discursive, ruminating thought" (Shapiro, 1980, p. 14). This definition has three important components. First the word *conscious* is used explicitly to introduce the importance of the *intention* to focus attention. Second, the definition is independent of religious framework or orientation (although not implying that meditation does not or cannot occur within a religious framework). Finally, the word *attempt* is used throughout, which places an emphasis on the *process*, as opposed to the specific end goals or results (Shapiro, 1980).

The "family" of techniques traditionally has been divided into concentrative meditation and mindfulness meditation (Goleman, 1972). In all types of concentrative meditation, there is an attempt to restrict awareness by focusing attention on a single object. The practitioner attempts to ignore other stimuli in the environment and focus complete attention on the object of meditation. Attention is focused in a non-analytical, unemotional way, in order to directly experience the object of meditation, which can be located in either the external or the internal environment. Examples of the object include the breath, a mantra, a single word (e.g., *one*; see Benson & Proctor, 1984) or specific sounds (see Carrington, 1998).

In mindfulness meditation, an attempt is made to attend nonjudgmentally to all stimuli in the internal and external environment but not to get caught up in (ruminate on) any particular stimulus. Mindfulness meditation is referred to as an opening-up meditation practice. Some meditation techniques involve integrated elements of both concentrative and opening-up types. For example, a person may focus on breathing (Zen and Vipassana meditation) or a mantra (e.g. transcendental meditation), but be willing to allow attention to focus on other stimuli if they become predominant and then return to the breathing (or mantra).

We suggest that a third category, contemplative meditation, needs to be introduced. Contemplative meditation involves opening and surrendering to a larger Self (e.g., God, benevolent other). From this receptive place one may ask questions and bring things unresolved. Kabat-Zinn proposes contemplating larger questions, for example, "What is my Way?" during meditation practice while remaining open to *not knowing* (Kabat-Zinn, 1994, p. 132). He suggests that "inquiry of this kind itself leads to openings, to new understandings and visions and actions" (p. 133). Contemplative meditation practices presuppose a certain degree of skill in both concentration and mindfulness meditation, as both the ability to focus and the ability to be open are essential. Examples of contemplative meditation include certain types of Jewish meditation, Centering Prayer, and Labyrinth meditations.

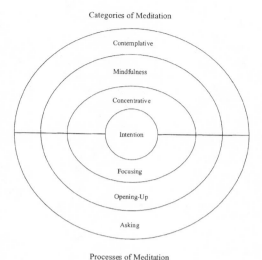

Figure 46.1 Categories and processes of meditation

It is important to categorize types of meditation for the sake of simplicity and clarity. It also is essential to realize that meditation is not a static category but a dynamic process. For this reason, we would like to propose parallel *process* levels to the three categorical levels of meditation discussed previously. In this way, we hope to clearly illustrate that meditation is a developmental process, beginning with concentration and continuing with the ability to open and contemplate. We suggest that each level transcends and includes the previous one. The core and center level is intention, which is a prerequisite to all meditation (albeit there are different levels of intention). Stemming from intention, there are three process levels that parallel the three categories of meditation. The three process levels include *focusing*, which reflects the concentrative meditation category; *opening up*, which reflects the category of mindfulness meditation; and *asking*, which reflects the category of contemplative meditation (see Figure 46.1).

Finally, in developing an understanding of meditation, it is crucial to note that meditation training differs both operationally and in its deep intentions from relaxation training (Kabat-Zinn, 1996). First, an emphasis of meditation is the development of greater understanding through the systematic cultivation of inquiry and insight, whereas the objective of relaxation training is to achieve a state of low autonomic arousal, with little or no emphasis on the cultivation of inquiry or insight. Relaxation is often a by-product of meditation, but it is not an objective of the process. Furthermore, relaxation is taught as a technique, to be used during stressful or anxiety-provoking situations. Meditation, in contrast, is not a technique whose use is contingent upon stressful situations; rather, it is conceived as a "way of being" that is to be cultivated daily regardless of circumstances (Kabat-Zinn, 1996). The formal mediation practice seeps into daily life, bringing greater nonjudgmental consciousness to everything that one does, feels, and experiences.

Original Intentions of Meditation

Walsh (1993b), a pioneer in the field of meditation research, states, "What we have called 'normality' is not the peak of human development but rather may represent a form of developmental arrest" (p. 130). The intention behind meditation is to "wake up" from this suboptimal state of consciousness, to wake up to our true nature.

From a psychological growth perspective, it is essential to learn ways to free ourselves from the artificial and unnecessary limits we impose, as well as to learn to expand our worldviews and consciousnesses. This liberation involves recognizing and letting go of old structures and boundaries and evolving to more complex worldviews. Meditation provides road maps to reach optimal openness, awareness, and insight.

According to Walsh and Vaughan (1993), the initial physical, psychological, and emotional benefits of meditation often are overemphasized, neglecting the traditionally more highly valued benefits. Walsh (1983) identified the ultimate aims of meditation practice as "the development of deep insight into the nature of mental processes, consciousness, identity, and reality, and the development of optimal states of psychological well-being and consciousness" (p. 19). These aims include but go beyond personal self-regulation and stress management. And yet research exploring the effects of meditation to attain these goals has been scarce. With few exceptions, meditation research has not measured the deeper levels of meditation's original intent. As Walsh (1993a) observes, "more attention has been given to heart rate than heart opening" (p. 66).

Meditation Research

Over the past three decades, there has been considerable research examining the psychological and physiological effects of meditation (Murphy, Donovan, & Taylor, 1997). Moreover, meditative practices now are being utilized in a variety of health care settings. The research demonstrates that meditation is an effective intervention for cardiovascular disease (Zamarra, Schneider, Besseghini, Robinson, & Salerno,1996); chronic pain (Kabat-Zinn, 1982); anxiety and panic disorder (Edwards, 1991; Miller, Fletcher, & Kabat-Zinn, 1995); substance abuse (Gelderloos, Walton, Orme-Johnson, & Alexander, 1991); dermatological disorders (Kabat-Zinn et al., 1998); and reduction of depressive symptoms in nonclinical populations (Shapiro, Schwartz, & Bonner, 1998). Few researchers have examined meditation's original purpose as a self-liberation strategy to enhance compassion, understanding, and wisdom. Despite this, a small number of pioneering studies have addressed the effects of meditation on positive psychological health. These studies provide a valuable foundation on which to build future research. This meditation research demonstrates improvements in self-actualization (Alexander, Rainforth, & Gelderlos, 1991); empathy (Shapiro et al., 1998); sense of coherence and stress-hardiness (Tate, 1994); increased autonomy and independence (Penner, Zingle, Dyck, & Truch, 1974); a positive sense of control (Astin, 1997); increased moral maturity (Nidich, Ryncarz, Abrams, Orme-Johnson, & Wallace, 1983); and spirituality (Shapiro et al., 1998). Positive behavioral effects documented in the literature include heightened perception (visual sensitivity, auditory acuity); improvements in reaction time and responsive motor skill; increased field independence; and increased concentration and attention (see Murphy et al., 1997).

These pioneering studies are not without limitations, however, and several caveats should be noted. Many of these studies are over a decade old, do not use rigorous research design (including lack of randomization, lack of follow-up, and imprecise measurement of constructs), and sometimes are based on small samples. Researchers often failed to report what type of meditation technique was taught, or the length and intensity of the practice. Also, several of the studies retrospectively compared meditating persons with those in control conditions, which yields correlational but not causal inferences.

Furthermore, most meditation research is derived from relative beginners of meditation practice.

Despite these limitations, the existing research provides a beginning. Subsequently, we review the specific studies examining the effects of meditation on positive psychological health, starting with the microlevel (physiological) and moving to the macrolevel (transpersonal; for a review, see Murphy et al., 1997).

Positive Physiological Findings

Human wellness is at once about the mind and the body and their interconnections (Ryff & Singer, 1998). Therefore, it is essential to note the research exploring the positive physiological states elicited through meditation in addition to the positive psychological findings. A profound state of physiological rest during meditation is indicated by changes on a wide range of parameters, including reduced respiration rate and plasma lactate levels and increased skin resistance. Statistical meta-analysis showed that changes in these particular variables are consistent across studies (Dillbeck & Orme-Johnson, 1987) and are twice as large as those associated with eyes-closed rest. Also, decline in blood cortisol and lactates (Jevning, Wilson, & Davidson, 1978) and more stable phasic skin resistance have been found (Alexander et al., 1991).

Although meditation is associated with physiological rest, several indicators also show that it simultaneously facilitates heightened alertness (Wallace, 1986). For example, these changes are marked by increased cerebral blood flow; enhanced alpha and theta EEG power and coherence in the frontal and central regions of the brain; marked increases in plasma arginine vasopressin; faster H-reflex recovery; and shorter latencies of auditory evoked potential (e.g., O'Halloran, Jevning, Wison, Skowsky, & Alexander, 1985; Orme-Johnson & Haynes, 1981; Wallace, 1986). EEG coherence is considered as being a measure of long-range spatial orderliness in the brain, and it is suggestive of enhanced functional integration of mental operations (Alexander et al., 1991). Furthermore, during meditation, there appears to be a greater equalization in the workload of the two cerebral hemispheres (Banquet, 1973). This may lessen the verbal, linear, time-linked thinking, which is processed through the left hemisphere (in the right-handed person), and enhance the holistic, intuitive, wordless thinking usually processed

through the right hemisphere. Indeed, it has been hypothesized that the therapeutic effects derived from meditation may reflect this relative shift in balance between the two hemispheres (Carrington, 1993).

Physiological Change and Mood

Harte, Eifert, and Smith (1995) examined the effects of running and meditation on beta-endorphin (beta-Ep), corticotropin-releasing hormone (CRH), cortisol, and mood change in 11 elite runners and 12 highly trained meditators matched in age, sex, and personality. Results demonstrated significant elevations of beta-EP and CRH after running and of CRH after meditation, but no significant differences in CRH increases between groups. CRH was correlated with positive mood changes after running and meditation.

Taylor (1995) evaluated the effects of a behavioral stress management program, including meditation, on T-cell count, anxiety, mood, and self-esteem in a group of HIV-positive men. After random assignment, 10 subjects were trained in meditation and stress-reduction techniques in 20 biweekly sessions. Analyses showed that, compared with the control group, the treatment group showed significant improvement on all dependent measures, and it was maintained at a 1-month follow-up.

Stress Reactivity and Recovery

Goleman and Schwartz (1976) compared 30 experienced meditators' and 30 control subjects' responses to laboratory stressors. Participants either meditated or relaxed with eyes closed or with eyes open, then watched a stressor film. Stress response was assessed by phasic skin conductance, heart rate, self-report, and personality scales. Meditators demonstrated heightened initial reactivity, but their heart rate and phasic skin-conductance responses habituated more quickly to the stressor impacts, and they experienced less subjective anxiety than the nonmeditators.

MacLean et al. (1997) extended the research in stress reactivity and recovery by conducting a prospective random assignment study to examine the effects of TM on responses to laboratory stressors by four hormones: cortisol, growth hormone, TSH, and testosterone. Healthy men were tested before and after 4 months of learning TM. The results indicated that basal cortisol level and average cortisol across the stress session decreased from pretest to posttest in the TM group but not in the control group. Cortisol responsiveness to stressors, however, increased in the TM group compared with controls. The baselines (stress responsiveness) for TSH and growth hormone as well as testosterone changed in opposite directions for the two groups. The authors suggest that, "overall, the cortisol and testosterone results appear to support previous data suggesting that repeated practice of TM reverses effects of chronic stress" (p. 277).

Positive Psychological Findings

Memory and Intelligence

Meditation appears to result in improvements in intelligence, school grades, learning ability, and short- and long-term recall (see Cranson et al., 1991; Dillbeck, Assimakis, & Raimondi, 1986; Lewis, 1978). The first study examined the effects of TM on performance on the Culture Fair Intelligence Test (CFIT) and reaction time (RT) as compared with a control group. Even when controlling for age, education level, level of interest in meditation, parents' education level, and annual income, the TM group improved significantly on both measures as compared with the control group. The authors suggest that TM meditation seems to be a "promising educational tool for enhancing a learner's ability to learn" (Cranson et al., 1991, p. 1105).

Hall (1999) randomly assigned 56 undergraduates to a meditation or no-meditation group. The intervention included a 1-hour session twice a week for the academic semester. The meditation group was instructed to meditate before and after studying and before exams. Significantly higher grades were found in the experimental group than in the control group.

There also is evidence that these improvements in memory and academic performance associated with meditation apply across the life span. Chang and Hiebert (1989), in a review of relaxation procedures with children, reported that teaching meditation to children in public schools increased academic performance. In another study of elderly adults who were taught meditation, there were significant improvements in cognitive flexibility as compared with a control group (Alexander, Langer, Newman, Chandler, & Davies, 1989).

Creativity

Creativity is a complex construct consisting of various traits and capacities, including perceptual skill, ideational fluency, openness to experience, and emotional flexibility. In some meditation studies, one or more of these traits have improved, whereas others have not, making interpretation difficult.

Cowger and Torrance (1982) studied 24 college undergraduates who were taught Zen meditation and 10 who were taught relaxation. The meditators attained statistically significant gains in creativity as defined by heightened consciousness of problems, perceived change, invention, sensory experience, expression of emotion/feeling, humor, and fantasy. Other TM researchers also have reported a link between TM and creativity (e.g., Margid, 1986).

Interpersonal Functioning

Tloczynski and Tantriella (1998) examined the effects of Zen breath meditation as compared with relaxation on college adjustment. Seventy-five undergraduates, matched on initial anxiety, were randomly assigned into meditation, relaxation, and control groups. The students received only 1 hour of instruction in either technique. Interestingly, after 6 weeks, interpersonal problem scores significantly decreased only in the meditation group; however, anxiety and depression scores significantly decreased in both meditation and relaxation groups as compared with the control group.

Personality and Self-Esteem

Based on correlational findings, meditation appears to be associated with positive personality characteristics. For example, when matched groups of nonmeditators, beginners, short-term meditators, and long-term meditators were compared, results indicated a significant increase in positive personality growth as a function of length of meditation (Sridevi, Rao, & Krisha, 1998). Also, Nystul and Garde (1977) reported that meditators had significantly more positive self-concepts than nonmeditators.

Emavardhana and Tori (1997) examined the effects of participation in a 7-day Vipassana meditation retreat as compared with a matched control group. The post-retreat meditators had significant increases in overall self-esteem, feelings of worth, benevolence, and self-acceptance as compared with the matched control group. Furthermore, those completing the meditation retreat reported significant changes in ego-defense mechanisms (characterized by a greater maturity in coping skills). The authors suggested that a 7-day Vipassana retreat "significantly changes ways the self is perceived and defended" (p. 200).

Van den Berg and Mulder (1976) conducted two studies to examine changes in personality brought about by the practice of TM. The first experiment, with 41 subjects, compared short-term meditators (mean practice time, 9 weeks) with nonmeditating controls and reported significant reductions in physical and social inadequacy, neuroticism, depression, and rigidity, whereas no change was found in the control condition. The second study, with 68 subjects, compared long-term meditators with nonmeditating controls. Long-term meditators showed remarkably higher levels of self-esteem, satisfaction, ego strength, self-actualization, and trust in others, as well as improved self-image.

Arguably, these results may be related to the finding that attrition from meditation practice is predicted by poor self-esteem (Rivers & Spanos, 1981) and a negative self-concept (Nystul & Garde, 1979). Those with positive self-esteem or self-concept initially, therefore, tend to continue practice. As noted previously, however, in a prospective study, Taylor (1995) found significant increases in self-esteem in HIV-positive men after an intervention involving meditation.

Happiness and Positive Affect

Smith, Compton, and West (1995) investigated the impact of adding meditation to Fordyce's (1983) Personal Happiness Enhancement Program (PHEP). Thirty-six subjects were randomly assigned to an experimental group or a no-treatment control group. Experimental subjects were divided into two groups, both of which received instruction on the PHEP, but one experimental group also was taught meditation exercises that resembled Benson's Relaxation Response (Benson, 1975). Groups met for 12 sessions, 1½ hours each, over a 6-week period. The meditation-plus-PHEP group significantly improved on measures of happiness, state-trait anxiety, and depression as compared with the PHEP-only group and the control

group. Frequent meditators also report a significantly higher level of positive affect, significantly fewer stressors and illness symptoms, and lower levels of anxiety, hostility, depression, and dysphoria (Beauchamp-Turner & Levinson, 1992).

Informal Practice: Assessment During Daily Life

Although very little research has been devoted to examining the effects of practicing meditation throughout the moment-to-moment experience of daily life (informal practice), this topic of research is crucial. Easterlin and Cardena (1999) evaluated effects of Vipassana meditation in the daily lives of beginning and advanced meditators. Participants consisted of 43 mediators, 19 of whom were beginning meditators, and 24 of whom were advanced meditators, who responded to daily random pager signals containing questions related to awareness, acceptance, affect, and cognitive style. Relative to the beginners, the advanced meditators reported greater awareness, positive mood, and acceptance and lower anxiety levels, lower stress, and a healthier sense of control.

Stress Hardiness and Sense of Coherence

Stress Hardiness (Kobasa, 1990) and Sense of Coherence (Antonovsky, 1987) refer to relatively stable personality characteristics that affect how one perceives and makes sense of the world. Stress Hardiness is composed of three distinct but intertwined qualities: commitment, control, and challenge. Sense of Coherence refers to the ability to find the world meaningful, comprehensible, and manageable. Kabat-Zinn and Skillings (1989) examined the effects of an 8-week mindfulness-based stress reduction program (MBSR) on Stress Hardiness and Sense of Coherence. The researchers found a 6% to 7% mean score improvement on measures of both Stress Hardiness and Sense of Coherence over the course of the intervention with 582 patients. Those with the largest improvement in Sense of Coherence made the largest improvements in psychological and physical symptom reduction. At 3-year follow-up (Kabat-Zinn & Skillings, 1992), the initial gains were maintained, and even further improvement was made in Sense of Coherence.

Empathy

All schools of meditation have emphasized concern for the condition of others and an intention to "promote an empathy with created things that leads toward oneness with them" (Murphy et al., 1997, p. 82). In a randomized controlled study, Shapiro et al. (1998) examined the effects of mindfulness meditation on 78 medical and premedical students. Results indicated increased levels of empathy and decreased levels of anxiety and depression in the meditation group as compared with the wait-list control group. Furthermore, these results held during the students' stressful exam period. The findings were replicated when participants in the wait-list control group received the mindfulness intervention.

Lesh (1970) studied Zen meditation and the development of empathy in counselors. The design included three groups: a meditation group, a control group of subjects who had volunteered to learn meditation, and a control group of students who were opposed to learning meditation. All subjects completed pre-test and post-test (4 weeks later) measures, including the Affective Sensitivity Scale, the Experience Inquiry, and the Personal Orientation Inventory. Results indicated that the group practicing meditation improved significantly in empathic ability, whereas the two control groups did not.

Self-Actualization

Meditation has been described as a "technique to actualize and integrate the personality of human kind to those fulfilled states of personal integration" (Ferguson, 1981, p. 68). Important positive characteristics demonstrating self-actualization include "increased acceptance of self, of others, and of nature's superior perception of reality" (Maslow, 1968, p. 26). These characteristics parallel some of the fundamental objectives of meditation. It is not surprising, therefore, that the most widely measured positive psychological outcome in the meditation literature is self-actualization (Alexander et al., 1991).

Alexander and colleagues (1991) performed a meta-analysis of studies examining the effects of TM and other meditation and relaxation interventions on self-actualization. The analysis included 42 independent treatment outcome studies (18 TM, 18 other meditation studies, 6 relaxation studies). The authors found significant improvements in self-actualization across the studies.

Affiliative Trust and Oneness Motivation

Weinberger, McLeod, McClelland, Santorelli, and Kabat-Zinn (1990) hypothesized that MBSR would promote development of affiliative trust and oneness motivation. Affiliative trust is characterized by a sense of basic trust, openness, and caring and can predict positive health outcomes (McClelland, 1989). Oneness motivation is characterized by a positive sense of being part of something larger than oneself, part of a larger whole. Weinberger and colleagues demonstrated in a controlled study design that affiliative trust and oneness motivation increased over the course of the mindfulness intervention.

Spirituality

Shapiro and colleagues (1998) conducted a randomized controlled study examining the effects of mindfulness meditation on premedical and medical students. Significantly higher scores were obtained on a measure of spiritual experience in the meditation group than in the control group. Furthermore, these results were replicated when the control group received the same intervention. Astin (1997) also demonstrated significant increases in spiritual experience after mindfulness meditation intervention in a group of undergraduate students.

Summary and Critique

Meditation appears to enhance physiological, psychological, and transpersonal well-being. Specific enhancements observed include physiological rest and increased happiness, acceptance, sense of coherence, stress hardiness, empathy, and self-actualization. Thus, meditation may help human beings identify and actualize their potential strengths.

The results of past research are qualified by their limitations in methodology. We suggest the following necessary and sufficient criteria to ensure rigorous design: (a) An adequate sample size of subjects should be randomized into experimental and control groups; (b) the type of meditation technique taught should be made explicit (e.g., mindfulness or concentrative); (c) frequency and duration of meditation practice should be recorded (e.g., meditation journals); (d) outcome variables should be included that are well established and consistent with the original intentions of meditation; (e) follow-up should include long-term as well as short-term assessment; and (f) researchers should include long-term meditators as well as beginning meditators. Also, when matching control subjects to long-term meditators in retrospective studies, in addition to age, gender, and education, it would be important to consider matching subjects on the dimension of an alternative attentional practice (e.g., playing a musical instrument). With such improvements, the inferences that we could make from results would be substantially strengthened.

Meditation and Context

We now turn to the context of meditation and the role of context in both research and clinical practice. We conclude this section with a discussion of a theoretical model, intentional systemic mindfulness (ISM), in which context is explicitly introduced into the practice of meditation.

When meditation was introduced to Western science, it was adapted to fit the current reductionistic scientific paradigm. Most scientists removed the cultural and religious context of meditation, which they judged to be extraneous or tangential to the "core" that might prove useful to the West (e.g., Woolfolk & Franks, 1984). These assumptions led to extracting the operational aspects of the technique of meditation that were measurable and replicable and developing secular forms of meditation that were accessible to a wide range of people with diverse religious values and beliefs (e.g., Benson, 1975). As a result, in the vast majority of meditation studies, the focus has been on the content of meditation as a generic, replicable technique that is independent of the religious and philosophical *context* within which it was embedded historically.

It has been argued that this strategy was necessary to establish meditation as a credible technique within Western scientific psychology (Shapiro, 1994). In fact, by removing the original context, researchers and clinicians have been able to tailor the technique to current health care needs. On the other hand, this lim-

itation may impede attainment of the original meditative intentions, such as achieving higher levels of meaning, purpose, and self-actualization. Although reductionistic research on the content of meditation can and should continue, it is equally important to reintroduce and examine issues of context.

It therefore seems critical to provide some explicit context for the meditation practice; moreover, we must preserve the integrity of the original intentions behind this wisdom tradition along with offering universal applicability. Based on these standards, we suggest ISM, a universal religion- and culture-neutral approach to meditation by which we can introduce both context and quality to the attentional practice of meditation.

Intentional Systemic Mindfulness

All meditation disciplines involve the cultivation of attention. The *intention* with which *attention* is directed, however, may be crucial in maximizing optimal health. By making intention explicit in meditation research and practice, the attainment of positive psychological qualities may be enhanced. Intention as defined by this model is composed of two elements: (a) the quality of attention referred to as *mindfulness qualities* and (b) the context of attention referred to as *systemic perspectives*. ISM addresses both the *nature of the attention* through the mindfulness qualities and the *framework within which the attention is practiced* through the systemic perspectives. In short, it examines two critical aspects of intention—how we attend and why we attend.

In the following sections we explore the importance of *how* we attend through a discussion of mindfulness qualities and the importance of *why* we attend through a discussion of systemic perspectives. Finally, we consider implications, hypotheses, and further directions.

How We Attend: Mindfulness Qualities

All meditation techniques are founded on the cultivation of attention. Attention by itself, however, is not enough. How one attends may be consequential in cultivating health, especially in an effort to cultivate health on multiple levels. For example, if a woman practices meditation in an attempt to lower her hypertension, and she attends to her blood pressure with fear that she will not be able to control it or with anger at herself for having high blood pressure, such attention may have deleterious effects on her health (or at least impede the potential healing effects of the self-regulation technique). On the other hand, if she focuses her attention with a conscious intention to infuse the attention with mindfulness qualities of acceptance, generosity, and nonjudgmentalness, this intention may indeed be health promoting.

Mindfulness qualities refers to the intention to incorporate and bring into conscious attention 12 mindfulness qualities, 7 initially defined by Kabat-Zinn (1990) and an additional 5 by Shapiro and Schwartz (2000). The 7 mindfulness qualities from Kabat-Zinn are nonstriving, nonjudging, acceptance, patience, trust, openness, and letting go. The 5 elaborated by Shapiro and Schwartz consist of gratitude, gentleness, generosity, empathy, and lovingkindness (see Table 46.1). The latter qualities are incorporated to address explicitly the affective (heart) qualities of mindfulness. All 12 qualities are described in Table 46.1.

Why We Attend: Systemic Perspectives

Intention can be applied to context as well as to attitudinal qualities—not only *how* one pays attention but *why* one is practicing a particular type of self-regulation attentional strategy. Therefore, we suggest that it is critical to discuss the larger *systemic perspectives* in order to address the question of why.

Without this larger contextual perspective, as we have discussed previously, meditation may focus on a symptom and ignore the larger system. A self-regulation technique practiced with the intention toward the systemic perspectives includes multiple levels of intention, each transcending and including the previous level (Wilber, 1993).

In the case of the woman practicing meditation to lower her blood pressure by directing intention toward the systemic perspectives, the intention may evolve to promote the well-being of the entire circulatory system. In turn, this may lead to enlarging the intention, recognizing that the heart is a system but also part of a larger system. From there the conception of the

Table 46.1 Mindfulness Qualities

Nonjudging: impartial witnessing, observing the present, moment by moment without evaluation and categorization

Nonstriving: non-goal-oriented, remaining unattached to outcome or achievement, not forcing things

Acceptance: open to seeing and acknowledging things as they are in the present moment, acceptance does not mean passivity or resignation, rather a clearer understanding of the present so one can more effectively respond

Patience: allowing things to unfold in their time, bringing patience to ourselves, to others, and to the present moment

Trust: trusting oneself, one's body, intuition, emotions, as well as trusting that life is unfolding as it is supposed to

Openness:[a] seeing things as if for the first time, creating possibility by paying attention to all feedback in the present moment

Letting go: nonattachment, not holding on to thoughts, feelings, experiences; however, letting go does not mean suppressing

Gentleness: characterized by a soft, considerate, and tender quality; however, not passive, undisciplined, or indulgent

Generosity: giving in the present moment within a context of love and compassion, without attachment to gain or thought of return

Empathy: the quality of feeling and understanding another person's situation in the present moment—their perspectives, emotions, actions (reactions)—and communicating this to the person.

Gratitude: the quality of reverence, appreciating and being thankful for the present moment

Lovingkindness: a quality embodying benevolence, compassion, and cherishing; a quality filled with forgiveness and unconditional love

Note: These categories are offered heuristically, reflecting the general idea that there are mindfulness qualities that should be part of the intention phase as well as the attention phase of the pathway model. A commitment (intention phase) is made to bring the qualities to the practice, and then the qualities are themselves cultivated throughout the self-regulation practice itself (attention phase). See Kabat-Zinn, 1990, pp. 33–40, for detailed definitions of the first seven qualities.

[a]Openness: derived from beginner's mind, defined as "a mind that is willing to see everything as if for the first time" (Kabat-Zinn, 1990, p. 35).

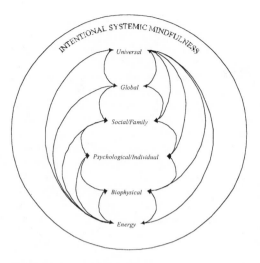

Figure 46.2 Systemic perspectives

body as a psychosomatic self may arise. The self may then be recognized as embedded within interpersonal relationships, family, and community. Consequently, the intention to heal interpersonal relationships also is added. That awareness may stimulate recognition that these relationships are part of a larger community (humankind), which may create the intention to acknowledge connectedness with all beings and with the earth itself.

Clearly, this process will not occur for everyone practicing self-regulation techniques within the framework of ISM. We use it, however, to exemplify the possibility of one's intentions spanning the micro to the macro. Furthermore, in this example we see the dynamic and developmental quality of intention, allowing for evolution based on continuous feedback. Through becoming aware and expanding one's scope of intentionality, deeper levels of previously unrecognized feedback are discovered and amplified. As one continues to practice a self-regulation technique within the model of ISM, one's intentions may move through concern for the specific symptom to concern for the larger context of one's symptoms. Put generally, *systemic perspectives* refers to the intention to incorporate into the self-regulation practice the awareness that symptoms themselves (intrapersonal) exist as part of larger systems (interpersonal and transpersonal), as illustrated in Figure 46.2. The arrows in Figure 46.2 indicate how each level is directly or indirectly connected to all others. Each level both sends and receives

direct or indirect feedback to all other levels as a dynamic process (not all possible arrows [interactions] are shown).

Meditation Techniques: Potential Limitations

By using ISM, we can address potential limitations of meditation techniques as taught within Western medicine. As noted previously, for many practitioners and patients, the context within which meditation interventions are implemented is a reductionist approach to "stress management," with a focus on symptom alleviation without regard for a larger perspective on health, including positive psychological qualities. Given such an approach, these meditation techniques share limitations that may prevent the individual from achieving "optimal health." As defined by the World Health Organization (1946), optimal health reflects a move beyond the absence of disease, to mental, physical, and social well-being.

In reductionistic self-regulation models, we cannot explicitly address the multiple levels that create and sustain optimal health. As such, the goal in numerous meditation techniques simply is to return things to normal (e.g., blood pressure). Although there is nothing wrong with using meditation to lower blood pressure, we hypothesize that meditation based on the ISM perspective may be more effective at promoting healing on systemic and symptom levels.

The model we have proposed is not just a vision for self-regulation and stress management but a vision for health enhancement and optimal positive psychological growth and development. Intentional systemic mindfulness provides the *context* to realize the original intentions of mediation, including self-actualization and greater meaning in life.

Applications of ISM to Meditation: Some Evidence

The positive impact of ISM on intrapersonal, interpersonal, and transpersonal levels is suggested by the preliminary findings of a well-controlled study exploring the effects of an ISM meditation intervention for medical and premedical students. A significant quantitative reduction in depression and anxiety occurred among experimental subjects relative to the control group (Shapiro et al., 1998). Furthermore, the experimental group demonstrated a significant quantitative increase in empathy and spiritual experience. Finally, based on qualitative data, the mindfulness intervention appears to have impacted the experimental group on intrapersonal, interpersonal, and transpersonal levels (Shapiro & Schwartz, 1998, in press). Because there was no comparison meditation group, the positive changes observed may be due to common effects of meditation practice rather than to the specific effects of ISM. Future research is needed before definitive conclusions can be drawn.

Summary: Intentional Systemic Mindfulness

Intentional systemic mindfulness is a theoretical model developed to explicitly reintroduce context into meditation research and practice. Through directing intention toward the mindfulness qualities and systemic perspectives, a more accepting, compassionate, and systemic approach may be brought to the study and practice of meditation. We maintain that by using ISM methods, meditation research may progress toward a more comprehensive and integrative approach to healing.

Future Directions

There are multiple directions for future research. Rigorous and sensitive designs are needed that assess the multifaceted nature of health, including both the negative and the positive. We briefly outline six directions for future research in meditation and positive psychology.

First, in our research designs, we must examine dependent variables so that they more closely parallel the original goals and objectives of meditation (e.g., self-actualization, cultivation of empathy, meaning, purpose). Second, we should explore the physiological states elicited during positive psychological experiences, including meditation practice, to further augment the emerging concept of the "physiological substrates of flourishing" (Ryff & Singer, 1998). Third, it is crucial to determine the most effective way to teach meditation in clinical settings by comparing differing lengths of meditation intervention, as well as different formats for the intervention (e.g., group vs. individual). Along these lines we must ask, What works best for whom? For example, are there specific types of meditation that fit better with specific individuals or specific goals? Different types "of meditation may have very different effects on the practitioner and thus may have different clinical applications" (Bogart 1991, p. 385). It is crucial to consider what therapeutic goals (e.g., stress management, self-exploration, or transformative transpersonal experiences) are being sought when determining which type of meditation is most appropriate. Bogart (1991) suggests that concentration methods may allow the participant to feel inner balance, calm, and the ability to transcend the continuous flow of cognitions and emotions, whereas opening-up meditation may encourage insights into maladaptive cognitive, emotional, and behavioral patterns.

A fourth direction for future research involves operationalizing experience levels of participants. Researchers must both assess length of practice and have some index of depth of practice (e.g., teacher ratings). Fifth, we should ask, What is the process through which meditation brings about positive psychological changes? The explanatory mechanisms of meditation are elusive, and more attention needs to be given to them. A sixth and final direction we propose is to determine the importance of context in teaching meditation. We suggest that meditation interventions that are grounded in ISM need to be compared with interventions as they are traditionally taught in Western medicine. We hypothesize that such an intervention would benefit the individual on multiple levels of health as compared with the traditional intervention. To determine this, future research needs to create both reliable and valid self-report measures to assess elements of ISM (e.g., one's intentions, the degree to which one understands and is able to integrate ISM into the meditation practice), as well as measures to assess systemic health (an assessment sensitive to the multiple levels of health).

Researchers in meditation have helped to expand our view of psychological health. The original intentions of meditation parallel, in many ways, the reemerging field of positive psychology. The need for further research in the area of meditation and positive psychology is clear. In this movement, researchers are encouraged to help in the evolution of meditation research from simple symptom reduction to more systemic and intentional approaches to health and healing.

Acknowledgments   The authors would like to thank Benedict Freedman for his invaluable suggestions and support. We further thank Deane and Johanna Shapiro, Alfred Kaszniak, and Richard Haier for their editorial assistance. Finally, we acknowledge all of the researchers who have contributed to developing an integrated vision of health.

References

Alexander, C. N., Druker, S. M., & Langer, E. J. (1990). Major issues in the exploration of adult growth. In C. N. Alexander & E. J. Langer (Eds.), *Higher stages of human development: Perspectives on adult growth* (pp. 3–32). New York: Oxford University Press.

Alexander, C. N., Langer, E. J., Newman, R. I., Chandler, H. M., & Davies, J. L. (1989). Transcendental meditation, mindfulness, and longevity: An experimental study with the elderly. *Journal of Personality and Social Psychology,* 57(6), 950–964.

Alexander, C. N., Rainforth, M. V., & Gelderloos, P. (1991). Transcendental meditation, self-actualization, and psychological health: A conceptual overview and statistical meta-analysis. *Journal of Social Behavior and Personality,* 6(5), 189–247.

Allport, G. W. (1961). *Pattern and growth in personality.* New York: Holt, Rinehart and Winston.

Antonovsky, A. (1987). *Unraveling the mystery of health: How people manage stress and stay well.* San Francisco: Jossey-Bass.

Astin, J. A. (1997). Stress reduction through mindfulness meditation: Effects on psychological symptomatology, sense of control, and spiritual experiences. *Psychotherapy and Psychosomatics,* 66, 97–106.

Banquet, J. (1973). Spectral analysis of the EEG in meditation. *Electroencephalography and Clinical Neurophysiology,* 35, 143–151.

Beauchamp-Turner, D. L., & Levinson, D. M. (1992). Effects of meditation on stress, health, and affect. *Medical Psychotherapy: An International Journal,* 5, 123–131.

Benson, H. (1975). *The relaxation response.* New York: Morrow.

Benson, H., & Proctor, W. (1984). *Beyond the relaxation response.* New York: Putnam/Berkley.

Bogart, G. (1991). The use of meditation in psychotherapy: A review of the literature. *American Journal of Psychotherapy,* 45(3), 383–412.

Carrington, P. (1993). Modern forms of meditation. In P. M. Lehrer & R. L. Woolfolk (Eds.), *Principles and practice of stress management* (2nd ed., pp. 139–168). New York: Guilford.

Carrington, P. (1998). *The book of meditation.* Boston: Element Books.

Chang, J., & Hiebert, B. (1989). Relaxation procedures with children: A review. *Medical Psychotherapy, An International Journal,* 2, 163–176.

Cowger, E. L., & Torrance, E. P. (1982). Further examination of the quality changes in creative functioning resulting from meditation (Zazen) training. *Creative Child and Adult Quarterly,* 7(4), 211–217.

Cranson, R. W., Orme-Johnson, D. W., Gackenbach, J., Dillbeck, M. C., Jones, C. H., & Alexander, C. N. (1991). Transcendental meditation and improved performance on intelligence-related measures: A longitudinal study. *Personality and Individual Differences,* 12(10), 1105–1116.

Dillbeck, M. C., Assimakis, P. D., & Raimondi, D. (1986). Longitudinal effects of the transcendental meditation and TM-Sidhi program on cognitive ability and cognitive style. *Perceptual Motor Skills,* 62(3), 731–738.

Dillbeck, M. C., & Orme-Johnson, D. W. (1987). Physiological differences between transcendental meditation and rest. *American Psychologist,* 42(9), 879–881.

Easterlin, B. L., & Cardena, E. (1999). Cognitive and emotional differences between short- and long-term Vipassana meditators. *Imagination, Cognition and Personality,* 18(1), 68–81.

Edwards, D. L. (1991). A meta-analysis of the effects of meditation and hypnosis on measures of anxiety. *Dissertation Abstracts International,* 52(2-B), 1039–1040.

Emavardhana, T., & Tori, C. D. (1997). Changes in self-concept, ego defense mechanisms, and religiosity following seven-day Vipassana meditation retreats. *Journal for the Scientific Study of Religion,* 36(2), 194–206.

Ferguson, P. C. (1981). An integrative meta-analysis of psychological studies investigating the treatment outcomes of meditation studies. (Doctoral dissertation, University of Colorado, 1981). *Dissertation Abstracts International,* 42(4-A), 1547.

Fordyce, M. W. (1983). A program to increase happiness: Further studies. *Journal of Counseling Psychology,* 30, 483–498.

Gelderloos, P., Walton, K., Orme-Johnson, D., & Alexander, C. (1991). Effectiveness of the transcendental meditation program in preventing and treating substance misuse: A review. *Inter-*

national Journal of the Addictions, 26(3), 293–325.

Goleman, D. (1972). The Buddha on meditation and states of consciousness: Part 1. The teaching; Part 2. A typology of meditation techniques. Journal of Transpersonal Psychology, 4(1–2), 1–44, 151–210.

Goleman, D. (1988). The meditation mind. Los Angeles: Tarcher.

Goleman, D. J., & Schwartz, G. E. (1976). Meditation as an intervention in stress reactivity. Journal of Consulting and Clinical Psychology, 44(3), 456–466.

Hall, P. D. (1999). The effect of meditation on the academic performance of African American college students. Journal of Black Studies, 29(3), 408–415.

Harte, J. L., Eifert, G. H., & Smith, R. (1995). The effects of running and meditation on beta-endorphin, corticotrophin-releasing hormone and cortisol in plasma, and on mood. Biological Psychology, 40(3), 251–265.

Jevning, R., Wilson, A. F., & Davidson, J. M. (1978). Adrenocortical activity during meditation. Hormones and Behavior, 10(1), 54–60.

Kabat-Zinn, J. (1982). An outpatient program in behavioral medicine for chronic pain patients based on the practice of mindfulness meditation: Theoretical considerations and preliminary results. General Hospital Psychiatry, 4, 33–47.

Kabat-Zinn, J. (1990). Full catastrophe living. New York: Delacorte Press.

Kabat-Zinn, J. (1994). Wherever you go, there you are. New York: Hyperion.

Kabat-Zinn, J. (1996). Mindfulness meditation: What it is, what it isn't, and its role in health care and medicine. In Y. Haruki, Y. Ishii, & M. Suzuki (Eds.), Comparative and psychological study on meditation (pp. 161–170). Netherlands: Eburon Publishers.

Kabat-Zinn, J., & Skillings, A. (1989, March). Sense of coherence and stress hardiness as predictors and measure of outcome of a stress reduction program. Poster presented at the meeting of the Society of Behavioral Medicine, San Francisco.

Kabat-Zinn, J., & Skillings, A. (1992). [Sense of coherence and stress hardiness as outcome measures of a mindfulness-based stress reduction program: Three-year follow-up]. Unpublished raw data. University of Massachusetts Medical Center.

Kabat-Zinn, J., Wheeler, E., Light, T., Skillings, A., Scharf, M. J., Cropley, T. G., Hosmer, D., & Bernhard, J. D. (1998). Influence of mindfulness meditation-based stress reduction intervention on rates of skin clearing in patients with moderate to severe psoriasis undergoing phototherapy (UVB) and photochemotherapy (PUVA). Psychosomatic Medicine, 60(5), 625–632.

Kobasa, S. C. O. (1990). Stress-resistant personality. In R. Ornstein & C. Swencionis (Eds.), The healing brain: A scientific reader (pp. 219–230). New York: Guilford.

Lesh, T. (1970). Zen meditation and the development of empathy in counselors. Journal of Humanistic Psychology, 10(1), 39–74.

Lewis, J. (1978). The effects of a group meditation technique upon degree of test anxiety and level of digit-letter retention in high school students. Dissertation Abstracts International, 38(10-A), 6015–6016.

MacLean, C., Walton, K. G., Wenneberg, S. R., Levitsky, D. K., Mandarino, J. P., Waziri, R., Hillis, S. L., & Schneider, R. H. (1997). Effects of the transcendental meditation program on adaptive mechanisms: Changes in hormone levels and responses to stress after 4 months of practice. Psychoneuroendocrinology, 22(4), 277–295.

Margid, S. (1986). Meditation, creativity, and the composing process of student writers. Dissertation Abstracts International, 46(9-A), 2603.

Maslow, A. H. (1968). Toward a psychology of being (2nd ed.). New York: Van Nostrand Reinhold.

McClelland, D. C. (1989). Motivational factors in health and disease. American Psychologist, 44, 675–683.

Miller, J., Fletcher, K., & Kabat-Zinn, J. (1995). Three-year follow-up and clinical implications of a mindfulness-based intervention in the treatment of anxiety disorders. General Hospital Psychiatry, 17, 192–200.

*Murphy, M., Donovan, S., & Taylor, E. (1997). The physical and psychological effects of meditation: A review of contemporary research with a comprehensive bibliography. Sausalito, CA: Institute of Noetic Sciences.

Nidich, S. I., Ryncarz, R. A., Abrams, A. I., Orme-Johnson, D. W., & Wallace, R. K. (1983). Kohlbergian cosmic perspective responses, EEG coherence, and the TM and TM-Sidhi program. Journal of Moral Education, 12, 166–173.

Nystul, M. S., & Garde, M. (1977). The self-concepts of transcendental meditators and nonmeditators. Psychological Reports, 41, 303–306.

Nystul, M. S., & Garde, M. (1979). The self-concepts of regular transcendental meditators, dropout meditators and nonmeditators. Journal of Psychology, 103, 15–18.

O'Halloran, J. P., Jevning, R. A., Wilson, A. F., Skowsky, R., & Alexander, C. N. (1985). Hormonal control in a state of decreased activation:

Potentiation of arginine vasopressin secretion. *Physiology and Behavior, 35,* 591–595.

Orme-Johnson, D. W., & Haynes, C. T. (1981). EEG phase coherence, pure consciousness, and TM-Sidhi experiences. *International Journal of Neuroscience, 13,* 211–217.

Penner, W. J., Zingle, H. W., Dyck, R., & Truch, S. (1974). Does an in-depth transcendental meditation course effect change in the personalities of the participants? *Western Psychologist, 4,* 104–111.

Rivers, S., & Spanos, N. P. (1981). Personal variables predicting voluntary participation in and attrition from a meditation program. *Psychological Reports, 49,* 795–801.

Ryff, C. D., & Singer, B. (1998). Human health: New directions for the next millennium. *Psychological Inquiry, 9*(1), 69–85.

Shapiro, D. H. (1980). *Meditation: Self-regulation strategy and altered state of consciousness.* New York: Aldine.

Shapiro, D. H. (1994). Examining the content and context of meditation: A challenge for psychology in the areas of stress management. *Journal of Humanistic Psychology, 34,* 101–135.

*Shapiro, D. H., & Walsh, R. N. (Eds.). (1984). *Meditation: Classic and contemporary perspectives.* New York: Aldine.

Shapiro, S. L., & Schwartz, G. E. (1998). Mindfulness in medical education: Fostering the health of physicians and medical practice. *Integrative Medicine, 1,* 93.

*Shapiro, S. L., & Schwartz, G. E. (2000). The role of intention in self-regulation: Toward intentional systemic mindfulness. In M. Boekaerts, P. R. Pintrich, & M. Zeidner (Eds.), *Handbook of self-regulation* (pp. 253–273). New York: Academic Press.

Shapiro, S. L., & Schwartz, G. E. (in press). Intentional systemic mindfulness: Implications for self-regulation and health. *Advances in Mind-Body Medicine.*

Shapiro, S. L., Schwartz, G. E. R., & Bonner, G. (1998). The effects of mindfulness-based stress reduction on medical and pre-medical students. *Journal of Behavioral Medicine, 21,* 581–599.

Smith, W. P., Compton, W. C., & West, W. B. (1995). Meditation as an adjunct to a happiness enhancement program. *Journal of Clinical Psychology, 51,* 269–273.

Sridevi, K., Rao, P., & Krisha, V. (1998). Temporal effects of meditation and personality. *Psychological Studies, 43*(3), 95–105.

Tate, D. B. (1994). Mindfulness meditation group training: Effects on medical and psychological symptoms and positive psychological characteristics. *Dissertation Abstracts International, 55*(55–B), 2018.

Taylor, D. N. (1995). Effects of a behavioral stress-management program on anxiety, mood, self-esteem, and T-cell count in HIV-positive men. *Psychological Reports, 76,* 451–457.

Tloczynski, J., & Tantriella, M. (1998). A comparison of the effects of Zen breath meditation or relaxation on college adjustment. *Psychologia: An International Journal of Psychology in the Orient, 41*(1), 32–43.

Van den Berg, W., & Mulder, B. (1976). Psychological research on the effects of the transcendental meditation technique on a number of personality variables. *Gedrag, Tijdschrift voor Psychologie, 4,* 206–218.

Wallace, R. K. (1986). *The Maharishi technology of the unified field: The neurophysiology of enlightenment.* Fairfield, IA: MIU Neuroscience Press.

Walsh, R. N. (1983). Meditation practice and research. *Journal of Humanistic Psychology, 23*(1), 18–50.

Walsh, R. (1993a). Meditation research: The state of the art. In R. Walsh & F. Vaughan (Eds.), *Paths beyond ego: The transpersonal vision* (pp. 60–66). Los Angeles: Tarcher/Perigee.

Walsh, R. (1993b). The transpersonal movement: A history and state of the art. *Journal of Transpersonal Psychology, 25*(2), 123–139.

*Walsh, R., & Vaughan, F. (1993). *Paths beyond ego: The transpersonal vision.* Los Angeles: Tarcher/Perigee.

Weinberger, J., McLeod, C., McClelland, D., Santorelli, S. F., & Kabat-Zinn, J. (1990). *Motivational change following a meditation-based stress reduction program for medical outpatients.* Poster presented at the First International Congress of Behavioral Medicine, Uppsala, Sweden.

Wilber, K. (1993). The spectrum of transpersonal development. In R. Walsh & F. Vaughan (Eds.), *Paths beyond ego: The transpersonal vision* (pp. 116–117). Los Angeles: Tarcher/Perigee.

Woolfolk, R. L., & Franks, C. M. (1984). Meditation and behavior therapy. In D. H. Shapiro & R. N. Walsh (Eds.), *Meditation: Classic and contemporary perspectives* (pp. 674–676). New York: Aldine.

World Health Organization. (1946). Constitution. Geneva, Switzerland.

Zamarra, J. W., Schneider, R. H., Besseghini, I., Robinson, D. K., & Salerno, J. W. (1996). Usefulness of the transcendental meditation program in the treatment of patients with coronary artery disease. *American Journal of Cardiology, 77,* 867–870.

47

Spirituality

Discovering and Conserving the Sacred

Kenneth I. Pargament & Annette Mahoney

A world without God would be a flat, mono-chromatic world, a world without color or tex-ture, a world in which all days would be the same. Marriage would be a matter of biology, not fidelity. Old age would be seen as a time of weakness, not of wisdom. In a world like that, we would cast about desperately for any sort of diversion, for any distraction from the emptiness of our lives, because we would never have learned the magic of making some days and some hours special.

(Kushner, 1989, p. 206)

G. Stanley Hall and William James would have been quite comfortable with Harold Kushner's bold assertions about the centrality of the sacred to human experience. To these founding fathers of psychology, spiritual phenomena represented critically important topics for psychological study. Since the early part of the 20th century, however, psychologists have tended to: (a) ignore spirituality; (b) view spirituality as pathological; or (c) treat spirituality as a process that can be reduced to more basic underlying psychological, social, and physiological functions.

Writers have suggested a number of reasons for this psychospiritual rift: the difficulty of studying phenomena as subjective and elusive as spirituality; a tendency to underestimate the power of spirituality by psychologists who, as a group, manifest considerably lower levels of religiousness than the general public; and competitiveness among psychological and religious communities in the values, worldviews, and resources they offer to their "consumers" (Pargament, 1997; Richards & Bergin, 1997; Shafranske & Malony, 1990).

Whatever the explanation for this rift, there are a number of good reasons that psychologists should attend to spirituality. First, spirituality is a "cultural fact" (cf. Shafranske & Malony, 1996): The vast majority of Americans believe in God (95%), believe that God can be reached through prayer (86%), and feel that religion is important or very important to them (86%, Gallup, 1995; Hoge, 1996). Second, in a growing empirical body of literature, the important implications of spirituality for a number of aspects of human functioning are being noted. Included in this list are mental health (Koenig, 1998); drug and alcohol use (Benson, 1992); marital functioning (Mahoney et al., 1999); parenting (Ellison & Sherkat, 1993); the outcomes of stressful life experiences (Pargament, 1997); and morbidity and mortality (Ellison & Levin, 1998; Hummer, Rogers, Nam, & Ellison, 1999). Finally, in a more practical vein, the American Psychological Association has defined religiousness as a "cultural diversity" variable. Although it has received relatively less attention than other diversity variables, psychologists are no less ethically obligated to attend to this dimension and reduce potential biases in their professional work with clients of diverse religious backgrounds (see Principal D, Ethical Principles of Psychologists and Code of Conduct; APA, 1992). There are, in short, some very good reasons that psychologists should attend more carefully to the spiritual dimension of people's lives.

In this chapter, we consider some of the intriguing findings that are emerging from the study of spirituality. Our review here will be selective rather than inclusive. We will discuss some of the ways that spirituality can be understood and studied from a psychological perspective. We will review some of the things we are beginning to learn from empirical studies of spirituality and its connections to well-being. Finally, we will illustrate some of the implications of spirituality for human functioning and positive psychology. In this process, we may encourage others to consider the spiritual dimension in their own psychological study and practice. We begin with a definition of spirituality.

Defining Spirituality

Although most people describe themselves as spiritual, they define the term in many different ways (Zinnbauer et al., 1997). Psychologists are no less diverse in their views (see Zinnbauer, Pargament, & Scott, 1999). Definitions of spirituality have ranged from the best of that which is human (Twerski, 1998), to a quest for existential meaning (Doyle, 1992), to the transcendent human dimension (Mauritzen, 1988). Even though any single definition of this rich, complex construct is unlikely to satisfy everyone, some definition is needed to provide boundaries and order to this literature.

In moving to a definition, it is particularly important to consider the relation between spirituality and religiousness. Traditionally, psychologists of religion did not distinguish be-

tween these constructs (Wulff, 1998). More recently, however, writers have begun to contrast the two, with some suggesting that religion is institutional, dogmatic, and restrictive, whereas spirituality is personal, subjective, and life-enhancing. Elsewhere, we have argued against this polarization of the two constructs. Empirical studies indicate that most people appear to define themselves as both religious and spiritual (Zinnbauer et al., 1997). Moreover, both religion and spirituality can be expressed individually and socially, and both have the capacity to foster or impede well-being (see Pargament, 1999; Zinnbauer, et al., 1999). In short, we believe there are important points of overlap between the two constructs. We prefer to use the term *religion* in its classic sense as a broad individual and institutional domain that serves a variety of purposes, secular as well as sacred. *Spirituality* represents the key and unique function of religion. In this chapter, spirituality is defined as "a search for the sacred" (Pargament, 1999, p. 12).

There are two key terms in this definition: *search* and the *sacred*. The term *search* indicates that spirituality is a process, one that involves efforts to discover the sacred and one that involves efforts to hold onto the sacred once it has been found. People can take a virtually limitless number of pathways in their attempts to discover and conserve the sacred. Spiritual pathways include social involvements that range from traditional religious institutions to nontraditional spiritual groups, programs, and associations (e.g., Twelve-Step, meditation centers, Scientology). Pathways involve systems of belief that include those of traditional organized religions (e.g., Protestant, Roman Catholic, Jewish, Hindu, Buddhist, Muslim), newer spirituality movements (e.g., feminist, goddess, ecological spiritualities), and more individualized worldviews. Pathways are also made up of traditional religious practices that include prayer, Bible reading, watching religious television, and rites of passage, as well as other human expressions that have as their goal the sacred, including yoga, music, art, and social action (see Streng, 1976). What these diverse pathways share is a common end—the sacred.

In the *Oxford English Dictionary*, the word *sacred* is defined as the holy, those things "set apart" from the ordinary and worthy of veneration and respect. The sacred includes concepts of God, the divine, and the transcendent. However, other objects can become sacred or take on extraordinary power by virtue of their association with, or representation of, divinity (Pargament, 1999). Sacred objects include time and space (the Sabbath, churches); events and transitions (birth, death); materials (wine, crucifix); cultural products (music, literature); people (saints, cult leaders); psychological attributes (self, meaning); social attributes (compassion, community); and roles (marriage, parenting, work). We would describe persons as spiritual to the extent that they are trying to find, know, experience, or relate to what they perceive as sacred.

As Pargament (1999) noted, this view of spirituality is broad enough to cover both traditional, theocentric, institutionally based spiritual expressions and nontheistic expressions that take place outside of traditional religious institutions, beliefs, and practices. The definition of spirituality, however, offers a basis for distinguishing between this construct and related phenomena. Unlike other psychological attributes, spirituality is centered around perceptions of the sacred. It overlaps with other human processes, many of which are described in this book (e.g., creativity, wisdom, forgiveness, meaning, hope, humility), only to the extent that they represent pathways to the sacred or become sacred in and of themselves. Of course, as we will see, many seemingly secular objects do, in fact, become sacred, and when they do, they become relevant topics for the study of spirituality.

Pargament's (1999) definition of spirituality does not assume that it is basically "good." In their search for the sacred, people can take destructive as well as constructive pathways. For example, in the effort to realize God's kingdom on earth, people may reach out to embrace or persecute others who hold different beliefs. Those things perceived as sacred may include the malevolent (e.g., a despotic religious leader), as well as the benign. Thus, spirituality is not inherently good. Rather, the value of spirituality depends on the specific form of the individual's search for the sacred, that is, the particular pathways that the person takes toward particular sacred ends.

Finally, although we have emphasized that it is a process, it also can be understood and evaluated as an outcome. At any point in time, we can assess how successful the individual has been in the search for the sacred by using spiritually oriented criteria, such as spiritual well-being (e.g., Paloutzian & Ellison, 1982). We also

can assess the implications of the search for the sacred and the success of this search for other psychological, social, and physical health outcomes. With this definition in mind, we now turn to the processes that are critical to spirituality: the discovery and conservation of the sacred.

The Discovery of the Sacred

Discovering God

The search for God begins in childhood. "How young we are when we start wondering about it all," Robert Coles (1990, p. 335) concludes from his study of the spiritual lives of children. Although some have questioned the child's capacity to grapple with religious abstractions (Goldman, 1964), social scientists have presented rich anecdotal accounts of children who appear to be engaged in a search for God. Consider the words of a 9-year-old Jewish boy:

> I'd like to find God! But He wouldn't just be there, waiting for some spaceship to land! He's not a person, you know! He's a spirit. He's like the fog and the mist. Maybe He's like something—something we've never seen here. So how can we know? You can't imagine Him, because He's so different—you've never seen anything like Him. . . . I should remember that God is God, and we're us. I guess I'm trying to get from me, from us, to Him with my ideas when I'm looking up at the sky! (Coles, 1990, pp. 141–142)

Social scientists have offered a variety of explanations for the propensity to seek the divine. Some have suggested that there is an innate, genetic basis for spirituality (e.g., Bouchard, Lykken, McGue, Segal, & Tellegen, 1990). Others have emphasized that conceptions of God are rooted in the child's intrapsychic capacity to symbolize, fantasize, and create superhuman beings (Rizzuto, 1979). Some have asserted that spirituality grows out of critical life events and challenges that reveal human limitations (Johnson, 1959; Pargament, 1997). And others have emphasized the importance of the social context (familial, institutional, cultural) in shaping the child's understanding of God (Kaufman, 1981).

Empirical research on the origins of spirituality is not plentiful. Lee Kirkpatrick's (1999) work is an exception to this rule. Elaborating on Bowlby's (1988) attachment theory, he suggests that the child's mental models of God are likely to correspond to the models of self and others that emerge out of repeated interactions with primary attachment figures. In support of this notion, Kirkpatrick cites a number of studies among children, adolescents, and adults that demonstrate parallels between the quality of attachments to God (e.g., secure or insecure) and the quality of attachments to parents. Children are not, however, passive sponges that simply absorb the spiritual views of their parents. In this vein, Kirkpatrick presents evidence of another dynamic that shapes the individual's relationship with God. Over time, he notes, people may look to the divine as compensation for the loss, unavailability, or inadequacy of a primary attachment figure. For example, in two longitudinal studies, he found that adult women and college students who reported insecure romantic attachment styles were more likely than their secure romantic counterparts to "find a new relationship with God" (Kirkpatrick, 1997, 1998, p. 962). Similarly, other researchers have found that individuals who have suffered a major trauma are more likely to experience a religious conversion (Ullman, 1982; Zinnbauer & Pargament, 1998).

Research such as that of Kirkpatrick suggests that the individual's path to God is shaped by a variety of personal, social, and contextual factors. Even so, this research cannot tell the full story, for the child's emerging spirituality is more than a reaction to his or her personal and social world. Interview studies of children underscore their capacity to reject, elaborate, or move well beyond the religious points of view of parents, teachers, and religious leaders. Listen to the words of one 10-year-old Brazilian girl whose mother is dying of tuberculosis:

> Mother used to tell us we'll go to heaven, because we're poor. I used to believe her. I don't think she really believes that herself. She just says that—it's a way of shutting us all up when we're hungry! Now, when I hear her say it, I look up at Him, and I ask Him: What do *You* say, Jesus? Do you believe her? (Coles, 1990, p. 91)

Accounts such as these suggest that many children are far from passive when it comes to matters of faith. Instead, they may be described more accurately as spiritual pilgrims or seekers of something beyond themselves, motivated by a desire that cannot be reduced to purely psychological or social drives.

What are the implications of this search for the divine? In a number of studies, psychologists have found that individuals who perceive God to be a loving, compassionate, and responsive figure also report higher levels of personal well-being (e.g., Kirkpatrick & Shaver, 1992; Pargament, Smith, Koenig, & Perez, 1998; Pollner, 1989). On the other hand, people who describe God in more distant, harsh, fearful, or punitive terms indicate higher levels of psychological distress (Pargament, Smith et al., 1998; Schwab & Petersen, 1990). In other studies of religious coping, people who see God as a partner in the problem-solving process report better mental health, whereas those who passively defer their problems to God, particularly in controllable situations, show lower levels of mental health (Hathaway & Pargament, 1990; Pargament et al., 1988). Based on these studies, it appears that the helpfulness or harmfulness of an individual's search for the divine depends on the kind of God the person discovers and the kind of relationship he or she forms with that God.

Discovering the Sacred

God is central to any understanding of spirituality. Spirituality involves more, however, than God. It has to do with the sacred, and the sacred can be found on earth as well as in heaven. As noted earlier, virtually any aspect of life can take on sacred status. We use the term *sanctification* to refer to the perception of an object as having spiritual significance and character (Mahoney et al., 1999; Pargament, 1999). Sanctification can occur in theistic and nontheistic ways. The divine may be linked to many human domains: God may be seen as manifest in marriage; work can be perceived as a divine calling or vocation; the environment can be viewed as God's creation. Ostensibly secular objects also can develop sacred character when they are imbued with divinelike qualities: Many parents perceive their children as blessings; others view the body as something holy; and many describe love as eternal (see Hendrick & Hendrick, this volume). Conceivably, even atheists could sanctify objects by imbuing them with divine attributes. In short, through the process of sanctification, people are able to discover the sacred in many spheres of life.

Indeed, according to some religious traditions, all life is sacred. Through scripture, education, and ritual, adherents of many traditions are encouraged to see God as manifest in all of life. Religious institutions are not the only source of education about sanctification, however, because the nature of what is and what is not sacred is shaped by personal experience, families, organizations, communities, and the larger culture.

Mahoney et al. (1999) and Pargament (1999) point to three important implications of sanctification. First, people are likely to preserve and protect sacred objects. Second, people are likely to invest more of themselves in the pursuit of things sacred. Third, people are likely to derive more meaning, strength, and satisfaction from sacred dimensions of their lives. In support of these assertions, Mahoney et al. (1999) studied a religiously representative sample of 97 White, married couples in the community and found that those who sanctified their marriages experienced a number of benefits, including greater marital satisfaction, more investment in the marriage, less marital conflict, and more effective marital problem-solving strategies. Similarly, mothers and fathers who sanctified the role of parenting reported less verbal aggression and more consistent discipline with their children (Swank, Mahoney, & Pargament, 1999). Research by Emmons, Cheung, and Tehrani (1998) also underscores the potential benefits of the search for the sacred. They analyzed the content of those things that college students said they strived for in their lives. Spiritual strivings were defined as personal goals that are concerned with ultimate purpose, ethics, commitment to a higher power, and a recognition of the transcendent (Emmons et al., 1998). Emmons et al. found that spiritual strivings were more highly correlated with measures of well-being than any other type of striving.

It appears that people who seek out the sacred also experience a number of psychological and social benefits. On the other hand, the discovery of the sacred may be associated with some problems, as in the case of the Heaven's Gate cult, in which members invested their leader with sacred status and followed him to their deaths. Individuals may also be more vulnerable to anxiety and depression when the path to the sacred is blocked or when the sacred is lost. Distress may be especially likely and severe when a sacred object has been violated. Historically, perceptions that the sacred has been desecrated have led to rage, violence, and war. Thus, it is important to keep in mind that the search for the sacred is not invariably successful. Nor is it without risks to the spiritual seeker and the larger community. And yet, for many people, the discovery of the sacred is accompanied by an enhanced sense of themselves, more satisfying relationships with others, and feelings of connectedness with the transcendent.

The Conservation of the Sacred

The search does not end after the sacred has been discovered. Once found, people strive to *hold on* to the sacred. Although social scientists have generally viewed religion and spirituality as mechanisms that help people maintain themselves physically, psychologically, and socially, the ultimate purpose of spiritual involvement for the religiously minded is not exclusively biological, psychological, or social (Pargament, 1997). Spiritual persons are, instead, concerned with developing, maintaining, and fostering their relationship with the sacred.

There is no shortage of examples of the human desire to hold on to the sacred, even at terrible costs. In a book aptly titled *With God in Hell*, Berkovits (1979) illustrates the great lengths many Jews went to preserve their faith in the ghettos and concentration camps of World War II. One Jewish couple hurried to complete a ritual circumcision of their newborn son as the Gestapo were breaking into their homes to take them away, with the mother shouting "Hurry up! . . . They have come to kill us. At least let my child die as a Jew" (p. 45). Another concentration camp inmate secretly searched for a place to worship in the camp. Ultimately, he found a place to pray in the vast open pits where people who had been murdered were buried.

These illustrations of spiritual perseverance are readily available. When people are confronted with major life stressors, spiritual stability rather than change appears to be the norm. Researchers find that levels of faith and religious beliefs and practices are largely unchanged or even strengthened following traumatic events such as accidents (Bahr & Harvey, 1979), war (Allport, Gillespie, & Young, 1948), and death of loved ones (Balk, 1983). For example, in their longitudinal study of people who had suffered heart attacks, Croog and Levine (1972) found that over two thirds of the group maintained the same reported levels of congregational attendance and religious importance over a 1-year period, before and after their heart attacks.

There are a number of spiritual methods for conserving the individual's relationship with the sacred. People sustain their relationship by prayer, meditation, and experiencing the spiritual dimension in daily life. There are many different forms of prayer. Although prayer often is viewed as an instrumental means through which individuals petition God for assistance, it also can be directed to maintaining a relationship with God. In this vein, Poloma and Gallup (1991) distinguish between four types of prayer: ritual (e.g., read from a book of prayers); petitionary (e.g., ask God for material things); conversation (e.g., ask God to forgive your sins); and meditative (e.g., spend time just "being in" the presence of God). In contrast to the other three types of prayer, the meditative form has as its goal the experience of a divine relationship. This type may be especially helpful. In a telephone survey of community residents, Poloma and Gallup (1991) report that the meditative form of prayer was more strongly related to measures of personal well-being and a sense of closeness to God than were the other three prayer types.

Studies of meditation techniques yield results consistent with studies of meditative prayer. Many people who practice meditation regularly do so with a spiritual mantra in mind. At least some of the well-documented beneficial effects of this technique may be attributable to the sense of the connection that the individual regularly experiences with the transcendent (Marlatt & Kristeller, 1999).

Finally, although many people experience a sense of the divine only in extraordinary times and circumstances, others routinely try to "practice the presence of God or the sacred." The sense of spirituality can be fostered and maintained by experiencing the transcendent in the everyday occurrences of life. Underwood (1999) has developed a Daily Spiritual Experiences measure that shows promise for assessing this construct. This 16-item instrument grew out of a recognition that many aspects of spirituality can be experienced regularly, including a sense of awe, perceptions of God's love, connectedness with the transcendent, feelings of inspiration, and a sense of wholeness.

In addition to these day-to-day forms of spiritual involvement, people can draw on a number of spiritual coping methods to help them conserve the sacred in times of stress. In the following we consider three of these spiritual methods of coping (see Pargament, 1997, for complete review).

Marking Boundaries

Life is filled with threats and challenges to an individual's personal and social world. Threats to the sacred, however, may be the most dangerous. As comparative religionist William Paden (1988) wrote, "If the sacred is the foundation of a world, then whatever denies that sacredness will be intolerable" (p. 61). Yet in our pluralistic culture, these threats may be fairly commonplace; they come in the form of exposure to individuals and groups that define God and the sacred in very different ways and challenge the basic assumption that the individual has a special knowledge of the truth.

Institutionally, some religious groups cope with these threats by "marking boundaries," that is, defining clear rules about what makes someone a member of a particular faith community, be it Protestantism, Catholicism, Hinduism, Islam, or Judaism. Wrapped in the distinctive beliefs, values, and practices of a particular religious tradition, members are able to conserve a sacred way of life in the face of competing and potentially threatening lifestyles. They also receive the benefits of a compelling worldview, a clear personal identity, and the support and approval of their coreligionists. In contrast, those who cross the boundary line may be sanctioned in degrees that range from criticism and disapproval to excommunication.

Individuals as well as institutions have ways to mark boundaries. People can selectively filter, block, or distort material that threatens their sacred beliefs, practices, and values. For example, Brock and Balloun (1967) presented groups of more and less religious people with messages that attacked hypocrisy within organized Christianity. The experimenters intentionally made the message difficult to hear by filling the background with a high level of static. In comparison to their less religious counterparts, participants who prayed and attended church more frequently were less likely to make the "Christianity is evil" message easier to hear by pressing a "static-eliminating button." These results were replicated in four separate experiments. In a related study, Pargament and DeRosa (1985) presented recorded religious messages that varied in their congruence with the religious beliefs of the listeners and then asked the listeners to recall the message. As the messages became more discordant, the listeners were more likely to distort their memory of the message to fit with their religious beliefs.

In the face of threat, people may even intensify their belief commitments. Batson (1975) illustrated this process in a study of groups of students who were asked to demonstrate their religious commitment publicly by choosing to sit with either a group of those who could affirm that Jesus Christ is the Son of God or a group of those who could not. Both groups were presented with an article that purportedly contained "conclusive proof" that the body of Jesus was actually stolen by his followers to justify their claims that he was resurrected. The religious beliefs of the students were measured before and after they read the article. As predicted, students who made a public commitment to their faith intensified their religious beliefs following their exposure to the disconfirming article. Through institutional or psychological mechanisms, many people build barriers against spiritual dangers. Paden (1988) summarized this process of marking boundaries well: "The subject matter here: worlds shut out, profanity shunned, bulwarks erected, lines not crossed, refusals to follow 'man's law, instead of God's law.' The results: existence unified, the sacred kept intact, integrity maintained" (p. 154).

Marking boundaries, however, may be accompanied by some negative consequences. When psychological boundaries are marked too strongly, people may refuse to accept important new information. When social boundaries are defined too strictly, people may treat those who lie outside those boundaries with prejudice and aggression. For example, Glock and Stark (1966) found that Christians who view themselves as "singularly possessed of the one true faith" (p. 21) were more likely to agree with the statements "Jews can never be forgiven for what they did to Jesus until they accept Him as the True Savior" and "The reason the Jews have so much trouble is because God is punishing them for rejecting Jesus" (pp. 96–97). Similarly, Altemeyer and Hunsberger (1992) reported higher levels of prejudice toward many minority groups by religious fundamentalists, a group that draws a clear line between members and outsiders. Particularly alarming were correlations between fundamentalism and a willingness to support the arrest, torture, and execu-

tion of political "radicals" and agreement with the statement that "the AIDS disease currently killing homosexuals is just what they deserve" (p. 123). Hunsberger (1996) adds three cautions. First, fundamentalism is not restricted to Christians; Hindu, Muslim, and Jewish fundamentalists also report higher levels of prejudice (Hunsberger, 1996). Second, the size of these relationships is not so great as to suggest that all fundamentalists are prejudiced. Third, the relationship between fundamentalism may be linked to prejudice by other critical variables, such as the degree to which the individual is personally or socially rigid. Nevertheless, based on empirical studies, there is a clear connection between fundamentalism and prejudice and aggression toward people and practices that are seen as threats to the faith.

Thus, the process of marking boundaries is one way people preserve and protect the sacred. When boundaries are "overmarked" though, the sacred may be protected at high cost to oneself or others. Of course, there are times when the boundary-marking process is unsuccessful, when something sacred is, in fact, harmed or violated. Even when the boundary is crossed, however, people can access other spiritual methods of coping to help them conserve the sacred.

Spiritual Purification

The religions of the world recognize that people occasionally stray from the spiritual path. This is not, however, taken lightly. Sins or transgressions are said to undermine the relationship between the individual and the sacred (Tillich, 1951), and for that reason they are condemned. Nevertheless, virtually every faith provides its adherents with ways to get back on the right path. Rituals of purification are coping methods that allow people to cleanse themselves of their sins and reconcile with God. The rituals can take many forms, drawing on any number of physical elements (e.g., water, fire, rain, ashes, sun, and blood) and a variety of behaviors (social isolation, repentance, sacrifice, punishment; Paden, 1988). As a group, however, they involve three steps: (a) a recognition of personal transgressions; (b) reparations for the misdeeds; and (c) a "cleaning of the slate," accompanied by divine acceptance, forgiveness, and reconciliation. For instance, within Roman Catholicism, the sacrament of reconciliation involves a confession of sins followed by absolution from a priest and penitential exercises to be performed. Although purification rituals such as the sacrament of penance are commonly performed throughout the world, researchers have not directly studied their impact on individual well-being.

Pennebaker and his colleagues, however, have conducted some research that bears, at least indirectly, on this topic. In one study, they asked a group of undergraduates to write about either the most traumatic event they had experienced or a set of unimportant assigned topics over 4 consecutive days (Pennebaker & Beall, 1986). The group of "trauma" participants were further subdivided into three subgroups that were asked to write: (a) only about their feelings related to the trauma (trauma-emotion); (b) only about the facts associated with the trauma (trauma-factual); or (c) both their feelings and the facts related to the trauma (trauma-combination). Although participants in the trauma-emotion and trauma-combinations groups were more upset than others after writing about the trauma, they reported fewer illnesses and less restricted activity as a result of their illnesses over the following 6-month period. Apparently, the process of "confession" increased distress for a short time but enhanced physical health over the long run (see Nieder-hoffer & Pennebaker, this volume).

There are important differences between the secular form of confession studied by Pennebaker and his colleagues and the spiritual forms of purification. For example, spiritual forms of purification typically involve an individual and a religious figure of authority, such as a confessor, which could conceivably inhibit emotional or enhance its beneficial effects. Spiritual forms of purification are also marked by a sense of acceptance and forgiveness from the divine. Potentially powerful spiritual experiences of this kind could magnify the impact of the confession on the individual's emotional and physical well-being. Empirical studies are clearly needed to develop a better understanding of this spiritual method of coping. Researchers who delve into this topic should keep a critical point in mind: The ultimate goal of spiritual purification is not simply to enhance the psychological or physical well-being of the individual but to bring the individual back to the sacred.

Spiritual Reframing

Many people in the United States believe in a loving God who watches over them to ensure that they will be protected and ultimately re-warded or punished for their good and bad behavior (Kushner, 1981). And yet, few people are able to go through their lives without encountering significant losses that threaten not only their sense of themselves and their just worldviews but also their beliefs in a God who is fair and benevolent. In the process of coping, the conservation of the sacred is as critical a task as the conservation of psychological or social ends.

One way to maintain beliefs in a just, loving God in the midst of trauma and loss is to see a larger, benign, spiritual purpose behind the negative event. This is a form of reframing in which crises become spiritually meaningful, or even opportunities for growth. For example, one parent was able to make sense of the death of her firstborn son this way: "They say there's a reason for God to do everything you know. I think that's very true because I think I love him (second child, born after the death of first child) a lot more than I would [have] had our first son been here" (Gilbert, 1989, p. 10). Benevolent religious appraisals of negative events such as this one are very common. For example, in their study of victims paralyzed by accidents to the spinal cord, Bulman and Wortman (1977) found that the most popular answer to the question Why me? was that God had a reason. Seeing a spiritual design beneath tragedy, interpreting negative events as opportunities for spiritual growth, or attributing loss to a loving God whose will cannot be fully understood are ways that people preserve their beliefs in the benevolence of the divine in the face of trauma.

In their empirical studies, researchers have shown that individuals who interpret negative life events within a more benevolent religious framework generally experience better adjustment to those crises (see Pargament, 1997, for a review). For example, Jenkins and Pargament (1988) asked patients with cancer about the degree to which they felt that God was in control of their illness. Attributions of control over the illness to God were tied to self-reports of greater self-esteem and nurses' reports of better patient adjustment. In another study of patients in India who were hospitalized as a result of an accident, attributions of the accident to karma were related positively to a measure of psychological recovery (Dalal & Pande, 1988).

In contrast, those who are unable to sustain their belief in a loving God following stressful events may be more vulnerable to problems. In a study of primary hospice caregivers for terminally ill patients, Mickley, Pargament, Brant, and Hipp (1998) found that benevolent religious reframing of the experience (e.g., viewing the situation in a spiritual light, attributions to God's will) was associated with perceptions of greater coping efficacy, more positive spiritual outcomes, and greater purpose in life. In contrast, beliefs that God was apathetic or unfair were linked to more depression and anxiety and lower purpose in life. These religious appraisals continued to be predictive of adjustment after controlling for the effects of nonreligious appraisals. Other researchers have reported similar findings (Exline, Yali, & Lobel, 1999; Fitchett, Rybarczyk, DeMarco, & Nicholas, 1999). For example, in a study of medical rehabilitation patients, anger toward God was predictive of declines in functional status over a 4-month period (Fitchett et al., 1999). These studies suggest that individuals who do not maintain a benevolent view of God in the midst of major life crises may be at risk for psychological or physical problems.

It should be noted, though, that there may be disadvantages associated with certain ways that people conserve their beliefs in a caring, just God. For example, negative events can be viewed as a caring but punishing God's effort to teach necessary lessons to those who have sinned. God's benevolence also can be preserved by attributions of negative events to a different, malevolent spiritual force, such as the devil. Although these forms of religious reframing may conserve the sacred, they may be purchased at the price of self-blame and guilt, victim-blame and derogation, or fear and anxiety. Consider the advice one woman gave her friend who had been diagnosed with cancer: "Surely, there's something in your life which is displeasing to God. . . . You must have stepped out of His will somewhere. These things don't just happen" (Yancey, 1977, p. 13). Researchers also have reported correlations between these negative forms of religious reframing and higher levels of depression, distress, physical symptomatology, and maladjustment to life stressors (Koenig, Pargament, & Nielsen, 1998; Pargament, Koenig, & Perez, in press; Pargament, Smith, et al., 1998; Pargament, Zinnbauer, et al., 1998). The struggle to conserve the sacred in the face of seemingly incomprehensible tragedy and injustice requires a delicate, tripartite balancing of the ways that people understand themselves, the world, and the sacred.

The Cycle of Discovery, Conservation, and Rediscovery of the Sacred over the Life Span

The search for the sacred does not end once the sacred has been discovered and conserved. Internal changes, developmental transitions, and external life events may precipitate a loss of the sacred or a change in the way the sacred is understood and experienced. At any point in life, the individual may experience periods in which the sacred is relinquished and rediscovered. Spiritual methods also are available to facilitate the process of transformation at these times (see Pargament, 1997, for a review). For example, religious rites of transition help people prepare for the deaths of those they hold most dear, acknowledge the loss, ease the deceased into the afterlife, incorporate the spiritual essence of the loved one into the inner experience of the survivors, and encourage the survivors to find new sources of sacred value in their lives once again. Spiritual conversion represents another transformational method in which those confronted by the limitations of their own self-contained worlds incorporate a sense of the sacred into themselves. The result is the discovery and experience of a force that goes beyond the self.

The process of discovering, conserving, and rediscovering the sacred is the essence of spirituality. It does not begin and end in childhood, nor does it conclude in early adulthood. It is a cycle that unfolds in different ways over the entire life span. Spirituality takes different forms for different people depending on a unique blend of biological, social, psychological, situational, and transcendent forces. It is, in short, a highly individualized phenomenon.

Conclusions and Implications

Spirituality is a process that speaks to the greatest of our potentials. The capacity to envision, seek, connect and hold on to, and transform the sacred may be what makes us uniquely human. In the past, psychologists often reduced spirituality to presumably more basic biological, psychological, or social motives. Certainly, spirituality may serve important psychosocial functions; as we have seen, the sacred can be fundamentally interconnected with virtually any dimension of life. Spirituality, however, cannot be reduced to purely biological, psychological, or social processes without distorting its essential character. Spirituality is an important human motive in and of itself (see also Emmons, 1999), one that deserves much greater study. Of course, we cannot speak to the actual existence of the sacred as social scientists. We have no instruments to measure God. We can learn, however, about the variety of ways that people try to discover and conserve what they perceive to be sacred. And we can examine how the search for the sacred impacts peoples' lives.

Psychologists and other social scientists are beginning to learn that spirituality holds a number of important, often positive implications for human functioning. But the study of spirituality is only beginning. Researchers have tended to study spirituality "from a distance," relying on surveys that contain global, distal measures, such as whether the individual believes in God, how often he or she goes to religious services, or prays, and his or her self-rated religiousness and spirituality. To develop a deeper understanding of this process, we will need to study it at closer hand by getting to know spiritually oriented people; learning about their worldview, values, and relationships; participating in and observing their institutions and settings; and examining the specific resources and methods of spirituality in much greater detail. It will be important to consider the full variety of spiritual pathways and destinations, not only those associated with traditional religious institutions but also those tied to smaller, newer, culturally diverse, and nontraditional groups. Given the history of tension, antipathy, and misunderstanding between psychological and spiritual communities, research of this kind may be far from easy. Researchers need to gain some basic education in the psychology of religion and spirituality and to examine their own preconceptions and attitudes toward spirituality before they engage in this type of study. And yet, research in this area may be well worth its initial costs and challenges, for the study of spirituality holds promise not only for understanding a neglected dimension of life but also for practical efforts to help people enhance their well-being.

Spirituality offers, in some respects, a unique set of resources for living. As Pargament (1997) has noted elsewhere, much of psychology in the United States is control oriented. Making the unconscious conscious, increasing behavioral and cognitive control, and empowering the disempowered are hallmarks of an American psychology that tries to help people develop greater control over their lives. And yet, there are aspects of our lives that are beyond our control. Birth, developmental transitions, accidents, illnesses, and death are immutable elements of existence. Try as we might to affect these elements, a significant portion of our lives remains beyond our immediate control. In spirituality, however, we can find ways to understand and deal with our fundamental human insufficiency, the fact that there are limits to our control. Unfortunately, the language of spirituality—the sacred, transcendence, letting go, forbearance, suffering, faith, mystery, finitude, sacrifice, grace, and transformation—is largely unfamiliar to psychologists. Even so, there may be much to be gained by bridging the worldviews, methods, and values of spirituality with those of psychology. Limitations and capacities are both a part of the human condition. After all, we grapple with both the possible and the impossible in any situation. Thus, a spirituality that helps us come to terms with our limits may complement rather than contradict a psychology that attempts to enhance our power and control.

Social scientists, health professionals, and mental health professionals already are starting to develop "psychospiritual interventions" that integrate spiritual resources into clinical practice. Spiritually oriented approaches have been interwoven with rational-emotive, cognitive-behavioral, psychoanalytic, marital-family, and existential therapies (see Shafranske, 1996). Although evaluations of the efficacy of these interventions are in short supply, initial results have been promising in several instances (e.g., McCullough, 1999; Propst, Ostrom, Watkins, Dean, & Mashburn, 1992).

Researchers and practitioners have also begun to study a host of "virtues," constructs that have clear roots in religious traditions, and apply these spiritually related themes to preventive, educative, and therapeutic interventions. For example, there is a burgeoning interest in the study of hope (Snyder, 1994; see also Snyder, Rand, & Sigmon, this volume), forgiveness (see McCullough, Pargament, & Thoresen, 2000; see also McCullough & Witvliet, this volume), love (Thoresen, 1998; see Hendrick & Hendrick, this volume); acceptance (Sanderson & Linehan, 1999); and serenity (Connors, Toscova, & Tonigan, 1999). In the future, psychologists should also turn their attention to "vices," such as narcissism (Emmons, 1987), evil (Baumeister, 1997; Peck, 1983), and spiritual struggles. Helping people grapple with this darker side to spirituality represents another important direction for psychological practice. However, lest we slip back into a "negative psychology," this focus needs to be balanced with an appreciation for the resource that spirituality represents for many people.

In our efforts to help people, we have to be especially sensitive to the diverse ways they experience and express their spirituality. In the search for the sacred, people take many different pathways toward many different destinations. As psychologists we must respect the full range of worldviews, practices, and communities that people form in their spiritual journeys. Perhaps the best antidote to our professional arrogance will come from a willingness to develop closer, collaborative relationships with spiritual individuals and communities. We have much to learn from and about each other. With a relationship founded on mutual respect and trust, we may be able to pool our resources and extend our ability to enhance the well-being of people. And with a willingness to learn about, learn from, and work with each other, we may set the stage for a spiritually enriched, positive psychology.

References

Allport, G. W., Gillespie, J. M., & Young, J. (1948). The religion of the post-war college student. *Journal of Psychology, 25,* 3–33.

Altemeyer, B., & Hunsberger, B. (1992). Authoritarianism, religious fundamentalism, quest, and prejudice. *International Journal for the Psychology of Religion, 2,* 113–133.

American Psychological Association (1992). Ethical principles of psychologists and code of conduct. *American Psychologist, 47,* 1597–1611.

Bahr, H. M., & Harvey, C. D. (1979). Widowhood and perceptions of change in quality of life: Evidence from the Sunshine Mine Widows. *Journal of Comparative Family Studies, 10,* 411–428.

Balk, D. (1983). Adolescents' grief reactions and self-concept perceptions following sibling death: A study of 33 teenagers. *Journal of Youth and Adolescence, 12,* 137–161.

Batson, C. D. (1975). Rational processing or rationalization? The effect of disconfirming evidence on a stated religious belief. *Journal of Personality and Social Psychology, 32,* 176–184.

Baumeister, R. F. (1997). *Evil: Inside human cruelty and violence.* New York: Freeman.

Benson, P. L. (1992). Religion and substance use. In J. F. Schumaker (Ed.), *Religion and mental health* (pp. 211–220). New York: Oxford University Press.

Berkovits, E. (1979). *With God in hell: Judaism in the ghettos and death camps.* New York: Sanhedrin Press.

Bouchard, R. J., Jr., Lykken, D. T., McGue, M., Segal, N. L., & Tellegen, A. (1990, October 12). Sources of human psychological differences: The Minnesota study of twins reared apart. *Science, 250,* 223–250.

Bowlby, J. (1988). *A secure base: Parent-child attachment and healthy human development.* New York: Basic Books.

Brock, T. C., & Balloun, J. L. (1967). Behavioral receptivity to dissonant information. *Journal of Personality and Social Psychology, 6,* 413–428.

Bulman, R. J., & Wortman, C. B. (1977). Attributions of blame and coping in the "real world": Severe accident victims react to their lot. *Journal of Personality and Social Psychology, 35,* 351–363.

Coles, R. (1990). *The spiritual life of children.* Boston: Houghton Mifflin.

Connors, G. J., Toscova, R. T., & Tonigan, J. S. (1999). Serenity. In W. R. Miller (Ed.), *Integrating spirituality into treatment: Resources for practitioners* (pp. 235–250). Washington, DC: American Psychological Association.

Croog, S. H., & Levine, S. (1972). Religious identity and response to serious illness: A report on heart patients. *Social Science and Medicine, 6,* 17–32.

Dalal, A. K., & Pande, N. (1988). Psychological recovery of accident victims with temporary and permanent disability. *International Journal of Psychology, 23,* 25–40.

Doyle, D. (1992). Have we looked beyond the physical and psychosocial? *Journal of Pain and Symptom Management, 7,* 302–311.

Ellison, C. G., & Levin, J. S. (1998). The religion-health connection: Evidence, theory, and future directions. *Health Education and Behavior, 25,* 700–726.

Ellison, C. G., & Sherkat, D. E. (1993). Obedience and autonomy: Religion and parenting values reconsidered. *Journal for the Scientific Study of Religion, 32,* 313–329.

Emmons, R. A. (1987). Narcissism: Theory and measurement. *Journal of Personality and Social Psychology, 52,* 11–17.

Emmons, R. A. (1999). *The psychology of ultimate concerns.* New York: Guilford.

Emmons, R. A., Cheung, C., & Tehrani, K. (1998). Assessing spirituality through personal goals: Implications for research on religion and subjective well-being. *Social Indicators Research, 45*, 391–422.

Exline, J. J., Yali, A. M., & Lobel, M. (1999). When God disappoints: Difficulty forgiving God and its role in negative emotion. *Journal of Health Psychology, 4*, 365–380.

Fitchett, G., Rybarczyk, B. D., DeMarco, G. A., & Nicholas, J. J. (1999). The role of religion in medical rehabilitation outcomes: A longitudinal study. *Rehabilitation Psychology, 44*, 1–22.

Gallup Poll Organization (1995). *Disciplining children in America: Survey of attitude and behavior of parents.* Project registration No. 104438. Princeton, NJ:

Gilbert, K. R. (1989, April). *Religion as a resource for bereaved parents as they cope with the death of their child.* Paper presented at the meeting of the National Council on Family Relations, New Orleans, LA.

Glock, C. Y., & Stark, R. (1966). *Christian beliefs and anti-Semitism.* New York: Harper and Row.

Goldman, R. (1964). *Religious thinking from childhood to adolescence.* New York: Seabury.

Hathaway, W., & Pargament, K. I. (1990). Intrinsic religiousness and competence: Inconsistent mediation by different religious coping styles. *Journal for the Scientific Study of Religion, 29*, 423–441.

Hoge, D. R. (1996). Religion in America: The demographics of belief and affiliation. In E. P. Shafranske (Ed.), *Religion and the clinical practice of psychology* (pp. 21–42). Washington, DC: American Psychological Association.

Hummer, R. A., Rogers, R. G., Nam, C. B., & Ellison, C. G. (1999). Religious involvement and U.S. adult mortality. *Demography, 36*, 273–285.

Hunsberger, B. (1996). Religious fundamentalism, right-wing authoritarianism, and hostility toward homosexuals in non-Christian religious groups. *International Journal for the Psychology of Religion, 6*, 39–49.

James, W. (1902). *The varieties of religious experience: A study in human nature.* New York: Modern Library.

Jenkins, R. A., & Pargament, K. I. (1988). Cognitive appraisals in cancer patients. *Social Science and Medicine, 26*, 625–633.

Johnson, P. E. (1959). *Psychology of religion.* Nashville, TN: Abingdon.

Kaufman, G. D. (1981). *The theological imagination: Constructing the concept of God.* Philadelphia: Westminster.

Kirkpatrick, L. A. (1997). A longitudinal study of changes in religious belief and behavior as a function of individual differences in adult attachment style. *Journal for the Scientific Study of Religion, 36*, 207–217.

Kirkpatrick, L. A. (1998). God as a substitute attachment figure: A longitudinal study of adult attachment style and religious change in college students. *Personality and Social Psychology Bulletin, 24*, 961–973.

Kirkpatrick, L. A. (1999). Attachment and religious representations and behavior. In J. Cassidy & P. R. Shaver (Eds.), *Handbook of attachment: Theory, research, and clinical applications* (pp. 803–822). New York: Guilford.

Kirkpatrick, L. A., & Shaver, P. R. (1992). Attachment theory and religion: Childhood attachments, religious beliefs, and conversion. *Journal for the Scientific Study of Religion, 29*, 315–334.

Koenig, H. G. (Ed.). (1998). *Handbook of religion and mental health.* San Diego, CA: Academic Press.

Koenig, H. G., Pargament, K. I., & Nielsen, J. (1998). Religious coping and health status in medically ill hospitalized older adults. *Journal of Nervous and Mental Disease, 186*, 513–521.

Kushner, H. S. (1981). *When bad things happen to good people.* New York: Schocken Books.

Kushner, H. S. (1989). *Who needs God?* New York: Summit Books.

Mahoney, A., Pargament, K. I., Jewell, T., Swank, A. B., Scott, E., Emery, E., & Rye, M. (1999). Marriage and the spiritual realm: The role of proximal and distal religious constructs in marital functioning. *Journal of Family Psychology, 13*, 321–338.

Marlatt, G. A., & Kristeller, J. L. (1999). Mindfulness and meditation. In W. R. Miller (Ed.), *Integrating spirituality into treatment: Resources for practitioners* (pp. 67–84). Washington, DC: American Psychological Association.

Mauritzen, J. (1988). Pastoral care for the dying and bereaved. *Death Studies, 12*, 111–122.

McCullough, M. E. (1999). Research on religion-accommodative counseling: Review and meta-analysis. *Journal of Counseling Psychology, 46*, 92–98.

McCullough, M. E., Pargament, K. I., & Thoresen, C. E. (Eds.). (2000). *Forgiveness: Theory, research, and practice.* New York: Guilford.

Mickley, J. R., Pargament, K. I., Brant, C. R., & Hipp, K. M. (1998). God and the search for meaning among hospice caregivers. *Hospice Journal, 13*, 1–18.

Paden, W. E. (1988). *Religious worlds: The comparative study of religion.* Boston: Beacon.

Paloutzian, R. F., & Ellison, C. W. (1982). Loneliness, spiritual well-being, and quality of life. In L. A. Peplau & D. Perlman (Eds.), *Loneliness: A sourcebook of current theory, research, and therapy* (pp. 224–237). New York: Wiley.

Pargament, K. I. (1997). *The psychology of religion and coping: Theory, research, practice.* New York: Guilford.

Pargament, K. I. (1999). The psychology of religion *and* spirituality? Yes and no. *International Journal for the Psychology of Religion, 9,* 3–16.

Pargament, K. I., & DeRosa, D. (1985). What was that sermon about? Predicting memory for religious messages from cognitive psychology theory. *Journal for the Scientific Study of Religion, 24,* 119–236.

Pargament, K. I., Kennell, J., Hathaway, W., Grevengoed, N., Newman, J., & Jones, W. (1988). Religion and the problem solving process: Three styles of coping. *Journal for the Scientific Study of Religion, 27,* 90–104.

Pargament, K. I., Koenig, H. G., & Perez, L. (2000). The many methods of religious coping: Development and initial validation of the RCOPE. *Journal of Clinical Psychology, 56,* 519–543.

Pargament, K. I., Smith, B., Koenig, H. G., & Perez, L. (1998). Patterns of positive and negative religious coping with major life stressors. *Journal for the Scientific Study of Religion, 37,* 711–725.

Pargament, K. I., Zinnbauer, B. J., Scott, A. B., Butter, E. M., Zerowin, J., & Stanik, P. (1998). Red flags and religious coping: Identifying some religious warning signals among people in crisis. *Journal of Clinical Psychology, 54,* 77–89.

Peck, M. S. (1983). *People of the lie.* New York: Simon and Schuster.

Pennebaker, J. W., & Beall, S. (1986). Confronting a traumatic event: Toward an understanding of inhibition and disease. *Journal of Abnormal Psychology, 95,* 274–281.

Pennebaker, J. W., Hughes, C. F., & O'Heeron, R. C. (1987). The psychophysiology of compassion: Linking inhibitory and psychosomatic processes. *Journal of Personality and Social Psychology, 52,* 781–793.

Pollner, M. (1989). Divine relations, social relations, and well-being. *Journal of Health and Social Behavior, 30,* 92–104.

Poloma, M. M., & Gallup, G. H., Jr. (1991). *Varieties of prayer: A survey report.* Philadelphia: Trinity Press International.

Propst, L. R., Ostrom, R., Watkins, P., Dean, T., & Mashburn, D. (1992). Comparative efficacy of religious and nonreligious cognitive-behavioral therapy for the treatment of clinical depression in religious individuals. *Journal of Consulting and Clinical Psychology, 60,* 94–103.

Richards, P. S., & Bergin, A. E. (1997). *A spiritual strategy for counseling and psychotherapy.* Washington, DC: American Psychological Association.

Rizzuto, A. M. (1979). *The birth of the living God: A psychoanalytic study.* Chicago: University of Chicago Press.

Sanderson, C., & Linehan, M. M. (1999). Acceptance and forgiveness. In W. R. Miller (Ed.), *Integrating spirituality into treatment: Resources for practitioners* (pp. 199–216). Washington, DC: American Psychological Association.

Schwab, R., & Petersen, K. U. (1990). Religiousness: Its relation to loneliness, neuroticism, and subjective well-being. *Journal for the Scientific Study of Religion, 29,* 335–345.

Shafranske, E. P. (Ed.). (1996). *Religion and the clinical practice of psychology.* Washington, DC: American Psychological Association.

Shafranske, E. P., & Malony, H. N. (1990). Clinical psychologists' religious and spiritual orientations and their practices of psychotherapy. *Psychotherapy: Theory, Research, Practice, Training, 27,* 72–78.

Shafranske, E. P., & Malony, H. N. (1996). Religion and the clinical practice of psychology: A case for inclusion. In E. P. Shafranske (Ed.), *Religion and the clinical practice of psychology* (pp. 561–586). Washington, DC: American Psychological Association.

Snyder, C. R. (1994). *The psychology of hope: You can get there from here.* New York: Free Press.

Streng, F. J. (1976). *Understanding religious life.* Encino, CA: Dickenson.

Swank, A., Mahoney, A., & Pargament, K. I. (1999, October). *The sanctification of parenting and its psychosocial implications.* Paper presented at the meeting of the Society of the Scientific Study of Religion, Boston.

Thoresen, C. E. (1998). Spirituality, health, and science: The coming revival? In S. Roth-Roemer, S. Kurpius Robinson, & C. Carmin (Eds.), *The emerging role of counseling psychology in health care* (pp. 409–431). New York: Norton.

Tillich, P. (1951). *Systematic theology* (Vol. 1). Chicago: University of Chicago Press.

Twerski, A. J. (1998). *Twerski on spirituality.* Brooklyn, NY: Shaar Press.

Ullman, C. (1982). Change of mind, change of heart: Some cognitive and emotional antecedents of religious conversion. *Journal of Personality and Social Psychology, 42,* 183–192.

Underwood, L. G. (1999). Daily spiritual experience. In *Multidimensional measurement of religiousness/spirituality for use in health research: A report of the Fetzer Institute/National Institute on Aging Working Group* (pp. 11–17). Kalamazoo, MI: Fetzer Institute.

Worthington, E. L., Jr., Kurusu, T. A., McCullough, M. E., & Sandage, S. J. (1996). Empirical research on religion and psychotherapeutic processes and outcomes: A 10-year review and research prospectus. *Psychological Bulletin, 119,* 448–487.

Wulff, D. (1998). *Psychology of religion: Classic and contemporary* (2nd ed.). New York: Wiley.

Yancey, P. (1977). *Where is God when it hurts?* Grand Rapids, MI: Zondervan.

Zinnbauer, B. J., & Pargament, K. I. (1998). Spiritual conversion: A study of religious change among college students. *Journal for the Scientific Study of Religion, 37,* 161–180.

Zinnbauer, B. J., Pargament, K. I., Cole, B., Rye, M. S., Butter, E. M., Belavich, T. G., Hipp, K. M., Scott, A. B., & Kadar, J. L. (1997). Religion and spirituality: Unfuzzying the fuzzy. *Journal for the Scientific Study of Religion, 36,* 549–564.

Zinnbauer, B. J., Pargament, K. I., & Scott, A. B. (1999). The emerging meanings of religiousness and spirituality: Problems and prospects. *Journal of Personality, 67,* 889–919.

IX

Special Populations and Settings

48

Positive Psychology for Children

Development, Prevention, and Promotion

Michael C. Roberts, Keri J. Brown, Rebecca J. Johnson, &
Janette Reinke

You have brains in your head
You have feet in your shoes
* You can steer yourself*
Any direction you choose.
                            —Dr. Seuss

Although the specialties of psychology dealing with children recognize the serious problems encountered during their development,
much of the recent orientation involves moving
away from viewing the psychological and behavioral deficits resulting from a developmental
challenge. Instead, the focus increasingly has
become one of perceiving the competence of the
child and his or her family and enhancing
growth in psychological domains. The clinical
child, school, and pediatric psychology literatures frequently address concepts of stress and
coping, generally accepting that coping is a positive response to the stress of a negative environmental situation or life event such as a
chronic illness or parental divorce.

As noted by Siegel (1992), "individual-
differences factors can influence both a child's

response to stress and his or her use of coping
strategies" (p. 4). He called for increased attention to the individual differences in children's
behavioral, emotional, and physiological responsiveness to their environment. Siegel indicated that each child may respond quite differently to an environmental stressor. An
important aspect of coping is that the same
mechanisms of responding to stress are involved
in life events that are not as significant as divorce or disease but are the daily hassles of human existence. For example, in pediatric psychology, several resilience and coping models
have emerged to frame issues of children who
have a chronic illness such as diabetes, cystic
fibrosis, or sickle-cell disease. In much of the
earlier literature and still to some extent today,
coping or resilience concepts are thought of
only as responses to a stressor, usually a major
one, not as a positive behavioral style of adjusting, adapting, accommodating, and assimi-
lating to an ever-changing environment in a
child's life. In a positive psychology orientation,
however, a comprehensive and inclusive conceptualization of coping views these adaptations as

normal developmental events with much common origin and function. Additionally, there is an increasing recognition that growth and enhancement to achieve physical and psychological well-being occur through these adaptations.

Others have noted the need, particularly working with adolescents, to examine the strengths and positive assets of the developmental stage rather than focusing on the multitude of stressors and potential negative outcomes (Johnson, Roberts, & Worell, 1999). Johnson and Roberts (1999) recognized that "looking at strengths rather than deficits, opportunities rather than risks, assets rather than liabilities is slowly becoming an increasing presence in the psychotherapy, education, and parenting literature" (p. 5). Similarly, Dryfoos (1998) reviewed the programs aimed at assisting adolescents and concluded that successful ones emphasized optimism and hope and were growth-enhancing for the adolescents and their families.

All too often, a "pathology model" has been applied to studying how children develop. That is, children with significant behavior disorders pose major problems for parents, teachers, and peers, such that their pathology gets the greatest attention. More recent conceptualizations have focused attention on more "normal" development for most children, but also to considering how pathology might be avoided through early intervention and enhanced environments for all children. Frequently the focus has been on taking children with problems and doing something to change them. Positive psychology has something to offer this process, but a larger application of positive psychology would be to view it in terms of prevention and promotion. Additionally, the pathology model typically takes an adult-oriented perspective. By assuming that the goal of all human development and any intervention is intended to produce a fully functioning adult, only adult outcomes are considered important. The positive psychology alternative is to focus on the child while a child is in development and attempt to enhance functioning, competence, and overall mental health at any particular time. Furthermore, psychological conceptualizations of pathology have historically been formulated for adults and then, in a downward extension, applied to children and adolescents (Maddux, Roberts, Sledden, & Wright, 1986). This application, all too frequently, does not fit. Adult-oriented theories and intervention techniques

"have never sufficed in other areas of mental health intervention. . . . work with children requires a developmental perspective which recognizes the process of continual change over time in the psychology of children" (Roberts & Peterson, 1984, p. 3). In our view, well-formulated positive psychology literature takes a developmental perspective.

In this chapter, we will describe the three major conceptualizations of optimism, hope, and quality of life as related to positive psychology for children and adolescents. This examination of the extant literature is descriptive and not exhaustive, but it does illustrate the potential utility of positive psychology in child development. In the final section, we propose that integrating a positive psychology orientation with a developmental perspective creates a catalyst for prevention.

Optimism

Definition and Concepts

One conception of optimism defines it in terms of explanatory style and how an individual thinks about causality of an event. That is, an optimist is defined as a person who sees defeat as temporary, confined to a particular case, and not his or her direct fault (Seligman, 1991). A pessimist, on the other hand, believes bad events will last a long time and undermine everything he or she does, and that these events were his or her fault. Thus, the way that a person explains positive or negative events to him or herself determines whether he or she is optimistic or pessimistic. This explanatory style is evident in how an individual thinks about the causes of events. A pessimist dwells on the most catastrophic causes for the event, whereas an optimist can see that there are other possible, less catastrophic causes for the same event. For example, two children may receive poor grades on a test. The pessimistic child might say to himself, "I'm stupid and can't get anything right," whereas the optimistic child might say to herself "I need to study a little harder next time." In summary, Seligman stated that the way in which a person explains events has three dimensions: permanent versus temporary, universal versus specific, and internal versus external. These dimensions determine whether a person is pessimistic or optimistic. This explanatory style can be acquired by children and adults and has been labeled *learned optimism.* Seligman and his colleagues have studied the concept of learned optimism with children as well as adults.

Considerable research has been conducted on the benefits of optimism and the costs of pessimism. Optimists tend to do better in school and college than pessimists. Optimists also perform well at work and in sports. The physical and mental health of optimists tends to be better, and optimists may even live longer than pessimists (Seligman, 1991). Optimists also tend to cope with adverse situations in more adaptive ways (Scheier & Carver, 1993). Adolescents who are optimistic tend to be less angry (Puskar, Sereika, Lamb, Tusaie-Mumford, & McGuiness, 1999) and abuse substances less often (Carvajal, Clair, Nash, & Evans, 1998). Conversely, pessimists tend to give up more easily, get depressed more often, have poorer health, be more passive (Seligman, 1991), have more failure in work and school, and have more social problems (Peterson, 2000).

Seligman, Reivich, Jaycox, and Gillham (1995) described four sources for the origins of optimism. The first possible source is genetics (Schulman, Keith, & Seligman, 1993; Seligman et al., 1995). A second source is the child's environment, in which parents seem to be a strong influence on the level of optimism in their children. Researchers have found that there is a strong relationship between a mother's explanatory style and that of her child (Seligman et al., 1995). Children may imitate parents' explanatory style. A third source for optimism is also an environmental influence, in the form of criticism that a child receives from parents, teachers, coaches, or other adults. If an adult criticizes a rather permanent ability of a child (e.g., "You just can't learn this"), the child is more likely to develop a pessimistic explanatory style. A fourth way in which optimism develops is through life experiences that promote either mastery or helplessness. Life events such as divorce, death in the family, or abuse can affect how a child describes causes to him- or herself. Events such as these tend to be permanent, and many times the child is unable to stop or reverse the event.

In light of all the benefits of being optimistic and the costs of being pessimistic, is it best for a child to be optimistic all the time? Seligman and other researchers have not advocated that parents mold their children to be the more extreme "Pollyanna." Instead, Seligman et al.

(1995) noted that there are limits to optimism. Children must see themselves in a realistic light in order for them to successfully challenge their automatic negative thoughts. Teaching children to be realistic helps them perceive the beginnings of negative self-attribution (e.g., "I flunked the test because I am stupid") and challenge that thought, and also to see where they might be able to overcome a fault (e.g., "I flunked the test because I didn't study enough. Next time I'll study harder"). Disputing automatic thoughts only works when the thoughts can be checked against reality.

Measurement

One assessment tool for measuring optimism in children is the Children's Attributional Style Questionnaire (CASQ; Seligman et al., 1995). This instrument is a 48-item forced-choice questionnaire that assesses explanatory style for both positive and negative hypothetical events. The questions measure whether the child's attributions about positive or negative events are stable or unstable, global or specific, and internal or external. Example items include: "You get good grades: (A) School work is simple; or (B) I am a hard worker." The CASQ gives an overall picture of the child's explanatory style and whether that style is positive or negative. The book *The Optimistic Child* (1995), by Seligman et al., contains an in-depth description of the CASQ, including administration, scoring, and interpretation. The Life Orientation Test (Scheier & Carver, 1985) is a measure developed for assessing optimism of adults and has been used with adolescents (e.g., Carvajal et al., 1998; Puskar et al., 1999)

Interventions

The Penn Prevention Program is an intervention-oriented research project that has investigated the costs of pessimism in children (Jaycox, Reivich, Gillham, & Seligman, 1994; Gillham, Reivich, Jaycox, & Seligman, 1995). The goal of this program has been to prevent depressive symptoms in children at risk for this pathology using a treatment that addresses the child's explanatory style and social-problem-solving skills. The children in the prevention group were taught to identify negative beliefs, to evaluate those beliefs by examining evidence for and against them, and to generate more realistic alternatives. They were also taught to identify pessimistic explanations for events and to generate alternative explanations that were more optimistic. These children also learned social problem solving, as well as ways to cope with parental conflict, and behavioral techniques to enhance negotiations, assertiveness, and relaxation. The results of this project are encouraging. The researchers found that the children who were in the prevention condition had half the rate of depression as the control group. Immediately after the prevention program, the control group had more depressed symptoms than the treated group. Also of considerable interest is the finding that the benefits of the program seemed to maintain over time. Children who completed the prevention program in preadolescence were able to deal with the challenges they faced in adolescence more effectively and had less depression than children in the control group. This study demonstrates the importance of teaching children the skills of learned optimism before they reach puberty, but late enough in childhood for them to understand the concepts.

The study of optimism in children is fairly new, and many areas have yet to be researched. Results thus far seem to indicate that optimism can be taught, and learned optimism can be helpful in alleviating and even preventing some of the problems of childhood and adolescence. Optimism may be a very valuable tool that children can use to negotiate the challenges and adversity they are sure to face.

Hope

Definition and Concept

Snyder and his colleagues have defined hope as a cognitive set involving an individual's beliefs in his or her capability to produce workable routes to goals (waypower or pathways) and beliefs in his or her own ability to initiate and sustain movement toward those goals (willpower or agency; Snyder, 1994; Snyder et al., 1991; Snyder, Hoza, et al., 1997). With this definition they have suggested that hope is an important construct in understanding how children deal with stressors in their lives, avoid becoming mired down in problem behaviors, and use past experiences to develop strategies for working toward goals in an adaptive, effective manner.

Hope is not correlated with intelligence, and Snyder, Hoza, et al. (1997) have proposed that most children have the intellectual capacity to use hopeful, goal-directed thinking. Children's hope does appear to moderately predict cognitive and school-related achievement. Boys and girls have similar levels of hope. Children tend to be biased somewhat positively in their perceptions of the future, although it has been argued that this is typical and rather adaptive (Snyder, Hoza, et al., 1997). This bias may be appropriate to help children develop and sustain positive outcome thoughts even if they are realistically untenable, because it appears that high-hope children do this as they successfully deal with stressful events in childhood. The research thus far indicates that, for most children, hope is relatively high, and that even children with comparatively low hope rarely indicate that they have no hope, and they tend to have hope in at least some of their thoughts (Snyder, McDermott, Cook, & Rapoff, 1997). Measures of children's hope correlate positively with self-reported competency, and children with higher levels of hope report feeling more positively about themselves and less depressed than children with lower levels of hope. Snyder, Feldman, Taylor, Schroeder, and Adams (2000) present some experimental evidence to support the idea that self-esteem results from the development of hope (through identification of goals and pathways).

Measurement

A measure of children's hope, the Children's Hope Scale (CHS), was developed by Snyder, Hoza, et al. (1997). The guiding assumption behind the development of the CHS and subsequent versions of the scale (Snyder, Hoza, et al., 1997) was that the acquisition and usage of goal-directed thinking are critical for effective functioning in children and adolescents. Therefore, the purpose of the measure is to identify children who need nurturance and education in order to improve their hopeful thinking, especially during times of illness and stress (Snyder, McDermott, et al., 1997). The scale also identifies children who exhibit hope at high levels and who can serve as models for other children. Several versions of the CHS have been designed for different age-groups and for different purposes. These versions include the Young Children's Hope Scale (YCHS) Story

Form (aged 5–8 years); the Young Children's Hope Scale (YCHS) Self-Report Form (aged 5–9 years); the Young Children's Hope Scale (YCHS) Observer Rating Form (for teachers, parents, and other adults), the Children's Hope Scale (CHS) Self-Report Form (aged 9–16 years); and the Children's Hope Scale (CHS) Observer Rating Form. Adolescents aged 16 and over can complete the Trait Hope Scale or the State Hope Scale, which have been designed for adults and also come with observer rating forms.

Data collected during the development of the original Children's Hope Scale indicate that the CHS demonstrates high test-retest reliability for intervals up to 1 month (Snyder, Hoza, et al., 1997). Research with the hope scales for children has shown that the agency (willpower) and pathways (waypower) subscales tend to correlate .50 to .70. Snyder, McDermott, et al. (1997) have labeled four different patterns of scores that tend to describe children's hope based on the combination of their agency and pathways subscores: small hope (low agency and low pathways), half hope (one low and one high), and high or large hope (high agency and high pathways). It has been suggested that interventions may be tailored to address either low agency or low pathways, or both, but research has not addressed this possibility (Snyder, McDermott, et al., 1997).

Increasingly more research has explored hope in children. In particular, hope has been introduced as a useful concept to examine in pediatric populations, because children who are seriously ill or injured are often required to cope with or adjust to difficult conditions. In this section, we will examine the handful of studies that have investigated hope in children.

In the first study, Lewis and Kliewer (1996) investigated the role that coping strategies play in the relationship between hope and adjustment in a group of children with sickle-cell disease (SCD). Results revealed that hope was negatively related to anxiety, but that coping strategies moderated this relationship. Specifically, hope was negatively related to anxiety when active support and distraction coping strategies were high. In other words, children with SCD who had high levels of hope and who reported using primarily active, support, and distraction coping strategies reported less anxiety. Hope did not appear to be associated with a reduction in anxiety by affecting coping ef-

forts. Hope and coping were related to anxiety but did not make unique contributions to functional adjustment or depression once control variables were considered. The authors concluded that knowing both a child's level of hope and the types of coping behaviors he or she is using may be important for understanding variations in psychological adjustment, especially when talking about a disorder like SCD, where stress and anxiety can exacerbate physical conditions.

In the second study, Barnum, Snyder, Rapoff, Mani, and Thompson (1998) hypothesized that high-hope thinking may serve a protective function, allowing children to function effectively in spite of obstacles and challenges in their lives. They examined predictors of adjustment in adolescents who suffered burns as children and their matched controls. Variables that were selected as possible predictors of adjustment included social support, family environment, burn characteristics, demographics, and hope. There were few differences between the burn survivors and the comparison group. For both groups, hope was the only significant predictor of externalizing behavior problem scores: Higher hope scores predicted lower externalizing behavior scores. In addition, social support and hope both significantly contributed to the prediction of global self-worth. Barnum et al. suggested that adolescents who report higher levels of hope may think in ways that generate positive solutions, and they may feel more capable of enacting a variety of behaviors to solve problems, possibly reducing the need to act out in problematic ways.

In a third study using the CHS, Hinton-Nelson, Roberts, and Snyder (1996) gathered information from junior high students attending a school in close proximity to a high crime area in order to explore the relationship between stressful life experiences, hope, and perceived vulnerability. In addition to measuring the children's hope, they also measured the children's exposure to violence and their perceptions of their vulnerability to victimization. Hinton-Nelson et al. hypothesized that children who had been exposed to violence would have lower levels of hope, but this was not the case. The children in this study reported levels of hope similar to that of other groups. Adolescents who had witnessed violence around them but had less personal or direct experience with violence reported the highest levels of hope, and adolescents with higher hope perceived that they would be less likely to die a violent death. Adolescents with direct exposure to violence tended to predict violent deaths for themselves. The authors concluded that, while these young people acknowledged the violence surrounding them, they were able to sustain high hope as long as they did not experience violence directly.

Intervention

A few preliminary projects are being reported in which an intervention has been designed to influence children's hope. Snyder, McDermott, et al. (1997) proposed that hopeful stories are important for constructing and maintaining a sense of hope in children. They viewed hopeful stories as reflections of past experiences and argued that these stories are used to guide future action. McDermott et al. (1996; and described in McDermott & Hastings, 2000) discussed a program in which schoolchildren (grades 1–6) were read stories of high-hope children, and classroom discussions addressed how these children might incorporate hope into their own lives. Modest positive changes were found on measures of hope. These authors noted that a more comprehensive inclusion of teaching hope in the classroom might have greater effect. Lopez (2000) conducted another pilot project in a junior high school in which hopeful stories (e.g., from a Harry Potter book) were read. Children were engaged in structured exercises, goal-oriented discussions, and the assignment of a "Hope Buddy" to discuss goals, pathways to achieve goals, and ways to navigate around barriers. Future research needs to examine the usefulness of hope-filled curriculum as an intervention technique.

Other projects have examined whether psychosocial interventions are associated with children's hope (but where hope was not the prime target of the intervention). McNeal (1998) conducted a study of children and adolescents' hope before and after they had been in psychological treatment in a residential setting over 6 months. He found that significantly higher levels of hope were developed over that period. In another study of hope with children in an intervention program, Brown and Roberts (2000) assessed hope in children who were participants in a summer day camp after being identified as being at risk for a number of psychosocial problems. In the 6-week camp, the children were given intensive training in dance and performing arts. They also participated in group sessions on a variety of psychosocial issues related to their life experiences. During the day camp, the participants wrote essays answering questions similar to those proposed by Snyder, McDermott et al. (1997). The results during the camp and afterward indicated that hope scores increased significantly as a result of the 6-week experience. Mean hope scores remained elevated and stable at a 4-month follow-up. The study could not isolate what contributed to the hope changes, so the comprehensive camp experience as a whole may be viewed as an intervention. These types of intervention can indicate the viability of hope as a dependent measure indicating change as a result. Most important, these studies into children's hope demonstrate that hope in children is an essential element of development.

Quality of Life

Definition and Concept

The concept of quality of life (QOL) takes a multidimensional view of well-being and includes physical, mental, spiritual, and social aspects (Institute for the Future, 2000). However, QOL has not been well defined or consistently utilized in the literature. Other terms, such as *psychological well-being* or *adjustment* are also used to represent constructs similar to QOL. Walker and Rosser (1988) defined QOL as "a concept encompassing a broad range of physical and psychological characteristics and limitations which describes an individual's ability to function and derive satisfaction from doing so" (p. xv). One QOL measure for pediatric cancer patients includes five domains: disease and treatment-related symptoms, physical functioning, social functioning, cognitive functioning, and psychological functioning (Varni, Seid, & Rode, 1999).

In addition to exploring QOL as a general concept, research has examined health-related quality of life (e.g., determination of whether new and invasive treatments to increase chances of survival are worthwhile given the deleterious nature of the treatment side effects). Health-related QOL reflects an individual's personal perceptions of his or her own well-being. For example, a child with asthma may successfully pass a pulmonary function test but may have fears of an attack and thus limit the physical activities he or she is willing to try. Those interested in the delegation of limited health resources also have recognized the utility of measuring health-related QOL. Measuring QOL in the medical setting may assist health professionals in demonstrating to third-party payers the effectiveness of particular interventions.

In addition to measuring QOL in health situations, QOL measures are used to assess impact of health-related diseases and procedures on one's daily life. However, one of the most frequently noted concerns is that the various QOL measures lack theoretical foundations. Much of the philosophy behind the measurement of health-related QOL has been based on the notion that the medical treatment itself is the primary determinant of a patient's QOL. Varni (1983) suggested that this biomedical model does not encompass all aspects of a pediatric patient's life or situation that might affect his or her perceptions of QOL. Varni proposed that, in addition to the traditional biomedical model, a biobehavioral conceptualization should guide assessment. In this model, a patient's problem-solving skills and ongoing level of symptom control are important. Kaplan, Sallis, and Patterson (1993) proposed a biopsychosocial model that emphasizes the important roles of social, psychological, and biological factors in the conceptualization of health-related QOL. To date, conceptualization and measurement of health-related QOL in children has lagged behind that of adults (Spieth & Harris, 1996).

Measurement

QOL measures were developed for adults, so many of the measures cover domains not applicable to children (e.g., economic independence, infertility) or base the psychometrics on adult responses. Thus, there is little information regarding the validity or reliability of these measures for use with children. When assessing a child's QOL, age and development should be considered. In addition, there is a lack of consensus in the literature regarding who is the best informant of a child's health-related QOL. Early measures did not take into account a child's perceptions, for example. Instead, parents, teachers, nurses, and doctors provided subjective information to define children's QOL. While some studies have suggested that proxy informants are similar to a child's own percep-

tions of his or her QOL, the majority of the research provides limited evidence for concordance between respondents (Vogels et al., 1998). Additionally, considerable difference in observer ratings provided by parents and teachers and the children's own self-ratings of health attitudes and behaviors has been reported (Pantell & Lewis, 1987).

Using parents to rate QOL is a widely implemented strategy in the literature, yet parents may not report all important aspects of their children's well-being. For example, parents of adolescents might underestimate the important role of peers. Health personnel also may serve as reporters for a child's QOL. One advantage of hospital staff is that these individuals can use other patients as points of reference. However, they may have limited knowledge regarding the child's functioning in other arenas of life, such as at home, in school, or with peers. In addition, they may overemphasize the importance of positive health outcomes versus social, psychological, or spiritual outcomes.

Guyatt and colleagues (1997) suggested that information should be obtained regarding perceived QOL from the children themselves. Although age-appropriate modifications are necessary, self-report QOL information can be reliably obtained from children as young as 7 (Feeny, Juniper, Ferry, Griffith, & Guyatt, 1998). Guyatt et al. noted that younger children have difficulty recalling events that occurred more than a week earlier. In addition, they found that the feeling thermometer, a measure often used to assess children's QOL, seemed more difficult for children to understand than interview-administered questionnaires. They suggested that feeling thermometers should only be used with children at a reading level of age 8 or grade 3.

One frequently used measure assesses both child and parent perceptions of health-related QOL. The Pediatric Cancer Quality of Life Inventory (PCQL) contains two parallel forms designed to define health-related QOL in terms of the impact of the disease and treatment on the child's physical, social, psychological, and cognitive functioning and disease or treatment-related symptoms as perceived by parent and child patient (Varni et al., 1998). In addition to issues of who is the best informant, a clinician must decide between general and disease-specific QOL measures. General measures of QOL can be used in many other instances as well, such as for children with low-incidence childhood diseases. Additionally, these general measures allow for cross-condition comparisons. These measures include the Child Health and Illness Profile—Adolescent Edition (Starfield et al., 1995); Child Health Questionnaire (Landgraf, Abetz, & Ware, 1996); Functional Status II-R (Stein & Jessop, 1990); and Play Performance Scale for Children (Mulhern, Faircough, Friedman, & Leigh, 1990).

Disease-specific measures of QOL may be more sensitive in determining the differential effects of treatments within one illness domain. Consequently, different QOL measures have been developed for use with various childhood conditions including pediatric cancer (Varni et al., 1998), diabetes (Diabetes Control and Complications Trial Research Group, 1988), asthma (Mishoe et al., 1998; Townsend et al., 1991), and children born with limb deficiencies (Pruitt, Seid, Varni, & Setoguchi, 1999). These measures demonstrate some utility in detecting changes in patients whose health status has changed due to fluctuations of their disease or as a result of treatment. In the case of children's asthma, a multidisciplinary team assesses QOL in the domains of symptomatology, activity limitations, and emotional functioning (Townsend et al., 1991). The QOL measure for diabetes assesses disease impact as well as school life and relationships with peers (Ingersoll & Marrero, 1991). Most of the better measures appear to use this multidimensional approach to assess not only physical symptoms but also health status, psychological and adaptive functioning, and family functioning.

Interventions

One purpose of studies examining QOL is to add clinical relevance to the results of outcome studies following medical or psychological interventions. Drotar and colleagues (1998) suggested that the use of health-related QOL measures could aid in the identification of children with chronic illness who may need additional psychological assessment and intervention. The use of these measures early in the initial identification of an illness may help improve parents' ability to report information regarding their child's mental and physical health earlier and more thoroughly. For example, for children diagnosed with cancer, Boggs and Durning (1998) reported using the Pediatric Oncology Quality of Life Scale as a screening measure to determine which children would be most likely

to benefit from psychological services. Another purpose of QOL studies is to identify the children who are experiencing health problems who are less likely to adhere to a treatment protocol (Drotar et al., 1998). For some children, the side effects of a treatment regimen may be seen as very aversive and may affect QOL. Information collected through the use of QOL measures may lead to additional support or intervention for the child. Psychosocial interventions designed to improve the adjustment and functioning of children undergoing medical treatment may also impact reported QOL.

Related Concepts of Positive Psychology

There are several psychological concepts related to positive psychology in children in addition to the concepts reviewed here. The movement in pediatric psychology away from an exclusive focus on children's deficits or pathology to a more affirming and strength-building approach exemplifies a positive psychology orientation (whether acknowledged or not). Clinicians and researchers are increasingly focused on enhancing and facilitating children's development whatever the setting or circumstances. In the psychosocial care of children with cancer, Noll and Kazak (1997) emphasized that while diagnosis and treatment "can be overwhelming, they can be managed in positive ways that encourage families to continue to function in the best possible fashion and facilitate personal growth" (p. 263). They recommended that in order to promote positive adaptations, certain psychologically directed actions can be taken by professionals, parents, and children themselves. Other aspects related to enhancing the psychosocial growth of children in medical settings involve making changes in the hospital architecture that welcome and support children and families, training staff to recognize and facilitate children's needs and development at all times, and following medical procedures that allow children appropriate input and control regarding what is done to them (Johnson, Jeppson, & Redburn, 1992).

Similarly, schools can be envisioned as settings where children can experience empowerment and enhanced development rather than places where the focus is on stresses and challenges (Donnelly, 1997; Schorr, 1997). For example, Spivack and Shure have developed and tested a model of teaching children and teachers to use interpersonal cognitive problem-solving skills in interactions (Shure, 1996). These skills enhance positive growth and development without focusing on any of a child's deficiencies.

Social support is also viewed as a potential element of positive psychology for children facing the challenges of stressful events as well as coping and adjusting in everyday living. Quittner (1992) noted that the accepted definition of social support includes several aspects such as "provision of direct assistance, information, emotional concern, and affirmation" (p. 87). Social support has not been fully conceptualized within a positive psychology framework but relates to it very well.

Faith is another aspect of positive psychology that has not been given significant attention. As noted by health researchers, "Spiritual factors promote good health . . . and contribute to the state of wellness that characterizes health" (Institute for the Future, 2000, p. 190). Additional consideration of faith and religion in the lives of children and adolescents may be an important aspect of positive psychology research.

Developmental Perspective

Because positive psychology is a newly developing field of research and application, there remain a large number of issues for children and adolescents that deserve greater attention. Although it is encouraging to have any research, the relative lack of empirical studies to review in this chapter indicates that there is much to be done. We strongly urge that positive psychology theorists and researchers consider a developmental perspective rather than focusing only on adults (and children as "smaller humans") or give minimal attention to development by considering childhood *only* as a period preceding adulthood. Maddux et al. (1986) suggested that two elements are important to a developmental approach. The first is a future orientation in which any effort at intervention or change is considered important because of its relationship to improving future health status (i.e., in adulthood). The second, and perhaps most neglected, element in a developmental perspective requires that "each period of life receive attention to the particular problems evident in that period" (p. 25). Thus, there should be a focus on the health status of children while they *are* children rather than recognizing children's

importance only because the children will become adults in the future. We think both elements are important in the positive psychology movement, but we want to emphasize the latter point. The uniqueness of children's development needs to be recognized in all theories, measurements, and application of positive psychology concepts.

Prevention and Promotion

Interlinked with the developmental perspective is a view that childhood may be the optimal time to promote healthy attitudes, behavior, adjustment, and prevention of problems (Roberts & Peterson, 1984). Roberts (1991) stated, "Prevention is basically taking action to avoid development of a problem and/or identify problems early enough in their development to minimize potential negative outcomes. Health promotion refers to increasing individuals' abilities to adopt health-enhancing life styles" (p. 95). Prevention and promotion efforts in childhood attempt to improve the quality of life for the child *during childhood* and for that child's *later* adulthood. As noted by Peterson and Roberts (1986), prevention efforts often take a developmental perspective and focus on competency enhancement that "is likely to be most effective when applied during the time of greatest competency acquisition, which is during childhood for many skills such as language, social abilities, or self-efficacy beliefs" (p. 623). Such enhancement of positive psychology thinking, such as encouraging hope, would similarly be most effective at these early stages of human development.

Future Research Directions

Studies of the positive psychology topics of hope and optimism, as examples, have typically utilized cross-sectional designs. Longitudinal models would elucidate the sequence of development and what influences change over time. Interventions and evaluations of programs to promote hope or optimism are also prime areas for further work. Interventions may enhance the positive frames for all children or for those with special stresses. In the latter case, applications may be necessary with children who have a chronic illness or with those experiencing psychological problems or disruptive life events, such as divorce, death, or relocation. Most important, because positive psychology seems inherently linked to preventive efforts to improve children's lives, these concepts need to be integrated into prevention theory and programming. Behavioral measures of positive psychology concepts, such as hope, need to be developed and integrated into the theories. These behaviors can then be used as affirmative outcome measures in prevention and intervention programs.

More research needs to be done with children with regard to happiness and positive well-being. So far, outcome measures in the study of optimism in children assess whether negative states are present or absent. Instruments need to be developed that also measure the positive aspects that children possess, like happiness, instead of just the absence of any negatives. Another area for future research is in pediatric psychology. Does enhancing hope and teaching children with a chronic illness the skills of learned optimism improve the course of their illness or the quality of their lives? Does a positive psychology approach help the family to cope with the child's illness?

Research is needed to determine more precisely when hope becomes a stable personality trait and whether hope is stable during childhood and adolescence. Additional research should determine what types of experiences are related to high or low hope, and under what circumstances children's levels of hope may be malleable to negative or positive circumstances. Further research may explore what types of interventions may help children to increase their level of hope or optimism. McNeal (1998) and Brown and Roberts (2000) found evidence suggesting that children and adolescents reported higher levels of hope after psychosocial interventions (but these interventions were not directly attempting to affect the children's hope). Pilot projects by Lopez (2000) and McDermott et al. (1996) are promising investigations directly targeting changes in children's hope. Whether such changes in hope subsequently affect other significant outcomes in children will be important to measure. As suggested by Snyder et al. (2000), ensuring that children have "hope coaches" early and consistently in their lives seems important to the development of hope. Books for parents and other caregivers that teach hope coaching skills, such as McDermott and Snyder, *The Great Big Book of Hope* (2000), should be empirically evaluated to assess their effectiveness.

Research is needed to examine whether other types of psychotherapy or psychosocial interventions might affect children's levels of hope or learned optimism (or whether these variables predict the influence of the psychological/behavioral interventions). Finally, future research needs to address the relationship between hope, coping, and adjustment. Studies need to examine whether preexisting levels of hope may influence the impact of life events on children's adjustment.

In their study of the effects of violence on hope, Hinton-Nelson et al. (1996) suggested that future research should investigate whether hope and perceptions of the future differentiate those young people who commit violent acts from those who do not. They also suggested that future research examine the relationship between hope and resiliency.

Quality-of-life issues are important when one is considering a multidimensional view of how a child (or adult) perceives the world and his or her functioning within it. Further refinement of the conceptual bases and measurement tools is clearly needed. Measurement of QOL in its general and situation-specific forms will aid in the conceptualization of how children develop their perspectives on their lives, what they define as important, and how they rate what they value. In its development the QOL concept derived from a deficit view, for example, negative life events diminish QOL. In newer conceptualizations, measuring QOL perceptions in children and adolescents may provide evidence of the positive effects of even negative life events (Cohen & Park, 1992). Thus, future research should also examine the adaptive and resiliency features in a child that may lead to greater satisfaction and enhanced or increased QOL.

The many benefits of a positive psychology orientation with children have been hinted at by the research thus far. The full contribution will be demonstrated through a better understanding of children's development and more effective interventions that also address prevention, treatment of problems, and the promotion of well-being.

References

Barnum, D. D., Snyder, C. R., Rapoff, M. A., Mani, M. M., & Thompson, R. (1998). Hope and social support in the psychological adjustment of children who have survived burn injuries and their matched controls. *Children's Health Care, 27,* 15–30.

Boggs, S. R., & Durning, P. (1998). The pediatric oncology quality of life scale: Development and validation of a disease-specific quality of life measure. In D. Drotar (Ed.), *Measuring health-related quality of life in children and adolescents* (pp. 187–202). Mahwah, NJ: Erlbaum.

Brown, K. J., & Roberts, M. C. (2000). *An evaluation of the Alvin Ailey Dance Camp, Kansas City Missouri.* Unpublished manuscript, University of Kansas, Lawrence, KS.

Carvajal, S. C., Clair, S. D., Nash, S. G., & Evans, R. I. (1998). Relating optimism, hope, and self-esteem to social influences in deterring substance use in adolescence. *Journal of Social and Clinical Psychology, 17,* 443–465.

Cohen, L. H., & Park, C. (1992). Life stress in children and adolescents: An overview of conceptual and methodological issues. In A. M. La Greca, L. J. Siegel, J. L. Wallander, & C. E. Walker (Eds.), *Stress and coping in child health* (pp. 25–43). New York: Guilford.

Diabetes Control and Complications Trial (DCCT) Research Group. (1988). Reliability and validity of a diabetes quality of life measure for the DCCT. *Diabetes Care, 11,* 725–732.

Donnelly, M. (1997). Changing schools for changing families. *Family Futures, 1,* 12–17.

Drotar, D. (1998). (Ed.). *Measuring health-related quality of life in children and adolescents.* Mahwah, NJ: Erlbaum.

Drotar, D., Levi, R., Palermo, T. M., Riekert, K. A., Robinson, J. R., & Walders, N. (1998). Clinical applications of health-related quality of life assessment for children and adolescents. In D. Drotar (Ed.), *Measuring health-related quality of life in children and adolescents* (pp. 329–339). Mahwah, NJ: Erlbaum.

Dryfoos, J. G. (1998). *Safe passages: Making it through adolescence in a risky society.* Oxford, England: Oxford University Press.

Feeny, D., Juniper, E., Ferry, P. J., Griffith, L. E., & Guyatt, G. H. (1998). Why not just ask the kids? Health-related quality of life in children with asthma. In D. Drotar (Ed.), *Measuring health-related quality of life in children and adolescents* (pp. 171–185). Mahwah, NJ: Erlbaum.

Gillham, J. E., Reivich, K. J., Jaycox, L. H., & Seligman, M. E. P. (1995). Prevention of depressive symptoms in school children: Two-year follow-up. *Psychological Science, 6,* 343–351.

Guyatt, G. H., Juniper, E. F., Griffith, L. E., Feeney, D. H., & Ferry, P. J. (1997). Children and adult perceptions of childhood asthma. *Pediatrics, 99,* 165–168.

Hinton-Nelson, M. D., Roberts, M. C., & Snyder, C. R. (1996). Early adolescents exposed to violence: Hope and vulnerability to victimization. *American Journal of Orthopsychiatry, 66,* 346–353.

Ingersoll, G. M., & Marrero, D. G. (1991). A modified quality of life measure for youths: Psychometric properties. *Diabetes Education, 17,* 114–118.

Institute for the Future. (2000). *Health and health care 2010: The forecast, the challenge.* San Francisco: Jossey-Bass.

Jaycox, L. H., Reivich, K. J., Gillham, J., & Seligman, M. E. P. (1994). Prevention of depressive symptoms in school children. *Behaviour Research and Therapy, 32,* 801–816.

Johnson, B. H., Jeppson, E. S., & Redburn, L. (1992). *Caring for children and families: Guidelines for hospitals.* Bethesda, MD: Association for the Care of Children's Health.

Johnson, N. G., & Roberts, M. C. (1999). Passage on the wild river of adolescence: Arriving safely. In N. G. Johnson, M. C. Roberts, & J. Worell (Eds.), *Beyond appearances: A new look at adolescent girls* (pp. 3–18). Washington, DC: American Psychological Association.

Johnson, N. G., Roberts, M. C., & Worell, J. (Eds.). (1999). *Beyond appearances: A new look at adolescent girls.* Washington, DC: American Psychological Association.

Kaplan, R. M., Sallis, J. F., Jr., & Patterson, T. L. (1993). *Health and human behavior.* New York: McGraw-Hill.

Landgraf, J. M., Abetz, L., & Ware, J. (1996). *The Child Health Questionnaire (CHQ): A user's manual.* Boston: Health Institute, New England Medical Center.

Lewis, H. A., & Kliewer, W. (1996). Hope, coping, and adjustment among children with sickle cell disease: Tests of mediator and moderator models. *Journal of Pediatric Psychology, 21,* 25–41.

Lopez, S. J. (2000). *Positive psychology in the schools: Identifying and strengthening our hidden resources.* Unpublished manuscript, University of Kansas, Lawrence, KS.

Maddux, J. E., Roberts, M. C., Sledden, E. A., & Wright, L. (1986). Developmental issues in child health psychology. *American Psychologist, 41,* 25–34.

McDermott, D., & Hastings, S. (2000). Children: Raising future hopes. In C. R. Snyder (Ed.), *Handbook of hope: Theory, measures, and applications* (pp. 185–199). San Diego, CA: Academic Press.

McDermott, D., Hastings, S., Gariglietti, K. P., Gingerich, K., Callahan, B., & Diamond, K. (1996, April). *Fostering hope in the classroom.*

Paper presented at the meeting of the Kansas Counseling Association, Salina.

McDermott, D., & Snyder, C. R. (2000). *The great big book of hope.* Oakland, CA: New Harbinger Publications.

McNeal, R. (1998). Pre- and post-treatment hope in children and adolescents in residential treatment: A further analysis of the effects of the Teaching Family Model. *Dissertation Abstracts International: Section B: The Sciences and Engineering, 59,* 2425.

Mishoe, S. C., Baker, R. R., Poole, S., Harrell, L. M., Arant, C. B., & Rupp, N. T. (1998). Development of an instrument to assess stress levels and quality of life in children with asthma. *Journal of Asthma, 35,* 553–563.

Mulhern, R. K., Faircough, D. L., Friedman, A. G., & Leigh, L. D. (1990). Play performance scale as an index of quality of life of children with cancer. *Psychological Assessment, 2,* 149–155.

Noll, R. B., & Kazak, A. (1997). Psychosocial care. In A. R. Ablin (Ed.), *Supportive care of children with cancer: Current therapy and guidelines from the Children's Cancer Group* (2nd ed., pp. 263–273). Baltimore: Johns Hopkins University Press.

Pantell, R. H., & Lewis, C. C. (1987). Measuring the impact of medical care on children. *Journal of Chronic Diseases, 40,* 99S–108S.

Peterson, C. (2000). The future of optimism. *American Psychologist, 55,* 44–55.

Peterson, L., & Roberts, M. C. (1986). Community intervention and prevention. In H. C. Quay & J. S. Werry (Eds.), *Psychopathological disorders of childhood* (3rd ed., pp. 620–660). New York: Wiley.

Pruitt, S. D., Seid, M., Varni, J. W., & Setoguchi, Y. (1999). Toddlers with limb deficiency: Conceptual basis and initial application of a functional status outcome measure. *Archives of Physical Medicine and Rehabilitation, 80,* 819–824.

Puskar, K. R., Sereika, S. M., Lamb, J., Tusaie-Mumford, K., & McGuiness, T. (1999). Optimism and its relationship to depression, coping, anger, and life events in rural adolescents. *Issues in Mental Health Nursing, 20,* 115–130.

Quittner, A. L. (1992). Re-examining research on stress and social support: The importance of contextual factors. In A. M. La Greca, L. J. Siegel, J. L. Wallander, & C. E. Walker (Eds.), *Stress and coping in child health* (pp. 85–115). New York: Guilford.

Roberts, M. C. (1991). Overview to prevention research: Where's the cat? Where's the cradle? In J. H. Johnson & S. B. Johnson (Eds.), *Advances in child health psychology* (pp. 95–107). Gainesville: University of Florida Press.

Roberts, M. C., & Peterson, L. (1984). Prevention models: Theoretical and practical implications. In M. C. Roberts & L. Peterson (Eds.), *Prevention of problems in childhood: Psychological research and applications* (pp. 1–39). New York: Wiley-Interscience.

Scheier, M. F., & Carver, C. S. (1985). Optimism, coping, and health: Assessment and implications of generalized outcome expectancies. *Health Psychology, 4,* 219–247.

Scheier, M. F., & Carver, C. S. (1993). On the power of positive thinking: The benefits of being optimistic. *Current Directions in Psychological Science, 2,* 26–30.

Schorr, L. B. (1997). *Common purpose: Strengthening families and neighborhoods to rebuild America.* New York: Anchor Books/Doubleday.

Schulman, P., Keith, D., & Seligman, M. E. P. (1993). Is optimism heritable? A study of twins. *Behaviour Research and Therapy, 31,* 569–574.

Seligman, M. E. P. (1991). *Learned optimism.* New York: Knopf.

Seligman, M. E. P., Reivich, K., Jaycox, L., & Gillham, J. (1995). *The optimistic child.* Boston: Houghton Mifflin.

Shure, M. B. (1996). I can problem-solve: An interpersonal cognitive problem solving program for children. In M. C. Roberts (Ed.), *Model programs in child and family mental health* (pp. 47–74). Mahwah, NJ: Erlbaum.

Siegel, L. J. (1992). Overview. In A. M. La Greca, L. J. Siegel, J. L. Wallander, & C. E. Walker (Eds.), *Stress and coping in child health* (pp. 3–6). New York: Guilford.

Snyder, C. R. (1994). *The psychology of hope: You can get there from here.* New York: Free Press.

Snyder, C. R., Feldman, D. B., Taylor, J. D., Schroeder, L. L., & Adams, V. (2000). The roles of hopeful thinking in preventing problems and promoting strategies. *Applied and Preventive Psychology, 15,* 262–295.

Snyder, C. R., Harris, C., Anderson, J. R., Holleran, S. A., Irving, L. M., Sigmon, S. T., Yoshinobu, L., Gibb, J., Langelle, C., & Harney, P. (1991). The will and the ways: The development and validation of an individual-differences measure of hope. *Journal of Personality and Social Psychology, 60,* 570–585.

Snyder, C. R., Hoza, B., Pelham, W. E., Rapoff, M., Ware, L., Danovsky, M., Highberger, L., Rubinstein, H., & Stahl, K. J. (1997). The development and validation of the Children's Hope Scale. *Journal of Pediatric Psychology, 22,* 399–421.

Snyder, C. R., McDermott, D., Cook, W., & Rapoff, M. A. (1997). *Hope for the journey: Helping children through good times and bad.* Boulder, CO: Westview.

Spieth, L. E., & Harris, C. V. (1996). Assessment
of quality-of-life outcomes in children and adolescents: An integrative review. *Journal of Pediatric Psychology, 21,* 175–193.

Starfield, B., Riley, A. W., Green, B. F., Ensminger,
M. E., Ryan, S. A., Kelleher, K., Kimharris, S.,
Johnston, D., & Vogel, K. (1995). The Adolescent Child Health and Illness Profile: A popu-
lation-based measure of health. *Medical Care,
33,* 553–566.

Stein, R. E., & Jessop, D. J. (1990). Functional
Status II(R): A measure of child health status.
Medical Care, 28, 1041–1055.

Townsend, M., Feeny, D., Guyatt, G., Furlong, W.,
Seip, A., & Dolovich, J. (1991). An evaluation of
the burden of illness for pediatric asthma patients and their parents. *Annals of Allergy, 67,*
403–408.

Varni, J. W. (1983). *Clinical behavioral pediatrics:*
An interdisciplinary biobehavioral approach.
New York: Pergamon.

Varni, J. W., Katz, E. R., Seid, M., Quiggins,
D. J. L., Friedman-Bender, A., & Castro, C. M.
(1998). The pediatric cancer quality of life inventory (PCQL): I. Instrument development,
descriptive statistics, and cross-informant variance. *Journal of Behavioral Medicine, 21,* 179–
204.

Varni, J. W., Seid, M., & Rode, C. A. (1999). The
PedsQL(tm): Measurement model for the pediatric quality of life inventory. *Medical Care, 37,*
126–139.

Vogels, T., Verrips, G. H. W., Verloove-Vanhorick,
S. P., Fekkes, M., Kamphuis, R. P., Koopman,
H. M., Theunissen, N. C. M., & Wit, J. M.
(1998). Measuring health-related quality of life
in children: The development of the TACQOL
parent form. *Quality of Life Research, 7,* 457–
465.

Walker, S. R., & Rosser, R. (1988). *Quality of life:
Assessment and application.* Lancaster, England:
MTP Press.

49

Aging Well

Outlook for the 21st Century

Gail M. Williamson

Getting old is something most people dread because they believe it portends the loss of functional capacities and the enjoyable aspects of life. But, as my grandfather often said in the last years of his life, "Being old is better than the only available alternative." Thus, if we are fortunate, we will age. Our best option, then, is to remain as vital as we can for as long as possible. In the last two decades, there has been a movement toward defining and fostering "successful aging" that, to judge by recent professional and popular press publications, has literally exploded.

It is a credit to our society that we are more concerned about old people than ever before. On the other hand, there never have been as many old people about whom to be concerned. An even greater worry is that the number of older Americans will increase dramatically in the next 10 years and beyond, as will their percentage of the population. Indeed, this demographic shift is the most salient explanation for the mushrooming interest in gerontological science.

History of Aging and Outlook for the Future

The population is "graying."[1] Put simply, people are living longer. Life expectancy in 1900 was 47 years; today, it is closer to 76 years. Over two thirds of people now live to at least age 65 (a threefold increase from 1900). And the fastest growing segment of the population is in the over age 85 category—4% in 1900 to over 10% today (e.g., Rowe & Kahn, 1998; U.S. Department of Health and Human Services [DHHS], 1992; Volz, 2000). Moreover, the first wave of the 76 million baby boomers born between 1946 and 1964 will approach traditional retirement age in 2010 (Binstock, 1999). In 30 years, there will be twice as many people 65 years of age and older, and these oldsters will constitute at least 20% of the total population (e.g., Hobbs, 1996). By 2050, the number of centenarians (those over age 100) in the United States may be as high as 4.2 million (Volz, 2000).

Historically, attitudes about aging have been fraught with mythical thinking, a shortsightedness we have yet to overcome. To give a few examples, old people are viewed as sick, cognitively inept, isolated, a financial drain on society, and depressed by their circumstances (e.g., Center for the Advancement of Health [CAH], 1998; Palmore, 1990; Rowe & Kahn, 1998). Traditional attitudes and the projected increase in elderly people within the next few years have seduced scholars, commentators, and policy makers into the doomsday philosophy that our society is about to be overwhelmed by people who are disabled, requiring constant care, and not making worthwhile contributions. With fewer children per capita than previous generations, a major concern is that when the baby boomers age into disability, there will be fewer adult children available to provide care, creating a demand for formal care that may severely (if not impossibly) tax the rest of societal resources.

Are we, in fact, on the brink of geriatric Armageddon? As with any substantial demographic shift, there are problems to be addressed. The central purpose of this chapter, however, is to summarize evidence that indicates things are not as grim as they might appear, and, indeed, that there are offsetting parallel, positive arguments to these catastrophic predictions. Many solutions revolve around actions that should be taken and, in some cases, already are being taken at governmental and societal levels. But I also argue that aging individuals and their immediate social networks can solve many problems without resorting to public assistance. The solution lies in changing their behaviors so that they can continue to engage in valued normal activities with each advancing year. First, however, we need to take a realistic look at today's elders and what future generations can expect as they age.

Are Old People Sick People?

An important truth, albeit persistently denied by much of the population, is that most adults over age 65 are remarkably healthy. Rates of disability, even among the very old (i.e., those over age 95), are steadily declining. Only 5.2% of older adults live in nursing homes and similar facilities, a drop of 1.1% since 1982 (CAH, 1998). In 1994, 73% of adults 78 to 84 years of age reported *no* disabling conditions, and among the "oldest old" (i.e., those over age 85), fully

40% had no functional disabilities (Manton, Stallard, & Corder, 1995).

Along with increasingly widespread public knowledge and acceptance of the behavioral aspects of chronic illness, advances in medical technology forecast an even rosier old age for baby boomers and subsequent generations (DHHS, 1992). Although no solution is in sight for the fact that, with age, physiological systems slow down and become less efficient (Birren & Birren, 1990), older adults are quite skilled in making gradual lifestyle changes to accommodate diminishing physical abilities (Williamson & Dooley, 2001). Through medical and psychological research, we also know that "nature is remarkably forgiving" (CAH, 1998). In other words, it is never too late to begin a healthful lifestyle. For example, regardless of age, duration of smoking, and magnitude of tobacco consumption, after 5 years of abstinence, ex-smokers have about the same risk for heart disease as those who never smoked. The same is true for a variety of other risk factors, including obesity and a sedentary lifestyle.

Are Old People Cognitively Deficient?

As with physiological functions, in the "normal" course of events, cognitive abilities slow down with increasing age (Horn & Hofer, 1992; Schaie, 1996). The "use it or lose it" adage about sexual functioning, however, applies to learning and memory abilities as well. Short of organic disorders (e.g., Alzheimer's disease) that increase with age (e.g., Gatz & Smyer, 1992), older adults in cognitively challenging environments show minimal, if any, declines in thinking and learning abilities. Similar to any other age group, when elderly people are less mentally challenged, their cognitive performance declines (e.g., CAH, 1998; Lawton & Nahemow, 1973). Although older adults may routinely encounter such challenges less frequently than the college students to whom they typically are compared (Williamson & Dooley, 2001), under the right conditions, they can learn new things—and learn them quite well (e.g., Schaie, 1996; also see Volz, 2000, for a review). Moreover, whether people *believe* they can learn and remember is crucial (Cavanaugh, 1996). The lesson here is that aging adults bear some responsibility for making sure that they engage in cognitively challenging activities (West, Crook, & Barron, 1992).

What about future generations? Being able to use current and emerging technologies should improve cognitive capacities of seniors, but those who make the effort to gain technological expertise will benefit most from these advances. The first step may involve no more than learning to use an ATM machine, but that effort can promote subsequent skills (Rogers, Fisk, Mead, Walker, & Cabrera, 1996). In addition, "neurobic exercises" both preserve and improve brain and memory functions (Katz, Rubin, & Suter, 1999). Routine activities that require little cognitive effort can exacerbate cognitive decline. Accordingly, Katz and colleagues recommend seeking offbeat and, simultaneously, fun experiences—not because they are difficult but because they are different.

Are Old People Isolated and Lonely?

Rowe and Kahn (1998) assert that "the common view of old age as a prolonged period of demanding support from an ever-diminishing number of overworked providers is wrong" (pp. 159–160). Citing evidence from the Mac-Arthur Foundation Study of Aging in America, these researchers argue that social networks remain remarkably stable in size throughout the life span, with the number of close relationships among noninstitutionalized older adults equaling those of younger people. Some elders are isolated and lonely, but people fail to realize that the same is true for other age groups as well. Network losses do occur over the life span through death, relocation, and retirement, but even among very old people, new social relationships are formed to replace lost ones.

What does the future bode for the baby boomers? Will they, with fewer offspring, be lonelier and more isolated than previous generations? Probably not. They should be just as capable of dealing with changes in network size as are today's elders. In addition, they will have the advantages afforded by technology and cyberspace. With their computer competencies, the majority of aging baby boomers will use e-mail to stay in touch with family members and friends. Furthermore, we already have evidence that they are more likely than their younger counterparts to access Internet information and support from a wide spectrum of people who share their needs and concerns (Kiyak & Hooyman, 1999).

Do Old People Drain Society's Resources?

According to the CAH report (1998), the common belief that old people drain society's resources is based on the assumption that "everybody who works for pay is pulling his or her weight, and those who do not are a burden" (p. 5). Contrary to past attitudes, the benefits elders receive are being scrutinized as potentially wasted and taking away from "more needy" groups and the overall economic well-being (Hendricks, Hatch, & Cutler, 1999). How accurate is the "emerging social construction of older Americans as 'greedy geezers' who are advantaged relative to younger age groups and who do not deserve such a large slice of the government pie" (Hendricks et al., 1999, p. 15; also see Hewitt, 1997; Steckenrider & Parrott, 1998)?

Evidence does not support such sweeping interpretations. First, lumping older adults into a homogeneous group is inappropriate. They vary as widely as their younger counterparts in health, financial security, and willingness to accept public support. Second, senior citizen benefits depend on social status and past work experience, favoring high-income earners with a continuous work history, that is, white middle-class men (Hendricks et al., 1999). The stereotype of these "advantaged" oldsters is used to justify reforms aimed at decreasing old-age benefits for all elders. Let us look at the actual scenario. The standard for living at or below the poverty level changes between age 64 and age 65; people 64 and younger qualify for poverty benefits with less income than do those 65 and older. Today, 12% of people over age 65 live in governmentally defined poverty (U.S. Senate Special Committee on Aging, 1997). Without Social Security, this percentage would increase to 50% or more (Moon & Mulvey, 1996). Thus, cuts in Social Security would hit hardest those who need it most.

Moreover, older adults do not drain societal resources. They may not engage in work for pay, but "paid" work tends to be overvalued in our society (e.g., CAH, 1998). By contrast, unpaid (e.g., in the home, volunteer efforts) and underpaid (e.g., working in fast-food restaurants and bagging groceries) activities contribute a great deal to the social enterprise. In fact, when given the opportunity, large numbers of seniors are eager to do volunteer work and take on low-paying part-time jobs.

The baby boomers and subsequent generations should be more advantaged in the work domain relative to the current cohort of oldsters. Attitudes about older workers are changing. More important, because of post–baby boom declines in birth rates, as the baby boomers age, the number of employable adults will decrease relative to the number of new jobs (DHHS, 1992; Kiyak & Hooyman, 1999). Following the law of supply and demand, older workers will be more valued and sought-after, and those who do not feel ready to retire are less likely to be compelled to do so. Many policy makers advocate raising the normal retirement age to 70. The reasoning is that, in terms of health and life expectancy, age 70 today is roughly the equivalent of age 65 in the 1930s when Social Security was established (e.g., Chen, 1994). Indeed, changing health status and attitudes have led to age 65 no longer being considered "old" (Kiyak & Hooyman, 1999). Although most individuals who have adequate (or better) financial resources will retire at the usual time or follow the trend toward early retirement (e.g., Quinn & Burkhauser, 1990), physically healthy elders will be able to choose to continue working either because they want to or because they feel the need to supplement their retirement benefits.

But the critical prerequisite for continuing to live as one pleases is good health. What about older adults who both are physically unable to continue working for pay and do not have the financial resources to live in a satisfactory fashion without working—that is, those whose primary, perhaps only, source of income is Social Security? Recognizing the needs of these people in an ever-aging population has fostered numerous governmental initiatives (U.S. Department of Housing and Urban Development, 1999; also see Hendricks et al., 1999).

The point to be made here revolves around personal choice. People who feel in control, who can make choices about the important aspects of their lives, are both physically healthier and less depressed than those who perceive that they lack personal control (e.g., Peterson, Seligman, & Vaillant, 1988; Taylor, 1983; Taylor & Brown, 1988).

Are Old People Depressed?

Despite Rowe and Kahn's (1998) allegation that "depression is . . . terribly prevalent in older people" (p. 106), the evidence is to the contrary. In fact, clinically diagnosable depression is *less* prevalent in older than younger adults (e.g., Rybash, Roodin, & Hoyer, 1995; Schulz & Ewen, 1993). Indeed, elders often cope more effectively with stressful life events than do younger adults (McCrae, 1989). Over the life course, through life experiences and successes in coping with a variety of stressors, the typical adult builds adaptive attitudes and beliefs that generalize to coping with new stressors (see Williamson & Dooley, 2001). Regardless of age, people are motivated to exercise personal control over the important aspects of their lives (Schulz & Heckhausen, 1996). Solving the problems that go along with getting older (e.g., death of a spouse, declines in health status), however, simply may not be possible. Consequently, those who adapt well will shift their focus from actively trying to change the situation to managing stress-related emotional reactions by, for example, accepting the situation and continuing to function as normally as possible.

Personal control often is limited by social and cultural expectations about appropriate roles for specific segments of the population. Today's trend toward less stigmatization of older adults should offer seniors more choices. Other societal changes will add impetus to this movement. For example, economic prosperity has created financial security for many current and future older Americans, enabling them to exercise control over how they spend their retirement years. The construct of personal control constitutes an important part of the foundation underlying the model described in the next sections.

The Activity Restriction Model of Depressed Affect

Activity restriction is the inability to continue normal activities (e.g., self-care, care of others, doing household chores, going shopping, visiting friends, working on hobbies, and maintaining friendships) that often follows stressful life events such as debilitating illness (e.g., Williamson & Schulz, 1992). According to the Activity Restriction Model of Depressed Affect, major life stressors lead to poorer mental health outcomes *because* they disrupt normal activities (e.g., Williamson, 1998). In other words, activity restriction mediates the association between stress and mental health (Walters & Williamson, 1999; Williamson, 2000; Williamson & Dooley, 2001; Williamson & Schulz, 1992, 1995; Williamson, Schulz, Bridges, & Behan, 1994; Williamson & Shaffer, 2000; Williamson, Shaffer, & Schulz, 1998; Williamson, Shaffer, and the Family Relationships in Late Life Project, 2000).

Individual Differences in Activity Restriction

Stressful life circumstances are not the only contributors to activity restriction. Rather, individual differences are important factors as well. Age is one of the ways that individuals differ. For example, older adults tolerate similar levels of pain better than do younger adults (Cassileth et al., 1984; Foley, 1985), a phenomenon most commonly attributed to the increased exposure to pain and disabling conditions that older people experience. Indeed, my colleagues and I have found that experience, rather than chronological age, matters more in terms of predicting those who will restrict their activities in the wake of stressful events (Walters & Williamson, 1999; Williamson & Schulz, 1995; Williamson et al., 1998). In other words, old age does *not* necessarily foster activity restriction or depression.

Another potentially important contributor to coping with stress is financial resources. Inadequate income interferes with normal activities (Merluzzi & Martinez Sanchez, 1997). Moreover, if financial resources are merely *perceived* as being less than adequate, activities are more restricted (see Williamson, 1998, for a review). Thus, when life becomes stressful, an understandable first line of defense may be to cut back on normal activities that involve spending money, for example, shopping, recreation, and hobbies (Williamson & Dooley, 2001).

Aside from demographic factors, aspects of the individual's personality also contribute to activity restriction. Some people cope in maladaptive ways across all situations throughout their lives. In contrast, there are those who are dispositionally inclined to face the situation, rationally evaluate possible solutions, seek help and information as appropriate, and, if all else fails, accept that the problem has occurred, deal with their emotional reactions (perhaps with help from others), and make every effort to resume life as usual.

As an example of how personality can affect adjustment, consider public self-consciousness as it relates to activity restriction and depression when an illness condition results in bodily disfigurement. Public self-consciousness is the stable tendency to be highly concerned about aspects of the self that are evident to others and from which others form impressions (Scheier & Carver, 1985). People high in this trait worry a great deal about their personal appearance and actively avoid disapproval and rejection from others. As would be expected, limb amputation and breast cancer patients who are high in public self-consciousness restrict their public activities (e.g., shopping, visiting friends) and experience more depression than their counterparts who are low in public self-consciousness (Williamson, 1995, 2000). Moreover, highly self-conscious individuals also restrict nonpublic activities such as household chores (Williamson, 1995). Thus, it appears that giving up activities conducted in the presence of others may generalize to acts conducted in private, thereby fostering an unnecessary "spread" of the disability. Reminiscent of findings in the self-presentation literature on anticipatory excuse-making (Snyder, Higgins, & Stucky, 1983), when confronting stressful life events, some people may forgo their usual activities because they have a justification for doing so (e.g., Parmelee, Katz, & Lawton, 1991). But this is not an adaptive strategy (Snyder & Higgins, 1988; Williamson & Dooley, 2001). Even after controlling for a wide variety of other factors, activity restriction remains the most proximal predictor of depression (e.g., Williamson, 1998).

Another important individual difference is social support resources. People with stronger social support networks cope better with all types of stressful life events (Mutran, Reitzes, Mossey, & Fernandez, 1995; Oxman & Hull, 1997), and routine activities are facilitated by social support (Williamson et al., 1994). Social support, however, appears to be a function of personality variables that, in turn, influence activity restriction (e.g., Williamson & Dooley, 2001). Those with more socially desirable or more socially proactive characteristics also have more supportive social ties and less activity restriction. Comparable benefits are seen in people who merely *perceive* that social support is available if it is needed, and the benefits of perceiving that one has supportive others remain after controlling for demographics (e.g., age, financial resources), illness severity, and personality variables such as public self-consciousness (Williamson, 2000).

Summary of Current Research Findings

The forecast for our aging population is that, more than ever before, older adults will be physically, cognitively, psychologically, and socially healthy. Still, substantial numbers of the elderly population will be disabled, socially isolated, and depressed. From accumulating evidence, it is now clear that people consistently become depressed in the wake of stressful life events largely because those events disrupt their ability to go about life as usual (see Williamson, 1998, 2000, for reviews), and that illness severity, younger age (or lack of experience), inadequate income, less social support, and higher public self-consciousness contribute to this effect (e.g., Walters & Williamson, 1999; Williamson, 1998, 2000; Williamson & Schulz, 1992, 1995; Williamson et al., 1998).

In their acclaimed book, *Successful Aging*, Rowe and Kahn (1998) propose that there are three components of successful aging: (a) avoiding disease, (b) engagement with life, and (c) maintaining high cognitive and physical function. They further propose that each of these factors is "to some extent independent of the others" (p. 38). My colleagues and I do not disagree with this categorization of contributors to successful aging. However, we argue that these factors are less inclusive and independent than Rowe and Kahn suggest. Not only do numerous other factors influence how well one ages, but also Rowe and Kahn's three components can be subsumed by the construct of maintaining a lifestyle that involves normal, valued, and beneficial activities.

Our first counterargument is that avoiding disease is largely a function of routine activities. Temperance in detrimental behaviors (e.g., smoking, drinking alcohol, eating a high-fat diet) is related to better physical health, less disability, and greater longevity (e.g., Cohen, Tyrrell, Russell, Jarvis, & Smith, 1993; McGinnis & Foege, 1993). Second, "engagement with life" (Rowe & Kahn, 1998) is virtually synonymous with continuing valued personal activities. People who feel engaged with life are those who engage in personally meaningful activities, but what qualifies as meaningful will vary according to each person's history. In the Activity Restriction Model, it is postulated that continuing to

be involved in personally relevant activities (whether intellectual, physical, or social) is what matters most.

Finally, Rowe and Kahn (1998) advocate maintaining high cognitive and physical functioning as the third key to aging successfully. When a person is confronted with seemingly overwhelming life events, the telling factor may well be the extent to which at least a semblance of normal activities can continue. What does this mean when, for example, disability precludes playing several sets of tennis every day? If this activity was driven by love of the sport, then the aging tennis addict can still participate by watching matches or, even better, by coaching others in the finer aspects of playing the game.

Interventions to Increase Activity and Decrease Depression

In the Activity Restriction Model, coping with stress is posited to be a complex, multifaceted process that is influenced by numerous factors. Stressors vary in nature across the life span, with those faced by older adults being at least as threatening as those confronted by young adults. Because physical and psychological stress differ (e.g., in terms of controllability) with increasing age, however, coping successfully may require replacing previously adaptive strategies with ones better suited to the demands of advancing age. Therefore, interventions may require convincing elders to shift from problem-focused to emotion-focused coping mechanisms (see Stanton, Parsa, & Austenfeld, this volume).

By acknowledging that depressed affect is a function of restricted normal activities, we can design interventions that reduce both activity restriction and depression. Simply encouraging older adults to engage in more of their normal activities, however, probably is not the best strategy. Rather, efforts to increase activity might take three (and probably several more) forms. First, therapists should carefully consider the (likely multiple) reasons that activities have become restricted and design their interventions accordingly. Second, they should target the individuals most at risk for poor adaptation. Third, identifying manageable activities and available resources means that programs can be implemented to engage aging adults in pastimes that not only meet their specific interests and needs but also fit their functional capacities.

As with younger adults, older adults' financial resources vary widely, but higher costs for insurance and health care in late life can sap the resources of even the most financially prepared seniors. Still, there are substantial individual differences in how financial circumstances impact activity restriction (Williamson, 1998). Those with low incomes do not necessarily see their financial resources as inadequate; likewise, people with higher incomes do not uniformly report that their financial resources are adequate (Williamson & Shaffer, 2000). Thus, perceptions of income adequacy appear to matter more than actual dollar amounts. Either way, older adults can be directed toward the community-based and inexpensive social and recreational resources that are available to them.

In addition to evaluating demographic characteristics such as age and financial resources, it is important to assess relevant personality dimensions. Although most personality traits are quite stable across the life span (Costa & McCrae, 1993; McCrae & Costa, 1986) and, consequently, should be difficult to change, identifying the traits that predispose people to restrict their normal activities can help determine those who are at risk for poor adaptation. For example, when an illness involves body disfigurement (e.g., limb amputation or breast cancer surgery), patients high in public self-consciousness can be targeted for interventions to improve self-esteem and sense of efficacy such as hope enhancement (see Snyder, Rand, & Sigmon, this volume), training in adaptive coping skills, and support groups.

Other personality traits also warrant consideration. For instance, people low in optimism do not cope effectively or adjust well to stress (Carver et al., 1993) and may be vulnerable to activity restriction. High levels of neuroticism are related to a maladaptive coping style (McCrae & Costa, 1986) that may include forgoing pleasurable activities. When faced with disruptive life events, individuals who are less agentically oriented and do not have a strong sense of mastery will have more difficulty finding ways to avoid restricting their rewarding activities (e.g., Femia, Zarit, & Johansson, 1997; Herzog, Franks, Markus, & Holmberg, 1998). In addition, those who are low in the dispositional predilection to hope for positive outcomes are less likely to conceptualize ways to continue (or replace) valued activities or to persist in their efforts to do so, particularly

when pathways to achieving these goals are blocked (e.g., Snyder, 1998). Although research in this area is in its infancy, personality factors should not be ignored—particularly when the goal is to identify those who are at risk for restricting their usual activities, are adapting poorly to stress, and are in need of early intervention.

Social support, like personality traits and experience with illness, interacts with health-related variables to influence normal activities. With stronger social support networks, activity restriction is less likely (Williamson et al., 1994). For example, disabled elders will attend church and visit friends more often if other people help with walking, transportation, and words of encouragement. Maintaining usual activities in the face of stress, in turn, reduces the possibility of negative emotional responses and further decrements in health and functioning. Thus, identifying community-residing older adults with deficits in social support is a good starting point for intervention. Before intervening, however, we need to specify which aspects of social support are absent or most distressing and target treatment accordingly (Oxman & Hull, 1997). Some older people may be depressed simply because they do not have enough social interaction. Others may have concrete needs for assistance that are not being met (e.g., getting out of bed or grocery shopping). Still others may be exposed to exploitative or abusive social contacts (Cohen & McKay, 1983; Suls, 1982; Williamson et al., 2000; Wortman, 1984).

Directions for Future Research

The Activity Restriction Model of Depressed Affect, like other models of stress and coping (e.g., Lazarus & Folkman, 1984), implies that the causal path is unidirectional—that is, that stress causes activity restriction, which, in turn, causes negative affect. Without doubt, this is an inadequate representation. Consider pain and depression as an example. According to unidirectional models, depression is an outcome of an inability to adjust to chronic pain. Yet substantial research suggests that depression fosters higher levels of reported pain (e.g., Lefebvre, 1981; Mathew, Weinman, & Mirabi, 1981; Parmelee et al., 1991). Similarly, the Activity Restriction Model of Depressed Affect can be turned on its head such that, as clinicians have long known, being depressed causes people to forgo many of their previously enjoyed activities. In fact, one of the better behavioral treatments for depression is to motivate patients to become more socially and physically active (e.g., Herzog et al., 1998). In a reciprocal fashion, for both physiological and psychological reasons, inactivity also increases levels of experienced pain (e.g., Williamson & Dooley, 2001).

Conducting controlled experimental studies can clarify previous results by demonstrating that strategies designed to increase activity level will, in fact, improve well-being. In addition, identifying differences between people who will tolerate discomfort in order to continue engaging in meaningful activities and those who will not voluntarily make such efforts under similar levels of discomfort will bring us closer to successful intervention programs.

Further complicating already complex associations, psychosocial predictors of activity restriction (e.g., poor social support, inadequate income) are sources of stress in their own right, but they also can be conceptualized as both coping mechanisms and outcomes. For instance, access to and perceptions of available support resources facilitate coping in multiple ways (e.g., Billings & Moos, 1984; Cohen & Wills, 1985). Declines in social support, however, can result from overtaxing support resources, particularly if stress is ongoing. Most people will rally round when a stressful event first occurs, but they tend to fade away as the situation becomes chronic—especially if the individual is perceived as doing little to either solve or adapt to the problem (e.g., see Williams, 1993). All illnesses tend to be viewed as acute rather than chronic, and the (often unrealistic) expectation is for a patient to get well (Arluke, 1988; Parsons, 1951, 1978). For older adults with chronic health conditions, declines in social support may be the result of this cognitive bias.

By considering several demographic, personality, psychosocial, and health-related factors, we can begin to explain why stress and activity restriction increase the possibility of experiencing negative emotions. It should be emphasized, however, that the list of variables studied thus far is by no means exhaustive. Other personal and social factors also bear investigation, and doing so will probably, at least initially, contribute more confusion than definitive answers. Nevertheless, in the Activity Restriction Model, we do have a foundation for intervention and further research.

Conclusions

Contrary to common belief, growing old in the 21st century is not likely to be an unpleasant experience for most people, nor are older adults likely to overwhelm societal resources with their needs. Clearly, physical, mental, social, and financial well-being are intertwined, and aging successfully depends, to a large extent, on effectively coping with age-related life events.

As specified in the Activity Restriction Model of Depressed Affect, people experience decrements in mental health in direct proportion to how stress interferes with their normal activities. Therefore, those who age well are those who feel in control of at least some of the important aspects of their lives and maintain (perhaps with the help of others) the normal activities that they value most. The association between stress and adjustment is multifaceted and complex. There are no simple solutions to what really happens, nor are there easy answers about ways to intervene. But if people continue at least some of their valued activities, they should be physically and psychologically healthier and depend less on others for assistance. Indeed, maintaining normal activities may be the key to aging well.

Acknowledgments Preparation of the manuscript was supported by the National Institute on Aging (AG15321, G. M. Williamson, principal investigator) and further facilitated by a fellowship from the Institute for Behavioral Research at the University of Georgia.

Note

1. Most of the data reported in this chapter are based on trends in the population of the United States. All industrialized countries are facing similar problems, however, and emerging nations soon may be dealing with even more extreme increases in the proportions of older adults in their populations (e.g., Hendricks, Hatch, & Cutler, 1999). I have chosen to focus on U.S.-based data, but the situation in other countries is either highly analogous to, or even more critical than, the one described in this chapter.

References

Arluke, A. (1988). The sick-role concept. In D. S. Gochman (Ed.), *Health behavior: Emerging re-*

search perspectives (pp. 169–180). New York: Plenum.

Billings, A. G., & Moos, R. H. (1984). Coping, stress, and social resources among adults with unipolar depression. *Journal of Personality and Social Psychology, 46,* 877–891.

Binstock, R. H. (1999). Challenges to United States policies on aging in the new millennium. *Hallym International Journal of Aging, 1,* 3–13.

Birren, J. E., & Birren, B. A. (1990). The concepts, models, and history in the psychology of aging. In J. E. Birren & K. W. Schaie (Eds.), *Handbook of the psychology of aging* (3rd ed., pp. 3–20). San Diego, CA: Academic Press.

Carver, C. S., Pozo, C., Harris, S. D., Noriega, V., Scheier, M. F., Robinson, D. S., Ketcham, A. S., Moffat, F. L., Jr., & Clark, K. C. (1993). How coping mediates the effect of optimism on distress: A study of women with early stage breast cancer. *Journal of Personality and Social Psychology, 65,* 375–390.

Cassileth, B. R., Lusk, E. J., Strouse, T. B., Miller, D. S., Brown, L. L., Cross, P. A., & Tenaglia, A. N. (1984). Psychosocial status in chronic illness: A comparative analysis of six diagnostic groups. *New England Journal of Medicine, 311,* 506–511.

Cavanaugh, J. C. (1996). Memory self-efficacy as a moderator of memory change. In F. Blanchard-Fields & T. M. Hess (Eds.), *Perspectives on cognitive change in adulthood and aging* (pp. 488–507). New York: McGraw-Hill.

*Center for the Advancement of Health. (1998). Getting old: A lot of it is in your head. *Facts of Life: An Issue Briefing for Health Reporters, 3.*

Chen, Y. P. (1994). "Equivalent retirement ages" and their implications for Social Security and Medicare financing. *Gerontologist, 34,* 731–735.

Cohen, S., & McKay, G. (1983). Interpersonal relationships as buffers of the impact of psychosocial stress on health. In A. Baum, S. E. Taylor, & J. E. Singer (Eds.), *Handbook of psychology and health* (Vol. 4, pp. 253–267). Hillsdale, NJ: Erlbaum.

Cohen, S., Tyrrell, D. A. J., Russell, M. A. H., Jarvis, M. J., & Smith, A. P. (1993). Smoking, alcohol consumption, and susceptibility to the common cold. *American Journal of Public Health, 83,* 1277–1283.

Cohen, S., & Wills, T. A. (1985). Stress, social support, and the buffering hypothesis. *Psychological Bulletin, 98,* 310–357.

Costa, P. T., & McCrae, R. R. (1993). Personality, defense, coping, and adaptation in older adulthood. In E. M. Cummings, A. L. Greene, & K. K. Karraker (Eds.), *Life span developmental psychology: Perspectives on stress and coping* (pp. 277–293). Hillsdale, NJ: Erlbaum.

Femia, E. E., Zarit, S. H., & Johansson, B. (1997). Predicting change in activities of daily living: A longitudinal study of the oldest old in Sweden. *Journal of Gerontology, 52,* 294–302.

Foley, K. M. (1985). The treatment of cancer pain. *New England Journal of Medicine, 313,* 84–95.

Gatz, M., & Smyer, M. A. (1992). The mental health system and older adults in the 1990s. *American Psychologist, 47,* 741–751.

Hendricks, J., Hatch, L. R., & Cutler, S. J. (1999). Entitlements, social compacts, and the trend toward retrenchment in U.S. old-age programs. *Hallym International Journal of Aging, 1,* 14–32.

Herzog, A. R., Franks, M. M., Markus, H. R., & Holmberg, D. (1998). Activities and well-being in older age: Effects of self-concept and educational attainment. *Psychology and Aging, 13,* 179–185.

Hewitt, P. S. (1997). Are the elderly benefitting at the expense of younger Americans? Yes. In A. E. Scharlach & L. W. Kaye (Eds.), *Controversial issues in aging* (pp. 70–79). Boston: Allyn and Bacon.

Hobbs, F. B. (1996). *65 + in the United States, U.S. Bureau of the Census, current population reports.* Washington, DC: U.S. Government Printing Office.

Horn, J. L., & Hofer, S. M. (1992). Major abilities and development in the adulthood period. In R. J. Sternberg & C. A. Berg (Eds.), *Intellectual development* (pp. 44–99). New York: Cambridge University Press.

*Katz, L., Rubin, M., & Suter, D. (1999). *Keep your brain alive: 83 neurobic exercises.* New York: Workman.

*Kiyak, H. A., & Hooyman, N. R. (1999). Aging in the twenty-first century. *Hallym International Journal of Aging, 1,* 56–66.

Lawton, M. P., & Nahemow, L. (1973). Ecology and the aging process. In C. Eisdorfer and M. P. Lawton (Eds.), *Psychology of adult development and aging* (pp. 619–674). Washington, DC: American Psychological Association.

Lazarus, R. S., & Folkman, S. (1984). *Stress, appraisal and coping.* New York: Springer.

Lefebvre, M. F. (1981). Cognitive distortion and cognitive errors in depressed psychiatric and low back pain patients. *Journal of Consulting and Clinical Psychology, 49,* 517–525.

Manton, K. G., Stallard, E., & Corder, L. (1995). Changes in morbidity and chronic disability in the U.S. elderly population: Evidence from the 1982, 1984, and 1989 National Long Term Care Surveys. *Journal of Gerontology, 50,* 194–204.

Mathew, R., Weinman, M., & Mirabi, M. (1981). Physical symptoms of depression. *British Journal of Psychiatry, 139,* 293–296.

McCrae, R. R. (1989). Age differences and changes in the use of coping mechanisms. *Journal of Gerontology, 44,* 161–164.

McCrae, R. R., & Costa, P. T., Jr. (1986). Personality, coping, and coping effectiveness in an adult sample. *Journal of Personality, 54,* 385–405.

McGinnis, J. M., & Foege, W. H. (1993). Actual causes of death in the United States. *Journal of the American Medical Association, 270,* 2207–2212.

Merluzzi, T. V., & Martinez Sanchez, M. A. (1997). Assessment of self-efficacy and coping with cancer: Development and validation of the Cancer Behavior Inventory. *Health Psychology, 16,* 163–170.

Moon, M., & Mulvey, J. (1996). *Entitlements and the elderly: Protecting promises, recognizing reality.* Washington, DC: Urban Institute Press.

Mutran, E. J., Reitzes, D. C., Mossey, J., & Fernandez, M. E. (1995). Social support, depression, and recovery of walking ability following hip fracture surgery. *Journal of Gerontology, 50,* 354–361.

Oxman, T. E., & Hull, J. G. (1997). Social support, depression, and activities of daily living in older heart surgery patients. *Journal of Gerontology, 52,* 1–14.

Palmore, E. (1990). *Ageism: Positive and negative.* New York: Springer.

Parmelee, P. A., Katz, I. R., & Lawton, M. P. (1991). The relation of pain to depression among institutionalized aged. *Journal of Gerontology, 46,* 15–21.

Parsons, T. (1951). *The social system.* New York: Free Press.

Parsons, T. (1978). *Action theory and the human condition.* New York: Free Press.

Peterson, C., Seligman, M. E. P., & Vaillant, G. E. (1988). Pessimistic explanatory style is a risk factor for physical illness: A thirty-five-year longitudinal study. *Journal of Personality and Social Psychology, 55,* 23–27.

Quinn, J. F., & Burkhauser, R. V. (1990). Work and retirement. In R. Binstock & L. K. George (Eds.), *Handbook of aging and the social sciences* (3rd ed., pp. 307–323). San Diego, CA: Academic Press.

Rogers, W. A., Fisk, A. D., Mead, S. E., Walker, N., & Cabrera, E. F. (1996). Training older adults to use automatic teller machines. *Human Factors, 38,* 425–433.

*Rowe, J. W., & Kahn, R. L. (1998). *Successful aging.* New York: Pantheon.

Rybash, J. M., Roodin, P. A., & Hoyer, W. J. (1995). *Adult development and aging* (3rd ed.). Madison, WI: Brown and Benchmark.

Schaie, K. W. (1996). Intellectual development in adulthood. In J. E. Birren & K. W. Schaie (Eds.), *Handbook of the psychology of aging* (4th ed., pp. 266–286). San Diego, CA: Academic Press.

Scheier, M. F., & Carver, C. S. (1985). The Self-Consciousness Scale: A revised version for use with general populations. *Journal of Applied Social Psychology, 15,* 687–699.

Schulz, R., & Ewen, R. B. (1993). *Adult development and aging: Myths and emerging realities* (2nd ed). New York: Macmillan.

Schulz, R., & Heckhausen, J. (1996). A life-span model of successful aging. *American Psychologist, 51,* 702–714.

*Snyder, C. R. (1998). A case for hope in pain, loss, and suffering. In J. H. Harvey, J. Omarza, & E. Miller (Eds.), *Perspectives on loss: A sourcebook* (pp. 63–79). Washington, DC: Taylor and Francis.

Snyder, C. R., & Higgins, R. L. (1988). From making to being the excuse: An analysis of deception and verbal/nonverbal issues. *Journal of Nonverbal Behavior, 12,* 237–252.

Snyder, C. R., Higgins, R. L., & Stucky, R. (1983). *Excuses: Masquerades in search of grace.* New York: Wiley.

*Steckenrider, J. S., & Parrott, T. M. (1998). Introduction: The political environment and the new face of aging policy. In J. S. Steckenrider & T. M. Parrott (Eds.), *New directions in old age policies* (pp. 1–10). Albany: State University of New York Press.

Suls, J. (1982). Social support, interpersonal relations, and health: Benefits and liabilities. In G. S. Saunders & J. Suls (Eds.), *Social psychology of health and illness* (pp. 255–277). Hillsdale, NJ: Erlbaum.

Taylor, S. E. (1983). Adjustment to threatening events: A theory of cognitive adaptation. *American Psychologist, 38,* 1161–1173.

Taylor, S. E., & Brown, J. D. (1988). Illusion and well-being: A social psychological perspective on mental health. *Psychological Bulletin, 103,* 193–210.

U.S. Department of Health and Human Services. (1992). *Healthy people 2000: Summary report.* Washington, DC: U.S. Government Printing Office.

U.S. Department of Housing and Urban Development. (1999). *Housing our elders: A report card on the housing conditions and needs of older Americans.* Washington, DC: U.S. Government Printing Office.

U.S. Senate Special Committee on Aging. (1997). *Developments in aging: 1996* Vol. 1. Washington, DC: U.S. Government Printing Office.

*Volz, J. (2000). Successful aging: The second 50. *Monitor on Psychology, 31,* 24–28.

Walters, A. S., & Williamson, G. M. (1999). The role of activity restriction in the association between pain and depressed affect: A study of pediatric patients with chronic pain. *Children's Health Care, 28,* 33–50.

West, R. L., Crook, T. H., & Barron, K. L. (1992). Everyday memory performance across the life span: Effects of age and noncognitive individual differences. *Psychology and Aging, 7,* 72–82.

Williams, H. A. (1993). A comparison of social support and social networks of black parents and white parents with chronically ill children. *Social Science Medicine, 37,* 1509–1520.

Williamson, G. M. (1995). Restriction of normal activities among older adult amputees: The role of public self-consciousness. *Journal of Clinical Geropsychology, 1,* 229–242.

Williamson, G. M. (1998). The central role of restricted normal activities in adjustment to illness and disability: A model of depressed affect. *Rehabilitation Psychology, 43,* 327–347.

Williamson, G. M. (2000). Extending the Activity Restriction Model of Depressed Affect: Evidence from a sample of breast cancer patients. *Health Psychology, 19,* 339–347.

Williamson, G. M., & Dooley, W. K. (2001). Aging and coping: The activity solution. In C. R. Snyder (Ed.), *Coping with stress: Effective people and processes* (pp. 240–258). New York: Oxford University Press.

Williamson, G. M., & Schulz, R. (1992). Pain, activity restriction, and symptoms of depression among community-residing elderly. *Journal of Gerontology, 47,* 367–372.

Williamson, G. M., & Schulz, R. (1995). Activity restriction mediates the association between pain and depressed affect: A study of younger and older adult cancer patients. *Psychology and Aging, 10,* 369–378.

Williamson, G. M., Schulz, R., Bridges, M., & Behan, A. (1994). Social and psychological factors in adjustment to limb amputation. *Journal of Social Behavior and Personality, 9,* 249–268.

*Williamson, G. M., & Shaffer, D. R. (2000). The Activity Restriction Model of Depressed Affect: Antecedents and consequences of restricted normal activities. In G. M. Williamson, D. R. Shaffer, & P. A. Parmelee (Eds.), *Physical illness and depression in older adults: A handbook of theory, research, and practice* (pp. 173–200). New York: Plenum.

Williamson, G. M., Shaffer, D. R., & Schulz, R. (1998). Activity restriction and prior relationship history as contributors to mental health outcomes among middle-aged and older caregivers. *Health Psychology, 17,* 152–162.

Williamson, G. M., Shaffer, D. R., & The Family Relationships in Late Life Project. (2000). Caregiver loss and quality of care provided: Preillness relationship makes a difference. In J. H. Harvey & E. D. Miller (Eds.), *Loss and trauma: General and close relationship perspectives* (pp. 307–330). Philadelphia: Brunner/Mazel.

Wortman, C. B. (1984). Social support and the cancer patient. *Cancer, 53,* 2339–2360.

50

Positive Growth Following Acquired Physical Disability

Timothy R. Elliott, Monica Kurylo, & Patricia Rivera

People acquire physical disabilities through aging and a multitude of mishaps, diseases, and infections. Although clinicians have offered many different explanations for the diverse psychological reactions that occur in the wake of physical disabilities, few have applied scientific tools to study these behaviors, and fewer still have presented heuristic and testable theoretical explanations. Moreover, most observers have overlooked the potentially valuable experience of acquiring a physical disability. Writers have given only scant attention to positive growth and optimal living with chronic health problems, as well as the related searches for meaning, purpose, and fulfillment.

In this chapter, we first will review the historical perspectives regarding adjustment to the onset of physical disability. We then will present a model for understanding such adjustment, along with supporting evidence. Finally, we will discuss relevant measures and intervention practices that merit use in practice and research and will propose directions for future study.

Historical Perspectives

In most conceptualizations of psychological adjustment following the onset of physical disa-

bility, researchers have focused primarily on the negative emotional reactions; rarely have they mentioned the potential for psychological growth. For many years, the prevailing models of adjustment were Freudian ones in which people were presumed to pass through predictable stages in reaction to severe loss (Grzesiak & Hicock, 1994). With the losses accompanying the disability, the individual was posited to sustain a severe blow, and only with the passage of time could the ego permit recognition of that loss. Thus, a person purportedly would manifest denial to defend against the anxiety precipitated by the disability and thereafter would gradually progress through depression, anger, and bargaining phases until the ego could rationally accept the permanence and severity of the disability (Mueller, 1962). Thus, optimal adjustment was conceptualized as the final acceptance of the reality of permanent disability.

In contrast to this rather fatalistic perspective, students of Kurt Lewin (1939) observed great variation in reactions to physical disability. They recognized that many people manage the negative implications of the disability by shifting their values so as to experience increased personal worth (Barker, Wright, Meyerson, & Gonick, 1953; Dembo, Leviton, & Wright, 1956; Meyerson, 1948). Additionally, these researchers demonstrated how physical settings and societal attitudes impede personal growth and adjustment following the onset of a disability. These views facilitated the recognition of the potential for optimal positive adjustment following physical disability; moreover, they influenced a generation of psychologists, counselors, physicians, and policy makers. Finally, these views shed light on the limitations imposed by the physical environment and the ways in which the environment can define a person as "handicapped" (Shontz & Wright, 1980).

Learning principles also have been applied to identify environmental contingencies that reinforce and shape "disabled" behaviors and produce impairment that is beyond what can be directly attributable to a physical condition (Fordyce, 1976). These applications have been expanded to take into account specific beliefs people develop in interactions with the environment, and the way people find meaning in their daily experiences (Fordyce, 1988). In other models steeped in a learning tradition, the theorists consider the interactions of both the characteristics of the disability and personal coping behaviors in influencing adjustment (Thompson, Gil, Burbach, Keith, & Kinney, 1993; Wallander & Varni, 1989).

In much of the available empirical research, the approaches have been largely descriptive, detached from overarching theoretical models, and centered upon the measurement of distress and other negative emotional reactions (Livneh & Antonak, 1997). Unfortunately, this work does not increase our understanding of how people can experience positive growth and meaning following disability. Indeed, psychological models in which persons with a disability are portrayed as recipients of care or victims of misfortune preoccupied with matters of health cannot inform us about positive growth following disability (Fine & Asch, 1988a).

Positive Growth Following Disability

Several theorists now acknowledge that stress does not always result in negative outcomes; some people may experience positive shifts in values, attitudes, and beliefs that were generated in part by the changes imposed by a stressful event (Somerfield & McCrae, 2000). These changes have been described as positive illusions (Taylor & Brown, 1988), benefit-finding (Tennen & Affleck, 1999), positive reinterpretation

(Scheier, Weintraub, & Carver, 1986), and posttraumatic growth (Tedeschi, Park, & Calhoun, 1998). These concepts signify the possible occurrence of positive growth in response to a stressful incident, but at times the labels and definitions of these constructs seem condescending, suggesting that observed behaviors may not be "real" or reflective of genuine change.

As early as 1956, Dembo and her colleagues pointed out that for some persons, disability is neither the "core" of their self-worth nor the center of their daily activities. In fact, many believe that their disabilities have helped them to find meaning or to take a more adaptive perspective of life (Wright, 1983). These individuals reported (a) appreciating personal worth regardless of appearance or ability; (b) valuing time spent in family activities; and (c) becoming more spiritual, thoughtful, or understanding (Taylor, 1983; Wright, 1983). According to Wright (1983), persons who have developed greater acceptance of disability will demonstrate a sense of meaning in their circumstances, value their selfhood, and maintain positive beliefs about themselves. Such changes may be construed as both process and outcome and may be reflected in a heightened sense of priorities, a greater appreciation of the preciousness of life, and an inner strength and meaning that permeates daily decisions and activities (Tedeschi et al., 1998). Thus, individuals who incur a physical disability may do more than "survive" their condition; their resilience and clarity of purpose may result in a greater resolve for pursuing personal goals (Snyder, 1998) and an attainment of spiritual awareness and psychological adjustment that surpasses their previous level of adaptation (Wright, 1983).

Families, too, may experience positive changes in the wake of disability. Olkin (1999) observes that acquired disability can force family members to directly confront issues of trust, mortality, and values, which in turn compel them to develop deeper commitments and restructure the meaning of marriage or kinship. Some family members report a greater sense of closeness, a greater emphasis on family and personal relationships, and positive changes in shared family values (Crewe, 1993).

Positive growth can be reflected in a greater sense of well-being and satisfaction with life and also may be associated with fewer psychological problems such as depression, anxiety, social isolation, and loneliness. Presumably, positive growth should be associated with a decreased risk and infrequent occurrence of secondary complications (e.g., pressure sores, urinary tract infections, respiratory problems), that may be prevented in part by observing regimens for personal care, avoidance of possible damaging stimuli, and other health-promoting behaviors. We believe that persons who attain a greater degree of positive growth following disability would be more likely to engage in behaviors conducive to general well-being and optimal physical health.

An Integrative and Dynamic Model

To appreciate the potential for positive growth and optimal adjustment following physical disability, it is necessary to review several basic tenets in rehabilitation psychology. First, disability does not occur in a vacuum: It is defined in part by the immediate environment and the historical and societal context in which it occurs. According to the Lewinian equation, $B = f(P,E)$, observed behavior following disability (e.g., passivity, aggression, well-being, search for meaning) is a function of the person *and* the environment (Wright, 1983). Stage models, learning principles, and field-theory perspectives also acknowledge that dynamic processes occur in ongoing interactions between the person and the environment. Through transactional models in which the focus is on the interplay between the person and the environment, we have increased our understanding of stress and coping processes (Lazarus & Folkman, 1984). Unfortunately, researchers and clinicians often have failed to attend to within-person dynamic growth that may occur with aging (Trieschmann, 1987), the cognitive adaptations to a physical condition over time (Rape, Bush, & Slavin, 1992), as well as the interpersonal world changes that follow a disability (Frank et al., 1998). This dynamic, developmental aspect is a powerful, albeit long neglected element of the adjustment process following disability.

Second, in stage theories and Lewinian concepts it is assumed that the unique characteristics of the individual are involved in the adjustment process. Whereas in Lewinian psychology, individual characteristics are conceptualized as "the person" in the previous equation, competing stage models identify an individual difference construct (i.e., the "ego") as having a bearing on adjustment. In contemporary parlance, these constructs represent the domain of enduring personality characteristics that can predispose an individual toward certain behaviors.

As depicted in Figure 50.1, we conceptualize adjustment following disability in several broad-based domains, each of which has considerable influence on two areas of adjustment. The primary components involve individual characteristics and the immediate social and interpersonal environment (see left side of Figure 50.1). These influence the phenomenological and appraisal processes that constitute elements of positive growth and, in turn, predict psychological and physical health outcomes (see far right side of Figure 50.1). These components are framed within the developmental continuum that flows left to right and is shown at the bottom of the figure. The dynamic continuum encompasses changes in any of the aforementioned five areas as people age, as technologies advance, as relationships shift, and as health and public policies evolve. This continuum reflects the ongoing process of growth, adaptation, and development in the person and the environment, and the subsequent alterations in interactions between these entities. Thus, in our model, we adopt a collectivistic approach in which behavior results from the combined interactions of individual, situational, and environmental factors that function in an integrated and fluid manner.

Enduring Characteristics and Individual Differences

Many variables are subsumed within this aspect of the model. Enduring characteristics are defined as demographic characteristics, disability-related characteristics (e.g., level of injury and pain), predisability behavioral patterns, and personality characteristics.

Demographic Characteristics

Few researchers have taken a priori theoretical perspectives in examining racial, gender, age, or socioeconomic status (SES) differences as they relate to adjustment following disability (Elliott & Uswatte, 2000; Fine & Asch, 1988b). Most demographic characteristics are included in clinical studies for descriptive purposes only, and their relation usually is examined within the context of maladjustment. Of those studies that included analyses of race, gender, age, and SES, these variables appeared to account for a very

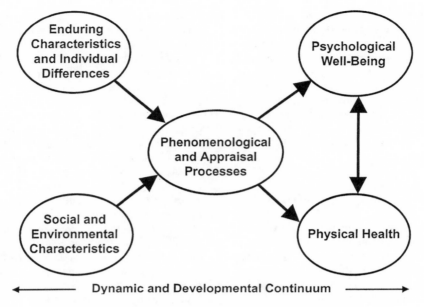

Figure 50.1 Model for understanding positive growth following disability.

small portion of variance in adjustment following disability. It should be noted that the socially defined constructs such as race, gender, ethnicity, SES, and age share considerable overlap with the social and environment component of our model.

Disability-Related Characteristics

Aspects of any specific disability (e.g., level of spinal cord injury) do not reliably predict subsequent adjustment, although some differences may be observed between groups of people with different types of disabilities. Changes in the physical condition itself can influence routine activities, available resources, and ongoing behavioral patterns, thereby affecting adjustment. For example, research has demonstrated that the presence of chronic, unresolved pain can be distressing to persons with physical disability, and it can compromise their abilities to come to terms with their condition and find meaning and purpose in life (Li & Moore, 1998; Summers, Rapoff, Varghese, Porter, & Palmer, 1991).

Predisability Behavioral Patterns

People who engage in health-compromising behaviors and have problems in interpersonal adjustment prior to their disabilities often have difficulty coming to terms with disability. Previous researchers have demonstrated a link between these characteristics and behavior, but a theoretical model has not been developed to facilitate understanding of this relationship within the context of disability. Some persons have complicated histories of alcohol and substance abuse that may have contributed to the injury (Bombardier, 2000). These persons are at risk for developing secondary complications (e.g., urinary tract infections, pressure sores) that might be prevented in part by behavioral self-care regimens (Hawkins & Heinemann, 1998; Kurylo, Elliott, & Crawford, 2000).

Personality Characteristics

Many psychological constructs have been related to adjustment following disability. For example, persons who have an internal locus of control often report less distress than those with more external expectancies (Frank et al., 1987). Persons with a disability who have effective social-problem-solving skills and who have positive orientations toward solving problems are more assertive, more psychosocially mobile, more accepting of their disability, and less depressed than their counterparts who lack these skills (Elliott, 1999; Elliott, Godshall, Herrick, Witty, & Spruell, 1991). There also is evidence that people with a physical disability who develop preventable medical complications secondary to the disability lack effective problem-solving skills (Herrick, Elliott, & Crow, 1994).

Snyder's (1989) conceptualization of hope, which incorporates one's perceived ability to identify and pursue personally meaningful goals under times of duress, also is a useful construct in understanding positive growth after acquired disability (see Snyder, Rand, & Sigmon, this volume). Persons who are hopeful selectively attend to certain aspects of their situation following the onset of disability (Elliott, Witty, Herrick, & Hoffman, 1991). Moreover, persons who have higher levels of hope seem to have a greater sense of control over their symptoms and report a greater sense of personal, positive growth in reaction to their condition (Tennen & Affleck, 1999). Higher levels of hope and goal-directed energy are associated with less distress, greater use of more confident and sociable coping styles, and higher self-reported functional abilities (Elliott & Kurylo, 2000; Elliott, Witty, et al., 1991; Jackson, Taylor, Palmatier, Elliott, & Elliott, 1998; Laird, Snyder, & Green, 2001). Generally, people who have greater tendencies to utilize denial and who have greater psychological defensiveness are less distressed and less angry and have fewer handicaps throughout the first year of acquired disability (Elliott & Richards, 1999).

Snyder (1989; Snyder, Rand, & Sigmon, this volume) has repeatedly emphasized that hope is goal-oriented and goal-based. Goal orientation is also significant in contemporary neo-Freudian conceptualizations of the self and personal adjustment. A greater goal orientation is associated with less depression, greater acceptance of disability, and increased life satisfaction 1 year later among persons with recent-onset physical disability. Goal orientation also is associated with less perceived social stigma and increased mobility among these persons (Elliott, Uswatte, Lewis, & Palmatier, 2000). Among persons with chronic disabilities, those who have many rather than few goals evidence more optimal adjustment (Kemp & Vash, 1971).

Other personality traits are predictive of adjustment as well. Krause and Rohe (1998) found that elements of neuroticism and extraversion were associated with life satisfaction among community-residing persons with spinal cord injuries. Specifically, a greater proclivity for negative emotions and decreased tendency for positive emotions were predictive of less life satisfaction. Similarly, Rivera and Elliott (2000) found that lower neuroticism and higher agreeableness (measured by the NEO; Costa & McRae, 1991) were predictive of greater acceptance of disability among persons with a spinal cord injury after controlling for level of injury, completeness of injury, depression, and demographic variables. Thus, the personality traits that are stable and unlikely to change over time appear to be significant correlates of depression and acceptance of disability in persons with an acquired spinal cord injury.

Social and Interpersonal Environment

Elements of interest within the interpersonal and social environment portion of our model include social support, environmental barriers, and social stereotypes. Social support has been associated with well-being among persons with acquired disabilities (Rintala, Young, Hart, Clearman, & Fuhrer, 1992). The fluid nature of social support may reflect the various types of assistance (e.g., informational, emotional) required to complement specific coping efforts (McColl, Lei, & Skinner, 1995). Family members may shift in their own adjustments and abilities to cope with the caregiving demands, thereby affecting the care recipients' abilities to cope (Chaney, Mullins, Frank, & Peterson, 1997; Frank et al., 1998). There also is evidence that elements of social support can have positive and negative effects on other aspects of adjustment. For example, assertive persons may be able to marshal available social support in certain situations; however, this direct style also may alienate others in the social support system (Elliott, Herrick, et al., 1991). Similarly, goal-directed persons who voice their aspirations and do not assume a passive role in rehabilitation might encounter negative and resistant attitudes from professional staff (Elliott & Kurylo, 2000).

Marital satisfaction following disability is associated with greater satisfaction in leisure activities (Urey & Henggeler, 1987), and satisfaction with recreational activities is a major component of overall life satisfaction following disability (Kinney & Coyle, 1992; Krause & Crewe, 1987). But significant others also can have a negative impact in the way they may reinforce disabled behaviors, undermine self-care efforts, restrict activity, and compromise the health of a person with disability (Turk, Kerns, & Rosenberg, 1992). In some situations, family members have to make a conscious choice between the personal goals of the person with a disability and contradictory goals espoused by health care professionals (Elliott & Kurylo, 2000). In other cases, family members may be unable to adjust to the changes imposed by the disability and display more distress than the person with the condition (Elliott & Shewchuk, in press).

We also are learning that family members in caregiving roles can have an impact on the psychological and physical adjustments of persons with disabilities. In a recent study, caregiver tendencies to solve problems carelessly and impulsively were significantly predictive of lower acceptance of disability among patients who were leaving a rehabilitation hospital (Elliott, Shewchuk, & Richards, 1999). When a group of these patients were evaluated a year later for the occurrence of pressure sores, caregiver impulsive and careless styles *assessed 1 year earlier* correctly classified 87.88% of those persons with and without a sore. It is conceivable that the persons with disabilities were aware of their caregivers' problem-solving styles and recognized that their caregivers could care less about working to help them in adhering to self-care regimens.

The social environment can yield considerable stress because persons with disabilities are impeded from being integrated and mobile in society at large. Factors ranging from architectural barriers to negative social stereotypes contribute to this stress. Perceived independence, personal transportation, and personal living arrangements are strong predictors of good self-concepts among persons with a physical disability who reside in a community (Green, Pratt, & Grigsby, 1984). Some persons with disabilities may become very uncomfortable in anticipation of potentially embarrassing situations associated with interacting and resuming social roles (Dunn, 1977). To compound the problems, these concerns may be internalized as social stigmas. On this point, persons with higher levels of perceived stigma report more problems coming to terms with their disabilities (Li & Moore, 1998; Rybarczyk, Nyenhuis, Nicholas, Cash, & Kaiser, 1995).

Phenomenological and Appraisal Processes

We must understand the unique perspective of the person with disability. In contemporary perspectives of adjustment, an emphasis is placed on the importance of appraisals in understanding individual experiences. For example, there is a focus on the primary appraisal of events as the mediators of stress effects in transactional models of stress and coping. In concert with these views, rather than the disability itself, the research focus has shifted to the person's perceptions of disability and interference with personal goals and desired activities as the source of stress (Williamson, 1998; see also Williamson, this volume). Thus, we focus on the perception and appraisal of stress in our model and do not make assumptions about the discrete nature of stressful incidents among people with disabilities.

The appraisal component, then, is the centerpiece of our model because its processes have considerable influence on subsequent adjustment. We believe that elements of positive growth are first evident in how people evaluate and interpret their situation and circumstances. Following disabilities, adaptive people often look inward to exercise control over internal states rather than trying to exert behavioral control over external events, some of which they realistically cannot affect (Heckenhausen & Schulz, 1995). Individuals then actively process aspects of their situations to find positive meanings and side benefits (Dunn, 1996, 2000). We can observe how people try to accept, positively reinterpret, and seek personal growth soon after the onset of disabilities (Kennedy et al., 2000). Those who are successful in realizing these aspects will have better adjustment (Thompson, 1991). Appraisal processes also may help to explain why persons with disabilities who are distressed exhibit many different coping behaviors, whereas those who are less distressed reported fewer coping efforts and a greater sense of internal locus of control (Frank et al., 1987). This also may account for the beneficial sequelae of acceptance coping and cognitive restructuring on the adjustments of persons with spinal cord injuries who are returning to their communities (Hanson, Buckelew, Hewitt, & O'Neal, 1993; Kennedy, Lowe, Grey, & Short, 1995).

Specific beliefs about the disability (e.g., "I will walk again") and attributions of responsibility and blame are unstable over time and have been found not to be consistently related to objective and subjective measures of adjustment (Elliott & Richards, 1999; Hanson et al., 1993; Reidy & Caplan, 1994; Richards, Elliott, Shewchuk, & Fine, 1997; Schulz & Decker, 1985). People who ruminate about their perceived victimization, however, may do so at the expense of finding meaning and direction in their circumstances. Thus, they may compromise their adjustments (Davis, Lehman, Wortman, Silver, & Thompson, 1995). Yet others may interpret information in a manner that exacerbates their problems (Smith, Peck, Milano, & Ward, 1988). Dunn (1994) observes that adaptive personality and interpersonal characteristics predispose some individuals toward more functional cognitive appraisals, and that people lacking in these personal and social resources will be more likely to exhibit difficulties in accepting their condition and their circumstances.

Dynamic and Developmental Processes

Changes in a person's belief system, interpersonal environment, and physical health may occur over time. Advances in medical therapies and public policy can facilitate adjustment. One hundred years ago, Helen Keller gave Americans an example of functional adaptation to multiple "limitations" (blindness, deafness, and gender). Were it not for the zeitgeist, her success as a speaker and educator may not have been realized. The sociopolitical climate at the time, including the suffragist movement, supported her efforts to integrate and prosper in mainstream society. Other examples of social advocacy led to the passage of the Rehabilitation Act of 1973 and the Americans with Disabilities Act of 1990. More recently, attention has turned to actor Christopher Reeve, resulting in increased public awareness about—and federal and private funding for—spinal cord injury research. Today's advocacy movement demands consideration for the relationship between individuals and their physical, social, and cultural environments.

People typically navigate developmental changes with the intention of minimizing their discomforts and activity restrictions and maintaining or improving ability levels, senses of well-being, and volitions (Williamson, 1998). Persons with physical disabilities may grow positively over time as they develop adaptive beliefs and experience shifts in their values. Some of these positive aspects may take time to be realized or appreciated. All of these changes represent developmental processes that can be understood within the context of our model. Observations of such adjustments can be made with tools that are sensitive to individual trajectories of adaptation over time.

There are many different measures of specific beliefs, values, and attitudes that represent certain appraisal processes, but we advocate the use of instruments such as the Acceptance of Disability Scale (Linkowski, 1971), which was developed to assess acceptance as defined by Wright (1983). Other instruments that assess aspects of positive growth are available (e.g., the Posttraumatic Growth Scale; Tedeschi & Calhoun, 1996), but we are unaware of any previous application of these among persons with physical disability. To understand specific and phenomenological processes that underpin positive growth and subsequent adjustment, we believe sophisticated qualitative devices (e.g., Q-sorts, focus groups, structured interviews) are required.

Adjustment Following Disability

Paralleling the indices of adjustment for people in general, we posit two broad areas of optimal adjustment for persons with physical disability: psychological and physical health. These domains share considerable overlap. Traditionally, researchers have attended to negative indicators of adjustment by using measures of distress, depression, anxiety, psychosocial impairment, and divorce. Some measures of physical health also are construed in fairly negative terms (e.g., Sickness Impact Profile; Bergner, Bobbitt, Carter, & Gilson, 1981). Some outcomes—returning to work or receiving vocational rehabilitation services—are associated with reports of well-being. For those persons who have these options, these are important, discrete indicators of psychological adjustment (Szymanski, 2000). Meaningful social and leisure activities also are important indicators of adjustment that fit within this domain (Krause & Crewe, 1987).

We advocate using measures that draw on positive aspects of adjustment after acquired physical disability. In this regard, we would suggest the Satisfaction With Life Scale (Diener, Emmons, Larsen, & Griffin, 1985) and the Life Satisfaction Index (Adams, 1969), where the respondent is provided with an opportunity to consider positive growth and meaning in the face of significant personal change.

In sum, the individual, social, environmental, and phenomenological factors in our model are likely to have significant effects on psychological and physical health. Overall health, in turn, appears to contribute significantly to variation in positively valenced outcomes such as self-esteem, acceptance of disability, and life satisfaction. Greater recognition and attention to the factors in this model will aid our understanding of the potential for optimal adjustment among persons with acquired physical disabilities.

Psychological Interventions

With the decreasing financial support for psychosocial programs for persons with disabilities in the last decade, there has been a shift in intervention policies (Frank, 1997). The opinions, goals, and aspirations of the person with disability must be primary in developing strategic interventions (Wright, 1983). When these personal goals and aims are addressed, interventions are more likely to be effective (Glueckauf & Quittner, 1992; Webb & Glueckauf, 1994). Wright (1983) recommended that services to people with disabilities include efforts to eliminate societal barriers, increase accommodations, improve medical and psychosocial services where indicated, develop and provide assistive devices and technologies, and aid in the learning of new skills. For example, programs such as interpersonal and social-skills training and innovative interventions such as aerobic exercise training have led to an increase in abilities, sense of well-being, and acceptance of disabilities among persons with physical disabilities (Coyle & Santiago, 1995; Dunn, Van Horn, & Herman, 1981; Glueckauf & Quittner, 1992; Morgan & Leung, 1980). Cognitive-behavioral interventions designed to enhance coping effectiveness may have beneficial effects on people's ability to positively reappraise their situations and to increase their senses of hope, with corresponding improvements in psychological adjustment (King & Kennedy, 1999). Strategies that include family members as an integral part of the rehabilitation process may be particularly effective (Moore, 1989); moreover, these approaches may be couched within cognitive-behavioral frameworks and delivered in innovative, home-based programs (e.g., Roberts et al., 1995). Formal vocational rehabilitation intervention programs that support a return to career-related activities—broadly defined to include support for independent living, assistive devices, and meaningful social activities—remain important despite the constant threat of decreasing federal and state funding.

To appreciate the unique perspectives of persons living with disabilities, it is prudent to hire staff members who have disabilities. This not only will enhance service provisions but also will model professionalism, independence, and self-sufficiency for the individuals served. Additionally, clinicians should solicit input from persons with disabilities and their families so that useful and desired services are developed (Shewchuk & Elliott, 2000). With qualitative assessment devices, we can measure participants' goals and needs and expedite their inclusion in the evaluations of the intervention programs. Health professionals also must advocate legislation and seek new funding sources in order to create accessible and affordable community-based programs (e.g., support groups, educational interventions, recreational activities, and training for individuals with disabilities). Likewise, clinicians should strengthen their multidisciplinary collaboration so as to offer community-based services, including respite and home health care. For example, professionals can work together to develop neighborhood centers in rural, underserved areas or use technology such as telecommunication devices to deliver a variety of services and therapies to participants at home (Temkin & Jones, 1999). Other technologies and assistive devices can have immense effects on positive growth (Scherer, 2000). Virtual-reality technologies can be used to help individuals learn specific coping skills (e.g., coping with persistent pain; Hoffman, Doctor, Patterson, Carrougher, & Furness, 2000) and attain greater mobility and independence (learning driving skills; Schultheis & Rizzo, in press). These technologies will eventually prove to be cost-effective and, accordingly, should be subsidized by health insurance, state or federal funds, or a combination of sources.

As increasing numbers of Americans are affected by the need to care for an older adult relative, states are feeling the burden of financing long-term care services. Fortunately, policy makers are beginning to recognize the value of supporting family caregivers as an extension of the formal health care system. In fact, in a recent study by California's Family Caregiver Alliance, it was found that five states (California, New Jersey, New York, Oregon, and Pennsylvania) now offer a variety of innovative and cost-effective services to support caregivers of family members with dementia (Feinberg & Pilisuk, 1999). Similar solutions may decrease the concerns that rehabilitation professionals have regarding the lack of input and choice of health care services available to persons with disabilities. Likewise, a more consumer-oriented system of care may evolve (Kosciulek, 2000).

Future Directions

Many correlates of adjustment following disability have been identified in research to date. This work should continue so that we can identify those persons who are at risk for poor adjustment; moreover, we need to recognize the characteristics of those persons with disabilities who should experience greater satisfaction, health, and well-being over time. Nevertheless, several issues warrant our attention in future research programs pertaining to beneficial interventions, service delivery, and policy formation.

First, participants' perspectives, opinions, beliefs, and appraisals have not been consistently taken into account in research and practice. To assess and use this rich but subjective information, more sophisticated qualitative measurements are necessary. Too often researchers and clinicians eschew this approach, opting to bind participants' life experiences to some a priori Procrustean bed of theory and lore. To understand the cognitive mechanisms underlying optimal adjustment—and the precursors of such processes—it is imperative that we develop and use qualitative devices that are sensitive to the perceptions and beliefs through which people find meaning rather than despair following disability. We have yet to determine what kind of value shifts occur following disability, how and why these occur, and the relationship of such shifts to a sense of acceptance and well-being (Keany & Glueckauf, 1993).

Second, through more sophisticated statistical methods we now can uncover the dynamic processes of adjustment as they unfold over time. Designs that incorporate constructs from our model can be used to predict individual trajectories of adaptation. Included in this statistical armamentarium are hierarchical linear modeling, structural equation modeling, and other complex multilevel modeling techniques that trace various characteristics and measures over time, as well as intraindividual change trajectories in intervention research (Drotar, 1997; Elliott & Shewchuk, in press). These elegant tools are particularly attractive for theory building and program evaluation because they can accommodate dichotomous and ordinal-level variables. Additionally, these techniques allow us to revisit old notions of adjustment that never have truly been tested (e.g., Do people experience a series of stagelike processes in reaction to the disability onset?) and refine predictive models that are essential for resource allocation (e.g., What are the psychological characteristics of those who benefit optimally from interventions? Who is at greatest risk for rehospitalizations?).

By using these new statistical procedures in tandem with qualitative devices, we also may illuminate how people cognitively process information about their disabling conditions, their lives, and their environments; likewise, we may better appreciate how such changes in perceptions relate to long-term adjustment. This information is crucial for improving our theoretical understanding of life beyond disability and for developing policies and service delivery systems to ensure that persons with disabilities may participate fully in a positive psychology in the 21st century. Everyone deserves a chance at "the good life," and this is the spirit in which we have advocated new and better science, interventions, and environs for persons with disabilities.

Acknowledgments   This chapter was supported in part by the National Center for Injury Prevention and Control and the Disabilities Prevention Program, National Center for Environmental Health Grant R49/CCR412718-01, the National Institute on Disability and Rehabilitation Research Grant H133B980016A, and the National Center for Medical Rehabilitation Research, National Institute of Child Health and Human Development, National Institutes of Health, Grant T32 HD07420. The contents of this article are solely the authors' responsibility and do not necessarily represent the official views of the funding agencies.

References

Adams, D. (1969). Analysis of a life satisfaction index. *Journal of Gerontology, 24,* 470–474.

American With Disabilities Act of 1990, Pub. L. No. 101–336, 42 U.S.C. 12111, 12112.

Barker, R. G., Wright, B. A., Meyerson, L., & Gonick, M. R. (1953). *Adjustment to physical handicap and illness: A survey of the social psychology of physique and disability* (2nd ed.).

New York: Social Science Research Council Bulletin.

Bergner, M., Bobbitt, R., Carter, W., & Gilson, B. S. (1981). The sickness impact profile: Development and final revision of a health status measure. *Medical Care, 19,* 787–805.

Bombardier, C. H. (2000). Alcohol and traumatic disability. In R. G. Frank & T. Elliott (Eds.), *Handbook of rehabilitation psychology* (pp. 399–416). Washington, DC: American Psychological Association.

Chaney, J., Mullins, L. L., Frank, R. G., & Peterson, L. (1997). Transactional patterns of child, mother, and father adjustment in insulin-dependent diabetes mellitus: A prospective study. *Journal of Pediatric Psychology, 22,* 229–244.

Costa, P. T., & McCrae, R. R. (1991). *NEO Five Factor Inventory—Form S.* Odessa, FL: Psychological Assessment Resources.

Coyle, C. P., & Santiago, M. C. (1995). Aerobic exercise training and depressive symptomology in adults with physical disabilities. *Archives of Physical Medicine and Rehabilitation, 76,* 647–652.

Crewe, N. (1993). Spousal relationships and disability. In F. P. Haseltine, S. Cole, & D. Gray (Eds.), *Reproductive issues for persons with physical disabilities* (pp. 141–151). Baltimore: Paul H. Brookes.

Davis, C. G., Lehman, D. R., Wortman, C., Silver, R. C., & Thompson, S. (1995). The undoing of traumatic life events. *Personality and Social Psychology Bulletin, 21,* 109–124.

*Dembo, T., Leviton, G. L., & Wright, B. A. (1956). Adjustment to misfortune: A problem of social-psychological rehabilitation. *Artificial Limbs, 3*(2), 4–62.

Diener, E., Emmons, R. A., Larsen, R., & Griffin, S. (1985). The satisfaction with life scale. *Journal of Personality Assessment, 49,* 71–75.

Drotar, D. (1997). Relating parent and family functioning to the psychological adjustment of children with chronic health conditions: What have we learned? What do we need to know? *Journal of Pediatric Psychology, 22,* 149–165.

*Dunn, D. S. (1994). Positive meaning and illusions following disability: Reality negotiation, normative interpretation, and value change. *Journal of Social Behavior and Personality, 9,* 123–138.

Dunn, D. S. (1996). Well-being following amputation: Salutary effects of positive meaning, optimism, and control. *Rehabilitation Psychology, 41,* 285–302.

*Dunn, D. S. (2000). Matters of perspective: Some social psychological issues in disability and rehabilitation. In R. G. Frank & T. Elliott (Eds.), *Handbook of rehabilitation psychology* (pp. 565–584). Washington, DC: American Psychological Association.

Dunn, M. (1977). Social discomfort in the patient with SCI. *Archives of Physical Medicine and Rehabilitation, 58,* 257–260.

Dunn, M., Van Horn, E., & Herman, S. (1981). Social skills and spinal cord injury: A comparison of three training procedures. *Behavior Therapy, 12,* 153–164.

Elliott, T. (1999). Social problem-solving abilities and adjustment to recent-onset physical disability. *Rehabilitation Psychology, 44,* 315–352.

Elliott, T., Godshall, F., Herrick, S., Witty, T., & Spruell, M. (1991). Problem-solving appraisal and psychological adjustment following spinal cord injury. *Cognitive Therapy and Research, 15,* 387–398.

Elliott, T., Herrick, S., Patti, A., Witty, T., Godshall, F., & Spruell, M. (1991). Assertiveness, social support, and psychological adjustment of persons with spinal cord injury. *Behaviour Research and Therapy, 29,* 485–493.

*Elliott, T., & Kurylo, M. (2000). Hope over disability: Lessons from one young woman's triumph. In C. R. Snyder (Ed.), *The handbook of hope: Theory, measures, and applications* (pp. 373–386). New York: Academic Press.

Elliott, T., & Richards, J. S. (1999). Living with the facts, negotiating the terms: Unrealistic beliefs, denial and adjustment in the first year of acquired disability. *Journal of Personal and Interpersonal Loss, 4,* 361–381.

Elliott, T., & Shewchuk, R. (in press). Family adaptation in illness, disease, and disability: Implications for research, policy, and practice. In J. Racynski, L. Bradley, & L. Leviton (Eds.), *Health and behavior handbook* (Vol. 2). Washington, DC: American Psychological Association.

Elliott, T., Shewchuk, R., & Richards, J. S. (1999). Caregiver social problem-solving abilities and family member adjustment to recent-onset physical disability. *Rehabilitation Psychology, 44,* 104–123.

Elliott, T., & Uswatte, G. (2000). Ethnic and minority issues in physical medicine and rehabilitation. In M. Grabois, S. J., Garrison, K. A. Hart, & L. D. Lehmukuhl (Eds.), *Physical medicine and rehabilitation: The complete approach* (pp. 1820–1828). Franklin, NY: Blackwell Science.

Elliott, T., Uswatte, G., Lewis, L., & Palmatier, A. (2000). Goal instability and adjustment to physical disability. *Journal of Counseling Psychology, 47,* 251–265.

*Elliott, T., Witty, T., Herrick, S., & Hoffman, J. (1991). Negotiating reality after physical loss: Hope, depression, and disability. *Journal of Personality and Social Psychology, 61,* 608–613.

Feinberg, L. F., & Pilisuk, T. (1999). *Survey of fifteen states' caregiver support programs: Final report.* Long Beach, CA: Archstone Foundation.

*Fine, M., & Asch, A. (1988a). Disability beyond stigma: Social interaction, discrimination, and activism. *Journal of Social Issues, 44,* 3–21.

Fine, M., & Asch, A. (1988b). *Women with disabilities: Essays in psychology, culture, and politics.* Philadelphia: Temple University Press.

Fordyce, W. E. (1976). *Behavioral methods in chronic pain and illness.* St. Louis, MO: Mosby.

*Fordyce, W. E. (1988). Pain and suffering. *American Psychologist, 43,* 276–283.

Frank, R. G. (1997). Lessons from the great battle: Health care reform 1992–1994. *Archives of Physical Medicine and Rehabilitation, 78,* 120–124.

*Frank, R. G., Thayer, J., Hagglund, K., Veith, A., Schopp, L., Beck, N., Kashani, J., Goldstein, D., Cassidy, J. T., Clay, D., Chaney, J., Hewett, J., & Johnson, J. (1998). Trajectories of adaptation in pediatric chronic illness: The importance of the individual. *Journal of Consulting and Clinical Psychology, 66,* 521–532.

Frank, R. G., Umlauf, R. L., Wonderlich, S. A., Ashkanazi, G., Buckelew, S. A., & Elliott, T. (1987). Coping differences among persons with spinal cord injury: A cluster analytic approach. *Journal of Consulting and Clinical Psychology, 55,* 727–731.

Glueckauf, R. L., & Quittner, A. L. (1992). Assertiveness training for disabled adults in wheelchairs: Self-report, role-play, and activity pattern outcomes. *Journal of Consulting and Clinical Psychology, 60,* 419–425.

Green, A., Pratt, C., & Grigsby, T. (1984). Self-concept among persons with long-term spinal cord injury. *Archives of Physical Medicine and Rehabilitation, 65,* 751–754.

Grzesiak, R. C., & Hicock, D. A. (1994). A brief history of psychotherapy in physical disability. *American Journal of Psychotherapy, 48,* 240–250.

Hanson, S., Buckelew, S. P., Hewett, J., & O'Neal, G. (1993). The relationship between coping and adjustment after spinal cord injury: A 5-year follow-up study. *Rehabilitation Psychology, 38,* 41–51.

Hawkins, D. A., & Heinemann, A. W. (1998). Substance abuse and medical complications following spinal cord injury. *Rehabilitation Psychology, 43,* 219–231.

Heckenhausen, J., & Schulz, R. (1995). A life-span theory of control. *Psychological Review, 102,* 284–304.

Herrick, S., Elliott, T., & Crow, F. (1994). Self-appraised problem-solving skills and the prediction of secondary complications among persons with spinal cord injury. *Journal of Clinical Psychology in Medical Settings, 1,* 269–283.

Hoffman, H. G., Doctor, J., Patterson, D., Carrougher, G., & Furness, T. (2000). Use of virtual reality for adjunctive treatment of adolescent burn pain during wound care: A case report. *Pain, 85,* 305–309.

Jackson, W. T., Taylor, R., Palmatier, A., Elliott, T., & Elliott, J. L. (1998). Negotiating the reality of visual impairment: Hope, coping, and functional ability. *Journal of Clinical Psychology in Medical Settings, 5,* 173–185.

*Keany, C. M.-H., & Glueckauf, R. L. (1993). Disability and value change: An overview and reanalysis of acceptance of loss theory. *Rehabilitation Psychology, 38,* 199–210.

Kemp, B. J., & Vash, C. L. (1971). Productivity after injury in a sample of spinal cord injured persons: A pilot study. *Journal of Chronic Disease, 24,* 259–275.

Kennedy, P., Lowe, R., Grey, N., & Short, E. (1995). Traumatic spinal cord injury and psychological impact: A cross-sectional analysis of coping strategies. *British Journal of Clinical Psychology, 34,* 627–639.

Kennedy, P., Marsh, N., Lowe, R., Grey, N., Short, E., & Rogers, B. (2000). A longitudinal analysis of psychological impact and coping strategies following spinal cord injury. *British Journal of Health Psychology, 5,* 157–172.

King, C., & Kennedy, P. (1999). Coping effectiveness training for people with spinal cord injury: Preliminary results of a controlled trial. *British Journal of Clinical Psychology, 38,* 5–14.

Kinney, W. B., & Coyle, C. (1992). Predicting life satisfaction among adults with physical disabilities. *Archives of Physical Medicine and Rehabilitation, 73,* 863–869.

Kosciulek, J. F. (2000). Implications of consumer direction for disability policy development and rehabilitation service delivery. *Journal of Disability Policy Studies, 11*(2), 82–89.

Krause, J. S., & Crewe, N. (1987). Prediction of long-term survival of persons with spinal cord injury: An 11-year prospective study. *Rehabilitation Psychology, 32,* 205–213.

Krause, J. S., & Rohe, D. (1998). Personality and life adjustment after spinal cord injury: An exploratory study. *Rehabilitation Psychology, 43,* 118–130.

Kurylo, M., Elliott, T., & Crawford, D. (2000, August). *Alcohol use history and secondary complications following spinal cord injury.* Paper presented at the meeting of the American Psychological Association, Washington, DC.

Laird, S., Snyder, C. R., & Green, S. (2001, August). *Development and validation of the multidimentional prayer inventory.* Paper presented at the meeting of the American Psychological Association, San Francisco, CA.

Lazarus, R., & Folkman, S. (1984). *Stress, appraisal, and coping.* New York: Springer.

Lewin, K. (1939). Field theory and experiment in social psychology: Concepts and methods. *American Journal of Sociology, 44,* 868–896.

Li, L., & Moore, D. (1998). Acceptance of disability and its correlates. *Journal of Social Psychology, 138,* 13–25.

Linkowski, D. C. (1971). A scale to measure acceptance of disability. *Rehabilitation Counseling Bulletin, 14,* 236–244.

Livneh, H., & Antonak, R. (1997). *Psychosocial adaptation to chronic illness and disability.* Gaithersburg, MD: Aspen.

McColl, M. A., Lei, H., & Skinner, H. (1995). Structural relationships between social support and coping. *Social Science and Medicine, 41,* 395–407.

Meyerson, L. (1948). Physical disability as a social psychological problem. *Journal of Social Issues, 4,* 2–10.

Moore, L. I. (1989). *Behavioral changes in male spinal cord injured following two types of psychosocial rehabilitation experience.* Unpublished doctoral dissertation, St. Louis University, St. Louis, MO.

Morgan, B., & Leung, P. (1980). Effects of assertion training on acceptance of disability by physically disabled university students. *Journal of Counseling Psychology, 27,* 209–212.

Mueller, A. D. (1962). Psychologic factors in rehabilitation of paraplegic patients. *Archives of Physical Medicine and Rehabilitation, 43,* 151–159.

Olkin, R. (1999). *What psychotherapists should know about disability.* New York: Guilford.

Rape, R., Bush, J., & Slavin, L. (1992). Toward a conceptualization of the family's adaptation to a member's head injury: A critique of developmental stage models. *Rehabilitation Psychology, 37,* 3–22.

Rehabilitation Act of 1973, Pub. L. No. 93–112.

Reidy, K., & Caplan, B. (1994). Causal factors in spinal cord injury: Patients evolving perceptions and association with depression. *Archives of Physical Medicine and Rehabilitation, 75,* 837–842.

Richards, J. S., Elliott, T., Shewchuk, R., & Fine, P. (1997). Attribution of responsibility for onset of spinal cord injury and psychosocial outcomes in the first year post-injury. *Rehabilitation Psychology, 42,* 115–124.

Rintala, D., Young, J., Hart, K., Clearman, R., & Fuhrer, M. (1992). Social support and the well-being of persons with spinal cord injury living in the community. *Archives of Physical Medicine and Rehabilitation, 37,* 155–163.

Rivera, P., & Elliott, T. (2000, September). *Personality style as a predictor of adjustment to disability following spinal cord injury.* Paper presented at the meeting of the American Association of Spinal Cord Injury Psychologists and Social Workers, Las Vegas, NV.

Roberts, J., Brown, G. B., Streiner, D., Gafni, A., Pallister, R., Hoxby, H., Drummond-Young, M., LeGris, J., & Meichenbaum, D. (1995). Problem-solving counselling or phone-call support for outpatients with chronic illness: Effective for whom? *Canadian Journal of Nursing Research, 27*(3), 111–137.

Rybarczyk, B. D., Nyenhuis, D. L., Nicholas, J., Cash, S., & Kaiser, J. (1995). Body image, perceived social stigma, and the prediction of psychosocial adjustment to leg amputation. *Rehabilitation Psychology, 40,* 95–110.

Scheier, M. F., Weintraub, J. K., & Carver, C. S. (1986). Coping with stress: Divergent strategies of optimists and pessimists. *Journal of Personality and Social Psychology, 51,* 1257–1264.

Scherer, M. J. (2000). *Living in the state of stuck: How technology impacts the lives of people with disabilities* (3rd ed.). Cambridge, MA: Brookline Books.

Schultheis, M. T., & Rizzo, A. A. (in press). The application of virtual reality technology for rehabilitation. *Rehabilitation Psychology.*

Schulz, R., & Decker, S. (1985). Long-term adjustment to physical disability: The role of social support, perceived control, and self-blame. *Journal of Personality and Social Psychology, 48,* 1162–1172.

Shewchuk, R., & Elliott, T. (2000). Family caregiving in chronic disease and disability: Implications for rehabilitation psychology. In R. G. Frank & T. Elliott (Eds.), *Handbook of rehabilitation psychology* (pp. 553–563). Washington, DC: American Psychological Association.

Shontz, F. C., & Wright, B. A. (1980). The distinctiveness of rehabilitation psychology. *Professional Psychology, 11,* 919–924.

Smith, T. W., Peck, J. R., Milano, R. A., & Ward, J. R. (1988). Cognitive distortion in rheumatoid arthritis: Relation to depression and disability.

Journal of Consulting and Clinical Psychology, 56, 412–416.

Snyder, C. R. (1989). Reality negotiation: From excuses to hope and beyond. *Journal of Social and Clinical Psychology, 8,* 130–157.

Snyder, C. R. (1998). A case for hope in pain, loss, and suffering. In J. H. Harvey, J. Omarzu, & E. Miller (Eds.), *Perspectives on loss: A sourcebook* (pp. 63–79). Washington, DC: Taylor and Francis.

Somerfield, M. R., & McCrae, R. R. (2000). Stress and coping research: Methodological challenges, theoretical advances, and clinical applications. *American Psychologist, 55,* 620–625.

Summers, J. D., Rapoff, M. A., Varghese, G., Porter, K., & Palmer, R. (1991). Psychosocial factors in chronic spinal cord injury pain. *Pain, 47,* 183–189.

Szymanski, E. M. (2000). Disability and vocational behavior. In R. G. Frank & T. Elliott (Eds.), *Handbook of rehabilitation psychology* (pp. 499–517). Washington, DC: American Psychological Association.

Taylor, S. E. (1983). Adjustment to threatening events: A theory of cognitive adaptation. *American Psychologist, 38,* 1161–1173.

Taylor, S. E., & Brown, J. D. (1988). Illusion and well-being: A social psychological perspective on mental health. *Psychological Bulletin, 103,* 193–210.

Tedeschi, R. G., & Calhoun, L. G. (1996). The posttraumatic growth inventory: Measuring the positive legacy of trauma. *Journal of Traumatic Stress, 9,* 455–471.

Tedeschi, R. G., Park, C. L., & Calhoun, L. G. (1998). Posttraumatic growth: Conceptual issues. In R. G. Tedeschi, C. L. Park, & L. G. Calhoun (Eds.), *Posttraumatic growth: Positive changes in the aftermath of crisis* (pp. 1–22). Mahwah, NJ: Erlbaum.

Temkin, A. J., & Jones, M. L. (1999). Electronic medicine: Experience and implications for treatment of SCI. *Topics in Spinal Cord Injury Rehabilitation, 5*(3), 1–74.

Tennen, H., & Affleck, G. (1999). Finding benefits in adversity. In C. R. Snyder (Ed.), *Coping: The psychology of what works* (pp. 279–304). New York: Oxford University Press.

Thompson, R. J., Gil, K., Burbach, D., Keith, B., & Kinney, T. (1993). Role of child and maternal processes in the psychological adjustment of children with sickle cell disease. *Journal of Consulting and Clinical Psychology, 61,* 468–474.

Thompson, S. C. (1991). The search for meaning following a stroke. *Basic and Applied Social Psychology, 12,* 81–96.

Trieschmann, R. (1987). *Aging with a disability.* New York: Demos Publications.

Turk, D. C., Kerns, R., & Rosenberg, R. (1992). Effects of marital interaction on chronic pain and disability: Examining the down side of social support. *Rehabilitation Psychology, 37,* 259–274.

Urey, J. R., & Henggeler, S. (1987). Marital adjustment following spinal cord injury. *Archives of Physical Medicine and Rehabilitation, 68,* 69–74.

Wallander, J. L., & Varni, J. (1989). Social support and adjustment in chronically ill and handicapped children. *American Journal of Community Psychology, 17,* 185–201.

Webb, P. M., & Glueckauf, R. L. (1994). The effects of direct involvement in goal setting on rehabilitation outcome for persons with traumatic brain injuries. *Rehabilitation Psychology, 39,* 179–188.

Williamson, G. M. (1998). The central role of restricted normal activities in adjustment to illness and disability: A model of depressed affect. *Rehabilitation Psychology, 43,* 327–347.

*Wright, B. A. (1983). *Physical disability: A psychosocial approach.* New York: Harper and Row.

51

Putting Positive Psychology in a Multicultural Context

Shane J. Lopez, Ellie C. Prosser, Lisa M. Edwards,
Jeana L. Magyar-Moe, Jason E. Neufeld, &
Heather N. Rasmussen

"Competition and prejudice clutter the landscape of virtually every town. Imagine, however, if we had more people of all races, ethnicities, or cultures, who were allowed to contribute. Imagine the enormous advances we could make in enhancing communication and increasing knowledge, and in realizing our basic needs for connectedness. Together, by drawing on the strengths of each other, we can build an American community where the word 'equality' truly can be applied to the abilities of all citizens to pursue their goals" (Lopez et al., 2000, p. 238). Behavioral scientists and practitioners who identify the strengths of all people and value diverse meanings of the good life can encourage optimal functioning of individuals and communities.

In this chapter, we examine cognitive, philosophical, emotional, and interpersonal frameworks that can be used to understand and foster healthy functioning. We also discuss a diversity of specific coping approaches. This critical review of literature places positive psychology in a multicultural context and identifies the diverse psychological strengths of individuals and cultural groups. We also call on scientists and practitioners to examine the magnitude and equivalence of constructs across cultures, to recognize the value of religious practices, spirituality, and diverse constructions of life meaning, to search for the clues to the good life that cultural experiences might provide, to find exemplars (individuals or subgroups) who function within positive psychological frameworks, and to clarify what works in the lives of people.

The Wise Man of the Gulf

The following story sets the stage for discussing positive psychology as it exists in a multicultural society:

> An American businessman, Woody, was at the pier of a small Mexican village when a boat with just one fisherman docked. Inside the boat were many pounds of large gulf shrimp.

The American complimented the Mexican on the quality of his catch and asked about the mesh of his cast net, "Why is the mesh so large? Couldn't you catch more with a tighter weave?" Hector, the fisherman, replied, "I catch what I need *señor*. And the net, the net is a fine net. I was taught how to weave this net by my father, who was taught by his father. I work on the net everyday to keep it strong."

Woody then asked how long it took to seine for his catch. Hector replied, "Only a little while." The American questioned, "So what do you do with the rest of your time?" The Mexican fisherman said, "I sleep late, I pray, go shrimping for a while, play with my children, take siesta with my wife, Maria, examine and repair the net, stroll into the village each evening to sip wine and play guitar with my amigos. On Sundays, I go to mass and spend the rest of the day with *la familia*. I have a full and busy life *señor*. I am very happy."

After hearing the fisherman's account of his week, Woody scoffed, "I am a Harvard MBA and could help you be more successful. You should use a net with a smaller weave and spend more time fishing and, with the proceeds, buy a bigger boat with a larger net you could troll for many miles. With the profits from the bigger boat you could buy several boats; eventually you would have a fleet of boats. Instead of selling your catch to a middle man, you would sell directly to the processor and then open your own plant. You would control the product, processing, and distribution. You would need to leave the small coastal fishing village and move to Mexico City, then Houston and then Los Angeles. There you will run your expanding enterprise."

Hector was somewhat taken aback by the complicated plan and asked, "But *señor*, how long will all this take?" Woody replied, "Fifteen to 20 years." "But what then, *señor*?" The American laughed and said, "That's the best part. When the time is right, you would sell your company stock to the public and become very rich; you would make millions." "Millions, *señor*? Then what?" Hector questioned. The American said, "Then you would retire, move to a small coastal fishing village where you would sleep late, pray, fish a little, play with your grandkids, take a siesta with your

wife, stroll in the village in the evenings to sip wine and spend time with *la familia*."

Positive Psychology in a Multicultural Context

Positive psychology's emphasis on the scientific pursuit of optimal human functioning draws scientists' attention to protective factors, assets, resources, and strengths. To date, however, there has been little effort to highlight the cultural factors that influence health and the meaning of the good life. Researchers and practitioners must remember that the societal and cultural context of life affects how individuals pursue identity development, goals, and happiness. The Basic Behavioral Science Task Force of the National Advisory Mental Health Council (1996) highlighted the context within which mental health exists, stating that "social, cultural, and environmental forces shape who we are and how well we function in the everyday world. . . . Together, those contextual factors, interacting with our individual biological and psychological characteristics, color our experience, limit or enhance our options, and even affect our conceptions of mental illness and mental health" (p. 722).

Psychological models and diagnostic frameworks provide clinicians and scientists with means to conceptualize observations and communicate about functioning. Models and frameworks also provide schema through which professionals discern differences and similarities and offer perspectives on diversity. Not all these explanatory models have incorporated positive and negative views of difference, however. More recent models are increasingly culturally responsive because they highlight the diversity of strengths and weaknesses. Thus, as a field we are beginning to understand how culture relates to health, but there is still a need to develop new conceptual frameworks recognizing and capitalizing on individual and group strengths (Chin, 1993; Sue, 1996).

Models of Inferiority to Models Recognizing Strengths in Diversity

Early psychological models examined differences from a deficiency perspective. Deviation from the characteristics of the dominant culture were viewed through an ethnocentric lens that interpreted any differences negatively and as indicative of weakness.

Inferiority Model

An early paradigm used to explain ethnic differences was based on a history of racist rationalization. This model (as described in a review by Kaplan & Sue, 1997) attributed variability in functioning to biological differences. The "natural inferiority" argument contended that if members of ethnic groups were inherently incapable of advancing in society, it was useless to attempt to adjust the existing environment to provide equal or favorable opportunities. Of course, the fundamental attribution errors inherent in this model were illuminated when biological explanations for racial and ethnic differences were not supported by human genetic research (see reviews of related research in Jackson, 1992; Zuckerman, 1990).

Deficit Model

In the deficit model it was proposed that ethnic differences were the result of immutable environmental mechanisms rather than biological factors (Allport, 1954). Prejudice was purported to be a key factor in creating stress that adversely affected minority group members' ability to excel (Sue, 1983). Higher rates of distress in minorities were attributed to hostile environmental circumstances (Carter, 1994), which elicited inferior or self-destructive coping strategies. Although this model focused greater attention on the effects of prejudice and unequal social conditions, it still cast minority group members in the shadow of inferiority (Kaplan & Sue, 1997) and did not adequately address the complexity of individual differences.

Cultural Pluralism

The field of psychology moved away from deficiency or inferiority models to explanatory models that recognized the importance of culture. These models acknowledge that specific cultural experiences contribute to healthy functioning and engender unique strengths.

In the cultural pluralism model, it is proposed that ethnic groups should remain distinct cultural entities, while simultaneously promoting traditional American values such as individualism. This is not a reflection of the melting pot idea (i.e., ethnic groups combine with the dominant American culture to produce a universal American identity). Instead this model champions a "unity in diversity" position, which, according to Kaplan and Sue (1997), succeeds more as an idealized description of cultural group relations than as an explanatory model for viewing and working with multicultural populations.

Cultural Grid

Pedersen and Pedersen (1989) proposed that, rather than characterizing cultural groups in rigid categories, there is a need to combine the many different *cultural identities* each person presents in distinct situations. The cultural grid is an open-ended model that matches social system variables (i.e., demographics, status, and affiliation) with patterns of cognitive variables (i.e., expectations and values). It was developed to help identify and describe the cultural aspects of a situation, assisting researchers and clinicians in forming hypotheses that include complex cultural perspectives, as well as intercultural differences and explanations. The result is an orientation that allows group variables to be combined with individual cognitive perspectives in a single framework for the purpose of anticipating an individual's "personal cultural" response to specific situations.

Human Diversity

The emerging model in ethnic psychology establishes that each person has a unique culture, both independently and connected to the larger society (Chin, 1993). The human diversity model broadens the focus of research beyond merely racial, ethnic, and cultural issues to include varied groups and populations with unique differences, strengths, and histories. The umbrella of human diversity allows researchers to focus on patterns unique to specific groups or populations, and/or universal group processes. This expands conceptualization options unequivocally, allowing recognition of the importance of cultural variables upon functioning.

Chin (1993) makes strides in the direction of understanding diversity by elucidating a "psychology of difference" to invoke changes in assumptive models to develop a more comprehensive framework, valuing differences and the context of culture. This requires that clinicians and researchers actively engage in (a) displaying a positive presentation of values, potentials, and lifestyle of the culturally different client; (b) shifting from a deficit hypothesis to a difference hypothesis; (c) recognizing that cultural differences exist; (d) examining frameworks that are biased against these differences; and (e) acknowledging that cultural behaviors are adaptive and have withstood the test of time. Thus, cultural behaviors should be examined for their inherent health-promoting values.

A full explanatory model that not only recognizes individual cultural strengths and weaknesses but also potentially sheds light on factors that would help maximize the strengths of all individuals will require further expansion. It is our contention that such a model will flow out of a psychological science committed to studying what works. Thus, we will cluster observations about manifestations of psychological processes so that we can clarify what works for individuals and the broader community. This scientific review, along with the recommendations offered, will provide a framework for positive human diversity models.

Cognitive Aspects of Positive Psychology: Examining Magnitude and Equivalence Across Cultures

The cognitive components of positive psychology have received considerable research attention in recent years. For example, the constructs of optimism, self-efficacy, and hope have been examined extensively to discover the roles they play in human functioning. Despite this growth of literature, however, relatively little can be found concerning the manifestation of these constructs across cultures.

Examining the Magnitude of Cognitive Constructs Across Cultures

When researchers choose to investigate the nature of constructs across cultures, they often look at group differences in the magnitude of these constructs. In one such study, Halpin, Halpin, and Whiddon (1981) examined differences in locus of control between Native Americans and white. Their results indicated that locus of control did not differ significantly. In an ethnically diverse sample, Munoz-Dunbar's (1993) examination of hope profiles of college students revealed that Native Americans had significantly higher dispositional hope and Asian Americans had significantly lower levels

of hope than the other ethnic groups in the sample.[1] This straightforward method of comparing personal characteristics frequently is used in an attempt to discover how groups may or may not differ regarding the specific constructs under investigation. Implicit in this method of examining "how much" are assumptions and questions regarding How much of what? and Is more of X necessarily a good thing?

Examining the Equivalence of Cognitive Constructs Across Cultures

When investigating psychological constructs in a multicultural context, should investigators assume that the constructs represent the same thing across cultures? Correlational procedures provide two avenues for examining construct equivalence. The question, How much of what? is addressed via factor analysis of group data. For example, the studies by Halpin et al. (1981) and Munoz-Dunbar (1993) would have been strengthened had the researchers determined if "apple to apple" comparisons were being made. The question of Is more of X necessarily a good thing? is indirectly addressed by considering the relationships between scores on positive psychology measures and some indicator of positive outcome or well-being.

Surprisingly, few attempts have been made to directly evaluate the cross-cultural equivalence of constructs such as hope and optimism. Though over 20 studies have confirmed the two-factor model of hope, data from a diverse sample have not been analyzed (this issue is the focus of two studies that currently are under way). Optimism, or explanatory style, soon will undergo cross-cultural examination by Peterson and colleagues, but to date, studies examining the construct equivalence of optimism have not been completed.

Currently, most of the research examining positive psychology constructs has focused predominantly on white samples. Thus, relatively little is known about the real-world usefulness (and the concurrent and predictive validity of related measures) of these cognitive processes with non-white cultural groups. Without this knowledge, the interpretation of the results from any investigation focusing solely on the levels at which these positive psychology constructs manifest in various cultural groups becomes highly questionable. Some of the literature examining cognitive constructs across cultures has taken into account the stability of the construct of interest. For example, Carvajal, Garner, and Evans (1998) investigated levels of dispositional optimism in sexually active inner-city minority adolescents. The results of this study indicated that dispositional optimism functions as a protective factor for this specific cultural group (e.g., correlating with higher intentions to avoid unsafe sex). This is consistent with other studies that have found that increased levels of dispositional optimism have health-promoting benefits (Scheier & Carver, 1992; Snyder, Irving, & Anderson, 1991).

A second study that investigated the equivalence of a cognitive construct across cultural groups looked specifically at career self-efficacy and its correlates in a multicultural context (Hackett, Betz, Casas, & Rocha-Singh, 1992). It was concluded from this study that, irrespective of ethnicity, career self-efficacy was an important factor in the educational and career progress of students. Furthermore, because this relationship between self-efficacy and educational and career progress was confirmed across the groups used in the study, the lower self-efficacy scores of Mexican-Americans as compared with Caucasians could be interpreted with greater confidence.

Apples and Oranges?
A Tale of an Exemplar Study

Chang (1996a) has done an excellent job in his research of taking into consideration the stability of positive psychology constructs. The researcher emphasizes that making the assumption that constructs are equivalent potentially can have negative consequences. This was demonstrated in a study in which Chang investigated, among other variables, optimism and pessimism in Asian Americans and Caucasians. Furthermore, this study examined the utility of optimism and pessimism in predicting problem-solving behaviors, depressive symptoms, general psychological symptoms, and physical symptoms. In general, the results revealed that Asian Americans were significantly more pessimistic than Caucasians (according to the Extended Life Orientation Test; Chang, Maydeu-Olivares, & D'Zurilla, 1997) but not significantly different in their level of optimism. These findings were corroborated when data from an independent sample were examined (Chang, 1996b). Chang astutely points out that

his findings might suggest that Asian Americans are generally more negative in their affectivity than Caucasian Americans; however, he found that there were no significant differences in reported depressive symptoms between the two groups. In fact, optimism was negatively correlated with both general psychological symptoms and physical symptoms for Asian Americans but not for Caucasians. Also, problem solving was found to be negatively correlated with depressive symptoms for Asian Americans but unrelated for Caucasians. Finally, whereas pessimism was negatively correlated with problem-solving behaviors, for Caucasians, it was positively correlated for Asian Americans.

Differences Across Cultures?
How Much and How Stable?

Though we cannot summarize the research on group differences in the manifestation of optimism and similar constructs, some of the cross-cultural research could lead clinicians and researchers to develop negative generalizations about certain groups or mask the heterogeneity that exists within groups (Mann & Kato, 1996). Conversely, benefits of conducting and reviewing group difference research include recognition of group strengths and potential areas of weakness or difficulty, as well as recognition of the importance of cultural variables and influence in the development of interventions.

Despite the utility of group difference multicultural research, Chang (1996a, 1996b) revealed the need to assess the equivalence of specific constructs across cultures rather than merely measure differences in levels of the construct. This need clearly can be understood if one were to suggest an intervention focused on reducing pessimism in the Asian-American participants in Chang's study without knowing the psychological correlates of pessimism in Asian-American samples. In this case, reducing pessimism levels for Asian Americans could conceivably lead to a decreased utilization of problem-solving behaviors. These constructs must be understood in a multicultural framework in order to interpret their magnitudes in terms of their utility for the cultural group. Only after they are placed in this framework can the development of culturally appropriate interventions proceed in a responsible manner.

Philosophical Foundations of the Good Life: Recognizing the Value of Religion, Spirituality, and Diverse Constructions of Meaning

The establishment of meaningful existence requires "an overall organizational framework that unites separate goal strivings into a coherent structure" (Emmons, 1999, p. 113). Baumeister (1991) contends that one must be able to see the possible connections among things, events, and relationships in order to achieve life meaning. For many people in today's society, religiosity and spirituality provide a foundation on which a framework of personal meaning is built. According to Burke and Miranti (1995), "Throughout history, each culture, civilization, and nation has adopted practices considered to be sacred and life sustaining. The forms that these practices take are expressions of religiosity. The beliefs are said to be one's individual spirituality" (p. ix)[2]

If we are to truly value diverse constructions of meaning and individual perspectives of what is the "good life," an appreciation of the differences in philosophies that exist among people across the country and world is essential. Drawing upon religion and/or spirituality may provide a person with the courage and strength needed to cope with everyday stressors as well as life crises and ultimately live up to his or her own conventions (Burke & Miranti, 1995).

Religion

Religion often is the foundation upon which disadvantaged and estranged groups of people are able to build strength and meaning. Faith can be enlisted to prevent problems from occurring and to aid in recovery from adversity. Thus, faith serves as a coping mechanism, a source of emotional and social support, and a basis for hope (Maton & Wells, 1995).

Though people of all races and ethnicities practice religion, studies demonstrate that religious faith is enlisted in coping processes to a greater extent by some groups. Rosen (1982) found that although both impoverished African Americans and Caucasians reported practicing religion as a means of coping with everyday problems and depression, the African-American participants turned to faith more often. In addition, the African-American participants reported a more positive outlook on their lives than their counterparts in spite of living in objectively poorer circumstances. Rosen concluded that the African Americans seemed to use religion as a medium for finding meaning and purpose in their lives. Likewise, Blaine and Crocker (1995) found that the psychological well-being of African-American individuals (but not Caucasians) was predicted by religiosity. Religiosity (i.e., public and private religious behaviors, including meaning-enhancing attributions to God and positive social identification based on one's religious affiliation) in African-American participants was positively correlated with self-esteem and satisfaction with life and negatively correlated with depression and hopelessness.[3]

Spirituality

"We are a diverse and increasingly complex nation of cultures, races, and ethnic groups who strive to coexist. . . . whether it be our search for personal meaning of life or deep religious affiliation and conviction, we share spirituality regardless of our historical roots or heritage" (Sweeney, 1995, p. vii). The spiritual grounding of cultural groups serves as a model for how life can be when one is able to look beyond traditional Western beliefs. Native-American spirituality involves the belief that all things are connected and are worthy of respect. In order to be spiritual, people must seek their place in the world, and all else will follow. Purpose and direction in life for Native Americans are derived by seeking harmony and balance among interrelated thoughts, emotions, and behaviors. Living a meaningful life involves "making constructive and creative choices through clear intention (wisdom) to fulfill one's purpose in the Greater Circle of Life by maintaining and contributing to the reciprocal balance of family, clan, tribe, and community in the context of personal, social, and natural environment" (Garrett & Myers, 1996, p. 99). This description reflects how spirituality influences a Native American's search for meaning and purpose. We all must become more familiar and comfortable with diverse constructions of religion, spirituality, and meaning in order to be able to research these constructs and, in turn, feel more confident addressing these issues in practice.

The Value of Religion, Spirituality, and Diverse Constructions of Meaning

Religion, spirituality, and the diverse constructions of meaning held by various populations across the world can serve as sources of comfort and support for those who are searching for the good life but are unable to find it within their current cultural milieu. Chandler, Holden, and Kolander (1992) contend that spirituality is an "innate capacity" of all people, that is, a capacity "found in humans, albeit realized to different degrees by different people at different times" (p. 171). Thus, a goal of clinicians could be to increase client awareness regarding their innate personal spirituality so that they may reap the benefits. Hopefully we can all become open to new ideas and willing to try new things as we continue to discover the benefits others are achieving via these tools.

Cross-Cultural Research on Emotion-Focused Approaches: Clues to the Good Life

Just as certain approaches to life and interpretations of events can constrict or limit the potential for well-being, other processes open a realm of possibilities and suggest many opportunities for positive experience. Self-esteem, happiness, subjective well-being, and resilience often are researched to provide insight into people's interpretation of the world and themselves. Though several of these emotion-based constructs have been examined empirically, little research has focused on their role in a multicultural context. Recognizing that individuals from diverse backgrounds face unique issues that invariably affect their experiences, it is necessary to further explore these constructs and evaluate how they might provide clues to the good life.

Happiness and Subjective Well-Being

How we experience life is fundamental to our growth and motivation, and humans interminably seek to feel satisfied and happy. While happiness is "the fundamental goal of life" (Csikszentmihalyi, 1999, p. 821), laypersons and scientists alike struggle to find what happiness is and how to identify the factors that produce it. When considering members of different cultures and acknowledging the fact that minorities might be subject to the widespread effects of prejudice, questions can emerge: Does happiness fluctuate along lines of culture and group membership? What characteristics lead to satisfaction and well-being for members of diverse cultures?

A large body of research exists that looks at differences in subjective well-being (SWB) across groups in nations (Diener & Diener, 1995; Diener, Diener, & Diener, 1995; Suh, Diener, Oishi, & Triandis, 1998), providing clues to correlates of life satisfaction in diverse cultures. In a review of national differences in SWB, Diener and Suh (1999) reported that people living in individualistic cultures have higher levels of life satisfaction than those in collectivist cultures. While collectivist cultures give priority to the in-group and define the self in relational terms, individualist cultures, such as that of the United States, encourage independence, attention to personal opinions and feelings, and autonomy. The distinctions between these cultural variables suggest that SWB may be more salient to individualists, and that attributes traditionally associated with well-being may not be as relevant for members of collectivist cultures (Suh, 2000). Recognizing that certain constructs may hold different cultural meaning is especially significant for work in a multicultural setting.

Research looking at SWB across nations also has shown that individuals in wealthier nations report higher levels of life satisfaction, though the processes by which national wealth and well-being are connected are unclear, and there are exceptions to this relationship (Diener & Suh, 1999). According to Csikszentmihalyi (1999), who explored factors related to happiness, findings based on Americans suggest weaker relationships between wealth and subjective reports of well-being, with some of the wealthiest individuals reporting levels of happiness not far greater than those of people with average incomes (Diener, Horwitz, & Emmons, 1985). Material poverty should not preclude the attainment of well-being for individuals who are disadvantaged and relegated to lower socioeconomic levels in society, and finding other approaches to happiness, including such avenues as spirituality, optimism, and flow, is essential for these individuals to reach their maximum potential (Csikszentmihalyi, 1999).

Resilience

How to cope and utilize positive behavioral patterns under stress constitutes the idea of resilience. Gordon (1996) defined resilience comprehensively as "the ability to thrive, mature, and increase competence in the face of adverse circumstances or obstacles" (p. 63). Indeed, the importance of this ability to adapt to stress is highlighted in the lives of children and adolescents as they grow and adjust to the challenges of development and their environments. Those who are resilient generally have a much greater chance of thriving when life circumstances are difficult.

Previous research has explored the individual and environmental characteristics that contribute to resilience in people, particularly in children and adolescents. Gordon's (1996) review of characteristics that contribute to resilience in adolescents indicated that five personal factors were stable across ethnic groups: intelligence, androgyny, independence (autonomy), social skills, and internal locus of control. Children and adolescents who exhibited sociability as well as a sense of independence, who had hobbies and creative interests, and who engaged in activities that were not narrowly sex-typed also were better able to adjust to life stressors.

Gordon (1996) highlighted the impact of the school environment on ethnic minority students. In general, findings suggest that schools that have high standards and expectations that are supportive of the student and his or her entire family, and that are integrated and conflict free help to foster resilience in children. Within these schools, it appears that the teachers serve as role models and mentors, give effective feedback and ample praise, and work to understand and accept their students' culture, language, and communication style. Rak and Patterson (1996) and Werner (1984) also address the important role of environment, including teachers, school counselors, coaches, mental health workers, clergy, and good neighbors, in the lives of resilient children.

Group or Collective Self-esteem

Self-esteem has been operationalized in the psychological literature as a construct related to how an individual values him- or herself (Porter & Washington, 1993) and can be explored as a personal, individual construct, as well as a collective self-esteem, or "aspects of the self concept relating to race, ethnic background, religion, feelings of belonging in one's community, and the like" (Luhtanen & Crocker, 1992, p. 302). Many researchers (Blash & Unger, 1995; Lorenzo-Hernandez & Ouellette, 1998; Martinez & Dukes, 1997; Phinney, 1991; Phinney, Cantu, & Kurtz, 1997) have suggested that there is a link between collective self-esteem and personal self-esteem, and indeed it seems

logical that individuals with positive feelings toward their group affiliation also will feel positively about themselves. Some theorists have speculated that when other people view an individual's group in a negative manner, it may lead to negative self-evaluations or self-esteem. For ethnic or other minority groups, this social identity theory has particularly powerful implications and has been the subject of several studies. Crocker, Luhtanen, Blaine, and Broadnax (1994) studied the distinction between public appraisals of African Americans and personal self-esteem, finding that there was no significant relationship between the two. This suggests African Americans separate personal feelings about their groups from how they believe society values them. A study by Phinney et al. (1997) of African-American, Latino, and Caucasian adolescents also appears to disconfirm the ideas behind social identity theory, instead demonstrating that members of ethnic groups may distance themselves from negative perceptions that others may hold. Looking at how members of stigmatized groups guard their self-esteem, Crocker and Major (1989) found that individuals make attributions that are protective, such as assuming that prejudiced or stereotyped reactions by others are aimed toward the collective group rather than the individual. Perhaps these attributions, as well as the sense of a broader identity source (personal and group), help to lessen the impact of negative stereotypes and social denigration of minority group members (Martinez & Dukes, 1997).

Because research suggests collective self-esteem is related to higher personal self-esteem and minority group members seem able to distinguish between others' perceptions of their group and their own feelings of personal identity, the individual's development of ethnic or other minority group identity could be quite valuable to personal well-being. In a longitudinal study of ethnic identity and self-esteem in Asian-American, African-American, and Hispanic adolescents, Phinney and Chavira (1992) found that the exploration of cultural background appeared to promote personal self-esteem and, in turn, exploration of ethnic issues. In a study of college students, Phinney and Alipuria (1990) found that ethnic identity search was positively related to self-esteem for African-American males, and less strongly for both Asian Americans and Caucasians. These results suggest that for members of certain minority groups, self-esteem may be influenced by exploration and learning about one's culture (Phinney, 1991).

Clues to the Good Life

Recognizing the variety of protective emotional factors in the lives of individuals further illustrates the crucial role of family, group, school, and community as mechanisms for increasing resilience, happiness and well-being, and self-esteem. As children and adults are faced with a variety of misfortunes and inequities, increasing their sources of support and personal competencies is fundamental. Emotion-focused approaches can build on existing abilities within a person, as well as aid in the process of developing a larger repertoire of strengths. When considering people from diverse backgrounds, it is essential to realize that standards for satisfaction may differ from culture to culture, and assumptions based on majority groups may not be adequate to describe the desired characteristics or goals of members of other cultures. As researchers continue to explore emotion-focused constructs in their search for clues to the good life, a broad lens of investigation should be used, along with clinicians' appreciation of the unique nature of diverse people in all societies.

Interpersonal Connection: Finding Exemplars

The quotation that begins this chapter refers to "our basic needs for connectedness" (Lopez et al., 2000, p. 238). In our scientific and clinical pursuit of optimal human functioning, the importance of interpersonal connection cannot be underestimated. We know that a sound therapeutic relationship promotes change (Hubble, Duncan, & Miller, 1999), that the number of friendships correlates with positive affectivity and health (Moore & Isen, 1990), and that disconnection leads to despair and despondency (Joiner & Coyne, 1999).

Many positive psychology scholars believe that healthy interpersonal and social functioning pave the way to the discovery of health and fulfillment. The same scholars are challenged to operationalize constructs and processes that would facilitate the testing of the basic assumption that the Golden Rule facilitates good living. The authors in this volume describe the science related to interpersonal processes of love, compassion, forgiveness, gratitude, and altruism and make a strong case for the personal benefits of interpersonal goodness. Despite the progress that has been made, the answer to questions such as Why are these people/families able to maintain such good relationships? and Why are members of this particular group in such good health? remain difficult to answer. Finding exemplars of health and "good living" may reveal some of the answers.

Libben' de Good Life

The Gullah people are African Americans who were brought to the sea islands off the coast of South Carolina during the slave trade. (Gullah is actually the name of the pidgin language that incorporates English, Wolof, and Fula languages. The dialect name has evolved into a common reference to the people living in the sea islands off Charleston.) Historical and anthropological accounts suggest that Gullah forefathers lived in the Sierra Leone region in Africa and were well known as rice farmers. Numerous situational factors resulted in the families and other tribespeople remaining together rather than being separated when they were sold as slaves. Thus, the Gullah people, although trapped by the atrocities of slavery, were able to maintain interpersonal connections and cultural mechanisms that allowed them to thrive in a region that was similar to their West African homeland.

The ethnic enclave of the Gullahs has fostered rich traditions, a unique language, and a respect for family and tribe that is manifested in the manner in which homes of descendants are built around the home of a family elder, and interpersonal relations are viewed as personal priorities. Could the Gullah people offer insight into the value of interpersonal connection, compassion, altruism, and other relational aspects of the good life?

Though the Gullahs' ability to maintain strong interpersonal ties and care for friends and extended family may serve as an exemplar for healthy interpersonal living, social science has not sought to discover the strengths in this culture. How did the cultural traditions and strong interpersonal frameworks survive the environmental conditions and demoralization associated with slave life? There are few scientific answers to this question, yet there are some signs that the Gullahs established means of "libben' de good life" (i.e., "living the good life") even though they were enslaved.

Numerous cultural groups have managed to maintain strong connections with others from similar backgrounds so that they are able to thrive under difficult circumstances. The French Acadians, or Cajuns, of southern Louisiana have developed the community mantra of "laissez les bon temps rouler" (i.e., let the good times roll), which suggests that the people may have insight into how to have collective good times. The mystique of the "no problem" Jamaican lifestyle also may offer clues to how a lifestyle of a people produces a relaxed attitude.

Studying the Best of the Best

We do not mean to imply that psychology has not attempted to study the best of the best. Clearly, projects such as the Harvard Study (Vaillant, 1977) and the Terman Studies (Holahan & Sears, 1995; Terman & Oden, 1959) have yielded amazing discoveries regarding how healthy, bright people develop and manage war-related stress and physical illness. The correlates of good health and success, and conversely, illness and adversity, continue to be illuminated by these longitudinal studies and their offshoots (see Peterson, Seligman, & Vaillant, 1988). Yet efforts to be inclusive in studying the best of the best and the interpersonal processes that contribute to individuals being the best have been limited. Researchers must turn their energies to finding examples of individuals and groups that translate *connection* into health and well-being.

Finding Representative Exemplars

How do single-parent families maintain cohesiveness and strong community connections? What are the sequelae of positive interpersonal interactions? Do altruism and compassion provide mutually positive effects for the giver and the receiver of kindness? Do people from all cultural backgrounds benefit from interpersonal connection in the same manner? Does living with *la familia* have the same type of effects as living with a family? An Irish proverb provides a possible answer to all these questions: In the shelter of each other is where the people *live*. Studying all types of psychological shelters, the shelters in which people of all backgrounds exist and live, is an important aspect of putting positive psychology in a multicultural context.

Coping: Clarifying What Works

We know little about the pattern of coping behaviors utilized in groups other than Caucasians. Thus, the coping strategies of each multicultural subpopulation cannot be explored individually in this chapter. In addition, it is important to remember that within each subgroup, whether it be Caucasians or Hispanic Americans, there are probably as many similarities as there are differences. Keeping this within-group diversity in mind, when a single subgroup's coping behaviors are examined, it is not to imply that every person within that group will behave the same when faced with a similar stressor.

The Influence of Cultural Values and Coping Models

When exploring how people cope, one must consider the cultural values that may influence how a person thinks, acts, and feels. For instance, many psychologists distinguish between collectivist and individualistic cultures when exploring behavior (Chang, 2001; Triandis, 1995). As noted previously, collectivist cultures value fitting in, group and family interdependence, and filial piety, whereas individualistic cultures value personal independence and assertiveness (Sue, 1998). These individualistic values often are found in Western society; hence, the research that has been conducted with Caucasians may not paint an accurate picture of the coping behaviors of persons in other cultures; thus comparing apples and oranges comes to mind. Although some argue that coping is neither inherently adaptive nor maladaptive (Lazarus & Folkman, 1984; Stanton & Franz, 1999), some researchers have made this distinction, and researchers and clinicians should question the generalizability of findings (e.g., X generally is an adaptive coping mechanism for Caucasians). Finally, the coping model that is utilized as the framework for a particular study also could affect how a specific cultural group's coping behaviors differ from those of Caucasians.

Coping in Multicultural Populations

There is little consensus among researchers regarding coping factors and the association of these factors with well-being and mental and physical health outcomes, but research is beginning to clarify what works for different people in diverse situations. In the Shaw et al. (1997) study of the coping processes of family caregivers of Alzheimer's disease patients in Shanghai, China, and San Diego, California, results indicated that four coping factors were utilized consistently across samples: (a) behavioral confronting (taking action); (b) behavioral distancing/social support (utilizing social support); (c) cognitive confronting (cognitive reappraisal and intellectualization); and (d) cognitive distancing (denying the problem or avoiding thoughts about it). They hypothesized that these four strategies transcend culture; however, they found that while coping strategies may be similar in different cultures, the application of strategies and the relationship of coping to psychological distress may differ substantially for different groups. These results are consistent with other research indicating that different coping strategies can be adaptive and can affect well-being differently depending on the cultural background of the person (Chang, in press; Liu, 1986).

Other researchers have found support for the hypothesis that culture also can influence the interpretation of an event and the coping strategies utilized. Strong (1984) conducted a study comparing the coping behaviors of Native-American and Caucasian families who care for elderly relatives. The results indicate that the two groups differed on the use of control and expression of anger. More of the Caucasian caretakers felt they had control over the situation, while expressing anger and frustration more often than the Native-American caretakers. Strong suggests that perhaps since the Native-American caretakers felt less control, they coped by emphasizing acceptance of the way things are rather than by becoming frustrated. This is consistent with the concept of noninterference, which is considered a traditional Native-American value (Garrett & Garrett, 1998). The results also indicated, though, that respondents did not differ significantly on other dimensions such as emotional involvement, feelings of apprehension about caretaking, and a sense of duty or responsibility to their elder.

Chang (2001) suggests that most Asian Americans use a collectivist frame of reference, whereas Caucasians act from an individualistic one, and that these cultural differences should influence how each group copes with stress. Three coping models were examined, and significant differences were found between the groups. Yet even when differences were not found on a specific coping dimension, differences emerged in relation to measures of adjustment. For example, as previously mentioned, Asian Americans had higher optimism, but scores were not significantly associated with life satisfaction or depression. With Caucasian Americans, optimism was related to greater life satisfaction. Chang suggests that cultural differences do not necessarily influence coping directly, but that culture can affect other factors such as personality, which in turn could influence coping behaviors.

Like researchers previously referenced, Conway (1985) found many similarities in coping responses between groups but also found some significant differences. When examining African American and Caucasian elderly women faced with a medical problem, both action-oriented coping (in the form of prayer) and cognitive-oriented coping (making positive self-statements) responses were utilized in the two groups. The African-American women seemed to be more advantaged in terms of social support than the Caucasian women. More specifically, church members, friends, and family were additional sources of support for the African-American women. This finding is consistent with the importance of kinship and church support systems within traditional African-American values of affiliation and spirituality (Wilson & Stith, 1998).

The use of family or additional support systems seems to be an essential coping response for other groups as well. De La Rosa (1988) found that Puerto Rican adolescents with strong support systems were better able to handle stressful situations and were less likely to become ill, regardless of age, gender, socioeconomic status, or health status. Consistent with De La Rosa's findings, Colomba, Santiago, and Rossello (1999) also found support for the hypothesis that the more frequently Puerto Rican adolescents engage in strategies such as seeking family and other social support, the lower the probability that they will develop depressive symptoms when faced with a stressful situation. Finally, the results of Kim and McKenry's (1998) study, comparing the use of social networks and social support between African Americans, Asian Americans, Caucasians, and Hispanics, indicated that there were far more similarities than differences in use of social support when education was controlled. The differences they did find suggested the support systems utilized by Caucasians may not be helpful for ethnic minority families.

Clarifying What Works

This overview of coping literature with multi-cultural populations indicates that while there are many similarities between the coping behaviors of Caucasians and other groups, there are many differences as well. Thus, the current models of stress and coping may not be sufficient to address the unique strategies and styles of groups other than Caucasians. To understand coping behaviors of multicultural groups, more research needs to be conducted to consider the role of development, within-group differences, and the specific coping behaviors contributing to better adjustment within the diverse groups.

Casting a Good Net: Recommendations for Putting Positive Psychology in a Multicultural Context

Hector, the protagonist in this chapter's introductory story, used a "fine net" as the tool of his trade. We believe that we have a science, a fine science, capable of elucidating the characteristics and psychological processes that potentially could have salutogenic effects for members of our diverse society.[4] Continued efforts to build the scientific base for positive psychology should guarantee that the net of science be of the right weave. In discussing psychological frameworks and coping, we have attempted to highlight the awareness and procedures that help put positive psychology in a multicultural context:

- Examining the magnitude and equivalence of constructs across cultures
- Recognizing the value of religious practices, spirituality, and diverse constructions of life meaning
- Searching for the clues to the good life that cultural experiences might provide
- Finding exemplars who function within a positive psychological framework
- Clarifying what works in the lives of people

Prescribing the Good Life: What Is Good for One Is Not Good for All

Woody, the Harvard MBA, spoke with confidence, as if he knew the path to the good life. Hector, spoke with contentment and listened with respect, yet he did not seem to question his own path. Clearly, what is good for one is not good for all, nor is there one path to the good life.

In building a positive psychology, scientists have made amazing discoveries, including what induces positive affect (see Isen, in this volume) and what promotes happiness and subjective well-being (see Diener, Lucas, & Oishi, this volume). In this chapter we repeatedly have referred to the "good life" in a manner that implied it is the ultimate goal in life, yet we offered no definition or recipe for the reference. Scientists have not yet operationalized "*the* good life," and most are acutely aware that a morally pluralistic society engenders not a general definition of the good life but an individual opportunity to define it and pursue it. We dare not prescribe a "good life" or an approach to health that is good for all humankind. It is our hope, however, that research and practice will help to illuminate a path for those individuals pursuing their self-defined good life and provide the psychological tools necessary for clearing the way.

Extending the Science and Practice of Positive Psychology

We wrote this chapter with the goal of encouraging professionals in social science and clinical practice to extend and enhance their work by putting positive psychology in a multicultural context. Darwinian statements seem to frame this as a natural progression: "As man advances in civilization and small tribes are united into larger communities . . . he ought to extend his social instincts and sympathies to all members of the same nation. . . . This point being reached there is only an artificial barrier to prevent his sympathies extending to men of all nations and races" (Darwin, 1998, p. 126).

Notes

1. Despite the significant differences, it is important to note that, on average, all groups reported hopeful thinking most of the time.

2. It should be noted that though religious faith and spirituality may lead to similar human ends, the two are not the same. "Spirituality is not a religion. Spirituality has to do with experience; religion has to do with the conceptualization of that experience. Spirituality focuses on what happens in the heart; religion tries to codify and capture

that experience in a system" (Legere, 1984, p. 376). Thus, individuals who do not practice a particular religion can establish the foundation for meaning through a nonreligious form of spirituality.

3. Although religious faith appears to be a source of strength individuals can enlist to enhance well-being, we would be remiss if we did not acknowledge that faith also can have negative effects. For example, some religious beliefs and values can invoke a sense of inappropriate guilt, shame, or worry in an individual and thus do more harm than good (Maton & Wells, 1995). In addition, some religious groups blatantly deny membership to persons of particular ethnic groups and sexual orientations, which can be detrimental for those who are excluded. For instance, many gay men and lesbian women have been turned away and even shamed by traditional Western religious groups (Ritter & O'Neill, 1989). Thus, many homosexuals view religion in a negative light and become disillusioned by an institution that claims to be committed to helping the oppressed while hypocritically being an oppressor itself.

4. The bodies of work of psychologists such as Dean Simonton, Mihaly Csikszentmihalyi, and Susan Harter serve as exemplars to other researchers who are trying to determine the multicultural context of their work.

References

Allport, G. W. (1954). *The nature of prejudice.* Reading, MA: Addison-Wesley.

Basic Behavioral Science Task Force of the National Advisory Mental Health Council. (1996). Basic behavioral science research for mental health. *American Psychologist, 51,* 722–731.

Baumeister, R. F. (1991). *Meanings in life.* New York: Guilford.

Blaine, B., & Crocker, J. (1995). Religiousness, race, and psychological well-being: Exploring social psychological mediators. *Personality and Social Psychology Bulletin, 21,* 1031–1041.

Blash, R., & Unger, D. G. (1995). Self-concept of African American male youth: Self-esteem and ethnic identity. *Journal of Child and Family Studies, 4,* 359–373.

Burke, M. T., & Miranti, J. G. (Eds.). (1995). *Counseling: The spiritual dimension.* Alexandria, VA: American Counseling Association.

Carter J. H. (1994). Racism's impact on mental health. *Journal of the National Medical Association, 86,* 543–547.

Carvajal, S. C., Garner, R. L., & Evans, R. I. (1998). Dispositional optimism as a protective factor in resisting HIV exposure in sexually active inner-city minority adolescents. *Journal of Applied Social Psychology, 28,* 2196–2211.

Chandler, C., Holden, J., & Kolander, C. (1992). Counseling for spiritual wellness: Theory and practice. *Journal of Counseling and Development, 71,* 168–175.

Chang, E. C. (1996a). Cultural differences in optimism, pessimism, and coping: Predictors of subsequent adjustment in Asian American and Caucasian American college students. *Journal of Counseling Psychology, 43,* 113–123.

Chang, E. C. (1996b). Evidence for the cultural specificity of pessimism in Asians vs. Caucasians: A test of a general negativity hypothesis. *Personality and Individual Differences, 21,* 819–822.

Chang, E. C. (2001). A look at the coping strategies and styles of Asian Americans: Similar and different? In C. R. Snyder (Ed.), *Coping and copers: Adaptive processes and people* (pp. 222–239). New York: Oxford University Press.

Chang, E. C., Maydeu-Olivares, A., & D'Zurilla, T. J. (1997). Optimism and pessimism as partially independent constructs: Relationship to positive and negative affectivity and psychological well-being. *Personality and Individual Differences, 23*(3), 433–440.

Chin, J. L. (1993). Toward a psychology of difference: Psychotherapy for a culturally diverse population. In J. L. Chin, V. De La Cancela, & Y. M. Jenkins (Eds.), *Diversity in psychotherapy: The politics of race, ethnicity, and gender* (pp. 69–91). Westport, CT: Praeger.

Colomba, M. V., Santiago, E. S., & Rossello, J. (1999). Coping strategies and depression in Puerto Rican adolescents: An exploratory study. *Cultural Diversity and Ethnic Minority Psychology, 5,* 65–75.

Conway, K. (1985). Coping with the stress of medical problems among black and white elderly. *International Journal of Aging and Human Development, 21,* 39–48.

Crandall, V. C., Katkovsky, W., & Crandall, V. J. (1965). Children's beliefs in their own control of reinforcements in intellectual-academic situations. *Child Development, 36,* 91–109.

Crocker, J., Luhtanen, R., Blaine, B., & Broadnax, S. (1994). Collective self-esteem and psychological well-being among White, Black, and Asian college students. *Personality and Social Psychology Bulletin, 20,* 503–513.

Crocker, J., & Major, B. (1989). Social stigma and self-esteem: The self-protective properties of stigma. *Psychological Review, 96,* 608–630.

Csikszentmihalyi, M. (1999). If we are so rich, why aren't we happy? *American Psychologist, 54,* 821–827.

Darwin, C. (1998). *The descent of man.* Amherst, MA: Prometheus Press.

De La Rosa, M. (1988). Natural support systems of Puerto Ricans: A key dimension for well-being. *Health and Social Work, 13,* 181–190.

Diener, E., & Diener, M. (1995). Cross-cultural correlates of life satisfaction and self-esteem. *Journal of Personality and Social Psychology, 68,* 653–663.

Diener, E., Diener, M., & Diener, C. (1995). Factors predicting the subjective well-being of nations. *Journal of Personality and Social Psychology, 69,* 851–864.

Diener, E., Horwitz, J., & Emmons, R. A. (1985). Happiness of the very wealthy. *Social Indicators, 16,* 263–274.

Diener, E., & Suh, E. M. (1999). National differences in subjective well-being. In D. Kahneman, E. Diener, & N. Schwarz (Eds.), *Well-being: The foundations of hedonic psychology.* New York: Russell Sage Foundation.

Emmons, R. A. (1999). *The psychology of ultimate concerns: Motivation and spirituality in personality.* New York: Guilford.

Garrett, J. T., & Garrett, M. W. (1998). The path of good medicine: Understanding and counseling Native American Indians. In D. R. Atkinson, G. Morten, & D. W. Sue (Eds.), *Counseling American minorities: A cross-cultural perspective* (pp. 183–192). Boston: McGraw-Hill.

Garrett, M. T., & Myers, J. E. (1996). The rule of opposites: A paradigm for counseling Native Americans. *Journal of Multicultural Counseling and Development, 24,* 89–104.

Gauvain, M. (1998). Cognitive development in social and cultural context. *Current Directions in Psychological Science, 7,* 188–192.

Gordon, K. A. (1996). Resilient Hispanic youths, self-concept and motivational patterns. *Hispanic Journal of Behavioral Sciences, 18,* 63–73.

Hackett, G., Betz, N. E., Casas, J. M., & Rocha-Singh, I. A. (1992). Gender, ethnicity, and social cognitive factors predicting the academic achievement of students in engineering. *Journal of Counseling Psychology, 39,* 527–538.

Halpin, G., Halpin, G., & Whiddon, T. (1981). Locus of control and self-esteem among American Indians and whites: A cross-cultural comparison. *Psychological Reports, 48,* 91–98.

Holahan, C. K., & Sears, R. R. (1995). *The gifted group in later maturity.* Stanford, CA: Stanford University Press.

Hubble, M. A., Duncan, B. L., & Miller, S. D. (1999). *The heart and soul of change: What works in therapy.* Washington, DC: American Psychological Association.

Jackson, F. L. C. (1992). Race and ethnicity as biological constructs. *Race and Ethnicity, 2,* 120–125.

Joiner, T., & Coyne, J. C. (1999). *The interactional nature of depression: Advances in interpersonal approaches.* Washington, DC: American Psychological Association.

Kaplan, J. S., & Sue, S. (1997). Ethnic psychology in the United States. In D. F. Halpern & A. E. Voiskounsky (Eds.), *States of mind: American and post-Soviet perspectives on contemporary issues in psychotherapy* (pp. 349–369). New York: Oxford University Press.

Kim, H. K., & McKenry, P. C. (1998). Social networks and social support: A comparison of African Americans, Asian Americans, Caucasians, and Hispanics. *Journal of Comparative Family Studies, 29,* 313–334.

Lazarus, R. S., & Folkman, S. (1984). *Stress, appraisal, and coping.* New York: Springer.

Legere, T. E. (1984). A spirituality for today. *Studies in Formative Spirituality, 5,* 375–388.

Liu, W. T. (1986). Culture and social support. *Research on Aging, 8,* 57–83.

Lopez, S. J., Gariglietti, K. P., McDermott, D., Sherwin, E. D., Floyd, R. K., Rand, K., & Snyder, C. R. (2000). Hope for the evolution of diversity: On leveling the field of dreams. In C. R. Snyder (Ed.), *The handbook of hope* (pp. 220–240). San Diego, CA: Academic Press.

Lorenzo-Hernandez, J., & Ouellette, S. (1998). Ethnic identity, self-esteem, and values in Dominicans, Puerto Ricans, and African Americans. *Journal of Applied Social Psychology, 28,* 2007–2024.

Luhtanen, R., & Crocker, J. (1992). A collective self-esteem scale: Self-evaluation of one's social identity. *Personality and Social Psychology Bulletin, 18,* 302–318.

Mann, T., & Kato, P. (1996). *Handbook of diversity issues in health psychology.* New York: Plenum.

Marsella, A. J. (1998). Toward a "global-community psychology": Meeting the needs of a changing world. *American Psychologist, 53,* 1282–1291.

Martinez, R. O., & Dukes, R. L. (1997). The effects of ethnic identity, ethnicity, and gender on adolescent well-being. *Journal of Youth and Adolescence, 26,* 503–516.

Maton, K. I., & Wells, E. A. (1995). Religion as a community resource for well-being: Prevention, healing, and empowerment pathways. *Journal of Social Issues, 51,* 177–193.

Moore, B. S., & Isen, A. (Eds.). (1990). *Affect and social behavior.* New York: Cambridge University Press.

Munoz-Dunbar, R. (1993). *Hope: A cross-cultural assessment of American college students*. Unpublished master's thesis, University of Kansas, Lawrence.

Pedersen, A., & Pedersen, P. (1989). The cultural grid: A framework for multicultural counseling. *International Journal for the Advancement of Counselling, 12*, 299–307.

Peterson, C., Seligman, M. E. P., & Vaillant, G. E. (1988). Pessimistic explanatory style is a risk factor for physical illness: A thirty-five-year longitudinal study. *Journal of Personality and Social Psychology, 55*(1), 23–27.

Phinney, J. (1991). Ethnic identity and self-esteem: A review and integration. *Hispanic Journal of Behavioral Sciences, 13*, 193–208.

Phinney, J., & Alipuria, L. (1990). Ethnic identity in college students from four ethnic groups. *Journal of Adolescent Research, 13*, 171–183.

Phinney, J. S., Cantu, C. L., & Kurtz, D. A. (1997). Ethnic and American identity as predictors of self-esteem among African American, Latino, and White adolescents. *Journal of Youth and Adolescence, 26*, 165–185.

Phinney, J. S., & Chavira, V. (1992). Ethnic identity and self-esteem: An exploratory longitudinal study. *Journal of Adolescence, 15*, 271–281.

Porter, J. R., & Washington, R. E. (1993). Minority identity and self-esteem. *Annual Review of Sociology, 19*, 139–161.

Rak, C. F., & Patterson, L. E. (1996). Promoting resilience in at-risk children. *Journal of Counseling and Development, 74*(4), 368–373.

Ritter, K. Y., & O'Neill, C. W. (1989). Moving through loss: The spiritual journey of gay men and lesbian women. *Journal of Counseling and Development, 68*, 9–15.

Rosen, C. E. (1982). Ethnic differences among impoverished rural elderly in use of religion as a coping mechanism. *Journal of Rural Community Psychology, 3*, 27–34.

Scheier, M. F., & Carver, C. S. (1992). Effects of optimism on psychological and physical well-being: Theoretical overview and empirical update. *Cognitive Therapy and Research, 16*(2), 201–228.

Shaw, W. S., Patterson, T. L., Semple, S. J., Grant, I., Yu, E. S. H., Zhang, M. Y., He, Y., & Wu, W. Y. (1997). A cross-cultural validation of coping strategies and their associations with caregiving distress. *The Gerontologist, 37*, 490–504.

Snyder, C. R., Irving, L. M., & Anderson, J. R. (1991). Hope and health. In C. R. Snyder &

D. R. Forsyth (Eds.), *Handbook of social and clinical psychology: The health perspective* (pp. 285–305). New York: Pergamon.

Stanton, A. L., & Franz, R. (1999). Focusing on emotion: An adaptive coping strategy? In C. R. Snyder (Ed.), *Coping: The psychology of what works* (pp. 90–118). Oxford: Oxford University Press.

Strong, C. (1984). Stress and caring for the elderly relatives: Interpretations and coping strategies in an American Indian and White sample. *The Gerontologist, 24*, 251–256.

Sue, D. W. (1996). Multicultural counseling: Models, methods, and actions. *Counseling Psychologist, 24*, 279–284.

Sue, D. W. (1998). The interplay of sociocultural factors on the psychological development of Asians in America. In D. R. Atkinson, G. Morten, & D. W. Sue (Eds.), *Counseling American minorities: A cross-cultural perspective* (pp. 205–213). Boston: McGraw-Hill.

Sue, S. (1983). Ethnic minority issues in psychology: A reexamination. *American Psychologist, 38*, 583–592.

Suh, E. (2000). *Culture, identity consistency, and subjective well-being*. Unpublished manuscript.

Suh, E., Diener, E., Oishi, S., & Triandis, H. C. (1998). The shifting basis of life satisfaction judgments across cultures: Emotions versus norms. *Journal of Personality and Social Psychology, 74*, 482–493.

Sweeney, T. J. (1995). Foreword. In M. T. Burke & J. G. Miranti (Eds.), *Counseling: The spiritual dimension* (pp. vii–viii). Alexandria, VA: American Counseling Association.

Terman, L. M., & Oden, M. H. (1959). *Genetic study of genius: Vol. 5. The gifted group at midlife*. Stanford, CA: Stanford University Press.

Triandis, H. C. (1995). *Individualism and collectivism*. Boulder, CO: Westview.

Vaillant, G. E. (1977). *Adaptation to life*. Boston: Little, Brown.

Werner, E. (1984). Resilient children. *Young Children, 40*, 68–72.

Wilson, L., & Stith, S. M. (1998). Culturally sensitive therapy with Black clients. In D. R. Atkinson, G. Morten, & D. W. Sue (Eds.), *Counseling American minorities: A cross-cultural perspective* (pp. 116–126). Boston: McGraw-Hill.

Zuckerman, M. (1990). Some dubious premises in research and theory on racial differences: Scientific, social, and ethical issues. *American Psychologist, 45*, 1297–1303.

52

Positive Psychology at Work

Nick Turner, Julian Barling, & Anthea Zacharatos

The move to push psychology toward "the best things in life" (Seligman, 1998) comes at an interesting time with regard to the changing nature of work and the role psychology can play in helping us understand it. As researchers, we have only recently started to examine the shape of new employment relations (Barling, 1999; Tetrick & Barling, 1995), focusing mainly on the negative implications in our studies. Stress and burnout, violations of psychological contracts, workplace violence, job insecurity, and downsizing, to name but a few, remain the most popular topics for study. To some degree, these are appropriate subjects for research as failing to recognize the detrimental effects of organizational decisions on workers would be an injustice to their circumstances. However, failing to recognize the positive aspects of work in our research is also inappropriate. Thus, we strongly believe it is time to extend our research focus and explore more fully the positive sides, so as to gain a full understanding of the meaning and effects of working.

We firmly believe that a healthy and positive work focus is achievable. Indeed, we will argue that, in its truest sense, "healthy" work means the promotion of both psychological and physical well-being. Given the scope of this short chapter, however, we concentrate here on job-

related well-being for two reasons. First, the conceptualization of job-related well-being is well established in research, and it provides a positive foundation for examining the determinants of healthy work. Warr (1987, 1990, 1994, 1999), in his triaxial approach to measuring well-being, characterizes general well-being as an "active state" consisting of positive affect and high arousal. In the work context more specifically, Warr considers job satisfaction, job involvement, and organizational commitment (reflections of how employees feel about their jobs) as but a few of many measures of job-related well-being. What determines job-related well-being cuts across many areas of industrial/organizational (I/O) research and is a very relevant question to this chapter on positive psychology at work.

The second reason for our focus on job-related well-being is that work experiences translate directly into other mental health outcomes (e.g., Kelloway & Barling, 1991) and indirectly affect employees' life satisfaction (e.g., Hart, 1999; Higginbottom, Barling, & Kelloway, 1993; Judge & Watanabe, 1993). This interdependence between work and nonwork domains deserves prominent attention and remains an important research area. Our focus, however, will be on how to promote well-being in the workplace, and, as such, we examine people "at work."

By using our model of healthy work as a framework, we aim to show how employment practices and processes can make work positive and enjoyable. Our goal is to encourage others to take a similar positive psychology approach to the study of work and to further our understanding of the many benefits work can provide, as well as to learn about how these practices and processes interact to achieve this.

We begin by examining how today's competitive environment and the nature of the employment relationship are very different from what they were as recently as a decade ago. Trends include increases in part-time and contingent work, and the general intensification of labor through layoffs and other "lean" strategies. Against this backdrop, we then begin to outline our model of healthy work—one that includes organizational, group, dyadic, and individual perspectives on job-related well-being. First, we examine how organizational-level work processes, such as work redesign, can promote positive psychological development. We argue that high-quality work (e.g., jobs with high levels of control and social support to match job demands) complements the benefits of teamworking (a group-level process) and transformational leadership (a dyadic-level process). We then examine how these practices can help to develop more flexible employee role orientations, which we believe enable individual employees to face change with greater resilience and optimism.

In discussing the different levels at which healthy work can be promoted, we also illustrate how these perspectives indirectly result in positive outcomes through psychological mechanisms such as trust, interpersonal justice, and organizational commitment. Last, we argue that the proponents of organizational psychology are in a strong position to help promote positive psychological goals.

The Changing Nature of Work

Although patterns of work are complex and often difficult to disentangle, their direct effects on workers are more readily understood. What is clear is how recent employment trends affect the quantity and quality of work (Barling, 1999); and, more broadly, how the changing na-

ture of competition creates contradictions in the work experience.

The employment relationship has changed dramatically in recent decades, altering not only the type of work that people do but also when they work and how much they do (Barling, 1999; Sennett, 1998). For most of today's older population, long-term employment was the norm, whereas much of today's workforce faces a very different situation. For many people today, work increasingly involves part-time employment, contingent employment, and multiple careers. Furthermore, not only are more workers holding multiple jobs, but there is a parallel increase in the overtime worked by these individuals.

Against this backdrop of a larger number of hours worked and more temporary employment, some employees also face diminished choice and control in that they are forced to take on hours and working arrangements that are against their preferences. As we will discuss subsequently, perceptions of personal control play a key role in the way work is experienced. Yet additional unpredictability results as many employers move toward greater functional flexibility by expanding and shrinking the workforce to correspond with shifting production and service demands. For many employees, there has been not only a loss of control over working hours but also a sense of job and employment insecurity (Canadian Auto Workers, 1996; Martin, 1997).

For many organizations, the struggle to compete has meant adopting practices that attempt to reduce costs and increase productivity—a "do-more-with-less" mentality that favors profits over the welfare of people. Now-familiar mantras like "reengineering," "downsizing," and "lean production" provide the illusion of organizational efficiency to the outside world while often placing greater demands on remaining employees and failing to increase productivity (Cascio, 1993; De Meuse, Vanderheiden, & Bergmann, 1994; Patterson, Wall, & West, 1999). Furthermore, occupational safety and health may even be compromised (Landsbergis, Cahill, & Schnall, 1999). Sennett (1998) describes this situation as one in which "perfectly viable businesses are gutted or abandoned, capable employees are set adrift rather than rewarded, simply because the organization must prove to the market that it is capable of change" (p. 51).

The challenges that employers and employees face not only reflect their relations with the external environment but also guide and influence the inner life of organizations. A combination of contingent employment relationships and continually changing competitive structures can make the nature of work more intensive for both employers and employees. Amid these conditions, it is hardly surprising that workers are becoming disheartened at the decreasing quality of work life and are searching for the meaning that underlies their efforts.

It is this work environment that provides a starting point for our examination of how positive psychology goals can be integrated into the way we experience and understand work. We argue that to make the experience of work more positive in today's confusing occupational environment, there must be a commitment from both the individual and the organization to improve the quality of work life. On the one hand, managers must design the organization in a way that allows employees to do meaningful work in a healthy way; on the other hand, employees must embrace opportunities that make the most of unstable situations.

Work Redesign

We believe that one of the most important ways of improving the experience of work is to design jobs so as to encourage workers to engage actively with their tasks and work environment. By providing workers with autonomy in performing their jobs, challenging work, and the opportunity for social interaction, we encourage them to exert choice and to feel competent. It is this form of work redesign that maximizes employee effectiveness and well-being. In this section, we focus on key aspects of work design research, basing our discussion in two influential approaches: the job characteristics model and the demand/control model. Both approaches also help to show how the way work is designed can affect the way people perceive their work roles. Furthermore, we will discuss the implications of job characteristics for employee well-being.

Job Characteristics Model

The job characteristics model (JCM) is one of the most influential theories of work design

(Hackman & Oldham, 1980; Oldham, 1996). In the JCM, five characteristics—skill variety, task identity, task significance, task autonomy, and task feedback—are identified in order to capture the general content and structure of jobs. The presence of these core job dimensions leads to three psychological states—perceived meaningfulness of work, felt responsibility for outcomes, and knowledge of results. In turn, it is argued that employees with a need for personal growth and development, as well as knowledge and skill, will display a range of positive personal and work outcomes, including greater work motivation, performance, satisfaction with work, and lower absenteeism and turnover as a result of job quality (Hackman & Oldham, 1980; Oldham, 1996) (see Figure 52.1). Although this theory has been criticized (see Parker & Wall, 1998, for an overview), and some aspects remain to be tested in integrative ways (Oldham, 1996), researchers and practitioners continue to use the JCM as a psychological framework for understanding how enriching jobs can be designed.

By combining aspects of the JCM, a Motivating Potential Score (MPS) can be generated to provide a comparative metric of job enrichment (Fried & Ferris, 1987; Hackman & Oldham, 1976). One form of the MPS is calculated as follows: (skill variety + task significance + task identity) ÷ 3 × task autonomy × task feedback, such that higher scores reflect a more enriched job. It is worth noting that a low score on any one of the core variables can appreciably reduce a job's potential quality, with high degrees of autonomy and feedback being essential to designing high-quality work.

According to the JCM, high task control and feedback are crucial for maximizing the motivational and learning potential of a job. Being engaged in a quality job results in feelings of meaningfulness and significance for employees while also encouraging their acquisition of greater knowledge, a sense of mastery, and overall well-being.

Demand/Control Model

Researchers and practitioners also have used the demand/control model (Karasek, 1979; Karasek & Theorell, 1990) to design jobs that enhance psychological and physical well-being. According to this model, healthy work environments are those in which appropriate demands (e.g.,

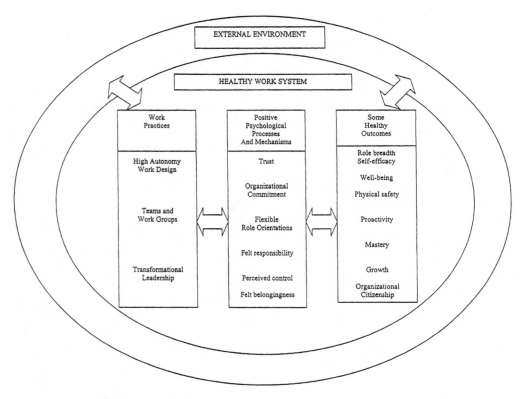

Figure 52.1 A model of healthy work.

production goals) are made of workers who are given correspondingly suitable amounts of decision latitude (e.g., the ability to control the pace or method of work).

In the more recent dynamic version of this model (see Figure 52.2), Karasek and Theorell (1990) propose "spirals of behavior" (Parker & Wall, 1998, p. 48) to explain the effects of work design on well-being through a learning and development mechanism. Jobs with high demands and high control (termed "active" jobs in the demand/control model) can inhibit strain by promoting both employee confidence and active learning. Stated differently, workers with active jobs are more likely to apply coping strategies and seek challenging situations that promote mastery, thereby further encouraging skill and knowledge acquisition. On the other hand, a "relaxed" job (low demands and high control) does not provide employees with such intrinsic motivation. Similarly, "high strain" jobs (high demands and low control) are likely to overwhelm employees and encourage a form of helplessness that can undermine employees' sense of mastery and dissuade them from de-

veloping and using skills. Last, a "passive" job (low demands and low control) does not encourage skill development and can result in employee helplessness, similar to that found in a higher strain job (Karasek & Theorell, 1990).

A final extension to the demand/control model recognizes the importance of social support in promoting psychosocial health (Karasek & Theorell, 1990). As defined by Karasek and Theorell, social support reflects the quality of helpful interactions provided by colleagues and supervisors. These and other researchers (e.g., Beehr, 1995) argue that high social support and trust between coworkers can promote a sense of identity, group cohesion, and better well-being when combined with the characteristics of an active job.

Despite its intuitive appeal, however, the demand/control model lacks evidence for the interaction between demands and control (for exceptions, see Barling & Kelloway, 1996; Parker & Sprigg, 1999; Wall, Jackson, Mullarkey, & Parker, 1996); yet the hypothesized direct relationships between demands, control, and well-being remain founded. Typically, high amounts

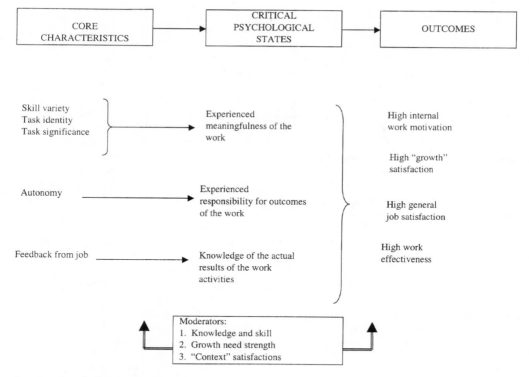

Figure 52.2 Job characteristics model.

of job control are associated with increases in job satisfaction and decreased depression, whereas higher demands independent of adequate control are more modestly correlated with increased anxiety (Warr, 1990; Xie, 1996).

Role Clarity, Role Agreement, and Role Load

In the same manner that social support can aid in coping with or buffering strain, the way in which workers, coworkers, and supervisors "enact" their work roles is related to their experience of work (Weick, 1979). We will focus on three job characteristics that relate to how work is experienced—role clarity, role agreement, and role load.

Ideally, employees should have challenging jobs designed with considerable latitude, as typically a job that is perceived by the incumbent to be clearly defined and of an appropriate load is the most beneficial to both the worker and the organization. This proves to be especially important under conditions where coworkers expect different things from one another, or when employees report to multiple supervisors.

These conditions can sometimes make it difficult for employees to feel comfortable and confident in their roles. In the longer term, a clear fit between employees and their roles is critical for employees' sense of commitment to the organization and indirectly their ability to work toward organizational goals.

While role clarity, role agreement, and role load are conceptually distinct (Beehr, 1995), they frequently co-occur. A broad base of research (e.g., Beehr, 1995; Jackson & Schuler, 1985; Kahn, Wolfe, Quinn, Snoek, & Rosenthal, 1964) has explored how having sufficient information and predictability in one's work (i.e., role clarity), restricted sets of demands and expectations (i.e., role agreement), and work that is challenging yet manageable (i.e., role load) can affect employee morale and job-related well-being. In terms of role clarity and role agreement, Jackson and Schuler's (1985) meta-analysis of these properties across a range of individual outcomes is informative. Job satisfaction and organizational commitment are consistently positively related to role clarity, as is a lack of anxiety and employee well-being. Furthermore, the same analysis finds that satisfaction with pay, supervisors, and coworkers is positively related to role agreement.

Also of considerable importance within the new employment relationship is the extent of role load, given the increase in the amount and pace of work facing many workers (Barling, 1999). This is especially salient given that there is a consistent trend for an appropriate workload to be positively associated with physical health (Sparks, Cooper, Fried, & Shirom, 1997) and positive mood (Bolger, DeLongis, Kessler, & Schilling, 1989). Through the mediating effect of mood, appropriate workload has a positive effect on marital relations (MacEwen, Barling, & Kelloway, 1992) and interpersonal job performance (Stewart & Barling, 1996). It becomes critical, therefore, to ensure that the quality of work is more likely to leave individuals in a positive mood.

Teams and Work Groups

So far, we have considered the effect of individual job quality on mental health. More specifically, we have concentrated on how characteristics of the job (e.g., sufficient control over methods and timing of work to meet demands) can promote employee well-being. In the previous section, we discussed how aspects of job design influence the way people take up their work roles, particularly as people interact with others to meet organizational goals. Indeed, a long-standing reality of work is that people meet work demands together. Nevertheless, only relatively recently have academics and practitioners taken interest in work groups as a means of increasing personal and organizational effectiveness (Guzzo & Dickson, 1996).

While there are many definitions of a "team," and many variations on teams' exact purposes (e.g., self-managing teams, project teams, cross-functional teams), we consider the concept broadly. In line with Guzzo and Dickson's (1996) review of team effectiveness, we define a work group as an entity comprising individuals who perform tasks in an interdependent fashion to meet the goals of an organization; and who can readily distinguish themselves from other work groups. The components of this definition, as we will see, serve as key ingredients in linking the benefits of cooperative working to mental health.

Studies conducted in a range of contexts have associated teamworking with better individual

well-being (e.g., Greller, Parsons, & Mitchell, 1992; Sonnentag, 1996). There are a number of reasons for such benefits. First, working with a group of people provides a social network, and, as Jahoda (1982) notes, this is a critical latent function of employment. In line with our previous discussion of social support, group members can provide companionship, as well as the emotional and practical assistance that can help themselves and others cope successfully with task and interpersonal demands. Still more fundamentally, work groups can help to fulfill our individual need to belong (Baumeister & Leary, 1995).

Collective evidence for these inclusive benefits of teamworking is provided by Carter and West (1999), who report on the well-being of employees working in health care teams in the United Kingdom. In a cross-sectional analysis of 71 health care teams, Carter and West found that higher levels of team clarity and team commitment to group goals, and otherwise positive processes such as task reflexivity and task orientation, predicted better team-level well-being. In a larger scale study, a sample of 2,263 health care workers was divided into three categories: those who felt they were a member of a well-defined team (56.9%); those who reported being in an ambiguously defined team (30.6%), termed a "pseudo team"; and those who worked alone (12.5%). Using the General Health Questionnaire (GHQ-12; Goldberg, 1972) as the measure of mental health, members of the more well-defined teams reported better psychological health than did the employees who either were members of a less well-defined team or who worked alone. Such findings reinforce Jahoda's (1982) notion of the importance of the social context at work to the psychological well-being of employees.

One interesting implication of promoting healthy work through teams involves the employees' emotional reactions toward their work groups and their organization. Specifically, are employees who are highly committed to their team also highly committed to the organization? Allen (1996) contends that research thus far has yet to demonstrate what she calls this "group-organization congruence" (p. 376). We do know, however, that employees' greater attachment to their work groups is modestly correlated (correlations of .36 to .45) with more positive affective commitment to the larger organization, and that there is a positive link between positive affective organizational commitment and better well-being (e.g., Begley & Czajka, 1993; Romzek, 1989). Developing a further understanding of this link should be on the future agenda of work group researchers.

Transformational Leadership

Although few academics or business practitioners would argue with the notion that effective leadership contributes to the positive health of an organization, precious little research has focused on the extent to which leadership might make a difference for individual well-being. This is shortsighted, in our estimation, and it has resulted in a limited appreciation of the real value of positive leadership within the context of organizations. More important, we extend this general argument and suggest that transformational leadership in particular has the potential to contribute considerably to individual well-being. Transformational leadership occurs when leaders increase followers' awareness of the mission or vision toward which they are working, thereby creating a situation where followers feel excited and interested in common goals. In such a situation, followers are rewarded internally with achievement and self-actualization rather than externally with safety and security (Bass, 1985; Burns, 1978). In particular, the elements of transformational leadership (idealized influence, inspirational motivation, intellectual stimulation, and individualized consideration; Avolio, 1999; Bass, 1998) have the potential for enhancing well-being.

Idealized influence reflects the extent to which leaders choose to do what is right rather than what is simple or expedient. When leaders act in a way that reflects idealized influence consistently, and such actions become predictable to employees, mutual trust and respect are built between management and employees. Positive perceptions of interpersonal justice, which are critical for the organization, would follow from such leader behavior (e.g., Greenberg, 1990).

Leaders display inspirational motivation when they challenge employees to be their very best and convince both employees and work groups that they can perform beyond expectations. Therefore, the use of inspirational motivation would enhance employees' feelings of self-confidence and self-efficacy, thereby enabling employees to perform optimally in their jobs.

Intellectual stimulation consists of encouraging employees to think for themselves, to challenge cherished assumptions about the way in which work takes place, and to think about old problems in new ways. By providing intellectual stimulation, leaders foster employee growth in the workplace. To paraphrase a comment attributed to Ralph Nader in 1976, the function of leadership is to produce more leaders, not followers.

Last, leaders manifest individualized consideration when they care for the work-related development of their employees. For instance, when leaders listen and demonstrate empathy for given employees, they are extending a special personalized form of social support.

Transformational leadership has been associated with superior performance in both correlational (Howell & Avolio, 1993; Howell & Hall-Merenda, 1999) and quasi-experimental research (Barling, Kelloway, & Weber, 1996). Of much greater importance from the perspective of positive psychology, however, is how transformational leadership affects performance. Barling et al., (1996) for example, hypothesized that the effect of transformational leadership on performance is indirect, being mediated by different aspects of employee morale. They showed some support for this notion, illustrating how affective commitment to the organization mediated this relationship. Barling, Moutinho, and Kelloway (1999) extended this finding to show that transformational leadership also is associated with higher levels of trust in management and group cohesion, both of which predicted affective commitment to the organization. Furthermore, the only factor to directly influence group performance was affective commitment.

There is also a substantial body of literature demonstrating the effects of transformational leadership on positive employee morale. In general, transformational leadership is associated consistently with higher levels of satisfaction with leadership, trust in the leader, and perceptions of fairness (Bass, 1998; Hater & Bass, 1988; Pillai, Schriesheim, & Williams, 1999).

We believe these findings are important for several reasons. First, and most generally, they identify how transformational leadership positively affects performance. Specifically, transformational leadership does not exert any direct effects on performance outcomes (see Barling et al., 1996). Instead, it raises performance to the extent to which it elevates employee morale in general and affective commitment to the organization in particular. In turn, employees who are more committed to the organization manifest behaviors that are more likely to help the organization achieve its goals (e.g., Barling et al., 1996; Meyer & Allen, 1997). Second, and more germane to this chapter on positive psychology, all the mediating factors that themselves are affected positively by transformational leadership (e.g., affective commitment, trust in management, perceived fairness, self-efficacy) are manifestations of context-specific mental health. Transformational leadership, therefore, has the potential to result in positive employee well-being.

There are several other reasons for emphasizing the role of transformational leadership in promoting healthy work. In technical terms, researchers of transformational leadership have found support for the "augmentation hypothesis": that transactional leadership is a necessary but insufficient condition for superior performance. Instead, superior performance would require that transformational leadership is present above and beyond the basic exchanges or constructive transactions between management and employees that constitute good management. Empirical findings support the augmentation hypothesis (Bass, 1998; Brown & Dodd, 1999). Again, we see that optimal employee well-being is a precondition for superior performance.

Furthermore, one of the more recent fascinating developments within psychology in general has been the emergence of the concept of emotional intelligence (Mayer & Salovey, 1997; Salovey & Mayer, 1990; also see Salovey, Mayer, & Caruso, this volume). In short, emotional intelligence consists of self-awareness and the ability to control one's own emotions, empathy for others and the corresponding ability to influence others' emotions, and the willingness and ability to delay gratification. Furthermore, success within organizations is thought to be more a function of emotional intelligence levels than of classical cognitive intelligence. Early research findings provide some support for this notion. Barling, Slater, and Kelloway (2000) have shown that there is considerable overlap between emotional intelligence and three of the components of transformational leadership (namely, idealized influence, inspirational motivation, and individualized consideration) but not with the fourth (i.e., intellectual stimulation). The clear differentiating

factor is that the former three components of transformational leadership are substantially more emotive than cognitive, whereas intellectual stimulation is more cognitive than emotive.

It also appears that transformational leadership is related to aspects of cognitive development. Akin to the relationship between emotional intelligence and transformational leadership, Turner, Barling, Epitropaki, Butcher, and Milner (in press) found that those supervisors who were rated by their subordinates as having higher levels of idealized influence, inspirational motivation, and intellectual stimulation reported higher levels of moral reasoning. Individualized consideration was unrelated to moral reasoning, perhaps due to its more emotive roots. Nevertheless, we speculate that leaders who recognize a greater range of social cooperation strategies (indicative of more sophisticated moral development) are also more likely to recognize the benefits of and use transformational leadership behaviors. Although the direction of causality for the relationships between transformational leadership, emotional intelligence, and cognitive moral development remains unproven, these links complement the evidence that transformational leadership behaviors can be developed in the workplace.

In regard to this latter point, Barling et al. (1996) conducted a controlled-outcome study in which one group of bank managers received training in the use of transformational leadership while a control group received no such training. The managers' subordinates were assessed before, immediately after, and 4 months following the leadership training. Despite the fact that the employees themselves received no intervention at all, indicators of branch-level financial performance in the group that received transformational leadership exceeded those of the employees whose managers did not receive such training. Equally important, the effects of the training were shown to be mediated by a change in employees' affective commitment to the organization.

Consequently, to the extent that organizations choose to adopt a transformational leadership framework, or individual leaders manifest these behaviors, performance objectives will be achieved by elevating employees—or, to paraphrase the title of Pfeffer's (1998) book, by "putting people first." Presumably, this would also result in a workforce that is more likely to display higher levels of psychological well-being.

Developing Proactive Role Orientations and Behaviors

In the previous sections, we have outlined some key ingredients for promoting healthy work. For example, from an organizational point of view, a healthy workplace is based on designing work to maximize employees' control over challenging work. We also described the significant potential for improving well-being that rests in the functions and structures of clearly defined teams. Finally, we reasoned that there are benefits for employee morale and mental health that stem from the inspiration and personal attention provided by transformational leaders.

In line with our model of healthy work, several commentators (e.g., Barling & Zacharatos, 2000; Pfeffer, 1998) contend that such practices have benefits for both employee health and organizational productivity, and that they ideally represent a systematic approach by managers for improving individual and organizational outcomes. We extend this line of thought by proposing that employees bear some responsibility for making these healthy work systems succeed. High-quality job design, teamworking, and transformational leadership provide the potential for healthy work, which can only be realized when employees take an active role in making these practices work. Fortunately, these same work practices provide a motivating context in which employees can do something about making the workplace better. Simply stated, there is a mutual obligation between employers and employees to make work more positive, and we believe the same work practices allow both parties to do their share.

Given the unstable nature of the modern workplace, however, changing how organizational members approach this responsibility in the face of uncertainty will undoubtedly be challenging. Fortunately, it appears that opportunities to promote broader employee role orientations and more proactive behavior can stem from some of the same practices that promote healthy work. We describe some illustrative research in more detail next.

Parker, Wall, and Jackson (1997) examined how the introduction of new manufacturing practices (e.g., just-in-time manufacturing, total quality management) affects employee attitudes and outcomes. First, they demonstrated that employees' appreciation of wider production issues (e.g., preventative problem solving, responsiveness to customer demands) does increase with the changes in production practices. More important, however, is the relationship between these changes and corresponding changes in work design. When the changes were accompanied by an increasing amount of job control, employees reported incorporating these broader issues into their core job responsibilities. Indeed, developing a more strategic orientation to workplace change appears to be different from developing a more flexible role orientation. It is not enough to implement workplace changes and expect employees to embrace the implications without building sufficient autonomy into work design. Employees may be able to conceive the importance of more proactive behaviors (what Parker and colleagues call a "strategic orientation"); but, with insufficient autonomy, they will be unlikely to accept these broader tasks as an important part of their roles (a "flexible role orientation").

With evidence that active jobs can help employees incorporate broader organizational issues into their role orientations, Parker (1998) subsequently explored how work characteristics (such as autonomy) affected employees' confidence (or self-efficacy) that they actually could carry out a broader set of role responsibilities. Using a longitudinal design, Parker found that employees who had high amounts of task control in an environment with high-quality communication exhibit greater confidence in their ability to undertake a more proactive set of work tasks than do employees with fewer of these job characteristics. Furthermore, Parker (1998, 2000) demonstrated that "role breadth self-efficacy" (RBSE) is both different from a proactive personality (cf. Bateman & Crant, 1993), and distinct from commonly used affective outcomes such as organizational commitment and job satisfaction.

Taken together, broader role orientations and enhanced RBSE have several implications for healthy work and positive psychology more generally. First, these two constructs go beyond measures of job-related well-being traditionally considered in the work design domain. Although there is some evidence that broader role orientations and RBSE are related to increased job satisfaction and organizational commitment (Parker, in press), it is noteworthy that other constructs closely related to proactive role orientations and RBSE positively relate to proactive behavior and job-related well-being. Recently, Morrison and Phelps (1999) found that white-collar employees were more likely to initiate change when they possessed higher levels of self-efficacy and felt responsibility for bringing about change. Similarly, longitudinal research suggests that job complexity and enhanced self-efficacy are related to employees exhibiting initiative (Frese, Kring, Soose, & Zempel, 1996; Spier & Frese, 1997). Finally, Birdi, Gardner, and Warr (1998) have shown that when encountering changing organizational conditions, employees who voluntarily undertake more training and initiate personal development projects report better job satisfaction.

The second major implication, and one that is closely related to the research we highlighted before, is that flexible role orientations and RBSE point to the important developmental effects of high-quality work design. From a research point of view, the notion that people's role orientation can change through supportive

work characteristics has implications for the way we measure variables such as job satisfaction and other aspects of job-related well-being (Parker, in press; Parker et al., 1997). Morrison's (1994) finding that employees' role orientations affect their perceptions of what constitutes in- and extra-role behaviors has an important parallel for the measurement of job-related well-being. It makes sense, therefore, for future positive psychology researchers to reexamine the conceptual bases of job-related well-being so as to reflect the way employees with differing role orientations perceive, interpret, and deal with the positive and negative consequences of work.

Conclusions

In sum, our aim in this chapter was to provide a sense of how healthy work can contribute to

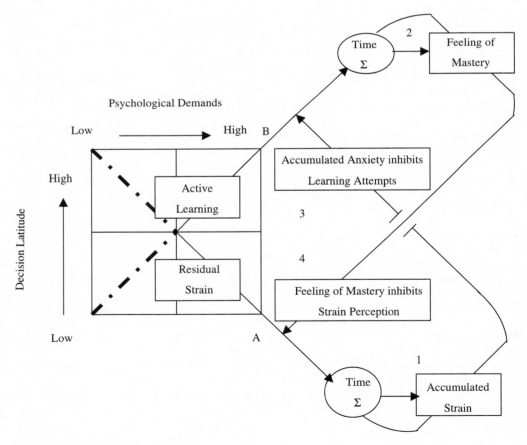

Figure 52.3 Demand/control model.

the positive psychology ethic, and to motivate researchers in the field to keep positive psychology in mind when considering their own research agendas. Although many important topics in the field are intrinsically negative, we should recognize that even they are allied in a broad way with promoting employee well-being and effectiveness. In this respect, the growing recognition of occupational health psychology as a unique discipline can only reinforce the role that understanding healthy work can play in building a positive psychology (Sauter, Hurrell, Fox, Tetrick, & Barling, 1999). As a community of researchers, we need to explore how different work practices and processes can help to create more positive workplaces. In this chapter, we have provided a framework from which to start doing this (see Figure 52.3).

We believe Figure 52.3 aptly summarizes how healthy work can contribute to a more positive organizational experience and to positive psychology more generally. Specifically, high-quality work (i.e., work that offers employees autonomy), in conjunction with transformational leadership in a team-based context, is likely to result in greater trust in management, organizational commitment, perceptions of fairness, perceived control, and belongingness and to contribute to the development of flexible employee role orientations. In turn, these positive psychological processes and mechanisms will result in healthy outcomes, such as job satisfaction, higher levels of psychological well-being, physical safety, a greater sense of mastery and role breadth self-efficacy, proactivity, and other opportunities for growth. This state of health and well-being represents an ideal target for organizational interventions, offers employees a context in which they can excel, and is a worthy objective for both organizational research and practice. In our estimation, these ideas are at the very heart of promoting healthy and positive work in the 21st century.

Acknowledgments We are grateful to Angela Carter, Kevin Kelloway, Catherine Loughlin, Sharon Parker, and Toby Wall for constructive feedback on an earlier draft of this chapter. We also would like to acknowledge the financial support of the UK Health and Safety Executive, the Queen's School of Business, and the Social Sciences and Humanities Research Council of Canada.

References

Allen, N. J. (1996). Affective reactions to the group and the organization. In M. A. West (Ed.), *Handbook of work group psychology* (pp. 371–396). Chichester, England: Wiley.

*Avolio, B. J. (1999). *Full leadership development: Building the vital forces in organizations.* London: Sage.

Barling, J. (1999). Changing employment relations: Empirical data, social perspectives and policy options. In D. B. Knight & A. Joseph (Eds.), *Restructuring societies: Insights from the social sciences* (pp. 59–82). Ottawa, Ontario: Carlton University Press.

Barling, J., & Kelloway, E. K. (1996). Job security and health: The moderating role of workplace control. *Stress Medicine, 12,* 253–260.

Barling, J., Kelloway, E. K., & Weber, T. (1996). Effects of transformational leadership training on attitudinal and financial outcomes: A field experiment. *Journal of Applied Psychology, 81,* 827–832.

Barling, J., Moutinho, K., & Kelloway, E. K. (1999). *Transformational leadership and group performance: The mediating role of affective commitment.* Revised manuscript submitted for publication.

Barling, J., Slater, F., & Kelloway, E. K. (2001). Transformational leadership and emotional intelligence: An exploratory study. *Leadership and Organization Development Journal, 21*(3), 157–161.

Barling, J., & Zacharatos, A. (2000). *High performance safety systems: Ten management practices to create safe organizations.* Manuscript in preparation, Queen's University.

Bass, B. M. (1985). *Leadership and performance beyond expectations.* New York: Free Press.

*Bass, B. M. (1998). *Transformational leadership: Industry, military and educational impact.* Mahwah, NJ: Erlbaum.

Bateman, T. S., & Crant, J. M. (1993). The proactive component of organizational behavior: A measure and correlates. *Journal of Organizational Behavior, 14,* 103–118.

Baumeister, R. F., & Leary, M. R. (1995). The need to belong: Desire for interpersonal attachments as a fundamental human motivation. *Psychological Bulletin, 117,* 497–529.

Beehr, T. A. (1995). *Psychological stress in the workplace.* London: Routledge.

Begley, T. A., & Czajka, J. M. (1993). Panel analysis of the moderating effects of commitment on job satisfaction, intent to quit, and health following organizational change. *Journal of Applied Psychology, 78,* 552–556.

Birdi, K. S., Gardner, C. R., & Warr, P. B. (1998). Correlates and perceived outcomes of four types of employee development activity. *Journal of Applied Psychology, 82,* 845–857.

Bolger, N., DeLongis, A., Kessler, R. C., & Schilling, E. A. (1989). Effects of daily stress on negative mood. *Journal of Personality and Social Psychology, 57,* 808–818.

Brown, F. W., & Dodd, N. G. (1999). Rally the troops or make the train run on time: The relative importance of contingent reward and transformational leadership. *Leadership and Organizational Development Journal, 20,* 291–299.

Burns, J. M. (1978). *Leadership.* New York: Harper and Row.

Canadian Auto Workers. (1996, May). *Working condition study: Benchmarking auto assembly plants.* Willowdale, Ontario: Canadian Auto Workers.

Carter, A. J., & West, M. A. (1999). Sharing the burden: Teamwork in health care settings. In R. L. Payne & J. Firth-Cozens (Eds.), *Stress in health care professionals* (pp. 191–202). Chichester, England: Wiley.

Cascio, W. F. (1993). Downsizing: What do we know? What have we learned? *Academy of Management Executive, 7,* 95–104.

De Meuse, K. P., Vanderheiden, P. A., & Bergmann, T. J. (1994). Announced layoffs: Their effect on corporate financial performance. *Human Resource Management, 33,* 509–530.

Frese, M., Kring, W., Soose, A., & Zempel, J. (1996). Personal initiative at work: Differences between East and West Germany. *Academy of Management Journal, 39,* 37–63.

Fried, Y., & Ferris, G. R. (1987). The validity of the job characteristics model: A review and meta-analysis. *Personnel Psychology, 40,* 287–322.

Goldberg, D. P. (1972). *The detection of minor psychiatric illness by questionnaire.* Oxford, England: Oxford University Press.

Greenberg, J. (1990). Employee theft as a reaction to underpayment inequity: The hidden cost of pay cuts. *Journal of Applied Psychology, 75,* 561–568.

Greller, M. M., Parsons, C. K., & Mitchell, D. R. D. (1992). Additive effects and beyond: Occupational stressors and social buffers in a police organization. In J. C. Quick, L. R. Murphy, and J. J. Hurrell Jr. (Eds.), *Stress and well-being at work: Assessments and interventions for occupational mental health* (pp. 33–47). Washington, DC: American Psychological Association.

*Guzzo, R. A., & Dickson, M. W. (1996). Teams in organizations: Recent research on performance and effectiveness. *Annual Review of Psychology, 47,* 307–338.

Hackman, J. R., & Oldham, G. R. (1976). Motivation through the design of work: Test of a theory. *Organizational Behavior and Human Performance, 16,* 250–279.

Hackman, J. R., & Oldham, G. R. (1980). *Work redesign.* Reading, MA: Addison-Wesley.

Hart, P. M. (1999). Predicting employee life satisfaction: A coherent model of personality, work and non-work experiences, and domain satisfaction. *Journal of Applied Psychology, 84,* 564–584.

Hater, J. J., & Bass, B. M. (1988). Superiors' evaluations and subordinates' perceptions of transformational and transactional leadership. *Journal of Applied Psychology, 73,* 695–702.

Higginbottom, S., Barling, J., & Kelloway, E. K. (1993). Linking retirement experiences and marital satisfaction: A mediational model. *Psychology and Aging, 8,* 508–516.

Howell, J. M., & Avolio, B. J. (1993). Predicting consolidated unit performance: Leadership behavior, locus of control and support for innovation. *Journal of Applied Psychology, 78,* 891–902.

Howell, J. M., & Hall-Merenda, K. E. (1999). The ties that bind: The impact of leader-member exchange, transformational and transactional leadership, and distance on predicting follower performance. *Journal of Applied Psychology, 84,* 680–694.

Jackson, S. E., & Schuler, R. S. (1985). A meta-analysis and conceptual critique of research on role ambiguity and role conflict in work settings. *Organizational Behavior and Human Decision Processes, 36,* 16–78.

Jahoda, M. (1982). *Employment and unemployment: A social psychological analysis.* Cambridge, England: Cambridge University Press.

Judge, T. A., & Watanabe, S. (1993). Another look at the job satisfaction–life satisfaction relationship. *Journal of Applied Psychology, 78,* 939–948.

Kahn, R. L., Wolfe, D. M., Quinn, R. P., Snoek, J. D., & Rosenthal, R. A. (1964). *Organizational stress: Studies in role conflict and ambiguity.* New York: Wiley.

Karasek, R. A. (1979). Job demands, job decision latitude, and mental strain: Implications for job redesign. *Administrative Science Quarterly, 24,* 285–308.

*Karasek, R. A., & Theorell, T. (1990). *Healthy work: Stress, productivity, and the reconstruction of working life.* New York: Basic Books.

Kelloway, E. K., & Barling, J. (1991). Job characteristics, role stress and mental health. *Journal of Occupational Psychology, 64,* 291–304.

Landsbergis, P. A., Cahill, J., & Schnall, P. (1999). The impact of lean production and related new systems of work organization on worker health. *Journal of Occupational Health Psychology, 4,* 108–130.

MacEwen, K. E., Barling, J., & Kelloway, E. K. (1992). Effects of short-term role overload on marital interactions. *Work and Stress, 6,* 117–126.

Martin, P. (1997). *The sickening mind: Brain, behaviour, immunity, and disease.* London: HarperCollins.

Mayer, J. D., & Salovey, P. (1997). What is emotional intelligence? In P. Salovey & D. J. Sluyter (Eds.), *Emotional development and emotional intelligence* (pp. 3–31). New York: Basic Books.

Meyer, J. P., & Allen, N. J. (1997). *Commitment in the workplace: Theory, research, and application.* London: Sage.

Morrison, E. W. (1994). Role definitions and organizational citizenship behavior: The importance of the employee's perspective. *Academy of Management Journal, 37,* 1543–1567.

Morrison, E. W., & Phelps, C. C. (1999). Taking charge at work: Extrarole efforts to initiate workplace change. *Academy of Management Journal, 42,* 403–419.

Oldham, G. R. (1996). Job design. In C. L. Cooper & I. T. Robertson (Eds.), *International review of industrial and organizational psychology* (Vol. 11, pp. 33–60). Chichester, England: Wiley.

Parker, S. K. (1998). Enhancing role breadth self-efficacy: The role of job enrichment and other organizational interventions. *Journal of Applied Psychology, 83,* 835–852.

Parker, S. K. (2000). From passive to proactive motivation: The importance of flexible role orientations and role breadth self-efficacy. *Applied Psychology: An International Review, 49,* 447–469.

Parker, S. K., & Sprigg, C. A. (1999). Minimizing strain and maximizing learning: The role of job demands, job control, and proactive personality. *Journal of Applied Psychology, 84,* 925–939.

*Parker, S. K., & Wall, T. D. (1998). *Job and work design: Organizing work to promote well-being and effectiveness.* London: Sage.

Parker, S. K., Wall, T. D., & Jackson, P. R. (1997). "That's not my job": Developing flexible employee work orientations. *Academy of Management Journal, 40,* 899–929.

Patterson, M. G., West, M. A., & Wall, T. D. (2001). *Integrated manufacturing, empower-* ment, and company performance. Manuscript submitted for publication.

*Pfeffer, J. (1998). *The human equation: Building profits by putting people first.* Cambridge, MA: Harvard Business School Press.

Pillai, R., Schriesheim, C. A., & Williams, E. S. (1999). Fairness perceptions and trust as mediators for transformational and transactional leadership: A two-sample study. *Journal of Management, 25,* 897–933.

Romzek, B. S. (1989). Personal consequences of employee commitment. *Academy of Management Journal, 32,* 649–661.

Salovey, P., & Mayer, J. D. (1990). Emotional intelligence. *Imagination, Cognition, and Personality, 9,* 185–211.

Sauter, S. L., Hurrell, J. J., Fox, H., Tetrick, L. E., & Barling, J. (1999). Occupational health psychology: An emerging discipline. *Industrial Health, 37,* 199–211.

Seligman, M. E. P. (1998, April). Positive social science. *APA Monitor, 29,* 2.

*Sennett, R. (1998). *Corrosion of character: The personal consequences of work in the new capitalism.* New York: Norton.

Sonnentag, S. (1996). Work group factors and individual well-being. In M. A. West (Ed.), *The handbook of work group psychology* (pp. 346–367). Chichester, England: Wiley.

Sparks, K., Cooper, C. L., Fried, Y., & Shirom, A. (1997). The effects of hours of work on health: A meta-analytic review. *Journal of Occupational and Organizational Psychology, 70,* 391–408.

Spier, C., & Frese, M. (1997). Generalized self-efficacy as a mediator and moderator between control and complexity at work and personal initiative: A longitudinal study in East Germany. *Human Performance, 10,* 171–192.

Stewart, W., & Barling, J. (1996). Daily work stress, mood and interpersonal job performance: A mediational model. *Work and Stress, 10,* 336–351.

*Tetrick, L. E., & Barling, J. (Eds.). (1995). *Changing employment relations: Behavioral and social perspectives.* Washington, DC: American Psychological Association.

Turner, N., Barling, J., Epitropaki, O., Butcher, V., & Milner, C. (in press). Transformational leadership and moral reasoning. *Journal of Applied Psychology.*

Wall, T. D., Jackson, P. R., Mullarkey, S., & Parker, S. K. (1996). The demands-control model of job strain: A more specific test. *Journal of Occupational and Organizational Psychology, 69,* 153–166.

Warr, P. B. (1987). *Work, unemployment, and mental health*. Oxford, England: Oxford University Press.

Warr, P. B. (1990). The measurement of well-being and other aspects of mental health. *Journal of Occupational Psychology, 63,* 193–210.

Warr, P. B. (1994). A conceptual framework for the study of work and mental health. *Work and Stress, 8,* 84–97.

*Warr, P. B. (1999). Well-being and the workplace. In D. Kahneman, E. Diener, & N. Schwarz (Eds.), *Well-being: The foundation of hedonic psychology* (pp. 392–412). New York: Russell Sage Foundation.

Weick, K. E. (1979). *The social psychology of organizing*. Reading, MA: Addison-Wesley.

Xie, J. L. (1996). Karasek's model in the People's Republic of China: Effects of job demands, control, and individual differences. *Academy of Management Journal, 39,* 1594–1618.

X

The Future of the Field

53

Positive Ethics

Mitchell M. Handelsman, Samuel Knapp, &
Michael C. Gottlieb

The goals of positive ethics are to shift the ethics of psychologists from an almost exclusive focus on wrongdoing and disciplinary responses to a more balanced and integrative approach that includes encouraging psychologists to aspire to their highest ethical potential (Knapp, 2000; Small & Knapp, 1999). Consider the following vignette:

A clinical psychologist has worked at a university for years, and she has always conformed her behavior to the requirements of the Ethical Standards of the American Psychological Association (APA, 1992), the policies of her institutional review board (IRB), and state law. Now she has developed a set of deep personal beliefs (which could be due to factors such as philosophy, life experience, or religion) and has tried to integrate some new concepts into her daily life. At the same time, she is aware of the application of these concepts to her professional behavior. Consequently, she has discontinued using deception in her research, even though her IRB previously had approved such designs. She also has made special arrangements for her graduate students to do practicum work at agencies such as the local domestic abuse shelter, even though it means an increase in her supervisory responsibilities.

This psychologist made a conscientious effort to develop a deep ethical philosophy and to implement it in both her personal and her professional life. For her, decisions about ethical behavior did not occur solely as a result of studying the disciplinary rules of her profession. Instead, they came from an awareness of a long-standing and well-thought-out philosophical tradition. She did not adopt changes in her research and teaching to avoid disciplinary sanctions; rather, she made these changes to actualize her core values and to improve the welfare of those with whom she worked, as well as people in the larger society.

The psychologist in this vignette may find it very hard to explore her integrative and aspirational ethical thinking with other psychologists because those discussions seem to focus on negative behaviors or defensive strategies. For example:

• Discussions of ethics get bogged down quickly on the topic of prohibitions against sexual relationships with clients.

- Presentations about research ethics seem to become workshops on how to complete IRB forms.
- Seminars on academic ethics degenerate into discussions of student cheating.
- "Ethics" workshops become forums for discussing the differences between subpoenas and court orders.
- The ethics portions of continuing education courses on good clinical service consist of rules for keeping records to avoid malpractice suits.

Nothing is wrong with learning about the prohibitions against sexual misconduct, the intricacies of IRB forms, remedies for student cheating, and other such issues. These important topics need to be presented and discussed, but problems develop if ethics is seen as relevant only in situations in which disciplinary actions could occur.

Generally, the current notions of professional ethics focus too heavily on avoiding or punishing misconduct rather than promoting the highest ethical conduct. We contend that, similar to the pathology perspective, the prevailing models of ethics often are too rule-bound or defensive. Thus, we believe it is beneficial to explore more positive and aspirational ethics as an alternative to models of ethical "sickness."

The hallmark of positive ethics is that psychologists consider ethics in a multifaceted context, with greater awareness of both internal (e.g., personal and professional values) and external (e.g., societal influences on professional behavior) perspectives. Such an expanded awareness should help psychologists integrate specific rules with aspirational principles and to formulate their own personal and professional moral identities.

In this chapter, we first consider some of the factors that contribute to a focus on negative (defensive or rule-bound) ethics. We then explore some major aspects of positive ethics, which integrates several levels of ethical thought. Finally, we suggest some implications of positive ethics.

Factors Contributing to Negative Approaches to Ethics

Ethics Codes, Licensing Boards, and Regulation

Just as research and clinical activities traditionally have focused on suffering, pathology, and other negative issues, so, too, have ethical issues in psychology focused on deficiencies in ethical behavior, bad actions, and bad actors. Historically, no significant impetus for the regulation of professional behavior or for an ethics code existed before World War II (Strickland, 1998). In fact, in 1938 a committee of the APA met to discuss a code of ethics for psychology and "concluded that any attempt to legislate a complete code would have been premature but recommended that a standing committee be appointed to consider complaints of unethical conduct" (Kimmel, 1988, p. 58). In regard to this recommendation, it is interesting that complaints of unethical conduct were handled before any document defined ethical conduct. Furthermore, when the APA was ready to develop an ethics code in 1948, it did so by soliciting examples of problematic situations rather than creating or developing ethical ideals or aspirations (Kimmel, 1988; Pope & Vetter, 1992).

Nazi atrocities in the name of research led to several documents regarding research ethics, from the Nuremberg Code of 1947, to the Declaration of Helsinki in 1964 (Levine, 1986), to the establishment of rules governing IRBs in 1966 (Kimmel, 1988). These codes and regulations were designed to curb the power of researchers and to protect research participants from abuses (Appelbaum, Lidz, & Meisel, 1987). Accounts of the history of research ethics routinely cite lists of celebrated cases of misconduct—such as the Tuskegee syphilis study (Jones, 1981) and Cyril Burt's fabrication of data (Hearnshaw, 1979)—as the impetus for codes and regulations.

Another outgrowth of World War II was an increase in the clinical roles for psychologists. In turn, this contributed to the need for state regulation of psychological practice. In 1945, Connecticut became the first state to enact licensure for psychologists; most states followed suit by the end of the 1960s (Strickland, 1998). Licensure laws, similar to professional ethics and research codes, became restrictive. The major purpose of state boards was (and is) to protect the public by sanctioning psychologists who have been found guilty of professional misconduct (Handelsman & Uhlemann, 1998).

Discussions of ethics in graduate schools (e.g., Johnson & Corser, 1998), in continuing education courses, and in much of the professional literature (e.g., Canter, Bennett, Jones, & Nagy, 1994; Koocher & Keith-Spiegel, 1998; VandeCreek & Knapp, 1993) emphasize laws, codes of conduct, court cases, and disciplinary sanctions. Consequently, some psychologists erroneously believe that ethics consists solely of the rules of their licensing board, the APA code of conduct (APA, 1992), case law, or the adjudication processes of disciplinary bodies. This emphasis on ethical rules may cause the adoption of a purely defensive, or "Thou shalt not," perspective through which psychologists consider ethics as a list of prohibitions they must follow without considering the underlying spirit or philosophy. Indeed, in 1992 the APA ethics code was divided into two sections: the aspirational ethical principles and the enforceable standards of conduct. As a practical matter, however, psychologists generally equate the ethics code with the standards of conduct and ignore the aspirational ethical principles. On this point, Bersoff (1994) has written, "The current code, at best, builds an ethical floor but hardly urges us to reach for the ceiling" (p. 385). It is useful and appropriate for a profession to define harmful behaviors and to provide sanctions for them, but the benefits of a narrow focus on punitive actions are limited. Although the ethics code does address more flagrant conduct (Bersoff, 1994), it does not address subtle acts of harm or substandard care. Only a few of the 102 standards within the code are absolute (e.g., do not have sex with clients, do not abandon clients, and do not falsify insurance forms); the other standards allow professionals considerable discretion in their interpretations.

Opportunities for such professional discretion—some would say loopholes (Keith-Spiegel, 1994)—were noted by Bersoff (1994) as he pointed out that the term *reasonableness* or some variation occurs 40 times in the code, and the term *feasible* appears 15 times. For example, the APA code states that patients should be informed about the nature of therapy "as soon as feasible." The application of this rule, however, requires a considerable amount of judgment concerning the state of the patients, their abilities to attend to the information given, and both the long-term and the short-term usefulness of reviewing informed consent procedures at a given time. Indeed, an approach to ethics that relies only on interpreting the code may identify minimally acceptable behaviors that will avoid disciplinary actions. Furthermore, this approach may cause psychologists to dislike, ignore, or avoid discussions of ethics, and it moves the focus away from developing more positive ethical and professional practices. Rather than being driven only by the motivations to avoid misbehavior, positive ethics allows psychologists to look beyond the immediate situation to include, for example, aspirational principles and their own professional and moral values.

In the regulatory arena, state laws also have focused on minimally acceptable behaviors. During the early years of licensure, the APA ethics code was written into many state laws so as to make psychologists legally accountable to ethical standards, but courts have struck down these more aspirational provisions on the grounds that they are unenforceable (*White v. North Carolina State Board of Examiners of Practicing Psychologists*, 1990). Consequently, the recent legal trend has been toward the listing of specific prohibited behaviors rather than aspirational guides for mental health professionals.

Alienation From Core Professional Values

Negative approaches to ethics may create or exacerbate alienation among psychologists who feel that their values no longer are reflected in their institutional or societal norms. From our work in professional associations and ethics committees, we get the impression that many psychologists believe that licensing boards and ethics committees do not represent or enforce the values that they endorse or hold dear. They perceive that IRBs, licensing boards, and the APA Ethics Office enforce exceedingly narrow and restrictive interpretations of principles and behavior, thereby undercutting the effective professional activities of the great majority of psychologists. These committees and boards focus on the relatively small number of psychologists who have complaints filed against them, and not on the majority. Thus, many psychologists may fail to see the relevance of such bodies for their own professional activities.

Another type of alienation that psychologists may feel from a rule-bound approach to ethics is a "disconnect" between their professional roles and their personal moral philosophies. A focus on conforming professional behavior to minimum standards may create the impression that professional ethics are separate from our intuitive moral sense. Moreover, our moral sense sometimes does not lead to good professional decisions (Kitchener, 1984). To discard personal philosophies entirely, however, is not appropriate or feasible. For example, the APA code includes aspirational principles that are considered optional. The personal philosophy of a particular individual, however, may make those principles obligatory. Pro bono work, for example, is optional according to the APA code but obligatory according to the personal moral code of many psychologists. Focusing exclusively on rules may make it difficult to integrate personal sources of moral judgment.

Difficulties With Open Discussions of Ethics

Professional alienation appears to be increasing at a time when the profession needs more, rather than less, open discussion of ethical issues. Psychology is becoming more complex and moving in new directions (Gottlieb & Cooper, in press). New practice areas and funding patterns (Acuff et al., 1999; Cooper & Gottlieb, 2000) mean new issues regarding competence, along with new ethical problems in areas such as relationship boundaries, consent, and confidentiality. For example, many clinical psychologists have considered working in conjunction with the legal system (e.g., conducting custody evaluations, testifying as an expert witness) as an attractive alternative to dealing with managed care. Such practice, however, is fraught with ethical complexity; one must be very familiar with the legal system, its ethical issues, and how these evolved within an adversarial system (Committee on Ethical Guidelines for Forensic Psychologists, 1991), where the values routinely conflict with psychology's original professional ideals of helping those in distress. Well-intentioned but ignorant efforts to practice ethically in this legal environment can be counterproductive and, in some cases, harmful. For example, psychologists have no control over how their testimony may be used—no matter how they qualify it. Seemingly noble behaviors such as divulging information in an effort to resolve a dispute may violate attorney-client privilege, and volunteering information on the witness stand may give the appearance of prejudice in the eyes of jury members.

Many psychologists feel angst over the ethical decisions they have to make in an ever more complex professional environment, but they may be hesitant to discuss ethical issues with colleagues because of the increased vulnerability to complaints, suits, and sanctions from clients, research participants, and students. Similarly, trainees very much may want their professors to articulate their ethical decision-making processes but may hesitate to raise questions about the ethics of their professors' behaviors for fear that they would react negatively; Veatch and Sollitto (1976) wrote that supervisors and professors may feel that such questions are "ethical insults." Thus, current approaches to ethics may constrain rather than facilitate open exploration.

Aspects of Positive Ethics

Historical, societal, regulatory, and professional factors have contributed to negative approaches to ethics. These very factors, however, make it all the more important to develop an understanding of positive ethics. Throughout the history of psychology, a number of trends and ideas have laid a foundation for a positive approach to ethics. This positive approach, in turn, may allow psychologists to discuss issues more openly, to reduce their alienation, and to aspire to an optimal level of ethical functioning (see Table 53.1 for a comparison of some attributes of negative and positive approaches to ethics). In fact, positive ethics spans several philosophical traditions; positive ethicists can be found among psychologists who rely primarily on virtue, deontological, principle-based, utilitarian, feminist, or other ethical theories, including religious traditions.

Our view of positive ethics encompasses a broad context of ethical behavior—including aspirational elements that range from the personal to the societal—which goes beyond a focus on rules and risk. We propose that the morality of professional actions can be explored without emphasizing the prohibitions or potential sanctions found within psychology's disciplinary codes. At the same time, we are not advocating the abandonment of ethical rules and prohibitions; they do have a basis in morality that psychologists need to understand. Likewise, psychologists should know the laws that govern the practice of psychology and the ways to reduce legal risk. We are suggesting that whereas rules and good risk management strategies are not antithetical to positive ethics, they are not sufficient to ensure optimal ethical practice. What is necessary is an awareness of several interacting perspectives.

Seven Themes of Positive Ethics

We present our perspectives about positive ethics in the form of seven basic themes, which

Table 53.1 Comparison of Attributes of Negative and Positive Approaches to Ethics

Negative Ethics	Positive Ethics
Narrow focus: limited to codes, laws	Comprehensive focus: integration of codes with personal ethics, other ethical traditions
Enforceable rules, standards	Aspirational principles, virtues, and values
Focused on misconduct, problems	Focused on conduct, positive behaviors, ethical ideals
Identifying specific prohibited activities	Identifying positive virtues
Screening out bad actors	Helping psychologists take care of themselves so they can care for others
Sanctions for misconduct	Personal and professional benefits of ethical reasoning and behavior; prevention of negative behaviors and promotion of positive ones
Limited discussion of ethical issues	Broadened discussions of ethical issues
Independence of each code, policy, law	Integration of aspects of positive ethics (e.g., values, decision making, prevention) into a consistent whole
Focused on constraint of behavior	Focused on integrated awareness of levels of thought and behavior
Separation of personal and professional	Integration of personal and professional ethical principles
Denial or devaluation of self-interest	Recognition and integration of appropriate self-interest (positive motivations for optimal professional behavior)

start with the more internal and progress to more external considerations. An awareness of these themes can be quite beneficial to psychologists in articulating a meaningful and consistent ethical perspective. Also, these themes do not constitute a linear model; each informs and influences all the others.

Values and Virtues: Inspiring Psychologists Toward the Ethical Ideals of Their Profession

We start with the most personal level of analysis. For psychologists to understand and integrate principles, codes, laws, reasoning procedures, and other external sources of guidance, they need to start with a personal inventory of their own values, including the virtues they want to develop.

Knowledge of Our Own Values and Aspirational Goals

Abeles (1980) urged psychologists to teach ethics, as least in part, by means of value confrontations. In one scenario, for example, students are asked to put themselves in the position of a therapist who is asked by a client to write a letter detailing the treatment in an effort to avoid a shoplifting charge. Such situational discussions often lead students to examine their own motivations and self-perceptions and to ask basic questions: Why did we go into this profession in the first place (remember your graduate school essay)? How do we see ourselves as professionals? How do we understand the concept of being helpful?

Confronting and articulating their values may set apart the outstanding teachers, psychotherapists, or researchers from the average ones. The outstanding ones seem to place great value on their professional activities. They put self-interest into perspective, they do not allow financial interests to compromise or cloud their judgments, they exemplify virtues, convey their caring for others, and so on. Also, outstanding psychologists may have what Rest (1986) called *moral motivation*, the ability to prioritize moral values relative to other values. In an era of regulation, managed care, litigation, and rapidly expanding opportunities and pitfalls, keeping our eyes on our own values may be especially difficult, but it also is more necessary.

Additionally, clarifying our moral and ethical values and making them prominent in our thinking may help realign our behaviors. For example, researchers are paying more attention to the social impact of their work (Sales & Folkman, 1998; Sieber, 1992). In the forensic area, trends are now toward more positive models of dispute resolution, including mediation and developing shared parenting responsibilities rather than custody. These approaches may move us closer to our basic professional value of considering the best interests of the child.

One example of a positive trend in family law is "collaborative law" (Webb, 1996), in which the attorneys for both sides agree to assist in resolving conflict using cooperative rather than adversarial strategies. There is a most intriguing aspect of this notion that departs from mediation. Namely, both parties agree that, should the cooperative process fail, then the current attorneys will not be the ones to pursue litigation. Instead, the parties must go to the additional expense and inconvenience of hiring new lawyers to try the case. Such a systemic change in the process places great weight on cooperation and settlement. Likewise, mental health professionals can be deeply involved and are much freer to work on behalf of what is best for everyone concerned.

Developing Our Selves: Virtues

Rule-based or principle-based ethics invites us to ask the question, What should (or shouldn't) I do? Values clarification invites us to ask, What do I believe? And virtue ethics (Jordan & Meara, 1990; Meara, Schmidt, & Day, 1996) takes us to the next step, inviting us to ask, Who should I be? The personal qualities that enable positive ethical behavior include, but are not limited to, humility, prudence, respectfulness, integrity, and benevolence. The reader will recognize these latter issues as being key components of a positive psychological framework. These virtues do not exist independently of principles and rules but instead complement them.

The virtues represent the most personal aspect of our ethical life, what Rest (1986) called moral character. Psychologists need to persist in the face of distractions, to implement skills, and to have courage to act ethically in the face of competing forces. The empirical evidence is not encouraging, however, as psychology students and practitioners routinely report that they would not do all they know they should in difficult situations (Bernard, Murphy, & Lit-

tle, 1987). For example, they might not intervene to help a colleague whom they know to be impaired because they "do not want to get involved." A focus on positive ethics may help psychologists integrate their values, virtues, and behaviors so that they become more consistent.

Sensitivity and Integration

Rest (1986) identified moral sensitivity as the first of four components that determine moral behavior. Sensitivity, a cornerstone of positive ethics, refers to interpreting a situation as having moral or ethical aspects and implications, even when no explicit dilemma exists. We argue that ethical sensitivity is a necessary step toward integrating ethical dimensions and ethical reasoning into all professional activities. Positive ethics is not just an add-on or a set of constraints on teaching, research, and clinical practice. Instead, positive ethics sensitizes psychologists to the needs of those with whom they work, and it emphasizes ethical thinking as a means to that end. For example, Sullivan, Martin, and Handelsman (1993) found that practicing good ethics by providing comprehensive informed consent increased participants' perceptions that psychotherapists would provide better outcomes.

A focus on positives also should help professional psychologists become better at identifying and understanding the ethical dilemmas that they and their clients encounter during psychotherapy (Tjeltveit, 1999). Will psychotherapy lead a submissive woman to want a divorce from her husband (despite her present statement that she "does not believe in divorce")? Will a therapeutic goal of making the authoritarian father from Pakistan more democratic in his household represent cultural imperialism? Using a positive approach may help psychologists see these issues as integral parts of ongoing ethical processing rather than aberrations that lead to crises.

Ethics and Ongoing Self-Care

In negative ethics approaches, self-care may be ignored because psychologists should simply strive toward meeting the needs of clients (research participants, students, etc.); personal well-being is at best irrelevant and at worst in conflict with clients' interests. However, to argue that we have no personal stake in the process or outcome of our work, or to neglect psychologists' interests in their deliberation of ethical issues, is to create an alienation between values and professional work. In positive ethics, we strive to incorporate notions of appropriate self-interest into what we do, recognizing that we do get satisfaction from our professional behavior. Such appropriate satisfactions include using our skills and creativity, interacting directly with others for their benefit, seeing progress, and indirectly benefiting society. Cultivating that satisfaction leads both to a greater awareness of the boundaries of our professional relationships and to a greater ability to actualize our values and virtues within professional relationships. The twin goals of becoming more aware of the implications of their behavior for others and becoming better at caring for themselves are not mutually exclusive.

Our model of positive ethics recognizes two complementary notions: (a) Some types of satisfaction are derived from our work and need to be recognized, appreciated, and cultivated; and (b) other types of satisfaction must be cultivated elsewhere, beyond the boundaries of our professional roles. Part of positive ethics is appreciating the legitimacy of both types of needs, along with the differences between them.

Psychologists who are good at self-care are sensitive to their own needs: They balance their workload and their personal lives, develop strong social networks, seek and accept help from others when needed, and offer help to other psychologists when appropriate (Knapp & Pincus, 1999). These activities are intrinsically worthwhile, but there also is a utilitarian aspect to psychologists' self-care. According to the informal impressions of Koocher and Keith-Spiegel (1998), about one half of the psychologists brought before the APA Ethics Committee appeared to have an emotional disorder related to their alleged misdeeds. Conceivably, therefore, one half of the ethical violations by psychologists could be eliminated if these professionals were taking care of their own needs more effectively. Of course self-care, in and of itself, is not sufficient for psychologists to understand and comply with either aspirational or mandatory ethical standards. At a minimum, however, psychologists who engage in effective self-care are less likely to have their ethical skills clouded by personal problems, distress, or

conflicts and are more likely to be engaging in behavior that is benevolent and consistent with their values.

Ethical Reasoning and Decision Making

Such personal activities as recognition of values and needs and sensitivity to ethical concerns are necessary but clearly not sufficient to ensure optimal ethical behavior. Psychologists also need to be aware of the shared values of the profession. All major health professions have created ethics codes embodying the shared values to which their members are expected to adhere. Although they vary in degree of specificity, all codes have two things in common: First, they all strive to help professionals make good decisions; second, none are able to help professionals make decisions about specific ethical dilemmas except in the most obvious situations. For example, the APA code clearly states that psychotherapists do not engage in sexual relationships with their current patients; there is no dispute about the matter and no competing concerns that must be weighed.

In the daily life of psychologists, however, numerous gray area situations and dilemmas arise for which good reasons exist to justify two or more mutually exclusive actions. For example, a therapist might have to decide whether to violate confidentiality to warn a possible victim that his or her patient may attempt harm. In this example, the therapist must weigh the importance of confidentiality and respect for the patient's autonomy against the potential harm that might come to a third party.

Ethics codes do little to assist psychologists in vexing situations when ethical standards and principles are pitted against each other. Codes are limited to specific prohibitions and a few aspirational goals. Furthermore, deducing specific actions from aspirational goals or understanding how specific prohibitions may generalize across differing situations can be quite difficult. Thus, we see the importance of ethical reasoning, a process designed to help the decision maker arrive at the best possible result based on sound ethical principles and explicit, careful thinking.

Several models of ethical reasoning exist in the literature (Haas & Malouf, 1989; Handelsman, 1998; Kitchener, 1984, 2000; Tymchuk, 1981). Kitchener (1984, 2000) developed a model that starts with the information about the situation and one's own moral sense of the right thing to do. This "immediate" level of reasoning reminds us of the importance of exploring our affective responses to the ethical components of our work. The immediate impression is then examined at what Kitchener called the "critical-evaluative level," which entails ethics codes, more general ethical principles, and ethical theory. Haas and Malouf (1989) developed a more elaborate flow chart that helps decision makers weigh alternatives, consider possible outcomes, and evaluate the impact of their decisions.

Other decision-making procedures have been developed to address more specific ethical dilemmas. The best examples are two procedures applied to questions surrounding dual relationships (Gottlieb, 1993; Kitchener, 1988); these authors encouraged psychologists to think proactively and to account for such factors as power differences, duration of the relationship, and differential expectations of the parties involved. Clearly, all reasoning approaches share one important attribute of positive ethics: They broaden the context of ethical thinking beyond immediate circumstances and simplistic calculations.

There has been some research on ethical reasoning in psychology and other professions (Rest & Narváez, 1994). However, we have much to learn about this complex process that combines individual emotions, cognitions, values, knowledge, and outcomes in a myriad of ways. For instance, we do not know how focusing on positive issues rather than ethical rules and risk management issues may lead to different decision-making processes and outcomes.

Appreciation of the Moral Traditions That Underlie Ethical Principles

To the extent that psychologists feel alienated, their ethical rules and regulations may seem arbitrary and meaningless. An awareness of the ethical "roots" of our profession and its rules may decrease such feelings. Kitchener (1984, 2000) has written extensively on the importance of understanding and applying the foundational ethical principles, which have been discussed by our colleagues in medicine. On this point, Beauchamp and Childress (1994) have identified autonomy, beneficence, nonmaleficence, and justice as the major principles. Kitchener (1984, 2000) added fidelity to the list.

In discussing the foundational principles, Kitchener argued that "when psychologists are conducting research or therapy ethically, these are the implicit principles they share" (2000, p. 21). The foundational principles underlie specific rules and can lend clarity to discussions of the justification for rules about issues such as consent and record keeping. Indeed, the 1992 revision of the APA ethics code contains a section of such principles, including those referring to respect for rights (autonomy) and concern for others' welfare (beneficence, nonmaleficence). Understanding the foundational principles can help psychologists work through potential conflicts among rules by providing criteria by which to judge which rules take precedence in specific situations.

Principle-based ethical theory is not the only source for understanding the foundations of positive ethical practice. More recent work includes the ethics of care (Carse, 1991), feminist ethics (Feminist Therapy Institute, 1990; Lerman & Porter, 1990), virtue ethics (Meara et al., 1996), and utilitarianism (Knapp, 1999), all of which move the focus of ethical reasoning beyond defensive concerns.

Prevention of Misconduct and Promotion of Positive Behaviors

As a profession, psychology is moving toward prevention of ethical misconduct through education. Since 1979, APA-accredited doctoral programs have required instruction in ethics (APA Council of Representatives, 1979). Ethics committees in many states are emphasizing education and prevention and are ceasing their investigation and adjudication functions (Honaker, 2000; Nagy, 1996). Also, 14 state licensing boards now require continuing education in ethics as a condition of licensure renewal. In this section, we describe the ways that graduate schools of psychology, continuing education courses, and licensing boards can promote the highest levels of professional conduct, as well as prevent harmful misconduct by psychologists.

Promoting Ethics in Training Programs

Empirical data suggest that the quality of ethical decision making, and perhaps ethical behavior, would improve if ethics were taught more explicitly within graduate training programs (e.g., Baldick, 1980; Rest, 1994). Currently in professional training programs, ethics is taught both formally through courses and informally or incidentally through an "implicit" curriculum (i.e., the institutional atmosphere within the program). In implicit curricula, students absorb the ethical lessons within the milieu of their institutions (Branstetter & Handelsman, 2000) and learn what they need to survive or thrive within this environment. Students will notice whether the faculty members are courteous, promote student welfare, and model collegiality, integrity, and hard work. In some cases, this environmental influence may teach students more about ethics than the courses they take. Even good departments, however, can do better by talking *explicitly* about the values that motivate their behavior, along with integrating ethics into all of their classes. Students may benefit when faculty or supervisors point out ethical implications of their own work, particularly when they judiciously disclose their decision-making processes.

For information regarding how to implement "ethics across the curriculum," we would recommend programs such as those at Duke University (http://kenan.ethics.duke.edu/curriculum.html), the University of San Diego (http://ethics.acusd.edu/eac/), and Saint Louis University (http://www.slu.edu/centers/ethics/). Although these programs vary in content, they all require students to take a certain number of classes wherein ethics constitutes a substantial portion of the class grade. Furthermore, these programs openly articulate the goal of teaching ethics as being primary to their educational mission.

We strongly believe that ethics across the curriculum should focus on positive ethics. If ethics is viewed from a "Thou shalt not" perspective, then ethics across the curriculum would be unpleasant for all parties. Both students and faculty would be continually policing each other and pointing out ethical violations and shortcomings. If viewed as a positive and supportive experience, however, ethics across the curriculum would invigorate both students and faculty to be supportive and encouraging of each other, to discuss and share perspectives, and to strive to do their best.

As part of positive ethics, faculty will model ethical behavior through their sensitive treatment of students and their willingness to talk openly about their ethical ideals and conflicts. The goal should be to create a pattern of ethical

awareness that would be sustained across students' careers (Handelsman, in press). A positive training program also will challenge students to strive to reach their highest ethical potential and to talk openly about their own ethical ideals and conflicts. In this educational atmosphere, students will become aware that they are not merely passive recipients, but that they, too, are responsible for improving the training program through their attitudes and conduct.

Continuing Education Programs

Continuing education workshops and other training opportunities often try to prevent misconduct by pointing out the financial, professional, and personal hardships that can result from being the subject of a disciplinary action. They also try to dissuade misconduct by engendering fear or guilt over the possibility of harming patients or embarrassing the profession, although such fear-based efforts may not work and may even backfire (Gleicher & Petty, 1992; Jepson & Chaiken, 1990). Another view of continuing education is that it may be more effective in promoting behaviors that are incompatible with ethical misconduct. This approach would encourage prudent forethought, caring, conscientiousness, and other virtues that should reduce the likelihood of misconduct. We would emphasize, however, that promoting positive ethics has a purpose beyond avoiding misconduct. Promoting prudent forethought and virtuous behavior can improve the day-to-day quality of services provided by all psychologists. As such, the average psychologist could be transformed into a better one.

Regulatory Boards

Licensing boards, even when functioning at their best, are designed to protect the public by enforcing only the minimal standards of ethical behavior. They establish minimal standards of competence for entry into the profession, they often require a minimal number of continuing education credits as a condition of licensure renewal, and they punish psychologists who fail to follow minimal standards of conduct. Although effective in the screening of licensure applicants, state licensing boards do little, if anything, to promote higher levels of conduct among psychologists who already are licensed.

Obviously, the boards do not focus on positive ethics.

Perhaps licensing boards could be restructured to promote higher levels of competence and conduct, as opposed to merely preventing blatantly substandard behavior through the threat of punishment. For example, boards could reduce renewal fees for those psychologists who obtain a proficiency certificate or diplomate status, or who receive substantially more than the minimum amount of high-quality continuing education.

Furthermore, the disciplinary system could be reformed so as no longer to focus exclusively on the public exposure of all psychologists who are found guilty of infractions. Perhaps state boards could adopt different strategies for first-time minor offenders. In such a system, the first offenders would undergo strong continuing education or monitoring requirements; moreover, if they successfully complete these processes, no public finding of violations would be made. Aggrieved patients or colleagues may be more willing to report the misconduct of psychologists if they knew that the consequences would be truly rehabilitative and not result in a public and potentially career-shattering ethics violation.

A more radical preventive approach would be for state boards to require relicensure after approximately 10 years—a point at which psychologists seem to be especially at risk for ethical misconduct (Handelsman, 1997). Rather than taking a test as they did the first time, psychologists would be required to undergo a practice audit that would focus on elements of ethical practice. As part of the audit, psychologists would have the opportunity to (re)examine the ethical bases of their professional lives to avoid potential problems. We are not aware of any states that have adopted such a strategy.

Sensitivity to Our Larger Professional Contexts

The last element of positive ethics broadens our perspective to include the social context within which psychologists work. Psychologists operate in many different arenas, and behaving with ethical excellence may mean understanding the differing traditions and values that may be salient in the academic, business, legal, and scientific settings. The professional context also includes the similarities and differences between psychologists and other professionals (Appelbaum & Lawton, 1990; Rest & Narváez, 1994).

Understanding the ethical values and traditions of others may inform and enrich our own ethical thinking, behaving, and training.

In addition to exploring relationships with other professionals, psychologists need to recognize their roles in the society more generally. In large measure, psychologists owe their livelihood (and their relatively high social status) to the general public—even though they serve relatively few students or clients. Many professors teach in public colleges and universities, and their research is funded by government agencies. Even those who work for private firms, foundations, or agencies are likely to have been trained in public institutions. Licenses to practice are granted by the states as part of a social contract. The nature of that contract is complex and has ramifications for how we create, disseminate, and use psychological knowledge with a wide range of populations (APA, 1991; APA, Public Interest Directorate, 1998; Clark, 1993).

In addition to providing direct services, psychologists fulfill their social contract through involvement in public policy (Fainberg, 1994; Lorion, Iscoe, DeLeon, & VandenBos, 1996). A more controversial element is encouraging and participating in political action (Brown, 1997). One of the goals of psychology is to promote human welfare, which may require attacking laws and regulations that discriminate against women and others, that restrict access to psychological services among populations who need them, or that permit poor practices by health care organizations. These options are controversial because psychologists hold differing beliefs concerning the desirability of political action. Nonetheless, they are ways that psychologists can remain true to their values and act on their moral beliefs. At the very least, a positive approach to ethics includes an awareness of how our professional actions influence public perceptions and how we fit into both the positive and the negative aspects of the culture that sustains us.

Recommendations

In this chapter we have illustrated some of the ways in which psychology can move beyond a narrow rule-bound approach toward an ethics that is based on an integrated awareness of both internal and external themes. Increasing our scope of awareness can help us explore who we are—professionally and personally—in the service of the people with whom we interact. Although some goals are easier to accomplish than others, we conclude with recommendations that—in the spirit of positive ethics—are aspirational and beneficial.

Training

When considering applicants for graduate training in psychology, it would be helpful to evaluate candidates' general ethical sensitivity, and/or ethical reasoning skills, as part of the selection process. For example, training program materials could clearly identify the public service mission of the department. In their biographical statements students could be asked to specify how their undergraduate experiences and career goals are consistent with the department's mission. Moral motivation also could be assessed by asking students to identify the charitable or volunteer activities in which they have participated.

More specific assessment might focus on different issues depending on the emphasis of the program. Some programs might be more practically oriented and assess awareness of boundary issues, whereas others might focus on the applicants' understanding of the expectations and obligations of professionals who function as researchers, consultants, or teachers in society. We recognize that evaluating moral motivation potentially could be challenged on legal, empirical, and other grounds. We believe, however, that even considering the possibilities would raise the level of discourse about ethics, training, and selection.

Consistent with positive ethics is the view that, regardless of the focus or theoretical orientation of training programs, students should be specifically trained in the limitations of our knowledge base and its applications. We are dismayed that ethics is sometimes taught in a haphazard, compartmentalized, and/or incidental manner. Teaching ethics in this fashion is simply not adequate. Programs should make an affirmative effort to teach ethical sensitivity not only by integrating ethical processes and concerns into other courses (cf., Handelsman, 1986), but also by including specific ethics courses that cover theory, method, and technique. Programs should emphasize the importance of ethics codes, risk management, and positive ethics—all of which are integral to good ethical decision making and do not contradict one another. Furthermore, this recommendation should not be restricted to professional

training programs. In our view, experimental and other research programs have no less of a burden in this regard.

Continuing Education

The trend toward mandating continuing education in ethics exposes many psychologists to ethical issues about which they would not otherwise be aware. Ideally, these programs will help psychologists achieve acceptable standards of ethics competence. Competent psychologists should know the relevant ethical standards, laws, court cases, and risk management procedures. However, thorough ethical competence also requires ethical sensitivity, an appreciation of the moral traditions that underlie the ethical standards, ethical decision-making skills, and a commitment to develop moral character.

As noted previously, we believe that too many ethics workshops focus on instilling anxiety to enhance rule compliance. Although psychologists may inevitably feel some anxiety as they learn about the rules or the disciplinary process, we see no reason that risk management cannot be taught from a supportive perspective that encourages people to do their best rather than seeing their actions through a "lens of defensiveness." In addition, teaching positive ethics requires a safe and supportive environment in which psychologists feel free to reflect on their underlying values, past behaviors, and ways that they can elevate the levels of their professional (and perhaps personal) conduct. Thus, ethics workshops have the possibility of being uplifting experiences.

Peer Consultation

We believe that consultation is fertile ground for change based on positive ethics. Currently, consultation often is used primarily in emergency situations or as a risk management tool to document that one is covering the necessary bases. This need not be so. We believe a model could be developed that asks psychologists to consult on a regular basis, and to do so before problems emerge. Under these conditions, consultants could help psychologists think through their policies in advance and strive to do (and be) better. In our view, consultants would have the responsibility of bringing both risk management and aspirational issues to the attention of those with whom they consult. As mentioned previously, such a model might be tied to licensure (e.g., licensure renewal could include documentation of a thorough ethics consultation in addition to the fee). Agencies could institute "ethics rounds," which would be routine discussions of ethical issues in nonemergency situations. Private practitioners could form consultation groups that meet regularly to discuss ethics.

A Broader Perspective

Ethics training and behavior that focus only on particular actions in specific cases are too narrow. We suggest that the ethical camera not only zoom in on details but also use a wide-angle lens for a fuller view of the professional, cultural, and societal contexts within which actions are considered.

"Zooming in" means paying explicit attention to personal values and personal distress as they affect psychologists' abilities to work. Self-reflection and self-care are integral parts of positive ethics; moreover, if they were reinforced in training, continuing education, professional associations, and regulatory agencies, they could improve not only our lives but also the lives of those we serve and the society in which we live.

In a climate where risk management dominates our thinking, working for the greater good often is sacrificed in the service of self-protection. The "wide-angle" lens, however, allows us to consider social justice, a concept that should not be left only to those few psychologists who work explicitly in the realm of public policy. We believe that just as self-care improves us and our work, so does working for the benefit of our community, country, and fellow human beings.

Acknowledgment   The authors wish to thank Margie Krest, whose expert comments on several drafts of this chapter can best be called "positive edits."

References

Abeles, N. (1980). Teaching ethical principles by means of values confrontations. *Psychotherapy: Theory, Research and Practice, 17,* 384–391.

Acuff, C., Bennett, B. E., Bricklin, P. M., Canter, M. B., Knapp, S. J., Moldawsky, S., & Phelps, R. (1999). Considerations for ethical practice in managed care. *Professional Psychology: Research and Practice, 30,* 563–575.

American Psychological Association. (1991). *Guidelines for providers of psychological services to ethnic, linguistic, and culturally diverse populations.* Washington, DC: Author.

American Psychological Association. (1992). Ethical principles of psychologists and code of conduct. *American Psychologist, 47,* 1597–1611.

American Psychological Association Council of Representatives. (1979). *Criteria for accreditation of doctoral training programs and internships in professional psychology.* Washington, DC: American Psychological Association.

American Psychological Association, Public Interest Directorate. (1998). *About the public interest directorate.* Retrieved from World Wide Web: http://www.apa.org/pi/about.html.

Appelbaum, D., & Lawton, S. V. (1990). *Ethics and the professions.* Englewood Cliffs, NJ: Prentice-Hall.

Appelbaum, P. S., Lidz, C. W., & Meisel, A. (1987). *Informed consent: Legal theory and clinical practice.* New York: Oxford University Press.

Baldick, T. L. (1980). Ethical discrimination ability of intern psychologists: A function of training in ethics. *Professional Psychology, 11,* 276–282.

Beauchamp, T. L., & Childress, J. F. (1994). *Principles of biomedical ethics* (4th ed.). New York: Oxford University Press.

Bernard, J. L., Murphy, M., & Little, M. (1987). The failure of clinical psychologists to apply understood ethical principles. *Professional Psychology: Research and Practice, 18,* 489–491.

Bersoff, D. (1994). Explicit ambiguity: The 1992 Ethics Code as oxymoron. *Professional Psychology: Research and Practice, 25,* 382–387.

Branstetter, S. A., & Handelsman, M. M. (2000). Graduate teaching assistants: Ethical training, beliefs, and practices. *Ethics and Behavior, 10,* 27–50.

Brown, L. S. (1997). The private practice of subversion: Psychology at *tikkun olam. American Psychologist, 52,* 449–462.

Canter, M. B., Bennett, B. E., Jones, S. E., & Nagy, T. F. (1994). *Ethics for psychologists: A commentary on the APA ethics code.* Washington, DC: American Psychological Association.

Carse, A. L. (1991). The "voice of care": Implications for bioethical education. *Journal of Medicine and Philosophy, 16,* 5–28.

Clark, C. R. (1993). Social responsibility ethics: Doing right, doing good, doing well. *Ethics and Behavior, 3,* 303–328.

Committee on Ethical Guidelines for Forensic Psychologists. (1991). Specialty guidelines for forensic psychologists. *Law and Human Behavior, 15,* 655–665.

Cooper, C. C., & Gottlieb, M. C. (2000). Ethical issues in managed care: Challenges facing counseling psychologists. *Counseling Psychologist, 28,* 179–236.

Fainberg, A. (Ed.). (1994). *From the lab to the hill.* Washington, DC: American Association for the Advancement of Science.

Feminist Therapy Institute. (1990). Feminist Therapy Institute Code of Ethics. In H. Lerman & N. Porter (Eds.), *Feminist ethics in psychotherapy* (pp. 38–40). New York: Springer.

Gleicher, F., & Petty, R. E. (1992). Expectations of reassurance influence the nature of fear-stimulated attitude change. *Journal of Experimental Social Psychology, 28,* 86–100.

Gottlieb, M. C. (1993). Avoiding exploitive dual relationships: A decision-making model. *Psychotherapy, 30,* 41–48.

Gottlieb, M. C., & Cooper, C. C. (in press). Ethical issues in integrative therapies. In J. Lebow (Ed.), *Comprehensive handbook of psychotherapy: Vol. 4. Integrative and eclectic therapies.* New York: Wiley.

Haas, L. J., & Malouf, J. L. (1989). *Keeping up the good work: A practitioner's guide to mental health ethics.* Sarasota, FL: Professional Resource Exchange.

Handelsman, M. M. (1986). Problems with ethics training by "osmosis." *Professional Psychology: Research and Practice, 17,* 371–372.

Handelsman, M. M. (1997, March 14). *Colorado Grievance Board Sanctions.* (Available from the Colorado State Mental Health Boards, 1560 Broadway, Suite 1370, Denver, CO 80202)

Handelsman, M. M. (1998). Ethics and ethical reasoning. In S. Cullari (Ed.), *Foundations of clinical psychology* (pp. 80–111). Needham Heights, MA: Allyn and Bacon.

Handelsman, M. M. (in press). Learning to become ethical. In S. Walfish & A. K. Hess (Eds.), *Succeeding in graduate school: The compleat career guide for the psychology student.* Mahwah, NJ: Erlbaum.

Handelsman, M. M., & Uhlemann, M. R. (1998). Be careful what you wish for: Issues in the statutory regulation of counsellors. *Canadian Journal of Counselling, 32,* 315–331.

Hearnshaw, L. S. (1979). *Cyril Burt, psychologist.* London: Hodder and Stoughton.

Honaker, L. M. (2000, July 7). Memo from APA Ethics Office.

Jepson, C., & Chaiken, S. (1990). Chronic issue-specific fear inhibits systematic processing of persuasive communications. *Journal of Social Behavior and Personality, 5,* 61–84.

Johnson, W. B., & Corser, R. (1998). Learning ethics the hard way: Facing the ethics committee. *Teaching of Psychology, 25,* 26–28.

Jones, J. H. (1981). *Bad blood.* New York: Free Press.

Jordan, A. E., & Meara, N. M. (1990). Ethics and professional practice of psychologists: The role of virtues and principles. *Professional Psychology: Research and Practice, 21,* 107–114.

Keith-Spiegel, P. (Ed.). (1994). The 1992 ethics code: Boon or bane? *Professional Psychology: Research and Practice, 25,* 315–387.

Kimmel, A. J. (1988). *Ethics and values in applied social research.* Newbury Park, CA: Sage.

Kitchener, K. S. (1984). Intuition, critical evaluation and ethical principles: The foundation for ethical decisions in counseling psychology. *Counseling Psychologist, 12,* 43–55.

Kitchener, K. S. (1988). Dual role relationships: What makes them so problematic? *Journal of Counseling and Development, 67,* 217–221.

Kitchener, K. S. (2000). *Foundations of ethical practice, research, and teaching in psychology.* Mahwah, NJ: Erlbaum.

Knapp, S. (1999). Utilitarianism and the ethics of professional psychologists. *Ethics and Behavior, 9,* 383–392.

Knapp, S. (2000). Positive ethics in psychology. *Pennsylvania Psychologist, 60* (4), 31.

Knapp, S., & Pincus, J. (1999, September). Self-care and ethical theories. *Pennsylvania Psychologist, 59*(9), 10.

Koocher, G. P., & Keith-Spiegel, P. (1998). *Ethics in psychology: Professional standards and cases* (2nd ed.). New York: Oxford University Press.

Lerman, H., & Porter, N. (Eds.). (1990). *Feminist ethics in psychotherapy.* New York: Springer.

Levine, R. (1986). *Ethics and regulation of clinical research* (2nd ed.). Baltimore: Urban and Schwarzenber.

Lorion, R. P., Iscoe, I., DeLeon, P. H., & VandenBos, G. R. (Eds.). (1996). *Psychology and public policy: Balancing public service and professional need.* Washington, DC: American Psychological Association.

Meara, N. M., Schmidt, L. D., & Day, J. D. (1996). Principles and virtues: A foundation for ethical decisions, policies, and character. *Counseling Psychologist, 24*(1), 4–77.

Nagy, T. F. (1996, January/February). Ethics committees: Investigate or educate? *National Psychologist, 5*(1), 615–616.

Pope, K. S., & Vetter, V. A. (1992). Ethical dilemmas encountered by members of the American Psychological Association: A national survey. *American Psychologist, 47,* 397–411.

Rest, J. R. (1986). *Moral development: Advances in research and theory.* New York: Praeger.

Rest, J. R. (1994). Background: Theory and research. In J. R. Rest & D. Narváez (Eds.), *Moral development in the professions: Psychology and applied ethics* (pp. 1–26). Hillsdale, NJ: Erlbaum.

Rest, J. R., & Narváez, D. (Eds.). (1994). *Moral development in the professions: Psychology and applied ethics.* Hillsdale, NJ: Erlbaum.

Sales, B. D., & Folkman, S. (Eds.). (1998). *The ethics of research with human participants* (Draft copy). Washington, DC: American Psychological Association, Board of Scientific Affairs Task Force.

Sieber, J. E. (1992). *Planning ethically responsible research: A guide for students and internal review boards.* Newbury Park, CA: Sage.

Small, R., & Knapp, S. (1999, October). *Ethics is more than a code.* Workshop presented at the Second Annual Fall Ethics Workshop, Fort Washington, PA.

Strickland, B. R. (1998). History and introduction to clinical psychology. In S. Cullari (Ed.), *Foundations of clinical psychology* (pp. 1–25). Needham Heights, MA: Allyn and Bacon.

Sullivan, T., Martin, W. L., Jr., & Handelsman, M. M. (1993). Practical benefits of an informed consent procedure: An empirical investigation. *Professional Psychology: Research and Practice, 24,* 160–163.

Tjeltveit, A. (1999). *Ethics and values in psychotherapy.* London: Routledge.

Tymchuk, A. J. (1981). Ethical decision-making and psychological treatment. *Journal of Psychiatric Treatment and Evaluation, 3,* 507–513.

VandeCreek, L., & Knapp, S. (1993). *Tarasoff and beyond* (2nd ed.). Sarasota, FL: Professional Resource Press.

Veatch, R. M., & Sollitto, S. (1976). Medical ethics teaching: Report of a national medical school survey. *Journal of the American Medical Association, 235,* 1030–1033.

Webb, S. (1996, July–August). Collaborative law— A Conversation: Why aren't those divorce lawyers going to court? *Hennepin Lawyer,* 26–28.

White v. North Carolina State Board of Examiners of Practicing Psychologists, 97 N.C. App. 144, 388 S.E.2d 148 (1990), *review denied,* 326 N.C. 601, 393 S.E.2d 891 (1990).

54

Constructivism and Positive Psychology

Michael J. Mahoney

Although the term *positive psychology* is of recent coinage, it shares a rich legacy with humanism, health psychology, constructivism, and spiritual studies. Perhaps reflecting its close ties to medical models and metaphors of illness in human adaptation, much of applied psychology had developed a decidedly pathological emphasis. A growing awareness of the liabilities and limitations of this deficiency- and disease-oriented trend sparked more vocal expressions of the other side of human experience. This other, more positive side is still being defined (see the various chapters in this volume), but it includes such themes as altruism, caring, compassion, consciousness, coping, creativity, emotional intelligence, forgiveness, hope, humor, resilience, resourcefulness, self-efficacy, and spirituality. Psychology's preoccupation with human frailties must now compete with strong interests in human capacities, healthy inclinations, and virtuous possibilities. This shift in our view of human nature has important implications for future theory, research, and practice, as well as welcome possibilities for changes in the public image and everyday application of psychology.

For most of the 20th century, a common lay assumption was that psychologists were persons who were assumed to be always analyzing, scrutinizing, and labeling the neurotic pathologies of everyone they encountered. Given the prevalence of this stereotype, it is remarkable that professional life counseling has enjoyed such growth in 20th-century culture. With the positive psychology movement such stereotypes are losing ground to more balanced characterizations of what psychology is and how psychologists may serve future generations. Instead of being stereotyped as pessimistic pathologists, perhaps psychologists of the future will be viewed as promoters of the human spirit and professionals adept at seeing possibility and promise in our individual and collective development. This is, in part, what positive psychology aspires to accomplish, as does constructivism, which is essentially a philosophy of human process and potential.

This chapter is devoted to the philosophy of constructivism and its expression of perennial interests in both possibility and human potential. Similar to positive psychology, *constructivism* is a term that has only recently emerged. Archival analyses of word frequencies in PsychLit between 1974 and 1994 reflect an exponential increase in references to constructivism and constructivists (Mahoney & Albert, 1996). But constructivism is a philosophy that is at least three centuries old in Western cultures and more than two millennia old in the wisdom traditions of Asia and India.

A Brief History of Constructivism

Studies of the historical roots of constructivism have pointed toward both classical Asian-Indian and Greek voices. Gautama Buddha (560–477 B.C.E.) should be counted as an early (if not the original) constructivist if only because of the opening words of his teachings, which emphasized the role we play in who we are and how we find our world: "We are what we think. All that we are arises with our thoughts. With our thoughts we make the world" (Walsh, 1999, p. 45). His contemporary Lao-Tzu in the sixth century B.C.E. was the founder of Taoism, a philosophy that emphasized the dialectical tension of contrasts and the primacy of process. These same insights lay at the heart of the teachings of the pre-Socratic philosopher Heraclitus (540–475 B.C.E.). Heraclitus is famous for his sayings that one "cannot step into the same river twice" because "all is flux; all is becoming" (i.e., neither the person nor the river is ever the same). The pioneer of process philosophy in Western traditions, Heraclitus believed that there was a "tension of opposites" in all things, and that life reflects the ever-changing dynamics of these interactive contrasts.

In Western philosophy, the pioneers of constructivism are generally deemed to include three individuals: Giambattista Vico (1668–1744), Immanuel Kant (1724–1804), and Hans Vaihinger (1852–1933). Both Vico and Kant were writing in response to the growing popularity of British empiricism, which became the primary vehicle for the scientific revolution. Vico said that human knowing involves an imaginary construction of order in experience, thus implying that the knower cannot be separated from what is presumed to be known. Kant went even further by describing the mind as an active organ "which transforms the chaotic multiplicity of experience into the orderly unity of thought" (Durant, 1926, p. 291). Although Kant is often classified as an Idealist (emphasizing the primacy of ideas in human experience), he was decidedly a constructivist in granting the mind an active role in giving form to experience.

In Kant's *Critique of Pure Reason*, he devoted brief reflections to the provocative dimension of "as if," which dealt with possibility and imagi-

nation. Vaihinger focused on this dimension in his studies. In *The Philosophy of "As If,"* Vaihinger described the mind as an organic, formative, and constructive force whose function is not to portray or mirror reality but to serve the individual in navigations through life circumstances. Where Vico had emphasized the role of "fantasia" and myth in human adaptation, Vaihinger (1911) suggested that we live our lives via personally and collectively "functional fictions": "The mind is not merely appropriative, it is also assimilative and constructive" (p. 2). Furthermore, it was Vaihinger who supervised the dissertation of one of the most influential early American psychologists, James Rowland Angell, who had already completed two master's degrees under John Dewey and William James (Hilgard, 1987). Angell's students and the students of his students read like a "who's who" of 20th century American psychology: John B. Watson, Harvey A. Carr, Karl S. Lashley, Walter S. Hunter, L. L. Thurstone, Carney Landis, Arthur Benton, and Albert Bandura, among others.

When Alfred Adler broke with Freud in 1911, he adopted Vaihinger's principle of functional fictions as the cornerstone of his theory of individual psychology. Contemporary Adlerian scholars maintain that Adler is more accurately portrayed as a pioneer in constructivist thinking rather than as a reactionary neo-Freudian (Carson & Sperry, 1998; Oberst, 1998). Vaihinger's writings also inspired George A. Kelly, whose personal construct psychology became a classic expression of constructivism. After Vaihinger, pioneering contributions to constructivism were made by Sir Frederic Bartlett, Jean Piaget, Friedrich Hayek, and Kelly. Bartlett's (1932) work on perception and memory showed that both of these are fundamentally constructive and reconstructive processes. Although Jean Piaget often is remembered for his proposed stages of intellectual development, he made important contributions to the view that all life forms are fundamentally self-organizing. Piaget believed that the child organizes her world by first organizing herself. This reflects a basic premise of constructivism (see later discussion). Self-organization is inseparable from the experience of reality. Piaget also elaborated the equilibration theory of Johann Herbart (1776–1841), which offered one of the first dynamic theories of human learning and development. Equilibration theory portrays knowing as a quest for a dynamic and developing balance between what is familiar and what is novel. This is accomplished by the counterbalancing processes of assimilation and accommodation—distorting an experience in order to assimilate it into existing (familiar) epistemological structures and processes or modifying those structures and processes such that they can accommodate the novelty that they have encountered.

In 1952 Friedrich A. Hayek published perhaps the most powerful theoretical outline of constructivism. Hayek received the Nobel Prize in Economics for his brilliant analysis of distributed wisdom in complex and spontaneously self-organizing systems (such as the market economy). His writing of *The Sensory Order* was mostly an avocational project, although personal interviews late in his life suggested that his award-winning economic theories emerged out of his theoretical conjectures in psychology (Mahoney & Weimer, 1994). In *The Sensory Order,* Hayek showed that the particulars of perception—including the most basic of sensations—can become particulars only in the context of an ongoing classification or ordering process that is fundamentally abstract.

George A. Kelly's (1955) publication of *The Psychology of Personal Constructs* was a landmark in the development of constructivism. Kelly's theory of *constructive alternativism,* better known as *personal construct theory,* emphasized both possibility and pattern in the self-organization of personality. Kelly elaborated a truly original theory of personality built around constructs, which he described as basically dichotomous processes of self-organization that varied in such dimensions as their permeability and their tightness and looseness. Kelly translated his theory into a novel approach to psychotherapy, in which the role of the therapist is to skillfully challenge the client's ways of construing self, others, the world, and their possible relationships.

Influences from and contributions to constructivism continued to increase at exponential rates throughout the last quarter of the 20th century. In 1996 the Society for Constructivism in the Human Sciences was formed to encourage and communicate developments in theory, research, and practices that reflect an appreciation for "human beings as actively complex, socially-embedded, and developmentally dynamic self-organizing systems" (CONSTRUCTIVISM, UNT Box 311280, Denton, TX 76203). The society honored Walter Truett Anderson, Albert Bandura, Jerome S. Bruner, James F. T. Bugen-

tal, Donald H. Ford, Viktor E. Frankl, Humberto R. Maturana, Joseph F. Rychlak, Francisco J. Varela, Heinz von Foerster, Ernst von Glaserfeld, and Walter B. Weimer as pioneering contributors to constructivism. What exactly is constructivism, and how does it relate to positive psychology? These are the themes of the next two sections.

The Defining Themes of Constructivism

A central thesis of constructivism is that we participate in cocreating the universe that we experience and the realities to which we respond. The heart of constructivism is expressed in five basic themes: activity, order, identity, social-symbolic processes, and dynamic, dialectical development. Constructivism views the living system as a proactive agent that participates in its own life dynamics. This portrayal is in contrast to traditional physical science renditions, in which the living system is a passive conduit of energies, forces, and masses that are moved or modified only by being impacted by other external entities. In constructivism, complex systems—and certainly those that we call "living" systems—are organic processes expressing self-movement and ongoing self-organization.

The activity of the organism is her or his primary means of expressing attempts to adapt to prevailing circumstances. This is a basic assumption of constructivism. The relevance of activity to positive psychology is readily apparent: An active and motivated organism is one that remains engaged with the challenges of life and the developmental opportunities that those challenges present. Learned optimism, learned resourcefulness, and hope, for example, are expressions of such engagement. Constructivism maintains not only that living systems are active but also that their activity is primarily directed toward self-organization—toward establishing, maintaining, and elaborating a patterned order (coherent continuity) in their experience. Ordering patterns that "work" for us become our "personal realities." They are not conceptual abstractions so much as they are embodied and continuously enacted theories of life. This is part of the reason they are often so difficult to change.

Emotional processes are among the most powerful and primitive of human self-organizing processes. Emotions involve preparations to act. Through emotional and symbolic processes, we actively "project" our past onto our future. In the process of such anticipatory projection, we shape every present moment. The practical significance of this can be seen daily in mental health clinics. Clients have difficulty imagining—let alone hoping for and working toward—patterns of experiencing that might be healthy and satisfying. If they have never felt safe or loved or capable, it is very difficult for them to explore or maintain activity patterns that might foster these experiences. Combined with responsible action, the processes of hope, fantasy, and imagination figure prominently in constructive and positive approaches to life counseling.

But there is more to constructivism than self-organizing activity. Disorder—the conceptual opposite of order—is a necessary element in the development of all complex systems. Disorder and order are defined by and relative to one another, of course. One of the more promising of the tenets of constructivism is that processes of disorder are not pathologized as enemies of health. Rather, as Herbart and Piaget anticipated, disordering processes are natural and necessary expressions of a complex system's attempts to reorganize its life. New life patterns emerge out of the chaos and dysfunction that ensue when old patterns are no longer viable (Mahoney, 1991, 2000). Similar to positive psychology, constructivism cautions against judgmental and pejorative portrayals of disorder and dysfunction.

The third theme of constructivism pays homage to the complex dynamics of the system we call a self. We humans actively order our own experiencing, and our self-organizing processes tend to orbit around distinctions based in our embodiment and the contrast between "self" and "other." The boundaries of the individual system serve to define that system as a fundamentally personal and phenomenological undertaking. It is more than coincidental that Alfred Adler called his approach "individual psychology," that Albert Bandura has championed "self-efficacy," that Vittorio Guidano focused on the "complexity of self" and "the self in process," or that George Kelly focused on "personal constructs." From a constructive perspective, all psychotherapy is psychotherapy of the self (Guidano, 1987, 1991). But constructivism is far from a narcissistic, self-absorbed, or solipsistic philosophy. It honors the mysteries of selfhood as emergent expressions of social consciousness. Constructivism does not view the self as an entity, a possession, or an enduring collection of personality traits. Rather, the self is considered to be an embodied and emerging process—indeed, a complex system of active and interactive self-organizing processes. As such, the self exhibits a rich fabric of simultaneous unity (consistency) and diversity. The complexity of the idea of a simultaneously changing and changeless self is daunting. It seems increasingly clear that individual selves exhibit multiple facets, levels, and capacities (Anderson, 1998). We are only now beginning to explore language forms that may allow us to better understand this complexity and the mysteries of a self seeking to understand itself. It is, as Allen Wheelis (1971) says, "like a man before a mirror asking the man he sees what the man in the mirror is asking" (p. 57).

The fourth theme of constructivism reflects a strong convergence with cultural studies, ecological ethics, feminist theory, linguistics, and the human rights movements in their recognition that everyone and everything is connected. Constructivism maintains that human self-organizing activities are embedded in social and symbolic contexts. Symbol systems—such as languages and mathematics—are expressions of the social fabric of experiencing. If we artificially separate these two for the sake of closer examination, we quickly see that the social or "intersubjective" dimension of human experience is fundamental. We live in and from relationships with other human beings. The self—although uniquely personal and largely "self-centered"—is always socially embedded. Personal identities—the experience of who one is, what one is capable of, and personal worth—develop *within* human relationships. Changes in the sense of self also develop within such relationships: relationships with parents, family, friends, teachers, and, sometimes, therapists.

Symbolic processes allow us to transcend space and time. How they do this is still mostly a mystery, and this is reflected by the diversity of views in cognitive science, communications studies, linguistics, philosophy, and semiotics (theory of signs). It is clear, however, that our symbolic capacities allow us to "play with reality" and to dream, fantasize, hope, imagine, pretend, and remember. Much of positive psychology invokes such processes as promising paths toward health and well-being. Our understanding in these dimensions is still barely rudimentary, but it is clear that communication, in all its diversity, is an expression of our fundamental connection to one another.

The fifth working principle of constructivism is that human development is a lifelong process that is dynamic (always changing) and dialectical (generated by contrasts). This theme envelops the first four principles and also elaborates them into metaphors that may help us to understand the complexities of an open, active system that is both changing and self-stabilizing over time. Our development—both as a species and as individuals—reflects complexly interactive and distributed processes. We are always changing, if only to stay the same. We are actively participating in the ordering—the structuring and, therefore, the construction—of our own continuing existence. And we are rarely (and even then only barely) aware of what we are doing and how we do it.

Another way to convey the spirit of the developmental principle in constructivism is to say that it reflects the lifelong quest to achieve a delicate balance between ordering and disordering processes. Ordering processes literally allow us to maintain life support and our coherence as a life-form. Disordering processes present challenges to our overall balance. They disrupt our familiar ways of being in the world. In so doing, they challenge us to learn—to revise our ordering patterns. When they challenge us too much, however, disordering processes may threaten our viability as a living system. Disorder does not guarantee development. When we do survive, however—when we learn new skills and elaborate our systems of meanings— we are said to "develop." Such development is called "dialectical" because it emerges out of the interaction of contrasts. The cardinal dialectical contrast in human development is between the "old" (familiar, order) and the "new" (novel, chaos), but it can be experienced and expressed in a variety of ways (good/bad, me/not-me, true/false, right/wrong, real/illusory, etc.).

Constructivist views of life span human development are fundamentally complex and dynamic. That is to say, they are generally organic portrayals that acknowledge that human development can be meaningfully glimpsed at the level of abstract principles, but that it can never be completely predicted or engineered. Such views are noteworthy in their assertion that cycles (oscillations) are natural and common as-

pects of human experiencing. Variability in experience and action are critical to the selection processes that both protect old patterns and promote novel possibilities. This is why disorder is an essential aspect of development (Neimeyer & Raskin, 2000). But ordering processes are the favored children of biological life. Like all other life forms, we humans are fundamentally conservative. We often resist change more vigorously than we seek it (although both processes coexist in all of us, all the time).

Positive Psychology, Human Potential, and Spirituality

In the larger scheme of postmodern thought, constructivism emphasizes agency, choice, possibility, and complex dynamics. Like the positive psychology that it reflects, constructivism recognizes the central importance of meaning in the quality and continuing emergence of human life. Meaning reflects a basic human need for order, relationship, and hope. These needs are not satisfied without being actively sought, co-created, and nurtured. Contrary to Alexander Pope's assurance that "hope springs eternal in the human breast," it is only the seeds of such hope that remain perennial. To flower and bear fruit, they must be carefully tended. I believe that this is where constructivism and positive psychology embrace the promise offered by the world's spiritual and wisdom traditions.

This is not the place to trace the indebtedness of positive or constructivist psychology to Renaissance humanism, the "mind cure" or "healthy-mindedness" that so fascinated William James, the popularity of "positive thinking" (and its contemporary cognitive expressions), or the contributions of humanistic psychology and the human potential movement. What does warrant at least brief mention in these closing remarks, however, is the fundamental resonance among constructivism, positive psychology, and contemporary inquiries into the spiritual dimensions of human experience and meaning-making. Until recently, spirituality was an unwelcome topic of discussion in mainstream psychological writing. This has changed dramatically in the past quarter century. Also changing are the meanings and correlates of the term *spiritual* (Mahoney & Graci, 1999). Where it was once a synonym for *religious*, the word *spiritual* has taken on meanings that echo many of the themes emphasized in positive psychology (e.g., caring, compassion, forgiveness, generosity, hope, love, meaning, nonviolence [peace], responsibility, and wisdom).

Constructivism and positive psychology are not Pollyannaish perspectives. They do not argue that all life stories can end happily or that all life circumstances can be reframed in positive hues. They do, however, encourage an authentic engagement with the living moment, and in this encouragement they share important themes with existential humanism and transpersonal spirituality. A large part of their promise may therefore stem from their openness to a more holistic conceptualization of what it means to be human and to be partially and developmentally conscious.

References

Anderson, W. T. (1997). *The future of the self: Inventing the postmodern person*. New York: Tarcher and Putnam.

Bartlett, F. C. (1932). *Remembering*. Cambridge: Cambridge University Press.

Carlson, J., & Sperry, L. (1998). Adlerian psychotherapy as a constructivist psychotherapy. In M. F. Hoyt (Ed.), *The handbook of constructivist therapies* (pp. 68–82). San Francisco: Jossey-Bass.

Durant, W. (1926). *The story of philosophy*. Garden City, NY: Garden City Publishing.

Guidano, V. F. (1987). *Complexity of the self*. New York: Guilford.

Guidano, V. F. (1991). *The self in process*. New York: Guilford.

Hayek, F. A. (1952). *The sensory order*. Chicago: University of Chicago Press.

Hilgard, E. R. (1987). *Psychology in America: A historical survey*. San Diego, CA: Harcourt Brace Jovanovich.

Kelly, G. A. (1955). *The psychology of personal constructs*. New York: Norton.

Mahoney, M. J. (1991). *Human change processes*. New York: Basic Books.

Mahoney, M. J. (2000). *Constructive psychotherapy: The heart of positive practice*. New York: Guilford.

Mahoney, M. J., & Albert, C. J. (1996). Worlds of words: The changing vocabulary of psychology. *Constructivism in the Human Sciences, 1*(3–4), 22–26.

Mahoney, M. J., & Graci, G. M. (1999). The meanings and correlates of spirituality: Suggestions from an exploratory survey of experts. *Death Studies, 23*, 521–528.

Mahoney, M. J., & Weimer. W. B. (1994). Friedrich A. Hayek 1899–1992. *American Psychologist, 49*, 63.

Neimeyer, R. A., & Raskin, J. D. (Eds.). *Constructions of disorder*. Washington, DC: American Psychological Association.

Oberst, U. E. (1998). Alfred Adler's Individual Psychology in the context of constructivism. *Constructivism in the Human Sciences, 3*, 153–176.

Vaihinger, H. (1911). *The philosophy of "as if."* Berlin: Reuther and Reichard.

Walsh, R. N. (1999). *Essential spirituality*. New York: Wiley.

Wheelis, A. (1971). *The end of the modern age*. New York: Harper.

55

The Future of Positive Psychology

A Declaration of Independence

C. R. Snyder & Shane J. Lopez

With contributions from Lisa Aspinwall, Barbara L. Fredrickson, Jon Haidt, Dacher Keltner, Christine Robitschek, Michael Wehmeyer, and Amy Wrzesniewski

In thinking about preparing this handbook, we were driven by a basic question. What has psychology previously contributed to our understanding of human strengths such as forgiveness, love, kindness, courage, hope, sharing, caring, cooperation, sacrifice, spirituality, friendship, and so on? The answer, regrettably, is not very much. Although we can debate the underlying causes for the attraction to the "dark side" of human experience, that strikes us as an unproductive exercise. Our focus, we would argue, should be looking into the future of positive psychology.

So, what does lie ahead for positive psychology? That is the question that sparks excitement in both of us because the positive psychology perspective presents opportunities to address philosophical issues (e.g., What is the good life?) and practical questions (e.g., "How do positive emotions affect us over time?"). Positive psychological science could guide us in our pursuit of mental health at the personal and community levels. Toward this end, over 100 con-

tributing scholars in this volume offer their visions of how human strengths can foster health, well-being, and a sense of community.

In this chapter, we describe the declaration of independence that has been made from the weakness model in psychology. We have partitioned this declaration of independence into four parts. The first involves a brief review of what has transpired and its significance; the second, third, and fourth sections explore issues pertaining to the science, application, and training in positive psychology. Additionally, we have interspersed the views of some emerging leaders in positive psychology at various points in the chapter.

On Breaking Away

Some have characterized the positive psychology perspective as a recent phenomenon. Others see it as a slow accretion of work that has been building for years. In this section, we will argue that it is probably most accurate to describe the emergence as involving both of these forces. Additionally, we will comment on the practical implications of the growth of positive psychology.

The Positive Psychology Movement

Positive psychology will not supplant the weakness model, but it will grow as a necessary and complementary scientific quest. The study of mental illness and its treatment will continue as researchers delve into the etiology of disorders, the nature of suffering, and the remediation of psychological illness with psychotherapeutic and pharmacological treatments. But should we look only to the weaknesses of people? Concerning this lack of balance in our foci, Bandura (1998) observes that we have been "more heavily invested in intricate theories of failure than in theories of success" (p. 3). But increasing numbers of social scientists in general, and psychologists in particular, agree that the sole focus on human problems is not sufficient (Seligman & Csikszentmihalyi, 2000). There is no need, however, for battles over the superiority of either the pathology or the strength approach. Indeed, at this juncture of living history, what positive psychology seeks is not so much a confrontation but rather recognition as a viable, new paradigm—a rigorous science on the positive side of what it means to be human.

We would hasten to emphasize that this positive psychology perspective is not a brand-new one (Snyder & McCullough, 2000). Indeed, pioneering thinkers over the past several decades have provided compelling exemplars of positive psychology in their theories and research endeavors. Therefore, what appears to be a phenomenon that suddenly jumped into our awareness actually has been growing steadily through the efforts of these theorists and bench scientists. Consider the names of the authors in this volume. They are recognized, first and foremost, as being outstanding psychological scientists. Although these scientists previously were not called "positive psychologists," their efforts over the last two decades have laid a strong foundation for the building of this perspective.

It was Martin Seligman who provided a necessary spark for positive psychology. From the bully pulpit of his 1998 presidency of the American Psychological Association, he trumpeted the essential principle of positive psy-

chology—the need to recognize and study the very best in people (see Seligman, this volume). He did this not once but time and again, in one forum and another, spreading the word about positive psychology.

Since that watershed year of 1998, what has happened in regard to the progressive spread of attention to and knowledge about positive psychology? Certainly, there have been recent notable gains. One network television special, exchanges on National Public Radio, countless articles in magazines and newspapers, two national summits, small gatherings of prominent scholars, and $37 million of funding (Seligman, 2000) (and $300 million being recommended by the surgeon general for mental *health* research) have attracted attention inside and outside of psychology.

It is our view, therefore, that the first stage of a scientific movement—*one that we would characterize as a declaration of independence from the pathology model*—has been completed. The broader field now realizes that the positive psychology perspective exists. This handbook, which is built on our belief that a vital science and practice of positive psychology should grow alongside the science and practice of the pathology model, is yet another marker of this declaration of independence.

The Significance of Adding the Positive Psychology Perspective

The pathology model delimits the search for knowledge on at least two levels. First, suppose the psychologist begins the study of a given person or phenomenon within the pathology model, and the evidence begins to point to a human strength issue. With the dominance of the pathology model, the investigator does not pursue the strength. We are reminded here of a common scene in American cowboy movies where the posse is in hot pursuit but must pull up when the suspect rides across the border. With the acceptance of the positive psychology approach, it would be more likely that such boundaries would not halt the pursuit of knowledge.

Second, even when a psychologist is operating from a strength model and the data clearly point to the scholarly search of human strength, the pathology focus may prevail. Consider the example of the positive psychology researcher who was explaining his struggle to apply his talents and scientific skill to developing an understanding of optimal health. After sharing a synopsis of two decades of his research, he took questions from the audience. One question is of particular importance in the present context. Namely, this researcher was asked why most of his studies had examined the relationships between "his" positive psychology construct *and mental illness.* The questioner continued, "Why haven't you examined the connection to *mental health?"* First our researcher was puzzled, and then he candidly replied, *"I don't know how to measure health!"*

The positive psychology perspective also may aid in the discovery of aspects of human nature that previously have been undetected by social scientists. For example, Jon Haidt, who once focused his efforts on researching moral disgust, has become captivated by moral beauty and its effects. His ideas about awe and elevation in particular and about positive emotions more generally exemplify the emergence of positive psychology.

The Positive Emotion of Elevation—
Jon Haidt

The emotions have generally been thought of as self-interest monitors. Emotions force our minds and bodies to care about what's good for us. Yet it is a curious, beautiful, and understudied fact about human nature that we can be deeply moved by the sight of a stranger doing a good deed for another stranger. I have been studying this emotional response for the past few years, and I find enough similarities in the way people talk about it that I have given it a name: "elevation." Elevation has most of the hallmarks of a basic emotion: It has an eliciting condition (acts of moral beauty), a physiological effect (something in the chest, probably involving the vagus nerve, which gives a warm, open, and pleasant feeling), and an action tendency (the desire to be a better person oneself—to be more loving or helpful toward others). Elevation can be best thought of as the opposite of social disgust. Elevation lacks a specific facial expression (which may be why it has not previously been studied), and it is not as discrete as the negative emotions (it appears to overlap with awe, love, and gratitude). So elevation is harder to study than emotions such as anger and fear. But it can be studied. Ongoing research with Sara Algoe and Dacher Keltner finds that this emotional responsiveness

to moral beauty can be clearly identified in American sixth graders and in members of non-Western cultures. The exploration of positive emotions such as elevation, awe, and gratitude is an important area in which positive psychology can reshape and brighten the picture of human nature.

In our estimation, the positive psychology perspective unfetters the search for understanding all aspects of human nature, it opens the eyes of skilled researchers to new questions concerning health and well-being, and it sets the stage for future scientific discovery.

Breaking Away: Issues for the Science of Positive Psychology

In this section, we explore some of the major issues that will be involved in the science of positive psychology in the coming years. Although these issues would apply to any rigorous new branch of psychological science as it establishes its identity, it is important to discuss these as they apply to positive psychology.

Building on Science, Peer Review, and Prudent Claims

What is obvious in the previous pages of this volume is that the scholars want to construct a positive psychology on a foundation of scientific principles and methods. All of the advances that have been made in experimental design and sophisticated statistical analyses within the pathology paradigm can be used in the service of positive psychology science. A viable and enduring positive psychology will be founded not on armchair philosophical speculations but rather on carefully crafted hypotheses that can be tested empirically and analyzed with the latest statistical procedures.

With the spread of positive psychology experimentation, the gatekeepers—the journal editors—will be seeing more studies that explore the strengths of people. When this happens, however, the authors of positive psychology manuscripts should be prepared to have their writing undergo extra scrutiny. Namely, journal editors may well ask that results cast within a positive psychology framework be compared and contrasted with various pathology explanations. On this point, Snyder and McCullough (2000) have written about the activities at many psychology journals in the 1980s that "authors who submitted manuscripts often were forced to prove that their results were not explicable in terms of negative affectivity counter explanations. . . . [the] prevailing lens through which reality was seen was strongly ruled by the negative affectivity construct to the exclusion of other tenable *and more positive constructions*" (p. 154).

As a new paradigm becomes more successful and gathers proponents, it usually is the case in science that it no longer must be tested routinely in relation to the old paradigm (Kuhn, 1970). We have yet to reach this stage in positive psychology. Thus, in the near future, we must be prepared to have our ideas met with skepticism. There are those who will try to cast positive psychology ideas as being whimsical and lacking in merit. Consider Lisa Aspinwall's retort to such views.

Happier and Wiser: Optimism and Positive Affect Promote Careful Realistic Thinking and Behavior—Lisa Aspinwall

Perhaps one of the most important advances that could be made in positive psychology is to incorporate into the field's thinking the wealth of evidence suggesting that positive beliefs and states foster careful realistic thinking and constructive behavior (Armor & Taylor, 1998; Ashby, Isen, & Turken, 1999; Aspinwall, 1998, in press; Aspinwall, Richter, & Hoffman, 2000; Isen, 1993). Characterizations of positive thinking as empty-headed, delusional, wishful, or Pollyannish are at odds with a great deal of evidence suggesting considerable benefits of optimism and positive affect, including (a) more thorough, efficient, and flexible decision making, (b) careful attention to negative information that suggests the possibility of harm or loss, and (c) consistent relations to adaptive coping efforts and good outcomes in a wide range of settings.

People can be—and frequently are—both happier and wiser. What are the implications of this assertion for research and application in positive psychology? I believe there are several.

First, in our efforts to send Pollyanna home, we should not oversimplify the study of positive beliefs and states. It would be premature— and likely incorrect—to say that all positive beliefs and states are salutary. Instead, it may be

more reasonable to say that one should no longer assume that positive beliefs and states are harmful. Understanding how and when such beliefs are linked to constructive future-oriented behaviors—as well as when they are not—will yield a more nuanced and accurate view (see, e.g., Armor & Taylor, 1998).

What is needed in future research are studies in which the nature and consequences of different positive states and beliefs are evaluated in diverse and meaningful contexts, such as achievement, development, close relationships, intergroup processes, coping, work, and health (see Aspinwall & Staudinger, in press). An essential element of such efforts will be to jettison widespread assumptions regarding the symmetrical effects of positive and negative affect on cognition and behavior (see Isen, 1993, for discussion). In its strong form, this assumption may yield misleading conclusions—for example, if depression leads people to think carefully, then happiness must promote careless thinking; or if people in a negative mood are sensitive to risk information in the environment, then people in a positive mood must be insensitive to it. Again, such conclusions are at odds with a great deal of evidence, yet they frequently influence the design and interpretation of research.

Across the exciting spectrum of "positive" topics that will be examined in the coming years, efforts to take positive beliefs, feelings, and attributes seriously—and to elucidate their neurological, cognitive, developmental, social, and therapeutic functions in their own right— are likely to yield many findings with important implications for human health and well-being.

In the excitement that may be associated with this new and invigorating approach, it may be tempting to overextrapolate so as to convey a sense of the progress that is being made. This can be even more possible when a person from the news media is almost putting words in our mouths about the supposed discoveries and advances that already have occurred. Contrary to this "breakthrough" mentality, however, science typically advances in the context of slow, incremental increases in knowledge. Therefore, in the processes of conducting positive psychology research, getting it published, and describing such work in public forums, researchers must be very careful to make appropriate inferences from their data. Claims that go beyond the data never are appropriate, and they can be especially damaging to the credibility of a new field. When one positive psychologist makes an unwarranted claim, this undermines the trustworthiness of all positive psychologists and the "movement" more generally. Accordingly, we must carefully monitor both our colleagues and ourselves.

The Need for a Classification of Human Strengths

Positive psychology needs to have a classification of human strengths and civic virtues. To be able to measure human strengths not only will facilitate our understanding of those strengths but also will help in our efforts to increase these strengths. Classification is absolutely crucial to scientific ventures, and, as such, positive psychology must be careful and thorough in fulfilling this need. We turn to this and related issues in this section.

Classification Systems as Foundations of Science

Classifications exist in every scientific discipline (recall the periodic table of elements learned in high school chemistry class), and it could be argued that it would be difficult to have a science without a system for categorizing the phenomena being examined. For psychology, a classification system is needed to build a greater understanding of psychological strengths, to promote research, and to foster positive psychology practice focused on inculcating strengths. Though we do not view the *Diagnostic and Statistical Manual of Mental Disorders* (known as the *DSM*; American Psychiatric Association, 1952, 1968, 1980, 1987, 1994, 2000) system as a good example of a classification system (see Maddux, this volume), it has served as a profoundly influential framework for the research and practice arms of psychology. The new system in positive psychology will have to gain widespread acceptance of the same level as that exhibited by the *DSM*.

A Classification System in Development

Developing a classification system is a daunting task that involves the collaboration of experts, along with field testing in practice communities. The skills of psychologists are being put to good use as Christopher Peterson, Martin Seligman, and a team of consultants develop a classification system for strengths. In an early draft of this taxonomy, Peterson and Seligman (2000) wrote: "Psychology is not the only field now concerned with the striving and thriving end of the human continuum. . . . psychology has come late to this perspective. The unique contribution of psychology to the study of positive traits, we believe, is its century-old concern with the measurement of individual differences" (p. 3).

By the time this handbook is published, this classification system may be completed; moreover, it may serve positive psychology in a manner akin to how the *DSM* has served the pathology model. In the interim, however, it is not as if we are lacking in theory-based, individual differences measures that tap the most visible constructs in the field. Indeed, we already have several such measures. We turn next to the role of individual differences in positive psychology.

Individual Differences

Brief Measures of Positive Psychological Constructs

Based on the chapters in this handbook, it appears that there already have been strides made in the measurement of individual differences in various positive psychology constructs. Even at this early stage in the positive psychology movement, scholars have established sophisticated and well-articulated theories, along with the accompanying reliable and valid self-report indices.

Personal Growth Initiative—
Christine Robitschek

Personal Growth Initiative (PGI; Robitschek, 1998, 1999) is defined as active, intentional involvement in changing and developing as a person. Not only must the growth or change be in the person's awareness; it also must be an intentional process. People who have high levels of PGI recognize and capitalize on opportunities for personal growth. They also seek out and create situations that will facilitate their growth. In contrast, people with low levels of PGI have little or no awareness that they are changing and might actively avoid situations that might challenge them to grow.

The Personal Growth Initiative Scale (PGIS; Robitschek, 1998, 1999) measures this construct. Research to date has supported a unitary factor structure and strong internal consistency and construct validity. No significant differences have been found on mean scores for the PGIS between women and men or between ethnic minority and majority groups. Scores on the PGIS are positively related to assertiveness, internal locus of control, instrumentality, and growth that is in awareness and intentional. Also, PGI appears to be related to environmental career exploration and vocational identity (Robitschek & Cook, 1999). When PGI was combined with another measure of personal growth (Ryff, 1989), the latent construct of personal growth orientation fully mediated the relation of family functioning to psychological distress (Robitschek & Kashubeck, 1999). We have hypothesized that PGI (i.e., including a willingness to change and grow) might protect against psychological distress when stressful events occur and might lead people to seek help earlier in the process of experiencing psychological distress, thus reducing the extent and effects of distress. Research is under way to examine these hypotheses. Additional current research is testing the validity of the PGI construct with an ethnic minority population and is distinguishing between PGI, openness to experience, and risk-taking attitudes. PGI appears to be an important construct that is related to many aspects of human behavior.

Having such instruments available should help to bring further attention to the positive psychology approach as researchers increasingly use these measures of strength, health, and well-being in their studies. Indeed, because of the ease of giving these questionnaires, we predict an outpouring of instrument-driven research (Snyder, 1997).

Although considerable research has been conducted on the moderation and mediation roles of weakness-oriented individual differences measures such as depression, neuroticism, and hostility, there has been relatively little work on strength-oriented variables as moderators (Snyder & Pulvers, 2001). Accordingly, the role of positive psychology individual differences as moderators and mediators should receive increasing attention as the 21st century unfolds.

The "Other" Positive Psychology Variables

Just as there have been psychological variables wherein the associated individual differences variable have been examined, there also are individual differences in nonpsychological "resources" that warrant our positive psychology attention. These "other" variables often are tapped in the demographics portion of various questionnaires. In this list of beneficial individual differences, we would call the reader's attention to higher income and education (Diener, 1984; Veroff, Douvan, & Kulka, 1981), higher socioeconomic status (Dohrenwend, 1998; Pearlin, 1989; Wills & DePaulo, 1991), and better physical health (Williamson, Parmelee, & Shaffer, 2000). Positive psychology would be well advised to embrace these concepts, as well as environmental variables (see Wright and Lopez, this volume), as being part of our territory in plotting the strengths of people. Of interest would be research on the predictive powers of these variables for important life outcomes, as well as how these variables moderate or mediate other relationships of interest.

Unique Aspects of Optimal Functioning

In advancing positive psychology constructs and their associated individual differences instruments, it will be important to learn a lesson from problems that emerged in the pathology model. In particular, there has been a proliferation of pathology concepts without the appropriate attention to how those concepts are similar to, and different from, existing ones. Positive psychology researchers must constrain their natural tendencies to see their constructs as unique (Snyder & Fromkin, 1980). What this means is that greater attention needs to be paid to the overlap of constructs so as to ascertain shared operative processes and the shared variance in optimal functioning. Furthermore, positive psychology researchers must document the discriminant validity of their measures. Thus, the proliferation of positive psychology ideas and measures should proceed with careful attention to what is common or shared, as well as what is unique.

Sampling Issues

At the risk of oversimplification, the positive psychology research to date may be falling into a sampling pattern of emphasizing Caucasian college students as research participants. In a recent survey that we (Snyder, Tennen, Affleck, & Cheavens, 2000) conducted of 100 articles taken from the 1998 issues of six journals that provide major outlets for positive psychology research, the percentages of research participants recruited for the studies from various sources were as follows: college students, 45%; community residents, 24%; outpatients, 13%; children/adolescents, 9%; hospital health patients, 8%; and psychiatric inpatients, 1%.

In total, there were 56.4% females and 43.6% males in this sample, a finding that reverses the predominance of male over female participants that has been found in previous research. We would encourage positive psychology researchers to continue to include women *and* men in their research. Because approximately 80% of the present Ph.D. graduates in counseling and clinical psychology are women (see Snyder, McDermott, Leibowitz, & Cheavens, 2000), it is our prediction that the female investigators in these fields will include female research participants along with males.

Only half of the articles in this survey reported racial composition, and the breakdown in those articles was as follows: Caucasians, 75.6%; African Americans, 18.9%; Hispanics, 4.6%; Asians, 2.8%; and other, 1.8%. It is difficult to infer the reasons for the omission of these racial identification data in half of the studies that were sampled. For positive psychology researchers who will be living in the increasingly diverse and multiracial United States of the 21st century, it will be crucial to have persons of color participating in research and to determine acculturation levels of those participants (see Lopez et al., this volume). The same applies to positive psychology researchers in other countries around the globe. Positive psychology research should be tested with various ethnic groups to examine whether similar or different processes are operative. At this point in the research, we would be just as premature in assuming that positive psychology principles apply to all ethnic groups as we would be in inferring that different processes apply only to particular racial groups.

Children were not participants in the studies that made up this sample. Granting that there are special journals dedicated to developmental and child issues, we nevertheless find this omission to be problematic because of its similarity to pathology research. We should be careful, in our estimation, to avoid what has happened in the weakness model, where research is best characterized as being "trickle-down" in that anything about children appears only as an afterthought. It is crucial, we believe, to build etiology into our theory and research.

Having made the case that we attend to developmental issues, we also would emphasize that positive psychology is not just pertinent to the young. Indeed, much more attention needs to be given to research with the elderly. In this regard, the age of research participants was reported in only 35% of the studies in the Snyder, Tennen, et al. (2000) sample. Positive psychology researchers should routinely report on the age of their research participants. Moreover, older persons need to be targeted for study from a positive psychology perspective. Because life expectancies are increasing and American baby boomers are maturing from their 50s to 60s, positive psychology research will be needed on this segment of our population (see Williamson, this volume).

Overall, we hold that the scientific foci of positive psychology, along with its applications, should be on the full age range and ethnic backgrounds of humankind. A guiding premise, therefore, is that positive psychology is for the many rather than the few.

Longitudinal Research

Louis Terman (Terman, 1926, 1959; Terman & Oden, 1947) devoted decades to tracing what can be learned from examining the unfolding lives of exceedingly intelligent people. Similarly, Emmy Werner (Werner & Smith, 1982, 1992) followed children who were born into difficult circumstances and yet were resilient and adaptive throughout their lives. It is this kind of longitudinal research that will be needed to provide insights that simply cannot be examined by the cross-sectional, snapshot methodology.

We also acknowledge the methodological and financial challenges of conducting longitudinal research. We call for this form of study because longitudinal designs offer enduring answers to the questions about how psychological strengths can make our futures brighter, buffer us against the ills of the world, and assist us in coping with the adventures of daily living.

Breaking Away: Issues for the Applications of Positive Psychology

As positive psychological science develops, so, too, must a parallel application of the principles and findings from such research. In this section, we review some of the major issues pertaining to applications.

Making Changes to Practice

Primary and Secondary Enhancement

Elsewhere, we have proposed that it may prove useful for the purposes of research and applications to divide positive psychology practice into primary and secondary enhancement (Snyder, Feldman, Taylor, Schroeder, & Adams, 2000). Primary enhancement includes activities geared to achieve optimal functioning and satisfaction—the topics that previously have been invoked to define positive psychology. Secondary enhancement represents those additional efforts that are taken over time to obtain peak functioning and satisfaction. Thus, secondary enhancement pertains to reaching beyond the already positive levels of functioning and satisfaction of primary enhancement. Such secondary enhancement efforts typically occur after a primary or basic level of enhancement has been achieved. Thus, as can be seen in Figure 55.1, the enhancement activities of positive psychology can be conceptualized as occurring over time, with establishing optimal functioning and satisfaction (primary enhancement) progressing to peak levels of functioning and well-being (secondary enhancement).

Let us consider some examples of the difference between primary and secondary enhancement. Suppose a person decides to undertake a regimen of exercise involving rigorous workouts at three differing times per week. Such a person will achieve a level of physical functioning and psychological wellness that we would characterize as exemplifying primary enhance-

ment. But then suppose that the person undertakes an even more rigorous regimen of exercise so as to obtain a level far beyond that which would be considered typical of a well-conditioned person. This latter training approach may yield truly superb levels of physical functional and its associated psychological wellness. Such a person would be described as reaching secondary enhancement. Or, in another example, a person may gain primary enhancement through his or her interchanges with other people, but the peak of such experiences would involve intensive human interaction events such as passionate love, the birth of a child, a wedding, the graduation of a loved one, and so on.

It may be that primary enhancement is a more easily attained and widely applicable positive psychology focus than secondary enhancement. On the other hand, some types of primary enhancement activities may lend themselves most readily to progression into secondary enhancement. Another possibility is that that our attentions need to be focused on understanding and promoting secondary enhancement—even though it is more difficult to attain than primary enhancement. This latter scenario would be driven by the fact that secondary enhancement is such a profoundly intense and gratifying experience.

Intervention Issues

Relative to the amount of inquiry into theory and individual differences variables in positive psychology, there has been less research on how to induce positive change in people. (In fairness, however, it should be acknowledged that the intervention work has begun in some of the positive psychology research programs.)

An in-depth understanding of any positive psychology concept also should involve comprehension of how to enhance it. Thus, positive psychology should be careful to avoid the separation of diagnosis and intervention that has happened in the pathology model. For example, even with its pervasive influence, the *DSM* does not provide links to appropriate interventions for each diagnostic category. As we come to define a classification system in positive psychology, it should have obvious leads to appropriate interventions. Of special interest will be experiments on how to increase the strengths of people who are low on one or more of the positive psychology individual differences measures.

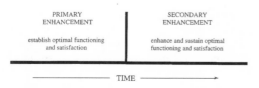

Figure 55.1 Primary and secondary enhancement in positive psychology.

These latter designs enable one to explore the important person (individual differences) by environment (change interventions) interactions that are crucial for both understanding a given positive psychology concept and providing an appropriate intervention.

As we more fully comprehend the underlying dynamics of positive psychology change processes (see Mahoney, this volume), the ultimate beneficiaries will be the people with whom those interventions can be used. To facilitate the discovery of change processes, we believe that positive psychology should reach out to the present psychotherapy outcome investigators who typically are operating under a pathology model (Snyder & Ingram, 2000).

Delivery Issues

Caution will be necessary, however, when attempting to translate positive psychological science into practice. We encourage researchers and innovative practitioners to be sure to ground interventions in theory and science, and to submit these interventions to careful and extensive empirical examination before sharing them with the broader community of scientists and practitioners.

To make appropriate applied translations of our findings, we not only will need to conduct the basic research aimed at understanding the positive change processes but also will need to undertake programs of research to see how such interventions actually can be effectively delivered to maximal numbers of people. Eventually, we will want to know how to impart strengths to people in the context of families, schools, works settings, and so on.

Likewise, officials in government and private granting agencies must be kept apprised of the benefits derived from the science and applications of positive psychology principles. Obviously, there will be an ongoing need for streams of funding related to positive psychology research and action programs. Similarly, it will be crucial to keep policy makers and the general public apprised of the usefulness of positive psychology research and applications.

Broadening the Philosophy and Scope of Practice

There is a saying in journalistic circles that "bad news sells papers." Obviously, however, bad news is not the full story. Compelling recounts about the strength of human will, the bonds of a loving family, the deeds of a caring community, and the like, are worthy of telling if balanced reporting is the goal. Such tales also can raise our spirits and give us models to emulate. Unfortunately, the "bad news" approach is likely to create a self-fulfilling bunker mentality in which people expect things to be bad, think in terms of protection, and to some extent passively allow bad things to happen.

Although there may be happy endings that are begotten from the pathology approach, such as a person being successfully treated for depression, in such instances it still is the negative framework that retains the power to command our attention. It is as if this weakness perspective is the default option to which we automatically turn. For all its contributions, and there have been many significant ones, the pathology model leaves us reactive. With some notable exceptions, the weakness model of psychology can foster a passive, avoidant approach to life. Positive psychology, on the other hand, starts with the premise that human beings have an immense storehouse of remarkable talents and skills. Many of these strengths, however, have lain fallow as we implicitly accept a passive view about human capabilities. What positive psychology offers is a more comprehensive view of humankind.

Self-Determination and Causal Agency Theory—Michael Wehmeyer

Over the last decade there has been considerable focus in the field of special education on the importance of promoting the self-determination of students with disabilities to enable them to successfully transition from school to adulthood. That focus, which has been applied to other populations of youth at risk for school failure and negative adult outcomes, including youth in foster care and children and youth in urban settings, is predicated on the contention that students who leave school as self-determined young people will be better able to become self-sufficient, self-reliant adults. We have developed a functional model of self-determination, also referred to as causal agency theory, which defines self-determined behavior as acting as the primary causal agent in one's life and making choices and decisions regarding one's quality of life free from undue external influence or interference (Wehmeyer, 1996).

Drawing on work in personality, community and motivational psychology, the functional model identifies four essential characteristics of self-determined behavior: (a) the person acted autonomously; (b) the action was self-regulated; (c) the person initiated and responded to the event(s) in a psychologically empowered manner; and (d) the person acted in a self-realizing manner. The model posits that people become self-determined as they develop or acquire a set of component elements of self-determined behavior, including learning to set goals, solve problems, make decisions, and advocate for one's needs as well as by having opportunities to make choices and experience control in life. Our research has empirically validated this framework (Wehmeyer, Kelchner, & Richards, 1996), explored the relative self-determination of youth with disabilities (Wehmeyer & Metzler, 1995), provided evidence of the relationship between student self-determination and positive adult outcomes (Wehmeyer & Schwartz, 1997, 1998), and examined environmental barriers to self-determination (Wehmeyer & Bolding, 1999). We have identified instructional methods and materials to promote self-determination (Wehmeyer, Agran, & Hughes, 1998) and have developed and empirically validated an instructional model to enable educators to teach youth to become more self-determined and to become self-regulated problem solvers (Wehmeyer, Palmer, Agran, Mithaug, & Martin, 2000). Current research is examining key operators in why people become causal agents in their lives, including exploring the development and acquisition of causal and agentic capability and examining how such capability is used to respond to opportunities and threats to create causal action and, in turn, enable individuals to become more self-determined. While our earliest work was with youth with cognitive and other disabilities, later work, including the instructional model and our efforts to examine the key operators in causal and agentic action, is applied to all youth, though not excluding youth with disabilities or other at-risk groups.

Positive Bodies

Positive psychology will need to go "under the hood," so to speak. Whereas most positive psychology researchers are focused at the cognitive and behavioral levels, we believe that a growing group of researchers will trace human strengths to the neurological (see Isen, this volume), bi-ological (see Ryff & Singer, this volume; Taylor, Dickerson, & Klein, this volume), and physiological (see Dienstbier & Zillig, this volume) levels.

From a positive psychology perspective, the investigative focus turns to those bodily structures and processes that enable humans to thrive and flourish. With the exciting advances that are being made at the juncture of psychology and the neurosciences, we look forward to discoveries about brain structures and functions that are implicated in the manifestation of human strengths. This approach has received little attention to date, but it holds enormous promise for stimulating future advances in understanding and applying positive psychology concepts.

Positive Families

What are the characteristics of families that produce happy, well-adjusted offspring who contribute meaningfully to society? Admittedly, this is a very complex question; nevertheless, it needs to be addressed by positive psychology scholars. One place to start in such positive family research would be to examine the role of family rituals in the inculcation of values. Another line would be to determine how families explain everyday adversity, how they set goals for the future, and how they engender hope in their offspring (McDermott & Hastings, 2000; McDermott & Snyder, 2000; Snyder, McDermott, Cook, & Rapoff, 1997). In addition to the traditional male and female two-parent and child(ren) model, positive psychology also would be wise to examine the various forms that families are taking in the 21st century. Whatever the structure, however, the family will be a crucial arena for fostering the tenets of positive psychology. For these reasons, and countless others, the family should capture the attentions of positive psychology researchers.

Positive psychology also should open its doors to child psychology and any other discipline that focuses on research aimed at understanding and promoting the welfare of children. The training of clinical child psychologists, for example, would focus on helping children in areas of their weakness *and* enhancing the strengths of all children (see Brown, Johnson, Roberts, & Reinke, this volume).

Positive Schools

Although families are expected to provide the necessary stimulation and nurturing for healthy development, the reality is that many families struggle to meet the very basic food and shelter needs of their children. Therefore, school becomes a place where adjunctive instruction and services are offered. In our experience, the school and families embrace such psychological and physical health programs. Some critics argue that such programs take precious time away from "real learning," but we contend that positive psychological support sets the stage for better learning. It is not an either-or issue, in our estimation, but rather one in which children deserve excellent instruction in both life skills and content areas.

School psychologists often have been identified as being responsible for making sure that the children with special needs (e.g., learning disabilities, behavioral problems, physical problems), are given optimal environments for learning. These professionals play a key role in our schools, and positive psychology should reach out to them. The tenets of positive psychology should prove very attractive to school psychologists in their work to facilitate the very best in children with special needs, as well as all children. This approach is based on adding various positive psychology experiences to classroom activities. For example, the junior editor of this volume (SJL) has established a series of classroom experiences to enhance the hope of junior high-school students (Lopez, Bouwkamp, Edwards, & Teramoto Pedrotti, 2000). Furthermore, assuming that such educational activities prove to be beneficial for both the psychological and the academic development of students, we believe that positive psychology principles and applications should become a part of the teacher instruction curricula in colleges. We look forward to the day in which teachers systematically use such positive psychology approaches. Our guess is that the very best of teachers already weave positive psychology into their teaching plans and styles.

Youth Development

Benjamin Franklin said that wasted strengths are like sundials in the shade. This is particularly true about the untapped assets of children because they often are in need of help to realize their potentials. As adults, we are entrusted with promoting youth development. This requires that we view all children as needing some support or guidance, not just those who are gifted or at risk for problems (Snyder, Tran, et al., 2000). Positive psychology does not point an

accusing finger of "look at those lousy kids and the problems they have created." Rather, positive psychology views all children as *our* children and asks what we can do to help bring out the best in them. In this regard, perhaps the greatest gift we can give to children is our time. As adults, we sometimes get caught up in own activities, and we do not carve out enough time to spend with our children and those in the neighborhood. Children hunger for positive models. To accomplish this, it is far better if children have the option of turning to real people than to the television screen that is filled with people committing violence against each other.

Positive Workplaces

Turner, Barling, and Zacharatos (this volume) explain how the work setting can be a more positive place that yields better outcomes related to both the financial bottom line and the development of healthy people. The work of industrial/organizational and vocational psychologists also points to how the workplace provides an arena for workers to develop resources, find meaning, and pursue social, emotional, and psychological well-being. We must not neglect the nurturing of human potential in today's workplace.

Jobs, Careers, and Callings: The Meaning of Work—Amy Wrzesniewski

How do people differ in their experience of work? This is an important question, given that people spend more than one third of their waking life at work and increasingly define themselves by what they do for a living. Research has shown that most people have one of three distinct relations to their work, seeing it as a Job, Career, or Calling (Bellah, Madsen, Sullivan, Swidler, & Tipton, 1985; see also Schwartz, 1986, 1994; Wrzesniewski, McCauley, Rozin, & Schwartz, 1997). The distinctions, drawn starkly, are these: People with Jobs focus on financial rewards for working, rather than pleasure or fulfillment, those with Careers focus primarily on advancement, and those with Callings focus on enjoyment of fulfilling, socially useful work. Employees in a wide range of occupations, from clerical to professional, were unambiguous in seeing their work primarily in one of these three ways. Jobs, Careers, and Callings are each represented within occupations as well. Having a Calling was associated with the highest life and job satisfaction and with missing the fewest days of work (Wrzesniewski et al., 1997). Jobs, Careers, and Callings as general orientations toward work also predicted the goals people pursue in a job search, as well as quality of and occupational level in the new job (Wrzesniewski, 1999). Recent research has shown that people in menial jobs can transform their relations to their work and do so by shaping the tasks and relationships that are part of the job in ways that make the work more meaningful (Wrzesniewski & Dutton, 2000). As a conceptual approach to studying work, Jobs, Careers, and Callings offer a rich opportunity for understanding the meaning of work.

Positive Communities

Vibrant communities are ones that pull together for the purpose of fostering the development of healthy children. Cultural and historical preservation unite yet other communities. Irrespective of the nature of the community mission, effective communities share unifying goals (Bellah, Madsen, Sullivan, Swidler, & Tipton, 1992). Moreover, when such community pursuits result in goal attainments, celebrations are warranted to mark the accomplishments. We mention this because we believe that community striving leads to the development of positive connections, and community-wide celebration increases the likelihood of future striving.

The area of community psychology has yet to receive the scholarly attention that it deserves. Perhaps with the assistance of their colleagues in positive psychology, and with further attention to making good things happen rather than solely trying to prevent bad things (see Snyder, Feldman, et al., 2000), there may be an increase in research focusing on community forces. Community is a concept that positive psychology can and should embrace.

Breaking Away: Issues for Training in Positive Psychology

For decades, psychology students have been taught about human foibles, and the pathology model spread across generations of young, malleable minds. In turn, those students took academic and applied jobs and imparted the same psychology of the negative to their intellectual offspring. The positive psychology mission to illuminate and promote human flourishing can be accomplished only when a critical mass of positive psychology professionals collaborate with laypeople who have identified their strengths and acknowledged the role of their abilities and talents in their daily functioning. For this to happen, psychologists assume that health rather than illness is the natural state of the human condition. In the immediate future, however, our goal is to ensure that there is balance between the two psychologies—positive and negative.

We encourage readers to think about the assumptions they make about their research participants, their clients, their partners, children, and themselves. Psychological science has suggested that we use a negative lens for viewing people. When it comes to your view of human behavior, you concern yourself with what you think is most important to developing a better understanding of a person. What *you* see determines what working hypotheses you develop and test. The Aristotle-Galileo "pendulum debate" demonstrates this point. Aristotle assumed that a stone suspended by a string realized its natural state when it was at rest. Therefore, he concerned himself with the "time to come to rest" and built hypotheses related to the "swinging stone" around this metric. On the other hand, Galileo was more interested in the "time per swing" because he believed that the swinging state was natural in the absence of friction. Thus, what you believe and therefore see influences what you examine. So, if on first blush a researcher or clinician sees symptoms of illness instead of a person's strengths, this will determine the hypotheses that are constructed.

Another Side to Human Nature— Dacher Keltner

The future of positive psychology is bright and promises to include an impassioned cadre of young scholars across the disciplines of psychology, as this volume suggests. The advances this field will bring are numerous, from new ideas about relationships to studies of well-being and virtue. Perhaps the most lasting of these contributions is the opportunity positive psychology creates to contemplate the more positive, beneficent nature of human nature.

Many of the great traditions in the behavioral sciences have portrayed human nature in a rather unflattering light. For Freud, humans were conflicted, defensive, and neurotic. For utilitarian approaches that have shaped social psychology, humans were rational seekers of outcomes that maximize self-interest—an assumption that is echoed in certain versions of evolutionary psychology. Other branches of psychology have placed greater emphasis on the negative: We study aggression and not peace-making; we study negative emotion and not positive emotion; we study relationship dissatisfaction and dissolution rather than satisfaction.

These, of course, are just assumptions about human nature. Positive psychology offers an alternative, scientific approach to human nature. In many ways it has the power of the cognitive revolution in psychology, which simply raised the question of how thought guides behavior. Positive psychology asks about positive human nature.

This emphasis is already producing scientific advances in at least three ways. First, researchers are now studying what was underrepresented in psychology. This is clearly seen in the study of positive emotions. Early emotion theorists widely assumed that the number of negative emotions outnumbered the positive ones (for no real reasons). Inspired in part by the work of Fredrickson, we are now discovering that there are numerous positive emotions, including awe, love, desire, relief, hope, pride, and joy. These states may operate in different ways than the negative ones, and they certainly are embedded in many activities humans cherish most. Were it not for positive psychology, these states might still continue to be ignored.

Second, many widespread assumptions about human nature are being challenged by research within positive psychology. For example, it was widely assumed as part of a Freudian legacy in the understanding of bereavement that people who are grieving are best served by working through their negative emotions, such as anger and guilt. My own research with George Bonanno has shown this to be an erroneous assumption (and one worries about clinical treatments based on this assumption). We have found that bereaved individuals who express a great deal of anger do worse over the long haul, whereas those individuals who laugh and gain some distance from the loss do better.

Finally, research within positive psychology will help develop a more nuanced view of many phenomena that have largely been viewed through a more "negative" lens. For example, the literature on teasing has largely focused on its hostile content and antisocial outcomes, as evident in the literature on bullying and victimization. This is no doubt true and one facet to teasing. Yet it would be erroneous to assume that these extreme kinds of teasing represent the teasing of most people in their day-to-day lives. My own research on teasing starts from a different assumption: that most teasing reflects the human capacity to play and pretend, and that it serves a variety of pro-social functions, from expressing affection to socialization.

As positive psychology progresses, it will generate many inspiring insights about human nature, from the inspiration people find in virtue and beauty to the ways people devote themselves to community. These insights will originate in a simple scientific question positive psychology asks: What is good about human nature?

Undoubtedly, personal and professional experiences determine what you "see." Thus, your view of human nature may be influenced by your training (Snyder, 1977). The paradigm within which you have been professionally trained guides what you see in human behavior and the routes that you take to positively influence human change. For positive psychology to become fully viable, there will need to be rigorous graduate programs with faculty and courses devoted to this perspective. The same will be necessary for internships in positive psychology. Clinical, counseling, personality, and social psychology programs, or interfaces of scholars from two or more such programs, offer possible arenas for the teaching of positive psychology at the graduate level. To further awareness, however, there will need to be undergraduate courses in positive psychology.

At the organizational level, there eventually will need to be organizations and conventions devoted to positive psychology perspectives. Likewise, as with the scholarly and educational evolution of any area, there will need to be books that give voice to the key ideas in positive psychology, as well as journals that serve as outlets for research. All of these matters, and more, are necessary for the proper education in positive psychology.

The Future of Positive Psychology—
Barbara Fredrickson

Positive psychology shows tremendous promise. Although many of the ideas central to the field predate the emergence of the positive psy-

chology movement, only now—in response to the movement and with resources like this handbook—have these various ideas been united under the common mission of developing the science of human flourishing. To realize this promise fully, the field needs to broaden the range of phenomena targeted for study. For instance, here and elsewhere I have pointed out that the scientific study of positive emotions lags far behind the study of negative emotions. Plus, some positive emotions have hardly basked in the empirical spotlight at all, namely, awe, serenity, gratitude, and elevation. Although this handbook is impressively comprehensive, in this early moment, positive psychology no doubt carries significant gaps. I encourage interested readers to locate those gaps, see them as opportunities, and make empirical contributions to fill them.

Even more important, to realize its full potential the field needs to build the ranks of scientific psychologists who devote their careers to understanding what makes people thrive. Recruiting graduate students and reorienting recent Ph.D.s to become active, contributing positive psychologists is perhaps the first hurdle. Such efforts are already under way, with both the Positive Psychology Summer Institute and the Positive Psychology Young Scholars Grants Program. While these programs begin to institutionalize training and outreach within positive psychology, more widespread efforts to cultivate the next generation of positive psychologists are needed. For instance, doctoral programs with multiple faculty working as positive psychologists could develop graduate and postdoctoral training programs in positive psychology. These training programs would need to cross boundaries within psychology, drawing on the strengths of multiple subdisciplines within psychology and related fields. With these and other active efforts to "broaden-and-build" itself, the field of positive psychology will flourish.

Closing Thoughts on Breaking Away: Advice From a Grandmother

As the other passengers were slowly boarding the plane, a white-haired woman sat down next to one of the editors (CRS). As we came to cruising altitude, we began a lively conversation that was to continue across the skies from Philadelphia to Kansas City. I learned that, because

of a mandatory age retirement rule, this woman had to quit her teaching position over 15 years ago. She fondly recounted how she had spent those postretirement years with her grandchildren. In fact, on this occasion, she was going to visit her brand-new great-grandson. "What do you do for a living?" she asked. I recounted the short version of my life as a professor and mentioned my work in positive psychology. Upon hearing about this, she became very animated, asking question after question about positive psychology. The time passed quickly, and we soon were off the plane, walking up the ramp to the terminal building. She turned and opined, "Positive psychology, that's a good way to spend your time." With that, she waved and disappeared into the outstretched arms of smiling family members. *Positive psychology, that's a good way to spend your time.* We agree. Please join us.

References

American Psychiatric Association. (1952). *Diagnostic and statistical manual of mental disorders*. Washington, DC: Author.

American Psychiatric Association. (1968). *Diagnostic and statistical manual of mental disorders* (2nd ed.). Washington, DC: Author.

American Psychiatric Association. (1980). *Diagnostic and statistical manual of mental disorders* (3rd ed.). Washington, DC: Author.

American Psychiatric Association. (1987). *Diagnostic and statistical manual of mental disorders* (3rd ed., Rev.). Washington, DC: Author.

American Psychiatric Association. (1994). *Diagnostic and statistical manual of mental disorders* (4th ed.). Washington, DC: Author.

American Psychiatric Association. (2000). *Diagnostic and statistical manual of mental disorders* (4th ed., text revision). Washington, DC: Author.

Armor, D. A., & Taylor, S. E. (1998). Situated optimism: Specific outcome expectancies and self-regulation. In M. P. Zanna (Ed.), *Advances in experimental social psychology* (Vol. 30, pp. 309–379). New York: Academic Press.

Ashby, F. G., Isen, A. M., & Turken, A. U. (1999). A neurological theory of positive affect and its influence on cognition. *Psychological Review, 106,* 529–550.

Aspinwall, L. G. (1998). Rethinking the role of positive affect in self-regulation. *Motivation and Emotion, 22,* 1–32.

Aspinwall, L. G. (in press). Dealing with adversity: Self-regulation, coping, adaptation, and health.

In A. Tesser & N. Schwarz (Eds.), *The Blackwell handbook of social psychology: Vol. 1, Intraindividual processes*. Oxford, England: Blackwell.

Aspinwall, L. G., Richter, L., & Hoffman, R. R., III, (2000). Understanding how optimism "works": An examination of optimists' adaptive moderation of belief and behavior. In E. C. Chang (Ed.), *Optimism and pessimism: Theory, research, and practice* (pp. 217–238). Washington, DC: American Psychological Association.

Aspinwall, L. G., & Staudinger, U. M. (Eds.) (in press). *A psychology of human strengths: Perspectives on an emerging field*. Washington, DC: American Psychological Association.

Bandura, A. (1998, August). *Swimming against the mainstream: Accenting the positive aspects of humanity*. Invited address presented at the annual meeting of the American Psychological Association, San Francisco.

Bellah, R. N., Madsen, R., Sullivan, W. M., Swidler, A., & Tipton, S. M. (1985). *Habits of the heart: Individualism and commitment in American life*. New York: Harper and Row.

Bellah, R. N., Madsen, R., Sullivan, W. M., Swidler, A., & Tipton, S. M. (1992). *The good society*. New York: Vintage.

Diener, E. (1984). Subjective well-being. *Psychological Bulletin, 95*, 542–575.

Dohrenwend, B. P. (1998). Theoretical integration. In B. P. Dohrenwend (Ed.), *Adversity, stress, and psychopathology* (pp. 539–555). New York: Oxford University Press.

Isen, A. M. (1993). Positive affect and decision making. In M. Lewis & J. M. Haviland (Eds.), *Handbook of emotions* (pp. 261–277). New York: Guilford.

Kuhn, T. S. (1970). *The structure of scientific revolutions*. Chicago: University of Chicago Press.

Langer, E., & Abelson, R. (1974). A patient by any other name . . . : Clinician group differences in labeling bias. *Journal of Consulting and Clinical Psychology, 42*, 4–9.

Lopez, S. J., Bouwkamp, J., Edwards, L. E., & Teramoto Pedrotti, J. (2000, October). *Making hope happen via brief interventions*. Presented at the Second Positive Psychology Summit, Washington, DC.

McDermott, D. S., & Hastings, S. (2000). Children: Raising future hopes. In C. R. Snyder (Ed.), *Handbook of hope: Theory, measures, and applications* (pp. 185–200). San Diego: CA: Academic Press.

McDermott, D., & Snyder, C. R. (2000). *The great big book of hope: Help your children reach their dreams*. Oakland, CA: New Harbinger.

Pearlin, L. I. (1989). The sociological study of stress. *Journal of Health and Social Behavior, 30*, 241–256.

Peterson, C., & Seligman, M. E. P. (2000). *The VIA taxonomy of human strengths and virtues*. Unpublished manuscript, University of Pennsylvania, Philadelphia.

Robitschek, C. (1998). Personal growth initiative: The construct and its measure. *Measurement and Evaluation in Counseling and Development, 30*, 183–198.

Robitschek, C. (1999). Further validation of the Personal Growth Initiative Scale. *Measurement and Evaluation in Counseling and Development, 31*, 197–210.

Robitschek, C., & Cook, S. W. (1999). The influence of personal growth initiative and coping styles on career exploration and vocational identity. *Journal of Vocational Behavior, 54*, 127–141.

Robitschek, C., & Kashubeck, S. (1999). A structural model of parental alcoholism, family functioning, and psychological health: The mediating effects of hardiness and personal growth orientation. *Journal of Counseling Psychology, 46*, 159–172.

Ryff, C. D. (1989). Happiness is everything, or is it? Explorations on the meaning of psychological well-being. *Journal of Personality and Social Psychology, 57*, 1069–1081.

Schwartz, B. (1986). *The battle for human nature: Science, morality, and modern life*. New York: Norton.

Schwartz, B. (1994). *The costs of living: How market freedom erodes the best things in life*. New York: Norton.

Seligman, M. E. P. (2000, October). *Positive psychology: A progress report*. Presented at the Second Positive Psychology Summit, Washington, DC.

Seligman, M. E. P., & Csikszentmihalyi, M. (2000). Positive psychology: An introduction. *American Psychologist, 55*, 5–14.

Snyder, C. R. (1977). "A patient by any other name" revisited: Maladjustment or attributional locus of problem? *Journal of Consulting and Clinical Psychology, 45*, 101–103.

Snyder, C. R. (1997). The state of the interface. *Journal of Social and Clinical Psychology, 16*, 1–13.

Snyder, C. R. (2000). The past and possible futures of hope. *Journal of Social and Clinical Psychology, 19*, 11–28.

Snyder, C. R., Feldman, D. B., Taylor, J. D., Schroeder, L. L., & Adams, V., III. (2000). The roles of hopeful thinking in preventing problems and promoting strengths. *Applied and Pre-*

ventive Psychology: Current Scientific Perspectives, 15, 262–295.

Snyder, C. R., & Fromkin. H. L. (1980). *Uniqueness: The human pursuit of difference.* New York: Plenum.

Snyder, C. R., & Ingram, R. E. (2000). Psychotherapy: Questions for an evolving field. In C. R. Snyder & R. E. Ingram (Eds.), *Handbook of psychological change: Psychotherapy processes and practices for the 21st century* (pp. 707–726). New York: Wiley.

Snyder, C. R., & McCullough, M. (2000). A positive psychology field of dreams: "If you build it, they will come. . . ." *Journal of Social and Clinical Psychology, 19,* 151–160.

Snyder, C. R., McDermott, D., Cook, W., & Rapoff, M. (1997). *Hope for the journey: Helping children through the good times and the bad.* Boulder, CO: Westview; San Francisco: HarperCollins.

Snyder, C. R., McDermott, D. S., Leibowitz, R. Q., & Cheavens, J. (2000). The roles of female clinical psychologists in changing the field of psychotherapy. In C. R. Snyder & R. E. Ingram (Eds.), *Handbook of psychological change: Psychotherapy processes and practices for the 21st century* (pp. 639–659). New York: Wiley.

Snyder, C. R., & Pulvers, K. (2001). Dr. Seuss, the coping machine, and "Oh, the places you will go." In C. R. Snyder (Ed.) *Coping and copers: Adaptive processes and people* (pp. 3–29). New York: Oxford University Press.

Snyder, C. R., Tennen, H., Affleck, G., & Cheavens, J. (2000). Social, personality, clinical, and health psychology tributaries: The merging of a scholarly "river of dreams." *Personality and Social Psychology Review, 4,* 16–29.

Snyder, C. R., Tran, T., Schroeder, L. L., Pulvers, K. M., Adams, V., III, & Laub. L. (2000). Teaching children the hope recipe: Setting goals, finding routes to those goals, and getting motivated. *Today's Youth, 4,* 46–50.

Terman, L. M. (1926). *Genetic studies of genius: Vol. 1. Mental and physical traits of a thousand gifted children.* Stanford, CA: Stanford University Press.

Terman, L. M. (1959). *Genetic studies of genius: Vol. 5. The gifted group at mid-life.* Stanford, CA: Stanford University Press.

Terman, L. M., & Oden, M. H. (1947). *Genetic studies of genius: Vol. 4. The gifted child grows up.* Stanford, CA: Stanford University Press.

Veroff, J. B., Douvan, E., & Kulka, R. A. (1981). *The inner American: A self-portrait from 1957 to 1976.* New York: Basic Books.

Wehmeyer, M. L. (1996). Self-determination as an educational outcome: Why is it important to children, youth and adults with disabilities? In D. J. Sands & M. L. Wehmeyer (Eds.), *Self-determination across the life span: Independence and choice for people with disabilities* (pp. 15–34). Baltimore: Paul H. Brookes.

Wehmeyer, M. L., Agran, M., & Hughes, C. (1998). *Teaching self-determination to students with disabilities: Basic skills for successful transition.* Baltimore: Paul H. Brookes.

Wehmeyer, M. L., & Bolding, N. (1999). Self-determination across living and working environments: A matched-samples study of adults with mental retardation. *Mental Retardation, 37,* 353–363.

Wehmeyer, M. L., Kelchner, K., & Richards, S. (1996). Essential characteristics of self-determined behaviors of adults with mental retardation and developmental disabilities. *American Journal on Mental Retardation, 100,* 632–642.

Wehmeyer, M. L., & Metzler, C. (1995). How self-determined are people with mental retardation? The National Consumer Survey. *Mental Retardation, 33,* 111–119.

Wehmeyer, M. L., Palmer, S., Agran, M., Mithaug, D., & Martin, J. (2000). Promoting causal agency: The Self-Determined Learning Model of Instruction. *Exceptional Children, 66,* 439–453.

Wehmeyer, M. L., & Schwartz, M. (1997). Self-determination and positive adult outcomes: A follow-up study of youth with mental retardation or learning disabilities. *Exceptional Children, 63,* 245–255.

Wehmeyer, M. L., & Schwartz, M. (1998). The relationship between self-determination, quality of life, and life satisfaction for adults with mental retardation. *Education and Training in Mental Retardation and Developmental Disabilities, 33,* 3–12.

Werner, E. E., & Smith, R. S. (1982). *Vulnerable but invincible: A study of resilient children.* New York: McGraw-Hill.

Werner, E. E., & Smith, R. S. (1992). *Overcoming the odds: High risk children from birth to adulthood.* Ithaca, NY: Cornell University Press.

Williamson, G. M., Parmelee, P. A., & Shaffer, D. R. (Eds.). (2000). *Physical illness and depression in older adults: A handbook of theory, research, and practice.* New York: Plenum.

Wills, T. A., & DePaulo, B. M. (1991). Interpersonal analysis of the help-seeking process. In C. R. Snyder & D. R. Forsyth (Eds.), *Handbook of social and clinical psychology: The health perspective* (pp. 350–375). Elmsford, NY: Pergamon.

Wrzesniewski, A. (1999). *Jobs, careers, and callings: Work orientation and job transitions.* Unpublished doctoral dissertation, University of Michigan.

Wrzesniewski, A., & Dutton, J. E. (in press). Crafting a job: Revisioning employees as active crafters of their work. *Academy of Management Review.*

Wrzesniewski, A., McCauley, C. R., Rozin, P., & Schwartz, B. (1997). Jobs, careers, and callings: People's relations to their work. *Journal of Research in Personality, 31,* 21–33.

Author Index

Irvine, M. J., 208
Irving, L., 53, 54, 258, 264, 267, 270n.3, 354, 355, 704
Isaacowitz, D. M., 181
Iscoe, I., 740
Isen, Alice M., 31, 51, 124, 141, 142, 528–37, 708, 711, 754, 760
Isom, J., 535, 537
Itard, J., 619
Ito, T. A., 122
Iverson, R. D., 115
Ivey, A. E., 39
Ivey, M. B., 39
Ivry, R., 338
Iyer, V. C., 448
Izard, C. E., 107

Jackson, D. N., 448
Jackson, F. L. C., 702
Jackson, J. S., 358
Jackson, M., 208
Jackson, P. R., 718, 723
Jackson, S., 90, 93, 94, 95, 96, 99
Jackson, S. E., 719
Jackson, W. T., 265, 691
Jacobson, N. S., 427, 429
Jacoby, S., 480
Jaffe, J., 29
Jahoda, Marie, 48, 542, 720
James, William, 91, 92, 135, 140, 173, 190, 278, 390, 399, 492, 542, 646, 746, 749
Jamison, K. R., 161, 183n.5, 194
Jamner, L. D., 563
Janes, L. M., 622, 629
Jang, K. L., 20, 109, 112
Janigian, A. S., 601
Janis, I. L., 228, 289, 404, 414, 626
Janiszewski, C. A., 450
Janoff-Bulman, R., 353, 357, 584, 589, 590, 591, 599, 600, 601
Jarvis, M. J., 681
Jarymowicz, M., 492
Jaycox, L. H., 5, 53, 69, 248, 250, 665
Jeffries, V., 462
Jemmott, J. B., 403
Jenkins, J. M., 20, 121, 461, 464
Jenkins, R. A., 653
Jensen, A. L., 166
Jensen, A. M., 506
Jensen, K., 203
Jeppson, E. S., 670
Jepson, C., 338, 739
Jessop, D. J., 670
Jetten, J., 398–99
Jevning, R. A., 635
Jezova, D., 562
Johansson, B., 682
John, O. P., 109, 151, 449

John of the Cross, Saint, 180
Johnsen, T. B., 518
Johnson, B. H., 670
Johnson, C. A., 165
Johnson, D., 294
Johnson, E., 532
Johnson, J. D., 494
Johnson, J. L., 77, 249, 451
Johnson, J. T., 383, 416
Johnson, L. B., 292
Johnson, M. M. S., 124, 530
Johnson, N. G., 664
Johnson, P. E., 648
Johnson, Rebecca J., 663–72, 760
Johnson, S. M., 154
Johnson, W. B., 732
Johnson-Laird, P. N., 197, 368
Johnston, M., 208
Joiner, T. E., 109, 126, 127, 131, 416, 708
Jones, E., 220
Jones, E. E., 29, 353, 355, 366, 416, 425
Jones, J. E., 448
Jones, J. H., 732
Jones, M. L., 694
Jones, R. A., 354
Jones, S. C., 366
Jones, S. E., 732
Jones, S. M., 166
Jones, W. H., 448
Jordan, A. E., 736
Jordan, J. V., 389
Jorgenson, P. F., 461
Josephs, R. A., 370
Joss, J., 217
Jost, J. T., 371
Joubert, L., 620
Jourard, S. M., 573
Joyce, James, 227
Juda, A., 194
Judge, T. A., 307, 715
Jung, Carl, 542
Juniper, E., 669
Jurankova, E., 562

Kabat-Zinn, J., 633, 634, 637, 638, 640
Kaczala, C. M., 249
Kaemingk, K., 559
Kagan, J., 613
Kahle, K., 266
Kahn, B. E., 124, 529, 530, 531, 533
Kahn, D., 99
Kahn, R. L., 545, 676, 677, 678, 679, 681, 719
Kahneman, D., 64, 65, 224, 337
Kaiser, J., 692
Kalmar, K., 291
Kamarck, T., 626
Kameda, M., 450

Kamen-Siegel, L., 253
Kameoka, V. A., 208
Kampf, H. C., 492
Kanouse, D. E., 31
Kant, Immanuel, 352, 439, 463, 491, 746
Kaplan, B. H., 452
Kaplan, D., 476
Kaplan, J. S., 702
Kaplan, M., 284
Kaplan, R. M., 53, 264, 669
Kaplan, S., 208
Karasek, R. A., 717, 718
Karlson, J. I., 194
Karney, B. R., 115
Karniol, R., 320
Kashiwagi, K., 249
Kashubeck, S., 756
Kaslow, F. W., 22
Kaslow, N. J., 249
Katkovsky, W., 205
Kato, P., 704
Katz, I. R., 680
Katz, J., 208, 370, 453
Katz, L., 678
Katz, L. D., 536
Katz, S. T., 183n.4
Kaufman, G. D., 648
Kawachi, I., 560
Kaye, K., 321
Kazak, A., 670
Kazdin, A. E., 283
Keane, S. P., 283
Keany, C. M.-H., 695
Keasey, C. B., 320
Keating, D., 78
Keating, D. P., 316
Keating, J. P., 490
Keener, A. D., 107, 112
Keith, B., 688
Keith, D., 248, 665
Keith, P. M., 370
Keith-Spiegel, P., 732, 733, 737
Kekes, J., 327, 329, 339, 341
Kelchner, K., 760
Keller, Helen, 693
Keller, M. B., 46
Kelley, Harold H., 33, 247, 319, 354, 355, 423, 429, 431, 599
Kelloway, E. K., 715, 718, 720, 721, 722
Kelly, A. E., 386, 577
Kelly, E. L., 115
Kelly, G. A., 367, 368
Kelly, George A., 746, 747, 748
Keltner, Dacher, 622, 625, 753, 762–63
Kemeny, M. E., 206, 237, 586, 593, 601, 615
Kemp, B. J., 691
Kemper, T. D., 461
Kendall, P. C., 283, 289

Subject Index

SNS. *See* sympathetic nervous system
SNS-adrenal medullary system, 516–20, 523, 524
social acceptance, 48, 398, 404
social actualization, 48
social agents, reality negotiation role of, 356
social behavior, positive affectivity and, 113, 114, 116, 528, 529, 534, 536
social-cognitive theory, 279, 281, 284, 285, 306
social coherence, 48, 577
social collaboration, wisdom and, 336–37
social comparison, 366
    benefit-finding and, 593
    evaluation and, 219, 221, 226–27, 228
    self-esteem and, 353
social-constructionist theory, 173, 352
social constructions, 15, 18–19, 23
    of love, 475
    of self-esteem, 135–46
social contribution, 48
social desirability, 41, 266
social emotions, 464
social equality, 137, 139, 143
social harmony, 449
social identity theory, 707
social integration, 48, 266, 577, 579–80
social isolation, 563, 564
    aging and, 678
    as health risk, 549, 556, 577, 579
    pessimistic explanatory style and, 253
    physical disability and, 688
socialization, 499
    authenticity development, 383, 384, 385, 391
    empathy-related issues, 489, 493
social justice, 742
social learning, 278
social participation, 66, 622, 636
social perception, 136
social phobia, 114, 416
Social Problem Solving Inventory, 290
Social Readjustment Rating Questionnaire, 194
social referencing, 314–15, 316
social relationships
    older people and, 678
    self-verification and, 367–77
    social support issues and, 556, 558, 562, 564, 565
    as well-being factor, 549–50, 553
social responsibility, 528, 529, 536
social science, 8, 404, 447, 542, 752
Social Security, 678, 679
social structure, well-being and, 541, 553
social support, 236, 556–65
    aging and, 680–81, 682, 683
    attachment and separation issues, 556, 557–59, 561, 562, 563, 564
    benefit-finding in loss and, 603, 605
    for children, 671
    cultural perspectives on, 710
    as health factor, 549, 556, 557, 559–60, 562–65, 577, 579
    hope theory issues and, 266, 667
    optimistic explanatory style and, 253

physical disability adjustment and, 691, 694
    reality negotiation and, 351, 356, 357–59
    religion as source of, 705
    stress-related biobehavioral responses, 559–64
    work-related, 718, 720, 721
social values, 340
social workers, 37
Society for Constructivism in the Human Sciences, 747
socioeconomic status
    cultural issues, 706
    physical disability adjustment and, 689–90
    positive affectivity and, 113
    as positive psychology research variable, 756
    as resilience factor, 82
    well-being and, 545–48, 550, 553
sociology, 82, 404
software, computer, 96
soul, 4, 308
specific action tendencies, 121, 122
specificity, goal setting and, 305
spending, pathological, 16
spirit, 437
spirituality, 151, 646–56
    conservation of the sacred, 650–54
    constructivist view of, 749–50
    cultural perspectives on, 705–6
    definition of, 647–48
    discovery of the sacred and, 648–50, 654
    emotional creativity and, 179–80
    future research considerations, 655–56
    as life-span process, 654
    meditation's enhancement of, 634, 638, 642
    positive affectivity and, 113–14
    resilience and, 82
spiritualization of passions, 173, 176, 179–80, 182
spiritual reframing, 653–54
sports
    collective efficacy in, 284
    flow and, 91, 96
    hope theory and, 263–64
    self-efficacy and, 280
SPSI. *See* Social Problem Solving Inventory
S-S learning, 317
SSRIs. *See* selective serotonin reuptake inhibitors
stability, in life, 609
staleness syndrome, 521
Stanford Bereavement Project, 600
State Hope Scale, 260, 667
state measurements, 414, 415
statistical deviation, 20, 22
statistical significance, 41
stereotypes, 26, 707
    attitude tests of, 41–42
    "good woman," 388–89
    physical disability and, 692
    of psychologists, 745
stimulus discrimination, 314, 316
stockmarket day trading, pathological, 17
stoicism, 237
Stoics, 160, 464

optimistic outlook's effects on, 235–36
proactive orientation development and, 723–24
problem-solving appraisal issues and, 294
teams and work groups, 716, 720–21, 723
transformational leadership and, 716, 721–22, 723, 725
unemployment and, 247
as wisdom factor, 335
work ethic, 3, 5
working memory, 534
working through a problem, 579, 590
World Health Organization, 48, 548, 641

writing
benefits of disclosure and, 163, 574–75
emotional approach coping and, 149, 153, 154
journaling, 153
meaning-making research and, 614
story sharing, 574–75, 577–82, 615

YCHS. *See* Young Children's Hope Scale
yoga, 129
Young Children's Hope Scale, 666–67

Zen meditation, 632, 633, 636, 638
Zung depression inventory, 48